TABLE OF CONTENTS

*The contents of this strategy guide are based solely on the research of BradyGames

INTRODUCTION

And so there came a day like no other.

When the very fabric of two universes began to unravel and collide.

And yet, the cause of this disastrous occurrence was not a natural one. Rather, it was the result of a most unholy alliance...

...as villains from these two very different worlds united with an eye on conquering both.

Their vile scheme would throw their respective realities into chaos...

...by meddling with forces they could not even possibly comprehend. By angering a god.

"I am that god. I... Galactus! And now, because of this great insolence...the FATE OF TWO WORLDS hangs in the balance!"

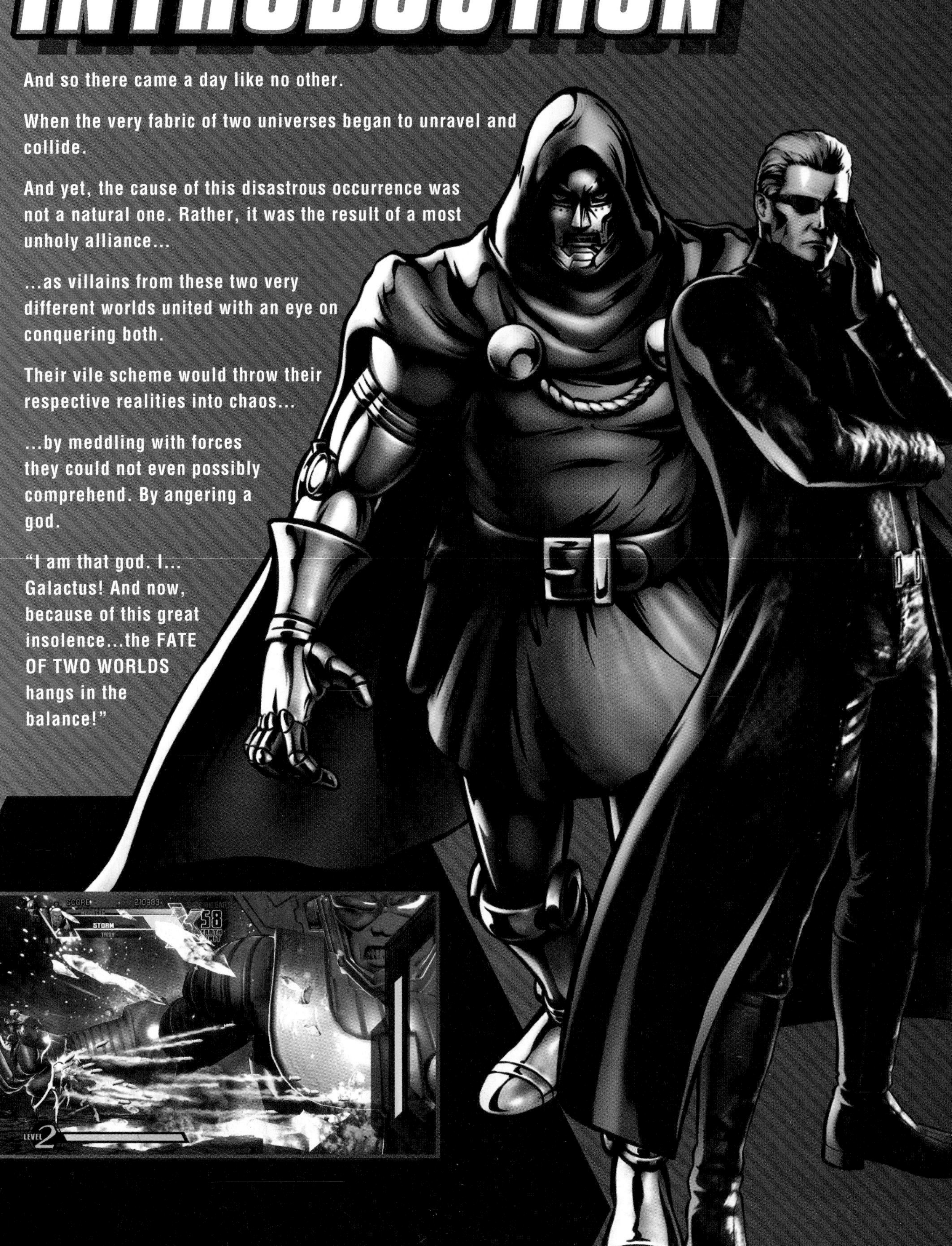

About This Guide

WELCOME BACK!

Ultimate Marvel vs. Capcom 3 is like a director's cut—the definitive version of the game. *UMvC3* producer Ryota Niitsuma has said as much himself, indicating that *UMvC3* includes ideas and characters his team didn't have time to cram into original *MvC3*. *Ultimate Marvel vs. Capcom 3* is bigger, better, with a shinier wrapper.

That's how we feel about this guide, too. We didn't know how *MvC3* would actually shake out in the wild. We had to sort of rely on our collective, extensive knowledge of previous fighting games. After that, we had to guess.

Readers of the original guide may wonder what's different now, whether we've just trotted out the same old pony. The answer is no! No, we didn't. We've re-examined *UMvC3* with the same attention to detail with which we looked at *MvC3*... even more detail, in fact. Just like everyone else, we benefitted from exposure to the game once it was released officially into the unpredictable hands of hardcore gamers, who found many things we (and Capcom!) missed. And furthermore, *UMvC3* is not just the previous version with a new paintjob. In addition to new costumes, missions, and gameplay alterations for every returning character, there are a dozen new heroes joining the fray. That is a huge upgrade!

MvC3 released on February 15th, 2011. Online, there are thousands of high-level match videos, combo videos, tutorials, Mission mode completion guides, viral videos, funny videos, salty videos, and all manner of other media dedicated to the game. The Evolution 2011 World Finals, held annually in Las Vegas and organized by the staff of shoryuken.com, set records for tournament attendance (in the thousands) and for online stream viewership (in the *millions*). The way is not quite as dark as it once was for new or inexperienced players.

We knew what our opportunities were for an even better guide to accompany an even better game. There were things in that guide we would change even without a new game. But there is indeed a new game, and with more characters and content, and changes to every existing hero, we brought back everyone who worked on the original book, along with three more authors to help us make it to the finish line in an incredibly short time in one piece.

So, we're going a little less easy on you this time. Everyone is acclimated, yes? Our goal with the original guidebook was to give a generation of new players, who were mostly NOT weaned on *MvC2* and other Capcom arcade classics, a comprehensive primer. Our goal this time is simply to be as indispensable to the *UMvC3* fan as the game disc itself.

We hope you think we succeeded.

THIS GUIDE: TUNING SINCE ORIGINAL MVC3

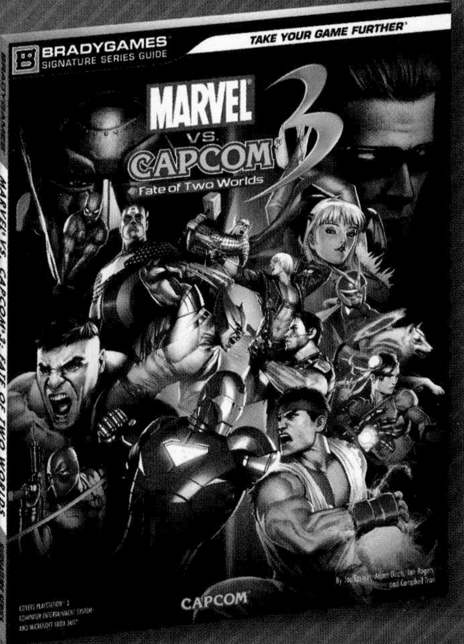

The experience of putting together the first *MvC3* guide with the same team has allowed us to get more familiar with the game after release, while thinking about how to improve the guide if we got the chance. As it turns out, here we are, and so we've put most of our ideas into practice. Certainly, as expansive as this book is at an unprecedented 592 pages, we've left some things out. Hitbox illustrations, for the most obvious example, and delving further into team setups or mix-ups against certain characters in increasingly specific situations, for another. But the perfect is the enemy of the good, and some things fall outside the circumstances of available time, space, and resources.

Full coverage for all 12 new characters! Extensive data, devastating combos, and winning tactics from a team of fighting game experts, all on day one!

Every returning character revisited: changes large and small since original *MvC3* detailed, with data reviewed and expanded, and revised and expanded discussion! No cut and paste here!

Layout tweaks to ease readability; character overviews and changelists placed right at the beginning with their art and biography; character battle plans treated as organic articles tailored to given characters rather than universally separated into a grounded section, an aerial section, and an assist section (which worked better for some characters than others); combo transcriptions stretched farther horizontally where possible to ease eye tracking

Revisited peripheral and system-oriented chapters that are more focused for reader ease-of-use and quick reference

Quick Reference

ALL COMMANDS IN THIS GUIDE ASSUME YOUR CHARACTER IS STANDING ON THE LEFT SIDE OF THE SCREEN, ON THE PLAYER 1 SIDE, FACING RIGHT TOWARD THE PLAYER 2 SIDE. FORWARD IS THUS EXPRESSED AS ➔, BACKWARD AS ←. FOR A CHARACTER ON THE RIGHT, FACING LEFT TOWARD THE PLAYER 1 SIDE, REVERSE ANY DIRECTIONAL INPUTS.

UMvC3 can be played with a variety of gamepads and joysticks (though unfortunately, or really perhaps fortunately, there's no Microsoft Kinect or PlayStation Move support, so you won't be trying to super jump in real life). To accommodate all sorts of potential input devices, you can customize your control scheme from within the options menu.

DEFAULT BUTTON CONFIGURATIONS

The default control schemes on both PlayStation® 3 and Xbox 360® assign the buttons to similar locations. Although you can assign whichever buttons you like, we recommend disabling the button assigned by default to register both assist buttons. This removes the risk of accidentally triggering a crossover combination with stray fingers in the heat of battle.

To simulate the arcade experience, many players prefer using a joystick. Having a truly great home stick used to mean going the custom route with old independent companies like MAS Systems, but now there are excellent, widely available joysticks for each console, most notably variations of the MadCatz Tournament Edition joystick or the Hori Real Arcade Pro VXSA and V3SA. These sticks are made from high-quality arcade parts, and they are extremely durable and accurate. They are also extremely friendly to players who wish to modify their own sticks, whether for different parts or custom aesthetics. Some independent stick manufacturers, such as Project GiantSword, build custom sticks to client specifications, for those looking for something personally tailored and unique.

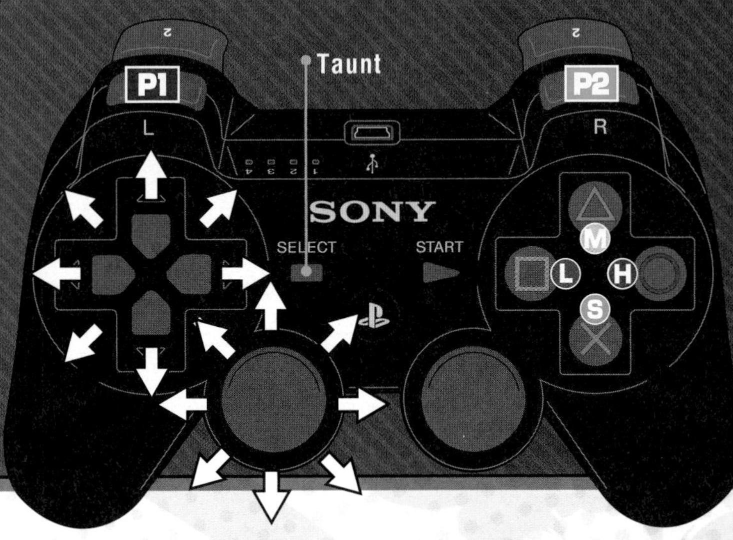

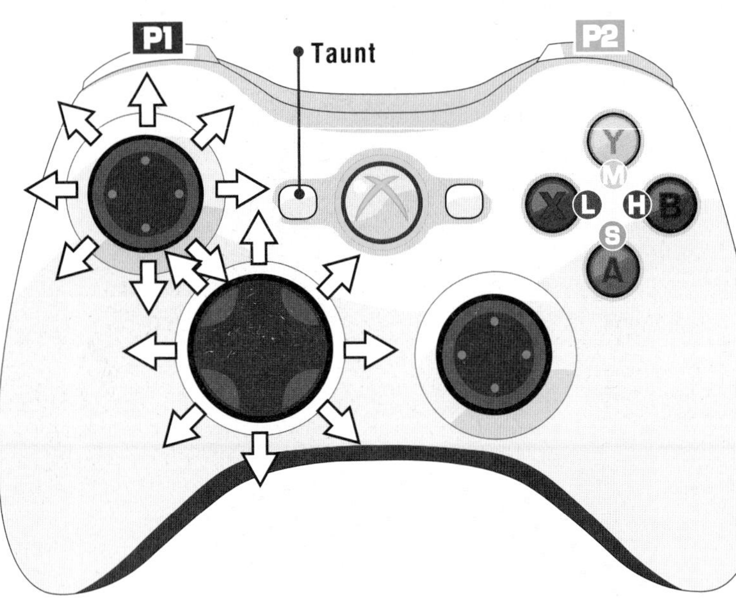

Variations of the excellent MadCatz sticks available since *Street Fighter IV*, which revived the fighting game scene in recent years, have replaced the old sight of MAS Systems custom stick (also pictured) as the standard-bearer of the modern tournament crowd. Not pictured: Joe Epstein's girlfriend, who somehow approves of this.

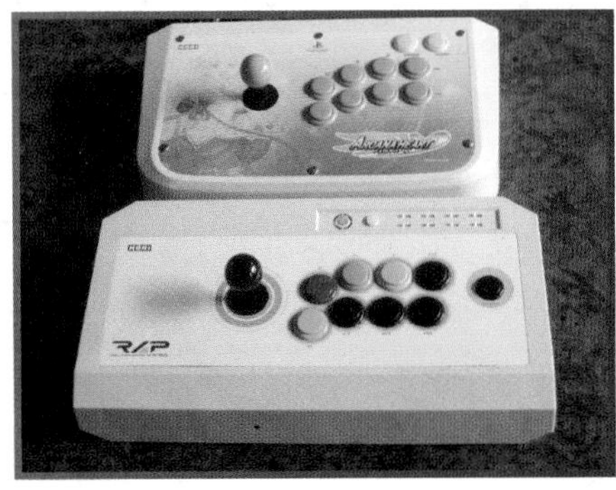

Hori has been a Japanese standard-bearer for durable, top-shelf joysticks for years. Some players prefer Hori's recent HRAP VXSA/V3SA sticks to variants of the MadCatz Tournament Edition sticks because of the wider base. In terms of functioning hardware, the sticks are virtually identical. Photo courtesy Nathan Roach.

While the old custom standard MAS Systems is now defunct, outfits like Project GiantSword have sprung up, offering custom-made premium joysticks. Photo courtesy Daniel Maniago.

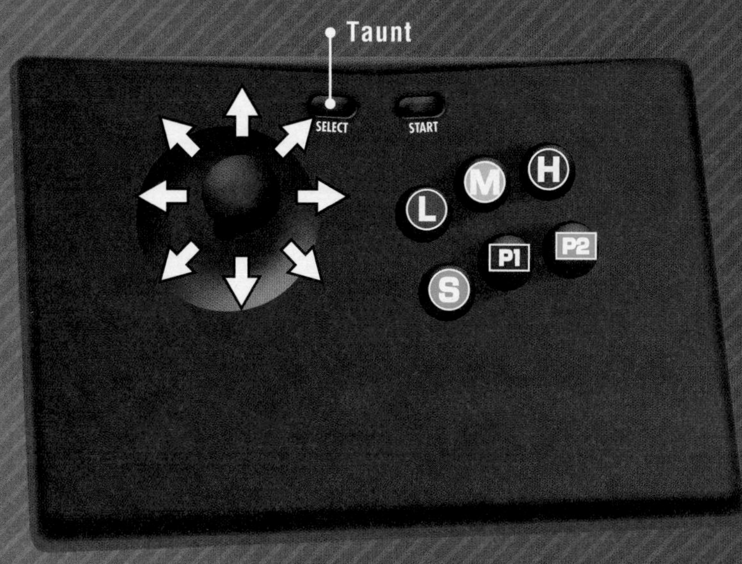

The intended configuration for a six-button joystick. Depending on your joystick, this is almost certainly NOT the default mapping. Check in options, and customize as needed. For a MadCatz, it's as easy as setting controller type to β. For any Hori joystick, you'll need to configure a custom controller setup. Of course, for online play, you can map your buttons however you like, and most tournaments also allow button mapping. Some players frown on multiple inputs mapped to one button (used to make dashes and whatnot easier), but others view concern as much ado about nothing. However, almost all players SERIOUSLY frown on the use of turbo or macro functions on controllers, and every tournament worth its salt bans them, as well, for good reason in a game that relies so heavily on dexterous execution. You can get away with using turbo functions online, but you're doing yourself and your opponents a disservice.

The use of a gamepad or joystick comes down to preference, ultimately. When almost all tournaments were in arcades, players had no choice—if you weren't used to playing on a stick, you weren't playing. But now, with the preeminence of console and online play, there is no forced specialization. PlayStation joypads have been competent for fighting games since their inception, and Xbox 360 has a special edition silver gamepad available with a twisting adjustable d-pad, released specifically to better cater to finely tuned games like fighters. More and more tournament-winning players perform perfectly well on pads where that was never the case before (outside of scenes like *Tekken*, which had arcade cabinets that allowed for PlayStation pads to be plugged in), so any stigma you might hear about sticks being better than pads is just about obsolete (though certain techniques like plinking do just end up being easier for most people to perform on a stick with larger, more sensitive buttons than a pad. Your mileage may vary).

SIMPLE MODE

Simple mode allows special moves and hyper combos to be performed simply by pressing single buttons, and chain combos can be executed by repetitiously pressing the same button, but the full arsenal of attacks for any given character is unavailable. The button configuration in simple mode can be configured to your liking. Note that all it takes to activate X-Factor in simple mode is pressing the chain combo and special attack buttons simultaneously. This guide assumes that the player is using normal mode for maximum potential. The same strategies described for normal mode also work for simple mode, but within the limitations of simple mode's diminished movelist.

Simple Play Button Configuration

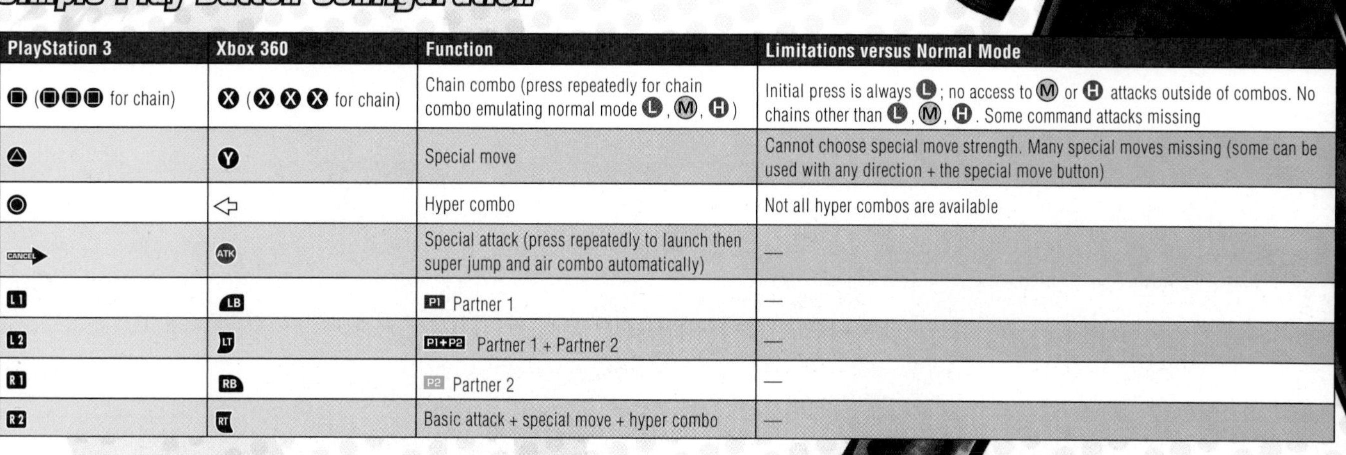

PlayStation 3	Xbox 360	Function	Limitations versus Normal Mode
■ (■■■ for chain)	Ⓧ (ⓍⓍⓍ for chain)	Chain combo (press repeatedly for chain combo emulating normal mode Ⓛ, Ⓜ, Ⓗ)	Initial press is always Ⓛ; no access to Ⓜ or Ⓗ attacks outside of combos. No chains other than Ⓛ, Ⓜ, Ⓗ. Some command attacks missing
▲	Ⓨ	Special move	Cannot choose special move strength. Many special moves missing (some can be used with any direction + the special move button)
●	⇦	Hyper combo	Not all hyper combos are available
CANCEL	ATK	Special attack (press repeatedly to launch then super jump and air combo automatically)	—
L1	LB	P1 Partner 1	—
L2	LT	P1+P2 Partner 1 + Partner 2	—
R1	RB	P2 Partner 2	—
R2	RT	Basic attack + special move + hyper combo	—

Notations

Many icons are used throughout this guide to indicate button presses and techniques. **DIRECTIONS ASSUME A CHARACTER IS FACING RIGHT**. Guarding is always relative to the other team's point character—the enemy's assist behind your point character doesn't alter how you guard.

Icon	Description	May Also Be Called
→	Indicates forward. Hold → to walk forward, tap → → (or ATK ATK) to dash forward	—
↘	Diagonally down-forward	Offensive crouch
↓	Down. Hold ↓ to crouch. You must also tap ↓ before tapping any upward direction for a super jump	Crouch
↙	Diagonally down-back. Hold ↙ for crouching guard when low or mid attacks are incoming	Defensive crouch
←	Back. Hold ← to walk backward, or for standing guard against high and mid attacks. Tap ← ← (or ← + ATK ATK) to backdash.	—
↖	Up-back. Starts a backward jump. Hold any backward direction to guard while airborne	Defensive jump
↑	Up. Starts a jump. Tap ↓ first before any upward direction for a super jump. After jump-cancelable actions, like S launchers, simply hold any upward direction to jump or super jump (the result is move-dependent)	Jump
↗	Up-forward. Starts a forward jump	Offensive jump
L	Light attack, or L	1 or A, as a holdover from *Tatsunoko vs. Capcom All-Stars*; jab or short, as a holdover from *Street Fighter*
M	Medium attack, or M	2 or B, as a holdover from *Tatsunoko vs. Capcom All-Stars*; strong or forward, as a holdover from *Street Fighter*
H	Heavy attack, or H	3 or C, as a holdover from *Tatsunoko vs. Capcom All-Stars*; fierce or roundhouse, as a holdover from *Street Fighter*
ATK	Attack icon. Indicates any of L, M, or H may be used. Most hyper combos require ATK ATK (any two attack buttons together) following the right motion; dashes can also be performed with ATK ATK. Many moves allow ATK inputs to be mashed for more damage	Basic attacks, normal moves
S	Special attack, or S	Exchange, as a holdover from *MvC3's* pre-final development
P1	Partner 1. Partners can be called while standing or crouching, and during normal jumps, flight modes starting from normal jumps, and during basic attacks starting from any of those positions	Assist 1
P2	Partner 2. Partners cannot be called while guarding, nor while executing special moves or hyper combos, nor during super jumps or flight modes originating from super jumps	Assist 2
P1 or P2	Partner 1 *or* 2 (but not both!). This is used often in our notation of combos, as the right assist for a combo or tactic may be in a different slot depending on your overall team makeup and the flow of the match	—
P1+P2	Partner 1 + Partner 2, resulting in a crossover combination if the hyper meter has at least 1 bar	Team hyper combo, as a holdover from *MvC2*. Here, team hyper combo means what delayed hyper combo, or DHC, used to mean in *MvC2*
CANCEL ▶	Cancel icon. Indicates the action preceding CANCEL ▶ is interrupted with the following action, e.g., crouching M CANCEL ▶ ↓ ↘ → + H	Buffer
L))), M))), H))), ATK)))	Icon indicating a move that requires at least three rapid inputs to activate. Some of these moves are sustainable, given continued inputs	Pressing an input rapidly is often called "mashing"
X-Factor	X-Factor. Executed by pressing L + M + H + S all together while standing. The activation of X-Factor cancels almost any action, even guarding or most hyper combos, and X-Factor itself increases speed and power for a limited time. Can only be used once per match	—

Glossary of Terms

Don't worry, Nemesis. We'll help you understand.

The lexicon of fighting game terms has roots stretching as far back as 1991, the year that *Street Fighter II: The World Warrior* took the arcade world by storm and essentially created the competitive fighting game. The popularity of this then-fledgling genre was instrumental in ushering in more complex video games in general, and fighting games remain among the most complicated. A lot of information must be understood in order to be successful. If you're new to fighting games, or maybe just *Marvel Vs. Capcom* and the larger "*Vs.*" series, this section is designed to clear up any questions on jargon, terms and concepts as quickly as possible. For more in-depth discussion, check out the **System and Gameplay** chapter, or consult the sections for individual characters. Many terms included here match official in-game terms, but some non-standard definitions are included. These are appropriated from other games, or from the consensus of the competitive community, in the interests of thoroughness and clarity.

active frames	Related to **frame data.** Active frames are the period of time during which an attack can strike the opponent. After this period, a move enters its **recovery** phase.
advancing guard	Perform by pressing ATK ATK while **guarding** the opponent's attack. Creates separation from the opposing character, which is invaluable for breathing room. Can also be called **pushblock**.
advantage	The opportunity to act first, between two combatants acting as soon as possible after some sort of interaction. Converse — **disadvantage**. See **frame advantage/frame disadvantage**.
aerial rave	Synonym for **air combo**; a holdover from *MvC1*.
air	One of the three main states, or stances, of any character (with the other two being **standing** and **crouching**). "Air" generically refers to actions performed while your character is airborne, not grounded.
air combo	A **combo** performed in the air, after **launching** with Ⓢ **special attack**. During an air combo following a launcher, air Ⓢ (with no direction input) causes **flying screen** and a **hard knockdown**, while directional input + Ⓢ starts a **team aerial combo**, or **TAC**. Air combo can also be used to refer to a combo that simply occurs between two characters who are both in midair, but it is usually intended to refer to **launcher combos**.
air control	The ability to alter a character's airborne jump arc by holding ⇦ or ⇨. Not every character allows for the same degree of air control.
airdash	A dash performed in midair. Having extra mobility is never a bad thing. Some characters can airdash in any direction, but others can only airdash backward, forward, or both. Characters like Morrigan and Amaterasu have irregular airdashes, while characters like Firebrand and Rocket Raccoon have special moves that amount to airdashes. The ability to airdash opens the door for movement techniques like **triangle** and **square jumps**.
air exchange	A class of **special attacks** used in **launcher air combos** by pressing direction + Ⓢ. On contact, the next available ally will be tagged in in midair to continue the air combo. Combos using air exchange hits to swap heroes are called **team aerial combos**, or **TACs**. May also be called air tags.
air recovery	A **knockdown** that ends with the victim airborne results in air recovery. Air recovery occurs in place automatically with no input, but ⇨ or ⇦ can be held to choose a direction in which to recover. Characters who are recovering are invincible, and **crossover assists** can be called. After air recovery, a character is considered to be in a **normal jump** state.
air throw	**Throw** performed air-to-air. Accomplished with air ⇦ or ⇨ + Ⓗ. Some characters have midair **command throws**. Usually leads to a **hard knockdown** and thus an **OTG** opportunity.
anchor	The character who represents your last resort. Usually, this naturally ends up being the third character on a team (unless the third character is forced into the mix earlier by a three-stage **TAC/THC**, a **crossover attack,** or a **snap back**). In *UMvC3*, with the potential of many characters and the incredible boost of level 3 **X-Factor**, even a last-hero-standing cannot be counted out, so building around a solid anchor can make all the difference. Hope for the best… plan for the worst.
anti-air	Any attack or action used to stop a **jump-in** or otherwise counter an airborne adversary.
assist type	Types for **crossover assists** are organized by the first three letters of the Greek alphabet: alpha—α, beta—β, gamma—γ. Assist types are further described by their characteristics. Shot type means that the character fires a **projectile** or **beam**, while direct type means they attack using their body, for example.
backward	Action, movement, or directional input away from the opponent.
backward dash	A quick backward movement, accomplished with ⇦⇦ or ⇦ + ATK ATK. Usually just called **backdash**.
backward jump	A defensive leap away from a foe. Tap ⇖ to jump backward. Tap ⇩ first for a backward **super jump**.
basic attack	An attack performed with just Ⓛ, Ⓜ, or Ⓗ. Differs depending on whether **standing**, **crouching**, or airborne. Basic attacks can be **canceled** into one another with **chain combos**; they can also be canceled with just about anything else, including command attacks, special moves, hyper combos, and crossover combinations. Some characters can even cancel basic attacks into jumps, dashes, or airdashes, opening new avenues for offensive pressure and combo potential. Basic attacks can also be called **normal moves.**
battery	A character whose primary purpose on a team is to build up the **hyper combo gauge**.
beam	**Projectile**-like blast of energy that behaves a bit differently than standard projectiles. Beams usually hit many more times than projectiles, and they disappear instantly if the beamer is **counterhit** in the act of firing the beam. When beams clash with other beams or projectiles, they'll exchange **durability points** from the opposing beam or projectile every **frame** for a certain number of frames, until one or the other is depleted of durability points and thus destroyed.
block	Synonymous with **guard**.
block damage	Damage taken from an attack even if **guarded**. Most **special moves** and **hyper combos**, and even a few **basic attacks**, inflict block damage. Block damage is sometimes also called **chip damage**, or just chip. This damage is 30% that of an actual hit.
blockstun	Synonymous with **guardstun**.
bread and butter	The main tactic or **combo** that drives a particular character is often referred to as their bread and butter, or "BNB."
break away	A break away is a **throw** escape (sometimes called a "tech throw"). A throw can be broken by inputting ⇦ or ⇨ + Ⓗ within 7 **frames** of being thrown. Note that **command throws** cannot be escaped! After a break away, both characters end up next to each other in a neutral situation, with neither side having **frame advantage**.
buffering	Multiple definitions. Can refer to using the commands or motion for one action to also count for another; used frequently in **cancels** and **combos**. Buffering can also refer to entering the command for your next action while a current action is still underway. In both instances, you're taking advantage of a game engine feature that allows inputs to account for multiple actions.
bug	Unintended game feature. Synonymous with **glitch**. Sometimes enhances or detracts from gameplay.
cancel	Interrupting one action before its recovery period ends by starting another action. This is key to lots of advanced gameplay and **combos** in general. "Cancelable" is often used as a characteristic of important attacks; for example, a move that is "jump-cancelable" can be interrupted with a jump.
capture	**Hit state** caused by certain attacks, in which the victim is snared, unable to act or guard for several seconds, and thus vulnerable to a **combo**. Examples of moves that induce this state include Spider-Man's Web Ball, Magneto's throw, and Magneto's Hyper Gravitation.
chain combo	A string of **basic attacks,** canceled into one another. The ultimate rules are character-dependent and fall under a few archetypes, but generally, attacks can always be chained upward in strength, and they can almost always chain to Ⓢ **special attack**. Chain combos are accomplished simply by pressing the button for the next basic attack while the current one is in progress. Usually just called **chains**.
chip damage	Synonymous with **block damage**. Usually just called **chip**.
close range	Characters right next to each other, in range of each other's **launchers** and **throws**, are at close range. Close-range combat is usually focused on **mix-ups** between **overheads**, **low** attacks, and **throws**, each of which must be dealt with differently.

combo — A sequence of attacks that is guaranteed if the first attack is not **guarded**. Works because of **hitstun**.

command throw — A **special move throw** that requires a motion to accomplish. **Command throws** cannot be escaped, and they sometimes have other properties that distinguish them from normal throws, such as increased range, damage, or follow-up opportunities. Normal throws grab on the first frame, while many—but not all—command throws are slower to activate. Some command throws (like Thor's Mighty Hurricane H, or Wesker's Mustang Kick) also grab on the first frame.

corner — The side of a stage. Cornering a rival usually grants a huge advantage; cornered opponents can no longer move backward, are usually susceptible to larger combos, and have limited, predictable options for escaping the corner. **Advancing guard**, normally a cornerstone of defense, is also much less effective when cornered. Being cornered is generally bad, unless you are intentionally going for something like a backward **throw** into corner-only **combo**.

corner-only — Refers to a **combo** or tactic that only works with the foe pushed against into a corner.

counter — Counter can refer generally to any action that is used to **reverse** the opponent's intentions, or specifically to refer to **special moves** that deflect incoming attacks, such as Wesker's Tiger Uppercut or Amaterasu's Solar Flare.

counterhit — Striking the opponent while they try to attack results in a counterhit. Counterhits do not have an across-the-board damage increase in *UMvC3* as they do in most fighting games; rather, counterhits create 2 additional frames of **hitstun** and occasionally cause special **hit states** on a case-by-case basis, based on a given move.

crossover assist — Call for help from a partner by tapping (and immediately releasing!) P1 or P2. Every character has three assist types, which dictate the attack they perform when called. Assist type also dictates which **hyper combo** they perform during a **crossover combination**. Crossover assists are usually just called **assists.**

crossover attack — Accomplished by holding P1 or P2. If available, the requested partner tags in with a quick **overhead** attack before becoming the **point character**. You'll usually hear this referred to simply as a "**tag-out**" or "tag."

crossover combination — Performed by pressing P1+P2. Requires one bar of **hyper combo gauge** for every partner participating. Depending on how many characters remain, and how much hyper combo gauge is available, one to three characters come on screen simultaneously to perform **hyper combos** together. The hyper combo each character executes is dictated by their **crossover assist** type.

crossover counter — Accomplished by **blocking**, then inputting → + P1 or P2. One bar of **hyper combo gauge** is consumed, and the chosen ally tags in with a **crossover assist**.

cross-up — An attack that must be guarded in the opposite direction. **Cross-ups** are usually set up by **jumping** just over an opponent's head, so that you cross over at the last second. Cross-ups are particularly effective when used against a character forced to fall in after their teammate is knocked out, or against an adversary recovering from a **knockdown**.

crouching — A ducking position accomplished by holding any downward direction. A crouching character is a shorter target than a **standing** one, but he or she is susceptible to **overheads** and certain "pass-through" tricks that don't work on standing characters (for example, Hulk's forward **dash** actually passes *over* many crouching characters). When crouching basic attacks are required for combos, we'll notate "CROUCHING" or "CR." in our combo transcriptions.

crouching guard — A defensive stance that guards against incoming **low** and **mid** attacks. Vulnerable to **throws** and **overheads**.

crumple — Special hit effect caused by certain attacks, like C. Viper's EX Thunder Knuckle or her Focus Attack. The target slumps slowly to the floor and is vulnerable to continued punishment on the way down. Victims hit during a crumple are then **juggled** into aerial **hitstun**.

damage scaling — A safety feature innate to **combos** wherein successive hits deal a dwindling percentage of base damage. Prevents combos from being totally overpowering. Damage scaling is considerably lessened with **X-Factor** active, and it doesn't apply to **level 3 hyper combos** at all.

dash — A quick movement. Dashes are vital to covering distance quickly, regaining positioning after being pushed back with **advancing guard**, and keeping your competitor on their toes. Can be accomplished either by tapping ← ← or → →, or by pressing ← or → + ATK ATK.

delay — Delaying move execution either to **hit-confirm** before continuing a **chain combo**, or to bait the opponent into attempting to attack. Coaxing the opponent to stick out attacks when they don't really have time to do so is called a **frame trap**, and this is a prime way to cause **counterhits**. For example, if your opponent **guards** your opening of crouching L, crouching M, yet they do not use **advancing guard** to push you out, you can recognize this and wait longer than usual before chaining into H very late. Challengers who see the small gap and attempt to take the initiative back with a **poke** of their own end up eating the late chained H as a counterhit.

disadvantage — Refers to a situation in which your earliest possible action occurs after your opponent's. The opposite of **advantage**. See also **frame advantage/frame disadvantage**. Usually expressed as a number; for example, a disadvantage of -4 means your rival can act four frames before you.

dizzy — A **hit state** created by certain moves, such as Haggar's air ↑ + H, that **counterhits** a standing opponent, or She-Hulk's ↓ ↘ → + H **command throw**. The victim reels, stunned and unable to act until dizzy ends. Victims cannot **mash** inputs in order to shorten the dizzy period, and it is also unaffected by **hitstun decay**.

draw — The result if both teams have an equal percentage of life remaining when the timer runs out. Neither team wins.

durability points — A hidden value, different for each **projectile** or **beam**, which helps determine what happens when projectiles of equal **projectile priority** collide. When two **projectiles** or **beams** of equal projectile priority collide, they mutually deplete each other's durability points frame after frame (by a set amount per frame—the actual durability points value—which varies per projectile) until the loser projectile is destroyed and the victor projectile continues forward as normal. The winning projectile will have a depleted reserve of remaining durability points, which becomes relevant if another projectile is encountered.

empty jump — A **jump** performed without any attack. Usually followed by a fast **low** attack upon landing. Since most jumping attacks are **overheads** (meaning they must be **guarded** while standing), an opponent's defensive reaction to recognizing a jump should be to guard standing, which makes them susceptible to low attacks.

fireball — Generic term that applies to **projectiles** and **beams**.

flight — The power to fly is possessed by many members of the cast. Flight modes are both started and stopped with ↓ ↙ ← + S. The properties of flight are slightly different depending on whether flight was activated during a **super jump**, or from a **normal jump** or a **standing** position. Mobility is increased during flight, at the cost of not being able to **guard**. Flight ends naturally after roughly two seconds (character depending), after using air S, after receiving a hit, after particular moves, or after another input of ↓ ↙ ← + S. The **startup** of flight and its manual **cancelation** can both be used to cancel **basic attacks**.

flight cancel — **Canceling** a **basic attack** into **flight**, or using the manual cancelation of flight to cancel a basic attack. Some characters can use flight-canceling to prolong **air combos**, or to suddenly switch from ground attacks that must be guarded crouching to air attacks that must be guarded standing.

float — Ability possessed only by Rocket Raccoon and Storm. Hold ↑ in midair to slow their descent. As a consequence of this ability, these characters can execute extremely fast air **overhead** attacks just off the ground; see their chapters for details.

flying screen — The unique event that occurs after **launching** the opponent with S, then ending the subsequent **air combo** with air S. The character struck by the combo is hurled to the ground in a **hard knockdown**, and the screen shifts quickly as the aggressive character falls downward to catch up. Since flying screen leaves the victim in a hard knockdown, **OTG**s are possible.

footsies — Refers to positional game that usually takes place at the edge of each character's range, in which players try to **poke,** counter-**poke,** and score **knockdowns**. The "*Vs.*" games are unique among fighters in how much this takes place in the air as much as on the ground, thanks to the aerial mobility exhibited by so much of the cast, and because of the flexibility offered by team dynamics and **crossover assists**.

"for free" — A catch-all fighting game term that indicates an action is guaranteed and risk-free, e.g., "after guarding X move, you can land Y combo for free."

forward — Refers to directions toward your opponent. This guide assumes your character is on the left side of the screen (often called the 1P side), facing your adversary on the right, for forward is represented as →.

forward dash — An aggressive movement toward the opponent. Accomplished with → → or → + ATK ATK. Most characters can cancel their dash at any time with most actions, but a few characters can only cancel their dash after a certain point, and some characters can't cancel their dashes at all.

forward jump — Sometimes called offensive jump. Tap ↗ to jump forward. Tap ↓ first for a forward **super jump**.

frame	The game's unit of time measurement. 60 frames is equal to one second.
frame advantage / frame disadvantage	Most encounters in the game result in one character ready to act slightly before the other. Being able to act before your opponent is called frame advantage, or simply advantage. When your competitor can act first, you are at a frame disadvantage, or simply disadvantage. The concept of frame advantage or disadvantage can be expressed with a number—for example, +6 would indicate a frame advantage of +6, meaning you can act six frames before the opposition.
frame trap	Intentionally placing very small, educated gaps in an offense so the opponent has time to stick out an attack, just in time to be **counterhit**. You want these gaps to be very small, just a few frames; long enough for your rival's attack to **startup**, but not long enough for it to be **active**.

FRAME DATA: A BRIEF PRIMER

Throughout this guide, we refer specifically to frame data figures that illustrate the actual period of time taken up by attacks and actions. This information may seem daunting at first, especially if you're unfamiliar with frame data up until now, but as you play the game while referring to this guide, you'll quickly grasp the ideas involved and appreciate the usefulness of the data.

STARTUP frames always include the first **active** frame, for ease of reading to find possible links. For example, a character with a +8 advantage will be able to link any move with 8 or fewer startup frames, thus creating or perpetuating a combo.

ACTIVE FRAMES represent the number of frames in which an attack can actually contact the opponent.

RECOVERY FRAMES start 1 frame after the last active frame of non-projectile moves and end the frame before the character returns to a neutral state. Once recovery is complete, the character is free to perform another action.

PROJECTILE RECOVERY starts one frame after the last projectile released becomes active and ends the frame before the character can perform another action. For example, if Ryu's Hadoken has a 10 frame startup, recovery starts on frame 11.

FRAME ADVANTAGE is always shown assuming that the *first* active frame is the one to make contact with the opposing character. In effect, this makes the remaining active frames a part of recovery, as well. Timing attacks to strike during the end of active frames (a "meaty" attack) results in more frame advantage, but this is not always feasible.

Frame advantage usually (but not always!) differs depending on whether the opponent eats an attack or guards it. If your adversary guards properly and pushes your character away with advancing guard, the issue of frame advantage or disadvantage is usually rendered irrelevant due to the separation created, though some characters have methods to keep advantage even when pushed out with advancing guard.

SPECIFIC NOTATIONS USED IN HIT, DAMAGE, AND FRAME DATA.

Parentheses indicate inactive frames in the active frame column. For example, 5(3)5 would indicate that there are 5 active frames, then 3 inactive frames that cannot interact with the opposing character, and then 5 more active frames.

When the tilde (~) is used, it means that the values can be either one of the listed values or somewhere in between, depending on the move and situation. A common example is for moves that can be charged. Other examples include moves that can require repeated button presses to increase the number of hits by a limited amount, or moves that have some other mechanic that can cause any of the data to be variable within a fixed range of values.

Similarly, when / is used, it indicates values for different states of the same move. For example, charge moves that have multiple stages that increase the power in each stage, such as Zero's Hyper Zero Blaster. When a character is in a powered-up state that drastically alters a majority of a character's data, such as Wolverine's Berserker Charge, *italics* are used to indicate the altered data while that character is in the powered-up state.

**The contents of this strategy guide are based solely on the research of BradyGames*

glitch	Synonymous with **bug**.
ground bounce	**Hit state** in which a character is ricocheted forcibly off the ground. Victim is vulnerable to further punishment. Only one ground bounce is normally allowed per **combo,** though exceptions to this rule exist.
ground recovery	After **knockdowns at ground level**, the target springs back up to their feet instantly and automatically. By holding ⇦ or ⇨, this recovery can be directed. Victims are momentarily invincible while recovering from the floor, and **crossover assists** can be called.
guard	A critical defensive action that negates some or all of the damage sustained from incoming attacks. In the air, guarding is accomplished simply by holding any backward direction, relative the opponent's **point character**—⇙, ⇦, or ⇖, it doesn't matter. On the ground, you must choose to guard either standing by holding ⇦, or crouching by holding ⇙. **Standing guard** will block incoming **high** and **mid** attacks, while **crouching guard** will block incoming mid and **low** attacks. Guarding is not impenetrable—**unguardable** attacks and **throws** ignore guard. Also called **blocking.**
guard break	In previous *Vs.* series titles, speaking very generally, characters could only act once per normal jump. This meant that characters who attacked while normal jumping were then unable to guard until landing; more significantly, it meant that characters who guarded something in the air and then stopped guarding *could not guard again until landing.* It turned out to be very easy to create situations where this was exploitable—take every single time a partner character fell in to replace a knocked out point, for example. However, in *UMvC3*, normal jumps are not restricted in the same way, and guard breaks are no longer a threat.
guardstun	The period of time a character spends stuck in a defensive animation while successfully **guarding**. While engaged in guardstun, the only actions possible are **crossover counters**, **advancing guard**, and **X-Factor**. Characters stuck in guardstun cannot be **thrown** until the fifth frame after guardstun ends.
guessing game	Any situation where you cannot be sure what will happen, and you are forced to take a guess. It is beneficial to set these situations up in your favor, and avoid them yourself.
hard knockdown	An unrecoverable knockdown that creates an **OTG** opportunity by forcing the victim to lie still for a moment. OTG-capable attacks can strike foes who are lying prone. Hard knockdowns occur after most **throws**, some **special moves** and **hyper combos**, and after Ⓢ **launcher combos** that end with Ⓢ **special attack**. Victims of hard knockdowns eventually recover in place like after a **knockdown**, or they can opt to roll to one side or the other by holding ⇦ or ⇨.
high attack	An attack that strikes crouching opponents and must be **guarded** standing. Commonly called **overheads**. Most air attacks are overheads, along with some **command attacks**, some **special moves,** and Akuma—γ and C. Viper—γ **assists**.
hitbox	Hitboxes are hidden engine mechanics that dictate how interactions between characters play out. They're called hitboxes because of their rectangular appearance in most fighting games, but in *UMvC3*, they are actually "hitovals" rather than hitboxes. There are three types—attacking hitboxes, which dictate the area of an attack that can actually impact the opponent; defending hitboxes (sometimes called "hurtboxes"), which dictate the areas of a character's body that can actually be struck; and push hitboxes, which dictate how characters push against or pass around one another in physical space. Hitboxes are not visible to the player, and they are not necessarily tied directly to the animation of a given attack or the posture of a character.
hit confirmation	Visually confirming that an attack is successful before initiating follow-up attacks. Crucial to avoid putting yourself at too much risk when attacking and to avoid wasting opportunities. Also called **verification**.
hit state	Certain attacks cause types of hitstun that is different than the normal reeling animation. These states include **capture**, **crumple**, **hard knockdown, ground bounce, spinning knockdown, stagger**, and **wall bounce.**
hitstun	The period of time a character reels after being struck by an attack. No actions are possible during hitstun. Being struck again during hitstun creates or perpetuates a **combo**. Also called **hitreel**.
hitstun decay	Safety mechanism in place to help prevent the **infinites** that have (to a degree) characterized the *Vs.* series up to this point. As hits pile up in a combo, eventually a threshold is crossed where the length of time that **hitstun** lasts begins to degrade (character and situation depending, this usually begins after 6~12 hits, with less leeway for ground and **normal jump combos** than **super jump air combos**). This dwindling hitstun naturally makes combos harder as they go on, eventually making it impossible to continue. Works hand-in-hand with **damage scaling** to somewhat limit the potential of **combos**. Some **hit states**, such as **capture**-type moves or **dizzies**, are immune to hitstun decay.

hyper combo
The apex of a character's power is deployed during a hyper combo. Hyper combos require bars from the **hyper combo gauge**—most hyper combos cost one level, though some characters have more powerful **level 3 hyper combos**. Phoenix has a unique hyper combo that activates automatically if she is knocked out while possessing five bars. As holdovers from *Street Fighter*, sometimes also called supers or ultras. Most hyper combos deal direct damage to the target, though some hyper combos are intended to enhance abilities for a limited period of time or activate other effects. Team members can chain hyper combos one after another while also tagging out with **team hyper combos**, or perform hyper combos simultaneously through **crossover combinations.**

hyper combo gauge
Meter at the bottom of the screen that displays how many levels of energy you have available for use on powerful techniques. Built up primarily by interacting with your rival, with hits or blocked attacks. The hyper combo gauge powers **hyper combos**, **level 3 hyper combos**, **crossover counters**, **snap backs**, **team hyper combos**, **crossover combinations**, C. Viper's EX **special moves**, and Phoenix's Dark Phoenix Rising.

hyper meter
A common shorthand for **hyper combo gauge**. Also **super meter**.

infinite
A never-ending **combo**. **Hitstun decay** in *UMvC3* prevents most infinites in the traditional sense, though inevitably some infinites are still possible, whether because of experiencing increased speed during **X-Factor**, using **special moves** that ignore hitstun decay, or employing extremely exacting techniques.

instant overhead
No attack is truly "instant," but some air **basic attacks** performed just after leaving the ground for a **jump** do a good impression.

judgment
When a match ends by time-out, with neither side having won outright, the winner is determined by remaining **vitality**. This is called judgment.

juggle
Jargon referring to a character striking an opponent who is in the air, stuck in aerial **hitstun**. Used in very many, if not most, **combos**.

jump
See **normal jump** and **super jump**.

jump cancel / super jump cancel
Refers to canceling an attack with a jump of some sort. Everyone can super jump cancel (S) on hit (but not on block) simply by holding any upward direction. Some characters have basic attacks that can be canceled with a jump simply by tapping any upward direction.

jump-in
An air attack performed while jumping or flying at a grounded opponent. Useful for putting on pressure, beginning **combos**, and setting up **throws**.

kara-cancel
The Japanese term for **canceling** a move very quickly after activation, within a fraction of a second. Frequently, this is done before a move even perceptibly animates. Properties of the move **canceled** can sometimes be transferred to the follow-up move, such as forward movement.

knockdown
A knockdown is when a character is either knocked off their feet on the ground, or off-balance in the air. After being knocked down, a character automatically either **air recovers** or **ground recovers**, depending on proximity to the earth. The stricken character recovers in place automatically; they can also be directed to recover forward or backward by holding ⇨ or ⇦. Not every knockdown is created equal… while most moves cause knockdowns that lead to recovery after just a moment, some knockdowns last much longer before the character recovers. In these cases, the reeling character is still vulnerable. Once the recovery portion of a knockdown begins, reeling characters are then invincible until they are able to act (**assists** can be called during recovery, though). **Hard knockdowns** are an effect, distinct from knockdowns, in which the stricken character does not recover immediately and is instead susceptible to **OTG**-capable attacks while lying prone. Guessing games employed against recovering adversaries are called **okizeme**.

knockdown follow-up
Synonymous with **OTG**.

knockdown recovery
Hold ⇦ or ⇨ while being knocked down to use knockdown recovery to rise from the floor in the desired direction. Without directional input, characters recover in place. Characters are invincible during knockdown recovery, and **crossover assists** can be called.

launcher combo
A ground combo that leads to (S), which launches the opponent. From here, you can hold any upward direction to **super jump cancel** (S), then you can continue with an **air combo** (with "auto super jump" set to ON under operation mode options, you can simply hold down (S) to launch and then super jump automatically). Air combos that start with (S) **launcher** and end with air (S) cause **flying screen** and a **hard knockdown**. Air combos that start with (S) launcher then proceed to a directional input + (S) lead into **team aerial combos**.

level 3 hyper combo
A powerful **hyper combo** that requires three bars of **hyper meter** to use. A big reason that these hyper combos are so strong is that they are unaffected by **damage scaling,** so they make ideal **combo** enders. You can **THC** *to*, but not *from*, a lv.3 hyper combo, and lv.3 hyper combos cannot be **canceled** with **X-Factor**.

link
Perpetuating a **combo** using moves that have completely recovered rather than **canceling** or **chaining** moves. As an example, Spencer's ⇨ + (H) **overhead** can't be canceled into ⇩ ⇘ ⇨ + (S) for a combo, but the second move can be linked after the first by performing it as soon as possible.

long range
All the way across the screen, out of the immediate range of any opposing attacks. Combat at this distance is based on either **zoning** the opponent out or trying to find a way back in. The quickest threat from this distance is a fast **beam hyper combo** like Akuma's ⇩ ⇘ ⇨ + (ATK)(ATK), hold (H). The fastest way in from here is for **teleport**-capable characters to call an assist that gives them some cover, so they can teleport behind or on top of the opposing character.

low attack
An attack that must be guarded **crouching**. Many crouching attacks hit low, along with a handful of **crossover assists** (Deadpool—α, Felicia—α, Phoenix Wright—γ, She-Hulk—α, Wesker—β, X-23—β).

magic series
The combination of basic attacks a character can use to **chain combo**. Also called **chain combo archetype**.

mashing
Several definitions; can refer to pressing **basic attack** button inputs rapidly (as is required to execute certain **special moves**, or to maximize the damage of some **hyper combos**). Can also refer to unseasoned play that does not involve premeditation, reads, thinking, or **guarding**. Also slang to refer to repetitive tactics, e.g., "mashing out fireballs." (In that case, synonymous with **spamming**.)

meaty
An attack performed so that it hits very late during its **active** period. In effect, this shortens the move's **recovery** period since earlier active frames have already elapsed (the **frame advantage/disadvantage** shown in this guide assumes that a move strikes on the first possible active frame). Landing an attack "meaty" results in greater frame advantage, and thus, follow-ups/**combos** are not normally possible.

mid attack
An attack that can be **guarded** both **standing** and **crouching**. This is different from **low** and **high**/**overhead** attacks, which must be guarded either **crouching** or **standing**, respectively. Most standing **basic attacks** are mids. Mid attacks go mostly unspoken when talking about 2D fighting games, as they are a much more important concept in 3D fighting franchises like *Dead or Alive, Soul Calibur, Tekken,* and *Virtua Fighter.*

mid range
Refers to where characters stand on the edge of each others' **poke** range. Not as far apart as **long range**, but neither is it fighting in a phone booth at **close range**.

midscreen only
Refers to a tactic that only works midscreen and doesn't function properly in a corner. Usually, this is because of reasons of spacing, like an **assist** behaving differently in a combo in the corner rather than midscreen, or Captain America's shield having varied travel time depending on screen position.

mix-up
Presenting the opponent with a situation where they have to guess between oncoming threats. A good mix-up demands that options be defended against differently, such as deciding between **guarding low**, **high**, or breaking a **throw**.

negative edge
Button presses in *Street Fighter* register on release as well as the initial press, for purposes of **special moves**. **Negative edge** refers to using the release to activate special moves. Negative edge is *NOT* an engine feature in *UMvC3*.

normal attack
An attack performed by pressing (L), (M), or (H). The resulting normal attack varies depending on whether a character is crouching, standing, or airborne. Synonymous with **basic attack**.

normal jump
An upward leap into the air, accomplished by tapping any upward direction. Sometimes called normal jump to distinguish from **super jump**, the latter of which is accomplished by tapping ⇩ just before any upward direction. **Crossover assists** can be called during normal jumps, unlike super jumps. Some characters cannot perform the full air **chain combo** during a normal jump. **Flight** activated during a normal jump adopts the properties of a normal jump. Characters struck in midair will be in a normal jump state after **air recovery**.

OCV
Initials meaning **o**ne-**c**haracter **v**ictory. Refers to winning without swapping out the first point character. Typically quite embarrassing for the victim! The only fate worse is getting **perfected**…

option select — An advanced fighting game concept, critical to successfully employing and defending against **mix-ups** and **guessing games**. An **option select** is a combination of inputs or actions that can defeat or defend against multiple options at once, removing some of the guesswork from playing. An example would be always performing (H) **basic attacks** as ← or → + (H). Doing this means that you sometimes score **throws** or **break away** just because you happened to be doing the throw input also. Without being in position to throw, or without a throw incoming to break, you'll simply perform a heavy attack, which is what you wanted to do anyway—"accidentally" scoring a throw, or breaking one, is just icing on the cake.

OTG — Initials meaning **o**ff **t**he **g**round. While opponents are floored from a hard **knockdown**, they can only be hit by OTG-capable attacks. It is possible to OTG repeatedly in the same combo. Situations where **OTGs** are possible occur after any **hard knockdown**. While some characters are capable of OTG combos on their own (an extremely valuable ability), other characters require the services of OTG-capable **crossover assists**.

overhead — Synonymous with **high attack**. Most air attacks are overheads, as well as some **command attacks, special moves**, and **crossover assists** (Akuma—γ, C. Viper—γ, and Nova—β).

partner — An ally waiting in the wings, ready to assist. Call them in for a **crossover assist** by tapping (P1 or P2). Hold (P1 or P2) for a **crossover attack**, an **overhead** strike that also replaces the **point character** with the chosen partner. While **guarding** on the ground, tap → + (P1 or P2) for a **crossover counter**, which also swaps control to the partner. **Team aerial combos** also employ partners, as do **team hyper combos** and **crossover combinations**.

partner's vitality gauge — The **vitality gauges** for **partners** are displayed above and below the vitality gauge for the current **point character**. "ASSIST OK!!" is displayed on this gauge whenever a partner is ready to be called again, though assists can actually be summoned again a few frames before ASSIST OK!! appears.

perfect — A win achieved without sustaining *any* damage (or by sustaining **red damage**, but having it regenerate before the match ends). The chaotic team-based nature of *MvC3* makes perfects *exceedingly* rare compared to other fighting games—the vast majority of players will never score a perfect in *MvC* titles! As with **OCV**, it's pretty humiliating to be on the receiving end!

plink — A term that refers to pushing a button exactly one frame after another button. Originated from *Street Fighter IV*, where plinking allowed for much easier **linking**. In *UMvC3*, plinking has various uses, the most prominent of which is to **kara-cancel dashes** or **airdashes** into one another. Plinking is indicated by button presses separated by a tilde, as in (M)~(H) (in that example, press (H) immediately after (M)).

point character — The character currently being directly controlled on-screen. The directional inputs, **basic attack** buttons, and **special attack** button are used to issue commands to the point character. **Partners** wait in the background, ready to be summoned as **crossover assists** by tapping (P1 or P2).

poke — An attack that, because of speed, priority, or range, is relatively safe to use for pressuring or **zoning** your opponent.

primary assist — A character whose primary purpose on your team is to provide the main **crossover assist**.

primary user — A character whose primary purpose on your team is to expend **hyper meter**.

priority — The likelihood that one attack is going to beat another.

projectile — A ranged attack that is a distinct object, separate from the character who produces it. Many characters have **projectiles**, which are valuable for both **long range** tactics and **close range** pressure. **Beams** have similar function, but they work slightly differently. When projectiles clash with other projectiles or beams, the projectile that wins the exchange and continues forward is determined by hidden values called **projectile priority** and **durability points.**

projectile priority — When **projectiles** or **beams** (or attacks that can destroy projectiles, such as some of Dormammu's or Sentinel's **basic attacks**) strike each other, hidden properties dictate which projectile wins. The first check is **projectile priority.** Projectiles either have low, medium, or high priority against other projectiles or projectile-like attacks. Higher-priority projectiles destroy lower-priority projectiles outright. When equal-priority projectiles collide, **durability points** come into play, and the two projectiles chew away at each other's durability points until the lesser projectile is destroyed.

pushblock — Another term for **advancing guard**.

recovery — The period during which a move is still animating but is no longer **active**. Characters are vulnerable during this period. **Canceling** a move avoids this period altogether.

red damage — Damage that has been sustained but is not yet permanent. Half of initial damage on **point characters**, and all damage on **partner characters**, is inflicted as red damage. Partner characters recover red damage over time, and point characters recover red damage during **X-Factor** (and a few other methods, such as Dante's Devil Trigger **hyper combo**). A partner's red damage becomes permanent if they become the new point character via: a crossover attack (hold (P1 or P2)); the previous character is knocked out; the opponent forces them in with a **snap back** (↓ ↘ → + (P1 or P2)).

reset — Intentionally ending a **combo** in a confusing manner, such that another combo or **mix-up** can be started up. Often attempted in order to circumvent **damage scaling**, since starting a new combo resets the combo meter and thus the scaling.

recovery roll — After being **knocked down**, stricken characters rise in place automatically, but they can also be made to roll by holding either ← or →. Rolling to one side or the other keeps the waiting opponent on their toes, forcing them to act differently than if they could be sure of where you'd stand. Crafty competitors often have **mix-ups** ready to spring on rolls, however, so watch out. Also called **knockdown recovery**. Characters rolling to their feet are invulnerable, and **crossover assists** can be called while rolling! The aerial counterpart to recovery roll is **air recovery**.

reversal — Performing a move at the first possible frame following the end of **guardstun/hitstun/knockdown** states. Moves that are invincible on the first frame make the best reversals, as nothing beats them out. Reversal is also used as a generic term describing any situation in which you thwart (or reverse) the opposing player's intentions.

safe on guard/block — Refers to attacks that do not leave the user open to guaranteed punishment if **guarded**.

simple mode — A simplified control scheme that can be selected instead of normal mode. **Special moves** and **hyper combos** do not require motions and can instead be activated with the press of a button. Not all attacks and tactics are available in simple mode, however. This guide assumes the use of normal mode, but the tactics do translate to simple mode, as long as the recommended options are actually available. Simple mode is detailed more thoroughly earlier in this chapter.

spamming — Refers to repeated use of a given move or tactic, e.g., "spamming **triangle jumps**" or "spamming **fireballs**." Can be synonymous with **mashing**.

special attack — An attack performed with (S). Differs depending on whether your character is grounded or airborne. (S) can be chained into from almost any **basic attack**. Grounded (S) will **launch** the opponent. During a launcher combo, neutral air (S) causes a **hard knockdown**, while direction + (S) causes an **air exchange** hit that leads to a **team aerial combo.** The special attack button is also used for some **special moves**, such as ↓ ↙ ← + (S) **flight** and the (S) + (ATK) specials possessed by much of the cast.

special move — An attack or action performed with a sequence of commands, ending in an attack button press. Most **basic attacks** can be **canceled** into special moves, which forms the backbone of **combos**. Specials themselves can (mostly) be canceled into **hyper combos**.

spinning knockdown — **Knockdown** effect caused by certain moves. The duration of the spinning knockdown varies depending on the move used to cause it. After the spinning effect, the victim **air recovers** or **ground recovers**, depending on where they end up.

square jump — Refers to using lateral **airdashes** performed very low to the ground. Can also be called an instant airdash, squaredash, or box jump. Square jumps are used to strike the target with a fast **overhead** attack, to pass just over their heads with a **cross-up**, or to pass clean over the foe, hopefully after having called a **crossover assist** that lands on the side your character just vacated. Doing the same thing but using a diagonal airdash rather than a lateral one is called a **triangle jump**.

stagger — **Hit state** caused by certain attacks, like Amaterasu's Thunder Edge → → + (H) (hold). Victim staggers on their feet and is vulnerable to further punishment.

standing — A character idling, walking, or **dashing** on the ground is in a standing state. This is distinct from **crouching** or **jumping**. **Basic attacks** performed are the standing variants, and any **flight** mode initiated has the characteristics of a normal jump. Characters must **guard** while standing to block **overhead** attacks; **low** attacks crush standing guard. When standing basic attacks are required for **combos,** we will preface these attacks with "STANDING," or the abbreviation "ST." in our combo transcriptions.

standing guard — Accomplished by holding ←. **High** and **mid** attacks can be guarded standing. **Low** attacks will not be guarded, and **throws** cannot be guarded.

startup	The length of time a move takes to become **active** and capable of connecting, assuming it strikes on the first possible active **frame**. The fastest attacks are active in as few as 2 to 4 frames, and **throws** are active in 1 frame.
super armor	Property innate to certain moves, in which one incoming hit will be absorbed without interrupting the attack.
super jump	Performed by quickly tapping down, then any upward direction within 9 frames. Super jumps go much higher and travel farther than normal jumps. **Chain combos** and **command attack** use are unrestricted during super jumps. **Crossover assists** cannot be called during a super jump, however. **Flight** activated during a super jump inherits the properties of a super jump.
tag-in	On the ground: see **crossover attack.** In the air: see **air exchange** and **team aerial combos.** Using **hyper combos**: see **team hyper combos**. Using **guard**: see **crossover counter.**
taunt	Activated by pressing Select or Back, this is a humorous action designed to rile your opponent. No other effect. Cannot be **canceled** with other actions, except **X-Factor** activation.
team aerial combo (TAC)	An **air combo** in which the next partner is swapped in to continue the aerial assault. Accomplished by **chaining** into ⇧ or ⇩ or ⇦ or ⇨ + Ⓢ after **launching** an opponent. These **special attacks** are often called **air exchange** or **air tags.** ⇩ + Ⓢ builds an entire bar of **hyper meter**, while ⇨ or ⇦ + Ⓢ ERASES one of your *opponent's* hyper meter bars! ⇧ + Ⓢ deals slightly more damage and puts your competitor into better **juggle** position (but has no unusual hyper meter consequence). For each character who tags in during a **TAC**, normal **hitstun decay** is ignored, allowing extended **air combos** that are otherwise impossible.
team aerial counter	**Team aerial combo** (TAC) attempts can be thwarted by pressing the same command your opponent used to execute the combo within 15 frames: either ⇧ + Ⓢ, ⇩ + Ⓢ, or ⇦ or ⇨ + Ⓢ (the game does not differentiate between ⇦ or ⇨ + Ⓢ in air combos). You are only allowed one escape "guess" per TAC break window, and inputting neutral Ⓢ (which itself does not count as a potential team aerial counter command) prevents a correct direction + Ⓢ input afterward! The different **air exchange** hits are actually color-coded to aid the potential escapee: upward is red, sideways is green, and downward is blue.
team hyper combo (THC)	While a **hyper combo** is in progress, input a hyper combo command for the next character in the team order, and that character will tag in with that hyper combo. This is called a team hyper combo. You can continue to team hyper combo until you either run out of **hyper meter** or until all three characters have participated. Team hyper combos are invaluable for extending **combos** and for tagging out ailing characters safely.
tech	Generic term referring to an escape action, such as "tech throws" or "tech rolls."
teleport	A warping movement power possessed by many characters. Teleports are vital for offense and cross-ups.
throw	An **unguardable** attack performed with ⇨ or ⇦ + Ⓗ at close range. Throws are possible both on the ground and airborne, and they are active in 1 frame. Almost all throws result in a hard **knockdown** that the opponent can't quickly recover from, which often allows an **OTG** follow-up depending on character and position. Normal throws can be escaped if the victim inputs ⇨ or ⇦ + Ⓗ within 7 frames of the start of the throw. **Special move** throws, often called **command throws**, are executed with directional sequences followed by a button press, and these are not escapable.
tick	A quick move used to incite a particular reaction. For example, most crouching **light attacks** give an opponent the expectation that more crouching attacks are coming, inducing them to hold down-back passively. This presents an ideal opening to step forward and **throw**. Unsurprisingly, this common tactic is called a "**tick-throw**." Once your adversary is conditioned to expect a throw after the tick, you can then chain into **delayed** attacks after the tick to potentially **counterhit** their throw **reversal** attempt—this kind of layered baiting, with measured, intentional gaps, is called a **frame trap**.
tiger knee	Originated with *SFII*'s Sagat, whose Tiger Knee **special move** required a command of ⇩ ⇘ ⇨ ⇗ + kick. In *UMvC3*, tiger knee motions are usually used to combine the commands for a **jump** with a special move, so the special is performed at low altitude just after a character leaves the ground for a jump.
timer	The clock ticking away remaining match time at the top-center of the screen. When this hits 0, the team with the most vitality remaining is declared the winner. If both teams have the same exact amount of life left (based on percentage of **vitality gauges** still full), the match is declared a **draw**. (In *MvC* games, a draw is even more rare than a **perfect**!)
triangle jump	Refers to using diagonal **airdashes** immediately after a jump to return to the ground quickly, potentially with a **high**-hitting air attack. Fast mix-ups between triangle jump air hits and **low** attacks are very hard to **guard** consistently. Using lateral airdashes to achieve the same effect is called **square jumping**.
unfly	Generically, simply refers to ceasing **flight** by re-inputting the command ⇩ ⇗ ⇦ + Ⓢ. Unfly can also refer to using the manual cancelation of Flight to **cancel** the **recovery** of an air **basic attack**. Unfly allows for extended **air combos** after flight expires. Characters can also unfly and **guard** in midair while falling to the ground to block incoming attacks.
unguardable	An attack that cannot be guarded. **Throws** are unguardable, as are some moves like C. Viper's fully charged Focus Attack. Also called **unblockable.** Situations that are unblockable, or close enough to be indistinguishable, can also be created by striking simultaneously with **overhead** attacks along with a **low**-hitting **crossover assist**, or vice-versa (Deadpool—α, Felicia—α, Phoenix Wright—γ, She-Hulk—α, Wesker—β, and X-23—β hit low; Akuma—γ, C. Viper—γ, and Nova—β are overheads).
unsafe on guard	Refers to attacks that are risky when blocked because an alert opponent is assured an opportunity to punish you.
verification	Refers to insuring that an action is successful before performed desired follow-ups. Success is dependent of the speed of the attacks and the reaction time of the player. Also called **hit confirmation**. Verification is a vital skill to avoid needlessly using resources or putting yourself at unnecessary risk.
vitality gauge	The meter at the top of the screen that displays remaining health. When this is depleted, a character is knocked out. **Red damage** is not permanent, and it can be recovered.
wakeup	This refers to the frequent situation where one character is standing and another is floored, waiting to rise with **ground recovery**. The standing character has a large advantage here, since mix-ups can be staged against a floored foe as they recover from the ground. The Japanese term for mix-ups staged against a rising foe is **okizeme**.
wall bounce	Hit effect in which a character is ricocheted forcibly off the wall. Victim is vulnerable to further punishment. Only one wall bounce is allowed per **combo**.
wavedash	**Canceling** one **dash** into another to cover space more quickly. Required for certain combos and more or less just required for movement in high-level play, which is characterized among other things for its speed. Wavedashing is accomplished by interrupting a dash by tapping down to **crouch**, then dashing again. It's faster to use command dashes (ATK ATK) than double taps for this (alternating ATK ATK, ⇩, ATK ATK is by nature faster than ⇨⇨, ⇩, ⇨⇨; it's basically three inputs versus five).
whiff	Missed attacks, whether intentional or not.
X-Factor	System new to the *MvC3* series in which, once per match, a team can unleash its true potential for a brief period. Activated with Ⓛ + Ⓜ + Ⓗ + Ⓢ. Speed and damage output are increased, and **red damage** recovers more quickly. The effect is more substantial with fewer characters still standing. New to *UMvC3*, X-Factor can be activated at *any time*, whether grounded or airborne, except during **hitstun**, **throws**, or **lv.3 hyper combos**.
X-Factor cancel	**X-Factor** can cancel almost any action, at almost any time. X-Factor can therefore be used to create otherwise-impossible **combos** and setups. **Canceling** other actions with X-Factor is indicated in our combo transcriptions with .
zoning	Refers to keeping your opponent in a particular range that is beneficial to your characters and gameplan, while being detrimental to theirs.

Gonna Take You For A Ride: The History of *Marvel vs. Capcom* (Updated!)

1994: *X-MEN: CHILDREN OF THE ATOM*

1995: *MARVEL SUPER HEROES*

1996: *X-MEN VS. STREET FIGHTER*

1997: *MARVEL SUPER HEROES VS. STREET FIGHTER*

1998: *MARVEL VS. CAPCOM: CLASH OF SUPER HEROES*

2000: *MARVEL VS. CAPCOM 2: NEW AGE OF HEROES*

FEBRUARY 15TH, 2011: *MARVEL VS. CAPCOM 3: FATE OF TWO WORLDS*

NOW: *ULTIMATE MARVEL VS. CAPCOM 3*

Video games haven't been around for very long. Their tenure as an accepted and important part of modern culture is even shorter. Their utility as a forum for recognized, skilled competition is briefer still. This is easy to take for granted now in the days of photo-realistic blockbuster games that reproduce settings real and imagined to the finest detail, which foster and support international competitive scenes and tournaments, while sometimes out-grossing Hollywood films. Where games started as rudimentary text interfaces, or a paddle wheel, or a directional control and a single button, we now have controls sometimes approaching the nuance of a musical instrument.

Of course, things didn't start out that way. During its infancy, gaming was regarded as a single-player diversion for children. Controls were simple, by and large. Direct competition between players was non-existent outside of competing for high scores, which themselves were attained mostly through memorization, pattern recognition, and sheer endurance. Dallas-based id had not yet essentially created both online competitive play and catapulted the fledgling FPS genre with *DOOM*. Midway's *NBA Jam* had not yet saturated every place it would fit into. Blizzard's monster franchises *Diablo* and *Starcraft* were years away, *World of Warcraft* further still. Arcades existed to inhale quarters with punishing games like *Double Dragon*, *Final Fight*, *Shinobi*, and *TMNT*.

But then, in 1991, Capcom released *Street Fighter II: The World Warrior*. The "*II*" in the title may as well be apocryphal; *Street Fighter* the first bears little resemblance to its revolutionary sequel. Most games used a button or three (the original *Street Fighter* famously had arcade cabinets with only one large pressure-sensitive button, the primary purpose of which seemed to be to break). This game used *six*, all of which had many different contextual results (jumping, standing, crouching). Does that seem quaint now? It wasn't, then. In action games at the time, player-controlled characters had an arsenal of actions numbering in the single-digits. In *Street Fighter II*, every single character had dozens of moves, and there were a dozen distinct characters. With a few exceptions, most characters were decidedly different, creating an interlocking web made of dozens of different matchups, each with their own ins and outs.

SFII was, simply put, the quickest and most complex video game yet seen for head-to-head competition, requiring for success the highest dexterity, along with the most practice and foreknowledge. A new genre was born, and the purpose of arcades (and gas stations, and convenience stores, and pizza places, and bus stops, and bowling alleys) changed entirely. If you wanted to play Pop-A-Shot, ski-ball, a skill crane, or pinball, you'd have to shoulder past dozens of players crowded around *SFII* cabinets, players clutching their dot-matrix-printed move sheets or their now-ancient issues of *GamePro* filled with movelists and ProTips; players unbridled in their enthusiasm to see who was the best.

Arcade machines then still represented the cutting edge; not until the Sega Dreamcast and Sony PlayStation 2 did consoles start to catch up to the experience of the best arcade titles, and not until the Xbox 360 did the online experience begin to catch up to the social feel of the arcade. For a time, arcades were not the fringe establishment they are now: absent in most places, usually corporate or gimmick-driven where they remain. Instead, arcades were *the* definitive gaming experience. Only a few bastions remain in North America to remind us of what once was...Game Galaxy in Nashville, or Arcade UFO in Austin, or Family Fun Arcade in Los Angeles, to name a few that hold out against the proverbial dying of the light.

But, while traditional arcades are largely a relic today, those players are still around, still huddled, still boisterous in their passion and razor-sharp in their skill. The difference is that now you'll find them online, or at tournaments, or at your cousin's house, or you'll invite them over, or meet up with them at websites like shoryuken.com. And *SFII* is now not the only game in town (though, amazingly, it's still around—see the recent success *Super Street Fighter II: HD Remix!*). Competitors from other developers sprang up more or less immediately, and *SFII* itself directly spawned dozens more fighting games from Capcom. The core of most of these games is not so different—controls are generally still rooted in the fundamentals laid down by *SFII*—but the important aspects of gameplay in each title and series differ greatly.

Almost all of these titles, even today, feature one-on-one battles with mechanics and pacing that resemble *SFII*. But in 1994, Capcom went for something a little looser, less rigid and disciplined than the *SFII* series. Drawing on the massive treasure trove of beloved Marvel Comics creations, Capcom released ***X-Men: Children of the Atom*** (usually referred to in fighting game circles as, simply, ***COTA***). This was the first game in a string of beefed-up fighters that kept the bedrock concepts of *SFII*, but, in the details, spun off in a new direction entirely. This was the beginning of what is now known as the "***Vs.***" series, the fighting game taxonomy that leads directly to ***Marvel vs. Capcom 3: Fate of Two Worlds***. Foreshadowing the fully fledged crossover games that later defined the *Vs.* series, Capcom's Akuma was even present as a secret character!

X-Men: Children of the Atom *Roster*

- Akuma (secret character)
- Colossus
- Cyclops
- Iceman
- Juggernaut (sub-boss)
- Magneto (boss)
- Omega Red
- Psylocke
- Sentinel
- Silver Samurai
- Spiral
- Storm
- Wolverine

The next year, in 1995, COTA would get an indirect sequel in the form of ***Marvel Super Heroes*** (or ***MSH***). New heroes and villains appeared, and gameplay was spiced up further with the introduction of Infinity Gems, Thanos-related power-ups that could be picked up to enhance the power of your character.

Marvel Super Heroes *Roster*

Blackheart
Captain America
Doctor Doom (sub-boss)
Hulk
Iron Man
Juggernaut
Magneto
Psylocke
Shuma-Gorath
Spider-Man
Thanos (boss)
Wolverine

Another year brought another update, and ***X-Men vs. Street Fighter*** released in 1996. Now, things were heating up! Fulfilling the potential hinted at with secret Akuma in *COTA*, *X-Men vs. Street Fighter* (predictably usually just called ***XvSF***) was a full crossover battle between Capcom and Marvel characters! Not only was this the first crossover fighting game, but it was also the first game to forgo one-on-one fighting for team combat. As the first team-based fighter, it also blazed a trail in the sense that characters fought together, rather than simply one after the other (as is the case in most team-based fighting games since). Battles were fast and fluid, and deep team dynamics emerged—with two characters to your team, you could have some match-ups that were bad for one hero, but good for the other; you could have one character that you preferred to use hyper combo gauge with, while the other primarily built it up; and so on. *XvSF* was very popular, but this popularity underscored the disparity that then existed between arcades and consoles—the eventual PlayStation 1 version was stripped down, removing the tag battle feature that made *XvSF* stand out. Home consoles at the time simply lacked the memory to handle all the action and characters! However, the Japanese release of the Sega Saturn version actually came with a RAM cartridge that upped the system's capabilities specifically to run *XvSF* at full potential. Fighting games would not just increase the complexity of gaming—they pushed the envelope for hardware requirements, as well!

X-Men vs. Street Fighter *Roster*

Marvel	Capcom
Apocalypse (boss)	Akuma
Cyclops	Cammy
Gambit	Charlie
Juggernaut	Chun-Li
Magneto	Dhalsim
Rogue	Ken
Sabretooth	M. Bison
Storm	Ryu
Wolverine	Zangief

XvSF earned the first direct sequel in the *Vs.* series with 1997's ***Marvel Super Heroes vs. Street Fighter***. This title retained the tag-team fighting of its progenitor, while adding the ability to directly call your off-screen teammate to briefly assist in battle—apart from the initial tag-team concept in the first place, this would become *the* defining trait of the then-forthcoming *MvC* series. Like *XvSF*, ***MSHvSF*** would require the services of the Sega Saturn's RAM cart for a faithful home version, and even then only in Japan, as the PlayStation 1 port again excised features. Happily, with the release of the Sega Dreamcast around the corner, this kind of feature-stripping to squeeze arcade games onto home ports was close to being a thing of the past.

Marvel Super Heroes vs. Street Fighter *Roster*

The full promise and breadth of ideas attempted in *COTA*, *MSH*, *XvSF*, and *MSHvSF* were then synthesized into the first of a new series that would become a sensation. ***Marvel vs. Capcom: Clash of Super Heroes*** released in early 1998, with a Dreamcast port following around a year later that was, for the first time, virtually indistinguishable from the arcade version. ***MvC1*** retained the tag combat of *XvSF* and *MSHvSF*, while casting the Capcom net wider to include characters from throughout Capcom's franchises rather than just *Street Fighter*. Assists, first present in *MSHvSF*, returned, though tweaked—rather than use the off-screen partner as an assist, an assist-only helper character was selected along with the two actual point characters for a team. This helper was selected from a random reel, though secret codes allowed precise selection of a desired assist. Assists could only be used a limited number of times per match; a limitation that did not apply to MSHvSF or subsequent titles in the *MvC* series. *MvC1* also introduced Duo Attacks—tremendous displays of power in which both characters on a team came on screen simultaneously, both controlled by the player at once, both capable of infinite hyper combos for the duration of the Duo Attack!

Marvel	Capcom
Apocalypse (sub-boss)	Akuma
Blackheart (secret version: Mephisto)	Chun-Li
Captain America (secret version: U.S. Agent)	Dan
Cyclops	Dhalsim
Hulk	Ken
Omega Red	M. Bison
Shuma-Gorath	Ryu
Spider-Man (secret version: Armored Spider-Man)	Sakura (secret version: Evil Sakura)
Wolverine	Shadow (Evil Charlie)
	Zangief (secret version: Mecha-Zangief)
	Cyber-Akuma (boss)

Marvel vs. Capcom: Clash of Super Heroes *Roster*

Marvel Point Characters	Marvel Assist Characters (not available as point characters)	Capcom Point Characters	Capcom Assist Characters (not available as point characters)
Captain America	Colossus	Captain Commando	Anita
Gambit	Cyclops	Chun-Li	Arthur
Gold War Machine (secret character)	Iceman	Jin	Devilotte
Hulk	Jubilee	Lilith (secret character)	Lou & Siva
Onslaught (boss)	Juggernaut	Mega Man	Michelle Heart
Orange Hulk (secret character)	Magneto	Morrigan	Pure & Fur
Red Venom (secret character)	Psylocke	Roll (secret character)	Saki Omokane
Spider-Man	Rogue	Ryu	Shadow
Venom	Sentinel	Shadow Lady (secret character)	Ton Pooh
War Machine	Storm	Strider Hiryu	Unknown Soldier
Wolverine	Thor	Zangief	
	U.S. Agent		

For most gamers, the Sega Dreamcast represents a quirky footnote in console gaming history. In both chronology and horsepower, it was sandwiched ahead of the original PlayStation, N64, and Sega's own Saturn, and behind the PlayStation 2. The PlayStation 2 did the Dreamcast no favors by releasing not very long into the Dreamcast's abbreviated lifecycle. By the time the original Xbox rose to compete with the PlayStation 2, the Dreamcast was already becoming a memory—to be sure, the home of some truly memorable titles like *Seaman* and *Shenmue*, but ultimately proof of the growing pains of nascent high-fidelity console gaming.

For fighting game enthusiasts, though, the Dreamcast was the most important console yet produced; it might still be. Finally, compromises did not have to be made when bringing arcade fighting games into the living room, and a veritable deluge of Capcom titles followed, to say nothing of offerings from other developers. From Capcom alone, the Dreamcast hosted *MvC1, Street Fighter Alpha 3,* every version of *Street Fighter III* (*New Generation, 2nd Impact,* and *3rd Strike*), *Power Stone* and *Power Stone 2, Plasma Sword, Rival Schools: Project Justice*, and both *Capcom vs. SNK: Millennium Fight 2000* and *Capcom vs. SNK 2: Mark of the Millennium.* To this day, some gamers maintain working Dreamcast consoles to play the best versions of some fighting titles. Nowhere else is this more the case than with ***Marvel vs. Capcom 2: New Age of Heroes*** (or, simply, ***MvC2***). This sequel to *MvC1* released in 2000 with an *enormous* roster and greatly expanded mechanics over its predecessors. Teams were three characters instead of two; the hyper meter topped out at five bars; the entire team could attack at once with what were then called team hyper combos (in *MvC3*, this has become the crossover combination); assist calls were potentially limitless and performed directly by the point character's teammates. In general, the team dynamics introduced in earlier *Vs.* titles were emphasized even further, while the over-the-top nature of the combat itself was highlighted, as well.

INTRODUCTION

Marvel vs. Capcom 2: New Age of Heroes *Roster*

Somewhat simultaneously, several things happened. The internet came truly into form in the late 1990s and early 'aughts, leaving behind the detritus of bulletin board systems, usenet groups, and IRC channels for fully formed websites and forums. Two brothers from California, fans of fighting games, started the seminal website shoryuken.com, the natural and more concrete extension of usenet's alt. games.SFII, where serious fighters gathered for mutual discussion, debate, and derision. The rise of SRK (the shorthand by which readers refer to shoryuken.com) as a meeting place made *MvC2* the first, and most important, competitive fighting game of the online era. Never before had detailed information been available so readily, and never before had match videos been so easily attainable. The eventual inception of YouTube only enhanced this synergy. Fighting games had flagged somewhat in the face of burgeoning online play, drifting arcade revenue, and home consoles that finally matched the capabilities of dedicated arcade boards. *Marvel vs. Capcom 2* re-energized the scene, while elevating the general level of play and the number of skilled players to previously unseen heights.

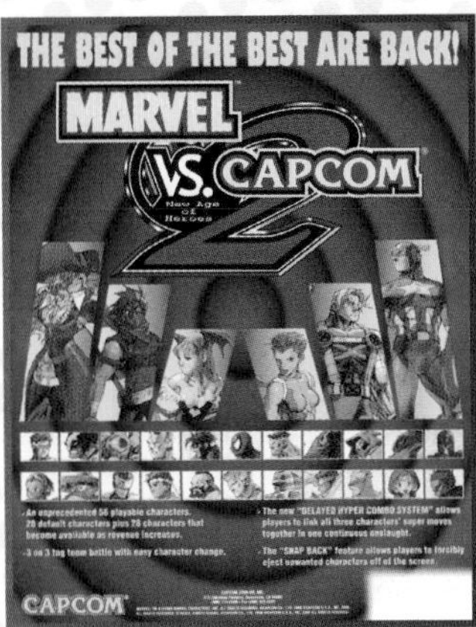

Marvel

- Blackheart
- Cable
- Captain America
- Colossus
- Cyclops
- Doctor Doom
- Gambit
- Hulk
- Iceman
- Iron Man
- Juggernaut
- Magneto
- Marrow
- Omega Red
- Psylocke
- Rogue
- Sabretooth
- Sentinel
- Shuma-Gorath
- Silver Samurai
- Spider-Man
- Spiral
- Storm
- Thanos
- Venom
- War Machine
- Wolverine (Adamantium claws)
- Wolverine (Bone claws)

Capcom

- Abyss (boss)
- Akuma
- Amingo
- Anakaris
- B.B. Hood
- Cammy
- Captain Commando
- Charlie
- Chun-Li
- Dan
- Dhalsim
- Felicia
- Guile
- Hayato
- Jill Valentine
- Jin
- Ken
- M. Bison
- Mega Man
- Morrigan
- Roll
- Ruby Heart
- Ryu
- Sakura
- Servbot
- SonSon
- Strider Hiryu
- Tron Bonne
- Zangief

But it was not just this synergy that propelled *MvC2* to a decade of competitive and commercial success. The game is astounding in its own right. Unrestrained in its action, polarizing in its immense and heavily stratified roster, seemingly accessible on the surface but with a gameplay rabbit hole that goes down further than the Challenger Deep, everyone knew about *Marvel vs. Capcom 2*. It became the reason to own a Dreamcast long after the Dreamcast presses stopped, whether you were a casual gamer who wanted to mash out fun with your friends or a hardcore tournament "head" looking to perfect your Magneto resets and Sentinel fast flies at home. Upon its triumphant re-release on Xbox Live Arcade and PlayStation Network in 2009, *MvC2* immediately shot up the charts as one of the most-bought and most-played titles... *10 years after its initial release*, and in direct competition with ridiculously successful modern online franchises like *Halo* and *Call of Duty*.

While *Street Fighter II* has its following and its tournament players to this day, and now *Street Fighter IV* has performed its own trick of revitalizing the scene yet again, there is something of a public relations problem with the keystone fighting game franchise. It can be difficult or even impossible for a casual fan to tell the difference between two pros engaging in an intense, measured zoning war, versus just two players who happen to know how to throw fireballs at each other. Apart from the happy happenstance of the release of *MvC2*, the rise of the internet, and the start of shoryuken.com, the mark of the *Vs.* franchise, *Marvel vs. Capcom 2* in particular, and now *Marvel vs. Capcom 3*, is that there is nothing subtle about it. It is blatantly obvious, and in the most excessive, wonderful, outrageous way possible, when someone knows what they are doing. Using the most open movement and combo systems of any fighting game to date, some players truly reach for the heights of artistry with their play, elevating as far above and beyond average players as professional musicians and athletes do beyond the amateur hobbyist. *Marvel vs. Capcom* is not Kurt Rambis doing the small things to win basketball games...it is Michael Jordan issuing a clarion call, making the gulf obvious beyond a shadow of a doubt, and making it seem effortless in the process.

That is the ultimate legacy of *Marvel vs. Capcom*—combat unmatched in excess, unquestionable in depth, unrivaled in breadth. If *Street Fighter 1* was klondike, and *Street Fighter II* is poker (a comparison we are hardly the first to make; incidentally, many tournament SF players make great cardslingers!), *Marvel vs. Capcom* is a wild variant—let's say pineapple with 4s, 8s, and queens wild.

You didn't think it could happen, we didn't think it could happen, but here we are. A decade later, beyond the death of arcades and the predominance of online play, after three console generations and legal wrangling unimaginable between juggernaut intellectual properties, no one is happier than your humble authors to say:

WELCOME TO *MARVEL VS. CAPCOM 3*!

EVOLUTION OF THE METAGAME: THE ROAD TO ULTIMATE MARVEL VS. CAPCOM 3

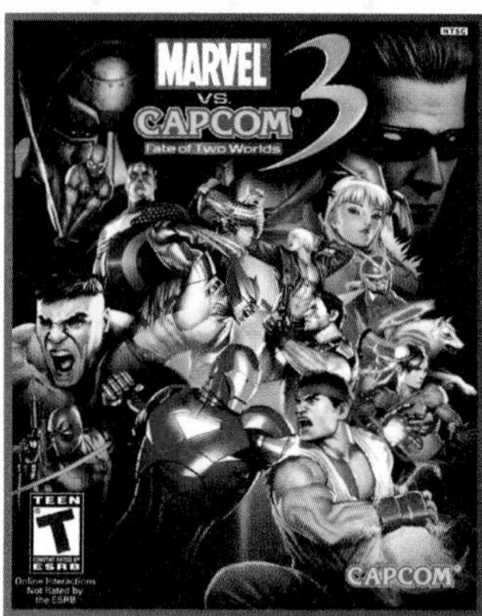

A game is constituted of a set of rules designed to determine the outcome of a friendly competition. In a game like chess, the rules of the game, and therefore the game itself, is constituted of things like the way the pieces are allowed to move, the ways the pieces are allowed to interact with each other, and the requirements for the game to end. That's not any different than in *UMvC3*: the outcome is determined, one way or another, by the vitality gauges and the timer, and players interact with each other through the capabilities of the characters.

So, in chess, pawns typically move in a straight line but capture diagonally and usually not more than one square at a time (with exceptions), while bishops can move only diagonally but with no restriction on the number of spaces at a time; in *UMvC3*, Frank West can send zombies after his opponent and roll through them to generate confusion, while Doctor Strange can harness magic projectile attacks, flight, and teleportation. And in chess, a king may be checkmated, or a player may resign, or the situation may devolve such that no side can really win, and a stalemate is achieved. In *UMvC3*, one side can have the vitality drained from all three heroes and lose, or they can have a lower percentage of overall vitality remaining than the opposing team when time expires; in rare cases, time will expire and both sides will have the exact same percentage of remaining vitality, and a draw occurs.

The metagame is the deeper game that springs into being because players produce unpredictable results inside the ecosystem of hard rules. If there's a weak point in the wall of the game's design, people will find a way to break it down and produce unintended consequences. Knowing the rules of the game and the capabilities of the pieces or characters is no longer enough. You have to know what your opponent knows. Ideally, you know more than he or she does.

In chess, ideas and knowledge have evolved for hundreds of years and have become consensus truisms like: control the center of the board; array your pieces in complementary arrangements (such as pawns in triangle formations); playing as the white side is better (the only asymmetrical design feature in chess being, after all, that the white side goes first).

TESTING GROUNDS

In *MvC3*, ideas and knowledge have evolved throughout the game's development, during which it was shown to fans in advance of release numerous times, in varying states of completion. Consensus knowledge began to develop in earnest upon the game's release, of course, which precipitated a robust competitive scene. There were already tournaments pre-release at Capcom Fight Club events and gaming conventions like PAX, and release day tournaments at some GameStop retail locations. This continued on with events like Final Round in Atlanta, tournaments at The Box Arena in San Diego, the NorCal and SoCal Regionals, and ReveLAtions in L.A., among many others, such as the Wednesday Night Fights streaming tournament series. Ideas about the way *MvC3* plays out had fresh cement poured on their foundation at Evo 2011, the biggest tournament of the year.

These events serve as touchstones in the evolution of *MvC3*'s metagame. Early tournaments featured heavy use of Sentinel, thus prompting strong, innovative players like Justin Wong to create a plethora of anti-Sentinel strategies, ultimately weakening Sentinel's viability in future competitions. Local scenes across the country spawned countless Wolverine players spamming dive kicks; the proliferation of such a consistent and easy offensive tactic led to popularizing of dive kick punishment through canceling block with X-Factor, allowing for instant retaliation. The real reason Wolverine was so good had not been truly popularized yet! At Final Round in Atlanta, Peter "Combofiend" Rosas demonstrated the importance of a strong anchor that meshes well with level 3 X-Factor (in this case, Spencer, in many cases coming back all by his lonesome in some of *MvC3*'s most exciting matches). This caused scores of players to re-evaluate their own team configurations. Needing to have a very powerful back pocket character who was ready to spend lv.3 X-Factor and a ton of meter became a given, and fighters like Wesker, Taskmaster, Dormammu, Spencer, Akuma, and Phoenix fit the role perfectly.

Another powerful tactic to emerge was the THC glitch. When performing a THC out of a capture/grab state (such as Jill's Raven Spike, Magneto's Hyper Grav, or Storm's Elemental Rage), the following combo would receive no damage scaling or hitstun decay penalty if performed correctly. This enabled easy 100% damage combos for many characters in the game, top tier and lower-tier alike. Characters such as Spencer, Magneto, Jill, Amaterasu, X-23, and Storm could start the trick, while characters such as Wolverine, Wesker, Taskmaster, Arthur, Dante, Sentinel, and Hsien-Ko could end it with an extremely damaging combo. Team configurations such as Magneto/Wolverine/Akuma and Magneto/Storm/Sentinel relied heavily on the use of this glitch and saw moderate success in tournament play; the THC glitch (now removed in *UMvC3*) was a method to deal big damage while hoarding X-Factor for later in the match.

Eventually, Phoenix set major tournaments ablaze, with simultaneous wins at CEO in Orlando, Florida and ReveLAtions in Los Angeles, California. Winners Hajime "Tokido" Taniguchi and Jay "Viscant" Snyder showed that the quest for Dark Phoenix, either for her or against her, is the defining conflict in *MvC3*. Phoenix's capabilities on both offense and defense end up being so great that her unapproachably low vitality is often a non-issue; fragile or not, Jean Grey is essentially unbeatable in Dark Phoenix form. Saving hyper meter and X-Factor for Dark Phoenix became the apex version of the lv.3 comeback, with the consensus view in Phoenix matches being that the match hadn't even really started yet before Dark Phoenix Rising. Dark Phoenix was *that* powerful, especially with X-Factor.

But, at the same time, Tokido and Justin Wong were already bucking the new conventional wisdom that X-Factor was a precious gem that must be squirreled away until absolutely necessary. By starting Wolverine and activating X-Factor the first time they landed *any* clean hit or throw, sure, they'd only have lv.1 X-Factor, but because of Wolverine's damage output there was still enough time to K.O. the first character, then put the next character in a nauseating mix-up with X-Factor to spare. Very quickly, onlookers and fellow competitors went from asking, "Did he mean to spend X-Factor that early...?" to, "I wonder if there are other ways I can spend X-Factor opportunistically, instead of just saving it for a rainy day?"

Eventually, while other viable tactics and characters emerged throughout *MvC3*'s span of competitive play, Viscant's team of Wesker/Haggar/Phoenix proved to be unstoppable at Evo 2011, the biggest tournament in fighting games. In a competitive landscape that had become overrun with Wolverines looking to pop X-Factor at a stiff breeze, Magnetos who could transition from being the best rushdown and grappling character to being an unbeatable zoner in the same match, and high-execution, 40-second combo Dante specialists, adopting Haggar into the team was key to keeping the rushing masses at bay. Despite being universally thought of as one of the worst characters in *MvC3*, the benefits of Haggar's invincible assist far outweighed the cons of his point game.

What *MvC3*'s development revealed was a lively game in which almost every character can be used with some success, even though (no different from every asymmetrical game ever) some characters and tactics end up being more effective most of the time.

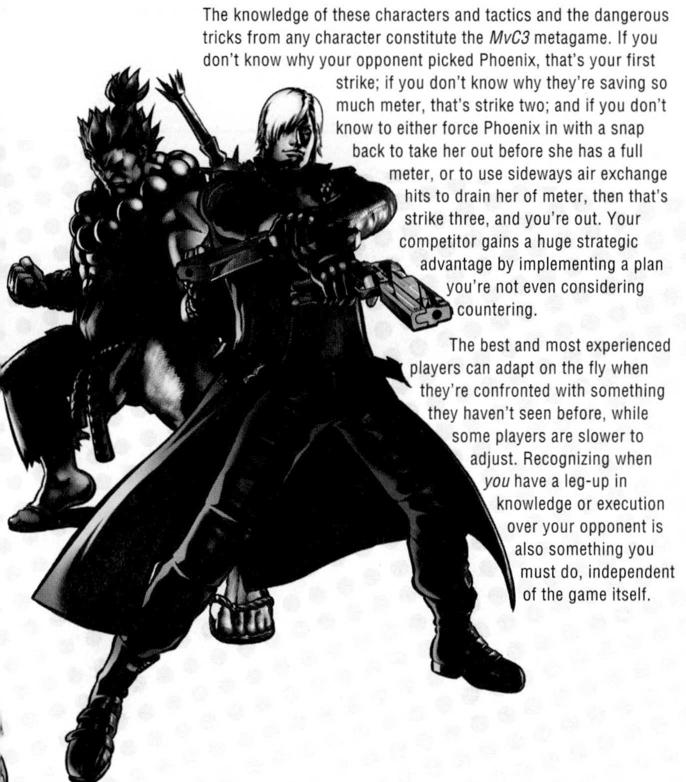

The knowledge of these characters and tactics and the dangerous tricks from any character constitute the *MvC3* metagame. If you don't know why your opponent picked Phoenix, that's your first strike; if you don't know why they're saving so much meter, that's strike two; and if you don't know to either force Phoenix in with a snap back to take her out before she has a full meter, or to use sideways air exchange hits to drain her of meter, then that's strike three, and you're out. Your competitor gains a huge strategic advantage by implementing a plan you're not even considering countering.

The best and most experienced players can adapt on the fly when they're confronted with something they haven't seen before, while some players are slower to adjust. Recognizing when *you* have a leg-up in knowledge or execution over your opponent is also something you must do, independent of the game itself.

PARSING THE DATA

Few players really know everything about every matchup. Usually, players grow familiar with the most relevant matchups they run into frequently, and after some time, this information is disseminated around the community and congealed into tier lists. Now, you can find "tier lists" all over the internet for just about any game in existence; somewhere, someone probably has a tier list already up for ideal controls in *Modern Warfare 3*. There is a great deal of misunderstanding out there about what a tier list is, and how it can be applied.

The first caveat is simply that anyone's idea of a tier list is an opinion. Some opinions are certainly grounded more firmly than others, but they're still just opinions, and one can never be sure when everything is unearthed in a game, or when a particular player is the best arbiter of that knowledge.

The best use of a tier list is to show characters who generally have even matches with each other but are separate from the rest of the cast. So characters in a purported "top tier" tend to be dominant over non-top tier cast members, but they also tend to have more or less neutralizing matchups amongst each other. If discussion arises about whether a character is "good enough" to be in a particular tier, yet that character doesn't do well against those characters, that's a clue they aren't quite there. If they belong, why do they have trouble among their peers?

A "mid-tier" or "upper-mid tier" if a game's cast is diverse for enough divisions is then characters who aren't quite dominant but are still serviceable against each other. They aren't hopeless against the top characters, and they have winning advantages against characters under them.

And so it goes, until we arrive at a "bottom tier," if it exists, consisting of characters who generally just don't have favorable matchups. In *Super Street Fighter IV*, someone like Hakan fits this description, whereas in *MvC3*, you can look to Hsien-Ko or Captain America as combatants with clear deficiencies in many, or most, matchups. It's important to note that "low tier" is not synonymous with "bad" or "unplayable." In particular, the *SFIV* series and *MvC3* have terrific parity through the cast, even though some deltas are obvious. And we've already seen in *MvC3* how ostensibly "bad" characters can make all the difference!

A tier list can perhaps be most useful when it gives you some idea of how to prepare, even for matchups you're not familiar with. Even if you never get to play Morrigan players, for example, perhaps you've perused our guide, watched some videos online, checked out the forums at SRK. You have an idea of what people generally think of her: not awful, not dominant. Why could that be? Where do your characters tend to fall in the court of public opinion? What could that tell you about how to prepare for matches?

If you love Haggar, Captain America, and Ryu, you then have some idea of what you're getting yourself into. These characters are far from worthless, but they very obviously lack the flexibility of characters like Dante and Magneto, and they don't exploit system features to an outsized degree like Phoenix or Dormammu. They must simply be played patiently, you must pick their spots, and fight it out, accepting and even relishing the uphill battle. In this way, a tier list can be useful.

On the other hand, many players, especially new ones, tend to drastically overvalue tier lists. Characters at the top are "broken," while the bottom tier is "worthless" and "unplayable." This remains prevalent, despite the fact that balance issues were unquestionably worse in previous generations of fighting games than they are in the *SFIV* and *MvC3* series. And this exists, ignoring the issue that tier lists only tend to matter at high levels of play, when playing for keeps. When playing casually, playing for fun with friends, or playing online, being slave to general opinions about what's good or bad can hold back players creativity. Look how fast things change, after all: at the release of *MvC3*, numerous well-known players claimed that Sentinel ruined the game. However, after only a few weeks of hardcore play, even disregarding the vitality nerf that Sentinel received shortly in, the feared robot was already regarded as maybe having lost the hallowed "top tier" status (and indeed, ultimately Sentinel is now considered about 10th best or so overall, as *MvC3* shook out). And this happens all the time: Rolento and Dhalsim were going to ruin *Street Fighter Alpha 3*. Rock was going to ruin *CvS2*. Zangief was going to ruin *SFIV*. Dudley was going to ruin *SSFIV*.

Tier lists are a useful tool to stay aware of the most relevant matches you'll see, since if characters are really better, then you naturally see much more of them. But they're not the be-all end-all. *Ultimate Marvel vs. Capcom 3* might be said to have what a couple members of our authoring team affectionately refer to as "*Guilty Gear* balance". That is, sure, Haggar can't really compete with Phoenix. But *if* you can be patient and get a little lucky, you can still make lemons out of lemonade.

There is no character who cannot be made threatening or who cannot squeeze fatal damage out of their ideal setups in a game as open as this. It's telling that, for both of our guides, we've kind of set the bar for the sort of combos we'd even consider putting down by asking, "Does this deal at least half damage to most characters?" Everyone in the game is powerful, especially if you build around them, especially if you use X-Factor judiciously, and especially if you leave behind the notion that you can only have success by playing characters that some player or group of players claim "breaks the game." The only sure thing in life is that things change; in the Cro-Magnon pre-YouTube era, *MvC2* was basically a different game every year for almost a half-decade. Now, in the age of smartphones and streaming video, *MvC3* still managed multiple sea changes across an exciting roster free of filler.

Often times, losses are blamed heavily on character choice. The question is begged: are you really losing to the character, or are you merely losing to the player? The overemphasis on character selection can become a red herring, a distraction.

TRAINING HARD VS. TRAINING SMART

We are often taught that hard work is the cousin of success; this does not always hold true to fighting games! Your time is best spent not training hard, but training *smart*.

Take for example the mismatch between Amaterasu vs. Sentinel, where Amaterasu has severe advantage. No amount of brute-force matches played makes it any easier to use Sentinel in this match. Rather, it is only through recognition of why Sentinel has a hard time in this match that insight can be gained on what can be done for you to get a fighting chance. Pinpoint exactly why your Sentinel is losing; how are you getting opened up? How is your opponent avoiding your attacks? What can be done to stop Amaterasu's most powerful anti-Sentinel tools, such as Solar Flare's instant overhead air Ⓗ? Keeping questions like these in mind while actually playing the match-up can reveal solutions that would otherwise have been overlooked—it's easier to just play mindlessly and just go through the motions, even when losing repeatedly. Perhaps you'll notice that you are usually falling prey to instant overhead air Ⓗ, let's say, in which case you can adjust and play more of a long-range game with projectiles and crossover assists. Pinpoint what exactly is making you lose, and go from there. And the reason can't be "I lost because they chose X character or I missed Y combo!"

CASUAL MATCHES VS. SERIOUS MATCHES

The attitude you take toward casual games (both online and offline) and tournament matches helps greatly in improving your game overall. If your goal is to become a better player, you should view casual matches as a learning experience. Matches where nothing is necessarily "on the line" are an opportune time to try different attacks or tactics that you are unsure of or don't normally use; frequently, it is helpful simply to see what happens when X action is used in Y situation. This is also a great time to experiment with different combos to test their merit, such as corner-carrying combos or meter-building combos. Experimenting with alternative combos and strategies during casual matches may cause you to lose more than usual, but it is beneficial in the long run. Given this, it is important to not be discouraged by losses in casual matches. So long as something is learned, whether it's "don't use cr. Ⓜ as anti-air" or "She-Hulk is too heavy for this combo to land properly," then the match can be considered a success. In casual matches, learning should take precedence over winning.

Matches in a competitive environment, such as a tournament, are a different story. In important matches where something *is* on the line (such as your tournament entry fee), you should utilize everything in your arsenal to win: every sneaky setup, every dirty trick, every crazy gimmick, the most damaging combos, the "cheapest" chip damage sequence. Experimentation should not be considered during a tournament match. (Even though some players will disagree!) However, sometimes it's best to simply outplay your opponent with solid, safe gameplay during an important match, saving your best tricks and setups for circumstances and match flarepoints that require clutch play. The ace up your sleeve is for a dire situation!

GAME MODES

In *Ultimate Marvel vs. Capcom 3*, every character is available right from the get-go. Shuma-Gorath and Jill are available as DLC; if you already acquired those characters for use in vanilla *MvC3*, they'll be available in *UMvC3*, as well. In addition to the six color schemes available for each hero to flaunt, a seventh alternate costume will be available for each character through various pre-order and DLC channels.

Player Points and Unlockable Rewards

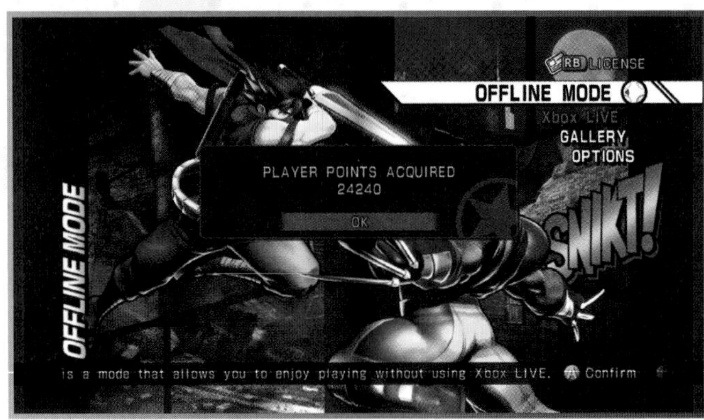

Playing any mode of *UMvC3* lets you garner player points, which are tabulated on the license card. The license card can be viewed from the main menu. The license card displays lots of data related to battle history, and it allows for a little customization.

The license card allows you to:

View accumulated player points, online rank and rank points, overall wins and losses, and recent accomplishments.
Set the icon and title, which are visible to other players in online modes.
Examine frequency of character use.
Set up to three reserve units for quick selection of favorite teams.
Examine battle data for both offline and online play.

Gallery Goodies:

Quite a few goodies can be accessed right from the beginning in the gallery:

Character bios and a model viewer
Stage art
Special art
Concept art
The Fate of Two Worlds comic
The sound gallery

Unlockables:

You can view the credits movie in the gallery any time after defeating Arcade Mode.
Land the final blow on Arcade Mode Galactus with a character to unlock that character's ending, as well as extra artwork.
Galactus Mode is unlocked by accumulating 30,000 player points.
Defeat Galactus Mode to unlock art and an ending for Galactus.
(Or, *lose* the last Arcade Mode stage to Galactus for his ending!)

Icons and Titles

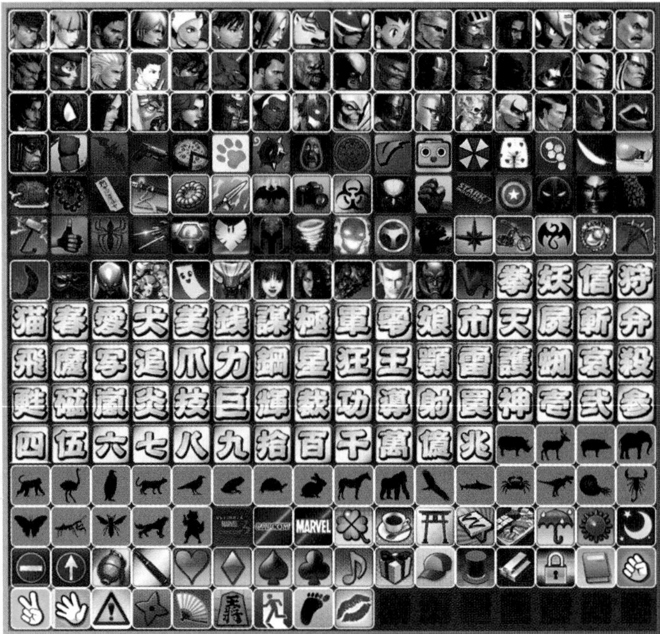

Icons are available right away, but titles must be earned.

The icon and title you set appear to other players online. Initially, you won't have access to any cool titles; just the *UMvC3* logo. You'll unlock up to 443 titles in all. 300 of the titles are unlocked by accomplishing various feats with specific characters:

- **Clear Arcade Mode on any difficulty with a given character**
- **Clear Arcade Mode on Very Hard difficulty with a given character**
- **Complete five trials in Mission Mode with a given character**
- **Complete all the trials in Mission Mode with a given character**
- **Use a given character 30 times**
- **Use a given character 100 times**

The rest of the titles are unlocked by accomplishments like the following:

- **Winning up to 1000 matches online**
- **Completing various things a certain amount of times: 200 hyper combo wins or first attack bonuses, 10 wins via block damage, acquiring up to 999,999 player points, completing Galactus Mode, and so on.**
- **Completing various tasks in Heroes & Heralds Mode, an upcoming addition to the game planned as free post-release DLC**

Achievements and Trophies

There are 47 achievements and trophies. Their unlock conditions are self-explanatory.

Title	Gamerscore (Xbox 360)	Trophies (PS3)	Requirement
The Ultimate	50 points	Platinum	Unlock all achievements
Waiting for the Trade	50 points	Gold	View all endings in Arcade Mode (Does not include Shuma-Gorath/Jill)
The Best There Is	10 points	Bronze	Beat Arcade Mode on the hardest difficulty
Saving My Quarters	10 points	Bronze	Beat Arcade Mode without using any continues
The Points Do Matter	20 points	Bronze	Earn 400,000 points in Arcade Mode
High-Score Hero	30 points	Silver	Earn 500,000 points in Arcade Mode
Missions? Possible.	20 points	Bronze	Clear 120 missions in Mission Mode
Up to the Challenge	30 points	Silver	Clear 240 missions in Mission Mode
Master of Tasks	40 points	Silver	Clear 480 missions in Mission Mode
Above Average Joe	10 points	Bronze	Land a Viewtiful Combo (Arcade/Online)
Mutant Master	10 points	Bronze	Land an Uncanny Combo (Arcade/Online)
Mega Buster	20 points	Bronze	Use 1,000 hyper combo gauge bars (Arcade/Online)
Defender	10 points	Bronze	Block 100 times (Arcade/Online)
Advancing Guardian	10 points	Bronze	Perform 100 advancing guards (Arcade/Online)
A Friend in Need	20 points	Bronze	Perform 100 crossover assists (Arcade/Online)
First Strike	10 points	Bronze	Land 50 first attacks (Arcade/Online)
Savage Playing	10 points	Bronze	Perform 50 snap backs. (Arcade/Online)
Quick Change-Up	10 points	Bronze	Perform 50 crossover counters (Arcade/Online)
Perfect X-ample	10 points	Bronze	Use X-Factor 50 times (Arcade/Online)
Gravity? Please...	10 points	Bronze	Land 50 team aerial combos (Arcade/Online)
Mighty Teamwork	10 points	Bronze	Land 30 team aerial counters (Arcade/Online)
Big Bang Theory	15 points	Bronze	Perform 30 hyper combo finishes (Arcade/Online)
Hard Corps	15 points	Bronze	Perform 30 crossover combination finishes (Arcade/Online)
Training Montage	20 points	Bronze	Play in Offline Mode for more than 5 hours
Training in Isolation	30 points	Silver	Play in Offline Mode for more than 30 hours
Seductive Embrace	20 points	Bronze	Play Online for more than 5 hours
Rivals Welcome	30 points	Silver	Play Online for more than 30 hours
Brave New World	10 points	Bronze	Participate in any mode over Online
Hellbent	20 points	Bronze	Participate in 100 matches Online
Dreaded Opponent	20 points	Bronze	Participate in 200 matches Online
Forged from Steel	30 points	Silver	Participate in 300 matches Online
Full Roster	30 points	Silver	Battle against all characters over Online
Incredible	20 points	Bronze	Win without calling your partners or switching out in a Online match
Need a Healing Factor	20 points	Bronze	Win without blocking in an Online match
Crazy Good	10 points	Bronze	Surpass the rank of Fighter
Mega Good	40 points	Silver	Surpass the sixth rank of any class
Hotshot	15 points	Bronze	Win 10 battles in Ranked Match
Slam Master	20 points	Bronze	Win 50 battles in Ranked Match
Fighting Machine	40 points	Silver	Win 100 battles in Ranked Match
Noble Effort	15 points	Bronze	Get a five-game win streak in Ranked Match
Assemble!	15 points	Bronze	Participate in an eight-player Lobby over Online
Dominator	30 points	Silver	Collect 100 titles
A Warrior Born	10 points	Bronze	Earn 5,000 Player Points (PP)
Devil with a Blue Coat	15 points	Bronze	Earn 30,000 Player Points (PP)
Divine Brawler	50 points	Silver	Earn 100,000 Player Points (PP)
Comic Collector	50 points	Gold	Unlock all items in the gallery
Passport to Beatdown Country	10 points	Bronze	Fight in all of the stages

Stages

Bonne Wonderland

Kattelox Island

Demon Village Redux

Demon Village

Chaos at Tricell

Tricell Laboratory

Days of Future Past

Metro City

S.H.I.E.L.D. Helicarrier

City That Never Sleeps

Shadowland

The Daily Bugle

Hand Hideout

Asgard: Sea of Space

Danger Room

Asgard

Training Room

S.H.I.E.L.D. Air Show

Fate of the Earth (Galactus only)

Arcade

In Arcade Mode, you'll choose your team, difficulty, time limit, damage level, and fight request status before embarking on a seven-stage quest with a goal of saving both Earths. When you've cleared Arcade Mode, only the character who lands the final blow on Galactus gets credit for completing the game.

Six preliminary battles are waged against random CPU-controlled teams.

At lower difficulties, the CPU is fairly passive and hapless, and it can be cowed by repetitive, relatively safe tactics. At the highest difficulty, the CPU guards, reacts, and punishes with inhuman speed and accuracy, to an unrealistic degree. This is not the best practice for actually thinking about playing human opponents, but it *is* good practice for learning to play for keeps. If your team is knocked out, you can continue and try again without penalty. You can even switch teams, if desired. With fight request on, online opponents may interrupt your Arcade Mode bouts with a match challenge.

You'll still get credit for beating the game if you lose and continue, even if you switch teams.

Defeat the opposing team, and you'll advance to the next stage.

Versus

With two controllers, you can play local matches against friends in this mode. You'll both select teams, and then the stage, time, damage, and individual handicaps can be altered before the match. Immediately after each match, you can opt to rematch instantly with the same teams and settings, or you can opt to head back to the character select screen to re-pick teams and options. Like any other mode, playing in versus garners PP, so be sure to exit to the main menu when you're done with your session.

A lowered handicap results in more damage taken. This is on top of the damage rating, so with damage set to highest and the handicap all the way down, characters are knocked out by three or four-hit chain combos! This is a good way for experienced players to still have good casual fun with players who don't take the game as seriously.

Training

Ultimate Marvel vs. Capcom 3 thankfully includes an excellent Training Mode. Virtually everyone who picks up the game is going to spend significant time here, and with good reason—experimenting with different teams, assist types, combos, and overall strategies is not only a crucial part of getting better, but it's at least half the fun of playing a fighting game in the first place.

Video games aren't often thought of as a physical endeavor, but there is definitely a high dexterity bar set for fighting games at large, and the Vs. series specifically. The *MvC3* series is a littler friendlier to newcomers than its predecessors, but it's still filled with exacting techniques, precise sequences, and elaborate combos. Different aspects of execution come more naturally to different players, but everyone must spend at least some time honing muscle memory and practicing important tactics.

YOU COULD LEARN A LOT FROM A DUMMY

Training Mode features extra commands that can be assigned beyond the normal attack and assist buttons. These commands allow you to control the training dummy directly, and to set up recorded sequences that you can play back from either team. This is most useful if you happen to play on a pad, where extra shoulder buttons and even the left and right analog stick buttons can be used for these functions. If you have a joystick, the amount of utility you can get out of these features is dependent on how many buttons are on the stick, basically. If you have a six-button stick, there's no room to assign extra functions; with an eight-button stick, you can assign a recording button and a playback button. If you prefer using those buttons for macros, like to have a one-button dash, then something's gotta give, at least when you're practicing in Training Mode.

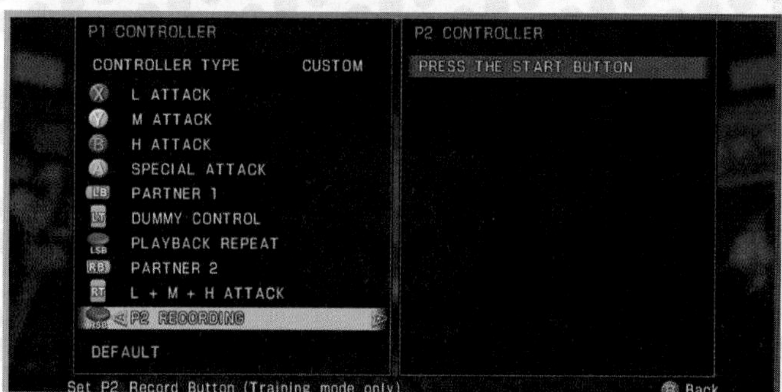

Dummy Control: If this is assigned to a button, hold that button, and you'll have full control of the dummy. If it's possible to assign this to button that's comfortable for you to just hold (or weigh) down, then you can effectively practice with two different teams, six different characters, and 18 different assist types at once. It's also very useful for repositioning the dummy, like when you want to move it slightly out of a corner so you can squeeze your point character behind the dummy for the maximum possible distance to practice midscreen combos.

P1 / P2 Recording; Playback / Playback Repeat: You can record up to 10 seconds of action for either team to repeat, and this series of actions can play back at your beck and call, or on a repeat loop. The recording function is the best feature of Training Mode. This lets you test out anything you want in a controlled environment, with no pressure.

Do you wonder if your team's zoning can hold up? Match them up against teams made of characters like Doctor Doom, Taskmaster, Magneto, Hawkeye, and Arthur, then record that team chucking as much stuff as you can manage at your side of the screen. Now play it back, and see if you can keep up.

Not sure if a mix-up, reset attempt, or rushdown sequence you've come up with can actually pass muster? Do it to yourself. Record one team going through the motions of your discovery, then play it back while you control the other team and try to guard or otherwise thwart it.

Do you want to practice punishing and juggling assists? Record the dummy doing nothing but blocking and calling assists.

Do you want to practice pressuring defensive characters who come in post-K.O. or after snap backs? Record the dummy doing nothing but walking backward, play it back on repeat, then dash in and start a low combo into a snap back. When the new character drops in, the walking backward input simply causes air blocking; add in the random advancing guard setting to better simulate player behavior.

Do you want to practice midscreen combos, but get annoyed that you can't just jump into the corner over the dummy for the maximum distance to the other corner? Just set the dummy to do nothing but walk forward; if you carry it to the corner while practicing your midscreen juggles, you can just jump forward over it.

While recording functions are invaluable, they do come with a caveat. Remember that the game is doing nothing other than playing back your inputs, exactly as you recorded them. It won't make any concessions to insuring that the results are exactly what you intend. This may come up if you perform actions that require meter while the dummy doesn't have any, and especially if you interrupt the dummy in progress somehow, and the duration of the playback is messed up as the dummy never ends up being in quite the right state for whatever input it's receiving. For the best controlled experiments, keep recorded clips brief and to-the-point, with a dead period afterward where the character is just standing around. This keeps the playback from becoming counterproductive or annoying if playback repeat is on.

Dummy Forward / Dummy Jump: Sets a button to either make the dummy jump or walk forward. The Dummy Control setting is more of a comprehensive catch-all. Using Dummy Control instead means if you want the dummy to walk forward or jump, you can, but you can also make them do anything else. That said, while holding a button to trigger Dummy Control, you *cannot* control your own team, so these functions can be useful for testing situations where you want the dummy to jump or move while still controlling your character, too.

TRAINING SETTINGS

After setting Dummy Control of some kind, check out the Dummy Options page of the Training Mode pause menu:

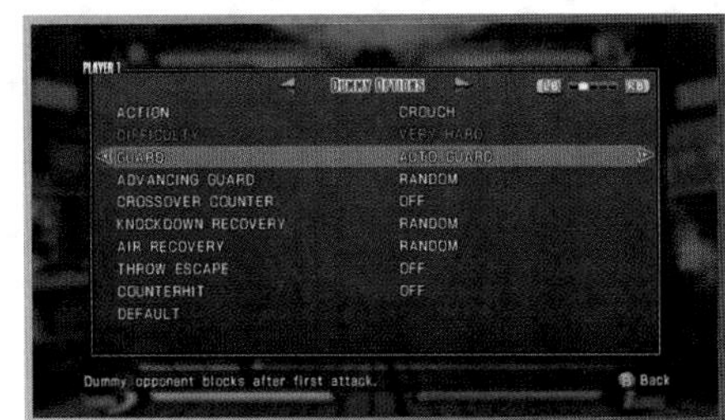

Action: Set the dummy to stand when you are practicing combos you expect to land on a standing opponent. These kind of situations include against competitors dashing, attempting a throw, or trying to anti-air from the ground. Set the dummy to crouch when practicing combos for other situations, like when pinning a foe with an assist, or after using a fast overhead (such as a triangle jump, square jump, or instant overhead jumping attack). Set the dummy to jump or super jump when practicing air throw combos or anti-air combos.

Difficulty: This applies to CPU control, which allows you to spar against a moving target. Focus on combo execution and confident movement against computer opponents, but do not rely on CPU sparring to make you a better strategist. Over-reliance on playing the CPU can be detrimental for playing human adversaries, as you unconsciously train tactics that work on the CPU rather than being deliberate about each action while reading your thinking challenger.

Guard: At the very least, set this to Auto Guard so the dummy blocks if you start hitting it but fail to keep a combo going. This is useful for perfecting your execution of basic ground chains. Later, when you're practicing tactics instead of just execution, set this to Random Guard. Then, if the dummy guards, practice stopping after your opening attacks on reaction, so you can shift to plan B instead of just getting punished or pushed away with advancing guard.

Advancing Guard: And speaking of advancing guard, it's a big deal. Proper guarding, followed by advancing guard once a successful block is confirmed, is the main universal defensive tactic in *UMvC3*. Midscreen, the defending character pushes back the aggressor almost a full screen away! So you have to be ready to react when your offensive momentum is stunted by advancing guard. Set the dummy to some kind of guard (usually Auto Guard or Random Guard) and turn advancing guard on; you can work on regaining lost momentum quickly, or bypassing advancing guard in the first place by timing attacks and assists to strike the opponent simultaneously. It's important to note that with advancing guard set to on, the training dummy uses advancing guard with the fastest possible timing, every time. This is not how humans play—it's not even conceivable that a person could pushblock on the first frame of blocking as a baseline approach, so keep that in mind when practicing with the dummy.

Crossover Counter: With this setting on, the dummy crossover counters to the next character whenever the dummy's team has at least one bar of hyper meter available. For general training purposes, it is actually more annoying than helpful to turn on this setting—opponents simply won't be using crossover counters that much, and most assists don't make great crossover counters against a point-blank aggressive character anyway (though certainly some do). Instead, turn this on periodically when you want to specifically check how vulnerable your close range tactics are to some of the better crossover counters, especially invincible ones like Haggar—α or Captain America—β. If you're practicing zoning patterns, you can also turn this on to see what happens when your adversary uses your fullscreen attacks as an opportunity to crossover counter and switch characters safely... perhaps you have some way to punish them for that on reaction, like with a quick beam hyper combo.

Knockdown Recovery / Air Recovery: The recovery settings should usually be set to "random" unless you are testing something specific. When opponents are knocked to the turf or flip out in midair, after all, the direction they recover in—left, right, or neutral—won't be the same every time. Characters in the process of recovering are invincible, but you should practice going for a throw or reset attempt right as their invulnerability expires.

Throw Escape: Throws (accomplished with ⇨ or ⇦ + Ⓗ, whether on the ground or in the air) grab on the first frame after input, and they create OTG openings for most characters. This means that throws are great and a required part of anyone's gameplan. However, throws can be broken, which leads to a situation where both characters are standing next to each other ready to act, with nothing having actually happened. It's important to be able to react to throw breaks—they happen *extremely* quickly, faster than in any other fighting game—so turn this on periodically to train yourself to be ready with instant follow-ups or evasive actions when characters face off at close range after a throw break.

Counterhit: Hits against characters who are winding up an attack are counterhits and cause a distinctive red hit spark. +2 frames are added to the hitstun created, and for certain moves, an entirely different effect than normal hitstun occurs, such as causing the opposing character to stagger. Certain combos and links are only possible after a successful counterhit, so turn this on when practicing such tactics. You can even set this to random, which you should probably do eventually so you actually get a feel for trying to react to the red spark rather than just doing a counterhit setup on auto-pilot. This is difficult, but possible.

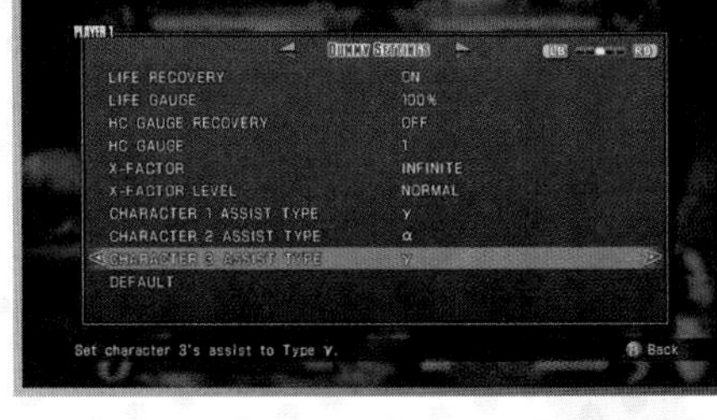

Apart from setting the dummy's behavior, there are general settings that can be adjusted for both teams to scale how closely a real match is simulated.

Life Recovery: Determines whether characters regenerate health. With this on, characters in Training Mode cannot be knocked out. You'll usually want this on, unless you're trying to simulate real matches.

H.C. Gauge Recovery: Determines whether the hyper combo gauge (which we refer to as the hyper meter) automatically refills whenever bar is expended. When training execution, you'll want this on. If you're trying to get a sense of how quickly you actually build hyper meter when attacking, turn this off. You'll also want this off if you're trying to simulate match settings.

X-Factor Settings: You can adjust both whether X-Factor can be used repeatedly in Training Mode, and what level it will register as when it is activated. With both settings on normal, X-Factor behaves as it does in matches—only one use per session (unless Training Mode is reset by holding Back or Select, then pressing Start), with X-Factor strength determined by how many characters are left on your team (with Life Recovery set to on, X-Factor will always registered as level 1, since none of your characters will ever be knocked out). When practicing X-Factor setups and hit-confirm combos, set X-Factor use to infinity. When trying to simulate real matches in Training Mode, set it to normal. Setting X-Factor to a level higher than normal/1 can be useful for practicing combos and movement in last-ditch, lv.3 X-Factor scenarios, which are commonplace.

Assist Types: Beautifully, and unlike previous Vs. titles, you do not have to back all the way out to the character select screen to try out different assist types! Simply change the assist types for each character on either team here. Hooray!

When training execution (practicing inputs and combos) or matchup difficulties (using record and dummy control functions to simulate troublesome situations), you'll probably want the timer set to infinite. You'll likely also want hyper meter recovery on, along with life recovery. Attack Data is an extremely useful tool—with this window active, you'll see how much damage your combos do in real-time. The Input Display is equally valuable for being able to see where you went wrong with execution errors.

Match settings can be simulated in Training Mode; when one side or the other is totally depleted or the timer expires, the "round" simply resets immediately. To simulate match settings whether with a friend or against the CPU:

Set Training Mode to 99 seconds when picking teams

Assign dummy control to either the CPU or player 2

Turn life and hyper meter recovery off for both sides, and set X-Factor use to normal

Nothing in Training Mode counts toward trophies or achievements, and wins/losses aren't tabulated as in Versus Mode, but if you exit properly (instead of simply shutting off the console) after a session, you earn tons of player points!

Mission

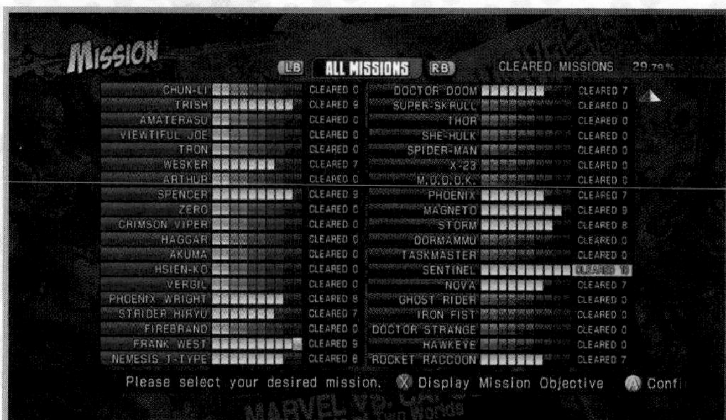

Mission Mode contains 10 trials for each character, for 480 trials total (500 if you have access to Jill and Shuma-Gorath, as well). For every character, the first four missions are simply performing basic motions or simple combos. The fifth mission is the universal combo (L, M, H, S CANCEL forward super jump, air M, M, H, S, or close to it), and after that, the last four trials exhibit combos and techniques serious players of that character should be familiar with. Doing the first five trials for every character, which is easy enough, nets 240 total, unlocking the second of three achievements. The last one requires 480 trials, or at least every trial for every non-DLC character. (Jill and Shuma-Gorath can count toward those totals, but you don't need to have them to get there.) Clearing just about every trial is difficult, obviously, but if you can perform the bread and butters we discuss throughout this guide, you should be more than capable of completing Mission Mode (though some combos are definitely tough!).

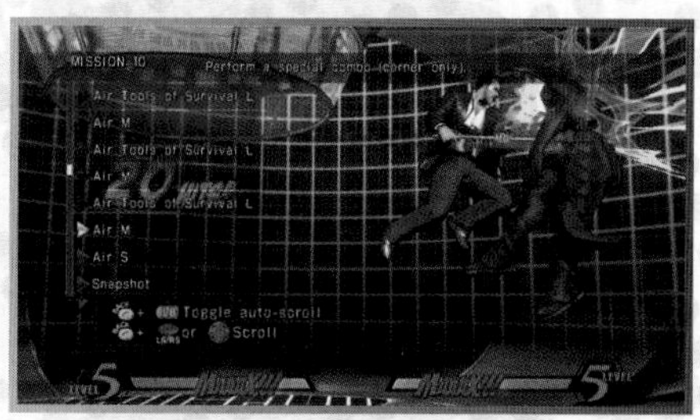

Because the Mission Mode combo commands are listed in the game, because inevitable YouTube videos of Mission completion tend to be more useful to help you through trouble spots than any advice we can impart in text and screenshots, and because we've chosen to focus our limited pages and time on discussing strategy for using characters against your friends and players online, we have not included transcripts of the Mission Mode combos. Instead, you'll find that the combos we list for every character are actually much better.

Online

There are several online modes you can enter to test your mettle against other fans of *UMvC3* . Whether engaging in player matches for fun or ranked matches that go toward your overall record and ranking, this is where many players spend the vast majority of their time.

By participating in ranked matches, you'll have a chance to jockey for position on the leaderboards across several metrics. There are separate leaderboards for win streaks, win/loss record, and overall ranking. There is also a leaderboard for Arcade Mode high score, though of course that's not an online mode.

Gallery

As indicated earlier in this chapter, a great many fan-friendly unlockables are available for your perusal. These include intro cinemas, art pieces, sound effects, and background music, and a model viewer to check out various characters up close.

Options

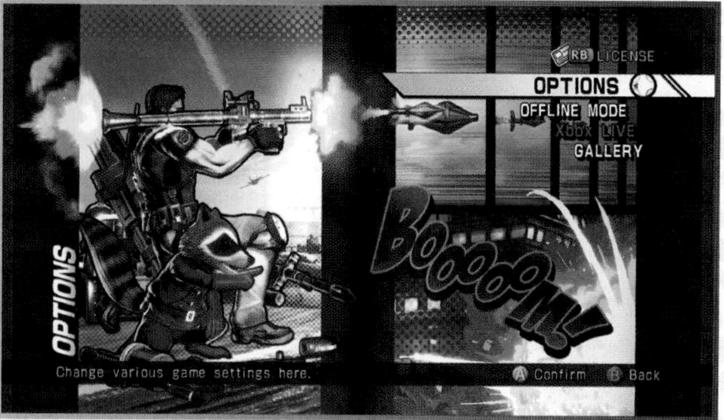

You can tailor general settings to your preference here.

Controller: Command inputs can be customized here. Note that Training Mode has more controller options than other modes, and those controls can only be set while in Training Mode.

Operation Mode: Here, you can choose between Normal or Simple controls, and whether this choice appears before every match. Only the most casual fans should stick to Simple Mode for very long. Auto Super Jump is a new option in *Ultimate Marvel vs. Capcom 3:* with this on, you can launch someone with S and then simply hold S for the follow-up super jump.

HUD Position: Here, you can adjust the position of the vitality gauges and timer, as well as the hyper meters. You can even position them both entirely offscreen if you want to enjoy the visuals unfettered by UI elements.

Sound: Here, you can adjust various sound options. With Classic BGM selected, theme music for various characters plays when they appear!

Character Voice: Here, you can choose between Japanese or English voiceovers for several characters, as you like.

System: Turn notifications on or off. You may want to set this to off if you'd prefer no distractions while playing matches online, but then you won't see match invites from friends, either!

Reset Battle Records: This allows you to scrub your play data and start over, should you desire.

GALACTUS

"NO AMOUNT OF TRAINING CAN PREPARE YOU FOR GALACTUS."

After successfully clearing six stages in Arcade Mode, you'll be face-to-face (or, face-to-chest, really) against this colossal entity. Your team of three must topple almighty Galactus to save the Earth! As the only survivor of the universe previous to ours, and wielding the Power Cosmic, Galactus stands on even keel with the deities. The machinations of Doctor Doom and Albert Wesker to control the fates of their parallel Earths have drawn the attention of this towering, unfathomable being, who consumes entire worlds filled with sentient beings for his nourishment. For Galactus, there is not necessarily malice, only need...but that's little consolation to his scores of victims.

Galactus can manifest himself at any size he likes. He's thinking big in Ultimate Marvel vs. Capcom 3, *clearly.*

PHASE 1

"YOUR PLANET WILL PROVIDE ME WITH SOME MUCH-NEEDED NOURISHMENT."

During phase 1, Galactus summons his heralds to fight in his stead, as he glowers over Earth in the background. The heralds are silver copies of Akuma, Doctor Doom, Dormammu, Super-Skrull, and Wesker. At first, Galactus summons one herald from this evil quintet to aid him...after nine ticks off the timer (or about 17 seconds), he'll summon a second herald. (Although if you manage to deplete the vitality gauge before about 17 seconds have elapsed, you won't have to deal with a second herald at all.) Once both of Galactus' minions are drawn out, they'll attack in tandem—veterans of Capcom fighting games will be reminded of the "Dramatic Battle" modes present in *Street Fighter Alpha* and some versions of *Street Fighter Alpha 3*. (And we'll all be seeing a lot more of this kind of thing soon in *Street Fighter X Tekken!)*

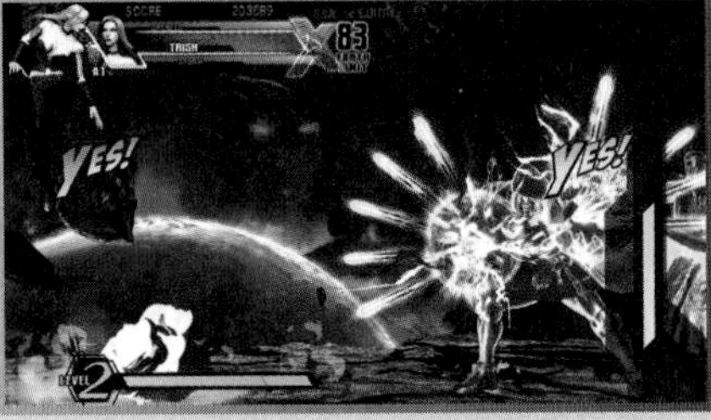

Try to stay out from between the two heralds, as it can be tricky trying to block when standing between two foes who are both considered point characters!

The heralds share one vitality gauge, which is visible on the right edge of the screen. Catch both heralds at once with a combo into hyper, and you'll destroy them very quickly on any difficulty. Save X-Factor for Galactus! Once the heralds return to dirt, Galactus himself takes a moment from his coveting of Earth to step to the foreground and personally dispense with your pesky team.

PHASE 2

"ONLY THE ULTIMATE NULLIFIER WOULD GIVE ME PAUSE."

As they say, you want something done right? You have to do it yourself. Galactus shifts his attention from his celestial meal to your team. Galactus takes up the entire right half of the playing field. Like his heralds, his vitality gauge occupies the right edge of the screen. Any part of Galactus is a viable target, and he cannot guard! Any attack that touches him deals damage. Galactus attacks more frequently on higher difficulties.

Most of his attacks are heavily telegraphed, either with visual or audio cues. This allows you to cease attacking so you can guard or dodge as necessary. Because of the high power of his entire arsenal and the damage penalty crossover assists sustain when hit, don't call assists unless you're absolutely sure they'll leave before Galactus strikes. Some of his attacks are able to one-shot full-vitality assists!

While he retains over 50% vitality, Galactus' barnburner is his throw. He telegraphs it by stepping into the background...

...so stop attacking, and super jump above it!

At first, Galactus holds back his full power, and he just attacks with brute force. He'll go for overhand smashes, backhand swats, and snap back flicks against you. Squeeze in a chain and special or two in between his attacks, except when he occasionally starts doing overhand attacks over and over. When he steps to the background to ready his throw, stop whatever you're doing and get to the top of super jump height before he brings his hands together. After he whiffs his grab, he's vulnerable for a long time.

With over 50% vitality, Galactus uses a limited arsenal:

Attack	Hit Area	Safe Area	Tell Quotes
Backhand swat	Ground level to mid range	Super jump height or far away	—
Snap back flick	Ground level at close range	Super jump height or far away	—
Right arm smash	Downward arc at mid to long range	Hugging Galactus	Insolent whelp. Fall. Submit.
Left arm smash	Downward arc full screen	—	Insolent whelp. Fall. Submit.
Hyper smash	Downward arc full screen	—	Enough!
Haymaker punch	Ground level	Super jump height	Insignificant. Yield. I am a force of nature.
Throw	Ground level	Super jump height	Feel my wrath. You will know pain.

PHASE 3

"YOU ARE LIKE AN ANT, FIGHTING THE SUN."

Characters capable of hovering at super jump height, whether with flight or special moves, can get free shots in at Galactus' face as he spams ground-level lasers.

Galactus' fullscreen laser shower can severely chip any character when guarded. Think Gill's "Blesser of All Souls" super art from SF3: Third Strike! Activate X-Factor to guard safely.

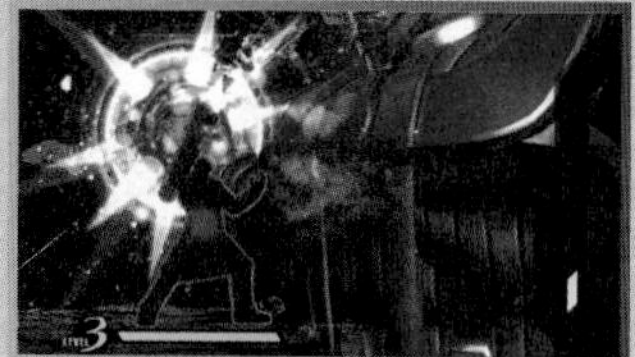

The fully charged hyper hand smash that Galactus employs when he's desperate is a guaranteed knockout. Strike him repeatedly as he winds it up to interrupt it.

Take Galactus below half vitality, and he staggers briefly. Apparently, he's underestimated your team! He becomes far more aggressive afterward, and he soon unleashes some deadly new attacks. Galactus grows more urgent as he nears the unimaginable prospect of defeat. He starts to unleash his full power, flooding the screen with powerful energy blasts. Continue to strike whenever it's safe to do so, but err on the side of caution—Galactus can hurt you a lot faster than you can hurt him, so don't get greedy. Don't use laggy attacks, and cut chain combos short if it seems like he's about to attack.

Attacks used only under 50% vitality:

Attack	Hit Area	Safe Area	Tell Quotes
Fingerlaser	Ground level	Super jump height	Die. You may die now.
Hyper laser	Ground level	Super jump height	Enough! You will rue this day.
Eyelaser	Fullscreen	Crouch close to Galactus	Away with you! You cannot hide from me!
Full-screen hyper laser	Everywhere	Guard and activate X-Factor	Yield to me... you are broken.
Final smash	Everywhere	Interrupt Galactus!	There is no hope for you... this charade is over.

X-Factor boosts damage considerably against Galactus, especially with only one character left. X-Factor is also vital to negate the extreme chip damage dealt by a couple of his final attacks. When Galactus is defeated, the current point character is declared the winner.

Since only one character can earn an ending per playthrough, don't fret if you lose a character or two, unless you're going for a high score. Instead, decide whose ending you're after, then consider the other two characters expendable; use them to push aside the heralds and get a start on Galactus himself, but don't be too careful with them—let them fall to Galactus so the character whose ending you'd like can come in, hulk up (so to speak) with lv.3 X-Factor, then finish Galactus off easily with a flurry of hyper combos built up by expendable partners.

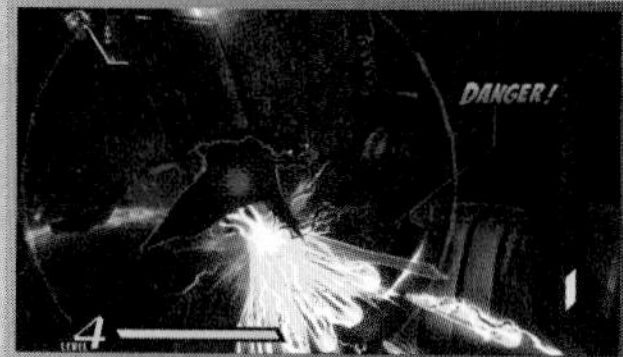

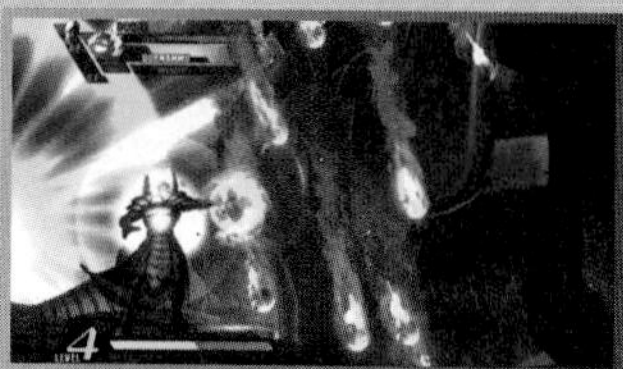

During lv.3 X-Factor, many moves and hyper combos can inflict incredible damage on Galactus. Good examples include Dormammu's Creation/Destruction mix meteors and Stalking Flare, Doctor Doom's Sphere Flame and Photon Array, Spencer's Armor Piercer and Bionic Lancer, and anything Phoenix Wright does with both X-Factor and Turnabout mode active.

You don't need the Ultimate Nullifier to defeat Galactus. You just need a good lawyer.

There are rewards both for beating Arcade Mode with every character, and for getting to Galactus but *losing!* After all, Galactus himself has an ending, but the residents of the respective worlds of Marvel and Capcom aren't going to like it too much...

If you manage to just never lose to Galactus, his ending can also be unlocked by defeating Galactus Mode.

Galactus Mode

"I AM NOT WITHOUT MERCY. YOU MAY SERVE AS MY HERALD."

Galactus Mode is unlocked by building up at least 30,000 player points. This is quickly accomplished simply by taking different characters through Arcade or Mission Modes, playing versus or online with friends, or messing around in Training Mode. Make sure to exit to the main menu to save your PP progress before shutting off the console.

In Galactus Mode, you control Galactus! You'll have to fend off six teams of increasingly skillful heroes as they attempt to stop you from utterly destroying their worlds. The first few trios of heroes should fall easily, but the last couple actually try their hardest to interrupt Galactus as he's winding up his lengthy attacks.

The game's best four-hit combo.

Galactus Mode is a pretty good way to blow off some steam because Galactus is, rightfully, *ridiculously strong*. On top of having most of Arcade Mode boss Galactus' moveset, Galactus Mode Galactus can simply lean on the ← + ATK haymaker punch. This attack causes a hard knockdown and can be canceled after hit into another attack... most usefully, right back into itself, for another hard knockdown. And then another. And then another. And then repeat for the next bothersome would-be hero. And the next. You can beat Galactus Mode easily with nothing other than ← + ATK, if you want the quickest path.

Galactus has most of the attacks of the boss version:

Command	Attack
L	Backhand swat

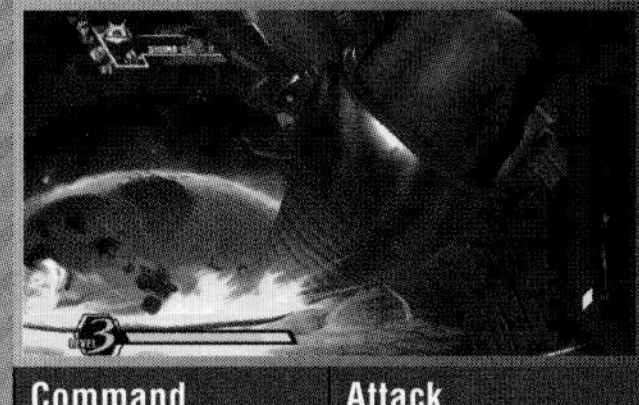

Command	Attack
M	Left hand smash

Command	Attack
H	Snap back flick

Command	Attack
⇧ + ATK	Fingerlaser

Command	Attack
⇦ + ATK	Haymaker punch

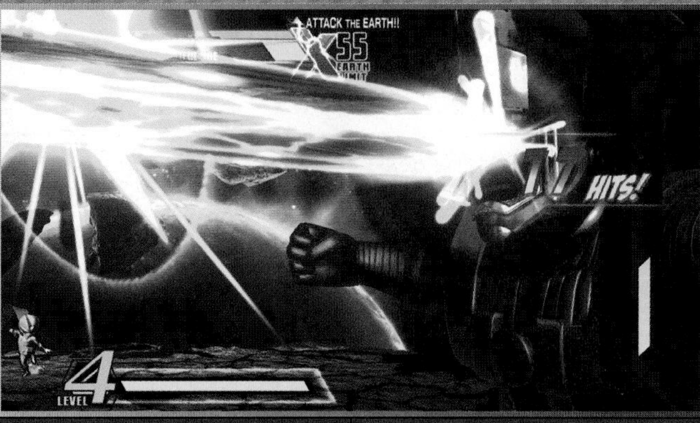

Command	Attack
⇨ + ATK	Eyelaser

Command	Attack
⇩ + ATK	Right arm smash

Command	Attack
S	Hyper smash

Command	Attack
P1+P2	Hyper laser

SYSTEM AND GAMEPLAY

ULTIMATE MARVEL VS. CAPCOM 3: TUNING SINCE ORIGINAL MVC3

As with the transition from *SFIV* to *SSFIV*, *Ultimate MvC3* has undergone a ton of changes to get here. None of the changes in particular is drastic, but the aggregate is a new game that is much more than a fresh coat of paint. Considering the sheer amount of fresh 3D animations, art, and character models involved in getting the total character count of *Ultimate Marvel vs. Capcom 3* up to 50 distinct characters, the accomplishment is kind of spectacular... remember that *MvC2*, with its unsurpassed roster of 56 characters, had the advantage of drawing upon art and ideas from almost a dozen games (*Darkstalkers* titles, earlier *Vs.* games, and the *Street Fighter Alpha* series).

New challengers have appeared!

Marvel	Capcom
Ghost Rider	Strider
Hawkeye	Firebrand
Doctor Strange	Nemesis T-Type
Iron Fist	Vergil
Nova	Phoenix Wright
Rocket Raccoon	Frank West

12 new challengers!

Nine new stages!

Galactus Mode—destroy pesky heroes as Galactus!

Spectator Mode and an enhanced Online experience

Numerous new moves and tweaks to existing moves for all 36 returning characters, and the two DLC characters, Shuma-Gorath and Jill (if you acquired the DLC characters for use in original *MvC3*, they will also work in *UMvC3*)

Display tweaked—the point character's vitality gauge shows in the center, with partner 2 (the anchor) above and partner 1 (the next in line) below. The X-Factor indicator is much more prominent

X-Factor tweaked—X-Factor values tweaked for all characters, X-Factor damage scaling adjusted, X-Factor is now possible in midair!

Team aerial combos tweaked—sideways TAC now erases one of the opponent's hyper meter bars! (In original *MvC3*, it built half a bar of meter)

THC glitch removed—when team hyper combo canceling from capture/cutscene hyper combos to indirect hyper combos, damage scaling and hitstun decay will now be properly applied

TAC glitch removed—characters like Amaterasu and She-Hulk can no longer use late air exchange hits just off the ground for relaunch opportunities

Meter gain for attacks in general lowered by about 10% (with some characters affected more severely than others)

Hitstun decay now applies to assist hits

Combos against assists now damage scale correctly if the point character is guarding, rather than the assist taking unscaled damage from every hit

In a return to the mechanics from previous *Vs.* games, airdash characters can no longer block while airdashing!

Inputting ATK rapidly now increases the number of hits and consequently the damage of many hyper combos

P1 can be used to call the last remaining teammate's assist when one partner is knocked out

New option: auto super jump! Just hold S to have your character super jump automatically after a launcher. BY DEFAULT, THIS SETTING IS ON! So if you don't want to super jump after a launcher with immediate timing, take care only to tap S and never to hold it down for long

Rumor Control: These are the Facts! Clearing up Some Common Misconceptions

X-Factor timers are *not* different between characters! Each character has the same amount of X-Factor frames at each level of X-Factor, and these values are unchanged from original *MvC3*. Characters may *seem* to *look like* they have different X-Factor timers, but that's both because: a) you aren't going to be able to activate X-Factor for two characters at roughly the same moment, since the first activation causes a 30-frame "X-Factor freeze;" the likelihood that you activate the opposite character's X-Factor on the very next few frames for a relatively precise test is low, and b) the actual X-Factor icon effects at the top of the screen are asymmetrical!

You *cannot* "mash" out of team aerial combos! You are allowed one input of S during the 15-frame window, which starts on the very frame where the TAC "flash" happens. If the first S input registered in this window is wrong—even if you just input neutral S, which isn't even an escape input—you will not break the TAC, even if you input the correct escape command immediately afterward.

Marvel Characters at a Glance

Name	Vitality	Alpha—α Assist Type	Beta—β Assist Type	Gamma—γ Assist Type	Chain Combo Archetype	OTG-Capable Attacks	Power-Up State	Flight	Airdash	Teleport/ Passthrough	Extra Air Mobility
Captain America	1050000	Projectile	Invulnerable counter	—	Marvel Series	↓↘→ + L	—	—	—	S + ATK	Double jump
Deadpool	900000	Low, spinning knockdown, invulnerable counter	OTG-capable, ground bounce	Projectile	Hunter Series	→↓↘ + H, air ↓↘→ + L	—	—	—	←↓↙ + ATK	Double jump, wall jump
Doctor Doom	1000000	Beam	Unique projectile	Projectile	Marvel Series	st. M, st. H, air ↓↘→ + ATK, air ↓↙← + ATK ATK	—	Yes	8-way	—	—
Doctor Strange	850000	Homing projectile	Hovering projectile	Double beam	Marvel Series	↓↙← + H (after Grace of Hoggoth), ↓↘→ + ATK ATK	—	Yes	—	←↓↙ + ATK	—
Dormammu	1000000	Projectile	Vertical beam, OTG-capable	Varies based on Destruction / Creation points	Marvel Series	↘ + H, →↓↘ + ATK, ↓↙← + H (mixed), →↓↘ + ATK ATK	↓↙← + L/M	Yes	8-way	←↓↙ + ATK	—
Ghost Rider	1000000	Wall bounce	OTG-capable	OTG-capable	2-Hit Limited	← + H, ↓↘→ + L, →↓↘ + ATK ATK	—	—	—	—	—
Hawkeye	900000	Projectile	Projectile, OTG-capable, poisons target	Projectile, OTG-capable	2-Hit Limited	↓↙← + L, L/M/H; →↓↘ + M, →↓↘ + ATK ATK, ↓↙← + ATK ATK	—	—	—	—	—
Hulk	1200000	Projectile, OTG-capable	Super armor	Super armor	2-Hit Limited	← (charge) → + ATK, ↓↘→ + ATK ATK	—	—	—	—	—
Iron Fist	1000000	Crumple (vs. ground), hard knockdown (vs. air)	OTG-capable, overhead attack, ground bounce	Wall bounce, destroys medium priority projectiles	Hunter Series	↓↙← + M	→↓↘ + ATK	—	—	—	Wall jump
Iron Man	950000	Beam	Local beam	High-durability double projectile, OTG-capable	Hunter Series	→↓↘ + ATK	—	Yes	8-way	—	—
M.O.D.O.K.	950000	Shield	Spinning knockdown	Beam	Marvel Series	cr. M	Strike with Analysis Cubes to gain Levels of Understanding	Yes	8-way	—	—
Magneto	850000	Beam	Capture projectile	Counter	Marvel Series	↓↘→ + ATK ATK, →↓↘ + ATK ATK	—	Yes	8-way	—	—
Nova	900000	Local beam / shield	Overhead attack, ground bounces against airborne target	Wall bounce	Marvel Series	→ + H, →↓↘ + L	Certain attacks are more powerful the more red vitality Nova has	Yes	8-way	—	—
Phoenix	375000	Projectile	—	Trap projectile	Hunter Series	air ↓↘→ + L/M	↓↙← + ATK ATK	Yes	8-way	←↓↙ + ATK	—
Rocket Raccoon	750000	Double projectile	Landmine	Wall bounce	Hunter Series	Oil Bomb air/ground explosion, →↓↘ + M, air ↓↘→ + L, →↓↘ + ATK ATK	—	—	Air M or S + ATK	↓↓ + ATK	Float
Sentinel	900000	Triple projectile	Projectile rain, OTG-capable	OTG-capable	2-Hit Limited	↓↘→ + L	—	Yes	—	—	Double jump
She-Hulk	1150000	Low attack, OTG-capable	Crumple, super armor	Invulnerable counter	Marvel Series	L (during Chariot), air ↓ + H	—	—	—	—	Wall jump
Shuma-Gorath (DLC)	950000	Beam, OTG-capable	Projectile	Knockdown against aerial target	Hunter Series	↓ (charge) ↑ + ATK, ↓↙← + ATK ATK	—	—	2-way (forward/ backward)	—	—
Spider-Man	900000	Capture projectile	—	Invulnerable counter	Marvel Series	air ↘ + ATK + S	—	—	1-way (forward), 4-way (diagonal + ATK + S)	—	Wall jump
Storm	850000	Projectile sequence	Vertical beam, OTG-capable	—	Hunter Series	↓↙← + ATK, ↓↙← + ATK ATK, →↓↘ + ATK ATK	—	Yes	8-way	—	Float
Super-Skrull	1000000	OTG-capable, wall bounce	Super Armor	—	Hunter Series	st./cr. H (hold), ↓↓ + H, air ↓ + H, L))), →↓↘ + ATK, →↓↘ + ATK ATK	—	—	Up-forward only	→↓↘ + ATK	→↓↘ + ATK
Taskmaster	1100000	Projectile	Projectile	Projectile	Marvel Series	air ↓↘→ + M/H, air ↓↘→ + LH/MH	—	—	—	—	—
Thor	1250000	Beam	Invulnerable counter, ground bounce	—	2-Hit Limited	→↓↘ + ATK, →↓↘ + ATK ATK	—	Yes	8-way	—	—
Wolverine	950000	Invulnerable counter	—	—	Hunter Series	↘ + M	↓↓ + ATK ATK	—	—	↓↙← + ATK	Wall jump
X-23	830000	—	Low attack, OTG-capable	Invulnerable counter	Hunter Series	↓↘→ + M (hold)	↓↙← + ATK ATK	—	—	↓↙← + ATK	Wall jump

Capcom Characters at a Glance

Capcom	Vitality	Alpha—α Assist Type	Beta—β Assist Type	Gamma—γ Assist Type	Chain Combo Archetype	OTG-Capable Attacks	Power-Up State	Flight	Airdash	Teleport/ Passthrough	Extra Air Mobility
Akuma	750000	Projectile	Goes through medium priority projectiles	Overhead attack, OTG-capable, ground bounce	Marvel Series	⇦⇩⇙ + (ATK) (CANCEL)→ (M) air ⇩⇘⇨ + (ATK)(ATK) (hold (H))	—	—	—	⇨⇩⇘ or ⇦⇩⇙ + (S)	—
Amaterasu	800000	Projectile reflector	Pinning projectile	30% meter gain	Marvel Series	Thunder Edge air ⇘ + (H), ⇩⇘⇨ + (ATK)(ATK) (ice/lightning)	⇩⇙⇦ + (ATK)(ATK)	—	3-way (forward, up-forward, down-forward)	—	—
Arthur	850000	Invulnerable counter	Triple projectile	Staggers, OTG-capable	Marvel Series	air (S), ⇩⇙⇦ + (L), ⇨⇩⇘ + (ATK)(ATK)	⇩⇙⇦ + (ATK)(ATK)	—	—	—	Double jump
C. Viper	900000	—	OTG-capable	Overhead attack	Marvel Series	⇨⇩⇘ + (ATK), ⇨⇩⇘ + (S), ⇩⇙⇦ + (ATK)(ATK)	—	—	8-way	—	Double jump
Chris	1100000	Invulnerable counter, hard knockdown	Projectile	Landmine, spinning knockdown	Marvel Series	cr. (H), ⇨ + (M), air ⇩⇘⇨ + (M) or (H), ⇩⇘⇨ + (ATK)(ATK) (1st hit), ⇩⇙⇦ + (ATK)(ATK), ⇨⇩⇘ + (ATK)(ATK) (Uzi)	—	—	—	—	—
Chun-Li	850000	Projectile	Invulnerable counter	Pinning kicks	Marvel Series	air ⇩ + (M)	—	—	1-way (forward, twice per jump)	—	Triple jump, wall jump
Dante	900000	Pinning vertical beam	OTG-capable	Projectile	3-Hit Alternating	⇨⇩⇘ + (M), ⇘ + (H)(H), ⇩⇘⇨ + (M)	⇩⇙⇦ + (ATK)(ATK)	Devil Trigger only	2-way (forward/ backward)	⇩⇩ + (S)	Double jump (Triple jump in Devil Trigger)
Felicia	880000	Invulnerable counter, low attack	Projectile, OTG-capable	—	Hunter Series	⇘ + (M)	⇨⇩⇘ + (ATK)(ATK)	—	—	(S) + (ATK)	Wall cling
Firebrand	850000	OTG-capable, knocks down	—	—	Hunter Series	⇩⇘⇨ + (H), ⇩⇘⇨ + (ATK)(ATK)	⇩⇙⇦ + (ATK)(ATK)	Yes	3-way (⇩⇙⇦ + (ATK))	—	Wall cling
Frank West	1050000	—	Pinning poke	30% meter gain	Hunter Series	⇩⇘⇨ + (S), ⇩⇘⇨ + (H), ⇨⇩⇘ + (H) (lv.2), ⇩⇘⇨ + (ATK)(ATK)	Use Snapshots late in combos to level up	—	—	(S) + (ATK) (lv.2+)	—
Haggar	1200000	Invulnerable assist, invulnerable counter, knockdown	Spinning knockdown	Ground bounce, hard knockdown	Marvel Series	cr. (H), ⇨⇩⇘ + (ATK)(ATK)	—	—	—	Roll after cr. (H)	—
Hsien-Ko	900000	—	Projectile reflector	Projectile	Hunter Series	⇩⇘⇨ + (ATK)(ATK), ⇩⇙⇦ + (ATK)(ATK)	⇨⇩⇘ + (ATK)(ATK)	—	2-way (forward/ backward)	Teleport dash	—
Jill (DLC)	850000	Ground bounce	Wall bounce	Invulnerable counter	Hunter Series	⇨⇩⇘ + (L), ⇩⇘⇨ + (ATK)(ATK)	⇩⇙⇦ + (ATK)(ATK)	—	8-way (Mad Beast only)	Any direction during Feral Crouch	—
Morrigan	950000	Invulnerable counter	Projectile	30% meter gain	Hunter Series	⇨⇩⇘ + (ATK)(ATK)	⇩⇩ + (ATK)(ATK)	Yes	4-way (forward/ backward/up/ down)	—	—
Nemesis T-Type	1150000	Wall bounce (first hit)	Ground bounce	Projectile	Marvel Series	⇩⇘⇨ + (ATK)(ATK)	—	—	—	—	—
Phoenix Wright	1000000	Projectile series; during Turnabout: invulnerable assist, invulnerable counter	Pinning assist, knockdown; during Turnabout: wall bounce, invulnerable assist, invulnerable counter	Low attack, OTG-capable	Marvel Series	⇩⇘⇨ + (M)/(H) (Investigation), ⇩⇙⇦ + (ATK)(ATK) (Trial/Turnabout), ⇨⇩⇘ + (ATK)(ATK) (Turnabout)	With three pieces of evidence, Trial ⇨ + (H) or air ⇩ + (H)	—	—	—	—
Ryu	1000000	Invulnerable counter	Projectile	—	Marvel Series	air ⇩⇘⇨ + (ATK)(ATK) (aim down)	⇩⇩ + (ATK)(ATK)	—	—	—	—
Spencer	1050000	Hard knockdown	Places target standing upright	Wall bounce	Marvel Series	air ⇩⇘⇨ + (M)/(H)/(S)	—	—	5-way (in air, non-upward directions + (ATK) + (S))	—	In air, upward direction + (S) + (ATK)
Strider	750000	Ground bounce	Wall bounce	Hard knockdown	Hunter Series	⇘ + (H), ⇩⇙⇦ + (S) (shot), ⇩⇘⇨ + (ATK)(ATK)	⇩⇙⇦ + (ATK)(ATK)	—	—	⇦⇩⇙ + (ATK)	Double jump, wall jump
Trish	850000	Vertical projectile trap	Capture trap	Projectile	3-Hits Alternating	Air ⇩⇘⇨ + (ATK)(ATK)	—	Yes	8-way	—	Double jump
Tron	1200000	Knockdown	Nullifies medium priority projectiles, invulnerable counter	Projectile	Marvel Series	cr. + (H)	—	—	2-way (forward/ backward)	—	—
Vergil	850000	Projectile	—	Spinning knockdown	Marvel Series	⇘ + (H), ⇩⇙⇦ + (ATK)(ATK) (during Devil Trigger)	⇩⇙⇦ + (ATK)(ATK)	—	2-way (backward/ forward) (Devil Trigger only)	⇩⇙⇦ + (ATK)	Double jump (Devil Trigger only), wall jump
Viewtiful Joe	950000	Projectile	Invulnerable counter	Bomb projectile, OTG-capable	Hunter Series	⇩⇘⇨ + (ATK), air ⇩⇘⇨ + (ATK)(ATK)	⇩⇙⇦ + (ATK)(ATK)	—	2-way (forward/ backward) twice per jump	—	Triple jump
Wesker	1000000	Wall bounce	Low attack, OTG-capable	Spinning knockdown	Marvel Series	⇘ + (H)	Lose sunglasses	—	—	⇨⇩⇘ + (ATK)	—
Zero	830000	Invulnerable counter	Projectile	Pinning slash	Marvel Series	air ⇩⇘⇨ + (M)/(H), ⇩⇘⇨ + (ATK)(ATK)	⇩⇙⇦ + (ATK)(ATK)	—	2-way (forward/ backward), 3-way (⇩⇙⇦ + (ATK))	⇩⇙⇦ + (ATK)	—

Display Essentials

VITALITY GAUGES AND TIMER

The display has been reworked from original *MvC3*. The vitality gauge of the current point character occupies the center slot. The next character in line, partner 1, is shown below the center slot and labeled as A1. Partner 2 is shown above the point character and labeled as A2. Commands for the assist characters correspond to whichever buttons are assigned to P1 and P2. The A1/A2 labels dim when those characters are unavailable. "ASSIST OK!!" indicators appear over a given character's vitality gauge when they've recovered and are ready to take part in team actions again.

Between the vitality gauges for both teams are the X-Factor indicators and the timer. The X-Factor indicator's pulsing effects make it obvious whether or not X-Factor has been expended. The timer counts down 99 game ticks, which translates to 180 seconds.

If every member of a team is drained of vitality, that team loses. If the timer runs all the way down, the team with more vitality remaining *by percentage* is declared the winner. A draw is possible if both teams have an identical percentage of vitality remaining. For example, if Thor and Phoenix both have full vitality when time expires, the match is a draw even though Thor has *far* more actual vitality than Phoenix.

We recommend playing with the timer on the default setting of 99, and with damage set on medium. Not only will most, if not all, tournaments use these setting, but this is also the setting most experienced players favor online. The timer serves a useful purpose within gameplay—most matches between competent players will not actually go the distance, but the very threat of a time over victory forces players to take action eventually and prevents eternal staring contests. And the attacks of the game are balanced with medium damage in mind—other settings can be amusing, but they are not the product working as intended.

The UMvC3 Jobs Program

The vitality gauge order isn't just a grinder for different characters to rotate through. You should have some idea of the roles and responsibilities of each member of your team, both under ideal conditions and when serious problems arise.

Your starting point character's job should typically be to build a vitality lead or to build a significant amount of hyper meter, or both. For most teams, your ultimate goal is to create a solid handoff to partner 1 through either a powerful THC or TAC, which probably knocks one or two of their characters out while putting you in solid control of the match.

So naturally, your A1 character should synch up well with your point choice. Having complementary assists and hyper combos that handoff well (especially if the THC swaps are safe even if guarded) enables the characters on the first two slots of a team to just trade places fluidly, while keeping partner 2 in the back slot. This partner can be used as the primary assist, since the plan isn't to swap them in, or they can be relied upon as a level 3 X-Factor anchor, ready to spend the full resources of the team in a supercharged last gasp if it comes to that.

You may choose to use partner 2 more directly through three-stage team hyper combos (which are now much more powerful if you use mashable hypers!) or team aerial combos. Especially with the increased threat and more heavily weighted guessing game TACs represent in *UMvC3*, this approach can be extremely valuable with some characters. Characters with long corner carry air combos like Magneto, Storm, and Doctor Doom benefit tremendously from being incorporated into TACs, and a few characters, such as M.O.D.O.K., Viewtiful Joe, and Chun-Li, are much less scary *without* them!

You may have an alternate path to success, such as if your opening plan consists of saving hyper meter for Phoenix, building up evidence for Phoenix Wright, or leveling up Frank West's photography level. Regardless, you should be going into a match with some sense of the jobs of each member of your team and with alternatives planned in case your competitor doesn't cooperate with your wishes.

Actions That Change Team Order (and thus Vitality Gauge Order):

Crossover attack (red damage becomes permanent)
Crossover counter
Point character knocked out (red damage becomes permanent)
Struck with opponent's snap back (red damage becomes permanent)
Team aerial combo
Team hyper combo

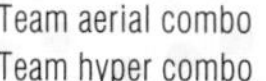

Marvel Character Vitality

Name	Vitality
Thor	1250000
Hulk	1200000
She-Hulk	1150000
Taskmaster	1100000
Captain America	1050000
Doctor Doom	1000000
Dormammu	1000000
Ghost Rider	1000000
Iron Fist	1000000
Super-Skrull	1000000
Iron Man	950000
M.O.D.O.K.	950000
Shuma-Gorath (DLC)	950000
Wolverine	950000
Deadpool	900000
Hawkeye	900000
Nova	900000
Sentinel	900000
Spider-Man	900000
Doctor Strange	850000
Magneto	850000
Storm	850000
X-23	830000
Rocket Raccoon	750000
Phoenix	375000

Capcom Character Vitality

Name	Vitality
Haggar	1200000
Tron	1200000
Nemesis T-Type	1150000
Chris	1100000
Frank West	1050000
Spencer	1050000
Phoenix Wright	1000000
Ryu	1000000
Wesker	1000000
Morrigan	950000
Viewtiful Joe	950000
C. Viper	900000
Dante	900000
Hsien-Ko	900000
Felicia	880000
Arthur	850000
Chun-Li	850000
Firebrand	850000
Jill (DLC)	850000
Trish	850000
Vergil	850000
Zero	830000
Amaterasu	800000
Akuma	750000
Strider	750000

RED VITALITY

Initially, half of the damage received against point characters, and *any* damage inflicted against assists, is red damage. Red damage is not permanent! Partners recover red damage slowly over time whenever they are not directly engaged in a team action. Inactive assists recover 200 red vitality per frame, or 12,000 red vitality per second. Under the influence of X-Factor, point characters recover red damage, as well (except when being hit), and partner characters recover red damage faster than normal, alternating between 400 and 500 vitality recovered every other frame for 27,000 red vitality recovered per second!

The rate of red vitality recovery is a straight line, rather than being different for characters with different vitality totals. This means that partners with lower maximum vitality refill max vitality more quickly. Thor with 99% red vitality takes about 103 seconds to heal fully, while Phoenix with 99% red vitality is fully healed in 31 seconds.

Red damage becomes permanent when a partner character is tagged in via a crossover attack (hold P1 or P2), or when a character is forced to come in when their partner is knocked or snapped out. This is where snap backs come in most handy strategically—if you inflict heavy red damage to one of your opponent's assists, use the next clean hit you land on their point character to combo to a snap back, forcing that character in and making the red damage permanent! This is often the most efficient use of hyper meter—snapping in a character who has 90% red vitality does a lot more overall than a hyper combo to add 15-30% damage to a regular combo. Similarly, be wary when you have partner characters who've sustained severe red damage, especially if it's partner 1 (shown below the point character's vitality gauge)... that red damage is only a snap back away from becoming permanent, and if your point character succumbs, partner 1 will be forced in, as well.

When partner 1 has sustained severe red damage, avoid using their ***crossover assist*** (tap P1) or tagging them in with a ***crossover attack*** (hold P1). Be extra cautious to avoid having your point character knocked out, which would force partner 1 to replace them and make red damage permanent. If your point character's vitality is low in addition to significant red damage on partner 1, look for ways to bring in partner 2 safely. This may buy time for both ailing characters to heal red vitality, lessening your immediate risk of having two low-health characters in jeopardy back-to-back. The fastest method is a crossover attack to partner 2 (hold P2), but your rival may expect this and wait for it, eager to punish your new point character while they pose after the tag-in. A three-stage ***team hyper combo*** all the way to partner 2 or a ***team aerial combo*** involving all three characters are safer ways to accomplish getting partner 2 in. You can also guard your opponent's attack and use a ***crossover counter*** (tap → + P2 while guarding, requires one bar of meter).

When partner 2 has sustained severe red damage, refrain from further P2 assist calls. At least partner 2 isn't in imminent danger of having all that red damage become permanent yet if your point character is knocked out—partner 1 will drop in, not partner 2, so as long as you lay off assist 2 for a while, you should be fine. Beware of accidentally hitting → + P2 while blocking, as this causes an inadvertent ***crossover counter*** that swaps in partner 2, which is the last thing you want. This won't make the red damage permanent, but it does put the character in further jeopardy, since knockouts are dependent on depleting regular vitality, not red damage. You shouldn't be calling an assist this battered anyway, so just consider the P2 button off-limits for a while.

If both partner 1 and 2 are in bad shape, with deep red damage, then you could be in trouble. Any poorly timed partner call could just get them knocked out, yet your point character can't afford to get knocked out, either. You also cannot afford to tag either character in with a ***crossover attack***, as this just makes a lot of red damage permanent and compounds a difficult situation. Furthermore, playing sheepishly without assists is usually just delaying the inevitable, unless your capacity for stalling is confident and immaculate. Although ***X-Factor*** is at its least potent with three characters still standing, consider using it here. Getting health back for all three ailing characters, and thus breathing room, can help right the ship in a match gone wrong early. Be aware that later on in the match, as characters start to fall on both sides and the stakes and risks rise, your opponent may still have X-Factor available, while you will not. Some matches boil down to damned-if-you-do, damned-if-you-don't; you'll just have to feel it out.

You can squeeze the maximum amount of vitality possible out of your team with proper red vitality management, forcing your opponent to work even harder for the win. By letting your team rest as needed with character rotations through crossover attacks, THCs, and crossover counters, 300% vitality essentially becomes 450% vitality! Building a team that has plenty of safe THC options or invincible crossover counters helps you get injured comrades to the sidelines without risk, aiding your red vitality management overall. Vitality management is just as important as hyper meter management, so be vigilant in paying close attention to both!

VITALITY: SEALING THE DEAL

Sometimes at the end of a combo, your competitor will have only a sliver of life left. You can decide to do one of two things: either burn an extra bar of hyper meter for a THC to seal the K.O., or save it in an attempt to K.O. the weakened character via a mix-up or chip damage. In this scenario, it is almost always better to finish with a THC, even if your rival has close to zero vitality left.

UMvC3 is a team game, in which team dynamics are a core element of gameplay and strategy. Given this, losing a character is a big deal. Dealing 33% to all three characters of an opposing team is not nearly as significant as dealing 100% damage to a single foe, though the vitality lost is the same. If you let an opponent survive by not burning meter to THC for an assured knockout, you risk letting that character get away. If that character escapes to the sidelines, said character can possibly heal back all red vitality while being used as a crossover assist and THC/TAC partner. That character may even exact revenge later in the match with level 3 X-Factor after they've fully healed and returned at the end!

Hyper meter is much easier to come by than knockouts, so you'll almost never regret spending meter to THC and finish a character off, especially given that a knockout leads to an immediate mix-up opportunity against your competitor's next character. If you have limited hyper combo to spare, be mindful of the capabilities of the character you're trying to knock out, and the tendencies of your human opponent. It's always a good idea to K.O. the character your opponent can play best, but on the other hand, saving meter might be best if meter is tight and one of their less dangerous characters is the target. Of course, throw caution to the wind and burn all hyper meter if it's your rival's last character.

VITALITY: POST-KNOCKOUT

When an opponent's assist character is being forced out after a K.O. or a snap back, they are extremely vulnerable. Crossover assists cannot be called and THCs cannot be performed for roughly four seconds, and the opposing character is in a disadvantageous position. This time is crucial; a successful mix-up gives you the momentum you need to control the rest of the match or to come back after a bad start. Enemies in this position are highly susceptible to cross-under cross-ups, performed by dashing under their character as they fall in at normal jump height. Almost every character can perform some type of cross-under by dashing underneath the adversary and performing standing or crouching (L). New characters coming in after a K.O. or snap back are often already cornered, allowing even more mix-up and pressure opportunities.

In the case of snap backs, be wary of opponents eager to use crossover attacks to tag back out! This is especially important when performing a snap back to bring in Phoenix or your character's primary crossover assist character, like Akuma or Haggar. Frequently, opponents are itching to tag back out as soon as possible, so they'll be holding P1 or P2 from the get-go. If your mix-up attempt fails, be ready to guard high to block the crossover attack, so you can punish them with a combo and snap them right back out.

HYPER METER

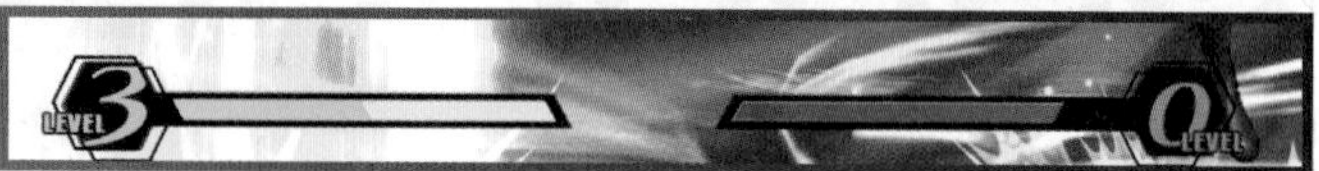

While team members have individual **vitality gauges**, they all share the hyper meter. The hyper meter is built up by interacting with opposing characters. Building and using hyper meter effectively is a key aspect of team management. With three characters on a team, there's rarely enough hyper meter to go around for everyone. But a team isn't just a slapping together of three characters who then operate in individual vacuums—consideration should be paid to who builds the meter well, who needs to expend the meter to be effective, who is present mostly for their assist, who is a good **THC** (team hyper combo) partner, and so on.

It is beneficial to decide on the general roles of each member of your team ahead of time. Will one character primarily serve as a battery, building hyper meter early on without needing to use much? Which character makes the best use of hyper meter? Are any of your characters utterly dependent on using the hyper meter to be effective? Should one character be considered a primary user? What tactics do you have available for building bar—will you rush your rival and rely on melee hits to build gauge? Or will you try to whittle away at the foe from afar with blocked attacks, slowly but safely stockpiling? You can also be aggressive and go for **team aerial combos** with air ⇩ + (S), or construct a team around point Felicia or Thor (who possess special moves that build hyper meter at will), or use a bar-building crossover assist (Morrigan, Frank West, or Amaterasu—γ).

Building hyper meter is inevitable—just about any interaction generates bar. So, plan for it or not, you'll have bar to burn. With just a little forethought as to where that hyper meter will come from, and where it ultimately actually goes, you'll gain a slightly more firm grip on the match. The various uses of hyper meter are covered in further depth later on in this chapter and throughout the chapters on character strategy, as appropriate.

The most effective way to build hyper meter is with a downward-aimed ***team air combo*** *(launch the target with (S), then super jump and air combo into ⇩ + (S); this tags in your next character while granting one full bar of the hyper meter!*

Building Hyper Meter (in Order of Effectiveness):

Perform a team aerial combo by launching with (S), then chaining into air ⇩ + (S)
Call Morrigan, Frank West, or Amaterasu—γ
Use ⇩ ⇩ + (H) (hold) with Felicia or Thor
Hit opponent
Receive an attack from adversary
Hit rival (guarded)
Guard foe's attack

Hyper Meter Usage

Ability	Hyper Meter Bar Cost	Purpose
C. Viper EX moves	1	Special properties
Crossover combination	1~3	Damage, combo extension
Crossover counter	1	Safely swap partners, retaliate against blocked attacks, avoid chip damage K.O.
Hyper combo	1~3, 5 for Dark Phoenix Rising	Damage, combo extension, enhancement
Snap back	1	Mess up opposing team order, force in an opposing character who has low vitality or significant red damage
Team hyper combo	2~5 (lv.3 hyper combos can finish THCs)	Damage, combo extension, safely swap partners

Hyper Meter Gain

Each bar of hyper meter represents 10000 meter points. We've listed the meter gain for every move in the game; a move that gains 1000 meter is gaining a tenth of a bar. When attacks are blocked, the aggressor earns 62.5% of the usual meter gain value.

X-FACTOR

L + M + H + S (ONCE PER MATCH; NOTATED THROUGHOUT GUIDE IN COMBOS AND SEQUENCES AS)

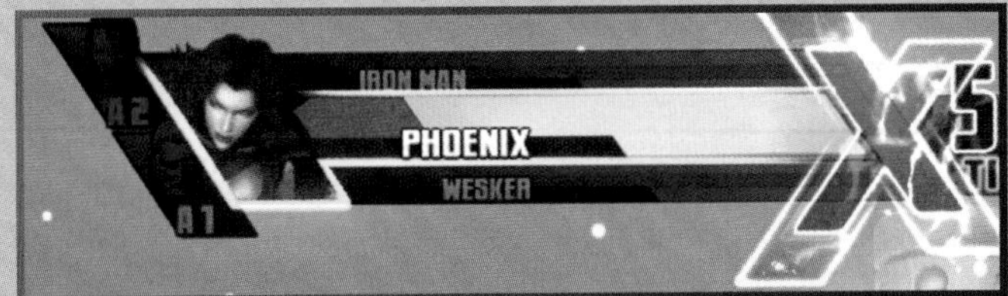

X-Factor available; press L + M + H + S ( ).

X-Factor activated!

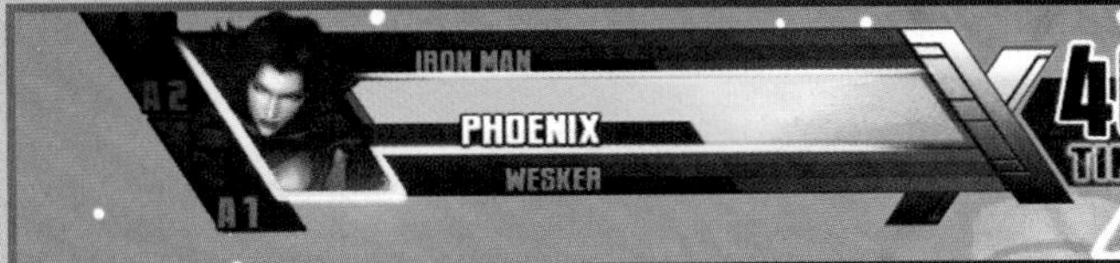

X-Factor unavailable; X-Factor can only be used once per match. The potential and duration of X-Factor is greater the fewer partners you have remaining, and the X-Factor indicator itself becomes more pronounced if you haven't yet used X-Factor with only one character left.

Between the vitality gauges of both teams is the X-Factor indicator. A glowing cross indicates that X-Factor is available or in use; a sterile, gray X indicates that X-Factor has been expended. X-Factor cannot be activated while knocked down, nor in hitstun, nor during hyper combos with cutscenes, lv.3 hyper combos, or throws. Otherwise, X-Factor can be activated at any time. New to *UMvC3*, it can be activated in the air as well as on the ground!

Actions Cancelable with X-Factor Activation:

- Basic Attacks L, M, H
- Special Attacks S
- Command Attacks → + H, etc.
- Special Moves ↓ ↘ → + ATK, etc.
- Hyper Combos ↓ ↘ → + ATK ATK, etc.; not including lv.3 hyper combos or cutscene hypers
- Guardstun

X-Factor can be used once per match, and it applies to an entire team at a time, including crossover assists. During X-Factor's duration, characters for that team will be encased in a shadowy galactic glow. The strength and speed of the point character, along with the strength of assists, are greatly increased during X-Factor. The speed boost means that attacks used during X-Factor often have shorter startup and faster recovery than outside of X-Factor, which leads to opportunities for link combos that are impossible otherwise, and makes hitstun decay less of a limiting factor. Both the strength and speed boosts innate to X-Factor vary from character to character.

The remaining duration of X-Factor is indicated by a glowing, shrinking red border around the vitality gauge.

Both partner characters and the point character recover 27,000 red vitality per second as long as they're not actively being hit by the adversary and no chip damage is received during X-Factor. This last point is extremely important, since some late-game strategies revolve around dealing tremendous chip damage from characters like Akuma, Dormammu, or Storm using hyper combos repeatedly. Using X-Factor to negate the unavoidable hits may often be the only way to avoid being knocked out.

Teammates Remaining	X-Factor Level	Duration (identical for all characters)	Damage Increase (character dependent)	Speed Increase (character dependent)
Three characters standing	X-Factor level 1	10 seconds	115~140%	100~125%
Two characters standing	X-Factor level 2	15 seconds	135~170%	105~130%
One character standing	X-Factor level 3	20 seconds	150~200%	110~145%

Marvel Character X-Factor Data

Name	Lv.1 Damage %	Lv.2 Damage %	Lv.3 Damage %	Lv.1 Speed %	Lv.2 Speed %	Lv.3 Speed %
Captain America	135	160	185	105	110	115
Deadpool	125	145	165	115	125	135
Doctor Doom	130	150	175	110	120	130
Doctor Strange	120	145	170	120	125	130
Dormammu	130	155	180	110	115	120
Ghost Rider	135	160	185	105	110	115
Hawkeye	120	140	160	120	130	140
Hulk	140	170	200	100	100	100
Iron Fist	130	150	170	110	120	130
Iron Man	125	150	175	115	120	125
M.O.D.O.K.	135	160	185	105	110	115
Magneto	125	147.5	170	115	122.5	130
Nova	130	150	170	110	120	130
Phoenix/Dark Phoenix	120/135	135/170	150/200	110/115	120/130	130/145
Rocket Raccoon	120	140	160	120	130	140
Sentinel	130	150	170	110	120	130
She-Hulk	130	150	170	110	120	130
Shuma-Gorath (DLC)	127.5	144.9	162.4	112.5	125	137.5
Spider-Man	125	145	165	115	125	135
Storm	125	140	155	115	130	145
Super-Skrull	130	147.5	165	110	122.5	135
Taskmaster	130	155	180	110	115	120
Thor	140	170	200	100	100	100
Wolverine	125	145	165	115	125	135
X-23	120	140	160	120	130	140

Capcom Character X-Factor Data

Name	Lv.1 Damage %	Lv.2 Damage %	Lv.3 Damage %	Lv.1 Speed %	Lv.2 Speed %	Lv.3 Speed %
Akuma	132.5	155	177.5	107.5	115	122.5
Amaterasu	120	140	160	120	130	140
Arthur	125	145	165	115	125	135
C. Viper	125	147.5	170	115	122.5	130
Chris	140	165	190	100	105	110
Chun-Li	120	135	150	120	135	150
Dante	130	150	170	110	120	130
Felicia	115	135	155	125	135	145
Firebrand	115	135	155	125	135	145
Frank West	135	160	185	105	110	115
Haggar	140	165	190	100	105	110
Hsien-Ko	125	145	165	115	125	135
Jill (DLC)	125	140	155	115	130	145
Morrigan	120	137.5	155	120	132.5	145
Nemesis T-Type	140	165	190	100	105	110
Phoenix Wright	135	160	185	105	110	115
Ryu	135	160	185	105	110	115
Spencer	135	160	185	105	110	115
Strider	120	135	155	120	135	145
Trish	120	140	160	120	130	140
Tron	135	160	185	105	110	115
Vergil	125	150	175	115	120	125
Viewtiful Joe	120	140	160	120	130	140
Wesker	130	150	170	110	120	130
Zero	120	140	160	120	130	140

X-Factor's purpose and potential uses are multifaceted:

Since X-Factor activation can cancel any action, you can hit-confirm into X-Factor from any combo. The ideal application for a hit-confirmed X-Factor combo is when you recognize that you've nailed both the opponent's point and partner character at once—a solid X-Factor combo, even at X-Factor level 1, can easily knock out any full-life assist, and most full-life point characters! Two-for-one is just about the best deal you'll find in *UMvC3*.

The ability to X-Factor cancel actions in otherwise-impossible places means you can create new set-ups by canceling the recovery of certain projectiles and hyper combos with X-Factor. This is analogous to using FADC in *Super Street Fighter IV* (or "roman canceling" in *Guilty Gear XX* and its sequels) to throw a fireball, then dash immediately behind it.

Similarly, you can use X-Factor to achieve otherwise impossible, outrageous combos by canceling a ground hyper combo partway through into another hyper combo. This is great when you want to ensure that a combo results in a knockout, rather than simply a severely damaged foe. Interestingly, if you X-Factor cancel a mashable hyper combo, your inputs after your character recovers from the X-Factor cancel still influence the hits of the canceled hyper combo!

You can also use X-Factor to cut guardstun short after blocking a recovery-heavy attack—your punishment becomes much stronger with X-Factor active, and you can access it sooner without waiting for guardstun to decay naturally. This can be ideal for harshly punishing some predictable tactics, like dive kicks, square jumps, and crossover assists.

X-Factor can also be used during guardstun to avoid a chip damage knockout, such as while blocking a beam like Iron Man's Proton Cannon. Depending on the situation, this can be a lot more palatable than using a crossover counter out of desperation, which wastes a bar of meter and often just means you trade the knockout of one character for another. And, crossover counters aren't available while blocking in midair, making air X-Factor activation the only recourse sometimes.

Expanding on this medical role, if your point character and partners have banged-up vitality gauges filled with red damage, you can activate X-Factor and run away from your attacker for a bit while red damage replenishes more quickly than normal.

Finally, you can simply keep X-Factor in reserve to deploy in last-man-standing scenarios. X-Factor is tremendously powerful when used by a single, unassisted character, greatly increasing comeback potential if you find yourself sliding down the slippery slope of dwindling numbers!

It's easy to recommend knocking out two characters at once—both a point character and an assist—as the most efficient and dominant proactive use of X-Factor. In effect, this resembles the "double snap back" assist infinites that became one of the most deadly high-level tactics in *MvC2*—you receive an outsized reward for an incidental, or even *accidental*, hit. And in some ways, this is even *more* powerful—here, you don't just knock out one character and gain tremendous momentum against the next; instead, you just outright demolish two characters! However, that situation may not come up in a given match, or you may not have time to react to glancing blows that strike two opposing characters. How you use X-Factor in each match is ultimately a judgment call, and the factors for that judgment differ from bout to bout and opponent to opponent. The only sure thing regarding X-Factor is that it's far too powerful to overlook. So, at the very least, don't neglect to use it if you're down to your last character—there is no reason not to, at that point—but also look for efficient opportunities to use X-Factor that come sooner than a last-ditch comeback effort!

X-FACTOR COMEBACKS

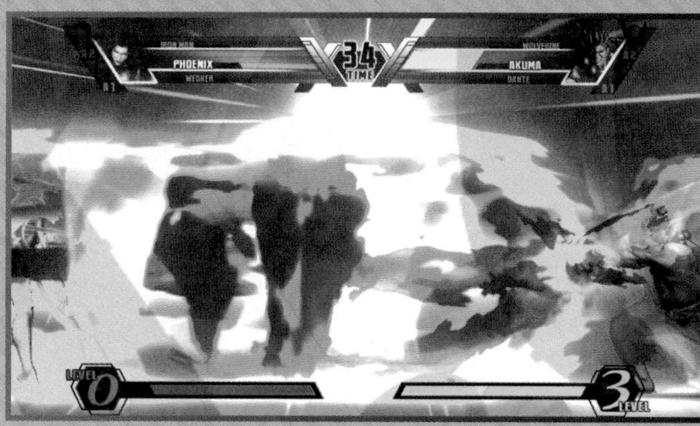

If you have only one character left against an entire team of three, don't lose hope just yet! Sometimes, level 3 X-Factor is all you need to stage a comeback. Don't be hasty with your activation, however. Activating X-Factor without having the initiative isn't always the best choice. Quickly analyze the opposing team's characters and remaining vitality. For example, if the remaining team is 40% Storm, 90% Wesker, and 100% Nemesis, you should aim to K.O. Storm without the use of X-Factor if possible, since the remaining two characters have high vitality.

Usually, players respond to a level 3 X-Factor activation by fleeing, making it harder to stage a comeback; it's less likely for them to run away from your last remaining character that has yet to activate X-Factor because you have no remaining characters to call on for help. In this case, especially if the opposing team is healthy overall, save your X-Factor for a guard cancel attempt. After the first K.O., perform a mix-up on the next character coming in; if successful, any character should score 100% off the resulting combo. Level 3 X-Factor hits *hard!* You then get *another* mix-up opportunity on the last character, which hopefully seals the comeback! It's important in this situation to perform combos that are not only specifically tailored for a K.O. in level 3 X-Factor, but that are also reliable and consistent. Securing a combo opportunity only to mess it up because of X-Factor's speed increase kills your momentum while precious X-Factor time bleeds away.

If you are having trouble finding a good opportunity to activate X-Factor level 3, create the opportunity yourself. Hyper combos like Dormammu's Stalking Flare, Strider's Ouroboros, or Firebrand's Chaos Tide are great to use right before activating X-Factor. Special moves like Vergil's Rapid Slash, Super-Skrull's Meteor Smash, or Phoenix's TK Overdrive can be used and canceled into X-Factor for positioning or fishing for hits. Similarly, invincible and long-reaching hyper combos like Spencer's Bionic Lancer and Iron Fist's Iron Rage give you high-damage openings to use seemingly at random; if your cold hyper combo hits, great! Either pop X-Factor and turn the hit into a knockout if it's their last character, or save X-Factor and keep the threat handy; if your "random" hyper combo is blocked, X-Factor cancel the recovery to keep safe and enable an immediate follow-up attack!

In short, don't just use X-Factor randomly because you have one character remaining. Being strategic with your X-Factor use in a dire situation can mean the difference between staging an epic comeback or losing horribly. Save your X-Factor for a good opportunity, or if you're on your last legs and need to save yourself from a chip damage K.O.

Foundation: Guarding

The most important thing you can do to improve at any fighting game is to guard properly. And yet the number one thing that novice and intermediate players neglect to develop is defense. For the most part, whenever you are in doubt in *UMvC3*, the prime directive is to rely on solid guarding, while staying calm and looking for a way to turn momentum to your favor. None of that works if you didn't block correctly in the first place, however. Guarding an attack negates most or all of its damage, and it allows you to input ATK ATK to push the attacker away with **advancing guard**. Many attacks, including most **special moves** and **hyper combos**, deal damage even when guarded—this is called **chip damage**. Chip damage amounts to 30% of the damage an attack would have caused if it wasn't blocked. Guarding is accomplished by holding a backward direction while your character is not otherwise occupied performing an action.

Ground Guarding

Defensive Input	Result without Incoming Attack	Result with Incoming Attack
⇖	Backward jump	Standing guard during 3 pre-jump frames / air guard after 4th frame*
⇦	Backward walk	Standing guard
⇙	Crouch	Crouching guard

** M.O.D.O.K. leaves the ground on the first frame after an upward input, so he cannot block during pre-jump frames; he doesn't have any!*

Air Guarding (Not Possible while Airdashing or Flying)

Defensive Input	Result without Incoming Attack	Result with Incoming Attack
⇖, ⇦, or ⇙	Air control backward (if possible)	Air guard

Guarding Types

Guard Type	Guards Against	Vulnerable To	Actions Available during Guardstun
Standing Guard	Overhead attacks, mids	Low attacks, throws	Advancing guard, crossover counter, X-Factor
Crouching Guard	Low attacks, mids	Overhead attacks, throws	Advancing guard, crossover counter, X-Factor
Air Guard	—	Air throws, anti-air special throws	Advancing guard, X-Factor

The speed of the action in the *MvC* series is unsurpassed among fighting games, and many offensive tactics are based on creating situations where it's difficult, or close to impossible, to guard properly. This makes guarding under pressure an absolutely crucial skill. Because of the nature of *MvC*, your success is occasionally based on sheer reactions and skill, but much of the time, it is based on solid guesswork and knowledge of your opponent. Sure, understanding how to block is key in any fighting game, but few games have you pay so heavy a price for getting it wrong.

Wrong.

Wrong.

Right! ***Low*** *attacks must be guarded crouching. Many crouching basic attacks are low attacks, along with certain crossover assists and other moves.*

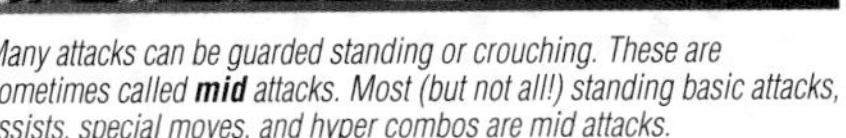

Many attacks can be guarded standing or crouching. These are sometimes called ***mid*** *attacks. Most (but not all!) standing basic attacks, assists, special moves, and hyper combos are mid attacks.*

Right! Overhead attacks *must be guarded standing. Also called* high attacks. *Most air basic attacks are overheads, as are some command attacks and special moves. Crossover attacks, accomplished by holding* P1 or P2 *to switch characters, are overheads.*

Guarding correctly places your character in **guardstun**. The duration of guardstun is dependent upon the attack that caused it; heavier attacks tend to inflict lengthier guardstun. While on the ground, many attacks can be guarded either standing or crouching, but low attacks can only be guarded while crouching, and overhead attacks can only be guarded while standing. Some assists strike either high or low and are very useful as a result, since they allow virtually unguardable setups when used in tandem with point character attacks that must be blocked the other way.

MARVEL LOW HITTING ASSISTS (MUST BE GUARDED CROUCHING!)

Deadpool—α
She-Hulk—α
X-23—β

CAPCOM LOW HITTING ASSISTS (MUST BE GUARDED CROUCHING!)

Felicia—α
Phoenix Wright—γ
Wesker—β

MARVEL OVERHEAD ASSISTS (MUST BE GUARDED STANDING!)

Iron Fist—β
Nova—β

CAPCOM OVERHEAD ASSISTS (MUST BE GUARDED STANDING!)

Akuma—γ
C. Viper—γ

Guarding in the air is done by holding any backward direction.

You don't have to worry about high or low attacks when guarding in midair. You can use this to your advantage, jumping defensively to reduce the number of blocking variables from four to two. Jump defensively with caution, though. Before jumping, you risk being hit by a low attack during the three pre-jump frames, and once off the ground, you risk eating an **air throw**. As with guarding on the ground, guarding in midair puts you into **guardstun**, your character's blocking animation. During aerial guardstun, the only things you can do are press ATK ATK to push your rival away with **advancing guard** and use all four attack buttons to cancel guard with **X-Factor.**

Flying characters cannot guard. Guarding is possible the rest of the time while airborne, but using some moves means you can't guard (or act in general) until that character lands on the ground again. Examples include Storm's S + ATK Lightning Attack (used outside of flight) and Wolverine's S + ATK Drill Claw. Do not use these moves carelessly, since watchful opponents will recognize that your character is vulnerable all the way down; all they have to do is launch your character or start a hyper combo before your hero lands.

No Proximity Blocking!

MvC3* and *UMvC3 do not have "proximity blocking," a feature found in many Capcom fighting games where nearby whiffed attacks force you into **guardstun**. Here, characters only enter guardstun when they are actually guarding an attack.

Active Blocking / Absolute Guard

Attacks that strike quickly enough to leave no gaps for the defender to move or act are all guarded automatically if the first attack is blocked correctly, since the defending character is stuck in **guardstun**. These gapless sequences, which prevent the defender from surprising the aggressor with a **reversal** or similar escape tactic, are often called **true blockstrings**. As an example, block the beginning of Iron Man's Proton Cannon **hyper combo**, then stop holding back. Your character still guards the entire hyper combo. This is called **active blocking**, or **absolute guard**. Don't rely on active blocking, though—this can get you into trouble if competitors switch from low to high (or vice-versa) in a series of attacks, or if attacks are delayed.

ADVANCING GUARD

ATK ATK DURING GUARDSTUN

Advancing guard pushes both the aggressive and defensive characters apart. When cornered, advancing guard is less effective because only the aggressor character is pushed back—the defensive character has nowhere to go!

Advancing guard (also called **pushblock**) can be performed at any time during **guardstun** by pressing ATK ATK. Against multi-hit attacks, advancing guard can be performed many times successively. Advancing guard pushes the defender and the attacker away from each other, and it may reduce some of the **chip damage** received from blocked attacks, depending on positioning. *UMvC3* is full of fast characters equipped with devious options to compromise your blocking and score a hit, so when you do block correctly, it's almost always crucial to buy yourself some space with advancing guard. The only reason you wouldn't want to employ advancing guard is if your opponent has let you guard something that has enough recovery so you can punish for free—in these instances, advancing guard is actually detrimental, as you waste a punish opportunity! Savvy competitors won't hand it over for free very frequently, though, so err on the side of using advancing guard to repel any enemy offensive, and always perform advancing guard repeatedly when guarding a continual attack like a beam hyper combo.

Don't be overzealous trying to use advancing guard right away, though—if you start pressing ATK ATK in anticipation of advancing guard rather than actually reacting to your successful blocking, you'll inevitably produce errant attacks or dashes when the opponent actually doesn't do anything. When your challenger realizes you're using advancing guard early, they can simply act aggressively and bait you into whiffing unintentional attacks, which they then punish. Slow yourself down slightly, and force yourself to *react* with advancing guard, rather than just *hoping* for it. Likewise, when you realize someone is using advancing guard a little too quickly after blocking, start delaying your follow-up hits to counterhit them.

Advancing guard can be activated at any time during guardstun, even down to the last frame

Once the "push" actually happens, advancing guard recovers from guardstun after 21 frames, regardless of the attack that caused guardstun

The earliest time a "push" happens is after one-third of an attack's guardstun has passed. You can input advancing guard earlier and the game will register it, but the push won't actually happen until this timeframe has passed

Advancing guard almost always results in *more* guardstun than simply blocking, unless the guarded move causes abnormally lengthy guardstun, like more than 35 frames

Both characters are pushed away from a central point during advancing guard, though the attacker is pushed back farther. This is why advancing guard means less in the corner

COUNTERS TO ADVANCING GUARD

Advancing guard doesn't work against certain moves, and it is less effective against some tactics that force you to block separate attacks simultaneously.

Advancing guard does not represent an unassailable wall. Advancing guard is far less potent when cornered. Some moves, like Storm's Lightning Sphere or Dante's Devil Trigger specials, are actually immune to advancing guard. And if you are made to guard against attacks from both a point character and assist at the same time, advancing guard gets diminished in effect. This is especially troublesome if the opposing point character manages to drop an assist on one side, then attack from the other—a situation some **teleport** and **square jump**-capable characters can create at will.

Characters who have thrown a projectile and fully recovered can negate advancing guard with precise timing. Wait until just as your rival guards and begins to use advancing guard with a projectile, then dash forward. If you dash a little early, you'll just get pushed back as normal. With perfect timing, your character simply appears to dash forward, as if advancing guard had no effect at all! With slightly late timing, you'll have your character get pushed backward for a split-second before initiating the forward dash, which means that your character will probably maintain roughly the same overall position.

Input a dash JUST as your opponent's advancing guard animation begins.

Projectile characters can ignore advancing guard entirely by dashing just as the competitor initiates advancing guard against a projectile.

The same kind of thing can be done with flight activation. From a move that your opponent has blocked and pushblocked, cancel into flight; the state change halts the backward momentum of advancing guard. Similarly, certain special moves and actions can circumvent advancing guard. With Trish, you can chain cancel from a blocked air attack to her Stiletto Kick to negate advancing guard, whereas with Doctor Doom, you can cancel blocked basic attacks into forward dashes, achieving the same effect.

Take care not to simply mash on ATK ATK when you expect to block an attack. In other words, try very hard to react to attacks before using advancing guard, rather than anticipating attacks and pressing ATK ATK on autopilot. If your rival doesn't actually produce an attack for you to guard, you either accidentally trigger either a dash or an unintentional attack. Either result can be disastrous against an attentive foe.

THE THEORY OF RELATIVITY (FOR GUARDING, AT LEAST)

No matter where your opponent's assist is, block away from their point character. Assist characters have PLAYER 1 or PLAYER 2 above their heads, depending on the team to which they belong.

If your competitor manages to place their crossover assist far behind you, you must block both the assist's attack and anything from the point character by holding **away from the point**. Do not be confused by the crossover assist!

With all the mayhem possible in a match, with up to six characters on the screen amidst effects and explosions innumerable, it's important to keep yourself oriented. No matter where characters are positioned, no matter where crossover assists are being called, no matter what's going on, guarding is **always** relative the opposing team's **point character**. So, if the opposing point character is to the right, block with ⇦ or ⇙. If they're to the left, block with ⇨ or ⇘.

Many tactics are devised to be confusing specifically to put the onus on the defensive player to block properly. For example, say a teleport-capable character calls a pinning crossover assist on one side of the opponent, then teleports to the other side. The defensive opponent not only has to process that the teleporting point character swapped sides, and that the crossover assist now stuck to their backs is irrelevant (though it still must be guarded!), but they also have to be watchful for that point character to mix up between overheads and low attacks, or maybe even another side switch. Often in these kinds of situations, the presence of a pinning assist disables advancing guard, so it's important to have good guarding fundamentals for when the issue is forced upon you. Don't panic or worry about chip damage—just try to react to what the offense executes, and guard accordingly until you have an opportunity to use advancing guard to begin an escape. Keep in mind that if you are set up for solid **crossover counters**, an adversary trying to pin you with an assist from the front while also attacking represents the best time to counter—catching two characters is better than one, and it can turn the tide of a match instantly!

CROSSOVER COUNTERS

⇨ + P1 or P2 DURING GROUND GUARDSTUN (REQUIRES ONE BAR OF HYPER METER AND AN AVAILABLE PARTNER)

Crossover counters can be used like variable counters from *MvC2*, to block and hit back opponents, or to escape chip damage knockouts.

Counters are a team-oriented defensive measure from blocking. When guarding on the ground, you can perform a crossover counter by pressing ⇨ + P1 or P2. If a partner is present and hyper meter is available, the chosen character tags in and performs their crossover assist. The incoming character becomes the point character immediately, and the move performed adopts the characteristics of a special move rather than a crossover assist—meaning it can be hyper combo canceled or interrupted with X-Factor. C. Viper's crossover counters can be canceled with a feint by pressing Ⓢ, just like her special moves.

The most obvious use of crossover counters is in desperation—you can crossover counter to avoid a chip damage knockout. You have to weigh whether it's worth eating some guaranteed damage on the character coming in against letting the low-health character expire. This is always a case-by-case decision, as countering in a character to eat the end of a hyper combo for someone else may just lead to them getting knocked out instead.

You can also employ crossover counters more proactively on defense, timing the tag in to hit your opponent while they're still recovering from their blocked attack. If you used a good crossover assist for this, you'll have the chance to hit-confirm and cancel into the new character's hyper combo!

Interestingly, after initiating a crossover counter, you can actually perform any air hyper combo the incoming character has before they actually touch down and perform their assist attack as a counter! This costs yet another bar of meter, so it's an expensive trick, but it's worth keeping in mind; for example, Trish and Sentinel don't have great crossover counters for taking back momentum or punishing enemy attacks safely, but they *can* perform relatively safe hyper combos in midair. Counter to Trish or Sentinel, then perform air Maximum Voltage or Hard Drive before landing to fry your aggressor.

Some assist types are invulnerable, but only when they are used as a crossover counter! Most "uppercut" type assists fit this bill... they aren't actually invincible when used as crossover assists, but counter into them, and all these attacks are invincible and guaranteed to make it to at least the first hitting frame. The only assists in the game with invulnerability *as assists* are Haggar—α and (Turnabout) Phoenix Wright—α or Phoenix Wright—β.

MARVEL INVULNERABLE CROSSOVER COUNTERS

Captain America—β
Deadpool—α
She-Hulk—γ
Spider-Man—γ
Thor—β
Wolverine—α
X-23—γ

CAPCOM INVULNERABLE CROSSOVER COUNTERS

Arthur—α
Chris—α
Felicia—α
Haggar—α
Morrigan—α
Phoenix Wright—α/—β (Turnabout)
Ryu—α
Tron—β
Viewtiful Joe—β
Zero—α

Crossover counters can be performed during guardstun, whether standing or crouching.

Input ⇨ + P1 or P2, and the new character tags in with their crossover assist! They become your new point character immediately. You can even cancel their tag-in into an air hyper combo before they even touch down!

Character-depending, you have follow-up options if this crossover assist hits...for example, canceling into a hyper combo!

Movement

WALKING

HOLD ⇦ OR ⇨

The most basic way to move. Holding ⇦ also doubles as standing guard if your rival decides to attack. Apart from fine positioning, or using Arthur on point, you probably won't be doing a lot of sustained walking. The pace of the game is simply too fast for this to be a viable primary method of locomotion.

DASHING

⇨⇨ OR ⇦⇦ (WITH NO MORE THAN 9 FRAMES SEPARATING THE INPUTS); ATK ATK OR ⇦ + ATK ATK (WITH NO MORE THAN 1 FRAME SEPARATING THE BUTTON PRESSES; REFERRED TO AS "COMMAND DASH")

A dash on the ground is a fast movement either backward or forward. This is likely how you'll travel most of the time on the ground, unless you plan to focus on Arthur, Hsien-Ko, or Morrigan (Arthur cannot dash, Hsien-Ko warps forward rather than dashes, and Morrigan airdashes up from the ground). Dashes allow you to either close distance with a foe or to retreat very quickly. Most characters can cancel a dash with other actions (such as an attack or blocking) after only 4 frames, and you should get in the habit of being ready to guard, jump, or attack immediately after starting a dash. Dashing forward and then guarding immediately is one of the best ways to cautiously gain ground and test your opponent's defensive reactions without running into enemy assists or attacks carelessly.

Ground dashes can be canceled into attacks or guarding after frame 4, unless otherwise noted. All dashes (except irregular ones) can be canceled into jumps instantly.

While most characters can cancel a dash with any other action after frame 4, some characters can't cancel a dash for a longer period at the beginning, and a handful of characters can't cancel a dash at all! Players using these characters must be more careful with their use of dashes than with the rest of the cast, who have the luxury of being able to cancel their dashes with attacks or (more importantly) by guarding. Characters who cannot cancel their dashes early or at all also occasionally run into problems with jump-in combo positioning. Other characters may land a jump-in hit from far away, land, then dash and immediately cancel the dash with an attack to hit the target point-blank and continue into a full combo. Characters who can't interrupt dashes can't do that, however: by the time their dash is cancelable or ended, the defensive character is able to guard. Thus, in addition to taking extra care with movement, players of these characters must be more precise with their air-to-ground offense.

Marvel Character Ground Dash Data

Name	Forward Dash	Backdash	Notes
Captain America	40	33	—
Deadpool	31	35	—
Doctor Doom	35	33	Cannot cancel dash
Doctor Strange	35	35	—
Dormammu	19	33	Cannot cancel dash
Ghost Rider	20	25	—
Hawkeye	30	30	—
Hulk	40	40	Cannot cancel dash
Iron Fist	30	33	—
Iron Man	35	35	Ground dashes can be canceled after frame 11
Magneto	45	45	—
M.O.D.O.K.	19	33	—
Nova	35	25	—
Phoenix	38	39	—
Rocket Raccoon	15	15	—
Sentinel	30	27	—
She-Hulk	19	33	—
Shuma-Gorath	45	54	Backdash: frames 12-31 invulnerable
Spider-Man	41	40	—
Storm	19	33	—
Super-Skrull	32	32	—
Taskmaster	35	35	Movement starts on frame 6
Thor	19	39	—
Wolverine	20	34	—
X-23	16	21	—

Capcom Character Ground Dash Data

Name	Forward Dash	Backdash	Notes
Akuma	28	28	—
Amaterasu	73	32	—
Arthur	—	—	No dash ability
Chris Redfield	39	40	—
Chun-Li	22	29	—
C. Viper	15	23	—
Dante	19	31	—
Felicia	25	24	—
Firebrand	22	22	—
Frank West	30	30	—
Haggar	30	31	—
Hsien-Ko	50	33	Forward dash: frames 16-30 invincible, can pass through foe
Jill	19	23	—
Morrigan	46	23	Morrigan airdashes instead of ground dashing. Hold input to dash for longer. Can cancel forward dash into air attack after frame 15. Backdash cannot be canceled
Nemesis T-Type	45	37	Can cancel ground dashes after frame 10
Phoenix Wright	35	35	—
Ryu	20	25	—
Spencer	30	35	—
Strider	54	38	—
Trish	25	25	—
Tron	34	42	Can cancel ground dashes after frame 11
Vergil	21	39	—
Viewtiful Joe	26	26	—
Wesker	18	24	—
Zero	41	35	—

DASH INPUT LENIENCY, AND BACKDASH FEINTS

When dashing using tap commands, you must leave a gap of no more than 9 frames between ⇨ or ⇦ inputs. With a gap of 10 frames, no dash is produced. This is true of airdashes, as well.

When dashing using attack button presses (L, M, and H —although any of these work, we notate ATK throughout this guide), things work differently. To simply dash forward, press any two basic attack buttons together (this does not include S). There is *very* slight leniency here—the inputs are intended to be simultaneous, but they do not have to be, exactly. Press one attack button, then another attack button on the *very next frame*, and a dash is still produced. As a side effect, this enables plink wavedashing. (See the following note.)

To backdash with attack buttons, press ⇦ + ATK ATK. You MUST hit ⇦ at the same time as at least one attack button, and the same tiny leniency applies for the other attack button press—a gap of one frame is allowed, and the dash still registers.

However, if you tap ⇦, then wait at least 1 frame but up to 8 frames before inputting ATK ATK, something strange happens: your character backdashes for 4 frames, then automatically cancels into a forward dash! This can be useful as a visual feint when you want to dash forward anyway—if your character has a particularly distinctive backward dash animation (such as Haggar's, or M.O.D.O.K.'s, or Sentinel's) this trick may incite reactions from an opponent who expects a backdash. However, this is not useful for characters without distinctive animations at the beginning of a backdash.

Note that this backdash feint trick does not work for the characters who cannot cancel dashes immediately (Chris, Doctor Doom, Dormammu, Hulk, Iron Man, Ryu, and Tron). For them, tapping ⇦ then ATK ATK within 8 frames simply results in a backdash. With a gap of 9 frames or larger, a forward dash is produced.

Wavedashing

Wavedashing refers to canceling a dash into another dash. There are two ways to do this.

Crouch-cancel dashes into one another. Input → → or ATK ATK for the first dash, then quickly repeat ↓ , ATK ATK, ↓ , ATK ATK. You're tapping down ever so briefly to interrupt one dash before returning the pad or stick to neutral and inputting the dash command again for a new one.

Plinking dash inputs. This causes a dash to cancel to a basic attack, which is then instantly kara-canceled into another dash. To perform this, first dash with → → or ATK ATK, then input ATK~ATK, with only one frame separating the attack inputs. If performed correctly, you'll seem to seamlessly cancel one dash into another, without a crouch cancel. Bonus points if you perform this with → + H~ATK, → + H~ATK to install option select throw break attempts into each dash!

Mastery of wavedashing allows you to have your characters cross the ground much more quickly—useful if your competitor is trying to run away or zone from the air, or if they leave themselves vulnerable from far away. It can also open up extra combo and OTG possibilities from farther out than is possible with a single dash.

Characters who cannot cancel a dash also cannot wavedash; characters who can only cancel a dash midway through cannot wavedash as quickly as the rest of the cast. Every character's dash duration and acceleration is a little different, so the ideal time to actually cancel dashes to wavedash for maximum speed and distance varies from character to character.

JUMPS, SUPER JUMPS, DOUBLE JUMPS, TRIPLE JUMPS, WALL JUMPS, AND FLIGHT

In most fighting series, it's imprudent to spend too much time in the air. That's definitely not the case here; *UMvC3* battles can take place as much in the air as on the ground. Characters vary wildly in their aerial capabilities; some should be played so they are in the air a majority of the time, while others are best used while they are grounded.

The screen will shift to super jump height to track an ascending character, and the ground is not visible. Point characters who are still grounded will be represented by "1P" and "2P" indicators, and can still move around and act as normal. Assist characters are ***not indicated*** visually from super jump height! The only way to know if an assist was called is by audio cues and the disappearance of assist button icons over vitality gauges.

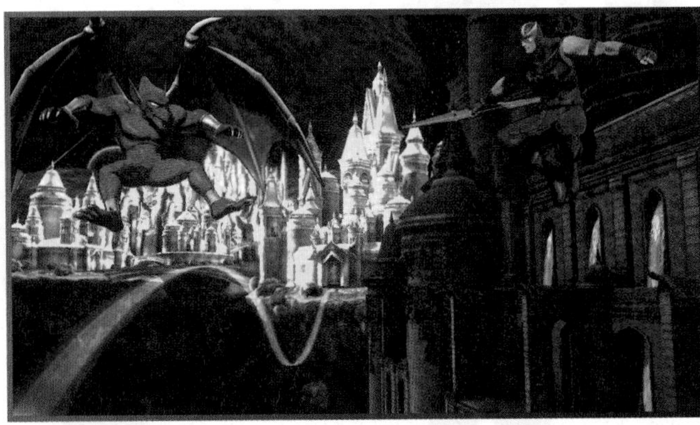

In a departure from previous *Vs.* titles, characters *do not* turn around on their own when **jumping**! That is to say, if you jump over an opposing **point character**, you will *not* automatically turn back to face them until landing again. While you can still air **guard**, or air **throw** an opponent with ⇨ or ⇦ + H if close enough, this does mean aerial **basic attacks** will whiff in the wrong direction! The only way around this is to use a **special move** after you've crossed over your foe—this will re-orient your character properly. Like guarding, the commands for special moves are *always* relative the opponent's character, no matter which direction your character is actually facing.

Flight characters have it best here, as activating flight will re-orient them with more freedom to maneuver. Additionally, passing over an opponent during flight will automatically auto-correct a character's orientation.

While airborne, you won't need to worry about whether to guard ***high*** or ***low***; only holding backward, away from the opposing point character, matters. You are still susceptible to air throws, however, most of which lead to ***OTG*** opportunities. Also, flying/airdashing characters cannot block, and certain characters cannot block until landing after using certain attacks.

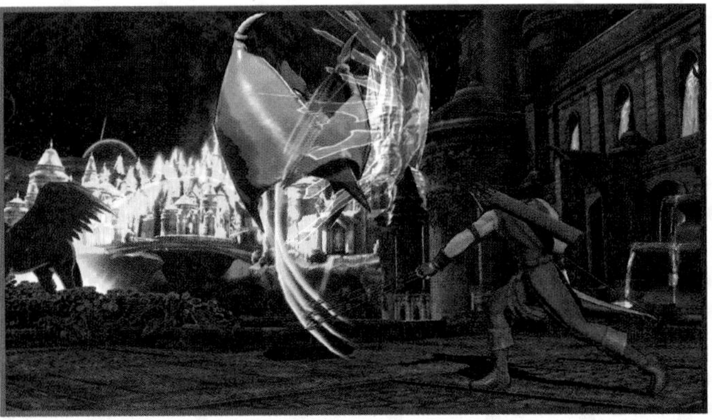

Limitation on Special Moves During Airborne Periods

In a given airborne period, which is defined as the time between when your character leaves the ground and when they land again, no more than three **special moves** can be used. There is one way around this: flight-capable characters can use as many special moves as they want while flying, provided that you actually activate flight before *already* using three special moves—flight activation itself counts as a special move, so your character can't start flying if you've already used three specials! Once activated, flight is its own distinct state, which allows the use of as many special moves as you can perform. Once flight expires, you'll only be able to use a special move again if you *haven't* used more than two special moves already, including flight activation itself, and any specials used during flight.

Except for M.O.D.O.K. jumps have 3 grounded startup frames before becoming airborne on the 4th frame after input. They have 1 frame of recovery upon landing. Values for double/triple jumps indicate added frames of vertical movement. By holding ⇦ or ⇨ during a super jump you can alter your character's trajectory slightly with air control, though some characters are better at this than others. For flight frames, the first number is the startup of flight mode, and the second number is the duration.

Marvel Character Jump Data

Name	Jump Frames	Super Jump Frames	Double/ Triple Jump Frames	Flight Frames (startup / duration)	Notes
Captain America	44	81	+17	—	—
Deadpool	37	81	+19	—	Wall jump capable
Doctor Doom	44	81	—	15 / 106	—
Doctor Strange	43	81	—	22 / 99	—
Dormammu	42	81	—	21 / 100	—
Ghost Rider	40	81	—	—	—
Hawkeye	49	81	—	—	—
Hulk	40	81	—	—	—
Iron Fist	40	81	—	—	Wall jump capable
Iron Man	46	79	—	12 / 108	—
Magneto	48	81	—	15 / 106	—
M.O.D.O.K.	5	81	—	5~7 / 300	Normal jump flight mode starts 5 frames after pressing ⇧
Nova	40	81	—	10 / 110	—
Phoenix	42	81	—	19 / 102	—
Rocket Raccoon	40	81	—	—	Hold ⇧ during jump to float
Sentinel	47	81	+24	17 / 104	—
She-Hulk	40	81	—	—	Wall jump capable
Shuma-Gorath	46	81	—	—	—
Spider-Man	52	81	—	—	Wall jump capable
Storm	43	81	—	22 / 99	Hold ⇧ during jump to float
Super-Skrull	40	81	—	—	—
Taskmaster	46	81	—	—	—
Thor	43	81	—	30 / 90	—
Wolverine	39	80	—	—	Wall jump capable
X-23	45	80	—	—	Wall jump capable

Capcom Character Jump Data

Name	Jump Frames	Super Jump Frames	Double/ Triple Jump Frames	Flight Frames (startup / duration)	Notes
Akuma	42	81	—	—	—
Amaterasu	46	81	—	—	—
Arthur	58	81	+25	—	—
Chris Redfield	40	81	—	—	—
Chun-Li	46	82	+22 DJ / +22 TJ	—	Wall jump
C. Viper	49	81	+22	—	—
Dante	44	81	+20 DJ / +20 TJ	170	Triple jump only available in Devil Trigger mode
Felicia	44	85	—	—	Wall cling capable
Firebrand	40	81	—	30 / 90	Wall cling capable
Frank West	44	81	—	—	—
Haggar	36	81	—	—	—
Hsien-Ko	46	81	—	—	—
Jill	40	81	—	—	—
Morrigan	43	80	—	111	—
Nemesis T-Type	44	81	—	—	—
Phoenix Wright	40	81	—	—	—
Ryu	40	81	—	—	—
Spencer	40	81	—	—	Air upward + (S) + (ATK) functions somewhat like a double jump
Strider	43	81	+13	—	Wall jump
Trish	45	81	+20	21 / 100	—
Tron	43	81	—	—	—
Vergil	41	81	+16	—	Double jump only available in Devil Trigger mode
Viewtiful Joe	50	81	+21 DJ / +22 TJ	—	—
Wesker	41	81	—	—	—
Zero	46	81	—	—	—

NORMAL JUMPS

NORMAL JUMP: TAP ANY UPWARD DIRECTION

Some attacks can also be canceled into a normal or super jump simply by holding any upward direction; for example every character's (S) special attack launcher on hit. With AUTO SUPER JUMP set to ON in options, you can also simply hold (S) down to super jump cancel after a successful launcher

The most direct way to get a character airborne is through jumping. There are two kinds of jumps: jumps, and super jumps. Both types of jumps have 3 pre-jump frames after input, before they actually leave the ground on the 4th frame. Input the command for a basic attack during pre-jump frames, and the command will be buffered and executed as early as possible during the jump. However, if the command for a ground-based special move or hyper combo is finished during pre-jump frames, the jump will be canceled into the ground-based action, and never even animate!

Normal jumps keep the battle at normal jump height, and they do not shift the playing field focus upward. Assists can be called.

A normal jump keeps the screen focused on ground level, and doesn't travel as fast or as far as a super jump (though both leave the ground at the same speed, on the 4th frame after the upward input). The following rules apply to normal jumps:

- **Air chain combos are restricted to three hits for certain characters**
- **Crossover assists can be called**
- **Some ground attacks can be canceled into a normal jump by simply holding any upward direction as the attack connects. Examples include Iron Fist's ⇨ + (H), Chun-Li's standing or crouching (H), Storm's standing (M) and crouching (H), Dante's ⇨⇩⇘ + (M), Morrigan's ⇨ + (H), and Phoenix Wright's (Trial) standing (H), (H)**
- **Hitstun produced by a successful air attack is less during a normal jump than the hitstun produced by that exact same attack during a super jump. In effect, this makes some air combos harder, if not impossible, during a normal jump state**
- **Flight modes started while either standing or normal jumping will follow the rules of a normal jump: assists can be called, but certain characters have limited chain combos, and hitstun produced by attacks is shorter**

Air Recovery

Some hits or knockdowns will make the victim recover by flipping out in midair, rather than by being floored, then rolling up off the ground. Air recovery occurs automatically when applicable, but characters can also be directed to recover in a desired direction by holding forward or backward. After air recovery, a character is considered to be normal jumping—even if air recovery leaves them at the top of the playing field! Being in a normal jump state after air recovery means crossover assists can be called to help regain momentum.

M.O.D.O.K. AND NORMAL JUMP FLIGHT

The diabolical M.O.D.O.K. doesn't have a normal jump. Instead, tapping any upward direction while grounded causes M.O.D.O.K. to fly. M.O.D.O.K.'s exclusive normal jump flight is the fastest way to get from the ground to the air *in the game*—M.O.D.O.K. is airborne the *next frame* after input! He's ready to act after 5 frames of floating up from the ground. Standard jumps are not airborne until the 4th frame after input, and activating flight from the ground for any other flight-capable character requires at least 11 frames.

M.O.D.O.K.'s normal jump Flight shares the rules of any normal jump state, with three exceptions: M.O.D.O.K.'s flight ends if an airdash is used, it lasts much longer than for other flight characters (five seconds, compared to around two for most others, and three for Devil Trigger Dante), and M.O.D.O.K. is the only character who can fly twice in one airborne period (start with normal jump flight by tapping up from the ground, then activate ⇩ ⇙ ⇦ + Ⓢ flight after the first flight period ends).

SUPER JUMPS

SUPER JUMP: TAP DOWN, THEN ANY UPWARD DIRECTION WITHIN 9 FRAMES

Can also super jump cancel launchers by holding any upward direction or Ⓢ after scoring a hit

Super jumps take the fight to the skies. The screen drags upward to super jump height, and assists cannot be called.

During a super jump a character soars to the top of the playing field, and the screen shifts to follow. Super jumping characters can alter their airborne trajectory in a way that normal jumping characters cannot via **air control**—simply hold left or right to influence the jump arc (different characters can exert different degrees of air control). Grounded point characters aren't shown while the screen is following super jumping characters, and will instead have their positions marked with "1P" or "2P" indicators. Super jump rules:

- **The full air chain combo is possible for every character during a super jump**
- **Crossover assists *cannot* be called during super jumps**
- **Super jumps for most characters can be "steered" with air control by holding ⇦ or ⇨**
- **Hitstun produced by a successful attack during a super jump is 5 frames longer than the same attack during a normal jump. This means many air combos are easier, or only possible, during a super jump. This includes super jump flight mode!**
- **Flight modes started during a super jump will follow super jump rules. That is, assists cannot be called, but full chain combos are allowed for every character, and hitstun produced by attacks is longer**

DOUBLE & TRIPLE JUMPS

DOUBLE AND TRIPLE JUMPS: TAP ANY UPWARD DIRECTION WHILE AIRBORNE

Some characters, having left the ground with a jump already, can then jump one or twice more from midair. Double and triple jumps follow the rules of the jump they started from, just as flight does. Most significantly, this means you can normal jump, then double or triple jump to achieve great height, while still being capable of calling assists!

For each double or triple jump capable character, some air basic attacks are cancelable by double or triple jumps. Simply tap an upward direction during these moves and the character will immediately cancel the attack with the double or triple jump. This grants great potential during air combos (particularly **team air combos**, where they shine especially), but also allows for unorthodox mix-ups. For example, against a standing opponent, you can jump-in with an attack, then double jump cancel it on impact. Normally, opponents expect a character falling in with an attack to land, so this may throw them off. Depending on whether you double jump straight up or forward over the opponent (and whether they advancing guard your initial assault), you can either go for another overhead attack, or call an assist to land on the side you started from, while you land behind the enemy!

Be careful with upward inputs on these characters: double jumping can be accomplished on frame 1 when a jump is airborne, so if you get an extraneous double jump input in early, you may use up a double jump immediately and not even realize it until you need it later! Be particularly careful about this after landing a launcher and super jumping by holding Ⓢ ; if you tap up to super jump out of habit from older games, you'll get an immediate double jump.

Double jump canceling air attacks also allows for hit confirms at low altitude. You can jump forward, perform air pokes in anticipation of enemy movement, then hit confirm and jump cancel the attacks and transition to a combo when they're successful.

Double and triple jumps add air mobility, and increase the potential of both combos and mix-ups. Many air basic attacks can be canceled by a double jump, leading to devious tactics like late, second-chance overheads, or overheads canceled into a double jump over the opponent while your assist arrives on the original side.

WALL JUMPS

WALL JUMPS: NORMAL JUMP BACKWARDS ALONG THE SCREEN EDGE AND PRESS DIAGONALLY UP-FORWARD

Some characters can jump forward off of the edge of the screen during a normal jump. To accomplish this, simply normal jump backward along a screen edge, then press up-forward. Jumping straight up won't work, even in a corner; you *must* jump diagonally backward. The wall jumps for Felicia and Firebrand work slightly differently; first, normal jump diagonally backward against a screen edge, then tap ← to initiate wall cling. From here, simply release ← to wall jump. Wall jumps aren't possible during super jumps, but characters with double jumps can normal jump (in any direction), then double jump backward against a screen edge in order to wall jump at higher altitude. In general, wall jumps are useful for these characters for surprise maneuvering, and for escaping corners. Since wall jumps occur during normal jumps only, it's also always possible to call **crossover assists**!

FLIGHT

↓↙← + Ⓢ (IN AIR OK)

One-third of the cast is capable of flight. Flight is activated by inputting ↓↙← + Ⓢ, and can be started on the ground or in the air. The activation (or manual cancelation) of flight can be used to cancel basic attacks. There is a brief dead period of 5~30 frames (character dependent) during which no inputs are accepted while the flight animation begins, but afterward characters can act as they normally can in midair.

All flight modes are both activated and canceled with ↓↙← + Ⓢ. (M.O.D.O.K. can also activate flight with ↑ from the ground)

Movement during flight is enhanced—characters can be made to simply flit about as you please, in any direction. You can use as many **special moves** as you can manage while flight is active—the normal limit of three special moves per airborne period doesn't apply during flight. This applies to **airdashes** too—flight-capable characters can airdash over and over during flight! (M.O.D.O.K. again excepted.) Flight ends after any of a handful of things happens:

- **Receiving the enemy's attack (characters cannot block while flying)**
- **↓↙← + Ⓢ is input again (flight deactivation can be used to cancel basic attack recovery, and Morrigan special move recovery)**
- **Attacking with air Ⓢ during flight, or certain other attacks (like M.O.D.O.K. air Ⓛ or Ⓢ + ATK Body Attack)**
- **Flight expires naturally (occurs after about two seconds for most characters, three seconds for Devil Trigger Dante, five seconds for M.O.D.O.K.)**

Flight can only be activated once per airborne period. The exception here, once again, is M.O.D.O.K., whose normal jump flight (activated simply by tapping any upward direction while grounded; M.O.D.O.K. does not have a normal jump!) does not preclude him from using special move flight later in the same airborne period.

Flight and airdash characters are able to airdash after flight expires only if they didn't airdash at all before *or during* flight mode. Likewise, flight and double jump characters retain their double jump after flight only if they didn't double jump before. Characters that can both airdash *and* double jump can do one or the other after flight expires only if they used neither during the airborne period prior to flight ending. These details of what's left after flight ends are most important when using flight in air combos, but are also useful to know for positioning and zoning sequences.

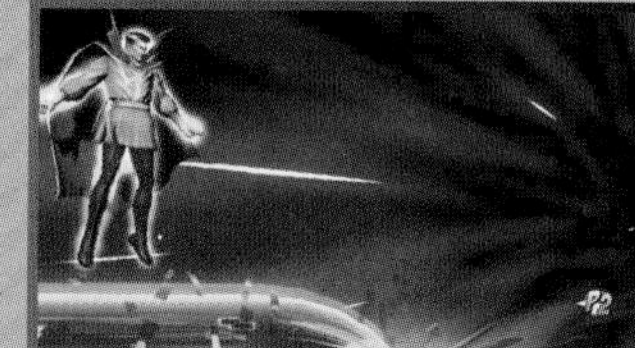

It's not as big a deal as it sounds that you cannot guard during flight—after all, the point of flight is to be unpredictable and evade attacks in the first place.

Normal jump flight can be used to place crossover assists behind foes while flying or airdashing over them. Flying characters correct their orientation after switching sides, allowing you to sandwich them between you and your assist.

The properties of flight are different depending on when flight was activated. Flight that begins during a normal jump, while a character is grounded, or after air recovery, can be thought of as **normal jump flight**. Flight that begins during a super jump can be thought of as **super jump flight**. The differences between normal jump flight and super jump flight are similar to the differences between normal and super jumps themselves. During normal jump flight crossover assists can be called, and certain characters are restricted to three-hit air chain combos. The hitstun produced by successful attacks is also shorter than during super jump flight. During super jump flight, crossover assists *cannot* be called, but the full air chain combo is available for all flight characters, and the hitstun produced by attacks is longer than during normal jump flight.

AIRDASHES

DIRECTION + ATK ATK OR DIRECTIONAL DOUBLE-TAP, DIRECTIONS AVAILABLE AND AIRDASH BEHAVIOR VARIES PER CHARACTER

The ability to airdash is a great boon to many characters. Airdashes are what they sound like—dashes in midair! Airdashes are accomplished like ground dashes. To airdash in a particular direction, hold that direction while pressing ATK ATK. Alternatively, double-tap the desired direction. Use whichever is easier and more consistent for you, but note that double-tapping a diagonal input is much less consistent than simply pressing that diagonal plus ATK ATK.

Airdashes have a height restriction—below a certain altitude, airdashes aren't possible. From a standing start, it's faster to get over this floor with a super jump than a normal jump, as a super jump moves upward more quickly. In this table, the earliest frame before airdashing during a normal or super jump is counting airborne frames only. The three pre-jump frames before leaving the ground are separate. Numbers in parentheses indicate how many frames of airdash must elapse before attack is possible

Marvel Character Airdash Data

Name	Airdash Type	First Frame Airdash is Possible After Leaving Ground For a Normal Jump	First Frame Airdash is Possible After Leaving Ground For a Super Jump	Up	Up-Forward	Forward	Down-Forward	Down	Down-Back	Back	Up-Back	Notes
Doctor Doom	8-Way	6	3	30(5)	30(5)	38(7)	30(5)	30(5)	30(5)	37(7)	30(5)	—
Dormammu	8-Way	10	5	30(5)	30(5)	38(4)	20(5)	30(5)	20(7)	37(4)	30(5)	Down-back airdash movement starts on frame 6
Iron Man	8-Way	3	3	40(5)	25(11)	38(11)	35(11)	34(5)	25(11)	38(7)	25(11)	Diagonal and lateral airdash movement starts on frame 10; up and down airdashes move instantly but hover at finish
Magneto	8-Way	7	4	24(3)	24(3)	40(7)	24(4)	24(3)	24(7)	42(7)	24(3)	Down-back airdash movement starts on frame 6
M.O.D.O.K.	8-Way	1	1	30(5)	30(5)	38(5)	30(4)	30(5)	30(5)	37(4)	30(5)	Airdashing ends flight
Nova	8-Way	8	4	24(3)	24(9)	30(7)	29(10)	24(3)	24(10)	37(7)	24(10)	Forward and backward airdash movement starts on frame 6; diagonal airdash movement starts on frame 9
Phoenix	8-Way	9	4	20(7)	20(7)	38(7)	37(7)	20(7)	20(7)	37(7)	20(7)	—
Shuma-Gorath	2-Way	7	3	—	—	38(7)	—	—	—	38(7)	—	—
Spider-Man	1-Way	6	3	—	—	38(7)	—	—	—	—	—	Forward airdash movement starts on frame 6
Storm	8-Way	7	3	40(5)	22(7)	26(4)	23(7)	23(7)	23(7)	25(4)	23(7)	—
Super-Skrull	1-Way	4	1	—	—	38(7)	—	—	—	—	—	Airdash travels up-forward
Thor	8-Way	10	4	40(7)	38(7)	38(7)	30(7)	40(7)	38(11)	37(7)	38(7)	—

Capcom Character Airdash Data

Name	Airdash Type	First Frame Airdash is Possible After Leaving Ground For a Normal Jump	First Frame Airdash is Possible After Leaving Ground For a Super Jump	Up	Up-Forward	Forward	Down-Forward	Down	Down-Back	Back	Up-Back	Notes
Amaterasu	1-Way	7	3	—	—	40(7)	—	—	—	—	—	Forward airdash movement starts on frame 13th
Chun-Li	1-Way	6	3	—	—	20(7)	—	—	—	—	—	Forward airdash travels at slight downward angle.
C. Viper	8-Way	8	4	38(5)	30(9)	38(7)	Until grounded(9)	38(5)	Until grounded(9)	37(7)	30(9)	Diagonal airdash movement starts on frame 9
Dante	2-Way	6	3	—	—	38(4)	—	—	—	37(4)	—	Gains double airdash in Devil Trigger mode
Hsien-Ko	2-Way	4	2	—	—	60(7)	—	—	—	60(7)	—	—
Morrigan	4-Way	7	4	34(9)	—	23(9)	—	34(9)	—	23(7)	—	Upward airdash: Morrigan swoops in a vertical arc forward; downward airdash: Morrigan swoops in a downward-dipping parabola
Trish	8-Way	8	4	30(7)	25(7)	38(4)	20(7)	30(7)	20(7)	37(4)	20(7)	—
Tron	2-Way	8	4	—	—	30(7)	—	—	—	30(7)	—	—
Vergil	None/2-Way	3	2	—	—	33(5)	—	—	—	29(7)	—	Gains 2-Way air dash in Devil Trigger mode
Viewtiful Joe	2-Way	7	3	—	—	38(7)	—	—	—	37(7)	—	—
Zero	2-Way	8	4	—	—	29(7)	—	—	—	29(7)	—	Airdash movement starts on frame 9

Airdashing has myriad applications:

Some air basic attacks can be canceled with an airdash. This allows for combo extension, and for enhanced air zoning tactics

Airdashes allow quick retreat from the enemy by jumping and airdashing back or down-back. Like double jumps and flight, airdashes keep the properties of the jump they originated from, so if you retreat with an airdash from a normal jump, you can also call a crossover assist to cover your tracks. Similarly, if you normal jump, then airdash upward, you'll achieve super jump height while remaining in a normal jump state.

Airdashes allow you to advance laterally from long or mid range at a trajectory different than a ground dash (but without the ability to guard).

Flight characters can airdash repeatedly while flight is active (except M.O.D.O.K.), allowing for even faster retreats or advances

Airdashes can be used diagonally or straight down to return to the ground as quickly as possible after jumping at close range, usually with a quick overhead attack—this is usually called a triangle jump. Strong mix-ups between low-hitting combos, triangle/square jump overheads, and cross-ups can be essentially impossible to block consistently. Opponents will often have to rely at least in part on luck and guesswork to resist a truly furious and varied offensive attack.

Lateral airdashes just after jumping near the opponent, going over their heads, can be used to square jump over them, while placing an assist on the side you just vacated. Do this a little bit lower with an air attack, so you don't actually pass over their head, and the effect is a very fast overhead just like a triangle jump.

Lateral airdashes at normal jump height allow you to advance while calling an assist along a different horizontal plane. An opponent is unlikely to be capable of attacks that hit both of your characters cleanly.

In a big change from original *MvC3*, characters *cannot* air guard while airdashing, unlike almost all ground dashes. Airdashes can be canceled with air attacks, though. This includes throws, basic attacks, special moves, and hyper combos. Moves executed during an airdash will often continue the inertia of the airdash, which may make certain attacks more or less useful in certain positions.

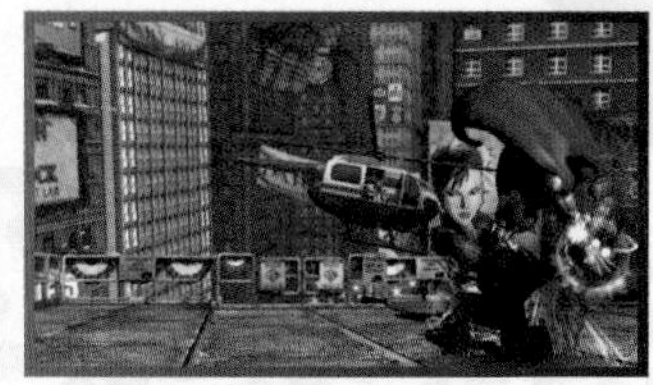

Air attacks from low altitude lateral airdashes make great overheads. Some airdash attacks can cross up, if you dash over the opposing character's head. Low lateral airdashes are often called square jumps, as opposed to triangle jumps for low diagonal airdashes.

An airdash-capable character that can also fly, falling after flight expires naturally, can only airdash if they didn't airdash previously in the airborne period; if they airdashed at all either before or during flight, attempting to airdash after flight expires won't work.

Additionally, characters who can both double jump and airdash can only do one or the other per airborne period. The exceptions are Chun-Li, Devil Trigger Dante, and Viewtiful Joe, the triple jump characters—they can both airdash and double jump in the same airborne period (or do a double jump and triple jump, or two airdashes).

Option Select Air Throw / Airdash

You can actually build-in an option select air throw to any airdash that isn't straight up or down, by performing airdashes with direction ✚ Ⓗ ~ ATK. Press the desired direction for the airdash at the same time as Ⓗ, then drum another ATK input one frame later. This plink input causes the game to register an air throw/ air Ⓗ attempt for 1 frame, before "correcting" itself by kara-canceling into an airdash when the other input is received.

ADVANCED AIRDASHING: TRIANGLE AND SQUARE JUMPING

Airdashes are perhaps most useful, and most infamous, in their capacity for enabling fast overhead attacks. By jumping near the opposing character, then immediately airdashing straight down or down-forward, you can leave the ground and return almost immediately. Remember that most attacks used while airborne are overheads—if you can get an attack out before landing, it's impossible for most players to guard standing on reaction.

You're just as liable to have this problem as anyone, so here's a tip: when faced with tricky air overheads, watch for the dust that explodes up when a character jumps. With a little practice looking for it, that dust can be an extra visual cue that alerts you a triangle jump overhead is coming. This isn't foolproof, since some other moves make dust puffs too, some characters (like Magneto, and Storm) do not produce dust effects when they leave the ground, and opponents may mix it up by landing without attacking then striking low, but it's better than nothing. As another cue, you can realize that the screen is shifting upward if the opponent is super jumping before their triangle jumps... but again, this might just be bait, and they might empty triangle jump, land, and go low. You'll have to either make a good read to escape unscathed, or avoid the situation in the first place.

Diagonal triangle jumps have the most notoriety, but lateral airdashes have similar uses. Super jumping into a quick lateral airdash is one of the safest ways to gain a little ground on an adversary, as long as they don't have a hyper combo ready they can use on reaction to cover that space (you cannot block while airdashing, after all). But apart from some dangerous beam hyper combos, you only have to watch out for a few assists, like Dante—α, Dormammu—β, and Rocket Raccoon—γ; you'll be done with the airdash and able to air block long before most characters can do anything about it on reaction.

The biggest worry is when your opponent uses an anti-air command throw, or simply jumps and air throws you. The problem of being air thrown can be somewhat obviated by making air ⇨ + Ⓗ your airborne attack of choice, if that's at all workable for your characters. Using this command will produce a heavy air attack under most circumstances, but if the foe happens to be in throw range it will instead produce an air throw. As a bonus, you may happen to break away from foes who air throw you first, essentially on accident. Using one input to cover several options, as is the case here, is called an option select.

Lateral airdashes can also be used just off the ground right in an opponent's face, as overheads with the same purpose as triangle jumps. Use air ⇨ + Ⓗ when possible; this can result in either an attack, or an air throw.

Used from a slightly higher altitude, a square jump can make you pass just over the opponent's head. This forces them to switch the direction they're blocking in. You can take advantage of this by creating confusing situations—get near the opposing character, jump straight up or up-forward near their heads, then call an assist before airdashing to the other side. Depending which assist you call, when you airdash, and what you do during the airdash, this can force the opponent to have to block more or less at random, if you vary how you approach the setup.

Utilizing airdashes effectively is incredibly powerful. Offensive tactics this good essentially mean the trick is to be never put into bad defensive situations in the first place, rather than getting out of them consistently once you're trapped.

REPEATED FLYING AIRDASHES

During flight, restrictions on the number of special moves or airdashes which can be used per airborne period vanish, and you can perform as many actions as you can manage to squeeze into the flight window. For characters with fast airdashes, this can provide an invaluable tool for running away or approaching very quickly. Activate flight, then cancel airdashes into one another very quickly with one of two methods:

- **Never repeat the same airdash direction. During flight, airdashes can be canceled into other airdashes naturally, by simply inputting direction + ATK ATK repeatedly, as long as you don't repeat the same direction. So, for example, ⇗ + ATK ATK CANCEL ➡ ⇘ + ATK ATK CANCEL ➡ ⇗ + ATK ATK CANCEL ➡ ⇘ + ATK ATK would work.**

- **Use plink inputs for airdashes. Any combination of attack buttons works, but the ideal command is direction + Ⓗ ~ ATK, so an option select air throw is built-in. The second attack input must follow the first on the very next frame. This method allows you to cancel the same-direction airdash into itself rapidly, but it also requires a fair bit more precision than simply performing different-direction airdashes.**

After you've flitted about and arrived wherever you'd like to be, either manually unfly by inputting ⇩ ⇙ ⇦ + Ⓢ, or use air Ⓢ to automatically fall from flight with an overhead attack if the enemy is nearby. Note that M.O.D.O.K. leaves flight by airdashing at all, so you cannot apply this trick with him.

Attacking on Point

So, we now come to the proverbial meat-and-potatoes of combat, the actual fighting. There are numerous ways to attack in *UMvC3*, and this section aims to help you understand how it all works.

THROWS

⇦ OR ⇨ + Ⓗ (ON GROUND OR IN AIR)

Active in 1 frame, throws are extremely quick.

*The throw victim has 7 frames to input ⇦ or ⇨ + Ⓗ in order to **break away** from the throw. Most throws lead to an opportunity to OTG the throw victim, leading to even more damage.*

As an **unblockable** close range attack, throws are ideal for assaulting a **guarding** opponent. Throws cannot snag an adversary who is stuck in **guardstun**, actively guarding something, but they can grab passive enemies who *expect* to guard (throws are also not possible for 4 frames after guardstun or hitstun ends). If you throw as your opponent's assist comes on screen, your point character will be invulnerable to whatever that assist does as long as the throw is actually being performed. Normal throws from any position can be broken by the target, no matter what they were doing when the throw started. When a throw is broken, both characters end up right next to each other 12 frames later, with neither side having an advantage.

Throws are very important for breaking down the defense of passive, defensive opponents (who are sometimes called turtles; depending on whom it's coming from, this title can be bestowed with either admiration or scorn!). The threat of throws (along with the threat of chip damage, and the threat of a time-out loss) prevent guarding from being an impenetrable bulwark against damage.

BASIC ATTACK

Ⓛ Ⓜ Ⓗ

Basic attacks are the building blocks of chain combos and the foundation of any poking gameplan.

Basic attacks, sometimes called normal moves, are the basis of offense. Basic attacks are performed by pressing Ⓛ, Ⓜ, or Ⓗ. The outcome differs depending on whether your character is airborne, standing, or crouching. Basic attacks can be canceled into one another with **chain combos**, which are detailed later in this chapter.

Basic attacks can all chain to **command attacks** and **special attacks**, and are all cancelable to **special moves** and **hyper combos**. Specific basic attacks can also be canceled with jumps or dashes.

Basic Attack Notation

Throughout this guide, basic attacks are discussed as being performed crouching, standing, or airborne. Crouching and standing are sometimes abbreviated as cr. and st. for space. If a state is not provided for a move, assume it follows the same state as the previous one; for example, air Ⓜ, Ⓜ, Ⓗ, Ⓢ refers to a chain of basic attacks in the air.

SPECIAL ATTACK

Ⓢ

Special attack was referred to as "exchange" for much of original MvC3's development.

On the ground, Ⓢ is a **launcher** attack that can be chained into from almost any **basic attack**, and which launches the opponent on hit. On a successful Ⓢ hit, you can simply hold any upward direction to automatically **cancel** into a **super jump**, which takes your character into position to **air combo** the target. With AUTO SUPER JUMP set to ON in Options, you can also just opt to keep holding Ⓢ.

In the air, Ⓢ is an aerial attack that has a unique property if used within an **air combo** that started from a grounded Ⓢ **launcher**. Used at the end of a launcher combo, air Ⓢ causes **flying screen**, an effect in which the air combo victim is tossed into a **hard knockdown** while the attacking character falls to pursue. This is an opportunity to pop the floored character up **o**ff **t**he **g**round with an **OTG-capable** attack. Most characters have *something* that can OTG, and many crossover assists do, as well—most (but not all) assists labeled as TILT DW type are intended as OTG tools.

Ⓢ is also used as an input for several **special moves**, such as ⇩ ⇙ ⇦ + Ⓢ flight for many characters, She-Hulk's ⇩ ⇩ + Ⓢ charging stance, or variations of a direct body attack move with Ⓢ + (ATK). With many more special moves added to *UMvC3*, the Ⓢ button gets a lot more special move use.

COMMAND ATTACK

Command attacks extend chains, or possess special properties.

A command attack is a sort of specialized **basic attack** that often has special properties, but special restrictions, as well. Some command attacks are **overheads**. Some command attacks cannot be **canceled**, or can only be chained into a particular way. Other command attacks basically function as another hit in ground chains before launching with (S). Some characters don't have command attacks at all. For specifics on command attacks for a particular character, visit that character's chapter.

SPECIAL MOVE

Special moves are powerful attacks and abilities that are performed by inputting a directional sequence before pressing the appropriate button. There are motion special moves, charge special moves, and tap special moves.

After inputting the motion for a special move, you must press the button within 9 frames. This might not sound like a long time—it's less than 1/6th of a second—but this allows for some interesting execution tricks. As just one example, let's say you want to perform an air special move that has a command of ⇩ ⇘ ⇨ + (ATK), but you want to do it as soon as possible after leaving the ground. To accomplish this, you can "tiger knee" a motion while standing on the ground, combining the move's directional sequence with an upward direction: ⇩ ⇘ ⇨ ⇗ . Now, jumps aren't airborne until the 4th frame after the upward input, so you must wait at least 4 frames before pressing (ATK) in this instance, but no longer than 9 frames total.

Special moves have all sorts of uses.

As another example, this 9 frame grace period can also be used for **option selects**, covering more than one option intentionally. Let's say Felicia is pressuring Ryu with ground attacks, with the intent of landing her special move throw (⇨ ⇘ ⇩ ⇙ ⇦ + (ATK)). A common method of attempting a throw is what is known as a tick throw. First, you "tick" the opposing with a single light attack, which creates the expectation in the opposing player that a **chain combo** is coming. Then, while they continue to hold back in anticipation of further attacks, you throw them. This trick has been around since time immemorial (or, ok, since 1991, in *Street Fighter II: The World Warrior*), and here, as in other Capcom fighting games, you can add a twist. Felicia's standing (L), when blocked, leaves her at a -2 frame disadvantage—in this case, Ryu can act 2 frames sooner than Felicia after guarding her attack. Furthermore, a character in guardstun cannot be thrown for 4 frames after guardstun ends. Further still, Ryu has perhaps the best attack in the game for negating this situation: his Shoryuken is invincible starting with the very first frame. If Felicia is made to go for her throw as soon as possible, Ryu will still be unthrowable because of guardstun. If the Felicia player performs it as soon as possible with a normal input method, Ryu might just Shoryuken Felicia in the face. So, what does that player do? If, instead of going for a throw right away, the Felicia player **ticks** with standing (L), then immediately inputs ⇨ ⇘ ⇩ ⇙ ⇦, but then *waits* as long as possible before pressing (ATK) to activate the throw, one of two things will happen. If Ryu comes out of guardstun with Shoryuken as fast as he can, Felicia will guard! After all, the motion ⇨ ⇘ ⇩ ⇙ ⇦ ends in a ⇦ input, which counts as blocking. But if the Ryu player *doesn't* Shoryuken, and instead just waits, the Felicia player's late (ATK) press will engage her throw and snag Ryu.

HYPER COMBO

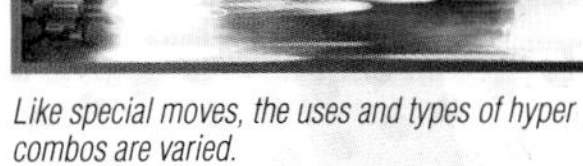
Like special moves, the uses and types of hyper combos are varied.

Hyper combos are powered-up versions of special moves, which require hyper meter to use. Hyper combos have many uses. Most damaging combos feature hyper combos in some way. Many deal direct damage, whether through physical hits or an inescapable command throw. Some create high priority projectile threats or high priority fullscreen beams. A few hyper combos serve to enhance your team with bonuses: Amaterasu and Viewtiful Joe have hyper combos that slow down the opposing characters, while Strider, Firebrand, Arthur, Felicia, Hsien-Ko, and several others have hyper combos that temporarily enhance their own abilities in some way. These enhancements are as varied as speed and ability boosts, shadow or kitty helpers, a healing aura, or hyper armor.

Hyper Combo Cutscenes

Each hyper combo progresses in a particular manner: the very first few frames of the hyper combo play out, accompanied by the distinctive hyper combo "flash." Then, the action briefly freezes, while a cutscene of the character gathering energy for the attack plays. Then, action starts back up again as the character actually winds up to release their hyper combo. Nothing is actually transpiring in the background during these hyper combo cutscenes—the action picks back up after the close-up shot.

SNAP BACK

⇩ ⇦ ⇨ + P1 or P2 **(REQUIRES ONE BAR OF HYPER METER)**

Snap backs are 2 frame attacks that require one bar of hyper meter to perform. Faster than any other physical attack, the purpose of snap backs is to rearrange the opponent's team order. Partner characters who are snapped in with red damage have the damage become permanent. Partner actions are not possible for a few seconds between teammates who've been swapped with a snap back.

⇩ ⇦ ⇨ + P1 snaps in their first partner, while ⇩ ⇦ ⇨ + P2 snaps in their second partner. If you read that a desperate challenger will crossover attack to tag out a character near defeat, you can block their incoming tag standing, then punish the new character with a full combo that ends in a snap back right back to the character they tried to save! This leads to a natural chance to finish off their ailing, would-be escapee when they're forced to return—either chip them out before they can even touch the ground, or stage a devious mix-up reserved for new characters falling in after K.O.s and snaps.

If your challenger has a lot of red damage, or a deadly THC order, or a weak character they're using just for the assist, snap backs can be your best friend.

You have a good shot at knocking out the original ailing character AND getting another mix-up on the character after that! Or, at least you'll force the enemy to burn their X-Factor earlier than they would on their terms. Coaxing foes to pop X-Factor before they really want to is a victory in and of itself. This is doubly true if they use X-Factor to save a low-health character from chip, but then take a hit and get knocked out anyway. Not only have they lost a character, but their quickly-dwindling X-Factor is a level lower in power than it would have been if they'd just waited!

Go for snap backs aggressively against:

- **Extra dangerous X-Factor lv.3 anchors**
- **Characters who provide an assist or crossover combination hyper that the rest of the team depends on**
- **A character like Phoenix or Phoenix Wright, who requires preparation to be dominant, but doesn't quite have the right resources yet**
- **Teams with deadly THCs/TACs that require a particular order**

Attacking with a Team

PARTNERS

Partner characters, usually just called **partners** or **assists**, are a huge part of what makes *UMvC3* the unique beast it is. In this game, teammates are active participants in a battle, and they can contribute their efforts or tag in and become the point character in a variety of ways.

Each teammate has his or her (or its) own vitality gauge, visible at the top of the screen. Partners not actively performing an action slowly regenerate **red vitality**. Red vitality regeneration speeds up during **X-Factor**.

The basis of partner gameplay is the crossover assist, usually just called assist. For each of the three heroes you select, you'll also have to pick one of three assist types—either —α, —β, or —γ. The type you select determines which attack that character is going to use when called upon to perform a crossover assist (tap P1 or P2), or crossover counter (during ground guardstun, tap ⇨ + P1 or P2 with at least one bar of hyper meter available). Assist type also determines which hyper combo gets used within a crossover combination (P1+P2).

CROSSOVER ASSIST

TAP P1 or P2 (P1 FOR PARTNER 1; P2 FOR PARTNER 2)

Tapping P1 or P2 calls an assist. The chosen partner character leaps onto the playing field and performs the crossover assist selected before the match. Most assists have no invulnerability whatsoever, and they are vulnerable the entire time they're attacking. Only Haggar—α and (Turnabout) Phoenix Wright—α or Phoenix Wright—β have invulnerability as assists. For almost all assists, being hit stops whatever action the assist character had in progress. If a point character gets hit after calling an assist, but before the assist performs their attack, the assist attacks anyway—striking the point doesn't stop an assist from acting the way it did in *MvC2*!

Assist characters take 50% more damage than point characters. The damage scaling quirk from original *MvC3* that caused assists to take unscaled damage if their point character was blocking is now corrected, so your assists won't be punished quite so hard just for eating hyper combos or whatever else while you block.

Assists Can be Called:

When standing, crouching, or normal jumping
During flight, dashes, or airdashes that began while standing or performing a normal jump
With basic attacks performed during any of the preceding states
During ground or air recovery

Assists Cannot be Called:

When stuck in hitstun or guardstun
When performing a special move, hyper combo, or throw (though there are exceptions, such as during Wolverine's ⇦ + Ⓗ throw)
During a super jump, nor during any airdash or flight mode that starts from a super jump
When assist characters are not ready, due to other assists or partner actions. "ASSIST READY!!" displays momentarily across each team member's vitality gauge to indicate when they are ready for action

The safeguard preventing assists from being called during special moves or hyper combos is very thorough—if you hit an assist button while performing a move motion, then hit the button to finish the move, but the assist is not yet on screen, then the assist never comes out! Thus, if you plan to call assists before using special moves or hyper combos, make sure your inputs are very clean, and ensure that you've pushed P1 or P2 a little early to guarantee that your special move motion doesn't eat up the input.

Assist Labels	Description
Direct	Character attempts a direct attack.
Shot	Character produces a projectile or beam of some sort.
Extra	Irregular effects.
Instant	Action occurs immediately.
Front	Attack is directed laterally.
Tilt Dw	Attack is aimed at the ground.
Tilt Up	Attack is aimed up in the air.
Upward	Attack is aimed straight up; likely comes right back down.

Assists, Hitstun, and Screen Position

Assists follow mostly the same rules as point characters when it comes to getting hit, but they can't block, and any knockdown move causes a hard knockdown on them, allowing for OTG hits. Hitstun decay doesn't apply, nor do the normal rules about having only one ground bounce and wall bounce per combo. Basically, if you can keep the assist from having a chance to get up and leave the playing field, you can keep hitting them. Unlike in original *MvC3*, damage scaling functions properly against assists now, though they still take 150% normal damage as a straight penalty.

If the opposing point character leaves the playing field while you're juggling their assist, whether through a snap back hit or knockout or whatever, you'll still be able to hit the assist for a couple seconds, but then they'll become invulnerable and fall to safety. This prevents "helper infinites" from being possible by batting aside opposing point characters and going after assists, *MvC2*-style.

Interestingly, one of the best ways to juggle opposing assists is to use air exchange hits. Launch an assist, then combo into an upward exchange hit with air direction ✚ Ⓢ. The TAC flash happens, but the opponent can't counter it—you're not hitting their point character! The assist gets lofted high in the air or spiked hard with a ground bounce, and not only will you be able to keep hitting them, but your competitor can't use assists again until you stop juggling the one that's already out!

Assists are not restricted to remain within the lateral bounds of the screen and on the playing field, as point characters are. Call an assist that normally comes out far behind your point character (most prominently Phoenix—α) while backed against a screen edge, and the assist still tosses their attack onscreen, but never goes onscreen or becomes vulnerable themselves!

Similarly, if a crossover assist is hit hard by an attack that tosses them off the screen, follow-up attacks won't continue punishing the assist (even fullscreen attacks like Storm's Hail Storm or Amaterasu's Okami Shuffle).

What Assists Are For

Assists are best used to close the gaps in an offense, as well as for combo extension. Some characters who can't stage offense safely on their own are dependent upon assists to create frame advantage to work behind. Assists are also useful for space control, as in ranged warfare. What assists are not so great for, generally, is defense. Using assists while at a disadvantage means you run the risk of getting two characters hit at once. This is the absolute worst thing that can happen, since both characters could be nuked rather easily, depending on your opponent's reactions and resources. Calling assists in a panic is a bad reaction. Good players try to bait assists specifically to fry them or to go for two-for-one by mixing up your point character while hitting your assist, too.

Assists can facilitate mix-ups. Low-hitting assists can be timed to hit just as you also attack high, and overhead assists can be timed to hit just as you go low. With a teleport character, you'll frequently call an assist on one side of your foe, then teleport to the other.

Assists are also great for covering slower attacks. Vergil's Rapid Slash is a cross-up attack that you can follow with a big combo. Unfortunately, Vergil is extremely punishable if this special move is guarded. To alleviate this problem, a crossover assist called immediately before performing Rapid Slash serves as protection from punishment; a beam assist like Doctor Doom—α works well in this situation. Another example is Strider's Gram H. This attack covers almost the entire distance of the screen and causes a wall bounce, which you can follow with a combo. However, Gram H suffers from a long period of startup time, making it easy for your challengers to interrupt with an opposing attack. A solution to this is to call an assist a moment before performing Gram H, thwarting attempts to interrupt the attack; Ghost Rider—β works well in this scenario. Assists can be used to protect air throw attempts, as well. Going for air throws is very valuable, but if you anticipate a chance for an air throw and jump forward with air ⇨ + Ⓗ, yet no air throw opportunity actually materializes, you'll just whiff air Ⓗ, a dangerous proposition. But by calling an assist just as you go for a throw, you can provide cover for yourself in case there's no air throw.

In original *MvC3*, the best assists, speaking very generally, ended up being:

- Akuma—β
- Amaterasu—β
- Arthur—β
- Dante (take your pick, really)
- Doctor Doom (again, they're all good)
- Haggar—α
- Iron Man—α
- Magneto—α
- Morrigan—γ
- Ryu—γ
- Sentinel—α
- Tron—β
- Wesker—β

It's not that other assists weren't good, or that they couldn't be used for the same things. These are just great examples of tools that fill very valuable niches. Nearly any character can benefit with the staggered hits and horizontal screen control offered by Sentinel—α or Doctor Doom—γ. Any character had much added to their defense by packing Tron—β or Haggar—α, not to mention the drastically increased ability to safely go for air throws offensively. (Tron—β has now lost the invulnerability that made it so useful for this in original *MvC3*). And just about anyone can benefit from the fullscreen control and chip offered by great beams and long range assists like Iron Man—α, Doctor Doom—α, and Dante—γ. Some assists are multi-function, like Amaterasu—β and Dante—α; one of them looks like it's a projectile, and it kind of is, and the other looks like it's a defensive pillar, and that's also sort of true, but what these assists are both really for is to pin your adversary in a huge amount of blockstun so that your point character is free to mix them up without worrying about advancing guard.

CROSSOVER ATTACK

HOLD P1 or P2 FOR 14 FRAMES (P1 FOR PARTNER 1; P2 FOR PARTNER 2)

Crossover attacks are overheads that swoop in and send victims into a small, spinning knockdown. Incoming characters pose briefly after a crossover attack, making them briefly vulnerable if the attack whiffs.

A crossover attack is the most direct way to swap a partner character in for the current point character. In order to accomplish a crossover attack, you must hold down P1 or P2 for 14 frames. On the 15th frame after continuous input, your point character becomes invincible and leaps away and is then replaced by the chosen incoming character. Holding P1 or P2 can be buffered behind other actions to mask your intention, but it does require that the decision to swap be at least somewhat premeditated. If incoming characters have any red damage, it becomes permanent after a crossover attack.

During a crossover attack, the incoming partner strikes with an overhead attack that soars out to mid-screen, deals 27,000 damage, and causes a spinning knockdown on hit. Victims are vulnerable until they hit the ground during a spinning knockdown, but because characters pose briefly at the end of a crossover attack, this knockdown is usually difficult or impossible to take advantage of.

Crossover Attack Data—Marvel Side

Name	Active	Recovery	Advantage if Guarded
Captain America	22	36	-17
Deadpool	22	32	-14
Doctor Doom	24	34	-15
Doctor Strange	20	35	-15
Dormammu	20	33	-15
Ghost Rider	19	33	-13
Hawkeye	20	33	-9
Hulk	21	35	-11
Iron Fist	19	35	-14
Iron Man	20	33	-17
Magneto	20	34	-14
M.O.D.O.K.	20	35	-11
Nova	20	35	-16
Phoenix	20	34	-17
Rocket Raccoon	18	33	-14
Sentinel	20	39	-17
She-Hulk	20	34	-16
Shuma-Gorath (DLC)	22	34	-17
Spider-Man	20	34	-16
Storm	20	32	-19
Super-Skrull	20	34	-16
Taskmaster	20	34	-16
Thor	20	34	-15
Wolverine	20	34	-15
X-23	17	34	-13

Crossover Attack Data—Capcom Side

Name	Active	Recovery	Advantage if Guarded
Akuma	20	34	-16
Amaterasu	20	32	-13
Arthur	20	35	-15
Chris	20	34	-16
Chun-Li	24	34	-17
C. Viper	20	33	-15
Dante	21	34	-17
Felicia	20	34	-17
Firebrand	20	33	-13
Frank West	21	33	-12
Haggar	20	31	-11
Hsien-Ko	20	34	-16
Jill (DLC)	21	33	-17
Morrigan	21	34	-18
Nemesis T-Type	19	32	-12
Phoenix Wright	20	33	-15
Ryu	20	34	-13
Spencer	20	33	-15
Strider	18	31	-12
Trish	20	34	-9
Tron	23	34	-16
Vergil	19	33	-14
Viewtiful Joe	20	33	-15
Wesker	20	34	-13
Zero	20	33	-15

Novice players almost always make the mistake of using crossover attacks too often. Switching characters repeatedly takes away cohesion and momentum from your team. Not to mention that you are taking a risk every time you perform a crossover attack—yes, it's an overhead, but it's a remarkably weak one, and you are always vulnerable for at least a little bit at the end. If your opponent anticipates a crossover attack, they may wait and simply look to punish one. Find another way to swap a character in if you really must, or surprise your foe by dashing in with a low attack.

But when used sparingly or from far away, it's pretty safe to tag a character in with a crossover attack. Some characters have moves that can cover the vanity of a posing character. Phoenix's homing TK Shot H is an example. You also wait until your opponent super jumps, and tag in as soon as possible—their upward trajectory not only visually masks your tag, but it also more or less guarantees that they don't have an angle to punish. Finally, if your rival is all over you, it can sometimes pay off to use crossover attacks as a kind of high-risk reversal, though this should be done very sparingly.

CROSSOVER COMBINATION

P1+P2

With at least three hyper meters and three characters, your whole team joins in. With only two bars or two characters, only two join in. With only one bar or character, your character still performs their crossover combination hyper combo, but no one else joins in.

As is true elsewhere in combos, keeping the number of hits low helps boost combo damage by virtue of smaller combos having less damage scaling.

Trish—α and Trish—β on point starting a crossover combination can still move as normal and mix it up during Round Harvest, while her partners help hold the adversary in place and deal chip damage with their hyper combos.

During a crossover combination, as many characters as possible join their efforts to generate a tremendous attack. Each character performs the hyper combo dictated by the assist type you chose for them. One bar of hyper meter is expended for each character participating.

The startup, damage, and other characteristics of your crossover combination are dictated by the hyper combos of the characters on your team. So, for example, if you have a character like Iron Man or Spencer, whose hyper combos hit faster than most, or a hyper combo that returns control of the point character early, your crossover combination shares that advantage. If one of the hyper combos is OTG-capable, the entire crossover combination can be considered an OTG-capable attack. After all, you can just cause a hard knockdown by a throw or air combo, then P1+P2 for easy, big damage, if your team is set up correctly for it.

You can cancel into a crossover combination from grounded basic attacks, but not from special moves or hyper combos. (Unless you use X-Factor canceling as a bridge!) You can cancel *out* of a crossover combination with X-Factor, and your point character will be free to act while your partners continue to finish their hyper combos!

CROSSOVER COUNTER

DURING GUARDSTUN, ⇨ + P1 or P2 WITH AT LEAST ONE BAR OF HYPER METER AVAILABLE

Crossover counters allow you to take advantage of guardstun by tagging in a partner, who then immediately performs their crossover assist while becoming the point character. Crossover counters can be good to avoid chip damage knockouts or to surprise aggressive foes with invulnerable reversal crossover assists like Haggar—α. Crossover counters can be canceled into hyper combos or character-specific actions; for example, C. Viper crossover counters can be made into feints by pressing Ⓢ, same as her special move versions of those attacks, while Morrigan can fly-cancel her crossover counters. More on crossover counters can be found earlier in this chapter, in the section on guarding.

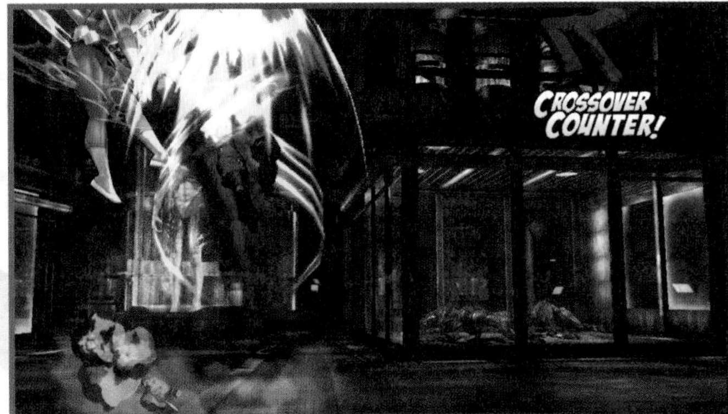

Crossover counters allow you to turn the tables on aggressors.

TEAM AERIAL COMBOS

Air ⇧ + Ⓢ during launcher combo: upward air tag; glows red.

Air ⇨ or ⇦ + Ⓢ during launcher combo: erases one of the opponent's hyper meter bars, sideways air tag; glows green.

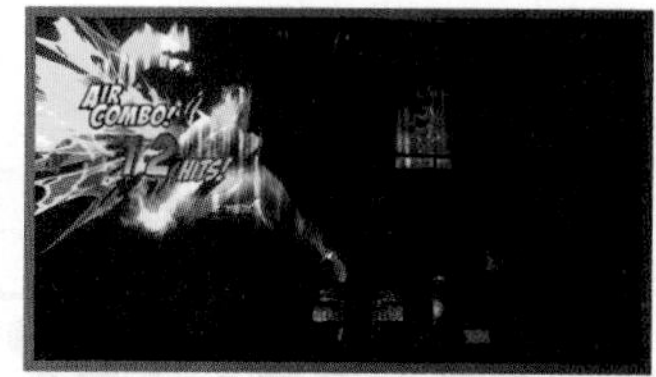

Air ⇩ + Ⓢ during launcher combo: generates a hyper meter bar for your team, ground bounce air tag; glows blue.

After the actual team aerial combo tag flash, the victim has 15 frames to input the same command as the air tag used in order to break out with a team aerial counter.

New to the *MvC3* series are team aerial combos, or **TAC**s. A team aerial combo starts by landing Ⓢ launcher, then super jumping with the victim and performing at least one air basic attack before chaining into direction + Ⓢ. (Diagonal directional inputs are interpreted as upward or downward) The direction you input dictates which kind of team aerial combo you'll initiate. Upward offers the best juggle position and a slight damage boost on the tag hit, downward causes a ground bounce while building a full bar of meter for your team, and sideways juggles the enemy with a wall bounce, while erasing one of the opponent's bars of meter!

After the first tag hand-off in midair, the next character can perform an air chain as they normally can during a launcher combo. The new incoming character can also hand off to the second partner by using direction + Ⓢ again. No need to do at least one basic attack after the first tag, either; for the second tag, you can potentially just do air ⇧ or ⇨ or ⇩ + Ⓢ right away.

When direction + Ⓢ is input to spark a team aerial combo during an air combo, the victim has 15 frames following the brief freeze to input the break command. The correct break command is exactly the command used to start the air tag: ⇧ + Ⓢ if that's the air tag incoming, ⇩ + Ⓢ for the down air tag, and ⇨ or ⇦ + Ⓢ for the sideways air tag (either direction works). Only one Ⓢ input is accepted during this 15-frame window—a victim who can potentially perfectly input every possible escape during the 15-frame window is *not* guaranteed to break every team aerial combo; he'll only break them at random, if the first input he uses during the window happens to be right. Interestingly, a neutral Ⓢ input during the window *prevents* a correct input right afterward from being used, even if accomplished during the break window.

A successful team aerial counter tosses the character who attempted to air tag off of the victim, while dealing 50,000 damage. The offender is invincible off the wall bounce caused by a team aerial counter, so neither side is guaranteed anything—it's essentially a match reset.

The primary purpose of team aerial combos is to stave off hitstun decay and build tons of hyper meter. (Or to erase your enemy's meter!) Team aerial combos are weighted heavily in favor of the aggressor—you get far more out of successful team aerial combos than you do out of successful team aerial counters. Solid team aerial combos build/erase multiple meters while easily dealing more than 500,000 damage, before any potential hyper combo or THC enders. Just like any other air combos, team aerial combos can lead to OTG opportunities right afterward, since flying screen is still possible.

Team Aerial Combo Order Quirk

Normally, team aerial combos simply tag to the next character in line. On a team of three heroes, the first tag swaps teammate A for teammate B, and the second tag then swaps teammate B for teammate C.

If teammate B is not available for some reason when a team aerial combo is attempted (most likely because their assist was called too recently), something interesting happens. Teammate A air tags to teammate C instead. If teammate C is then made to air tag again, the air switch goes *back* to teammate A! Teammate B never comes into play, the team's order ultimately stays the same, and teammate A gets to do *two* air combos in the same combo!

The easiest way to set this up is to use teammate B as an assist in teammate A's combo that leads up to Ⓢ launcher. Then, quickly chain to an air tag before teammate B's crossover assist is ready again.

TEAM HYPER COMBO

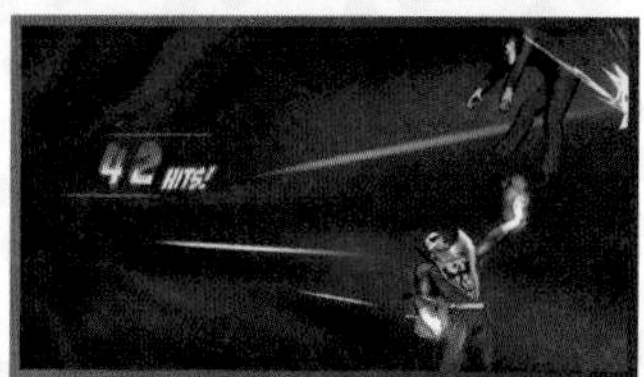

THCs greatly expand damage and combo potential, and they are also key to swapping in characters with less risk.

During level 1 hyper combos, you can team hyper combo cancel to the next character's hyper combo simply by inputting the command for the desired hyper while the current hyper combo is in progress. You can THC at a single stretch up to twice, ultimately using one hyper combo from each partner. Level 3 hyper combos can finish, but not start, team hyper combos. When called into a THC, characters leap on screen and perform their hyper combo cutscene as usual, but all their lead-in frames *before* the cutscene are truncated, resulting in a hyper combo that's much faster than usual.

Team hyper combos are obviously useful for their damage and chip potential; for example, any combo ending in a beam hyper combo can easily be made much more powerful simply by team hyper combo canceling to another beam hyper combo. But team hyper combos are also important because of the safety you're potentially afforded. In most situations, tagging in a new point character with a crossover attack or crossover counter is risky. By burning a few bars of hyper meter, you can perform your current point character's safest hyper combo, then THC to the safest hyper combo for your next teammate.

And, in combos, THC handoffs are better than ever thanks to the return of mashable damage on many hyper combos. Team hyper combo cancel a mashable hyper into another mashable hyper, and get as many ATK inputs as possible in for both, and you'll definitely be doing much better damage than equivalent combos did in original *MvC3*!

PROJECTILES AND BEAMS

Projectiles and beams have their own hidden durability priorities and values that dictate what happens when different projectiles collide.

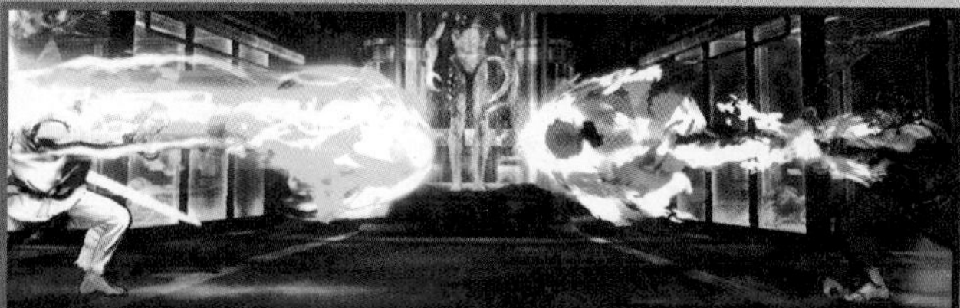

PROJECTILE PRIORITY

The first check is priority. There are three projectile priorities: low, medium, and high. Most standard projectiles and beams are low priority, while certain attacks, like Arthur's Golden Armor Lance, are medium priority. Projectile or beam hyper combos are high priority.

When projectiles of higher priority run into projectiles of lower priority, the higher priority projectile wins outright. It doesn't matter how many low priority projectiles a medium priority projectile plows through, for example: as long as it only encounters lower priority projectiles, it always wins.

DURABILITY POINTS

Durability points come into play when projectiles of the same priority collide. Projectiles pack their durability points into a single punch, while beams distribute their durability points across a certain number of frames. When projectiles collide, they mutually deplete durability according to their durability point ratings; projectiles as one blast of DP, beams as DP distributed evenly across their number of frames.

Frame Data

Going from a complete novice to an intermediate player requires grasping the fundamental concepts of the game—moving, guarding, attacking, things like that. Taking the extra step to becoming an expert player, to some degree, requires digging a little deeper and internalizing some rather more esoteric concepts. The most prominent, measureable, and ultimately meaningful of these is the idea of frame advantage. Getting into this can be a little intimidating for a new player, so rest assured that Rome wasn't built in a day, and neither do you have to incorporate all this information and somehow translate it into improved gameplay all at once. As in any hobby or skill with depth, serious players measure the time they've put into fighting games in *years*, not days, weeks, or months. So don't fret if this seems overwhelming at first. A salad bar approach can work wonders here: take a little of what seems to help you at a time.

FRAMES

A frame is the game's unit of time measurement. Like most modern games, *UMvC3* runs at 60 frames per second. Regarding the game using the actual frame data, when available, takes the discussion to a deeper, more useful place. The actual utility of a given move, for example, becomes much more apparent when looking at the frame data for that move. Visually, there is very little difference between a move that hits in 4 frames versus a move that hits in 8 frames. To most human observers, there is not a difference at all—for this example, we're talking about the difference between "just under a tenth of a second" and "just over a tenth of a second." But in terms of the game, this miniscule, barely perceptible difference can amount to a vast gulf.

STARTUP FRAMES

This is the number of frames it takes for an attack to become "active," or capable of hitting an opponent, after the command for the move is correctly input. The fastest moves in the game have 1 to 4 frames of startup, and these are mostly throw attacks. For the purposes of this guide, startup frames naturally include the first frame of the active period. This is for ease of looking for links under frame advantage: if something lists an advantage of +6, then any attack with a startup of 6 frames or lower works. This does mean, however, that if you add up the startup, active, and recovery frames, the sum is actually 1 frame longer than the real duration of the move.

ACTIVE FRAMES

This is the number of frames in which a move is actually capable of striking. For basic attacks, this number tends to be very small—usually no more than 3-5 frames. Exceptions apply, of course, and it's always worth noting when a move has an unusually high number of active frames.

RECOVERY FRAMES

This is the number of frames in which an attack is recovering and is no longer active. Characters can't guard or perform other actions while recovering, so they are vulnerable to retaliation if the recovery period is lengthy. The recovery period is the portion that is circumvented when using any kind of cancel into other moves. For projectile attacks, recovery begins the moment the projectile is actually released.

ADVANTAGE ON HIT / ADVANTAGE IF GUARDED

When an attack strikes an opponent, two things happen: the attacking character's move goes through its recovery period, and the defending character either goes through their animation of guardstun or hitstun (depending, of course, on whether the attack was blocked). Different attacks have different recovery periods and inflict different amounts of guardstun or hitstun. The attacking character eventually fully recovers from their attack and is ready to act again, just as the defending character eventually leaves the animation of guardstun or hitstun, ready to act again, as well. The discrepancy between when the attacker and the defender can act is expressed exactly with the concept of frame advantage. A frame advantage of +10 means that the attacker can act a full 10 frames before the defender—no small advantage at all. Many attacks are active in less than 10 frames, so in this hypothetical scenario, the attacker can actually link any move faster than 10 frames, and there's nothing the defender can do about it. On the other hand, a frame advantage of +1 is not particularly noteworthy; yes, the attacker can act a whole single frame before the competitor, and the opportunity to act first is never a bad thing, but nothing is guaranteed. (Except a throw attempt, if close enough!)

So, how is this useful? In this guide, we've compiled almost complete frame data for every single character. The only data we did not manage to complete, due to time restrictions and logistical difficulties, was frame advantage on hit/guard for air-to-air attacks (these are variable both from normal to super jump, but they are also harder to determine because of the less exact nature of air-to-air combat and the exigencies of air recovery).

What is here, however, should be a treasure trove to the novice gamer and the hardened tournament veteran alike.

HITSTUN

Hitstun is the counterpoint to **guardstun**. As guardstun is the state in which defending characters are actually blocking, hitstun is the state in which the victim on the receiving end of an attack is actually reeling. At least during guardstun, the defensive character still has some ability; during hitstun, victimized characters cannot do *anything*. The length and nature of hitstun depends on the attack that caused it. Generally, heavier attacks cause more hitstun than lighter ones. Strike a character again while they're still in hitstun, and you'll create a **combo**.

Hitstop

Hitstop is the brief effect that happens almost imperceptibly whenever two characters contact each other. In order to subtly highlight the force of their blows, any hit exchange is depicted through the game freezing for a small number of frames. This occurs whenever attacks are exchanged, whether on hit or block, and it can account for some minor difficulties with timing or execution in some cases.

NORMAL HITS AND COUNTERHITS

Normal hits occur when a character is struck while standing, crouching, moving, but not performing an attack. Throughout this book, you'll find references to the frame advantage created "on hit"—in all cases, unless otherwise noted, the frame advantage referenced describes a normal hit.

Our frame data figures assume a normal hit.

A counterhit occurs when a character is struck during their own attack, whether during startup, active, or recovery frames. A counterhit is visually indicated by a red hit effect. Counterhits sometimes create hit states that normal hits don't, such as **crumples** or **knockdowns** where a normal hit would just cause standard hitstun. Counterhits—all counterhits—also add +2 to the frame advantage conferred on hit. This means that landing a counterhit can lead to **link** combo opportunities that are not available with normal hits.

Counterhits are indicated by a special red spark and grant +2 frame advantage. Some counterhits result in special hit states.

SPECIAL HIT STATES

Most attacks just cause characters to reel, whether on normal or counterhit. Some attacks cause special hit states that do different things.

Soft Knockdown (ground or air)

Nothing is guaranteed after a knockdown, but if you guess right on which way your foe is going to recover, you can keep offensive momentum going.

Ground Recovery Frames:	
Neutral	19
Forward	33
Backward	33

Air Recovery Frames	
Neutral / Forward / Back	10

The idea of a "knockdown" is a little different in *UMvC3* than in other fighting games. Most knockdown-capable moves result in the victim recovering more or less immediately and automatically. With no controller input, characters who are knocked down simply rise in place right away. Characters can be made to recover in a desired direction by holding ⇦ or ⇨ as they recover. This is called **ground recovery** or **air recovery**, depending on where it takes place—not all knockdowns in *UMvC3* knock the opponent to the turf! Very many attacks cause victims to be "knocked down" into aerial hitstun, after which they perform an air recovery. After an air recovery, the airborne character is considered to be normal jumping, with all the attendant benefits (crossover assist calls allowed) and limitations (chain combos may be limited; hitstun from attacks is shorter) that entails.

During ground or air recovery, your point character is invulnerable, and assists can be called. Beware of mix-ups designed intentionally to be confusing or difficult to defend against just as you become vulnerable after recovery ends. Getting an assist out can help run interference, but if you're careless, it can just result in two characters getting hit instead of one.

Hard Knockdown

Spencer ends an air combo with air Ⓢ, causing flying screen.

Immediately upon landing, he dashes forward, then performs Wire Grapple H just off the ground to OTG his target.

The universal way to cause a hard knockdown is flying screen—start a launcher combo with Ⓢ, then chain to air Ⓢ. Most throws also cause hard knockdowns, as do some other attacks. OTG-capable attacks can hit opponents stuck in a hard knockdown.

Hard knockdowns prevent immediate ground or air recovery and instead leave the victim laid out on the floor, unable to move. During this period, the floored victim of the hard knockdown is vulnerable to **off the ground** (**OTG**) hits. Technically, there is no limit on the number of hard knockdowns and OTG hits that can be used in a single combo...the limiting factors are player creativity and **hitstun decay**.

MARVEL OTG-CAPABLE CROSSOVER ASSISTS

Deadpool—β
Dormammu—β
Ghost Rider—β/—γ
Hawkeye—β/—γ
Hulk—α
Iron Fist—β
Iron Man—γ
Sentinel—β/—γ
She-Hulk—α
Shuma-Gorath—α (DLC)
Storm—β
Super-Skrull—α
X-23—β

CAPCOM OTG-CAPABLE CROSSOVER ASSISTS

Akuma—γ
Arthur—γ
C. Viper—β
Dante—β
Felicia—β
Firebrand—α
Phoenix Wright—γ
Viewtiful Joe—γ
Wesker—β

Ground Bounce

Some attacks cause the victim to bounce off the floor forcibly. Before the target lands on the ground a second time, they are vulnerable to continued attacks. For the most part, only one ground bounce is possible per combo. Using another ground bounce attack will only cause a hard or soft knockdown, depending on the attack.

One ground bounce can be used per combo.

Wall Bounce

Some attacks cause the victim to bounce forcibly off the side of the screen, rather than the floor. This is a wall bounce. Characters subjected to a wall bounce are vulnerable until they hit the ground. Only one wall bounce is possible per combo.

One wall bounce can be used per combo. Subsequent wall bounce moves simply cause a knockdown.

Spinning Knockdown

Some attacks cause a violent spinning knockdown, which hurls the victim across the screen. Whether characters can recover out of the spinning knockdown before hitting the ground is dependent on the move that started the spinning knockdown; some moves always cause spinning foes to be vulnerable until they hit the ground, paving the way for juggle opportunities, while other moves that cause a spinning knockdown are only different from a regular knockdown in terms of aesthetics. Spinning characters cannot do anything or recover until they hit the ground, so, as with both types of bounces, victims are open to more punishment. The difference is that there's no innate limit on the number of spinning knockdowns allowed during a combo.

The spinning knockdown effect looks more violent than a soft knockdown, but the behavior is mostly the same.

Stagger

Some attacks, like Thunder Edge Amaterasu's ⇨ + Ⓗ (hold), cause a lengthy stagger rather than regular hitstun. This stagger lasts a set length of time, allowing further ground hits. Multiple staggers can be used in the same combo without diminishing the effect.

A stagger is just a rare, move-specific, lengthy hitstun. Technically, staggers can be linked in perpetuity; the victim stays grounded.

Crumple

When a character eats an attack like C. Viper's Ⓢ + ATK Focus Attack or Iron Fist's ⇩ ⬂ ⇨ + Ⓜ Dragon's Touch, they crumple slowly to the ground, vulnerable on the way down. Hitting the opponent during this time juggles them into the air. Only one crumple is possible per combo, because only standing targets can be crumpled. An aerial or juggled target will react differently.

Certain attacks cause a crumple. Characters hit during crumples are juggled into the air.

Capture and Dizzy

Capture, or incapacitation, states are created by certain moves, like Spider-Man's Web Ball. During capture, the victim is tied up one way or another and cannot act for a set period of time. After this time has elapsed, the opposing character recovers normally, but in the meantime, they are completely vulnerable. Dizzy is different from capture states because it can end with characters in a hard knockdown, during which any attack will pop the enemy up, whether OTG-capable or not.

As many capture and dizzy moves can be used in the same combo as you can manage.

Combos

Back in 1991, intended input leniency for special moves in *Street Fighter II: The World Warrior* accidentally allowed basic attacks to strike before canceling into an unavoidable special. This afterthought became an official feature with the introduction of the combo meter in *Super Street Fighter II*. In the mid-'90s, series like *Darkstalkers* and *Street Fighter Alpha*, along with the games *X-Men: Children of the Atom*, *Marvel Super Heroes*, *X-Men vs. Street Fighter*, and *Marvel Super Heroes vs. Street Fighter* (these the seeds of the *MvC* series) began to take combos to a whole different level. Outrageous, over-the-top, outstanding combos represent the number one source of serious damage in the *MvC* franchise and the *Vs.* games in general, as well as a good portion of their heart and soul.

The classics never die.

So, in fighting game terms, what is a combo? A combo is a sequence of hits that is guaranteed if the first attack is not blocked. Combos work because of **hitstun**, which is the period of time a character reels when struck by an attack. During hitstun, no actions are possible, blocking included. Hit your opponent, then during their hitstun, cancel your current move into another or link into another move after the initial one is fully recovered, and you'll create a combo. Combos are vital for the obvious purpose of dealing lots of damage, but they are more important in that good combos allow you, after two or three initial attacks, to **verify** whether your attacks are being guarded. Many combos and tactics are vulnerable to guaranteed retaliation if blocked—the (S) launcher possessed by every character is the best example—so confirming your hits before you reach the unsafe parts of a combo is a vital skill. Instead of finishing the combo, you can stop and switch to a back-up plan, or rethink your positioning if the blocking adversary pushes you away with advancing guard.

Number of Hits	Combo
3-4	YES!
5-6	COOL!
7-9	GOOD!
10-12	GREAT!
13-16	DUDE!

Number of Hits	Combo
17-20	SWEET!
21-25	AWESOME!
26-30	WONDERFUL!
31-35	VIEWTIFUL!
36-42	EXCELLENT!

Number of Hits	Combo
43-49	STYLISH!
50-55	FANTASTIC!
56-64	AMAZING!
65-74	INCREDIBLE!
75-81	MIGHTY!

Number of Hits	Combo
82-90	MARVELOUS!
91-100	UNCANNY!
101-110	CRAZY!
111-199	GALACTIC!
200+	UNSTOPPABLE!

Combo Limitations

Plenty of combos are capable of knocking out any character outright. Certain safeguards are in place, however, to prevent certain repetitious infinite combos from occurring, as well as to prevent combos with high numbers of hits from doing disproportionate damage compared to less sizable combos.

Great for style and building hyper meter? Yes. Good for damage or hitstun deterioration? No.

DAMAGE SCALING

As the first hit in a combo, all attacks deal their full damage. With each hit added to the combo, however, attacks deal a diminishing percentage of their full damage.

Damage scaling somewhat devalues certain attacks that do lots of hits quickly, such as Sentinel's standing and crouching (H) mouth lasers and Morrigan's standing (H). These moves can still be excellent for other reasons, like the extra time they grant you to hit-confirm a combo, but the damage of your follow-up suffers.

DAMAGE = (BASE_DAMAGE * MODIFIER ^ COMBO_COUNTER) / 100

BASE_DAMAGE is the listed base damage of an attack. COMBO_COUNTER is the current hit number in the combo. The "MODIFIER" value is as follows:

- **(L) basic attacks = 0.75**
- **(M) basic attacks = 0.8**
- **(H) basic attacks = 0.85**
- **(S) attacks, special moves, and hyper combos = 0.9**

Damage cannot be less than 10% of base damage. (S) attacks, special moves, and hyper combos reach the scaling cap on hit 23. The other attack strengths reach the scaling cap progressively earlier.

Because scaling is weighted by button and based on the current number of hits, light attacks don't adversely affect scaling for the entire combo; scaling for only the current move is affected. This is unlike many modern fighting games, where opening with a light attack is detrimental to scaling on down the line.

Throws (and capture moves) scale damage heavily, which is noticeable if you throw your opponent, then start a combo off the throw. This is possible with most throws by landing an OTG-capable attack.

During X-Factor, the effects of damage scaling are reduced, but not negated.

HITSTUN DECAY

As discussed before, **hitstun** is the period of time during which a struck character reels, unable to block. Hitstun lasts for a certain period of time depending on the move used to inflict the blow. As a general rule, the heavier the attack, the longer the hitstun. However, as hits pile up within a combo, this hitstun period begins to shrink. Hitstun decay is rapidly accelerated in combos that start after a throw.

- **Attacks against grounded characters will eventually cause ground hitstun to drop by 5 frames, air hitstun to drop by 1 frame**
- **Attacks against airborne characters will cause both ground and air hitstun to drop by 5 frames**
- **The amount of attacks needed before hitstun decay occurs is variable per move**
- **Hitstun decay can occur multiple times within a combo!**
- **Some attacks are not affected by hitstun decay; Doctor Strange's Impact Palm will always inflict 35 frames of hitstun, hard knockdown attacks will always cause hard knockdown, hyper combos are unaffected by damage scaling, etc.**
- **TACs cause hitstun decay to revert back to normal and not advance at all until the attacker touches the ground. After touching the ground all decay is applied**

X-Factor Infinites

Some special knockdown states ignore hitstun decay. These effects are going to be the same no matter how many times they're applied in the same combo. During certain levels of X-Factor, due to speed boosts, some characters are able to link special moves together in such a way as to skirt around the issue of hitstun decay altogether.

Arthur, Captain America, Dante, Deadpool, Felicia, Wolverine, and X-23 have infinites that work only by linking certain special moves together indefinitely during particular levels of X-Factor. (Captain America and Wolverine have extra safeguards in place that prevent truly infinite X-Factor combos, but by the time those safeguards have kicked in, their opponent is probably knocked out regardless.)

CHAIN COMBOS

Chain combos are sequences of basic attacks chained together by pressing attack buttons one after another. Most basic attacks chain upward in strength, from Ⓛ light to Ⓜ medium to Ⓗ heavy, and most basic attacks can be chained into Ⓢ special attack. Ⓢ special attacks cannot be chained into anything else. Chains are possible when crouching, standing, or airborne. Not every character can perform the same chain combos—there are a handful of chain combo archetypes under which various characters fall.

Marvel Character Chain Combo Data

Name	Chain Combo Archetype	Full Normal Jump Chains	Rapid Fire Ⓛ Attacks
Captain America	Marvel Series	Yes	Standing Ⓛ
Deadpool	Hunter Series	Yes	Standing/crouching Ⓛ
Doctor Doom	Marvel Series	No	Crouching Ⓛ
Doctor Strange	Marvel Series	No	Crouching Ⓛ
Dormammu	Marvel Series	No	—
Ghost Rider	2-Hit Limited	No	—
Hawkeye	2-Hit Limited	No	—
Hulk	2-Hit Limited	No	—
Iron Fist	Hunter Series	No	Standing/crouching Ⓛ
Iron Man	Hunter Series	Yes	Standing/crouching Ⓛ
M.O.D.O.K.	Marvel Series	No	Standing/crouching Ⓛ
Magneto	Marvel Series	No	Standing/crouching Ⓛ
Nova	Marvel Series	No	Standing Ⓛ
Phoenix	Hunter Series	Yes	Standing/crouching Ⓛ
Rocket Raccoon	Hunter Series	Yes	Standing/crouching Ⓛ
Sentinel	2-Hit Limited	No	Crouching Ⓛ
She-Hulk	Marvel Series	No	—
Shuma-Gorath (DLC)	Hunter Series	Yes	Standing/crouching Ⓛ
Spider-Man	Marvel Series	Yes	Standing/crouching Ⓛ
Storm	Hunter Series	Yes	Crouching Ⓛ
Super-Skrull	Hunter Series	Yes	Standing/crouching Ⓛ
Taskmaster	Marvel Series	No	—
Thor	2-Hit Limited	No	—
Wolverine	Hunter Series	Yes	Crouching Ⓛ
X-23	Hunter Series	Yes	Standing/crouching Ⓛ

Capcom Character Chain Combo Data

Name	Chain Combo Archetype	Full Normal Jump Chains	Rapid Fire Ⓛ Attacks
Akuma	Marvel Series	No	Standing/crouching Ⓛ
Amaterasu	Marvel Series	No	Standing/crouching Ⓛ
Arthur	Marvel Series	No	Standing/crouching Ⓛ
C. Viper	Marvel Series	Yes	Crouching Ⓛ
Chris	Marvel Series	No	—
Chun-Li	Marvel Series	Yes	Standing/crouching Ⓛ
Dante	3-Hit Alternating	Yes	Crouching Ⓛ
Felicia	Hunter Series	Yes	Standing/crouching Ⓛ
Firebrand	Hunter Series	Yes	Standing/crouching Ⓛ
Frank West	Hunter Series	Yes	—
Haggar	Marvel Series	No	—
Hsien-Ko	Hunter Series	Yes	Standing/crouching Ⓛ
Jill (DLC)	Hunter Series	Yes	Standing/crouching Ⓛ
Morrigan	Hunter Series	Yes	Crouching Ⓛ
Nemesis T-Type	Marvel Series	No	—
Phoenix Wright	Marvel Series	No	—
Ryu	Marvel Series	No	Standing/crouching Ⓛ
Spencer	Marvel Series	No	Standing Ⓛ
Strider	Hunter Series	Yes	Standing/crouching Ⓛ
Trish	3-Hit Alternating	Yes	Standing/crouching Ⓛ
Tron	Marvel Series	No	—
Vergil	Marvel Series	No	—
Viewtiful Joe	Hunter Series	Yes	Standing/crouching Ⓛ
Wesker	Marvel Series	No	—
Zero	Marvel Series	Yes	—

GROUND CHAIN COMBO ARCHETYPES

HUNTER SERIES (FULL ALTERNATING)

A style of chaining that originated from the *Darkstalker* series, it is no surprise that Hsien-Ko, Felicia, and Morrigan all use this archetype. Characters with this type may chain one of each ground attack together from weakest to strongest. Attacks of the same strength can also be chained together only when alternating from the standing to crouching position (for example, Super Skrull may chain standing Ⓛ, crouching Ⓛ, standing Ⓜ, crouching Ⓜ, standing Ⓗ, crouching Ⓗ).

MARVEL SERIES (STRAIGHT AHEAD)

This chain archetype only allows three attacks chained together from weakest to strongest. This chain set may NOT alternate from a standing to crouching attack of the same strength, unlike the Hunter series (with some exceptions like Chun-Li, who can chain standing Ⓗ into crouching Ⓗ, and Trish, who can chain standing Ⓜ to crouching Ⓜ).

2-HITS LIMITED

This chain set allows the player to only chain two attacks together. The sequence must start with a light attack (crouching or standing) before chaining into any medium or heavy attack. Afterward, you must chain to a launcher or cancel into a special move to keep the combo going.

3-HIT ALTERNATING

This chain type has the chaining properties of the Hunter series; you can string together attacks from weakest to strongest while also alternating from standing to crouching attacks of the same strength. The difference here is that you can only chain up to three attacks together within these limitations. Dante can normally chain crouching Ⓜ, standing Ⓗ, then crouching Ⓗ. However, if the combo is started with an additional attack, like standing Ⓜ, crouching Ⓜ, and then standing Ⓗ, you cannot follow up with the final crouching Ⓗ.

AERIAL CHAIN ARCHETYPES

There exist only two types of air chains: a "Hunter Series" style of chaining where the player can chain two attacks each of light and medium before chaining to stronger attacks (air L, L, M, M, H, S), and a limited air chain where the player follows the same rules as the Hunter Series alternating chain method but can only chain up to three attacks together. The full Hunter Series style of chaining is available to all characters during a super jump, but only to some characters during a normal jump. The 3-Hit Limited style of air chaining is seen only on some characters during their normal jump.

OTHER CHAIN TYPES

RAPID FIRE LIGHT ATTACKS

Some characters can chain light attacks into each other repeatedly. Whenever desired, you can transition from rapid fire light attacks to their regular chain combo.

TARGET COMBOS (CHARACTER-SPECIFIC CHAIN COMBOS)

Some characters have unique chain combos. Though all characters initially fall into a chain archetype of some sort, these special combos, also known as target combos, bypass the normal rules of their chain structure. For example, Amaterasu may chain H into crouching H, but only within a three-attack chain limit, however you may chain air H three times consecutively (this ability bypasses the three-attack normal jump chain limit). Similarly, Dante can chain crouching L into standing L, and this chain does not interfere with the three-hit alternating rule.

COMMAND ATTACK CHAINS

Command attacks are much like basic attacks in a lot of ways but do not fit into chain combos in the same way. Command attacks play by their own rules, on a case by case basis: some command attacks can be chained into or out of, while some can't be used in chain combos at all.

LINKS

A link occurs when you wait until an attack has fully recovered before striking again. This is distinct from **chain combos**, in which ATK buttons are simply pressed in sequence, or **cancel** combos, in which recovery periods are interrupted with new actions. *UMvC3* is not as link-intensive as some fighters, like *Super Street Fighter IV*, but links are still present. In absolute terms, links are present all over the place, just in a different form. When chaining into S to launch then performing an air combo, you are technically canceling S with a super jump, then linking into an aerial chain.

Spencer ⇨ + H, linked into Armor Piercer, is a simple example of a link combo.

CANCELS

To cancel means to interrupt the recovery of one action with another action. Most ATK basic attacks are chain-cancelable into other basic attacks or command attacks, or command movements such as flight or teleportation. Some basic attacks are jump, double/triple jump, or super jump-cancelable—that is, the attack can be interrupted simply by holding an upward direction. S special attacks are cancelable only on hit, and then only into super jump, while air S is not cancelable when used after a launch into an air combo (though air S is cancelable if used in an air combo that begins without a launch). Most ATK basic attacks and command attacks are cancelable into special moves and hyper combos, and most level 1 hyper combos can themselves be canceled into a team hyper combo (THC), in which the next partner tags in to continue the hyper combo punishment. Finally, X-Factor activation can be used to cancel nearly any action, whether on the ground or in the air.

Smart Bomb L OTG CANCEL ▶ Proton Cannon X ▶ Proton Cannon CANCEL ▶ Okami Shuffle

CROSSOVER ASSISTS IN COMBOS

P1 or P2

The openings for using assists in combos are too numerous to bother listing many examples. The possibilities offered by Vs. games have driven hardcore experimenters and combo video producers for more than a decade and a half.

Apart from their utility for zoning, protection, and distraction, crossover assists are invaluable combo tools. Each partner can be called once per combo. Partners cannot be called during hitstun, guardstun, special moves, super jumps, or super jump flight. They can be called during normal jumps, normal jump flight, during or after ground and air recovery, and while on the ground performing ATK basic attacks or S special attacks. And basic attacks on the ground or off of jump-ins (or advanced jump-ins like triangle jumps or square jumps) are where most combos begin.

You can't use the same crossover assist twice in one combo, but you *can* use each assist once. Assists can be used in combos to help with verification, to extend combos on the ground, and to OTG after a launcher combo that leads to flying screen. Combos can start off of errant or grazing hit from a crossover assist—an opponent may get clipped by, for example, the edge of Doctor Doom's Molecular Shield or Iron Man's Unibeam, allowing you to start a combo if you juggle them in time. Sometimes, this can be as simple as starting up a long range hyper combo or linking S launcher, or it can be more complex.

Only one general possibility of many for the use of both assists in one combo: catching a stray hit with a close range assist, then following up with a chain combo ending in S to launch your foe into an air combo, ending in S to create flying screen, where then an OTG-capable partner can be called to continue further.

SPECIAL HIT STATES IN COMBOS

Using special states is a great way to perpetuate combos. This also enables you to think of combos as somewhat modular pieces, although hitstun decay prevents this from working perfectly—before floor bounce, after floor bounce, after flying screen, and so on. Certain hit states can only show up once per combo—these are ground bounce, wall bounce, and crumple (although multiple ground bounces are possible if you follow a ground bounce with a downward team aerial combo). There are technically no restrictions on the number of staggers, spinning knockdowns, hard knockdowns, capture type moves, and OTG hits, however. Those are limited in combos only by team makeup and hitstun decay.

The most universal special state is flying screen, caused by landing air S in a launcher combo. After flying screen, the combo victim is left in a hard knockdown state, during which OTG-capable attacks hit. OTGs are possible after flying screen, after most throws, and after certain special moves and hyper combos. While many characters can OTG without any help, some characters require an assist to OTG.

COMPOSING STRONG COMBOS

A large part of being successful in fighting games is making the most of the opportunities you have. Good opponents give up little for free, so when a solid chance comes your way, make it count. The ways in which attacks **chain**, **cancel**, and **link** into one another, along with the limitations imposed by **damage scaling** and **hitstun deterioration**, suggest a certain approach to eking out the most damage when you score a hard-earned first hit.

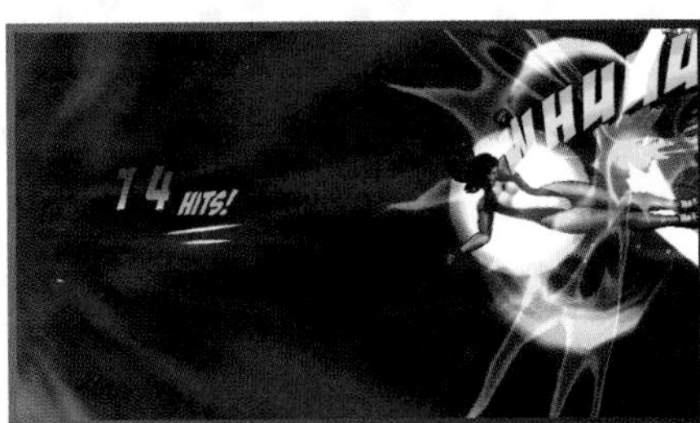

Combos need to start somewhere. Call a **crossover assist** and wait to see if the attack is successful. If yes, start a combo. Bonus points here if you can put the assist in a place that makes it difficult to deal with—the best example is dropping an assist on one side of your competitor before **jumping**, **airdashing**, **flying**, or **teleporting** to the other.

Alternatively, attack your opponent directly. Vary your opening attacks between low attacks that must be guarded crouching, overheads and quick airborne attacks (of which there are many, most of which must be blocked standing), and throws. Each can lead to combos, and each must be defended against differently.

When you start your **chain combo**, get to a point where you can cause a **wall bounce** or **ground bounce** with the fewest, hardest hits possible. Off the bounce, chain into Ⓢ launcher, then perform a brief **air combo** into Ⓢ to cause **flying screen**. Many attacks cause bounces, whereas flying screen is caused by air Ⓢ in a launcher combo. If you don't have attacks or assists available to create a wall or floor bounce, proceed directly to flying screen.

When performing air chain combos into air Ⓢ for flying screen, it's usually best to cause flying screen as low to the ground as possible. This is because the faster you land, the more likely it is you'll be able to OTG your rival, which is what you want to do after flying screen. The best way to cause flying screen low enough to OTG afterward, before the opponent can get up, varies from character to character. For some, it's as simple as chaining very slowly or using one air Ⓜ instead of two during air chains. For others, using flight in an air combo helps. And sometimes, because of the larger distance involved, following up with an OTG after flying screen is more difficult, requiring longer-range OTG-capable assists and deft wavedashing for fine repositioning. Securing an OTG is much easier in a corner.

After the OTG, you're probably approaching 15 or 20 hits, the point at which **hitstun decay** starts to mean that combo extension is impossible soon. Get as close as you can to this limit as possible, then finish with something that either causes lots of damage or sets you up to keep momentum. Ending with flying screen again is fine—at this point, you might not be able to score another OTG into anything, but you'll be able to drop an assist right on top of your foe as they recover, perhaps starting another combo. Otherwise, if you can, finish with a powerful **hyper combo**. From here, if necessary for the knockout, an **X-Factor cancel** into another hyper combo and/or a **team hyper combo** are strong options. Although damage scaling is at its heaviest by this point, many hyper combos add on enough total hits to add up damage quickly regardless, especially now that many can be mashed for more damage. And while **THC**s from **level 3 hyper combos** aren't allowed, these costly maneuvers make great combo or THC enders, as level 3 hyper combos are unaffected by damage scaling!

The combo engine in *UMvC3* manages to keep the outrageousness of the *Vs.* series combos alive, while mostly eliminating one of the lingering problems with the openness of the *Vs.* series combo rules: the previous preponderance of infinite combos. The use of infinites in high-level play for previous installments is the rule, rather than the exception. One of the best characters in *MvC1*, Red Venom, was essentially a hideously fast, walking infinite combo whose only deficiency was low stamina, and in *MvC2*, Magneto continued that tradition. But that's only two examples. *MvC2* alone had Iron Man as a slower, more air-based version of Magneto. Between his flight modes, normal jump infinite, and guard break potential, he could turn one glancing aerial counterhit into three dusted characters. Here, there are still high-risk, high-reward offensive characters, and there are certainly incredible, high damage combos that annihilate any character's health bar (usually from X-Factor or using heavy resources). But between hitstun decay, the removal of guard breaks against normal jumps, and the ability to roll forward or backward with invulnerability from any wakeup, the frustration of eating a single random accident into a lost round is removed.

This is not to say *UMvC3* won't be full of huge swings and ridiculous damage; it wouldn't be *MvC* without it, would it? Getting your point and assist character both caught in a strong team hyper combo, crossover combination, or X-Factor combo is perhaps even worse then eating a double snap back into anti-assist infinite in *MvC2*...instead of losing one character to an accident, then perhaps being guard broken when your next character falls in, you just lose two characters simultaneously! At least your own X-Factor gets beefed up with only one character left, if you still have it...never give up!

THE PURPOSE OF A COMBO

A combo is a series of attacks that cannot be guarded once the initial attack connects, and it is the fastest way to deal large amounts of damage in *UMvC3*. However, the most damaging combo is not always the best; different combos serve different purposes in ways that are beneficial beyond just doing the most damage possible.

Some combos are designed to gain maximum horizontal distance, with the goal of carrying the opposing character to the corner. In most cases, corner combos deal much more damage than their midscreen counterparts, so adjusting the beginning of a combo in hopes that the combo eventually gets to the corner can possibly yield more damage than if the combo is performed normally.

Other combos are designed with THCs in mind, as is demonstrated by Ghost Rider. Combos ending in Ghost Rider's Hellfire Maelstrom are slightly more powerful than combos ending in Spirit of Vengeance. However, Hellfire Maelstrom causes a hard knockdown, and it is not as THC-friendly as Spirit of Vengeance. Therefore, sometimes it is better to go with the lower damage of combos ending with Spirit of Vengeance because their THC potential is much higher.

Characters like Zero or Dante have access to long, drawn-out combos that take particularly long to finish. Combos such as these are great for stalling the timer on your rival's X-Factor or power-up hyper, such as Strider's Ouroboros. Extended combos like these also double-up as a means of building hyper meter for characters who are meter-hungry, such as Phoenix or Dormammu.

Special combos must be used against smaller characters such as Rocket Raccoon, or characters with an abnormal hitbox such as Shuma-Gorath or Tron. It's best to have these combos in mind before the match even starts. There's nothing worse than getting a combo opportunity only to have it fail because it wasn't suited for your opponent's character!

The positioning in which a combo leaves the competitor is also an important factor to consider. Though it's obvious that the corner is the ideal position for a combo to end in, midscreen combos that end in a position that allows for a throw reset or mix-up can possibly lead to significantly more damage than a combo designed solely to maximize damage.

Being able to make a quick decision about what combo to use in any given situation on the fly is a skill that must be mastered when learning the ins-and-outs of your team. Take a quick glance at your opponent's vitality gauge when starting a combo. If your most damaging bread and butter combo guarantees a K.O. given their current vitality, then go for it. Otherwise, using a combo with a purpose not necessarily bound to damage maximization might prove to yield more damage overall as a result.

DEVELOPING STRONG SET-UPS

Combos obviously deal damage, but they'll also frequently leave you in an ideal position to mount a continued assault. If successful, following a solid combo with a mix-up or trick that allows you to start a combo up again usually spells defeat for most characters. There is nothing better than having an opponent fall victim to a carefully crafted set-up. Ideally, it only takes one or two successful set-ups to secure victory in a match! Great set-ups can take some planning and creativity to come up with, given the freedom of the battle engine and variety of characters and attacks. The set-up potential of certain attacks is sometimes very apparent (such as Wolverine's Berserker Slash or X-23's Mirage Feint), while other moves' set-up potential might not be so obvious (such as Doctor Strange's Daggers of Denak or Amaterasu's Power Slash). Take this Vergil set-up as an example:

Call Iron Man—α, then perform Vergil's Rapid Slash.

Vergil crosses up with Rapid Slash while Iron Man Unibeam covers from the original direction.

This set-up fulfills several criteria that a good set-up consists of. A good set-up deals a worthwhile amount of damage. In this case, any of Vergil's follow-ups to Rapid Slash can lead to good damage.

Flexibility is also key: upon connecting, a set-up that allows for multiple follow-up options is ideal so that you can decide what to do depending on characters, vitality, time remaining, and so on. In this situation, Vergil can cancel Rapid Slash into Dimension Slash or into Devil Trigger for a combo that can end in either Dimension Slash or even a TAC if desired. Flexibility also refers to positional, character, and meter requirements. This particular set-up works midscreen and in the corner, requires no hyper meter (though having at least one increases its effectiveness considerably), and works on most characters.

Safety is as important. Good set-ups should be as risk-free as possible. If your set-up is guarded, ideally, you should be at least safe from retaliation or have a backup plan to avoid punishment. In the example given, the recovery on Vergil's Rapid Slash is protected by Iron Man's Unibeam, making it safe if guarded. In addition, Rapid Slash can be canceled into Devil Trigger, which puts Vergil in a position to mount a follow-up offense.

Deception: no competent opponent falls for an obvious set-up! Be sure your set-up is tricky enough to fool a competitor, giving them as few visual/audio cues as possible. The speed in which the set-up is performed adds to its deceptiveness—the faster, the better. In this example, Rapid Slash is a fairly quick move and doesn't necessarily need preparation or pinning down to use effectively. Adding several layers of depth to your set-up is ideal, so be sure that doing so does not make your set-up more obvious than it has to be!

You likely won't have one end-all set-up that works in every situation, against every character, and deals 100% damage every time; given the variety of systems and characters in the game, this is nearly an impossible task (though Wolverine's Berserker Slash canceled into Berserker Charge in original *Marvel Vs. Capcom 3* came close!). For every great set-up you create, make sure to have an alternative that covers up any shortcomings of other set-ups in your arsenal. Explore the different options your team has to offer, and keep an open mind!

Practice and Execution

Not every tactic is created equal, and neither is every technique equally easy to perform.

As in chess, the best defense is a good offense. An adversary who is pinned or being hit is an adversary who cannot retaliate.

Don't come in with the goal of winning every game. To begin, you won't. And that's not the point, anyway. The point is to improve. Winning is a consequence. Losses are a chance to learn.

Consider the levels of expertise:

- **Unconscious incompetence: The player isn't experienced enough to make an honest self-appraisal (and almost certainly overrates their abilities as a result)**
- **Conscious incompetence: The player has now gained the experience to see their initial shortcomings**
- **Conscious competence: With practice and preparation, the player is much more comfortable and develops a sense of their own effectiveness, but diligence is required to stay focused**
- **Unconscious competence: Concepts are fully ingrained, muscle memory is established, and the process of thinking about what to do during a match is largely unconscious**

The key is to realize that every match is a chance to try new things and experience new situations, rather than to win at all costs every time.

Team Building and Space Control

Ultimate Marvel vs. Capcom 3 requires you to think of your team as a whole entity, rather than simply a trio of different characters. The nature and character of a team stems not just from what each character is capable of, but also what each enables for the others. When building a team, always consider the following:

Any character can and absolutely should team up with partners whose crossover assists (tap P1orP2) help close gaps in offense or defense, or which emphasize strengths. For example, characters without options to OTG by themselves can team up with characters who have OTG-capable crossover assists. Characters who are good at zoning with long-range projectiles can choose assists partners who further press that advantage. Rushdown-oriented characters can pick assists that make blocking problematic—flying and airdashing characters can couple with low-hitting assists, while teleport-capable characters can drop pinning assists on one side, then easily cross to the other, which makes blocking tricky and safe retaliation almost impossible.

Some crossover assists also make great crossover counters (during guardstun, tap ⇨ + P1orP2). One could build an entire strategy around gaining meter and biding time to turn a match on its head with one solid crossover counter that hits both the foe's point and their assist. Guard their pinning pressure tactics, then crossover counter, catch both characters, and cancel to hyper combo; now, with either an X-Factor cancel to another hyper combo or a THC to your next partner, you've taken out two characters just from being patient and letting your opponent think they were getting what they wanted!

A solid team order should take into account team hyper combos. It is *much* more valuable to knock an opposing character out completely rather than just deal heavy damage. If you don't maximize the opportunities that come your way and try to put characters down whenever possible, you're leaving the door open for them to heal up in reserve and waste your efforts. Solid team hyper combos are often the only way to continue a combo, the only way left to get that *last* little bit of damage to knock out a point or assist. It is *extremely* valuable to take your rivals out completely when given the chance, no matter the cost.

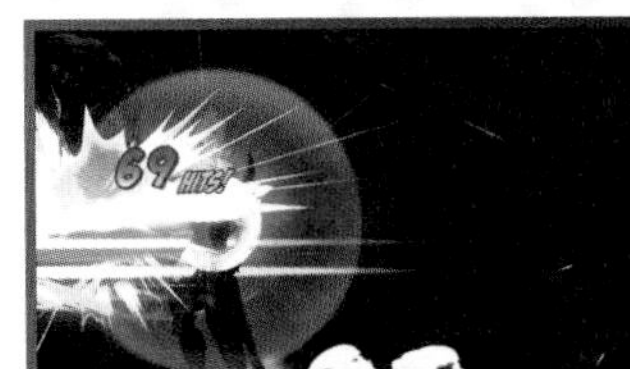

Of course, in addition to combo extension, team hyper combos also serve to rotate in a new point character. While there are several ways to switch characters, you will inevitably find yourself in a situation where most options are unavailable or unsafe. Crossover attacks can be read and punished; crossover counters aren't possible if your competitor doesn't give you anything to guard, which they won't if they're on the lookout for some sort of switch in the first place. Team aerial combos require a clean hit, and what's more, they require that the opponent doesn't properly team aerial counter. Often, the only remotely safe option to tag in a new character is to activate the current character's fastest-activating hyper combo, then starting the next character's safest hyper combo. There are many hyper combos that are completely safe when guarded, which is the best quality for this purpose. The archetypal example here, of course, is Storm's Hail Storm.

Characters who lack great air combos on their own can score a launcher, then hand off the air combo to more combo-capable teammates with team aerial combos. Team aerial combos not only allow more flexibility in teammate switching and team construction, but they also provide terrific damage and potentially insane hyper meter rewards, in addition to the new ability to erase the opponent's meter!

Of course, a lot of these techniques cost hyper meter. So here, too, there are decisions. How are you going to build hyper meter? Of the characters you favor, who is best suited to a "battery" role? Will you stockpile hyper meter primarily for one purpose, such as a particular THC, a hyper combo that is safe to guess/chip with, or a crossover counter to hyper combo? Or, you might save hyper meter for a particular character. For example, so Phoenix can be ready to rise as Dark Phoenix, so Dormammu can unleash repeated Stalking Flares, or so characters like Ryu and Akuma can land their level 3 hyper combos. Perhaps you've picked a trio with a solid crossover combination; some pairings of characters and assist types create crossover combinations that knock many character out outright, or which deal incredible chip damage.

Regardless of your ultimate plans with team chemistry and construction or with hyper meter consumption, the point is mainly that you should have plans in the first place. Of course, things won't always go according to plan—inevitably, you will lose a partner to assist damage prematurely, or a character or two will disappear in seconds to a nasty X-Factor combo or THC, but you can control a lot more of your fate if you've at least thought about what you'll do ahead of time.

Controlling the Ground

Although super jump height greatly expands the field of play, *UMvC3* isn't as air-centric as *MvC2*. Characters no longer turn around automatically after they pass over their opponents in midair. Basic attacks performed then often whiff (making special moves such as Akuma's Hyakkishu or Jill's Teleport ↗ valuable because they always face you in the correct direction). Additionally, whiffed air attacks are not cancelable into airdashes. This means characters cannot play "air footsies" by quickly doing whiffed super jump attacks dash-canceled into more air attacks.

Additionally, flight-capable characters don't stay airborne nearly as long as in previous titles, and characters who fly while super jumping can't call assists.

All this means is that *UMvC3* is played more at normal jump height and ground level, rather than up at super jump height. For most characters, controlling the ground is much more likely and valuable than controlling the air.

OVERCOMING BAD MATCHUPS

It is inevitable in a game with so much variance that some characters have the tools to utterly shut down others. But this does not make those matches, or other impossible-looking situations, hopeless. Bad matchups are disadvantageous on paper—we still play the matches after the select screen for a reason. But overcoming bad matchups and situations requires a certain mentality.

You must accept that a lot of the time, maybe even most of the time, you will not be allowed to do what you want to do. This often translates into being forced to guard, as the opposition pins your character with something like a beam character firing while calling Doctor Doom—β. For a character like Haggar, Tron, or Nemesis, this can be demoralizing. If you respond by flailing or panicking, throwing stuff at the wall to see if anything sticks, then you have no chance whatever beyond dumb luck.

Accepting that you have no obvious way to attack and no direct path to victory is what makes the match playable in the first place. In this case, simply super jumping forward while blocking is often the best, or even the only action possible. Now, that isn't why you picked those characters. Further, super jumping itself isn't the best idea for most characters—not everyone is mobile or possesses decent options at super jump height, and crossover assist calls and tag-outs become unavailable. But, we aren't talking about ideal circumstances to begin with. We are talking about finding the branch on the failure tree that doesn't break. Super jumping makes you vulnerable to air throws and cross-under cross-up antics, but it helps you interrupt your competitor's pinning attempts by repositioning all the characters. Perhaps your rival just reorients to a similar position and resumes attack, forcing you to block or try super jumping again. But, maybe you end up gaining ground and getting in range of your own character's options.

If the opponent reads your attempts to super jump over their offense, they may preemptively super jump themselves—a character like Iron Man can transition pretty easily between horizontal space control at ground height to horizontal space control at super jump height, after all. If you read their adjustment, you can dash forward instead of super jumping, and go for cross-under tricks or air throws of your own.

The key is to be patient and careful when going for your shot. After all, it's *MvC*, so with the right resources and team structure, one shot is often all it takes. Along those lines, if you do manage to earn your shot, don't let it go to waste! You must make your opportunities count, especially when they're so hard to come by.

In addition, *MvC* is a team game; a well-balanced team consists of characters that cover each other's weaknesses. For example, Chris has trouble against opponents who rain down projectiles from the air at a distance since he has no attack that aims upwards at an angle. However, pairing Chris with Strider effectively covers up this problem, as Strider—β Vajra homes in on even aerial adversaries. Any bad matchups that Chris has due to aerial challengers are suddenly not so bad anymore with the proper tools. Be sure to keep bad matchups in mind when deciding what team to use, which crossover assists to choose, and what order to place them in.

SET-UPS, MIX-UPS, AND THE HUMAN ELEMENT

Frequently, a player's strength is owed to not only their fighting game fundamentals, but also their set-ups and mix-ups. A well-crafted set-up sends your opponent a strong message: either guard or escape this set-up, or face a possible K.O. However, not all set-ups and mix-ups are created equal.

For example, if you are playing as Dark Phoenix, a typical set-up you can utilize is to perform TK Trap M as a new character is coming in after a K.O., then use Teleport M just as the trap is triggered for a cross-up. This set-up can be modified as follows: before a new character comes in, set TK Trap M, set TK Trap H (timed so that the character comes in a moment after it launches), and then perform Teleport M as TK Trap M is triggered. The core of both set-ups is basically the same: cross-up TK Trap M. Both set-ups also have the same end result: use the hitstun from the projectile to start a combo. However, the latter scenario has additional "smoke and mirrors" to confuse your foe. TK Trap H launches by itself without being triggered, and it is not actually meant to connect on the opponent. Instead, it is used to initiate a preemptive reaction out of them; in this case, holding ⇦ to get their aerial guard ready. While they are preoccupied with worrying about TK Trap H, their reaction time to the real cross-up attack, TK Trap M, is decreased due to the ruse. A super jump can be added after setting TK Trap H to further confuse your competitor, since they can no longer see TK Trap M **or** their character as they enter the screen.

Another example involves a Doctor Doom mix-up in the corner. Using a guardstun-heavy crossover assist such as Amaterasu—β Cold Star holds the opponent in place while you are free to perform square jump air Ⓜ as an overhead. The set-up can be modified into: call Amaterasu—β, then perform two *empty* triangle jumps before performing square jump air Ⓜ. Normally, adversaries try to react to either square jump air Ⓜ or empty triangle jump crouching Ⓛ. However, by performing two empty triangle jumps first, the opponent is tricked into attempting to guard low, making them more susceptible to an overhead attack.

Both examples detail two set-ups for each character that are fundamentally the same. The difference is that the second variation of the set-ups have added layers of complexity—more than a mere high/low or left/right mix-up. With these set-ups, the opponent's eyes are diverted elsewhere, similar to when magicians use sleight of hand to distract the audience while the real trick goes unnoticed. The more layers of complexity added to a set-up, the more deceptive it can be.

However, complex set-ups are often slightly more difficult to perform. In the case of the Dark Phoenix set-up, you must either memorize the timing in which TK Trap M is going to trigger or use an audio cue to know when to perform Teleport M, since you are subject to the same ground-level blindness as your opponent during a super jump! With the Doctor Doom set-up, extra inputs are required for the two empty triangle jumps before square jump Ⓜ, and these must be performed as quickly as possible; these also introduce more chances to screw up with an execution error.

When crafting mix-ups, taking the easy road isn't necessarily the best choice. Take into account all the tools your character possesses so that you can make your set-up as tricky as possible, even if it requires more work and a higher level of execution than normal. Basic attacks and special moves that you might think have little use (such as Phoenix's TK Trap H) might prove to be useful in a specific set-up. In addition, the human element must be taken into consideration when creating a mix-up or set-up. Punish your opponent for being human; that is, take advantage of the fact that a well-crafted set-up or well timed cross-up cannot be reacted to with human reflexes. Although anticipation often heightens a competitor's reaction time, adding extra "fluff" to a set-up can throw your opponent off, hampering their ability to react in time and causing them to question their instincts. In essence, the strongest set-ups are designed to punish your rival for being human!

NEW

DOCTOR STRANGE

"ONE DOES NOT REQUIRE THE EYE OF AGAMOTTO TO SEE THIS OUTCOME."

Bio

REAL NAME

Stephen Vincent Strange

OCCUPATION

Sorcerer Supreme, former physician

ABILITIES

One of the most powerful sorcerers in existence. Powers include astral manipulation, astral projection, teleportation, illusions, and more.

WEAPONS

Utilizes a variety of magical items, such as the Eye of Agamotto and the Cloak of Levitation.

PROFILE

Having studied under the tutelage of the Ancient One, Strange became the Earth's greatest sorcerer and hero. Having gained superior insight and knowledge through his studies, as well as obtaining valuable knowledge and consultation from other heroes, Strange acts as a consultant for all things related to the paranormal.

FIRST APPEARANCE

Strange Tales #110 (1963)

POWER GRID

4	INTELLIGENCE
2	STRENGTH
2	SPEED
3	STAMINA
6	ENERGY PROJECTION
3	FIGHTING ABILITY

*This is biographical, and does not represent an evaluation of the in-game combat potential of this hero.

Vitality	850,000
Chain Combo Archetype	Marvel Series

X-Factor Boost	Damage	Speed
Level 1 (3 teammates remaining)	120%	120%
Level 2 (2 teammates remaining)	145%	125%
Level 3 (1 teammate remaining)	170%	130%

Unlike a purely offensive or defensive character, your goal with Doctor Strange is to create situations where you can perform his special moves unimpeded. In other words, you need to buy time.

When given time, you can perform several attacks with Doctor Strange that can lead into a Teleportation mix-up:

- **Eye of Agamotto is great defensive tool and a key component of his mix-ups. It places Strange's opponent in guardstun for a huge amount of time and inflicts sizeable chip damage**
- **Daggers of Denak M has slow startup speed but allows for tricky Teleportation mix-ups when safely pulled off**
- **Finding time to create Grace of Hoggoth L orbs allows for an unavoidable mix-up using Flames of the Faltine**
- **Cross-ups using crossover assists and Teleportation M are nearly impossible for adversaries to see coming, as long as you have time for Strange to safely teleport**

How do you buy time to set up Doctor Strange's Teleportation mix-ups?

- **Impact Palm and Mystic Sword L lead to big damage when they connect, making competitors think twice about approaching on the ground**
- **Mystic Sword M projectiles are quick and difficult to stop, allowing Doctor Strange to fight from long range, control the ground, and force his rival to jump**
- **Once opponents have taken to the skies, air ← + Ⓗ option-selects to either air throw the foe or release an air Ⓗ attack that can be converted into a big combo**
- **Teleportation M and H can be used to evade attacks and create space away from the attacker**
- **Crossover assists are great for tying up the opponent long enough to let Doctor Strange safely set up a mix-up**

Attack Set

Standing Basic Attacks

Screen	Command	Hits	Damage	Meter Gain	Startup	Active	Recovery	Advantage on Hit	Advantage if Guarded	Notes
1	Standing Ⓛ	1	45,000	360	4	3	20	-10	-11	Chains into crouching Ⓛ
2	Standing Ⓜ	1	53,000	424	6	3	30	-15	-16	—
3	Standing Ⓗ	1	70,000	560	8	4	35	-16	-17	—

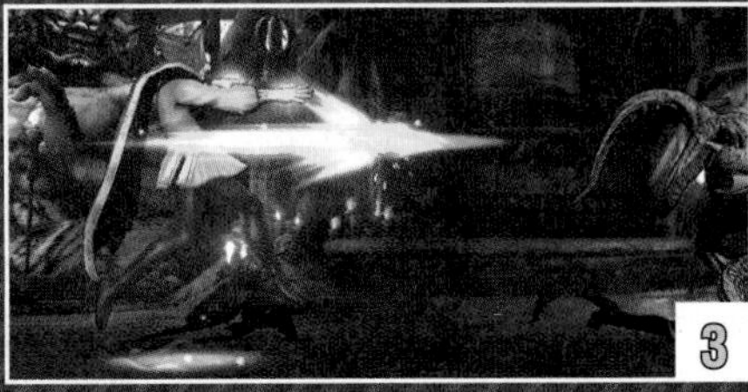

Crouching Basic Attacks

Screen	Command	Hits	Damage	Meter Gain	Startup	Active	Recovery	Advantage on Hit	Advantage if Guarded	Notes
1	Crouching Ⓛ	1	43,000	344	5	2	17	-6	-7	—
2	Crouching Ⓜ	1	50,000	400	8	5	25	-13	-14	—
3	Crouching Ⓗ	1	68,000	544	9	4	27	—	-9	Low attack, knocks down

Ground Special Attack—Launcher

Screen	Command	Hits	Damage	Meter Gain	Startup	Active	Recovery	Advantage on Hit	Advantage if Guarded	Notes
1	Ⓢ (while standing or crouching)	1	75,000	600	8	5	38	—	-21	Launcher, not special- or hyper combo-cancelable

Air Basic Attacks

Screen	Command	Hits	Damage	Meter Gain	Startup	Active	Recovery	Advantage on Hit	Advantage if Guarded	Notes
1	Air Ⓛ	1	48,000	384	5	8	15	+11	+10	Overhead attack
2	Air Ⓜ	1	58,000	464	7	3	25	+16	+15	Overhead attack
3	Air Ⓗ	1	68,000	544	8	3	34	+18	+17	Overhead attack

Air Special Attacks—Flying Screen and Air Exchange

Air (S) causes a hard knockdown when used in a launcher combo (this is sometimes called flying screen). When used outside of a launcher combo, air (S) behaves mostly like another basic attack. Air exchange attacks, performed by inputting a direction plus (S), are only possible during a launcher combo. Exchange hits initiate team aerial combos by tagging in the next available character to continue the air combo.

Screen	Command	Hits	Damage	Meter Gain	Startup	Active	Recovery	Advantage on Hit	Advantage if Guarded	Notes
1	Air (S)	1	73,000	584	9	4	28	+18	+17	Causes hard knockdown if used in launcher combo, overhead attack
2	Air ⇧ + (S) (during launcher combo)	2	105,00	880	8	4	39	—	—	Tags in next available ally while lofting opponent upward
3	Air ⇨ or ⇦ + (S) (during launcher combo)	2	95,000	800	8	6	33	—	—	Tags in next available ally while causing wall bounce, erases 1 hyper meter bar from foe
4	Air ⇩ + (S) (during launcher combo)	2	95,000	800	9	4	28	—	—	Tags in next available ally while causing ground bounce, generates 1 hyper meter bar

1

2

3

4

Command Attacks

Command attacks resemble basic attacks but have different chaining and canceling properties. It's usually possible to chain *into* a command attack from basic attacks, but most command attacks cannot be chained from or canceled themselves.

Screen	Name	Command	Hits	Damage	Meter Gain	Startup	Active	Recovery	Advantage on Hit	Advantage if Guarded	Notes
1	Illusion	⇦ + (H)	—	—		4	21	1	—	—	Teleports if contact is made with non-low physical attacks, not applicable to hyper combo attacks, not special- or hyper combo-cancelable
2	Illusion Teleport	—	—	—	—	1	10	15	—	—	Frames 1-20 invincible
3	Impact Palm (in air OK)	⇨ + (H)	1	75,000	600	6	5	35	—	-18	Crumples rival

1

2

3

Throws

Throws are for snagging passive or blocking opponents. Since throws are active so quickly, you can also use them to preemptively toss opposing characters out of their offense. Combos are usually possible after throws, one way or another.

Screen	Command	Hits	Damage	Meter Gain	Startup	Active	Notes
1	⇨ + (H) (ground)	1	80,000	800	1	1	Hard knockdown
	⇦ + (H) (ground)	1	80,000	800	1	1	Hard knockdown
2	⇨ + (H) (air)	1	80,000	800	1	1	Hard knockdown
	⇦ + (H) (air)	1	80,000	800	1	1	Hard knockdown

1

2

DOCTOR STRANGE

NEW

As a Partner—Crossover Assists

Screen	Type	P1+P2 Crossover Combination Hyper Combo	Description	Hits	Damage	Meter Gain	Startup	Active	Recovery (this crossover assist)	Recovery (other partner)	Notes
1	Doctor Strange—α	Spell of Vishanti	Daggers of Denak M	3	50,000 x 3	400 x 3	55	—	106	76	3 projectiles become active after 45 frames, each projectiles have 3 low priority durability points each, aim toward foe's current location
2	Doctor Strange —β	Spell of Vishanti	Eye of Agamotto	10	97,300	1200	49	—	112	82	Projectile lasts 120 frames, beam durability: 10 frames x 1 low priority durability points
3	Doctor Strange —γ	Spell of Vishanti	Bolts of Balthakk	2	60,000 x 2	480 x 2	43	15(29)15	139	109	First hit staggers, 2 projectiles with 8 low priority durability points each

Doctor Strange—β Eye of Agamotto assist is great for any team: the projectile keeps the opposing character in an enormous amount of hitstun and guardstun, allowing offensive characters to easily keep momentum and establish mix-ups. Defensive characters can use this assist to escape danger while the huge orb takes up space on the screen for almost two seconds!

Doctor Strange—α Daggers of Denak is a great all-purpose assist, as well: it's able to attack characters anywhere on the screen, making it useful for long range fights. It hits only three times thus causing less damage scaling in combos, making it a natural fit for characters who can cross up the competitor with teleports or rapid movement.

Doctor Strange—γ Bolts of Balthakk isn't recommended. While it is an unusual beam assist that fires twice, most characters can crouch directly under the beams, making it impractical to use effectively against the majority of the cast.

Snap Back

Screen	Command	Hits	Damage	Meter Gain	Startup	Active	Recovery	Advantage on Hit	Advantage if Guarded
1	↓↘→ + P1 or P2	1	50,000	500 (-1 hyper meter bar)	2	3	37	—	-18

Notes

On hit, snap back forces the opposing point character to be replaced by an assist. Opposing assist calls or tag outs are also locked out for 4 seconds

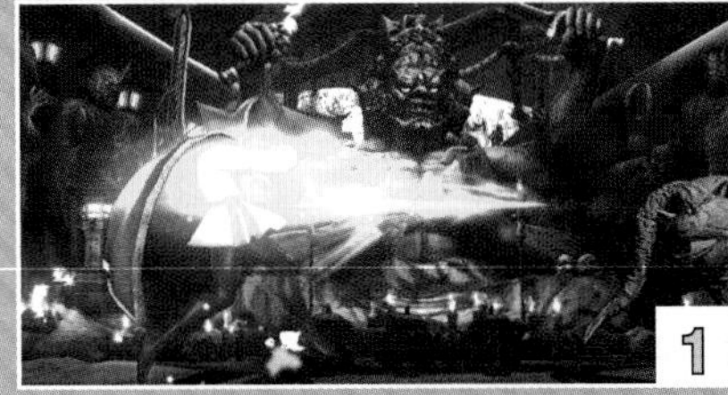

Special Moves

Screen	Name	Command	Hits	Damage	Meter Gain	Startup	Active	Recovery	Advantage on Hit	Advantage if Guarded	Notes
1	Daggers of Denak L (in air OK)	↓↘→ + L	1	50,000	400	11	—	34 (air: until grounded)	—	—	Projectile active after 15 frames, aims toward foe's current location , projectile has 3 low priority durability points
2	Daggers of Denak M (in air OK)	↓↘→ + M	3	50,000 x 3	400 x 3	31	—	29 (air: until grounded)	—	—	3 projectiles active after 45 frames, each projectile has 5 low priority durability points, aim toward opponent's current location
3	Eye of Agamotto (in air OK)	↓↘→ + H	10	97,300	1200	31	—	14 (air: until grounded)	+53	+52	Can be sent toward adversary using Impact Palm, has homing capabilities once sent, Eye of Agamotto disappears if Doctor Strange gets hit or creates another one, beam durability: 10 frames x 1 low priority durability points, active for 120 frames
4	Mystic Sword L	→↓↘ + L	3	50,000 x 3	400 x 3	8	3(1)4 (8)4	18	—	0	Knocks down
5	Mystic Sword M	→↓↘ + M	2	50,000 + 80,000	400 + 640	11 (projectile: 13)	4	36	-15	-16	Projectile has 8 low priority durability points
6	Mystic Sword H	→↓↘ + H	2	50,000 + 80,000	400 + 640	11 (projectile: 13)	4	36	-15	-16	Projectile has 8 low priority durability points
7	Grace of Hoggoth L (in air OK)	↓↙← + L	—	—	—	26	—	14	—	—	Increases strength of Flames of the Faltine on contact
8	Grace of Hoggoth M (in air OK)	↓↙← + M	—	—	—	26	—	14	—	—	Explodes on contact with Flames of Faltine
9	Flames of the Faltine (in air OK) (empty)	↓↙← + H	1	50,000	400	12	—	18	+4	+3	Projectile has 3 low priority durability points
10	Flames of the Faltine (Grace of Hoggoth L 1) (in air OK)	↓↙← + H	1	80,000	640	—	—	—	—	—	Projectile has 5 low priority durability points

Special Moves continued

Screen	Name	Command	Hits	Damage	Meter Gain	Startup	Active	Recovery	Advantage on Hit	Advantage if Guarded	Notes
11	Flames of the Faltine (Grace of Hoggoth L 2) (in air OK)	↓↙← + H	1	100,000	800	—	—	—	—	—	Projectile has 8 low priority durability points
12	Flames of the Faltine (Grace of Hoggoth L 3) (in air OK)	↓↙← + H	1	130,000	1040	—	—	—	—	—	Projectile has 10 low priority durability points, crumples
13	Flames of the Faltine (Grace of Hoggoth M) (Explosion)	—	1	90,000	720	—	—	—	—	—	OTG-capable, explosion has 3 low priority durability points, lasts 20 frames
14	Flight (in air OK)	↓↙← + S	—	—	—	22	—	—	—	—	Lasts 99 frames, input command again to cancel flight
15	Teleportation L (in air OK)	←↓↙ + L	—	—	—	11	—	19	—	—	—
16	Teleportation M (in air OK)	←↓↙ + M	—	—	—	11	—	19	—	—	—
17	Teleportation H (in air OK)	←↓↙ + H	—	—	—	11	—	14	—	—	—
18	Bolts of Balthakk	ATK + S	2	60,000 x 2	480 x 2	19	15(29) 15	14	-6	-7	First hit staggers, 2 projectiles with 8 low priority durability points each

Daggers of Denak: The Daggers of Denak are projectiles that hover in the air before homing in on the target. The L version fires a single projectile that pauses in the air momentarily before flying toward an opponent's current location.

The M version fires three projectiles that pause in the air for much longer before flying out. The gap before the daggers fly toward your competitor is long enough to use Teleportation M to position Doctor Strange behind his foe before the daggers hit, creating a cross-up situation. The M version takes substantially more time for Doctor Strange to recover, so generally, you'll have to call a crossover assist first to cover him.

The Daggers of Denak usually miss if your adversary is in the air and far away, so make sure your opponent is on the ground before you fire them off. Also, the M version disappears if Doctor Strange is hit before the daggers make contact with his rival, so make sure Doctor Strange is relatively safe before performing the attack.

Be careful when using the Daggers of Denak in the air, since Doctor Strange is vulnerable after performing the attack until he touches the ground! Use aerial Daggers of Denak L from fullscreen to protect Doctor Strange, or use them to punish projectiles from fullscreen — jump over your opponent's projectile, then send Daggers of Denak L back their way!

Eye of Agamotto: Doctor Strange creates a large projectile that sits in place for 120 frames (two seconds), hitting the opposition 10 times. The Eye of Agamotto is one of the focal points of Doctor Strange's gameplan—having one in play almost guarantees control of the match for the next few moments, and the move allows you to set up offense with the good Doctor while dealing heavy chip damage to the opposing character. The existence of an Eye of Agamotto on the screen can hinder the advance of offense based competitors, giving you time to create space and remove Strange from a dangerous attacker or prepare your own offense.

When the Eye of Agamotto projectile is hit with Doctor Strange's Impact Palm, the projectile slowly homes in on the target, making it great for mix-ups using Teleportation. This actually creates a brand new Eye of Agamotto projectile with 10 more hits; with proper timing, you can hit your opponent with 20 hits of Eye of Agamotto for 90,000 points of chip damage! The projectile loses hits the farther it travels, reducing guardstun and hitstun.

Mystic Sword L: This attack creates a quick flurry of three attacks in front of Doctor Strange and is most useful in combos against airborne opponents; if it hits, the opposing character is left in hitstun long enough for you to dash in and continue your combo! You can also use Mystic Sword L to make Doctor Strange's basic attacks safe against larger characters. Canceling into Mystic Sword L is completely safe against large characters and inflicts 45,000 points of chip damage. However, smaller characters can crouch under the second and third hits, making it incredibly unsafe when used against them.

Mystic Sword M and H: These quick projectiles are Doctor Strange's only traditional projectile attacks. Mystic Sword M is a solid long range attack tool and also has 8 low priority durability points for use in firefights against other long range characters who have trouble outputting as many durability points. It's also typically the safest way to cancel guarded basic attacks, since no characters can crouch under it and are pushed too far away to counter-attack during the attack's recovery. Mystic Sword H is an upward-angled projectile primarily used against other long range characters who can attack from super jump height, such as Trish, Firebrand, and Morrigan.

Grace of Hoggoth: Doctor Strange sets down orbs that interact with the Flames of the Faltine projectile. Up to three can be in play at any given time, and creating a new one while three are already out destroys the oldest one.

The yellow orbs created by Grace of Hoggoth L power up the projectile, giving it increased speed, hitstun, and damage. Two yellow orbs are sufficient to make the projectile fast enough to be unavoidable in most cases, and they cause enough hitstun to convert any stray hit into a combo. Three orbs changes Flames of the Faltine into a beam that causes crumple stun on hit. Having yellow orbs available greatly enhances Doctor Strange's mix-up potential, and the orbs comprise a significant part of his offense.

Grace of Hoggoth M creates red orbs that do not directly power up Flames of the Faltine. Instead, the red orbs create a high-damage explosion when hit by the projectile, making them primarily a combo tool.

Both orbs allow for OTG combos: yellow orbs cause the projectile itself to become OTG-capable, while red orbs create an OTG-capable explosion, so you can use each in different situations.

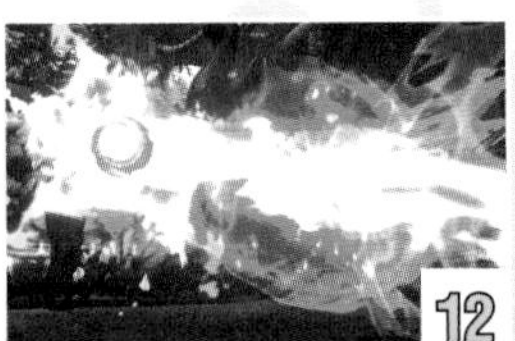

Flames of the Faltine: This move fires a projectile with extremely fast recovery that most characters can duck under, and only one can be in play at a time. However, if any Grace of Hoggoth orbs are in play, Flames of the Faltine instead seeks out the nearest one. Once the projectile hits an orb, the projectile looks for another orb, and if no other orbs are available, it directs itself toward your adversary's current location! Flames of the Faltine becomes a very powerful attack when powered up by Grace of Hoggoth L orbs, and you can use it to create unavoidable mix-ups!

Flight: Activating flight mode with Doctor Strange doesn't come with the usual benefits: having no airdash, you cannot use airdash cancels to make him fly across the screen quickly, and he is still completely vulnerable after using Daggers of Denak or Eye of Agamotto in the air. You should mainly use flight alongside Impact Palm to squeeze a bit more damage out of corner combos.

Teleportation: The source of Doctor Strange's offense, Teleportation M makes the Doctor appear behind his opponent in an instant. When used with slow, homing projectiles like Daggers of Denak M, Eye of Agamotto, or Flames of the Faltine (boosted by yellow orbs), Strange can put his competitor in a cross-up mix-up at almost any time without the use of an assist!

Teleportation L puts Doctor Strange on the ground directly in front of the opposing character, Teleportation M places him behind his rival, and Teleportation H positions Strange in the air directly above his adversary. You can also perform Doctor Strange's Teleport in the air, giving him great aerial mobility without needing airdashes or double jumps. Teleport is also useful defensively—you can use Teleportation M or H to evade incoming opponents and get Strange away from the corner. One drawback to Teleportation M is that when your attacker is in the corner, the maneuver instead places Doctor Strange directly in front of his foe, preventing you from crossing up the opposing character with Eye of Agamotto or Daggers of Denak.

Bolts of Balthakk: This move fires two consecutive beams—the first causes a stagger, and the second combos off the first and leaves your rival standing. Its relatively fast startup for a beam makes it useful for long range firefights, but it's only useful in certain situations because most characters can crouch under both beams.

Hyper Combos

Screen	Name	Command	Hits	Damage	Startup	Active	Recovery	Advantage on Hit	Advantage if Guarded	Notes
1	Spell of Vishanti (in air OK)	⇩⇘⇨ + ATK ATK	10~20	264,200~ 317,400	10+1	30	45 (air: until grounded)	-17	-26	OTG-capable, appears directly under foe's current location, can be mashed for additional hits/damage, beam durability: 5 frames x 3 high priority durability points
2	Seven Rings of Raggador	⇩⇙⇦ + ATK ATK	—	—	15+1	25	19	—	—	Frames 1-15 invincible, activate beam attack when struck by projectile or beam
3	Seven Rings of Raggador (Beam)	⇩⇙⇦ + ATK ATK	15~30	300,000~ 360,000	11	65	39	—	-24	Knocks down, frames 1-114 invincible, can be mashed for additional hits/damage, beam durability: 15 frames x 1 high priority durability point
4	Astral Magic (Level 3 Hyper Combo)	⇨⇩⇘ + ATK ATK	1	450,000	10+1	30	49	—	-57	Frames 1-33 invincible, hard knockdown, projectile has 3 high priority durability points

Spell of Vishanti: This move quickly appears directly under an opponent's current location and creates a pillar of light that starts hitting within 11 frames. You can also perform Spell of Vishanti in the air, which lets you use it to reactively hit your competitor out of almost anything! However, Spell of Vishanti is very unsafe if guarded, and the air version is really unsafe because Doctor Strange does not recover until he touches the ground, so make sure the hyper will hit before firing it off.

You can also mash Spell of Vishanti for additional damage, making it an excellent move for punishing whiffed attacks. It is also OTG-capable, so most combos with Doctor Strange conclude with this hyper.

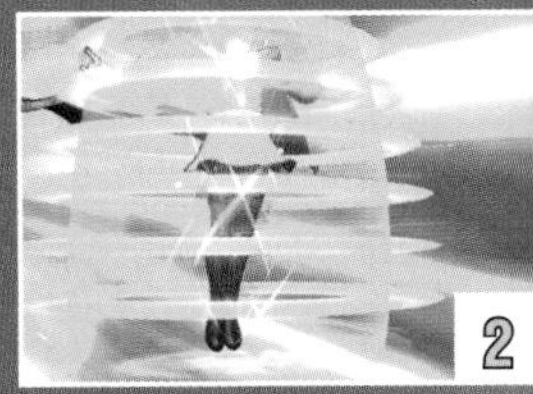

Seven Rings of Raggador: This is a unique hyper combo that functions as a counter for projectiles only. If successfully triggered, Doctor Strange fires a retaliatory beam while being completely invulnerable, and the beam can be mashed for additional damage. Unfortunately, Seven Rings of Raggador is generally only effective against hyper combo projectiles because the earliest the beam can hit an opponent is 27 frames, so normal projectiles typically have recovered by the time the beam is fired.

Astral Magic: This fully invincible level 3 hyper combo fires a slow projectile that causes huge unscaled damage if it hits the target. Doctor Strange is fully invincible for 33 frames after casting Astral Magic, making it an excellent tool for countering aggressive opponents or for countering heavily telegraphed attacks. After Astral Magic has finished, the opposing character is placed in hard knockdown state, allowing you to tack on Strange's Spell of Vishanti for additional damage. Astral Magic is incredibly unsafe if blocked, so only use it in situations where it's guaranteed to hit.

Battle Plan

Doctor Strange has several ways to cross an opponent up with projectiles using Teleportation M.

After using Grace of Hoggoth L, you can set up a Teleportation mix-up even during a super jump!

From fullscreen, Doctor Strange is at his strongest, and you generally have time for at least one action before your opponent can close the distance. From full screen, using Eye of Agamotto is recommended; once the projectile is in play, the opponent either must play passively until it's gone or find a way to get behind Doctor Strange. What you do here depends on the range:

If your competitor is already guarding Eye of Agamotto, call a crossover assist simultaneously with Impact Palm, then cancel to Daggers of Denak M

If your rival is barely out of range of the Eye of Agamotto, simply hit with Impact Palm and immediately cancel into Teleportation M or H

From medium range, simply cancel Impact Palm into Daggers of Denak M

From long range, call a long range crossover assist before using Grace of Hoggoth L, then perform Eye of Agamotto again. Repeat until your opponent gets closer

Whenever the ground version of Daggers of Denak M can safely be summoned into play at medium range, you can easily set up a mix-up—simply summon the projectiles, then immediately use Teleportation M to cross-up your opponent, or Teleportation H to stay in front. If your adversary guards in the wrong direction they'll get hit by the daggers, allowing you to easily transition into a combo!

With at least one Grace of Hoggoth L orb out, Flames of the Faltine also sets up its own mix-up. To make up for the requirement of having orbs in play, Flames of the Faltine can be used to set up a mix-up at super jump height, and it reliably hits adversaries jumping around. Simply fire the projectile, then use Teleportation M or H right before the redirected projectile is going to hit the opposing character. Having two or three yellow orbs out is preferred; when the Flames of the Faltine projectile is powered up twice, it becomes nearly impossible for your competitor to avoid. It also causes much more hitstun, since an opponent getting hit out of the air remains stuck in hitstun all the way until hitting the ground, giving plenty of time for you to convert the hit into a juggle combo.

Long range crossover assists are a simple, fast, and unpredictable way to set up a mix-up: simply call the assist and immediately teleport! This is reason enough to team Doctor Strange up with strong projectile assists like Doctor Doom—α or Rocket Raccoon—α because these assists allow you to create a Teleportation M mix-up without creating a set up for a mix-up with Daggers of Denak M or Eye of Agamotto.

Jumping into the air and pressing ⇦ + Ⓗ is a strong option-select: you'll either get an air throw or air Ⓗ. If air Ⓗ hits, you can easily react and cancel into Impact Palm to start a combo!

Impact Palm is fast and has a great hitbox in front of it; use it to stop attackers from dashing in.

Doctor Strange's offense hinges on your ability to mix-up your opponent by using Teleport M while a crossover assist's attack or his own magical tools strike from where he used to be. Unfortunately, performing Daggers of Denak M and Eye of Agamotto take time, and if Doctor Strange is hit while performing these attacks, not only do they not appear, but he stands to sustain significant damage. As such, when using Doctor Strange, creating the chance to safely summon these attacks is as important as hitting your target with them.

The most consistent way to gain control of a match at medium range is to use crossover assists: simply making contact with an assist gives Doctor Strange enough time to use Daggers of Denak M or Eye of Agamotto. Recognize when the opponent will be forced to guard an assist's attack and react by immediately casting one of these two spells! Afterward, your rival will be in the perfect range for an immediate mix-up!

Without the immediate aid of a crossover assist you often won't have enough time to use Eye of Agamotto or Daggers of Denak M; competitors can react to the start-up of these moves and punish Doctor Strange with a combo. Instead, pressure your opponent into taking to the air by using Mystic Sword M. Once your adversary is in the air, meet them in the air with ⇦ + Ⓗ; you'll either get an air throw or air Ⓗ. If air Ⓗ hits your foe, cancel into air Impact Palm for a combo; see the Combo Usage section for details. If the attacks are guarded, come down on the target with air Ⓢ while simultaneously calling a crossover assist. Once on the ground, the opposing character is forced to block, giving you the chance to call a crossover assist and perform a Teleportation mix-up.

If you don't have enough time to use Mystic Sword M, things get a little dicey. Against opponents approaching on the ground, sticking out Impact Palm is great for interrupting their attack and starting a combo. Press ⇨ + Ⓗ and see what happens:

If Impact Palm is guarded, call a crossover assist before using Mystic Sword M; almost everything else is unsafe. Alternatively, perform a late chain cancel to the Ⓢ launcher to catch adversaries trying to retaliate. The Ⓢ launcher is incredibly unsafe, so this tactic is best used sparingly

If Impact Palm hits, cancel to Mystic Sword L, then dash forward to get a full combo

If the Impact Palm whiffs completely, cancel to Mystic Sword M to prevent your competitor from dashing in and hitting Doctor Strange with a combo

Against opponents approaching from the air, Doctor Strange has a few strong options besides the aforementioned air ⇦ + Ⓗ. Standing Ⓛ only has 4 frames of startup and has a displaced attacking hitbox far in front of Doctor Strange, making it a strong anti-air against rivals approaching at a slightly low angle. Impact Palm works great against aerial attacks coming at extremely low angles that would make contact at chest-level or lower. Strange can stop attackers coming in from directly above with crouching Ⓜ, but in this case, sticking to air throws is preferable.

One of the best ways to prevent your opponent from coming in is with Spell of Vishanti; evade incoming attacks by jumping or Teleportation, then punish their recovery with the powerful hyper combo.

You can't use Strange's Teleportation M to get behind cornered opponents, severely limiting his offensive capabilities. You have to resort to a good old-fashioned crouching Ⓛ or throw mix-up to force damage quickly.

If you have more time to work with, try keeping your rival pinned in the corner with Eye of Agamotto and crossover assists.

While Doctor Strange's midscreen offense is strong, his offense comes to a screeching halt when his foe has been pushed into the corner. Doctor Strange cannot teleport behind cornered opponents using Teleportation M, and crouching Ⓗ is his only low-hitting attack. Furthermore, he cannot setup particularly effective or fast overheads, allowing cornered competitors to easily guard and prepare their counterattack. So, you must rely on different methods of attack in order to break the defenses of a cornered adversary.

If you must force damage quickly, perform a simple crouching Ⓛ or throw mix-up—stagger the timing on crouching Ⓛ attacks to prevent your opponent from using advancing guard or pressing buttons, or mix in a throw after one or two crouching Ⓛ attacks, then tack on a Spell of Vishanti after the throw for some quick damage.

If you think the opposing player may try to break the throw, cancel crouching Ⓛ into Teleportation H: your rival will whiff a standing Ⓗ attack instead of breaking the throw, allowing Doctor Strange to drop down so you can land a big combo!

If there's plenty of time left on the clock to work with, try concentrating on chipping your foe with Eye of Agamotto instead. Keeping a steady offense going using Eye of Agamotto and crossover assists stacks up chip damage quickly, forcing your opponent to make a move that you can counter for big damage.

COMBO USAGE

I. CR. Ⓛ, ST. Ⓗ, → + Ⓗ CANCEL ↓↙← + Ⓜ, ↓↙← + Ⓜ, ↓↙←↖ + Ⓗ, AIR → + Ⓗ, LAND, ST. Ⓜ, Ⓗ, → + Ⓗ, Ⓢ CANCEL SUPER JUMP FORWARD, AIR Ⓜ, Ⓜ, Ⓗ, → + Ⓗ, Ⓢ, LAND, ↓↘→ + ATK ATK, MASH ATK

644,300 damage, 4% meter gain

This combo relies on the crumple stun of Impact Palm, but it only works against opponents who aren't already in the air and are very close, since challengers in the air cannot be crumpled.

After laying down the two Grace of Hoggoth M orbs, perform a low-altitude air Flames of the Faltine by inputting ↓↙←↖ + Ⓗ. This lets you tack on an additional air Impact Palm on the way down for some extra damage!

This combo uses four Impact Palms, which are fast and unaffected by hitstun scaling; Impact Palm always causes 35 frames of hitstun against an airborne character, no matter how many hits are in the combo, letting you do some long, damaging combos with the Sorcerer Supreme!

All of Doctor Strange's basic attacks are unsafe if guarded; perform the first two attacks, and verify the hits. If hit, a late chain cancel to Impact Palm still connects, so you can cancel into Grace of Hoggoth M on reaction. If guarded, delay the chain to Impact Palm while simultaneously using a crossover assist to keep safe and maintain pressure. Alternatively, after calling a crossover assist, cancel to Teleportation M to cross up your adversary and create an opportunity for additional offense!

II. ST. Ⓛ, Ⓗ, → + Ⓗ CANCEL →↓↘ + Ⓛ, DASH, → + Ⓗ, Ⓢ CANCEL SUPER JUMP FORWARD, AIR Ⓗ, → + Ⓗ CANCEL ←↓↙ + Ⓜ, ST. Ⓛ, Ⓜ, Ⓗ, → + Ⓗ, Ⓢ CANCEL SUPER JUMP FORWARD, AIR Ⓜ, Ⓜ, Ⓗ, → + Ⓗ, Ⓢ, LAND, ↓↘→ + ATK ATK, MASH ATK

631,300 damage, 12% meter gain

This combo is used generally when using Teleportation cross-ups or in other situations when you cannot crumple your rival, such as when they're in the air.

Doctor Strange's standing Ⓛ has only 4 frames of startup and also has a large displaced hitbox in front of him, making it good anti-air against low-angled aerial attacks. If your standing Ⓛ hits, you can go straight into this combo to punish your opponent for jumping with big damage!

When cancelling Impact Palm into Mystic Sword L, wait a moment to allow your foe to get lower to the ground to connect with all hits and ensure maximum damage in this combo.

III. (AGAINST AIRBORNE OPPONENT) JUMP FORWARD, Ⓗ, → + Ⓗ, DELAYED Ⓢ, LAND, ST. Ⓜ, Ⓗ, → + Ⓗ, Ⓢ CANCEL SUPER JUMP FORWARD, AIR Ⓜ, Ⓜ, Ⓗ, → + Ⓗ CANCEL ←↓↙ + Ⓜ, ST. Ⓛ, Ⓜ, Ⓗ, → + Ⓗ, Ⓢ CANCEL SUPER JUMP FORWARD, AIR Ⓜ, Ⓜ, Ⓗ, → + Ⓗ, Ⓢ, LAND, ↓↘→ + ATK ATK, MASH ATK

632,600 damage, 11% meter gain

This is an air to air combo starting from option-select air throw attempt. When jumping, option select with ← + Ⓗ; either your opponent is thrown and you can combo with Spell of Vishanti, or air Ⓗ comes out. If air Ⓗ comes out, continue chaining to Impact Palm and the delayed Ⓢ; if the Ⓗ hits, you can continue on to the full combo for huge damage, and if it's blocked, you can keep your adversary blocking onto the ground, where you can set them up for a mix-up with Daggers of Denak H and Teleportation M or H!

ADVANCED TACTICS

LONG RANGE MAGICKIN'

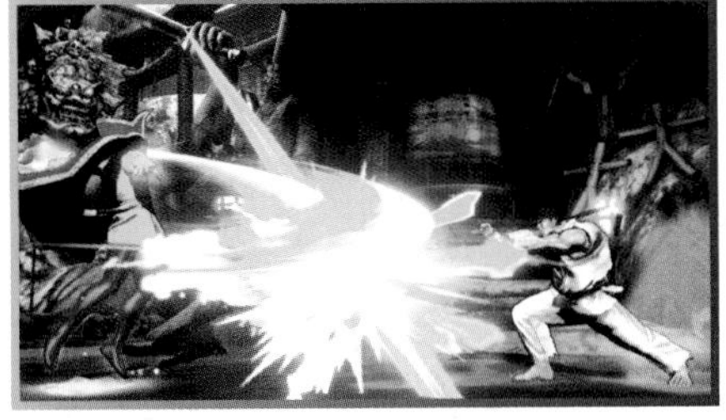

Mystic Sword M is fast and has 8 low priority durability points, which is great for long range firefights!

While Doctor Strange has access to many projectiles, many of them disappear before they have the chance to attack an opponent when he is hit. This makes them difficult to use in a long range firefight. In situations where you need to attack an adversary at a distance, Mystic Sword M is a valuable tool that can shut down many characters' long range attacks. Mystic Sword M has 8 low priority durability points, which is enough to overpower several characters' projectiles.

Projectiles that can overpower Mystic Sword M are typically slow and have a lot of recovery, like Iron Man's Unibeam, Doctor Doom's Plasma Beam, or any projectile hyper combo. Counter these by hyper combo canceling Mystic Sword M into Seven Rings of Raggador, which counters projectiles by destroying them and firing a high-powered beam at the target!

If you absolutely can't win the long range game with Mystic Sword M, use Teleportation H to drop Doctor Strange on the opposing character's head with a big combo during the recovery of their projectile. However, this tactic is risky, and opposing players can counter it with an air throw.

For quick damage against a projectile-thrower, jump over their projectile and send back your own Daggers of Denak L, which homes in on the foe and flies over most projectiles.

You can also use projectile wars to your advantage by using Strange's Grace of Hoggoth during a super jump. If your opponent doesn't move in to come after Doctor Strange, create one yellow orb, fire Flames of the Faltine, then use Teleportation M or H to start a quick mix-up using the powered-up projectile.

IV. (OPPONENT IN CORNER) CR. Ⓛ, ST. Ⓗ, → + Ⓗ [CANCEL] ↓↙← + Ⓜ, ↓↙← + Ⓢ, FLY DOWN-FORWARD SLIGHTLY, AIR Ⓗ, → + Ⓗ, Ⓢ, LAND, JUMP FORWARD, AIR Ⓜ, Ⓗ, → + Ⓗ, DELAYED Ⓢ, LAND, ST. Ⓜ, Ⓗ, → + Ⓗ, Ⓢ [CANCEL] SUPER JUMP, AIR Ⓜ, Ⓜ, Ⓗ, → + Ⓗ, Ⓢ, LAND, ↓↙← + Ⓗ, → + Ⓗ, Ⓢ [CANCEL] SUPER JUMP, AIR Ⓗ, → + Ⓗ, Ⓢ, ↓↘→ + [ATK][ATK], MASH [ATK]

684,100 damage, 43% meter gain

Doctor Strange can score big damage with this corner combo that uses the OTG-capable properties of Grace of Hoggoth M. After Flames of the Faltine hits a red orb, the explosion caused can OTG opponents, allowing this combo to work. Notice that this combo has seven Impact Palms! Doctor Strange is gunning for Magneto in the "I use one move a dozen times in the same combo" department.

V. CR. Ⓛ, ST. Ⓗ, → + Ⓗ [CANCEL] ↓↙← + Ⓜ, ↓↙← + Ⓜ, ↓↙←↖ + Ⓗ, AIR → + Ⓗ, LAND, ST. Ⓜ, Ⓗ, → + Ⓗ, →↓↘ + [ATK][ATK], ↓↘→ + [ATK][ATK], MASH [ATK]

1,026,600 damage, 333% meter loss

The Astral Magic level 3 hyper combo is unaffected by damage scaling and leaves the target in a hard knockdown state. Use this combo when you absolutely need to knock out an adversary, no matter the cost in meter. You can get even more damage to finish off high-health rivals by tacking on an extra Spell of Vishanti at the end of the combo!

VI. CR. Ⓛ, ST. Ⓗ. → + Ⓗ [CANCEL] ↓↙← + Ⓜ [CANCEL] [X-FACTOR], ↓↙← + Ⓜ, ↓↙← + Ⓜ, ↓↙← + Ⓗ, ST. Ⓜ, Ⓗ, → + Ⓗ, Ⓢ [CANCEL] SUPER JUMP FORWARD, AIR Ⓜ, Ⓗ, → + Ⓗ [CANCEL] ←↓↙ + Ⓗ, {ST. Ⓗ, → + Ⓗ, Ⓢ [CANCEL] SUPER JUMP FORWARD, AIR Ⓗ, → + Ⓗ [CANCEL] ←↓↙ + Ⓜ} X3, {→ + Ⓗ, Ⓢ [CANCEL] SUPER JUMP, AIR → + Ⓗ [CANCEL] ←↓↙ + Ⓜ} X2, → + Ⓗ, Ⓢ [CANCEL] SUPER JUMP, AIR → + Ⓗ, Ⓢ

1,371,800 damage, 267% meter gain

When Impact Palm is combined with the extra speed from X-Factor, you can loop Doctor Strange's Impact Palms indefinitely until X-Factor runs out, inflicting well over 100% damage against any character in the game without using any meter!

COMBO APPENDIX

GENERAL EXECUTION TIPS

Impact Palms on the ground create a ridiculous amount of hitstun; delay canceling into Mystic Sword L or Ⓢ launcher to allow your opponent to drop a little lower

Successfully juggling a standing Ⓛ after hitting air Impact Palm into Teleportation M has a two-frame window; there's nothing that can help here besides practice!

A timing aid to get all 10 hits out of Eye of Agamotto before using Impact Palm: time the → + Ⓗ right when Doctor Strange says the "mo" in "Agamotto". Mo' Agamotto, *less* problems.

THROW OR AIR THROW, ↓↘→ + [ATK][ATK], MASH [ATK]

Notes	Damage
Simple combo from any throw	381,500 damage, 92% meter loss

CR. Ⓛ, Ⓗ, → + Ⓗ [CANCEL] →↓↘ + Ⓛ, DASH FORWARD, ST. Ⓗ, → + Ⓗ, DELAYED Ⓢ [CANCEL] SUPER JUMP FORWARD, AIR Ⓜ, Ⓜ, Ⓗ, → + Ⓗ [CANCEL] ←↓↙ + Ⓜ, ST. Ⓛ, Ⓜ, Ⓗ, → + Ⓗ, DELAYED Ⓢ [CANCEL] SUPER JUMP, AIR Ⓜ, Ⓜ, Ⓗ, → + Ⓗ, Ⓢ, LAND, ↓↘→ + [ATK][ATK], MASH [ATK]

Notes	Damage
Alternate combo that works against both airborne and grounded adversaries	626,000 damage, 8% meter gain

[P1 or P2], ←↓↙ + Ⓜ, ST. Ⓛ, Ⓗ, → + Ⓗ [CANCEL] →↓↘ + Ⓛ, DASH, → + Ⓗ, Ⓢ [CANCEL] SUPER JUMP FORWARD, AIR Ⓗ, → + Ⓗ [CANCEL] ←↓↙ + Ⓜ, ST. Ⓛ, Ⓜ, Ⓗ, → + Ⓗ, Ⓢ [CANCEL] SUPER JUMP FORWARD, AIR Ⓜ, Ⓜ, Ⓗ, → + Ⓗ, Ⓢ, LAND, ↓↘→ + [ATK][ATK], MASH [ATK]

Notes	Damage
Beam cross-up combo using Doctor Doom—α	496,800 damage, 15% meter gain

(OPPONENT IN AIR) CR. Ⓜ, Ⓢ [CANCEL] SUPER JUMP [CANCEL] ←↓↙ + Ⓗ, AIR Ⓗ, → + Ⓗ [CANCEL] ↓↙← + Ⓗ [CANCEL] ↓↘→ + [ATK][ATK], MASH [ATK]

Notes	Damage
Combo from anti-air crouching Ⓜ, super jump cancel Ⓢ into Teleportation H	490,900 damage, 75% meter loss

NEW

GHOST RIDER

"I WOULD PRAY NOW. A LOT."

Bio

REAL NAME

Jonathan "Johnny" Blaze

OCCUPATION

Former Stuntman

ABILITIES

Can summon Hellfire, and is a world-class motorcyclist. Anyone who falls victim to his Penance Stare will experience first-hand all the pain and suffering they have inflicted on others.

WEAPONS

Enchanted Chain, Hell Bike

PROFILE

Bonded to the demon Zarathos through Mephisto's manipulations, Ghost Rider can project and control Hellfire. He manipulates mystical chains that can transform into other weapons.

FIRST APPEARANCE

Marvel Spotlight #5 (1972)

POWER GRID

- 2 INTELLIGENCE
- 4 STRENGTH

- 2 SPEED
- 5 STAMINA

- 4 ENERGY PROJECTION

- 2 FIGHTING ABILITY

*This is biographical, and does not represent an evaluation of the in-game combat potential of this hero.

Vitality	1,000,000
Chain Combo Archetype	2-Hit Limited

X-Factor Boost	Damage	Speed
Level 1 (3 teammates remaining)	135%	105%
Level 2 (2 teammates remaining)	160%	110%
Level 3 (1 teammate remaining)	185%	115%

Ghost Rider specializes in long range fighting. Many of his basic attacks and special attacks reach just short of fullscreen, and his most damaging combos are performed from a distance. When playing as Ghost Rider, your main objective is to keep your opponent at a distance, with the secondary goal of cornering your adversary. With a good understanding of Ghost Rider's ranged attacks and enough patience, you can defeat enemies without them ever reaching melee range. Why these two goals?

- **Ghost Rider's most damaging combos start from the long-reaching standing Ⓗ, Ⓗ attack sequence. You can perform entire combos off standing Ⓗ from across the screen**
- **Ghost Rider's chains are not an extension of his body and therefore cannot be traded with**
- **Most of Ghost Rider's tools are designed for long-distance fighting**
- **Combos started from close range are often weaker than their long range counterparts**
- **Ghost Rider has no attacks that reach fullscreen besides his hyper combos. A cornered opponent cannot retreat, ensuring that Ghost Rider is always within attack range while maintaining a safe distance**

How can you achieve these goals?

- **Using the massive range and hitstun/guardstun of standing Ⓗ, Ⓗ to threaten adversaries at mid to long range**
- **Utilizing air Ⓢ both offensively as an instant overhead and defensively as a means to cover a retreat**
- **Creating breathing room from overly aggressive competitors with ← + Ⓗ**

Attack Set

Standing Basic Attacks

Screen	Command	Hits	Damage	Meter Gain	Startup	Active	Recovery	Advantage on Hit	Advantage if Guarded	Notes
1	Standing L	1	55,000	440	7	3	12	+1	-1	—
2	Standing M	1	75,000	600	10	3	16	+2	0	—
3	Standing H	1	90,000	720	15	4	27	-5	-7	—

1

2

3

Crouching Basic Attacks

Screen	Command	Hits	Damage	Meter Gain	Startup	Active	Recovery	Advantage on Hit	Advantage if Guarded	Notes
1	Crouching L	1	45,000	360	7	3	13	0	-2	Low attack
2	Crouching M	1	80,000	640	12	4	15	+2	0	—
3	Crouching H	1	80,000	640	17	4	28	—	-8	Low attack, knocks down

1

2

3

Ground Special Attack—Launcher

Screen	Command	Hits	Damage	Meter Gain	Startup	Active	Recovery	Advantage on Hit	Advantage if Guarded	Notes
1	S (while standing or crouching)	1	100,000	800	15	6	25	—	-7	Launcher, not special- or hyper combo-cancelable

1

Air Basic Attacks

Screen	Command	Hits	Damage	Meter Gain	Startup	Active	Recovery	Advantage on Hit	Advantage if Guarded	Notes
1	Air L	1	55,000	440	7	3	16	+14	+12	Overhead attack
2	Air M	1	78,000	624	10	5	23	+18	+16	Overhead attack
3	Air H	1	90,000	720	17	3	31	+21	+19	Overhead attack

1

2

3

Air SpecialAttacks—Flying Screen and Air Exchange

Air (S) causes a hard knockdown when used in a launcher combo (this is sometimes called flying screen). When used outside of a launcher combo, air (S) behaves mostly like another basic attack. Air exchange attacks, performed by inputting a direction plus (S), are only possible during a launcher combo. Exchange hits initiate team aerial combos by tagging in the next available character to continue the air combo.

Screen	Command	Hits	Damage	Meter Gain	Startup	Active	Recovery	Advantage on Hit	Advantage if Guard	Notes
1	Air (S)	3	128,600	1200	15	10	36	+21	+18	Causes hard knockdown if used in launcher combo, overhead attack
2	Air ↑ + (S) (during launcher combo)	2	105,00	880	17	6	28	—	—	Tags in next available ally while lofting opponent upward
3	Air → or ← + (S) (during launcher combo)	2	95,000	800	10	5	23	—	—	Tags in next available ally while causing wall bounce, steals 1 hyper meter bar from foe
4	Air ↓ + (S) (during launcher combo)	2	95,000	800	15	10	36	—	—	Tags in next available ally while causing ground bounce, generates 1 hyper meter bar

Command Attacks

Command attacks resemble basic attacks but have different chaining and canceling properties. It's usually possible to chain *into* a command attack from basic attacks, but most command attacks cannot be chained from or canceled themselves.

Screen	Name	Command	Hits	Damage	Meter Gain	Startup	Active	Recovery	Advantage on Hit	Advantage if Guarded	Notes
1	Rage Whip	(during standing (H) on contact) (H)	1	95,000	760	5	3	18	+5	+3	—
2	Heartless Spire	← + (H)	3	94,800	840	15	—	25	+6	+4	OTG-capable, beam durability: 3 frames x 5 low priority durability points, projectile active for 32 frames, not special- or hyper combo-cancelable

Throws

Throws are for snagging passive or blocking opponents. Since throws are active so quickly, you can also use them to preemptively toss opposing characters out of their offense. Combos are usually possible after throws, one way or another.

Screen	Command	Hits	Damage	Meter Gain	Startup	Active	Notes
1	→ + (H) (ground)	2	80,000	800	1	1	Hard knockdown
	← + (H) (ground)	2	80,000	800	1	1	Hard knockdown
2	→ + (H) (air)	2	80,000	800	1	1	Hard knockdown
	← + (H) (air)	2	80,000	800	1	1	Hard knockdown

As a Partner—Crossover Assists

Screen	Type	P1+P2 Crossover Combination Hyper Combo	Description	Hits	Damage	Meter Gain	Startup	Active	Recovery (this crossover assist)	Recovery (other partner)	Notes
1	Ghost Rider—α	Hellfire Maelstrom	Chain of Rebuttal	3	135,400	1200	39	7	120	90	Wall bounces foe
2	Ghost Rider—β	Hellfire Maelstrom	Heartless Spire	3	94,800	840	39	—	117	87	OTG-capable, beam durability: 3 frames x 5 low priority durability points, projectile active for 32 frames
3	Ghost Rider—γ	Hellfire Maelstrom	Hellfire L	10	129,900	1600	44	28	109	79	OTG-capable, beam durability: 10 frames x 5 low priority durability points

1

2

3

Ghost Rider has three useful crossover assists to choose from, depending on your team's needs. Ghost Rider—α Chain of Rebuttal is a quick, far-reaching attack that causes a wall bounce. Its speed and range are great for catching opponents off-guard, and it can be followed with a combo after the wall bounce. Ghost Rider—β Heartless Spire is a projectile attack that emerges from the ground and is useful as a defensive crossover assist. Ghost Rider—γ Hellfire L is OTG-capable and is useful for extending standard air combos.

Snap Back

Screen	Command	Hits	Damage	Meter Gain	Startup	Active	Recovery	Advantage on Hit	Advantage if Guarded
1	↓↘→ + P1onP2	1	50,000	500- (-1 hyper meter bar)	2	4	27	—	-7

Notes

On hit, snap back forces the opposing point character to be replaced by an assist. Opposing assist calls or tag outs are also locked out for 4 seconds

1

Special Moves

Screen	Name	Command	Hits	Damage	Meter Gain	Startup	Active	Recovery	Advantage on Hit	Advantage if Guarded	Notes
1	Hellfire L	↓↘→ + L	10	129,900	1600	20	28	18	-2	-4	OTG-capable, beam durability: 10 frames x 5 low priority durability points
2	Hellfire M	↓↘→ + M	10	129,900	1600	21	27	18	-1	-3	Beam durability: 10 frames x 5 low priority durability points
3	Hellfire H	↓↘→ + H	10	129,900	1600	21	27	18	-1	-3	Beam durability: 10 frames x 5 low priority durability points
4	Chain of Rebuttal	→↓↘ + L	3	135,400	1200	15	7	29	—	-8	Wall bounces foe
5	Chain of Punishment	→↓↘ + M	3	135,400	1200	15	7	29	—	-8	Wall bounces opponent
6	Judgment Strike	→↓↘ + H	10	25,000 x 10	200 x 10	25	—	30	-5	-7	Each projectile has 5 low priority durability points
7	Chaos Bringer	↓↙← + L	2	110,400	1104	15	3	43	—	-22	Hard knockdown
8	Hell's Embrace	↓↙← + M	7	143,000	1430	15	3	43	—	-22	Hard knockdown
9	Conviction Slam	↓↙← + H	2	154,500	1545	15	3	43	—	-22	Hard knockdown

1

2

3

Hellfire: Ghost Rider belches flames at his rivals. Hellfire is considered a projectile and has 5 low-durability points to stop opposing projectiles. It has three different versions. Hellfire L fires down at an angle and is OTG-capable, making it ideal for ending combos when canceled into Hellfire Maelstrom. Hellfire M fires straight ahead and can be used to stop incoming projectiles and apply pressure against a cornered opponent. Hellfire H fires up diagonally, but it must be performed early to be used as an anti-air because of its slow startup.

4

Chain of Rebuttal: Ghost Rider quickly attacks from a distance with his chain. If connected, Chain of Rebuttal causes a wall bounce, which you can follow with a combo. This attack is most frequently used after connecting standing (H), (H), and it is integral to Ghost Rider's bread and butter combos. Though it has fairly quick startup considering the range it boasts, the angle of the chain is very straightforward and can be jumped over or even ducked under by characters who crouch low, such as Vergil or Spider-Man. Given this, you should only use Chain of Rebuttal during combos or with the cover of a crossover assist.

5

Chain of Punishment: Chain of Punishment is identical to Chain of Rebuttal in its frame data and wall-bouncing effect. The main difference is that Chain of Punishment attacks at an upwards angle, tagging opponents approaching at normal jump height. If performed early, it can serve as a decent anti-air that leads to a combo opportunity. If you react quickly enough to an adversary jumping over standing (H), swiftly cancel into Chain of Punishment to stop your foe's attempt at a punish.

6

Judgment Strike: Ghost Rider fires a spread of projectiles from his chain that reaches nearly the entire horizontal length of the screen. This fan-shaped attack controls a massive amount of space, stopping all frontal advances from the ground and normal jump height. Judgment Strike pushes the opposing character back a fair amount if guarded, so cancel it from standing (H), (H) to push your rival away. Judgment Strike is -7 if guarded, meaning it is punished only by fast attacks if guarded at close range and safe if guarded at a distance. Judgment Strike's main weakness is its slow startup, making it easily interrupted by attacks if performed at close range. To mitigate this, use it at mid to long range, or create breathing room first with standing (H), (H) before canceling into it. Make liberal use of this attack from a distance to frustrate opponents while chipping away at their vitality.

7

Chaos Bringer: Ghost Rider latches onto his target with his chain and brings them to his feet with a hard knockdown. If successfully connected, you can follow with Hellfire L OTG into Hellfire Maelstrom or Spirit of Vengeance for additional damage. Like Chain of Rebuttal, Chaos Bringer is easily used in combos and starts up fairly quickly given its massive range. Its hitbox goes lower than Chain of Rebuttal's, however, so it cannot be avoided by crouching. If you connect standing (H), (H) on a crouching foe, canceling into Chaos Bringer always connects, unlike Chain of Rebuttal. As a consequence, Chaos Bringer has a long period of recovery time, making it risky to use outside of combos.

8

Hell's Embrace: Hell's Embrace snatches competitors out of the sky for a hard knockdown. The range in which it usually connects causes an opponent to be grounded far away, so use Spirit of Vengeance OTG to follow up. If connected at point-blank range in the corner, you can use Hellfire L OTG before canceling into a hyper combo for more damage, although this situation is rare. Hell's Embrace attacks at an upward angle slightly higher than that of Chain of Punishment, covering another angle from which your challengers might attempt to approach. It suffers from a long period of recovery time, so use it only when you are sure it is going to connect, or with the cover of a crossover assist.

9

Conviction Slam: Ghost Rider slams his opponent down with his chain for a hard knockdown. By itself, Conviction Slam does the most damage of all of Ghost Rider's chain-based special moves, and you can follow it with Spirit of Vengeance OTG for even more damage. Like Hell's Embrace and Chaos Bringer, Conviction Slam has a staggering 43 frames of recovery, so use it only as a combo-ender or as a mid to long-range poke with the cover of a crossover assist.

Hyper Combos

Screen	Name	Command	Hits	Damage	Startup	Active	Recovery	Advantage on Hit	Advantage if Guarded	Notes
1	Hellfire Maelstrom	↓↘→ + ATK ATK	20~42	290,200~355,100	13+1	85(12)32	50	—	-42	Can be mashed for extra damage, knocks down, projectile has 5 high priority durability points
2	Spirit of Vengeance (no inputs)	→↓↘ + ATK ATK	12	189,000	20+1	56	53	—	-42	OTG-capable, knocks down, Hyper Armor frames 21-79, press (L), (M), (H), or (S) for extra attacks
3	Spirit of Vengeance (L)	(during Spirit of Vengeance) (L)	1	150,000	1	30	50	—	-56	Hard knockdown, Hyper Armor frames 1-30
4	Spirit of Vengeance (M)	(during Spirit of Vengeance) (M)	1	160,000	15	26	65	—	-62	Hard knockdown, Hyper Armor frames 1-40
5	Spirit of Vengeance (H)	(during Spirit of Vengeance) (H)	1	200,000	8	12	81	—	-57	Wall bounces foe, hard knockdown, Hyper Armor frames 1-50
6	Spirit of Vengeance (S)	(during Spirit of Vengeance) (S)	9	258,500	15	25	46	—	-73	Hard knockdown, Hyper Armor frames 1-85
7	Penance Stare (Level 3 Hyper Combo)	→↘↓↙← + ATK ATK	1	450,000	3+0	2	28	—	—	Throw, frames 1-10 invincible, crumples adversary

1

Hellfire Maelstrom: Ghost Rider swings his chain in fiery fashion before causing a huge explosion at a distance. Hellfire Maelstrom is often canceled from Hellfire L OTG and can be mashed for increased damage. This attack has an interesting hitbox: the first swing reaches a little farther than two characters' length in front of Ghost Rider and cannot be crouched under, the next four swings have farther reach but can be crouched under, and the last swing reaches the entire horizontal distance of the screen. The flames around Ghost Rider are active the entire time, as well. Though Hellfire Maelstrom controls the ground quite effectively, foes can avoid it completely with a super jump for an easy punish. Given this, you should only use it in combos or with a safe THC ready to avoid punishment.

Hyper Combos continued

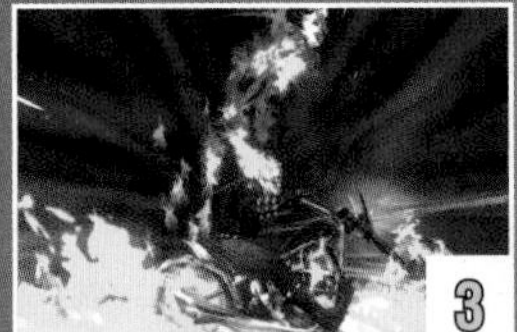

Spirit of Vengeance: Spirit of Vengeance summons Ghost Rider's bike to damage opponents and is OTG-capable. This hyper combo sports a long window of hyper armor, so Ghost Rider will not succumb to hitstun if he is attacked (though damage will still be incurred). While the hyper armor allows Spirit of Vengeance to be used to plow through enemy attacks, it has no invincibility on startup, limiting its ability to counter opposing hyper combos. Inputting an attack during Spirit of Vengeance cancels into different attacks depending on the strength used: Ⓛ causes Ghost Rider to simply run over his rival, Ⓜ performs a wheelie that knocks the opposing character upward, Ⓗ performs a turn for a wall bounce and Ⓢ performs a wheelie with multiple hits. Before canceling with one of these attacks, Spirit of Vengeance should be allowed to hit as many times as it can (10 hits from a distance, 12 hits at close range). Canceling towards the end of the hyper combo (as opposed to the very end) is your best bet; getting the damage from the extensions is much more important than the minimal damage gained from getting every hit possible of the initial bike ride. Be mindful of your next character's THC when deciding which attack to end the hyper combo with. Some THCs require the wheelie, while others are better suited with the turn. If you opt to not use a THC, performing the wheelie with Ⓢ yields the most damage.

It is important to perform → ↓ ↘ + ATK ATK with no additional inputs afterward. Any attack inputs during the hyper combo flash perform the Spirit of Vengeance follow-ups preemptively. None of the follow-ups are OTG-capable, so accidentally performing one causes the hyper combo to whiff entirely if performed on an opponent in a hard knockdown state.

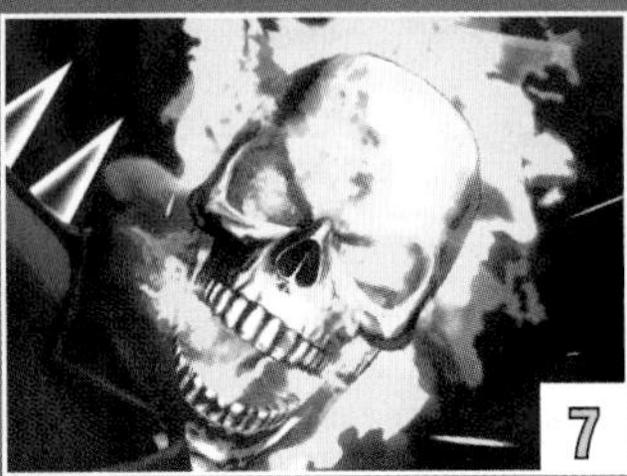

Penance Stare: His signature attack, Ghost Rider stares his foes down for unguardable damage. Penance Stare requires three levels of hyper meter, and it leaves the opponent in a crumple state. Because it is only one hit, combos following Penance Stare are not yet heavily affected by hit decay and frequently lead to a K.O. if your opponent's vitality isn't already completely depleted from the throw. This hyper combo has a short window of invulnerability during its startup, so you can cancel your guard with X-Factor and blow through your competitor's attack at close range. Because Penance Stare is considered a throw, it will not connect on opponents who are in hitstun or guardstun, nor will it work against airborne adversaries. A whiffed Penance Stare is easily punished, especially by challengers jumping straight up to avoid it. You can drastically increase the range of Penance Stare with the use of kara-canceling—see the Advanced Tactics section for more details.

Battle Plan

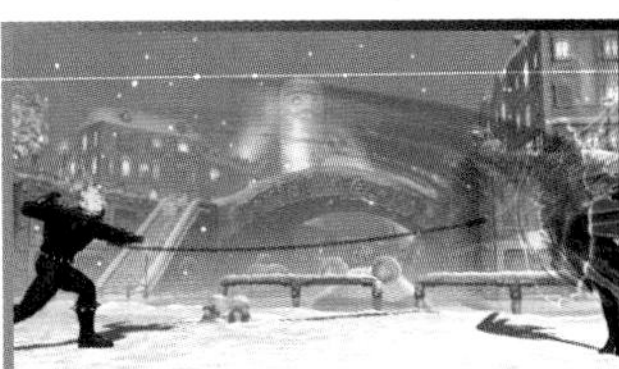

Standing Ⓗ is your main weapon at mid to long range, and it leads to powerful combos if connected. If your opponent jumps over the chain, cancel into Chain of Punishment to counter.

Judgment Strike covers a great amount of vertical and horizontal space. Use it liberally (but safely) with a long range crossover assist to chip away at your rival's vitality.

Input Ⓢ + P1 or P2 the moment Ghost Rider leaves the ground with a normal jump for an instant overhead attack. Continue the combo with a long range crossover assist.

Once your competitors become accustomed to guarding high to defend against air Ⓢ, mix up with the low-hitting crouching Ⓗ to sweep them off their feet!

Your main objective when using Ghost Rider is to keep your opponents at bay with his long range basic attacks and special moves. Unlike most characters, Ghost Rider does not need to be within close range to deal large amounts of damage. Combos starting with standing Ⓗ easily break the 600,000 damage mark! Learning to effectively use Ghost Rider's various defensive tools and long range offensive attacks is the key to success.

Despite being a long range monster, Ghost Rider has no attacks that reach the entire length of the screen besides hyper combos. An adversary with attacks that reach the entire length of the screen can attack at maximum range, where Ghost Rider cannot reach. Given this, try to keep Ghost Rider at a distance where you can threaten with standing Ⓗ and Judgment Strike, eventually pushing your opponent into the corner so that they cannot back up out of range of Ghost Rider's attacks. To mitigate this weakness, try choosing a teammate with a crossover assist that reaches fullscreen in order to make Ghost Rider a threat at any distance.

From a distance, your main attack should be standing Ⓗ. Ghost Rider's chain reaches just short of fullscreen and has a startup of 15 frames, which is quite fast given its far reach. If standing Ⓗ makes contact with a foe , it can be canceled into another Ⓗ Rage Whip, which can then be canceled into a special move. Standing Ⓗ produces a great deal of hitstun, giving you plenty of time to hit-confirm into Rage Whip. A guarded Rage Whip gives you +3 frames of advantage and pulls the opponent toward Ghost Rider. If standing Ⓗ, Ⓗ connects, cancel into Chain of Rebuttal or Chaos Bringer for a combo. If guarded, cancel into Judgment Strike to keep your challengers at bay. Canceling standing Ⓗ into Rage Whip can be delayed extremely late to create a basic frame trap; if your opponent attempts to do anything but guard between a guarded standing Ⓗ and a delayed Rage Whip, they'll be caught with the second attack. Note that you can also use this tactic when canceling Rage Whip into any of Ghost Rider's special moves. Mix up your cancel timing to throw your competitors off. If you have a long range crossover assist at your disposal, use standing Ⓗ + P1 or P2 to give your foe even more to deal with from a distance. The following characters can crouch under Ghost Rider's standing Ⓗ from a distance:

Strider	**Hawkeye**	**Felicia**	**Viewtiful Joe**
Firebrand	**Frank West**	**X-23**	**Spider-Man**
Arthur	**Deadpool**	**Hsien-Ko**	**Phoenix**
	Wolverine		**Jill**

Morrigan and Amaterasu can avoid standing Ⓗ completely at any range by crouching, so make use of air Ⓢ instead to deal with these characters.

Your secondary go-to attack is air Ⓢ. This air-to-ground attack reaches half a screen's length and must be guarded high. This allows you another angle of attack to be used in conjunction with standing Ⓗ and Judgment Strike. If performed slightly after the apex of a normal jump, you can follow into a combo with standing Ⓗ after Ghost Rider lands. Learning the range and angle of air Ⓢ is extremely important! With proper positioning, air Ⓢ acts as an instant overhead if performed immediately after Ghost Rider leaves the ground, and it can be extremely difficult for opponents to guard on reaction. If you have a long range crossover assist like Doctor Doom—α or Strider—α, you can input P1 or P2 at the same time as air Ⓢ for a combo. A compatible crossover assist will combo off air Ⓢ, allowing you to have Ghost Rider land and continue with standing Ⓗ into a bread and butter combo. Once your rival is conditioned to guard this attack high, you can utilize crouching Ⓗ to check the opponent's low guard. Crouching Ⓗ connects at the same horizontal range in which air Ⓢ connects and can be canceled into Chain of Rebuttal for a damaging combo. Like standing Ⓗ, cancel into Judgment Strike if crouching Ⓗ is guarded to keep the enemy out. Though standing Ⓗ and crouching Ⓗ have extremely long reach, competitors can easily jump over them if you become too predictable. If an opponent manages to avoid these chain attacks with a normal jump forward, quickly cancel into Chain of Rebuttal or Hell's Embrace to cut off their approach and avoid punishment.

Since fighting at a distance is ideal for Ghost Rider, learning to retreat safely is great for resetting positioning and maintaining the pace of the battle. While air Ⓢ is good for long range offense and pressure, you can also use it as a way to cover a retreat. You can normal jump backward with air Ⓢ while calling a crossover assist, then land and attack with standing Ⓗ, Ⓗ into Judgment Strike to push your foe away. Air Ⓢ effectively cuts off frontal assaults and can even lead to a combo depending on your crossover assist. For opponents attempting to approach at higher altitudes, jump back with air Ⓗ to knock adversaries out of the sky. The chain covers the area directly above Ghost Rider's head as well as slightly above diagonally, making it great as a defensive attack to cover the avenues of attack that air Ⓢ does not reach. While on the ground, you can use Ⓢ to cover the area directly above Ghost Rider's head.

Battle Plan continued

Heartless Spire does not disappear if Ghost Rider is attacked, which makes it great for interrupting your adversary's offense.

Use Heartless Spire to nullify incoming projectiles.

If foes do manage to get close, Ghost Rider has several close range options to utilize, the most effective being Heartless Spire (performed with ← + (H)). Heartless Spire is a stationary projectile attack that has 5 low durability points and is OTG-capable. Though it takes 15 frames to startup and recovers in 25 frames, it stays active for 35 frames and does not disappear if Ghost Rider is attacked while it is active. At a distance, you can employ it to nullify projectile attacks, giving Ghost Rider a way to deal with projectiles at maximum range. At close range, use this attack as a sort of "get off me" maneuver. If guarded, Heartless Spire creates enough distance between Ghost Rider and his opponent to perform standing (H) in an attempt to push them back out. The drawback to Heartless Spire is that it is not special move or hyper combo-cancelable, so a connected Heartless Spire must be followed with a pre-summoned crossover assist or X-Factor activation to get a substantial amount of damage from it. Heartless Spire gives you frame advantage if guarded on the ground, so you can cancel into it from any guarded ground basic attack strings for safe pressure.

Crouching (M) is another option to consider if your competitor manages to get past Ghost Rider's chains. Though it doesn't have the quickest startup, it has decent priority and range. With this attack, you can perform a basic option select with (S). Input crouching (M), (S) just outside of your rival's range, guaranteeing the shoulder attack will not be guarded. If crouching (M) whiffs, the (S) input is ignored. If your adversary tries to attack or advance forward, the shoulder connects and can then be canceled into a launcher. Alternatively, (S) can be substituted for ← + (H), though it is more defense-oriented than (S). Note that a whiffed crouching (M) can be punished, so don't abuse this tactic.

As a last resort against an overly aggressive attacker, cancel your guard with X-Factor and immediately perform Penance Stare. The window of invulnerability on startup allows Penance Stare to interrupt your opponent's offense with the throw and likely leads to a K.O. Make sure to use this tactic only when your target is right next to you on the ground. There's nothing worse than activating X-Factor and burning three bars of hyper meter only to have the throw not be in range or avoided with a jump!

Special mention must be made of Ghost Rider's snap back. Even though it isn't slower or faster than any other character's snap back, it shares the same animation as standing (H), making it the longest reaching snap back in the game! It can even be connected after Heartless Spire, which is not normally cancelable. If you have hyper meter to spare, you can use Ghost Rider's snap back as a long range punish against slower attacks.

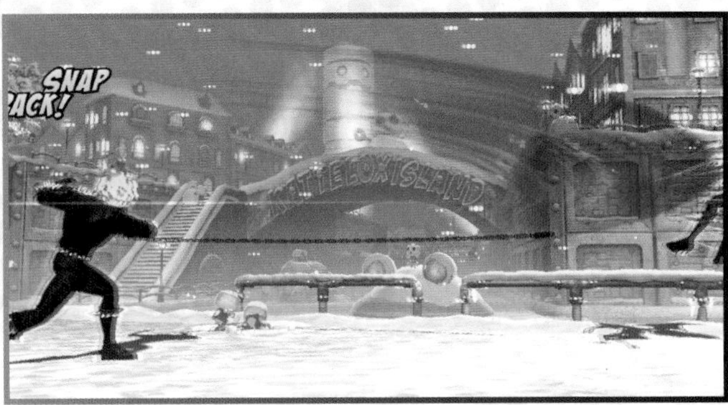

Ghost Rider's snap back starts up in 2 frames, making it a lightning-fast attack that reaches nearly fullscreen!

COMBO USAGE

I. (WHEN 3/4 OF THE SCREEN AWAY FROM THE ENEMY) ST. (H), (H) CANCEL → ↓ ↘ + (L), FORWARD DASH, ST. (H), (H) CANCEL ↓ ↙ ← + (L), ↓ ↘ → + (L) (2 HITS) CANCEL ↓ ↘ → + (ATK)(ATK) (MASH (ATK))

623,900 damage, 48% meter loss

Here's a basic long range combo that's relatively easy to do. Verify if standing (H), (H) connects or not before canceling into Chain of Rebuttal, which has a heavy recovery period. After the Chain of Rebuttal makes contact, dash forward and juggle with (H), (H). At close ranges, the forward dash may be substituted with a small step forward, or omitted entirely. You can replace the standing (H), (H) chain starter with crouching (H) to start the combo off of a fullscreen low attack (536,900 damage).

II. (WHEN 3/4 OF THE SCREEN AWAY FROM THE ENEMY) ST. (H), (H) CANCEL → ↓ ↘ + (L), FORWARD DASH, ST. (H), (H), DELAYED (S) CANCEL FORWARD SUPER JUMP, AIR (M), (M), (S), LAND, FORWARD DASH, ↓ ↘ → + (L) (2 HITS) CANCEL ↓ ↘ → + (ATK)(ATK) (MASH (ATK))

633,900 damage, 17% meter loss

This is a slightly harder variation of **Combo I** that builds more meter and inflicts additional damage. When juggling with standing (H), (H), make sure to hit your opponent as low to the ground as possible to ensure that you can have Ghost Rider follow his rival into the sky after (S) connects. After hitting with air (S), dash forward when Ghost Rider lands by hitting (ATK)(ATK) instead of → →. This prevents you from accidentally getting → ↓ ↘ + (L) over Hellfire L. You can replace the standing (H), (H) chain starter with crouching (H) to start the combo off of a fullscreen low attack (lowering the damage to 584,600).

III. CR. (L), (M), (S) CANCEL FORWARD SUPER JUMP, AIR (M), (M), (S), LAND, FORWARD DASH, ↓ ↘ → + (L) (2 HITS) CANCEL ↓ ↘ → + (ATK)(ATK) (MASH (ATK))

524,500 damage, 48% meter loss

Surprisingly, Ghost Rider's long range combos are more damaging than his close range ones. Nevertheless, use this lower-damage combo if you manage to connect with crouching (L). If crouching (L), (M) is guarded, chain into ← + (H) to leave Ghost Rider at a sizeable frame advantage.

COMBO USAGE CONT.

IV. CR.(L), (M) CANCEL → ↓ ↘ + (L), ST. (H), (H), DELAYED (S) CANCEL FORWARD SUPER JUMP, AIR (M), (M), (S), LAND, FORWARD DASH, ↓ ↘ → + (L) (2 HITS) CANCEL ↓ ↘ → + (ATK)(ATK) (MASH (ATK))

563,800 damage, 22% meter loss

This inflicts slightly more damage than **Combo III**, but → ↓ ↘ + (L) whiffs against small crouching characters like Amaterasu, Morrigan, Rocket Raccoon, Arthur, and Viewtiful Joe. Use it only against those characters if they are standing. If these smaller characters are attacked while crouching, substitute → ↓ ↘ + (L) with ↓ ↙ ← + (L), which connects on all characters.

V. BACK THROW, → ↓ ↘ + (ATK)(ATK), ON THE 10TH HIT, INPUT (S)

332,900 damage, 92% meter loss

Ghost Rider can consistently OTG an opposing character off of his back throw. If you are performing this combo without a THC, use the (S) extension at the end of → ↓ ↘ + (ATK)(ATK) for maximum damage.

VI. (REQUIRES CORNER) FRONT THROW OR FRONT AIR THROW, ↓ ↘ → + (L) CANCEL ↓ ↘ → + (ATK)(ATK) (MASH (ATK))

309,300 damage, 92% meter loss

This is an OTG combo off of Ghost Rider's air throw that can only be performed near corners.

VII. (A LITTLE CLOSER THAN 3/4 OF THE SCREEN AWAY FROM THE ENEMY) FORWARD JUMP, INSTANT AIR (S) + (P1 or P2), LAND, ST. (H), (H) CANCEL → ↓ ↘ + (L), FORWARD DASH, ST. (H), (H), DELAYED (S) CANCEL FORWARD SUPER JUMP, AIR (M), (M), (S), LAND, ↓ ↘ → + (L) CANCEL ↓ ↘ → + (ATK)(ATK) (MASH (ATK))

629,800 damage, 5% meter gain (or self-sufficient for Hellfire Maelstrom ender)

This is an assist-oriented combo starting off of an instant overhead air (S). Many different crossover assists can be used with instant overhead air (S) including Doctor Doom—α, Strider—α, Iron Man—α, and Hawkeye—α. If guarded, use the cover from the crossover assist to mount a secondary offensive.

VIII. (AGAINST AN AIRBORNE ENEMY) FORWARD JUMP, AIR (M), (S), ST. (M) CANCEL → ↓ ↘ + (L), FORWARD DASH, ST. (H), (H), DELAYED (S) CANCEL FORWARD SUPER JUMP, AIR (M), (M), (S), LAND, FORWARD DASH, ↓ ↘ → + (L) (2 HITS) CANCEL ↓ ↘ → + (ATK)(ATK) (MASH (ATK))

599,500 damage, 7% meter loss

Here's a basic air-to-air combo. Air (M), (S) is safe when blocked in the air, so have no fear when landing. It's only dangerous if the first attack misses altogether, in which case, Ghost Rider is left open to punishment.

IX. → ↘ ↓ ↙ ← + (ATK)(ATK), ST. (H), (H) CANCEL → ↓ ↘ + (L), FORWARD DASH, ST. (H), (H), DELAYED (S) CANCEL FORWARD SUPER JUMP, AIR (M), (M), (S), LAND, FORWARD DASH, ↓ ↘ → + (L) (2 HITS) CANCEL ↓ ↘ → + (ATK)(ATK)

982,400 damage, 325% meter loss

Ghost Rider's level 3 hyper combo is a fully invincible throw. Because the throw is only one hit, you can perform a full combo afterward without being heavily affected by hit decay. Use this defensively to deal a death blow to an adversary attacking Ghost Rider at close range.

X. (WHEN 3/4 OF THE SCREEN AWAY FROM THE ENEMY) ST. (H), (H) CANCEL (X-FACTOR), ST. (H), (H) CANCEL → ↓ ↘ + (L), FORWARD DASH, ST. (H), (H), DELAYED (S) CANCEL FORWARD SUPER JUMP, AIR (M), (M), (S), LAND, FORWARD DASH, ↓ ↘ → + (L) (2 HITS) CANCEL ↓ ↘ → + (ATK)(ATK) (MASH (ATK))

986,100~1,223,500 damage, 27~75% meter gain (or self-sufficient for the Hellfire Maelstrom ender)

This is a basic long-range X-Factor combo. Use this combo when in need of a K.O. with X-Factor still available.

ADVANCED TACTICS

BIKE OR CHAIN?

The last hit of Hellfire Maelstrom causes a hard knockdown, making it difficult to connect a THC afterward.

Combos ending in Hellfire Maelstrom often deal slightly more damage than combos ending in Spirit of Vengeance. However, Spirit of Vengeance is much more THC-friendly than Hellfire Maelstrom because of the hard knockdown that Hellfire Maelstrom produces. If you cancel Hellfire Maelstrom early for THC purposes, you miss the damaging last hit of the hyper combo. However, it's the last hit of the maelstrom that causes the hard knockdown, which makes Hellfire Maelstrom less than stellar for THCs. Keep your hyper meter and Ghost Rider's partners in mind when choosing what combo to perform in any given situation. If you have meter to spare, performing the initially weaker Spirit of Vengeance at the end of combos might be better if your next character can THC well from it, while combos ending with Hellfire Maelstrom are best used if hyper meter is scarce.

LOOK INTO MY EYES: KARA-THROW

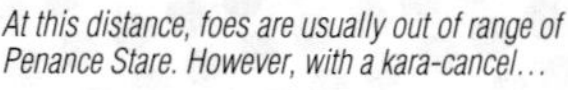

At this distance, foes are usually out of range of Penance Stare. However, with a kara-cancel...

... you can grab opponents from much farther than usual!

Penance Stare is Ghost Rider's most powerful attack, and it often leads to a K.O. if successfully landed. You can extend the range on this hyper combo throw drastically with kara-canceling. A kara-cancel is a technique that increases the range on an attack by canceling it from a basic attack that has forward movement. In this case, the range on Ghost Rider's standing Ⓜ can be added onto Penance Stare with a quick kara-cancel.

To perform this, cancel Penance Stare from standing Ⓜ as Ghost Rider begins to stake a step forward but before the active frames of the knee occur. ⇨ ⇘ ⇩ ⇙ ⇦ + ATK ATK must be performed immediately after standing Ⓜ; cancel it faster than you would normally cancel an attack into a hyper combo. If you are having trouble executing this, input Penance Stare normally with ⇨ ⇘ ⇩ ⇙ ⇦ + ATK ATK, but add standing Ⓜ at the beginning of the input so that the entire sequence looks like this: ⇨ + Ⓜ, ⇘ ⇩ ⇙ ⇦ + ATK ATK, all in one smooth motion. The maximum range of a kara-canceled Penance Stare is roughly two characters' length away from the opponent, a distance in which adversaries would normally feel safe from a throw.

COMBO APPENDIX

GENERAL EXECUTION TIPS

During ⇨ ⇩ ⇘ + ATK ATK, allow at least nine hits of the hyper combo before canceling into one of the three extensions

When performing standing Ⓗ, Ⓗ, delayed Ⓢ, make sure to attack your rival as low to the ground as possible to allow the rest of the combo to connect properly.

(GHOST RIDER COMES IN) AIR Ⓜ, Ⓢ, LAND, ⇨ ⇩ ⇘ + ATK ATK

Notes	Damage
⇧ + Ⓢ or ⇨ + Ⓢ or ⇩ + Ⓢ TAC to Ghost Rider	—

FRONT THROW, ⇦ + Ⓗ, ST. Ⓗ, Ⓗ CANCEL➡ ⇨ ⇩ ⇘ + Ⓛ, ST. Ⓗ, Ⓗ, Ⓢ CANCEL➡ FORWARD SUPER JUMP, AIR Ⓜ, Ⓜ, Ⓢ, LAND, ⇩ ⇘ ⇨ + Ⓛ CANCEL➡ ⇩ ⇘ ⇨ + ATK ATK (MASH ATK)

Notes	Damage
Requires corner. The final hit of ⇦ + Ⓗ hits late against middle to lightweight characters if the first hit connects from as far away as possible. This means that against some characters, you must back up a step before initiating ⇦ + Ⓗ. If done correctly, the flames keep the opponent airborne long enough for standing Ⓗ to juggle	438,400 damage, 11% meter loss

CR. Ⓛ, CR. Ⓜ CANCEL➡ X-FACTOR, ST. Ⓗ, Ⓗ CANCEL➡ ⇨ ⇩ ⇘ + Ⓛ, FORWARD DASH, ST. Ⓗ, Ⓗ, DELAYED Ⓢ CANCEL➡ FORWARD SUPER JUMP, AIR Ⓜ, Ⓜ, Ⓢ, LAND, FORWARD DASH, ⇩ ⇘ ⇨ + Ⓛ (2 HITS) CANCEL➡ ⇩ ⇘ ⇨ + ATK ATK (MASH ATK)

Notes	Damage
—	942,800~1,234,100 damage, 25~61% meter gain

"HELL HATH NO FURY LIKE A FLAMING SKELETON ON A MOTORCYCLE."

GHOST RIDER

NEW

NEW

HAWKEYE

"WORLD'S GREATEST MARKSMAN, AT YOUR SERVICE."

Bio

REAL NAME

Clinton Francis "Clint" Barton

OCCUPATION

Adventurer

ABILITIES

Possesses the ability to fire arrows with precision and at incredible speeds, even in the worst conditions.

WEAPONS

Custom-made bow with specially equipped arrows.

PROFILE

Trained to be a master archer by a traveling circus at an early age, Hawkeye joined the Avengers in order to protect the world from evil. While a bit overconfident and rash to act, on the battlefield, he is often the catalyst that raises everyone's spirits.

FIRST APPEARANCE

Tales of Suspense #57 (1964)

POWER GRID

 2 INTELLIGENCE

 2 STRENGTH

 2 SPEED

 2 STAMINA

 1 ENERGY PROJECTION

 4 FIGHTING ABILITY

*This is biographical, and does not represent an evaluation of the in-game combat potential of this hero.

ALTERNATE COSTUMES

Overview

Vitality	900,000
Chain Combo Archetype	2-Hit Limited

X-Factor Boost	Damage	Speed
Level 1 (3 teammates remaining)	120%	120%
Level 2 (2 teammates remaining)	140%	130%
Level 3 (1 teammate remaining)	160%	140%

Hawkeye is a pure zoning character. While you are playing him you should want nothing more than to keep him across the screen at all times, bombarding the opposing character with his many different arrow attacks.

What good is it being so far away?

- **Hawkeye can pile up chip damage with a variety of ranged arrow attacks, including standing Ⓗ, Quick Shot (Greyhound), and Ragtime Shot (Balalaika)**
- **Any hits from afar can be easily verified and hyper combo canceled into Gimlet**
- **The angles of Hawkeye's attacks make him much better suited to prevent forward movement at fullscreen when compared to medium range**

How does one keep the opposing character away when using Hawkeye?

- **Using standing Ⓗ in tandem with long range crossover assists, then canceling into Trick Shot or Ragtime Shot to push your competitor backward while dealing chip damage**
- **Using Ragtime Shot preemptively from afar to prevent your adversary from jumping**
- **Using air Quick Shot (Greyhound) and air throws to prevent your rival's advances at closer ranges**
- **Using Slide (↘ + Ⓗ) simultaneously with a crossover assist, then canceling into Trick Maneuver H to get over the foe and away from the corner**

Attack Set

Standing Basic Attacks

Screen	Command	Hits	Damage	Meter Gain	Startup	Active	Recovery	Advantage on Hit	Advantage if Guarded	Notes
1	Standing L	1	45,000	360	5	2	11	0	-1	—
2	Standing M	1	60,000	480	7	3	17	-2	-3	—
3	Standing H	1~3	50,000 per arrow	400 per arrow	10/29/39	1/4/7	30/20/12	-5/+5/+13	-6/+4/+12	Hold H to fire extra shots (2 shots — 28 frames, 38 frames — 3 shots), each projectile has 3 low priority durability points, can be directed by holding ⇧ or ⇩, inflicts chip damage

Crouching Basic Attacks

Screen	Command	Hits	Damage	Meter Gain	Startup	Active	Recovery	Advantage on Hit	Advantage if Guarded	Notes
1	Crouching L	1	43,000	344	5	2	15	-4	-5	Low attack
2	Crouching M	1	55,000	440	9	4	19	-5	-6	Low attack
3	Crouching H	1	70,000	560	12	3	26	—	-7	Low attack, knocks down

Ground Special Attack—Launcher

Screen	Command	Hits	Damage	Meter Gain	Startup	Active	Recovery	Advantage on Hit	Advantage if Guarded	Notes
1	S (while standing or crouching)	1	80,000	640	9	3	29	—	-10	Launcher, not special- or hyper combo-cancelable

Air Basic Attacks

Screen	Command	Hits	Damage	Meter Gain	Startup	Active	Recovery	Advantage on Hit	Advantage if Guarded	Notes
1	Air L	1	45,000	360	5	3	19	+11	+10	Overhead attack
2	Air M	1	55,000	440	8	4	24	+16	+15	Overhead attack
3	Air H	2	74,000	640	9	11	25	+18	+17	Overhead attack

Air Special Attacks—Flying Screen and Air Exchange

Air Ⓢ causes a hard knockdown when used in a launcher combo (this is sometimes called flying screen). When used outside of a launcher combo, air Ⓢ behaves mostly like another basic attack. Air exchange attacks, performed by inputting a direction plus Ⓢ, are only possible during a launcher combo. Exchange hits initiate team aerial combos by tagging in the next available character to continue the air combo.

Screen	Command	Hits	Damage	Meter Gain	Startup	Active	Recovery	Advantage on Hit	Advantage if Guarded	Notes
1	Air Ⓢ	1	75,000	600	11	4	26	+15	+14	Causes hard knockdown if used in launcher combo
2	Air ⇧ + Ⓢ (during launcher combo)	2	105,00	880	9	7	29	—	—	Tags in next available ally while lofting opponent upward
3	Air ⇨ or ⇦ + Ⓢ (during launcher combo)	2	95,000	800	8	4	24	—	—	Tags in next available ally while causing wall bounce, erases 1 hyper meter bar from foe
4	Air ⇩ + Ⓢ (during launcher combo)	2	95,000	800	11	4	26	—	—	Tags in next available ally while causing ground bounce, generates 1 hyper meter bar

1

2

3

4

Command Attacks

Command attacks resemble basic attacks but have different chaining and canceling properties. It's usually possible to chain *into* a command attack from basic attacks, but most command attacks cannot be chained from or canceled themselves.

Screen	Name	Command	Hits	Damage	Meter Gain	Startup	Active	Recovery	Advantage on Hit	Advantage if Guarded	Notes
1	Shock Value	⇨ + Ⓜ	1	64,200	600	13	—	27	0	-1	Inflicts chip damage
2	Double Roundhouse	⇨ + Ⓗ	2	35,000 + 40,000	280+320	9	3(13)4	27	—	-9	Second hit knocks down
3	Slide	⬂ + Ⓗ	1	70,000	560	11	11	24	—	-13	Low attack, knocks down

1

2

3

Throws

Throws are for snagging passive or blocking opponents. Since throws are active so quickly, you can also use them to preemptively toss opposing characters out of their offense. Combos are usually possible after throws, one way or another.

Screen	Command	Hits	Damage	Meter Gain	Startup	Active	Notes
1	⇨ + Ⓗ (ground)	2	80,000	800	1	1	Hard knockdown
	⇦ + Ⓗ (ground)	1	80,000	800	1	1	Hard knockdown
2	⇨ + Ⓗ (air)	2	80,000	800	1	1	Hard knockdown
	⇦ + Ⓗ (air)	1	80,000	800	1	1	Hard knockdown

1

2

As a Partner—Crossover Assists

Screen	Type	P1+P2 Crossover Combination Hyper Combo	Description	Hits	Damage	Meter Gain	Startup	Active	Recovery (this crossover assist)	Recovery (other partner)	Notes
1	Hawkeye—α	Gimlet	Quick Shot (Greyhound)	3	50,000 x 3	400 x 3	34	9	118	88	Each projectile has 3 low priority durability points
2	Hawkeye—β	Gimlet	Trick Shot (Violet Fizz)	1	50,000	400	49	—	136	106	OTG-capable, projectile has 3 low priority durability points
3	Hawkeye—γ	Gimlet	Ragtime Shot (Kamikaze)	10	25,000 x 10	200 x 10	39	—	126	96	OTG-capable, each projectile has 5 low priority durability points

1

2

3

Hawkeye—α Quick Shot (Greyhound) is a great all-around crossover assist that can be used effectively for almost any purpose! Long range characters can bolster their firepower with additional projectiles, offensive characters can get the covering fire they need to begin an attack, and since Quick Shot (Greyhound) only hits three times, teleporting characters can call Hawkeye, then teleport to create cross-up mix-ups that don't cause a lot of damage scaling. Unfortunately, some characters can crouch under Quick Shot (Greyhound), hampering its effectiveness against some of the cast.

Hawkeye—β Trick Shot (Violet Fizz) is an OTG-capable assist and the only assist in the game that can poison the opponent, which can cause up to 90,000 points of unscaled damage! While the poison damage is good, it's generally too slow to be of use outside of combos, so players need to develop specific combos to best make use of it.

Hawkeye—γ Ragtime Shot (Kamikaze) is a barrage of arrows that can cut off parts of the screen, keeping the adversary away from your character. However, the assist only cuts off a very specific portion of the screen, making it only useful in a few particular situations. Ragtime Shot (Kamikaze) is also OTG-capable, but it is generally much too slow to be used in most OTG situations. While this assist isn't as versatile as OTG-capable assists like Wesker's Samurai Edge (Lower Shot), it can create new combos for many characters: call Hawkeye—γ simultaneously with an Ⓢ launcher, then perform an air Ⓜ, Ⓜ, Ⓗ chain. The Ragtime Shot (Kamikaze) then begins to hit the target and drag them down to the floor, allowing for easy additional juggles!

Snap Back

Screen	Command	Hits	Damage	Meter Gain	Startup	Active	Recovery	Advantage on Hit	Advantage if Guarded
1	↓↘→ + P1⇔P2	1	50,000	500 (-1 hyper meter bar)	2	3	29	—	-10

Notes

On hit, snap back forces the opposing point character to be replaced by an assist. Opposing assist calls or tag outs are also locked out for 4 seconds

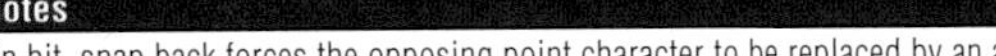

1

Special Moves

Screen	Name	Command	Hits	Damage	Meter Gain	Startup	Active	Recovery	Advantage on Hit	Advantage if Guarded	Notes
1	Quick Shot (Greyhound) (in air OK)	↓↘→ + Ⓛ	3	50,000 x 3	400 x 3	10	9	35 (air: until grounded)	-13	-14	3 projectiles each have 3 low priority durability points
2	Quick Shot (Hunter) (in air OK)	↓↘→ + Ⓜ	1	50,000	500	20	—	30 (air: until grounded)	+12	-9	Captures adversary, projectile has 3 low priority durability points
3	Quick Shot (Spritzer) (in air OK)	↓↘→ + Ⓗ	3	149,000	1320	20	—	40 (air: until grounded)	-11	-13	Piercing, cannot be destroyed by low priority projectiles, projectile has 3 low priority durability points
4	Trick Maneuver L	↓↙← + Ⓛ	—	—	—	Violet Fizz:8, Ice Breaker: 14, Ice Breaker: 16	27	14	—	—	Hawkeye is airborne from the 6th frame, on the ground from frames 40-45 if uncanceled
5	Trick Maneuver M	↓↙← + Ⓜ	—	—	—	11	19	6	—	—	—
6	Trick Maneuver H	↓↙← + Ⓗ	—	—	—	16	19	12	—	—	Hawkeye is airborne from the 6th frame
7	Trick Shot (Violet Fizz)	(during Trick Maneuver) Ⓛ	1	50,000	400	5	—	30 or until grounded	+5/-8/-3	+5/-6/-3	Causes poison status effect if hit, poison inflicts 300 damage per frame for 300 frames, hitting Hawkeye removes the poison status, is OTG-capable if used from Trick Maneuver L or H, projectile has 3 low priority durability points

Special Moves continued

Screen	Name	Command	Hits	Damage	Meter Gain	Startup	Active	Recovery	Advantage on Hit	Advantage if Guarded	Notes
8	Trick Shot (Ice Breaker)	(during Trick Maneuver) Ⓜ	1	80,000	640	5	—	30 or until grounded	+11/+6/+11	-3/-9/-4	Is OTG-capable if used from Trick Maneuver L or H and ground bounces airborne or grounded foes, projectile has 3 low priority durability points
9	Trick Shot (Rusty Nail)	(during Trick Maneuver) Ⓗ	3	108,300	960	5	—	30 or until grounded	0/0/0	+1/+3/+1	Is OTG-capable if used from Trick Maneuver L or H, projectile has beam durability: 3 frames x 3 low priority durability points
10	Ragtime Shot (Jack Rose)	→↓↘ + Ⓛ	2	102,000	880	13	—	37	—	—	Projectile has 3 low priority durability points, arrow grounded and inactive at 37 frames, arrow explodes on contact, explosion has 99 low priority durability frames and lasts 8 frames when destroyed or 121 frames after grounded
11	Ragtime Shot (Kamikaze)	→↓↘ + Ⓜ	10	25,000 x 10	200 x 10	15	—	45	—	—	OTG-capable, first projectile has 5 low priority durability points, spreads into 10 arrows that descend after 35 frames, each of these projectiles has 5 low priority durability points
12	Ragtime Shot (Balalaika)	→↓↘ + Ⓗ	9	81,200 x 3	720 x 3	21	10	35	—	—	3 projectiles with 5 low priority durability points each

1

Quick Shot (Greyhound): This attack is a quick horizontal volley of three projectiles that cause a total of 45,000 chip damage! Quick Shot (Greyhound) is one of the staples of Hawkeye's keepaway game, since it causes great chip damage and starts up quickly, allowing Hawkeye to pile on pressure from across the screen. The attack also has 9 total low priority projectile durability points, allowing Hawkeye to win firefights against most characters with ease. On hit, you can hyper combo cancel into Gimlet on reaction for quick, fullscreen damage. Unfortunately, several characters can crouch under Quick Shot (Greyhound), limiting its usefulness against them. Those characters include:

Amaterasu	**Firebrand**	**Phoenix**	**Spider-Man**	**Wolverine**
Arthur	**Frank West**	**Rocket Raccoon**	**Strider Hiryu**	**X-23**
Felicia	**Morrigan**		**Viewtiful Joe**	

There are several other characters who duck under one or two of the arrows in the attack, so against them, Quick Shot (Spritzer) may be a better choice to keep pressure because those characters are forced to block all three hits of that arrow attack.

The air version of Quick Shot (Greyhound) follows Hawkeye's jump trajectory, making it the most reliable way of stopping adversaries from normal jumping toward him. With Hawkeye normal jumping backwards and firing Quick Shot (Greyhound) after the peak of the jump, three projectiles cover normal jumping space, keeping opponents away from him.

If you have Hawkeye jump backwards and notice that your rival is not in the air with him, then perform Quick Shot (Greyhound) slightly later; performed late enough, the arrows make contact with standing competitors and can hit characters trying to dash in during Hawkeye's jump. Hawkeye instantly recovers upon landing, allowing you to further push the opposing character away with standing Ⓗ, crossover assists, and more Quick Shots.

2

Quick Shot (Hunter): This projectile attack is unique in that, on hit, it places the opponent in a state similar to a dizzy, completely incapacitating grounded foes and allowing for ground combos from fullscreen! If Quick Shot (Hunter) hits an aerial adversary, they are placed in a hard knockdown state during which all attacks are OTG-capable, allowing you to convert Hawkeye's standing Ⓗ into big damage.

Unlike Quick Shot (Greyhound) and Quick Shot (Spritzer), Quick Shot (Hunter) has low projectile durability, making it fairly useless in a long range firefight, so you should only use it in guaranteed punish situations or in combos. However, no characters can crouch under Quick Shot (Hunter), so it can always lead to a combo if a small crouching character is hit by a standing Ⓗ.

The aerial version can be useful as a high-risk air-to-air counter; meet your rival in the air with air Ⓜ, Ⓗ, then cancel into Quick Shot (Hunter) for a big combo. However, if the opposing player blocks the Quick Shot (Hunter), Hawkeye is completely vulnerable. To keep Hawkeye safe, perform the first two attacks while buffering the ↓↘→ motion; if it hits, verify and cancel into Quick Shot (Hunter). If not, simply press Ⓢ to continue attacking your target.

3

Quick Shot (Spritzer): This attack is unique in that it destroys all other low priority projectiles, yet loses to all medium priority projectiles. Even if Quick Shot (Spritzer) hits another projectile, it still makes contact for all three hits and snags both the opponent's point character and assist, making it incredibly powerful while Hawkeye is attacking from long range.

Even though Quick Shot (Spritzer) starts up slower than Quick Shot (Greyhound), Quick Shot (Spritzer) is generally the more useful attack because it can destroy most characters' projectiles and causes 49,500 chip damage when blocked. This is slightly more than Quick Shot (Greyhound). Unfortunately, the same characters who can crouch under Quick Shot (Greyhound) can also crouch under Quick Shot (Spritzer), hindering its effectiveness against those characters. However, characters who can only duck under one or two of Quick Shot (Greyhound)'s projectiles must block all three hits of Quick Shot (Spritzer)!

When Hawkeye is forced to meet his challenger in the air, Quick Shot (Spritzer) isn't recommended when compared to Quick Shot (Greyhound), since Quick Shot (Greyhound) releases faster and covers a larger area than Quick Shot (Spritzer).

Trick Maneuver**:** These attacks, which give Hawkeye special movement options, are the only way to access his sneaky Trick Shot attacks.

Trick Maneuver L makes Hawkeye perform a quick backwards jump that travels faster and farther than his standard jump. You can use this maneuver to cancel the recovery of standing H and jump backwards away from opponents who jump over the initial projectile, or jumps that are getting too close for comfort. Trick Shots performed during Trick Maneuver L cover a lot of horizontal range and are OTG-capable, making them integral during most of Hawkeye's combos.

Unlike the other Trick Maneuvers, which send Hawkeye into the air, Trick Maneuver M causes Hawkeye to roll forward across the ground. Hawkeye always fires a Trick Shot toward his adversary during the move, so rolling under an opponent jumping toward Hawkeye and shooting them in the back can sometimes be a good option. Trick Maneuver M is mainly used when you need fullscreen versions of the Trick Shots in combos, particularly Violet Fizz.

Trick Maneuver H makes Hawkeye jump forward and should be mainly used to jump over the opposing character when they have Hawkeye in the corner. During Trick Maneuver H, Hawkeye shoots at a much steeper angle than Trick Maneuver L during the forward jump, and the move can only hit competitors who are close to Hawkeye. Like Trick Maneuver M, Hawkeye always aims in the proper direction during the jump; if he jumps over an adversary during Trick Maneuver H, he'll turn around and aim toward his foe, allowing Hawkeye to quickly strike behind his opponent. Trick Maneuver H comprises a large part of Hawkeye's offense because you can call a crossover assist before performing Trick Maneuver H to confuse and mix up your opponent.

Trick Shot (Violet Fizz): This attack can only be performed during a Trick Maneuver, and it packs a nasty punch because it keeps dealing damage after the attack is over! When Violet Fizz hits an opponent, they become poisoned and lose health over time. Poison deals 300 damage per frame for 300 frames, which adds up to 18,000 damage per second and up to 90,000 damage over five seconds! If Hawkeye or any other point character on his team is hit, then poison status disappears, but assists can be hit, and the target will remain poisoned. Even if the opposing character has no life, they cannot be finished off from poison, so Hawkeye or another member of his team must finish off the rival . If a poisoned character tags out, they are still poisoned when they return to the battlefield as a point character, but the poison does not deal damage while the character is off the playing field or used as an assist.

During Trick Maneuver L or H, you can use Violet Fizz to OTG your opponent and add unscaled poison damage to a combo before hyper combo canceling to Gimlet, increasing Hawkeye's damage during a combo! You can also tack on a Violet Fizz during fullscreen standing H combos to poison and pressure your foe into advancing before they lose too much life to the poison. This gives you a chance to land additional damage against reckless advances.

Trick Shot (Violet Fizz) can also be performed from Trick Maneuver L much faster than the other two Trick Shots, only 8 frames after initiating the attack. This lets you throw surprise Violet Fizz attacks during standing H and also makes it easy for you to use Violet Fizz as an OTG during combos.

Trick Shot (Ice Breaker): When this shot hits an opponent, it encases them in ice for a brief period of time, allowing you to occasionally land a ground combo after a successful hit. Unfortunately, the time the adversary is stuck in ice is very short, so linking attacks after this shot connects can be difficult.

When this attack is performed from Trick Maneuver L or H, and hits an airborne target or one stuck in hard knockdown state, Ice Breaker causes ground bounce, which allows you to extend Hawkeye's combos. This makes it an essential combat tool. Outside of combos, you should stick to using Violet Fizz in most situations.

Trick Shot (Rusty Nail): Unlike the other Trick Shots, Rusty Nail is a straightforward attack that doesn't cause any unique status ailments to the opposing character. It is, however, the fastest traveling of all the Trick Shots, and it causes the most chip—36,000 points of damage. This attack also has the longest range of all the Trick Shots when used from Trick Maneuver L, making it a valuable weapon when your rival is just out of range of Violet Fizz.

Rusty Nail also causes the most guardstun of any of the Trick Shots, making it the best Trick Shot to use when jumping over competitors with Trick Maneuver H.

Ragtime Shot (Jack Rose): Unlike Hawkeye's other arrows, the Ragtime Shot attacks fly straight into the air before coming down on opponents from the top of the screen. During Jack Rose, Hawkeye fires an explosive arrow straight up into the air, which arcs around and then falls straight down a short distance in front of Hawkeye. If the arrow hits the target while it's in the air, it explodes on contact, damaging your foe. This attack is best used to control aerial space if your adversary is attempting to super jump at close range.

After the arrow hits the ground, it becomes almost a different move entirely, as it becomes a bomb that explodes after two seconds, damaging any competitors in the blast range. The bomb cannot harm the opponent until it explodes. Unfortunately, it's tough to rely on the bomb explosion to happen when necessary during a match because the timing is so awkward; it's too long to easily combo into, and its duration is too short to use as a ground deterrent like Chris' landmines or Viewtiful Joe's Shocking Pink bombs. Instead, it's best regarded as a "nice if it happens" sort of thing. If your opponent is in the vicinity of the explosive when it's about to go off, be ready to capitalize with Quick Shot (Hunter) for a big combo!

Ragtime Shot (Kamikaze): After this attack is fired into the air, it releases a volley of arrows that rain down on your opponent at a steep angle, covering the far third of the screen with projectiles. This attack is mainly used to prevent attacks from characters jumping forward, while Hawkeye fires standing Ⓗ projectiles at his target from across the screen.

If Ragtime Shot (Kamikaze) makes contact with your competitor in the air, they are placed back into Hawkeye's optimal range and forced to guard a standing Ⓗ arrow, which you can also cancel into Quick Shot (Spritzer) for big chip damage!

Kamikaze is one of the most important tools in Hawkeye's arsenal because combining standing Ⓗ arrows into Ragtime Shot (Kamikaze) with crossover assists mixed in keeps the opposing character away from Hawkeye while causing tons of chip damage! The amount of chip damage caused by Kamikaze depends on where the opponent is and how the arrows randomly fall, but if a foe is forced to block all hits of Kamikaze, it can deal up to 67,500 points of chip damage!

Ragtime Shot (Balalaika): This attack fires three arrows straight into the air, which arc at around the peak of super jump height before dropping down, covering the far third of the screen in arrows. This attack is best used as a guess to keep opponents from super jumping toward Hawkeye, since it stops any super jumping character from being able to advance, keeping them in Hawkeye's optimum range. Balalaika only deals 27,000 points of chip damage, however, and it should only be used as a predictive move against competitors looking to super jump away from Hawkeye's barrage of arrows.

HAWKEYE

NEW

Hyper Combos

Screen	Name	Command	Hits	Damage	Startup	Active	Recovery	Advantage on Hit	Advantage if Guarded	Notes
1	Gimlet (in air OK)	↓↘→ + ATK ATK	1	250,000	8+1	—	50	-8	-29	Projectile has 3 high priority durability points, piercing
2	Kiss of Fire	→↓↘ + ATK ATK	7	50,000 per arrow	9+1	—	58	—	—	OTG-capable, 7 projectiles with 3 high priority durability points each
3	Tag Team Special (Level 3 Hyper Combo)	↓↙← + ATK ATK	4	430,000	10+1	37	37	—	-45	OTG-capable, frames 1-19 invincible

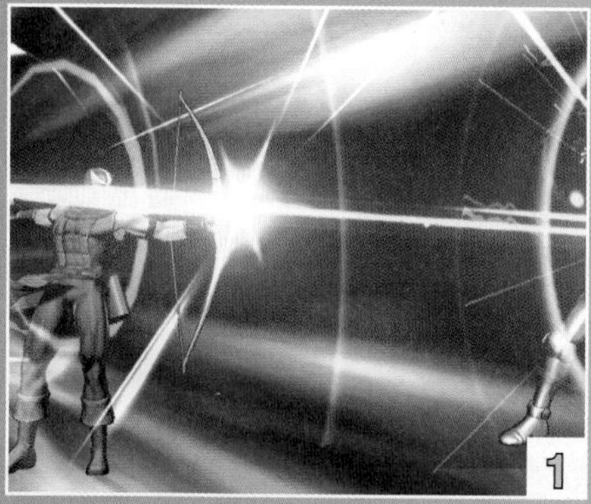

Gimlet: During this hyper combo, Hawkeye quickly fires an incredibly fast arrow at his opponent's position, no matter where they are on screen, making it an excellent tool that you can use on reaction to punish nearly anything your rival does because it instantly homes to wherever the opposing character is! Hawkeye can evade his adversary's attacks, then quickly strike back with Gimlet from wherever he is, even at super jump height against a grounded attacker. Gimlet itself doesn't inflict much damage and its damage is concentrated in a single hit, causing its damage to scale fairly heavily and making it a relatively mediocre combo ender. The optimal way to use Gimlet is to punish your opponent's whiffed attacks, following it up with a suitable THC hyper combo.

Be careful when using Gimlet in the corner: ending combos against a cornered competitor with Gimlet can often put Hawkeye in a position to be punished, as it has a frame disadvantage of -8 even on hit! When ending combos in the corner, make sure Hawkeye has enough meter to follow up Gimlet with a THC to ensure that Hawkeye stays safe after landing this hyper combo.

2

Kiss of Fire: When this hyper combo is performed, Hawkeye fires numerous, OTG-capable explosive arrows into the air that then fall on to the ground, one after another, covering the playing field in projectiles. Kiss of Fire is best used to push opponents away from Hawkeye while also dealing chip damage, since while the arrows are falling, you can tack on additional standing Ⓗ arrows canceled into a Quick Shot attack to push an adversary farther away while inflicting chip damage. If Kiss of Fire hits an opponent, you can easily tack on Gimlet for an extra chunk of damage.

While it looks similar to Magneto's Magnetic Shockwave, this hyper combo cannot be used in certain situations where that hyper combo excels. If the opposing character is too close to Hawkeye, they can throw him, negating the hyper combo as they become invincible to the arrows as they rain onto the ground. Also, once the arrows hit a competitor or an assist, they immediately explode; if the arrows hit an assist, the assist shields the point character by taking all hits of the super, allowing the point character to move in and punish Hawkeye.

Tag Team Special: In this level 3 hyper combo, Hawkeye jumps into the air and shoots an arrow onto the ground, creating a cloud of smoke that can hit his foe. If an opponent is hit, Hawkeye enlists the help of fellow Avenger Ant Man to pummel the attacker and inflict huge amounts of unscaled damage! During Tag Team Special, Hawkeye is completely invincible and fairly fast, so you can use it as a last-ditch, defensive counter-measure. Tag Team Special is also OTG-capable, allowing Hawkeye to end combos with it, which is also his only way to inflict really big damage. However, beware if your competitor blocks Tag Team Special, as Hawkeye is incredibly unsafe if blocked.

Battle Plan

Hawkeye's ranged game revolves almost entirely around standing H used with long range crossover assists.

After making contact with a standing H arrow, canceling into Ragtime Shot (Kamikaze) almost guarantees that your opponent will not be able to advance for a brief moment.

Your goal with Hawkeye is to keep adversaries away from him at all times. His strengths lie in being able to deal large amounts of chip damage from fullscreen distances with a variety of arrow attacks; once opponents get in, those arrow attacks become ineffective. As such, you must prevent your rival from moving forward at all costs.

When choosing an assist for Hawkeye, note that he is best when teamed up with an assist who can supplement his onslaught of projectiles like Doctor Doom—α or Arthur—β. These assists not only add chip damage on to Hawkeye's projectile assault, but they also fill in holes in Hawkeye's offense, allowing you to keep opponents locked down without a chance to escape.

All of Hawkeye's offense revolves around the usage of his standing H arrow attack, which is a fast, cancelable projectile that inflicts chip damage and allows you to tack on additional arrow attacks from across the screen. To keep offense working effectively, press H while simultaneously calling a long range crossover assist, then cancel to Quick Shot (Greyhound) or (Spritzer) to deal big chip damage while keeping your adversary away and keeping Hawkeye safe. Note that some characters can avoid Greyhound and Spritzer by crouching; if they can, use Quick Shot (Hunter) instead. It doesn't do as much chip damage, but it keeps rivals from advancing to Hawkeye's position.

After the Quick Shot makes contact with the target, your crossover assist's attack should begin making contact, further pinning the opponent in place. From here, you can add on another standing H attack canceled into Ragtime Shot (Kamikaze) to prevent the your foe from moving forward.

From here, Hawkeye's offense can stall, and your opponent has a chance to attack, so you have to make a choice while the crossover assist is recharging—if you think your competitor is going to approach by the air, jump backwards and use air Quick Shot (Greyhound) to push your challenger back. While this still doesn't give you enough time to fully recharge the most recently used assist, your other assist may be ready for action; if that assist is also a long range assist, simply press H and the assist button again, and resume your fullscreen space control. If you think your opponent may approach on the ground, fire off standing H canceled into Quick Shot. This won't push the opposing character back very far, so you'll generally have to shift into the medium range mindset afterwards.

Unfortunately for Hawkeye, the height that the standing H arrow flies is somewhat random: if the arrow is angled too high, many characters can crouch directly under the projectile. You'll have to put in a bit more effort by manually aiming the arrow downward, right before releasing it. To guarantee a properly aimed standing H, press H and hold it very briefly while inputting the ⇩ ⇘ ⇨ motion for Quick Shot, then immediately release H. If performed correctly, Hawkeye aims the arrow downward very slightly, preventing any characters from crouching under it.

If any of the above tactics hit the opposing character, you can react and hyper combo cancel to Gimlet (and THC if applicable), getting big damage and forcing your foe back into a position where they must defend against Hawkeye's projectiles.

Like many zoning characters, Hawkeye's long range offense struggles against teleport-enabled characters. To keep Hawkeye safe against teleporters, you'll want to stick with only using standing H and crossover assists; don't cancel into Quick Shots or Ragtime Shots, since teleporting characters can bypass Hawkeye's projectiles and punish him while he's defenseless. Since standing H is cancelable, Hawkeye can remain safe while firing arrows by canceling the standing H into Trick Maneuver if you see the opposing character teleport. If your adversary only has teleports that appear in the air like Dante and Dormammu, it's a little safer to fire Quick Shot and Ragtime Shot arrows; if you see the teleport, instantly react by hyper combo canceling Quick Shot into Gimlet. You can do this against grounded opponents, as well. However, while Gimlet is safe against airborne competitors, it's generally unsafe against grounded characters even on hit, unless Hawkeye has the meter and teammates remaining to follow Gimlet with a THC.

Once your challenger has broken through Hawkeye's long range offense, everything starts to become much more risky. A single wrong guess puts Hawkeye in a position for punishment. You have to be a bit more *slippery* at this range and attempt to increase the distance between Hawkeye and his adversary.

At medium ranges, standing H while calling crossover assist is still strong, but if you see your rival jump over it, you'll need to be ready to cancel into Trick Maneuver L at a moment's notice to get away from your foe. In cases when you don't have an assist ready, cancel to Trick Maneuver L anyway to increase the distance so you can get back to shooting projectiles at your target.

Jumping back and using Quick Shot (Greyhound) is the most reliable anti-air Hawkeye has outside of air throw range.

Trick Maneuver H is vital to get behind opponents and draw them away from the corner; call a crossover assist first both to make it safe and a sneaky cross-up!

Up close, Hawkeye is very weak to jumping opponents. While standing M occasionally works as an anti-air, it isn't consistent, and Hawkeye stands to take incredible damage if it fails. Outside of air throw range, jumping backwards and using air Quick Shot (Greyhound) is Hawkeye's most reliable anti-air. If an attacker jumps while you're firing Greyhound, they'll be stuck in blockstun long enough for you to tack on an additional standing H canceled into another Quick Shot or a Trick Maneuver to create more distance from your opponent.

If you have Hawkeye jump backwards and his competitor isn't in the air with him, you can still convert the situation into an opportunity by firing off a late Greyhound or air S, depending on distance. If it hits, you can convert into a combo by using standing H canceled into Quick Shot (Hunter) from far or ⇘ + H (Slide) into S launcher when close!

However, when at medium range, your main focus should be using Trick Maneuver to create a cross-up situation and to escape from the corner. This is best accomplished by using Slide while simultaneously calling an assist, then canceling the Slide into Trick Maneuver H without releasing a Trick Shot. Your assist then crosses up your rival, and if it hits, you can convert into a combo! If the assist doesn't hit, you'll have frame advantage, allowing you to perform a guarded chain combo into Trick Maneuvers L to increase distance from your foe.

If you don't have a crossover assist available, use Slide into Trick Maneuver H, then attack from the other side with Trick Shot (Rusty Nail); this leaves Hawkeye at nearly even frame advantage, although this isn't necessarily recommended since Hawkeye excels when at long ranges, not so much close range. As such, it's generally better not to use Trick Maneuver H to jump over your opponent unless you have an assist ready, with an exception being if Hawkeye is in danger of being trapped in the corner.

Kiss of Fire is a reliable way to force your adversary backwards because Kiss of Fire projectiles move down the screen in sequential fashion, one after the other, and they can carry guarding or hit opponents all the way across the playing field! However, Kiss of Fire cannot be used when the target is too close, as they can throw Hawkeye out of the attack's startup before the arrows come in to play. After the arrows are guarded, use standing H combined with a crossover assist and resume fullscreen offense. This attack costs a bar, so try to get by without it. However, it's Hawkeye's most reliable option in many situations.

Hawkeye's defensive options aren't great, so you could be in trouble when opponents do manage to get near Hawkeye and force you to guard. When on defense, you should look for guaranteed chances to use advancing guard to push the opposing character away and look for opportunities to air throw or use Slide with an assist call, canceled into Trick Maneuvers H. Super jumping forward can be ok in a bind, but you'll almost definitely land into another mix-up when coming down, so only use it when in a severe emergency.

Using Hawkeye's S launcher isn't terrible as a panic button to catch both aerial and grounded adversaries, but it is crazy unsafe if guarded and should only be used as a last ditch attack. Using a crossover assist simultaneously helps mitigate risk, but throwing out a random S should only be used in the most dire of situations.

Quick Shot (Spritzer) absolutely dominates most long-range firefights!

Against most characters, Hawkeye can easily dominate a long range firefight due to the sheer volume of projectiles you can throw out at a time with him. While you are in a projectile war, you can generally treat the battle like any other match by liberally firing standing Ⓗ arrows canceled into Quick Shot (Spritzer), since this move overpowers any low priority projectiles and continues on to hit Hawkeye's opponent. If you see a Quick Shot projectile hit, hyper combo cancel into Gimlet for good, fullscreen damage. Also, when in a firefight, make sure to call projectile assists often, as their added firepower can help wear down your adversary more quickly.

Hawkeye's arrows generally only cover the horizontal space in front of him, so you should take extra precaution when opposing characters take to the air. The best way to keep rivals on the ground is by mixing in Ragtime Shot (Balalaika), which hits most characters from a fullscreen distance away. If a competitor does manage to get into the air, Hawkeye is not helpless, however. Against opponents who fire angled projectiles from normal jump height, like Morrigan and Taskmaster, preemptively jump and meet them in the air with Quick Shot (Hunter), which can lead to a big damage combo once Hawkeye reaches the ground! When fighting characters like Trish, who fire angled projectiles from super jump height, Quick Shot (Hunter) cannot be used because the opponent will break free of Hunter's net before Hawkeye reaches the ground. Instead, use Quick Shot (Greyhound) in those situations to score some quick damage while knocking your foe back to the ground.

Hawkeye can also instantly punish all normal projectiles by firing off Gimlet, if you have the bar to burn. This projectile is fast enough to hit any character out of the startup of their projectiles, making it a useful tool to win firefights against characters with medium durability projectiles that can overpower Quick Shot (Spritzer).

While Hawkeye can generally come out ahead of most other characters in a long range firefight, most long range characters also have access to a projectile hyper combo that can swiftly put an end to Hawkeye's projectile assault. Unfortunately, Hawkeye doesn't have many ways to defeat projectile hyper combos other than baiting his opponent into using them. If you think a random hyper combo might be coming, super jump to avoid it entirely, and then punish with a quick Gimlet. Most supers can even be punished when they are guarded because Gimlet is so fast, but it would be wiser to avoid the chip damage altogether.

COMBO USAGE

I. CR. Ⓛ, Ⓜ, ↘ + Ⓗ, Ⓢ CANCEL FORWARD SUPER JUMP, AIR Ⓜ, Ⓜ, Ⓗ (2 HITS), Ⓢ, LAND, ↓ ↙ ← + Ⓗ (DURING TRICK MANEUVER) Ⓜ, LAND, CR. Ⓗ, ↘ + Ⓗ, Ⓢ CANCEL FORWARD SUPER JUMP, AIR Ⓜ, Ⓜ, Ⓗ (2 HITS), Ⓢ, LAND, {↓ ↙ ← + Ⓛ (DURING TRICK MANEUVER) Ⓛ CANCEL ↓ ↘ → + ATK ATK} OR {↓ ↙ ← + ATK ATK}

491,600~819,800 damage (first variation is 581,600 after poison runs its course), 10% meter loss

As a pure zoning character, Hawkeye's combos deal less than average damage, since he is expected to get most of his damage by chipping away at his opponent with projectiles. When you do get a chance to land a clean crouching Ⓛ, you can at least convert it into decent damage.

When Hawkeye is near the corner, you must dash backwards before doing Trick Shot (Ice Breaker) to ensure it hits. To help with timing, input ←, ↓ ↙ ← when performing Trick Maneuver L to easily create the proper spacing needed to OTG with Ice Breaker.

Ending the combo in the corner with Gimlet should only be performed if it will K.O., since some characters can punish Gimlet even on hit. In most situations, it's better to simply end the combo with Violet Fizz, back up, and reestablish Hawkeye's projectile pressure.

If the initial hits are guarded, cancel into Trick Maneuver L and use Trick Shot (Rusty Nail) to stay safe and create some distance from your adversary. Alternatively, call a crossover assist simultaneously with Slide and cancel into Trick Maneuver H for a cross up attempt (and to get away from the corner). If your rival is in the corner, this tactic won't work because Trick Maneuver H cannot cross up an opponent in the corner.

II. ST. Ⓗ CANCEL ↓ ↘ → + Ⓛ CANCEL ↓ ↘ → + ATK ATK

375,400 damage, 84% meter loss

This is an easy, verifiable fullscreen combo from standing Ⓗ. Since Gimlet is so fast, you can delay hyper combo canceling until you're absolutely sure the Quick Shot hits.

If you have a partner with a long range hyper that can hit the target from the distance you're at when performing this combo, cancel Gimlet into a THC to add additional damage. Not bad for a fullscreen projectile!

III. ST. Ⓗ CANCEL ↓ ↘ → + Ⓜ, ST. Ⓗ CANCEL ↓ ↘ → + Ⓜ, ST. Ⓗ CANCEL ↓ ↙ ← + Ⓜ (DURING TRICK MANEUVER) Ⓛ CANCEL ↓ ↘ → + ATK ATK

417,800 damage (507,800 after poison distributes), 74% meter loss

This is a much bigger combo from fullscreen, useful in situations when you think the opposing character might dash into standing Ⓗ or if you have a guaranteed fullscreen punish.

After Quick Shot (Hunter) grabs the foe, linking the next standing Ⓗ is fairly difficult; the timing window is only 4 frames long, and the recovery on Hunter is somewhat misleading. The linked standing Ⓗ must be canceled into Hunter as soon as possible to ensure that this full combo connects.

It's best not to guess with this combo, as Quick Shot (Hunter) does far less chip damage than Quick Shot (Greyhound) and (Spritzer), so only try for this combo in guaranteed situations.

COMBO USAGE CONT.

IV. THROW OR AIR THROW, ↓↙← + (H) (DURING TRICK MANEUVER) (M), LAND, {ST. (H) [CANCEL] ↓↘→ + (M)} X 3, {↘ + (H), (S) [CANCEL] FORWARD SUPER JUMP, AIR (M), (M), (H) (2 HITS), (S), LAND, ↓↙← + (L) (DURING TRICK MANEUVER) (L) [CANCEL] ↓↘→ + (ATK ATK)} OR {[CANCEL] ↓↙← + (ATK ATK), ↓↘→ + (ATK ATK)}

357,900~484,800 damage (first variation is 447,900 after poison distributes), 22~159% meter loss

After doing ↓↙← + (H) [CANCEL] (M), you must time Ice Breaker very low to the ground to give yourself enough time to link standing (H) afterwards.

V. (REQUIRES CORNER) FRONT THROW, {ST. (H) [CANCEL] ↓↘→ + (M)} X 6, CR. (H), ↘ + (H), (S) [CANCEL] FORWARD SUPER JUMP, AIR (M), (M), (H) (2 HITS), (S), LAND, ↓↙← + (L) (DURING TRICK MANEUVER) (L) [CANCEL] ↓↘→ + (ATK ATK)

358,700 damage (448,700 after poison distributes), 4% meter gain

When you're very close to your adversary, Quick Shot (Hunter) loops are much easier and can lead to bigger much bigger damage.

VI. (AGAINST AIRBORNE ENEMY) FORWARD JUMP, AIR (M), (H) (2 HITS) [CANCEL] ↓↘→ + (M), {ST. (H) [CANCEL] ↓↘→ + (M)} X 3, ↘ + (H), (S) [CANCEL] FORWARD SUPER JUMP, AIR (M), (M), (H) (2 HITS), (S), LAND, {IF ENEMY IS CORNERED, BACKWARDS DASH, ↓↙← + (H) (DURING TRICK MANEUVER) (L) [CANCEL] ↓↘→ + (ATK ATK)} OR {IF MIDSCREEN, →↓↘ + (ATK ATK), ↓↘→ + (ATK ATK)}

484,000~536,500 damage (first variation is 574,000 after poison distributes), 15~118% meter loss

This combo is best used when your opponent is normal jumping toward Hawkeye, and he can meet them in the air with jumping air (M).

Verify to see if the first two attacks of this combo are guarded. If so, chain into air (S) instead of performing Quick Shot (Hunter) to remain safe. If the first two attacks hit, cancel into Quick Shot (Hunter) and punish your competitor with a decent air-to-air combo!

VII. CR. (L), (M), ↘ + (H), (S) [CANCEL] FORWARD SUPER JUMP, AIR (M), (M), (H) (2 HITS), (S), LAND, FORWARD DASH, ↓↙← + (L) (DURING TRICK MANEUVER) (L) [CANCEL] (ATK ATK) [CANCEL] [X-FACTOR], LAND, ↘ + (H), (S) [CANCEL] FORWARD SUPER JUMP, AIR (M), (M), (H) (2 HITS), (S), LAND, BACKWARDS DASH, ↓↙← + (H) (DURING TRICK MANEUVER) (M), LAND, (S) [CANCEL] VERTICAL SUPER JUMP, AIR (H) (2 HITS) [CANCEL] ↓↘→ + (ATK ATK)

825,500~949,600 damage, 93~72% meter loss

This is a fairly standard X-Factor combo, but it should only be used when it will K.O. the opposing character. At maximum damage, this combo isn't enough to kill several characters, so be sure that your opponent has been weakened enough for this combo to put them out of commission.

Before activating, perform Trick Shot (Violet Fizz) as quickly as possible so Gimlet hits close enough to the ground for the X-Factor cancel into Slide to work. If executed too slowly, your rival recovers, and you'll have wasted your X-Factor activation.

VIII. ST. (H) [CANCEL] ↓↘→ + (M), ST. (H) [CANCEL] ↓↘→ + (M), ST. (H) [CANCEL] ↓↘→ + (L) [CANCEL] ↓↘→ + (ATK ATK) [CANCEL] [X-FACTOR], ST. (H) [CANCEL] ↓↘→ + (L) [CANCEL] ↓↘→ + (ATK ATK)

690,500~770,500 damage, 147~141% meter loss

You can perform this X-Factor combo from fullscreen, giving Hawkeye a chance to put a pesky character away off of a standing (H). This combo doesn't do huge damage, however, so make sure your target will be knocked out before activating X-Factor.

ADVANCED TACTICS

TAKE OVER THE SKIES!

With the proper timing, you can use Hawkeye's charged standing Ⓗ shot to cover several angles!

When you hold Ⓗ while performing standing Ⓗ, you can aim the direction of the arrows by inputting up or down during the charging period.

Unfortunately, aiming these arrows is fairly difficult because aiming is very sensitive; releasing the arrows at the wrong time can cause all three arrows to shoot harmlessly into the ground!

However, pressing up at the last second allows you to aim arrows in a wide spread that not only sends an arrow toward grounded opponents, but also sends arrows both at normal jump and super jump height!

The best way to guarantee this powerful spread is to find a timing aid: tap the controller, hit extra buttons, or just count in your head! The best way to remember the timing is to find something that works for you, so experiment!

Charging standing Ⓗ does take time, however, so call a crossover assist during the long startup of standing Ⓗ to protect Hawkeye, or cancel the shots into a Quick Shot attack or Trick Maneuver L to maintain safety.

SIDEBUSTIN'

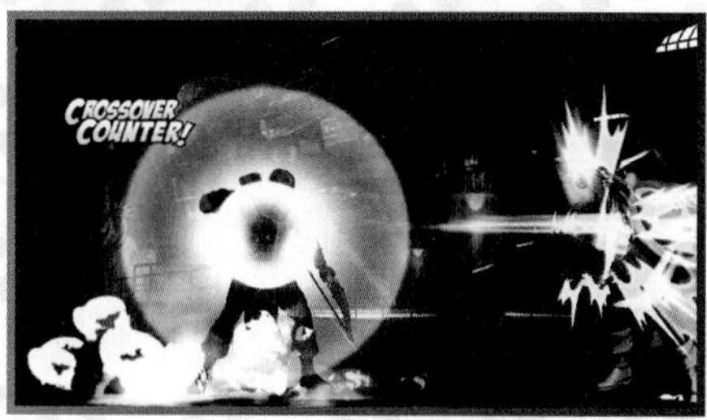

Gimlet is incredibly fast and can be performed in the air. Using it immediately after tagging in Hawkeye with a crossover counter is often free damage!

When a crossover counter is performed, the character who has been tagged in first appears in the air before performing their crossover attack. While in the air, you can hyper combo cancel into an aerial hyper combo to attack your foe while their attack is still recovering!

Since Gimlet is super fast, hyper combo canceling into Gimlet when performing a crossover counter to Hawkeye often results in guaranteed damage because your adversary must be attacking in order for you to perform the crossover counter.

If you have the meter to spare, you can THC to another hyper combo to do big damage off of a blocked attack, or activate X-Factor after releasing Gimlet to get a sudden surprise K.O.!

HAWKEYE

NEW

COMBO APPENDIX

GENERAL EXECUTION TIPS

During corner combos, you'll need to have Hawkeye dash backwards before using Trick Shot (Ice Breaker); otherwise, the move goes completely behind the opponent

When performing Quick Shot (Hunter) loops, press standing Ⓗ a little earlier than you think you are able to

After ground bouncing adversaries with Trick Shot (Ice Breaker), omit the crouching Ⓗ and just use Slide to make the combo a little easier

AS HAWKEYE COMES IN: AIR Ⓜ, Ⓜ, Ⓢ, LAND, ↓↙← + Ⓗ (DURING TRICK MANEUVER) Ⓜ, LAND, Ⓢ CANCEL➡ FORWARD SUPER JUMP, AIR Ⓜ, Ⓜ, Ⓗ (2 HITS), Ⓢ, LAND, ↓↙← + Ⓛ CANCEL➡ ↓↘→ + ATK ATK

Notes	Damage
↑ + Ⓢ or → + Ⓢ or ↓ + Ⓢ TAC to Hawkeye	Varies based on damage scaling

ST. Ⓗ CANCEL➡ ↓↘→ + Ⓜ, ST. Ⓗ CANCEL➡ ↓↘→ + Ⓜ, ST. Ⓗ CANCEL➡ →↓↘ + Ⓜ CANCEL➡ ↓↘→ + ATK ATK, ↓↘→ + ATK ATK

Notes	Damage
Requires corner, must be at a distance from the foe. After canceling into →↓↘ + Ⓜ, super cancel into ↓↘→ + ATK ATK as soon as Hawkeye releases the upward arrows	595,200 damage, 62% meter loss

(CORNER REQUIRED, OPPONENT MUST BE CROUCHING) CR. Ⓛ, ST. Ⓜ, → + Ⓗ CANCEL➡ ↓↙← + Ⓛ CANCEL➡ Ⓛ, LAND, CR. Ⓛ, Ⓜ, ↘ + Ⓗ, Ⓢ CANCEL➡ SUPER JUMP, AIR Ⓜ, Ⓜ, Ⓗ, Ⓢ, LAND, BACKDASH, ↓↙← + Ⓗ CANCEL➡ Ⓜ, LAND, ↘ + Ⓗ, Ⓢ CANCEL➡ SUPER JUMP, AIR Ⓜ, Ⓜ, Ⓗ, Ⓢ, LAND, ↓↙← + Ⓛ CANCEL➡ Ⓛ CANCEL➡ ↓↘→ + ATK ATK

Notes	Damage
A corner poison combo, works against smaller crouching characters	538,900 damage, with an additional 90,000 points of poison damage

ST. Ⓗ CANCEL➡ ↓↘→ + Ⓜ, ST. Ⓗ CANCEL➡ ↓↘→ + Ⓜ, ST. Ⓗ (CALL M.O.D.O.K.—γ) CANCEL➡ ↓↘→ + Ⓜ, {ST. Ⓗ CANCEL➡ ↓↘→ + Ⓜ} X 3, WAVEDASH FORWARD TWICE, ↘ + Ⓗ, Ⓢ CANCEL➡ FORWARD SUPER JUMP, AIR Ⓜ, Ⓜ, Ⓗ (2 HITS), Ⓢ, LAND, ↓↙← + Ⓛ (DURING TRICK MANEUVER) Ⓛ CANCEL➡ ↓↘→ + ATK ATK

Notes	Damage
A long range combo that uses an assist to keep Quick Shot (Hunter) loops going for several repetitions	499,500 damage, 0% meter loss

NEW

IRON FIST

"THE SCRIBES IN K'UN-LUN WILL WRITE OF THIS BATTLE FOR YEARS TO COME."

Bio

REAL NAME

Daniel "Danny" Thomas Rand-K'ai

OCCUPATION

Adventurer, formerly co-owner of Rand-Meachum, Inc.

ABILITIES

Master of hand-to-hand combat, specializing in close combat. Having mastered the secret arts of the K'un-Lun, he can harness his spiritual energy, or "chi". He can also use his powers to heal people.

WEAPONS

None

PROFILE

Having studied martial arts in the mystic city of K'un-Lun for 10 years, Daniel was their strongest student. Defeating the dragon known as Shou-Lao the Undying, he gained the title of Iron Fist. He is good friends with fellow martial artist hero Luke Cage.

FIRST APPEARANCE

Marvel Premiere #15 (1974)

POWER GRID

3 INTELLIGENCE

2 STRENGTH

2 SPEED

3 STAMINA

3 ENERGY PROJECTION

6 FIGHTING ABILITY

*This is biographical, and does not represent an evaluation of the in-game combat potential of this hero.

ALTERNATE COSTUMES

Overview

Vitality	1,000,000
Chain Combo Archetype	Hunter Series

X-Factor Boost	Damage	Speed
Level 1 (3 teammates remaining)	130%	110%
Level 2 (2 teammates remaining)	150%	120%
Level 3 (1 teammate remaining)	170%	130%

Iron Fist appears in *Ultimate Marvel vs. Capcom 3* as an out-and-out brawler, armed with a class of moves that seem instantly familiar to fans of Fei-Long, Karin, Rolento, and Yang. The Rekka Ken finally comes to *MvC*! Well, sort of: naturally, since this is *MvC*, Iron Fist's "Rekkas" are intended for combos and mix-ups, rather than to be used in the same kind of measured, counter-poking way Yang and Fei-Long apply their ↓ ↘ → + ATK x3 attacks. In this way, he's a bit more like Street Fighter Alpha 3's Karin than the others. Also, Iron Fist has eight of these moves!

Your goal when playing with Iron Fist should be to achieve point-blank range with frame advantage. Why?

- **More than any other aggressive character, Iron Fist is lacking in the non-universal options department for movement. No airdash, no teleport, no flight, no roll; the only special Iron Fist has to move him an appreciable distance is Rising Fang, which can only be accessed in a sequence of moves, and while his Iron Rage hyper combo travels forward quickly, it costs meter and it's unsafe guarded. Otherwise, Iron Fist can dash, wavedash, jump, and wall jump, and that's it**
- **Iron Fist lacks a quick opening high/low mix-up (or a comparable left/right side switch trick). Only crouching Ⓗ, Ⓢ launcher, and ↓ ↙ ← + Ⓛ Dragon Tail are low-hitting attacks, and none of these attacks makes a good opening gambit on its own; in order to mix up an opponent, Iron Fist must have already attacked, essentially**

At close range, you can work on coaxing out and taking advantage of your adversary's bad defensive reactions. How do you get there?

- **By having Iron Fist carefully dash, wavedash, and jump toward the opposing character, when backed by crossover assists**
- **By aggressively going for air throws and cross-up air Ⓗ**
- **By staying twitchy, always ready to unleash the invincible Iron Rage hyper combo right through your opponent's attacks on reaction (see also: Spencer's Bionic Lancer)**
- **By either patiently avoiding your rival's efforts to keep Iron Fist at bay with projectiles, or nullifying them with ← + Ⓗ Dual Palm or Chi**

Finally, you've closed the distance and achieved close range against your foe. How do you crack their shell?

- **By delaying chain combos and tricky Rekka special moves in close, exploiting your opponent's natural desire to press buttons either for advancing guard, or to take back initiative by attacking in perceived gaps in your offense**
- **By forcing your competitor to respect the low attacks Iron Fist does possess by occasionally opening up with a naked sweep rather than a chain combo into sweep, and by varying between ↓ ↙ ← + Ⓛ (which hits low) and ↓ ↙ ← + Ⓜ (which is an overhead) when the chance presents itself**
- **By filling gaps in your offense with Chi activations; these quick power-up actions each make Iron Fist much more powerful in different ways, and they actually have a substantial super armor period, meaning they can function like parries up close**

Attack Set

Standing Basic Attacks

Screen	Command	Hits	Damage	Meter Gain	Startup	Active	Recovery	Advantage on Hit	Advantage if Guarded	Notes
1	Standing Ⓛ	1	45,000	360	5	2	11	+3	+1	Chainable into Ⓛ attacks
2	Standing Ⓜ	1	73,000	584	7	4	16	+1	-1	—
3	Standing Ⓗ	1	83,000	664	11	5	19	+2	0	—

Crouching Basic Attacks

Screen	Command	Hits	Damage	Meter Gain	Startup	Active	Recovery	Advantage on Hit	Advantage if Guarded	Notes
1	Crouching Ⓛ	1	43,000	344	5	2	12	+2	0	Chainable into Ⓛ attacks
2	Crouching Ⓜ	1	70,000	560	8	4	17	0	-2	—
3	Crouching Ⓗ	1	75,00	600	10	4	25	—	-5	Low attack

Ground Special Attack—Launcher

Screen	Command	Hits	Damage	Meter Gain	Startup	Active	Recovery	Advantage on Hit	Advantage if Guarded	Notes
1	Ⓢ (while standing or crouching)	1	90,000	720	12	2	27	—	-5	Launcher, not special- or hyper combo-cancelable, cannot juggle airborne opponents, low attack!

Air Basic Attacks

Screen	Command	Hits	Damage	Meter Gain	Startup	Active	Recovery	Advantage on Hit	Advantage if Guarded	Notes
1	Air Ⓛ	1	50,000	400	6	8	12	+14	+12	Overhead attack
2	Air Ⓜ	1	65,000	520	8	3	20	+19	+17	Overhead attack
3	Air Ⓗ	1	80,000	640	9	3	29	+20	+17	Overhead attack

Air Special Attacks—Flying Screen and Air Exchange

Air Ⓢ causes a hard knockdown when used in a launcher combo (this is sometimes called flying screen). When used outside of a launcher combo, air Ⓢ behaves mostly like another basic attack. Air exchange attacks, performed by inputting a direction plus Ⓢ, are only possible during a launcher combo. Exchange hits initiate team aerial combos by tagging in the next available character to continue the air combo.

Screen	Command	Hits	Damage	Meter Gain	Startup	Active	Recovery	Advantage on Hit	Advantage if Guarded	Notes
1	Air Ⓢ	1	83,000	664	10	4	27	+18	+16	Causes hard knockdown if used in launcher combo, overhead attack
2	Air ⇧ + Ⓢ (during launcher combo)	2	105,00	880	9	3	29	—	—	Tags in next available ally while lofting opponent upward
3	Air ⇨ or ⇦ + Ⓢ (during launcher combo)	2	95,000	800	8	3	20	—	—	Tags in next available ally while causing wall bounce, erases 1 hyper meter bar from foe
4	Air ⇩ + Ⓢ (during launcher combo)	2	95,000	800	10	4	27	—	—	Tags in next available ally while causing ground bounce, generates 1 hyper meter bar

1

2

3

4

Command Attacks

Command attacks resemble basic attacks but have different chaining and canceling properties. It's usually possible to chain *into* a command attack from basic attacks, but most command attacks cannot be chained from or canceled themselves.

Screen	Name	Command	Hits	Damage	Meter Gain	Startup	Active	Recovery	Advantage on Hit	Advantage if Guarded	Notes
1	Dual Palm	⇦ + Ⓗ	1	70,000	560	9	4	21	+4	+2	Nullifies medium priority beams and projectiles
2	Quick Kick	⇨ + Ⓗ	1	80,000	640	12	7	25	-6	-8	Jump-cancelable

1

2

Throws

Throws are for snagging passive or blocking opponents. Since throws are active so quickly, you can also use them to preemptively toss opposing characters out of their offense. Combos are usually possible after throws, one way or another.

Screen	Command	Hits	Damage	Meter Gain	Startup	Active	Notes
1	⇨ + Ⓗ (ground)	2	80,000	800	1	1	Hard knockdown
	⇦ + Ⓗ (ground)	1	80,000	800	1	1	Hard knockdown
2	⇨ + Ⓗ (air)	2	80,000	800	1	1	Hard knockdown
	⇦ + Ⓗ (air)	1	80,000	800	1	1	Hard knockdown

1

2

As a Partner—Crossover Assists

Screen	Type	P1+P2 Crossover Combination Hyper Combo	Description	Hits	Damage	Meter Gain	Startup	Active	Recovery (this crossover assist)	Recovery (other partner)	Notes
1	Iron Fist—α	Iron Rage	Dragon's Touch	1	100,000	800	34	2	125	95	Crumples grounded foe, hard knockdown against airborne rival
2	Iron Fist—β	Iron Rage	Crescent Heel	1	85,000	680	45	5	119	89	OTG-capable, ground bounces adversary, overhead attack
3	Iron Fist—γ	Iron Rage	Rising Fang	1	130,000	1040	34	10	122	92	Wall bounces competitor, destroys low priority projectiles, mutually nullifies medium priority projectiles

1

2

3

Iron Fist—α causes a crumple stun against grounded enemies and a hard knockdown against airborne ones; either way, you can capitalize with a combo. The range is pitiful, but it is at least faster than Iron Fist—β.

Iron Fist—β has a few appealing properties. It's both OTG-capable and a close range overhead—in some ways, this seems like a high-hitting counterpart to Wesker—β. However, Crescent Heel has much less range than other OTG-capable and/or overhead assists. It's also noticeably slower than the fastest OTG assists. Coupled with the small range, this means some characters have trouble applying Iron Fist—β to extend combos even after throws and simple flying screen enders.

Iron Fist—γ sends Iron Fist soaring forward with a wall-bouncing kick. During active frames, this kick can plow through any low priority projectiles; it mutually nullifies with any medium priority projectile. Unless you are desperate for a close range crumple, overhead, or OTG assist, this is his best overall assist. He hits very quickly out to about half of the screen distance, and after that, he continues to travel the full length of his kick arc, like he does during the special move version. He's completely vulnerable at this time, although (amusingly) if you're aiming Iron Fist—γ at the right distance from an opponent (from close range to midscreen distance), then he will almost always rocket completely over their heads and land *off screen* behind them, making him functionally unpunishable! His rising trajectory at the beginning of the move means he'll whiff over many crouching characters from only a few steps away, but if your challenger is crouching in anticipation of this Iron Fist assist, then they are susceptible to overheads.

Although none of Iron Fist's assists is invincible when used as crossover counters, with two bars of meter, you can achieve the same effect by countering in Iron Fist, then *immediately* canceling to Iron Rage the instant he touches the ground. You can even do this with Iron Fist—γ. Since he's invincible while countering in and invincible during Iron Rage, the only vulnerable period is any gap you leave between landing and starting the hyper combo. If your opponent is still recovering from whatever they did that you countered, Iron Rage is assured of hitting.

Snap Back

Screen	Command	Hits	Damage	Meter Gain	Startup	Active	Recovery	Advantage on Hit	Advantage if Guarded
1	↓↘→ + P1 or P2	1	50,000	500 (-1 hyper meter bar)	2	7	16	—	+1

Notes

On hit, snap back forces the opposing point character to be replaced by an assist. Opposing assist calls or tag outs are also locked out for 4 seconds

1

Special Moves

Screen	Name	Command	Hits	Damage	Meter Gain	Startup	Active	Recovery	Advantage on Hit	Advantage if Guarded	Notes
1	Lotus Whip	↓↘→ + L	1	80,000	640	15	3	21	+2	0	—
2	Dragon's Touch	↓↘→ + M	1	100,000	800	10	2	39	—	-17	Crumples grounded foe, hard knockdown on airborne opponent
3	Surging Fist	↓↘→ + H	1	115,000	920	20	3	28	—	-7	Hard knockdown
4	Wall of K'un-Lun	(after 2nd special move) ↓↘→ + S	1	130,000	1040	15	5	41	—	-22	Wall bounces rival, hard knockdown, frames 5-17 super armor
5	Chi L	→↓↘ + L	—	—	—	1	—	29	—	—	Frames 5-20 super armor, Iron Fist gains 20% increasing damage, lasts 300 frames
6	Chi M	→↓↘ + M	—	—	—	1	29	—	—	—	Frames 5-20 super armor, Iron Fist takes 20% less damage, lasts 300 frames
7	Chi H	→↓↘ + H	—	—	—	1	29	—	—	—	Frames 5-20 super armor, Iron Fist gains 20% more hyper gauge from attacks, lasts 300 frames
8	Dragon Tail	↓↙← + L	1	70,000	560	13	3	25	-2	-4	Low attack
9	Crescent Heel	↓↙← + M	1	85,000	680	21	5	33	—	-14	OTG-capable, overhead attack, ground bounces competitor
10	Twin Snakes	↓↙← + H	2	101,000	880	15	3(3)4	36	—	-16	Knocks down
11	Rising Fang	(after 2nd special move) ↓↙← + S	1	130,000	1040	20	10	33	—	-19	Wall bounces target, destroys low priority projectiles, mutually nullifies medium priority projectiles

Iron Fist's "Rekka" specials (so called because of the similarity to Fei-Long's classic three-stage rushing punch Rekka Ken) are all executed with quarter-circle motions. You can make Iron Fist seamlessly cancel between up to three Rekka specials, as though he were simply chain canceling basic attacks. This eliminates the long recovery periods of most of the Rekkas, and it allows all of them to combo together. It also enables mix-ups, since you can cancel into high or low-hitting attacks, or ones with brief super armor. There are eight in all; a different one for each combination of ↓↙← or ↓↘→ with each attack button, and two more that are executed with ↓↘→ or ↓↙← + Ⓢ and are only possible as the third Rekka special in a sequence. After three Rekka specials, the third cannot be canceled into another Rekka (though it's still hyper combo-cancelable). In addition to canceling Rekka-type specials into more Rekkas, you can also cancel them into Chi activations.

1

Lotus Whip: Lotus Whip is Iron Fist's safest special move. If blocked, it leaves him frame neutral—neither he nor his opponent has frame advantage. In contrast, every other special move that Iron Fist has leaves him at a mild to gross frame disadvantage. When Rekka chains are blocked, Lotus Whip is the only safe third-Rekka-move finisher. It provides no mix-up potential, but it at least keeps Iron Fist in close proximity if the challenger guards and doesn't happen to pushblock. Using Dragon Tail or Crescent Heel (or Wall of K'un-Lun) as the third blocked Rekka is trickier, but it is riskier, as well (the former two might fool the opponent's guard, while the latter might absorb and plow through their counter poke if they try one).

Like the rest of Iron Fist's specials, Lotus Whip is also a staple of his combos. It's the most consistent of the Rekka moves to use as a first or second stage, so when in doubt early in the match, you should choose Lotus Whip. Other specials make much better third stages when you're actually hitting your rival.

From just outside the range of Lotus Whip, you can use the move as a sort of feint: whiff Lotus Whip in your foe's face, then immediately cancel into ↓↙← + Ⓛ Dragon Tail, which hits low. This trick is most viable when your opponent is busy blocking your assist from a few steps away.

2

Dragon's Touch: Iron Fist unleashes his version of a one-inch gut punch. The range is miniscule, but Dragon's Touch crumples grounded enemies on contact! (Against airborne or juggled foes, it causes a hard knockdown.) Dragon's Touch is best used in combos, where it opens up many possibilities. You can make Iron Fist activate Chi L or H (for a damage or meter building boost) and still have plenty of time to continue the combo. You don't even have to cancel from Dragon's Touch to Chi; Dragon's Touch can fully recover, then you can perform Chi, and you'll STILL have time to strike the crumpling adversary. You can even hold down P1 or P2 immediately after landing Dragon's Touch, and Iron Fist will tag out to the chosen teammate while the opposing character is still slumping to the ground! In this way, similar to some characters like She-Hulk, you can start combos with Iron Fist and hand them off to teammates without spending hyper meter on THCs, and without taking a chance on your competitor successfully breaking your TAC.

3

Surging Fist: Surging Fist is a two-sided palm strike that sends adversaries into a hard knockdown on contact. After landing Surging Fist, there's time to dash forward and OTG with ↓↙← + Ⓜ Crescent Heel to pop your rival right back up into a hyper combo or another Rekka sequence. Surging Fist is relatively slow to start for what it looks like and is horribly unsafe when guarded, so save it for the third stage of Rekka combos when you're going after a hard knockdown.

4

Wall of K'un-Lun: After Iron Fist performs the first and second stage of a Rekka sequence (which can be made up of any two of his six Rekka attacks that are performed with a basic attack button), he's charged to perform a special Rekka ender, of which he has two: Wall of K'un-Lun with ↓↘→ + Ⓢ, and Rising Fang with ↓↙← + Ⓢ. Wall of K'un-Lun is a tremendous shoulder check that causes a wall bounce on contact. Naturally, this allows you to perpetuate the combo with more juggles, or use the Volcanic Roar hyper combo.

If you initiate a Rekka sequence that is guarded, Wall of K'un-Lun can make a slightly effective delayed Rekka ender, because it has super armor that begins on frame 5 and extends all the way into K'un-Lun's active frames. If the slight delay before K'un-Lun baits your competitor into pressing a button, their attack is eaten up, and Iron Fist slams them into the wall. This is naturally very unsafe if guarded, so use this tactic sparingly just to remind your opponent that you have it (unless they have bad habits and try to attack right away whenever they can; in which case, knock yourself out shooting Wall of K'un-Lun into their face). If it's guarded, be prepared to cancel to Iron Rage, then to THC away to a teammate's safer hyper combo. Just as you canceled into Wall of K'un-Lun late, hyper cancel into Iron Rage late, as well; as the super armor on K'un-Lun may eat up the opponent's overeager pokes, the invincibility at the beginning of Iron Rage can do the same thing. When you perform a guarded Rekka sequence into delayed Wall of K'un-Lun, then delayed Iron Rage, you're essentially giving the opposing player multiple chances to make a fool out of themselves. Getting them to eat this even just once or twice can cause them to hesitate up close against your unpredictable Iron Fist from then on, basically.

Chi: Many characters have power-up hypers that grant them special abilities and stat bonuses for five or ten seconds, like Morrigan's Astral Vision or Ryu's Hado Kakusei. In the Chi series of special moves, Iron Fist has three different five-second power-up states, and they don't cost him any meter! Chi is activated with →↓↘, followed by an attack button. The attack button used determines which power-up state Iron Fist enters:

> **Chi L causes Iron Fist's fists to glow red, and it confers a 20% damage boost to him; an ideal time to activate this is just after hitting the target with Dragon's Touch for a crumple, but before continuing the combo**
>
> **Chi M causes Iron Fist's fists to glow blue, and it reduces the damage he takes by 20%. Whenever Iron Fist is far from his opponent, waiting for a chance to get inside, this is the Chi to rely upon if you find a free moment to buff up. This doesn't go quite so far as making Iron Fist's sturdiness equal to Hulk, She-Hulk, Thor, and so on, since most good combos last longer than five seconds, so Iron Fist will be taking full damage sooner rather than later anyway. But to help soak up incidental hits while jockeying for position, you'll never regret taking four-fifths normal damage just for keeping a free buff active.**
>
> **Chi H makes his fists glow yellow-green, and it increases Iron Fist's meter gain by 50%. Note that this only applies to the attacks of Iron Fist himself, and it won't extend to the meter-building assists (Amaterasu, Frank West, or Morrigan—γ). Chi H is most useful in combos; while you can't go wrong with Chi L's 20% damage boost, sometimes Chi H becomes more valuable because it can more or less guarantee that Iron Fist builds enough meter by himself to end a combo with a THC every time. (See *Combo III*.)**

Every version of Chi can absorb one incoming attack from frames 5 to 20. Chi activations can thus be used like parries, essentially: you can simply absorb fireballs from far away, or you can end blocked chain combos or Rekka strings up close by canceling into Chi activations. This technically doesn't do anything and leaves Iron Fist at a disadvantage, but in between the super armor of Wall of K'un-Lun and Chi activations, and Iron Fist's other tricks and tactics designed to combat counter pokes and advancing guard, your opponent should be very hesitant to try to take back momentum with physical strikes while Iron Fist is within close range. If you DO happen to "parry" an incoming strike with Chi, you can visually confirm the hit and cancel into Iron Rage to start a combo!

5

Although Chi L in this situation leads to more damage, it's best to use Chi M when fishing for Chi parries for the obvious reason that if you fail and start getting hit, the penalty is less severe than if you'd used Chi L or H.

6

While Chi activations aren't Rekkas, and the only thing you can cancel Chi with is a hyper combo or X-Factor, you can actually cancel from the first or second Rekka in a sequence directly into Chi. This can be useful for all of Iron Fist's Rekka moves besides Lotus Whip and Dragon Tail, which recover relatively quickly; the rest are all pretty laggy and leave Iron Fist vulnerable on block. Canceling into Chi (almost certainly Chi M) in those situations basically trades your regular recovery period with a period of super armor. Sure, there are still 10 frames after super armor wears off where Iron Fist is vulnerable, but that's STILL safer than simply letting any Rekka except the two fastest ones recover naturally... and even if your adversary waits out the super armor frames, you can still make them nervous if you're willing to blow through whatever they do with point-blank Iron Rage.

7

Like most power-up moves, the effects of Chi still linger even after tagging Iron Fist out. While all three effects still work in this instance, the 20% damage boost of Chi L is the obvious choice for boosting Iron Fist's assist attack.

Dragon Tail: This low-hitting kick is one of Iron Fist's most important attacks. It's one of his only three low moves (along with his launcher and his sweep), and since it's one of his Rekka moves, it can naturally cancel into other Rekkas, so it's vital to work it into your game somehow. It's also his "safest" Rekka after Lotus Whip, but that's only in relative terms; Lotus Whip leaves him neutral if guarded, while Dragon Tail ends up at -4, punishable by 4 frame attacks and throws. As long as Dragon Tail wasn't the third Rekka in a sequence, you can avoid this by canceling to another one—Lotus Whip to be safe, Crescent Heel for a low-high switch, or (if Dragon Tail was the second Rekka) Wall of K'un-Lun (which plows through attacks from foes who think they can mash out their attacks to take back initiative after blocking Iron Fist's first two Rekkas). You can also just cancel Dragon Tail with Chi activation as long as Dragon Tail wasn't the third Rekka.

13 frames of startup for a low attack isn't quick (by contrast, some characters have lows that are active in 4 frames), so you won't usually be using Dragon Tail as an opener on its own. You'll need to either mix it into blockstrings as a counterpoint to Crescent Heel, or mix up between Dragon Tail and Crescent Heel when you've first forced your opponent to block an assist. When opening with Dragon Tail, always cancel to Lotus Fist; this is tantamount to opening a basic attack blockstring with standing or crouching Ⓛ x2, which gives you time to confirm the hits. If your rival blocked Dragon Tail, Lotus Whip gives you time to verify their guard and halt your offense while keeping Iron Fist up close and safe. If Dragon Tail to Lotus Whip is successful, you have time to confirm and then cancel Lotus Whip to Dragon's Touch for a crumple. (See **Combo IV**.)

Crescent Heel: This overhead axe kick is Iron Fist's only OTG-capable move, and it is also his only overhead attack besides air basic attacks. It's a little slower to strike than Dragon Tail and is much less safe if guarded, so take the same contingency measures when it's blocked: cancel to Lotus Fist for safety, Dragon Tail to follow the high hit with a low strike, Wall of K'un-Lun as the third and final Rekka to fish for a super armor hit and wall bounce, or Chi activation to change gears. Using Chi activations point-blank when your Rekkas are guarded becomes more appealing for moves other than Lotus Whip or Dragon Tail, which recover quickly; every other Rekka move has notable, very punishable recovery.

As with Dragon Tail, the speed means that it's most appropriate to use when your opponent is pinned by one of your assists. This allows you to get close and open with either Dragon Tail or Crescent Heel, without worrying about advancing guard pushing Iron Fist away if you open up with one of Iron Fist's basic attacks or other Rekka moves. Cancel into Lotus Whip regardless; if Crescent Heel succeeded in cracking your competitor's guard, the Lotus Whip hit gives you time to confirm and cancel to Dragon's Touch. (See **Combo V**.)

Dragon Tail is also used to OTG enemies; although it's very hard, you have time to dash forward and perform ⇩⇙⇦ + Ⓜ for an OTG after any Iron Fist throw. You can also go for OTG Crescent Heel after any flying screen air combo, after causing a hard knockdown with Dragon's Touch (against an airborne target) or Surging Fist (always applicable). For consistency after you OTG with Crescent Heel midscreen, you'll usually want to cancel to Lotus Whip and then Surging Fist, which puts the foe right back down. In corners, you'll want to OTG with Crescent Heel to Surging Fist to Dragon's Touch, which also ends in another hard knockdown.

Twin Snakes: During this rising double-kick, Iron Fist is never actually considered airborne, although low attacks can whiff under him as he appears to hop slightly (this is similar to a move like Phoenix Wright's ⇨ + Ⓜ overhead; lots of low moves whiff under these attacks, but if your rival cleanly counterhits you, your character gets placed in standing hitstun rather than juggled off the ground). Twin Snakes is primarily a combo tool; while it might seem like it would be good for causing low counter pokes to whiff up close, if you're going for that kind of result, you might as well use Chi or Wall of K'un-Lun, which each can achieve the same effect (punishing the target for hitting a button while Iron Fist is in their face), with better follow-ups and less risk.

Rising Fang: Iron Fist rockets with a kick at head level across most of the playing field. The actual kick is active for only about the length of a dash and a half; you can't use this to hit someone who's far away, even though Iron Fist might make it to them. On hit, this causes a wall bounce and allows for further juggling. If your adversary blocks and Iron Fist doesn't manage to pass through or over them, he's highly punishable; if he somehow manages to soar past them, he's probably safe.

Like Wall of K'un-Lun, this attack is only possible as the third stage in a Rekka sequence. This is virtually Iron Fist's only mobile move at all, but using it requires canceling from other Rekka moves first, meaning that its use must be more premeditated rather than on a whim. The fastest way to execute it for its own sake is to perform Dragon's Touch to Dragon Tail to Rising Fang. The combined startup of each Rekka means that Rising Fang's true startup is about 43 frames. Just before performing Rising Fang to move in, call an assist that occupies lateral space for a while, like Captain America—α, Rocket Raccoon—α, or Sentinel—α. This prevents your challenger from simply hitting Iron Fist, allowing Iron Fist to close the distance from fullscreen.

During active frames, Rising Fang obliterates any low priority projectiles and keeps going. If Rising Fang encounters a medium priority projectile, like Arthur's Golden Armor Lance or M.O.D.O.K.'s Balloon Bomb, both Rising Fang and the projectile nullify each other, though Iron Fist continues toward his destination as normal.

Hyper Combos

Screen	Name	Command	Hits	Damage	Startup	Active	Recovery	Advantage on Hit	Advantage if Guarded	Notes
1	Iron Rage	⇩⇘⇨ + ATK ATK	10~20	244,200~293,300	3+3	46	34	—	-14	Frames 1-11 invincible, last hit wall bounces foe, can be mashed for additional damage
2	Volcanic Roar	⇨⇩⇘ + ATK ATK	25~50	261,700~313,900	9+1	90	38	-17	-35	Beam durability: 25 frames x 1 high priority durability point, can be mashed for additional damage
3	Dragon's Prey (Level 3 Hyper Combo)	⇩⇙⇦ + ATK ATK	1	400,000	10+10	21	38	—	-35	Frames 1-30 invincible, hard knockdown

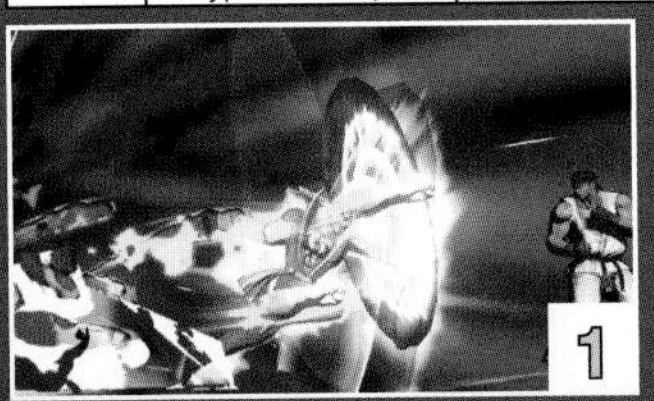

Iron Rage: On its face, this is Iron Fist's scariest attack. Think Spencer's Bionic Lancer with more hits and a wall bounce. Iron Rage has 11 frames of invulnerability and strikes on frame 6; it doesn't quite travel as fast laterally as Spencer's hyper punch, but it travels plenty fast for use at the range you'll want Iron Fist to be: breathing down his foe's neck. The purpose of Iron Rage is to pass through projectiles and punish the thrower at mid range, and to overpower the opponent's attacks at close range: Iron Rage will only lose out to attacks that have longer invulnerability periods, which is a list almost entirely comprised of other hyper combos. The speed and invulnerability mean that you can use Iron Rage on reaction to your competitor's hyper combo freeze, just like Spencer does with Bionic Lancer; the opposing character may have started their hyper combo first, but it doesn't matter. Iron Rage is mashable for more hits and damage.

After the wall bounce of Iron Rage, you can juggle your opponent. Whether you'll need to dash or wavedash to reposition Iron Fist and juggle after Iron Rage depends on where the corner is relative to Iron Fist. Since Iron Fist's Ⓢ launcher cannot juggle, you can't just go for easy-mode relaunches like any other character in this situation, but that doesn't mean you can't make Iron Fist take advantage. The simplest juggle is to catch your adversaries as they fall with ⇦ + Ⓗ Dual Palm, then cancel to Volcanic Roar. For a little more flavor, see **Combo VIII**.

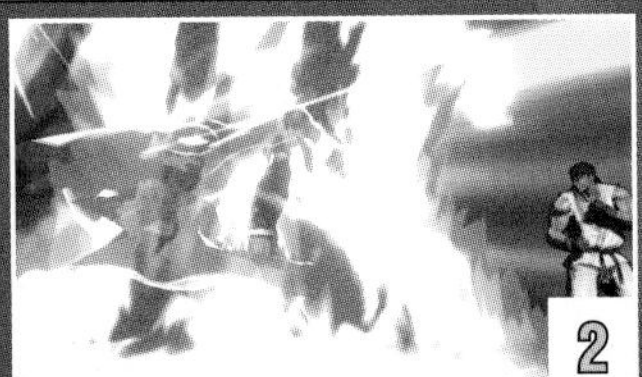

Volcanic Roar: Volcanic Roar is Iron Fist's main combo finisher. The intense column created around Iron Fist by a dragon made of chi energy is actually a big hyper beam, with high priority projectile durability. This ends up eating up any of the opposing projectiles that happen to be around, but by the very nature of this hyper combo (close range, intended to end combos and juggles), this doesn't provide extra utility.

Dragon's Prey: Iron Fist's level 3 hyper combo is a single brutal close range hit that strikes in a circle all around him (it can even hit targets who are behind him or airborne). Like other level 3 hypers, it's immune to damage scaling. The activation of Dragon's Prey erases any currently active Chi buff; this unfortunately prevents Chi L from automatically dragging the damage up from 400,000 to 500,000! Ah, well...

Dragon's Prey functions well in the same role as most lv.3 hypers: ending a long combo with 400,000 points of unscaled damage, assuring a knockout. If you're not going to send a character to dirt with Dragon's Prey, use one (or perhaps both!) of Iron Fist's other hypers to end the combo instead, for far better efficiency.

For many characters, their lv.3 hyper combo serves as their best reversal because of large invulnerability periods; this isn't as important to Iron Fist because he already has Iron Rage for this purpose, which is faster, has much more range, costs less hyper meter, and leads to more damage overall anyway. (**Combo VIII**, which involves Iron Rage as a reversal into Volcanic Roar as a juggle, does the same thing faster, from farther away, while dealing more damage, *and* costing less hyper meter! Sorry, Dragon's Prey.)

Battle Plan

⇦ + Ⓗ and the super armor on Chi can be used to negate the opposing character's projectiles, preventing them from building meter or chipping Iron Fist while buying you time to find an angle to move in.

With the right cover, you can use Rising Fang to easily achieve close range.

The Iron Fist player has two simple but unavoidable challenges to overcome in most matchups. From far away, you must find a way to thread the needle around the opposing team's zoning strategy. Once that's accomplished, you must then find a way around advancing guard up close. And that's it, in a nutshell—that's what Iron Fist is meant to do. His simplicity approaches zen for a character in an *MvC* title, no?

First things first: moving in. The only concession to non-universal movement possessed by Iron Fist apart from Rising Fang and Iron Rage is his wall jump, which can only be done by normal jumping backward against the screen edge. Useful if you happen to be near a corner already with your rival nearby, but not as much when they're at fullscreen distance, hurling every projectile and assist they have between them and Iron Fist.

Iron Fist has a fast wavedash, but his dashing posture is a little unfortunate—he's one of the "widest" characters while dashing, so dashing can sometimes get you into trouble because Iron Fist becomes more vulnerable to cross-ups and projectiles than characters with smaller wavedashing profiles. And, with the exceptions of standing Ⓜ / Ⓗ and crouching Ⓗ, his attacks from a dash have meager range, forcing you to have him dash in completely flush with his foe if you want to use a standard hit confirm opener like crouching Ⓛ x2. This may only take two or three frames longer than attacking earlier in the dash, but that's still plenty of time for an opponent's attack/throw to beat Iron Fist to the proverbial punch.

Jumping or super jumping forward is an option, but as with most characters, this has a high element of risk. Opponents may simply move out from under a super jump and just reset their positioning, or they may actively go for an air throw, which tends to be difficult to avoid because Iron Fist has no air mobility options—basic attacks only. When you do have him take to the air, be ready to fall on adversaries with air ⇨ + Ⓗ, so you have the opportunity for a jump-in attack, a cross-up, or an air throw. Note that by dashing forward *just* before jumping forward, you can transfer some of the momentum from Iron Fist's ground dash to his forward jump, which causes a noticeable and useful improvement on his jumping distance.

You simply have to be patient and move around your competitor's ranged threats and assists by using basic movement. You can bat aside incoming projectiles with ⇦ + Ⓗ Dual Palm or by timing the super armor of Chi activations to absorb projectiles. If you have an assist to back the attempt up, you can also use Rising Fang to move in much more easily from fullscreen! Call your assist, whiff Dragon's Touch into Dragon Tail, then cancel to Rising Fang to accomplish this in the quickest way possible. If there happen to be projectiles in the way, the Rising Fang kick can take care of them. Make sure Chi M is active first if you'd like a little extra security blanket (the Security Blanket of K'un-Lun?), and remember that trying this without an assist backing up Iron Fist is suicide.

Fighting aggressive opponents won't be a problem; they'll come to you. Against zoning characters, you'll just have to dodge their projectiles while forging a way in. Adversaries may also engage in outright runaway, however. The alpha example is Trish, who can airdash, fly, and set traps and fire projectiles all from super jump height, where Iron Fist is least threatening. Against characters who try to spend time up there, looking to stall against Iron Fist, remember that his Volcanic Roar hyper combo extends all the way to the ceiling—have him wavedash under the flying or running foe and activate Volcanic Roar to punish their cowardice. Against rivals trying to jump away at normal jump height, keep Iron Fist's air throw firmly in mind. He's no Magneto for landing it—he has to play more like She-Hulk—but Iron Fist has one of the most damaging combos off an air throw (or a ground throw, for that matter) in the game. After any throw, OTG with Crescent Heel as soon as possible to start a combo that deals over 600,000 damage! (See **Combo VII**.)

Once you're in close, your approach should be dictated by Iron Fist's position. In the case of using Rising Fang while covered by an assist to bully your way in, you'll usually end up with Iron Fist on the other side of his rival while they're forced to guard the end of the assist from behind. This presents an ideal opportunity to strike with either Dragon Tail or Crescent Heel, for either a low or high hit.

If you pushed your way into close range by patiently moving Iron Fist forward, your opponent won't necessarily already be pinned with an assist. In this case, Crescent Heel and Dragon Tail both make poor openers. Instead, make Iron Fist dash toward the adversary while poking with basic attacks chains. If you are close enough to have him dash all the way into point-blank range, open up with standing or crouching Ⓛ x2. Iron Fist's light attacks have poor range by design, so if you're too far for that, dash in with standing Ⓜ, Ⓗ instead.

After either basic attack double-tap, you'll have time to verify the result. A hit in either case can lead directly into **Combo I, II,** or **III**. If light attacks are guarded, Iron Fist remains positioned right next to the opposing character, but you shouldn't just keep right on chaining blocked basic attacks because that only insures that Iron Fist is going to get pushed away with advancing guard. Go for a throw, or pause and go for crouching Ⓛ x2 again, which can counterhit your opponent's attempts to take back momentum with their own close-range pokes. You need to frequently stagger light basic attacks when rushing up close for this exact purpose; between delayed chain attacks and Rekka specials, Chi activations, and the threat of random/reactionary Iron Rage, you want your competitor

When you chain to blocked ⇨ + Ⓗ...

...call an assist and jump cancel over your target for a cross-up opportunity.

discouraged from both using advancing guard and trying to counter poke Iron Fist. They should basically be taught not to press buttons when you are pressuring them with Iron Fist. The solution to Iron Fist is to keep him away; not to try beating him at his own game!

In the case of having dash-in standing Ⓜ, Ⓗ guarded, chain to crouching Ⓗ, ⇨ + Ⓗ, then jump cancel. You want to work in sweeps to your blockstrings to dissuade opponents from just holding up-back once they block Iron Fist's opening strike; if they do this, hoping to jump away as soon as possible, the sweep catches them, and ⇨ + Ⓗ Quick Kick successfully combos. On hit or block, the jump cancel after Quick Kick allows for follow-ups; on hit, strike with air Ⓗ at the peak of Iron Fist's jump, then wait as long as possible before juggling with air Ⓢ on the way down. Upon landing, if you spaced this correctly, standing Ⓜ catches the target for continued juggling. If Quick Kick is guarded, the forward jump cancel puts Iron Fist right over their heads. Call your pinning assist during Quick Kick, then either cross up with air Ⓗ or empty jump to the other side with no attack and land, then go for sweep or Dragon Tail. These low attacks are normally way, way too slow to work after an empty jump, which is why you must call an assist that occupies the adversary from behind. If your opponent uses advancing guard against Quick Kick, this prevents the cross-up attempt, but the jump cancel at least allows Iron Fist to regain some of the lost space.

Without a decent pinning assist to facilitate jumping over his challenger after guarded Quick Kick (or after fullscreen Rising Fang), Iron Fist is really susceptible to being pushblocked, so you'll have to use staggered Ⓛ attacks, Ⓛ ticks into throw attempts, and occasional point-blank Chi activations (fishing for a move you can absorb before canceling to Iron Rage) to discourage advancing guard. Delayed chains and super armor moves can work against advancing guard simply because advancing guard use requires the opponent to push two attack buttons; if you bait them into trying this when you *aren't actually attacking,* they'll produce a point-blank Ⓜ or Ⓗ attack instead (or a dash; whoops!), which almost certainly loses out to a delayed chain combo starting with Ⓛ. Strongly resist the temptation to use Rekka sequences as blockstrings on purpose, unless you've already conditioned your competitor to be terrified of trying to use advancing guard. In this case, mixing in Dragon Tail or Crescent Heel into blocked Rekka sequences becomes valuable. But if you just dash in, perform a chain combo, then perform a Rekka sequence hoping for the best, you're just going to give up the ground you gained by being pushblocked nine times out of ten.

Once your opponent is conditioned against spamming advancing guard every time they block, ⇦ + Ⓗ Dual Palm starts to really shine. This attack, normally used to punch projectiles into dust from long range, leaves Iron Fist at +2 even if guarded, and it doesn't push him away from the opposing character whatsoever. This gives you an alternative to ending chains with Quick Kick into a jump cancel; you can end chains with delayed Dual Palm and stay on the same side, ready to immediately go for Ⓛ attacks or a throw. If the delayed Dual Palm manages to coax your adversary into getting hit, you have ages to verify the hit and chain to Ⓢ for a launcher, or to cancel into Rekkas for a ground combo.

Iron Fist doesn't have an default opening low attack like most characters, so opening enemies up requires delayed chain cancels, which may coerce opponents to hit buttons prematurely...

... allowing a staggered attack to counterhit!

Iron Fist is particularly intriguing as an X-Factor anchor. As both teams dwindle down to their last one or two members, the opponent naturally loses some of their ranged capability and stability; if it happens to end up in a one-on-one fight, their ability to keep Iron Fist out is effectively eliminated. Meanwhile, Iron Fist is actually an above-average character in terms of vitality, and Chi M only enhances that. He is perfectly suited to a last-man-standing, down-and-dirty brawl, especially considering the brinksmanship you can levy in activating X-Factor in the first place.

For example, although Rising Fang executed from fullscreen without an assist covering it is folly, if you have X-Factor left, you can actually turn this into a brutal, virtually unguardable cross-up. Whiff Dragon's Touch to Dragon Tail fullscreen, cancel to Rising Fang, then activate X-Factor in the air *just* as Iron Fist is passing right over the opposing character's head. Iron Fist ends up falling straight down right over the foe, and air ⇨ + Ⓗ performed here can both function as an air throw if they jump or a cross-up if they don't. Rising Fang travels so fast laterally that it's difficult to even pick which side Iron Fist ends up on consistently, and if you don't know which side you'll be on, your competitor sure doesn't. Of course, a successful cross-up air Ⓗ hit just after activating higher levels of X-Factor should lead to a dusted opposing character, guaranteed. (See **Combo IX**.)

In Iron Rage, Iron Fist has another perfect means of activating X-Factor. Simply put, just get close to the target and "randomly" perform Iron Rage when you have a feeling they'll try to do something. If it hits, fantastic: keep the combo going after the wall bounce (**Combo VIII**) and save your X-Factor; if your foe blocks, X-Factor cancel during the last hit to keep Iron Fist from getting punished severely.

COMBO USAGE

I. ST. Ⓜ, Ⓗ, → + Ⓗ CANCEL ↓↘→ + Ⓛ CANCEL ↓↘→ + Ⓜ CANCEL →↓↘ + Ⓛ, Ⓢ CANCEL FORWARD SUPER JUMP, AIR Ⓜ, Ⓜ, Ⓗ, Ⓢ, LAND, FORWARD DASH, ↓↙← + Ⓜ OTG CANCEL ↓↘→ + Ⓛ CANCEL ↓↙← + Ⓗ CANCEL →↓↘ + ATK ATK (MASH ATK)

743,200 damage, 4% meter loss

Iron Fist combos are easier than they might look at first, but you have to be careful. It's easy to accidentally get Chi activations instead of Rekka specials if you're not controlled with your motions; it's also easy to cause Chi activation instead of a Rekka after → + Ⓗ. Insert a brief pause after → + Ⓗ and be sure to let the controller register a neutral input before you perform ↓↘→ to avoid the game reading the whole thing as →↓↘; the same advice holds true when performing Rekkas back-to-back. Don't mash out ↓↘→ inputs the way one might with Rolento, Fei-Long, or Yang (which just guarantees an accidental Chi activation); instead, perform Rekkas deliberately with an intentional, subtle gap between the motion of each. Master staying calm with these combos so you won't spazz out and mess up when you actually start one up in the heat of battle. Once you're solid on actually executing Rekkas in the proper places without causing errant Chi activations, it's just a matter of going through the motions confidently and nimbly.

You may add crouching or standing Ⓛ x 2 to the beginning of this combo to increase its offensive flexibility. This lowers the max damage to 661,200, but if your opponent is guarding, the remainder of the combo can be halted after these light attacks have been blocked, which keeps Iron Fist directly next to his opponent and ready to fish for a hit some other way.

II. ST. Ⓜ, Ⓗ, → + Ⓗ CANCEL ↓↘→ + Ⓛ CANCEL ↓↘→ + Ⓜ CANCEL →↓↘ + Ⓛ, ST. Ⓗ, CR. Ⓗ, → + Ⓗ CANCEL FORWARD JUMP, LATE AIR Ⓗ, DELAYED Ⓢ, LAND, ST. Ⓜ, Ⓗ, ← + Ⓗ CANCEL ↓↙← + Ⓛ CANCEL ↓↘→ + Ⓛ CANCEL ↓↘→ + Ⓗ, FORWARD DASH, ↓↙← + Ⓜ OTG CANCEL ↓↘→ + Ⓗ CANCEL ↓↘→ + Ⓜ CANCEL {→↓↘ + ATK ATK (MASH ATK)} OR {↓↘→ + ATK ATK (MASH ATK), ← + Ⓗ CANCEL →↓↘ + ATK ATK (MASH ATK)}

765,400~908,400 damage, 47% meter gain or 43% meter loss (both variations are self-sufficient for the first hyper combo used)

This devastating combo in all its glory carries your adversary from one end of the screen to another, cornering them instantly from any position. It also builds roughly one and a half bars of meter on its own, meaning that you only need to start with about half a meter in order to land the second max-damage variation, following up Iron Rage with Volcanic Roar. Though this combo does cause a wide variety of hit and juggle states, you can lead in with a jump attack instead without hitstun decay affecting it.

Opening with crouching Ⓛ x 2 increases flexibility, but it lowers max damage to 835,200.

III. ST. Ⓜ, Ⓗ, → + Ⓗ CANCEL ↓↘→ + Ⓛ CANCEL ↓↘→ + Ⓜ CANCEL →↓↘ + Ⓗ, ST. Ⓗ, CR. Ⓗ, → + Ⓗ CANCEL FORWARD JUMP, LATE AIR Ⓗ, DELAYED Ⓢ, LAND, ST. Ⓜ, Ⓗ, ← + Ⓗ CANCEL ↓↙← + Ⓛ CANCEL ↓↘→ + Ⓛ CANCEL ↓↘→ + Ⓗ, FORWARD DASH, ↓↙← + Ⓜ OTG CANCEL ↓↙← + Ⓗ CANCEL ↓↙← + Ⓢ, BACK OUT OF THE CORNER, ← + Ⓗ CANCEL ↓↙← + Ⓛ CANCEL ↓↘→ + Ⓗ CANCEL ↓↘→ + Ⓜ CANCEL →↓↘ + ATK ATK (MASH ATK)

745,700 damage, 103% meter gain (self sufficient for Volcanic Roar ender)

This slight deviation from **Combo II** is designed to build as much meter as possible. Even after canceling into Volcanic Roar, you'll *still* have one entire bar of hyper meter left over! This is the *perfect* combo to go for when you want to THC into another teammate for huge damage.

IV. ↓↙← + Ⓛ CANCEL ↓↘→ + Ⓛ CANCEL ↓↘→ + Ⓜ, →↓↘ + Ⓛ, ST. Ⓗ, CR. Ⓗ, → + Ⓗ CANCEL FORWARD JUMP, LATE AIR Ⓗ, DELAYED Ⓢ, LAND, ST. Ⓜ, Ⓗ, ← + Ⓗ CANCEL ↓↙← + Ⓛ CANCEL ↓↘→ + Ⓛ CANCEL ↓↘→ + Ⓗ, FORWARD DASH, ↓↙← + Ⓜ OTG CANCEL ↓↘→ + Ⓗ CANCEL ↓↘→ + Ⓜ CANCEL {→↓↘ + ATK ATK (MASH ATK)} OR {↓↘→ + ATK ATK (MASH ATK), ← + Ⓗ CANCEL →↓↘ + ATK ATK (MASH ATK)}

763,700~907,400 damage, 34% meter gain or 60% meter loss

This is Iron Fist's most damaging low combo option, but the opening attack is fairly slow and unwieldy. Pin your opponent with an assist first for max effectiveness. You can't cancel ↓↘→ + Ⓜ into →↓↘ + Ⓛ in this situation, but you don't need to. There's enough time to buff up with Chi after Dragon's Touch recovers and still hit the target.

When ↓↙← + Ⓛ, ↓↘→ + Ⓛ is guarded, you can cancel into either ↓↙← + Ⓛ or ↓↙← + Ⓜ to stage a basic low/high mix-up. A successful hit in either case can be hit confirmed into ↓↘→ + ATK ATK, but Iron Fist is left vulnerable if your foe blocks. When in doubt, stop at ↓↘→ + Ⓛ when guarded.

COMBO APPENDIX

GENERAL EXECUTION TIPS

Be precise when performing repeated ↓↘→ motions to avoid accidental Chi activations in place of Rekka specials

Also take care when canceling from → + Ⓗ into Rekka specials for the same reason; insert a slight pause between → + Ⓗ and ↓↘→ to avoid registering →↓↘

Against smaller characters, replace standing Ⓗ, crouching Ⓗ, → + Ⓗ after a successful Dragon's Touch with crouching Ⓗ, → + Ⓗ

AS IRON FIST COMES IN: AIR Ⓜ, Ⓜ, Ⓢ, LAND, FORWARD DASH, ↓↙← + Ⓜ CANCEL ↓↙← + Ⓛ CANCEL ↓↘→ + Ⓗ CANCEL ↓↘→ + ATK ATK (MASH ATK), ← + Ⓗ CANCEL →↓↘ + ATK ATK (MASH ATK)

Notes	Damage
⇧ + Ⓢ or ⇨ + Ⓢ or ⇩ + Ⓢ TAC to Iron Fist	Varies based on damage scaling

VI. ↓↙← + (M) CANCEL ⇨ ↓↘→ + (L) CANCEL ⇨ ↓↙← + (S), WAVEDASH FORWARD TWICE, CR. (M), ST. (H), CR. (H), → + (H) CANCEL ⇨ ↓↘→ + (L) CANCEL ⇨ ↓↙← + (H) CANCEL ⇨ →↓↘ + (L) CANCEL ⇨ →↓↘ + (ATK)(ATK) (MASH (ATK))

701,700 damage, 37% meter loss

This is the high-hitting counterpart to the previous combo, and it's one of the few combos that uses Rising Fang effectively. After ↓↙← + (H), you must cancel into →↓↘ + (L) just as the second hit connects, then kara-cancel the power-up immediately into →↓↘ + (ATK)(ATK). This is there only to gain the attack buff before the juggle.

VII. (MUST BE WITHIN ¾ OF PLAYING FIELD DISTANCE TO CORNER OR CLOSER) CR. (H), → + (H) CANCEL ⇨ FORWARD JUMP, LATE AIR (H), DELAYED (S), LAND, ST. (M), ST. (H), ← + (H) CANCEL ⇨ ↓↙← + (L) CANCEL ⇨ ↓↘→ + (L) CANCEL ⇨ ↓↘→ + (H), FORWARD DASH, ↓↙← + (M) OTG CANCEL ⇨ ↓↘→ + (H) CANCEL ⇨ ↓↘→ + (M) CANCEL ⇨ {→↓↘ + (ATK)(ATK) (MASH (ATK)) OR {↓↘→ + (ATK)(ATK) (MASH (ATK)), ← + (H) CANCEL ⇨ →↓↘ + (ATK)(ATK) (MASH (ATK))}

667,400~811,200 damage, 22~106% meter loss

The positioning requirement is minimal; for this combo to fail, Iron Fist has to be cornered, or nearly cornered at the beginning, to be too far for the OTG follow-up. If you think he is too far from his competitor, cancel the first ↓↘→ + (H) into ↓↘→ + (ATK)(ATK), then proceed with the remainder of the combo from there.

VIII. FRONT OR BACK THROW OR FRONT AIR THROW, ↓↙← + (M) CANCEL ⇨ ↓↘→ + (L) CANCEL ⇨ ↓↘→ + (H) CANCEL ⇨ ↓↘→ + (ATK)(ATK) (MASH (ATK)), FORWARD DASH, CR. (H), → + (H) CANCEL ⇨ ↓↘→ + (L) CANCEL ⇨ ↓↙← + (H) CANCEL ⇨ →↓↘ + (L) CANCEL ⇨ →↓↘ + (ATK)(ATK) (MASH (ATK))

643,900 damage, 142% meter loss

From the air throw, simply land and perform ↓↙← + (M) to start the combo. From the ground throw, you must input a dash with (ATK)(ATK) as soon as you're able, and then ↓↙← + (M) immediately after. This must all be done in one smooth motion as fast as possible, or else you'll miss.

VIIII. ↓↘→ + (ATK)(ATK) (MASH (ATK)), WAVEDASH FORWARD TWICE, ST. (M), (H), ← + (H) CANCEL ⇨ ↓↙← + (L) CANCEL ⇨ ↓↘→ + (L) CANCEL ⇨ ↓↘→ + (H), FORWARD DASH, ↓↙← + (M) OTG CANCEL ⇨ ↓↘→ + (H) CANCEL ⇨ ↓↘→ + (S) CANCEL ⇨ →↓↘ + (ATK)(ATK) (MASH (ATK))

574,200 damage, 137% meter loss

Here's a combo starting off of the invincible Iron Rage hyper combo. You should primarily use this one to punish projectiles or to intimidate opponents up close. THC to a safe hyper combo if Iron Rage is guarded.

IX. ST. (M), (H), → + (H) CANCEL ⇨ ↓↘→ + (L) CANCEL ⇨ ↓↘→ + (M) CANCEL ⇨ →↓↘ + (L) CANCEL ⇨ X-FACTOR, ST. (H), CR. (H), → + (H) CANCEL ⇨ FORWARD JUMP, LATE AIR (H), DELAYED (S), LAND, ST. (H), ← + (H) CANCEL ⇨ ↓↙← + (L) CANCEL ⇨ ↓↘→ + (L) CANCEL ⇨ ↓↘→ + (H), FORWARD DASH, ↓↙← + (M) OTG CANCEL ⇨ ↓↙← + (H) CANCEL ⇨ ↓↙← + (S), BACK OUT OF THE CORNER, ← + (H) CANCEL ⇨ ↓↙← + (L) CANCEL ⇨ ↓↘→ + (H) CANCEL ⇨ ↓↘→ + (S)

1,116,900~1,204,500 damage, 215~310% meter gain

This is a no-meter X-Factor combo where Chi L is stacked with the X-Factor damage boost for devastating results. If you're in X-Factor level 1 and you're certain the last hit will not K.O. your rival, hyper cancel the very last command into →↓↘ + (ATK)(ATK). At X-Factor level 2 and 3, replace →↓↘ + (L) with →↓↘ + (H); any further damage boosts at those levels is usually unnecessary, and you should focus on netting additional hyper combo meter instead.

ADVANCED TACTICS

GET LOW

In addition to restraining yourself from using Rekkas until the deck is already stacked in your favor, don't make a habit out of dashing in with a naked launcher, even though it is a low attack and consequently works at least occasionally. That's because Iron Fist is left at a punishable disadvantage when his foes guard (S), and guarded launchers can't be canceled into anything else as a contingency plan. If your challenger has an attack that's active in 5 frames or less, or if they just feel like throwing you, you're going to eat it. Instead, when you want to threaten low right off the bat, dash in with the tip of crouching (H), chain to → + (H) Quick Kick, then jump cancel Quick Kick. There's no hit confirmation involved; just do it. Crouching (H) and Quick Kick are both just as vulnerable when guarded as (S), but you're skipping over that by jump canceling.

If your competitor happens to block and use advancing guard against crouching (H), Iron Fist gets pushed back out, but advancing guard against all but the slowest single attacks is a fluke and should not discourage you—an adversary pushblocking against single attacks is a target who is ripe for walking right into your delayed chain frame traps. The more they're doing this, the more often they'll mash (ATK) inputs for advancing guard when you're either not doing anything or intentionally delaying attacks fishing for a counterhit. When you *do* get pushed out, accept that the situation is reset and cancel your whiffed → + (H) into a Chi power-up, then go about patiently looking for a way inside again.

If they happen to block crouching (H) and then use advancing guard on reaction to Quick Kick, at least you remain safe and can have Iron Fist gain back a little bit of ground with the forward jump cancel. If they *don't* use advancing guard at all, your forward jump creates the *perfect* cross-up shot—call an assist during the jump cancel, then fall on the other side of them with air (H)!

Similar to Doctor Strange, Iron Fist's lack of quick low attacks forces a player to get creative in order to give an opponent a reason to block low.

Air (H) can be performed *extremely* late and still hit overhead as a cross-up before Iron Fist lands.

In situations where your opponent is still managing to guard properly even after the cross-up, your options get better depending on whether you did indeed pin them with an assist from the back before jumping over them. Assists called from the first side like Dante—α, Chun-Li—γ, Phoenix Wright—β, Sentinel—α, and Rocket Raccoon—α can turn your prey into a brief captive audience, with Iron Fist on one side of the opposing character, and his assist on the other. This is the ideal time to mix your opponent up between cross-up air (H) or an empty jump over them, followed by either a naked Dragon Tail or Crescent Heel. These are Iron Fist's two most important "Rekka" attacks. ↓↙← + (L) Tail hits low, while ↓↙← + (M) Heel hits high, and there is not enough time for humans to consistently tell the difference between them on short notice, especially while their character is pinned from behind by one of Iron Fist's partners.

While challengers won't be able to react consistently by blocking either Dragon Tail or Crescent Heel correctly, these attacks aren't as fast as they look, and Iron Fist can easily be hit or thrown out of the startup periods at close range. That's why pinning with an assist first is so important to making this mix-up truly work. Just trying to dash in with ↓↙← + (L) (or a launcher) won't get you anywhere… but then, that's what dashing in with crouching (H), → + (H) is for!

NEW

NOVA

"I'M THE ONLY GUARDIAN THE GALAXY NEEDS."

REAL NAME

Richard Rider

OCCUPATION

Soldier, Adventurer

ABILITIES

In addition to superhuman strength and durability, he can also fly through space at supersonic speeds. He can also absorb and reflect energy attacks.

WEAPONS

None

PROFILE

Chosen by the dying alien Rhomann Dey to receive his Nova Corps powers, Richard began his new life as a super hero. His battles take him throughout the universe, fighting evil wherever he is needed.

FIRST APPEARANCE

Nova #1 (1976)

2	INTELLIGENCE
7	STRENGTH
7	SPEED
7	STAMINA
5	ENERGY PROJECTION
4	FIGHTING ABILITY

*This is biographical, and does not represent an evaluation of the in-game combat potential of this hero.

ALTERNATE COSTUMES

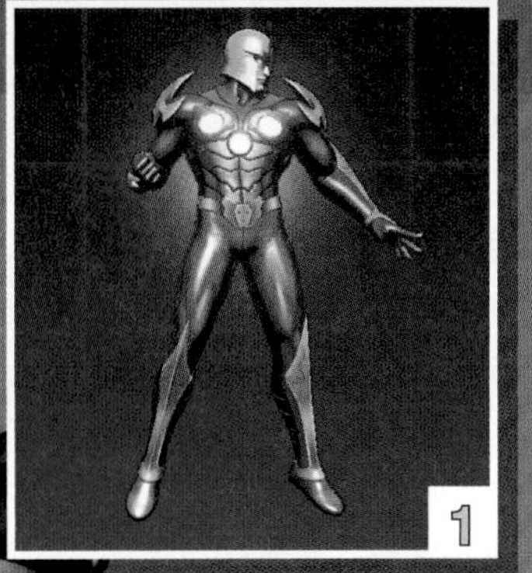

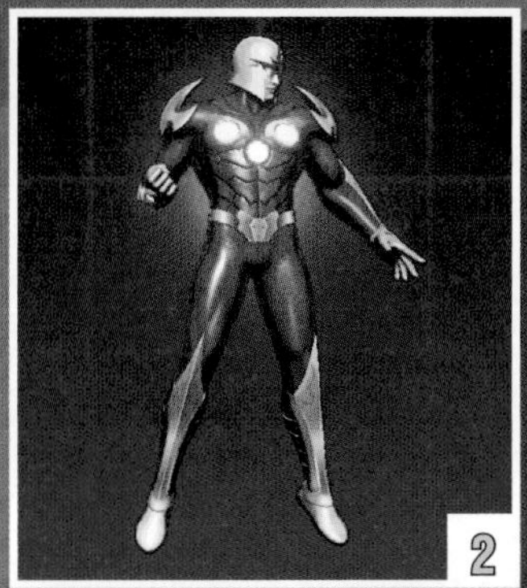

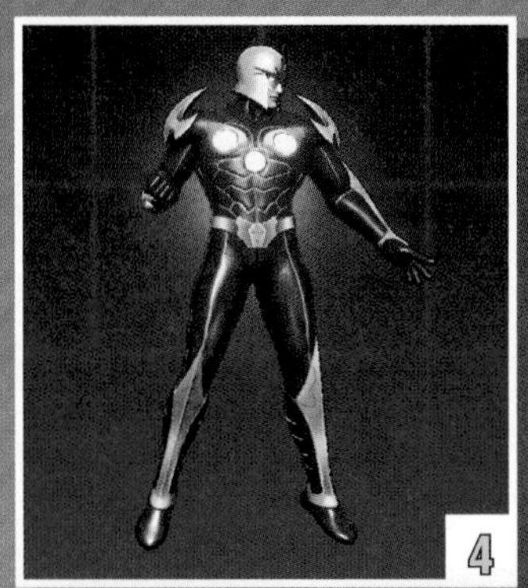

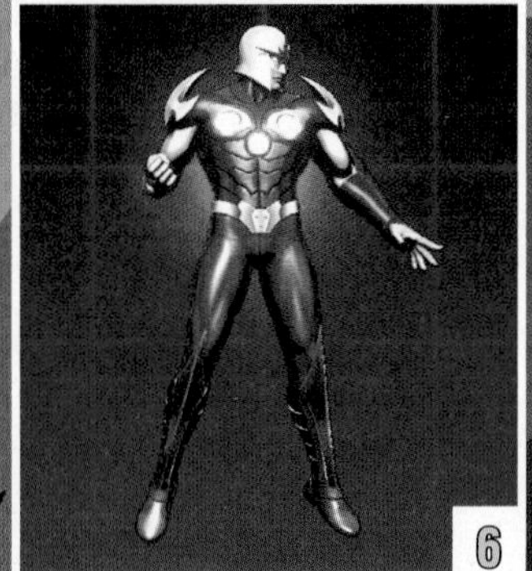

Overview

Vitality	900,000
Chain Combo Archetype	Marvel Series

X-Factor Boost	Damage	Speed
Level 1 (3 teammates remaining)	130%	110%
Level 2 (2 teammates remaining)	150%	120%
Level 3 (1 teammate remaining)	170%	130%

Your main goal with Nova is to simply land a hit, with a secondary goal of cornering your opponent. In certain match-ups (against melee-heavy characters), you don't need to approach with Nova; you simply need to lure the opposing character in by raining Energy Javelins while hiding behind Gravimetric Pulse H.

Why the dual goal?

- **Nova deals a massive amount of damage. His combos easily inflict over 600,000 damage, both midscreen and in the corner**
- **Super Nova, the hyper combo typically used to end combos, causes a hard knockdown and is easy to THC from. Adding a THC to Nova's already damaging combos is likely to K.O. his competitor**

How is this goal achieved?

- **By luring opponents near with Energy Javelins with the cover of Gravimetric Pulse H**
- **By utilizing Nova's strong midscreen game to take advantage of combo opportunities**
- **By forcing rivals into the corner with Nova's forward-moving attacks such as crouching Ⓜ, Centurion Rush, and Nova Strike**

Attack Set

Standing Basic Attacks

Screen	Command	Hits	Damage	Meter Gain	Startup	Active	Recovery	Advantage on Hit	Advantage if Guarded	Notes
1	Standing L	1	55,000	440	5	3	13	-1	-3	Rapid fire, chains to crouching L
2	Standing M	1	80,000	640	9	3	17	0	-2	—
3	Standing H	1	85,000	680	11	3	24	-2	-4	—

Crouching Basic Attacks

Screen	Command	Hits	Damage	Meter Gain	Startup	Active	Recovery	Advantage on Hit	Advantage if Guarded	Notes
1	Crouching L	1	50,000	400	6	3	12	0	-2	Chains to standing L
2	Crouching M	1	75,000	600	11	8	20	-8	-10	Low attack
3	Crouching H	1	80,000	640	13	3	23	—	-3	Low attack, knocks down

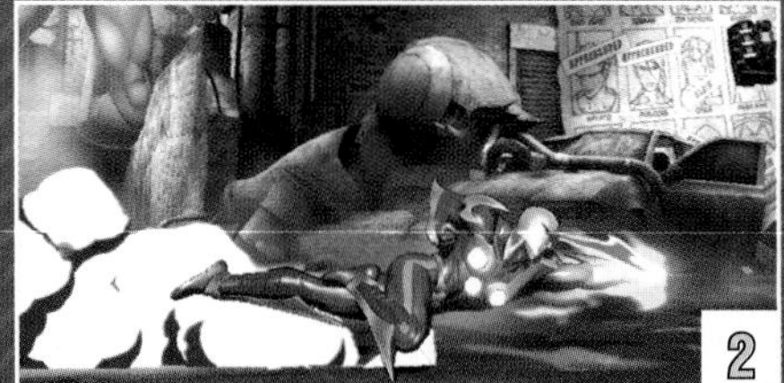

Ground Special Attack—Launcher

Screen	Command	Hits	Damage	Meter Gain	Startup	Active	Recovery	Advantage on Hit	Advantage if Guarded	Notes
1	S (while standing or crouching)	1	100,000	800	15	4	26	—	-7	Launcher, not special- or hyper combo-cancelable

Air Basic Attacks

Screen	Command	Hits	Damage	Meter Gain	Startup	Active	Recovery	Advantage on Hit	Advantage if Guarded	Notes
1	Air L	1	55,000	440	5	2	16	+13	+11	Overhead attack
2	Air M	1	75,000	600	8	4	18	+17	+15	Overhead attack
3	Air H	1	90,000	720	10	6	25	+20	+18	Overhead attack

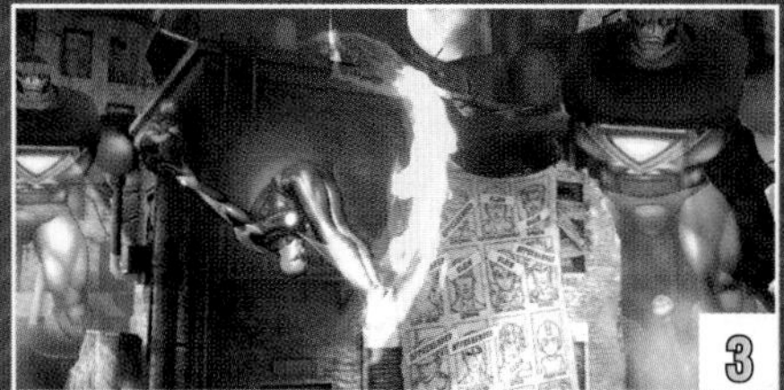

Air Special Attacks—Flying Screen and Air Exchange

Air Ⓢ causes a hard knockdown when used in a launcher combo (this is sometimes called flying screen). When used outside of a launcher combo, air Ⓢ behaves mostly like another basic attack. Air exchange attacks, performed by inputting a direction plus Ⓢ, are only possible during a launcher combo. Exchange hits initiate team aerial combos by tagging in the next available character to continue the air combo.

Screen	Command	Hits	Damage	Meter Gain	Startup	Active	Recovery	Advantage on Hit	Advantage if Guarded	Notes
1	Air Ⓢ	1	40,000	320	22	Until grounded	30	—	-9	Causes hard knockdown if used in launcher combo, overhead attack
2	Air ⇧ + Ⓢ (during launcher combo)	2	105,00	880	10	3	28	—	—	Tags in next available ally while lofting opponent upward
3	Air ⇨ or ⇦ + Ⓢ (during launcher combo)	2	95,000	800	10	3	28	—	—	Tags in next available ally while causing wall bounce, steals 1 hyper meter from foe
4	Air ⇩ + Ⓢ (during launcher combo)	2	95,000	800	10	3	28	—	—	Tags in next available ally while causing ground bounce, generates 1 hyper meter

1

2

3

4

Command Attacks

Command attacks resemble basic attacks but have different chaining and canceling properties. It's usually possible to chain *into* a command attack from basic attacks, but most command attacks cannot be chained from or canceled themselves.

Screen	Name	Command	Hits	Damage	Meter Gain	Startup	Active	Recovery	Advantage on Hit	Advantage if Guarded	Notes
1	Nova Slam	⇨ + Ⓗ	24	100,000	800	24	4	24	—	-5	Overhead attack, ground bounces rival, OTG-capable

1

Throws

Throws are for snagging passive or blocking opponents. Since throws are active so quickly, you can also use them to preemptively toss opposing characters out of their offense. Combos are usually possible after throws, one way or another.

Screen	Command	Hits	Damage	Meter Gain	Startup	Active	Notes
1	⇨ + Ⓗ (ground)	1	80,000	800	1	1	Hard knockdown
	⇦ + Ⓗ (ground)	1	80,000	800	1	1	Hard knockdown
2	⇨ + Ⓗ (air)	1	80,000	800	1	1	Hard knockdown
	⇦ + Ⓗ (air)	1	80,000	800	1	1	Hard knockdown

1

2

NOVA

NEW

As a Partner—Crossover Assists

Screen	Type	P1+P2 Crossover Combination Hyper Combo	Description	Hits	Damage	Meter Gain	Startup	Active	Recovery (this crossover assist)	Recovery (other partner)	Notes
1	Nova—α	Gravimetric Blaster	Gravimetric Pulse H	3	94,800	840	52	—	118	88	Beam durability: 3 frames x 3 low priority durability points, lasts for 180 frames
2	Nova—β	Gravimetric Blaster	Centurion Rush M	1	100,000	800	52	13	106	76	Overhead attack
3	Nova—γ	Gravimetric Blaster	Centurion Rush L	3	97,400	880	47	13	116	86	Wall bounces foe

1

2

3

Nova has three useful crossover assists that can suit any team configuration. Nova—α Gravimetric Pulse creates an energy shield that stays on screen for 180 frames. The drawback to this crossover assist is that it automatically depletes any red vitality Nova might have while on the sidelines. Nova—β Centurion Rush is one of the few overhead crossover assists in the game and is useful for any character's offense. Nova—γ Nova Strike is a quick attack that wall bounces and is useful for combos. However, Nova Strike has no projectile immunity: Nova can be interrupted by any projectiles during the attack.

Snap Back

Screen	Command	Hits	Damage	Meter Gain	Startup	Active	Recovery	Advantage on Hit	Advantage if Guarded
1	↓↘→ + P1 or P2	1	50,000	500 (-1 hyper meter bar)	2	3	19	—	+1
Notes									
On hit, snap back forces the opposing point character to be replaced by an assist. Opposing assist calls or tag outs are also locked out for 4 seconds									

1

Special Moves

Screen	Name	Command	Hits	Damage	Meter Gain	Startup	Active	Recovery	Advantage on Hit	Advantage if Guarded	Notes
1	Gravimetric Pulse L (in air OK)	↓↘→ + L	1	90,000	720	16	15	21	-5	-7	Projectile has 5 low priority durability points
	Gravimetric Pulse L (in air OK) (with less than 200,000 red life)	↓↘→ + L	3	135,400	1200	16	15	21	+7	+5	Depletes Nova's red life, beam durability: 3 frames x 5 low priority durability points
	Gravimetric Pulse L (in air OK) (with at least 200,000 red life)	↓↘→ + L	5	204,600	2000	26	—	29	+26	+7	Depletes Nova's red life, beam durability: 5 frames x 5 low priority durability points
2	Gravimetric Pulse M (in air OK)	↓↘→ + M	1	90,000	720	16	15	21	-3	-5	Projectile has 5 low priority durability points
	Gravimetric Pulse M (in air OK) (with less than 200,000 red life)	↓↘→ + M	3	135,400	1200	16	15	21	+5	-2	Depletes Nova's red life, beam durability: 3 frames x 5 low priority durability points
	Gravimetric Pulse M (in air OK) (with at least 200,000 red life)	↓↘→ + M	5	204,600	2000	26	—	29	+26	+1	Depletes Nova's red life, beam durability: 5 frames x 5 low priority durability points
3	Gravimetric Pulse H (in air OK)	↓↘→ + H	3	94,800	840	26	—	29	+1	-1	Beam durability: 3 frames x 3 low priority durability points, lasts 180 frames
4	Gravimetric Pulse H (in air OK) (with less than 200,000 red life)	↓↘→ + H	4	120,300	1120	26	—	29	+1	-1	Depletes Nova's red life, beam durability: 4 frames x 3 low priority durability points, lasts 180 frames, allows placement of a second weaker Gravimetric Pulse H
5	Gravimetric Pulse H (in air OK) (with at least 200,000 red life)	↓↘→ + H	5	143,200	1400	26	—	29	+25	+1	Depletes Nova's red life, beam durability: 5 frames x 3 low priority durability points, lasts 300 frames, allows placement of second weaker Gravimetric Pulse H
6	Centurion Rush L	→↓↘ + L	1	90,000	720	18	15	20	—	-12	OTG-capable, low attack, knocks down
7	Centurion Rush M	→↓↘ + M	1	100,000	800	28	13	15	-3	-5	Overhead attack, ground bounces airborne adversaries
8	Centurion Rush H	→↓↘ + H	3	35,000 x 2 + 80,000	280 x 2 + 640	23	10(15)6	30	—	-13	Launcher, frames 22-46 super armor

Special Moves continued

Screen	Name	Command	Hits	Damage	Meter Gain	Startup	Active	Recovery	Advantage on Hit	Advantage if Guarded	Notes
9	Nova Strike L (in air OK)	↓↙← + L	1	75,000	600	18	8	25	—	-10	Knocks down
	Nova Strike M (in air OK)	↓↙← + M	3	97,400	880	23	16	25	—	-9	Wall bounces foe
	Nova Strike H (in air OK)	↓↙← + H	1	110,000	880	30	20	16 (air: 15)	—	-13 (air: -12)	Crumples opponent, wall bounces airborne competitors
10	Flight (in air OK)	↓↙← + S	—	—	—	10	—	—	—	—	Lasts 110 frames
11	Energy Javelin	ATK + S	1	70,000	560	26	—	24	—	—	OTG-capable, projectile has 5 low priority durability points

1

2

Gravimetric Pulse L & M: With this move, Nova fires a close range blast of energy. Gravimetric Pulse L fires forward and can be used in combos. Gravimetric Pulse M fires upwards at an angle, but the timing to use it as an anti-air is strict. Both versions cause a soft knockdown when connecting with an aerial opponent. The blast is equipped with 5 low durability points and can stop incoming projectiles. You can use these attacks in the air, as well.

Gravimetric Pulse L and M are augmented depending on the amount of red vitality Nova has. Any amount of red health between none and 200,000 powers Gravimetric Pulse up by one level, increasing its hitstun and damage. Any amount 200,000 and over power this attack up by two levels, resulting in a dramatic change in hitstun and damage, as well as a soft knockdown on aerial opponents. Remember that these attacks wall bounce if connected on an aerial adversary near the corner. Powered up Gravimetric Pulses have a larger hitbox, as well.

3

4

5

Gravimetric Pulse H: Gravimetric Pulse H is different than the weaker versions in that it deploys a shield of energy on the screen that stays stationary for 180 frames before disappearing. This shield damages opponents who come into contact with it, causing it to disappear after three hits. The shield is equipped with 3 low durability points to absorb opposing projectiles with.

Having a Gravimetric Pulse shield on the screen limits your adversary's advances on the ground. This can be especially difficult for melee-oriented characters who do not have a projectile to dissipate the energy shield. Once it's on the screen, opponents must either deal with it or avoid it completely, and either option leaves them at a disadvantage.

Using Gravimetric Pulse H depletes any red vitality Nova has. Having any amount of red vitality below 200,000 increases the size and durability of the energy shield. If Nova has over 200,000 points of red vitality, the energy shield becomes larger, its durability is strengthened, and its duration is increased to 300 frames. In addition, it is possible to have two Gravimetric Pulse shields on the screen at once, as long as they are of differing levels. After depleting Nova's red vitality with Gravimetric Pulse H, you can perform another one right after it for even more space control.

6

7

8

Centurion Rush: Centurion Rush L is a slide attack that is OTG-capable and must be guarded low. If connected at any range besides point-blank, Centurion Rush can be followed with basic attacks for a combo. In combos where a ground bounce has already been used, you can perform Centurion Rush L canceled into Super Nova on a grounded foe for extra damage.

Centurion Rush M sends Nova flying down at an angle for an overhead attack. Nova is unable to combo basic attacks if connected, but it leaves him in a position to start an offense or attempt to throw. This attack is relatively safe if guarded on the ground, but it is easily punishable if your competitor jumps at the last moment to guard the dive in the air. You can use this attack safely with a crossover assist covering. If connected on an aerial opponent, Centurion Rush M causes a ground bounce that you can follow with a combo. It also has the unique property of infinite ground bounces, which you can utilize as a 100% damage combo in X-Factor. Consult the Combo Appendix for more details.

Centurion Rush H causes Nova to perform a shoulder charge into a launcher attack, which can be super jump canceled into an air combo. Centurion Rush H has super armor for 24 frames during the charge and absorbs any attacks that manage to get past its high priority. Even though no hitstun will be incurred, Nova still takes damage from absorbed attacks. You can use Centurion Rush H to blow through enemy attacks and projectiles to start a damaging combo. This attack is extremely unsafe if guarded, so using a crossover assist to cover is ideal.

9

Nova Strike: Nova charges toward the opposing character with a punch. Nova Strike covers a wide horizontal area, and you can use the move in the air, as well. Nova Strike L travels half a screen's length and causes a soft knockdown. Nova Strike M reaches near the end of the screen, causing a wall bounce. Nova Strike H travels the entire distance of the screen and causes a crumple if connected. Nova Strike H also can wall bounce an aerial opponent, making it possible to connect two consecutively to start a combo. All versions of Nova Strike are extremely unsafe, so only use Nova Strike if you are certain it is going to connect, or if you have a long range crossover assist covering you.

10

Flight: Nova's flight lasts for 110 frames. While Nova is in flight, you can perform an unlimited amount of airdashes during the duration of flight. If performed on the ground with a tiger knee motion, Nova floats much lower than if you had performed the move regularly off the ground. If used near your adversary, you can set up a quick overhead attack with ↓↙←↖ + S, air L, L, H (CANCEL) ↓↙← + S. After Nova lands, you may continue the combo with crouching L.

11

Energy Javelin: Nova launches a javelin into the sky, far above super jump height. It then homes in on the opponent's position and causes a ground bounce if connected on an aerial adversary. The javelin disappears if Nova is attacked during its flight.

Energy Javelin's tracking is fairly accurate and is especially useful for dealing with competitors who like to rain projectiles from the sky. If you are sure the projectile can tag an aerial opponent, follow the ground bounce with Gravimetric Blaster or Nova Strike H. The javelin is able to reach targets at fullscreen, as well, making up for Nova's lack of a "real" projectile. Several Energy Javelins thrown behind a Gravimetric Pulse H shield can be extremely annoying for opposing players to deal with!

Hyper Combos

Screen	Name	Command	Hits	Damage	Startup	Active	Recovery	Advantage on Hit	Advantage if Guarded	Notes
1	Gravimetric Blaster (in air OK)	↓↘→ + ATK ATK	25~50	217,800~ 261,700	20+1	80	30	—	-18	Can be mashed for extra damage, knocks down, beam durability: 25 frames x 1 high priority durability points
2	Gravimetric Blaster (in air OK) (with less than 200,000 red life)	↓↘→ + ATK ATK	25~50	261,700~ 313,900	20+1	80	30	—	-18	Depletes Nova's red life, can be mashed for extra damage, knocks down, beam durability: 25 frames x 2 high priority durability points
3	Gravimetric Blaster (in air OK) (with at least 200,000 red life)	↓↘→ + ATK ATK	25~50	319,800~ 384,200	20+1	80	30	—	-18	Depletes Nova's red life, can be mashed for extra damage, knocks down, beam durability: 25 frames x 3 high priority durability points
4	Super Nova (in air OK)	→↓↘ + ATK ATK	40~79	237,000~ 283,000	10+1	45	29 or until grounded	—	-32	Can be mashed for extra damage, knocks down, beam durability: 40 frames x 3 high priority durability points
5	Human Rocket (in air OK)	↓↙← + ATK ATK	1~3	100,000 per hit	13+1	16	53 or until grounded	-28	-44	Can direct additional attacks by pressing a direction + ATK

Gravimetric Blaster: Nova fires a beam of energy at his opponent. Like Gravimetric Pulse, Gravimetric Blaster can be strengthened at the cost of Nova's red vitality. Performing this hyper combo with any amount of red life between none and 200,000 increases the blaster's size and strength. Sacrificing 200,000 red vitality or more yields an even stronger beam that fills up a large portion of the screen. This hyper combo is mashable for more damage.

Gravimetric Blaster is difficult to punish if guarded because it pushes your competitor to a safe distance. However, a blaster not augmented by red vitality can be crouched under by the majority of the characters in the game, leaving Nova susceptible to heavy punishment. Your best bet is to use Gravimetric Blaster for combos or as fullscreen punishment for situations where Nova Strike H is too slow. You can use this hyper combo in the air, as well.

Super Nova: With this attack, Nova creates a sphere of energy, damaging all adversaries within its radius. This hyper combo is typically used to end combos, and it can be mashed for extra damage. Since the damage from this hyper combo comes mostly from the number of hits it produces, it is great when used to end long combos or to THC into. Super Nova has a long period of recovery time, making it highly punishable; use it only in situations where it is guaranteed to hit!

Human Rocket: With Human Rocket, Nova rockets into opponents for big damage. You can control Human Rocket slightly by pressing any ATK with whatever direction you wish Nova to rocket to next, for a total of three hits. It also is projectile-immune and can be used to blow through projectile-based hyper combos, but its startup time must be taken into consideration. Human Rocket takes a long time to recover, so use it only in combos or if you are certain that it is going to connect.

"BLUE BLAZES, I'M AWESOME!"

Battle Plan

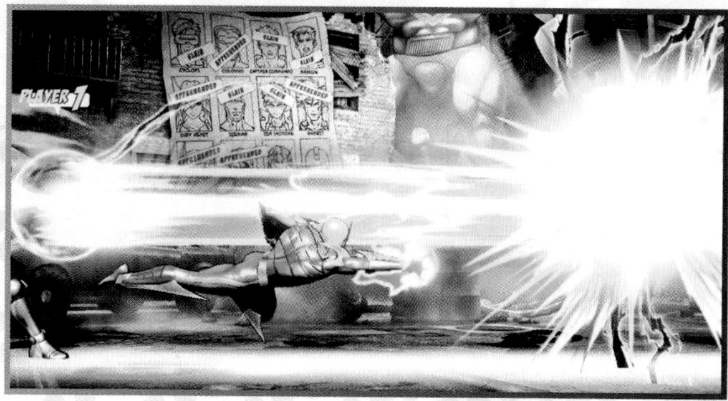

Protect yourself from frontal assaults with Gravimetric Pulse H while firing multiple Energy Javelins.

Use a long range crossover assist to cover slower attacks like Nova Strike H.

Nova's main strength lies in his ability to dish out damage. Simple bread and butter combos can deal upwards of 600,000 damage with minimal effort, and these combos can be started in several different ways. Learning to use long range crossover assists to cover the recovery of Nova's more powerful attacks is paramount to his offense. Given this, Nova is best placed first or second on a team so you can make use of crossover assists to shield these attacks.

At long range, you can take advantage of the tracking ability of Energy Javelin to harass your competitor. Cover yourself from ground advances with Gravimetric Pulse H, then throw Energy Javelins from fullscreen. This tactic is effective in that it forces the opposing player to make a move; if they are content in sitting back during the javelin rain, add in a long range crossover assist to add damage to your assault. If your adversary tries a forward advance, energy shield and all, you can interrupt their attack with a well-timed crouching Ⓜ or Centurion Rush L. You can also use Centurion Rush H if your foe attempts to negate the shield with a projectile of their own. If your rival starts approaching from the air, this is a good chance to utilize Nova's air throw. All of Nova's throws can be followed with full combos from any location on the screen. Once an opponent's movement is made predictable with Nova's ground control, air throws become a viable tool in starting combos. See the Combo Appendix section for more details on how to combo off an air throw.

While this technique is useful against melee-oriented characters, characters with the ability to destroy the energy shield easily are more of a problem. In this case, try throwing only one or two javelins and reacting to whatever the opposing player does in retaliation. You can always cancel Energy Javelin into Gravimetric Blaster, so this can be an effective way to create an opportunity to connect it from a distance. If you see your foe readying a long range attack as a counter to the Energy Javelins, immediately cancel into Gravimetric Blaster to keep them under control. A long range crossover assist can help a lot against long range fighters to help set up the shield and javelins.

The angle in which air Ⓗ attacks makes it useful for square jumps.

Use the priority of crouching Ⓜ to counter your adversary's offense.

When you are ready to go in for a K.O., Nova has several options in terms of approach. Even though Nova's mobility is highly versatile, it is somewhat slow compared to other flying characters such as Magneto or Storm. Many of his forward-moving airdashes and special attacks have startup frames, making it difficult to use them as a means of approach. As such, your best bet in approaching is to use a crossover assist to cover advancing attacks such as crouching Ⓜ, Centurion Rush, and Nova Strike. An airdash forward canceled late air Ⓗ is also a great way in closing the gap between Nova and the opposing character. You can employ these attacks at mid to long range, so Nova doesn't necessarily need to be close to be a threat.

Learning to use Nova's crouching Ⓜ is key to doing damage. This attack launches Nova low to the ground as a torpedo and must be guarded low. Nova extends his fist far outward, giving this attack great priority. Its speed and priority make it ideal for use at mid range. If it connects, you can continue into a full combo for huge damage. If guarded, you can cancel into Gravimetric Pulse L, which isn't particularly easy to punish at -7 frames of advantage. Against more defensive competitors, crouching Ⓜ can be canceled into Nova Slam, performed with ⇨ + Ⓗ. Nova Slam must be guarded high and is a good way of keeping foes on their toes with guarding. Mix this up with a delayed crouching Ⓗ for a basic high-low mix-up game (delay the crouching Ⓗ to mimic the slight startup of Nova Slam). For rivals who are advancing guard-happy, cancel crouching Ⓜ into Gravimetric Pulse H and either continue with offense or throw a few Energy Javelins. For the best results, use crouching Ⓜ with a crossover assist that can help pin the opponent down for tighter mix-up opportunities.

If you manage to get close to the opposing character, standing Ⓛ is your fastest basic attack to use, starting up in 5 frames. However, this attack is easily ducked by most characters, decreasing its usefulness. Another option is crouching Ⓛ, which takes one frame longer to start. Unlike most characters, Nova's crouching Ⓛ can be guarded high, so your go-to low attack at close range is crouching Ⓜ.

Up-close is a good position to sneak in a Nova Slam. Nova Slam must be guarded high and can be used to start one of Nova's powerful combos. Keep in mind that Nova steps forward when performing this attack, so he does not have to be at point-blank range to use it effectively. Once your target is conditioned to blocking crouching Ⓜ, throw in a Nova Slam for an unexpected overhead.

Nova can convert throws into huge damage.

Mix between crouching Ⓜ and ⇨ + Ⓗ to cover both high and low guarding from your opponent.

You can use Nova's airdashes as a means to set up an offensive, as well. You can perform a square jump by quickly canceling Nova's forward airdash from a normal jump with air Ⓗ. The angle of air Ⓗ is great for square jumping, and you can even use it as a deep cross-up if properly positioned. Nova's triangle jump is best performed with an airdash straight down, since his down-forward airdash has too much startup to be good for a triangle jump. A triangle jump Ⓛ is a quick overhead and also has a great angle for an air-to-ground attack. Nova does not have a quick low attack to mix up with, so go for an empty triangle jump into a throw instead.

Against a cornered competitor, mix up between crouching Ⓜ, triangle jumps, square jumps, Nova Slam, and throws to lead into your high-damage combos. Deploying a Gravimetric Pulse H energy shield against a cornered opponent limits their options further. Any attempts at advance guarding your offense can be countered with crouching Ⓜ, Nova Strike, or Centurion Rush to move back in, ideally with the cover of a crossover assist. If you get a forward throw or air throw on a cornered attacker, the regular Centurion Rush Ⓛ OTG can only be followed with a hyper combo. For maximum damage, use Nova Slam to OTG instead, since it can be followed by basic attacks into a launcher.

COMBO USAGE

I. CR. Ⓜ, CR. Ⓗ, Ⓢ CANCEL FORWARD SUPER JUMP, AIR Ⓗ CANCEL ↓↙← + Ⓢ, Ⓜ, Ⓜ, Ⓗ, Ⓢ, LAND, → + Ⓗ, Ⓢ CANCEL FORWARD SUPER JUMP, AIR Ⓜ, Ⓜ, Ⓗ CANCEL ↓↘→ + Ⓛ CANCEL →↓↘ + ATK ATK (MASH ATK)

696,800 damage, 2% meter loss

After canceling Ⓢ into a forward super jump, let your character glide closely to the opposing character before doing air Ⓗ. Doing so makes certain that you'll be in range for the link afterward.

You may add crouching Ⓛ to the beginning of this combo for flexibility at that loss of damage (which drops to 670,300) and low attack opening. If crouching Ⓛ, crouching Ⓜ is blocked, you can chain into → + Ⓗ or crouching Ⓗ to stage a basic high or low guessing game.

II. CR. Ⓜ, ST. Ⓗ, Ⓢ CANCEL FORWARD SUPER JUMP, AIR Ⓗ CANCEL ↓↙← + Ⓢ, Ⓗ CANCEL ↓↙← + Ⓢ, DELAYED Ⓗ, LAND, FORWARD DASH, ST. Ⓗ, Ⓢ CANCEL FORWARD SUPER JUMP, AIR Ⓗ CANCEL ↓↙← + Ⓢ, Ⓗ, Ⓢ, LAND, → + Ⓗ, Ⓢ CANCEL FORWARD SUPER JUMP, AIR Ⓗ CANCEL →↓↘ + ATK ATK (MASH ATK)

760,500 damage, 4% meter gain (or self sufficient for Super Nova ender)

Due to hitstun decay, this combo does not work if it's started from a jump attack or crouching Ⓛ. To ensure that you can still do most of the combo if you start it with an air attack, remove the standing Ⓗ done just after Nova lands from air Ⓗ. After air Ⓗ CANCEL ↓↙← + Ⓢ, Ⓗ CANCEL ↓↙← + Ⓢ, fall a bit before doing air Ⓗ. The later it hits, the easier it is to do the dashing standing Ⓗ.

III. → + Ⓗ, Ⓢ CANCEL FORWARD SUPER JUMP, AIR Ⓗ CANCEL ↓↙← + Ⓢ, AIR Ⓗ CANCEL ↓↙← + Ⓢ, DELAYED Ⓗ, LAND, FORWARD DASH, ST. Ⓗ, Ⓢ CANCEL FORWARD SUPER JUMP, AIR Ⓗ CANCEL ↓↙← + Ⓢ, Ⓗ, Ⓢ, LAND, →↓↘ + Ⓛ CANCEL →↓↘ + ATK ATK (MASH ATK)

754,000 damage, 26% meter loss

This combo is similar to **Combo II** but begins with the Nova Slam overhead.

IV. FRONT OR BACK THROW OR FRONT OR BACK AIR THROW, {FORWARD DASH} OR {FORWARD AIRDASH, LAND}, → + Ⓗ, ST. Ⓗ, Ⓢ CANCEL FORWARD SUPER JUMP, Ⓗ CANCEL ↓↙← + Ⓢ, Ⓗ, Ⓢ, LAND, →↓↘ + Ⓛ CANCEL →↓↘ + ATK ATK (MASH ATK)

488,100 damage, 42% meter loss

Off of a ground throw midscreen, you must dash and do → + Ⓗ as quickly as possible. This is difficult; if you can't do this consistently, you may opt to do →↓↘ + Ⓛ instead, which can be juggled after midscreen. After an air throw, you must airdash all the way to your adversary and land before doing → + Ⓗ.

V. (AGAINST AN AIRBORNE OPPONENT) FORWARD JUMP, AIR Ⓜ, Ⓜ, DELAYED Ⓗ, LAND, FORWARD JUMP, AIR Ⓜ, Ⓗ, Ⓢ, LAND, → + Ⓗ, Ⓢ CANCEL FORWARD SUPER JUMP, AIR Ⓜ, Ⓜ, Ⓗ CANCEL →↓↘ + ATK ATK (MASH ATK)

667,900 damage, 0% meter loss (or self sufficient for Super Nova ender)

Air Ⓗ should be delayed slightly to make this combo easier. To make the combo easier, omit the first part and go straight into air Ⓜ, Ⓗ, Ⓢ.

VI. CR. Ⓛ, Ⓜ, ST. Ⓗ CANCEL X-FACTOR, CR. Ⓜ, ST. Ⓗ, Ⓢ CANCEL FORWARD SUPER JUMP, AIR Ⓗ CANCEL ↓↙← + Ⓢ, Ⓗ CANCEL ↓↙← + Ⓢ, DELAYED Ⓗ, LAND, FORWARD DASH, Ⓢ CANCEL FORWARD SUPER JUMP, AIR Ⓗ, Ⓢ, LAND, → + Ⓗ, Ⓢ CANCEL FORWARD SUPER JUMP, AIR Ⓗ CANCEL →↓↘ + ATK ATK (MASH ATK)

1,021,000~1,261,000 damage, 34~65% meter gain (or self sufficient for Super Nova ender)

Here's a standard X-Factor combo that you can use as a guaranteed K.O. against your opponent. While some characters' combos become difficult or different in X-Factor, Nova's combos actually become easier due to his increased speed.

ADVANCED TACTICS

NOVA CATAPULT

Cancel a forward airdash with air Ⓗ to perform a square jump.

Canceling a forward airdash at the last possible moment to catapult Nova to the other side of the screen!

Nova's different airdashes all accelerate at different speeds. Airdashing diagonally in any direction has a noticeable pause before accelerating, while airdashing straight up or down is instant. Airdashing backward is quick enough to be useful as a method of escape.

Most unique is Nova's forward airdash. After a bit of startup, Nova charges forward, steadily accelerating before coming to a complete halt. You can cancel this airdash with any basic attack, adding with it the momentum of the airdash. Canceling early results in less forward momentum, while canceling late yields a greater speed.

The very last part of Nova's airdash is when he is moving the fastest. Waiting as long as possible before canceling the airdash results in Nova moving fast enough to reach the other side of the screen in one airdash! With the cover of a crossover assist, a well-timed forward airdash canceled into air Ⓗ can be an effective way to get close to your target.

GRAVIMETRIC TRAP

Perform Gravimetric Pulse H, then slide underneath your opponent to complete the cross-up.

After a knock out, you can mix up the incoming character with an ambiguous Gravimetric Pulse H energy shield cross-up. Place the shield in or near the corner so that the next character will land directly on top of it. As they come in, use crouching Ⓜ to slide underneath your rival, causing the shield to attack from the other side! You can also fake the cross-up by delaying the crouching Ⓜ so that your adversary lands on the shield right before Nova crosses up with the slide.

Characters who can airdash are going to be inclined to airdash away to avoid the shield altogether. In this case, an air throw is the perfect way to counter their escape. Note that the air throw must be input after the opponent airdashes because an incoming character cannot be thrown until they have performed an action of their own. This setup works midscreen, as well, but it is more difficult for foes to escape when executed in the corner.

NOVA

NEW

COMBO APPENDIX

GENERAL EXECUTION TIPS

When performing air combos, make sure to delay air Ⓜ, Ⓜ, Ⓗ, so that all the hits of air Ⓢ connect.

Try double tapping Ⓢ after the → + Ⓗ OTG to ensure that the launcher connects.

(AFTER A TAC) AIR Ⓗ (CANCEL) ↓↙← + Ⓢ, Ⓜ, Ⓜ, Ⓗ, Ⓢ, LAND, →↓↘ + Ⓛ (CANCEL) →↓↘ + (ATK)(ATK) (MASH (ATK))

Notes	Damage
↑ + Ⓢ or → + Ⓢ or ↓ + Ⓢ TAC to Nova	Varies based on damage scaling

→ + Ⓗ (CANCEL) (X-FACTOR), →↓↘ + Ⓜ, ↓↙← + Ⓗ, Ⓢ (CANCEL) FORWARD SUPER JUMP, AIR Ⓗ (CANCEL) ↓↙← + (CANCEL), Ⓗ, Ⓢ, LAND, →↓↘ + Ⓛ (CANCEL) →↓↘ + (ATK)(ATK) (MASH (ATK))

Notes	Damage
—	925,400~1,179,300 damage, 20~3% meter loss

FRONT/BACK THROW OR FRONT/BACK AIR THROW, {FORWARD DASH} OR {FORWARD AIRDASH}, → + Ⓗ (CANCEL) (X-FACTOR), →↓↘ + Ⓜ, ↓↙← + Ⓗ, Ⓢ (CANCEL) FORWARD SUPER JUMP, AIR Ⓗ (CANCEL) ↓↙← + Ⓢ (CANCEL), Ⓗ, Ⓢ, LAND, →↓↘ + Ⓛ (CANCEL) →↓↘ + (ATK)(ATK) (MASH (ATK))

Notes	Damage
—	692,800~851,400 damage, 21~7% meter loss

CR. Ⓜ, ST. Ⓗ, Ⓢ (CANCEL) FORWARD SUPER JUMP, AIR Ⓗ (CANCEL) ↓↙← + Ⓢ, Ⓗ (CANCEL) ↓↙← + Ⓢ, Ⓗ, LAND, FORWARD DASH, ST. Ⓗ, Ⓢ (CANCEL) FORWARD SUPER JUMP, AIR Ⓗ (CANCEL) ↓↙← + Ⓢ, Ⓗ (CANCEL) ↓↙← + Ⓛ, DOWNWARD AIRDASH, AIR Ⓗ (CANCEL) ↓↘→ + Ⓛ (CANCEL) →↓↘ + (ATK)(ATK) (MASH (ATK))

Notes	Damage
Requires corner	770,300 damage, 8% meter loss

↓↙← + Ⓗ, (ATK) + Ⓢ, ST. Ⓗ (CANCEL) ↓↙← + Ⓗ, →↓↘ + Ⓜ, ST. Ⓗ, Ⓢ (CANCEL) FORWARD SUPER JUMP, AIR Ⓜ, Ⓜ, Ⓗ (CANCEL) ↓↘→ + Ⓛ (CANCEL) →↓↘ + (ATK)(ATK) (MASH (ATK))

Notes	Damage
Nova's back must be facing corner	770,000 damage

→ + Ⓗ (CANCEL) LEVEL 3 (X-FACTOR), {→↓↘ + Ⓜ, →↓↘ + Ⓜ} X ∞

Notes	Damage
This combo takes advantage of Centurion Rush M's indefinite ground bounce property, which is only possible during X-Factor level 3	100%

NEW

ROCKET RACCOON

"THE RACCOON'S THE KING OF THE BEASTS. SCREW THE LION."

Bio

REAL NAME
Rocket Raccoon

OCCUPATION
Interplanetary explorer

ABILITIES
Rocket Raccoon possesses the same heightened sense and speed as a raccoon on our world, but can also handle various weapons freely and possesses high intelligence that helps on the battlefield.

WEAPONS
Rocket skates that allow for flights of short distance, as well as a laser pistol. He can also use a variety of heavy firearms.

PROFILE
Rocket Raccoon is a raccoon from the planet Halfworld that has received several enhancements, upping his intelligence and battle awareness. He protects the colony as a ranger, and currently explores the realm outside of Halfworld as an interplanetary explorer.

FIRST APPEARANCE
Marvel Preview #7 (1976)

POWER GRID

3 INTELLIGENCE

2 STRENGTH

2 SPEED

2 STAMINA

1 ENERGY PROJECTION

4 FIGHTING ABILITY

*This is biographical, and does not represent an evaluation of the in-game combat potential of this hero.

Vitality	750,000
Chain Combo Archetype	Hunter Series

X-Factor Boost	Damage	Speed
Level 1 (3 teammates remaining)	120%	120%
Level 2 (2 teammates remaining)	140%	130%
Level 3 (1 teammate remaining)	160%	140%

Contrary to what his arsenal of traps and firearms would have you believe, Rocket Raccoon is at is his best when he is able to perform mix-ups against an opponent. It can be difficult to keep your competitor still long enough to perform a mix-up, so your objective when playing with Rocket Raccoon is a unique one: make contact with a crossover assist's attack.

When a crossover assist is about to make contact with the target, you can use the following mix-up tactics:

- **Use Tunnel Rat M or L before the assist hits to create a cross-up mix-up from anywhere on the screen**
- **Use air Ⓛ from a low-altitude hover to perform an incredibly fast overhead attack while your rival is dealing with the assist**
- **Use crouching Ⓛ to pepper in some low-hitting attacks so that your adversary won't know when to guard high**

How do you go about ensuring that the opposing character is in position to connect with your crossover assists?

- **Force your foe to wade through Rocket Raccoon's long range options such as crouching Ⓗ, Spitfire, and Pendulum, then attack with a crossover assist when your rival moves into the proper position**
- **Recognize when your opponent is going to land on top of an Oil Bomb or Claymore trap, and summon an assist while your competitor is stuck in place**
- **Keep your foe in guardstun when up close using aerial chains starting from a low-altitude air Ⓜ and simultaneously call an assist**
- **End combos in the corner without using the Rock 'n' Roll hyper combo, and instead set up your adversary to guard a crossover assist as they stand**

Attack Set

Standing Basic Attacks

Screen	Command	Hits	Damage	Meter Gain	Startup	Active	Recovery	Advantage on Hit	Advantage if Guarded	Notes
1	Standing Ⓛ	1	31,000	248	4	2	10	-1	-1	Chains into Ⓛ attacks
2	Standing Ⓜ	1	42,000	336	6	3	15	-2	-2	—
3	Standing Ⓗ	1	60,000	480	10	8	18	-5	-5	Inflicts chip damage, beam durability: 5 frames x 2 low priority durability points

Crouching Basic Attacks

Screen	Command	Hits	Damage	Meter Gain	Startup	Active	Recovery	Advantage on Hit	Advantage if Guarded	Notes
1	Crouching Ⓛ	1	30,000	240	4	2	11	-2	-2	Low attack, chains into Ⓛ attacks
2	Crouching Ⓜ	1	45,000	360	6	4	16	—	-4	Low attack, knocks down
3	Crouching Ⓗ	1	60,000	480	12	8	19	-6	-6	Inflicts chip damage, beam durability: 5 frames x 2 low priority durability points

Ground Special Attack—Launcher

Screen	Command	Hits	Damage	Meter Gain	Startup	Active	Recovery	Advantage on Hit	Advantage if Guarded	Notes
1	Ⓢ (while standing or crouching)	1	60,000	480	8	4	26	—	-9	Launcher, not special- or hyper combo-cancelable

Air Basic Attacks

Screen	Command	Hits	Damage	Meter Gain	Startup	Active	Recovery	Advantage on Hit	Advantage if Guarded	Notes
1	Air Ⓛ	1	33,000	264	5	3	14	+9	+9	Overhead attack
2	Air Ⓜ	1	45,000	360	6	5	23	-2	-2	—
3	Air Ⓗ	1	60,000	480	8	4	24	+16	+16	Overhead attack

Air Special Attacks—Flying Screen and Air Exchange

Air Ⓢ causes a hard knockdown when used in a launcher combo (this is sometimes called flying screen). When used outside of a launcher combo, air Ⓢ behaves mostly like another basic attack. Air exchange attacks, performed by inputting a direction plus Ⓢ, are only possible during a launcher combo. Exchange hits initiate team aerial combos by tagging in the next available character to continue the air combo.

Screen	Command	Hits	Damage	Meter Gain	Startup	Active	Recovery	Advantage on Hit	Advantage if Guarded	Notes
1	Air Ⓢ	1	70,000	560	9	4	23	+14	+13	Inflicts chip damage, causes hard knockdown if used in launcher combo, projectile has 5 low priority durability points
2	Air ⇧ + Ⓢ (during launcher combo)	2	105,00	880	8	4	29	—	—	Tags in next available ally while lofting opponent upward
3	Air ⇨ or ⇦ + Ⓢ (during launcher combo)	2	95,000	800	6	5	23	—	—	Tags in next available ally while causing wall bounce, steals 1 hyper meter from foe
4	Air ⇩ + Ⓢ (during launcher combo)	2	95,000	800	9	4	29	—	—	Tags in next available ally while causing ground bounce, generates 1 hyper meter

1

2

3

4

Command Attacks

Command attacks resemble basic attacks but have different chaining and canceling properties. It's usually possible to chain *into* a command attack from basic attacks, but most command attacks cannot be chained from or canceled themselves.

Screen	Wild Ripper	Command	Hits	Damage	Meter Gain	Startup	Active	Recovery	Advantage on Hit	Advantage if Guarded	Notes
1	Wild Ripper	⇨ + Ⓗ	1	65,000	520	9	6	26	-11	-11	—

1

Throws

Throws are for snagging passive or blocking opponents. Since throws are active so quickly, you can also use them to preemptively toss opponents out of their offense. Combos are usually possible after throws, one way or another.

Screen	Command	Hits	Damage	Meter Gain	Startup	Active	Notes
1	⇨ + Ⓗ (ground)	4	80,000	800	1	1	Hard knockdown
	⇦ + Ⓗ (ground)	4	80,000	800	1	1	Hard knockdown
2	⇨ + Ⓗ (air)	4	80,000	800	1	1	Hard knockdown
	⇦ + Ⓗ (air)	4	80,000	800	1	1	Hard knockdown

1

2

As a Partner—Crossover Assists

Screen	Type	P1+P2 Crossover Combination Hyper Combo	Description	Hits	Damage	Meter Gain	Startup	Active	Recovery (this crossover assist)	Recovery (other partner)	Notes
1	Rocket Raccoon—α	Rock 'n' Roll	Spitfire M	2	50,000 x 2	400 x 2	39	20	126	96	Each projectile has 4 low priority durability points
2	Rocket Raccoon—β	Rock 'n' Roll	Claymore	10	97,300	1200	39	—	106	76	Claymore lasts for 180 frames, projectile has 5 low priority durability points, creates explosion on contact with beam durability: 10 frames x 1 low priority durability points, can be destroyed by attacks, absorbs attack on contact
3	Rocket Raccoon—γ	Rock 'n' Roll	Pendulum	1	80,000	640	44	—	122	91	Wall bounces foe, projectile active for 31 frames and has 10 low priority durability points

1

2

3

All three of Rocket Raccoon's assists are exceptional and allow him to fill different roles on different teams from the bench.

Rocket Raccoon—α functions similarly to the popular Sentinel—α crossover assist, with the added bonus that the projectiles won't disappear if Rocket Raccoon is hit, making it an excellent assist for offensive teams and a great fit for any other team! The assist variation of Spitfire Twice slightly varies from the special move, since it has more projectile durability points and fires shots farther apart than Rocket Raccoon can on his own. This gap benefits offensive characters because opponents who guard one projectile emerge from guardstun before the second hits, making them susceptible targets for cross-up mix-ups. Thanks to Rocket Raccoon's small stature, the projectiles fire low enough to pass under many opposing projectiles, which can penetrate zoning walls and give offensive characters an opening to blitz their rival!

Rocket Raccoon—β is Rocket Raccoon's Claymore mine attack and is an excellent tool on offense and defense. When an adversary makes contact with the mine, they are sprayed with a 10-hit blast of shrapnel, locking them in guardstun long enough for an offensive character to set up a mix-up or hit them, opening them up for a combo! A mine placed over a knocked down foe explodes when they stand up, mitigating their options and allowing offensive characters to continue applying pressure. Defensively, this assist can intimidate a competitor and make them hesitant to rush in, even if they hit your point character, the mine stays in play, forcing the opposing player to deal with the assist. Claymore can absorb a single attack, so opponents cannot easily destroy a mine without putting themselves at risk for a big punish.

Rocket Raccoon—γ gives a character instant access to the powerful Pendulum log trap attack, making it great for long range teams since it covers a huge portion of the screen. The log trap causes wall bounce on hit and can easily be converted into a combo, discouraging offensive characters from rushing in while giving zoning characters more time to chip away at their target.

Snap Back

Screen	Command	Hits	Damage	Meter Gain	Startup	Active	Recovery	Advantage on Hit	Advantage if Guarded
1	↓↘→ + P1 or P2	1	50,000	500 (-1 hyper meter bar)	2	6	26	—	-11

Notes

On hit, snap back forces the opposing point character to be replaced by an assist. Opposing assist calls or tag outs are also locked out for 4 seconds

1

Special Moves

Screen	Name	Command	Hits	Damage	Meter Gain	Startup	Active	Recovery	Advantage on Hit	Advantage if Guarded	Notes
1, 2, 3, 4, 5, 6	Spitfire (in air OK)	↓↘→ + ATK	1	40,000	320	15	—	35 (air: until grounded)	-10 (air: +10)	-10 (air: +10)	L version is OTG-capable, projectile has 3 low priority durability points
	Spitfire Twice (in air OK)	(during Spitfire) ATK	1	40,000	320	10-14+3	—	35 (air: until grounded)	-10 (air: +3)	-10 (air: +3)	L version is OTG-capable, projectile has 3 low priority durability points
7	Oil Bomb	→↓↘ + L	—	—	—	15	—	13	—	—	Bomb hits ground after 39 frames, creates a patch of oil upon contact with ground that lasts 300 frames, can be detonated in air or on the ground by Spitfire, standing H, or crouching H
8	Oil Bomb Air Explosion	—	1	70,000	560	1	8	—	—	—	OTG-capable, knocks down, projectile has 5 medium priority durability points
9	Oil Bomb Ground Explosion	—	10	10,000 x 10	80 x 10	1	100	—	—	—	OTG-capable, disappears if Rocket Raccoon is hit
10	Mr. Flapper	→↓↘ + M	1	70,000	560	27	—	8	+22	+22	OTG-capable, active for 10 frames, ground bounces airborne and knocked down foes, disappears if Rocket Raccoon is hit
11	Pendulum	→↓↘ + H	1	90,000	720	20	—	30	—	+3	Wall bounces adversaries, projectile active for 28 frames and has 5 low priority durability points, no longer hits opponent if Rocket Raccoon is hit

Special Moves continued

Screen	Name	Command	Hits	Damage	Meter Gain	Startup	Active	Recovery	Advantage on Hit	Advantage if Guarded	Notes
12, 13	Angel Gift	↓↙← + L	1	80,000	640	3	—	17	+36	+36	Trap has 5 low priority durability points and lasts 180 frames, rock falls toward rival on contact with them, rock has 5 low priority durability points, trap disappears if Rocket Raccoon is hit
14, 15	Claymore	↓↙← + M	10	97,300	1200	15	—	25	+16	+16	Claymore has 5 low priority durability points and lasts 180 frames, creates explosion upon contact with competitor with beam durability 10 frames x 1 low priority durability points, can be destroyed by attacks, absorbs attack on contact, trap disappears if Rocket Raccoon is hit
16, 17	Grab Bag	↓↙← + H	1	56,000	800	25	—	15	—	+5	Hard knockdown, trap has 5 low priority durability points and lasts 180 frames, captures rival upon contact, trap disappears if Rocket Raccoon is hit
18	Rocket Skate (can be directed)	(→ and ←) + ATK + S	—	—	—	30	—	—	—	—	Special-cancelable
19	Rocket Skate (can be directed)	(↖, ↑, and ↗) + ATK + S	—	—	—	22	—	—	—	—	Special-cancelable, airborne from frame 11
20	Air Rocket Skate (can be directed)	(in air) (↙, ←, ↖, ↑, ↗, and →) + ATK + S	—	—	—	22	—	—	—	—	Special-cancelable, has an additional 11 frames of recovery if directed into the ground
21	Air Rocket Skate (can be directed)	(in air) (↘ and ↓) + ATK + S	—	—	—	14	—	—	—	—	Special-cancelable, has an additional 11 frames of recovery if directed into the ground
22	Tunnel Rat	↓↓ + L	—	—	—	13	—	27	—	—	Invincible from frames 13-21
23	Tunnel Rat	↓↓ + M	—	—	—	13	—	27	—	—	Invincible from frames 13-21
24	Tunnel Rat	↓↓ + H	—	—	—	13	5~126	9~8	—	—	Invincible from frames 13-17~138, hold H to stay underground longer, can move while underground using the controller

1

2

3

4

5

6

Spitfire and Spitfire Twice: Rocket Raccoon can fire his unique projectile in three different directions, then instantly fire another projectile in a different direction at the press of a button. The button used when performing this attack determines where Rocket Raccoon fires his gun: L fires an angled shot downwards, M fires in a straight horizontal line, and H fires an angled shot toward the air. You can fire Spitfire a second time by pressing a button after the first shot is fired, and you can aim it in a different direction than the original shot. This lets you use Spitfire H to fire into the air, then Spitfire Twice to shoot across the ground, allowing Rocket Raccoon to cover a large portion of the screen.

Spitfire projectiles are fired incredibly low to the ground, allowing them to pass under other projectiles that would normally nullify them. If forced to trade, Rocket Raccoon isn't likely to overpower an opponent even with Spitfire Twice because each projectile only has 3 low priority durability points. Rocket Raccoon's aerial Spitfire aborts his jump trajectory and causes him to stop in the air, so jumping over your foe's projectiles and firing back with aerial Spitfire L is a much safer way to deal with other long range characters.

The aerial version of Spitfire recovers as soon as Rocket Raccoon lands on the ground. This results in very quick recovery when fired at low altitudes, giving you more time to establish your defense or set up a crossover assist. Avoid trying to use Spitfire from super jump height, since Rocket Raccoon can only use Spitfire once in the air and is completely vulnerable until he lands. Spitfire L doesn't fire low enough to keep your foe from dashing in, so your adversary can easily punish you before Rocket Raccoon hits the ground.

The L version of Spitfire is OTG-capable, but it lets your rival recover in the air before Rocket Raccoon can attack again, limiting its usefulness as a combo extender.

Oil Bomb: In this unique attack, Rocket Raccoon throws a bomb in the air that lands and then causes a puddle of oil to appear on the ground. By itself, Oil Bomb cannot hit an opponent at all, and it completely passes through them on contact. If Oil Bomb lands on the ground when a puddle of oil is on the ground, the earliest puddle of oil is removed from the screen.

7

8

9

When Oil Bomb is detonated in the air, it cases a small OTG-capable explosion that knocks your attacker down. If you cause Oil Bomb to detonate with crouching H and the explosion hits the enemy, you can then chain into Wild Ripper (→ + H) and start a combo!

When the puddle of oil is ignited, it causes an OTG-capable inferno on the ground for 100 frames. This fire creates a huge amount of hitstun and guardstun, giving you plenty of time to set up a mix-up. If Rocket Raccoon is hit while an ignited puddle of oil is out, the inferno disappears, so make sure Rocket Raccoon is safe from danger before setting it up.

No one but the Rocket Raccoon that threw the Oil Bomb can explode or ignite it, not even an opposing Rocket Raccoon.

Mr. Flapper: A massive, OTG-capable bear trap emerges from the ground and swipes a large area in front of Rocket Raccoon, causing a massive amount of hitstun against your foe. If Mr. Flapper hits an airborne opponent it causes a ground bounce, making it an essential component of Rocket Raccoon's combos.

If the bear trap successfully hits the enemy, you have plenty of time to dash in and start a combo. During X-Factor, Rocket Raccoon is fast enough to link several bear traps together! Even when guarded, Mr. Flapper leaves Rocket Raccoon at a +22 frame advantage, giving you ample time to perform a mix-up or Rocket Skate to safety. The bear trap extends high enough to hit characters who often take to the air, and it can hit adversaries even at the peak of normal jump height. It is a good tool to punish aerial enemies because it covers an angle that Pendulum misses.

Mr. Flapper has 27 frames of startup and disappears if Rocket Raccoon is hit before the bear trap comes out, so avoid using it when under heavy duress.

Pendulum: A log trap flies from behind Rocket Raccoon and swings forward in an arc, covering most of the screen, and causes wall bounce on hit, which you can convert into a combo from anywhere on the screen! The arc of Pendulum covers almost the entirety of normal jump space and most of the ground in front of Rocket Raccoon, making it a good deterrent against opponents trying to rush in.

Pendulum has long startup, so it's best used when Rocket Raccoon is covered by a crossover assist or his own Spitfire. There are dead spots in the log trap's arc that can be avoided if a rival jumps toward it, crouches under it from across the screen, or in front of Rocket Raccoon. Keep in mind that if Rocket Raccoon is hit before Pendulum connects with the opposing character, the log trap no longer hits its target; make sure Rocket Raccoon has ample distance from his foe before throwing it out.

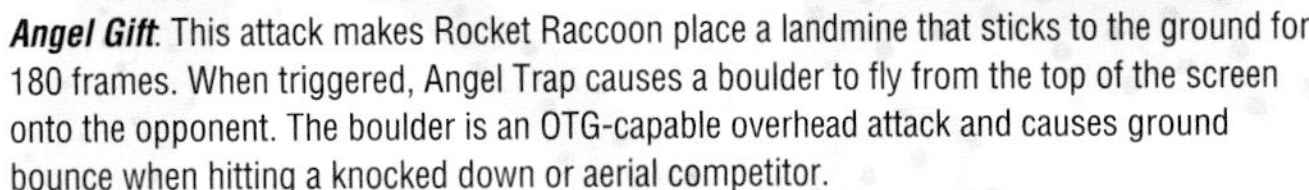

Angel Gift: This attack makes Rocket Raccoon place a landmine that sticks to the ground for 180 frames. When triggered, Angel Trap causes a boulder to fly from the top of the screen onto the opponent. The boulder is an OTG-capable overhead attack and causes ground bounce when hitting a knocked down or aerial competitor.

Unlike Trish's ground traps, a rival who jumps over Angel Gift can avoid the mine, as Rocket Raccoon's landmines are only triggered when an opponent makes contact with them on the ground. Angel Gift recovers very quickly and causes Rocket Raccoon to hop backward after placing it, making it a very safe move to throw out and take up space on the ground.

It takes 30 frames for the boulder to reach a grounded opponent after the mine is triggered, so challengers can quickly dash through the mine and avoid the boulder completely. This mine is best used when an adversary is guarding Rocket Raccoon's basic attack chains, so you can quickly maneuver Rocket Raccoon to safety.

Angel Gift disappears if Rocket Raccoon is hit or if he attempts to place more than one on the ground, although you can place his other landmines while Angel Gift is already out.

Claymore: This landmine attack places a mine that (when activated) sends a blast of shrapnel at the target, locking them in place! Claymore is a very useful tool on offense and defense, as it can function as both an anti-air as well as a lockdown tool, much like Oil Bomb. This landmine is slower than Angel Gift, making it less useful as a safety tool, but it is faster than Grab Bag, so you can use it in more offensive and defensive situations.

The shrapnel released by Claymore keeps the opponent in guardstun or hitstun for a very long time, leaving Rocket Raccoon at +16 frame advantage and gives you plenty of time to mix up your competitor. Place one over a knocked down opponent, forcing them to stand up into it, which keeps them locked down!

Claymore's unique properties make it very effective on defense, both as an anti-air and a shield. If an opponent jumps at Rocket Raccoon while a Claymore is out and they do not hit him, they must block the Claymore explosion. Claymore can be destroyed if it is hit by a basic attack, but Claymore completely absorbs the hit, making it whiff through Rocket Raccoon and giving you time to punish the opposing player for whiffing a move!

Like Rocket Raccoon's other landmine attacks, Claymore is only triggered when an opponent touches it on the ground, and you can only place one of each type of mine on the screen at the time. If Rocket Raccoon is hit before the landmine explodes, it disappears from the screen.

Grab Bag: Rocket Raccoon's final landmine is the slowest of them all, but has the highest reward: if Grab Bag successfully hits the opposing character it will trap them in a net in the air for 45 frames, allowing you to easily react and land a full combo.

This landmine is best used completely as a defensive tool, since it has the longest startup of any of the three landmine attacks. Lay one on the ground while firing Spitfire and Pendulums to further deter opponents from rushing in.

If the Grab Bag net hits an opponent, you can land a fairly sizable combo, but this trap has significant damage scaling, so it deals as much damage as a combo starting from a throw. If your target is released before they are hit out of the trap they get dumped onto the ground in a hard knockdown state. This still allows you plenty of time to capitalize with Mr. Flapper for a ground bounce combo! Like the other mines, Grab Bag only connects if an opponent touches it on the ground, disappears if Rocket Raccoon places another one, and is destroyed if Rocket Raccoon is hit.

Rocket Skate: Using his rocket-powered boots, this move allows Rocket Raccoon to quickly dash around the screen in five directions on the ground and eight directions in the air! Rocket Skates are cancelable from basic attacks and greatly increase Rocket Raccoon's mobility; making for an especially powerful tool when canceled into from crouching H or jumping S. Even better, Rocket Skate can be canceled at any point into a special move! This has several applications: safely place a landmine far in front of Rocket Raccoon by using Rocket Skate forward, then cancel into Claymore to hop back safely; quickly retreat while littering the ground with traps by using backwards Rocket Skate and canceling into landmines; gain space to establish momentum by using backwards Rocket Skate, cancel into up-back Rocket Skate, then cancel *that* into a low-altitude Spitfire. The possibilities are endless!

In the air, you can use Rocket Skate to quickly move Rocket Raccoon across the screen. The down-forward version, however, recovers substantially faster than the rest, allowing Rocket Raccoon to dash in and attack his opponent with an overhead air L, or quickly land and attack with a low-hitting crouching L! Rocket Skate has an additional 11 frames of recovery if Rocket Skate is still active when Rocket Raccoon touches the ground, so ensure you're at the proper height before attacking with the down-forward version.

Rocket Skates forward and backward have more recovery than the others, and moving forward in particular is unsafe if canceled into from basic attacks, so you should generally cancel into backward Rocket Skate to create distance from an attacker.

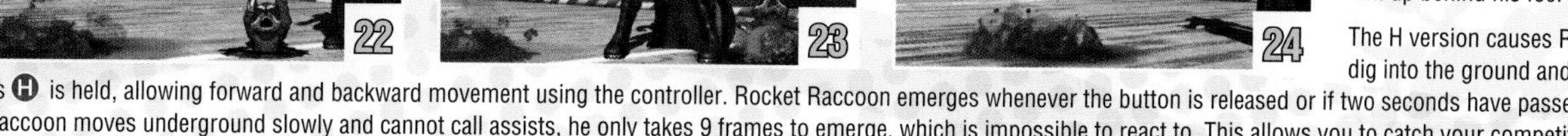

Tunnel Rat: This attack causes Rocket Raccoon to dig under the ground, then reemerge in a location depending on the button pressed. The L version causes Rocket Raccoon to emerge directly in front of his opponent, while the M version pops him up behind his foe.

The H version causes Rocket Raccoon to dig into the ground and stay there as long as (H) is held, allowing forward and backward movement using the controller. Rocket Raccoon emerges whenever the button is released or if two seconds have passed. While Rocket Raccoon moves underground slowly and cannot call assists, he only takes 9 frames to emerge, which is impossible to react to. This allows you to catch your competitor off guard with a throw or crouching (L), or hyper combo cancel into Mad Hopper to stop your adversary from attacking you as you emerge!

The M version is one of Rocket Raccoon's most useful mix-up tools because it always goes behind the opposing character, even in the corner. When used in combination with crossover assists, you can have Rocket Raccoon perform a nearly invisible fullscreen cross-up! If the assist hits, you can capitalize for a combo, and if it's blocked, Rocket Raccoon will remain next to the target even if they use advancing guard, allowing you to further mix up your rival!

Hyper Combos

Screen	Name	Command	Hits	Damage	Startup	Active	Recovery	Advantage on Hit	Advantage if Guarded	Notes
1	Rock 'n' Roll	↓↘→ + ATK ATK	35~69	246,800~ 288,800	8+2	67(82)1	36	-5	-15	Can be mashed for extra damage, 34th hit places opponent in spinning knockdown, final hit has homing capability and knocks down, each projectile has 1 high priority durability point, final projectile has 5 high priority durability points
2	Mad Hopper	↓↙← + ATK ATK	1	220,000	10+1	—	28	—	+8	Knocks down, projectile has 5 high priority durability frames and lasts 600 frames, activates on contact with foe
3	Rocky Raccoon (Level 3 Hyper Combo)	→↓↘ + ATK ATK	15~50	370,000~ 412,000	8+1	15	5	—	+1	OTG-capable, can be mashed for extra damage, hard knockdown, projectile has 5 high priority durability points

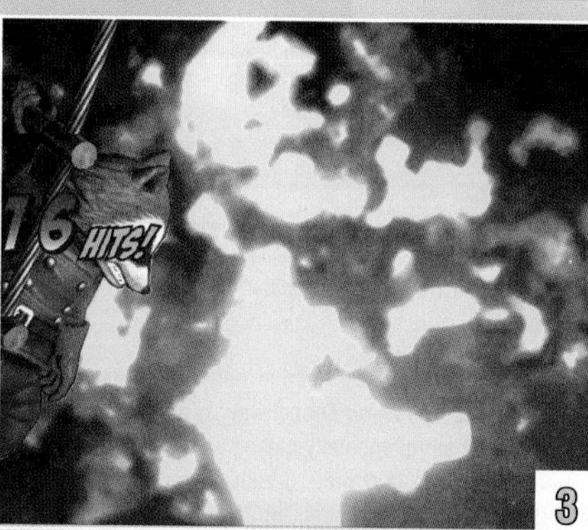
16 HITS!

Rock 'n' Roll: During this hyper combo, Rocket Raccoon unloads a barrage of chain gun bullets into his opponent, which can be mashed for up to 42,000 points of additional damage. This move sends foes spinning into the air, then finishes them off with an enormous homing energy ball. This hyper combo reaches to a fullscreen distance, making it useful as a THC into or out of other long range projectile hyper combos. It's also great as a crossover combination, since the last hit leaves your opponent in a slow, completely vulnerable spinning state that a point character can convert into a full combo!

It's best to only use Rock 'n' Roll during combos because it is incredibly unsafe if guarded; the delay between the chain gun and homing shot is long enough for nearly every character to dash in and punish, even from all the way across screen. When using it in a combo, make sure your adversary isn't bouncing too high, because this hyper combo fires so low to the ground that it can completely whiff if used after certain anti-air attacks.

Mad Hopper: This hyper combo causes Rocket Raccoon to place an enormous landmine on the ground that sends the opposing character hurtling through the air after it hits them! Depending on the buttons pressed to perform this hyper combo, the landmine sends your foe in different directions: (L) + (M) sends them to the left, (M) + (H) bounces them to the right, and (L) + (H) ejects them straight into the air. It's best to mostly use the (L) + (H) version, as you can always combo off it if Rocket Raccoon is close to his rival. The others should be used if you're trying to create a very specific situation; if you switch sides with your foe, an opponent hit by Mad Hopper gets sent farther from Rocket Raccoon, preventing you from converting the hit into a combo.

Unlike with Rocket Raccoon's other mines, you can place multiple Mad Hoppers at the same time, allowing Rocket Raccoon to literally create a minefield out of the screen! If Rocket Raccoon has plenty of meter, consider spending some meter to place a landmine on the ground; landmines stay on screen for 10 seconds, creating a hazard that competitors must carefully avoid. Mad Hopper stays on screen if Rocket Raccoon tags out, allowing Rocket Raccoon to safely tag out and allow your teammates to pressure while under the cover of the mine.

Rocky Raccoon: When this hyper combo is performed, a hole opens up directly under your opponent, no matter where they are in the screen. If this hyper combo hits, it can be mashed for 42,000 additional points of damage and can OTG from anywhere on the screen, dealing huge unscaled damage.

The hole may be in the ground, but this hyper combo can hit foes in the air, as well, and you can use it as anti-air from afar. Rocket Raccoon has no invulnerability during this hyper combo, making other options better choices from close range. In general, Rocky Raccoon should mostly be used at the end of long combos.

"LET'S SEE HOW CUTE I AM AFTER I STRANGLE YOU WITH YOUR OWN INTESTINES."

Battle Plan

While Rocket Raccoon has many zoning tools, he's not an exceptional fullscreen character; he generally loses long range battles to other zoning characters due to his low projectile durability output, and his keepaway tools against aggressive characters generally don't add up to enough damage to base a consistent gameplan around.

Rocket Raccoon's primary goal is to simply make contact with an assist. You should use his projectiles and traps to corral your opponent where you want them to be, call a crossover assist, and use Tunnel Rat M to cross up your adversary before the assist hits.

Begin by preventing your foe's forward movement by using an upward-angled Spitfire H followed by Spitfire Twice M to cover both the ground and the air. This tactic works even better when performed right off the ground by inputting ⇩ ⬂ ⇨ ⬀ + Ⓗ, Ⓜ to reduce Spitfire's recovery time! After Spitfire, immediately fire off a Pendulum to further cover the screen and push your competitor back. If Pendulum hits, you can follow up with a combo by using Rocket Skate to dash toward your rival, then pick them up out of the sky with an Ⓢ launcher!

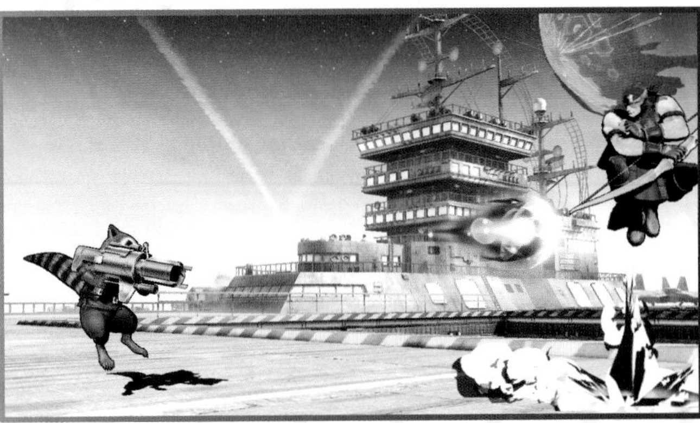

Spitfire fired immediately after jumping recovers faster than if performed on the ground. Use the H version followed by the M version to cut off a huge chunk of the screen!

Rocket Raccoon becomes tiny when using Spitfire, so he can sometimes go toe-to-toe against characters that can dwarf his projectile durability output.

Tunnel Rat M is very difficult to see and can be used alongside crossover assists to create a powerful mix-up.

Rocket Raccoon becomes much stronger when using a long range crossover assist that travels across the screen quickly, such as Doctor Doom—α or Hawkeye—α. These allow you to set up cross-ups using Tunnel Rat M from anywhere on the screen! After firing a low-altitude Spitfire wall, substitute Pendulum with crouching Ⓗ to prevent your opponent from jumping while simultaneously calling a crossover assist, then cancel the crouching Ⓗ into Tunnel Rat M to cross up your foe before the assist makes contact. If the assist hits the target, immediately go into a combo. If your adversary is catching on to your tactics making Rocket Raccoon tunnel behind them, mix it up with Tunnel Rat L and stay in front of your opponent to keep them guessing. If the mix-up fails and your challenger blocks the assist, Rocket Raccoon will generally be directly next to your opponent at frame advantage, where you can go directly into his close range mix-ups! Consult the gameplay sections further for more details on how to confound an attacker at close ranges.

If your foe is trying to super jump over your Spitfire, place a Claymore for him or her to land into instead of throwing out Pendulum. If your opponent attacks on their way down, they'll get hit by the Claymore, which you can convert into a combo. If they manage to block the Claymore, dash in and attack while calling a crossover assist, then go into a mix-up. If your competitor is getting used to your use of Claymore and constantly blocking, jump up and surprise them with an air throw, which can be converted into a combo.

While Rocket Raccoon is fullscreen, you generally have time to send out an Oil Bomb and create another defensive obstacle. You can set one up while keeping up your Spitfire wall by throwing out an Oil Bomb, then igniting it with standing Ⓗ canceled into Spitfire! This is especially effective against aggressive foes who have to close the distance on Rocket Raccoon in order to attack, since they eventually must deal with the wall of flames. If they jump and guard the flames, call an assist, and use this guardstun as an opportunity for a mix-up! If the other player is deterred by the flames and camps in front of them, punish this passive gameplay by calling a long range crossover assist and perform a Tunnel Rat mix-up. While Oil Bomb creates a small hole in your Spitfire zoning, it can create a solid defensive wall that is particularly effective against characters who have to super jump to close the distance on Rocket Raccoon. Against characters with more mobility, avoid using this tactic too often, as it gives them an opportunity to break through your Spitfire defense.

Against other long range characters, Rocket Raccoon will likely get beat in a firefight because Spitfire can't keep up with the durability point output of other long range characters. Against some, Rocket Raccoon can go under their attacks using Spitfire M shots. Alternatively, Rocket Raccoon can avoid projectiles and respond with air Spitfire L relatively safely, but his low health and damage output generally cause you to lose out in the end in a war of attrition. Instead of engaging in firefights at a tactical disadvantage, look for opportunities to call a long range crossover assist and get behind your opponent using Tunnel Rat M. Beam assists make great partners for Rocket Raccoon because they help you use Tunnel Rat to cross up your adversary and also provide additional firepower in a long range firefight.

Without a long range crossover assist, Rocket Raccoon tends to have trouble storming in against other long range characters and using Tunnel Rat M in general. While Tunnel Rat M can be difficult to see, the recovery is long enough to get him punished without cover, and his low health ensures that most characters can put him out of commission in a single combo. In situations where you can't win a firefight, work your way to get Rocket Raccoon to mid range by methodically super jumping and using hover or Rocket Skates, or use Tunnel Rat H to slowly close the distance against your competitor.

When at a range where challengers can normal jump at Rocket Raccoon, he's at his weakest—Spitfire becomes very risky if it misses and opposing characters can avoid Pendulum completely. Calling out crossover assists at this range also becomes incredibly risky because both Rocket Raccoon and his assist can get knocked out if called at an improper time. If you can't safely get out an assist, concentrate on closing the distance from your rival or getting back into long range to continue chipping away with projectiles.

Against characters trying to keep Rocket Raccoon away, you should generally look for a way to close the distance and have him get in close. Using Rocket Skate, Rocket Raccoon can quickly close the distance and initiate offense by super jumping, then canceling into aerial down-forward Rocket Skate when halfway to the apex of the jump. If performed properly, Rocket Raccoon can attack with an air Ⓛ just barely before hitting the ground, creating a particularly strong mix-up. Dash down with air Ⓛ, then immediately follow up with crouching Ⓛ to force your opponent to guard from high to low extremely quickly, if they can even block the air Ⓛ at all! Mix this up by performing air Ⓜ out of the airdash followed by an air Ⓢ, changing the second hit to an overhead attack. These attacks are too fast to guard on reaction, so the opposing player is forced to guess which attack is coming second, which makes for a strong mix-up.

Rocket Skates can't be canceled into basic attacks...

...but when performed at the right height, Rocket Raccoon can throw out a crouching (L) just before landing!

Opponents who are trying to attack Rocket Raccoon from mid range have much less predictable movement patterns, making it much more difficult for you to land this mix-up. Adversaries who approach from the ground can be cut off by using Rocket Skates downward instead of down-forwards into the same mix-up to evade their attack and drop down with an attack of your own.

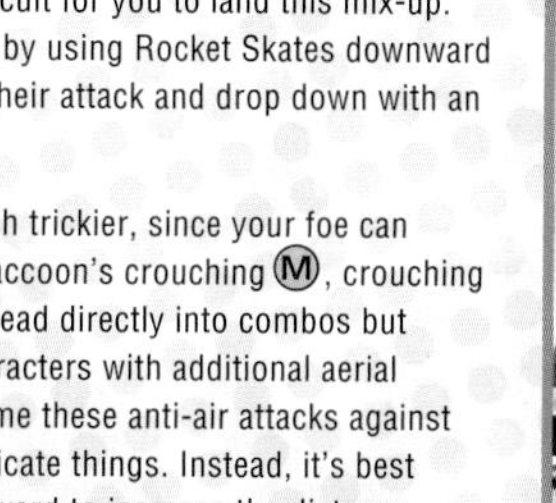

Dealing with a competitor approaching from the air is much trickier, since your foe can easily hit Rocket Raccoon out of Rocket Skates. Rocket Raccoon's crouching (M), crouching (H) and (S) launcher are all excellent anti-air attacks that lead directly into combos but are difficult to use consistently in this manner against characters with additional aerial movement options. While it's relatively easy to properly time these anti-air attacks against a standard jump, trajectory-altering abilities greatly complicate things. Instead, it's best to avoid your rival completely by using Rocket Skate backward to increase the distance between Rocket Raccoon and his foe. Create some cover with crouching (H) while calling a crossover assist, then cancel into backward Rocket Skates, and then cancel the Rocket Skates with Claymore or Angel Gift. By placing a mine at the end, Rocket Raccoon hops even farther backward while placing additional cover on the screen! Your crossover assist may be placed in danger if your opponent evades the crouching (H) projectile, but a Claymore can protect your assist from massive damage by absorbing a hit, allowing them to escape a full combo. Use the time earned from escaping to place another Claymore or lay down a quick, low-altitude spitfire wall.

Force an airborne opponent to land into a Claymore, which keeps them in guardstun long enough to mix them up!

Air throws are always a solid way to deal with opponents approaching from the air, and you can easily convert a connected throw into a solid combo with Rocket Raccoon. Unfortunately, Rocket Raccoon can't easily convert into a combo if an accidental air (H) hits an adversary during an air throw attempt. Instead, option-select an air down-backwards Rocket Skates during every air throw attempt to cruise back to the ground in an attempt to make it safer. Calling a crossover assist that can function decently as an anti-air when attempting an air throw also works well because if the opposing player breaks the air throw or guards the air (H), they'll be forced to land on the assist, allowing you to immediately go into a mix-up.

If it's too difficult to start an offense or easily escape your opponent from medium range, safely laying a Claymore should be the next focus. Once Claymore is out, Rocket Raccoon's safety is almost ensured, buying you time to plan your next move.

When Rocket Raccoon's hover is performed very low to the ground...

...he can perform a nearly instant overhead!

Once at close range, you can have Rocket Raccoon overwhelm his opponent using an incredibly fast mix-up featuring his hover ability! By pressing ⇧ ⇧ , Rocket Raccoon alters his jump trajectory and uses his tail to slowly float toward the ground. This can be performed almost immediately off the ground and then canceled into a jumping attack by inputting ⇧ ⇧ + (L), giving Rocket Raccoon a ridiculously fast overhead that you can chain into air (M), (S) for a combo! Challengers must guess in order to block this overhead properly, so mix this up by simply attacking with crouching (L). If either of the mix-up's option are guarded, you can simply do it again if your competitor doesn't use advancing guard.

Rocket Raccoon's crouching (L) has very short range, and a rival can counter a hovering (L) by sticking out attacks, so it's best to set this mix-up by forcing your opponent to block a crossover assist. If you have a crossover assist that can put your foe in guardstun for an extended period, like Chun-Li—γ or Dante—β, pepper in crouching (L) attacks to keep your opponent guessing when you're going to pull out the overhead.

If your adversary is successfully blocking your mix-up and pushing you out using advancing guard, try to maintain your momentum using air (M). Rocket Raccoon's air (M) propels him forward in the air, allowing him to attack while advancing, occasionally avoiding advancing guard altogether. It also comes out quickly and can chain into air (H) or (S), allowing you to maintain the attack on your target. Even though it's an aerial attack, your competitor can guard it standing or crouching, but no characters can avoid it by ducking under it. The aerial chain gives Rocket Raccoon huge frame advantage, making it a great tool to maintain proximity to his rival. If you're too far to use air (M), you can use that as an opportunity to set up a mix-up with down-forward Rocket Skates. Be sure to call a crossover assist immediately after landing to give Rocket Raccoon cover on his way toward his foe.

While in close range, have Rocket Raccoon make liberal use of his crossover assists and summon them whenever possible. From anywhere outside of point-blank range, your goal should still be to force your opponent to guard a crossover assist so you can perform a hover mix-up.

Whenever an adversary is successfully mixed up, you can convert into a combo that can carry your opponent very far across the screen toward the corner. If your challenger ends up in the corner and finishing a combo with Rock 'n' Roll won't vanquish them, save the meter and prepare a mix-up using your crossover assist instead. Maintaining your corner pressure is often more valuable than the damage caused by the hyper combo, as it is not uncommon for Rocket Raccoon to keep momentum for two to three combos and defeat a character without using a hyper combo at all!

COMBO USAGE CONT.

I. CR. (M), ST. (H), CR. (H), (S) [CANCEL] FORWARD SUPER JUMP, AIR (M), (S), LAND, →↓↘ + (M), →↓↘ + (H), (ATK) + (S), (S) [CANCEL] FORWARD SUPER JUMP, AIR (M), (S), LAND, {→↓↘ + (M) [CANCEL] ↓↘→ + (ATK)(ATK) (MASH (ATK))} OR {→↓↘ + (ATK)(ATK), →↓↘ + (M) [CANCEL] ↓↘→ + (ATK)(ATK) (MASH (ATK))}

618,100~1,012,600 damage, 41~341% meter loss

This combo may be started off of Rocket Raccoon's commonly used instant air (M), (S) attack opening, which can be linked into twice in a row before proceeding into **Combo II** (for 631,500 total damage).

Rocket Skates is used after Pendulum to move Rocket Raccoon into position to launch after the wall bounce. This puts him exactly where you need him to be and is easier than trying to time a forward dash, which might not even get him close enough to hit smaller opponents.

The final OTG Mr. Flapper to Rock 'n' Roll must be super canceled well before the bear trap hits; the trap comes out even if super canceled early. If the bullets hit at the exact moment the trap hits, the combo works despite the ground bounce being previously used. This isn't as hard as it sounds, but it can be tricky if you're trying to cancel the hyper combo after seeing the bear trap hit.

Cancel into Spitfire M, Claymore, or backward Rocket Skate when the opening string is guarded. Claymore deals heavy chip damage when blocked and sticks your adversary in guardstun, allowing you to call a crossover assist and try another mix-up.

If you have the meter, you can end the combo with Rocket Raccoon's level 3 hyper combo to add a ton of unscaled damage, then tack on bear trap into Rock 'n' Roll at the end!

II. ↗↗, AIR (S), LAND, CR. (M), ST. (H), CR. (H), (S) [CANCEL] FORWARD SUPER JUMP, AIR (M), (S), LAND, →↓↘ + (M), →↓↘ + (H), (ATK) + (S), (S) [CANCEL] FORWARD SUPER JUMP, AIR (M), (S), LAND, {→↓↘ + (M) [CANCEL] ↓↘→ + (ATK)(ATK) (MASH (ATK))} OR {→↓↘ + (ATK)(ATK), →↓↘ + (M) [CANCEL] ↓↘→ + (ATK)(ATK) (MASH (ATK))}

633,400~1,032,800 damage, 35~335% meter loss

This combo starts off of a hovering instant overhead, which is nearly impossible to guard unless your competitor guesses that it's coming.

Otherwise, this combo has the same trouble spots as **Combo I**: cancel into Pendulum as soon as possible off of the Mr. Flapper ground bounce, and perform Rock 'n' Roll before the second Mr. Flapper hits.

III. FRONT OR BACK THROW, →↓↘ + (M) [CANCEL] ↓↘→ + (ATK)(ATK) (MASH (ATK))

351,800 damage, 87% meter loss

This combo can be hit whenever Rocket Raccoon lands a ground throw. There isn't enough time for a throw for Mr. Flapper to cause a ground bounce before the opposing character gets up, forcing a ground recover instead.

IV. FRONT OR BACK AIR THROW, →↓↘ + (M), →↓↘ + (H), (ATK) + (S), (S) [CANCEL] FORWARD SUPER JUMP, AIR (M), (S), LAND, →↓↘ + (M) [CANCEL] ↓↘→ + (ATK)(ATK) (MASH (ATK)

402,300 damage, 60% meter loss

An air throw leaves your opponent in a hard knockdown state long enough for Mr. Flapper to cause ground bounce, so you can go into half of Rocket Raccoon's basic combo.

Perform the first bear trap immediately after hitting the ground to ensure that it ground bounces. If performed too late, your opponent recovers instead, making you lose out on tons of damage.

V. ↓↙← + (H), FORWARD JUMP, AIR (H), (S), LAND, CR. (H), (S) [CANCEL] FORWARD SUPER JUMP, AIR (M), (S), LAND, →↓↘ + (M), →↓↘ + (H), (ATK) + (S), (S) [CANCEL] FORWARD SUPER JUMP, AIR (M), (S), LAND, →↓↘ + (M) [CANCEL] ↓↘→ + (ATK)(ATK) (MASH (ATK))

535,500 damage, 31% meter loss

This combo should be used whenever an adversary gets caught in Grab Bag's net.

Try to hit the first air (H) on the downward arc of your jump to make sure your rival doesn't pop too high into the air after getting hit by the first (S).

VI. →↓↘ + (H), (ATK) + (S), (S) [CANCEL] FORWARD SUPER JUMP, AIR (M), (S), LAND, →↓↘ + (M), (ATK) + (S), (S) [CANCEL] FORWARD SUPER JUMP, AIR (M), (S), LAND, →↓↘ + (M) [CANCEL] ↓↘→ + (ATK)(ATK) (MASH (ATK))

608,100 damage, 54% meter loss

Use this combo whenever Pendulum tags an opponent out of the air.

Since your wall bounce has already been used, you can't use Pendulum after the first Mr. Flapper, so use Rocket Skates to close the distance and immediately launch your foe after it hits.

ADVANCED TACTICS

FIRE DOWN BELOW!

When used as an anti-air, Oil Bomb forces your opponent to land in the inferno, giving time to set up a mix-up!

With some setup time, Oil Bomb can be a useful tool for keeping the opposing character out and setting up your offense, as it can both keep adversaries out from long ranges and keep your foe blocking up close!

Before using Oil Bomb, your rival can easily hit Rocket Raccoon while he's throwing it, so make sure Rocket Raccoon has enough time to get it out safely. The best times to throw an Oil Bomb are when Rocket Raccoon is safely across the screen or if your competitor is guarding a crossover assist from a distance too far away to start a mix-up. The latter scenario often happens against players who are quick to use advancing guard.

Once oil is on the ground, Rocket Raccoon's ground game becomes much more threatening. There are four ways to ignite oil: Spitfire L, exploding an Oil Bomb in mid-air with Spitfire H, or crouching (H) and standing (H). Of these options, standing (H) is the most useful because it allows you to ignite the oil during a chain combo! Throw an Oil Bomb over an opponent and ignite with a crouching (L) to stand (H) chain combo, or simply standing (H)!

From fullscreen, ignited oil serves best as a deterrent, as it cuts off the ground from your opponent, forcing them to approach Rocket Raccoon from the air and then making them more likely to run into an anti-air Pendulum! Rocket Raccoon can also anti-air his adversaries with his (S) launcher, or simply allow them to jump in, forcing them to block the fire.

If the oil is over the target, quickly perform a hover overhead before they can use advancing guard; while ignited oil can keep your rival stuck blocking, they can also advancing guard the attack until it is over, forcing Rocket Raccoon to the far side of the screen. To counter, wait until the fire is almost finished, then use Tunnel Rat M while calling a crossover assist to mix up your competitor!

THUNDER FROM DOWN UNDER

Tunnel Rat H is completely invincible for up to two seconds, allowing Rocket Raccoon to avoid anything thrown at him!

During Tunnel Rat H, Rocket Raccoon is completely invincible, giving you the chance to have him perform some particularly sneaky tricks.

When emerging from Tunnel Rat H, Rocket Raccoon only has 9 frames of vulnerability, which is impossible to react to. The easiest way to punish Rocket Raccoon is by mashing chainable crouching (L) attacks, which many characters don't have access to, which forces your opponent to guess when Rocket Raccoon might emerge. You can perform a quick mix up when Rocket Raccoon emerges: throwing your opponent is the recommended option, but you can gamble and go for much more damage by emerging and using crouching (L) or a float overhead. In either case, be sure to call a crossover assist while performing your basic attacks; if the opposing character guards, the assist pins them in place long enough for you to perform another mix-up!

Against characters with chainable crouching (L) attacks, you can counter this with big damage by hyper combo canceling Tunnel Rat into Mad Hopper. Mad Hopper has no invincibility, so move Rocket Raccoon just out of the range of his challenger's attacks at the last second before performing the hyper combo. Since you're holding down (H), you can only perform the variation of Mad Hopper using (L) + (M); performing a different variation requires Rocket Raccoon to emerge first, slightly lengthening the time for the hyper combo to come out. If the foe is still mashing (L) before the hyper combo freeze, the hyper combo hits before the opponent can block, giving Rocket Raccoon a free combo!

Opposing players typically try to get away from Tunnel Rat H by having their character jump away. In this case, you can have Rocket Raccoon chase after them while underground until they reach mid range, then quickly emerge, super jump straight up, and attack with a down-forward Rocket Skate mix-up.

COMBO APPENDIX

GENERAL EXECUTION TIPS

After hitting the (S) launcher attack, hit with the air (M), (S) chain as early as possible to keep the opposing character in range for the OTG-capable Mr. Flapper

If you're having trouble juggling the Pendulum attack after the Mr. Flapper ground bounce, input the command much earlier than you think you can

Practice the timing to properly hyper combo cancel the OTG-capable Mr. Flapper to Rock 'n' Roll; the special move must be hyper combo canceled before the bear trap hits the target, but not before the bear trap appears on the screen

AS ROCKET RACCOON COMES IN: AIR (H), (S)

Notes	Damage
↑ + (S) or → + (S) or ↓ + (S) TAC to Rocket Raccoon	Varies based on damage scaling

CR. (M), ST. (H), CR. (H), (S) CANCEL→ FORWARD SUPER JUMP, AIR (M), (S), LAND, →↓↘ + (M), →↓↘ + (L), CR. (H) CANCEL→ →↓↘ + (L), CR. (H) CANCEL→ →↓↘ + (H), FORWARD DASH, (S) CANCEL→ FORWARD SUPER JUMP, AIR (H), (S), LAND, →↓↘ + ATK ATK, →↓↘ + (M)

Notes	Damage
Requires corner	816,200 damage, 219% meter loss

CR. (M), ST. (H), CR. (H) CANCEL→ ↓↙← + (L) + (H), FORWARD DASH, (S) CANCEL→ FORWARD SUPER JUMP, AIR (M), (S), LAND, →↓↘ + (M), →↓↘ + (H), ATK + (S), (S) CANCEL→ FORWARD SUPER JUMP, AIR (H), (S), LAND, →↓↘ + ATK ATK, →↓↘ + (M) CANCEL→ ↓↘→ + ATK ATK (MASH ATK)

Notes	Damage
After air (H), (S), you must perform Rocky Raccoon as soon as Rocket Raccoon lands from the jump	1,105,300 damage, 453% meter loss

↓↘→ + ATK ATK (MASH ATK), BEFORE FINAL HIT X-FACTOR ↓↓ + (L), →↓↘ + (M), →↓↘ + (H), (S) CANCEL→ FORWARD SUPER JUMP, AIR (M), (S), LAND, →↓↘ + (M) CANCEL→ ↓↘→ + ATK ATK (MASH ATK)

Notes	Damage
Requires X-Factor	669,900~808,600 damage, 158~144% meter loss

CR. (M), ST. (H), CR. (H) X-FACTOR (S) CANCEL→ FORWARD SUPER JUMP, AIR (M), (S), LAND, →↓↘ + (M), →↓↘ + (H), ATK + (S), (S) CANCEL→ FORWARD SUPER JUMP, AIR (M), (S), LAND, →↓↘ + (M) CANCEL→ ↓↘→ + ATK ATK (MASH ATK)

Notes	Damage
Requires X-Factor	728,900~925,500 damage, 32~13% meter loss

NEW

FIREBRAND

"THIS TIME, IT'S YOU THAT'LL TURN INTO A PILE OF BONES!"

Bio

REAL NAME

Firebrand

OCCUPATION

Demon World Knight

ABILITIES

Can spit fireballs from his mouth, fly (hover) and cling to walls (Hell Climb).

WEAPONS

None

PROFILE

Firebrand is a type of gargoyle known as a Red Arremer. He will stand up to any threat posed to his home, the Demon Village, without any fear. Firebrand is considered to be an elite warrior among the Red Arremers, gaining him hero status among his peers.

FIRST APPEARANCE

Ghosts 'n Goblins (1985)

POWER GRID

2	INTELLIGENCE
3	STRENGTH
3	SPEED
3	STAMINA
5	ENERGY PROJECTION
4	FIGHTING ABILITY

*This is biographical, and does not represent an evaluation of the in-game combat potential of this hero.

ALTERNATE COSTUMES

Overview

Vitality	850,000
Chain Combo Archetype	Hunter Series

X-Factor Boost	Damage	Speed
Level 1 (3 teammates remaining)	115%	125%
Level 2 (2 teammates remaining)	135%	135%
Level 3 (1 teammate remaining)	155%	145%

While you have many ways to take to the air and swoop around the screen when using Firebrand, he is primarily an offensive character whose ultimate goal is to get close to his adversary.

Once Firebrand gets close, you can use his many aerial movement options to attack the opposing character by:

- **Switching sides using Hell's Elevator M and Hell Dive M and a crossover assist**
- **Using Hell Dive L to perform high-low mix-ups**
- **Performing instant overheads using the Luminous Body hyper combo, jumping Ⓛ, and air Bon Voyage**
- **Activating Chaos Tide to continuously assault your rival**

How do you get close with Firebrand?

- **Using air Bon Voyage, which has advantage on guard**
- **Dashing through the air using Hell Dive M under the cover of a crossover assist**
- **Advance while attacking using Demon Missile H and a crossover assist**

Attack Set

Standing Basic Attacks

Screen	Command	Hits	Damage	Meter Gain	Startup	Active	Recovery	Advantage on Hit	Advantage if Guarded	Notes
1	Standing Ⓛ	1	33,000	264	5	3	9	+6	+6	Chains into Ⓛ attacks
2	Standing Ⓜ	1	45,000	360	8	3	15	+1	0	—
3	Standing Ⓗ	2	73,200	640	10	2(7)4	18	+2	+1	—

Crouching Basic Attacks

Screen	Command	Hits	Damage	Meter Gain	Startup	Active	Recovery	Advantage on Hit	Advantage if Guarded	Notes
1	Crouching Ⓛ	1	33,000	264	4	2	12	0	-1	Low attack, chains into Ⓛ attacks
2	Crouching Ⓜ	1	48,000	384	8	4	17	-2	-3	Low attack
3	Crouching Ⓗ	1	65,000	520	10	8	26	—	-11	Low attack, knocks down

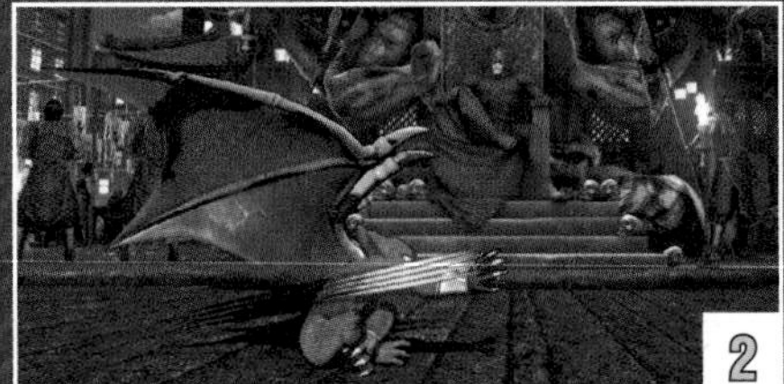

Ground Special Attack—Launcher

Screen	Command	Hits	Damage	Meter Gain	Startup	Active	Recovery	Advantage on Hit	Advantage if Guarded	Notes
1	Ⓢ (while standing or crouching)	1	75,000	600	9	5	30	—	-12	Launcher, not special- or hyper combo-cancelable

Air Basic Attacks

Screen	Command	Hits	Damage	Meter Gain	Startup	Active	Recovery	Advantage on Hit	Advantage if Guarded	Notes
1	Air Ⓛ	1	35,000	280	5	3	17	+12	+11	Overhead attack
2	Air Ⓜ	1	48,000	384	8	4	22	+17	+16	Overhead attack
3	Air Ⓗ	2	74,000	640	8	3(2)4	29	+19	+18	Overhead attack

Air Special Attacks—Flying Screen and Air Exchange

Air Ⓢ causes a hard knockdown when used in a launcher combo (this is sometimes called flying screen). When used outside of a launcher combo, air Ⓢ behaves mostly like another basic attack. Air exchange attacks, performed by inputting a direction plus Ⓢ, are only possible during a launcher combo. Exchange hits initiate team aerial combos by tagging in the next available character to continue the air combo.

Screen	Command	Hits	Damage	Meter Gain	Startup	Active	Recovery	Advantage on Hit	Advantage if Guarded	Notes
1	Air Ⓢ	1	70,000	560	10	4	32	+15	+14	Causes hard knockdown if used in launcher combo, overhead attack
2	Air ⇧ + Ⓢ (during launcher combo)	2	105,00	880	9	5	30	—	—	Tags in next available ally while lofting opponent upward
3	Air ⇨ or ⇦ + Ⓢ (during launcher combo)	2	95,000	800	8	4	22	—	—	Tags in next available ally while causing wall bounce, erases 1 hyper meter bar from foe
4	Air ⇩ + Ⓢ (during launcher combo)	2	95,000	800	10	4	32	—	—	Tags in next available ally while causing ground bounce, generates 1 hyper meter bar

Command Attacks

Command attacks resemble basic attacks but have different chaining and canceling properties. It's usually possible to chain *into* a command attack from basic attacks, but most command attacks cannot be chained from or canceled themselves.

Screen	Name	Command	Hits	Damage	Meter Gain	Startup	Active	Recovery	Advantage on Hit	Advantage if Guarded	Notes
1	Devil's Claw	(in air) ⇩ + Ⓗ	1	70,000	560	18	Until grounded	11	—	+11	Ground bounces foe, enters Hover on contact

Throws

Throws are for snagging passive or blocking opponents. Since throws are active so quickly, you can also use them to preemptively toss opposing characters out of their offense. Combos are usually possible after throws, one way or another.

Screen	Command	Hits	Damage	Meter Gain	Startup	Active	Notes
1	⇨ + Ⓗ (ground)	2	80,000	800	1	1	Hard knockdown
	⇦ + Ⓗ (ground)	2	80,000	800	1	1	Hard knockdown
2	⇨ + Ⓗ (air)	2	80,000	800	1	1	Hard knockdown
	⇦ + Ⓗ (air)	2	80,000	800	1	1	Hard knockdown

As a Partner—Crossover Assists

Screen	Type	P1+P2 Crossover Combination Hyper Combo	Description	Hits	Damage	Meter Gain	Startup	Active	Recovery (this crossover assist)	Recovery (other partner)	Notes
1	Firebrand—α	Dark Fire	Hell Spitfire H	6	100,000 + 15,000 x 5	800 + 120 x 5	50	—	111	81	Knocks down, first projectile active for 4 frames and has 3 low priority durability points, following projectiles become active 2 frames later for 62 frames and have 2 low priority durability points
2	Firebrand—β	Dark Fire	Demon Missile M	1	100,000	800	39	20	112	82	—
3	Firebrand—γ	Dark Fire	Demon Missile H	1	80,000	640	50	31	112	82	—

1

2

3

When Firebrand—α is called, he performs his Hell Spitfire H attack. This is useful to any character who doesn't have their own OTG attack because it only hits three times as an OTG, so it won't influence hitstun and damage-scaling that much. It's also very easily converted to a combo! It comes out fairly slowly, however, so it can be difficult to use. Outside of a combo, you can keep an opponent stuck in guardstun without the threat of getting pushed out by advancing guard, allowing characters to keep up aggression while limiting your competitor's options.

Firebrand—β makes Firebrand perform his Demon Missile M attack, which causes him to cruise across the screen horizontally. This assist covers the screen very quickly, which allows it to extend combos when used in combination with an OTG attack, or tack on some extra damage to a flying adversary. Outside of combos, its usefulness is fairly limited, since Firebrand is completely vulnerable as he charges across the screen, making him an easy target for a rival who sees him coming.

During Firebrand—γ, Firebrand bursts onto the screen and performs his Devil Missile H attack, which causes him to swoop across the screen like he does in the classic *Ghosts 'n Goblins* games. This assist is useful for characters who like to keep the opponent in guardstun, since it covers most of the screen while it attacks. Firebrand is completely vulnerable from the time he jumps out to the time he jumps back and performs the attack, so make sure you have plenty of safety before you call him out.

Snap Back

Screen	Command	Hits	Damage	Meter Gain	Startup	Active	Recovery	Advantage on Hit	Advantage if Guarded
1	↓↘→ + P1 or P2	1	50,000	500 (-1 hyper meter bar)	2	3	24	—	-4

Notes

On hit, snap back forces the opposing point character to be replaced by an assist. Opposing assist calls or tag outs are also locked out for 4 seconds

1

Special Moves

Screen	Name	Command	Hits	Damage	Meter Gain	Startup	Active	Recovery	Advantage on Hit	Advantage if Guarded	Notes
1, 2	Hell Spitfire L (in air OK)	↓↘→ + L	1	100,000	800	16	—	29	0	-1	Projectile has 5 low priority durability points
3, 4	Hell Spitfire M (in air OK)	↓↘→ + M	1	100,000	800	16	—	29	0	-1	Projectile has 5 low priority durability points
5, 6	Hell Spitfire H (in air OK)	↓↘→ + H	6	100,000 + 15,000 x 5	800 + 120 x 5	26	—	20 (air: until grounded)	—	+54 (air: +41)	First projectile has 3 (air: 5) low priority durability points, upon contact with ground, the first projectile produces 5 more projectiles with 3 low priority durability points that travel along the ground for 62 frames
7	Bon Voyage (in air OK)	↓↘→ + S	9	144,000	1440	13	15	28	—	-30 (air: +10)	Wall bounces foe, hard knockdown if wall bounce occurs
8	Demon Missile L	→↓↘ + L	1	100,000	800	15	20	21	+2	+1	Enters Hover upon contact
9	Demon Missile M	→↓↘ + M	1	100,000	800	15	20	21	-17	-18	Can pass through adversaries
10	Demon Missile H	→↓↘ + H	1	80,000	640	23	30	0	-4	-4	Enters Hover after recovery
11, 12, 13	Hell's Elevator	↓↙← + ATK	—	—	—	26	—	1	—	—	Enters Hover after recovery
14, 15, 16	Hell Dive	(in air) ↓↙← + ATK	—	—	—	15	—	—	—	—	—
17	Hover	↓↙← + S	—	—	—	30	—	—	—	—	Lasts 90 frames

1

2

3

4

Hell Spitfire L: During this attack, Firebrand spits a ball of fire straight forward, whether he's on the ground or in the air. This attack deals pretty big damage for a projectile, inflicting 100,000 on hit and 30,000 points of chip damage when guarded. This move is best used against characters who must come to Firebrand; spit some fire at them, and force them to get closer to him.

Unfortunately, Hell Spitfire isn't great in a projectile war, as each projectile only has 5 low priority projectile durability points, meaning it'll get crushed by more dedicated zoning characters and those with beam attacks. The recovery is also fairly long. In a projectile war, think about using Hell Spitfire M from the air instead!

Hell Spitfire M: This version of Hell Spitfire causes Firebrand to summon a ball of fire from his mouth and shoot it at an angle, either at the air while he's on the ground or toward the ground while he's in the air. This attack inflicts the same damage as Hell Spitfire L, dealing 100,000 damage on hit and 30,000 points of chip damage when guarded. On the ground, its uses are fairly limited because Firebrand shoots the fireball very high; at fullscreen, he shoots it at the timer! This can hit characters from close range, but you'll have to be fairly omniscient to use it well: if you do it too late or too early, you'll pay with a combo, and if your opponent doesn't jump at all, they can dash in and destroy you.

In the air, however, it's a great tool for taking potshots at long range characters since the angle it fires at is great for hitting targets on the ground from normal jump and super jump height. If you need to get Firebrand a little closer to his opponent to hit them, use Hell Dive M to have him dash toward a projectile-flinging competitor and blast them in the face with Hell Spitfire M. Air Hell Spitfire M is also good against aggressive adversaries trying to rush in, because it's angled to cut off a good portion of the screen from the opposing character.

5

6

Hell Spitfire H: Unlike the other versions of Hell Spitfire, the H version shoots a projectile straight into the ground on land or in the air. After hitting the ground, the fireball erupts into an inferno of flames that travels a very short distance and is capable of hitting your rival. If an opponent is forced to guard all hits of the attack, it'll deal 43,500 points of chip damage and 146,300 points of damage on hit. While it's not quite as good as Dormammu's Flame Carpet, you can use this similarly to keep your challengers stuck in guardstun or to prevent enemies from rushing in at you. However, its effectiveness is mitigated if your foe hits Firebrand while the projectiles are out, because the flames disappear if Firebrand is hit.

Furthermore, unlike the other version of Hell Spitfire, Firebrand can only spit one Hell Spitfire H in the air; after you perform the attack, you cannot have him act again until he hits the ground. Hell Spitfire is best used as an OTG, since it allows you to easily OTG after most of Firebrand's throws and if a random hit forces your opponent on the ground.

Bon Voyage: When this attack is performed, Firebrand rushes toward his rival at a 45-degree angle. If he connects, he drags them across the ground, setting them on fire with the friction created and then wall bouncing them, leaving them open for a combo! No matter where he is on the screen, Firebrand will try to take his opponent to the corner, and he can succeed from everywhere but the far side of the screen. The farther he drags his adversary, the more the move hits and the more damage is dealt, which is actually disadvantageous because it makes the following combo more difficult and more affected by damage-scaling.

On the ground, this move is best used as a whiff punisher against big misses because it travels across the ground incredibly quickly. It's unsafe if the opposing player guards it, however, so try not to throw it out that often. The air version is one of his greatest assets and an excellent tool to both attack and approach your target, as it's +10 frame advantage on guard and hits the competitor the same as it does on the ground! Use it to avoid projectiles or rivals rushing in at Firebrand; even if it's guarded, it's fine because you're at an advantage and get to make the next move first!

7

8

Demon Missile L: This attack causes Firebrand to propel himself at his opponent by charging toward them. If this attack connects with the opposing character, Firebrand jumps backward and starts Hovering automatically, making it a good way to both attack the target and start going into flight.

While this attack can quickly close distance against a grounded opponent, if your challenger guards it and uses advancing guard, Firebrand is pushed completely across the screen. This is very disadvantageous for Firebrand, so you should use this attack sparingly.

9

Demon Missile M: Similarly to Demon Missile L, in this move, Firebrand launches himself toward his opponent with a charging attack. Unlike the L version, Firebrand does not launch himself into the air after this attack connects.

Demon Missile M quickly covers the ground, giving you an easy way to close distances on the ground and get Firebrand next to his rival. Even if an adversary uses advancing guard, Firebrand continues advancing toward his foe, allowing him to get close to them while attacking. Demon Missile M is very unsafe if guarded at most distances; call a crossover assist that will cover Firebrand's recovery before performing this attack.

10

Demon Missile H: During this attack, Firebrand jumps backward into the air, then swoops in an arc while slashing at his target. After attacking his rival, Firebrand stays in the air in Hover state, allowing you to move Firebrand closer to his opponent with Hell Dive M or air Bon Voyage. Demon Missile H is a great tool for quickly moving Firebrand close to his opponent while attacking, since this attack moves very quickly and mitigates the effectiveness of advancing guard when guarded.

When used under the cover of a crossover assist, you can combo if Demon Missile H hits, and you can even cross your adversary up if Firebrand passes over them! Unlike Demon Missile L, Firebrand ends up close to his competitor even when the move is used from close range, meaning that you can convert Hover into additional pressure on Firebrand's enemy by using an additional attack.

Hell's Elevator: When performed, this special move causes Firebrand to jump into the air and immediately activate Hover, essentially functioning as a jump that can be canceled into from basic attacks. Firebrand moves in a different direction depending on the button pressed: Firebrand jumps straight in the air during the L version, he jumps toward his opponent with the M version, and he jumps away from his adversary with the H version.

11

12

13

The M version in particular is an excellent offensive tool. When jumping forward, Firebrand negates the effects of advancing guard, allowing him to stay close to his rival while putting him into position to attack from the air! If used next to his foe at midscreen, Firebrand jumps behind his target, which you can then use in combination with a crossover assist to cross your competitor up.

14

15

16

Hell Dive: This aerial special move causes Firebrand to quickly move toward his opponent. Like Hell's Elevator, the button pressed determines the direction Firebrand travels: the L version moves him downwards, the M version moves him toward his opponent, and the H version moves him away from his attacker.

Hell Dive M gives Firebrand additional mobility in the air, allowing him to get close to his adversary. While each individual Hell Dive M doesn't travel particularly far, you can use Hell Dive M up to three times when Firebrand is in the air, which is enough to have him travel the entire screen during a super jump!

Hell Dive L causes Firebrand to quickly reach the ground from the air, which you can use to quickly mix up your challenger. Attack with a jumping attack, then immediately cancel into Hell Dive L to put Firebrand back on the ground, then mix up your opponent with another jumping attack or a crouching (L)!

Since Hell Dive H moves backward, it's not as useful for Firebrand as the others, as he is best when close to his opponent. While Hell Dive H is useful when you need to create distance from your foe, you can also use it in conjunction with Hell Dive M to mix up your approach against an enemy with a defensive assist, like Haggar. In this situation, dash toward your opponent with Hell Dive M to bait out the assist, then avoid it with Hell Dive H, giving you an opportunity to attack.

17

Hover: This special move causes Firebrand to instantly enter Hover state without using Hell's Elevator or Demon Missile L or H. Since Firebrand does not have a standard airdash, he can't use Hover to quickly traverse the screen like Magneto or Storm, limiting Hover's usefulness as an approach tool. When used from the ground, Firebrand flies low enough to hit his opponent with an overhead air (S) against a crouching foe, or he can mix up an adversary expecting the overhead by immediately performing Hell Dive L and attacking the opposing character with crouching (L)!

Hyper Combos

Screen	Name	Command	Hits	Damage	Startup	Active	Recovery	Advantage on Hit	Advantage if Guarded	Notes
1	Dark Fire (in air OK)	↓↘→ + ATK ATK	20~40	294,200~353,100	12+1	50	33 (air: 33 + until grounded)	-14	-25	Can be mashed for extra damage, beam durability: 20 frames x 3 high priority durability points, OTG-capable
2	Luminous Body (in air OK)	↓↙← + ATK ATK	—	—	9+11	—	—	—	—	Firebrand gains a 25% speed increase, lasts for 593 frames
3	Chaos Tide (Level 3 Hyper Combo)	→↓↘ + ATK ATK	—	—	9+0	—	20	—	—	Summons a hovering Red Arremer that perform 3 attacks based on button pressed, (L) = Hell Spitfire M, (M) = Demon Missile M, (H) = Demon Missile H, lasts for 598 frames, Red Arremer accepts inputs for 579 frames

1

Dark Fire: During this hyper combo, a stream of fire emerges from Firebrand's mouth, which he uses to sweep the screen in an inferno of hellfire! This attack is OTG-capable, and it can be mashed for up to 58,900 additional points of damage. Dark Fire is best used to end combos, since Firebrand spends most of this hyper combo spitting fire below him instead of toward his opponent.

If you use this move when Firebrand is too far away from his adversary, Firebrand misses out on a ton of extra damage since a large portion of this hyper combo's attack is aimed toward the ground. It's best to perform this hyper combo directly next to your rival when used as an OTG.

Luminous Body: This hyper combo causes Firebrand to turn a solid white, and it gives him a massive 25% speed boost for about 10 seconds! When in Luminous Body, you can have Firebrand perform an instant overhead combo not normally possible by performing jumping (L) immediately after jumping, then canceling into air Bon Voyage! Unlike many power-up hyper combos, Firebrand continues to gain meter while in Luminous Body, allowing you to continue to gain meter while quickly attacking your opponent.

2

While in Luminous Body, you need to alter the timing when performing Firebrand's combos because his increased speed causes him to travel through the air faster when jumping. If you land a combo in Luminous Body and still have time remaining, consider ending a combo with Hell Spitfire H instead of Dark Fire to give yourself a chance to perform an additional mix-up on your adversary.

3

Chaos Tide: When this level 3 hyper combo is performed, Firebrand summons an additional Red Arremer that can attack his opponent for nine and a half seconds! The way your Red Arremer buddy attacks depends on the button pressed: (L) causes it to spit an air Hell Spitfire M, (M) causes it to perform Demon Missile M, and (H) causes it to swoop through the air using Demon Missile H.

Of the three Red Arremer attacks, (H) is the most useful, as (M) flies too high to hit crouching characters and many standing characters, and (L) can only hit characters close to the Red Arremer. To most effectively use Chaos Tide, try to press (H) as much as possible to keep Red Arremer constantly swooping on your rival. For additional strategies involving Chaos Tide, check the Advanced Tactics section.

Battle Plan

Calling an assist and using Demon Missile M lets Firebrand cross the screen quickly and safely.

Hell Spitfire M shoots downward at an angle that can go over projectiles from fullscreen.

Although Firebrand has quite an array of projectile attacks, you should avoid having him fight at long range as much as possible. On the ground, Firebrand's Hell Spitfire attacks have relatively low projectile durability, making it difficult to win a firefight. They also have fairly long recovery and travel slowly, making them incredibly risky against characters with a teleport.

If stuck behind a projectile wall, Hell Spitfire M is a good way to strike at projectile characters from the air. From super jump height, Hell Spitfire M can travel across the screen on a projectile-thrower while blocking off attackers trying to advance by dashing on the ground or through the air. Hell Spitfire deals 100,000 points of damage for every hit, which is pretty big damage for a projectile, especially against characters with low life. While it may be difficult to knock out an opponent with just Hell Spitfire, you can deal enough damage to force your competitor off their zoning game in an effort to make up the damage. Dark Fire is good for blowing through an enemy's projectile assault, but it won't do much damage because Firebrand spends most of the hyper combo shooting fire on the ground instead of toward his rival.

If your opponent doesn't have projectiles but is still acting defensively, Firebrand can ignore any posturing and easily zip toward his opponent with Demon Missile M, which covers fullscreen distance while attacking and is mostly unaffected by advancing guard, leaving Firebrand right next to his adversary. If Demon Missile M whiffs, Firebrand is left near his target completely vulnerable, so call a crossover assist before firing it off. Demon Missile H can leave Firebrand right next to his challenger, as well, but it misses the opponent and leaves Firebrand stuck in Hover above his foe, unable to guard. When combined with a crossover assist to cover Firebrand's advance, Firebrand is above his opponent at an advantage, allowing him to drop down on his competitor and start his offense with (S) or Hell Dive L.

Firebrand can also easily cross the screen with Hell Dive M. From super jump height, you can perform Hell Dive M three times, and this leaves Firebrand next to his opponent with enough time to come down with an attack. This approach is very obvious, as your opponent has plenty of time to react to Firebrand diving downward with an attack of their own. While Firebrand can guard after Hell Dive, having to guard in that situation places Firebrand on the defensive, which is not recommended! Instead of using Hell Dive M three times, mix up your approach with Hell Dive H or L. If an adversary has a defensive assist, Hell Dive H can dash back far enough to avoid it, giving you a chance to potentially hit both your target and their assist, while Hell Dive L drops Firebrand straight down, putting him in range to whiff punish with crouching (H)!

The air version of Bon Voyage gives Firebrand frame advantage, making it an excellent pressure and advancing tool.

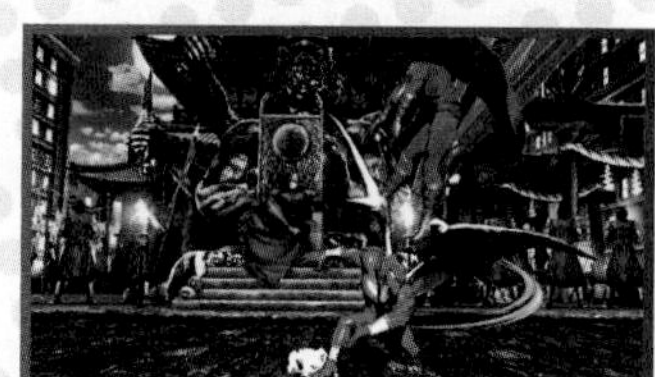

Firebrand's standing (M) has a huge hitbox above it while he gets smaller, making it an excellent anti-air attack!

As Firebrand gets closer to his foe, you can start making liberal use of aerial Bon Voyage. If Bon Voyage hits the opposing character, you can convert it into a combo, and when it's guarded, it leaves Firebrand at +10 frame advantage, safely getting him close to his rival and giving him plenty of time to start an offense! From fullscreen, it's best not to try using Bon Voyage to advance, since at peak super jump height, which is required to reach a fullscreen opponent, it stops attacking shortly before hitting, leaving Firebrand stranded in midair and vulnerable to attack. Once in range, pressure your competitor by super jumping and quickly performing Bon Voyage; it is incredibly difficult to beat Bon Voyage with basic attacks, and trying to do so generally gives Firebrand the chance for a big combo!

Once at mid range, Spitfire becomes a much more risky attack. An opponent who jumps over Spitfire can put Firebrand in big trouble, and a character with a fast horizontal airdash can destroy him. When you think your adversary might jump, you can keep them back with Spitfire M, but if it whiffs, or you guess wrong and your attacker stays on the ground, you'll be in big trouble.

It's better to rely on Firebrand's other special moves, since they become much more versatile at mid range, allowing him to advance on his opponent while attacking. From mid range, Demon Missile M not only moves to his foe, but depending on the range, it can leave Firebrand behind his challenger! The difference is only a few steps and impossible to tell before the attack has finished. While this won't make Demon Missile M itself cross up, it can catch your opponent off guard if they aren't expecting it. If used alongside a crossover assist, Firebrand is left at huge advantage, and you can convert a hit into a combo.

Demon Missile H won't whiff at mid range, making it a good tool to close the remaining distance between Firebrand and his opponent. Even if your adversary uses advancing guard, Firebrand is left hovering right above his competitor, where he can mix them up by falling to the ground with (S) or quickly moving to the ground with Hell Dive L. At the end of Demon Missile H when Firebrand is in Hover, you can call a crossover assist before attacking to keep Firebrand covered during your mix-up.

If you have to strike back at an aggressive opponent, Firebrand's standing (M) and (H) are both excellent defensive attacks. Firebrand shrinks slightly during standing (M), which makes him harder to hit, while the hitboxes on the attack are higher than the move's animation makes it seem. This allows the move to connect with enemies at normal jump height while Firebrand is generally safe. Standing (H) has long startup, but it hits way above Firebrand in an area he can't be hit at all, making it a great anti-air if you have time to use it. Using either attack as anti-air requires very strict timing because both attacks only have one to two active frames where they hit above Firebrand's head, so make sure you can get the hit instead of taking a risk.

You can perform Hell Dive M incredibly low to the ground, giving Firebrand a makeshift triangle jump...

...that can hit overhead with Devil's Claw or low with crouching (L)!

Your ultimate goal with Firebrand should be to get him close to his opponent and stay there as long as possible. Up close, his special moves become much more effective, allowing him to use each one of them in a different wacky mix-up!

Once Firebrand is next to his competitor, Hell's Elevator M can quickly jump over the target, which can create a cross-up using a crossover assist. This can be set up fairly easily, as well: call an assist during a basic attack chain combo, then cancel into Hell's Elevator M to make Firebrand jump over his rival! Depending on when you cancel into Hell's Elevator and how close Firebrand is, Firebrand might still jump over his opponent. If not, have Firebrand remain above the opposing character at a distance close enough to mix them up. Once Firebrand is in the air, you can perform another mix-up on your challenger using Hell Dive.

You can use Demon Missile H similarly to Hell's Elevator M, as when used up close, Firebrand ends up on the other side of his opponent! It's set up similarly, too: during a chain combo or just a crouching (L), call a crossover assist and cancel into Demon Missile H. Even if your adversary guards the cross-up, Firebrand is left at advantage, so use that opportunity to keep on the pressure by canceling the Hover at the end of Demon Missile H with (S), Bon Voyage, or Hell Dive L or M.

At close range, you can use Hell Dive L and M to mix up the opposing character if you find Firebrand in the air or stuck in Hover next to his rival in the air after Hell's Elevator or Demon Missile H. Hell Dive L sends Firebrand directly to the ground, where he can quickly attack with a low-hitting crouching (L). Most players instinctively guard high when they see their opponent in the air, allowing you to catch them off guard with the speed of Hell Dive L. The effectiveness of Hell Dive M up close depends on whether or not you can call a crossover assist; if you can't, getting behind your competitor won't accomplish much since Firebrand can only turn around to perform a special attack. If you do have a crossover assist available, Hell Dive M becomes a decent, if not fairly gimmicky, cross-up tool. Simply call a crossover assist, then jump and perform Hell Dive M, and the assist hits on the opposite side of Firebrand. If you want to be extra sneaky, jump over your foe and then perform Hell Dive M; you'll dash back to your original side, hitting opponents who think you're going to cross-up. Your opposition can shut down this tactic by mashing, so stick out a jumping (M) before calling an assist to cover yourself.

You can also use Hell Dive M as a makeshift triangle jump by performing it directly off the ground by inputting the motion ↓↘→↗ + (M). This isn't as effective as many other triangle jumps in the game since Firebrand can't perform very many attacks out of it, but he can mix up overhead by either using ↓ + (H) while still in the air or using crouching (L) after landing! Either hit can be easily converted into combo, giving Firebrand a quick surprise overhead he can pull out at any time.

Jumping and instantly pressing (L) can create an overhead that your opponent can only guard if they expect it coming, forcing them to randomly stand up! In Luminous Body and X-Factor, (L) into air Bon Voyage is a combo that can lead to big damage off an overhead your competitor can't see! Outside of X-Factor and Luminous Body, mix up your adversary by calling an assist while performing jumping (L), then cancel into Hell Dive L or M; M goes over your foe, allowing the assist to hit as Firebrand dives past them, while L drops Firebrand to the ground quick enough to slip in a crouching (L).

If Firebrand is getting pushed out of close range by advancing guard, use Demon Missile M or H. Demon Missile M and H ignore advancing guard as they move forward, leaving Firebrand close to the opposing player at the end of the move! Firebrand can also delay the timing on his crouching (L) attacks to bait his rival into using advancing guard; simply press a single (L), wait a moment, then go into a chain combo. If your competitor tries to use advancing guard while they're not in guardstun, they'll throw out a crouching attack that your crouching attacks can beat!

Hell Elevator M always jumps toward the opponent...

... which you can use with a crossover assist that can cross up your target!

COMBO USAGE

I. CR. M, CR. H, S [CANCEL] FORWARD SUPER JUMP, AIR M, M, ↓ + H, FLIGHT, ↓ ↙ ← + L, LAND, CR. H, S [CANCEL] FORWARD SUPER JUMP, AIR M, M, H (2 HITS) [CANCEL] ↓ ↘ → + S, LAND, S [CANCEL] FORWARD SUPER JUMP, AIR M, M, H (2 HITS), S, LAND, FORWARD DASH, ↓ ↘ → + ATK ATK (MASH ATK)

584,400 damage, 24% meter loss

You can start this combo with crouching L once or twice for a more flexible opening, but you'll lose out on some damage. When you start with crouching L, don't go into the rest of the combo, and instead wait a moment, then go for another crouching L to beat advancing guard or try to throw. If your throw connects, go into **Combo II**!

In Luminous Body, you have an additional option, as you can perform an instant overhead with jumping L canceled into Bon Voyage!

Firebrand automatically enters flight after Devil's Claw connects, causing a short delay before you can activate Hell Dive L.

If Bon Voyage drags the opposing character completely into the corner, Firebrand ends up in the corner himself, so backdash immediately to keep your rival in the corner. Dark Fire damage midscreen can be incredibly finicky, so it's best to make sure that Firebrand is as close as possible before firing it off.

If you do end up with your adversary at midscreen, quickly wavedash forward twice to move Firebrand closer to his opponent after the knockdown in order to get as much damage from Dark Fire as you can.

II. FORWARD THROW OR AIR THROW, ↓ ↘ → + H, DASH FORWARD, S [CANCEL] FORWARD SUPER JUMP, AIR M, M, H (2 HITS), ↓ + H, FLIGHT, ↓ ↙ ← + L, LAND, CR. H, S [CANCEL] FORWARD SUPER JUMP, AIR M, M, H (2 HITS) [CANCEL] ↓ ↘ → + S, LAND, S [CANCEL] FORWARD SUPER JUMP, AIR S, LAND, ↓ ↘ → + ATK ATK (MASH ATK)

406,900 damage, 25% meter loss

Firebrand can only OTG his opponent without an assist after either of his air throws or his forward throw; his back throw has too much delay. If you land a back throw, he can still combo with Dark Fire as soon as he lands. This actually does about the same damage as his full throw combo, but he doesn't gain any meter.

After the backward version of his air throw, you must perform air Hell Dive M to move close enough to your competitor to OTG with Hell Spitfire H.

After the OTG, perform this combo as you would **Combo I**, just much faster; opponents will flip out much easier if you take too long to perform any individual step.

Since you're ending the combo with an air S by itself, you're not going to have much time to get Firebrand close to the opposing character by dashing on the ground, so you might lose out on some damage depending on where on the screen you performed this combo.

III. AIR ↓ ↘ → + S, WAVEDASH FORWARD TWICE, CR. H, S [CANCEL] FORWARD SUPER JUMP, AIR M, M, H (2 HITS), ↓ + H, FLIGHT, ↓ ↙ ← + L, LAND, CR. H, S [CANCEL] FORWARD SUPER JUMP, AIR M, M, H (2 HITS), S, LAND, WAVEDASH FORWARD TWICE, ↓ ↘ → + ATK ATK (MASH ATK)

446,200~561,000 damage, 24% meter loss

Air Bon Voyage is one of Firebrand's best offensive tools, as it allows him to counter projectiles and low-oriented attacks from the air, and it is totally safe when guarded!

If one randomly hits while you're trying to approach or if you have a chance to punish a whiff with it, go straight into this combo to maximize damage.

The farther Firebrand is from the corner, the farther he drags the opposing character against the ground, dealing more damage! Unfortunately, this tends to only decrease the entire combo's damage because of stun and damage reduction caused by the extra hits.

COMBO APPENDIX

GENERAL EXECUTION TIPS

- Get familiar with the ↓ ↙ ← ↖ motion required to perform Firebrand's instant Hell Dive M; if performed too quickly, you'll get Hell's Elevator
- Before using Dark Fire, make sure you can get right next to your opponent, or it'll do little damage. If you can't, end a combo by activating Luminous Body or Chaos Tide
- Many special moves and Devil's Claw leave Firebrand in Hover, so remember to cancel flight with S, Hell Dive, Bon Voyage, or Hover before trying to guard

WHEN USING AN ALTERNATE TEAMMATE, ACTIVATE A TAC WITH ↑ + S, THEN AS FIREBRAND COMES IN, PERFORM AIR M, M, ↓ + H, FLIGHT, ↓ ↙ ← + L, LAND, CR. H, S [CANCEL] FORWARD SUPER JUMP, AIR M, M, H (2 HITS) [CANCEL] ↓ ↘ → + S, LAND, S [CANCEL] FORWARD SUPER JUMP, AIR H (2 HITS), S, LAND, FORWARD DASH, ↓ ↘ → + ATK ATK (MASH)

Notes	Damage
—	Varies

WHEN USING AN ALTERNATE TEAMMATE, ACTIVATE A TAC WITH ↑ + S OR ↓ + S, THEN AS FIREBRAND COMES IN, PERFORM AIR M, M [CANCEL] ↓ ↘ → + S, FORWARD DASH, S [CANCEL] FORWARD SUPER JUMP, AIR, M, M, H (2 HITS), S, LAND, ↓ ↘ → + ATK ATK (MASH)

Notes	Damage
—	Varies

AGAINST A CORNERED ENEMY WHILE IN LUMINOUS BODY AND X-FACTOR, CR. M, CR. H [CANCEL] ↓ ↘ → + L, {CR. H [CANCEL] ↓ ↘ → + L} X 5, CR. H, S [CANCEL] FORWARD SUPER JUMP, AIR M, M, H (2 HITS) [CANCEL] ↓ ↘ → + S, LAND, S [CANCEL] FORWARD SUPER JUMP, AIR S, LAND, ↓ ↘ → + ATK ATK (MASH)

Notes	Damage
Requires X-Factor or Luminous Body	1,042,400

COMBO USAGE CONT.

IV. FORWARD JUMP, INSTANT AIR Ⓛ CANCEL X-FACTOR, Ⓢ, LAND, ST. Ⓜ, CR. Ⓜ, CR. Ⓗ, Ⓢ CANCEL FORWARD SUPER JUMP, AIR Ⓜ, Ⓜ, ↓ + Ⓗ, FLIGHT, ↓ ↙ ← + Ⓛ, LAND, CR. Ⓗ, Ⓢ CANCEL FORWARD SUPER JUMP, AIR Ⓜ, Ⓜ CANCEL ↓ ↘ → + Ⓢ, LAND, Ⓢ CANCEL FORWARD SUPER JUMP, AIR Ⓜ, Ⓜ, Ⓢ, LAND, FORWARD DASH, ↓ ↘ → + ATK ATK (MASH ATK)

763,900~1,016,500 damage, 9% meter loss~22% meter gain

You can hit this combo at any level of X-Factor with an instant overhead jump Ⓛ, which is nearly impossible for an opponent to react to! You won't have time to verify that your jump Ⓛ is hitting when you activate X-Factor, so this combo is really an all-or-nothing proposition: if you miss, you're a fool, but if you hit, you're a genius!

Try not to take a risk with this combo when Firebrand's allies are healthy. This is a versatile way to get Firebrand into X-Factor when he's on his own, however, so wait until he's in range to hit an instant overhead jumping Ⓛ instead of blindly activating.

V. CR. Ⓜ, CR. Ⓗ, Ⓢ CANCEL FORWARD SUPER JUMP, AIR Ⓜ, Ⓜ, ↓ + Ⓗ, FLIGHT, ↓ ↙ ← + Ⓛ, LAND, X-FACTOR, CR. Ⓗ, Ⓢ CANCEL FORWARD SUPER JUMP, AIR Ⓜ, Ⓜ, Ⓗ (2 HITS) CANCEL ↓ ↘ → + Ⓢ, LAND, Ⓢ CANCEL FORWARD SUPER JUMP, AIR Ⓜ, Ⓗ (2 HITS), Ⓢ, LAND, FORWARD DASH, ↓ ↘ → + ATK ATK (MASH ATK)

722,000~866,100 damage, 12% meter loss~8% meter gain

If you absolutely must knock out a character or catch two characters in a combo, you can activate X-Factor in the middle of this combo for some extra damage.

This combo doesn't deal a large amount of damage, even when X-Factor is activated, and at level 1, it isn't enough to knock out a character on its own. As with any X-Factor combo, it's best to only activate if you're absolutely sure you're going to K.O. your rival.

This move can probably knock out your opponent's assist if you catch them, depending on their maximum health and how much damage they've taken, so it's probably worth it in a scenario when you can leave your adversary without an assist.

VI. WHILE IN LUMINOUS BODY OR X-FACTOR, FORWARD JUMP, INSTANT AIR Ⓛ CANCEL ↓ ↘ → + Ⓢ, WAVEDASH FORWARD TWICE, CR. Ⓗ, Ⓢ CANCEL FORWARD SUPER JUMP, AIR Ⓜ, Ⓜ, ↓ + Ⓗ, FLIGHT, ↓ ↙ ← + Ⓛ, LAND, CR. Ⓗ, Ⓢ CANCEL FORWARD SUPER JUMP, AIR Ⓜ, Ⓜ, Ⓗ (2 HITS), Ⓢ, LAND, FORWARD DASH, ↓ ↘ → + ATK ATK (MASH ATK)

459,800~927,900 damage, 35% meter loss~0% meter gain

Firebrand's jumping Ⓛ is aimed low enough to the ground to work as an overhead against many characters in the game, and when Luminous Body or X-Factor is activated, it combos directly into an air Bon Voyage!

Instant overhead jumping Ⓛ is incredibly fast, and your opponent must guess in order to guard it. If your competitor is stuck looking for it, they'll need to randomly stand, opening them up for a low attack!

ADVANCED TACTICS

BEST FRIENDS FOREVER

Chaos Tide causes Firebrand to summon a Red Arremer buddy that lets Firebrand continuously put on pressure!

Firebrand's level 3 causes him to summon an additional Red Arremer buddy to attack alongside him, giving him the chance to really put on the pressure! The Red Arremer performs one of Firebrand's special moves whenever you press a basic attack button: Ⓛ fires a Hell Spitfire M, Ⓜ performs Demon Missile M, and Ⓗ performs Demon Missile H. Of these, Demon Missile H is the most useful, as it attacks while moving Firebrand forward. The Red Arremer friend performs the attack from wherever he is on the screen; generally, he floats around Firebrand, moving forward when he does.

This hyper combo can be very hard to control; if you are attacking a guarding opponent, it's best to start combos with Ⓜ instead of Ⓛ. Advancing guard pushes both Firebrand and the Red Arremer away, and the little guy's Hell Spitfire M has very limited range and generally misses if an opponent uses advancing guard against a crouching Ⓛ. To put your tiny tot in position to pressure your competitor, send him toward the foe using Ⓜ; his Demon Missile M flies too high to hit many crouching characters, but it can stop characters from jumping away and can put him in position to assault your opponent from behind!

When behind the target, advancing guard won't push the flying friend away from the opponent, so you can pelt them with fireballs from behind, even in the corner! When your best buddy is behind your adversary, he's unaffected by advancing guard, so you can pelt your rival with Hell Spitfires or Demon Missile H from off the screen!

Once the friend is close, you can use Firebrand's Demon Dive M to create cross-ups without requiring the use of a crossover assist! Perform a jumping Ⓗ to summon Demon Missile H, then immediately cancel into Demon Dive M; Firebrand quickly dashes behind the opposing character right as the Demon Missile is hitting! Whenever your Red Arremer is close, make liberal use of Demon Missile H, as it moves forward while attacking and can keep Firebrand's friend in range to keep aggressing.

Even without a strategy, simply mashing on Demon Missile H can be an effective gameplan! When used against a cornered foe, using advancing guard on Firebrand's friend is useless; as long as Firebrand doesn't hit the opponent, he'll be completely unaffected by the opposing character's advancing guard! Demon Missile H from Firebrand's buddy does 24,000 points of chip damage whenever it's guarded and can be performed 17 times during a single activation, which can deal 408,000 in guarded damage alone! Throw out your own Hell Spitfire H and Demon Missile H to deal additional chip.

LUMINOUS POWER!

When Luminous Body is active, jumping Ⓛ can combo into Bon Voyage for a big damage instant overhead!

Firebrand's Luminous Body power-up is one of his best assets, giving him a massive 25% increase in speed at the cost of a single meter. If that weren't enough, the power-up lasts slightly less than 10 seconds and lets him build meter while the power-up is activated, which makes the hyper combo completely free if you land a combo while it's active!

Since Firebrand builds meter during Luminous Body, there's very little reason not to have it active if you can safely get it out. It's not terribly difficult, either: any guarded crouching Ⓗ can be canceled into Luminous Body, leaving you safe. You can also perform Luminous Body in the air, so you can just have Firebrand jump away from his opponent and fire it off. You can also trade some damage at the end of a combo by activating Luminous Body instead of Dark Fire.

Once in Luminous Body, Firebrand is much faster, making most of his normal mix-ups harder to guard, and he gains new mix-ups using his jumping Ⓛ. During Luminous Body, Bon Voyage combos into a jumping Ⓛ performed just off the ground, creating an instant overhead to free damage! If an opponent is expecting you to overhead, mix them up by canceling the Ⓛ into Hell Dive L, then do the mix-up again, or just go low with crouching Ⓛ since your adversary has to guess if the overhead is coming.

All of Firebrand's special moves activate quicker and recover faster when Luminous Body is active, letting Firebrand excel at some areas where he couldn't before. If your opponent is keeping you out while Luminous Body is active, it's not a bad idea to resign yourself to throwing fireballs at them until the hyper combo ends, as they fire off incredibly quickly and recover early enough for Firebrand to get two out at a time, enough to at least irritate a character who can't obliterate his fireballs immediately! If you need to close distance, spit a Hell Spitfire L, then immediately use Bon Voyage on the ground: the fireball recovers quickly enough to let Firebrand glide in under the cover of his own fireball, sailing in safely right in front of his opponent.

NEW

FRANK WEST

"WHAT DO YOU MEAN I DON'T BELONG HERE? I'VE COVERED WARS, Y'KNOW."

Bio

REAL NAME

Frank West

OCCUPATION

Freelance Photographer

ABILITIES

Has a number of professional wrestling moves at his disposal. He's also covered wars, y'know. His tough spirit lets him survive under even the most extreme conditions.

WEAPONS

While he doesn't have a specific weapon, he can utilize objects in his surroundings, such as golf clubs, benches, bicycles—basically, whatever he can get his hands on.

PROFILE

Though he's armed only with his strength, if there's a scoop to be had, he's got the courage to take anyone on. His willingness to dive head-first into any dangerous situation has saved his life as many times as it has put him in mortal peril.

FIRST APPEARANCE

Dead Rising (2006)

POWER GRID

2 INTELLIGENCE

2 STRENGTH

2 SPEED

3 STAMINA

1 ENERGY PROJECTION

2 FIGHTING ABILITY

*This is biographical, and does not represent an evaluation of the in-game combat potential of this hero.

ALTERNATE COSTUMES

Overview

Vitality	1,050,000
Chain Combo Archetype	Hunter Series

X-Factor Boost	Damage	Speed
Level 1 (3 teammates remaining)	135%	105%
Level 2 (2 teammates remaining)	160%	110%
Level 3 (1 teammate remaining)	185%	115%

From the beginning of the match, your number one priority when using Frank is to level up through use of his Snapshot attack, which earns him XP based on the number of hits in a combo. Gaining experience points and levels is important because:

- **He unlocks key functionality, including the special moves Barrel Roll, Roundhouse Kick, and the anti-air hyper combo Funny Face Crasher**
- **Starting from level 3, he gains additional functionality during his basic attacks, including chip damage at level 4**
- **His Tools of Survival special moves and assist become greatly enhanced, as well as his Survival Techniques hyper combo**
- **With maxed-out XP, not only does he have terrific attacks, but they deal 10% additional damage**

How does Frank go about scoring Snapshot combos to increase his level? In order of effectiveness:

- **By using air exchange to tag Frank in during a team aerial combo, which allows his teammates to build up the combo meter while he's on the bench; his own portion of the TAC combo gets naturally capped off with Snapshot to convert the hits into big XP**
- **Mix-ups at level 2+ with crossover assists and Barrel Roll**
- **Mix-ups at level 2+ between Tools of Survival H and Roundhouse Kick H, or crouching Ⓗ when his opponent is guarding a crossover assist**
- **Going for cross-up air Ⓗ or Ⓜ, or starting combos with the invincible portion of Ⓜ attacks or the tip of crouching Ⓗ slide**
- **Off any clean hit, performing combos that emphasize number of hits instead of damage; more hits equals more XP**
- **Using assists with large numbers of hits to find easy places to tack on Snapshot (something as simple as watching for the enemy to run into Doctor Strange—β, then using Snapshot as it ends is worth up to 11 XP, or as much as double that with Bottoms Up active!)**

FRANK WEST STARTS EACH MATCH AT LEVEL 1. JUST LIKE IN DEAD RISING, HIS LEVEL CAN BE INCREASED THROUGH PHOTOGRAPHY:

Level	Level Perks	Total XP Required
Lv.1	Snap Shot, Object Throw, Tools of Survival, Giant Swing, Hammer Throw, Bottom's Up	0 XP (match start)
Lv.2	Barrel Roll, Roundhouse Kick	5 XP
Lv.3	Funny Face Crusher, improves all Ⓜ and Ⓢ attacks and st. Ⓗ, improves Object Toss / Tools of Survival / Survival Techniques	20 XP
Lv.4	Improves all Ⓜ and Ⓢ attacks and st. Ⓗ, improves Object Toss / Tools of Survival / Survival Techniques	50 XP
Lv.5	10% Damage Boost	100 XP

Attack Set

Standing Basic Attacks

Screen	Command	Hits	Damage	Meter Gain	Startup	Active	Recovery	Advantage on Hit	Advantage if Guarded	Notes
1	Standing L	1	48,000	384	6	3	12	+1	-1	—
2	Standing M (Level 1-2)	1	60,000	480	10	3	22	-4	-7	—
3	Standing M (Level 3)	1	68,000	544	10	3	22	-4	-7	—
4	Standing M (Level 4-5)	3	109,800	1080	10	5	22	-2	-5	Deals chip damage
5	Standing H (Level 1-2)	1	70,000	560	14	4	28	-6	-9	—
6	Standing H (Level 3)	1	90,000	720	14	3	29	-6	-9	—
7	Standing H (Level 4-5)	5	166,700	1800	14	7	30	-7	-10	Deals chip damage

1

2

3

4

5

6

7

Crouching Basic Attacks

Screen	Command	Hits	Damage	Meter Gain	Startup	Active	Recovery	Advantage on Hit	Advantage if Guarded	Notes
1	Crouching L	1	45,000	360	6	2	15	-1	-3	—
2	Crouching M (Level 1-2)	1	58,000	464	9	3	22	-4	-7	—
3	Crouching M (Level 3)	1	63,000	464	9	3	22	-4	-7	—
4	Crouching M (Level 4-5)	3	104,900	1032	9	7	20	-2	-5	Deals chip damage
5	Crouching H	1	63,000	504	10	12	19	—	-8	Low attack, knocks down

1

2

3

4

5

Ground Special Attack—Launcher

Screen	Command	Hits	Damage	Meter Gain	Startup	Active	Recovery	Advantage on Hit	Advantage if Guarded	Notes
1	S (while standing or crouching) (Level 1-2)	1	80,000	640	9	5	25	—	-7	Launcher, not special- or hyper combo-cancelable
2	S (while standing or crouching) (Level 3)	1	90,000	720	9	5	25	—	-7	Launcher, not special- or hyper combo-cancelable
3	S (while standing or crouching) (Level 4-5)	1	100,000	800	9	5	25	—	-7	Launcher, not special- or hyper combo-cancelable

1

2

3

Air Basic Attacks

Screen	Command	Hits	Damage	Meter Gain	Startup	Active	Recovery	Advantage on Hit	Advantage if Guarded	Notes
1	Air L	1	50,000	400	5	8	13	+13	+11	Overhead attack
2	Air M (Level 1-2)	1	63,000	504	7	3	22	+19	+16	Overhead attack
3	Air M (Level 3)	1	70,000	560	7	3	22	+19	+16	Overhead attack
4	Air M (Level 4-5)	3	109,800	1080	7	12	22	+18	+15	Overhead attack, deals chip damage
5	Air H	1	65,000	520	11	5	20	+21	+18	Overhead attack

1

2

3

4

5

Air Special Attacks—Flying Screen and Air Exchange

Air (S) causes a hard knockdown when used in a launcher combo (this is sometimes called flying screen). When used outside of a launcher combo, air (S) behaves mostly like another basic attack. Air exchange attacks, performed by inputting a direction plus (S), are only possible during a launcher combo. Exchange hits initiate team aerial combos by tagging in the next available character to continue the air combo.

Screen	Command	Hits	Damage	Meter Gain	Startup	Active	Recovery	Advantage on Hit	Advantage if Guarded	Notes
1	Air (S) (Level 1-2)	1	70,000	560	13	3	23	+16	+13	Causes hard knockdown if used in launcher combo
2	Air (S) (Level 3)	1	90,000	720	13	4	22	—	+18	Causes hard knockdown if used in launcher combo, ground bounces foe
3	Air (S) (Level 4-5)	1	110,000	880	13	4	22	—	+17	Causes hard knockdown if used in launcher combo, ground bounces opponent, deals chip damage
4	Air ⇧ + (S) (during launcher combo)	2	105,00	880	11	4	Until grounded	—	—	Tags in next available ally while lofting adversary upward
5	Air ⇨ or ⇦ + (S) (during launcher combo)	2	95,000	800	13	4	Until grounded	—	—	Tags in next available ally while causing wall bounce, erases 1 hyper meter bar from rival
6	Air ⇩ + (S) (during launcher combo)	2	95,000	800	13	4	Until grounded	—	—	Tags in next available ally while causing ground bounce, generates 1 hyper meter bar

1

2

3

4

5

6

Command Attacks

Command attacks resemble basic attacks but have different chaining and canceling properties. It's usually possible to chain *into* a command attack from basic attacks, but most command attacks cannot be chained from or canceled themselves.

Screen	Name	Command	Hits	Damage	Meter Gain	Startup	Active	Recovery	Advantage on Hit	Advantage if Guarded	Notes
1	Object Throw – Pie (Level 1-2)	⇨ + (H)	1	50,000	400	12	—	35	-10	-13	Projectile has 3 low priority durability points, deals chip damage
2	Object Throw - Juice (Level 3)	⇨ + (H)	1	80,000	640	12	—	35	-7	-10	Projectile has 4 low priority durability points, deals chip damage
3	Object Throw - Bottle (Level 4-5)	⇨ + (H)	1	100,000	800	12	—	35	-5	-8	Projectile has 5 low priority durability points, deals chip damage
4	Knee Drop	(in air) ⇩ + (H)	1	70,000	560	13	Until grounded	13	—	+4	Hard knockdown

1

2

3

4

Throws

Throws are for snagging passive or blocking opponents. Since throws are active so quickly, you can also use them to preemptively toss opposing characters out of their offense. Combos are usually possible after throws, one way or another.

Screen	Command	Hits	Damage	Meter Gain	Startup	Active	Notes
1	⇨ + (H) (ground)	1	80,000	800	1	1	Hard knockdown
	⇦ + (H) (ground)	1	80,000	800	1	1	Hard knockdown
2	⇨ + (H) (air)	1	80,000	800	1	1	Hard knockdown
	⇦ + (H) (air)	1	80,000	800	1	1	Hard knockdown

1

2

FRANK WEST

NEW

As a Partner—Crossover Assists

Screen	Type	P1+P2 Crossover Combination Hyper Combo	Description	Hits	Damage	Meter Gain	Startup	Active	Recovery (this crossover assist)	Recovery (other partner)	Notes
1	Frank West—α	Blue Light Special	Shopping Cart	7	104,100	1120	31	35	104	74	—
2	Frank West—β	Blue Light Special	Tools of Survival L	4	103,000	960	39	2(5)3(4) 3(4)3	134	104	Increases in strength with level ups, see special move list
3	Frank West—γ	Blue Light Special	Pick Me Up	—	—	3000	25	—	177	147	Adds 3000 points to hyper meter

1

2

3

You might find use for any of Frank's assists, but Frank West—α is the best all-around, with Frank West—β drawing honorable mention, especially if you level Frank up. On the other hand, a leveled-up Frank should really be out taking advantage of his powered-up attacks on point, making the usefulness of Frank West—β a bit of a catch-22.

Frank West—α is a unique attack that he himself does not have access to on point. In it, Frank runs out to midscreen with a shopping cart, dragging any targets he hits along the way. The shopping cart itself is covered in a large unbeatable hitbox, so even though Frank has no invulnerability, this attack usually beats other melee attacks your opponent throws out! Frank's shopping cart is weak to projectiles, as they simply pass through the shopping cart unfazed and hit Frank out of his attack.

Frank West—β functions a lot like other pinning melee assists, such as Chun-Li—γ and Dante—α, in that it allows your point character to approach and stage a mix-up while the opposing character is being held in place by Frank's survival tools, without you needing to worry about being pushed away by advancing guard. This assist gets better as Frank levels up since he uses whatever version of Tools of Survival he has equipped: a plunger at level 1, a push broom at level 3, and a chainsaw staff at level 4!

Frank West—γ causes Frank to jump out and down some juice, building 30% of a single meter very quickly. While it's comparable in speed to Amaterasu—γ, it is much slower than Morrigan—γ, which is really the assist you should go for if you really want to conjure hyper meter from thin air. Frank is just too slow and vulnerable during this assist and has more useful assists in general. Only consider this assist if your team is incredibly dependent on meter, and you absolutely must play Frank.

Snap Back

Screen	Command	Hits	Damage	Meter Gain	Startup	Active	Recovery	Advantage on Hit	Advantage if Guarded
1	↓↘→ + P1 or P2	1	50,000	500- (-1 hyper meter bar)	2	4	25	—	-6

Notes

On hit, snap back forces the opposing point character to be replaced by an assist. Opposing assist calls or tag outs are also locked out for 4 seconds

1

Special Moves

Screen	Name	Command	Hits	Damage	Meter Gain	Startup	Active	Recovery	Advantage on Hit	Advantage if Guarded	Notes
1	Tools of Survival L (Level 1-2)	↓↘→ + L	4	103,000	960	15	2(5)3(4) 3(4)3	22	+1	-2	Pulls foe toward Frank on contact
	Air Tools of Survival L (Level 1-2)	(in air) ↓↘→ + L	4	103,000	960	15	2(6)3(3) 3(4)3	7	+16	+13	Pulls opponent toward Frank on contact
2	Tools of Survival L (Level 3)	↓↘→ + L	8	130,700	1472	15	4(3)5(2) 5(2)5	20	—	-4	Knocks down
	Air Tools of Survival L (Level 3)	(in air) ↓↘→ + L	8	130,700	1472	15	4(3)5(2) 5(2)5	7	—	+12	Knocks down
3	Tools of Survival L (Level 4-5)	↓↘→ + L	10	162,400	2000	15	25	11	+8	+5	—
	Air Tools of Survival L (Level 4-5)	(in air) ↓↘→ + L	10	162,400	2000	15	25	8	+11	+8	—
4	Tools of Survival M (Level 1-2)	↓↘→ + M	1	90,000	720	20	3	33	—	-13	Wall bounces adversary
	Air Tools of Survival M (Level 1-2)	(in air) ↓↘→ + M	1	90,000	720	20	3	33	—	-8	Wall bounces rival
5	Tools of Survival M (Level 3)	↓↘→ + M	1	120,000	960	20	3	33	—	-13	Wall bounces competitor
	Air Tools of Survival M (Level 3)	(in air) ↓↘→ + M	1	120,000	960	20	3	33	—	-4	Wall bounces target
6	Tools of Survival M (Level 4-5)	↓↘→ + M	8	170,500	1920	20	11(1)2	22	—	-7	Wall bounces challenger
	Air Tools of Survival M (Level 4-5)	(in air) ↓↘→ + M	8	170,500	1920	20	11(1)2	22	—	-3	Wall bounces foe
7	Tools of Survival H (Level 1-2)	↓↘→ + H	1	80,000	640	27	3	31	—	-11	OTG-capable, knocks down
	Air Tools of Survival H (Level 1-2)	(in air) ↓↘→ + H	1	80,000	640	27	3	Until grounded	—	+21	OTG-capable, knocks down
8	Tools of Survival H (Level 3)	↓↘→ + H	1	110,000	880	27	4	30	—	-11	OTG-capable, ground bounces opponent
	Air Tools of Survival H (Level 3)	(in air) ↓↘→ + H	1	110,000	880	27	4	30	—	+21	OTG-capable, ground bounces adversary

Special Moves continued

Screen	Name	Command	Hits	Damage	Meter Gain	Startup	Active	Recovery	Advantage on Hit	Advantage if Guarded	Notes
9	Tools of Survival H (Level 4-5)	⇩⇘⇨ + H	1	150,000	1200	27	5	29	—	-11	OTG-capable, ground bounces rival
	Air Tools of Survival H (Level 4-5)	(in air) ⇩⇘⇨ + H	1	150,000	1200	27	5	29	—	+21	OTG-capable, ground bounces competitor
10	Snapshot (in air OK)	⇩⇘⇨ + S	1	10,000	80 (+500 on level up)	15	10	31	-25	-27	OTG-capable, gains XP based on number of hits in combo
11	Roundhouse Kick L	(at level 2 or higher) ⇨⇩⇘ + L	—	—	—	—	—	—	—	—	Fake kick, takes 25 frames
12	Roundhouse Kick M	(at level 2 or higher) ⇨⇩⇘ + M	1	70,000	560	16	5	24	—	-6	Hard knockdown
13	Roundhouse Kick H	(at level 2 or higher) ⇨⇩⇘ + H	1	70,000	560	18	5	32	—	-14	OTG-capable, knocks down, low attack
14	Giant Swing L	⇩⇙⇦ + L	2	50,000 + 80,000	400 + 640	28	21	8	—	+17	Thrown zombie is active for 31 frames, knocks down
	Giant Swing M	⇩⇙⇦ + M	3	50,000 x2 + 80,000	400 x2 + 640	38	21	8	—	+17	Thrown zombie is active for 34 frames, knocks down
	Giant Swing H	⇩⇙⇦ + H	4	50,000 x3 + 80,000	400 x3 + 640	48	31	8	—	+17	Thrown zombie is active for 30 frames, knocks down
15	Hammer Throw L	⇦ (charge) ⇨ + L	1	80,000	640	30	—	10	+15	+15	Zombie stops 1 low priority projectile
	Hammer Throw M	⇦ (charge) ⇨ + M	1	80,000	640	30	—	10	+15	+15	Zombie stops 1 low priority projectile
16	Hammer Throw H	⇦ (charge) ⇨ + H	1	80,000	800	40	—	10	+101	+15	Zombie stops 1 low priority projectile, captures foe for 111 frames
17	Bottoms Up	⇩⇩ + S	—	—	—	60	—	145 (after duration of power-up)	—	—	Gains double XP from Snapshot combos, lasts for 600 frames
18	Barrel Roll	(at level 2 or higher) ATK + S	—	—	—	—	—	—	—	—	Forward roll that travels for 30 frames, can pass through opponent

Tools of Survival L: During this attack, Frank quickly stabs at his opponent several times with one of his zombie-busting tools. This has wildly different functions, depending on Frank's level. At level 1, Frank plunges a plunger toward his foes, pulling them closer to him when it connects, while at level 3, he sweeps them away with a long push broom, and at level 4 and above, he slashes at his target once with a long chainsaw on a stick.

1

2

3

The level 1 version of this attack is best used in combos, where it piles on the hits and gives Frank more XP per combo. Outside of combos, it has little range, and the pulling functionality of the attack doesn't work if the opponent uses advancing guard, leaving Frank blindly stabbing at the air. Once at level 3, you can poke at your opponent more effectively because the move has much more range and knocks down your competitor if it hits, making it a decent poke from the ground and the air. It's not technically safe if guarded, but it basically is from the edge of its range. At level 4, this attack becomes a great tool for constantly attacking your opponent, as it deals 75,000 points of chip damage on block and a massive 164,000 points of damage on hit while creating frame advantage for Frank in either case!

4

5

6

Tools of Survival M: This weapon-based attack causes Frank to pull out a large bat on the ground or in the air and swing for the fences, bouncing his opponent off the wall when it hits. At level 1, Frank doesn't recover in time for you to combo off the wall bounce outside of corners without an assist or a hyper combo. But once at level 3 and above, you can have Frank combo off the wall bounce when it hits without a crossover assist, and it easily combos from other attacks, making it a great tool to add on hits for your level-building combos. Frank's mobility isn't the best, however, making it difficult for Frank players to convert this wall bounce into a combo outside of the corner.

This attack is unsafe when guarded, so try to avoid throwing it out blindly and keep it for use strictly in combos. Level 4 Tools of Survival M functions similarly to the level 3 version, except Frank throws away his bat and swings at his opponent using a chainsaw! The level 4 version deals chip damage when guarded, but it is still unsafe from punishment if an attentive adversary guards it.

7

8

9

Tools of Survival H: Frank swings downward at his opponent with an overhead attack, striking them with enough force to bounce them off the ground! This attack is unsafe on block, making it a fairly risky overhead that should only be thrown out in a combo or with a crossover assist to back it up; when the lv.1 overhead hits on the ground, it's very difficult to combo off the bounce. After air Tools of Survival H, you can easily pick your rival up with S launcher, making it one of Frank's best tools to extend combos at lower levels. This attack is also OTG-capable, making it a great combo-extending tool to add additional hits after flying screen!

At levels 3 and 4, your competitor bounces much higher when the attack hits, making follow-ups easy even on the ground. But remember that the attack is still unsafe when guarded, so you should only throw it out under the cover of a crossover assist.

10

Snapshot: During this attack, Frank pulls out his trusty camera to cover the war, quickly taking an OTG-capable photograph of the battlefield that reaches in a huge area in front of Frank. By itself, this attack is almost completely useless; it does very little damage and is unsafe even if it hits. But in combos, Snapshot becomes Frank's most important attack and the entire foundation of his character, since Frank only gains levels by hitting with it: Frank gains one point of experience for every hit in a combo, so the more hits in a combo, the more experience Frank gains! For example, a four-hit chain combo ending with Snapshot earns Frank 5 XP—four XP for the chain combo and an additional XP point for the Snapshot.

Essentially, Snapshot is how you should end every combo until Frank reaches level 4, as gaining levels is Frank's number one priority. After an OTG Snapshot hit, it can be hyper combo canceled into Blue Light Special or Survival Techniques for big additional damage! Be careful when ending a combo without a hyper combo cancel, as Frank is left at big disadvantage after it hits, so even if you can guard your opponent's counter-attack, Frank remains on the defensive, which is definitely not recommended.

Levels are gained at 5, 20, 50, and 100 XP. Frank really isn't a complete character until lv.3 (Barrel Roll and Funny Face Crusher being really important), and he isn't a great one until lv.4 (huge improvements to many moves), so you must make XP part of your gameplan. Until Frank is at lv.4, it's the only gameplan, really; damage along the way is incidental to the goal of getting Frank's hands all over Chuck Greene's chittering chainsaws.

Luckily, it's not that hard. Off a single clean hit, even by himself without the aid of assists, Frank should get at least lv.3. But there's an even better way. If you put Frank in the second slot, you can revolve your gameplan around having a previous character hand off the longest possible combo to Frank via a team aerial combo. Score at least a solid 20~30 hit combo with a character or two performing air exchanges before Frank, and then Frank himself can easily cap it off and finish with a Snapshot to START at lv.4! Obviously, this is ideal: lv.4 brings the chainsaw pain, and the lv.5 damage buff is just a nice luxury to attain (if you get there, you are probably not having many problems in a given match, anyway).

You can also speed level-ups by working multiple Snapshots into the same combo, which can give you essentially double credit for a long sequence; for example, by calling an assist (many will do) just before performing a Snapshot OTG after a lengthy air combo, you can usually recover and Snapshot again! (Of course, Snapshot is hyper-cancelable, and so you can also tack on solid damage with Blue Light Special or Survival Techniques in any case.) If the chips are down or you just smell blood, you can also use X-Factor to cancel one Snapshot into another and then immediately into a hyper combo; when this technique K.O.s one character while building instant lv.4/5 and an angry red Frank to mix up the next character with, it can be very much worth the effort.

11

Roundhouse Kick L: The Roundhouse Kick attacks are only available when Frank is at level 2 and above, and their function differs depending on the button pressed. During the L version, Frank hops toward his opponent with a feint, hopefully coaxing the foe to hesitate. Cancel into this from a blocked attack, performed at the same time as an opponent's advancing guard, and Frank bypasses the push back, leaving him in front of the opposing character.

This tactic might be punished if not covered by a crossover assist, however. Roundhouse Kick L becomes most useful once your adversary is aware of your Barrel Roll mix-ups; mix in a Roundhouse Kick L instead of a Barrel Roll to keep your competitor guessing!

12

Roundhouse Kick M: The M version of Roundhouse Kick causes Frank to rush toward his rival and kick straight at the target, causing a hard knockdown on hit. Since it places the opponent in hard knockdown, it leaves you in position to OTG the foe with Tools of Survival H or Snapshot! This attack is unsafe when guarded, so you should only use it inside of combos.

13

Roundhouse Kick H: During the H version of Roundhouse Kick, Frank hops and then performs an OTG-capable low-hitting kick, knocking his opponent back into a soft knockdown.

You can only combo after this attack when combined with a crossover assist or by canceling into a hyper combo, but this is Frank's only low attack aside from crouching Ⓗ, so you'll need to occasionally use it to keep your opponents from constantly guarding while standing. Use it as a mix-up along with Tools of Survival H; call an assist to mask your attack and place the foe into guardstun, then make your adversary guess whether to block the overhead or the Roundhouse Kick H low attack!

Roundhouse Kick H is also a good OTG to use in combos after you've already caused a ground bounce with Tools of Survival H; using Tools of Survival H a second time prevents you from hyper canceling and actually having it combo, but Roundhouse Kick H works. Of course, either case assumes that you don't need to end combos with Snapshot canceled into a hyper combo for photography XP anymore, which should only happen at level 4 at the earliest.

14

Giant Swing: This attack causes Frank to pick up a wayward zombie, then swing them in a classic pro-wrestling fashion toward his opponent. Each button pressed causes Frank to spin the zombie more: one spin during the L version, two spins during the M version, and three swings during the H version. While this attack has significant startup time, Frank is not only safe when his adversary guards this attack, but he's left at huge frame advantage, allowing him to pile on the pressure while attacking his rival; on hit, you can convert this into a combo by simply using his Ⓢ launcher! Frank gets more frame advantage and more chip damage depending on the button used, but at the risk of the opposing character's advancing guard: the more hits, the farther they can push Frank away with advancing guard, limiting his ability to exploit the massive frame advantage.

This attack is vital against characters who can keep Frank out with projectiles, since the thrown zombie completely ignores enemy projectiles, passing through all of them on the way toward the opponent! If the thrown zombie hits the target, it only places them in soft knockdown, limiting your chance to convert into a combo, but it completely stops an onslaught of projectiles for enough time to allow you to get Frank in and start his offense. If Frank is hit before he throws the zombie, the attack ends, so make sure you have an opportunity to let one fly before attempting to shut down a zoning onslaught.

15

Hammer Throw L & M: When this attack is performed, Frank pulls out a zombie and tosses them ambling toward his opponent. The L version of this attack throws a zombie that walks slowly, while the M version throws a faster-moving zombie. While this attack has only one point of low projectile durability, the zombie can completely stop any single projectile, and it recovers extremely quickly, fast enough to have multiple undead clambering toward your competitor! While strong against characters who fire single projectiles, characters with beam attacks are able to destroy the zombie and continue hitting Frank, limiting its usefulness against them.

When advancing guard is used, Frank isn't pushed back at all because these zombies count as different characters, much like an assist! From midscreen, Frank can Hammer Throw L zombies quicker than many opponents (even those with projectiles) can react! Characters without projectiles can do little to keep Frank from slinging the fiends, so use them to force an adversary to jump, then grab them out of the air with Funny Face Crusher. You can also employ slow-moving Hammer Throw L zombies sort of like how Guile uses slow Sonic Booms… toss one, then follow closely behind it for cover!

16

Hammer Throw H: This attack has more startup time than its lighter counterparts, but the quick zombie released grabs and briefly captures the opposing point character if they get hit by it, giving you time to have Frank wavedash across the screen and start a full combo. Unlike a throw, when the zombie grabs your opponent, it applies normal damage scaling, making the combo after a successful grab deal the same damage as a normal combo!

It's most useful to get Hammer Throw H zombies out there against foes lacking projectiles, when you've generated heavy frame advantage in a zoning war (such as through the use of an assist), or against new characters falling in to replace defeated allies.

17

Bottoms Up: When this special move is performed, Frank pulls out a bottle of adult refreshment and chugs it down, and, as long as the power-up is active, Frank gains experience twice as fast, gaining two points of experience for every hit in a combo. This boost comes with a price, however, because after 10 seconds have passed, Frank purges the liquid out of his body, leaving him vulnerable to attack.

Frank still must connect with Snapshot for this boost to be effective, so try to activate Bottoms Up under the cover of an assist that hits for a while; activate the power-up, then rush in on your opponent while they're still under attack from the assist! Frank can keep from barfing by tagging to a different character through a THC, TAC, crossover counter, or a crossover attack; as long as Frank leaves the playfield, he won't barf!

18

Barrel Roll: During this special move, Frank uses his war-covering experience and rolls toward his opponent. While this attack doesn't hit, it can be used in mix-ups along with a crossover assist since it only lasts 30 frames and can have Frank change sides with his rival, quickly crossing them up, even in the corner! Barrel Roll can be canceled at any time with a special move, allowing you to fake a cross-up by canceling into Tools of Survival L! Unlike many command-based special maneuvers, you can call a crossover assist during Barrel Roll, giving you more flexibility when timing an assist to cross up!

You can also utilize this attack to cancel the landing recovery of Knee Drop, giving Frank more time to mix up his adversary after a guarded overhead hit. While Frank has no invulnerability during the attack, he has a much smaller profile while rolling, making him harder for foes to hit. Even with a smaller profile, however, he is susceptible to a competitor pressing buttons, so be sure to call a crossover assist before using it to ensure Frank's safety.

Hyper Combos

Screen	Name	Command	Hits	Damage	Startup	Active	Recovery	Advantage on Hit	Advantage if Guarded	Notes
1	Blue Light Special	⇩ ⇘ ⇨ + ATK ATK	9~18	248,100~297,700	12+2	62	45	—	-35	OTG-capable, wall bounces foe, can be mashed for extra damage, shopping cart nullifies projectiles and some beam attacks
2	Funny Face Crusher	(at level 3 or higher) ⇨ ⇩ ⇘ + ATK ATK	8	260,000	6+4	5	21	—	—	Frames 1-12 invincible, throws airborne opponents, hard knockdown
3	Survival Techniques (Level 1-2)	⇩ ⇙ ⇦ + ATK ATK	7	253,100	8+4	15	21	—	-13	Knocks down
3	Survival Techniques (Level 3)	⇩ ⇙ ⇦ + ATK ATK	8	312,000	8+4	15	21	—	-13	Frames 1-17 invincible, knocks down
3	Survival Techniques (Level 4-5)	⇩ ⇙ ⇦ + ATK ATK	15	356,100	8+4	15	21	—	-13	Frames 1-25 invincible, knocks down

1

Blue Light Special: When this attack is performed, Frank loads up a shopping cart full of chainsaws and other assorted Tools of Survival and charges toward his opponent! This attack is best used as a combo ender when used after Snapshot at low levels, since it can be mashed for 49,600 additional points of damage, which is more than is dished out by low-level Survival Techniques.

While this hyper combo is OTG-capable, it's best to end your combos with Snapshot first anyway; when used as an OTG, Snapshot can be quickly hyper combo canceled into Blue Light Special, and it will still connect! If your competitor guards this attack, it's unsafe, so try to only use it in combos or to THC into a different character to put Frank back on the bench. This attack is great to use to THC Frank back onto the bench, as it hits several times against a guarding target and, on hit, wall bounces your foe, allowing most characters to fully connect their follow-up hyper combo.

2

Funny Face Crusher: This hyper combo causes Frank to jump in the air with a Servbot-shaped mask in an attempt to throw any opponents out of the skies. Funny Face Crusher is a partially invincible air-throw that can grab an adversary even if they're trying to block! This attack is one of Frank's only defensive attacks, but he can only use it at level 3 and above.

This attack is fully invulnerable for the first 12 frames, making it an excellent anti-air against predictable air movement. Frank can make use of this on the bench, too: if an opposing character is clearly jumping straight toward Frank, quickly perform your point character's fastest hyper combo and immediately THC into Funny Face Crusher, letting Frank jump in and grab his foe from the air!

3

Survival Techniques: Frank rushes toward his opponent, and if he connects, he unleashes a flurry of attacks on the target using a variety of different weapons! This hyper combo is best used in combos because if it whiffs or is guarded, Frank doesn't perform any additional attacks, leaving him completely unsafe. This attack can also only hit your opponent's point character; even if Frank runs into an assist, they won't be caught by the rest of the attack.

At level 1, it's best to avoid using this hyper combo and use Blue Light Special instead, as it deals more damage and can hit both point character and assist. Once you reach level 3, however, this hyper combo becomes Frank's most useful by far, as it gains 17 frames of invincibility, allowing you to use it as a reversal! The damage dealt by the level 3 and onwards versions also greatly eclipses that of Blue Light Special, making it the go-to hyper combo once you've had Frank get sufficiently leveled up.

"SOMEONE NEEDS TO GET THE TRUTH TO THE PEOPLE. I'LL DO WHATEVER IT TAKES TO SURVIVE FOR THAT PURPOSE."

Battle Plan

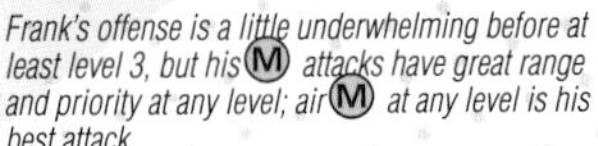

Frank's offense is a little underwhelming before at least level 3, but his (M) attacks have great range and priority at any level; air (M) at any level is his best attack.

Regardless of whatever else you're worrying about when using Frank, your main goal is to level him up.

Giant Swing tosses zombies clear through your opponent's projectiles, which is very useful to overcome hardcore zoning.

Against some teams and characters, sending a horde of zombies at your adversary with Hammer Throw can be very effective, coaxing foes into position to be hit by Frank's air (M) attacks, Barrel Roll cross-ups, and Funny Face Crusher.

To be perfectly honest, Frank West isn't a complete character at the start of any match, but that's by design. He has very limited reach, struggles to get in due to his poor mobility, gets destroyed by zoning characters, and can't mix up the opponent much at all—he has one low attack (his crouching (H) slide) and one slow overhead (which you can't convert into a combo without a hyper cancel or an assist). If Frank is at level 1, his best place is on the bench, helping the team with his assists, which can all be great on the right team. Your number one goal with Frank is to get him to at least level 2 so that he gains access to Barrel Roll and you can actually start mixing up your opponent.

But this does not make Frank a useless character; far from it, as he becomes a very strong fighter at level 3 and above. The easiest way to get there is through a TAC combo: Frank gains levels depending on the number of hits in the combo, but he doesn't actually have to perform those hits himself! If you build your team around landing a TAC combo into Frank, you can skip over his lesser levels entirely. For the team aerial combo lead-in to Frank, while more hits are better, if a character can perform a combo with 15 hits (and most can), Frank can pick up the slack by himself to get to at least level 3, and with an assist, straight to level 4 the first time Frank comes into the game! As long as you can build a combo with 19 hits before you use Snapshot, Frank will be able to enter the game as a very formidable combatant.

If you are ever forced to fight with low-level Frank, things aren't as bleak as they might seem. While Frank has a difficult time opening up an opponent by himself, his chances increase a lot with an assist; he only needs a five-hit combo to level up to level 2, which is easily achievable with assists. Since Frank needs as many hits in a combo as he can, multi-hitting and beam assists really help him out; Doctor Doom—α, Dante—β, and Chun-Li—γ are all great, since they apply at least six hits on their own before you start your combo. This means you can simply visually confirm whenever these assists hit your adversary (or their assist!) and tack on Snapshot for enough XP to ding to at least level 2, if not more! And, all of these characters have long combos they can hand off with an air exchange hit to TAC to Frank, making them perfect for bringing Frank in at level 3 or 4.

Keep in mind that Snapshot can hit assists and that combos against assists *do* count toward Frank's photography XP; if you happen to start hitting the opponent's assist but not their point character, perform as long a combo against the assist as you can without completely compromising Frank by overcommitting (for example, if the opposing player using Dormammu is waiting to Chaotic Flame you to death if you touch an assist, don't take the bait!), then call an assist to give Frank a little bit of cover and finish with Snapshot. Even something as simple as reacting with Snapshot whenever your beam assist catches their assist can go a long way toward getting Frank to more powerful levels! Note that Snapshot can't hit both their assist and point together, though, so put XP-gathering on hold if you catch two enemy characters in a combo at once, and replace Snapshot OTG with Tools of Survival H.

Even at low levels, Frank's (M) attacks are all worth mentioning. Think of a slightly slower, but much longer, version of Wesker's crouching (M). Whether on the ground standing or crouching, or jumping in the air, Frank's (M) pokes allow him to go toe-to-toe with the basic attacks and close-range tactics of just about anyone. And at higher levels, his (M) attacks number among the best basic attacks in the game, period.

Once Frank reaches level 2, he gains access to Barrel Roll, which gives you a chance to have him stage real mix-ups against his opponents. While Barrel Roll isn't great defensively (it has no actual invulnerability), it allows you to convert a blocked chain combo into a left/right mix-up when used with an assist, greatly improving your odds of having Frank actually land a hit. To use Barrel Roll effectively, simply get Frank next to his adversary and perform it while calling a crossover assist; this is a simple, generic mix-up, but all you're looking for is a single clean hit, which should easily translate into at least level 3 via simple combos. This is best done with frame advantage, such as by canceling a guarded basic attack into Barrel Roll. It can also be very useful for performing just under a rival as they're about to land from a jump.

If the crossover assist hits as Frank Barrel Rolls through them, go straight into a combo when Frank recovers—it doesn't need to be optimized for damage, just tailored to get enough hits before Snapshot to assure a level-up. With the right assist, a simple (S) launcher into air (M)(M)(H)(S), land OTG Snapshot combo should be enough to get Frank to level 3!

Combining Frank's Knee Drop air attack with Barrel Roll (and the Roundhouse Kick moves that are also learned at level 2) gives Frank his most potent mix-ups. See the Advanced Tactics section for more details. Barrel Roll mix-ups are also quite applicable to new characters falling in after a K.O. or snap back; have Frank dash into the corner briefly, call an assist that is going to face *out* of the corner just as the new challenger falls in, then have Frank Barrel Roll back *out* of the corner!

If you can get Frank to level 3, he becomes a very solid character whose goal should still be to gain more XP; while Frank is serviceable at level 3 and capable of handling most of the characters in the game off by himself, he becomes a true force to be reckoned with once he gets some wicked chainsaws at level 4. However, especially at levels 1 to 3, there are certain times when you are forced to deal with your opponent's long range game. From long range, Frank isn't great: his only projectile counters are Hammer Throw, Giant Swing, and Object Toss, and each has their own disadvantages. If Frank is being kept out by zoning tactics and your crossover assists can't win the fight for you, you need to remain calm and look for an opportunity to interrupt the opposition.

Unfortunately, there is no easy answer; Frank's projectiles all work best in extreme situations, and they need to be planned for accordingly. If your opponent is firing single projectiles without a beam, look for a chance to hold a charge and start trading with Hammer Throw; the zombies thrown by Hammer Throw eat up regular projectiles, giving you the chance to eventually win out because Hammer Throw recovers incredibly quickly! If you can get Hammer Throw L out and force your adversary to guard, you can use that time to close the distance and prepare a mix-up against your rival. You can also use Object Toss, depending on Frank's level, to force projectile trades long enough to get your opponent to react, letting you end the fireball war and prepare a chance to hit your target. Your foes can knock zombies over simply by hitting them, but if that's how they choose to react, have Frank wavedash in behind a zombie, and be ready to tag them with the tip of Frank's slide as they waste their time punching Frank's undead buddy.

If your opponent is overwhelming you with beams and assists, there's very little Frank can do other than try to get Giant Swing out. Giant Swing's zombie completely ignores all low and medium priority projectiles; Frank may take a little damage, but the zombie can stop the opposing character from throwing projectiles long enough for Frank to get in! If you can get a Giant Swing zombie out, prepare to have Frank immediately wavedash toward his rival while calling a crossover assist, as this is the best opportunity you'll have to mix up your competitor.

While being patient and waiting for a chance to interrupt a zoning character, keep in mind that Frank is one of the smallest characters in the game when he's crouching! Although Frank can't keep up with beam-oriented zoning characters in terms of projectile output or durability in any circumstance, he can very comfortably just crouch underneath many primary beams, like Iron Man's Unibeam, Doctor Doom's Plasma Beam, or Sentinel's (H) lasers! And, of course, you can call assists while crouching, or even use Frank's crouching (H) slide to gain a little ground.

Once Frank gets to level 3, he can start turning the tide on his opponent. Having access to Funny Face Crusher is enough; each of Frank's offensive tools becomes better when he can destroy an adversary when they jump! From mid range, get Frank into a position to keep throwing Hammer Throw L at your rival; you don't have to worry about enemies guarding Hammer Throw zombies and pushing Frank away with advancing guard because the game considers Frank's zombies separate from Frank, meaning that your opponent's advancing guard is only affecting them instead of Frank! This won't work against characters with a beam, as the beam can penetrate through the zombie and hit Frank, but enemies who lack beams must jump at some point in order to get away from the zombies. Once your opponent jumps, wait and see what they do: if they normal jump, immediately hyper combo cancel into Funny Face Crasher for some free damage! If they super jump, wait and see where they are going to land and prepare a cross-up mix-up with your crossover assists and Barrel Roll; call the crossover assist as the foe lands, and Barrel Roll to make them guess where they need to block! Barrel Roll can be canceled at any time with any special move, and you can call assists during Barrel Roll, giving you plenty of flexibility when mixing your challenger up. If they're getting used to your normal Barrel Roll with crossover assist timing, mix it up by canceling Barrel Roll into Tools of Survival L, or by calling your assist later or earlier during the Barrel Roll!

Foes who normal jump or attack at low altitude with triangle jumps and square jumps and similar attacks can also be met in midair with the tip of air (M). Press the (H) button right afterward to buffer air (H); if air (M) contacts the target, Frank chains to air (H) automatically, and you'll have time to confirm and score a delayed air (S), then have him land and proceed to juggle his opponent severely. Your follow-up options differ greatly depending on Frank's level; see Combo Usage section and the Combo Appendix for many reliable possibilities.

Frank's makeshift survivalist weapons become downright preposterous at lv.4+, with drastically increased range, damage, and hits.

Lv.4+ Object Toss actually makes Frank into one of the game's stronger regular projectile characters. Use Hammer Throw and Object Toss to complement each other and control ground level against non-beam characters.

Once you can get Frank to level 4, your gameplan should change significantly. No longer should you be concerned with trying to score clean hits and set up ideal Snapshot combos, but instead, you should be focused on simply pressuring your opponent! With *significant* upgrades conferred to all (M) and (S) attacks, standing (H), and Tools of Survival and Survival Techniques, Frank's damage output increases considerably. (M) attacks and standing (H) even deal chip damage to adversaries once Frank is at lv.4! While the chip damage isn't significant, it's plenty to pressure your competitor into striking back by pressing buttons, which is always advantageous.

Barrel Roll becomes more useful than ever; even if your foe guards everything, you're guaranteed at least some damage through chip from constant (M) attacks, making Frank all the more threatening. At level 4, you should make *extremely* liberal use of Tools of Survival L while attacking; Frank is left at a frame advantage even if guarded, making his offense low risk and high reward! Even Frank's jumping (M) deals chip damage when guarded, making him threatening whenever he blindly jumps! The arc of the chainsaws also makes air (M) into an instant overhead if you perform it just after jumping forward; chain into another air (M) after three hits, let the second one go for three more hits, then chain into air (H) before landing and starting a ground combo!

At level 3 and 4, Survival Techniques changes from a mere hyper combo to a completely invincible reversal technique; if your rival tries to use a raw hyper combo on Frank at all, simply cancel whatever you're doing into Survival Techniques for a reversal into big damage! (This is similar to Wesker using Rhino Charge, Spencer using Bionic Lancer, or Iron Fist using Iron Rage in retaliation to an opponent's close-range hyper combo.) At level 4, you don't need to be as fixated on landing a combo with Snapshot as you are with Frank at lower levels, but it's still worth using Snapshot as your OTG of choice until level 5. The only reason *not* to OTG with Snapshot in combos before level 5 (where you can replace it with the more damaging Tools of Survival H or Roundhouse Kick H OTG attacks) is if you've caught two characters at the same time. Snapshot won't hit both the opposing point and their assist at once, so you'll drop their assist out of the combo and forego tons of potential damage if you use Snapshot in that situation. For consistency, finish combos against two characters at once with a hard knockdown, then Roundhouse Kick H into Blue Light Special (Survival Techniques is a "cutscene" hyper combo that cannot hit multiple characters together).

While Frank is very strong at level 4 and above, he is not invincible, so you may still need to fall back on Hammer Throw and Giant Swing to get past zoning characters. Note that past level 3, Object Toss is upgraded quite a bit, becoming a very strong projectile with 5 points of low priority projectile durability, allowing Frank to overpower single projectile zoning characters with ease!

COMBO USAGE

I. (REQUIRES LEVEL 1~2 FRANK) CR. (M), ST. (H), CR. (H) CANCEL (S) FORWARD SUPER JUMP, AIR (M), (M), (H) CANCEL ↓ ↘ → + (H), LAND, CR. (H), (S) CANCEL FORWARD SUPER JUMP, AIR (M), (M), (H) CANCEL ↓ ↘ → + (L), (M), (S), LAND, WAVEDASH FORWARD TWICE, ↓ ↘ → + (S) OTG CANCEL ↓ ↙ ← + ATK ATK

592,200 damage, 1% meter gain, takes Frank from lv.1 to lv.3

The (M), (S) link after Tools of Survival L in midair does not work if this combo is started with a jump attack. Instead, just perform air (M), (M), (H), (S) when an additional hit precedes **Combo I**. This also means that Frank only reaches level 2 instead of 3, meaning ↓ ↙ ← + ATK ATK is not more damaging than ↓ ↘ → + ATK ATK. Cancel into ↓ ↘ → + ATK ATK instead when the combo doesn't ding Frank to lv.3.

Like with most of Frank's combos, the Snapshot OTG can be replaced by either Roundhouse Kick H or Tools of Survival H for more damage, though it's not worth passing up XP unless Frank is maxed out at level 5.

II. (REQUIRES LEVEL 1~2 FRANK) CR. (H), (S) CANCEL FORWARD SUPER JUMP, AIR (M), (M), (H) CANCEL ↓ ↘ → + (H), LAND, ST. (M), CR. (M), ST. (H), (S) CANCEL FORWARD SUPER JUMP, AIR (M), (M), (H) CANCEL ↓ ↘ → + (L), (M), (S), LAND, WAVEDASH FORWARD TWICE, ↓ ↘ → + (S) OTG CANCEL ↓ ↙ ← + ATK ATK

578,200 damage, 1% meter gain, takes Frank from lv.1 to lv.3

This is a modification of **Combo I** designed to take Frank to level 3 off a hit from his crouching (H) slide, which is his only low attack at level 1 (and the only low attack he can combo off of on his own at any level). The slide travels a fair distance, and if you hit with the last few active frames of it, Frank is actually left either neutral or at a tiny frame advantage. Couple this with Frank's tiny profile while crouching, and you may have ample opportunity to have him slide in under enemy attacks. Try to aim with just the tip of the slide, like how Rose players use her slide in the *Alpha* or *SFIV* series. Poke with it liberally from the tip of its range, ready to chain into (S) launcher and then this combo on a successful hit. At level 2 or higher, you can cancel slide into Barrel Roll for more trickery, like to call an assist, fake a slide, then cancel into a roll that passes through the foe; your assist now comes out against their back!

III. (REQUIRES LEVEL 1~2 FRANK) CR. (M), ST. (H), CR. (H), (S), CANCEL FORWARD SUPER JUMP, AIR (M), (M), (H), ↓ + (H), LAND, P1 or P2 (MAGNETO—β), ↓ ↘ → + (S) OTG (GRAV HITS), (S) CANCEL FORWARD SUPER JUMP, AIR (M), (M), (H), (S), LAND, P1 or P2 (GHOST RIDER—α), ↓ ↘ → + (S) OTG (GHOST RIDER HITS), CR. (H), CANCEL FORWARD SUPER JUMP, AIR (H), (S), LAND, ↓ ↘ → + (S) OTG CANCEL ↓ ↙ ← + ATK ATK

682,300 damage, 30% meter gain, takes Frank from lv.1 to lv.4

This combo, which requires Magneto and Ghost Rider, shows how you can use assists to prolong combos and get multiple Snapshots in one sequence. This combo takes Frank to lv.4 all the way from 0 XP... and it takes him clear to lv.5 if Bottoms Up is active! After air ↓ + (H) hits, call Magneto immediately, but wait a moment before doing ↓ ↘ → + (S). This ensures that the orbs hit directly after the camera flash.

COMBO USAGE CONT.

IV. (REQUIRES LEVEL 1~2 FRANK) AIR ↓ + H, ↓ ↘ → + S OTG CANCEL ↓ ↘ → + ATK ATK (MASH ATK)

347,400 damage, 94% meter loss

Here's a basic combo off of Frank's air ↓ + H Knee Drop overhead. You may replace ↓ ↘ → + S with ↓ ↘ → + H for additional damage (410,400 for the combo overall), and you're only giving up 2 XP because the combo before the hyper combo is so short. Verify whether knee drop has hit or not before continuing with an OTG in either case, and see the Advanced Tactics section for follow-ups if guarded. Once Frank is at level 3 or higher, it's better to end with Survival Techniques rather than Blue Light Special.

V. (REQUIRES LEVEL 3 FRANK) CR. M, ST. H, CR. H CANCEL S FORWARD SUPER JUMP, AIR M, M, H CANCEL ↓ ↘ → + L, M, S, LAND, WAVEDASH FORWARD, ↓ ↘ → + H, CR. H, S CANCEL FORWARD SUPER JUMP, AIR M, M, H, S, LAND, ↓ ↘ → + S CANCEL ↓ ↙ ← + ATK ATK

648,600 damage, 14% meter gain

This is Frank's bread and butter combo while he's at level 3.

VI. (REQUIRES LEVEL 4~5 FRANK) CR. M (3 HITS), ST. H (3 HITS), CR. H, S CANCEL FORWARD SUPER JUMP, AIR M (3 HITS), M (3 HITS) CANCEL ↓ ↘ → + L, M (3 HITS) CANCEL ↓ ↘ → + L, S, LAND, WAVEDASH FORWARD TWICE, ↓ ↘ → + H, ST. H (3 HITS), S CANCEL FORWARD SUPER JUMP, AIR H, S, LAND, ↓ ↘ → + S CANCEL ↓ ↙ ← + ATK ATK

774,400~834,100 damage, 80~92% meter gain, gains enough EXP to bring Frank from level 4 to level 5

A level 4 combo designed to max out Frank's XP at level 5, without the use of Bottoms Up. At level 5, you can replace the final Snapshot OTG with Roundhouse Kick H for slightly more damage if XP is no longer a goal.

VII. (REQUIRES LEVEL 1~2 FRANK) CR. M, ST. H, CR. H X-FACTOR ST. H, CR. H, S FORWARD SUPER JUMP, AIR M, M, H CANCEL ↓ ↘ → + H, LAND, ST. H, CR. H, S CANCEL FORWARD SUPER JUMP, AIR M, M, H, S, LAND, WAVEDASH FORWARD TWICE, ↓ ↘ → + S CANCEL ↓ ↘ → + ATK ATK (MASH ATK)

854,300~1,110,400 damage, 24~63% meter gain

This is a basic, hit-confirmable X-Factor combo. If you've caught two characters at once, use Roundhouse Kick H rather than Snapshot to OTG at the end; otherwise, the assist drops out before the hyper combo finishes.

ADVANCED TACTICS

KNEE DROP NIGHTMARE

Knee Drop sends Frank falling straight down with an overhead smash; on hit, this puts your rival into a hard knockdown. Mixing Knee Drop in various ways with the moves Frank acquires as he levels up leads to Frank's most effective mix-ups. Since Knee Drop travels straight down, it's easy to start the first layer to the mix-up by either whiffing Knee Drop in front of your adversary, or hitting them square. Knee Drop has a semi-long recovery period after Frank lands, but you can cancel this period with special moves! Depending on what kind of look you'd like to give your foe, there are many ways to apply this:

Between Frank's superior air M attacks and Funny Face Crusher, competitors should be wary of going toe-to-toe with Frank at low altitude, which paves the way for him to threaten with Knee Drop...

...cancel Knee Drop recovery into various tricks right next to your opponent to score hits, keep them guessing, and keep momentum.

- If the opponent is knocked down by Knee Drop, you can easily OTG them with Snapshot, Tools of Survival H, or Roundhouse Kick H, any of which can then be canceled into a hyper combo. If you would rather go for XP, knock them down with Knee Drop, then call an assist that can hold your challenger for a bit after the subsequent OTG. With the right assist, you'll be able to launch and keep a combo going for a bit before capping it off with OTG Snapshot into a hyper combo
- If your foe guards: you can cancel the recovery of Knee Drop into Roundhouse Kick L for a feint that leaves Frank right next to his target and in a good position to throw them
- If you have either an assist that hits high or low, call that assist while canceling landing recovery into Tools of Survival H or Roundhouse Kick H. Depending on your timing and the assist you're packing, this can be virtually unguardable
- Alternately, you can call an assist from the first side, then Barrel Roll to pass through to the other. If the assist hits your rival, start a combo as soon as Frank recovers from the roll; if guarded, you're point-blank on the other side of your foe, ready to keep up the pressure. Remember that in order to be unpredictable to an opposing player who is trying to guard properly, you can vary the timing of your assist calls during Barrel Roll, and you can also cancel Barrel Roll at any point into a special move

COMBO APPENDIX

GENERAL EXECUTION TIPS

In general, pause before super jumping to follow up a launcher, but after super jumping, attack on the way up as soon as possible

At any level, link after ↓ ↘ → + Ⓛ in midair as soon as possible. Frank recovers quickly; simply hit the next button in rhythm with his Tools of Survival L hits

When hitstun decay is adding up quickly, such as when starting combos with multiple jump-in attacks, omit air Ⓗ before repetitions of air Ⓜ CANCEL ▶ ↓ ↘ → + Ⓛ

Link air Ⓜ , Ⓢ after air Tools of Survival L as quickly as possible

AS FRANK COMES IN: AIR Ⓜ, Ⓗ CANCEL ▶ ↓ ↘ → + Ⓛ, AIR Ⓜ CANCEL ▶ ↓ ↘ → + Ⓛ, AIR Ⓜ CANCEL ▶ ↓ ↘ → + Ⓛ, Ⓢ, LAND, ↓ ↘ → + Ⓢ OTG CANCEL ▶ ↓ ↙ ← + ATK ATK

Notes	Damage
⇧ + Ⓢ or ⇨ + Ⓢ or ⇩ + Ⓢ TAC to Frank, Frank must be level 1~3	Varies based on damage scaling, gains enough XP to bring Frank to level 3

AS FRANK COMES IN: AIR Ⓜ (3 HITS), Ⓗ CANCEL ▶ ↓ ↘ → + Ⓛ, AIR Ⓜ (3 HITS) CANCEL ▶ ↓ ↘ → + Ⓛ, AIR Ⓜ (3 HITS) CANCEL ▶ ↓ ↘ → + Ⓛ, Ⓢ, LAND, ↓ ↘ → + Ⓢ OTG CANCEL ▶ ↓ ↙ ← + ATK ATK

Notes	Damage
⇧ + Ⓢ or ⇨ + Ⓢ or ⇩ + Ⓢ TAC to Frank, requires corner, Frank must be level 4~5; replace Snapshot OTG with ⇩ ⬂ ⇨ + Ⓗ for much more damage at lv.5	Varies based on damage scaling

FRONT AND BACK THROW OR FRONT AND BACK AIR THROW, ↓ ↘ → + Ⓢ CANCEL ▶ ↓ ↘ → + ATK ATK (MASH ATK)

Notes	Damage
Requires level 1~2 Frank	352,900 damage, 92% meter loss

FRONT AIR THROW, LAND, ↓ ↘ → + Ⓗ OTG, ST. Ⓗ, CR. Ⓗ, Ⓢ CANCEL ▶ FORWARD SUPER JUMP, AIR Ⓜ, Ⓜ, Ⓗ, Ⓢ, LAND, ↓ ↘ → + Ⓢ CANCEL ▶ ↓ ↘ → + ATK ATK (MASH ATK)

Notes	Damage
Requires level 3 Frank	449,700 damage, 39% meter loss

FORWARD JUMP, AIR Ⓜ, Ⓗ, DELAYED Ⓢ, LAND, Ⓢ CANCEL ▶ FORWARD SUPER JUMP, AIR Ⓜ, Ⓗ CANCEL ▶ ↓ ↘ → + Ⓗ, LAND, CR. Ⓗ, Ⓢ CANCEL ▶ FORWARD SUPER JUMP, AIR Ⓜ, Ⓜ, Ⓗ, Ⓢ, LAND, ↓ ↘ → + Ⓢ OTG CANCEL ▶ ↓ ↘ → + ATK ATK (MASH ATK)

Notes	Damage
Preemptive anti-air at low altitude, requires level 1~2 Frank	578,100 damage, 23% meter loss

FRONT AIR THROW, LAND, ↓ ↘ → + Ⓗ, ST. Ⓗ, CR. Ⓗ, Ⓢ CANCEL ▶ FORWARD SUPER JUMP, AIR Ⓜ, Ⓜ, Ⓗ, Ⓢ, LAND, ↓ ↘ → + Ⓢ OTG CANCEL ▶ ↓ ↘ → + ATK ATK (MASH ATK)

Notes	Damage
Requires level 3 Frank	449,700 damage, 39% meter loss

AIR ↓ + Ⓗ, LAND, ↓ ↘ → + Ⓗ, CR. Ⓗ, Ⓢ CANCEL ▶ FORWARD SUPER JUMP, AIR Ⓜ, Ⓜ, Ⓗ, Ⓢ, LAND, ↓ ↘ → + Ⓢ OTG CANCEL ▶ ↓ ↘ → + ATK ATK (MASH ATK)

Notes	Damage
Requires level 3 Frank	576,500 damage, 48% meter loss

FORWARD JUMP, AIR Ⓜ, Ⓗ CANCEL ▶ ↓ ↘ → + Ⓛ, ↓ ↘ → + Ⓛ, ↓ ↘ → + Ⓛ, Ⓢ, LAND, FORWARD DASH, ST. Ⓗ, Ⓢ CANCEL ▶ FORWARD SUPER JUMP, AIR Ⓜ, Ⓜ, Ⓗ, Ⓢ, LAND, ↓ ↘ → + Ⓢ OTG CANCEL ▶ ↓ ↘ → + ATK ATK (MASH ATK)

Notes	Damage
Preemptive anti-air at low altitude, requires level 3 Frank	589,800 damage, 0% meter loss, gains enough XP to bring Frank from level 3 to level 4

AIR ↓ + Ⓗ, LAND, ↓ ↘ → + Ⓗ, ↓ ↘ → + Ⓛ, ST. Ⓜ (3 HITS), ST. Ⓗ (3 HITS), Ⓢ CANCEL ▶ FORWARD SUPER JUMP, AIR Ⓜ (3 HITS), Ⓜ (3 HITS), Ⓗ, Ⓢ, LAND, ↓ ↘ → + Ⓢ OTG CANCEL ▶ ↓ ↙ ← + ATK ATK

Notes	Damage
Requires level 4~5 Frank, replace Snapshot OTG with ⇩ ⬂ ⇨ + Ⓗ for more damage at lv.5	679,900~747,900 damage, 11~21% meter gain

FORWARD JUMP, AIR Ⓜ (3 HITS), Ⓗ CANCEL ▶ ↓ ↘ → + Ⓛ, Ⓢ, LAND, ST. Ⓗ (3 HITS), Ⓢ CANCEL ▶ FORWARD SUPER JUMP, AIR Ⓜ (3 HITS), Ⓜ (3 HITS), Ⓗ, Ⓢ, ↓ ↘ → + Ⓢ OTG CANCEL ▶ ↓ ↙ ← + ATK ATK

Notes	Damage
Preemptive anti-air at low altitude, requires level 4~5 Frank, replace Snapshot OTG with ⇩ ⬂ ⇨ + Ⓗ for more damage at lv.5	596,500~653,900 damage, 12~14% meter gain

FRONT AIR THROW, LAND, ↓ ↘ → + Ⓗ, ↓ ↘ → + Ⓛ, ST. Ⓜ (3 HITS), ST. Ⓗ (3 HITS), Ⓢ CANCEL ▶ FORWARD SUPER JUMP, AIR Ⓜ (3 HITS), Ⓜ (3 HITS), Ⓗ, Ⓢ, LAND, ↓ ↘ → + Ⓢ CANCEL ▶ ↓ ↙ ← + ATK ATK

Notes	Damage
Requires level 4~5 Frank, replace Snapshot OTG with ⇩ ⬂ ⇨ + Ⓗ for more damage at lv.5	574,500~614,400 damage, 18~24% meter gain

→ ↓ ↘ + ATK ATK, ↓ ↘ → + Ⓗ OTG, ↓ ↘ → + Ⓛ, ST. Ⓜ, Ⓢ CANCEL ▶ FORWARD SUPER JUMP, AIR Ⓜ (3 HITS), Ⓜ (3 HITS), Ⓗ, Ⓢ, LAND, WAVEDASH FORWARD TWICE, ↓ ↘ → + Ⓢ OTG CANCEL ▶ ↓ ↙ ← + ATK ATK

Notes	Damage
Combo off of anti-air hyper combo, requires level 4~5 Frank, replace Snapshot OTG with ⇩ ⬂ ⇨ + Ⓗ for more damage at lv.5	688,200~756,900 damage, 113~105% meter loss

CR. Ⓜ (3 HITS), ST. Ⓗ (3 HITS), CR. Ⓗ, Ⓢ CANCEL ▶ FORWARD SUPER JUMP, AIR Ⓜ (3 HITS), Ⓜ (3 HITS), Ⓗ CANCEL ▶ ↓ ↘ → + Ⓛ, Ⓗ CANCEL ▶ ↓ ↘ → + Ⓜ, LAND, BACK UP A STEP, Ⓢ CANCEL ▶ FORWARD SUPER JUMP, AIR Ⓜ (3 HITS), Ⓜ (3 HITS), Ⓢ, LAND, ↓ ↘ → + Ⓗ OTG, ↓ ↘ → + Ⓜ (8 HITS) CANCEL ▶ ↓ ↙ ← + ATK ATK

Notes	Damage
Requires corner and level 4~5 Frank	788,400~852,800 damage, 87~100% meter gain

NEW

NEMESIS T-TYPE

"STAAAARS!"

Bio

REAL NAME

Unknown

OCCUPATION

B.O.W.

ABILITIES

This creature has monster-like super strength and enhanced stamina due to the Nemesis parasite. He can also spawn tentacles from his body, which are capable of stabbing or strangling.

WEAPONS

Rocket Launcher

PROFILE

Nemesis is a tyrant-type B.O.W. tasked with eliminating S.T.A.R.S. and anyone connected to them. Retaining a fair amount of intelligence due to the Nemesis parasite, he is able to effectively carry around a rocket launcher.

FIRST APPEARANCE

Resident Evil 3: Nemesis (1999)

POWER GRID

1	INTELLIGENCE
5	STRENGTH
1	SPEED
6	STAMINA
1	ENERGY PROJECTION
5	FIGHTING ABILITY

*This is biographical, and does not represent an evaluation of the in-game combat potential of this hero.

ALTERNATE COSTUMES

Overview

Vitality	1,150,000
Chain Combo Archetype	Marvel Series

X-Factor Boost	Damage	Speed
Level 1 (3 teammates remaining)	140%	100%
Level 2 (2 teammates remaining)	165%	105%
Level 3 (1 teammate remaining)	190%	110%

The primary objective with Nemesis is to dominate the opposing character from long range.

Why do you want to do this?

- **Nemesis has a number of great long range tools, such as his Air Rocket Launcher and Deadly Range attacks**
- **Nemesis often has a tough time getting near competitors because of his large size and limited mobility**
- **The large size and slow speed of Nemesis give him a number of liabilities on defense, instant overheads in particular**

How do you dominate from long range?

- **Using low-altitude Air Rocket Launcher to attack and inflict chip damage on an adversary from across the screen**
- **Using the three Deadly Range attacks to limit your foe's movements while interrupting attacks**
- **Supplementing Deadly Range and Air Rocket Launcher with long range crossover assists**

The secondary objective with Nemesis is to get within range of Tentacle Slam L.

Why should Nemesis be at this range?

- **Tentacle Slam L is a fast command throw with large range, and it leads into one of the most damaging post-throw combos in the game**
- **Opposing characters who attempt to counter Tentacle Slam L with attacks open themselves up to getting hit by Nemesis' assortment of armor-enabled attacks, some of which lead into huge damage**
- **Rivals who attempt to avoid Tentacle Slam L by jumping open themselves up to Nemesis' great anti-air attacks, which also lead into tons of damage!**

How do you effectively get within range of Tentacle Slam L?

- **Beating his opponent at long range with Air Rocket Launcher and Angled Deadly Reach, forcing them to come to him**
- **Jumping forward over ground-level threats while attacking with Air Deadly Reach, all while utilizing crossover assists**
- **Wavedashing forward while guarding incoming attacks**
- **Using the Bioweapon Assault hyper combo to cleanly beat out projectiles**
- **Using the armor-enabled properties of crouching Ⓗ to go through or under incoming attacks**

Attack Set

Standing Basic Attacks

Screen	Command	Hits	Damage	Meter Gain	Startup	Active	Recovery	Advantage on Hit	Advantage if Guarded	Notes
1	Standing L	1	70,000	560	8	3	13	+2	0	—
2	Standing M	1	90,000	720	12	3	21	-1	-3	—
3	Standing H	1	110,000	880	17	4	28	—	-6	Knocks down, super armor from frames 10-24

1

2

3

Crouching Basic Attacks

Screen	Command	Hits	Damage	Meter Gain	Startup	Active	Recovery	Advantage on Hit	Advantage if Guarded	Notes
1	Crouching L	1	65,000	520	9	3	12	+3	+1	Low attack
2	Crouching M	1	85,000	680	11	3	20	0	-1	—
3	Crouching H	1	100,000	800	18	4	29	—	-7	Knocks down, super armor from frames 16-27

1

2

3

Ground Special Attack—Launcher

Screen	Command	Hits	Damage	Meter Gain	Startup	Active	Recovery	Advantage on Hit	Advantage if Guarded	Notes
1	S (while standing or crouching)	1	100,000	800	10	5	34	—	-13	Launcher, not special- or hyper combo-cancelable

1

Air Basic Attacks

Screen	Command	Hits	Damage	Meter Gain	Startup	Active	Recovery	Advantage on Hit	Advantage if Guarded	Notes
1	Air L	1	75,000	600	9	3	19	+16	+14	Overhead attack
2	Air M	1	90,000	720	12	3	21	+21	+19	Overhead attack
3	Air H	1	100,000	800	15	11	15	+22	+20	Overhead attack

1

2

3

Air Special Attacks—Flying Screen and Air Exchange

Air (S) causes a hard knockdown when used in a launcher combo (this is sometimes called flying screen). When used outside of a launcher combo, air (S) behaves mostly like another basic attack. Air exchange attacks, performed by inputting a direction plus (S), are only possible during a launcher combo. Exchange hits initiate team aerial combos by tagging in the next available character to continue the air combo.

Screen	Command	Hits	Damage	Meter Gain	Startup	Active	Recovery	Advantage on Hit	Advantage if Guarded	Notes
1	Air (S)	1	110,000	880	17	4	25	—	+18	Causes hard knockdown if used in launcher combo, ground bounces foe
2	Air ⇧ + (S) (during launcher combo)	2	105,00	880	10	5	29	—	—	Tags in next available ally while lofting opponent upward
3	Air ⇨ or ⇦ + (S) (during launcher combo)	2	95,000	800	15	3	23	—	—	Tags in next available ally while causing wall bounce, steals 1 hyper meter from opposing character
4	Air ⇩ + (S) (during launcher combo)	2	95,000	800	17	4	20	—	—	Tags in next available ally while causing ground bounce, generates 1 hyper meter

1

2

3

4

Command Attacks

Command attacks resemble basic attacks but have different chaining and canceling properties. It's usually possible to chain *into* a command attack from basic attacks, but most command attacks cannot be chained from or canceled themselves.

Screen	Name	Command	Hits	Damage	Meter Gain	Startup	Active	Recovery	Advantage on Hit	Advantage if Guarded	Notes
1	Deadly Reach	⇨ + (H)	3	102,900	960	15	8	23	+1	-1	—
2	Air Deadly Reach	(in air) ⇨ + (H)	3	102,900	960	15	8	23	+23	+21	—
3	Angled Deadly Reach	(in air) ⇩ + (H)	3	102,900	960	15	8	23	+23	+21	—

1

2

3

Throws

Throws are for snagging passive or blocking opponents. Since throws are active so quickly, you can also use them to preemptively toss opposing characters out of their offense. Combos are usually possible after throws, one way or another.

Screen	Command	Hits	Damage	Meter Gain	Startup	Active	Notes
1	⇨ + (H) (ground)	1	80,000	800	1	1	Hard knockdown
1	⇦ + (H) (ground)	1	80,000	800	1	1	Hard knockdown
2	⇨ + (H) (air)	1	80,000	800	1	1	Hard knockdown
2	⇦ + (H) (air)	1	80,000	800	1	1	Hard knockdown

1

2

As a Partner—Crossover Assists

Screen	Type	P1+P2 Crossover Combination Hyper Combo	Description	Hits	Damage	Meter Gain	Startup	Active	Recovery (this crossover assist)	Recovery (other partner)	Notes
1	Nemesis—α	Bioweapon Assault	Clothesline Rocket M	2	80,000 + 150,000	640 + 1200	46	5(28)1	111	81	First hit wall bounces foe, second hit knocks down, projectile has 1 low priority durability point, creates explosion with 10 low priority durability points on contact
2	Nemesis—β	Bioweapon Assault	Launcher Slam M	1	130,000	1040	42	5	124	94	Ground bounces opponent
3	Nemesis—γ	Bioweapon Assault	Rocket Launcher	1	150,000	1200	44	—	136	106	Knocks down, projectile has 1 low priority durability point, creates explosion with 10 low priority durability points on contact

When deciding which crossover assist type to assign to Nemesis, it really just comes down to whether your team benefits more from an assist that can either wall bounce or ground bounce.

Nemesis—α is likely the most well-rounded of the three assist types, since it has a degree of utility outside of combos. The big punch of Clothesline Rocket M covers a fairly large chunk of the screen and causes wall bounce. However, the rocket blast afterward makes it difficult to convert a midscreen hit into a combo, and it also makes it much more difficult to protect Nemesis from his opponent. In this situation, the rocket likely sails right over the head of a crouching adversary, who can easily start hitting Nemesis with a combo unless you actively prevent this.

Nemesis—β performs Launcher Slam M, which causes a ground bounce state. Unfortunately, the attack does not retain any armor properties in its assist form. Select this crossover assist type if your teammate characters don't have a ground bounce in their combos.

Nemesis—γ performs his Rocket Launcher attack. While having an extra projectile assist is never a bad thing, the fact that about half of the characters in the game don't even need to crouch to be able to duck under the rocket make this a difficult assist type to use effectively.

Snap Back

Screen	Command	Hits	Damage	Meter Gain	Startup	Active	Recovery	Advantage on Hit	Advantage if Guarded
1	⇩⇙⇨ + P1⇔P2	1	50,000	500 (-1 hyper meter bar)	2	4	28	—	-6

Notes

On hit, snap back forces the opposing point character to be replaced by an assist. Opposing assist calls or tag outs are also locked out for 4 seconds

Special Moves

Screen	Name	Command	Hits	Damage	Meter Gain	Startup	Active	Recovery	Advantage on Hit	Advantage if Guarded	Notes
1	Clothesline Rocket L	⇩⇙⇨ + L	1	120,000	960	18	5	23	—	-2	Wall bounces foe
2	Clothesline Rocket M	⇩⇙⇨ + M	2	80,000 + 150,000	640 + 1200	22	5(28)1	20	—	+6	First hit wall bounces opponent, second hit knocks down adversaries, projectile has 1 low priority durability points, creates explosion with 10 low priority durability points on contact
3	Clothesline Rocket H	⇩⇙⇨ + H	2	80,000 + 150,000	640 + 1200	22	5(28)1	20	—	+6	First hit wall bounces foe, second hit knock down foe, projectile has 1 low priority durability points, creates explosion with 10 low priority durability points on contact

Special Moves continued

Screen	Name	Command	Hits	Damage	Meter Gain	Startup	Active	Recovery	Advantage on Hit	Advantage if Guarded	Notes
4	Rocket Launcher	↓↘→ + S	1	150,000	1200	20	—	45	—	-19	Knocks down, projectile has 1 low priority durability points, creates explosion with 10 low priority durability points on contact
5	Air Rocket launcher	(in air) ↓↘→ + S	1	150,000	1200	20	—	45	—	0	OTG-capable, knocks down, projectile has 1 low priority durability points, creates explosion with 10 low priority durability points on contact
6	Anti-Air Rocket Launcher	→↓↘ + S	1	150,000	1200	20	—	45	—	-19	Knocks down, projectile has 1 low priority durability points, creates explosion with 10 low priority durability points on contact
7	Launcher Slam L	→↓↘ + L	1	130,000	1040	15	5	29	+2	-8	Knocks down, super armor frames 10-24
8	Launcher Slam M	→↓↘ + M	1	130,000	1040	18	5	33	—	-12	Ground bounces rival, super armor frames 15-29
9	Launcher Slam H	→↓↘ + H	1	130,000	1040	22	5	39	—	-18	Wall bounces target, hard knockdown, super armor frames 11-30
10	Tentacle Slam L	→↘↓↙← + L	1	150,000	1500	7	1	48	—	—	Hard knockdown
11	Tentacle Slam M	→↘↓↙← + M	1	150,000	1500	20	1	45	—	—	Hard knockdown
12	Tentacle Slam H	→↘↓↙← + H	1	150,000	1500	20	1	45	—	—	Hard knockdown

***Clothesline Rocket L*:** Nemesis' primary attack for combos, Clothesline Rocket unleashes a large haymaker that wall bounces the opposing character. Nemesis has enough range on his attacks to be able to capitalize from this anywhere on the screen!

You can use Clothesline Rocket L to end guarded attack strings when fishing for counterhits; at -2 frame advantage, it's Nemesis' safest option after his L and M attacks. However, Nemesis is always within range for his rival to score a guaranteed throw afterward, even if you make contact with the very tip of the punch. Try to mitigate this by calling a crossover assist before using this attack.

It should be noted that Clothesline Rocket L can hit later against small crouching characters, resulting in even frame advantage.

***Clothesline Rocket M*:** Nemesis performs a haymaker that is immediately followed by a Rocket Launcher shot. While the animation for the rocket-firing portion of this attack recovers substantially faster than the stand-alone version, it's difficult to fit Clothesline Rocket M anywhere into your gameplan: unless used at an extremely specific distance from the corner, Clothesline Rocket L always results in better combos and is much safer if guarded. The frame data states that this attack is +6 if guarded, but that's if your competitor actually guards it—the rocket flies clear over the head of any crouching character besides Sentinel, leaving Nemesis wide open for punishment.

Hyper combo canceling Clothesline Rocket M into Fatal Mutation might seem like a fun trick to try now and then, but you can actually do the exact same thing with Clothesline Rocket L!

***Clothesline Rocket H*:** This version of the attack ends with the upward-angled Anti-Air Rocket Launcher. Like Clothesline Rocket M, it is very difficult to utilize this attack effectively.

***Rocket Launcher*:** Nemesis fires a rocket that has only a single low priority durability point but creates a lingering explosion with 10 low priority points upon impact. The rocket essentially trades with almost all low priority projectiles in the game.

Rocket Launcher inflicts 150,000 points of damage, which is an impressive amount for a single-hit projectile. Unfortunately, utility of this attack is very limited for one simple reason: every single character in the game besides Sentinel can crouch under the rocket.

The following characters don't even need to crouch; they can simply stand right under the rocket:

Firebrand	**Frank West**	**Chun-Li**	**Viewtiful Joe**	**Iron Fist**	**X-23**
Strider Hiryu	**Zero**	**Felicia**	**Hsien-Ko**	**Rocket Raccoon**	**Spider-Man**
Arthur	**Morrigan**	**Spencer**	**Amaterasu**	**Wolverine**	**Taskmaster**

5

Anti-Air Rocket Launcher: Nemesis fires a rocket 30 degrees upward. Unfortunately, this angle places the rocket at an awkward location, too high to catch opponents firing projectiles from normal jump height across the screen and still too low to catch adversaries firing projectiles at super jump height. While it's technically possible to intercept an opposing character normal jumping from across the screen with an Anti-Air Rocket Launcher, the exacting timing required makes it extremely unlikely.

6

Air Rocket Launcher: The aerial version of Rocket Launcher is one of Nemesis' most important tools: a fullscreen projectile that the opposing character cannot crouch under.

You can launch Air Rocket Launcher extremely low to the ground by executing it with a tiger knee motion: ↓↘→↗ + Ⓢ. While firing from this low altitude still allows the rocket to travel the length of the screen, it also lets Nemesis land on the ground much more quickly. Nemesis recovers as soon as he touches the ground, allowing him to immediately jump back up and tiger knee another Air Rocket Launcher!

Against a projectile-based character, you'll want to use Air Rocket Launcher at the apex of Nemesis' jump: this lets the rocket directly hit your target without being intercepted by another projectile!

7

Launcher Slam L: Nemesis swings his rocket launcher upward in a wide arc, covering a large portion of the screen. Launcher Slam L has armor properties beginning on frame 10, the fastest of all armor-enabled special attacks.

If Launcher Slam L hits your target, they are forced to air recover directly in front of Nemesis. If they air recover backwards, catching them out of the air with the Tentacle Slam throw attack is almost impossible to avoid. Air recovering forward gets them grabbed by Tentacle Slam H!

Launcher Slam L is very unsafe if guarded, though at its maximum range, it leaves Nemesis too far away for most characters to be able to capitalize. However, in terms of general usage, it's difficult to recommend Launcher Slam L over Nemesis' amazing Ⓢ launcher attack, and in terms of armor-enabled special attacks, Launcher Slam M results in a much higher reward.

8

Launcher Slam M: This attack becomes armor-enabled on frame 15, making it Nemesis' slowest armor attack. However, this is also the only Launcher Slam that naturally leads to a combo, so use it to try to catch rivals who are trying to punish Nemesis' unsafe normal attacks—perform a slightly delayed cancel to Launcher Slam M so that the armor kicks in just in time to absorb their retaliatory attacks. Hitting Launcher Slam M ground bounces the opponent, which usually results in a combo!

...usually? Launcher Slam M typically only gives Nemesis enough time to juggle additional hits if it hits either an airborne or a crouching adversary. If you hit your opponent out of the air with Launcher Slam M (usually during a juggle combo), great: follow it up with a crouching Ⓜ and continue into whatever combo you like. Against a crouching foe, you'll typically only barely have enough time to start a combo from crouching Ⓛ. Against most standing opponents, you won't have time to juggle anything at all. Fortunately, you'll generally be using the armor properties to absorb crouching Ⓛ attacks!

Launcher Slam M is very unsafe if guarded. If you make an incorrect guess and find yourself open to punishment, consider hyper combo canceling this into yet another armor-enabled attack: Biohazard Rush!

9

Launcher Slam H: The last version of Launcher Slam has armor frames kicking in on frame 11. This attack both wall bounces and causes a hard knockdown state, making it useful at the end of long combos aided by a crossover assist—simply tack on the Launcher Slam H to cause a hard knockdown, then hyper combo cancel it into the OTG-capable Bioweapon Assault!

While Launcher Slam H isn't used often outside of combos, be aware that many characters are able cleanly crouch under it.

10

Tentacle Slam L: This throw attack is the centerpiece of Nemesis' offensive threat. It has long range and great speed, and it leads into a very damaging combo.

It's important to note that Tentacle Slam L is actually Nemesis' fastest attack that isn't a snap back or a normal throw, and it should be used as such. In close range situations where frame advantage is near neutral, leading in with Tentacle Slam L is much more effective than a standing or crouching Ⓛ attack.

Similarly, Tentacle Slam L is generally the most reliable way for Nemesis to punish guarded attacks; it also has significantly more range than crouching Ⓛ!

11

Tentacle Slam M: A long range throw attack that grabs airborne opponents, Tentacle Slam is a very powerful yet risky tool. At 20 frames of startup, Tentacle Slam M is significantly slower than the Ⓛ version, and it can essentially only be used as a pure guess that your target will be in the air and in front of Nemesis. On a wrong guess, Nemesis is left wide open for punishment, so it's best to always call a crossover assist beforehand to cover the ground when performing Tentacle Slam M or H.

12

Tentacle Slam H: The last version of Tentacle Slam goes straight up, and it is just as slow as the Ⓜ version. But this throw is much more useful than it may seem, as it's great for countering opponents super jumping toward Nemesis. It's also great for adversaries who tend to air recover forward, trying get over the top of Nemesis and away from his offense.

Hyper Combos

Screen	Name	Command	Hits	Damage	Startup	Active	Recovery	Advantage on Hit	Advantage if Guarded	Notes
1	Bioweapon Assault	↓↘→ + ATK ATK	4	80,000 x 4	18+3	1(23) 1(24)1(93)7	82	—	-58	Rockets are OTG-capable, cause hard knockdown, last hit ground bounces foe, rockets have 1 high priority durability point, explodes on contact, explosions have 5 high priority durability points and last 3 frames
2	Biohazard Rush	→↓↘ + ATK ATK	6	312,400	15+3	10(23)11(26) 11(33)11 (50)20	69	—	-54	First three hits cause stagger state, fourth hit knocks down, last hit ground bounces opponent, has armor from frames 11-260, armor can absorb up to 10 hits
3	Fatal Mutation (Level 3 Hyper combo)	→↘↓↙← + ATK ATK	1	450,000	15+0	2	58	—	—	Throw attack, hard knockdown

Bioweapon Assault: Nemesis fires three rockets that are all OTG-capable and cause hard knockdown. Afterward, Nemesis leaps into the air and performs a final OTG-capable stomp with his rocket launcher on his target's current location.

Bioweapon Assault serves two vital purposes in Nemesis' gameplan: first and foremost, it's his primary combo ender. It's great for this purpose, easily converting a hard knockdown from anywhere on the screen into good damage. The final stomp propels the opposing character into the air slowly while Nemesis is standing in close proximity, making it extremely easy to team hyper combo to almost any other hyper combo in the game.

The three missiles are aimed toward your competitor's location at the time that Nemesis fires, adjusting up to a maximum of 45 degrees up or down. This can often cause issues with rockets missing against a quickly bouncing and juggled opponent, which in turn can lead to Nemesis performing the final unsafe stomp onto a guarding adversary. To prevent missing a rocket during a midscreen OTG combo, simply backdash immediately before using Bioweapon Assault.

You can also use Bioweapon Assault in long range fights against projectile-using characters. The rockets are high priority projectiles that can cleanly cut through everything besides other projectile hyper combos. With the startup frames of Bioweapon Assault included, it takes 36 frames for the first rocket to explode; this makes the move a difficult projectile counter to use on reaction. Instead, you'll usually have to make a read that the opposing player will use a projectile attack before using Bioweapon Assault.

Even though Nemesis is able to automatically aim his rocket launcher, it's generally best not to use Bioweapon Assault against aerial projectiles: the rocket typically flies past the projectile and causes both characters to get hit. Getting hit interrupts the rest of the hyper combo.

Biohazard Rush: This hyper combo has 10 hits worth of armor to blow through attacks at close range. Unfortunately, it also has 10 frames of completely vulnerable startup before the armor kicks in!

Biohazard Rush is used most effectively when your rival guards an unsafe Launcher Slam or avoids a Tentacle Slam; hyper combo cancel into Biohazard Rush with delayed timing to try to catch the opposing character's attempt at punishing your attacks. However, an incorrect guess leaves Nemesis extremely open for punishment, so be ready to THC to a teammate with a safer hyper combo if possible.

This is also Nemesis' most damaging combo ender, but it generally requires the help of a crossover assist to get the most out of it. Be aware that if your opponent isn't high enough when the first hit connects, the rest of the combo harmlessly whiffs and leaves Nemesis wide open for punishment.

Fatal Mutation: With three hyper combo gauge bars to spend, Nemesis can perform a throw attack with slightly more range than Tentacle Slam L. If it successfully grabs the target, you're rewarded with a cutscene in which... something gross happens? What's going on?

Fatal Mutation inflicts 450,000 points of damage and leaves your adversary in a hard knockdown state. You can then follow up with the OTG-capable Bioweapon Assault.

Contrary to what you may expect out of a level 3 throw hyper combo, Fatal Mutation has a very slow startup period and is not invincible at all; this relegates it to occasional usage as a hyper combo cancel after a guarded special attack. If your foe is guarding on the ground expecting a hyper combo cancel to Biohazard Rush, try surprising them with a Fatal Mutation instead!

Generally, it's better to limit your throw attempts to just Tentacle Slam L; it's much faster, has only slightly less range, and it usually even results in more damage dealt to the opposing character.

"WHOOOOOOOOAAAAAAAAH!"

Battle Plan

A rare sight in fighting games, Nemesis is a grappler-projectile hybrid character—he is perfectly at home fighting from long range with his Air Rocket Launcher and Deadly Reach attacks. Instead of incurring lots of damage trying to slog through projectiles in order to get near, a Nemesis player should try to dominate the ranged game and force competitors to come to close range!

Air Rocket Launcher from afar is a great forcing function to make your opponents feel like they have to come to you. Use it as low to the ground as possible!

Angled Deadly Reach is one of the best air attacks in the game, and it goes a long way toward frustrating projectile-based characters.

Air Rocket Launcher is the focal point of Nemesis' long-range game plan, as it is his only attack that can deal chip damage from afar. Make contact with this attack as often as possible by using it at an extremely low height. The tiger knee technique (named after one of the special attacks of a certain iconic Capcom character) helps out with this—input the command as ↓ ↘ → ↗ + Ⓢ. This cuts the total duration of the attack down to a minimum of 48 frames, allowing Nemesis to repeatedly let loose a barrage of rockets at the enemy!

Opponents without projectiles of their own generally are forced to jump in order to avoid the rockets. If they jump forward, stop them in their tracks with Deadly Range (→ + Ⓗ) or Air Deadly Range (→ + Ⓗ) while simultaneously calling a long-range crossover assist. While your rival is dealing with the crossover assist, force them to guard some more rockets! Attackers who are more passive about avoiding the rockets may opt to jump straight up over them. In this case, you'll want to advance forward just enough to threaten your foe with Angled Deadly Reach (air ↓ + Ⓗ) and Air Deadly Reach, all while calling more crossover assists. This lets you push your adversary back to the corner while still remaining at a safe range. Note that both of the aerial versions of Deadly Reach can also be canceled into Air Rocket Launcher for additional chip damage.

Against other long range characters, you'll have to take into account their angle of attack. If your foe's projectiles are mostly horizontal in nature, Nemesis can counter this by simply waiting until the apex of his jump before firing Air Rocket Launcher. This allows the rocket to proceed uninterrupted to the target, hopefully dealing a whopping 150,000 points of damage! Given Nemesis' large amount of health, especially when compared to most other long range characters, going even in projectile-trading eventually works in his favor. Against characters who can also attack from all the across the screen at normal jump height, you'll want to simply wait until they fire their own projectile before jumping over it and using Rocket Launcher, forcing them to guard it. Alternatively, you can preemptively super jump and use Air Rocket Launcher in an attempt to land a clean hit.

In either case, taking the fight just a little bit closer within the range of Deadly Reach is another strong option—jump over horizontal projectiles and try to score free hits with Angled Deadly Reach, or snag aerial projectile-firing competitors with Air Deadly Reach. Calling long range crossover assists simultaneously with Deadly Reach usage makes for a much more smothering threat.

Some characters are able to output spreads of projectiles that are difficult for Nemesis to deal with. In this case, you'll want to focus on interrupting your rival with the ground version of Deadly Reach before your opponent can release the projectiles: dash forward and guard a salvo of projectiles, then interrupt your attacker's next action by putting a bunch of tentacles in their face!

Deadly Reach becomes an extremely powerful tool if the opposing character cannot crouch under it. The following characters have this liability:

Nemesis	Tron	M.O.D.O.K.	Sentinel	Hulk

Competitors who can fire projectiles downward from super jump height are also tricky to deal with. Against these characters, you'll want to meet them in the air by super jumping and snagging them with Air Deadly Reach. If range permits, hitting air Ⓢ is even better—it causes a ground bounce and allows for a full combo. One combo from Nemesis and a team hyper combo is enough to finish off most characters!

Nemesis' Ⓢ launcher attack is among the best in the game: huge range, height, no vulnerable hitboxes around the tentacles, and surprisingly quick speed!

The armor properties of standing Ⓗ make it a great, safer alternative to the Ⓢ launcher. Cancel to Clothesline Slam L to help mitigate risk and allow for combos.

Opponents who are frustrated by Nemesis' long range game will inevitably try to close the distance. When this happens, you'll want to score as much free damage as you can by capitalizing on any openings that the opposing character gives you.

Most of the time, you'll perform said capitalizing with Nemesis' Ⓢ launcher. This attack has long horizontal range, enormous vertical range, and incredible speed, great for reacting when your competitor enters within its range. Nemesis does not have any vulnerable hitboxes where the tentacles are; to interrupt him out of the launcher, his adversary must have an attack that can actually reach Nemesis' body. If it hits, proceed into a simple launcher combo, then tack on a Bioweapon Assault for a quick 577,900 points of damage!

The Ⓢ attack is punishable if guarded, however, particularly if guarded in the air. At far ranges against opponents on the ground, it's difficult for most characters to punish unless they have fast dashes or long range. Rivals who try to lure you in using the Ⓢ launcher open themselves up in another way—dash in and grab them with a Tentacle Slam!

Standing Ⓗ is a moderately safer alternative to the Ⓢ launcher that has less range: the attack gains armor properties on the 10th frame, effectively making it the exact same speed as the 10-frame Ⓢ. When using Ⓗ defensively against airborne targets, also buffer a → ↘ ↓ ↙ ← motion during the attack: if your competitor gets hit by the attack, simply react and press Ⓢ to convert the hit into a combo. If the opponent guards, press Ⓛ with delayed timing to grab them right when they touch the ground!

If your rival manages to get within point-blank range and starts to attack, Nemesis' options are extremely limited. Most characters are able to rely on a combination of advancing guard and air throws for defense, but Nemesis has one huge threat to worry about—instant overheads! Due to his large size, many air attacks can be performed on the way up and still hit Nemesis in his attempts to guard crouching. Many characters are able to convert these hits into a full combo, making defense especially scary. The best policy is to simply not let the opposing player establish this momentum by putting up a strong mid-range defense based around the Ⓢ launcher and standing Ⓗ.

Some characters simply outmatch Nemesis at long range, forcing you to go in and establish an offensive threat. Approaching an adversary who already is able to dominate Nemesis at long range is a formidable task, since this already assumes that liberal use of Angled Deadly Reach combined with crossover assists wasn't doing the job.

Nemesis is a very large target, making it significantly more difficult for him to get around projectiles than with other characters. While Nemesis has a much better dash than you would expect for a grappler, Nemesis still has a major limitation: his forward dash cannot be canceled into attacks or guarded for the first 10 frames. This makes it much more difficult to reliably minimize damage by wavedashing forward and guarding attacks on reaction. However, you can cancel those first 10 frames with a jump, so it is possible to guard by pressing up and back on the controller. This results in a lot of unnecessary backward jumps when you inevitably react to false positives in this manner.

Outside of the standard dashing and jumping, there is one tool at your disposal to help close the distance—the crouching (H) attack. This attack performs two important functions: it gets Nemesis to crouch low while moving forward, and it has armor through a large portion of the attack. The armor comes in fairly late, though, starting at frame 16. This makes it difficult to use as a reactionary tool, but it is still occasionally useful as you can call a crossover assist simultaneously, which then allows you to safely perform Clothesline Launcher L to cover more distance.

Standing (H) is unsafe if guarded...

...but you can cancel into the armor-enabled Launcher Slam M to catch opponents trying to punish it!

Verify that your attacks are being guarded and chain into crouching (H) ...

...then cancel into Tentacle Slam L before the attack hits for a perfectly timed set-up!

Nemesis mostly relies on crossover assists to get near his rival. Sentinel—α is a great all-around partner for Nemesis to have, as are Doctor Doom—α and Iron Man—α. Advancing behind the cover of the assists also often traps the opposing character in guardstun as Nemesis gets near, allowing you to immediately place them in a mix-up.

When Nemesis finally does manage to get near his opponent, his offense revolves around Tentacle Slam L, Tentacle Slam M, and his armor-enabled attacks. To be able to establish the threat of the Tentacle Slam attacks, you first must get your adversary to stop attacking. The easiest way to accomplish this is to establish frame advantage with a crossover assist, then dash and attack with a crouching (L) to crouching (M) chain. From there, you can verify if the attacks hit, and perform one of the following options:

- **Chain to standing (H) and Launcher Slam M if the attacks hit**
- **Chain to crouching (H) and kara-cancel to Tentacle Slam L if your opponent remains guarding**
- **Chain to crouching (H) and kara-cancel to Tentacle Slam M to beat jumping**
- **Perform a delayed chain to the armor-enabled standing (H) to beat further attempts from the opposing player to press buttons**

Kara-cancel is an old Japanese *Street Fighter* term from the '90s, essentially meaning to cancel a normal attack into a special attack before it even hits an opponent. As it applies to the above scenario, you would chain to the crouching (H) attack on reaction to your rival guarding your initial two attacks. Before the attack actually hits your competitor, cancel it into Tentacle Slam L; this gives you a set-up with nice, intuitive timing that grabs your opponent at the earliest possible moment! Even better, this set-up cannot be interrupted by attacks slower than 5 frames; the opposing character must commit to jumping to avoid the Tentacle Slam L!

When fighting characters who have 5 frame startup attacks, you can counter their attempts to interrupt the Tentacle Slam L with the armor-enabled standing (H): delay the chain into standing (H) just enough to give them time to stick out their attack, then blast through the attack with your armor! Reacting to whether the standing (H) hit or not isn't reliable, so simply cancel to Clothesline Launcher whenever you attempt to use standing (H) in this way. If it hits, you can easily convert the wall bounce into a combo. If guarded, Nemesis is left at a -2 frame disadvantage and is vulnerable to throws, which generally result in much less damage than a normal combo.

Your rival can bypass the entire mix-up outlined above simply by using advancing guard early on. But Nemesis can counter this: see the Advanced Tactics section for details.

On offense, Nemesis is extremely likely to hit both the point and assist character with his huge Deadly Range attacks, armor-enabled Launcher Slams, and enormous (S) launcher. Don't be afraid to use X-Factor early in the combo to ensure that both characters get taken out!

COMBO USAGE

I. CR. (L), CR. (M), ST. (H) CANCEL → ↓ ↘ + (M), CR. (M), CR. (H) CANCEL ↓ ↘ → + (L), CR. (H), (S) CANCEL FORWARD SUPER JUMP, AIR (M), (H), (S), LAND, ↓ ↘ → + (ATK)(ATK) OTG

735,100 damage, 96% meter gain

If the first two opening attacks of this combo is blocked, stage a secondary offense that consists of a delayed Tentacle Slam L (into Combo III), delayed crouching (H) to Clothesline Launcher L, or Tentacle Slam M if your target attempts to jump away. Note that both crouching (M) and Clothesline Launcher L are -2 if guarded, but your foe is only in range for a throw. Crouching (L), crouching (M) is a actually a safe opening.

After the Clothesline Launcher L hits, your positioning may affect whether or not you can easily juggle a crouching (H) afterwards. If the opposing character bounces off of the wall and flies close by, omit the crouching (H) and just use (S). If Clothesline Launcher L connects when you're near a corner, you don't need to dash forward.

After Bioweapon Assault hits, your opponent flies into a long juggle state that's perfect for a THC. You can also pop X-Factor in this situation to score a finishing blow: juggle with Launcher Slam H, then hyper combo cancel into Bioweapon Assault again.

COMBO USAGE CONT.

II. AIR Ⓗ, Ⓢ, LAND, CR. Ⓜ, Ⓗ CANCEL ↓↘→ + Ⓛ, CR. Ⓗ, Ⓢ CANCEL SUPER JUMP, AIR Ⓜ, Ⓗ, Ⓢ, LAND, ↓↘→ + ATK ATK OTG

734,300 damage, 19% meter loss

A combo for air-to-air situations, such as against new characters entering the playing field.

III. →↘↓↙← + Ⓛ OR Ⓜ OR Ⓗ, CR. Ⓜ, ST. Ⓗ CANCEL ↓↘→ + Ⓛ, FORWARD DASH, CR. Ⓗ, Ⓢ CANCEL SUPER JUMP FORWARD, AIR Ⓜ, Ⓗ, Ⓢ, LAND, ↓↘→ + ATK ATK

638,900 damage, 80% meter gain

A high-damage combo off of the Tentacle Slam L command throw. In the event that you miss with the initial grab, you can counter incoming counterattacks by canceling its recovery into Biohazard Rush. You can alter this combo to ensure it always gains one meter by performing the following after the Clothesline Launcher L:

Forward dash, forward jump, air Ⓜ, Ⓜ, Ⓗ, land, Ⓢ CANCEL super jump forward, air Ⓜ, Ⓗ, Ⓢ, land, ↓↘→ + ATK ATK (101% meter gain, 626,800 damage).

IV. (CORNERED OPPONENT) AIR THROW, AIR Ⓜ, LAND, ST. Ⓜ, ST. Ⓗ CANCEL →↓↘ + Ⓜ, ST. Ⓜ, ST. Ⓗ CANCEL ↓↘→ + Ⓛ, CR. Ⓗ, Ⓢ CANCEL SUPER JUMP FORWARD, AIR Ⓜ, Ⓗ, Ⓢ, LAND, ↓↘→ + ATK ATK

500,200 damage, 107% meter gain

Nemesis recovers in the air after his air throw, allowing you to tack on an air Ⓜ as he's falling. Once you've landed, you can shift into any standard Nemesis combo.

V. AGAINST AIRBORNE ENEMY, ST. Ⓗ CANCEL →↓↘ + Ⓜ, CR. Ⓜ, CR. Ⓗ CANCEL ↓↘→ + Ⓛ, FORWARD DASH, CR. Ⓗ, Ⓢ CANCEL FORWARD SUPER JUMP, AIR Ⓜ, Ⓜ, Ⓗ, Ⓢ, LAND, ↓↘→ + ATK ATK

766,100 damage, 84% meter gain

Standing Ⓗ can plow through numerous jumping attacks due to its armor property. It's highly unsafe on guard, though, so be ready to cancel into either Tentacle Slam or Launcher Slam if guarded.

VI. CROUCHING Ⓗ ↓↘→ + Ⓛ, FORWARD DASH, CR. Ⓜ, CR. Ⓗ CANCEL →↓↘ + Ⓜ, ST. Ⓜ, Ⓢ CANCEL FORWARD SUPER JUMP, AIR Ⓜ, Ⓜ, Ⓗ, Ⓢ, LAND, ↓↘→ + ATK ATK

738,700 damage, 82% meter gain

You can use the armor properties of crouching Ⓗ to plow through mid-range attacks and single-hit projectiles. Unfortunately, Clothesline Launcher L is punishable by throws if guarded, so you may opt to cancel crouching Ⓗ into a delayed, verifiable Ⓢ launcher instead. Crouching Ⓗ and Ⓢ are both unsafe if guarded, but the delayed chain into the Ⓢ may catch competitors attempting to punish the crouching Ⓗ.

ADVANCED TACTICS

COMBATING ADVANCE GUARD

It's incredibly difficult to reliably use advancing guard against a crouching Ⓛ attack on reaction. If your adversary is attempting to do this…

…you can insert a small delay between crouching Ⓛ and Ⓜ. If the opposing player presses buttons, they'll get counterhit instead of guarding!

Nemesis has a strong mix-up from his crouching Ⓛ and Ⓜ chain, which can unfortunately be easily nullified simply by opponents using advancing guard. You can counter your rival's attempts to use advancing guard based on a simple idea—it's really tough to use advancing guard against a single crouching Ⓛ attack on reaction.

The first step is to condition your competitor into trying to use advancing guard against one crouching Ⓛ. To do this, simply use Tentacle Slam L and throw your target immediately after forcing them to guard a crouching Ⓛ attack. This allows you to perform a Tentacle Slam L or M mix-up right off the bat.

To reliably escape this mix-up, the opposing player must either use advancing guard or try to interrupt you with fast attacks. Either way, the counter is the same: insert a small delay between crouching Ⓛ and Ⓜ that gives your opponent enough time to leave guardstun. When this is done, an attacker trying to use advancing guard will simply press ⇦ + ATK ATK while not actually in guardstun: this results in a crouching Ⓜ or Ⓗ attack, which then proceeds to get counterhit by your own crouching Ⓜ and leads into a combo.

COMBO APPENDIX

GENERAL EXECUTION TIPS

When ending a midscreen combo, quickly dash backward upon landing from the launcher combo before using Bioweapon Assault to ensure that one of the rockets doesn't miss.

After hitting Clothesline Launcher L midscreen, input the forward dash earlier than you think you have to in order to be able to juggle the crouching Ⓗ attack.

Omitting the crouching Ⓗ and simply dashing forward and pressing Ⓢ is much easier, and it doesn't sacrifice much damage!

WHEN USING AN ALTERNATE TEAMMATE, ACTIVATE A TAC WITH ↑ + Ⓢ OR → + Ⓢ OR ↓ + Ⓢ, THEN AS NEMESIS COMES IN, PERFORM AIR Ⓗ, Ⓢ, LAND, ↓ ↘ → + ATK ATK

Notes	Damage
—	—

→ ↘ ↓ ↙ ← + ATK ATK, ↓ ↘ → + ATK ATK

Notes	Damage
—	731,800

FORWARD JUMP, INSTANT AIR Ⓜ, Ⓢ, LAND, ST. Ⓜ, ST. Ⓗ CANCEL ↓ ↘ → + Ⓛ, FORWARD DASH, CR. Ⓗ, Ⓢ CANCEL FORWARD SUPER JUMP, AIR Ⓜ, Ⓗ, Ⓢ, LAND, ↓ ↘ → + ATK ATK

Notes	Damage
This is intended to act as a very fast overhead against the following large characters: Sentinel, Hulk, MODOK, and Nemesis	733,600

CR. Ⓛ, CR. Ⓜ, ST. Ⓗ CANCEL → ↓ ↘ + Ⓜ, CR. Ⓜ, CR. Ⓗ CANCEL ↓ ↘ → + Ⓛ, FORWARD DASH, FORWARD JUMP, AIR Ⓜ, Ⓜ, Ⓗ, LAND, Ⓢ CANCEL FORWARD SUPER JUMP, AIR Ⓜ, Ⓗ, Ⓢ, LAND, ↓ ↘ → + ATK ATK

Notes	Damage
This is an alternate version of Combo I that inflicts 14,900 less points of overall damage but always builds enough gauge to use Bioweapon Assault	720,200 damage, 112% meter gain

THROW OR AIR THROW, ↓ ↘ → + ATK ATK CANCEL X-FACTOR, ST. Ⓗ CANCEL ↓ ↘ → + Ⓛ, CR. Ⓗ, Ⓢ CANCEL FORWARD SUPER JUMP, AIR Ⓜ, Ⓗ, Ⓢ, LAND, ↓ ↘ → + ATK ATK

Notes	Damage
A verifiable combo into X-Factor off of a ground or air throw	943,800~1,151,700 damage, 90%~118% meter gain

→ ↘ ↓ ↙ ← + Ⓛ OR Ⓜ OR Ⓗ, CR. Ⓜ, ST. Ⓗ CANCEL ↓ ↘ → + Ⓛ CANCEL X-FACTOR, FORWARD DASH, FORWARD JUMP, AIR Ⓜ, Ⓜ, Ⓗ, LAND, Ⓢ CANCEL FORWARD SUPER JUMP, AIR Ⓜ, Ⓗ, Ⓢ, LAND, ↓ ↘ → + ATK ATK

Notes	Damage
A verifiable combo into X-Factor off of Nemesis' Tentacle Slam	883,800~1,087,000 damage, 116~143% meter gain

CR. Ⓛ, CR. Ⓜ, ST. Ⓗ CANCEL → ↓ ↘ + Ⓜ CANCEL X-FACTOR, CR. Ⓜ, CR. Ⓗ CANCEL ↓ ↘ → + Ⓛ, FORWARD JUMP, AIR Ⓜ, Ⓜ, Ⓗ, LAND, Ⓢ CANCEL FORWARD SUPER JUMP, AIR Ⓜ, Ⓗ, Ⓢ, LAND, ↓ ↘ → + ATK ATK)

Notes	Damage
A verifiable combo into X-Factor off of a low attack. Note that the additional re-jump combo hits actually inflict more damage in X-Factor, instead of reducing it	1,042,700~1,176,700 damage, 142~181% meter gain

THROW OR AIR THROW, AIR ↓ ↘ → + Ⓢ OR ↓ ↘ → + ATK ATK

Notes	Damage
Basic air throw follow-ups	147,500~361,800 damage, 20% meter gain

X-FACTOR OPTION SELECT

When going for a Tentacle Slam...

...it's sometimes worth it to buffer an X-Factor activation at the moment the attack would grab your adversary. It doesn't activate if Nemesis actually grabs the foe, but it does if the opponent avoids the Tentacle Slam.

NEW

PHOENIX WRIGHT

"HEROES, VILLAINS, AND THIS HUGE GALACTUS GUY TRYING TO TAKE OVER... IT'S LIKE SOMETHING OUT OF MAYA'S FAVORITE SHOW!"

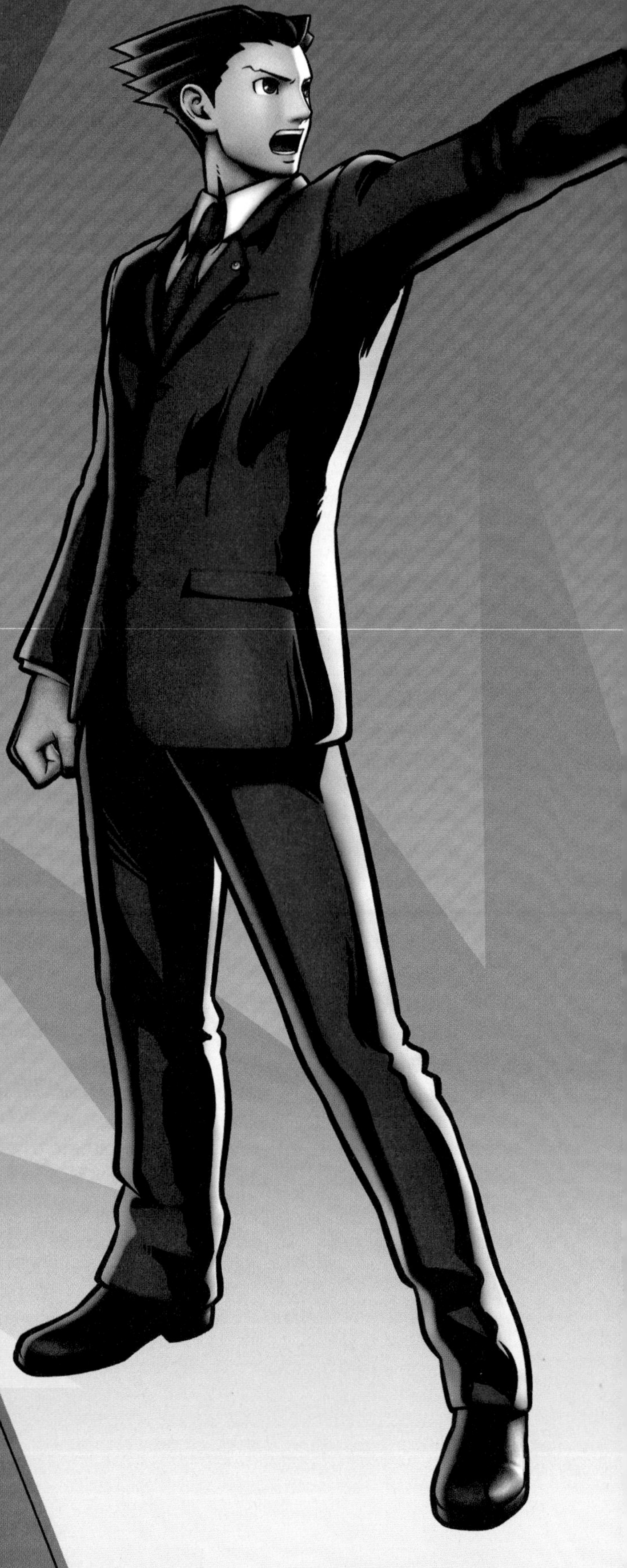

Bio

REAL NAME

Phoenix Wright

OCCUPATION

Lawyer

ABILITIES

Skilled legal defense and a keen sense of observation.

WEAPONS

None

PROFILE

Phoenix Wright is a defense attorney who specializes in criminal law at the Wright & Co. Law Offices. Although he has encountered several extremely difficult and mysterious cases, he has overcome overwhelming odds and turned the cases around for every one of his clients.

FIRST APPEARANCE

Phoenix Wright: Ace Attorney (2001)

POWER GRID

5	INTELLIGENCE
1	STRENGTH
1	SPEED
1	STAMINA
1	ENERGY PROJECTION
1	FIGHTING ABILITY

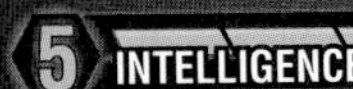

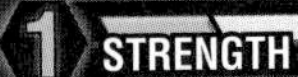

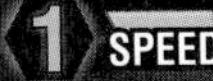

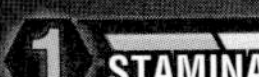

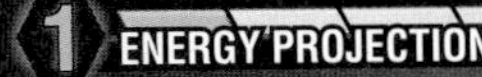

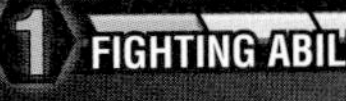

*This is biographical, and does not represent an evaluation of the in-game combat potential of this hero.

ALTERNATE COSTUMES

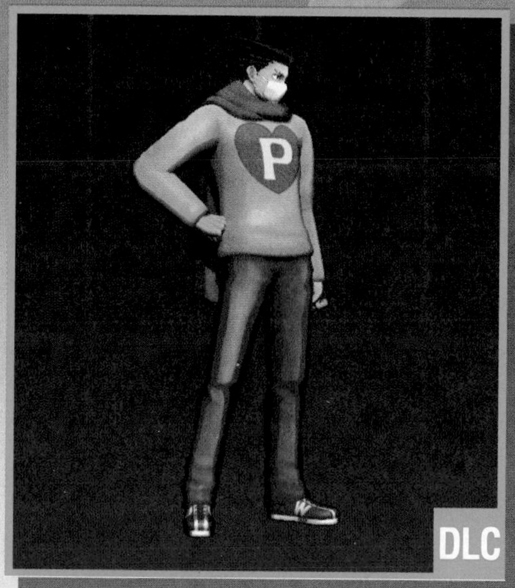

Overview

Vitality	1,000,000
Chain Combo Archetype	Marvel Series

X-Factor Boost	Damage	Speed
Level 1 (3 teammates remaining)	135%	105%
Level 2 (2 teammates remaining)	160%	110%
Level 3 (1 teammate remaining)	185%	115%

Phoenix Wright has stumbled into quite the legal conundrum here in *Ultimate Marvel vs. Capcom 3*. As you'll note from his canon stats, he's not the heartiest combatant—actually, he's the least hearty. He's a talker, not a fighter, and he's used to mounting a defense, not hurling chi energy from his fists and flying about like everyone else in the cast. So, instead of fitting a square peg into a round hole, Phoenix Wright goes with what he knows best—somewhat awkwardly building overwhelming evidence to refute the opposition's case.

Phoenix Wright has three stances, or modes: Investigation, Trial, and Turnabout. Turnabout, which can be entered during Trial mode by landing Wright's → + H or air ↓ + H while carrying three pieces of admissible evidence, boosts Phoenix Wright to the apex of his powers of counsel for an astonishing 20 seconds. For any of Wright's deficiencies outside of Turnabout, he is easily one of the most important characters in the game within Turnabout. What's the big deal with Turnabout?

- **Phoenix Wright gains a 20% boost to damage and speed**
- **Evidence on hand is increased in speed and power**
- **All Paperwork specials become Paperwork Storm; Press the Witness becomes Break the Witness; the same upgrades take place with Phoenix Wright—α and Phoenix Wright—β; these are the best special moves and assists in the game**
- **Ace Attorney, the single best attack in the game, becomes available**

So, how do we get there?

- **By using Investigations mode to compile evidence, while enlisting the help of Wright's legal assistant Maya, who basically functions like an extra assist**
- **By using Trial mode to leverage that evidence, keeping adversaries at bay with bolts of incrimination while waiting for a chance to score → + H or air ↓ + H when three pieces of evidence are held**

With Turnabout activated, Phoenix Wright not only becomes a tremendously powerful point character (who usually has a chance to K.O. whichever character he hit to enter Turnabout right away, leading to a mix-up against a fresh character too), but the game's best assist character with a bullet. There is not really a wrong way to go about exploiting Turnabout.

1	Standing Ⓛ (Investigation and Trial)	1	33,000	264	6	10	5	-1	-2	Chains into crouching Ⓛ
	Standing Ⓛ (Turnabout)	1	39,600	316	5	9	4	+3	+2	Chains into crouching Ⓛ
2	Standing Ⓜ (Investigation and Trial)	1	50,000	400	8	10	13	-4	-5	—
	Standing Ⓜ (Turnabout)	1	60,000	480	7	9	11	+1	0	—
3	Standing Ⓗ (Investigation)	1	60,000	480	12	10	17	-3	-4	—
4	Standing Ⓗ (Trial)	1	60,000	480	9	9	19	-4	-5	Press Ⓗ again to chain to Illuminating Point
5	Standing Ⓗ (Turnabout)	1	132,000	1056	12	10	11	—	+4	Knocks down, jump-cancellable, deals chip damage

1

2

3

4

5

Crouching Basic Attacks

Screen	Command	Hits	Damage	Meter Gain	Startup	Active	Recovery	Advantage on Hit	Advantage if Guarded	Notes
1	Crouching Ⓛ (Investigation and Trial)	1	33,000	264	7	10	6	-2	-3	Low attack
	Crouching Ⓛ (Turnabout)	1	39,600	316	6	9	5	+2	+1	Low attack
2	Crouching Ⓜ (Investigation)	1	45,000	360	9	10	15	-6	-7	—
3	Crouching Ⓜ (Trial)	1	55,000	440	8	10	13	-4	-5	—
	Crouching Ⓜ (Turnabout)	1	66,000	528	7	9	11	+1	0	—
4	Crouching Ⓗ (Investigation)	2	59,700	520	11	12	18	—	0	Low attack, second hit knocks down
5	Crouching Ⓗ (Trial)	1	65,000	520	10	10	16	-2	-3	Press Ⓗ again to chain to Note Scribbling
6	Crouching Ⓗ (Turnabout)	1	132,000	1056	11	10	12	—	+3	Knocks down, jump-cancellable, deals chip damage

1

2

3

4

5

6

Ground Special Attack—Launcher

Screen	Command	Hits	Damage	Meter Gain	Startup	Active	Recovery	Advantage on Hit	Advantage if Guarded	Notes
1	Ⓢ (while standing or crouching) (Investigation and Trial)	1	100,000	800	10	4	22	—	-3	Launcher, not special- or hyper combo-cancelable
	Ⓢ (while standing or crouching) (Turnabout)	1	120,000	960	9	4	18	—	+3	Launcher, not special- or hyper combo-cancelable

1

Air Basic Attacks

Screen	Command	Hits	Damage	Meter Gain	Startup	Active	Recovery	Advantage on Hit	Advantage if Guarded	Notes
1	Air Ⓛ (Investigation and Trial)	1	35,000	280	7	10	7	+11	+10	Overhead attack
	Air Ⓛ (Turnabout)	1	42,000	336	6	9	6	+13	+12	Overhead attack
2	Air Ⓜ (Investigation and Trial)	1	50,000	400	9	10	16	+17	+16	Overhead attack
	Air Ⓜ (Turnabout)	1	60,000	480	8	9	13	+19	+18	Overhead attack
3	Air Ⓗ (Investigation)	1	60,000	480	11	10	18	+19	+18	Overhead attack
4	Air Ⓗ (Trial)	1	60,000	480	9	10	18	+18	+17	Overhead attack, press Ⓗ again to chain to "Just a Little More…!"
5	Air Ⓗ (Turnabout)	1	132,000	1056	12	10	11	—	+23	Overhead attack, ground bounces foe, deals chip damage

1

2

3

4

5

Air Special Attacks—Flying Screen and Air Exchange

Air (S) causes a hard knockdown when used in a launcher combo (this is sometimes called flying screen). When used outside of a launcher combo, air (S) behaves mostly like another basic attack. Air exchange attacks, performed by inputting a direction plus (S), are only possible during a launcher combo. Exchange hits initiate team aerial combos by tagging in the next available character to continue the air combo.

Screen	Command	Hits	Damage	Meter Gain	Startup	Active	Recovery	Advantage on Hit	Advantage if Guarded	Notes
1	Air (S) (Investigation and Trial)	1	70,000	560	11	4	26	+20	+18	Causes hard knockdown if used in launcher combo.
	Air (S) (Turnabout)	1	64,000	672	10	4	21	+21	+20	Causes hard knockdown if used in launcher combo.
2	Air ↑ + (S) (during launcher combo) (Investigation and Trial)	2	105,00	880	10	4	27	—	—	Tags in next available hero while lofting opponent upward.
	Air ↑ + (S) (during launcher combo) (Turnabout)	2	117,000	976	9	4	22	—	—	Tags in next available hero while lofting opponent upward.
3	Air → or ← + (S) (during launcher combo) (Investigation and Trial)	2	95,000	800	10	4	27	—	—	Tags in next available hero while causing wall bounce, erases 1 hyper meter bar from foe
	Air → or ← + (S) (during launcher combo) (Turnabout)	2	105,000	880	9	4	22	—	—	Tags in next available hero while causing wall bounce, steals 1 hyper meter bar from foe
4	Air ↓ + (S) (during launcher combo) (Investigation and Trial)	2	95,000	800	10	4	27	—	—	Tags in next available hero while causing ground bounce, generates 1 hyper meter bar
	Air ↓ + (S) (during launcher combo) (Turnabout)	2	105,000	880	9	4	22	—	—	Tags in next available hero while causing ground bounce, generates 1 hyper meter bar

1

2

3

4

Command Attacks

Command attacks resemble basic attacks but have different chaining and canceling properties. It's usually possible to chain *into* a command attack from basic attacks, but most command attacks cannot be chained from or canceled themselves.

Screen	Name	Command	Hits	Damage	Meter Gain	Startup	Active	Recovery	Advantage on Hit	Advantage if Guarded	Notes
1	Slip-Up (Investigation and Trial)	→ + (M)	1	60,000	480	25	4	32	—	-13	Overhead attack, hard knockdown
	Slip-Up (Turnabout)	→ + (M)	1	72,000	576	21	4	27	—	-6	Overhead attack, hard knockdown
2	Questioning (Investigation)	→ + (H)	1	70,000	560	20	13	28	-17	-18	After 4 Questionings foe is stunned for 120 frames
3	Air Questioning (Investigation)	(in air) ↓ + (H)	1	70,000	560	20	13	28	+9	+8	After 4 Questionings foe is stunned for 120 frames
4	Illuminating Point (Trial)	(during standing (H) on contact) (H)	1	80,000	640	10	7	18	+6	-2	Knocks down, jump-cancelable
5	Note Scribbling (Trial)	(during crouching (H) on contact) ↓ + (H)	1	60,000	480	12	4	20	—	-1	Low attack, knocks down
6	"Just a Little More…!" (Trial)	(during air (H) on contact) (H)	1	70,000	560	11	10	16	+19	+18	Overhead attack
7	Cross-Examination (Trial)	→ + (H)	1	70,000	560	20	13	28	-17	-18	After 3 Cross- Examinations foe is stunned for 120 frames
8	Air Cross-Examination (Trial)	(in air) ↓ + (H)	1	70,000	560	20	13	28	+9	+8	After 3 Cross- Examinations foe is stunned for 120 frames
9	Bridge to the Turnabout (Trial)	(with 3 pieces of Evidence) → + (H)	1	100,000	800	27	20	24	+25	-11	On hit Phoenix Wright enters Turnabout, Wright's speed and damage increase by 20%, Turnabout lasts 1200 frames
10	Air Bridge to the Turnabout (Trial)	(with 3 pieces of Evidence) ↓ + (H)	1	100,000	800	27	20	24	+12	+8	On hit Phoenix Wright enters Turnabout, Wright's speed and damage increase by 20%, Turnabout lasts 1200 frames
11	Pursuit (Turnabout)	→ + (H)	1	120,000	960	17	17	18	+1	0	After 3 Pursuits foe is stunned for 120 frames
12	Air Pursuit (Turnabout)	(in air) ↓ + (H)	1	120,000	960	17	17	18	+12	+11	After 3 Pursuits foe is stunned for 120 frames

1

2

3

4

5

6

7

8

9

10

11

12

Throws

Throws are for snagging passive or blocking opponents. Since throws are active so quickly, you can also use them to preemptively toss opposing characters out of their offense. Combos are usually possible after throws, one way or another.

Screen	Command	Hits	Damage	Meter Gain	Startup	Active	Notes
1	→ + H (ground)	1	80,000	800	1	1	Hard knockdown
	← + H (ground)	1	80,000	800	1	1	Hard knockdown
2	→ + H (air)	1	80,000	800	1	1	Hard knockdown
	← + H (air)	1	80,000	800	1	1	Hard knockdown

1

2

As a Partner—Crossover Assists

Screen	Type	P1+P2 Crossover Combination Hyper Combo	Description	Hits	Damage	Meter Gain	Startup	Active	Recovery (this crossover assist)	Recovery (other partner)	Notes
1	Phoenix Wright—α	Steel Samurai Maya Smelting!	Paperwork (High) M	3	94,800	840	44	—	116	86	3 projectiles with 3 low priority durability points, each projectile lasts for 30 frames
2	Phoenix Wright—α (Turnabout)	Steel Samurai Maya Smelting!	Paperwork Storm (High) M	9	183,400	2160	38	—	102	72	3 projectiles with beam durability: 3 frames x 3 low priority durability points each, each projectile lasts for 25 frames
3	Phoenix Wright—β	Steel Samurai Maya Smelting!	Press the Witness M	5	114,800	1040	44	25(11)4	97	67	Knocks down
4	Phoenix Wright—β (Turnabout)	Steel Samurai Maya Smelting!	Break the Witness M	12	240,600	2592	37	21(11)4	84	54	Knocks down
5	Phoenix Wright—γ	Steel Samurai Maya Smelting!	"Get 'em, Missile!"	1	50,000	400	44	—	132	102	Low attack, OTG-capable, projectile has 5 low priority durability points
	Phoenix Wright—γ (Turnabout)	Steel Samurai Maya Smelting!	"Get 'em, Missile!"	1	60,000	480	37	—	115	85	Low attack, OTG-capable, projectile has 5 low priority durability points

1

2

3

4

5

There are two ways of looking at Phoenix Wright's roster of assists. One is to believe that Phoenix Wright has the best two crossover assists in the game, and the other is to be wrong. Phoenix Wright—α, which emulates Paperwork (High) M, and Phoenix Wright—β, which emulates Press the Witness M, are fine assists on their own. But the important part is that both are *drastically* improved when Turnabout is active. Paperwork becomes Paperwork Storm, covering most of the screen and becoming much more damaging and useful, while Press the Witness becomes Break the Witness, at once the best pinning assist or defensive assist in the game, as well as the most damaging assist on hit or block, period! Phoenix Wright—β during Turnabout even causes a wall bounce with the last hit.

But that's not all. Normally, none of Wright's assists have any kind of invulnerable period. But during Turnabout, both Phoenix Wright—α and Phoenix Wright—β are *100% invincible from start to finish.* That's right: Start. To. Finish. These incredible assists literally *cannot be stopped or punished* while Phoenix Wright has Turnabout active!! The other team can be Iron Man, Dormammu, and Akuma (and Ryu, and Nova, and Galactus, and the ghosts of Cable and Gold War Machine, it doesn't matter) all engaged in their beam hyper combos during a crossover combination, flooding the entire screen with an unbelievable torrent of destructive energy, but get Phoenix Wright riled up and the lawyer is unfazed by *anything*... he'll walk through it all to serve his papers during Turnabout. Then he'll leave, having never been vulnerable.

In *MvC2*, one way to make almost any character competent was to develop ways they could combo into Tron—γ (a different assist in that game than this one), which made any character capable of heavy damage. And in original *MvC3*, the most important assists ended up being Tron—β (what is it with Tron?) and Haggar—α, mostly because they were two of the only assists with any noteworthy period of invulnerability. Make no mistake, every other assist in *UMvC3* is fighting for third place at best against Phoenix Wright's über-assists. In fact, despite how powerful Turnabout is while Phoenix Wright is defending his case on point, it's arguable that supercharging Phoenix Wright—α or Phoenix Wright—β is the best overall application of the mode and character. There's nothing like having an ace attorney in your back pocket. Also note that these assists are also invulnerable when they are used as crossover counters, so countering to Turnabout Wright is an almost assured way to get him back on screen safely, and probably with a combo opportunity right off the bat!

Bringing up the rear with a regular-old assist is Phoenix Wright—γ, which somewhat emulates Wright's throw, in which Missile the trusty lawdog rushes out to surprise the enemy. The dog is OTG-capable and hits low, but the speed of this assist is lacking compared to others with similar useful traits. And, apart from the 20% damage and speed boost Phoenix Wright gains for all his attacks, the "Get 'em, Missile!" assist gains *no* benefit from Turnabout. The total invincibility granted to Phoenix Wright—α or Phoenix Wright—β during Turnabout is a reason all by itself to put the attorney on your team, and yet another reason not to pick Phoenix Wright—γ.

Snap Back

Screen	Command	Hits	Damage	Meter Gain	Startup	Active	Recovery	Advantage on Hit	Advantage if Guarded
1	↓↘→ + P1 or P2	1	50,000	500 (-1 hyper meter bar)	2	4	37	—	-18

Notes

On hit snap back forces the opposing point character to be replaced by an assist. Opposing assist calls or tag outs are also locked out for 4 seconds

1

Special Moves

Screen	Name	Command	Hits	Damage	Meter Gain	Startup	Active	Recovery	Advantage on Hit	Advantage if Guarded	Notes
1	"M-Maya!?" L (Investigation)	↓↘→ + L	—	—	—	27	—	13	—	—	Absorbs up to 250,000 damage, Phoenix Wright takes no damage if attack is absorbed by Maya, active for 152 frames
2	"M-Maya!?" M / H (Investigation)	↓↘→ + M or H	1	68,000	544	40	—	10	—	+15	Low attack, OTG-capable, hard knockdown, active for 20 frames
3	Investigate (Investigation)	ATK + S	—	—	—	30	—	5	—	—	Meat restores up to 150,000 red health, evidence usable for Trial and Turnabout are indicated by a highlighted folder
4	Discard (Investigation)	(possessing Evidence) ATK + S	1	70,000	560	12 (False evidence: 14)	—	23 (False evidence: 21)	0 (False evidence: +2)	-1 (False evidence: +1)	Tosses evidence in an arc
5	Mode Change (Investigation and Trial)	↓↓ + S	—	—	—	—	—	—	—	—	Switches between Investigation and Trial, stance change takes 20 frames
6	Paperwork (High) L (Trial)	↓↘→ + L	3	35,000 x3	280 x 3	15	—	25	+8	+7	3 projectiles with 3 low priority durability points each, each projectile lasts for 30 frames
7	Paperwork (High) M (Trial)	↓↘→ + M	3	35,000 x3	280 x 3	20	—	25	+8	+7	3 projectiles with 3 low priority durability points each, each projectile lasts for 30 frames
8	Paperwork (High) H (Trial)	↓↘→ + H	4	35,000 x 4	280 x 4	30	—	20	+8	+7	4 projectiles with 3 low priority durability points each, each projectile lasts for 30 frames
9	Paperwork Storm (High) L (Turnabout)	↓↘→ + L	9	183,400	2160	14	—	20	+17	+16	3 projectiles with beam durability: 3 frames x 3 low priority durability points each, each projectile lasts for 25 frames
10	Paperwork Storm (High) M (Turnabout)	↓↘→ + M	9	183,400	2160	18	—	21	+16	+15	3 projectiles with beam durability: 3 frames x 3 low priority durability points each, each projectile lasts for 25 frames
11	Paperwork Storm (High) H (Turnabout)	↓↘→ + H	12	214,800	2880	26	—	16	+25	+24	4 projectiles with beam durability: 3 frames x 3 low priority durability points each, each projectile lasts for 25 frames
12	Paperwork (Low) L (Trial)	↓↙← + L	3	35,000 x3	280 x 3	15	—	25	+8	+7	3 projectiles with 3 low priority durability points each, each projectile lasts for 30 frames
13	Paperwork (Low) M (Trial)	↓↙← + M	3	35,000 x3	280 x 3	20	—	25	+8	+7	3 projectiles with 3 low priority durability points each, each projectile lasts for 30 frames
14	Paperwork (Low) H (Trial)	↓↙← + H	4	35,000 x 4	280 x 4	30	—	20	+8	+7	4 projectiles with 3 low priority durability points each, each projectile lasts for 30 frames
15	Paperwork Storm (Low) L (Turnabout)	↓↙← + L	9	183,400	2160	14	—	20	+17	+16	3 projectiles with beam durability: 3 frames x 3 low priority durability points each, each projectile lasts for 25 frames
16	Paperwork Storm (Low) M (Turnabout)	↓↙← + M	9	183,400	2160	18	—	20	+17	+16	3 projectiles with beam durability: 3 frames x 3 low priority durability points each, each projectile lasts for 25 frames
17	Paperwork Storm (Low) H (Turnabout)	↓↙← + H	12	214,800	2880	26	—	16	+26	+25	4 projectiles with beam durability: 3 frames x 3 low priority durability points each, each projectile lasts for 25 frames
18	Present Evidence—Photograph (Trial)	ATK + S	5	102,300	1000	25	20	16	0	-1	Beam durability: 5 frames x 2 low priority durability points
	Present Evidence—Photograph (Turnabout)	ATK + S	5	122,600	1200	21	17	14	+7	+6	Beam durability: 5 frames x 2 low priority durability points
19	Present Evidence—Flower Vase (Trial)	ATK + S	1	100,000	800	15	—	20	+3	+2	Projectile has 5 low priority durability points
	Present Evidence—Flower Vase (Turnabout)	ATK + S	1	120,000	960	13	—	17	+8	+7	Projectile has 5 low priority durability points
20	Present Evidence (Documents) (Trial)	ATK + S	1	100,000	800	29	—	16	+20	+7	Knocks down, projectile has 5 low priority durability points, after 90 frames/contact with enemy/durability depletion the projectile explodes, explosion lasts for 8 frames and nullifies low priority projectiles
	Present Evidence (Documents) (Turnabout)	ATK + S	1	120,000	960	25	—	13	+23	+12	Knocks down, projectile has 5 low priority durability points, after 75 frames/contact with enemy/durability depletion the projectile explodes, explosion lasts for 7 frames and nullifies low priority projectiles
21	Present Evidence—Watch (Trial)	ATK + S	1	100,000	800	20	—	25	-2	-3	Projectile has 5 low priority durability points
	Present Evidence—Watch (Turnabout)	ATK + S	1	120,000	960	17	—	21	+4	+3	Projectile has 5 low priority durability points
22	Present Evidence—Knife (Trial)	ATK + S	3	40,000 x 3	320 x 3	20	—	30	-7	-8	Each projectile has 3 low priority durability points
	Present Evidence—Knife (Turnabout)	ATK + S	3	48,000 x 3	384 x 3	17	—	25	0	-1	Each projectile has 3 low priority durability points
23	Present Evidence—Cell Phone (Trial)	ATK + S	3	40,000 x 3	320 x 3	25	—	25	—	—	Each projectile has 5 low priority durability points, projectiles inactive for 60 frames then seek foe
	Present Evidence—Cell Phone (Turnabout)	ATK + S	3	48,000 x 3	384 x 3	21	—	21	—	—	Each projectile has 5 low priority durability points, projectiles inactive for 50 frames then seek foe

Special Moves continued

Screen	Name	Command	Hits	Damage	Meter Gain	Startup	Active	Recovery	Advantage on Hit	Advantage if Guarded	Notes
31	Press the Witness L (Trial)	→↓↘ + L	3	20,000 x 2 + 50,000	160 x 2 + 400	15	20(12)4	5	—	+14	Knocks down
	Press the Witness M (Trial)	→↓↘ + M	5	20,000 x 4 + 50,000	160 x 4 + 400	20	25(12)4	5	—	+14	Knocks down
	Press the Witness H (Trial)	→↓↘ + H	7	20,000 x 6 + 50,000	160 x 6 + 400	30	25(12)4	5	—	+14	Knocks down
32	Break the Witness L (Turnabout)	→↓↘ + L	7	171,000	1632	13	17(11)4	7	—	+14	Wall bounces foe
	Break the Witness M (Turnabout)	→↓↘ + M	12	240,600	2592	17	21(11)4	3	—	+18	Wall bounces foe
	Break the Witness H (Turnabout)	→↓↘ + H	20	320,700	4128	25	21(11)4	3	—	+18	Wall bounces foe

1

"M-Maya!?" L: Maya is summoned to aid Wright in his search for the truth. She rushes out to stand about a third of the way in from Wright's side of the screen, where she then generates a barrier that lasts for either 152 frames or until 250,000 damage absorbed, whichever comes first. While the barrier is active, anything that touches it is absorbed and cannot hit Wright, so standing just behind the barrier of "M-Maya!?" L is a pretty safe place to be; Wright won't be safe from characters who can teleport behind him or triangle jump down from sharp angles above, but all direct frontal assaults and shallow air assaults are more or less thwarted. Compliment calls of "M-Maya!?" L with assists that further protect Phoenix Wright's area of the screen, and use the safe time you're buying to Investigate for admissible evidence.

2

"M-Maya!?" M & H: As with "M-Maya!?" L, these versions are more like assists than special moves; in particular, these Maya attacks resemble She-Hulk—α, X-23—β, and Felicia—α. Maya rushes out, flummoxing a bewildered Wright as she runs by, before flopping on her belly and sliding in low at the enemy. This hits low and is OTG-capable. Wright is also free to move before it's over, so he'll have either a free chance to move forward, or to Investigate a new piece of evidence. Near corners and in some other situations, Wright can combo after "M-Maya!?" M or H!

3

Investigate: Phoenix Wright has three slots available for evidence. Each slot corresponds to a button combination: L + S for the first slot, M + S for the middle slot, and H + S for the right slot. While in Investigation mode, pressing a pair of buttons that matches an empty slot will cause Phoenix Wright to search for evidence to store in that slot. Admissible evidence which can contribute to accessing Turnabout will cause the slot it's in to become highlighted; false evidence, which cannot contribute to switching to Turnabout, will have the same drab folder background.

Investigating evidence is a quick process, but still certainly not a safe one; nearby foes can easily move in and hit Phoenix Wright as he digs for the truth. Save Investigate attempts for when the opposing character is either far away or preoccupied super jumping, or when Phoenix Wright is safely covered with Maya and/or crossover assists. If you score a hard knockdown, such as after an air combo or a throw, you might also intentionally forego the OTG opportunity and instead use the time to freely look for a couple pieces of evidence. For more on evidence gathering, see Advanced Tactics.

4

Discard: During Investigation mode, press S + ATK that matches a slot which already contains evidence, and Phoenix Wright will toss it in an arc across the screen. This is one of two ways to get rid of false evidence, which has no use other than to be thrown at the enemy with Discard. Take care not to accidentally Discard admissible, highlighted evidence, like knives, cell phones, and documents... you want to hold on to that stuff! Admissible pieces of evidence become powerful zoning tools in Trial mode, and are required in order to access Turnabout. False pieces of evidence actually make for slightly better Discard projectiles than real pieces of evidence, anyway.

In addition to being discarded with Discard, false evidence can also be destroyed simply by using the "Order in the Court!" hyper combo during Trial mode.

5

Mode Change: By tapping ↓, ↓ + S you can swap Phoenix Wright between Investigation and Trial mode at will. As a special move, Mode Change can be used to cancel basic and command attacks on the ground. Phoenix Wright recovers in 20 frames, having swapped modes. Investigation mode is intended primarily for the gathering of evidence, while Trial mode is more suited to general combat, and for activating Turnabout when three pieces of real evidence are on hand. Note that the recovery of Mode Change is hyper-cancelable; this is most useful after scoring a launcher in Investigation mode, as you can combo to a hard knockdown, swap to Trail mode, then immediately cancel to "Order in the Court!" for a strong OTG capper.

Paperwork (High) L 6

Paperwork (High) M 7

Paperwork (High) H 8

Paperwork Storm (High) L 9

Paperwork Storm (High) M 10

Paperwork Storm (High) H 11

Paperwork (Low) L 12

Paperwork (Low) M 13

Paperwork (Low) H 14

Paperwork Storm (Low) L 15

Paperwork Storm (Low) M 16

Paperwork Storm (Low) H 17

Paperwork & Paperwork Storm (High & Low): A career in law is about, among other things, being inundated with files, papers, records, documents and briefs—boxes upon boxes of them. During any version of Paperwork, Phoenix hurls some of the fruits of his meticulousness at the defendant. High (↓↘→) or Low (↓↙←) indicates the arc the papers take; for Paperwork (High) the papers rise in altitude, with the final paper being the highest, while Paperwork (Low) is the reverse, with the first paper starting near Wright's head, and the last one just off the ground. H versions create four distinct paper projectiles, while L and M versions create three.

The heavier the version, the further the papers are tossed; Paperwork H travels out to roughly mid screen. The papers persist for half a second, so while they're not quite Amaterasu's Power Slash papers for creating persistent on screen threats, they're slightly less transient than most projectiles. And each paper is itself a distinct projectile; in some ways, Paperwork functions like closer-range, more limited Sentinel drones, especially Paperwork (Low) H, the first paper of which starts out a little higher than Wright's head, providing some anti-air coverage. Note that small and mid-sized characters crouching near Phoenix Wright during Paperwork (Low) M or H can avoid his papers entirely.

During Turnabout, all versions of Paperwork become Paperwork Storm. Paperwork Storm reaches farther, faster, while dealing more damage. Each distinct paper projectile becomes a distinct beam with three frames of durability exchange possible, making Storm variants of Paperwork *three times* more durable against opposing projectiles! Coupled with the enhanced capabilities of Present Evidence and H attacks during Turnabout and it's easy to see how Phoenix Wright becomes a suffocating, full screen-dominant character under Turnabout.

Present Evidence—Photograph 18

Present Evidence—Flower Vase 19

Present Evidence—Documents 20

Present Evidence—Watch 21

Present Evidence—Knife 22

Present Evidence—Cell Phone 23

Present Evidence: Evidence gathered with Ⓢ + ATK during Investigation mode is presentable in Trial mode with the same command. Trying to present FALSE evidence will leave Wright disappointed at his own lack of preparation, and leave him a sitting duck for a moment. Presenting true evidence will trigger projectile attacks with varying behaviors. During Turnabout, these projectiles can be fired more quickly, one after another, and they deal more damage!

Photograph—enables Phoenix Wright's beam. While it's never bad to have a beam, this one can be crouched under by many characters, and it's a bit slow compared to many beams in Trial mode. In Turnabout mode, it's around the same speed as beams possessed by Iron Man and Doctor Doom. Coupled with the ability to immediately cancel it into itself again or a different Presenting move in Turnabout, it gets much more effective.

Flower Vase—enables a lofting, mortar-like projectile. Especially when used to immediately follow-up Paperwork (Low) H, this projectile asserts control of normal jump height across most of the playing field. It's also the Presenting move that can be used most rapidly outside of Turnabout.

Documents—launches a floating orb that goes to a random location in a 90 degree arc in front of Phoenix Wright. If nothing touches it, it will explode after a second and a half. If it encounters an enemy or object before then it will explode prematurely, sending any characters it hits into a brief spinning knockdown. Presenting Documents can be treated somewhat like Amaterasu's Power Slash papers (or like a somewhat random aerial Chris landmine, or like a faster M.O.D.O.K. Balloon Bomb), as it causes a stationary threat in front of Phoenix Wright that opponents are forced to either avoid or deal with. In Turnabout mode, Documents can be presented so fast that they'll combo into one another up close for a while, depending somewhat on their random nature.

Watch—enables Phoenix Wright's most conventional projectile. It shares similar behavior with other standard 5 point projectiles, and can be fired much more quickly in Turnabout.

Knife—may remind some old-school players of Michelle Heart's *MvC1* assist, which was one of the best in that game. Phoenix Wright shoots three knives in a 60 degree spread right in front of him, with one going horizontally and another two spreading out around it. This is his slowest-moving Presenting attack, and thus in some ways the most useful.

Cell Phone—summons three orbs that act a bit like Doctor Strange's Daggers of Denak; they don't do anything for a moment, but then they all fire simultaneously, homing in on the enemy. The orbs can be destroyed before they fire or while they're in transit, but it's very unlikely the enemy will destroy all of them. Especially when coupled with other Presenting moves, and with Paperwork (Low), this is one of the best tools for zoning an enemy and keeping them out.

Press the Witness (Trial) 31

Break the Witness (Turnabout) 32

Press/Break the Witness (Trial/Turnabout): Phoenix Wright marches forward to serve papers to his target. This move recovers more quickly than it looks; like most of Phoenix Wright's attacks, he has much more animation on the end of the action than you actually have to sit through. It grants big frame advantage even on block. This means you can link attacks just after scoring a Press the Witness hit, especially near corners. During Turnabout, Press the Witness becomes the utterly devastating Break the Witness, which causes a wall bounce with the last hit if successful. Fitting Break the Witness into Turnabout combos, like just after the ground bounce created by air Ⓗ, assures your damage will be outrageous. Add in X-Factor and it's downright preposterous… in Turnabout, with X-Factor lv.1, something as simple as crouching Ⓜ, ⇨ + Ⓗ CANCEL ⇨⇩⇘ + Ⓗ is already over 800,000 damage *before* the wall bounce!!

Hyper Combos

Screen	Name	Command	Hits	Damage	Startup	Active	Recovery	Advantage on Hit	Advantage if Guarded	Notes
1	Steel Samurai Maya Smelting!	⇩⇘⇨ + ATK ATK	11	270,400	10+4	—	35	—	+57	Last attack hits low, knocks down, active for 56(11)15 frames
2	"Order in the Court!" (Trial and Turnabout)	⇩⇙⇦ + ATK ATK	1	250,000	15+4	8	88	+18	-73	Frames 1-54 invincible, OTG-capable, hard knockdown on Wright and foe, projectile destroys most projectiles and beams, use of hyper destroys all false evidence
3	Ace Attorney (Level 3 hyper combo) (Turnabout)	⇨⇩⇘ + ATK ATK	17	600,000	10+0	3	32	—	-10	Invincible frames 1-18, OTG-capable, hard knockdown

1

Steel Samurai Maya Smelting!: The only hyper combo available to Phoenix Wright in every mode sends his assistant Maya forward in a swirling-armed frenzy. Like the Maya specials during Investigation, Steel Samurai Maya Smelting! is more like an assist attack than something Wright performs himself; he can move before it's over, and your opponent's use of advancing guard against Maya will only push their character back a little, while having no direct effect on Wright himself. Especially near corners this makes SSMS! a fantastic pressure hyper combo; if it hits, Wright can continue a combo afterward, and if it's guarded, you can attempt to mix your opponent up with a ⇨ + Ⓜ Slip-Up or a jumping basic attack overhead, or fake and go for a low attack. The opposing character is forced to try to guard correctly while Maya is holding them in place. If it's go-for-broke time, you can X-Factor cancel the startup to recover even earlier than usual, giving you more time to mix your opposition up while Maya holds them helplessly in place.

2

"Order in the Court!": This hyper combo, not available during Investigation mode, delivers one single damaging hit to most of the playing field from an enormous gavel of deep authority. All characters will be struck and tossed into hard knockdowns, even Phoenix Wright (though friendly characters don't actually take damage; this judge is just). The gavel smash is OTG-capable, which is a big reason why combo potential for Phoenix Wright is higher in Trial or Turnabout modes than in Investigation. "Order in the Court!" is also a great team hyper combo starter; most hyper combos can simply continue hitting the opposing character while they're spinning to the turf, and OTG-capable hyper combos can pick them up right after they're laid out.

One very useful, subtle feature of "Order in the Court!" is that it destroys all false evidence! Obviously you won't always have the luxury of hanging back to hide behind Maya and gather evidence; your opponent is going to try to stop you. You can always chuck false evidence at them in Investigation mode, but there are still good reasons to swap to Trial mode sometimes even when you don't have a full roster of admissible evidence, since Wright can go toe-to-toe a little bit better in his "presentation" mode. But, you can't discard undesirable evidence at will anymore. This problem goes away if you end combos with OTG "Order in the Court!" for solid damage and a one-smash-solution to destroying false evidence while leaving any admissible evidence in place. As both you and the opponent recover from the gavel, you're already back in Investigation mode automatically, so summon "M-Maya!?" L, then check for some real evidence.

3

Ace Attorney: Simply put, this is the best hyper combo in the game. It's only available during Turnabout, and after Ace Attorney all evidence is expended and Turnabout ends. After 10 pre-freeze frames, Ace Attorney strikes the enemy instantly post-freeze, no matter where they are. If the opponent was not ALREADY holding back to block before the hyper freeze, they cannot escape Ace Attorney. It's also OTG-capable… it's basically a faster, better version of Magneto's Gravity Squeeze. Ace Attorney is one of the two most damaging moves in the game, up there with Vergil's Spiral Swords level 3 hyper combo extension.

Ace Attorney is so fast that you can simply use it on reaction to the enemy doing all sorts of things from full screen; did a fireball character think they could get away with even starting to throw a projectile? Whoops, nope. And virtually any combo becomes a K.O. against any character if you unleash Ace Attorney at the end, causing 600,000 unscaled damage on top of the combo the preceded it. And if you get Phoenix Wright into Turnabout and then swap him for the next character before Turnabout ends, then you now have access to a 0-frame THC into Ace Attorney!

And, of course, Ace Attorney's advantages only become stronger with X-Factor. If Turnabout Phoenix Wright is the last counselor standing, Ace Attorney by itself during lv.3 X-Factor deals *over 1.1 million damage*! So if you'd tagged out Turnabout Phoenix Wright to harass your opponent with his unsurpassed assists, then they finally K.O. his teammates and force the lawyer back into the fray, they won't be able to afford a single slip-up for the duration of Turnabout, lest the match end in a resounding turnaround! Take that!

Battle Plan

Use "M-Maya?!" L and assists to provide cover for evidence-gathering in Investigation mode.

There is no doubt that your goal with Phoenix Wright is to achieve Turnabout mode. You have a few ways you can actually utilize Turnabout, but any of them is so much better than Phoenix Wright in Investigation or Trial mode that your modus operandi here is self-evident. The first step to activating Turnabout is collecting a full roster of highlighted evidence.

It's very likely that your opponent will be aware of how deadly Turnabout can be, so they won't be too eager to sit back and watch Phoenix Wright dig around for clues. If they do happen to sit back, well, okay. If they aren't pressuring from afar, call a long range assist if you have one (good examples for Phoenix Wright include staples like any Doctor Doom assist, Iron Man—α or Sentinel—α, and new assists like Rocket Raccoon—α), then dig for a piece of evidence or two. All the evidence items look distinct as Wright plucks them up, but *UMvC3* has a tendency to get chaotic, so if you aren't sure what's on hand then just check out Wright's inventory; highlighted folders are the important thing.

Against more aggressive opponents, you'll want to get "M-Maya!?" L out there, so Wright has a sturdy shield to stand behind. It's from the cover of this shield that you may find chances to attack your foe with Wright's short limbs safely, perhaps while they try foolishly to attack through Maya's shield. If it's Phoenix Wright's birthday and you happen to catch two characters at once, proceed to **Combo X** to do knockout-worthy damage to most point characters and all assists, even from Wright's least powerful mode.

Against foes who jump in over Maya's shield, note that Wright's standing basic attacks all make great anti-airs. There's a hitbox around any document Wright is reading, which extends above and in front of his head. So, although it may not look like it, that means Phoenix Wright's standing basic attacks can be used as anti-air like the standing Ⓛ attacks of Magneto or Dante. And both standing and air Ⓗ in Investigation have very large hitboxes that extend in a circle all the way around and above Wright. Enemies knocked out of the air at low altitudes by attacks like Investigation standing Ⓛ or Ⓗ can be chained into a launcher for a follow-up combo.

If your challenger gets around "M-Maya?!" L, like with a triangle jump or teleport...

...standing Ⓛ makes a surprisingly good anti-air! That paper must be heavy stock.

Wright is very limited in Investigation mode, especially in the moves that can be used to open up an enemy, and in the potential for combo embellishment. Still, the attorney isn't helpless even when he's still researching his case. If an opponent is made hesitant by the Maya barrier, or if they're forced to block your assist, you can stage a simple but effective mix-up. The baseline layer (or opening argument, if you will) is that you can dash in and attack with a chain of crouching Ⓛ, standing Ⓛ. This is your preferred opener when fishing for a hit. If the opponent is getting hit you can proceed to **Combo I** or **Combo II**. If they guard, halt the blocked chain and go for an alternative. Since crouching Ⓛ hits low, we need some counterpoints that hit high. ⇨ + Ⓜ is a command attack called Slip-Up in which Wright haplessly slips on a banana, thudding upon his enemy with an overhead attack that causes a knockdown. This can be canceled on hit or block to a "M-Maya?!" M attack, which hits low and will OTG from ⇨ + Ⓜ if it hit. (See **Combo III**.) If the overhead is guarded you can still cancel to Maya, or cancel to Mode Change to try slightly better up-close attacks with Trial mode.

Jumping toward the opposing character when there's a chance to attack can also lead to the same opportunities. Attack with Investigation air Ⓗ on the way in, which has a surprising cross-up hitbox; it doesn't matter which side you jump to, so just jump on top of them as ambiguously as possible! Mixing in an empty jump here and there so you can land and immediately go for crouching Ⓛ or a throw is also a strong option.

And although they don't help too much with the synergy of his team, since he's mostly kind of a zoning character, low-hitting OTG-capable assists go the longest way toward covering up Wright's offensive deficiencies, allowing for relaunches or ⇨ + Ⓗ hits in combos where they're otherwise impossible. The prototypical example is Wesker—β, still the all-around best OTG-capable assist in *UMvC3*.

Trial and Investigation modes can be toggled between with ⇩ ⇩ + Ⓢ. Once all three slots of evidence are filled, it's time to switch to Trial mode; not only is Phoenix Wright a better all-around accidental fighter in Trial mode, but landing any ⇨ + Ⓗ or air ⇩ + Ⓗ "OBJECTION!" attack will enter Turnabout.

Seeking Turnabout isn't the only reason to switch to Trial mode. If your challenger plays a style of constant offense trying to rush down Phoenix Wright, and especially if they have a teleport or similar pass-through tactic they're coupling with assist use, you won't have as much of a luxury of being able to search for evidence safely in Investigation mode. Trial has a few fighting upgrades over Investigation: standing, crouching, and air Ⓗ attacks can all be chained into an Ⓗ command extension, making for better chain combos, Wright's ⇨ + Ⓗ and air ⇩ + Ⓗ "HOLD IT!" questioning attacks cause a stun after three uses rather than four in Investigation, and the Paperwork and Press the Witness attacks become available. Also, any admissible evidence becomes a projectile weapon; these attacks are the saving grace of the mode when you have one or two pieces, but not enough to enter Turnabout.

Documents and Flower Vase are great pieces of defensive evidence.

Cell Phone coupled with Watch or Photograph allows you to fight at full screen.

When fighting in Trial mode without enough evidence for Turnabout, you should look at attack opportunities as chances to buy time to look for evidence, rather than strictly for damage dealing and meter building. Managing to score a hard knockdown from an air combo can lead to an "Order in the Court!" OTG hyper combo, sure, but you could also use the opportunity to swap back to Investigation mode, scoop up a piece of evidence, then call Maya out before scooping up another piece of evidence, all while they're still getting up. It can also be worth foregoing hyper combo use simply to conserve meter, since Phoenix Wright isn't the best battery in the world. In fact, since the majority of Phoenix Wright's useful damage potential comes from Turnabout anyway, you should consider saving most of your hyper meter for Wright's teammates, rather than spending too much of it for Phoenix Wright's below-average, non-Turnabout combos.

You can also buy chances to search for evidence by using some combinations of evidence and Maya calls. In order to use "M-Maya?!" during Trial mode, swap back to Investigations, summon Maya, then swap right back. Make sure you've actually swapped back before using evidence again; if you remain in Investigation thinking you're ready to use evidence, you'll just end up throwing it away. The pieces of evidence that provide the most long-term cover are Documents and Cell Phone. Fire either of them twice (or fire them each once, if you happen to have both), then swap back to Investigation and see about fixing up the remaining empty evidence slots. Using methods like these, you can also replace real pieces of evidence that you don't prefer. Beggars usually can't be choosers when it comes to which pieces of evidence to use due to the frantic pace of *UMvC3*, but if you get certain pieces of evidence right away (Cell Phone) then Wright's zoning and flexibility goes up in general, which grants you extra chances to be picky about remaining evidence.

OTG-capable assists make it possible to start Turnabout after throws, ⇨ + Ⓜ, or flying screen.

Three ⇨ + Ⓗ or air ⇩ + Ⓗ attacks puts the foe into a blue-tinted stupor (four hits are required in Investigation); the hit used to start Turnabout counts toward this total.

When you do have enough evidence to enter Turnabout, then it's time to find a way to score a hit with Trial mode ⇨ + Ⓗ or air ⇩ + Ⓗ. Either "OBJECTION!" attack will initiate Turnabout, which is far and away the longest timed power-up state in the game, lasting 20 seconds. These attacks (technically called Bridge to the Turnabout) can be easily worked into a combo; simply chain to ⇨ + Ⓗ after a standing Ⓗ, Ⓗ chain, or launch and super jump with air ⇩ + Ⓗ immediately. You can also cause a hard knockdown, like after an air combo, throw, or ⇨ + Ⓜ overhead, then call an OTG assist and juggle with ⇨ + Ⓗ off the OTG pop-up hit. (See **Combo IX**.)

It's very important to note that hitting an assist with these attacks still counts; you *can* enter Turnabout by using "OBJECTION!" against an assist. This can be hugely helpful if their point character is a stubborn nut to crack.

Turnabout starting with ⇨ + Ⓗ or air ⇩ + Ⓗ means that your foe will have a stun counter of at least one on them right as Turnabout begins. As with Trial mode, getting the stun counter up to three during Turnabout causes a special dizzy state in the enemy during which anything juggles, even launchers against prone foes. Try to keep in mind how many ⇨ + Ⓗ and ⇩ + Ⓗ attacks you've landed, to make the most of this if you can combo into the third attack, and thus the stun, under control. Note that it takes 4 of these attacks to stun during Investigation mode, but if you hit with one of them during Investigation, then swap to Trial and land two more, the third one will stun in this case, even though Investigation "HOLD IT!" attacks are worth less in terms of stun.

If you enter Turnabout off a clean hit, you should almost always be in position to perform a knockout combo, or very close to it. If you land ⇨ + Ⓗ against an opponent on the ground, dash forward immediately after the Turnabout freeze ends, and link crouching Ⓜ, ⇨ + Ⓗ CANCEL ⇨ ⇩ ⬂ + Ⓗ for heavy damage and a wall bounce from which you can easily juggle more Ⓗ attacks (see the last combo in the Combo Appendix). Crouching Ⓗ wall bounces, while air Ⓗ ground bounces, and standing Ⓗ causes enough lofting hitstun to allow you to dash forward and juggle standing Ⓗ again (or, near corners, to just stand still and juggle standing Ⓗ three or four times in a row). Meanwhile, both Paperwork and Press the Witness become much more powerful than normal, along with each piece of evidence.

Wright gains access to the most powerful attack in the game, Ace Attorney, but its use ends Turnabout. Super Samurai Maya Smelting! and "Order in the Court!" are also both still available, and don't do anything to shorten Turnabout's duration. "Order in the Court!" can add oomph to any combo that happens to end with a hard knockdown, while Super Samurai Maya Smelting! is

Battle Plan continued

extremely powerful near corners, *especially* during Turnabout—get Maya out there and your opposition will be pinned, forced to block her flailing arms in the corner, while you prepare whatever hellacious mix-up you like against them.

Once you activate Turnabout, you should think of the time it lasts as a commodity you can spend. Ideally, you enter Turnabout off a clean hit, and so you already have a chance to do serious damage, or outright eliminate, one character. Even if the chance presents itself to use Ace Attorney early on in Turnabout, even if it's for a knockout, you should consider passing it up. Instead, end Turnabout combos with "Order in the Court!" before using a team hyper combo cancel to hand off to Wright's next partner. This is virtually assured of doing at least 900,000 damage to the target, but more important it puts Wright on the sidelines with Turnabout assists active, and not very much Turnabout time expended off the clock!

Wright's partners can make serious use (and abuse) of Phoenix Wright—α and Phoenix Wright—β while he's in Turnabout; since the assists are never actually vulnerable, you can feel confident calling Wright even if he has only a sliver of life left on the sidelines. You can essentially get away with just attacking using your Phoenix Wright assist, and trying not to take risks otherwise!

If the chance presents itself here to turn the tide with a quick K.O., your point character backed by Phoenix Wright will have the option of landing a hyper combo, then using a THC to tack on Ace Attorney. Since Ace Attorney is instant after the hyper freeze and hits anywhere, there isn't a hyper combo this won't work with. You can even whiff punish your opposition from impossible positions by performing a quick hyper combo with your point character, then immediately THC canceling to Ace Attorney, for an anywhere-punish on short notice! This is costly, requiring four bars of meter, but it can be worthwhile if it will take the target out (and certainly is worthwhile if it will end the match).

If the character in front of Phoenix Wright is knocked or snapped out, he'll return with Turnabout still active. If you haven't used Ace Attorney you still have meter lying around, probably, so be patient and develop a sense of how long is left in Turnabout; if your opponent so much as flinches and time's running out, snag them from anywhere with the long arm of the law. Otherwise, if you have the chance, you can get Phoenix Wright out *again*, swapping to the other partner with a crossover attack or another "Order in the Court!" THC. Turnabout might be seconds or even frames from being over at this point, but the timer doesn't matter while Wright is off screen; with 1 frame or 1199 frames of Turnabout left, Phoenix Wright's powered-up assists are still unbelievable.

During Turnabout, Phoenix Wright—α and Phoenix Wright—β assists are never vulnerable...

...forcing even the most powerful opponent to be extremely respectful of Wright's team!

COMBO USAGE

I. IN INVESTIGATION, CR. L, ST. L, M, H, S (CANCEL) FORWARD SUPER JUMP, AIR M, M, H, S, LAND, P1 or P2 WESKER—β OTG, FORWARD DASH, S (CANCEL) FORWARD SUPER JUMP, AIR M, M, H, S, ↓↓ + S (TRIAL) (CANCEL) ↓↙← + ATK ATK OTG

526,900 damage, 27% meter loss

Phoenix Wright has a lot of trouble performing long combos in Investigation, so equipping a decent OTG assist helps. After the final air S knockdown, land and quickly perform ↓↓ + S (CANCEL) ↓↙← + ATK ATK to enter Trial and cancel its stance change recovery into the "Order in the Court!" hyper combo. Again, don't bother to wait for the stance to recover, you can just hyper cancel immediately.

If you choose to bypass swapping to Trial mode for the OTG hyper combo at the end, you can simply use the hard knockdown as an opportunity to summon "M-Maya!?" L, then Investigate for a couple pieces of evidence while your opponent is busy recovering from the hard knockdown. This nets 349,700 damage and a meter gain of 73%.

II. IN INVESTIGATION, CR. L, ST. L, M, H, → + H (CANCEL) ↓↘→ + ATK ATK, WAVEDASH TWICE, ST. M, H, S (CANCEL) FORWARD SUPER JUMP, AIR M, M, H, S, LAND, ↓↓ + S (TRIAL) (CANCEL) ↓↙← + ATK ATK OTG

552,500 damage, 45% meter loss

This short combo burns two bars of meter for a relatively small amount of damage, so it's only worth going for if you're sure it will K.O. the target. Otherwise, you're better off saving meter and using hard knockdowns as free chances to look for evidence. After Phoenix Wright recovers from ↓↘→ + ATK ATK, immediately wavedash forward twice to move into attack range; time your attack so that it hits the opposing character right as Maya finishes her assault.

If you happen to have any false evidence on hand, "Order in the Court!" destroys it, while switching Phoenix Wright back to Investigation from Trial mode.

III. IN INVESTIGATION, → + M (CANCEL) ↓↘→ + M OTG, ↓↓ + S (TRIAL) (CANCEL) ↓↙← + ATK ATK OTG

352,000 damage, 89% meter loss

→ + M Slip-Up is Phoenix Wright's overhead while standing, and it causes a hard knockdown on hit. It can be canceled into "M-Maya!?" M for an OTG; switch to Trial mode and perform "Order in the Court!" as fast as possible to add a third heavy hit after Maya OTGs your foe. You can call an assist to re-launch the opponent after Maya hits instead of doing the hyper combo, but the timing is pretty rough.

IV. IN INVESTIGATION, BACK THROW OR BACK AIR THROW, ↓↘→ + M OTG, ↓↓ + S (TRIAL) (CANCEL) ↓↙← + ATK ATK OTG

372,000 damage, 87% meter loss

It's easier to OTG after Phoenix's back throws, so use them over his forward throw unless your opponent is cornered. Since the target is closer, you can opt to sub out the hyper combo with an OTG assist for a re-launch instead.

COMBO USAGE CONT.

V. IN TRIAL, CR. Ⓛ, ST. Ⓛ, Ⓗ, Ⓗ CANCEL FORWARD JUMP, AIR ↓ + Ⓗ, DELAYED Ⓢ, LAND, ST. Ⓜ, Ⓗ, → + Ⓗ, Ⓢ CANCEL FORWARD SUPER JUMP, AIR Ⓜ, Ⓗ, Ⓗ, ↓ + Ⓗ (STUNNED), LAND, {Ⓢ CANCEL FORWARD SUPER JUMP, AIR Ⓜ, Ⓗ, Ⓗ, Ⓢ, LAND, FORWARD DASH, ↓ ↙ ← + ATK ATK} OR {↓ ↘ → + ATK ATK, WAIT FOR FINAL HYPER COMBO HIT, Ⓢ CANCEL FORWARD SUPER JUMP, AIR Ⓗ, Ⓗ, Ⓢ, LAND, ↓ ↙ ← + ATK ATK}

577,500~667,600 damage, 2~104% meter loss

This combo hits the enemy with → + Ⓗ/air ↓ + Ⓗ three times, resulting in a stun that allows for a relaunch after the super jumping portion. The opponent must not have been hit with → + Ⓗ before this, or else the stun timing will be off. Keep track of how many times you've landed → + Ⓗ or air ↓ + Ⓗ to better suit your combo needs. Note that the standing Ⓗ, Ⓗ chain whiffs against most crouching characters; it's only reliable against opponents who are standing (which they should be anyway, if crouching Ⓛ at the beginning hit them). Go for this after an empty jump in, or when the opponent is watching out for → + Ⓜ.

VI. IN TRIAL, → + Ⓜ CANCEL ↓ ↓ + Ⓢ (INVESTIGATION), ↓ ↘ → + Ⓜ, ↓ ↓ + Ⓢ (TRIAL) CANCEL ↓ ↙ ← + ATK ATK

352,000 damage, 90% meter loss

Even though it isn't necessary, you can cancel Trial's → + Ⓜ into a change to Investigation to summon "M-Maya!?" M, then change *back* to Trial for the "Order in the Court!" hyper combo OTG. You may also opt to simply cancel → + Ⓜ into ↓ ↙ ← + ATK ATK, however, skipping the stance-switching steps. As always, you can trade out the hyper combo for an OTG assist and a re-launch if your heart desires.

VII. IN TRIAL WITH THREE PIECES OF EVIDENCE, CR. Ⓛ, Ⓜ, ST. Ⓗ, Ⓢ CANCEL FORWARD SUPER JUMP, AIR Ⓜ, Ⓗ, Ⓗ, Ⓢ, LAND, P1 or P2 WESKER—β OTG, → + Ⓗ (TURNABOUT), CR. Ⓗ, FORWARD DASH INTO FORWARD JUMP, AIR Ⓗ, LAND, FORWARD DASH, Ⓢ CANCEL FORWARD SUPER JUMP, AIR Ⓜ, Ⓜ, Ⓢ, LAND, ↓ ↙ ← + ATK ATK OTG OR → ↓ ↘ + ATK ATK OTG

730,000~1,130,000 damage, 2% meter gain or 198% meter loss

A basic example of shifting into Turnabout mid-combo. After the Turnabout change, you can opt to enter X-Factor to ensure the remainder of the combo knocks out the opposing character (without having to use the level 3). This leaves you in both X-Factor and Turnabout for the incoming opponent. Alternatively, you can perform the first combo, ending with the gavel OTG, then THC to your next ally. The next character's hyper combo pours more damage onto the 730,000 Wright already did, and meanwhile he's now on the sideline, where you can abuse his astonishing Turnabout assists! If your point character ever has four bars of meter in reserve, almost any hyper combo can then easily lead back to Ace Attorney for huge, 0-frame damage, or you can simply wait for Wright to return, with the majority of his Turnabout still left, since he handed off the fight to a teammate almost immediately!

VIII. IN TRIAL WITH THREE PIECES OF EVIDENCE, CR. Ⓛ, ST. Ⓗ, Ⓗ, → + Ⓗ (TURNABOUT), FORWARD JUMP, AIR ↓ + Ⓗ, Ⓢ, LAND, Ⓢ CANCEL FORWARD SUPER JUMP, AIR Ⓜ, Ⓜ, Ⓗ, LAND, → ↓ ↘ + Ⓗ, WAVEDASH FORWARD FOUR TIMES, Ⓢ CANCEL FORWARD SUPER JUMP, AIR Ⓜ, Ⓜ, Ⓢ, LAND, ↓ ↙ ← + ATK ATK OR → ↓ ↘ + ATK ATK

882,300~1,355,500 damage, 35% meter gain or 164% meter loss

A devastating Turnabout combo. Performing the level 3 version instantly knocks out any character even from full vitality, but you'll have to weigh whether you actually want to end Turnabout this quick by using the level 3. Save this for when an opponent's final character enters the screen, so the strategic benefit of prolonging Turnabout is no longer relevant.

IX. IN TRIAL WITH THREE PIECES OF EVIDENCE, → + Ⓜ, WAIT A MOMENT, P1 or P2 WESKER—β OTG, → + Ⓗ (TURNABOUT), FORWARD DASH Ⓢ CANCEL FORWARD SUPER JUMP, AIR Ⓜ, Ⓜ, Ⓗ, LAND, → ↓ ↘ + Ⓗ, WAVEDASH FORWARD FOUR TIMES, Ⓢ CANCEL FORWARD SUPER JUMP, AIR Ⓜ, Ⓜ, Ⓢ, LAND, ↓ ↙ ← + ATK ATK OTG OR → ↓ ↘ + ATK ATK OTG

846,100~1,309,300 damage, 16% meter gain or 184% meter loss

This is a method of entering Turnabout off of an overhead attack. After → + Ⓜ hits, call Wesker—β a little later than you think you should to give yourself enough time to rise and connect → + Ⓗ. In the very likely event that using Ace Attorney here represents overkill, instead perform a team hyper combo from "Order in the Court!" to your next teammate's best hyper combo.

X. IN INVESTIGATION, CR. Ⓛ, ST. Ⓛ, Ⓜ, Ⓗ, Ⓢ CANCEL FORWARD SUPER JUMP, AIR Ⓜ, Ⓜ, Ⓗ, Ⓢ, LAND, ↓ ↓ + Ⓢ (TRIAL) CANCEL ↓ ↙ ← + ATK ATK OTG X-FACTOR, WAVEDASH FORWARD TWICE, ST. Ⓗ, Ⓢ CANCEL FORWARD SUPER JUMP, AIR Ⓜ, Ⓜ, Ⓗ, Ⓢ, LAND, ↓ ↓ + Ⓢ (TRIAL) CANCEL ↓ ↙ ← + ATK ATK OTG

867,700~1,019,300 damage depending on X-Factor level, 2~117% meter loss

A basic X-Factor combo that deals hellish damage. Go for this combo when you realize you've caught two characters at once; you may have this opportunity frequently if you call "M-Maya!?" L and the enemy attacks while calling their assist right into the barrier. In this way, Phoenix Wright is capable of dealing heavy damage to the other team even without his exclusive Turnabout mode. If you land the first crouching Ⓛ in Trial mode, change the air chain sequence to air Ⓜ, Ⓗ, Ⓗ Ⓢ for additional damage. Swapping to Trial mode manually after the first hard knockdown is also not required if you begin in Trial mode.

ADVANCED TACTICS

BODY OF EVIDENCE

Playing Phoenix Wright comes with a mild inventory management aspect. Six of his best special moves are all types of projectile attacks only available during Trial and Turnabout modes with the proper evidence in hand; there are also a half-dozen pieces of fake evidence lying about, which will trip Phoenix Wright up if you try to apply them during Trial mode. You can separate the wheat from the chaff with the Discard command, but be careful not to discard any real evidence unless you have a particular attack you absolutely want available in Trial and eventually Turnabout.

Since the results of Investigating are random, and since sometimes luck won't be on your side (and some opponents will be more aggressive and pesky than others), it may take a while to gather the right evidence to go for Turnabout. Patience and flexibility are invaluable here. Instead of just trying to force the issue digging for clues overzealously, eventually getting Wright overwhelmed, have a willingness to use him as an actual combatant, and play smart with the tools that he has. His range is pitiful, sure, but he still has solid anti-air attacks, high/low mix-ups, and totally competent solo combos, especially in Trial mode; you'll just have to rely on assists, evidence, and Maya to create openings, more than Wright's own "attacks". As a big advantage, combos landed in Trial mode can almost always end in "Order in the Court!" to destroy fake evidence less laboriously than actually discarding it. Additionally, the game will *never* allow you to have all three slots filled with fake evidence, so if you draw blanks on your first two searches, make sure to use the third slot for the third search (rather than discarding one of the two pieces of false evidence) and you'll guarantee that you get either real evidence, or at least healing meat.

Play within Phoenix Wright's means and you'll find more places to look for evidence naturally anyway, since you can use the huge frame advantage created by hard knockdowns to look for evidence for several seconds, uninterrupted.

Investigation mode

Trial mode

Turnabout mode

ADMISSIBLE EVIDENCE

Image	Item
	Photograph
	Flower Vase
	Documents
	Watch
	Knife
	Cell Phone

FAKE EVIDENCE

Image	Item
	Bottle
	Statue
	Plant
	Plunger
	Servbot
	Shades

LUNCH!

Image	Item
	Meat

COMBO APPENDIX

GENERAL EXECUTION TIPS

After scoring an S launcher hit, pause for a split second before super jumping to follow up with an air combo

Practice dashing or jumping as soon as possible after activating Turnabout, in order to link afterward

AS PHOENIX WRIGHT COMES IN: AIR H, H, S, LAND, {TRIAL ↓↙← + ATK ATK} OR {INVESTIGATION ↓↓ + S (CANCEL) ↓↙← + ATK ATK}

Notes	Damage
Activate a TAC with ↑ + S	Varies due to damage scaling, destroys fake evidence

AS PHOENIX WRIGHT COMES IN: AIR H, S, LAND, {TRIAL ↓↙← + ATK ATK} OR {INVESTIGATION ↓↓ + S (CANCEL) ↓↙← + ATK ATK}

Notes	Damage
Activate a TAC with → + S or ↓ + S	Varies due to damage scaling, destroys fake evidence

→ + M (CANCEL) ↓↘→ + M, ST. H, S (CANCEL) FORWARD SUPER JUMP, AIR M, M, H, S, LAND, ↓↓ + S (CANCEL) ↓↙← + ATK ATK

Notes	Damage
Investigation near cornered enemy	516,300, 59% meter loss, destroys fake evidence

FORWARD THROW, ST. H, H (CANCEL) FORWARD JUMP, AIR ↓ + H, DELAYED S, LAND, ST. M, H, → + H, S (CANCEL) FORWARD SUPER JUMP, AIR H, H, ↓ + H (STUNNED), LAND, ↓↘→ + ATK ATK, ON THE 23RD HIT S (CANCEL) FORWARD SUPER JUMP, AIR H, H, S, LAND, ↓↙← + ATK ATK

Notes	Damage
Trial near a corner, works only if no → + H or air ↓ + H stun counters are registered on the enemy	584,400, 106% meter loss, destroys fake evidence

FORWARD THROW, ST. H, S (CANCEL) FORWARD SUPER JUMP, AIR M, M, H, S, LAND, ↓↓ + S (TRIAL) (CANCEL) ↓↙← + ATK ATK

Notes	Damage
Investigation near a corner	404,700, 61% meter loss, destroys fake evidence

→ + H (TURNABOUT), FORWARD DASH, CR. M, → + H (CANCEL) →↓↘ + H, ST. H, H, H, VERTICAL JUMP, AIR H, LAND, FORWARD DASH, CR. H, S (CANCEL) SUPER JUMP, AIR M, M, H, S, LAND, →↓↘ + ATK ATK

Notes	Damage
Trial near a corner, each slot filled with evidence	1,449,100, 147% meter loss, ends Turnabout

"A COFFEE-LOVING PROSECUTOR ONCE SAID: ONCE YOU ELIMINATE THE IMPOSSIBLE, WHATEVER REMAINS MUST BE THE TRUTH."

NEW

STRIDER

"UNLESS YOU'RE A TARGET OF MINE, YOU WILL NEVER SEE ME. IF YOU DO SEE ME, THEN IT'S ALREADY TOO LATE."

Bio

REAL NAME

Unknown

OCCUPATION

A-Class Strider

ABILITIES

He has trained his body to its utmost physical limits. He also wields the Cypher, a plasma-generating broadsword capable of cutting through anything.

WEAPONS

Plasma sword "Cypher", sickle and chain, robotic animal helpers that he can summon at will.

PROFILE

He is a member of the Striders, a secret organization specializing in kidnapping, assassination, demolition, etc., that has worked behind the scenes throughout history. Having obtained A-Class status at a young age, he is the organization's best assassin.

FIRST APPEARANCE

Strider (1989)

POWER GRID

3	INTELLIGENCE
2	STRENGTH
4	SPEED
2	STAMINA
1	ENERGY PROJECTION
7	FIGHTING ABILITY

*This is biographical, and does not represent an evaluation of the in-game combat potential of this hero.

ALTERNATE COSTUMES

Overview

Vitality	750,000
Chain Combo Archetype	Hunter Series

X-Factor Boost	Damage	Speed
Level 1 (3 teammates remaining)	120%	120%
Level 2 (2 teammates remaining)	135%	135%
Level 3 (1 teammate remaining)	155%	145%

Strider is a versatile character that can be effective up close or from a distance. Your goal with Strider is to force your opponent into the corner. Why is this beneficial?

- **Strider's offense is comprised of quick, high-priority attacks that can be seamlessly interwoven. It is not easily dealt with while cornered**
- **Vajra M can cross up even cornered adversaries**
- **Strider has various tools for moving in after being pushed away including Vajra, Ame-no-Murakumo M or H, and his quick ground dash**

You can accomplish this goal by:

- **Using Strider's high-priority melee attacks at close to mid range**
- **Overpowering your competitor's long range game with Formation A1, Formation A2, Formation C, Gram H, and Vajra.**
- **Using forward-moving attacks such as Ame-no-Murakumo M/H or ↘ + Ⓗ to close the distance between Strider and his rival**

Attack Set

Standing Basic Attacks

Screen	Command	Hits	Damage	Meter Gain	Startup	Active	Recovery	Advantage on Hit	Advantage if Guarded	Notes
1	Standing L	1	35,000	280	4	2	11	0	-2	Chains into L attacks
2	Standing M	1	48,000	384	6	3	15	0	-2	—
3	Standing H	1	60,000	480	9	4	23	-4	-6	—

Crouching Basic Attacks

Screen	Command	Hits	Damage	Meter Gain	Startup	Active	Recovery	Advantage on Hit	Advantage if Guarded	Notes
1	Crouching L	1	33,000	264	5	2	11	0	-2	Low attack, chains into L attacks
2	Crouching M	1	50,000	400	8	3	15	0	-2	Low attack
3	Crouching H	1	60,000	480	10	3	26	—	-8	Low attack, knocks down

Ground Special Attack—Launcher

Screen	Command	Hits	Damage	Meter Gain	Startup	Active	Recovery	Advantage on Hit	Advantage if Guarded	Notes
1	S (while standing or crouching)	1	65,000	520	9	4	29	—	-12	Launcher, not special or hyper combo-cancelable

Air Basic Attacks

Screen	Command	Hits	Damage	Meter Gain	Startup	Active	Recovery	Advantage on Hit	Advantage if Guarded	Notes
1	Air L	1	40,000	320	5	3	15	+11	+9	Overhead attack
2	Air M	1	50,000	400	7	3	21	+16	+14	Overhead attack
3	Air H	1	60,000	480	9	4	23	+18	+16	Overhead attack

Air Special Attacks—Flying Screen and Air Exchange

Air Ⓢ causes a hard knockdown when used in a launcher combo (this is sometimes called flying screen). When used outside of a launcher combo, air Ⓢ behaves mostly like another basic attack. Air exchange attacks, performed by inputting a direction plus Ⓢ, are only possible during a launcher combo. Exchange hits initiate team aerial combos by tagging in the next available character to continue the air combo.

Screen	Command	Hits	Damage	Meter Gain	Startup	Active	Recovery	Advantage on Hit	Advantage if Guarded	Notes
1	Air Ⓢ	1	63,000	504	10	3	26	+14	+12	Causes hard knockdown if used in launcher combo, overhead attack
2	Air ⇧ + Ⓢ (during launcher combo)	2	105,00	880	9	4	23	—	—	Tags in next available ally while lofting opponent upward
3	Air ⇨ or ⇦ + Ⓢ (during launcher combo)	2	95,000	800	9	3	24	—	—	Tags in next available ally while causing wall bounce, erases 1 hyper meter bar from foe
4	Air ⇩ + Ⓢ (during launcher combo)	2	95,000	800	9	10	22	—	—	Tags in next available ally while causing ground bounce, generates 1 hyper meter bar

1

2

3

4

Command Attacks

Command attacks resemble basic attacks but have different chaining and canceling properties. It's usually possible to chain *into* a command attack from basic attacks, but most command attacks cannot be chained from or canceled themselves.

Screen	Name	Command	Hits	Damage	Meter Gain	Startup	Active	Recovery	Advantage on Hit	Advantage if Guarded	Notes
1	Arch Cut	⇨ + Ⓗ	1	63,000	504	10	4	22	-3	-5	—
2	Slide	⬂ + Ⓗ	1	55,000	440	9	10	22	—	-11	Knocks down, OTG-capable

1

2

Throws

Throws are for snagging passive or blocking opponents. Since throws are active so quickly, you can also use them to preemptively toss opposing characters out of their offense. Combos are usually possible after throws, one way or another.

Screen	Command	Hits	Damage	Meter Gain	Startup	Active	Notes
1	⇨ + Ⓗ (ground)	1	80,000	800	1	1	Hard knockdown
	⇦ + Ⓗ (ground)	1	80,000	800	1	1	Hard knockdown
2	⇨ + Ⓗ (air)	1	80,000	800	1	1	Hard knockdown
	⇦ + Ⓗ (air)	1	80,000	800	1	1	Hard knockdown

1

2

As a Partner—Crossover Assists

Screen	Type	P1+P2 Crossover Combination Hyper Combo	Description	Hits	Damage	Meter Gain	Startup	Active	Recovery (this crossover assist)	Recovery (other partner)	Notes
1	Strider—α	Legion	Ame-no-Murakumo M	1	80,000	640	47	4	116	86	Ground bounces foe
2	Strider—β	Legion	Gram M	1	90,000	720	49	5	118	88	Wall bounces adversary
3	Strider—γ	Legion	Vajra H	1	80,000	640	59	10	102	72	Hard knockdown against airborne opponents, Strider invincible from frames 37-53

1

2

3

Strider has three useful crossover assists to choose from. Strider—α Ame-no-Murakumo can be used to extend combos, but it can be dangerous to use otherwise because of Strider's forward movement. Strider—β Gram has decent speed and range, and it causes a wall bounce. Strider's best crossover assist is Strider—γ. When called, Strider performs Vajra H, which tracks down opponents regardless of their height, resulting in a hard knockdown on aerial targets. Adversaries can no longer attack from high in the sky with confidence when Strider has this crossover assist at the ready.

Even though Strider is useful as a crossover assist, extreme caution must be taken when calling him. Strider's vitality is tied for second-lowest in the game (Rocket Raccoon and Akuma are equally fragile; only Phoenix is flimsier), so a well-placed hyper combo can K.O. Strider instantly if he is called at an inopportune time.

Snap Back

Screen	Command	Hits	Damage	Meter Gain	Startup	Active	Recovery	Advantage on Hit	Advantage if Guarded
1	↓↘→ + P1onP2	1	50,000	500 (-1 hyper meter bar)	2	4	22	—	-5
Notes									
On hit, snap back forces the opposing point character to be replaced by an assist. Opposing assist calls or tag outs are also locked out for 4 seconds									

1

Special Moves

Screen	Name	Command	Hits	Damage	Meter Gain	Startup	Active	Recovery	Advantage on Hit	Advantage if Guarded	Notes
1	Ame-no-Murakumo L	↓↘→ + L	1	70,000	560	15	4	27	—	-10	Knocks down
	Ame-no-Murakumo M	↓↘→ + M	1	80,000	640	23	4	25	—	-8	Ground bounces foe
	Ame-no-Murakumo H	↓↘→ + H	1	90,000	720	31	4	22	—	-5	Ground bounces opponent
2	Excalibur L	(in air) ↓↘→ + L	4	30,000 x 4	240 x 4	10	15	11 or until grounded	+10	+8	—
3	Excalibur M	(in air) ↓↘→ + M	4	30,000 x 4	240 x 4	10	15	26	-9	-11	—
4	Excalibur H	(in air) ↓↘→ + H	4	30,000 x 4	240 x 4	10	15	26	-9	-11	—
5	Wall Cling	↓↘→ + S	—	—	—	Until wall	—	1	—	—	Lasts 295 frames
6	Ladder Kick	(during Wall Cling) L	1	55,000	440	8	11	16	-4	-6	Resumes Wall Cling upon recovery
7	Cypher Attack	(during Wall Cling) M	1	60,000	480	6	3	23	-3	-5	Resumes Wall Cling upon recovery
8	Jump Kick	(during Wall Cling) H	1	70,000	560	10	Until grounded	10	+12	+10	Overhead attack
9	Wall Exchange	(during Wall Cling) S	—	—	—	27	—	1	—	—	Resumes Wall Cling upon recovery
—	Dismount	(during Wall Cling) →	—	—	—	—	—	Until grounded	—	—	—
—	Climb	(during Wall Cling) ↑	—	—	—	—	—	1	—	—	—
—	Descend	(during Wall Cling) ↓	—	—	—	—	—	1	—	—	—
10	Gram L (in air OK)	→↓↘ + L	1	90,000	720	18	5	26 (air: until grounded)	—	-10 (air: 0)	Hard knockdown
11	Gram M (in air OK)	→↓↘ + M	1	90,000	720	25	5	26 (air: until grounded)	—	-10 (air: +8)	Wall bounces adversary
12	Gram H (in air OK)	→↓↘ + H	1	90,000	720	33	5	26 (air: until grounded)	—	-10 (air: +16)	Wall bounces rival
13	Formation A1	↓↙← + L	1	80,000	640	21	—	14	+13	+11	Projectile has 3 low priority durability points

Special Moves continued

Screen	Name	Command	Hits	Damage	Meter Gain	Startup	Active	Recovery	Advantage on Hit	Advantage if Guarded	Notes
14	Formation A2	↓↙← + (M)	1	40,000	320	21	—	14	+14	+12	Projectile has 3 low priority durability points
15	Formation C	↓↙← + (H)	1	90,000	720	36	—	4	—	—	Knocks down, first projectile has 3 low priority durability points, bomb projectile has 5 low priority durability points and falls toward ground after 21 frames, bomb explodes upon contact with rival or ground, explosion has 5 low priority durability points and is active for 30 frames
16	Formation B	↓↙← + (S)	—	—	—	11	—	9	—	—	Lasts 600 frames or until Strider is hit
17	Formation B (Shot)	(during Formation B) ↓↙← + (S)	1	80,000	640	2	—	18	+12	+8	OTG-capable, knocks down
18	Vajra L	←↓↙ + (L)	—	—	—	12	9	10	—	—	Frames 12-20 invincible
19	Vajra M	←↓↙ + (M)	—	—	—	12	9	10	—	—	Frames 12-20 invincible
20	Vajra H	←↓↙ + (H)	1	80,000	640	33	Until grounded	11	+2	-7	Frames 13-29 invincible, hard knockdown against airborne opponents

Ame-no-Murakumo: Strider performs a spinning slash that causes a ground bounce. Ame-no-Murakumo H and M send Strider running before slashing; the H version reaches almost the entirety of the screen. Because of their slow startup, these two versions of Ame-no-Murakumo cannot be used in typical combos. Despite this, you can link both versions after a Formation B shot. Ame-no-Murakumo L features no initial run, allowing it to combo off basic attacks such as standing or crouching M and H. All three versions have a varying degree of ground bounce; Ame-no-Murakumo H's ground bounce is the largest and allows for (H) attacks to combo afterward, while the L version only allows for faster (L) attacks as a follow up.

1

All three versions of Ame-no-Murakumo can be canceled into Formation B shot — even during recovery! If Formation B is active, you can make Ame-no-Murakumo unpunishable by canceling its recovery into the projectile. If the slash is successfully connected, the shot can be used to combo afterward, making this technique useful both on hit and guard. Note that Ame-no-Murakumo can only be canceled into Formation B shot, not activation.

Excalibur: Strider goes flying through the air in one of three directions: (H) goes up at an angle, (M) travels straight, and (L) shoots down at an angle. Upon recovering, Strider is in a jumping state in which special attacks (such as aerial Gram), double jumps, attacks, and guarding can still be performed. Excalibur is useful for changing Strider's aerial trajectory and causes decent damage if all four hits connect. Remember that you can only perform Excalibur once in the air.

2

3

4

Excalibur L is mostly used for combos and offensive pressure. Strider recovers almost immediately upon landing, making this attack only punishable via X-Factor if guarded. You can follow a connected Excalibur L with a standing (L) if connected on both grounded and aerial opponents. Because of its sharp angle, Excalibur L can also be used to counter an adversary's offense. If you see your foe rushing in for an attack, a quick jump or super jump into Excalibur L can counter their blitz, depending on the attack used.

Excalibur M covers a long distance horizontally and is most useful when you need to reset your positioning. Use Excalibur M to escape from the corner, or to close the distance between Strider and his challenger. Be careful in becoming too predictable with this attack, however, as Strider is vulnerable for 26 frames of recovery until guarding or attacking is possible. Opposing players who anticipate this attack or whose characters are in close proximity to Strider upon recovery can fully punish him.

Excalibur H sends Strider flying skyward, and he recovers near the top of the screen. Although it has the same recovery time as the punishable Excalibur M, its recovery frames begin as Strider is still ascending, reducing the chances of the attack being punished. If performed during a normal jump, a crossover assist can be called on the way down for a tricky surprise attack.

Wall Cling 5

Ladder Kick 6

Cypher Attack 7

Jump Attack 8

Wall Exchange 9

Wall Cling: Strider quickly jumps to the opposing wall. Strider is unable to guard not only during the initial jump but also during his time on the wall, making him extremely vulnerable. While he's on the wall, you can climb up and down with ↑ and ↓, respectively. You can also dismount from the wall by pressing the direction away from the wall. Several moves unique to Wall Cling become available: (L) performs Ladder Kick, a downwards stomp; (M) performs Cypher Attack, a quick slash; (H) performs Jump Kick, a diving kick off the wall that causes a ground bounce on aerial opponents; and (S) performs Wall Exchange, which causes Strider to leap to the opposite wall. All three Wall Cling attacks can be chained together just like basic attacks, and Jump Kick can be canceled into special moves while Strider is still in the air. Jump Kick must be guarded standing and is punishable only by guarding it in midair. Wall Exchange can be performed an unlimited amount of times throughout the entire duration of Wall Cling (just short of five seconds).

10

11

12

Gram: Strider performs a long, sweeping slash. The length of the slice is determined by the strength of the button used. Gram H covers almost the entirety of the screen, causing a wall bounce. Its startup is too slow for it to be used in most combos, but you can utilize its range to start hit-confirmable combos from long range. Gram M is similar to Gram H but with less range, hitstun, and startup. Gram L doesn't have the range of the M or H versions, but it has the quickest startup of the three, making it usable in most ground and air combos. Gram L is also different in that it causes a hard knockdown instead of a wall bounce.

You can cancel all three versions of Gram into Formation B shot at any time, whether in startup or recovery. The long startup of Gram H can be used as bait to surprise foes with Formation B shot into a combo. The recovery on Gram L can be covered up with Formation B shot during grounded offensive pressure. Note that Gram can only be canceled into Formation B shot, not activation.

13

Formation A1: Strider summons a mechanical tiger to attack his rival. Formation A1 behaves differently than other projectiles in that the tiger always emerges from the corner behind Strider and travels the entire distance of the screen, regardless of Strider's position. The tiger features 3 low durability points, leaving something to be desired in long range firefights. It can even be negated by almost any basic attack on reaction! Given this setback, Formation A should not be passed on as flimsy; the tiger absorbs whatever attack negated it, acting as a one-hit shield so long as the opposing attack connects either before or simultaneous to hitting Strider. Even though it is difficult to utilize this properly when defending yourself, it is an added bonus nonetheless.

14

Formation A2: Strider sends an eagle to attack his foes. Formation A2 is similar to Formation A1 in that the eagle always emerges from the corner behind Strider, regardless of his positioning. The eagle also has the low durability of the tiger, and it is easily destroyed with an attack or opposing projectile. However, Formation A2 is useful as a defensive tool when timed correctly, and this move possesses the same shielding property as Formation A1. Perform Formation A2 against opponents coming from the air to knock your foe out of their attack. If your adversary destroys the eagle instead, their aerial attack gets nullified. Though not useful against multiple strikes, standard one-hit air attacks using air (H) or (S) are rendered useless with a well-timed eagle.

15

Formation C: Strider sends an eagle armed with a bomb toward his opponent. Midway through its flight, the eagle drops the bomb toward the ground, and it then descends slowly until exploding. The bomb explodes if ever it comes into contact with any adversaries, whether it is during delivery or descent. You can use Formation C defensively in the same manner as Formation A2, though the timing is different because of the increased startup. You can also employ Formation C to complement Strider's long range attacks.

Formation B: Strider summons a satellite that floats nearby for 600 frames or until Strider is hit. With the satellite active, performing the ↓↙← + (S) motion again causes it to fire as a projectile. Both phases of Formation B have extremely fast startup and recovery—Formation B shot fires after a mere 2 frames of startup! Formation B shot can be used to start, end, and extend combos, while the satellite activation can be used to slightly decrease the recovery on slower attacks such as standing (H). Formation B shot always fires directly from Strider, as opposed to Formation A1 and A2. Because the projectile fires so quickly, Formation B shot is a vital tool in Strider's arsenal, both at long range and up close. It's so fast that in OTG situations, you often have enough time to not only summon the satellite, but fire it, as well!

16

17

Formation B shot has the special property of being usable during the startup and recovery of Gram and Ame-no-Murakumo. You can make these attacks safe on guard by canceling into the Formation B projectile, and you can extend combos through the use of the shot after either of these attacks successfully connects.

18

19

Vajra L & M: Vajra L and M are teleports that cause Strider to appear above his opponent, regardless of the opposing character's altitude. Vajra L always causes Strider to reappear in front of his rival, while Vajra M causes him to reappear behind his foe.

Vajra leaves Strider vulnerable for a short period of time immediately before teleporting and right after he reappears. Once fully recovered, Strider is in a jumping state in which basic attacks, special moves, double jumping, guarding, and crossover assists are available. You can use Vajra L and M to start an offense, avoid slower attacks, or punish slower recovering attacks from any distance. Try teleporting during projectile firefights or under the cover of a far-reaching crossover assist. However, don't overuse this move, since becoming too predictable with Vajra L or M leaves Strider open to punishment from air throws.

20

Vajra H: Vajra H is different than its L and M counterparts in that Strider comes out of the teleport already attacking with a flying kick. A successful Vajra H can lead into a well-timed standing (L) into a combo. If Vajra H connects on an airborne opponent, it causes a hard knockdown, which you can then follow with Formation B OTG. Like Vajra L and M, the teleport always tracks opponents regardless of their altitude, making Vajra H ideal for knocking aerial competitors out of the sky.

Vajra H is unpunishable if guarded standing or crouching. However, clever adversaries can punish Vajra H by jumping to guard the kick in the air, leaving Strider open to punishment as both characters land. This attack can also be punished after being guarded with X-Factor. To avoid these situations, try using Vajra H as a counter to ranged attacks rather than throwing it out randomly. Vajra H can also be made safe with many different crossover assists if called immediately before the teleport.

Hyper Combos

Screen	Name	Command	Hits	Damage	Startup	Active	Recovery	Advantage on Hit	Advantage if Guarded	Notes
1	Legion	↓↘→ + ATK ATK	15	25,000 x 15	9+1	—	76	+12	+6	OTG-capable
2	Ouroboros (Level 3 Hyper Combo)	↓↙← + ATK ATK	—	Projectiles: 15,000 Ouroboros: 40,000	13+2	—	7	—	—	Press (L), (M) or (H) to fire 2 projectiles, projectiles have 3 low priority durability points, lasts 420 frames, Strider does not gain meter while Ouroboros is active
3	Ragnarok (Level 3 Hyper Combo)	→↓↘ + ATK ATK	18	430,000	8+0	21	33	—	-33	Frames 1-20 invincible, hard knockdown

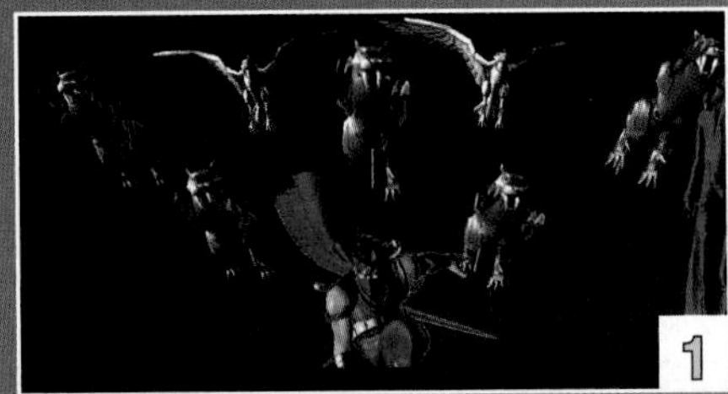
1

Legion: Strider summons a herd of mechanical tigers and eagles to fill the screen. Legion is OTG-capable and is commonly used as a combo ender. Once this hyper combo is activated, the animals are released regardless if Strider is hit while pointing. This means that a THC from Legion can be performed extremely early if need be. Legion is somewhat slow to start, and opponents can avoid it completely on reaction if they jump over the animals, so this hyper combo should only be used in combos and THCs.

Battle Plan

Combos can be started from fullscreen by occasionally using Gram H during long range battles.

Strider's strength lies in his effectiveness at both short and long range. He has some of the fastest attacks in the game, three different projectiles and teleports to choose from at a distance, and high-priority cypher swings at mid to close range. Strider has the tools to get close to his opponent easily, so waiting for the right moment is key.

Strider's main weakness is his low vitality. Coming in at 750,000, Strider's vitality ranks among the lowest in the game. Because of this, it is important to play Strider as safe as possible, covering any recovery time with crossover assists or a Formation B shot when possible. It is also prudent to not become too reliant on Vajra, as a poorly timed Vajra can lead to a K.O. on Strider.

As such, your best bet is to keep at a distance with Strider, attacking safely with Formation attacks combined with an occasional Gram H and crossover assist. Gram H can lead to huge damage, as long as Strider has the breathing room to perform it without being interrupted. The long slice gives enough time to dash in for a full combo, and it also goes unpunished if guarded anywhere besides point-blank range (and even then, it is difficult to punish). If you find your opponent trying to wade through the various projectiles Strider can throw, an unexpected Gram H on the ground or during a normal jump usually stops their advances cold.

Once your competitor starts firing back with ranged attacks of their own, you can then utilize Vajra to pass through their ranged game for positioning and combo opportunities. Vajra M is great for getting Strider behind his adversary during a firefight. Upon recovering, Strider can come down from the teleport with a falling air (H) or (S) into **Combo I**. If the situation changes and you find Strider teleporting into danger, you can guard on the way down and opt to attack with a crossover assist instead. For added safety, cover Vajra L or M with Formation A1, Formation B shot, or a crossover assist beforehand. If Vajra L or M go unpunished, use this positional advantage to start Strider's offense.

While Vajra L and M are used more for positioning and safe approach, Vajra H is best used to interrupt or punish slower ranged attacks, as well as vulnerable aerial attacks. This is especially useful against characters like Trish or Doctor Doom who love to rain down projectiles from the sky. Using Vajra H while your foe is attacking from a distance makes scoring a counterhit more likely, as well, easing up the leniency in connecting a standing (L) afterward. Vajra H is more of a commitment, however. Vajra L and M allow for several options upon Strider reappearing, while Vajra H leaves no option for anything except an X-Factor activation. Learning when to use each version of Vajra is important to Strider's overall success.

Wall Cling can be used not only as a way to get close to your target, but also for cross-ups with a timed Formation B shot. Time the Wall Cling so that Strider leaps past his opponent right before the projectile hits, and follow with a Wall Cling (L), (M), (H) for a ground bounce combo. You can perform this with a long-range crossover assist, as well.

Fire the Formation B shot, then perform a Wall Cling... then proceed to combo off of a successful hit with Ladder Kick, Cypher Attack, and Jump Kick!

If you feel the time is right to switch to offense, start by using a Formation B shot to cover a forward advance.

You can employ Strider's far-reaching basic attacks and special moves with the help of a crossover assist to push your way forward. You can use a forward dash to effectively increase the range of Strider's melee attacks (see the Advanced Tactics section), or cover ↘ + (H) or Ame-no-Murakumo M/H with a crossover assist to close the distance. A successful ↘ + (H) can always be canceled with an X-Factor activation for a possible K.O. combo, though simply performing the slide unpunished gives you the momentum needed to start an offense. Using a suitable crossover assist as cover, Excalibur M can also be used to get close. If the crossover assist can cover the 26 frames of recovery that plague Excalibur M, Strider will recover in the air safely, ready to come down with an attack.

While some characters must be at close range to bring their offense, Strider needs only to be in mid range for his offense to shine. The range and priority of standing (H) and → + (H) can be taken advantage of to start Strider's bread and butter combos. Formation B shot is also a great attack at mid range because of its extremely fast startup.

Once Strider is close, stay in the opposing character's face as best you can! Standing (L), crouching (L), and Formation B shot are the fastest attacks in your arsenal to use at close range. Any holes in your rival's offense should be taken advantage of with the speed of Strider's (L) attacks. Strider's air (L) acts as an instant overhead against mid to large-sized characters. Against a crouching opponent, perform an instant overhead air (L) canceled into Excalibur L for a full combo! Mix this up with crouching (L) to create a deadly 50/50 guessing game whenever Strider is close.

Strider has aerial options at close range, as well. Excalibur L is great for attacking at an unexpected angle, stopping any ground counter offenses with a diving attack. This attack is safe on guard and can be followed by continued pressure from the ground. Air (H) is an invaluable attack with many applications. The massive hitbox produced by Strider's slice puts opponents in a situation where they must either take a risk in attempting to counter it with an anti-air attempt or guard it, giving Strider positional advantage. Air (H) also serves as a cross-up when jumping over adversaries, and it can be delayed for a deep cross-up attack.

Be sure to cover Excalibur M with a long-range crossover assist.

You can take advantage of Strider's long reach and safe attack patterns to create strings of uninterrupted offense against opponents. For example, an attack string of cr. (L), (M), st. (H), cr. (H), → + (H) CANCEL ↓↙← + (S) can then be followed by a dash forward into st. (H), cr. (H), → + (H) CANCEL →↓↘ + (L) CANCEL ↓↙← + (S) into even more offense. To combat advancing guard, Ame-no-Murakumo M canceled into Formation B shot can be used at any time during attack strings.

When canceling a guarded Ame-no-Murakumo or Gram into Formation B shot, you can delay the Formation B shot cancel to interrupt your opponent's punishment attempt for a combo. Constantly vary the timing in which Formation B shot is canceled to throw your adversary off.

The strength of Strider's offense is only increased against a cornered target. Strider's dashing speed, long range, and substantial frame advantage can be used to corner his competitors and keep them cornered. Vajra M still crosses up cornered opponents and can be canceled from attack strings at any time to trick an adversary into guarding incorrectly. This can be mixed up with Vajra L, which looks similar to Vajra M when performed in the corner. If you find advancing guard to be a problem when trying to keep foes cornered, utilize Vajra L/M or the built-in dash feature of Ame-no-Murakumo M/H for constant pressure.

Start with a ground attack string ending with the Formation B satellite call. Follow this with another attack string ending in Ame-no-Murakumo L/M or Gram L, followed by the Formation B shot. Follow the Formation B shot with yet another ground string to apply pressure and build hyper meter!

Ouroboros: In Strider's signature attack, two satellites are summoned to orbit Strider during battle at the cost of three levels of hyper meter. Each satellite has active hit frames and can damage nearby foes. Pressing any (ATK) shoots one ring projectile from both satellites, and these can be fired rapidly as a combo. Strider is free to move, attack, and call crossover assists while Ouroboros is active.

You can use Ouroboros as a means to gain complete control of the match, leaving your opponent very few options. The rings have 3 low durability points and should be enough to clear out any opposing projectiles if fired rapidly. Vajra and Wall Cling are especially deadly during Ouroboros, since opponents are easily crossed up by the rings during these moves. Adversaries are forced to either run away or risk being crossed up during the storm of projectiles. Ouroboros is also an ideal way to employ instant overheads with air (L) CANCEL ↓↘→ + (L) and double jump air (H) (see the Advanced Tactics section for more details). Combined with X-Factor, Ouroboros is likely to K.O. a character or two.

Strider is not invulnerable to attacks during Ouroboros, however. Attacks that reach farther than the orbiting satellites are still able to hit Strider. During hitstun, the satellites have no active hit frames, making them useless while Strider is caught in a combo. Strider is also unable to fire rings while guarding or being hit. Even though Ouroboros is best used offensively, make sure to guard any incoming hyper combos that might be used in retaliation.

Ragnarok: Ragnarok causes Strider to dash toward his opponent for a devastating attack when it connects. At three levels of hyper meter, this hyper combo has 20 frames of invincibility on startup, is easily used in combos, and causes an unscaled 430,000 damage into a hard knockdown. Ragnarok is instant after the hyper combo flash, and it is immediately invincible. If performed at close range, the opposing character must be guarding before the hyper combo flashes, or else they will get hit. This invincibility is also great for plowing through an opposing hyper combo that is otherwise unavoidable.

COMBO USAGE

I. CR. Ⓜ, ST. Ⓗ, CR. Ⓗ, → + Ⓗ, Ⓢ CANCEL FORWARD SUPER JUMP, AIR Ⓜ, Ⓜ, Ⓗ CANCEL ↓ ↘ → + Ⓛ (3 HITS), LAND, FORWARD JUMP, AIR Ⓜ, Ⓗ CANCEL ↓ ↘ → + Ⓛ (3 HITS), LAND, Ⓢ CANCEL FORWARD SUPER JUMP, AIR Ⓜ, Ⓜ CANCEL FORWARD DOUBLE JUMP, Ⓗ, Ⓢ, LAND, ↓ ↘ → + ATK ATK

469,700 damage, 18% meter loss

Air ↓ ↘ → + Ⓛ must hit three times for the juggle after it to work.

II. (MIDSCREEN REQUIRED) CR. Ⓛ, Ⓜ, ST. Ⓗ, CR. Ⓗ, → + Ⓗ, Ⓢ CANCEL FORWARD SUPER JUMP, AIR Ⓜ CANCEL FORWARD DOUBLE JUMP, Ⓗ, Ⓢ, LAND, ↓ ↙ ← + Ⓢ, ↓ ↙ ← + Ⓢ, ↓ ↘ → + Ⓢ, WALL Ⓛ, Ⓜ, Ⓗ CANCEL → ↓ ↘ + Ⓗ, → ↓ ↘ + Ⓛ CANCEL ↓ ↘ → + ATK ATK

543,500 damage, 27% meter loss

The opposing character cannot be much closer than midscreen from the corner for this combo to work. Double jumping after air Ⓜ and performing air Ⓗ, Ⓢ causes Strider to fall to the ground faster, giving you more time to summon Formation B and fire it. Firing it, performing the wall cling, and then attacking all must be done as fast as humanly possible for it to work.

III. (CORNER REQUIRED) CR. Ⓜ, ST. Ⓗ, CR. Ⓗ, → + Ⓗ, Ⓢ CANCEL FORWARD SUPER JUMP, AIR Ⓜ CANCEL FORWARD DOUBLE JUMP, Ⓗ, Ⓢ, LAND, ↓ ↙ ← + Ⓢ, BACKWARDS DASH, ↓ ↙ ← + Ⓢ, FORWARD DASH, Ⓢ CANCEL FORWARD SUPER JUMP, AIR Ⓜ, Ⓜ CANCEL DOUBLE JUMP, Ⓗ, Ⓢ, LAND, ↓ ↘ → + ATK ATK

489,400 damage, 33% meter loss

Backdashing before firing Formation B ensures that the projectile hits late, giving you time to juggle after it. This will not work otherwise because of hitstun decay.

IV. (MIDSCREEN REQUIRED, FORMATION B SUMMONED) CR. Ⓜ, ST. Ⓗ, CR. Ⓗ, → + Ⓗ CANCEL → ↓ ↘ + Ⓛ CANCEL ↓ ↙ ← + Ⓢ, ↓ ↘ → + Ⓢ, WALL Ⓛ, Ⓜ, Ⓗ CANCEL → ↓ ↘ + Ⓗ, → ↓ ↘ + Ⓛ CANCEL ↓ ↘ → + ATK ATK

588,400 damage, 49% meter loss

You must start with Formation B summoned for this to work. The positioning for this combo is less strict than **Combo II**, as your opponent can be slightly closer to the corner than midscreen for it to work.

V. (REQUIRES MIDSCREEN) FORWARD JUMP, FORWARD DOUBLE JUMP, AIR Ⓗ, Ⓢ, LAND, CR. Ⓗ, → + Ⓗ, Ⓢ CANCEL FORWARD SUPER JUMP, AIR Ⓜ CANCEL DOUBLE JUMP, Ⓗ, Ⓢ, LAND, ↓ ↙ ← + Ⓢ, ↓ ↙ ← + Ⓢ, ↓ ↘ → + Ⓢ, WALL Ⓛ, Ⓜ, Ⓗ CANCEL → ↓ ↘ + Ⓗ, LAND → ↓ ↘ + Ⓛ CANCEL ↓ ↘ → + ATK ATK

541,000 damage, 26% meter loss

Double tapping ↗, ↗ quickly causes Strider to perform a shallow double jump very close to the ground. This mimics a very low jump that allows for near instant overhead jump attacks at close distances. This example shows a midscreen combo. Near corners, continue the combo after air Ⓗ, Ⓢ hits with something similar to **Combo III**.

ADVANCED TACTICS

NINJA 101: DOUBLE JUMPS

Strider's double jump stops any aerial momentum, performing instead a small jump either forward, backward, or straight up. Because the double jump covers less distance both vertically and horizontally, you can use it for tricky cross-up setups!

After performing Vajra L or M, fall with air Ⓛ. Right as your adversary guards it, immediately cancel the air Ⓛ into a double jump forward delayed air Ⓗ for a cross-up. The speed in which the air Ⓛ is canceled into the double jump paired with the tremendous hitbox of air Ⓗ make this cross-up extremely difficult for competitors to react to. If your opponent becomes accustomed to this setup, try changing it up by double jumping straight up instead, or falling from Vajra into a crouching Ⓛ to counter advancing guard.

Another way to utilize Strider's double jump is by performing a normal jump forward and immediately performing a double jump forward with air Ⓗ, Ⓢ. If performed successfully, the huge hitbox of air Ⓗ acts as an instant overhead against all characters, large or small. The timing used in this technique is similar to that of a forward dash: press ↗ ↗ in the same way you would press → → for a ground dash. The tighter the timing on your double jump is, the faster your air Ⓗ attacks overhead.

A-CLASS STRIDERS ONLY: MOMENTUM

Strider is unique in that the momentum he gains from his dashes is much greater than any other character. If you perform a forward ground dash and immediately cancel it into a crouch, you can see that momentum in motion. You can utilize this momentum to dramatically increase the range on some of Strider's attacks. Adding in a → → input right before performing ↙ + Ⓗ increases the slide's range to nearly fullscreen! The same treatment can be given to attacks such as standing Ⓗ or → + Ⓗ to increase their range. You can use the same principle when normal jumping forward, as well; adding a dash right before a forward jump causes Strider to cover a greater distance than without the dash.

Strider's standing Ⓗ has great range. However…

…its range can be further increased with the help of a forward dash!

VI. (AGAINST AIRBORNE ENEMY) FORWARD JUMP, AIR Ⓜ, Ⓜ, Ⓗ CANCEL ↓↘→ + Ⓛ, LAND, ST. Ⓜ, Ⓢ CANCEL FORWARD SUPER JUMP, AIR Ⓜ CANCEL FORWARD DOUBLE JUMP, AIR Ⓜ, Ⓗ, Ⓢ, LAND, ↓↙← + Ⓢ, ↓↙← + Ⓢ, ↓↘→ + Ⓢ, WALL Ⓛ, Ⓜ, Ⓗ CANCEL →↓↘ + Ⓗ, →↓↘ + Ⓛ CANCEL ↓↘→ + ATK ATK

488,500 damage, 24% meter loss

This is a midscreen combo starting off the low jump instant overhead trick. The jump attacks cannot be done as quickly as possible against very small crouching characters, like Rocket Raccoon, Amaterasu, and Morrigan.

VII. FRONT OR BACK THROW, ↓↙← + Ⓢ, ↓↙← + Ⓢ, ↓↘→ + Ⓢ, WALL Ⓛ, Ⓜ, Ⓗ CANCEL →↓↘ + Ⓗ, →↓↘ + Ⓛ CANCEL ↓↘→ + ATK ATK

411,500 damage, 57% meter loss

After Strider lands from the throw, you must summon and fire Formation B as quickly as possible.

VIII. FRONT OR BACK AIR THROW, ↓↙← + Ⓢ, ↓↙← + Ⓢ, FORWARD DASH, Ⓢ CANCEL FORWARD SUPER JUMP, AIR Ⓜ CANCEL FORWARD DOUBLE JUMP, Ⓗ, Ⓢ, LAND, ↓↘→ + ATK ATK

372,200 damage, 67% meter loss

Again, you must summon and fire Formation B as rapidly as possible for it to OTG properly.

IX. (REQUIRES MIDSCREEN) CR. Ⓛ, Ⓜ, ST. Ⓗ, CR. Ⓗ, → + Ⓗ, Ⓢ CANCEL FORWARD SUPER JUMP, AIR Ⓜ CANCEL FORWARD DOUBLE JUMP, Ⓗ, Ⓢ, LAND, ↓↙← + Ⓢ, ↓↙← + Ⓢ, ↓↘→ + Ⓢ, WALL Ⓛ, Ⓜ, Ⓗ CANCEL →↓↘ + Ⓗ, →↓↘ + Ⓛ CANCEL ↓↘→ + ATK ATK CANCEL X-FACTOR, ←↓↙ + Ⓗ, LAND, ↓↘→ + ATK ATK

716,900 damage, 120% meter loss

Here's an X-Factor combo that tacks on additional damage to **Combo I** when you need it and leaves a lot of X-Factor time left over for the next challenger if the previous is KO'd. Be sure to activate X-Factor just as you perform the first hyper combo to ensure its damage is buffed. Wait until about half of the robo animals hit, then perform ←↓↙ + Ⓗ. When Strider lands from Vajra, cancel its landing period into ↓↘→ + ATK ATK to ensure that the animals OTG in time.

X. CR. Ⓜ, ST. Ⓗ, → + Ⓗ CANCEL X-FACTOR, ST. Ⓗ, → + Ⓗ CANCEL →↓↘ + Ⓜ, ↓↘→ + Ⓗ, Ⓢ CANCEL FORWARD SUPER JUMP, AIR Ⓜ, Ⓜ CANCEL FORWARD DOUBLE JUMP, Ⓗ, Ⓢ, LAND, ↓↙← + Ⓢ, ↓↙← + Ⓢ, FORWARD DASH, Ⓢ FORWARD SUPER JUMP, AIR Ⓜ, Ⓜ CANCEL FORWARD DOUBLE JUMP, Ⓗ, Ⓢ, LAND, ↓↘→ + ATK ATK

771,500~941,600 damage, 5~32% meter gain

Omit ↓↘→ + Ⓗ when near corners.

STRIDER

NEW

COMBO APPENDIX

GENERAL EXECUTION TIPS

- Being able to perform two consecutive ↓↙← + Ⓢ motions is important to playing as Strider. Learn to time the second ↓↙← + Ⓢ so that the satellite is launched as fast as possible
- If you are having problems with Wall Cling Ⓛ, Ⓜ, Ⓗ, try chaining the three attacks slower. Inputting this combo too quickly prevents it from working properly

AS STRIDER COMES IN: AIR Ⓜ, Ⓜ CANCEL FORWARD DOUBLE JUMP, Ⓜ, Ⓗ CANCEL →↓↘ + Ⓛ

Notes	Damage
⇧ + Ⓢ or ⇨ + Ⓢ or ⇩ + Ⓢ TAC to Strider. Near corners, omit all Ⓜ attacks and just do Ⓗ CANCEL ⇨⇩⇘ + Ⓛ	Varies based on damage scaling

CR. Ⓛ, Ⓜ, ST. Ⓗ, CR. Ⓗ, → + Ⓗ, Ⓢ CANCEL FORWARD SUPER JUMP, AIR Ⓜ CANCEL FORWARD DOUBLE JUMP, Ⓗ, Ⓢ, LAND, ↓↙← + Ⓢ, ↓↙← + Ⓢ, ↓↘→ + Ⓢ, WALL Ⓛ, Ⓜ, Ⓗ (LET DIVE KICK FALL VERY CLOSE TO THE GROUND) CANCEL →↓↘ + Ⓗ, LAND, ↓↙← + Ⓢ, →↓↘ + Ⓛ CANCEL ↓↙← + Ⓢ, ←↓↙ + Ⓗ, CANCEL ↓↘→ + ATK ATK

Notes	Damage
—	559,300 damage, 12% meter loss

CR. Ⓜ, ST. Ⓗ, CR. Ⓗ, → + Ⓗ CANCEL →↓↘ + Ⓛ CANCEL ↓↙← + Ⓢ, ↓↘→ + Ⓢ, WALL Ⓛ, Ⓜ, Ⓗ (LET DIVE KICK FALL VERY CLOSE TO THE GROUND) CANCEL →↓↘ + Ⓗ, LAND, ↓↙← + Ⓢ, →↓↘ + Ⓛ CANCEL ↓↙← + Ⓢ, ←↓↙ + Ⓗ, LAND ↓↘→ + ATK ATK

Notes	Damage
Midscreen required, Formation B must already be summoned	615,800 damage, 26% meter loss

FRONT OR BACK THROW, ↓↙← + Ⓢ, ↓↙← + Ⓢ, ↓↘→ + Ⓢ, WALL Ⓛ, Ⓜ, Ⓗ (LET DIVE KICK FALL VERY CLOSE TO THE GROUND) CANCEL →↓↘ + Ⓗ, LAND, ↓↙← + Ⓢ, →↓↘ + Ⓛ CANCEL ↓↙← + Ⓢ, ←↓↙ + Ⓗ, LAND ↓↘→ + ATK ATK

Notes	Damage
After clinging to the wall, perform then Ⓛ, Ⓜ, Ⓗ chain, then as Ⓗ falls, cancel it just before the kick touches the ground. This reduces the recovery of ⇨⇩⇘ + Ⓗ, allowing you to fit in ⇩⇙⇦ + Ⓢ before the next juggle	430,400 damage, 44% meter loss

NEW

VERGIL

"POWER... I NEED MORE POWER..."

Bio

REAL NAME
Vergil

OCCUPATION
Dark Knight

ABILITIES
In addition to his super-human powers, he is also a skilled swordsman. Similar to Dante, his Devil Trigger allows him to transform for a limited time and gain access to demonic powers.

WEAPONS
Devil Arm "Yamato," which is a katana he inherited from his father, Sparda.

PROFILE
Son of the Legendary Dark Knight Sparda and Dante's twin brother. Vergil blames himself for not having been able to protect his mother at a young age, and believes that power is everything. Unlike Dante, he has embraced his demonic heritage and is willing to do whatever it takes to gain absolute power.

FIRST APPEARANCE
Devil May Cry 3 (2005)

POWER GRID

3	INTELLIGENCE
4	STRENGTH
3	SPEED
6	STAMINA
4	ENERGY PROJECTION
6	FIGHTING ABILITY

*This is biographical, and does not represent an evaluation of the in-game combat potential of this hero.

ALTERNATE COSTUMES

Overview

Vitality	850,000
Chain Combo Archetype	Marvel Series

X-Factor Boost	Damage	Speed
Level 1 (3 teammates remaining)	125%	115%
Level 2 (2 teammates remaining)	150%	120%
Level 3 (1 teammate remaining)	175%	125%

Your goal with Vergil is to set up a cross-up attempt. Why is this so important?

- **Rapid Slash hits the opposing character's backside from almost any position and leads to massive combos when canceled into Devil Trigger**
- **Trick Down teleports directly behind your adversary from any distance, while Trick teleports to their front; both can be used in combination with assists to sandwich your foe into an ambiguous side switch guessing game**
- **When meter is abundant, you can always force a guaranteed K.O. after a successful cross-up via Vergil's Dark Angel hyper combo**

How can you achieve this goal?

- **Use safe pressure stemming from standing Ⓗ, air Ⓜ, Stinger, and Judgment Cut to limit your adversary's mobility—this hinders their ability to jump and dash toward you, ultimately making it easier to keep them grounded for a cross-up attempt**
- **Force your opponent to block long range ➪ + Ⓗ while you call an assist to lock your rival down, and then cancel into Trick, Trick Down, or Rapid Slash**
- **Throw Round-Trip to lock your competitor in guardstun, then teleport next to them with Trick or Trick Down**
- **Activate Spiral Swords and teleport in with Trick or Trick Down**

Attack Set

Standing Basic Attacks

Screen	Command	Hits	Damage	Meter Gain	Startup	Active	Recovery	Advantage on Hit	Advantage if Guarded	Notes
1	Standing Ⓛ	1	40,000/48,000	320	6/6	3/3	12/10	-1/+1	-3/-1	—
2	Standing Ⓜ	8	60,000/72,000	480	8/7	3/3	23/20	-7/-4	-8/-5	—
3	Standing Ⓗ	1	85,000/102,000	680	10/9	3/3	33/29	-12/-8	-13/-9	—

Crouching Basic Attacks

Screen	Command	Hits	Damage	Meter Gain	Startup	Active	Recovery	Advantage on Hit	Advantage if Guarded	Notes
1	Crouching Ⓛ	1	45,000/54,000	360	5/5	2/2	16/14	-4/-2	-6/-4	Low attack
2	Crouching Ⓜ	1	63,000/75,600	504	8/7	2/2	24/21	-7/-4	-8/-5	Low attack
3	Crouching Ⓗ	1	80,000/96,000	640	12/11	3/3	26/22	—	-6/-2	Low attack, knocks down

Ground Special Attack—Launcher

Screen	Command	Hits	Damage	Meter Gain	Startup	Active	Recovery	Advantage on Hit	Advantage if Guarded	Notes
1	Ⓢ (while standing or crouching)	1	90,000/108,000	720	10/9	4/4	32/28	—	-13/-9	Launcher, not special- or hyper combo-cancelable

Air Basic Attacks

Screen	Command	Hits	Damage	Meter Gain	Startup	Active	Recovery	Advantage on Hit	Advantage if Guarded	Notes
1	Air Ⓛ	1	43,000/51,600	344	6/6	2/2	18/15	+12	+10	Overhead attack
2	Air Ⓜ	1	65,000/78,000	520	8/7	3/3	21/19	+17	+16	Overhead attack
3	Air Ⓗ	1	88,000/105,600	704	11/10	2/2	23/20	+19	+18	Overhead attack

Air Special Attacks—Flying Screen and Air Exchange

Air (S) causes a hard knockdown when used in a launcher combo (this is sometimes called flying screen). When used outside of a launcher combo, air (S) behaves mostly like another basic attack. Air exchange attacks, performed by inputting a direction plus (S), are only possible during a launcher combo. Exchange hits initiate team aerial combos by tagging in the next available character to continue the air combo.

Screen	Command	Hits	Damage	Meter Gain	Startup	Active	Recovery	Advantage on Hit	Advantage if Guarded	Notes
1	Air (S)	1	90,000/ 108,000	720	18/16	Until grounded	20/18	—	0	Causes hard knockdown if used in launcher combo, ground bounces foe
2	Air ⇧ + (S) (during launcher combo)	2	105,00/ 117,000	880	10/9	4/4	32/28	—	—	Tags in next available ally while lofting opponent upward
3	Air ⇨ or ⇦ + (S) (during launcher combo)	2	95,000/ 105,000	800	11/10	3/3	22/20	—	—	Tags in next available ally while causing wall bounce, erases 1 hyper meter bar from adversary
4	Air ⇩ + (S) (during launcher combo)	2	95,000/ 105,000	800	13/12	Until grounded	10/9	—	—	Tags in next available ally while causing ground bounce, generates 1 hyper meter bar

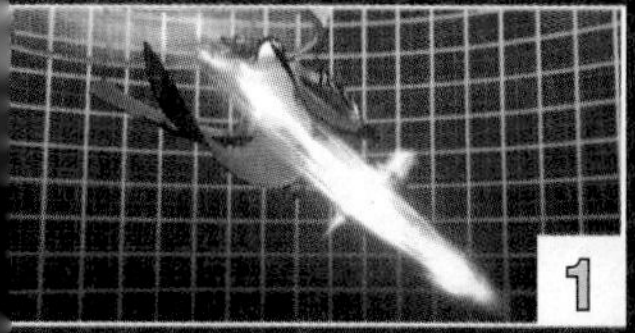
1

2

3

4

Command Attacks

Command attacks resemble basic attacks but have different chaining and canceling properties. It's usually possible to chain *into* a command attack from basic attacks, but most command attacks cannot be chained from or canceled themselves.

Screen	Name	Command	Hits	Damage	Meter Gain	Startup	Active	Recovery	Advantage on Hit	Advantage if Guarded	Notes
1	Stinger	⇨ + (H)	1	80,000/96,000	640	13/12	3/3	50/43	-29/-22	-30/-23	Wall bounces airborne foes
2	High Time	⇘ + (H)	1	100,000/120,000	800	9/8	10/9	31/27	0/+5	-17/-12	OTG-capable
3	Trick	(during High Time) (H)	—	—	—	11/10	5/5	10/8	—	—	Frames 11-15 (Devil Trigger: 10-14)invincible
4	Helmet Breaker	(in air) ⇩ + (H)	1	90,000/108,000	720	13/12	Until grounded + 2	18/16	—	0/+2	Hard knockdown
5	Trick L	(during Helmet Breaker) (L)	—	—	—	14/13	11/9	11/10	—	—	Frames 14-24(Devil Trigger: 13-21) invincible
6	Trick M	(during Helmet Breaker) (M)	—	—	—	16/15	7/6	13/11	—	—	Frames 15-22 (Devil Trigger: 15-20) invincible
7	Trick H	(during Helmet Breaker) (H)	—	—	—	16/15	5/4	10/9	—	—	Frames 16-20 (Devil Trigger: 15-18) invincible
8	Upper Slash	(during (S) on contact) (H)	1	75,000/90,000	600	5/5	3/3	28/24	—	-8/-4	Ground bounces opponent, chains into (S)

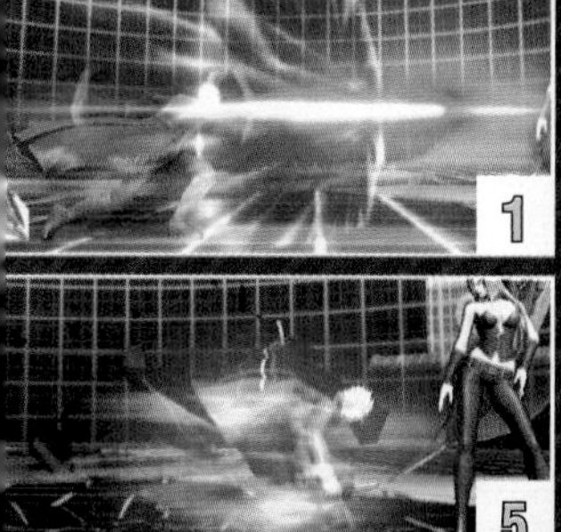
1

2

3

4

5

6

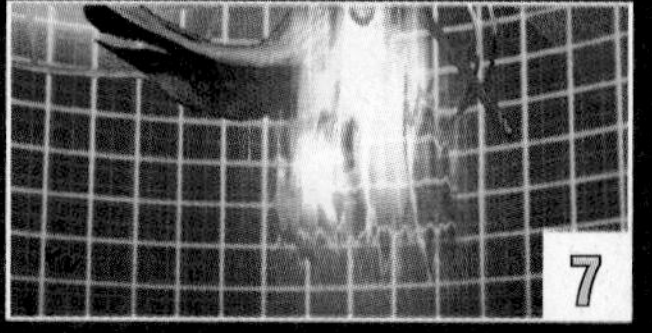
7

8

Throws

Throws are for snagging passive or blocking opponents. Since throws are active so quickly, you can also use them to preemptively toss opposing characters out of their offense. Combos are usually possible after throws, one way or another.

Screen	Command	Hits	Damage	Meter Gain	Startup	Active	Notes
1	⇨ + (H) (ground)	2	80,000/96,000	800	1	1	Hard knockdown
	⇦ + (H) (ground)	1	80,000/96,000	800	1	1	Hard knockdown
2	⇨ + (H) (air)	5	80,000/96,000	800	1	1	Hard knockdown
	⇦ + (H) (air)	5	80,000/96,000	800	1	1	Hard knockdown

1

2

As a Partner—Crossover Assists

Screen	Type	P1+P2 Crossover Combination Hyper Combo	Description	Hits	Damage	Meter Gain	Startup	Active	Recovery (this crossover assist)	Recovery (other partner)	Notes
1	Vergil—α	Dimension Slash	Judgment Cut	5	122,600/ 147,300	1200	49/44	—	121/111	91/81	Knocks down, projectile has 5 low priority durability points, projectile active for 30 frames
2	Vergil—β	Dimension Slash	Rising Sun	2	50,000 + 80,000/ 60,000 + 96,000	400 + 640	33/30	3(14)4/ 3(12)4	122/110	92/80	Brief spinning knockdown, air recovery
3	Vergil—γ	Dimension Slash	Rapid Slash	5	143,200/ 171,900	1400	52/48	16/14	123/111	93/81	First 3 projectiles have 99 low priority durability points, last projectile has 5 low priority durability points

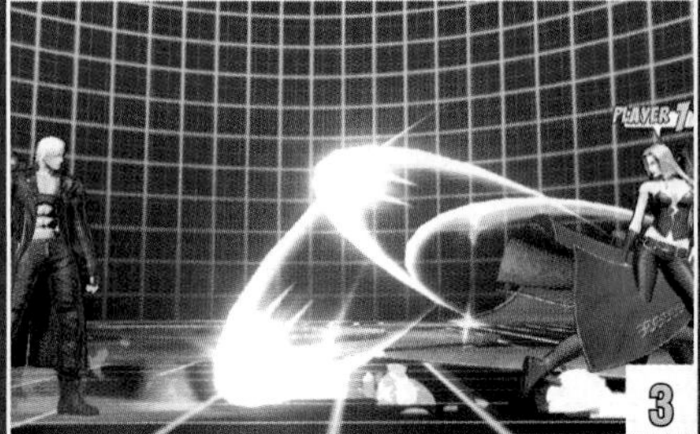

Vergil is great as a crossover assist. Vergil—β is decent for combos but lacks invincibility to be safely used as anti-air. Vergil—α is decent for helping offensive pressure and has good durability. Vergil—γ passes through opponents and can set up long-range hyper combos. If guarded, your rival is pushed to the far end of the screen, making it great for creating breathing space.

Snap Back

Screen	Command	Hits	Damage	Meter Gain	Startup	Active	Recovery	Advantage on Hit	Advantage if Guarded
1	↓↙← + P1 or P2	1	50,000	500 (-1 hyper meter bar)	2	3	33	—	-13

Notes

On hit, snap back forces the opposing point character to be replaced by an assist. Opposing assist calls or tag outs are also locked out for 4 seconds

"I AM A SON OF SPARDA, THE LEGENDARY DARK KNIGHT. YOU NEVER STOOD A CHANCE AGAINST ME."

Special Moves

Screen	Name	Command	Hits	Damage	Meter Gain	Startup	Active	Recovery	Advantage on Hit	Advantage if Guarded	Notes
1, 2, 3	Judgment Cut	↓↘→ + ATK	5	122,600/ 147,300	1200	25/22	—	30/26	—	+8/+12	Knocks down, projectile has 5 low priority durability points, active for 30 frames (Devil Trigger: 27)
4	Rising Sun	→↓↘ + L	2	50,000 + 80,000/ 60,000 + 96,000	400 + 640	9/8	5(12)4/ 5(10)4	30/26	+11/+15	-11/-7	Brief spinning knockdown, air recovery
5	Trick	(during Rising Sun) H	—	—	—	11/10	5/5	10/8	—	—	Frames 11-15 (Devil Trigger: 10-14) invincible
6	Lunar Phase	→↓↘ + M	9	25,000 x 8 + 50,000/ 28,600 x 8 + 60,000	200x 8 + 400	15/14	36(9)6/ 31(10)5	24/20	—	-7/-2	Ground bounces foe, hard knockdown
7	Rapid Slash	→↓↘ + H	5	143,200/ 171,900	1400	28/26	16/14	32/27	—	-8/-3	Knocks down, 4 projectiles with 5 low priority durability points each, each projectile active for 7 frames
8	Trick	↓↙← + L	—	—	—	14/13	11/9	11/10	—	—	Frames 14-24 (Devil Trigger: 13-21) invincible
9	Trick Down	↓↙← + M	—	—	—	16/15	7/6	13/11	—	—	Frames 16-22 (Devil Trigger: 15-20) invincible
10	Trick Up	↓↙← + H	—	—	—	16/15	5/4	10/9	—	—	Frames 16-20 (Devil Trigger: 15-18) invincible
11	Round-Trip (in air OK)	ATK (hold down for 90 frames)	17	20,000/ 24,000 per hit	160 per hit	30/27	—	15/13	+90/80	+89/+79	Projectile has 5 low priority durability points, active for 80/68 frames

Judgment Cut: Vergil takes a step back and performs a ranged slice attack. The strength of the button pressed determines the distance from which the flurry of slices appears: L attacks directly in front of Vergil, H appears about 4/5 of a full screen away, and M is right in between. Judgment Cut behaves more like a projectile than a melee attack, similar to Dormammu's Dark Hole. It has 5 points of low priority durability, making it possible to stop standard opposing projectiles.

Judgment Cut is great as a defensive attack and as a means of safe pressure. A well-timed Judgment Cut M or H cannot be punished by your opponent unless telegraphed. So long as the sphere makes contact with your rival, they will be hard-pressed to retaliate effectively. You can use Judgment Cut L to end blockstrings safely, such as after guarded standing H or Stinger.

During Devil Trigger, the size of the Judgment Cut sphere is increased dramatically.

Rising Sun and Trick: Vergil performs a pair of aerial kicks. Inputting H right after the second kick hits causes Vergil to perform Trick back down to the ground. Rising Sun is an integral part of Vergil's combos, so getting used to canceling it from Stinger is important for Vergil players. You can use the Trick cancel as a means to cut Rising Sun's recovery time, allowing for a combo. Upon Trick's recovery, immediately super jump forward with air M, H, S into a ground bounce for a continued combo opportunity (so long as you haven't used a ground bounce previously in the combo). If Rising Sun is blocked, perform Trick for a quick getaway. Only extremely quick attacks like throws or three-frame startup L attacks can punish the teleport.

During Devil Trigger, the hitbox on Rising Sun is increased dramatically, making it more viable to be used on its own.

Lunar Phase: Vergil flips forward with a slash, reminiscent of Dante. When successful, the opposing character is ground bounced and can be attacked further for a combo. It is possible to use this attack as a combo variation in Vergil's bread and butter combos. Unfortunately, Vergil floats high into the air for Lunar Phase, causing it to whiff easily against most crouching adversaries, even on hit. It is also easily punished when guarded.

During Devil Trigger, Lunar Phase's hitbox is increased, making it more likely to hit properly.

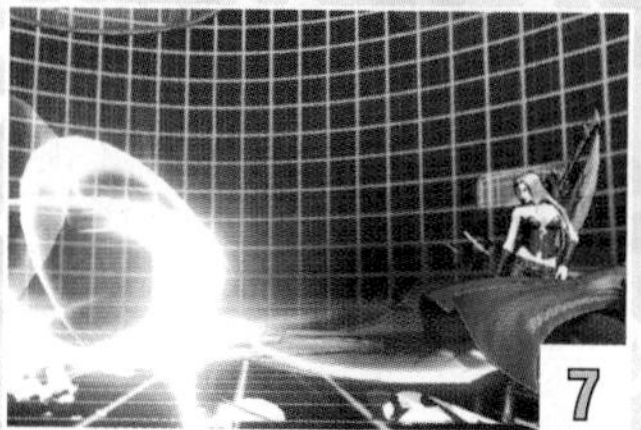

Rapid Slash: Vergil dashes through his rival and is followed by a flurry of sword slices for a cross-up and soft knockdown. Rapid Slash is difficult to guard on reaction (especially if performed unexpectedly) and can be used from close to mid range to cross foes up. You can cancel it into Devil Trigger for a powered up combo on hit or as a safety measure when the slash is guarded. If the opponent guards correctly, they are sucked in toward Vergil and can then punish him extremely easily. Remedy this situation by calling a crossover assist right before performing Rapid Slash to cover Vergil while he is recovering. You can also cancel a successfully landed Rapid Slash into Dimension Slash for easy damage. Note that only the last hit of Rapid Slash knocks your rivals off their feet; if Rapid Slash is canceled early into X-Factor, the foe gets sucked in toward Vergil in a standing state, ready for a possible K.O. combo!

Performing Rapid Slash during Devil Trigger increases its hitbox, giving it more vertical range.

Trick, Trick Down, and Trick Up: Performing Trick L causes Vergil to teleport and reappear directly in front of his opponent. Trick is a great way to cancel the recovery of special moves to allow for extended combos, as in the instance of Stinger or Rising Sun. Without Trick, you cannot follow the wall bounce from Stinger with any basic attacks. You can also employ Trick as a fake out for competitors expecting the cross-up of Trick Down. Train the opposing player to watch for Trick Down, and catch them off guard with Trick.

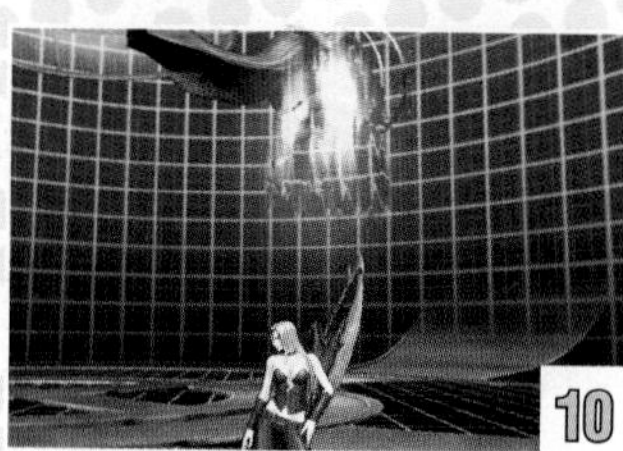

Trick Down places Vergil directly behind his adversary horizontally. Trick Down is great for cross-ups when used in tandem with crossover assists, or for escaping a big punish after a guarded attack. Trick Down is also useful for punishing long range attacks or slower hyper combos. Vergil's combos deal a heavy amount of damage, so opponents must always play cautiously with the constant threat of Trick Down. Don't become too predictable, however, since all versions of Trick can be punished upon recovery if opposing players react to the move with haste.

Trick Up sends Vergil directly above his rival, regardless of their current height. Afterward, Vergil is in a jumping state in which attacks can be performed, guarding is available, and crossover assists may be called. You can use a crossover assist in this situation to make a simultaneous ↓ + H Helmet Breaker safe if guarded. Trick Up is also available after certain special moves to reduce recovery time. You can mix it with the other two to get the drop on opponents unexpectedly. Be careful of abusing this move against characters who can land full combos off air throws, as the recovery on this teleport is very susceptible to a well-timed air throw.

Round-Trip: Round-Trip is a boomerang-like projectile that fires across the screen and back for a two-phase attack. Perform this move by holding any ATK input until Vergil's hand begins to glow. This attack can be charged even before the round begins! When launched, the projectile is constantly active, and can reach upwards of 15 hits. After the launch recovery, Vergil is able to move and attack freely, and you can follow the hits of Round-Trip for a combo or add to it with Judgment Cut. For the most damage, your opponent must get hit at mid range or so, ensuring hits from both the launch and the return. In the second phase of the attack, the sword tracks to Vergil's position, disappearing once it comes into contact with him. Given this, the projectile can be stalled a short time by performing Trick Down right before it comes back to Vergil, prolonging its screen time. Executing Trick while Round-Trip is out has the added benefit of making your teleport safe; varying between Trick L and M mounts a confusing side switch offense that's safe to enemy retaliation because of Round-Trip's presence. You can also use it as a combo variation, but its damage output is very low.

During Devil Trigger, the Round-Trip projectile is given an increase in size, making it more difficult to avoid.

Hyper Combos

Screen	Name	Command	Hits	Damage	Startup	Active	Recovery	Advantage on Hit	Advantage if Guarded	Notes
1	Dimension Slash (in air OK)	↓↘→ + ATK ATK	41 (varies)	341,000	8+3	106	65	—	-59	Hard knockdown, each projectile has 5 high priority durability points
2	Spiral Swords	→↓↘ + ATK ATK	18	15,000 per hit	13+1	—	10	—	—	Each sword has beam durability: 3 frames x 5 high priority durability frames, lasts 180 frames
3	Sword Storm	(during Spiral Swords) ↓↘→ + S	6	50,000 per hit	5	—	5	—	—	Burns 1 bar of meter, swords hover above foe for 190 frames before striking, each projectile has 5 high priority durability points, 1 projectile becomes active after 146 frames followed by 5 more every 20 frames afterwards
4	Blistering Swords (in air OK)	(during Spiral Swords) ATK + S	6	60,000 per hit	3	—	2	—	—	Burns 1 bar of meter, each projectile has 5 high priority durability point,
5	Summoned Swords (in air OK)	(during Blistering Swords) ATK + S	1	60,000	1	—	4	+27	+26	Projectile active after on frame 9, projectile has 5 high priority durability points
6	Devil Trigger	↓↙← + ATK ATK	—	—	6+0	—	4	—	—	Frames 3-6 invincible, Vergil gains a 15% speed increase and 20% damage increase, Vergil gains double jump and airdash, lasts 600 frames
7	Dark Angel (Level 3 Hyper Combo)	(during Devil Trigger) ↓↙← + ATK ATK	35	610,000	6+5	8	42	—	-27	Frames 1-19 invincible, crumples opponent, hard knockdown, OTG-capable

1

Dimension Slash: Vergil flies across the screen repeatedly, filling the screen with countless Judgment Cuts for a hard knockdown. Dimension Slash is Vergil's main combo ender, and it can inflict anywhere from a moderate to heavy amount of damage depending on the opposing character's position and size. It is typically canceled from High Time (which is performed with ↘ + H), Judgement Cut, or Rapid Slash. You can perform two of these in the air consecutively with the help of an aerial X-Factor activation, which is great for situations where you have both the point character and a crossover assist character caught in your combo!

Due to the random nature of Dimension Slash, enemies will sometimes get caught by an extra hit towards the end of the hyper combo, delaying their fall to the ground. If you see this occur, you can perform High Time OTG into another Dimension Slash as soon as you recover from the first Dimension Slash. With some luck and several bars of hyper meter, you can link together multiple Dimension Slashes for a substantial amount of damage.

For a sneaky trick, Dimension Slash can be performed with a tiger knee motion (↓↘→↗ + ATK ATK) right next to your opponent for a cross-up. You must be literally right next to your adversary for this to work properly; otherwise it can be guarded normally. Only attempt this against foes who you know for sure are unaware of this cross-up gimmick!

2

Spiral Swords: Vergil summons six floating swords to rotate around him, similar to Strider's Ouroboros. Foes within range suffer from a multi-hitting stream of sword attacks, while Vergil can continue attacking freely. Spiral Swords is great to use with Trick and Trick Down since the swords reappear with Vergil even before the teleport has recovered. Even though combos started from Spiral Swords suffer from heavy damage scaling, this hyper combo is still overwhelming for your opponent to deal with. When Spiral Swords is activated, your rival can only hope to attack safely from far away, so you can use this opportunity to look for chances to punish long range attacks with Trick Down.

Even though melee attacks are difficult to land on Vergil when Spiral Swords is activated, he is not invincible at any time during its activation or duration. Furthermore, the swords disappear as soon as Vergil is hit by any attack. Don't waste your hyper meter with a predictable Spiral Swords activation only to have it stuffed by an incoming attack!

3

Sword Storm: Performed during Spiral Swords, the swords reappear above the opposing character, creating a crown of swords ready to strike. After a short period of time, the swords begin to rain down automatically, interrupting whatever your adversary may be doing. Performing Sword Storm requires another bar of hyper meter, essentially making Spiral Swords to Sword Storm a level 2 hyper combo. The swords do not attack in a stream like Spiral Swords, so they do not combo on their own. However, each sword can easily be used as a means to start a damaging combo. Perform Trick Down right before the swords launch for a cross-up that is unguardable on reaction!

Unlike Spiral Swords, Sword Storm will not disappear if Vergil is hit by an attack. The only way the swords will disappear is if Vergil leaves the playing field (via crossover attack, THC, etc.) or if Vergil is knocked out. You can use this to your advantage by playing riskier while Sword Storm is active, since any retaliation will be met with a shower of swords.

Note that the timing in which Sword Storm is activated has no bearing on its duration. The swords always launch at the same time, regardless if you activated Sword Storm during the beginning or end of Spiral Swords. Maximize your meter spent by performing Sword Storm as late as possible!

4

5

Blistering Swords and Summoned Swords: Like Sword Storm, Blistering Swords can only be performed during Spiral Swords, and it requires one bar of hyper meter. Blistering Swords is also similar to Sword Storm in that it automatically launches projectiles after a certain amount of time directly in front of Vergil. Unlike Sword Storm, the swords during Blistering Swords combo naturally on their own, though the top swords sail over smaller characters at ground level. A well-timed Trick Down during Blistering Swords causes a tricky cross-up; swords released before Trick are coming from behind the target, after Vergil has swapped sides!

For players who are too impatient for the swords to launch during Blistering Swords, S + ATK can be input to perform Summoning Swords, which shoots each sword individually. S + L fires a sword straight ahead, S + M fire upwards at an angle, and S + H fires downwards at an angle, making it ideal to use from the air. Summoned Swords has almost no recovery, and you can fire the swords at a rapid rate both on the ground and in the air. The speed that the projectiles are released makes it great for combos, or as a defensive measure against aggressive opponents. Using Summoned Swords defensively can be worthwhile since the floating swords have no active hitbox, unlike Spiral Swords.

The duration of Blistering Swords is not affected by the timing in which you perform it during Spiral Swords. Get the most out of your meter by performing it as late as possible during Spiral Swords.

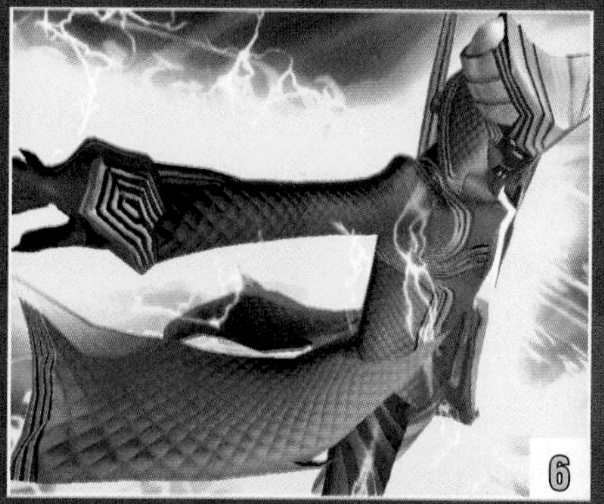

Devil Trigger: A signature move of Vergil's, Devil Trigger grants Vergil several improvements: a damage increase of 15%, health regeneration, a double jump and airdash, and increased speed. Having Devil Trigger activated also increases the hitboxes of Judgment Cut, Rapid Slash, Round-Trip, Lunar Phase, and Rising Sun. Devil Trigger can used both to start or finish a team hyper combo, and the move is great for making slow recovering attacks safe that are otherwise punishable, such as Stinger and Rapid Slash. It can be canceled into during most combo situations, improving the combo's overall damage. Gaining access to a double jump and airdash improve Vergil's mobility, and the airdashes travel fairly fast and far. Vergil retains these augmentations even as a crossover assist.

In addition to these benefits, Vergil also gains the ability to cancel whiffed basic attacks into special moves with Devil Trigger activated, something all other characters can normally do. This helps greatly, as whiffing an attack like Stinger results in huge recovery time.

Dark Angel: Dark Angel can only be performed while Devil Trigger is active (essentially making it a level 4 hyper combo), and it is performed with the same ↓ ↙ ← + ATK ATK input as Devil Trigger. Dark Angel not only causes tremendous damage (up there with Phoenix Wright's lv.3 hyper combo as the most damaging attacks in the game), but opponents are open to further attacks after being hit by it, guaranteeing a K.O. on most characters. You can use it to blow through an opposing hyper combo, since it has a lengthy window of invincibility on startup. This hyper combo is easily utilized in combos and is OTG- capable, as well. If hyper meter is not an issue, you should take advantage of any opportunity to land Dark Angel on a healthy adversary.

Battle Plan

Use Trick Down to get past long-range attacks.

Vergil's main strength lies in his cross-up game, his safe attacks, and his ability to be a relevant threat at any position on the screen. Opponents have to worry about Vergil's long range attacks, sneaky teleports, and high-priority basic attacks at all times. Vergil can transition from defense to offense easily, and any opening leads to any of Vergil's deadly combos. Mastering his offensive and defensive options and the range on his attacks are both key factors in playing Vergil effectively.

Vergil's main weakness lies in the slow recovery on several of his essential attacks, such as standing H and Stinger. Vergil takes his sweet time to sheath his sword after whiffing these attacks, leaving him vulnerable to severe punishment. Futhermore, Vergil is the only character in the game that is unable to cancel basic attacks and command attacks into special moves, making it imperative that your attacks at least come into contact with an enemy so that you can cancel into something safer such as Judgment Cut L. However, Vergil is still able to cancel whiffed attacks into hyper combos. If you react fast enough to a whiffed Stinger, for example, quickly cancel into Devil Trigger to regain control of Vergil. In addition, Devil Trigger grants the ability to cancel whiffed basic attacks and command attacks, so be sure to take advantage of this while Devil Trigger is active.

You have several options to choose from when attacking from a distance. If you've pre-charged Round-Trip, you can unleash it as soon as the round starts for a decent amount of chip damage or possible combo opportunity. You can harass your opponent with Judgment Cut H, and any successfully landed cut can be canceled into Dimension Slash for added damage. The hitstun on Judgment Cut is enough to comfortably hit-confirm into Dimension Slash. If competitors try to retaliate with ranged attacks of their own, use Trick Down to punish projectiles or slower recovering attacks. If you have a long range crossover assist at your disposal, you can use it with Trick Down for ambiguous cross-ups. Even if guarded, it's possible that the crossover assist can cover the teleport's recovery.

At mid to close range, Vergil's basic attacks come into play. Standing H has enormous range, and the sword hitbox does not trade hits with other character attacks. If used right after a forward dash, Vergil's swipe is able to reach more than halfway across the screen! You can then cancel this into Stinger into a massive combo. If you need something faster, standing M also has great range, albeit shorter than standing H.

This distance is also the perfect time for Stinger. Stinger is performed with ⇨ + H and can reach almost fullscreen with the help of a forward dash. Although it has quick startup considering its range, Vergil takes an awfully long time to sheath his sword thereafter, leaving him wide open for whatever punishment your rival plans to dish out! For this reason, Stinger must never be whiffed, since its recovery cannot be canceled into a special move if no contact with the opponent is made. If guarded, you can cancel into Trick Down for a great cross-up setup depending on your crossover assists. Input ⇨ + H + P1 or P2 canceled into Trick Down. This not only is great for cross-ups, but it can possibly make Stinger safe, as well. Another cross-up is Stinger canceled into Rapid Slash, which can be extremely difficult to block. Canceling into Judgment Cut, Rising Sun, or Devil Trigger are also great ways to mitigate Stinger's recovery. If Stinger connects, you can cancel into Rising Sun and continue to **Combo I** or into Devil Trigger to give your combo a welcome damage boost.

Vergil is fortunate to have two aerial attacks that are virtually safe if guarded. Helmet Breaker, performed with ⇩ + H in the air, stops Vergil's air trajectory and sends him straight down with a devastating sword attack. An input of L, M, or H right as Vergil touches the ground results in Trick, Trick Down, or Trick Up, respectively. Helmet Breaker is punishable by ground throws if guarded at a close distance, but the throw attempt can be avoided with a Trick cancel, causing your competitor to possibly whiff standing H instead. Cancel Helmet Breaker into Trick Up, and then follow it with yet another Helmet Splitter for a loop of aerial attacks! Combining this with a crossover assist call after Trick Up causes headaches for foes. If successfully connected, Helmet Breaker can then be followed with High Time into Dimension Slash, or Devil Trigger into Dark Angel if you have at least four bars of hyper meter.

Air S is another safe attack at your disposal. Coming down from the sky at an angle, air S causes a ground bounce on hit that can lead into a combo. It is often used in combos after air H and travels quickly after the initial startup. The higher altitude this attack is performed, the more horizontal range it covers. When in doubt, throw this move out for an easy combo attempt.

Rapid Slash and Trick Down still cross up on cornered opponents.

Keep in mind that both these air-to-ground attacks are susceptible to severe punishment via X-Factor activation upon an opponent's guard. Always take your challenger's remaining vitality, characters, and X-Factor availability in mind in calculating how likely it is for them blow their X-Factor to punish these attacks.

At close range, basic attack strings can be started with standing or crouching L. Standing L has great range and priority, and can be complemented with a forward dash at mid range to begin an offense. Crouching L doesn't quite have the range of standing L but must be guarded low. It is important to hit confirm using standing or crouching L, M rather than standing or crouching L, M, H because advancing guard will cause standing H to whiff, leaving you open to punishment because whiffed attacks cannot be canceled into a special move. Advancing guard will cause M to whiff after standing or crouching L only if the opponent uses advancing guard the first few frames of guarding L, which is nearly impossible to do on reaction. If your opponent tries to use advancing guard against your assault, cancel standing M into Stinger to get back close, then cancel Stinger into Judgment Cut L for safe pressure, Rapid Slash for a cross-up attempt, or Trick Up/Down with the help of a crossover assist to keep your offense flowing.

COMBO USAGE

I. CR. Ⓛ, Ⓜ, Ⓗ, → + Ⓗ CANCEL ↓ ↙ ← + Ⓛ, Ⓗ, Ⓢ CANCEL SUPER JUMP, AIR Ⓜ, Ⓜ, Ⓗ, ↓ + Ⓗ, LAND, {↘ + Ⓗ CANCEL Ⓗ CANCEL ↓ ↘ → + ATK ATK (MASH ATK)} OR {↓ ↙ ← + ATK ATK (DEVIL TRIGGER), ↓ ↙ ← + ATK ATK, FORWARD DASH, CR. Ⓗ CANCEL → ↓ ↘ + Ⓜ, ↘ + Ⓗ CANCEL Ⓗ CANCEL ↓ ↘ → + ATK ATK (MASH ATK)}

524,700~1,157,000 damage, 32%~268% meter loss

Here's a basic Vergil combo for beginners. After the OTG with ↘ + Ⓗ CANCEL Ⓗ, cancel to Dimension Slash afterward by hyper canceling Trick teleport while Vergil is still airborne. You can do this in one smooth motion by inputting ↘ + Ⓗ CANCEL ↓ ↘ → + ATK ATK ATK, which quickly activates the Trick teleport while also canceling it immediately.

Don't be wide-eyed about the second damage number; Vergil has to blow five meters to inflict that damage! It's usually worth knocking out opposing characters at any cost, but be mindful of how much hyper meter you're spending, depending on the circumstances and how many teammates Vergil has remaining.

II. CR. Ⓛ, Ⓜ, ST. Ⓗ, → + Ⓗ CANCEL → ↓ ↘ + Ⓛ CANCEL Ⓗ, AFTER LANDING FROM TRICK, IMMEDIATELY SUPER JUMP FORWARD, AIR Ⓜ, Ⓜ, Ⓗ, Ⓢ, LAND, ST. Ⓗ, → + Ⓗ CANCEL ↓ ↙ ← + Ⓛ, Ⓗ, Ⓢ CANCEL SUPER JUMP, AIR Ⓜ, Ⓜ, Ⓗ, ↓ + Ⓗ, LAND, {↘ + Ⓗ CANCEL Ⓗ CANCEL ↓ ↘ → + ATK ATK (MASH ATK)} OR {↓ ↙ ← + ATK ATK (DEVIL TRIGGER), ↓ ↙ ← + ATK ATK, FORWARD DASH, CR. Ⓗ CANCEL → ↓ ↘ + Ⓜ, ↘ + Ⓗ CANCEL Ⓗ CANCEL ↓ ↘ → + ATK ATK (MASH ATK)}

562,500~1,238,300 damage, 16% meter gain (or 459% meter loss!)

This is Vergil's standard combo. After landing → ↓ ↘ + Ⓛ CANCEL Ⓗ, Vergil recovers on the ground from Trick while the screen is still focused on super jump height, making it difficult to see when Vergil can act. There's no visual indicator for when you can have Vergil super jump, so you'll just have to practice the timing.

III. (AGAINST AIRBORNE OPPONENT) ST. Ⓛ, Ⓜ, Ⓗ CANCEL → ↓ ↘ + Ⓛ CANCEL Ⓗ, AFTER LANDING FROM TRICK, IMMEDIATELY SUPER JUMP FORWARD, AIR Ⓜ, Ⓜ, Ⓗ, Ⓢ, LAND, → + Ⓗ CANCEL ↓ ↙ ← + Ⓛ, Ⓗ, Ⓢ CANCEL SUPER JUMP, AIR Ⓜ, Ⓗ, ↓ + Ⓗ, LAND, {↘ + Ⓗ CANCEL Ⓗ CANCEL ↓ ↘ → + ATK ATK (MASH ATK)} OR {↓ ↙ ← + ATK ATK (DEVIL TRIGGER), ↓ ↙ ← + ATK ATK, FORWARD DASH, CR. Ⓗ CANCEL → ↓ ↘ + Ⓜ, ↘ + Ⓗ CANCEL Ⓗ CANCEL ↓ ↘ → + ATK ATK (MASH ATK)}

518,000~1,169,200 damage, 89% meter gain (or 478% meter loss)

The crouching opening attacks in **Combo II** hit low, which is necessary when varying between high and low attacks. However, Vergil's standing Ⓛ, standing Ⓜ opening is sometimes better because of its anti-air properties. This combo takes advantage of that, though at the expense of a small amount of damage.

IV. → ↓ ↘ + Ⓗ (3 HITS) CANCEL ↓ ↙ ← + ATK ATK (DEVIL TRIGGER), CR. Ⓜ, ST. Ⓗ, → + Ⓗ CANCEL → ↓ ↘ + Ⓛ CANCEL Ⓗ, AFTER LANDING FROM TRICK, IMMEDIATELY SUPER JUMP FORWARD, AIR Ⓜ, Ⓗ, Ⓢ, LAND, ST. Ⓗ, → + Ⓗ CANCEL ↓ ↙ ← + Ⓛ, Ⓗ, Ⓢ CANCEL SUPER JUMP, AIR Ⓜ, Ⓜ, Ⓗ, ↓ + Ⓗ, LAND, {↘ + Ⓗ CANCEL Ⓗ CANCEL ↓ ↘ → + ATK ATK (MASH ATK)} OR {↓ ↙ ← + ATK ATK (DEVIL TRIGGER), ↓ ↙ ← + ATK ATK, FORWARD DASH, CR. Ⓗ CANCEL → ↓ ↘ + Ⓜ, ↘ + Ⓗ CANCEL Ⓗ}

571,300~1,108,600 damage, 192~460% meter loss

V. THROW, {WAVEDASH FORWARD TWICE, ↘ + Ⓗ CANCEL Ⓗ CANCEL ↓ ↘ → + ATK ATK} OR {WHEN THE ENEMY IS CORNERED, ↓ ↙ ← + ATK ATK (DEVIL TRIGGER), ↓ ↙ ← + ATK ATK, ST. Ⓗ CANCEL → ↓ ↘ + Ⓛ CANCEL Ⓗ, AFTER LANDING FROM TRICK, IMMEDIATELY SUPER JUMP FORWARD, AIR Ⓜ, Ⓗ, Ⓢ, LAND, ST. Ⓗ, → + Ⓗ CANCEL ↓ ↙ ← + Ⓛ, Ⓗ, Ⓢ CANCEL SUPER JUMP, AIR Ⓗ, ↓ + Ⓗ, ↘ + Ⓗ CANCEL Ⓗ CANCEL ↓ ↘ → + ATK ATK

257,100~872,500 damage, 84~414% meter loss

The second combo is devastating, but it costs five meters to perform, exhausting your resources immediately. After the corner throw, you must time the shift into Devil Trigger and then the level 3 hyper combo as quickly as possible, or it will whiff entirely. This is exceedingly difficult to do unless you land the throw while in Devil Trigger mode already, in which case it's much easier.

VII. AIR THROW, LAND, → + (H) (CANCEL) ↓ ↙ ← + (L), ST. (H) (CANCEL) → ↓ ↘ + (L) (CANCEL) (H), AFTER LANDING FROM TRICK, IMMEDIATELY SUPER JUMP FORWARD, AIR (M), (M), (H), (S), LAND, ST. (H), (S) (CANCEL) SUPER JUMP, AIR (M), (M), (H), ↓ + (H), LAND, {↘ + (H) (CANCEL) (H) (CANCEL) ↓ ↘ → + (ATK)(ATK) (MASH (ATK))} OR {↓ ↙ ← + (ATK)(ATK) (DEVIL TRIGGER), ↓ ↙ ← + (ATK)(ATK), FORWARD DASH, CR. (H) (CANCEL) → ↓ ↘ + (M), ↘ + (H) (CANCEL) (H)}

318,200~982,700 damage, 2% meter gain or 373% meter loss

Vergil's air throw allows for a direct juggle after it. The variation required is only a slight alteration of his existing combo.

VIII. CR. (L), (M), ST. (H), → + (H) (CANCEL) (X-FACTOR), CR. (M), ST. (H), → + (H) (CANCEL) → ↓ ↘ + (L) (CANCEL) (H), AFTER LANDING FROM TRICK, IMMEDIATELY SUPER JUMP FORWARD, AIR (M), (H), (S), LAND, ST. (H), → + (H) (CANCEL) ↓ ↙ ← + (L), (H), (S) (CANCEL) SUPER JUMP, AIR (M), (M), (H), ↓ + (H), LAND, {↘ + (H) (CANCEL) (H) (CANCEL) ↓ ↘ → + (ATK)(ATK) (MASH (ATK))} OR {↓ ↙ ← + (ATK)(ATK) (DEVIL TRIGGER), ↓ ↙ ← + (ATK)(ATK), FORWARD DASH, CR. (H) (CANCEL) → ↓ ↘ + (M), ↘ + (H) (CANCEL) (H) (CANCEL) ↓ ↘ → + (ATK)(ATK) (MASH (ATK))}

938,200~1,263,600 damage, 156~210% meter gain or 422~344% meter loss

This is a verifiable combo off of a low attack. (mash (ATK))(mash (ATK))

VERGIL

NEW

ADVANCED TACTICS

PERKS OF BEING A DEMON

If you happen upon excess meter with Vergil on point, a good way to maximize meter usage is to activate Devil Trigger early on, and switch Vergil out. If later down the road, you gain a combo opportunity with a different character and have hyper meter in stock, perform a team aerial combo to get Vergil back in; preferably ↓ + (S) to build meter if you don't suspect your opponent is going to counter it. Upon entry, perform air (H), ↓ + (H) (CANCEL) ↓ ↙ ← + (ATK)(ATK). Because Devil Trigger was already active from before, you can use this combo to land huge damage with Dark Angel as an OTG. Save this tactic for healthy adversaries, as the high damage may be overkill on a competitor (and thus a waste of meter) with low vitality.

COMBO APPENDIX

GENERAL EXECUTION TIPS

To ensure that the Trick cancel from a special move is successful, try double tapping the desired (ATK) button to double your chances of teleporting.

After landing Rising Sun into Trick, super jump forward and input air (M) as quickly as possible so that Vergil doesn't get too high to continue the combo.

When using Stinger, always cancel it to avoid its awful recovery period.

When canceling ↘ + (H) into air ↓ ↘ → + (ATK)(ATK), use (L) + (H) or (M) + (H). Otherwise, High Time needs a Trick cancel before you can perform the aerial Dimension Slash.

AS VERGIL COMES IN: AIR (M), (H), ↓ + (H), LAND, ↘ + (H) (CANCEL) (H) (CANCEL) ↓ ↘ → + (ATK)(ATK)

Notes	Damage
↑ + (S) or → + (S) or ↓ + (S) TAC to Vergil	Varies based on damage scaling

THROW, WAVEDASH FORWARD TWICE, ↘ + (H) (CANCEL) (X-FACTOR) (WHILE VERGIL IS STILL GROUNDED), FORWARD SUPER JUMP, AIR (M), (M), (H), (S), LAND, ST. (H), → + (H) (CANCEL) ↓ ↙ ← + (L), ST. (H), (S) (CANCEL) SUPER JUMP, AIR (M), (M), (H), ↓ + (H), LAND, ↘ + (H) (CANCEL) (H) (CANCEL) ↓ ↘ → + (ATK)(ATK) (MASH (ATK))

Notes	Damage
Cancel into X-Factor just as ↘ + (H) OTGs the opponent; you must cancel before the uppercut rises into the air in order to stay grounded	723,200~872,500 damage, 121~163% meter gain

AIR THROW, LAND, → + (H) (CANCEL) ↓ ↙ ← + (L) (CANCEL) (X-FACTOR), ST. (H) (CANCEL) → ↓ ↘ + (L) (CANCEL) (H), AFTER LANDING FROM TRICK, IMMEDIATELY SUPER JUMP FORWARD, AIR (M), (M), (H), (S), LAND, ST. (H), (S) (CANCEL) SUPER JUMP, AIR (M), (M), (H), ↓ + (H), LAND, ↘ + (H) (CANCEL) (H) (CANCEL) ↓ ↘ → + (ATK)(ATK) (MASH (ATK))

Notes	Damage
X-Factor is activated during the Trick teleport	722,800~901,400 damage, 118~160% meter gain

CAPTAIN AMERICA

"I CONSIDER IT MY DUTY AND AN HONOR TO FIGHT FOR JUSTICE!"

Bio

REAL NAME

Steven "Steve" Rogers

OCCUPATION

Soldier, Adventurer

ABILITIES

Extremely proficient in boxing, judo, aikido, and various other fighting disciplines. He also utilizes weapons-based fighting styles using his shield.

WEAPONS

A shield made from vibranium-alloy; it is the only one in existence in the world.

PROFILE

The sole recipient of the Super Soldier Serum, Cap's deep love for his country and his unparalleled sense of justice make him one of the most respected heroes today. He has also been the long-time leader of the Avengers, a group dedicated to keeping the world safe from harm.

FIRST APPEARANCE

Captain America Comics #1 (1941)

POWER GRID

- 3 INTELLIGENCE
- 3 STRENGTH
- 2 SPEED
- 3 STAMINA
- 1 ENERGY PROJECTION
- 6 FIGHTING ABILITY

*This is biographical, and does not represent an evaluation of the in-game combat potential of this hero.

Vitality	1,050,000
Chain Combo Archetype	Marvel Series

X-Factor Boost	Damage	Speed
Level 1 (3 teammates remaining)	135%	105%
Level 2 (2 teammates remaining)	160%	110%
Level 3 (1 teammate remaining)	185%	115%

Your goal with Captain America is to close on an adversary and use his Backflip with a projectile or beam assist to cross up the opposing player.

Why do you want to do this?

- **Backflip can pass through adversaries and is now immune to all attacks except throws for 13 frames. This creates a situation where it is difficult for an opposing player to block when you use the Backflip in tandem with an assist**
- **Backflip can be used to "push" your competitor out of the corner, enabling Cap's more damaging Shield Slash combos**
- **Opponents attempting to guard Backflip cross-ups will get hit by simple crouching Ⓛ attacks and throws**

How do you get Captain America close to the opposing character in order to apply his Backflip mix-ups?

- **Using Charging Star and Hyper Charging Star to blow through beams and projectiles**
- **Using Shield Slash attacks at mid range and use the returning hit of Shield Slash to cover an approach**
- **Using slow projectile assists and wavedashing behind the cover of the assist, then using Backflip once close enough to cross up your opponent**

TUNING SINCE ORIGINAL MVC3

Captain America gained quite a few boosts in *Ultimate Marvel vs. Capcom 3*. His overall combo damage has increased due to the increase in damage of Shield Slash, the new OTG-capability of Shield Slash L, and Hyper Charging Star gaining extra damage when mashed. Shield Slash L's ability to OTG also greatly improves his previously mediocre corner combo damage. Double jump gives Captain America some more combo options and some added air mobility. Backflip gained immunity to nearly all attacks except throws, making his cross-up offense much safer . Charging Star M and H both received very minor damage reductions, but this has little effect on his combo damage or gameplay.

- Captain America can now double jump
- Shield Slash damage boost
- Shield Slash L is OTG-capable, both the ground and air version
- Charging Star M & H damage lowered
- Frames 1-13 of Backflip are immune to all attacks except throws
- Hyper Charging Star is now mashable for additional damage
- Charging Star causes more horizontal and less vertical knockback.
- Charging Star now causes soft knockdown.
- Shield Slash hit stun against airborne opponents has been decreased.
- Captain America—β and —γ damage increased.

Attack Set

Standing Basic Attacks

Screen	Command	Hits	Damage	Meter Gain	Startup	Active	Recovery	Advantage on Hit	Advantage if Guarded	Notes
1	Standing Ⓛ	1	46,000	368	5	3	12	0	-2	—
2	Standing Ⓜ	1	68,000	544	10	2	20	-2	-4	—
3	Standing Ⓗ	1	80,000	640	16	4	24	-4	-6	—

1

2

3

Crouching Basic Attacks

Screen	Command	Hits	Damage	Meter Gain	Startup	Active	Recovery	Advantage on Hit	Advantage if Guarded	Notes
1	Crouching Ⓛ	1	30,000	240	4	3	15	-3	-5	Low attack
2	Crouching Ⓜ	1	48,000	384	9	4	19	-3	-5	—
3	Crouching Ⓗ	1	75,000	600	13	4	26	—	-8	Low attack, knocks down

1

2

3

Ground Special Attack—Launcher

Screen	Command	Hits	Damage	Meter Gain	Startup	Active	Recovery	Advantage on Hit	Advantage if Guarded	Notes
1	Ⓢ (while standing or crouching)	1	90,000	720	10	4	22	—	-4	Launcher, not special- or hyper combo-cancelable

1

Air Basic Attacks

Screen	Command	Hits	Damage	Meter Gain	Startup	Active	Recovery	Advantage on Hit	Advantage if Guarded	Notes
1	Air Ⓛ	1	50,000	400	5	3	14	+12	+10	Overhead attack
2	Air Ⓜ	1	65,000	520	9	4	20	+17	+15	Overhead attack
3	Air Ⓗ	1	70,000	560	12	10	16	+19	+17	Overhead attack

1

2

3

Air Special Attacks—Flying Screen and Air Exchange

Air S causes a hard knockdown when used in a launcher combo (this is sometimes called flying screen). When used outside of a launcher combo, air S behaves mostly like another basic attack. Air exchange attacks, performed by inputting a direction plus S, are only possible during a launcher combo. Exchange hits initiate team aerial combos by tagging in the next available character to continue the air combo.

Screen	Command	Hits	Damage	Meter Gain	Startup	Active	Recovery	Advantage on Hit	Advantage if Guarded	Notes
1	Air S	1	85,000	680	15	5	21	+19	+17	Overhead attack, causes hard knockdown if used in launcher combo
2	Air ↑ + S (during launcher combo)	1	60,000	480	11	4	21	—	—	Tags in next available ally while lofting opponent upward
3	Air → or ← + S (during launcher combo)	1	60,000	480	12	10	Until grounded	—	—	Tags in next available ally while causing wall bounce, erases 1 hyper meter bar from foe
4	Air ↓ + S (during launcher combo)	1	60,000	480	11	5	17	—	—	Tags in next available ally while causing ground bounce, generates 1 hyper meter bar

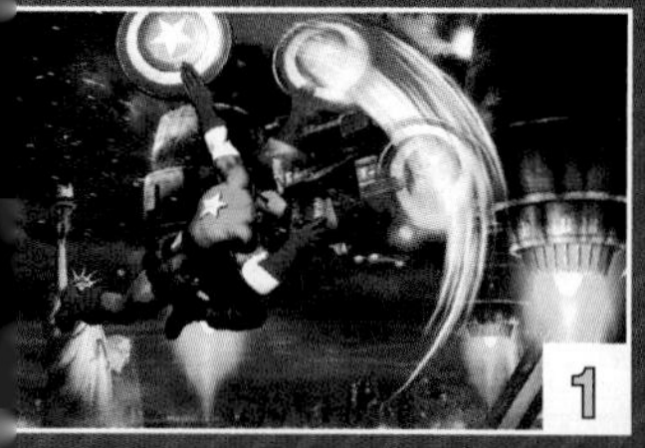
1

2

3

4

Command Attacks

Command attacks resemble basic attacks but have different chaining and canceling properties. It's usually possible to chain *into* a command attack from basic attacks, but most command attacks cannot be chained from or canceled themselves.

Screen	Name	Command	Hits	Damage	Meter Gain	Startup	Active	Recovery	Advantage on Hit	Advantage if Guarded	Notes
1	Middle Kick	(during st. M hit) M	1	48,000	480	9	4	19	-2	-5	—
2	Air-Rage Kick	Air ↑ + H	1	73,000	584	10	3	23	+19	+17	Overhead attack
3	Anti-Ground Kick	Air ↓ + H	1	70,000	560	11	5	16	+19	+17	Overhead attack

1

2

3

Throws

Throws are for snagging passive or blocking opponents. Since throws are active so quickly, you can also use them to preemptively toss opposing characters out of their offense. Combos are usually possible after throws, one way or another.

Screen	Command	Hits	Damage	Meter Gain	Startup	Active	Notes
1	→ + H (ground)	1	80,000	800	1	1	Hard knockdown
	← + H (ground)	1	80,000	800	1	1	Hard knockdown
2	→ + H (air)	1	80,000	800	1	1	Hard knockdown
	← + H (air)	1	80,000	800	1	1	Hard knockdown

1

2

As a Partner—Crossover Assists

Screen	Type	P1+P2 Crossover Combination Hyper Combo	Description	Hits	Damage	Meter Gain	Startup	Active	Recovery (this crossover assist)	Recovery (other partner)	Notes
1	Captain America—α	Hyper Charging Star	Shield Slash M	2	95,000	800	41	—	131	101	Shield is in play for 51 frames, each hit of Shield Slash has 5 low priority durability points
2	Captain America —β	Hyper Stars & Stripes	Stars & Stripes H	3	135,400	1200	29	12	145	115	Knocks down
3	Captain America —γ	Hyper Charging Star	Charging Star M	3	143,600	1272	29	11	138	108	Nullifies low and medium priority projectiles during frames 28-36, knocks down

1

2

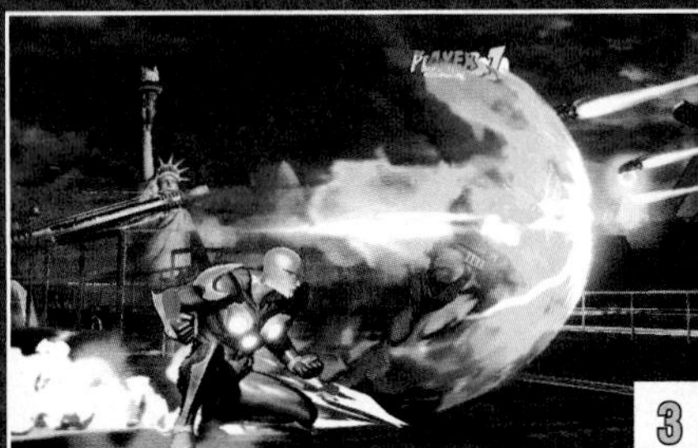

3

Captain America—α is a fairly good projectile assist that stays on screen for quite a bit of time, enabling it to virtually lock down an opponent for almost a full second in most cases. The second hit can actually work to push your adversary toward Cap, allowing for some interesting combo possibilities. It might appear to be a drawback that both hits only combo at certain distances, but this can actually help aggressive characters greatly, since the gap gives them an extra place to mess up their guarding, if you cross them up or switch from low to high attacks (or vice versa) in between hits of the shield.

Captain America—β does not have the invincibility of a normal Stars & Stripes attack, making it a poor defensive assist. It has very fast startup, but Captain America—γ has the same startup and more utility. It is not very useful as a combo tool, either, since the opposing character is carried upwards, making it difficult to convert this assist into a meaningful combo. However, it's important to note that when you use Captain America—β as a crossover counter, Captain America is invincible all the way up! This invulnerability period means you can crossover counter to Captain America and then cancel to Hyper Stars and Stripes against foes at close range, and into Hyper Charging Star to hit enemies throwing projectiles at long range! Performed correctly, Captain America comes in and performs his hyper combo seamlessly, and is invincible until the invulnerability period of his hyper combo wears off.

Captain America—γ has the ability to nullify low and medium priority projectiles, making it a very useful assist against zoning characters. It also provides a guaranteed knockdown, making it a useful assist to extend combos after an OTG in the corner. From a midscreen position, it tends to push the target too far away to combo afterwards.

Snap Back

Screen	Command	Hits	Damage	Meter Gain	Startup	Active	Recovery	Advantage on Hit	Advantage if Guarded
1	↓↘→ +  P1⇔P2	1	50,000	500 - (-1 hyper meter bar)	2	4	24	—	-6

Notes

On hit, snap back forces the opposing point character to be replaced by an assist. Opposing assist calls or tag outs are also locked out for 4 seconds

1

Special Moves

Screen	Name	Command	Hits	Damage	Meter Gain	Startup	Active	Recovery	Advantage on Hit	Advantage if Guarded	Notes
1	Shield Slash L	↓↘→ + L	2	114,000	960	21	—	30	—	—	Each hit of Shield Slash has 5 low priority durability points, shield is in play for 52 frames if Captain America does not move, disappears if Captain America gets hit, OTG-capable
2	Shield Slash M	↓↘→ + M	2	114,000	960	17	—	34	—	—	Each hit of Shield Slash has 5 low priority durability points, shield is in play for 51 frames if Captain America does not move, disappears if Captain America gets hit
3	Shield Slash H	↓↘→ + H	2	114,000	960	13	—	38	—	—	Each hit of Shield Slash has 5 low priority durability points, shield is in play for 50 frames if Captain America does not move, disappears if Captain America gets hit
4,5,6	Air Shield Slash	(in air) ↓↘→ + ATK	2	114,000	960	15	—	Until grounded	—	—	Each hit of Shield Slash has 5 low priority durability points, shield is in play for 51 frames if Captain America does not move, disappears if Captain America gets hit, L version is OTG-capable

Special Moves continued

Screen	Name	Command	Hits	Damage	Meter Gain	Startup	Active	Recovery	Advantage on Hit	Advantage if Guarded	Notes
7	Stars & Stripes L	→↓↘ + L	1	80,000	640	5	5	44	-12	-27	Invincible from frames 1-4, knocks down
	Stars & Stripes M	→↓↘ + M	2	104,500	880	5	11	50	-21	-39	Invincible from frames 1-6, knocks down
	Stars & Stripes H	→↓↘ + H	3	135,400	1200	5	12	57	-26	-47	Invincible from frames 1-9, knocks down
8	Charging Star L	↓↙← + L	1	100,000	800	5	9	30	+13	-17	Nullifies low and medium priority projectiles during frames 4-18, knocks down
	Charging Star M	↓↙← + M	2	123,500	1040	5	11	35	+4	-22	Nullifies low and medium priority projectiles during frames 4-18, knocks down
	Charging Star H	↓↙← + H	3	143,600	1272	5	13	43	-3	-17	Nullifies low and medium priority projectiles during frames 4-18, knocks down
9	Backflip	S + ATK	—	—	—	—	34	—	—	—	Invincible frames 1-13, can pass through opponents

Shield Slash L: This attack now has the ability to OTG, making it invaluable as a combo tool for Captain America. This allows you to dish out high damage anywhere on the screen regardless of Cap's positioning, whereas before, dealing significant damage in the corner or after air throws was difficult without the use of an assist. You can use this attack to start your offense at mid range against a grounded foe, allowing you to combo if the shield hits on the return trip.

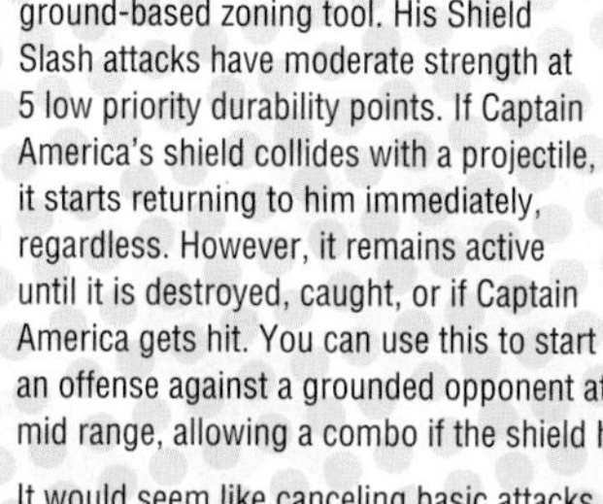
1

Shield Slash M: Captain America's main ground-based zoning tool. His Shield Slash attacks have moderate strength at 5 low priority durability points. If Captain America's shield collides with a projectile, it starts returning to him immediately, regardless. However, it remains active until it is destroyed, caught, or if Captain America gets hit. You can use this to start an offense against a grounded opponent at mid range, allowing a combo if the shield hits on the return trip.

2

It would seem like canceling basic attacks into Shield Slash would be an easy way to keep perpetual frame advantage against an opponent, but unfortunately this isn't the case: if any of the Shield Slash attacks are performed from up close, your opponent's character can actually land a guaranteed hit against you before the shield's return trip, causing the shield to disappear and giving your foe a free combo.

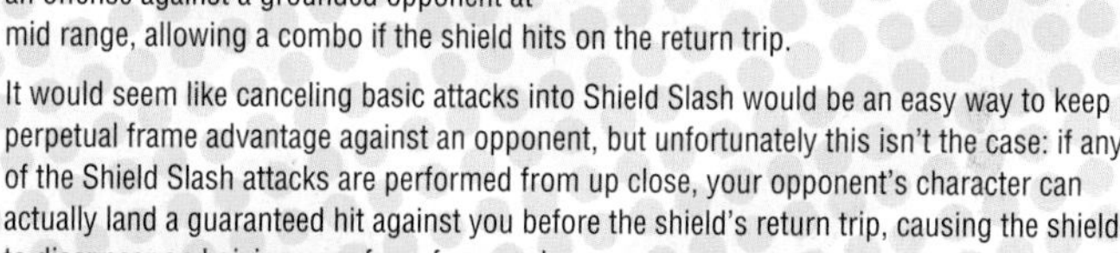

3

Shield Slash H: Employ this move as a ranged anti-air to deter the opposition from jumping in at Captain America. This is especially potent because if it hits an airborne adversary, it juggles with both hits (unless your target is cornered). This allows you to jump forward with Captain America and convert the attack into a full combo!

4

Air Shield Slash L: While the air version of Shield Slash L can OTG, it is far less practical for this purpose because it takes additional time for Captain America to start the attack due to jumping, and because it cannot be canceled into any hyper combos. However, it is excellent for starting his offense. The downward angle at which the shield is thrown makes it difficult for opponents to approach Captain America with a normal jump, and the returning shield locks the competitor down, allowing you to dash in with Cap and begin his offense, and then convert to a combo if the shield connects.

This is also a useful combo tool while both Captain America and his adversary are in the air at normal jump height. This tactic enables you to bring the opposing character lower to the ground, so you can combo into a launcher.

It is interesting to note that a height restriction exists for using air Shield Slash L, and it is much lower than the other two versions of the attack. A relatively low-altitude air Shield Slash L can be performed by inputting ↓↘→↗ + L, but that same input trick will not work for the other two versions.

5

Air Shield Slash M: This move is mainly used as a combo tool to keep the opposing character airborne at approximately the same height, allowing Captain America to land and jump forward with another attack. You can also use it against rivals who have airborne zoning tools.

6

Air Shield Slash H: Similar to the ground version of Shield Slash H, this move can be used against airborne opponents who are at an upward angle in front of Captain America. With the exception of extreme heights, if it connects, you can convert it into a full combo by having Captain America jump (or super jump if necessary) and continuing into further Shield Slash combos to bring your adversary closer to the ground. You can also use this tactic against airborne zoning competitors who are slightly above Cap.

Stars & Stripes: Stars & Stripes is one of the rare special moves with invincibility frames, making it a useful defensive option if opposing players become predictable with their attacks. Stars & Stripes M and H are the more useful versions because they have invincibility frames that last well into the active frames, while Stars & Stripes L invincibility fades 1 frame short of its first active frame.

Use this attack cautiously, since your opponent can easily punish a missed or guarded Stars & Stripes. If you are unsure that the attack will hit, make sure to use an assist to cover your recovery. Without an assist to cover you, attempting to make this attack safe can be costly, either requiring X-Factor or canceling into a hyper combo before Captain America leaves the ground, before a THC into a safe hyper combo.

Charging Star: Charging Star is the cornerstone of Captain America's strategy to combat zoning characters. This attack completely nullifies low and medium priority projectiles during frames 4-18. Higher strengths travel progressively farther distances and deal higher damage. However, Charging Star M & H knock the opposing character farther away, making the moves less useful for certain situations such as X-Factor usage (unless in the corner). The active frames are only active for a portion of the distance traveled, with Charging Star H only being active for about half the screen length.

Any time you hit with Charging Star, you can hyper combo cancel into Hyper Charging Star for an easy 400,000 or so damage. Keep in mind that Charging Star is easily punished when guarded, so use an assist to cover Captain America's recovery if possible.

Backflip: Although it inflicts no actual damage, Backflip is the primary means for Captain America to start his offense. Backflip is now immune to all attacks except throws during the first 13 frames and can pass through opponents for the entirety of the move. When used with an assist, you can time Backflip so that it can pass through your adversary immediately before the assist's attack hits, forcing your opponent to change the direction they are blocking. If they fail to block this attack, you can begin attacking and convert into a combo!

Backflip is very unsafe unless covered by an assist, canceled with X-Factor, or hyper combo canceled. No basic attacks are able to provide enough blockstun to prevent the opposing player from easily punishing Backflip.

Hyper Combos

Screen	Name	Command	Hits	Damage	Startup	Active	Recovery	Advantage on Hit	Advantage if Guarded	Notes
1	Hyper Stars & Stripes	→ ↓ ↘ + ATK ATK	5	290,800	12+0	11(7)12 (7)13	38	+11	-26	Invincible from frames 1-24, first two hits stagger the opponent
2	Hyper Charging Star	↓ ↙ ← + ATK ATK	10–20	274,100~ 328,800	5+2	11	45	—	-23	Destroys projectiles/ignores beams from frames 1-23, hard knockdown, can be mashed for additional damage
3	Final Justice (Level 3 Hyper Combo)	↓ ↘ → + ATK ATK	8	440,000	22+2	16	18	—	-12	Invincible from frames 16-36, hard knockdown

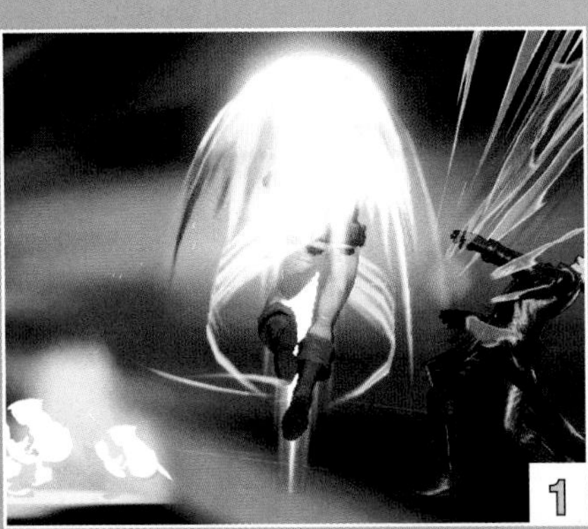

Hyper Stars & Stripes: This hyper combo's main use is to blow through an opponent's hyper combo at close range. With 24 invincibility frames, it will defeat most competitors' hyper combos on reaction. If it is somehow avoided or guarded, THC into a safe hyper combo.

Hyper Stars & Stripes hits instantly up close after the hyper screen freeze; if a foe is close enough and not already blocking before the freeze, so the first active frame of the hyper combo touches them, it's impossible for them to block if they weren't already guarding before the hyper freeze! This always works point blank against big characters, and works some of the time against smaller ones; even if it's not technically unblockable after the freeze when the first active frame doesn't touch the enemy right away, the invulnerability period will still be enough for Captain America to blow away most point-blank attacks.

Hyper Charging Star: This is Captain America's go-to combo ender, inflicting high damage for a level 1 hyper combo due to the fact that you can mash for extra damage. It does knock your opponent back quite far, so landing a combo with a THC can be tricky with some characters.

You can also employ this move to blow through any projectiles or beams at medium range, but you must be careful with this, since your adversary will likely cancel their attack into a hyper combo of their own in reaction to your hyper combo. It's best used in this manner to go straight through projectile hyper combos when the opponent does not have any additional meter to THC.

Final Justice: This is Captain America's level 3 hyper combo. Like other level 3 hyper combos, this is not subject to damage scaling, making it ideal to end long combos. Keep the long startup of this hyper combo in mind when using it in a juggle combo. While this hyper combo does have invincibility frames, it does not start until frame 16, meaning that Final Justice should be limited to combos.

"WE HAVE NO CHOICE. SO WE FIGHT—AND WE WIN. THERE ARE NO OTHER OPTIONS."

Battle Plan

Backflip is an extremely important part of Captain America's offense. Use it with well- timed assists to make it difficult for your opponent to block.

Use Charging Star to plow through enemy projectiles. If opponents attempt to punish Charging Star, cancel the recovery into a hyper combo!

Captain America's offense is highly reliant on crossover assists used with his Backflip, making him a less than ideal choice to be the anchor of your team. Captain America is best as a point character, allowing access to both assists and the ability to maintain cross-up Backflip pressure. Captain America is self-sufficient when it comes to hyper meter use in combos, and by refraining from spending meter on hypers he becomes a strong battery.

You want to get close enough to threaten with Backflip cross-ups, covered by an assist that will both enable the cross-up, and keep Captain America safe if the challenger guards properly. There are several ways to do this:

One method is to use low–altitude air Shield Slash L. You can perform this version of air Shield Slash much closer to the ground than Shield Slash M or H. The motion for this is ⇩ ⬂ ⇨ ⬃ + Ⓛ. Doing this immediately stops Captain America's ascent once the attack begins, and he slowly floats toward the ground. Upon landing, he immediately recovers, significantly reducing the recovery time of this attack. This allows you to easily follow up while the returning shield pulls the opposing character toward Captain America. If the shield connects, you can easily convert the attack into a full combo.

Another method of closing in against your adversary is by using a projectile assist who occupies the screen for a significant amount of time, such as Sentinel—α. The goal here is to wavedash in just behind the projectile assist and then attempt to Backflip past your competitor just as the projectiles are about to hit. You can also use this to follow up blockstrings, calling the assist as you get pushed out of range and then wavedashing behind the projectiles and attempting the Backflip cross-up. Captain America can rely on this strategy a little more heavily than most characters, however, because nearly any attempt to punish Captain America's assists can be potentially countered by Captain America's hyper combos. If your foe attempts to punish with a beam or projectile hyper combo, you can blow through it with Captain America's Hyper Charging Star. If the opposing player attempts a physical attack hyper combo, you can use the invincibility of Hyper Stars & Stripes to blow through this as well.

Zoning characters inevitably attempt to keep Captain America away from them. However, Captain America is well-equipped to deal with such characters. When at fullscreen, you can use Cap's Charging Star L to push through projectiles with relative safely due to the short distance traveled. At mid range or closer, you can use Charging Star H to go through any low or medium priority projectiles and hit your adversary. If any Charging Star hits, you can hyper combo cancel into Hyper Charging Star or even X-Factor cancel and score a very damaging combo, particularly if you catch two characters! It's a good idea to practice learning exactly how much range each version of his Charging Star has so you know the distance where you can punish projectiles and beams.

Even if your opponent attempts to punish this, you do have some options. If they attempt to punish your Charging Star L by canceling into a beam or projectile hyper, you can cancel the recovery of your Charging Star L into Hyper Charging Star to blow through their hyper combo. Some characters may have a slow projectile that they can follow in or cancel into a physical long range hyper combo, such as Wesker's Phantom Dance, and will attempt to punish you during the recovery of your Charging Star L. If they attempt this, you can use Hyper Stars & Stripes to cancel the recovery of Charging Star L, employing the invincibility of Hyper Stars & Stripes to win most situations!

Once up close you'll want to stay there and use assists to safely cross up your rival with Backflip. You can end blockstrings by calling an assist and using Shield Slash L or M to protect your assist and keep your opponent in blockstun, allowing you to follow your assist in an attempt to cross up the opposing character again.

When Captain America has to defend the onslaught of another offensive character, he has better options than most. His Stars & Stripes is one of the few special moves that provide invincibility. However, all versions are easily punished if guarded. Stars & Stripes L is vulnerable 1 frame before the first active frame, making it the riskiest option because you may get hit out of the attack. However, it is the easiest version to hyper combo cancel. Stars & Stripes has invincibility frames that last into active frames, but it's more difficult to hyper combo cancel into anything but Hyper Stars & Stripes, which does not actually combo. It can be useful to THC into a safe hyper combo, but you'll have to commit to this course of action without knowing whether the attack will hit, since the hyper combo cancel has to occur before the second hit of Stars & Stripes. An alternative to making the attack safe without using hyper meter or X-Factor is to use a projectile or beam assist that can cover Captain America during his recovery.

Hyper Stars & Stripes is one of the better defensive hyper combos; if your rival is close to Cap upon activation, and they are not *already* guarding or performing an invincible action before the screen freeze occurs, there's a good chance they will be *unable* to block on reaction! If they do manage to guard, THC into a safe hyper combo if possible.

COMBO USAGE

I. CR. Ⓛ, ST. Ⓜ, CR. Ⓗ ➡CANCEL ↓↘→ + Ⓗ, JUMP FORWARD, AIR ↑ + Ⓗ ➡CANCEL ↓↘→ + Ⓜ, LAND, JUMP FORWARD, AIR ↑ + Ⓗ ➡CANCEL ↓↘→ + Ⓛ, ST. Ⓗ, Ⓢ ➡CANCEL SUPER JUMP FORWARD, AIR Ⓜ, Ⓗ, ↑ + Ⓗ, Ⓢ, LAND, DASH FORWARD, ↓↘→ + Ⓛ ➡CANCEL ↓↙← + ATK ATK (MASH ATK)

Midscreen only, 728,300 damage, 1% meter gain

This is a modified version of Captain America's old midscreen combo using air Shield Slash juggling. The cr. Ⓗ is important because it puts your opponent in an airborne state, allowing Shield Slash H to juggle the foe upwards. From there, you'll jump forward and hit the ↑ + Ⓗ attacks as soon as your target is knocked back toward Captain America with the shield, approximately at the apex of his jump. After air Shield Slash L, the opponent should be bouncing back toward Cap at ground level. You'll want to start st. Ⓗ slightly early due to its lengthy startup. Once launched, you'll want to hit the air attacks as quickly as possible to avoid your opponent flipping out. Once landing, you may have to dash forward to get Hyper Charging Start to hit after the OTG Shield Slash L. After the OTG Shield Slash L, immediately cancel to Hyper Charging Star.

II. CR. Ⓛ, ST. Ⓜ, Ⓗ, Ⓢ ➡CANCEL SUPER JUMP FORWARD, AIR Ⓜ, Ⓜ, Ⓗ ➡CANCEL DOUBLE JUMP FORWARD, ↑ + Ⓗ, Ⓢ, LAND, ↓↘→ + Ⓛ ➡CANCEL ↓↙← + ATK ATK (MASH ATK)

630,100 damage, 40% meter loss

This is a combo you would use when your opponent is cornered, and you cannot juggle with Shield Slash. You'll want to cancel the first air Ⓗ with a double jump and continue to hold up to get the ↑ + Ⓗ. It's important to release up before you press Ⓢ, however, or you'll end up with a TAC instead. You can use an assist to combo after the OTG Shield Slash L and allow Captain America to relaunch into another double jump aerial combo and finish with Shield Slash L OTG into Hyper Charging Star on the second hard knockdown.

III. AIR THROW OR GROUND THROW, (LAND IF AIR THROW), ↓↘→ + Ⓛ ➡CANCEL ↓↙← + ATK ATK

436,200 damage, 82% meter loss

Without an assist or X-Factor, this is the most damage Captain America can get from a basic throw. This is still a huge improvement, as previously, he could not land any attacks following a throw without an OTG assist. On a ground throw, you'll want to use Shield Slash L immediately after recovering from the throw and immediately cancel into Hyper Charging Star. For air throws, you'll want to use Shield Slash L immediately after landing.

IV. FORWARD GROUND THROW, (LAND IF AIR THROW OR DASH IF BACK GROUND THROW), ↓↘→ + Ⓛ [X-FACTOR], ST. Ⓗ, CR. Ⓗ ➡CANCEL ↓↘→ + Ⓗ, JUMP FORWARD, AIR ↑ + Ⓗ ➡CANCEL ↓↘→ + Ⓛ, LAND, ST. Ⓗ, Ⓢ ➡CANCEL SUPER JUMP FORWARD, AIR Ⓜ, Ⓗ, ↑ + Ⓗ, Ⓢ, LAND, ↓↘→ + Ⓛ ➡CANCEL ↓↙← + ATK ATK (MASH ATK)

Midscreen only, X-Factor level 1, 944,800 damage, 33% meter gain

With X-Factor, you can convert a throw into a huge combo. Because of the automatic hitstun scaling after throws, you cannot do a full Shield Slash juggle combo, requiring you to launch earlier than normal. X-Factor as soon as the shield hits your adversary, which gives you time to confirm the hit but also makes sure you don't X-Factor before the projectile has come out. Immediately press Ⓗ after the X-Factor animation so that the opposing character does not hit the ground. This allows the returning Shield Slash L to juggle your competitor toward you and continue the combo.

V. AIR THROW OR GROUND THROW, (LAND IF AIR THROW, DASH FORWARD IF BACK GROUND THROW), ↓↘→ + Ⓛ [X-FACTOR], ST. Ⓗ, CR. Ⓗ, Ⓢ ➡CANCEL SUPER JUMP FORWARD, AIR Ⓜ, Ⓜ, Ⓗ ➡CANCEL DOUBLE JUMP FORWARD, ↑ + Ⓗ, Ⓢ, LAND, DASH FORWARD, ↓↘→ + Ⓛ ➡CANCEL ↓↙← + ATK ATK (MASH ATK)

X-Factor level 1, 823,800 damage, 3% meter loss

Hitstun decay is worse on all other throws, making them the inferior option most of the time. Avoid using back throws unless they are needed for specific positioning. This sequence also doubles as a corner throw combo when Shield Slash juggles are not possible.

VI. ↓↙← + Ⓛ [X-FACTOR], WALK FORWARD SLIGHTLY, ST. Ⓗ ➡CANCEL ↓↘→ + Ⓗ, JUMP FORWARD, AIR Ⓜ, ↑ + Ⓗ ➡CANCEL ↓↘→ + Ⓛ, LAND, ST. Ⓗ, Ⓢ ➡CANCEL SUPER JUMP FORWARD, AIR Ⓜ, Ⓜ, Ⓗ ➡CANCEL DOUBLE JUMP FORWARD, ↑ + Ⓗ, Ⓢ, LAND, DASH FORWARD, ↓↘→ + Ⓛ ➡CANCEL ↓↙← + ATK ATK (MASH ATK)

X-Factor level 1, 1,104,800 damage, 27% meter gain

Unlike the M and H versions, Charging Star L doesn't knock adversaries very far away. This allows you to X-Factor cancel on a hit confirm and continue into a combo that is able to K.O. all but full health, high-vitality characters. This combo is somewhat of a hybrid between **Combo I** and **Combo II**, with only two reps of Shield Slash juggles and a double jump launcher combo. There is no rush to land the st. Ⓗ after the X-Factor cancel; in fact, you should take a short moment to walk or dash forward so your combo is easier to perform.

ADVANCED TACTICS

SHIELD SLASH L OTG CORNER RESETS

You can use Shield Slash L to create deadly mix-ups in the corner when used as an OTG!

Since Shield Slash L can now OTG it creates a strong potential for resets. After a hard knockdown, Shield Slash OTG does not combo into the second hit without the use of an assist or a hyper combo cancel. However, the shield still remains active on the return trip. Depending on the hitstun decay, your adversary either falls to the ground, or if the hitstun decay is high, air recovers just above the ground.

When you have a competitor cornered after a hard knockdown, OTG with Shield Slash L. An option that can work regardless of hitstun decay is to Backflip after Shield Slash L. You then pass through the target, putting Cap in the corner. However, the shield still hits your foe upon its return to Captain America, forcing the attacker to block from the other side. With this tactic, you'll have to watch for a couple things, however.

If Shield Slash L knocks your opponent to the ground, they can roll forward on their recovery to avoid the cross-up. If you suspect that they might do this, you can counter by delaying your Backflip slightly until they roll underneath you. Your Backflip follows them and ends up on the other side, causing Captain America's shield to hit them! If your rival rolls backwards, they avoid the shield hit but still get crossed up. The best option if you are unsure what the opposing player might do is to simply delay your Backflip slightly and call a beam or projectile assist. This way, your Backflip comes out regardless, and your assist comes out behind your opponent, making it very difficult for your competitor to do anything!

If your opponent air recovers, you can still attempt the Backflip cross-up, but it is much riskier. Adversaries who air recover forward completely bypass the cross-up, and rivals who air recover backward do not get hit by the shield and may not even be crossed up. Even if you do cross up, opponents can air recover before Captain America is finished with Backflip, and they can punish you if they have a cross-up air attack. So instead, you have two viable options. One is to jump and attempt to air throw your challenger while calling projectile or beam assist. This allows you to continue pressure even if the throw is escaped. The other option is to use the delayed Backflip with a projectile or beam assist.

With these mix-ups, you can make Captain America's corner game much deadlier, making it difficult for the opposing player to be able to take the initiative!

COMBO APPENDIX

GENERAL EXECUTION TIPS

- When juggling with Charging Star and canceling into Hyper Charging Star, wait a moment so your adversary is closer to the ground and you get full damage
- Use st. Ⓜ over cr. Ⓜ. Cr. Ⓜ is not a low attack, and st. Ⓜ causes substantially more damage

↓↘→ + Ⓗ, JUMP FORWARD, AIR ↑ + Ⓗ CANCEL ↓↘→ + Ⓜ, LAND, JUMP FORWARD, AIR ↑ + Ⓗ CANCEL ↓↘→ + Ⓛ, LAND, ST. Ⓗ, Ⓢ CANCEL SUPER JUMP FORWARD, AIR Ⓜ, Ⓜ, Ⓗ CANCEL DOUBLE JUMP FORWARD, ↑ + Ⓗ, Ⓢ, LAND, DASH FORWARD, ↓↘→ + Ⓛ CANCEL ↓↙← + ATK ATK (MASH ATK)

Notes	Damage
Against airborne opponents only	728,600 damage, 8% meter loss

II. CR. Ⓛ, ST. Ⓜ, Ⓗ, Ⓢ CANCEL SUPER JUMP FORWARD, AIR Ⓜ, Ⓜ, Ⓗ CANCEL DOUBLE JUMP FORWARD, ↑ + Ⓗ, Ⓢ, LAND, CALL IRON MAN—α, ↓↘→ + Ⓛ, Ⓗ, Ⓢ CANCEL SUPER JUMP FORWARD, AIR Ⓜ, Ⓜ, Ⓗ CANCEL DOUBLE JUMP FORWARD, ↑ + Ⓗ, Ⓢ, LAND, ↓↘→ + Ⓛ CANCEL ↓↙← + ATK ATK (MASH ATK)

Notes	Damage
Corner combo with assist	742,200 damage, 24% meter gain

CR. Ⓛ, ST. Ⓜ, CR. Ⓗ CANCEL ↓↘→ + Ⓗ, JUMP FORWARD, AIR ↑ + Ⓗ CANCEL ↓↘→ + Ⓜ, LAND, JUMP FORWARD, AIR ↑ + Ⓗ CANCEL ↓↘→ + Ⓛ, ST. Ⓗ, Ⓢ CANCEL SUPER JUMP FORWARD, AIR Ⓜ, Ⓗ, ↑ + Ⓗ, Ⓢ, LAND, CALL IRON MAN—α, DASH FORWARD, ↓↘→ + Ⓛ CANCEL ↓↘→ + ATK ATK

Notes	Damage
Combo with assist and level 3 hyper combo. Can use Charging Star H before Final Justice in corner	Midscreen only, 990,100 damage, 186% meter loss

FORWARD THROW, CALL IRON MAN—α, ↓↘→ + Ⓛ, ST. Ⓗ CANCEL ↓↘→ + Ⓗ, JUMP FORWARD, AIR ↑ + Ⓗ CANCEL ↓↘→ + Ⓛ, LAND, ST. Ⓗ, Ⓢ CANCEL SUPER JUMP FORWARD, AIR Ⓜ, Ⓗ, ↑ + Ⓗ, Ⓢ, LAND, DASH FORWARD, ↓↘→ + Ⓛ CANCEL ↓↙← + ATK ATK (MASH ATK)

Notes	Damage
Forward ground throw OTG combo with assist	Midscreen only, 612,100 damage, 8% meter gain

GROUND THROW OR AIR THROW, (LAND IF AIR THROW, DASH FORWARD IF BACK GROUND THROW), CALL IRON MAN—α, ↓↘→ + Ⓛ, ST. Ⓗ, Ⓢ CANCEL SUPER JUMP FORWARD, AIR Ⓜ, Ⓜ, Ⓗ CANCEL DOUBLE JUMP FORWARD, ↑ + Ⓗ, Ⓢ, LAND, DASH FORWARD, ↓↘→ + Ⓛ CANCEL ↓↙← + ATK ATK (MASH ATK)

Notes	Damage
Throw OTG combo with assist, corner friendly	562,200 damage, 18% meter loss

DEADPOOL

"DO I KILL YOU WITH THE SLEEK BUT IMPERSONAL FIREARM, OR GO WITH THE COOL FACTOR OF A NICE KATANA?"

Bio

REAL NAME

Wade Wilson

OCCUPATION

Mercenary

ABILITIES

A healing factor coupled with enhanced physical conditioning. He is also a specialist in close-quarters combat, and his assassination skills are unparalleled.

WEAPONS

Uses various weapons, including handguns, machine guns, grenades, swords, nunchaku, etc. He also has a teleporting device on his belt, but it tends to malfunction easily.

PROFILE

To cure his terminal lung cancer, Wade attempted to obtain mutant powers artificially. However, the side effects of the procedure disfigured him and also caused psychological damage. Although he loves having cheerful conversations, because of his madness, no one really knows what he's saying.

FIRST APPEARANCE

The New Mutants #98 (1990)

POWER GRID

2	INTELLIGENCE
3	STRENGTH
2	SPEED
4	STAMINA
1	ENERGY PROJECTION
6	FIGHTING ABILITY

*This is biographical, and does not represent an evaluation of the in-game combat potential of this hero.

ALTERNATE COSTUMES

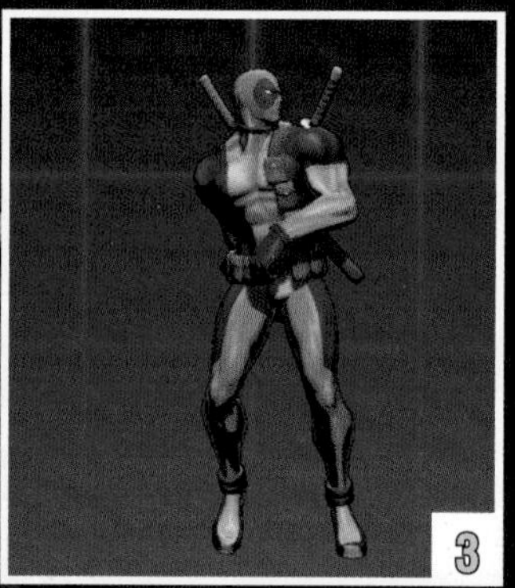

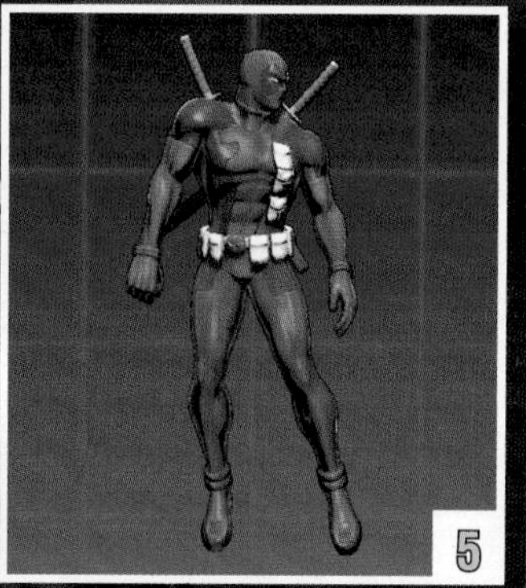

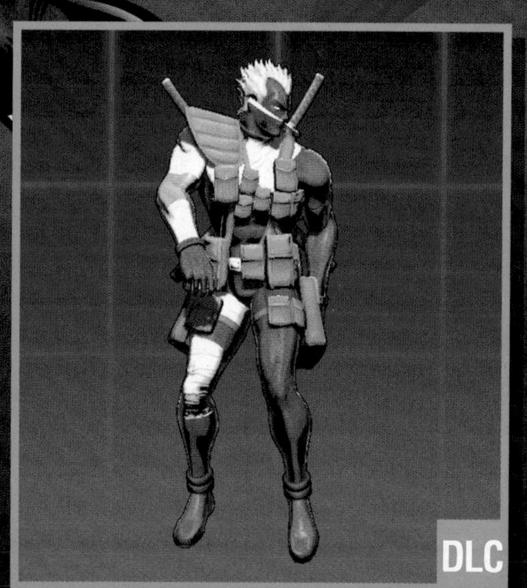

Overview

Vitality	900,000
Chain Combo Archetype	Hunter Series

X-Factor Boost	Damage	Speed
Level 1 (3 teammates remaining)	125%	115%
Level 2 (2 teammates remaining)	145%	125%
Level 3 (1 teammate remaining)	165%	135%

Your goal when using Deadpool is to keep his distance from the opponent by using his various zoning tools. You want to force your adversary to make mistakes to approach Deadpool, which puts your opposition in a disadvantageous position.

Keeping opponents at a distance is ideal when playing as Deadpool because:

- **He has a large array of zoning tools that allow him to stay mobile while still controlling space**
- **Deadpool's Ninja Gift attacks move him backward quickly while still allowing him to control space on the screen**
- **Trigger Happy can easily be linked into Happy-Happy Trigger via hit confirmation**
- **Deadpool's close range offense isn't as strong as dedicated offensive characters**

How do you keep your rivals at a distance when using Deadpool?

- **Jumping backward and using Air Trigger Happy M at the peak of the jump, followed by another Trigger Happy once Deadpool hits the ground to maximize damage**
- **Jumping over your foe's projectiles and punishing with Trigger Happy or Happy-Happy Trigger**
- **Using Ninja Gift when competitors start getting too close**

TUNING SINCE ORIGINAL MVC3

Deadpool's overhead attack can no longer by canceled except by X-Factor, forcing him to use an OTG to combo afterwards and limiting his solo combo potential off this command move. He gained extra damage on most of his combos because Happy-Happy Trigger can be mashed for extra damage. He can now cancel all basic attacks and special moves with Teleport, allowing him stronger zoning and mix-up options. His Teleport Malfunction now causes more damage, making it even riskier to use. Finally, the Ninja Gift H relaunch loop no longer works, and opponents recover immediately upon landing if hit with Ninja Gift H after approximately 8-10 hits. Being able to follow up Quick Work with Chimichangas!! allows for some interesting combo opportunities.

- Mad Wheel (→ + M) no longer chains into S and is no longer special or hyper combo-cancelable
- Happy-Happy Trigger can be mashed for extra damage
- Basic attacks and special moves can be canceled into Teleport
- Teleport Malfunction now causes 30,000 damage to Deadpool, up from 5,800
- Incapacitation caused by Ninja Gift H decreases with combo length.
- Chimichangas!! can be used during Quick Work.
- Ground basic attacks can be canceled with Taunt.
- Opponents stay grounded after throws slightly longer.

Attack Set

Standing Basic Attacks

Screen	Command	Hits	Damage	Meter Gain	Startup	Active	Recovery	Advantage on Hit	Advantage if Guarded	Notes
1	Standing L	1	43,000	344	4	3	11	-1	-2	—
2	Standing M	2	63,000	560	8	6	17	-3	-4	—
3	Standing H	1	80,000	640	11	4	19	+3	-1	—

Crouching Basic Attacks

Screen	Command	Hits	Damage	Meter Gain	Startup	Active	Recovery	Advantage on Hit	Advantage if Guarded	Notes
1	Crouching L	1	37,000	296	5	2	14	-3	-4	Low attack
2	Crouching M	1	60,000	480	7	3	19	-5	-5	Low attack
3	Crouching H	1	70,000	560	12	13	19	—	-10	Low attack, knocks down

Ground Special Attack—Launcher

Screen	Command	Hits	Damage	Meter Gain	Startup	Active	Recovery	Advantage on Hit	Advantage if Guarded	Notes
1	S (while standing or crouching)	1	80,000	640	5	6	34	—	-18	Launcher, not special- or hyper combo-cancelable

Air Basic Attacks

Screen	Command	Hits	Damage	Meter Gain	Startup	Active	Recovery	Advantage on Hit	Advantage if Guarded	Notes
1	Air L	1	44,000	352	5	3	15	+6	+5	Overhead attack
2	Air M	1	60,000	480	8	3	22	+12	+11	Overhead attack
3	Air H	1	75,000	600	12	8	11	+14	+13	Overhead attack

Air Special Attacks—Flying Screen and Air Exchange

Air (S) causes a hard knockdown when used in a launcher combo (this is sometimes called flying screen). When used outside of a launcher combo, air (S) behaves mostly like another basic attack. Air exchange attacks, performed by inputting a direction plus (S), are only possible during a launcher combo. Exchange hits initiate team aerial combos by tagging in the next available character to continue the air combo.

Screen	Command	Hits	Damage	Meter Gain	Startup	Active	Recovery	Advantage on Hit	Advantage if Guarded	Notes
1	Air (S)	1	80,000	640	13	3	20	+18	+16	Overhead attack, causes hard knockdown if used in launcher combo
2	Air ⇧ + (S) (during launcher combo)	1	60,000	480	12	3	16	—	—	Tags in next available ally while lofting opponent upward
3	Air ⇨ or ⇦ + (S) (during launcher combo)	1	50,000	400	8	3	22	—	—	Tags in next available ally while causing wall bounce, erases 1 hyper meter bar from foe
4	Air ⇩ + (S) (during launcher combo)	1	50,000	400	13	4	19	—	—	Tags in next available ally while causing ground bounce, generates 1 hyper meter bar

1

2

3

4

Command Attacks

Command attacks resemble basic attacks but have different chaining and canceling properties. It's usually possible to chain *into* a command attack from basic attacks, but most command attacks cannot be chained from or canceled themselves.

Screen	Name	Command	Hits	Damage	Meter Gain	Startup	Active	Recovery	Advantage on Hit	Advantage if Guarded	Notes
1	Mad Wheel	⇨ + (M)	2	63,000	560	25	7	14	—	+3	Overhead, hard knockdown, not special- or hyper-combo cancelable
2	Taunt	Select button	1	10,000	80	10	5	92	-74	-75	May be canceled into from any basic attack, cancelable into special moves, hyper combos, and (S)
3	Wall Jump	Jump backwards against wall, then press ⇙	—	—	—	8	—	—	—	—	Performs a wall jump, may initiate aerial attacks or movements after 8th frame

1

2

3

Throws

Throws are for snagging passive or blocking opponents. Since throws are active so quickly, you can also use them to preemptively toss opposing characters out of their offense. Combos are usually possible after throws, one way or another.

Screen	Command	Hits	Damage	Meter Gain	Startup	Active	Notes
1	⇨ + (H) (ground)	2	80,000	800	1	1	Hard knockdown
	⇦ + (H) (ground)	2	80,000	800	1	1	Hard knockdown
2	⇨ + (H) (air)	1	80,000	800	1	1	Hard knockdown
	⇦ + (H) (air)	1	80,000	800	1	1	Hard knockdown

1

2

As a Partner—Crossover Assists

Screen	Type	P1+P2 Crossover Combination Hyper Combo	Description	Hits	Damage	Meter Gain	Startup	Active	Recovery (this crossover assist)	Recovery (other partner)	Notes
1	Deadpool—α	Happy-Happy Trigger	Quick Work L	1	90,000	720	37	4	126	96	Low attack, ignores hitstun decay, knocks down
2	Deadpool—β	Happy-Happy Trigger	Katana-Rama! H	1	70,000	560	37	3	122	92	OTG-capable, ground bounce
3	Deadpool—γ	Happy-Happy Trigger	Trigger Happy H	10	97,300	1200	39	21	112	82	Each projectile has 1 low priority durability point

Deadpool—α is one of the few assists in the game that must be guarded low. This alone makes it very valuable, allowing you to set up simultaneous attacks with the assist that require low/high blocking at nearly the same time. The attack also ignores hitstun decay and knocks down, making it a very useful combo tool, especially during long combos to allow you those few extra hits. This is probably his best assist overall if you don't require an OTG-capable assist.

Deadpool—β is OTG-capable, making it useful primarily for partners who have poor or no OTG capability by themselves. This causes your opponent to ground bounce, allowing for an easy follow-up. However, this ground bounce can be detrimental to a few characters who rely on ground bounces in their combos, so keep that in mind when choosing this assist.

Deadpool—γ is a bit awkward because Deadpool uses Trigger Happy H, causing him to fire his guns forward at an upward angle. You can utilize it to assist a zoning character by covering jumping angles or to prevent an adversary from super jumping away from your projectiles.

Snap Back

Screen	Command	Hits	Damage	Meter Gain	Startup	Active	Recovery	Advantage on Hit	Advantage if Guarded
1	↓↘→ + P1 or P2	1	50,000	500 - (-1 hyper meter bar)	2	4	19	—	-1
Notes									
On hit, snap back forces the opposing point character to be replaced by an assist. Opposing assist calls or tag outs are also locked out for 4 seconds									

Special Moves

Screen	Name	Command	Hits	Damage	Meter Gain	Startup	Active	Recovery	Advantage on Hit	Advantage if Guarded	Notes
1, 2, 3	Trigger Happy	↓↘→ + ATK	10	97,300	1200	15	21	30	-8	-14	Each projectile has 0.8 low priority durability points
4	Air Trigger Happy L	(in air) ↓↘→ + L	10	97,300	1200	15	21	20 (or until grounded, then 8 frames recovery)	+12	+6	OTG-capable, each projectile has 1 low priority durability point
5	Air Trigger Happy M	(in air) ↓↘→ + M	10	97,300	1200	15	21	20 (or until grounded, then 8 frames recovery)	+12	+6	Each projectile has 0.8 low priority durability points
6	Air Trigger Happy H	(in air) ↓↘→ + H	10	97,300	1200	15	21	20 (or until grounded, then 8 frames recovery)	+12	+6	Each projectile has 0.8 low priority durability points
7	Ninja Gift L (in air OK)	(During Trigger Happy) L	3	108,300	860	10	—	35	-13	-14	Can cancel Trigger Happy from frames 3-15, each projectile has 2 low priority durability points
8	Ninja Gift M (in air OK)	(During Trigger Happy) M	1	80,000	640	10	—	35	+25	+3	Can cancel Trigger Happy from frames 3-15, grenade detonates on contact or after 100 frames, projectile has 1 medium priority durability point
9	Ninja Gift H (in air OK)	(During Trigger Happy) H	1	10,000	100	10	—	35	—	-23	Can cancel Trigger Happy from frames 3-15, projectile has 1 low priority durability point, captures grounded opponent for 72 frames, causes special hard knockdown state against airborne foes during which any attack is OTG-capable
10	Quick Work L	↓↙← + L	1	90,000	720	13	4	34	—	-16	Low attack, knocks down, ignores hitstun decay, can cancel to Chimichangas!! from frames 24-25
	Quick Work M	↓↙← + M	1	110,000	880	18	4	34	—	-16	Low attack, knocks down, ignores hitstun decay, can cancel to Chimichangas!! from frames 45-46
	Quick Work H	↓↙← + H	1	130,000	1040	23	4	34	—	-16	Low attack, knocks down, ignores hitstun decay, can cancel to Chimichangas!! from frames 55-56

Special Moves continued

Screen	Name	Command	Hits	Damage	Meter Gain	Startup	Active	Recovery	Advantage on Hit	Advantage if Guarded	Notes
11	Katana-Rama! L	→ ↓ ↘ + L	1	70,000	560	13	3	30	—	-11	Knocks down
	Katana-Rama! M	→ ↓ ↘ + M	1	70,000	560	13	3	30	—	-11	Knocks down
	Katana-Rama! H	→ ↓ ↘ + H	1	70,000	560	13	3	30	—	-11	OTG-capable, ground bounce
12	Chimichangas!!	(During Katana-Rama! or Quick Work) H	1	63,000	560	13	3	30	—	-11	Can cancel Katana-Rama! on hit/block during frames 15-20, can cancel Quick Work on hit/block, wall bounce
13	Teleport	← ↓ ↙ + ATK	—	—	—	25	—	—	—	—	Deadpool's teleporter will malfunction every third Teleport (see below)
14	Teleport Malfunction	—	1	100,000 (30,000 to Deadpool)	800	18	2	98	—	-79	Hard knockdown on both characters, OTG -capable

1

2

3

4

5

6

Trigger Happy: This is Deadpool's primary zoning tool. Trigger Happy L fires horizontally and low to the ground while grounded. This is primarily used against small to medium-sized characters when the opponent is unlikely to attempt to jump over your ranged attacks or when they are locked in blockstun, since most characters can duck under Trigger Happy M. When used in the air, Trigger Happy L fires at a downward angle with OTG-capable shots. Despite its use in combos, this is primarily used to safely counter an adversary's grounded anti-air attempts. From close distances, this leads into **Combo I** after Deadpool lands.

Trigger Happy M fires horizontally while Deadpool is grounded, but at a greater height than Trigger Happy L. This is always a superior option when fighting against opponents who cannot duck under Trigger Happy M. This is also useful when it's possible that your rival may attempt to normal jump over your Trigger Happy at long range. When used in the air, Trigger Happy M also fires horizontally but causes Deadpool to float, maintaining some of his airborne momentum when used. This is best used at the peak of his normal jump, causing him to float slightly slower to the ground than normal and put most, if not all, of his bullets onto the screen while descending, creating a wall of projectiles that is difficult for foes to bypass.

Trigger Happy H fires at an upward angle both while grounded and jumping. It can be useful to employ against competitors attempting to super jump toward Deadpool, or to take down challengers who are attempting to play a zoning game from the air.

7

8

9

Ninja Gift: Ninja Gift L is useful as a means of creating distance from opponents who are advancing from mid range. It is relatively safe, forcing the target to block while allowing Deadpool to create distance by jumping backward.

Ninja Gift M tosses a grenade that stays active for 100 frames or until it makes contact with an opponent or opponent's projectile. This makes it extremely useful for controlling the ground space, denying most adversaries the ability to dash toward Deadpool on the ground and allowing you to focus on denying your rival an avenue of approach through the air.

Ninja Gift H has a 72-frame capture against grounded foes, but it is nearly impossible to combo into anything other than an air Happy-Happy Trigger afterwards. This can be useful for tacking on extra damage with a THC. The real strength of this special move, however, is against airborne competitors. When the bolos hit an airborne foe, the foe falls to the ground in a special hard knockdown state. During this time, any attack is OTG-capable. However, this attack can be somewhat difficult to land because the projectile is rather small.

10

Quick Work: You should use this move primarily as a combo tool because it always knocks the opponent down regardless of hitstun decay. This attack also hits low and can be used to go under some projectiles, as well. Depending on the opposing character, Deadpool can use Quick Work M or H repeatedly during X-Factor 2 and 3 as an infinite. This attack can also be canceled into Chimichangas!! by pressing H during a precise 2 frame window. This window is different depending on which version of Quick Work you're canceling. Chimichangas!! is triggered by pressing H during frames 25-25 of Quick Work L, frames 45-46 of Quick Work M, and frames 55-56 of Quick Work H.

11

12

Katana-Rama!: The primary use of this move is Katana-Rama! H due to the ability of the attack to OTG and extend combos. This attack can be canceled into Chimichangas!!, which wall bounces your rival and is ideal for setting up a relaunch or hyper combo ender.

13

14

Teleport: This teleport transports Deadpool to a certain position on screen based on the button pressed. Pressing ← ↓ ↙ + L causes Deadpool to teleport to the left side of the screen, pressing ← ↓ ↙ + M causes Deadpool to teleport to the middle of the screen, and pressing ← ↓ ↙ + H causes Deadpool to teleport to the right side of the screen. You can use this either to keep distance from adversaries you want to zone or to cross up a competitor by teleporting behind the foe right before a projectile or beam assist connects.

Deadpool's Teleport is unique in that every third teleport malfunctions and causes an explosion, damaging and causing hard knockdown to Deadpool and any nearby opponents who are hit. However, if it misses the target or is blocked, it leaves Deadpool in a very vulnerable position where he can be easily be hit by any OTG his rival can muster. This can make Deadpool's Teleport unreliable, which is problematic because it's a core part of both his offense and zoning game.

Hyper Combos

Screen	Name	Command	Hits	Damage	Startup	Active	Recovery	Advantage on Hit	Advantage if Guarded	Notes
1	Happy-Happy Trigger (in air OK)	↓↘→ + ATK ATK	40~80	238,400~ 286,200	13+1	114	41	-11	-20	Each projectile has 1 high priority durability point, can be mashed for additional damage
1	Air Happy-Happy Trigger	(in air) ↓↘→ + ATK ATK	40~80	238,400~ 286,200	13+1	97	24 (or until grounded)	-2	-5	Each projectile has 1 high priority durability point, OTG-capable, can be mashed for additional damage
2	Cuttin' Time	↓↙← + ATK ATK	5	322,800	15+0	10	35	-6	-21	Frames 11-19 invincible
3	4th-Wall Crisis (Level 3 Hyper Combo)	→↓↘ + ATK ATK	3	400,000	5+1	80	24	—	—	5 frames invincibility, counters all attacks except beams/projectiles, hard knockdown

Happy-Happy Trigger: This is Deadpool's primary hyper combo. It is the ideal hyper to use at the end of combos, with fast startup and improved damage by mashing. You can also use it to cancel a hit-confirmed Trigger Happy L or M for extra damage. The air version of Happy-Happy Trigger is OTG-capable, so it can be useful to end combos if ground bounce is unavailable for Katana-Rama!

This hyper combo is also very useful for punishing poorly called assists. Even though this attack is a projectile, it hits all enemy characters in its path, allowing you to hit both an assist and the point character at the same time.

Cuttin' Time: Somewhat less useful now with the removal of the THC glitch, this attack will primarily be used if there is a need for a hyper combo early or to go through projectiles and beams at midscreen. You can also use it defensively to a limited extent, but the invincibility frames of that attack do not start until frame 11. It has no startup frames after the hyper freeze, so characters at close range may not always be able to block the attack if they were not already doing so before the hyper freeze.

4th-Wall Crisis: A counterattack hyper combo where Deadpool walks forward for 80 frames. If any attacks originating from the point character (aside from beams or projectiles) strike him, it activates the counterattack. Unfortunately, it has 1 frame of startup after the hyper freeze, so a quick opponent can easily cancel any attacks they were performing into a beam or projectile hyper combo during the hyper freeze animation.

"YOU WERE RECORDING THAT, WEREN'T YOU, PLAYER? NO? WHAT DO YOU MEAN YOU WEREN'T RECORDING THAT!"

Battle Plan

Using assists to augment Deadpool's zoning ability can be very helpful in locking down your rival.

Since Deadpool's preferred game plan is to stay at a distance and zone his adversary, his best role on the team is a meter builder as the first character on the team. This gives him access to his assists, which can greatly enhance his zoning game, either through increased zoning ability from projectile or beam assists or through protection from rushdown in the form of defensive assists. While Deadpool is decent as a meter user, he lacks the heavy damage and offensive ability needed to generate devastating combos, and his level 3 combo is unreliable. His X-Factor stats are average, and combined with his relatively weak offense, this makes him a weak anchor, though he does have an easy infinite in X-Factor levels 2 and 3 if you can manage to connect an attack.

As stated previously, your preferred game plan with Deadpool should be to keep your opponent at a distance and whittle them down with ranged attacks, or force them to take risks that put you in an advantageous situation. How you accomplish this with Deadpool varies depending on what type of competitor he is facing.

Battle Plan continued

Use Happy-Happy Triggers to punish opponents who recklessly call their assists.

Against offensive characters, Deadpool's primary means of zoning from mid to long range will be to normal jump, usually backward, and use Trigger Happy M at the peak of his jump. Ideally, you'll want the last shot to be low enough so your adversary cannot crouch under it. This allows Deadpool to control a wall of space from max jump height all the way to the ground, limiting the opposing character's options to super jump or use some other method to bypass the projectiles, such as invincibility or a stronger projectile or beam of their own. Always keep an eye on your rival's assist usage, as you can tag any careless assist usage with Happy-Happy Trigger to put massive damage on the assist.

Once Deadpool lands from air Trigger Happy M, you have options based on what the opposing player does or what you predict they might do. You can follow up with a Trigger Happy L or M for potentially added chip damage. However, opponents can escape this. Against large and some medium-sized characters, Trigger Happy M hits the target even if they are crouching. In these cases, this is your best option. However, against most medium-sized and smaller characters, Trigger Happy M simply goes over crouching competitors. Some can even simply walk under it, such as Amaterasu. In these cases, you need to decide whether your opponent will attempt to jump or not. If they aren't, Trigger Happy L is the better option, and Trigger Happy M or another jumping Trigger Happy M will be a less viable option. You can make this a completely inescapable blockstring if augmented by the use of a projectile or beam assist. You'll want to time the assist so that it hits between your air Trigger Happy M and your grounded Trigger Happy L or M. If your grounded Trigger Happy L or M connects in any of these situations, you can cancel into Happy-Happy Trigger for even more damage.

Ninja Gift L and M can be beneficial for deterring opponents from approaching Deadpool on the ground, as well. Ninja Gift M is especially useful at this because the grenades stays active for 100 frames, effectively preventing adversaries from dashing forward toward Deadpool, leaving you to protect other avenues of approach. If this grenade hits your attacker, you can usually follow up with a Trigger Happy L or M or even a Happy-Happy Trigger. You should use Ninja Gift L if your competitor is getting too close to Deadpool but is not yet attacking. Ninja Gift H can lead to big damage (see **Combo V**) if it hits an airborne rival, but it should not be relied upon heavily—use it sparingly.

If your opponent can correctly predict one of your zoning options and it seems as though they can punish before you have time to recover, you can now cancel any of Deadpool's special moves with Teleport. Use this to teleport him farther away or to the other side of the screen, and resume zoning. Just make sure to keep count of how many Teleports you have used, or you may find him on the ground setting up a free combo for your opposition.

If you have been doing a good job keeping your opponent away, they may attempt to super jump toward Deadpool in hopes of bypassing your zoning game. Luckily, Deadpool is well-equipped to handle this. If he is close to being cornered, the best option is to simply have him dash under the opposing character when they super jump. This puts him in the corner instead, giving you a ton of room to back up as needed and continue zoning your adversary. If dashing under your rival would be disadvantageous, you can use Trigger Happy H if the opponent is attempting to super jump toward Deadpool from fullscreen. If the opposing character is too close for Trigger Happy H, jumping back and using Ninja Gift L can help you gain some space, though this is risky because if your target dodges this attack, they can advance toward Deadpool and punish Deadpool's recovery.

When fighting other zoning characters, Deadpool needs to stay grounded more often in hopes of winning the distance fight. Trigger Happy L & M are typically the zoning tools of choice in this situation. While Deadpool has strong projectile strength, 8 durability points if he can get all 10 shots out, it takes a long time for him to fire all his shots. Characters with fast projectiles and beams with high durability are then able to overpower Deadpool in a zoning fight. Using projectile or beam assists may work in some situations, but against characters with quick beam attacks, this may end up just causing your assist to take unnecessary damage. In these cases, Deadpool needs to take the offensive.

When zoning is no longer a viable option because you are either facing a superior zoning character or time is running low and Deadpool has to make up a large health deficit, you must go on the offensive. While this is not the ideal situation for Deadpool, he does have a few ways to break his opponent's guard.

Using Teleport to cross up your adversary just as a projectile or beam assist hits the foe is one of Deadpool's few effective mix-ups.

While long or mid range, Deadpool can call long range assists and use his Teleport to appear behind an opponent right as the assist's projectile or beam is about to hit. If it connects, you can follow up with a full combo. Since Deadpool's Teleports are not relative to his rival's position, you'll need to learn the positions and distances he Teleports well in order for this to work. Once you have mastered his Teleport, you can perform these Teleports from distances that make it very difficult for your competitor to know which side Deadpool is going to appear on.

Use Quick Work or Cuttin' Time to bypass enemy projectiles.

You can use Quick Work to slide underneath some projectiles and beam attacks, either linking with crouching Ⓜ (**Combo VI**) if done from far away or canceling to Chimichangas!! (**Combo Appendix II**) if done close to convert into a full combo. This generally only works on ranged attacks that are above Deadpool's waist. Otherwise, you can have Deadpool perform his Cuttin' Time hyper combo before the projectile or beam reaches him and then use his invincibility to pass through the projectile.

Using assists with Mad Wheel can free up Deadpool's OTG Katana-Rama! for use later in a combo!

Once Deadpool is close to his opponent, you can use Deadpool's Mad Wheel (→ + Ⓜ) overhead attack. Like most overheads, this attack has slow startup. If it lands, you can follow up with an OTG attack (see **Combo IV**). You can use an assist to avoid using his OTG early in the combo in order to optimize damage. This overhead mixed with his chained crouching Ⓛ attacks can make it difficult for your competitor to know whether to block high or low.

Another option while close is to use staggered crouching Ⓛ attacks. These attacks can chain, but the timing can be changed up. Opponents frequently attempt to use advancing guard to push Deadpool away during blockstrings. Because light attacks cause very little blockstun, staggering the crouching Ⓛ attacks can cause your adversary to attempt to advancing guard when they are not in blockstun, causing them to attempt an attack. Your staggered crouching Ⓛ hits first and makes contact with the target, leading to a free combo (see **Combo I**).

Deadpool lacks any strong defensive tools and relies on zoning to stay out of harm's way. If a rival does manage to get close to Deadpool, Deadpool's main defense is going to be advancing guard. Aside from that, only his level 3 hyper combo, 4th-Wall Crisis, has complete startup invincibility, but it relies on the foe hitting Deadpool in order for it to work. This is mainly only useful if your challenger has no meter or lacks non-physical hyper combos. Most characters can completely negate the usefulness of this counter hyper combo by using the super freeze time to cancel any physical attacks in progress. Any projectiles, beams, or throws can beat this hyper combo handily.

COMBO USAGE

I. CR. Ⓛ, Ⓜ, ST. Ⓗ CANCEL ⇨ ↓ ↙ ← + Ⓗ(DURING QUICK WORK) Ⓗ, FORWARD DASH, CR. Ⓗ, Ⓢ, CANCEL ⇨ FORWARD SUPER JUMP, AIR Ⓜ, Ⓜ, Ⓗ, Ⓢ, LAND, FORWARD DASH, → ↓ ↘ + Ⓗ (DURING KATANA-RAMA!) Ⓗ CANCEL ⇨ ↓ ↘ → + ATK ATK (MASH ATK)

672,400 damage, 25% meter loss

Here's a basic combo for Deadpool from his cr. Ⓛ attack. You'll need to cancel his st. Ⓗ to Quick Work H very quickly, or the opponent air recovers. The hardest part of the combo is successfully canceling Quick Work H into the Chimichangas!! There is only a two- frame window for this input, so you'll want to press Ⓗ just after your adversary begins to descend. When canceling the final Chimichangas!! into Happy-Happy Trigger, you'll want to do it quickly since the wall bounce has already been used earlier in this combo.

You may tack on an additional crouching Ⓛ to the beginning of this combo for added flexibility but less overall damage. If crouching Ⓛ x 2 is blocked, stage a secondary attack by throwing your foe, canceling into → + Ⓜ, or attacking with **Combo I** again.

II. ↓ ↘ → + Ⓛ OR Ⓜ CANCEL ⇨ ← ↓ ↙ + Ⓗ, CR. Ⓛ, Ⓜ, ST. Ⓗ CANCEL ⇨ ↓ ↙ ← + Ⓗ(DURING KATANA-RAMA!) Ⓗ, FORWARD DASH, CR. Ⓗ, Ⓢ, CANCEL ⇨ FORWARD SUPER JUMP, AIR Ⓜ, Ⓜ, Ⓗ, Ⓢ, LAND, FORWARD DASH, → ↓ ↘ + Ⓗ (DURING KATANA-RAMA!) Ⓗ CANCEL ⇨ ↓ ↘ → + ATK ATK (MASH ATK)

439,600 damage, 3% meter loss

This converts Trigger Happy L or M into **Combo I** from great distances. Though its power is relatively low because of the damage reduction induced by the opening gun shots, this is still occasionally worth going for to maximize damage when a K.O. is needed. Note that the link into crouching Ⓛ after Teleport is very difficult; cancel into Teleport just as Deadpool's guns flare for the fifth time to ensure that you're following the very last shot fired as closely as possible.

III. FORWARD THROW, DASH FORWARD, → ↓ ↘ + Ⓗ(DURING KATANA-RAMA!) Ⓗ, FORWARD DASH, ST. Ⓗ CANCEL ⇨ ↓ ↙ ← + Ⓜ, Ⓢ CANCEL ⇨ FORWARD SUPER JUMP, AIR Ⓜ, Ⓗ, Ⓢ, LAND, ↓ ↘ → ↗ + ATK ATK (MASH ATK)

463,400 damage, 42% meter loss

Following the forward throw, you'll want to dash forward and then immediately cancel the dash into Katana-Rama! H. Deadpool only moves forward a short distance, but that's all he needs to get in range for the OTG. Following the wall bounce, dash forward and hit with st. Ⓗ as late as possible so that your adversary doesn't air recover before Quick Work hits. Quick Work M should place the target close enough that you don't need to dash to follow up with Ⓢ. If performing this combo in the corner, dash back after the Chimichangas!! so that you can combo properly after Quick Work. When attempting to OTG with Happy-Happy Trigger, make sure you get enough height so that both sets of bullets are hitting and you get full damage. You can also use Happy-Happy Trigger before Deadpool lands to OTG, if doing the ↓ ↘ → ↗ motion is troublesome.

IV. FORWARD AIR THROW, LAND, → ↓ ↘ + Ⓗ(DURING KATANA-RAMA!) Ⓗ, WALK FORWARD SLIGHTLY, ST. Ⓗ CANCEL ⇨ ↓ ↙ ← + Ⓜ, Ⓢ CANCEL ⇨ FORWARD SUPER JUMP, AIR Ⓗ, Ⓢ, LAND, ↓ ↘ → ↗ + ATK ATK (MASH ATK)

489,300 damage, 47% meter loss

This is similar to the previous combo, but the hit decay is worse after his air throw, allowing only an air Ⓗ, Ⓢ combo after the launcher.

V. → + Ⓜ, → ↓ ↘ + Ⓗ(DURING KATANA-RAMA!) Ⓗ, FORWARD DASH, CR. Ⓜ, ST, Ⓗ CANCEL ⇨ ↓ ↙ ← + Ⓜ, FORWARD DASH, Ⓢ CANCEL ⇨ FORWARD SUPER JUMP, AIR Ⓗ, Ⓢ, LAND, ↓ ↘ → ↗ + ATK ATK (MASH ATK)

595,600 damage, 45% meter loss

After landing a hard knockdown from his overhead, Deadpool can OTG to lead into a full combo. Having to use his OTG early in the combo limits his overall damage, using both his ground bounce and wall bounce very early in the combo.

VI. (AGAINST AIRBORNE OPPONENT) ↓ ↘ → + Ⓗ(DURING TRIGGER HAPPY) Ⓗ, FORWARD DASH, CR. Ⓜ, ST. Ⓗ CANCEL ⇨ ↓ ↙ ← + Ⓗ (DURING QUICK WORK) Ⓗ, FORWARD DASH, CR. Ⓗ, Ⓢ CANCEL ⇨ FORWARD SUPER JUMP, AIR Ⓗ, Ⓢ, LAND, → ↓ ↘ + Ⓗ (DURING KATANA-RAMA!) Ⓗ CANCEL ⇨ ↓ ↘ → + ATK ATK (MASH ATK)

652,700 damage, 34% meter loss

If Deadpool can manage to land Ninja Gift H against an airborne opponent, you can convert this into a full combo. Dash forward immediately upon landing and press cr. Ⓜ just before Deadpool gets in range. Deadpool then slides forward slightly, allowing his cr. Ⓜ to connect. The rest is identical to **Combo I**.

VII. ↓ ↙ ← + Ⓗ, FORWARD DASH, CR. Ⓜ, ST. Ⓗ CANCEL ⇨ ↓ ↙ ← + Ⓗ (DURING QUICK WORK) Ⓗ, FORWARD DASH, CR. Ⓗ, Ⓢ CANCEL ⇨ FORWARD SUPER JUMP, AIR Ⓗ, Ⓢ, LAND, → ↓ ↘ + Ⓗ (DURING KATANA-RAMA!) Ⓗ CANCEL ⇨ ↓ ↘ → + ATK ATK (MASH ATK)

772,700 damage, 27% meter loss

When Deadpool lands Quick Work H, he can easily convert into big damage. You'll want to hit the first cr. Ⓜ as low as possible so your challenger doesn't air recover, but otherwise, the combo is similar to **Combo I**.

ADVANCED TACTICS

CURSES! FOILED AGAIN. (TELEPORT MALFUNCTION MANAGEMENT)

Learning to manage Deadpool's Teleport Malfunction is important for mastering Deadpool and unlocking his full offensive potential.

Deadpool's Teleport can be an unreliable part of his game plan because every third Teleport malfunctions. Learning how to manage this aspect of his Teleport is key to mastering Deadpool. There are a few ways to deal with Teleport Malfunction. The optimal way is to end a combo with a hard knockdown followed by OTG Teleport Malfunction (possibly canceled into Air Happy-Happy Trigger, though not all hits will connect). This resets the Teleport count and also only causes marginally less damage than a similar Katana-Rama! OTG. Failing that, you can attempt to Teleport Malfunction behind the cover of a projectile or beam assist from fullscreen. Using assists that can keep your opponent locked down for a long period of time like Doctor Doom—β or Sentinel—α is your best option for this method. Another alternative is to simply use it at close range and cancel into Happy-Happy Trigger and THC to a safe hyper combo if it is blocked.

DEADPOOL

COMBO APPENDIX

GENERAL EXECUTION TIPS

- When using Happy-Happy Trigger after wall bounces and Quick Work, delay the hyper combo slightly so you get full damage
- Deadpool's basic attacks cause very little hitstun, so they must be chained quickly
- When canceling to Quick Work with Chimichangas!!, wait until just after your rival begins falling to press Ⓗ

AS DEADPOOL COMES IN: AIR Ⓜ, Ⓜ [CANCEL] FORWARD DOUBLE JUMP, AIR Ⓗ, Ⓢ, LAND, ↓↘→↗ + ATK ATK (MASH ATK)

Notes	Damage
⇧ + Ⓢ or ⇨ + Ⓢ or ⇩ + Ⓢ TAC to Deadpool	Varies based on damage scaling

CR. Ⓛ, Ⓜ, ST. Ⓗ [CANCEL] ↓↙← + Ⓗ, FORWARD DASH, CR. Ⓜ, ST. Ⓗ [CANCEL] ↓↙← + Ⓜ (DURING QUICK WORK) Ⓗ, FORWARD DASH, CR. Ⓗ, Ⓢ, [CANCEL] FORWARD SUPER JUMP, AIR Ⓗ, Ⓢ, LAND, FORWARD DASH, →↓↘ + Ⓗ (DURING KATANA-RAMA!) Ⓗ [CANCEL] ↓↘→ + ATK ATK (MASH ATK)

Notes	Damage
Harder version of **Combo I**	719,700 damage, 14% meter loss

↓↙← + Ⓗ (DURING QUICK WORK) Ⓗ, FORWARD DASH, CR. Ⓗ, Ⓢ [CANCEL] FORWARD SUPER JUMP, AIR Ⓜ, Ⓜ, Ⓗ, Ⓢ, LAND, →↓↘ + Ⓗ (DURING KATANA-RAMA!) Ⓗ [CANCEL] ↓↘→ + ATK ATK (MASH ATK)

Notes	Damage
Alternative, slightly easier combo for Quick Work combo starter	686,500 damage, 39% meter loss

→↓↘ + ATK ATK, COUNTERS ENEMY ATTACK, FORWARD DASH, →↓↘ + Ⓗ (DURING KATANA-RAMA!) Ⓗ, ST. Ⓗ [CANCEL] ↓↙← + Ⓜ, Ⓢ [CANCEL] FORWARD SUPER JUMP, AIR Ⓗ, Ⓢ, LAND, ↓↘→↗ + ATK ATK (MASH ATK)

Notes	Damage
Level 3 hyper combo follow-up	897,400 damage, 365% meter loss

↓↘→ + Ⓛ OR Ⓜ [X-FACTOR] ↓↙← + Ⓗ, ST. Ⓗ [CANCEL] ↓↙← + Ⓜ, ST. Ⓗ [CANCEL] ↓↙← + Ⓜ, CR. Ⓗ, Ⓢ [CANCEL] FORWARD SUPER JUMP, AIR Ⓜ, Ⓜ, Ⓗ, Ⓢ, LAND, →↓↘ + Ⓗ (DURING KATANA-RAMA!) Ⓗ, ↓↙← + Ⓗ [CANCEL] ↓↘→ + ATK ATK (MASH ATK)

Notes	Damage
Delay ⇩⬂⇨ + ATK ATK to get full damage; works from up to three-fourths of the screen away	Level 1 X-Factor, 871,000 damage, 33% meter gain

CR. Ⓛ, Ⓜ, ST. Ⓗ [CANCEL] ↓↙← + Ⓗ [X-FACTOR], ST. Ⓗ [CANCEL] ↓↙← + Ⓗ, (↓↙← + Ⓗ REPEAT AS NEEDED)

Notes	Damage
Infinite with Level 3 X-Factor. Works with Level 2 X-Factor, as well, but use ⇩⬃⇦ + Ⓜ instead for the repeating pattern	Level 3 X-Factor, 100% of enemy life, meter gain varies

CR. Ⓛ, Ⓜ, ST. Ⓗ [CANCEL] ↓↙← + Ⓗ (DURING QUICK WORK) Ⓗ, FORWARD DASH, CR. Ⓗ, Ⓢ, [CANCEL] FORWARD SUPER JUMP, AIR Ⓜ, Ⓜ, Ⓗ, Ⓢ, LAND, FORWARD DASH, ←↓↙ + ATK [CANCEL] ↓↘→ + ATK ATK (MASH ATK)

Notes	Damage
Combo ending with Teleport Malfunction OTG	617,600 damage, 28% meter loss

DOCTOR DOOM

"NO ONE DEFEATS DOOM!"

Bio

REAL NAME
Victor von Doom

OCCUPATION
Monarch of Latveria, Would-Be Conqueror

ABILITIES
Doom is a genius in physics, robotics, cybernetics, genetics, weapons technology, bio-chemistry, and time travel. He is also self-taught in the mystic arts. Doom is a natural leader, a brilliant strategist, and a sly deceiver.

WEAPONS
His armor is loaded with gimmicks, including a high-powered blaster on his waist holster. He also personally invented some nasty surprises.

PROFILE
The masked genius scientist who plots for world domination. While his physical strength is only average at best, the technologically advanced weapons he develops, as well as his sinister plans have given his super hero foes plenty to worry about.

FIRST APPEARANCE
Fantastic Four #5 (1962)

POWER GRID

6	INTELLIGENCE
4	STRENGTH
5	SPEED
6	STAMINA
6	ENERGY PROJECTION
4	FIGHTING ABILITY

*This is biographical, and does not represent an evaluation of the in-game combat potential of this hero.

1

2

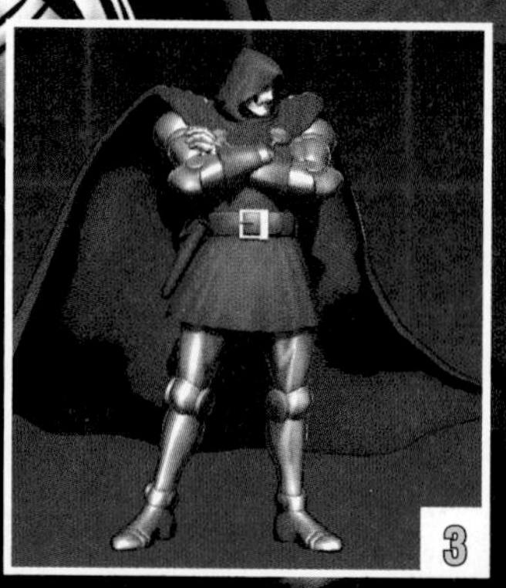
3

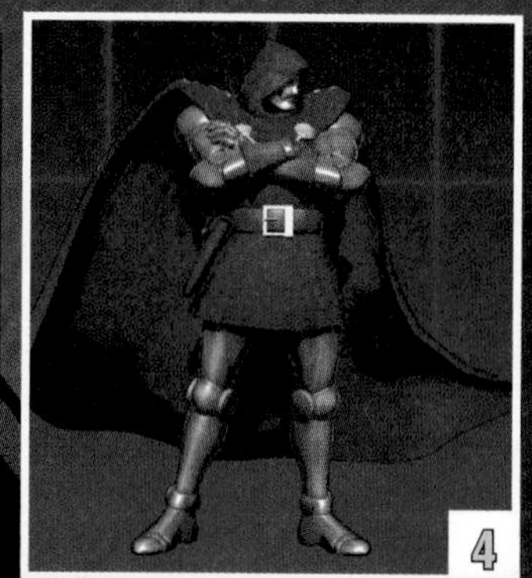
4

5

6

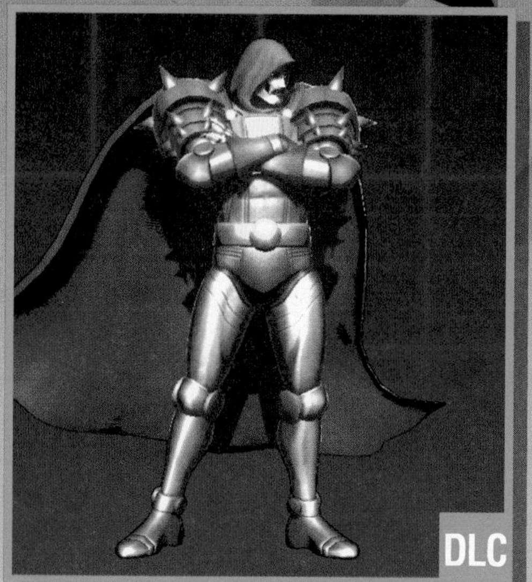
DLC

Vitality	1,000,000
Chain Combo Archetype	Marvel Series

X-Factor Boost	Damage	Speed
Level 1 (3 teammates remaining)	130%	110%
Level 2 (2 teammates remaining)	150%	120%
Level 3 (1 teammate remaining)	170%	130%

Doctor Doom is a well-rounded character who can be effective at both short and long range. Your goal when using him is to corner your opponent. Cornering foes with Doctor Doom is important because:

- **His mix-ups are much more difficult to defend against in the corner**
- **His corner combos are significantly more damaging than their midscreen counterparts**

Doctor Doom has numerous tools to achieve this goal, including:

- **Using air Ⓢ and air ➔ + Ⓗ as a means to approach.**
- **Utilizing dash canceling to combat advancing guard. Jumping forward and airdashing down-toward to cover horizontal distance quickly**
- **Super jumping and airdashing down-toward behind the cover of Air Photon Shot L**
- **Slowly pushing his opponent back toward the corner using his dominating array of projectile attacks**

Tuning Since Original MVC3

Already one of the most desired crossover assists to have on a team, as well as a perfectly capable point character, Doctor Doom still received several significant improvements to his game!

The most noteworthy change to Doctor Doom's arsenal is the improvements to his air Ⓢ attack: it now travels much more quickly and causes a hard knockdown state on opponents, allowing for easy conversions into combos using his OTG-capable standing Ⓗ attack. Doom's air Ⓗ laser beam now travels across the screen much more quickly, changing it from a liability into an important tool to close the distance and push Doom's rival back into the corner.

On the downside, Doctor Doom's Hidden Missiles crossover assist now fires two less missiles, making it slightly less infuriating for opponents to deal with.

- Hidden Missiles crossover assist now fires six missiles instead of eight
- Forward throw now causes hard knockdown but does not lift the opponent as high
- Forward air throw now causes hard knockdown but does not lift the target as high
- Air Ⓗ beam now travels across the screen much more quickly
- Air Ⓢ now travels much more quickly and causes hard knockdown
- Photon Array and Air Photon Array can now be mashed for additional hits and damage
- Doom's Time can now be mashed for additional hits and damage
- Glitch removed that allowed Doctor Doom to stack several silos of Hidden Missiles on top of each other
- Up-back and down-back airdashes can now be canceled with basic attacks or special moves

Attack Set

Standing Basic Attacks

Screen	Command	Hits	Damage	Meter Gain	Startup	Active	Recovery	Advantage on Hit	Advantage if Guarded	Notes
1	Standing L	1	55,000	440	5	3	12	+1	-1	Dash-cancelable
2	Standing M	2	72,000	640	10	4	17	+4	+2	OTG-capable, dash- cancelable
3	Standing H	2	101,700	880	15	7	21	+2	0	OTG-capable, dash-cancelable

1

2

3

Crouching Basic Attacks

Screen	Command	Hits	Damage	Meter Gain	Startup	Active	Recovery	Advantage on Hit	Advantage if Guarded	Notes
1	Crouching L	1	53,000	424	6	3	16	-3	-5	Low attack, chains into crouching L, dash-cancelable
2	Crouching M	1	70,000	560	9	4	21	-2	-4	Dash-cancelable
3	Crouching H	1	80,000	640	13	4	21	—	-1	Low attack, dash-cancelable, knocks down

1

2

3

Ground Special Attack—Launcher

Screen	Command	Hits	Damage	Meter Gain	Startup	Active	Recovery	Advantage on Hit	Advantage if Guarded	Notes
1	S (while standing or crouching)	1	100,000	800	11	4	21	—	-1	Launcher, not special- or hyper combo-cancelable

1

Air Basic Attacks

Screen	Command	Hits	Damage	Meter Gain	Startup	Active	Recovery	Advantage on Hit	Advantage if Guarded	Notes
1	Air L	1	55,000	440	6	3	20	+14	+12	Overhead attack
2	Air M	2	81,000	720	10	7	19	+21	+19	Overhead attack
3	Air H	4	120,300	1120	21	20	22	+24	+12	Inflicts chip damage, not special or hyper combo-cancelable, beam durability: 1 frame x 1 low priority durability points

1

2

3

Air Special Attacks—Flying Screen and Air Exchange

Air (S) causes a hard knockdown when used in a launcher combo (this is sometimes called flying screen). When used outside of a launcher combo, air (S) behaves mostly like another basic attack. Air exchange attacks, performed by inputting a direction plus (S), are only possible during a launcher combo. Exchange hits initiate team aerial combos by tagging in the next available character to continue the air combo.

Screen	Command	Hits	Damage	Meter Gain	Startup	Active	Recovery	Advantage on Hit	Advantage if Guarded	Notes
1	Air (S)	1	90,000	720	14	Until grounded or contact	1 or until grounded	—	-18	Causes hard knockdown
2	Air ↑ + (S) (during launcher combo)	2	105,00	880	10	4	27	—	—	Tags in next available ally while lofting opponent upward
3	Air → or ← + (S) (during launcher combo)	2	95,000	800	9	8	19	—	—	Tags in next available ally while causing wall bounce, erases 1 hyper meter bar from foe
4	Air ↓ + (S) (during launcher combo)	2	95,000	800	9	8	9	—	—	Tags in next available ally while causing ground bounce, generates 1 hyper meter bar

1

2

3

4

Command Attacks

Command attacks resemble basic attacks but have different chaining and canceling properties. It's usually possible to chain *into* a command attack from basic attacks, but most command attacks cannot be chained from or canceled themselves.

Screen	Name	Command	Hits	Damage	Meter Gain	Startup	Active	Recovery	Advantage on Hit	Advantage if Guarded	Notes
1	Hard Kick	→ + (H)	1	90,000	720	8	4	24	—	-4	Launcher attack, dash-cancelable
2	Hidden Missiles	← + (H)	1~8	20,000~113,600	160 per missile	25	—	30	—	—	Can press (H) rapidly for up to 7 extra missiles, OTG-capable, each missile has 1 low priority durability point
3	Foot Dive	(in air) → + (H)	1	90,000	720	12	Until grounded, contact with foe, or contact with screen edge	1	+21	+19	Can only be performed once per jump

1

2

3

Throws

Throws are for snagging passive or blocking opponents. Since throws are active so quickly, you can also use them to preemptively toss opposing characters out of their offense. Combos are usually possible after throws, one way or another.

Screen	Command	Hits	Damage	Meter Gain	Startup	Active	Notes
1	→ + (H) (ground)	1	80,000	800	1	1	Hard knockdown
	← + (H) (ground)	1	80,000	800	1	1	Hard knockdown
2	→ + (H) (air)	1	80,000	800	1	1	Hard knockdown
	← + (H) (air)	1	80,000	800	1	1	Hard knockdown

1

2

As a Partner—Crossover Assists

Screen	Type	P1+P2 Crossover Combination Hyper Combo	Description	Hits	Damage	Meter Gain	Startup	Active	Recovery (this crossover assist)	Recovery (other partner)	Notes
1	Doctor Doom—α	Photon Array	Plasma Beam M	8	113,600	1280	46	20	108	78	Beam durability: 8 frames x 1 low priority durability points
2	Doctor Doom—β	Photon Array	Hidden Missiles	6	93,500	160 per missile	50	37	147	117	OTG-capable, each missile has 1 durability point
3	Doctor Doom—γ	Sphere Flame	Molecular Shield M	9	111,800	1400	34	26	124	94	Initial barrier lasts for 25 frames, inflicts 1 low priority durability point of damage per frame, four rocks fired afterward, each rock has 1 low priority durability point

1

2

3

Doctor Doom is one of the best teammates to have in the game, since all three of his crossover assist types are top class. No matter which assist type you pick, calling Doctor Doom for backup as often as you can makes life significantly more difficult for the opposing player—just be sure to protect Doom!

Doctor Doom—α Plasma Beam is one of the best all-around assists in the game: it reaches fullscreen in an instant, dominates most other projectiles, places the opposing character in a long period of guardstun, and is perfect for cross-up mix-ups using teleports and other side-switching maneuvers!

Doctor Doom—β Hidden Missiles is a one-of-a-kind crossover assist, sending six missiles into the air to home in on the opponent at a later time. While this is a useful asset for any character to have, this crossover assist really shines when paired with a long range zoning character. Hidden Missiles is not only is effective at preventing adversaries from super jumping into the air, but it also makes the point character practically unassailable for a brief period of time; if the opponent tries to attack before the missiles come down, they get a host of explosives dumped on their head, allowing you to capitalize with a free combo!

Doctor Doom—γ Molecular Shield is slow, but in a good way: it remains an active threat on the screen for an extremely long period of time, making it awesome for use as covering fire for slower characters who struggle to get near their adversary.

Snap Back

Screen	Command	Hits	Damage	Meter Gain	Startup	Active	Recovery	Advantage on Hit	Advantage if Guarded
1	↓↘→ + P1 or P2	1	50,000	500 (-1 hyper meter bar)	2	4	24	—	-4

Notes

On hit, snap back forces the opposing point character to be replaced by an assist. Opposing assist calls or tag outs are also locked out for 4 seconds

1

Special Moves

Screen	Name	Command	Hits	Damage	Meter Gain	Startup	Active	Recovery	Advantage on Hit	Advantage if Guarded	Notes
1	Plasma Beam L	↓↘→ + L	5	81,700	800	22	15	14	—	+3	Knocks down, beam durability: 5 frames x 1 low priority durability points
	Plasma Beam M	↓↘→ + M	8	113,600	1280	22	20	17	—	+1	Knocks down, beam durability: 8 frames x 1 low priority durability points
	Plasma Beam H	↓↘→ + H	12	143,000	1920	22	25	19	—	+2	Knocks down, beam durability: 12 frames x 1 low priority durability points
2	Air Plasma Beam L	(in air) ↓↘→ + L	5	81,700	800	25	20	7	—	+4	Knocks down, OTG-capable, beam durability: 5 frames x 1 low priority durability points
	Air Plasma Beam M	(in air) ↓↘→ + M	8	113,600	1280	25	20	16	—	0	Knocks down, OTG-capable, beam durability: 8 frames x 1 low priority durability points
	Air Plasma Beam H	(in air) ↓↘→ + H	12	143,000	1920	25	25	21	—	-2	Knocks down, OTG-capable, beam durability: 12 frames x 1 low priority durability points
3	Photon Shot	↓↙← + ATK	5x2	30,000 per projectile	240 per projectile	27	—	33	-8	-10	Each projectile has 2 low priority durability points
4	Air Photon Shot L	(in air) ↓↙← + L	5	30,000 per projectile	240 per projectile	27	—	23	+19	+15	Each projectile has 2 low priority durability points
	Air Photon Shot M	(in air) ↓↙← + M	5	30,000 per projectile	240 per projectile	24	—	26	+14	+12	Each projectile has 2 low priority durability points
	Air Photon Shot H	(in air) ↓↙← + H	5	30,000 per projectile	240 per projectile	21	—	29	+11	+9	Each projectile has 2 low priority durability points

Special Moves continued

Screen	Name	Command	Hits	Damage	Meter Gain	Startup	Active	Recovery	Advantage on Hit	Advantage if Guarded	Notes
5	Molecular Shield L	⇨⇩⇘ + Ⓛ	7	103,100	1160	7	15(1)1	37	-13	-11	Initial barrier lasts for 15 frames, inflicts 1 low priority durability point of damage per frame, four rocks fired afterward, each rock has 1 low priority durability point
	Molecular Shield M	⇨⇩⇘ + Ⓜ	9	111,800	1400	10	26	33	-8	-8	Initial barrier lasts for 25 frames, inflicts 1 low priority durability point of damage per frame, four rocks fired afterward, each rock has 1 low priority durability point
	Molecular Shield H	⇨⇩⇘ + Ⓗ	11	118,900	1640	13	36	27	-1	-1	Initial barrier lasts for 35 frames, inflicts 1 low priority durability point of damage per frame, four rocks fired afterward, each rock has 1 low priority durability point
6	Flight (in air OK)	⇩⇙⇦ + Ⓢ	—	—	—	15	—	—	—	—	Activates flight mode, lasts for 106 frames

1

Plasma Beam: At a devastating 12 durability points, Doctor Doom's Plasma Beam cuts through most things in its path, including foes, opposing projectiles, and your enemy's crossover assists. For a projectile, Plasma Beam deals a substantial amount of regular damage and chip damage. Even though Plasma Beam H has the longest recovery of the three versions, it definitely packs the most punch and should be the primary version that Doom players use. Plasma Beam is one of the most damaging special attacks in the game in terms of chip damage, dealing a whopping 72,000 points of chip damage with each beam fired! Because of its high damage, Plasma Beam H is great for inflicting big damage to crossover assists. Tagging an assist with the beam definitely makes opposing players think twice about calling teammates for help! Plasma Beam can also be used in conjunction with Photon Array to finish off foes with low health. Cancel Plasma Beam into Photon Array into another Plasma Beam to K.O. a weakened opponent with massive chip damage.

If your adversary jumps over Plasma Beam H and is in range to hit Doctor Doom, react with a hyper combo cancel into Sphere Flame to quickly anti-air the foe for big damage.

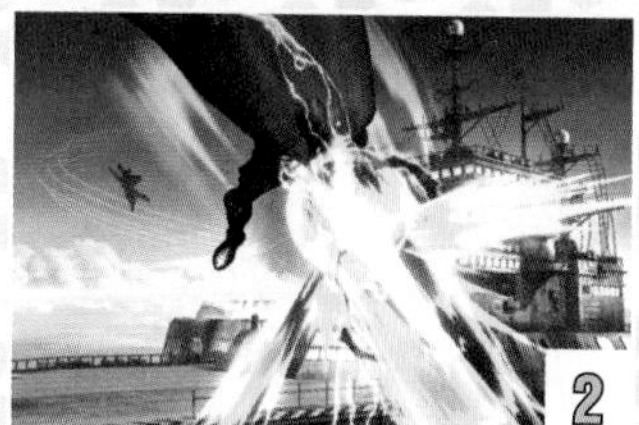
2

Air Plasma Beam: The aerial version of Plasma Beam fires at a little more than a 45-degree angle. It has the same properties as its ground counterpart, and it can be performed a total of three times when Doom is in the air. You can also utilize it to blast opponents approaching from below, as it creates a temporary wall that blocks ground-level advances.

You can use air Plasma Beam offensively, as well. Doctor Doom can quickly get into optimal firing range by normal jumping forward, then airdashing up-forward and performing air Plasma Beam. This can make for a surprising attack when used with a long range crossover assist: call your crossover assist during the normal jump so that once Doctor Doom is performing the air Plasma Beam, the crossover assist starts aiding in the firefight without being seen on screen.

Air Plasma Beam is an OTG-capable attack that can be used to lend huge damage at the end of long combos: after causing a hard knockdown state, hit your opponent with a low-altitude air Plasma Beam H and hyper combo cancel to air Photon Array. This leaves the opposing character at the perfect height to be further juggled with a THC combo.

3

Photon Shot: Doctor Doom fires five small lasers in both directions, controlling a fan-shaped space on the screen. While Photon Shot doesn't deal much damage, its utility is where it shines. Photon Shot can be used to bring down airborne opponents, shutting off the skies as a means to approach. Photon Shot also covers the space directly in front of Doctor Doom, impeding advances from the front. Given these angles, this projectile can be extremely difficult to avoid—this is particularly bad news for opposing characters who are low on life and trying to avoid a K.O. Photon Shot is also a nightmare for teleporting characters because it covers Doctor Doom's back from rear teleports, making competitors think twice about sneaking in from behind.

The speed of the photons changes based on the attack button used. Photon Shot L travels the slowest, the H version travels the fastest, and Photon Shot M is in-between. Players can use Photon Shot L both defensively and as a means of trapping rivals from across the screen. Photon Shot H is the fastest way to tag airborne opponents.

A drawback of Photon Shot is the "dead space" directly above Doctor Doom's head. A poorly timed Photon Shot against a quick foe can be a costly vulnerability. If you see the opposing character dropping in directly from above during Photon Shot, quickly hyper combo cancel it into Sphere Flame as a high-damage countermeasure.

4

Air Photon Shot: Doctor Doom creates the same fan-shape attack while in the air, except this version is aimed at the ground. Just like its ground version counterpart, air Photon Shot can be extremely difficult for opposing players to avoid, and it can be used for free chip damage. It also serves as a breather from the action below, resetting the pace of the battle. If an adversary jumps up to attack Doctor Doom and subsequently gets hit on the way up by air Photon Array, you can combo off the photons with a falling air Ⓜ if the opposing character is close enough. Keep in mind that you can only perform one air Photon Shot in the air before Doom lands, as opposed to air Plasma Beam and most other specials, which can be used three times in midair.

5

Molecular Shield: Molecular Shield is a two-phase move. It initially behaves as a shield, stopping incoming projectiles and damaging foes at point-blank range. The rocks are then launched as an offensive attack. This move should be primarily used as a combo ender in the corner. Molecular Shield boasts the fastest startup time of all Doctor Doom's special attacks. You can also use the initial shield of rocks to counter an incoming projectile in a pinch, nullifying the projectile before sending a wave of debris back at your rival. If you manage to pin your target down at mid to long range with a launched Molecular Shield, execute Plasma Beam H or even a quick advance to follow up.

6

Flight: Doctor Doom becomes airborne for 106 frames and has all of his air attacks at the ready, as well as unlimited airdashes throughout the duration of the flight. If flight mode is activated off the ground or during a normal jump, crossover assists may be used during the duration of the flight, which can make for an unorthodox style of attack. In addition, any air Ⓜ used during flight can be instantly unfly-canceled by inputting ⇩⇙⇦ + Ⓢ again, which can lead to another air Ⓜ while falling. Flight is also an opportune time to abuse air Ⓢ for foes waiting for Doctor Doom below.

Doctor Doom gains access to an unlimited amount of airdashes during the duration of flight mode, as well as the ability to cancel airdashes into each other (however, two consecutive dashes cannot be in the same direction, unless you use "plink" airdashing by pressing ATK~ATK on consecutive frames). So during flight mode, you can perform airdash down-forward, forward, then up-forward as a means to approach, then cancel flight mode into falling air Ⓜ or air Ⓢ to start Doctor Doom's strong up-close game.

If Flight is activated while grounded with a tiger knee motion of ⇩⇙⇦⇖ + Ⓢ, Doctor Doom will fly extremely low to the ground. This can be used to open your enemy up with an overhead air Ⓜ. Pin the opponent down with a crossover assist, dash in close and perform a tiger knee Flight, then perform air Ⓜ (2 hits), Ⓜ (2 hits) CANCEL ⇩⇙⇦ + Ⓢ, land, cr. Ⓛ, Ⓜ, Ⓗ into a combo.

Hyper Combos

Screen	Name	Command	Hits	Damage	Startup	Active	Recovery	Advantage on Hit	Advantage if Guarded	Notes
1	Photon Array	⇩⇙⇦ + ATK ATK	25~50x2	287,900~345,800 (20,000~24,000 per projectile)	10+1	40	34	+4	+2	Can be mashed for extra hits and damage, each projectile has 1 high priority durability point
2	Air Photon Array	(in air) ⇩⇙⇦ + ATK ATK	25~50	287,900~345,800 (20,000~24,000 per projectile)	10+1	40	59	-34	-35	OTG-capable, can be mashed for extra hits and damage, each projectile has 1 high priority durability point
3	Sphere Flame	⇨⇩⇘ + ATK ATK	57	340,000	8+1	—	47	+17	+35	First projectile rises for 40 frames, then disappears and produces 20 projectiles that spread and fall for 26 frames, first projectile has 1 high priority durability point, follow up projectiles have beam durability: 2 x 1 high priority durability points
4	Doom's Time (Level 3 Hyper Combo)	⇩⇘⇨ + ATK ATK	13	440,000	4+0	1	49	—	-27	Invincible from frames 1-9, unaffected by damage scaling

Photon Array: Photon Array covers the majority of the screen, making it almost impossible for opposing players to avoid. Because of its poor damage output, Photon Array is best used as a screen-clearing breather if you have an abundance of hyper meter to spare. If used at mid to long range, Doom recovers from the Photon Array earlier than a guarding opponent, giving you the initiative to begin an offensive or follow up with Plasma Beam H. You can also use Photon Array to punish foes who are predictable in their teleports, since Doom's photons end up covering the spots where most teleports typically wind up. New to *UMvC3*, Photon Array can now be mashed for extra damage!

Air Photon Array: Aside from using it as a combo ender, you can also employ air Photon Array the same way as air Photon Shot, as well as regular Photon Array. When you end combos with air Photon Array, your opponent is left in a prime position for a THC. Similar to the ground version of Photon Array, you can mash the air version for additional damage.

Sphere Flame: Doctor Doom fires a single projectile upward that explodes at the very top of the battlefield before sending a rain of projectiles down across the screen. The primary use of this hyper combo outside of combos is to protect the area directly above Doctor Doom's head. If Sphere Flame hits on the way up, the opposing character is sent to the top of the screen along with the projectile, causing them to eat every single additional projectile created by the explosion for massive damage! If it misses, the projectile rain generally ensures Doctor Doom's safety afterwards, allowing you set up more projectiles, advance toward your target, or even tag in a teammate. However, opponents who are close to Doctor Doom when Sphere Flame is activated can throw him before the projectile rain descends, making the projectiles harmlessly pass through them.

Doom's Time: This level 3 hyper combo is the fastest attack in Doctor Doom's arsenal. It is an ideal combo ender because it is not subject to damage scaling and it deals a significant amount of damage.

Doom Time's blinding speed and invulnerability make it great as a defensive tool against aggressive opponents. Furthermore, you can interrupt any offensive attempts by activating X-Factor and immediately performing Doom's Time. If your adversary is doing anything besides guarding upon the X-Factor activation, they will get caught by the hyper combo.

"YOU ARE BENEATH ME, AND IT SHOWED."

Battle Plan

Learning to properly maneuver with Doctor Doom is crucial. The main difference between his mobility and that of the rest of the cast is that he is unable to cancel his ground dash into basic attacks; it is only cancelable with normal jumps. Instead, Doctor Doom's primary method of getting around is through airdashes. By normal jumping forward and immediately airdashing down-forward, you gain the speed and momentum that normal dash attacks benefit from. Alternatively, retreating is as easy as normal jumping back and immediately airdashing down-back. Because Doctor Doom requires a lower minimum altitude to perform airdashes during normal jumps than other airdashing characters, this technique makes for a suitable alternative to ground dashing. Mix it up by normal jumping up-forward and airdashing down-back and vice versa, adding in lateral airdashes, as well.

Learning to triangle dash quickly is key with Doctor Doom.

Use ⇨ + H Foot Dive to close in on opponents.

Learning to manipulate Doctor Doom in the air is another important skill. The trajectory of Doctor Doom's air movement can be changed at any time by performing air Photon Shots, air Plasma Beams, airdashes, flight mode, and both Foot Dive and air S. You can employ both versions of Foot Dive as a means to approach, and you can cancel into flight mode to avoid diving into a dangerous situation.

Once you learn to properly manuever, the real fight begins! Doctor Doom is a force to be reckoned with from full screen. If you have the life lead, you can maintain it by keeping your opponent at bay with Plasma Beam H and Photon Shot L. Even without a lead in life, Doctor Doom can deal a significant amount of damage from full screen to turn the tides in battle. Plasma Beam H deals big damage on both hit and guard, and will cut through most opposing projectiles easily in a firefight. If your adversary manages to jump over your Plasma Beam H at close range, quickly cancel into Sphere Flame to counter their punishment attempt.

For defense, your main tools are Plasma Beam H, ground Photon Shots, and aerial Photon Shots. You can stay out of harm's way by super jumping, airdashing up-back, and canceling the airdash with Photon Shot L or H. The fan shape created by the Photon Shot cuts off your opposition's frontal advances. As a foe inches closer, surprise them by airdashing up-back and performing air S instead of Photon Shot into a combo. Or, you can airdash straight down instead of up-back after superjumping, and fall with air M to start a combo.

Once opponents are tired of dealing with Plasma Beam H, they are likely to look to the skies for another avenue of approach. To counter this, use Photon Shots to stop their advance. Even though Photon Shot doesn't do nearly as much damage as Plasma Beam, it covers a much larger amount of space and is difficult to avoid both on the ground and in the air. Aerial opponents can also be dealt with using Doctor Doom's back air throw. Combos performed off throws suffer from increased damage scaling, but Doctor Doom is so powerful that even combos from throws do massive amounts of damage! If opponents are approaching from super jump height, surprise them with a super jump of your own and back air throw them to the ground for a damaging combo.

Aerial assaults can also be defended against with air M. Air M causes a large amount of hitstun and has a hitbox useful for both air-to-air and air-to-ground situations. Opponents coming in from the sky can be countered by super jumping and performing air M (2 hits), ⇨ + H CANCEL ⇖ + ATK ATK, air M (2 hits), then land and continue the combo as you see fit. If your enemy is approaching with a normal jump, counter with normal jump air M (2 hits), M (2 hits), ⇨ + H CANCEL ⇖ + ATK ATK, land, standing L, crouching M, H, S into a combo. Learning to use the hitbox of air M to your advantage in situations such as these is imperative to playing Doctor Doom.

Once Doctor Doom is at close range, several offensive options become available. His close range game consists of interchanging between:

Use square jump air M for an overhead attack.

Empty triangle jump crouching L

Square jump air M

Triangle jump air L

Triangle jump air M

Empty triangle jump cross-up crouching L

Empty triangle jump into backwards throw

Empty triangle jump into crouching L is the primary method of starting combos. Typically when Doctor Doom leaves the ground, opponents start guarding high against overhead attacks. However, Doctor Doom can quickly dash back to the ground for a low-hitting crouching L, making for a difficult attack to guard. To be even more deceptive, you can give your opponent more time to react to the stimulus by normal jumping forward and waiting until the apex of the jump before quickly airdashing downwards and using crouching L to hit low. Keep in mind when using this technique that depending on your positioning, a combo of crouching L, M, H might not work because of the short distance of crouching M. Therefore, crouching L, H is more reliable. Lastly, the crouching L can be substituted for a back throw once foes become wary of the low attack.

Doctor Doom's air M is a great offensive tool, and its priority and hitstun shine when used in a square jump. For a quick overhead attack, perform a normal jump and quickly airdash forward and use air M, all in one swift motion. One air M for two hits is enough hitstun to land and continue the combo. Depending on positioning, you can even use a square jump air M as a cross-up!

Triangle jump L is a quick way to score an overhead attack on an opponent. This can be done by airdashing down-forward during a normal or super jump and performing an air L attack. Because it looks similar to the low-hitting empty jump triangle crouching L, it makes for a great mix-up when used in tandem with empty triangle jumps. Follow up with a crouching L to be able to capitalize with a combo.

Triangle jump air M is used mostly as a pressure and positioning technique. Execute this move by super jumping and quickly dashing down-forward with air M. Use this longer range technique to keep the momentum going against competitors insisting on escaping Doctor Doom's rushdown.

Against smaller characters, you can perform empty jump cross-up crouching L when your rival is at point-blank range. When a foe is right next to Doctor Doom, normal jump forward and airdash down-forward to the other side of the opponent with a crouching L from behind. Even the most seasoned opposing players tend to have a difficult time guarding this cross-up!

If your crouching H is guarded, you can dash cancel to keep your offense going.

Dash cancel your basic attacks to negate advancing guard!

Unique to Doctor Doom is his ability to cancel his grounded basic attacks into a ground dash. Perform this technique simply by inputting a dash during any ground basic attack.

Dash canceling can be used to combat advancing guard. If an opponent pushes away a guarded attack, quickly cancel the attack into a ground dash to stay close.

Foes can be caught off guard when dash canceling is used offensively. For example, if a rival guards a crouching L, H chain, you can cancel the crouching H into a forward dash, cancel the forward dash into a normal jump forward, and then airdash down-forward into a low-hitting crouching L, interrupting the opponent's next action with a surprise attack.

In some instances, a crossover assist can interrupt an attack already in progress. If you see an impending attack from a crossover assist during your own attack (such as crouching L, H chain), dash canceling backwards or even dash canceling to jumping guard can be a lifesaver!

COMBO USAGE

I. CR. Ⓛ, Ⓜ, Ⓗ, Ⓢ ⇒ FORWARD SUPER JUMP, AIR Ⓜ (2 HITS), → + Ⓗ ⇒ DOWN-FORWARD AIRDASH, AIR Ⓜ (2 HITS), LAND, CR. Ⓜ, Ⓗ, Ⓢ ⇒ FORWARD SUPER JUMP, AIR Ⓜ (2 HITS), → + Ⓗ ⇒ DOWN-FORWARD AIRDASH, AIR Ⓜ (2 HITS), LAND, CR. Ⓜ, Ⓗ, Ⓢ ⇒ FORWARD SUPER JUMP, AIR Ⓜ (2 HITS), Ⓜ (2 HITS), → + Ⓗ ⇒ FORWARD AIRDASH, AIR Ⓜ (2 HITS), Ⓜ (2 HITS) ⇒ ↓ ↙ ← + ATK ATK (MASH ATK)

712,300 damage, 36% meter gain

You can use this bread and butter combo midscreen for considerable damage. The key point to remember when learning this combo is to keep your opponent as low to the ground as possible: use air Ⓜ immediately after launching the target to prevent your foe from rising higher. The most difficult part is learning the timing on connecting the air Ⓜ after the airdash; you'll want to hit it as late as possible to keep the opposing character low to the ground.

II. (CORNER REQUIRED) CR. Ⓛ, Ⓜ, Ⓗ, [Ⓢ ⇒ FORWARD SUPER JUMP, AIR Ⓜ (1 HIT), → + Ⓗ, Ⓢ ⇒ DOWNWARD AIRDASH, LAND, ST. Ⓗ (2 HITS) OTG] REPEAT BRACKETS X3, Ⓢ ⇒ UPWARD SUPER JUMP, AIR Ⓜ (2 HITS), Ⓜ (2 HITS), → + Ⓗ, Ⓢ ⇒ DOWNWARD AIRDASH, LAND, ST. Ⓗ (2 HITS) OTG ⇒ ↓ ↘ → + ATK ATK (MASH ATK)

1,129,500, 134% meter loss

This combo inflicts enough damage to knock out almost any character in the game! Be careful not to accidentally perform an aerial exchange when during air → + Ⓗ, Ⓢ. During the downward airdashes, you can whiff an air Ⓗ to make Doom land faster, but it is not necessary. If you do not have three levels of hyper meter by the end of the combo, you can also end it with the OTG-capable air Plasma Beam H hyper combo canceled into air Photon Array for 837,500 points of damage.

III. AIR Ⓢ, LAND, ST. Ⓗ (2 HITS) OTG, Ⓢ ⇒ FORWARD SUPER JUMP, AIR Ⓜ (2 HITS), → + Ⓗ ⇒ DOWN-FORWARD AIRDASH, AIR Ⓜ (2 HITS), LAND, CR. Ⓜ, Ⓗ, Ⓢ ⇒ FORWARD SUPER JUMP, AIR Ⓜ (2 HITS), Ⓜ (2 HITS), → + Ⓗ ⇒ FORWARD AIRDASH, AIR Ⓜ (2 HITS) ⇒ ↓ ↙ ← + ATK ATK (MASH ATK)

620,100 damage, 6% meter loss

This combo can be used after a successful air Ⓢ. If you find it difficult to follow air Ⓢ with standing Ⓗ OTG, try triangle dashing forward before performing standing Ⓗ to get into a better position.

IV. (CORNER REQUIRED) AIR Ⓛ, Ⓜ (1 HIT), Ⓜ (1 HIT), → + Ⓗ ⇒ FORWARD AIRDASH, AIR Ⓜ (2 HITS), LAND, ST. Ⓛ, CR. Ⓜ, Ⓗ, Ⓢ ⇒ FORWARD SUPER JUMP, AIR Ⓜ (2 HITS), → + Ⓗ, Ⓢ ⇒ DOWNWARD AIRDASH, LAND, ST. Ⓗ (2 HITS) OTG, Ⓢ ⇒ SUPER JUMP, AIR Ⓜ (2 HITS), → + Ⓗ, Ⓢ ⇒ DOWNWARD AIRDASH, LAND, ST. Ⓗ (2 HITS) OTG, Ⓢ ⇒ FORWARD SUPER JUMP, AIR Ⓜ (2 HITS), Ⓜ (2 HITS), → + Ⓗ, Ⓢ ⇒ DOWNWARD AIRDASH, LAND, ST. Ⓗ (2 HITS) OTG ⇒ ↓ ↘ → + ATK ATK (MASH ATK)

1,044,100 damage, 143% meter loss

Use this combo on incoming enemies after a K.O. If you think the opposing player may come in attacking, interrupt their attack with a normal jump air Ⓛ into this damaging combo.

COMBO APPENDIX

GENERAL EXECUTION TIPS

For corner combos, you can whiff air Ⓗ on the way down from an airdash to reach the ground faster. This is helpful when coming down from a high altitude.

Air → + Ⓗ causes plenty of hitstun. Try delaying attacks after air → + Ⓗ to keep your opponent closer to the ground.

Return the controller to the neutral position between air → + Ⓗ and air Ⓢ so that you can eliminate any accidental aerial exchanges.

(AFTER TAC) AIR Ⓜ (2 HITS), AIR Ⓜ (2 HITS), ↓ ↙ ← + Ⓢ, AIR Ⓜ (2 HITS), Ⓜ (2 HITS) ⇒ FORWARD AIRDASH, AIR Ⓜ (2 HITS), Ⓜ (2 HITS) ⇒ FORWARD AIRDASH, AIR Ⓜ (2 HITS), Ⓜ (2 HITS) ⇒ FORWARD AIRDASH, AIR Ⓜ (2 HITS), Ⓜ (2 HITS), Ⓗ (5 HITS)

Notes:	Damage
Use this combo after an aerial exchange into Doctor Doom. Great for building meter	Damage varies based on damage scaling

CR. Ⓛ, Ⓜ, Ⓗ, Ⓢ, AIR Ⓜ (2 HITS), → + Ⓗ ⇒ DOWN-FORWARD AIRDASH, AIR Ⓜ (2 HITS), LAND, CR. Ⓜ, Ⓗ, Ⓢ, AIR Ⓜ (2 HITS), → + Ⓗ ⇒ DOWN-FORWARD AIRDASH, AIR Ⓜ (2 HITS), LAND, → ↓ ↘ + ATK ATK

Notes	Damage
A simplified bread and butter combo. Because X-Factor level 3 can be difficult to control, use this easy combo during X-Factor for big damage	641,900 damage, -13% meter gain

ADVANCED TACTICS

LATVERIAN STOMP

Combos starting with ⇨ + (H) against an aerial opponent differ depending on the altitude.

Doctor Doom's ⇨ + (H) Foot Dive is not only a great way to approach, but also can start combos at high altitudes. Attacks following ⇨ + (H) to continue the combo can vary depending on Doom's height.

At super jump height, cancel Foot Dive into ⇘ + (ATK)(ATK), air (M) (2 hits), land, forward normal jump, air (M) (2 hits), air (M) (2 hits), (S), land, triangle dash forward, st. (H), and proceed with the combo.

At normal jump height, cancel Foot Dive into ⇘ + (ATK)(ATK), air (L), land, forward normal jump, air (L), air (M) (2 hits), (M) (2 hits), ⇨ + (H) CANCEL ➡ ⇘ + (ATK)(ATK), land, cr. (L), (M), (H), (S), and proceed with the combo.

If Foot Dive lands on an opponent who is in the air but below normal jump height, cancel Foot Dive into ⇘ + (ATK)(ATK), land, cr. (L), (M), (H), (S) or ⇘ + (ATK)(ATK), air (L), land, cr. (L), (M), (H), (S) depending on your opponent's height.

If ⇨ + (H) is ever guarded, cancel into ⇘ + (ATK)(ATK) anyway to mount an offensive.

LATVERIAN STOMP CONTINUED

Air (S) is one of Doctor Doom's best attacks. Abuse it!

Possibly Doctor Doom's best attack in *Ultimate Marvel vs. Capcom 3*, the air (S) version of the Foot Dive now causes hard knockdown on both grounded and aerial opponents, leaving them susceptible to OTG-capable standing (H) into a full combo afterwards. Very rarely does the air (S) hit at an angle in which Doctor Doom is unable to follow up with an OTG after it connects. In cases where your target is too far for you to perform an immediate standing (H) OTG, it is possible to adjust your positioning by quickly jumping forward and airdashing down-forward before attempting a standing (H) or (M). Keep in mind that combos starting with air (S) are more susceptible to hit decay; use combos similar to those starting from a throw.

While air (S) cleanly stomps nearly anything in its path to allow for free combos, it leaves Doctor Doom in a precarious position if guarded. If you make contact with air (S) above Doctor Doom's minimum height required for an airdash, great: just cancel the air (S) into a downward airdash to quickly land on the ground with a substantial amount of frame advantage. If you make contact lower to the ground, Doom slowly bounces backwards in a completely vulnerable state. You can mitigate this by calling a crossover assist simultaneously with the air (S), or hyper combo canceling into air Photon Array. The hyper combo isn't safe either, so be ready to THC to a teammate afterward. You can also use air (S) as a mobility tool, since it descends from high altitudes faster than airdashing down. If used immediately after a high altitude Air Photon Shot L, you can touch the ground before the photons do! Follow this up with Plasma Beam H, another Air Photon Shot, or a dash to approach.

DOOM AWAITS

One wrong move, and the opposing player will lose another character!

Doom has several options against new characters coming in after their comrade is knocked out:

Against opponents who are coming in attacking, you can utilize a well-timed air (L) or (M) on the way up to combo into air (S), leading to a damaging corner combo. Alternatively, a safer method to counter opposing attacks is to use air (H). The range of the beam keeps you relatively safe, forcing your competitor to block. If they are hit, you can follow up with air (M), (S) after landing to continue the combo.

For foes sho are guarding on the way in, performing a quick airdash down-forward to get underneath them for a cross-up (S) that can be difficult to guard. Alternatively, performing a super jump into the corner and airdashing straight down into air (M) also causes a cross-up due to air (M)'s hitbox. As with any cross-up, you can adjust the timing on these setups to fake a cross-up, as well.

You can utilize Doctor Doom's airdash as a cross-up tool when paired with a crossover assist, depending on the timing of the airdash and the type of crossover assist available. In addition, calling a crossover assist during a guarded combo attempt can pin your opponent down for corner mix-ups.

Against other airdashing characters, a well-timed air (M) or air throw can stop any attempts to escape.

DORMAMMU

"WHO DARES DEFY THE DREAD LORD?"

Bio

REAL NAME

Dormammu

OCCUPATION

Despot, Conqueror

ABILITIES

Among his many abilities are matter transmutation, interdimensional teleportation, size and shape alteration, element control, telepathy, creation of artificial beings, and empowerment of others.

WEAPONS

None

PROFILE

Formerly a being made of energy residing in the Chaos Dimension, he gained a body made of metal and crossed over to the real world in the hopes of conquering it. Currently, he serves as the ruler of the mysterious Dark Dimension.

FIRST APPEARANCE

Strange Tales #126 (1964)

POWER GRID

6 INTELLIGENCE

7 STRENGTH

7 SPEED

7 STAMINA

7 ENERGY PROJECTION

4 FIGHTING ABILITY

*This is biographical, and does not represent an evaluation of the in-game combat potential of this hero.

ALTERNATE COSTUMES

1

2

3

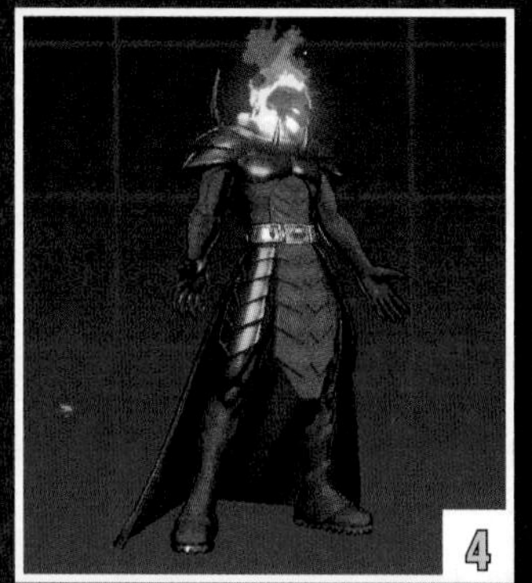

4

5

6

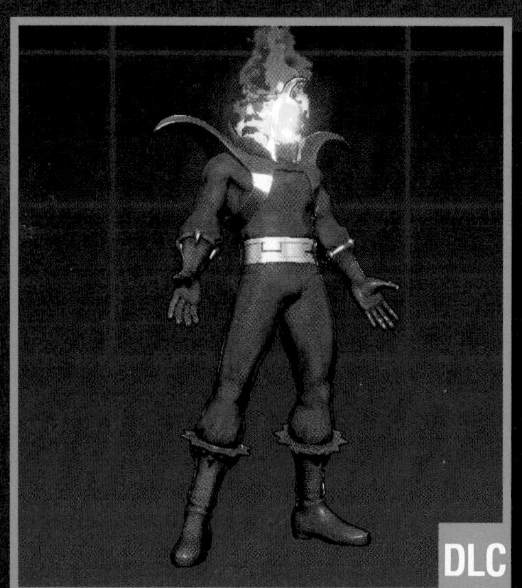

DLC

Overview

Vitality	1,000,000
Chain Combo Archetype	Marvel Series

X-Factor Boost	Damage	Speed
Level 1 (3 teammates remaining)	130%	110%
Level 2 (2 teammates remaining)	155%	115%
Level 3 (1 teammate remaining)	180%	120%

The goal when using Dormammu is a little more abstract than usual. Your goal is to create opportunities to perform actions unimpeded. In other words, you want to buy time.

When given time, you can safely pull off tactics with Dormammu that make him much more difficult to fight against:

- **Dark Spell points can be stored, giving access to game-altering special attacks**
- **The Flame Carpet can be created, making it a huge risk for opponents to attack Dormammu anywhere from the front**
- **The Stalking Flare hyper combo can be used to completely control the match for the next several moments**
- **Long range cross-ups can be set up using crossover assists and Mass Change M**

How do you go about buying time with Dormammu?

- **Discouraging the opposing character from advancing with well-placed Dark Matter and Liberation attacks, and capitalizing on your opponent's moment of hesitation**
- **Using Flame Carpet, Stalking Flare, or Liberation (Creation Mix)**
- **Using flight from super jump height to be able to use Dark Spell several times safely**

TUNING SINCE ORIGINAL MVC3

Already one of the more powerful characters, Dormammu surprisingly received a host of improvements in *Ultimate Marvel vs. Capcom 3*! These changes make Dormammu inflict much more damage with his combos, you can safely hit-confirm his combos instead of making a huge commitment, you can store Dark Spells much more easily and often, and use Dark Matter more freely to establish a stronger fullscreen presence!

On the flip side, Flame Carpet and crouching Ⓜ have been weakened significantly, lowering Dormammu's effectiveness in up-close defensive situations. Flame Carpet in particular was one of Dormammu's most dominating tools, so long-time Dormammu players have some adjustments to make.

- **Dormammu can now perform three-hit chain combos**
- **General reduction of hitstun scaling across the board**
- **Dormammu can now cancel ↙ and ↖ airdashes into attacks**
- **Ⓛ basic attacks push the enemy backwards a shorter distance**
- **Crouching Ⓜ now causes much less hitstun**
- **Dark Matter is special and hyper-cancelable**
- **Flame Carpet now disappears when Dormammu gets hit, and it knocks competitors farther away when used**
- **Forward and backward throws now cause hard knockdown state**
- **Dormammu—α Dark Hole assist now executes 2 frames faster**
- **Dormammu—β Purification assist now executes 2 frames faster**
- **Flight mode duration shortened to 100 frames from 120**
- **Dark Spell can now be performed in the air**
- **Liberation can now be performed in air**
- **Liberation (Destruction Mix) now creates the volcano even when Dormammu is interrupted, volcano hit now causes hard knockdown, individual rocks inflict more damage, rocks emit later**
- **Liberation (Creation Mix) now creates meteors even if Dormammu is interrupted**
- **Chaotic Flame can now be mashed for additional damage**

1	Standing L	1	48,000	384	6	2	12	0	-1	—
2	Standing M	1	70,000	560	8	10	16	-7	-8	Nullifies low and medium priority projectiles
3	Standing H	1	90,000	720	13	5	21	-2	-3	Nullifies low and medium priority projectiles, knocks opponent upward

Crouching Basic Attacks

Screen	Command	Hits	Damage	Meter Gain	Startup	Active	Recovery	Advantage on Hit	Advantage if Guarded	Notes
1	Crouching L	1	45,000	360	7	2	13	-1	-2	Low attack
2	Crouching M	1	70,000	560	9	8	17	+6	-7	Nullifies low and medium priority projectiles, launches foe slightly
3	Crouching H	1	90,000	720	13	4	24	—	-5	Nullifies low and medium priority projectiles, low attack, knocks down rival

Ground Special Attack—Launcher

Screen	Command	Hits	Damage	Meter Gain	Startup	Active	Recovery	Advantage on Hit	Advantage if Guarded	Notes
1	S (while standing or crouching)	1	95,000	760	9	20	12	—	-9	Nullifies low and medium priority projectiles, launcher, not special- or hyper combo-cancelable

Air Basic Attacks

Screen	Command	Hits	Damage	Meter Gain	Startup	Active	Recovery	Advantage on Hit	Advantage if Guarded	Notes
1	Air L	1	50,000	400	7	3	16	+14	+11	Overhead attack
2	Air M	1	70,000	560	10	11	15	+15	+15	Nullifies low and medium priority projectiles, overhead attack
3	Air H	1	85,000	680	10	5	29	+19	+18	Nullifies low and medium priority projectiles, overhead attack

Air (S) causes a hard knockdown when used in a launcher combo (this is sometimes called flying screen). When used outside of a launcher combo, air (S) behaves mostly like another basic attack. Air exchange attacks, performed by inputting a direction plus (S), are only possible during a launcher combo. Exchange hits initiate team aerial combos by tagging in the next available character to continue the air combo.

Screen	Command	Hits	Damage	Meter Gain	Startup	Active	Recovery	Advantage on Hit	Advantage if Guarded	Notes
1	Air (S)	1	90,000	720	14	5	27	+19	+15	Nullifies low and medium priority projectiles, causes hard knockdown if used in launcher combo
2	Air ⇧ + (S) (during launcher combo)	1	60,000	480	13	3	Until grounded	—	—	Tags in next available ally while lofting opponent upward
3	Air ⇨ or ⇦ + (S) (during launcher combo)	1	50,000	400	13	3	Until grounded	—	—	Tags in next available ally while causing wall bounce, erases 1 hyper meter bar from opposing character
4	Air ⇩ + (S) (during launcher combo)	1	50,000	400	13	3	Until grounded	—	—	Tags in next available ally while causing ground bounce, generates 1 hyper meter bar

1

2

3

4

Command Attacks

Command attacks resemble basic attacks but have different chaining and canceling properties. It's usually possible to chain *into* a command attack from basic attacks, but most command attacks cannot be chained from or canceled themselves.

Screen	Name	Command	Hits	Damage	Meter Gain	Startup	Active	Recovery	Advantage on Hit	Advantage if Guarded	Notes
1	Dark Matter	⇨ + (H)	1	80,000	640	20	—	26	—	-3	Wall bounces adversary, inflicts chip damage, projectile has 1 low priority durability point
2	Flame Carpet	⇘ + (H)	5	81,700	800	15	—	31	+5	+4	Creates pool of fire on the ground that lasts 180 frames, only one pool of fire per player can be in play at a time, OTG-capable, inflicts chip damage, not special- or hyper combo-cancelable, Flame Carpet disappears if Dormammu gets hit, beam durability: 5 frames x 1 low priority durability point

1

2

Throws

Throws are for snagging passive or blocking opponents. Since throws are active so quickly, you can also use them to preemptively toss opposing characters out of their offense. Combos are usually possible after throws, one way or another.

Screen	Command	Hits	Damage	Meter Gain	Startup	Active	Notes
1	⇨ + (H) (ground)	1	80,000	800	1	1	Hard knockdown
1	⇦ + (H) (ground)	1	80,000	800	1	1	Hard knockdown
2	⇨ + (H) (air)	1	80,000	800	1	1	Hard knockdown
2	⇦ + (H) (air)	1	80,000	800	1	1	Hard knockdown

1

2

As a Partner—Crossover Assists

Screen	Type	P1+P2 Crossover Combination Hyper Combo	Description	Hits	Damage	Meter Gain	Startup	Active	Recovery (this crossover assist)	Recovery (other partner)	Notes
1	Dormammu—α	Chaotic Flame	Dark Hole M	9	122,200	1440	50	33	98	68	Knocks down adversary, beam durability: 10 frames x 3 low priority durability points
2	Dormammu—β	Chaotic Flame	Purification L	4	120,300	1120	56	23	103	73	Spinning knockdown, OTG-capable, beam durability: 5 frames x 3 low priority durability points
3	Dormammu—γ	Stalking Flare	Liberation		Variable	Variable	Variable	Variable	Variable	Variable	Attack performed depends on how many Destruction or Creation points stored

1

2

3

Of all of Dormammu's crossover assist types, Dormammu—α's Dark Hole assist is the most recommended: it holds the opposing character in place for a long period of time, making it great for offensive characters to maintain their momentum. It can also be very useful in certain combos.

Dormammu—β's Purification is too slow to be used defensively for the most part. Being OTG-capable is a nice bonus, but it's usually difficult to capitalize on this due to the height that it launches the opponent to.

Dormammu—γ is potentially very useful as a crossover assist, giving Dormammu's powerful Liberation attacks to any character in the game for a single shot. In practice, it's simply too impractical to use often.

Snap Back

Screen	Command	Hits	Damage	Meter Gain	Startup	Active	Recovery	Advantage on Hit	Advantage if Guarded
1	↓↘→ + P1+P2	1	50,000	500 - (-1 hyper meter bar)	2	5	21	—	-3

Notes

On hit, snap back forces the opposing point character to be replaced by an assist. Opposing assist calls or tag outs are also locked out for 4 seconds

1

Special Moves

Screen	Name	Command	Hits	Damage	Meter Gain	Startup	Active	Recovery	Advantage on Hit	Advantage if Guarded	Notes
1	Dark Spell: Destruction (in air ok)	↓↙← + L	-	-	—	15	—	20	—	—	Stores 1 Destruction point. If 3 Dark Spell points already stored, then performs Liberation instead. Air version does not recover until grounded
2	Dark Spell: Creation (in air ok)	↓↙← + M	-	-	—	15	—	20	—	—	Stores 1 Creation point. If 3 Dark Spell points already stored, then performs Liberation instead. Air version does not recover until grounded
3	Liberation (empty)	↓↙← + H	1	80,000	640	15 (38 in air)	5	21	+5	-3	Performed with 0 stored points, knocks down opponent, air version teleports Dormammu, is invincible from frames 11-24, projectile has 5 low priority durability points
4	Liberation (Destruction 1)	↓↙← + H	3	94,800	840	15 (38 in air)	10	16	—	+1	Requires 1 Destruction point, uses all stored Dark Spell points, knocks down rival, air version teleports Dormammu, is invincible from frames 11-24, projectile has 5 low priority durability points
5	Liberation (Destruction 2)	↓↙← + H	6	163,800	1680	15 (38 in air)	10	16	—	+1	Requires 2 Destruction points, uses all stored Dark Spell points, knocks down foe , air version teleports Dormammu, is invincible from frames 11-24, beam durability: 6 frames x 1 low priority durability point
6	Liberation (Destruction 3)	↓↙← + H	10	195,000	2400	15 (38 in air)	15	21	—	-5	Requires 3 Destruction points, uses all stored Dark Spell points, OTG-capable, knocks down competitor , air version teleports Dormammu, is invincible from frames 11-24, beam durability: 10 frames x 1 low priority durability point

Special Moves

Screen	Name	Command	Hits	Damage	Meter Gain	Startup	Active	Recovery	Advantage on Hit	Advantage if Guarded	Notes
7	Liberation (Creation 1)	⇩⇙⇦ + H	3	108,300	960	12 (35 in air)	10	24	—	-10	Requires 1 Creation point, uses all stored Dark Spell points, knocks down opponent, air version teleports Dormammu, is invincible from frames 11-24, projectile has 5 low priority durability points
8	Liberation (Creation 2)	⇩⇙⇦ + H	9	183,400	2160	12 (35 in air)	10	24	—	-10	Requires 2 Creation points, uses all stored Dark Spell points, knocks down adversary , air version teleports Dormammu, is invincible from frames 11-24, projectile has 5 low priority durability points
9	Liberation (Creation 3)	⇩⇙⇦ + H	1	0	—	15 (38 in air)	—	36	-21	-23	Requires 3 Creation points, uses all stored Dark Spell points. On hit, opponent cannot jump for 300 frames. Air version teleports Dormammu, is invincible from frames 11-24
10	Liberation (Mixed)	⇩⇙⇦ + H	~24	~194,200	3840	10 (33 in air)	—	40	—	—	Requires 1 Destruction and 1 Creation point, meteors inflict hard knockdown on airborne adversaries , OTG-capable, air version teleports Dormammu, is invincible from frames 11-24, beam durability: each meteor has 3 frames x 3 low priority durability points
11	Liberation (Destruction Mix)	⇩⇙⇦ + H	variable	80,000 (flame pillar) 15,000 (per meteor)	variable	20 (43 in air)	20	21	—	—	Requires 2 Destruction points and 1 Creation point, meteors inflict hard knockdown on airborne rivals , all attacks are OTG-capable, flame pillar attack causes hard knockdown, air version teleports Dormammu, is invincible from frames 11-24, ground spike has 100 durability points, beam durability: each meteor has 1 frame x 1 low durability point
12	Liberation (Creation Mix)	⇩⇙⇦ + H	~40	~258,200	~6400	26 (29 in air)	—	14	—	—	Requires 2 Creation points and 1 Destruction point, meteors inflict hard knockdown on airborne competitors , OTG-capable, air version teleports Dormammu, is invincible from frames 11-24, each meteor has 3 frames x 3 low priority durability points
13	Dark Hole	⇩⇘⇨ + ATK (in air OK)	9	122,200	1440	26	34	6	—	+7	Knocks down target, Dark Hole disappears if Dormammu receives damage, air version does not recover until landing (unless in flight mode), beam durability: 10 frames x 3 low priority durability points
14	Purification	⇨⇩⇘ + ATK	4	120,300	1120	32	23	11	+11	+2	OTG-capable, spinning knockdown, beam durability: 5 frames x 3 low priority durability points
15	Mass Change	⇦⇩⇙ + ATK (in air OK)	-	-	—	13	—	17	—	—	—
16	Flight	⇩⇙⇦ + S (in air OK)	-	-	—	21	—	—	—	—	Activates flight mode, flight mode lasts for 100 frames, activating flight while already in flight mode cancels flight mode, has 0 recovery

1

Dark Spell: Destruction: Using Dark Spell: Destruction stores one destruction point, up to a total of three Dark Spell points. Attempting to store another Dark Spell while already having three points makes Dormammu automatically use Liberation instead, using up all of the points.

Visually, storing Destruction points causes Dormammu's hand to radiate with red flames. Having more Destruction points increases the size and intensity of the flames, so you can use that as a visual indicator of how many Dark Spells points you have stored. Additionally, the total number of Dark Spells stored affects Dormammu's head flames, causing them to grow larger!

New to *Ultimate Marvel vs. Capcom 3*, Dark Spells can now be used in the air! Performing Dark Spell in the air is actually slower, since it leaves Dormammu vulnerable all the way until he reaches the ground. However, when combined with flight mode, this is a major addition to Dormammu's toolset; during flight mode Dormammu can use Dark Spell up to three times and still drop down safely!

2

Dark Spell: Creation: The alternate version of Dark Spell stores one Creation point to access the Creation line of attacks, along with causing blue flames to show up on Dormammu's other hand.

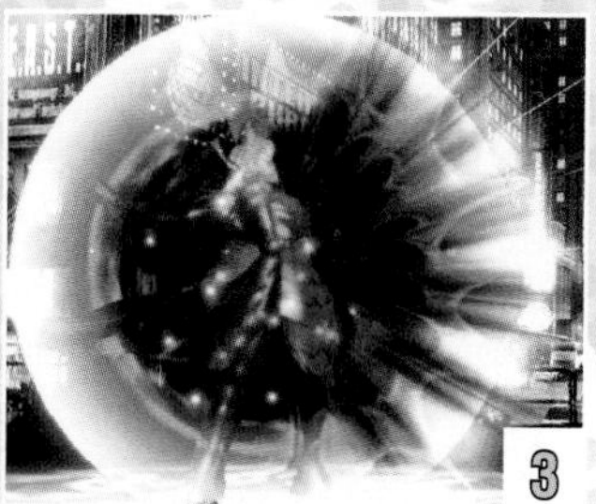
3

Liberation (empty): Liberation attacks cause Dormammu to release all Dark Spell points currently stored. New to *Ultimate Marvel vs. Capcom 3*, Liberation can be performed in the air! This makes Dormammu teleport back down to the ground before releasing all the Dark Spell points accrued.

When no Dark Spell points are stored, using Liberation causes Dormammu to attack with a spherical blast around his body. Surprisingly safe if guarded, this is the preferred way to use air Liberation as a teleport to the ground. Air Liberation (empty) from directly above your competitor is a surprisingly good way to begin an attack.

4

Liberation (Destruction 1): Using Liberation with one Destruction point stored changes the attack to create a small explosion in front of Dormammu. While it's generally better to just save up for better attacks, Liberation (Destruction 1) is best used in the air as a quick way to teleport back to the ground and counter forward movement from your adversary. Hitting with this explosion allows you to easily verify the hit and cancel into Chaotic Flame for a quick combo.

Liberation (Destruction 2): With two Destruction points, Liberation creates a larger explosion that knocks the target farther across the screen. It has mostly the same usage scenarios as Liberation (Destruction 1).

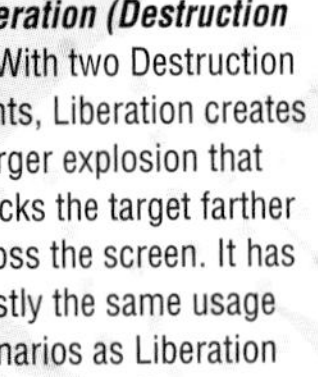

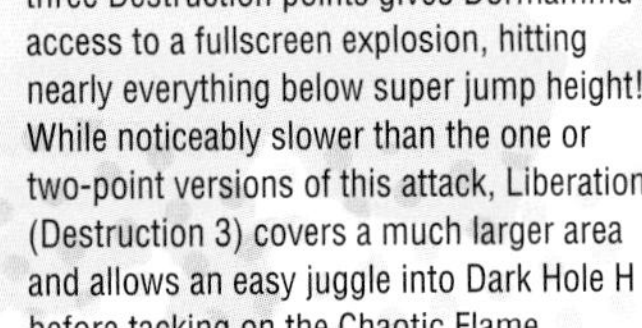

Liberation (Destruction 3): Loading up three Destruction points gives Dormammu access to a fullscreen explosion, hitting nearly everything below super jump height! While noticeably slower than the one or two-point versions of this attack, Liberation (Destruction 3) covers a much larger area and allows an easy juggle into Dark Hole H before tacking on the Chaotic Flame.

When Destruction 3 is primed, you can counter most attempts from opposing players to close the distance against you, as well as most projectiles, completely on reaction. Having this tool can completely change the tempo of a match because your opponent usually shifts gears to try to bait you into using the explosion at the wrong time.

Liberation (Creation 1): Storing a single Creation point causes Liberation to create a spike on the ground with essentially the same usage scenarios as Liberation (Destruction 1). Typically, your first Dark Spell point should always be a Destruction point because this move and the rest of the Creation attacks are rarely used.

Liberation (Creation 2): Having two Creation points creates a row of three spikes on the ground, but it still has the same usage scenarios as Liberation (Destruction 1) and (Destruction 2).

Liberation (Creation 3): Requiring three Creation points, Liberation (Creation 3) covers the entire ground area with an attack that causes zero damage but places a unique temporary status effect on your target—manually jumping cannot be performed at all for 300 frames. While this seems powerful in theory, the actual application of this is limited due to the short length of time of the status effect. It's generally best to save up your Dark Spell points for the other three-point options instead.

Liberation (Mixed): Having an even split of one Creation point and one Destruction point allows Dormammu to create a small meteor shower to fall in the entire area directly in front of him, creating a solid defensive wall. Of all of the Liberation attacks that require two Dark Spell points, Liberation (Mixed) is generally the most useful to have.

Liberation (Destruction Mix): A mix of two Destruction points and one Creation point allows Dormammu to create an OTG-capable eruption from the ground that spews OTG-capable meteors in random directions from the tip. Primarily used to add a ton of damage to Dormammu's combos when super jump-canceled from the Ⓢ launcher, the eruption and almost all of the meteors hit your competitor simultaneously and drag the opponent down, allowing you to continue the combo afterwards!

Liberation (Creation Mix): Requiring a cocktail of two Creation points and one Destruction point, Liberation (Creation Mix) creates a much larger meteor shower that potentially covers the whole screen, buying a lot of time while simultaneously attacking your adversary with chip damage.

The meteors strike areas completely at random, so while they typically interrupt an opponent hitting Dormammu and allow for a retaliatory combo, this just isn't always the case.

Dark Hole: This move creates a vortex in an area of the screen corresponding to the button pressed: Ⓛ creates a Dark Hole directly in front of Dormammu, Ⓜ places one at medium range, and Ⓗ creates a vortex almost all the way across the screen. It should be noted that Dark Hole H does not actually make contact against most characters who are all the way across the screen; for that, you have to use Purification H.

Dark Hole is faster and can be hit-confirmed into Chaotic Flame, but other than that, it is almost always better to use Purification attacks for the same purpose. Purification covers the entire vertical length of the screen and leaves your rival floundering in the air, while Dark Hole can be jumped over and allows your opponent to safely ground recover toward Dormammu if hit.

Dark Hole has a small amount of frame advantage if guarded, but if Dormammu gets hit while a Dark Hole is in play, it immediately disappears.

You can perform Dark Hole in the air, but its usefulness is questionable; Dormammu is completely vulnerable until he reaches the ground after using the attack, and cases where you would use an air Dark Hole over a Purification are rare.

Purification: The OTG-capable Purification is the foundation of Dormammu's fullscreen control. It creates a pillar that extends across the entire vertical length of the screen, placed in an area dependent on the button pressed in a manner similar to Dark Hole. The Ⓗ version actually can make contact with an adversary from fullscreen.

As opposed to relying on it for the purpose of inflicting chip damage against your rival, you should instead use Purification with the mindset of restricting forward movement. A well-placed pillar cuts off an entire section of the battlefield whether your foe is on the ground, at normal jump height, or at super jump height.

The OTG-capable Purification is also a major component of Dormammu's combos—nearly every combo ends with an OTG pillar hyper canceled into Chaotic Flame.

15

Mass Change: Dormammu teleports to an area relative to the opposing character based on the button pressed: (L) puts Dormammu in the air above and in front of the target, (M) warps him above and behind his foe, while (H) places him directly above his attacker.

Mass Change M is one of Dormammu's most important assets because it allows him to quickly get behind his adversary at relatively low risk. This is great both for fullscreen cross-up offense using crossover assists or Dark Matter, but you can also employ it defensively to evade an incoming attacker while simultaneously getting away from the corner.

The (H) version is primarily used a mix-up to the (M) version, keeping Dormammu in front of his competitor. It's also the only version of Mass Change that keeps Dormammu within range to easily attack his rival, making it ideal for countering projectile-based characters.

You can perform Mass Change in the air, as well, further increasing Dormammu's general evasiveness and unpredictability.

16

Flight: Due to the newly air-enabled versions of Dark Spell and Liberation, flight mode has a much more prominent role in Dormammu's gameplan in *Ultimate Marvel vs. Capcom 3*: all of these factors combined allow Dormammu to super jump high into the air, activate flight mode, store three Dark Spell points, then still remain safe on the way down!

As a result of this, the duration of flight mode has been reduced by 20 frames in the current game. This prevents Dormammu from activating flight mode at the peak of super jump height, flying higher out of enemy reach, then storing Dark Spells with relative impunity.

DORMAMMU

Hyper Combos

Screen	Name	Command	Hits	Damage	Startup	Active	Recovery	Advantage on Hit	Advantage if Guarded	Notes
1	Chaotic Flame	↓↘→ + ATK ATK	30~60	281,400~338,300	8+3	59	41	+8	-21	Knocks down opponent, beam durability: 30 frames x 1 high priority durability point, can be mashed for additional hits
2	Stalking Flare	↓↙← + ATK ATK	20	256,300	31+4	—	62	+19	+18	Projectile homes in on adversary, disappears if Dormammu gets hit, does not expire over time, beam durability: 20 frames x 5 high priority durability points
3	Dark Dimension	→↓↘ + ATK ATK (level 3 hyper combo)	1	400,000	8+0	20	72	—	-69	Invincible during frames 1-36, OTG-capable, hard knockdown, beam durability: 5 frames x 5 high priority durability points

1

Chaotic Flame: One of the best all-purpose "beam" hyper combos in the game, Chaotic Flame is incredibly fast and can be used on reaction to counter most threats; it's almost an "anti-everything" attack! Try using it to nuke both the opposing player's point and crossover assist characters simultaneously!

In *Ultimate Marvel vs. Capcom 3*, the Chaotic Flame is even better—now it can be mashed for additional 57,000 points of damage!

2

Stalking Flare: This hyper combo creates a slow-moving, homing projectile that relentlessly follows its target until it makes contact; it does not expire over time. For most characters, trying to avoid the Stalking Flare is a pointless endeavor; it's typically only possible with teleports or with projectile hyper combos that have more durability points. However, successfully hitting Dormammu while Stalking Flare is in play completely negates the projectile.

There is a tremendous amount of startup and recovery frames on the Stalking Flare hyper combo, so you should generally limit its use to situations where your adversary cannot move for a while—after getting hit by a Purification pillar, during a THC combo, or after knocking out one of the opponent's characters.

Once Stalking Flare is safely in play, it buys you a huge amount of time to do whatever you like: store some Dark Spells, safely tag in a teammate, call a crossover assist and Mass Change M behind the opposing character, or even rev up another Stalking Flare! Adversaries fruitlessly trying to avoid the Stalking Flare just give you more time; it's generally more prudent for them to just suck it up and quickly take the chip damage.

3

Dark Dimension: Dormammu's level 3 hyper combo is not only invincible, but it's also OTG-capable! This makes it great for general use, as well as for tacking on a huge amount of unscaled damage at the end of a long combo. After Dormammu welcomes his competitor to his realm, he unceremoniously dumps the foe on the floor in a hard knockdown state. This allows you to tack on an OTG-capable Liberation and combo into a Chaotic Flame afterward!

Battle Plan

Most character match-ups with Dormammu involve the opposing character being the aggressor trying to close the distance, while Dormammu is used to keep them away to buy time.

What should you be buying time for? The major examples are:

- **To lay down a Flame Carpet, completely closing off the ground route for your adversary**
- **To store Dark Spells, increasing your options and damage output**
- **To set up a cross-up mix-up using Mass Change M or H in tandem with either Dark Matter or a crossover assist**
- **To allow crossover assists to recharge**
- **To pressure your rival with Purification attacks to inflict chip damage**
- **To get Stalking Flare into play, attacking your opponent while buying more time**

Flame Carpet now disappears if Dormammu gets hit, so be careful not to leave him open to an obvious aerial attack.

The new cancelable properties of Dark Matter greatly increase its role in Dormammu's gameplan.

Super jumping into the air, activating flight mode, then storing multiple Dark Spell points is a real pain for any competitor to deal with.

The priority order of the above items fluctuates depending on several factors in a given match: the distance between Dormammu and the opposing character, the distance from the corner, the crossover assists available, and the amount of Dark Spell points stored are several factors you should be accounting for when making a decision.

Dark Matter (⇨ + H) and Purification comprise the backbone of Dormammu's ranged keepaway options. Tossing out Dark Matter ensures that your opponent must take to the air to advance forward, limiting their movement options. Immediately after the Dark Matter projectile is created, cancel into a Purification pillar placed directly *in front* of your rival. This is important—inflicting an insignificant amount of chip damage is much less valuable in the long run when compared to the time you earn by restricting forward movement. Once your adversary becomes hesitant to move forward for fear of running into a pillar, learn to recognize this and capitalize on it, and instead store Dark Spells and create Flame Carpets with the time that you have earned!

If the opposing character is hit by a Purification pillar, you should try to predict which direction your adversary will try to air recover in. If they air recover forward, cut them off with a Purification placed in front of them, or simply lay down a Flame Carpet if their aerial movement options aren't strong enough to get behind Dormammu. If your foe air recovers backwards, you've earned yourself a huge chunk of time to play around with; store a Dark Spell, plop down a Flame Carpet along with a crossover assist, then plan your next move!

Dark Matter becomes much more potent when used in tandem with a long range crossover assist: simply press ⇨ + H + P1 or P2 to send out multiple threats on the screen at once! Depending on the assist used, this gives you much more flexibility on viable options for canceling the Dark Matter projectile into: Dark Spell, Mass Change M to cross up your opponent, Stalking Flare— the possibilities really start to open up!

Flame Carpet has been significantly weakened in *Ultimate Marvel vs. Capcom 3*: it now disappears if Dormammu gets hit. This means that you can no longer act as if Dormammu is nearly invincible standing behind it, landing a huge combo from any attempt your competitor made to attack you. Flame Carpet is still an essential part of the Dormammu gameplan—it forces your adversary to take to the air to approach Dormammu, slowing them down and forcing them into a more predictable movement pattern. As long as you don't commit to anything that puts Dormammu in a situation to be hit by aerial attacks, this successfully buys you time! Opponents who can't get behind the Flame Carpet typically have to use projectiles to attack, jump into it while guarding, or simply wait it out. When your foe resorts to projectiles, counter by dropping on top of their head with Mass Change H. If successful, this leads into Dormammu's massive new combos! See the Combo Usage section for details. Jumping into Flame Carpet while guarding is a bad idea, since it lets the Dormammu player get away with anything: air throws, setting up a triangle jump air L overhead, setting up a cross-up using both a crossover assist and Mass Change M— all of these options are difficult to defend against and lead into big damage if successful! Trying to wait out the Flame Carpet is great for Dormammu users also: it gives you all the time in the world to do whatever you want!

Dark Spells are an easy, low-commitment thing to spend your free time on. When faced with the decision of storing Creation or Destruction points, it all depends on what you're trying to accomplish. You can't go wrong with storing Destruction points exclusively; all of the Destruction attacks are useful, and Liberation (Destruction 3) gives you access to a fullscreen attack that can be easily verified into a combo. Having Liberation (Destruction 3) locked and loaded allows you to counter nearly everything your adversary can do on reaction. This forces your opponent to completely shift their focus to baiting you to use the explosion as they advance toward you while guarding. This sort of passive play results in (you guessed it!) more time you've just earned for yourself! Most commonly, your competitors simply try to jump toward you while guarding to try to coax out the explosion; treat this situation the exact same way as you would if you had a Flame Carpet out.

Liberation (Destruction Mix) has a much more specialized role. Save up for the volcano when your aim is simply to inflict massive damage the next time you land a clean hit on your foe. Having a volcano in your back pocket makes it very possible to take out most characters in a single combo; check the Combo Usage section for details.

Liberation (Creation Mix) is great for more defensive-minded play, as it's essentially a Flame Carpet that covers the whole playing field! Once the meteors have been summoned, your adversary typically has no choice but to guard until the meteors have finished raining down. This lasts for a quite a while, and it usually allows you to store another two Dark Spell points! If your opponent hits Dormammu after you've summoned the meteors, they generally get snagged by a few rocks, which allows you to convert that into a combo. This isn't 100% consistent, however; the meteors land in completely random areas on the screen, so it's possible for your competitor to connect a full combo on you while escaping unscathed, especially if the combo involves a lot of forward movement.

An addition to *Ultimate Marvel vs. Capcom 3* makes it much easier for you to find time for Dormammu's Dark Spell. He can now store them in the air! But keep in mind that simply jumping into the air and storing a Dark Spell generally isn't a good idea—Dormammu is completely vulnerable all the way until touching the ground, making this method much more time-consuming than normal. However, super jumping into the air and activating flight mode at the peak of the super jump allows you to quickly store three Dark Spells and still drop down safely! Since Dormammu is a huge threat with three Dark Spell points, the opposing player must make an attempt to stop you. If your opponent is trying to wavedash forward first, you can surprise them storing a Dark Spell, then teleporting Dormammu back down to the ground with Liberation. If your adversary runs into any of the Liberation attacks, you can easily verify the hit and hyper combo cancel to Chaotic Flame! The other main counter to encroaching rivals is to simply use Mass Change M to evade them, then reestablish your defense.

Crouching M has a massive hitbox, making it perfect for anti-airs if given enough time.

Chaotic Flame is incredibly fast; using it immediately after advancing guard can net you some free damage if your opponent likes to perform full chain combos against guarding opponents!

When an aggressor manages to get close, you have stronger options than Dormammu's slow speed would imply. Crouching M has a huge displaced attacking hitbox above Dormammu, making it one of the very few basic attacks in the game that is a truly reliable anti-air if performed slightly early. The hitstun on crouching M has been drastically reduced in *Ultimate Marvel vs. Capcom 3*; it used to be possible to easily verify that it hit an opponent before canceling into an S launcher for a combo. While that anti-air combo is still possible, you must immediately commit to it for it to work now. If your rival jumps into the crouching M and guards, they'll be able to easily punish the launcher with a full combo; only execute the launcher if you are absolutely sure that this won't happen!

As an alternative, you can chain the crouching M to standing H and cancel to Purification L. The pillar does not actually combo the target, but it does prevent them from doing anything but guarding after the standing H hit. This leaves your foe in the air above you stuck guarding, perfectly setting up an air throw! If your opponent expects the air throw and tries to break it, simply perform anti-air with crouching M again!

As with most characters, relying on air throws is another solid way to counter air-based approaches with Dormammu. Jump forward and press ⇦ + H; if you get the air throw, great! If an aerial H attack comes out instead and makes contact with your opponent, perform a delayed chain into air S: if the air H hit your adversary, you'll be able to follow up with a full combo for huge damage; see the Combo Usage section for details. If the air H is guarded, the opposing character must also guard the air S on your way down. This gives you a lot of frame advantage to work with; call a crossover assist and cross your opponent up with Mass Change M!

When you are unsure if your rival is going to approach by the ground or air, simply sticking out the Ⓢ launcher is a strong option. Like crouching Ⓜ, the launcher has a huge displaced hitbox covering the area directly in front of Dormammu, making it very likely that it can beat whatever your adversary is trying to do. Follow up with a combo for a huge chunk of free damage!

Previously, Dormammu only needed enough time to just get the Flame Carpet in play; if the opponent hit him afterward they'd still get fried by the Flame Carpet and allow you to land a combo. This doesn't quite work anymore, making the Flame Carpet a much less attractive option when your competitor is within striking range.

Instead, try using advancing guard to push the opponent away, then immediately using Chaotic Flame. If your rival committed to performing a full guarded chain combo against you, the Chaotic Flame catches them while they are whiffing the next attack in their chain. Learn which attack patterns your opponent is using that can be punished this way, and take your free damage!

Another option is to use Mass Change M to get behind your adversary whenever the opportunity presents itself. Evade an incoming attack with Mass Change M, airdash down-back to get Dormammu back onto the ground quickly, then reestablish your defense!

Super jumping into the air is a relatively safe option, and from there, you can activate flight mode at the peak of the jump. Once activated, increase the distance from the opposing character by repeatedly canceling up-forward and down-forward airdashes into each other to travel across the screen, then use air Ⓢ to quickly drop down.

All of Dormammu's basic attacks besides Ⓛ can nullify projectiles. Use this to buy some time when being overwhelmed from afar!

Mass Change H is a high-risk but high-reward counter to projectile attacks.

Dormammu's long range attacks are slow and poorly suited to a firefight against other projectile-based characters. These character match-ups can create a situation where you can be overwhelmed from across the screen with the rapid output of projectiles that some characters can manage. Using Chaotic Flame is a simple way to gain the upper hand in these matches, since most likely, you won't have an infinite amount of hyper combo gauge bars to work with. If you do, stop cheating! Dormammu would never cheat!

The simplest counter to projectile usage is to just drop on your opponent's head using Mass Change H. If successful, you'll be able to land a whole combo and possibly take out the opposing character in one shot. Use this judiciously, though: this is the expected behavior for a Dormammu user, and experienced players can typically counter with an air throw that leads into a combo.

Another more stable answer is to simply super jump into the air, activate flight mode, then store three Destruction points. Having access to Liberation (Destruction 3) at the ready almost forces your rival to stop tossing projectiles; if they don't, just nuke them! Storing Dark Spell points from up in the air is something that most ranged characters have a lot of trouble dealing with, outside of simply coming after you. This will usually be much more in Dormammu's favor!

Some characters do have a strong answer to Dark Spell hoarding from above: Ryu, for example, can simply super jump along with you and use air Shinku Hadoken. In these cases, you'll have to do something that requires considerably more finesse: use Dormammu's basic attacks to buy yourself some time from across the screen! All of Dormammu's basic attacks besides Ⓛ have the special property of being able to nullify projectiles. Standing Ⓜ is best for this purpose due to its quick speed and generous amount of active frames. Call a long range crossover assist simultaneously with the standing Ⓜ attack to protect their entry, as well. Upon successfully nullifying a projectile, cancel the standing Ⓜ into a special attack to capitalize on the time earned: counterattacking with Dark Hole H or Purification H generally interrupts anything an opposing player tries, while canceling into Dark Spell: Destruction gets you one step closer to having access to a match-altering Liberation (Destruction 3).

DORMAMMU

COMBO USAGE

I. (OPPONENT CLOSER THAN HALFWAY TO CORNER) CR. Ⓛ, Ⓜ, ST. Ⓗ, → + Ⓗ CANCEL ➡ ← ↓ ↙ + Ⓜ, AIR Ⓗ, LAND, FORWARD JUMP, AIR Ⓜ, Ⓗ, Ⓢ, LAND, CR. Ⓜ, Ⓗ, Ⓢ CANCEL ➡ SUPER JUMP, AIR, Ⓜ, Ⓜ, Ⓗ, Ⓢ, LAND, → ↓ ↘ + Ⓜ CANCEL ➡ ↓ ↘ → + ATK ATK, MASH ATK

738,100 damage, 6% meter gain

Dormammu's new abilities of three-hit chains, cancelable Dark Matter, and mashable Chaotic Flame allow him to inflict truckloads of damage in *UMvC3*, albeit with a higher level of execution required. Dark Matter combos require constant awareness of the opposing character's distance to the corner, requiring one of three follow-ups to Dark Matter depending on that distance. If you're ever unsure, just omit the Dark Matter and use the reliable **Combo VII** instead.

Cancel Dark Matter into Mass Change M as soon as the projectile hits your rival to create the proper timing. After the Mass Change M, hit your competitor with air Ⓗ as late as possible to give yourself enough time for the subsequent normal jump and air Ⓜ. You can also just omit the normal jump air Ⓜ, Ⓗ, Ⓢ if that makes the combo too difficult.

Crouching Ⓜ goes right over many crouching characters; you can omit it from the initial hits entirely if you're not positive that the crouching Ⓛ will successfully hit. If guarded, you can still salvage the situation with a strong set-up—simply call a long range crossover assist simultaneously with → + Ⓗ, then cancel into Mass Change M or H for a cross-up mix-up. If no assist is available, you can still cancel to Mass Change H to continue the offense, but an alert adversary can easily counter with an air throw. Canceling Dark Matter into Dark Spell or Purification is usually the more prudent option.

II. (AGAINST CORNERED OPPONENT) CR. Ⓛ, Ⓜ, ST. Ⓗ, → + Ⓗ CANCEL ➡ ↓ ↙ ← + Ⓢ, AIR Ⓜ, Ⓗ, Ⓢ, LAND, JUMP FORWARD, AIR Ⓜ, Ⓗ, Ⓢ, LAND, CR. Ⓜ, Ⓗ, Ⓢ CANCEL ➡ SUPER JUMP, AIR, Ⓜ, Ⓜ, Ⓗ, Ⓢ, LAND, → ↓ ↘ + ATK CANCEL ➡ ↓ ↘ → + ATK ATK, MASH ATK

755,400 damage, 19% meter gain

The corner variant of Dormammu's new combo inflicts even more damage, using flight mode to get an additional aerial chain. The distance requirement to the corner for this combo is fairly generous—even if your attacker is a fair distance away from the corner, you can still perform the combo by simply flying forward after the flight cancel.

COMBO USAGE CONT.

III. (OPPONENT FARTHER THAN HALFWAY TO CORNER) CR. Ⓛ, Ⓜ, ST. Ⓗ, → + Ⓗ CANCEL ← ↓ ↙ + Ⓛ, AIRDASH DOWN, AIR Ⓗ, LAND, CR. Ⓜ, Ⓗ, Ⓢ CANCEL SUPER JUMP, AIR, Ⓜ, Ⓜ, Ⓗ, Ⓢ, LAND, → ↓ ↘ + ATK CANCEL ↓ ↘ → + ATK ATK, MASH ATK

700,500 damage, 14% meter loss

Considerably more difficult than the other two variations of the combo, this combo requires you to cancel Dark Matter into Mass Change L with an unintuitive timing: immediately before the opposing character is about to hit the wall. After Mass Change L, immediately airdash down and press Ⓗ to lift your challenger before they hit the ground.

IV. (OPPONENT IN AIR, CLOSER THAN HALFWAY TO CORNER) AIR Ⓗ, Ⓢ, LAND, CR. Ⓜ, ST. Ⓗ, → + Ⓗ CANCEL ← ↓ ↙ + Ⓜ, AIR Ⓢ, LAND, CR. Ⓜ, Ⓗ, Ⓢ CANCEL SUPER JUMP, AIR, Ⓜ, Ⓜ, Ⓗ, Ⓢ, LAND, → ↓ ↘ + Ⓜ CANCEL ↓ ↘ → + ATK ATK, MASH ATK

766,700 damage, 35% meter loss

An air-to-air combo that also doubles as an air throw attempt and pays huge dividends if it hits! Like the above combos, the most optimized combos in this situation involve Dark Matter, which require an awareness of your opponent's distance to the corner.

V. (OPPONENT IN AIR, CLOSER THAN HALFWAY TO CORNER) FORWARD OR BACKWARD AIR THROW, AIRDASH DOWN-FORWARD, LAND, ST. Ⓗ, → + Ⓗ CANCEL ← ↓ ↙ + Ⓛ, AIRDASH DOWN, AIR Ⓗ, LAND, CR. Ⓜ, Ⓗ, Ⓢ CANCEL SUPER JUMP, AIR, Ⓜ, Ⓜ, Ⓗ, Ⓢ, LAND, → ↓ ↘ + Ⓜ CANCEL ↓ ↘ → + ATK ATK, MASH ATK

565,800 damage, 15% meter loss

This air throw combo only works when you air throw the opponent from over Dormammu's airdash height restriction, which is almost at the peak of his jump.

If the air throw was performed too low to the ground, the simply use Purification M to Chaotic Flame: it still results in a solid 420,500 damage!

VI. CR. Ⓛ, Ⓜ, Ⓗ, Ⓢ CANCEL SUPER JUMP, AIR Ⓜ, Ⓜ, Ⓗ, Ⓢ, LAND, → ↓ ↘ + ATK CANCEL ↓ ↘ → + ATK ATK, MASH ATK

632,100 damage, 40% meter loss

A much easier combo than **Combo I, II, and III**, it doesn't require any fancy re-jumping or spatial awareness. It's also great for online play in sub-optimal conditions!

"A NEW WILL GRIPS THE EARTH! THE SKY, THE ETHER, MY WILL!"

ADVANCED TACTICS

DORMAMMU'S FAVORITE HOMIES

Beam-based crossover assists allow Dormammu to threaten with sudden cross-ups at almost any time!

One of the greatest assets Dormammu can have is a crossover assist who fires a beam projectile, like Doctor Doom—α or Iron Man—α. This gives you an incredible tool: the ability to put your opponent in a cross-up mix-up whenever they're on the ground! Simply call the assist immediately before performing Mass Change M or H: if the beam hits your rival, you'll be able to capitalize with a full combo! See the Combo Appendix section for details!

There are a number of common situations in which you can easily set up this mix-up:

- Perform a guarded chain combo to standing Ⓗ, use Dark Matter and crossover assist simultaneously, cancel to Mass Change M
- While your adversary is worrying about Flame Carpet or Liberation (Destruction 3)
- After forcing your competitor to guard Stalking Flare
- As your opponent is coming down from a jump

The only really reliable way for the opposing character to avoid this mix-up is to stay in the air, above the beam. Be ready to anti-air with crouching Ⓜ or air Ⓗ (which is also an air throw attempt). If your adversary is landing farther away, simply time your beam cross-up mix-up to hit as they land!

ADVANCED TACTICS CONTINUED

I SUMMON THE POWER (OF CHEAPNESS)

If your opponent has used their X-Factor already, Dormammu with level 3 X-Factor can get a nearly guaranteed K.O. using multiple Stalking Flares!

If your adversary uses their X-Factor before you do, a huge window of opportunity comes up—if Dormammu defeats the second character on their team, he can set up a multitude of Stalking Flare projectiles that the opponent cannot avoid. With the additional damage of level 3 X-Factor, each Stalking Flare guarded results in 216,000 points of chip damage. If you have enough hyper combo gauge bars to burn, you can stack a bunch of Stalking Flares on top of each other for an unavoidable K.O. before your rival even touches the ground!

When finishing off the opposing player's second character in a combo, end the combo by hyper combo canceling Purification into Stalking Flare instead of Chaotic Flame, then immediately activate X-Factor and perform another Stalking Flare. Try to get as many Stalking Flares as you can into play before your competitor's final character comes in. The first projectile roams over and hangs out directly in front of where the final character will spawn, forcing them to guard it. From there, the rest of the Stalking Flares home in on the opponent's character while they are guarding the first, resulting in a ridiculous amount of unavoidable chip damage!

COMBO APPENDIX

GENERAL EXECUTION TIPS

Hyper combo cancel the final OTG Purification in a combo within its first one to two hits to reliably get the Chaotic Flame to hit

Slightly delay the air Ⓢ in any normal jump chain to give Dormammu more time to reach the ground before his adversary

(AGAINST CLOSER THAN HALF-SCREEN TO THE CORNER) CR. Ⓛ, Ⓜ, ST. Ⓗ, → + Ⓗ [CANCEL] ← ↓ ↙ + Ⓜ, AIR Ⓢ, LAND, CR. Ⓗ, Ⓢ [CANCEL] SUPER JUMP [CANCEL] ↓ ↙ ← + Ⓗ, Ⓢ [CANCEL] SUPER JUMP, AIR, Ⓜ, Ⓜ, Ⓗ, Ⓢ, LAND, → ↓ ↘ + ATK [CANCEL] ↓ ↘ → + ATK ATK, MASH ATK

Notes	Damage
Requires 2 destruction points, 1 creation point. Jump-cancel the Ⓢ launcher into Liberation by performing ⇩ ⇙ ⇦ ⇖ + Ⓗ	886,300 damage, 59% meter gain

(AGAINST CORNERED OPPONENT) CR. Ⓛ, Ⓜ, ST. Ⓗ, → + Ⓗ [CANCEL] ↓ ↙ ← + Ⓢ, AIR Ⓜ, Ⓗ, Ⓢ, LAND, JUMP FORWARD, AIR Ⓜ, Ⓗ, Ⓢ, LAND, CR. Ⓗ, Ⓢ [CANCEL] SUPER JUMP [CANCEL] ↓ ↙ ← + Ⓗ, Ⓢ [CANCEL] SUPER JUMP, AIR, Ⓜ, Ⓜ, Ⓗ, Ⓢ, LAND, → ↓ ↘ + ATK [CANCEL] ↓ ↘ → + ATK ATK, MASH ATK

Notes	Damage
Requires 2 destruction points, 1 creation point. Super jump cancel the Ⓢ launcher to Liberation before Dormammu leaves the ground. Slightly delay canceling the crouching Ⓗ to Ⓢ to ensure that your target is low enough for Liberation (Destruction Mix) to hit	940,900 damage, 91% meter gain

P1+P2, ← ↓ ↙ + Ⓜ, AIR Ⓗ, LAND, ST. Ⓗ, → + Ⓗ [CANCEL] ← ↓ ↙ + Ⓛ, DOWNWARD AIRDASH, AIR Ⓗ, LAND, CR. Ⓜ, Ⓗ, Ⓢ [CANCEL] SUPER JUMP, AIR Ⓜ, Ⓜ, Ⓗ, Ⓢ, LAND, → ↓ ↘ + ATK [CANCEL] ↓ ↘ → + ATK ATK, MASH ATK

Notes	Damage
Combo from cross-up beam assist using Doctor Doom—α	566,100 damage, 3% meter loss

(OPPONENT CLOSER THAN HALFWAY TO CORNER) CR. Ⓛ, Ⓜ, ST. Ⓗ, → + Ⓗ [CANCEL] ← ↓ ↙ + Ⓜ, AIR Ⓗ, LAND, FORWARD JUMP, AIR Ⓜ, Ⓗ, Ⓢ, LAND, CR. Ⓜ, Ⓗ, Ⓢ [CANCEL] SUPER JUMP, AIR, Ⓜ, Ⓜ, Ⓗ, Ⓢ, LAND, → ↓ ↘ + ATK ATK, → ↓ ↘ + Ⓜ [CANCEL] ↓ ↘ → + ATK ATK, MASH ATK

Notes	Damage
4-bar combo using Dark Dimension	1,134,400 damage, 294% meter loss

↓ ↙ ← + Ⓗ, ↓ ↘ → + Ⓗ [CANCEL] ↓ ↘ → + ATK ATK, MASH ATK

Notes	Damage
Requires 3 Dark Spell points, fullscreen combo from any Liberation (Destruction 3) hit	460,500 damage, 63% meter loss

(OPPONENT CLOSER THAN HALFWAY TO CORNER) → + Ⓗ [CANCEL] ← ↓ ↙ + Ⓜ, AIRDASH DOWN, LAND, ↓ ↘ → + ATK [CANCEL] ↓ ↘ → + ATK ATK

Notes	Damage
Combo from cross-up Dark Matter	444,700 damage, 79% meter loss

HULK

"HULK SMASH! HULK WIN! HULK THE STRONGEST!"

Bio

REAL NAME

Bruce Banner

OCCUPATION

Former Nuclear Physicist

ABILITIES

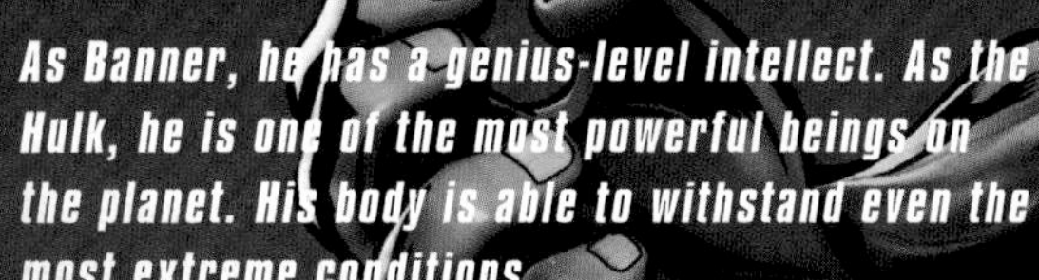

As Banner, he has a genius-level intellect. As the Hulk, he is one of the most powerful beings on the planet. His body is able to withstand even the most extreme conditions.

WEAPONS

None

PROFILE

A genius scientist, Bruce accidentally absorbed huge amounts of gamma radiation during a bomb test. As a result, when his anger or negative emotions reach a boiling point, he transforms into the green-skinned Hulk, complete with incredible power that sets the standard for strength.

FIRST APPEARANCE

The Incredible Hulk #1 (1962)

POWER GRID

6 INTELLIGENCE

7 STRENGTH

3 SPEED

7 STAMINA

1 ENERGY PROJECTION

4 FIGHTING ABILITY

*This is biographical, and does not represent an evaluation of the in-game combat potential of this hero.

Vitality	1,200,000
Chain Combo Archetype	2-Hit Limited

X-Factor Boost	Damage	Speed
Level 1 (3 teammates remaining)	140%	100%
Level 2 (2 teammates remaining)	170%	100%
Level 3 (1 teammate remaining)	200%	100%

Hulk's main strength lies in his ability to plow through his opponent's attacks with his numerous super armor-enabled attacks. As such, your goal when using Hulk is simple: get within striking range of his fearsome standing Ⓗ attack!

What's so great about being in range of standing Ⓗ?

- **Standing Ⓗ covers a large portion of the screen and has super armor properties to muscle through the opponent's attacks, often hitting both point and assist characters and leading into a damaging combo**
- **If the other player is wary of standing Ⓗ they will behave much more passively, opening up opportunities to catch them with Hulk's long range Gamma Tornado throw attacks**
- **Opponents that run away from Hulk's mix-up of standing Ⓗ and Gamma Tornado will often voluntarily run straight into the corner**

If Hulk is so big and slow, how does one maneuver him into position to threaten with standing Ⓗ?

- **Pestering them from afar with Gamma Wave H, coaxing the opponent to voluntarily move into Hulk's desired range**
- **Calling long range crossover assists while dashing forward or using Gamma Charge**
- **Patiently dashing and jumping forward while guarding attacks, attempting to push the enemy back into the corner**

TUNING SINCE ORIGINAL MVC3

Amusingly, Hulk's new tools in *Ultimate Marvel vs. Capcom 3* allow him to do even more damage than before! Gamma Charge 2nd M now wall bounces the enemy, adding a ridiculous amount of damage to his combos while pushing his foe much farther into the corner. If the opponent ends up in the corner after a combo, Hulk can easily inflict more than 900,000 points of damage with a single hyper combo bar!

Along with his increased damage potential, Gamma Charge now has super armor properties that greatly improve Hulk's chances at getting near an opponent with projectiles. Gamma Charge is still just as unsafe if guarded, so Hulk's reliance on long range crossover assists is still present, unfortunately.

Hulk also received a new command attack, the Impact Punch. This attack essentially gives Hulk a 3-hit chain combo, resulting in extra damage in combos in addition to making it easier to verify hits before committing to Gamma Charge (Anti-Air).

- **Recovery frames of standing Ⓛ decreased from 27 to 14**
- **Gamma Charge now has super armor properties, starting from frame 9, also bounces opponents slightly higher into the air**
- **Gamma Charge 2nd M (Anti-Air) now wall bounces opponent**
- **New command move, Impact Punch ➡ + Ⓜ: an attack that has armor properties and can be charged to cause a wall bounce**

Attack Set

Standing Basic Attacks

Screen	Command	Hits	Damage	Meter Gain	Startup	Active	Recovery	Advantage on Hit	Advantage if Guarded	Notes
1	Standing Ⓛ	1	85,000	680	9	3	14	+2	-1	—
2	Standing Ⓜ	1	90,000	720	13	3	33	-10	-10	1 hit of super armor during frames 3-15, knocks down foe
3	Standing Ⓗ	1	120,000	960	15	4	37	—	-15	1 hit of super armor during frames 6-18, ground bounces opponent, hard knockdown

1

2

3

Crouching Basic Attacks

Screen	Command	Hits	Damage	Meter Gain	Startup	Active	Recovery	Advantage on Hit	Advantage if Guarded	Notes
1	Crouching Ⓛ	1	58,000	464	9	3	19	-3	-6	Low attack
2	Crouching Ⓜ	1	85,000	680	14	3	26	-5	-9	—
3	Crouching Ⓗ	1	100,000	800	12	4	34	—	-12	Knocks down

1

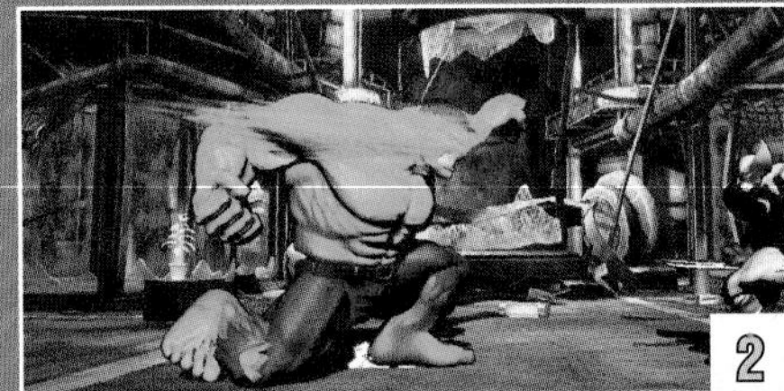
2

3

Ground Special Attack—Launcher

Screen	Command	Hits	Damage	Meter Gain	Startup	Active	Recovery	Advantage on Hit	Advantage if Guarded	Notes
1	Ⓢ (while standing or crouching)	2	121,000	1040	10	2(2)3	36	—	-13	Launcher, not special- or hyper combo-cancelable

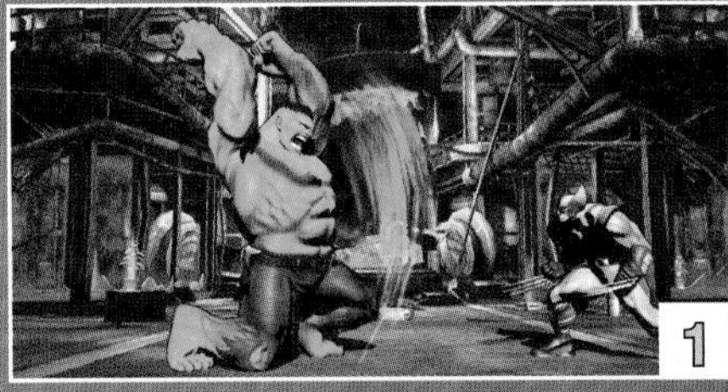
1

AAir Basic Attacks

Screen	Command	Hits	Damage	Meter Gain	Startup	Active	Recovery	Advantage on Hit	Advantage if Guarded	Notes
1	Air Ⓛ	1	60,000	480	7	3	18	+15	+13	Overhead attack
2	Air Ⓜ	1	90,000	720	13	3	19	+20	+16	Overhead attack
3	Air Ⓗ	1	110,000	880	16	5	18	—	-2	Overhead attack, staggers grounded foes for 49 frames

1

2

3

Air Special Attacks — Flying Screen and Air Exchange

Air Ⓢ causes a hard knockdown when used in a launcher combo (this is sometimes called flying screen). When used outside of a launcher combo, air Ⓢ behaves mostly like another basic attack. Air exchange attacks, performed by inputting a direction plus Ⓢ, are only possible during a launcher combo. Exchange hits initiate team aerial combos by tagging in the next available character to continue the air combo.

Screen	Command	Hits	Damage	Meter Gain	Startup	Active	Recovery	Advantage on Hit	Advantage if Guarded	Notes
1	Air Ⓢ	1	130,000	1040	17	3	36	—	+16	Causes hard knockdown if used in launcher combo, otherwise ground bounces adversary
2	Air ⇧ + Ⓢ (during launcher combo)	1	65,000	520	9	6	Until grounded	—	—	Tags in next available ally while lofting opponent upward
3	Air ⇨ or ⇦ + Ⓢ (during launcher combo)	1	65,000	520	9	6	Until grounded	—	—	Tags in next available ally while causing wall bounce, erases 1 hyper meter from foe
4	Air ⇩ + Ⓢ (during launcher combo)	1	35,000	280	9	6	Until grounded	—	—	Tags in next available ally while causing ground bounce, generates 1 hyper meter

1

2

3

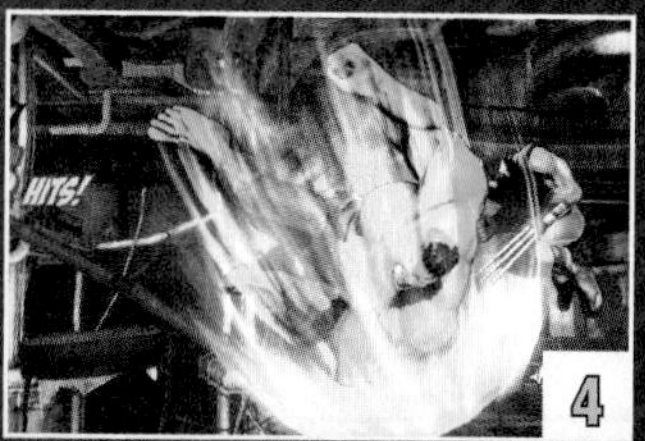

4

Command Attacks

Command attacks resemble basic attacks but have different chaining and canceling properties. It's usually possible to chain *into* a command attack from basic attacks, but most command attacks cannot be chained from or canceled themselves.

Screen	Name	Command	Hits	Damage	Meter Gain	Startup	Active	Recovery	Advantage on Hit	Advantage if Guarded	Notes
1	Impact Punch (can be charged)	⇨ + Ⓜ	1	115,000~140,000	920~1120	16~46	5	28	+4	-7	Knocks down, fully charged hit causes wall bounce, 1 hit of super armor during frames 10-19 (uncharged) or 10-48 (charged)

1

Throws

Throws are for snagging passive or blocking opponents. Since throws are active so quickly, you can also use them to preemptively toss opposing characters out of their offense. Combos are usually possible after throws, one way or another.

Screen	Command	Hits	Damage	Meter Gain	Startup	Active	Notes
1	⇨ + Ⓗ (ground)	1	100,000	1000	1	1	Hard knockdown
	⇦ + Ⓗ (ground)	1	100,000	1000	1	1	Hard knockdown
2	⇨ + Ⓗ (air)	1	100,000	1000	1	1	Hard knockdown
	⇦ + Ⓗ (air)	1	100,000	1000	1	1	Hard knockdown

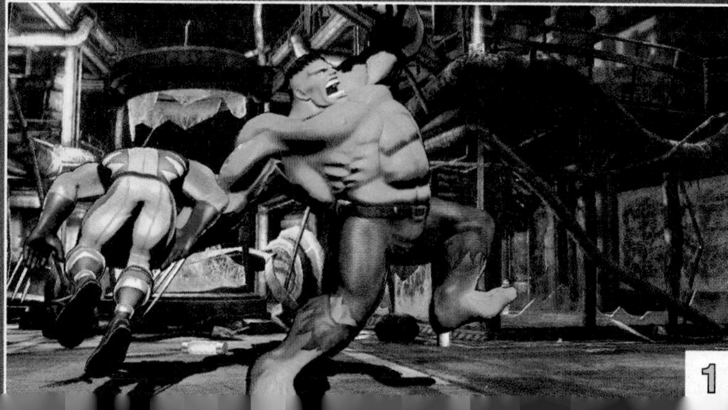
1

2

As a Partner—Crossover Assists

Screen	Type	P1+P2 Crossover Combination Hyper Combo	Description	Hits	Damage	Meter Gain	Startup	Active	Recovery (this crossover assist)	Recovery (other partner)	Notes
1	Hulk—α	Gamma Tsunami	Gamma Wave M	3	108,300	960	47	—	123	93	OTG-capable, knocks down, projectiles are in play a total of 28 frames, each projectile has 5 low priority durability points
2	Hulk—β	Gamma Quake	Gamma Charge M (Anti-Air)	4	137,400	1280	29	19	129	99	1 hit of super armor during frames 23-32
3	Hulk—γ	Gamma Crush	Gamma Charge M	4	137,400	1280	33	8	131	101	1 hit of super armor during frames 27-36

1

2

3

Hulk—α throws out three OTG-capable grounded projectiles, each with 5 low priority durability points. This assist is useful for chewing through enemy projectiles, pushing your opponent back, or forcing your foe into the air to avoid the attack. The main drawback of Hulk—α is its slow startup time, which tends to make it impractical for extended projectile battles or continuing combos off of enemies in a hard knockdown state. Overall, the long range capabilities of this assist make Hulk—α a good all-around fit for a lot of teams.

Hulk—β serves as an anti-air assist, launching Hulk upwards wherever he was called. It has the fastest startup of all of Hulk's assists, and also has super armor properties that activate as soon as Hulk comes into play. This makes the Gamma Charge (Anti-Air) assist an excellent defensive crossover assist that can be used in a similar manner to the dreaded Haggar—α Double Lariat! On the downside, Hulk—β only has a single hit of armor, which can sometimes result in situations where he will get stopped by multi-hit attacks. It is also much more difficult to convert an errant Hulk—β hit into a combo when compared to Haggar—α or a powered-up Hsien-Ko—γ. Regardless, having a dependable defensive crossover assist is an enormous asset!

Hulk—γ's Gamma Charge also has super armor properties to plow through attacks, but unfortunately Hulk is vulnerable for 2 frames before the effect kicks in. While this is still a strong asset, it isn't nearly as dependable as Hulk—β's assist. Having much more horizontal range and being easier to combo from is a huge asset however, and these factors should definitely be taken into account when deciding which crossover assist type to choose for Hulk.

Snap Back

Screen	Command	Hits	Damage	Meter Gain	Startup	Active	Recovery	Advantage on Hit	Advantage if Guarded
1	↓↘→ + P1 or P2	1	50,000	500 - (-1 hyper meter bar)	1	3	33	—	-10

Notes

On hit, snap back forces the opposing point character to be replaced by an assist. Opposing assist calls or tag outs are also locked out for 4 seconds

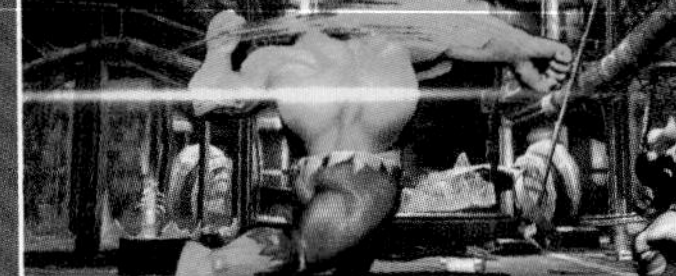
1

Special Moves

Screen	Name	Command	Hits	Damage	Meter Gain	Startup	Active	Recovery	Advantage on Hit	Advantage if Guarded	Notes
1	Gamma Wave L	← (charge), → + (L)	2	76,000	640	19	—	34	—	-1	OTG-capable, knocks down, projectiles are in play for a total of 23 frames, charge time required is 45 frames, each projectile has 5 low priority durability points
1	Gamma Wave M	← (charge), → + (M)	3	108,300	960	23	—	36	—	-5	OTG-capable, knocks down, projectiles are in play for a total of 28 frames, charge time required is 45 frames, each projectile has 5 low priority durability points
1	Gamma Wave H	← (charge), → + (H)	4	137,400	1280	27	—	36	—	-6	OTG-capable, knocks down, projectiles are in play for a total of 32 frames, charge time required is 45 frames, each projectile has 5 low priority durability points
2	Gamma Charge L	↓↘→ + (L)	3	135,400	1200	9	6	36	-12	-12	Knocks down, 1 hit of super armor from frames 9-15
2	Gamma Charge M	↓↘→ + (M)	4	171,800	1600	9	8	39	-15	-15	Knocks down, 1 hit of super armor from frames 9-17
2	Gamma Charge H	↓↘→ + (H)	5	204,600	2000	9	10	42	-18	-18	Knocks down, 1 hit of super armor from frames 9-19
3	Gamma Charge 2nd L	(During Gamma Charge) (L)	1	70,000	560	9	10	27	—	-11	1 hit of super armor during frames 3-15, must input command during frames 9-25 of Gamma Charge, knocks down
4	Gamma Charge 2nd M	(During Gamma Charge) (M)	1	70,000	560	7	19	35	—	-28	1 hit of super armor during frames 3-15, must input command during frames 9-25 of Gamma Charge, knocks down
5	Gamma Charge 2nd H	(During Gamma Charge) (H)	1	70,000	560	9	10	32	—	-16	1 hit of super armor during frames 3-15, must input command during frames 9-25 of Gamma Charge, knocks down

Special Moves continued

Screen	Name	Command	Hits	Damage	Meter Gain	Startup	Active	Recovery	Advantage on Hit	Advantage if Guarded	Notes
6	Gamma Charge L (Anti-Air)	→↓↘ + L	3	135,400	1200	5	6	44	-20	-22	1 hit of super armor during frames 6-11, knocks down
	Gamma Charge M (Anti-Air)	→↓↘ + M	4	171,800	1600	5	19	38	-25	-29	1 hit of super armor during frames 6-11, knocks down
	Gamma Charge H (Anti-Air)	→↓↘ + H	5	204,600	2000	5	25	48	-39	-43	1 hit of super armor during frames 6-11, knocks down
7	Gamma Charge 2nd L (Anti-Air)	(During Gamma Charge (Anti-Air)) L	1	70,000	560	10	6	Until grounded, 10 frames of recovery	+6	-28	Must input command during frames 5-25 of Gamma Charge (Anti-Air), knocks down
8	Gamma Charge 2nd M (Anti-Air)	(During Gamma Charge (Anti-Air)) M	1	70,000	560	10	6	Until grounded, 10 frames of recovery	—	+2	Wall bounces foe, must input command during frames 5-25 of Gamma Charge (Anti-Air), knocks down
9	Gamma Charge 2nd H (Anti-Air)	(During Gamma Charge (Anti-Air)) H	1	70,000	560	10	6	Until grounded, 10 frames of recovery	—	+8	Ground bounces opponent, causes hard knockdown, must input command during frames 5-25 of Gamma Charge (Anti-Air)
10	Gamma Tornado L	→↘↓↙← + L	2~11	92,000~200,000	920~2000	11	2	28	—	—	Throw attack, hard knockdown, can be mashed for additional damage
	Gamma Tornado M	→↘↓↙← + M	2~11	92,000~200,000	920~2000	16	2	23	—	—	Throw attack, hard knockdown, can be mashed for additional damage
11	Gamma Tornado H	→↘↓↙← + H	2~11	92,000~200,000	920~2000	18	2	21	—	—	Throw attack, hard knockdown, can be mashed for additional damage

1

Gamma Wave: As one of his few long range options, Gamma Wave is one of the greatest tools in Hulk's arsenal. Each projectile in Gamma Wave has 5 low priority durability points—enough to chew up a majority of standard projectiles in the game. Gamma Wave serves many different purposes: hitting foes from almost a full screen away, pushing characters back into the corner, or using its OTG properties to extend combos. Surprisingly, long range characters that are primarily based on the ground have a lot of trouble beating a Hulk player that is simply using Gamma Wave H repeatedly. If these characters don't have strong aerial projectile options they will have to take the initiative and move towards the Hulk, getting the dirty work done for you! As a combo ender, Gamma Wave is great for getting a few last hits in when either Gamma Tsunami or Gamma Quake is not viable. In the corner, Gamma Wave can be canceled into Gamma Crush for mega damage!

2

Gamma Charge: Hulk rushes forward toward his target, with the distance traveled dependent on the attack button used. You can use Gamma Charge to shore up Hulk's defensive positioning on a blocked normal hit: most of his normal attacks are very unsafe on block, so canceling into Gamma Charge and retreating with Gamma Charge 2nd H can give Hulk some much-needed breathing room. Attacking with Gamma Charge is a little trickier, but on hit, it can be canceled into Gamma Crush for some serious damage.

Arguably Hulk's biggest improvement in *Ultimate Marvel vs. Capcom 3*, the Gamma Charge attacks now have a single hit of armor starting from frame 9. This makes Hulk much more able to approach opponents that are trying to keep him out with long range single-hit projectiles: call a crossover assist for backup, then plow through the projectile with Gamma Charge H!

3

Gamma Charge 2nd L: After visually confirming the hit of Gamma Charge, you can use Gamma Charge 2nd L for an extra hit of damage and a knockdown. It can also be canceled into Gamma Crush to apply extra damage to your foe. While Gamma Charge 2nd L has super armor properties, it's impractical to try to leverage that in an actual match: having to first perform the preceding Gamma Charge makes it nearly impossible to properly time.

4

Gamma Charge 2nd M: This variation of Gamma Charge 2nd causes Hulk to attack straight up. You can employ this move to hit adversaries attempting to jump over Gamma Charge, but it is easily blocked and punished.

5

Gamma Charge 2nd H: Gamma Charge 2nd H causes Hulk to dash back in the direction he came from. This move is most useful for retreating when Gamma Charge is blocked, but fast, long range hyper combos can easily punish it. If this happens, react to the situation and hyper combo cancel into the invincible Gamma Crush to inflict huge damage on them instead!

6

Gamma Charge (Anti-Air): Hulk launches straight up with a powerful attack, the distance and damage determined by the attack button pressed. Gamma Charge has super armor properties, but they do not apply until the active frames have started. While this attack is serviceable as an anti-air, you'll generally want to use the trusty standing H attack instead for the same purpose; standing H covers a much larger area, activates super armor more quickly, and more consistently leads into a combo. As such, Gamma Charge (Anti-Air) is mainly used for its M and H follow-up attacks.

7

Gamma Charge 2nd L (Anti-Air): If Gamma Charge (Anti-Air) hits and your foe is too high to hit with Gamma Charge 2nd M (Anti-Air) or Gamma Charge 2nd H (Anti-Air), use the L version to score a free extra hit. With some practice, you can generally use Gamma Charge 2nd M (Anti-Air) as late as possible for a much high payoff, making it difficult to utilize to justify using this attack.

8

Gamma Charge 2nd M (Anti-Air): The M version of Gamma Charge 2nd (Anti-Air) has gained an enormous boost in *Ultimate Marvel vs. Capcom 3*: rivals are wall bounced on hit, opening up a whole new world of combo opportunities for Hulk!

Gamma Charge 2nd H (Anti-Air): Gamma Charge 2nd H (Anti-Air) is another very important tool for Hulk, serving a few different purposes in his gameplan. From an offensive standpoint, it ground bounces a competitor, leaving them open for huge combos. Perhaps more importantly, it is completely safe if guarded. When Hulk's basic attacks are guarded, if going for a Gamma Tornado throw seems too risky, cancel Gamma Charge 2nd H (Anti-Air) to leave Hulk right next to the opponent's character with frame advantage. While this will typically result in the Hulk getting pushed across the screen by advancing guard, it's still easily the safest option at your disposal.

Gamma Tornado L & M: Gamma Tornado L and M are throw attacks with great range and can be mashed for additional damage. All versions of Gamma Tornado leave the opponent in a hard knockdown state, allowing you to add one of Hulk's OTG-capable hyper combos or an OTG-capable assist to lead into a big combo. The main differences between these two versions of Gamma Tornado come down to range and speed. Gamma Tornado L is faster, but Gamma Tornado M has much longer reach. Both versions are horrendously slow however, so you must sufficiently scare your opponent into not pressing buttons to establish this threat.

If your adversary is guarding near you and expecting one of Hulk's super armor attacks, such as standing M, H, or Impact Punch, it can be a great opportunity to surprise them with Gamma Tornado. Whenever your challenger relies on advancing guard to push Hulk away, don't give them anything to guard in the first place: grab 'em with Gamma Tornado M!

Gamma Tornado H: Utilize Gamma Tornado H as a mix-up to the L and M versions when you think your opponent will try to jump to avoid being grabbed. It has a very slow startup time, but opposing characters cannot throw escape out of it. Grab guarding targets who are jumping away from you, or use it in situations where your foe has used air recovery. It can also work as an effective anti-air against adversaries super jumping toward you.

Hyper Combos

Screen	Name	Command	Hits	Damage	Startup	Active	Recovery	Advantage on Hit	Advantage if Guarded	Notes
1	Gamma Tsunami	↓↘→ + ATK ATK	5	327,400	6+15	24	39	—	-11	OTG-capable, knocks down, each projectile has 3 high priority durability points
2	Gamma Crush	↓↙← + ATK ATK	8	403,700	5+10	56	48	—	-25	Invincible from frames 1-73, hard knockdown
3	Gamma Quake	→↓↘ + ATK ATK	11	301,400	6+9	81	89	—	+13	OTG-capable, knocks down, rocks begin hitting a standing foe 34 frames after quake is initiated, each projectile has 3 high priority durability points

Gamma Tsunami: Gamma Tsunami is a projectile hyper combo that quickly covers the bottom of the screen and can be used to easily hit your opponent in many situations. It deals more damage the closer Hulk is to his foe, but it misses several hits if used while your rival is in the corner. This hyper combo is OTG-capable, making it the perfect ender for midscreen combos. In the corner, however, you'll want to go with Gamma Quake or land an OTG-capable Gamma Wave and hyper combo cancel into the massively damaging Gamma Crush.

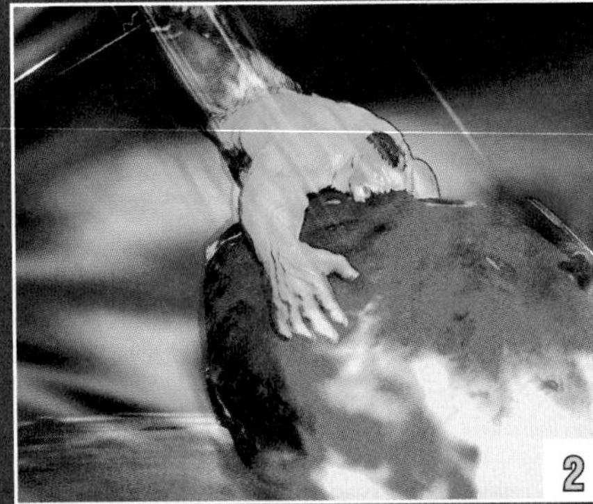

Gamma Crush: With Gamma Crush, Hulk flies high into the air and comes crashing down with giant red-hot boulder. It has a ton of invincibility, making it a great high-reward attack against other hyper combos and crossover combinations, dealing a whopping 400,000 damage on a successful hit. If a combo ends in the corner, pick up your adversary with an OTG assist or Gamma Wave L, and immediately cancel into Gamma Crush for a big damage boost. It's also a good option during team hyper combos, since any hyper combo that leaves the opponent high in the air is ripe pickings for this high-flying attack. Gamma Crush is very unsafe if guarded, so be sure you have enough meter to team hyper combo to something safer if you plan on using this move defensively.

Gamma Quake: This OTG-capable hyper is often used as a combo ender in the corner, where Gamma Tsunami misses most of its hits. Outside of combos, you can use Gamma Quake to hyper combo cancel out of a blocked Gamma Charge attack, giving you a positive frame advantage to continue your assault.

There are drawbacks to look for when using Gamma Quake—namely the large gap between the point when Hulk hits the ground and the rocks start hitting the opponent. If your foe is quick enough, they can counterattack Hulk before the rocks drop down: throws and level 3 hyper combos have several invincible frames that ignore the rocks completely, and teleporters can get right behind Hulk and make your life miserable with a combo. Conversely, you can use the gap it take for the rocks to appear to THC into another hyper combo, as the rocks still come out regardless of whether Hulk is in play or not.

Gamma Quake can be used effectively in team hyper combos: THC to Gamma Quake to safely tag in Hulk, or THC to another teammate immediately after Hulk pounds the ground to help cover their entrance.

"PUNY HUMAN TRY AND FIGHT HULK. AND THEY SAY IT HULK WHO NOT SMART!"

Battle Plan

Gamma Wave H can beat out most ranged attacks, and it is great for pushing grounded foes back into the corner.

Hulk's standing (M) and (H) attacks have super armor that can absorb attacks. Take advantage of this property to counterattack competitors and transition into deadly combos.

As the old saying goes, "Hulk's the strongest one there is!" With his high damage output and super armor attributes on a large number of his moves, Hulk is one of the heaviest hitters on the *Ultimate Marvel vs. Capcom 3* roster. However, adding Hulk to your team isn't without some drawbacks: Hulk is slow when it comes to mobility, attack speed and recovery, and his ability to gain meter. But with a bit of knowledge and proper assists (and a whole lot of standing (H)!), Hulk can strike fear into the hearts of many opposing players.

The first priority is to learn how to maneuver Hulk around the screen to cover large distances. His dash is great for covering ground, but you cannot cancel Hulk's dash into basic attacks or guard, leaving jump cancel as the only option. Simply dash forward, jump forward when you see an incoming threat, then immediately tap ← on the controller to guard in the air. Not only does this let you guard while dashing, guarding attacks in the air will almost always substantially reduce the amount of guardstun placed on a character; as soon as Hulk touches the ground he'll have recovered and be able to move again! This is Hulk's most stable way of advancing against opponents that are trying to keep him out; otherwise you'll have to resort to super jumping forward and hoping for the best.

An alternative method to cover ground involves canceling Hulk's pre-jump frames into Gamma Charge. Input ↓↘→↗ + (ATK) during a dash to cancel the dash straight into Gamma Charge H, allowing you to make contact with an opponent from full-screen quickly. A slow, long range projectile assist Rocket Raccoon—α works great here: call the assist while dashing, then perform the jump-canceled Gamma Charge H to make contact with the enemy. The projectiles will connect with your foe soon after, effectively giving you frame advantage after the Gamma Charge.

In the air, Hulk doesn't have any special attacks or movement options to rely on. In fact, the only way you can change his trajectory at all is by using air (H), which stops all of Hulk's forward momentum. You can use this technique to more precisely control Hulk's jumping height. Be sure to follow up an air (H) attack with (S), which covers a huge area below Hulk and results in a ground bounce on hit—and lets you combo your opponent into the corner.

Against some characters you won't even need to approach them; Gamma Wave can be an excellent tool to coax opponents into moving forward. Each rock on screen also has 5 low priority durability points, allowing Hulk to beat out most projectiles, even from a fullscreen distance. The startup is very slow, sometimes forcing Hulk to jump backwards to avoid a projectile before responding with Gamma Wave. However, once you get the rhythm down, you can output a successive string of Gamma Charge H projectiles that can triumph in firefights. Your challenger eventually gets forced to jump to avoid the rocks, to which they can respond by either throwing an air projectile (if they can) or jumping in for an attack. If they jump toward Hulk, respond with your armor-enabled standing (H) attack for a clean anti-air counter!

Many of Hulk's moves have super armor attributes—allowing him to soak up a hit of damage without going into hitstun, which completely changes the dynamics of a match when Hulk gets within striking distance. Standing (H) is much reliable overall due to its enormous area of effect. Opponents that refuse to respect these armor attacks will find themselves repeatedly getting bopped in the head, leading into Hulk's high-damage combos. See the Combo Usage section for details.

Standing (M) is Hulk's fastest super armor normal attack, having only three vulnerable frames before the armor kicks in. Compared to the mighty standing (H) attack standing (M) is best used in a pinch, where speed is of the essence; disregarding link combos and punishment situations, this attack can essentially be considered a 3-frame move! Unfortunately, standing (M) can be crouched under by the large number of the cast, making it best reserved for last-minute anti-air situations against them. The following characters cannot crouch under Hulk's standing (M):

Akuma	**Strange**	**M.O.D.O.K.**	**She-Hulk**
Captain America	**Ghost Rider**	**Nemesis**	**Spencer**
Chris	**Haggar**	**Nova**	**Taskmaster**
Doctor Doom	**Hulk**	**Ryu**	**Thor**
Doctor	**Iron Man**	**Sentinel**	**Wesker**

Always buffer a →↘↓↙← motion when using armor attacks as anti-air: if the attack hits the opponent, verifying the hit and pressing (S) to continue with a combo is a simple matter. If the attack is guarded, use the →↘↓↙← input and press (M) to perform a delayed cancel into Gamma Tornado M, grabbing the enemy right as they land. If your opponent wises up to this and starts immediately jumping after guarding, simply cancel into Gamma Tornado H to grab them out of the air instead!

Impact Punch has a completely different role in Hulk's toolset: aside from adding a bit of damage to Hulk's combos, it allows you three hits to visually confirm that Hulk's attacks are hitting the opponent before canceling into the proper attack. If your crouching (L), (M) combo starter is guarded, chain into Impact Punch and hold the button down. Any attempts to attack will get eaten up by the armor-enabled Impact Punch, which you can capitalize on by letting of the button to get a free retaliatory combo. Letting go of the button early also catches opponents trying to jump away; even if they guard Impact Punch in the air, you can cancel into Gamma Tornado for an immediate mix-up! If the opponent is respecting the charging Impact Punch and is sitting nearby, you can perform a goofy mix-up: cancel Impact Punch immediately after release into Gamma Tornado M or H. If performed properly, Hulk will grab your rival before the punch full extends!

The downside to Hulk's super armor attacks is they are all unsafe if guarded, and for good reason! To mitigate this, verify that your opponent is guarding, then cancel into Gamma Charge H (Anti-Air) H to Gamma Charge 2nd H (Anti-Air), leaving Hulk right next to the enemy with frame advantage. Opponents that use advancing guard against your armor attacks will leave Hulk all the way across the screen however. To mitigate this, simultaneously call a slow, long range crossover assist when armor attacks, then cancel into Gamma Charge H and Gamma Charge 2nd L; the assist will make contact immediately after Gamma Charge 2nd L, allowing you to resume pressure on your opponent.

The following characters can crouch under Impact Punch, rendering this tactic almost useless:

Amaterasu	**Hawkeye**	**Rocket Raccoon**	**Trish**
Arthur	**Magneto**	**Spider-Man**	**Viewtiful Joe**
Deadpool	**Morrigan**	**Storm**	**Wolverine**
Felicia	**Phoenix**	**Strider**	**X-23**
Firebrand	**Phoenix Wright**	**Super-Skrull**	
Frank West			

Your challengers may simply try to guard Hulk's super armored attacks when he's within range. Now is your chance to psych them out and grab them with Gamma Tornado instead! Opponents jumping backwards are a little trickier to deal with: dash forward, then jump cancel and catch them with a surprise air throw. If this proves difficult to pull off, continue pushing towards the opponent while decreasing their distance to the corner.

Gamma Charge 2nd (Anti-Air) H is one of Hulk's best tools to keep the pressure on in the corner.

Once you get your opponent in the corner, if can land a hit with Hulk, the opposing character is as good as knocked out. The best way to have Hulk apply corner pressure and keep his options open lies in Gamma Charge 2nd H (Anti-Air). Gamma Charge 2nd H (Anti-Air) is safe against a blocking opponent, allowing you to constantly loop →↓↘ + (L), (H) to keep your competitor pinned down. Any attempt to let go of a block or attack will result in a hit and a ground bounce, allowing you to unleash one of Hulk's powerful combos. Should your adversary attempt to use advancing guard to escape, the trajectory of Gamma Charge 2nd H (Anti-Air) keeps Hulk within striking distance of the target. Should they continue to block, mix it up with Gamma Tornado M, followed by a hyper combo, and pile on the damage!

Gamma Charge 2nd H pressure is countered by guarding it in the air, allowing the opponent to immediately move upon landing. Depending on the timing, this will allow them a free combo, or at the very least the initiative to interrupt your next attack. When your opponent begins trying to do this the answer is simple: jump up and grab them an air throw for a quick combo while keeping them stuck in the corner!

COMBO USAGE

I. (MIDSCREEN REQUIRED) CR. Ⓛ, Ⓜ, → + Ⓜ CANCEL ⇒ → ↓ ↘ + Ⓛ (DURING ANTI-AIR GAMMA CHARGE) Ⓜ, FORWARD DASH, FORWARD JUMP, AIR Ⓜ, Ⓗ, Ⓢ, LAND, ST. Ⓜ, → + Ⓜ, Ⓢ CANCEL ⇒ FORWARD SUPER JUMP, AIR Ⓜ, Ⓜ, Ⓗ, Ⓢ, LAND, {IF ENEMY IS MIDSCREEN, CHARGE ←, → + Ⓗ CANCEL ⇒ ↓ ↘ → + ATK ATK} OR {IF THE ENEMY IS LEAD TO A CORNER FROM MIDSCREEN, CHARGE ←, → + Ⓛ CANCEL ⇒ ↓ ↙ ← + ATK ATK}

793,000~913,000 damage, 28% meter gain

Hulk's new bread and butter combo takes full advantage of the buffs he's received in *Ultimate Marvel vs. Capcom 3*, including his new three-hit chain with → + Ⓜ and wall bounce abilities of Gamma Charge 2nd M (Anti-Air). This combo requires a slight modification when fighting smaller characters such as Rocket Raccoon or Amaterasu (See the Battle Plan section for a full list of characters who can crouch under Impact Punch). Both of these characters can simply duck under → + Ⓜ, so replace this command attack with crouching Ⓛ, Ⓜ before canceling into Gamma Charge L (Anti-Air).

When Hulk is three-fourths of the way from the corner or closer, Gamma Charge 2nd M (Anti-Air) can bounce his rival over his head, making it very difficult to juggle with the following air Ⓜ, Ⓗ, Ⓢ. From this position, use **Combo II** instead.

II. (CORNER REQUIRED) CR. Ⓛ, Ⓜ, → + Ⓜ CANCEL ⇒ → ↓ ↘ + Ⓛ (DURING ANTI-AIR GAMMA CHARGE) Ⓗ, ST. Ⓛ, Ⓜ, → + Ⓜ, Ⓢ CANCEL ⇒ FORWARD SUPER JUMP, AIR Ⓜ, Ⓜ, Ⓗ, Ⓢ, LAND, CHARGE ←, → + Ⓛ CANCEL ⇒ ↓ ↙ ← + ATK ATK

854,600 damage, 11% meter gain

This combo should be your go-to when you've got your adversary pinned in the corner. The ground bounce ability of Gamma Charge 2nd H (Anti-Air) ensures that your enemy stays in the corner and allows you to easily follow up with the highly damaging Gamma Crush hyper combo.

III. → ↘ ↓ ↙ ← + ATK, FORWARD DASH, FORWARD JUMP (CALL SHE-HULK—α), LAND, FORWARD JUMP, AIR Ⓗ, Ⓢ, LAND, ST. Ⓜ, → + Ⓜ, Ⓢ CANCEL ⇒ FORWARD SUPER JUMP, AIR Ⓜ, Ⓜ, Ⓗ, Ⓢ, LAND, {IF ENEMY IS MIDSCREEN, CHARGE ←, → + Ⓗ CANCEL ⇒ ↓ ↘ → + ATK ATK} OR {IF THE ENEMY IS CORNERED, CHARGE ←, → + Ⓛ CANCEL ⇒ ↓ ↙ ← + ATK ATK}

609,000~729,000 damage, 2% meter loss

Hulk's command throw can lead to some decent damage by simply performing ↓ ↘ → + ATK ATK, but with the right assist and mastery of his limited ability to move around quickly, you can increase Hulk's damage output dramatically. For this combo, you'll need to utilize She-Hulk—α for her long range OTG capability. Spend some time in the training room to get down the timing, and make your opponent fear the damage potential of Gamma Tornado.

ADVANCED TACTICS

HULK'S GOT HOPS

Hulk's unique dash allows him to hop over many characters when they are crouching. Use this ability with a crossover assist to cross up your opponent.

Hulk's dash has many drawbacks, but it does offer one distinct benefit— Hulk can dash straight over a large chunk of the cast while they're crouching. This gives you the opportunity to perform tricky cross-ups using assists, which can then lead into combos.

A slightly more realistic way to set this up is to force your opponent to guard an assist first, then dash over them at the last second. Since Hulk cannot attack normally out of his dash, perform a jump-canceled Gamma Charge (Anti-Air) by immediately inputting a ⇦ ⇩ ⇙ motion and pressing ATK while hopping over the opponent. If it connects, follow up with Gamma Charge 2nd M (Anti-Air) or Gamma Charge 2nd H (Anti-Air) to begin a damaging combo!

Hulk cannot dash over the following characters while they are crouching:

Akuma	**Doctor Doom**	**M.O.D.O.K.**	**She-Hulk**
Captain America	**Haggar**	**Nemesis**	**Spencer**
	Hulk	**Ryu**	**Thor**
Chris	**Iron Man**	**Sentinel**	**Wesker**

Some characters are easier to cross over than others: Rocket Raccoon can be crossed up from almost any point in Hulk's dash, while Taskmaster can only be cleared if the dash is started at a very close distance.

IV. FRONT OR BACK AIR THROW, LAND, CHARGE ←, → + Ⓛ CANCEL ↓ ↙ ← + ATK ATK

444,300 damage, 86% meter loss

This basic combo from Hulk's air throw is nothing to sneeze at. Begin holding ← to charge for Gamma Wave as soon as the throw animation begins to ensure that the move comes out in time. With an OTG-capable assist, you can transition into a variation similar to **Combo III** for even more damage.

V. ST. Ⓗ, Ⓢ CANCEL FORWARD SUPER JUMP, AIR Ⓜ, Ⓜ, Ⓗ, Ⓢ, LAND, {IF ENEMY IS MIDSCREEN, CHARGE ←, → + Ⓗ CANCEL ↓ ↘ → + ATK ATK} OR {IF THE ENEMY IS CORNERED, CHARGE ←, → + Ⓛ CANCEL ↓ ↙ ← + ATK ATK}

569,400~706,700 damage, 47~40% meter loss

The super armor and ground bounce properties of standing Ⓗ makes it one of Hulk's most important normal attacks. Should your opponent fall victim to its impressive hitbox, this simple combo leads to a massive amount of damage. To ensure that you land the final portion of the combo, begin charging ← as air Ⓢ connects with the target.

VI. (AGAINST AIRBORNE ENEMY) FORWARD JUMP, AIR Ⓜ, Ⓗ, Ⓢ, LAND, ST. Ⓜ, → + Ⓜ, Ⓢ CANCEL FORWARD SUPER JUMP, AIR Ⓜ, Ⓜ, Ⓗ, Ⓢ, LAND, {IF ENEMY IS MIDSCREEN, CHARGE ←, → + Ⓗ CANCEL ↓ ↘ → + ATK ATK} OR {IF THE ENEMY IS CORNERED, CHARGE ←, → + Ⓛ CANCEL ↓ ↙ ← + ATK ATK}

749,600~810,800 damage, 17~13% meter loss

Airborne opponents are not safe from the mighty Hulk! If you suspect that the opposing player is anticipating the attack, you can forgo the first air Ⓜ in the combo and hold → or ← to option select air Ⓗ with an air throw. If air Ⓗ connects, continue with the combo; if you connect the air throw instead, proceed to **Combo IV**.

VII. (MIDSCREEN REQUIRED) CR. Ⓛ, Ⓜ, → + Ⓜ CANCEL → ↓ ↘ + Ⓛ (DURING ANTI-AIR GAMMA CHARGE) Ⓜ X-FACTOR, LAND FORWARD DASH, FORWARD JUMP, AIR Ⓜ, Ⓗ, Ⓢ, LAND, ST. Ⓜ, → + Ⓜ, Ⓢ CANCEL FORWARD SUPER JUMP, AIR Ⓜ, Ⓜ, Ⓗ, Ⓢ, LAND, {IF ENEMY IS MIDSCREEN, CHARGE ←, → + Ⓗ CANCEL ↓ ↘ → + ATK ATK} OR {IF THE ENEMY IS CORNERED, CHARGE ←, → + Ⓛ CANCEL ↓ ↙ ← + ATK ATK}

1,018,300~1,391,000 or 1,222,700~1,603,000 damage, 68~124% or 64~118% meter gain

This meaty combo takes advantage of Hulk's new tools and air X-Factor cancel to ensure a K.O. against pretty much every character in the game. The trickiest part of this combo is landing the air Ⓜ, Ⓗ, Ⓢ chain after the forward dash following Gamma Charge 2nd M (Anti-Air). To ensure you have the maximum amount of time to get in, delay pressing Ⓜ until the last possible moment of → ↓ ↘ + Ⓛ. This way, your competitor reaches their maximum height from the wall bounce, which allows Hulk to connect all three hits of the air chain.

COMBO APPENDIX

GENERAL EXECUTION TIPS

When performing Impact Punch (→ + Ⓜ) in the middle of a combo, don't hold down Ⓜ at all. Otherwise, the delay caused by charging the attack drops the combo.

AS HULK COMES IN: AIR Ⓜ, Ⓗ, Ⓢ, LAND, FORWARD DASH CANCEL ↓ ↘ → ↗ + ATK ATK

Notes	Damage
⇧ + Ⓢ or ⇨ + Ⓢ or ⇩ + Ⓢ TAC to Hulk	Varies based on damage scaling

AS HULK COMES IN: AIR Ⓜ, Ⓗ, Ⓢ, LAND, CHARGE ←, → + Ⓛ CANCEL ↓ ↙ ← + ATK ATK

Notes	Damage
Requires corner, ⇧ + Ⓢ or ⇨ + Ⓢ or ⇩ + Ⓢ TAC to Hulk	Varies based on damage scaling

WHEN HULK'S BACK IS TO A CORNER, → ↘ ↓ ↙ ← + ATK, ST. Ⓜ, → + Ⓜ → ↓ ↘ + Ⓛ (DURING ANTI-AIR GAMMA CHARGE) Ⓗ, ST. Ⓜ, → + Ⓜ, Ⓢ CANCEL FORWARD SUPER JUMP, AIR Ⓜ, Ⓜ, Ⓗ, Ⓢ, LAND, CHARGE ←, → + Ⓛ CANCEL ↓ ↙ ← + ATK ATK

Notes	Damage
—	749,500 damage, 10% meter gain

→ ↘ ↓ ↙ ← + ATK, MASH ATK ↓ ↘ → + Ⓗ (WHIFF, BEGIN CHARGING ← FOR GAMMA WAVE), → + Ⓛ CANCEL ↓ ↙ ← + ATK ATK

Notes	Damage
Mid-screen combo from Gamma Tornado	434,800 damage, 74% meter lose

CR. Ⓛ, Ⓜ, → + Ⓜ CANCEL → ↓ ↘ + Ⓛ (DURING ANTI-AIR GAMMA CHARGE) Ⓗ, ST. Ⓛ, Ⓜ, → + Ⓜ, Ⓢ CANCEL FORWARD SUPER JUMP, AIR Ⓜ, Ⓜ, Ⓗ, Ⓢ, LAND, {CHARGE ←, → + Ⓛ, → ↓ ↘ + Ⓛ (DURING ANTI-AIR GAMMA CHARGE) Ⓗ} X ∞

Notes	Damage
Requires corner, works only against large characters like Sentinel, Dormammu, She-Hulk, and Hulk himself. Once started, the OTG segment of the combo can go on indefinitely	Damage varies depending on the amount of loops performed

IRON MAN

"I DON'T THINK I'M ALWAYS RIGHT. I KNOW IT."

Bio

REAL NAME

Anthony "Tony" Edward Stark

OCCUPATION

Adventurer, President Emeritus of Stark Industries

ABILITIES

Tony's sharp mind and technological know-how allow him to develop and maintain his own battle suit. As Iron Man, his armor is equipped with various weapons, as well as the ability to fly.

WEAPONS

He has various weapons, including the repulsor rays he can fire from both hands, anti-tank missiles, and the Unibeam he fires from his chest. He has several armors with different functionality.

PROFILE

Captured by a terrorist group in a war-torn region, Tony created a battle suit to help him escape. Afterwards, he improved the battle suit to become Iron Man, and has dedicated himself to protecting peace since.

FIRST APPEARANCE

Tales of Suspense #39 (1963)

POWER GRID

- 6 INTELLIGENCE
- 6 STRENGTH
- 5 SPEED
- 6 STAMINA
- 6 ENERGY PROJECTION
- 3 FIGHTING ABILITY

*This is biographical, and does not represent an evaluation of the in-game combat potential of this hero.

ALTERNATE COSTUMES

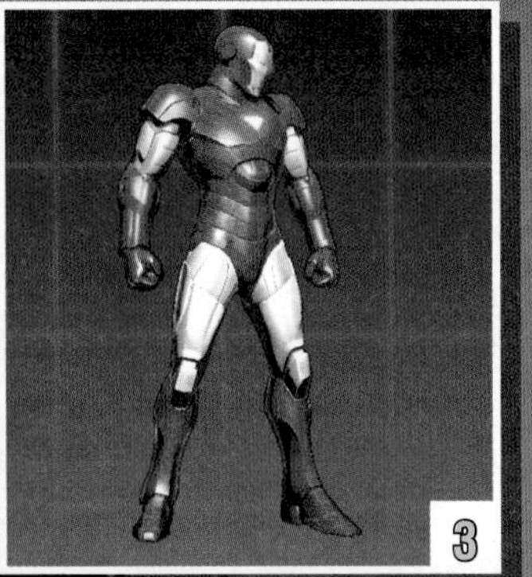

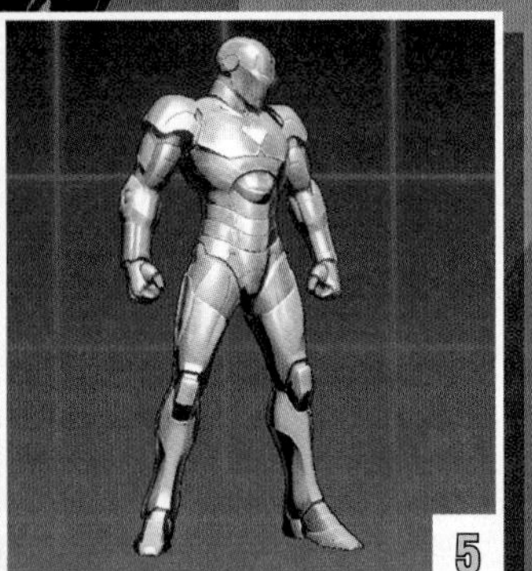

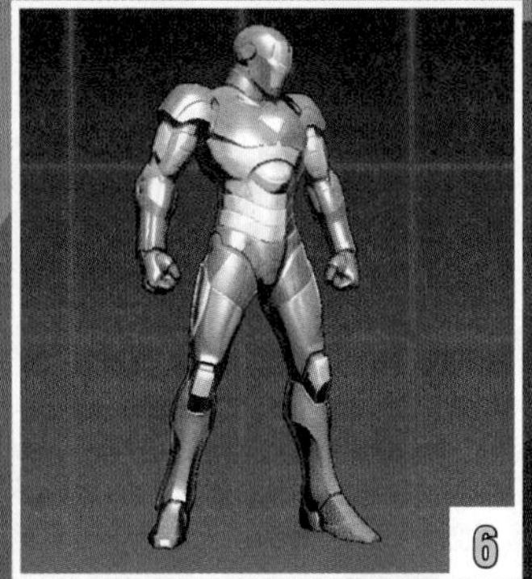

Overview

Vitality	950,000
Chain Combo Archetype	Hunter Series

X-Factor Boost	Damage	Speed
Level 1 (3 teammates remaining)	125%	115%
Level 2 (2 teammates remaining)	150%	120%
Level 3 (1 teammate remaining)	175%	125%

Your purpose when using Iron Man is to attack your opponent from mid range, and (in keeping with his attire) preferably from up above.

Why should an Iron Man player strive to control mid range?

- Iron Man's attack set is tailor-made to totally control the area that is about half the screen away, particularly below and in front of him
- Iron Man's ground dashes cannot be canceled for 11 frames, and any of his sideways airdashes aren't cancelable for 10 frames (and blocking isn't possible while airdashing, either); Iron Man doesn't have the best maneuverability for up-close fine positioning or sparring
- On the other hand, the hitting area of all of his attacks is fantastic, and although his airdash needs some space to get going, Iron Man travels a *huge* distance once it's underway

Why should Iron Man be used above an adversary?

- His air basic attacks have more range than those of almost anyone else (Sentinel and Ghost Rider can compete, and that's about the end of the list), especially his air Ⓗ which can be directed
- Using flight and airdashes to cancel air basic attacks allows Iron Man to out-poke almost anything in the air and convert stray hits to combos depending on positioning
- Smart Bomb allows Iron Man to hover in midair and attack in safety from a unique position, above and in front of his rival

How do you get Iron Man up there and use the space to an advantage?

- By using crouching Ⓗ, assists, Unibeam, and Repulsor Blast to control ground level
- By jumping or super jumping to dump Smart Bombs down on the target from above
- By using flight and airdashes to improve air mobility and follow-up options after Smart Bombs

TUNING SINCE ORIGINAL MVC3

Tony Stark has been tinkering with his armor quite a bit!

Airdashes in directions other than straight up or straight down now have a period of 10 frames at the beginning during which Iron Man's suit jets are firing up. You cannot attack during this time, and Iron Man doesn't actually start moving until the 10th frame. This ends up looking like a "hitch" at the beginning of his airdashes. You can still perform triangle jumps and square jumps with Iron Man, but you'll have to delay your button presses to be outside that window, or nothing happens. This also means his airdashing overhead attacks are slower by default. However, his airdash travels farther—Iron Man can airdash all the way back to the ground from super jump height! So, while Iron Man sort of lost a low altitude triangle jump in the Magneto/Storm tradition, he gained something no one else has: a triangle jump from super jump height.

The increase in size of the hitbox on standing Ⓗ makes chain combos after crouching Ⓜ sweep much more consistent. The drastically reduced recovery of grounded Smart Bombs makes them a more appealing close range zoning weapon, resulting in new combos entirely. Repulsor Spread now causes a brief hard knockdown, which also opens up new combo opportunities. Shorter startup on flight makes linking after flight in combos easier; it also makes Iron Man's aggressive use of flight more effective.

Iron Man, like Dante, has experienced enough small changes to make him almost like a new character, even if everything looks and acts about the same. The changes to his air mobility mechanics encourage Iron Man players to take full advantage of the reach and screen control his attacks produce air-to-air and air-to-ground, rather than trying to shoehorn him into being an inferior version of Doctor Doom or Magneto.

- Double jump removed (so that's where Captain America got it from...)
- Air basic attacks are airdash-cancelable
- Airdashes travels farther; diagonal and lateral airdashes have a 10-frame dead period before momentum begins. Up/down airdashes start up much faster and have a brief hovering period at the end
- Crouching Ⓗ is now cancelable and can also chain into Ⓢ
- Air Ⓢ active frames increases to 10 (from 6); air Ⓢ recovery shortened to 27 frames (from 29)
- Standing Ⓢ startup increased to 14 (from 13); recovery shortened to 30 (from 31)
- Hitboxes on standing Ⓗ, air Ⓢ, and Repulsor Spread increased slightly in size
- Repulsor Blast can be canceled into Repulsor Spread 3 frames sooner; Repulsor Spread causes brief hard knockdown; command simplified (just Ⓗ, rather than ↓ ↙ ← + Ⓗ)
- Smart Bomb damage increased; recovery on all versions of air Smart Bomb reduced by 1 frame; recovery of all versions of ground Smart Bomb reduced by roughly half
- Flight startup reduced to 12 frames (from 14); flight duration increased to 108 frames (from 106)
- Proton Cannon (both versions) and Iron Avenger are now mashable for more hits and damage

Attack Set

Standing Basic Attacks

Screen	Command	Hits	Damage	Meter Gain	Startup	Active	Recovery	Advantage on Hit	Advantage if Guarded	Notes
1	Standing L	1	47,000	376	5	3	8	+2	+1	Chains into standing L
2	Standing M	1	70,000	560	8	4	12	+1	0	—
3	Standing H	1	90,000	720	13	5	32	-14	-16	—

Crouching Basic Attacks

Screen	Command	Hits	Damage	Meter Gain	Startup	Active	Recovery	Advantage on Hit	Advantage if Guarded	Notes
1	Crouching L	1	45,000	360	5	3	11	-1	-2	Low attack, chains into crouching L
2	Crouching M	1	68,000	544	7	4	20	—	-3	Low attack, knocks down
3	Crouching H	1	80,000	640	20	—	17	+9	+4	Projectile has 5 low priority durability points, deals chip damage

Ground Special Attack—Launcher

Screen	Command	Hits	Damage	Meter Gain	Startup	Active	Recovery	Advantage on Hit	Advantage if Guarded	Notes
1	S (while standing or crouching)	1	80,000	640	14	3	30	—	-12	Launcher, not special- or hyper combo-cancelable

Air Basic Attacks

Screen	Command	Hits	Damage	Meter Gain	Startup	Active	Recovery	Advantage on Hit	Advantage if Guarded	Notes
1	Air L	1	50,000	400	4	3	17	+11	+10	Overhead attack
2	Air M	1	70,000	560	8	8	17	+15	+14	Overhead attack
3	Air H	1	80,000	640	11	6	29	+18	+16	Overhead attack

Air Special Attacks—Flying Screen and Air Exchange

Air Ⓢ causes a hard knockdown when used in a launcher combo (this is sometimes called flying screen). When used outside of a launcher combo, air Ⓢ behaves mostly like another basic attack. Air exchange attacks, performed by inputting a direction plus Ⓢ, are only possible during a launcher combo. Exchange hits initiate team aerial combos by tagging in the next available character to continue the air combo.

Screen	Command	Hits	Damage	Meter Gain	Startup	Active	Recovery	Advantage on Hit	Advantage if Guarded	Notes
1	Air Ⓢ	1	90,000	720	13	10	27	+15	+13	Causes hard knockdown if used in launcher combo
2	Air ⇧ + Ⓢ (during launcher combo)	1	60,000	480	11	4	Until grounded	—	—	Tags in next available ally while lofting foe upward
3	Air ⇨ or ⇦ + Ⓢ (during launcher combo)	1	50,000	400	11	4	Until grounded	—	—	Tags in next available ally while causing wall bounce, erases 1 hyper meter bar from opponent
4	Air ⇩ + Ⓢ (during launcher combo)	1	50,000	400 + 10,000	11	4	Until grounded	—	—	Tags in next available ally while causing ground bounce, generates 1 hyper meter bar

1

2

3

4

Command Attacks

Command attacks resemble basic attacks but have different chaining and canceling properties. It's usually possible to chain *into* a command attack from basic attacks, but most command attacks cannot be chained from or canceled themselves.

Screen	Name	Command	Hits	Damage	Meter Gain	Startup	Active	Recovery	Advantage on Hit	Advantage if Guarded	Notes
1	Focus Shot (higher shot)	Air ⇧ + Ⓗ	1	80,000	640	11	6	29	+18	+16	Overhead attack
2	Focus Shot (lower shot)	Air ⇩ + Ⓗ	1	80,000	640	11	6	29	+18	+16	Overhead attack

1

2

Throws

Throws are for snagging passive or blocking opponents. Since throws are active so quickly, you can also use them to preemptively toss opposing characters out of their offense. Combos are usually possible after throws, one way or another.

Screen	Command	Hits	Damage	Meter Gain	Startup	Active	Notes
1	⇨ + Ⓗ (ground)	4	80,000	800	1	1	Hard knockdown
	⇦ + Ⓗ (ground)	4	80,000	800	1	1	Hard knockdown
2	⇨ + Ⓗ (air)	1	80,000	800	1	1	Hard knockdown
	⇦ + Ⓗ (air)	1	80,000	800	1	1	Hard knockdown

1

2

As a Partner—Crossover Assists

Screen	Type	P1+P2 Crossover Combination Hyper Combo	Description	Hits	Damage	Meter Gain	Startup	Active	Recovery (this crossover assist)	Recovery (other partner)	Notes
1	Iron Man—α	Proton Cannon	Unibeam M	8	113,600	1280	47	25	108	78	Beam is fullscreen in 56 frames, beam durability: 8 frames x 1 low priority durability points
2	Iron Man —β	Angled Proton Cannon	Repulsor Blast M	5	122,600	1200	40	55	103	73	Knocks down foe, beam durability: 5 frames x 3 low priority durability points
3	Iron Man —γ	Proton Cannon	Smart Bomb H	10	129,900	1600	44	—	132	102	OTG-capable, two beam-like projectiles with 5 frames x 3 low priority durability points each

Each Iron Man assist has potential depending on the needs of your team, but Iron Man—α is easily the best all around. The Unibeam assist is one of the best in the game, period—it's relatively quick and not very telegraphed before it's active, it doesn't drastically increase hitstun scaling in combos, and it gives you plenty of time to combo or pressure your opponent. Any teleport or roll-capable character can easily use Iron Man—α to create cross-ups with their pass-through tricks, and any ranged character will love having Unibeam backing up their own firepower. The only mean thing to say about it is that eight hits from an assist naturally ramps up the damage scaling in a combo quite a bit, so if you employ Iron Man—α in combos, try to use it after you've already scored the brunt of your hits so that damage scaling is capped already anyway.

Iron Man—β returns from *MvC2*, where it was easily Iron Man's best assist then, but that's mostly because beam and projectile type assists weren't quite as useful in *MvC2* as they are in this game. It also happened to do outrageous damage—the most of any assist in the game, if all possible hits were scored. Here, it's more sedate. It can be useful to take up a large portion of the screen, especially nice as a preemptive defensive measure against aggressive teleporters, but beware if they anticipate this and just bait out your Iron Man calls so they can punish him safely from fullscreen instead of teleporting in the first place. Repulsor Blast's built-in juggling of the opposing character for several moments can also enable easy combo extension for any character.

Iron Man—γ is OTG-capable, which can be nice if Iron Man's teammates utterly lack any other means to pop competitors up from hard knockdowns. This assist version of Smart Bomb also packs an *absurd* amount of projectile durability points—*three times* more than Smart Bomb H on point! While ground Smart Bomb's limited trajectory makes it tough to utilize this practically to outmuscle opposing projectiles, it's at least worth pointing out. Like Tron—β, it sometimes happens to obliterate incoming projectiles without being called for that express purpose.

Snap Back

Screen	Command	Hits	Damage	Meter Gain	Startup	Active	Recovery	Advantage on Hit	Advantage if Guarded
1	↓↘→ + P1 or P2	1	50,000	500 - (-1 hyper meter bar)	2	4	12	—	+5

Notes

On hit, snap back forces the opposing point character to be replaced by an assist. Opposing assist calls or tag outs are also locked out for 4 seconds

Special Moves

Screen	Name	Command	Hits	Damage	Meter Gain	Startup	Active	Recovery	Advantage on Hit	Advantage if Guarded	Notes
1	Unibeam L (in air OK)	↓↘→ + L	5	81,700	800	18	20	15	0	-15	Beam is fullscreen in 26 frames, beam durability: 5 frames x 1 low priority durability points
	Unibeam M (in air OK)	↓↘→ + M	8	113,600	1280	23	25	15	+4	-11	Beam is fullscreen in 31 frames, beam durability: 8 frames x 1 low priority durability points
	Unibeam H (in air OK)	↓↘→ + H	10	129,900	1600	28	30	15	+5	-10	Beam is fullscreen in 36 frames, beam durability: 11 frames x 1 low priority durability points
2	Repulsor Blast L	↓↙← + L	5	81,700	800	11	50	10	—	-8	Knocks down foe, beam durability: 5 frames x 3 low priority durability points
3	Repulsor Blast M	↓↙← + M	5	102,300	1000	16	55	10	—	-13	Knocks down opponent, beam durability: 5 frames x 3 low priority durability points
4	Repulsor Blast H	↓↙← + H	5	122,600	1200	21	60	10	—	-18	Knocks down adversary, beam durability: 5 frames x 3 low priority durability points
5	Repulsor Spread	H during Repulsor Blast	1	80,000	640	(20~30+) 1	6	24	—	-9	Hard knockdown, explosion has 8 low priority durability points
6	Smart Bomb L	→↓↘ + L	2	66,500	560	20	—	12	+10	+8	OTG-capable, two projectiles with 1 low priority durability point each
	Smart Bomb M	→↓↘ + M	6	102,900	1056	20	—	16	+10	+8	OTG-capable, two beam-like projectiles with 3 frames x 1 low priority durability points each
	Smart Bomb H	→↓↘ + H	10	116,900	1440	20	—	24	+6	+4	OTG-capable, two beam-like projectiles with 5 frames x 1 low priority durability points each
	Air Smart Bomb L	→↓↘ + L	2	66,500	560	20	—	17	+4	+2	OTG-capable, two projectiles with 1 low priority durability point each
	Air Smart Bomb M	→↓↘ + M	6	102,900	1056	20	—	22	+3	+1	OTG-capable, two beam-like projectiles with 3 frames x 1 low priority durability points each
	Air Smart Bomb H	→↓↘ + H	10	116,900	1440	20	—	28	+7	+5	OTG-capable, two beam-like projectiles with 5 frames x 1 low priority durability points each
7	Flight	↓↙← + S	—	—	—	12	—	—	—	—	Flight lasts 108 frames

1

Unibeam: You can fire Iron Man's main projectile on the ground or in the air. Heavier versions have longer startup, but they also have more hits and damage. At 18 frames of startup, the L version is slightly faster than Doctor Doom's Plasma Beam but significantly slower than Magneto's Electromagnetic Disruptor, as examples of where Unibeam stands in comparison to other beams. It's a terrific beam, but you aren't going to win firefights on the strength of it alone unless the other team simply has no answer. Unibeam H is obviously much more durable and damaging, but it also occupies a lot more of Iron Man's time, making it less appealing unless your opponent is pinned by an assist.

If your competitors are capable of putting several slow-moving projectiles onscreen at once, like Ryu's Hadokens or Morrigan's Soul Fists, use Unibeam H to plow through these threats and hit the opposing fireball slinger; Unibeam L is fragile enough to just trade with most standard projectiles. With something like Rocket Raccoon's Double Spitfire, multiple Zero Hadangekis, or Sentinel Force drones, Unibeam L destroys one minor projectile before losing out to the rest. If your rivals have projectiles so fast that they can just shoot Iron Man before any of his Unibeams actually fire, such as Wesker with gunshots or Magneto with Disruptors, stick to using Unibeam L when you have a slight fullscreen advantage, such as after your competitor has guarded your Smart Bombs or crossover assist, or after the opposing player has performed a fullscreen action with minor recovery.

Repulsor Blast L 2

Repulsor Blast M 3

Repulsor Blast H 4

Repulsor Blast: Iron Man gathers energy in a warping cross around his raised hands. This energy is a beam rather than a direct physical attack, and it clashes with incoming projectiles and beams. As with beams, Repulsor Blast disappears instantly if Iron Man gets hit while performing it. By pressing H after a certain period of time during any version of Repulsor Blast, you can execute Repulsor Spread.

Successfully perform Repulsor Blast without being interrupted, and Iron Man is more or less immune to physical attacks until recovery. A long range beam or beam hyper combo may cut through, as do invincible attacks, but traditional aggressive actions like triangle jumps and dash in crouching L are cut off briefly. This means you can use Repulsor Blast as a poke from mid range with few repercussions. This can preempt and punish enemy movement or shield your own assist calls; call the desired assist, then perform Repulsor Blast. The closer the foe, the lighter the version you should use. Note that if your rival is at mid range, the forward-arcing tip of Repulsor Blast H actually hits them before heavier versions of Unibeam would!

Apart from its use as a mid range zoning tool and a shield for assists and Iron Man himself, Repulsor Blast can also be inserted into Iron Man combos; after just about any chain into the crouching H rocket, cancel to Repulsor Blast H to drag the opposing character on top of Iron Man after the rocket hits. If you're too far away for the crouching rocket, cancel standing H to Repulsor Blast M. From here, you can cancel directly into Proton Cannon for an easy finisher, or cancel to Repulsor Spread.

5

Repulsor Spread: Repulsor Spread is the built-in, instant follow-up to Repulsor Blast. Repulsor Spread is executed by pressing H after a certain amount of time has passed during Repulsor Blast; this is 20 frames for the L version, 25 frames for the M version, and 30 frames for the H version (this is 3 frames faster than Repulsor Spread could be executed for any version of Repulsor Blast in original *MvC3*; Repulsor Spread also used to require a repetition of the ↓↙← motion before the H press. Like Dante's alternate specials, this was simplified in the transition to *UMvC3*).

If Repulsor Blast hits the target, wait until just before the foe would fall out of Repulsor Blast to cancel to Repulsor Spread to attain the maximum number of hits. If Repulsor Blast doesn't hit your rival, use Repulsor Spread to make Iron Man much safer than after a whiffed Repulsor Blast; you're just trading Repulsor Blast's recovery for Repulsor Spread's, but it's still a decrease in vulnerability. By delaying the cancel to Repulsor Spread, you might even bait your opponent into rushing in, as they expect to punish Iron Man during the end of Repulsor Blast.

Like Repulsor Blast, Repulsor Spread is technically a localized beam attack, so it has projectile durability and can nullify incoming projectiles. If Repulsor Spread hits the adversary, they're sent spinning to the turf. New to *UMvC3*, this causes a brief hard knockdown! If you end up in position to get Iron Man close to the opposing character right away, you can start an OTG combo with Smart Bomb. You can also just cancel Repulsor Spread late into Iron Avenger to drag your competitor across the playing field for huge damage.

6

Smart Bomb: Iron Man releases two sets of bombs in a downward sloped path. These bombs are OTG-capable, and combos after OTG Smart Bomb are more flexible now that the recovery on grounded Smart Bombs has been reduced by a noticeable amount. Smart Bomb L shoots two distinct projectiles, while Smart Bomb M and H behave more like beams: two distinct bomb clusters are launched, each of which depletes opposing projectiles of their durability over time. Unlike beams, Smart Bombs do not disappear if Iron Man takes a hit while they're active.

Every version of Smart Bomb has identical startup; heavier versions have longer recovery periods, but they deal more damage with multi-hitting bombs. There is seldom a reason not to use Smart Bomb H, which builds roughly *three times* more hyper meter than Smart Bomb L while dealing more damage. You might use Smart Bomb L early in combos if you're trying to keep damage scaling down, but every Iron Man combo ends in Proton Cannon or Iron Avenger for a gajillion hits anyway, so it's not the biggest issue. And although Smart Bomb L has less recovery, Smart Bomb H holds and hits your opponent for longer, so speed comes out a wash.

Smart Bomb is a foundational tool for Iron Man. Other characters have better beams or faster airdashes, or both. But no other character has a ranged tool that controls quite the same bombing corridor as Smart Bomb, and Iron Man's tweaked airdash is totally complementary to converting Smart Bomb rain into aggressive air-to-ground offense.

7

Flight: Flight is used for mobility, for escapes, for secondary offense, and for combos. During flight, there is no restriction on the amount of times you can use special moves or airdashes.

Flight is crucial to Iron Man's combos, whether to fly cancel standing or crouching H into a low altitude air chain, or to extend air combos after a launcher. You can also utilize it to have Iron Man hang in the air tossing Smart Bombs for longer than otherwise possible, or to have him retreat from or advance upon his rival unexpectedly. And you'll end up using poke sequences like fly, air H canceled with unfly, falling air H, and crouching H canceled into flight, quite often.

Hyper Combos

Screen	Name	Command	Hits	Damage	Startup	Active	Recovery	Advantage on Hit	Advantage if Guarded	Notes
1	Proton Cannon	↓↘→ + ATK ATK	36~71	276,800~326,500	3*30+1	6*111	47	—	-47	Knocks down foe, beam durability: 35 frames x 1 high priority durability points, can be mashed for additional damage
2	Angled Proton Cannon	→↓↘ + ATK ATK	36~71	276,800~326,500	3*30+1	6*111	47	—	-47	Knocks down adversary, beam durability: 35 frames x 1 high priority durability points, can be mashed for additional damage
3	Iron Avenger	↓↙← + ATK ATK	68~98	430,000~460,000	10+3	11	41	—	-31	Level 3 hyper combo, hard knockdown, unaffected by damage scaling, frames 1-22 invulnerable, can be mashed for additional damage

Proton Cannon and Angled Proton Cannon: Iron Man's main hyper combo beam can be directed either straight ahead with a fireball motion or up-forward at a 30-degree slope with a →↓↘ motion. If the hyper beam strikes successfully during either version of Proton Cannon, mash ATK to increase the hits and damage. The startup of either version is identical: the Proton Cannon itself hits up close during frames 3 to 9 of startup in a circle all around Iron Man, but the hyper beam is not produced until the 30th frame after input. So, it's the reverse of what you might assume—Proton Cannon is wicked fast up close, and it's rather slow from far away. (It's not quite Hail Storm, but it also can't be used anything like the beam hypers of Ryu, Akuma, Dormammu, Nova, etc.)

After the Proton Cannon's up-close hit (which, if successful, guarantees the hyper beam will also hit, as long as nothing else interferes), there's a dead period between frames 10 and 30 during which Iron Man is just readying the beam. Even though Proton Cannon has no invincibility, the 3 frame startup up close makes for an appealing hyper combo to use as an occasional guess, but beware if your competitor blocks: they can easily start a chain combo in between guarding the initial hit and waiting for the hyper beam to actually fire. Be ready to THC to a teammate's safe hyper combo if this gamble doesn't pay off. Not that it's really recommended that you frequently guess on hyper combos up close; it's just something to keep in mind. Remember, if you can get your opponent to worry about a dangerous but risky trick, then you no longer have to actually do it; the effect has already been achieved.

Proton Cannon's primary purpose is to finish combos for heavy damage. You can accomplish this most easily by using close range Smart Bomb to OTG before canceling to Proton Cannon. Any combo that leads into Repulsor Blast can end in Proton Cannon, too. Virtually any basic attack chain into Proton Cannon works, provided your adversary is close enough. It's also an excellent THC and crossover combination tool. The long range and different angles of Proton Cannon and Angled Proton Cannon let it play well with just about any hyper combo. And the hit on frame 3 for Proton Cannon translates over to crossover combinations whether Iron Man is on point or on the sidelines, resulting in a crossover combination that hits up close MUCH sooner than usual!

If you have the meter to spend and you really want to K.O. a target (especially if you catch two opposing characters at once), combo into Proton Cannon, then X-Factor cancel just before the end, and either immediately perform Iron Avenger or dash forward and juggle with the early hit of another Proton Cannon!

Iron Avenger: Iron Man's level 3 hyper combo travels almost the fullscreen distance with 22 frames of invulnerability. Its primary purpose is to push long combos over the top for a knockout—Iron Avenger is immune to damage scaling, and it can even be mashed for a bit more damage. Iron Avenger's long reach and invulnerable period also mean that you can use it as a reversal to snag your foe out of almost anything they do.

After Iron Avenger, wavedash forward afterward and OTG the opposing character with Smart Bomb H... meter permitting, cancel to Proton Cannon! It's not the most efficient use of four meters, but 700,300 off a reversal is plenty good in many situations, and that already increases to 873,400 in only lv.1 X-Factor... in lv.3 X-Factor, it's 1,177,900! (And, of course, that's just assuming a naked Iron Avenger, with no combo leading up to it.) Of course, adding Iron Avenger into Proton Cannon on the end of any combo guarantees a K.O. against anyone.

Iron Avenger travels laterally so quickly that you have to be careful when trying to combo it. If you cancel into Iron Avenger immediately after attacks like crouching H or Repulsor Spread, Iron Man passes under his rival harmlessly at the cost of three bars of meter. Instead, take your time before canceling into Iron Avenger after those attacks. On the other hand, if you want to combo OTG Smart Bomb H into Iron Avenger, cancel as swiftly as possible.

Battle Plan

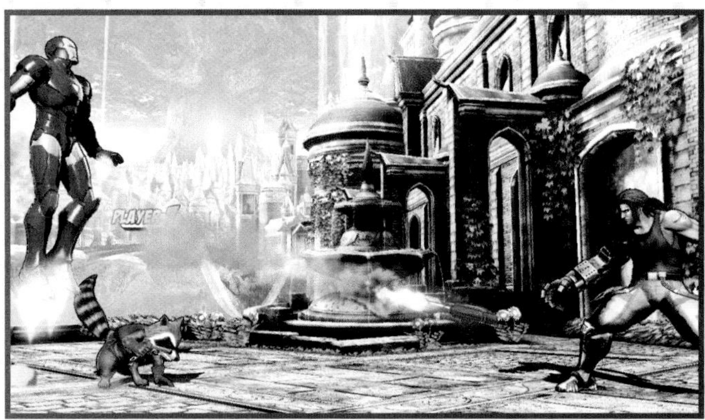
Newly cancelable, crouching H is now much more useful for both zoning and combos.

Iron Man is a character who isn't suited to total rushdown or keepaway; your goal with Iron Man should be to toe a line in the middle. The ideal place to begin operating from is a little closer to the opposing character than the edge of the range of crouching H. This is close enough to threaten with crouching H, the tips of air H attacks, the edges of Repulsor Blast, aerial Smart Bombs, and Unibeams.

You want to keep adversaries at around half-screen so you have enough separation to super jump and throw Smart Bombs to either build meter, stall, or transition to offense. If your rival is too close, you'll likely just get hit while jumping, or air thrown before Smart Bombs fire; even if you're able to release Smart Bombs, they'll probably land behind the target. So, you'll have to work at controlling ground level before you can control the sky. From far away, Unibeam alone can stalemate many characters who don't have their own dominant ranged tactics, forcing them to either try to jump over Unibeams, or to use their assists to try to close the gap. From mid range, these same characters can fall victim to crouching H, which you can fire much more liberally in *UMvC3* than before, secure in knowing that you can cancel the rocket into a number of other things depending on the situation (in original, crouching H was not cancelable and was generally only seen as an execution accident from Iron Man players who wanted *standing* H, which was easy to tell from their unprintable exclamations; now, a tiny bit of the glory of War Machine's "crouching fierce" from *MvC1* has been restored).

Crouching H is just slightly slower than Unibeam L while dealing comparable damage even if guarded and giving Iron Man more versatile follow-up options (whereas if your foe evades Unibeam, you might be in serious trouble, especially at mid range or closer). If competitors immediately get up over the path of the rocket, cancel it into Repulsor Blast to cover the area above and in front of Iron Man, preventing them from airdashing or teleporting in aggressively for a moment. If your adversary runs into any segment of Repulsor Blast, they'll be dragged on top of Iron Man, in position for you to cancel to Repulsor Spread (and then either a corner OTG combo if close enough, or a hyper combo anywhere else). If the attacker isn't baited by Repulsor Blast, hang onto Repulsor Spread and perform it with awkward timings to deter opponents who want to run in late to punish Repulsor Blast. Repulsor Spread isn't technically safe if whiffed or if your rival guards it, but by varying the timing, you can usually assure that the opposing character won't be ready to hit Iron Man properly right after.

Air ⒽＨ is one of the longest-reaching basic attacks in the game, and it is consequently excellent for keeping opponents away at low altitudes.

When you feel more in control of the situation (such as when adversaries are not immediately leaping over the rockets), cancel crouching Ⓗ to flight. From here, depending on what your foe is doing, you have a few options. If they went over the rocket, you can easily strike at them with enormous pokes to keep them at bay: perform flying air Ⓗ (direct it up or down as necessary, if the enemy isn't level with Iron Man), cancel it with flight deactivation, then perform falling air Ⓗ before Iron Man lands. Opponents jumping or airdashing forward frequently run into this, which causes a two-hit combo and gives Iron Man plenty of time to land, confirm, and jump forward to continue juggling them (see **Combo IV**).

If your competitor doesn't react to crouching Ⓗ canceled into flight by jumping forward, then immediately fly forward behind the rocket. If your challenger is in the habit of allowing rockets to actually *hit* them (lucky you), you can link after they're bounced upward by the explosion with forward-flying air Ⓜ, Ⓗ, ⇩ + Ⓗ, Ⓢ from a *huge* distance away, causing Iron Man to auto-land and again leading to a situation where you can immediately keep juggling them (see **Combo V**).

Remember that crouching Ⓗ is a basic attack, so assists can be called concurrently; Iron Man's zoning is vastly strengthened if you give him assists that can complement crouching Ⓗ and his other zoning tools, such as Doctor Doom—α or Doctor Doom—β. Depending on the assist, this can also help protect Iron Man against teleporting characters who can somewhat negate the threat of rockets and Unibeams by simply warping past them.

Repulsor Blast is a useful tool for controlling space around Iron Man, as well as for providing cover for assists.

If your adversary is eager to stay in the air and continually attack with air attacks, triangle jumps, or flight, using rockets and other projectiles to control ground level is obviously a less useful strategy. They're handing you an opportunity in another way, however: even though Repulsor Blasts take a long time, being able to discharge the energy with Repulsor Spread makes it a relatively low-commitment attack for Iron Man. If the screen shifts upward slightly as your rival takes to the sky, you can use this as your cue to activate Repulsor Blast and see what happens. The closer the foe is, the lighter the version you should use. If your competitor opts not to try to close in, cancel Blast with Spread as fast as you can to regain control of Iron Man. If they DO close in, wait for Repulsor Blast to either put them in hit or guardstun before canceling to Spread. At the very least, "poking" like this with Repulsor Blast to Spread reminds your opponent that Iron Man can control much of the screen around him, and although his up-close mobility is poor, he is not a soft target for rushdown-oriented blokes. Repulsor Blast's control area also means you can safely call an assist right before performing it; Iron Man himself provides 360-degree cover for assists that land near him (this is obviously not applicable if it's an assist that travels a long way from the point character, like Iron Fist—γ or Phoenix—γ).

Battle Plan continued

If you can keep opponents out from under Iron Man, Smart Bomb is very difficult for them to deal with.

You're also able to transition from this range to offense when the opportunity presents itself, such as right after you've dropped Smart Bomb H on your target from super jump height, or as they are forced to guard one of your crossover assists.

The point of all this, assuming you can't just outright bully your opponent to death with your ground-level zoning, is to gain clearance to have Iron Man take to the skies with your rival stuck behind the trajectory of Smart Bombs. Remember that teleport-capable characters can make instant short work of Smart Bomb use, and force Iron Man to go another direction. Against anyone else, though, just getting past a Smart Bomb wall can be difficult.

If you just want to harangue your opponent with Smart Bombs, the ideal way to take to super jump height to dump Smart Bombs on your challenger is to normal jump, airdash straight upward (this can be easily performed by double-tapping ⇧), then call an assist that can cover ground level and prevent foes from dashing, such as a projectile or pinning assist. Iron Man's vertical airdash doesn't have the 10-second momentum-building period at the very beginning, and he also lofts briefly as the top of it, so it's perfect for ascending and hovering quickly. Once Iron Man is at super jump height and you have called an assist, you can fire Smart Bomb H at your foe once or twice depending on their position. Smart Bombs deal great damage (improved since original!) and the Ⓗ version especially builds huge amounts of hyper meter, whether they hit or are guarded. You don't want to use all three air special actions on Smart Bombs—save one for activating flight. Now Iron Man is at super jump height having just bombarded his opponent, and you're ready to bomb two or three more times. Since you had Iron Man normal jump to take to the air, assist calls are still available.

Having a ground-level assist with lots of lateral range is immensely helpful for trapping and chipping the opposition even when they evade Smart Bombs (virtually any beam or projectile assist works for this purpose; even better are assists that force your adversary to guard in separate places, like Captain America—α, Rocket Raccoon—α, and Sentinel—α). If you're worried about competitors going over or under Smart Bombs, you might also consider an assist like Dante—α or Dormammu—β, which cover infinite vertical space and help prevent Iron Man's position from being compromised.

Calling an assist during flight also buys you a moment to decide where to have Iron Man touch down. If you're still in control of your side of the screen, you can simply have him descend. Like Iron Man's vertical airdash, his airdash straight down has no lag at the beginning. Airdash straight down near the ground, and Iron Man lands right away; airdash straight down from high altitude, and Iron Man hovers briefly at the end of the dash, as with the vertical airdash. Use any basic attack to skip over this hovering period and make him land more quickly.

If you aren't in control of your side of the screen, you'll want another landing zone. Iron Man's lateral airdashes travel quite far. Because of the 10-frame hitch at the beginning of any of Iron Man's airdashes that aren't straight up or straight down, you don't want to cancel airdashes into other airdashes right away while flying, like with other fliers; this makes him *slower*, not faster, since you're just forcing more 10-frame dead periods into his transit time (this is also true of Nova, who has a similar airdash). Instead, wait until Iron Man's airdashes during flight are almost totally over before starting up another one. With two or three airdashes across the top of the playing field, you'll have a chance to get Iron Man out from over an aggressive enemy so he can fall more safely, making him less susceptible to air throws or last-moment cross-under tactics.

After triangle jumping from super jump height, either strike with air Ⓜ or ⇘ + Ⓗ before landing, then go for a combo, or...

...do nothing, land without using an overhead attack, then strike with crouching L immediately!

Peppering enemies from mid range with rockets, Smart Bombs, and assists create opportunities to get in close and go for Iron Man's devastating combos. Once your rival expects you to bomb from above, change things up and super jump (instead of normal jumping then airdashing upward) to throw one instance of Smart Bomb H aimed squarely at the target, then airdash down-forward. Iron Man's airdash is so long now in *UMvC3* that he can effectively triangle jump from *super jump height!* What is a liability at normal jump height (his airdash hitches and distance) is a boon from farther up. The mix-up here is that you can either perform air ↘ + H for an overhead (which also doubles as an option select air throw, in addition to continuing a combo off the Smart Bombs if they hit), perform late air M as an overhead, or do nothing, land, and immediately go for crouching L into **Combo I**. That's right, being able to triangle jump from the top of the screen also means you can have Iron Man *empty* triangle jump from the top of the screen, and it's not possible for your competitor to react reliably to this! If they block correctly between airdash attacks and empty airdash into crouching L in this situation, it was basically luck or anticipation. It's Marvel, baby.

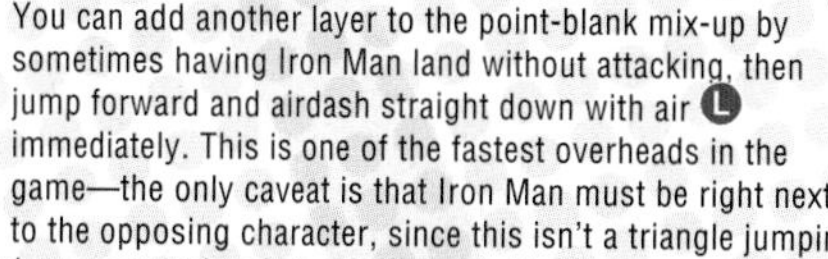

You can add another layer to the point-blank mix-up by sometimes having Iron Man land without attacking, then jump forward and airdash straight down with air L immediately. This is one of the fastest overheads in the game—the only caveat is that Iron Man must be right next to the opposing character, since this isn't a triangle jumping overhead that gains any ground. To attack with this, you must have essentially already earned close range position, either through an empty triangle jump, or by making your opponent guard an assist so that Iron Man can move in. Of course, you can perform this straight-down airdash without an attack so you can have Iron Man land and go low immediately for the same kind of trick as empty triangle jumping in.

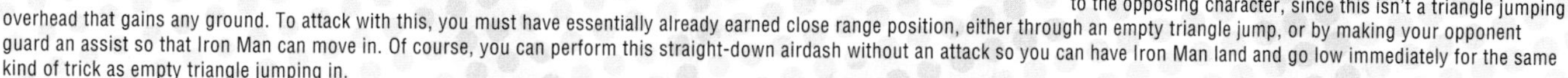

Remember that you can't block while using airdashes, so make sure to precede airdash attempts with either assist calls or Smart Bombs in order to score Iron Man some frame advantage to airdash in behind. Airdashing in with ↘ + H is at least a little safer because of how far Iron Man's air basic attacks reach, but you won't get away with many empty triangle jumps (at least without eating a hyper combo or getting launched or air thrown) unless there's nothing your opponent can do about them.

Off a successful close range hit, Iron Man gets to deal tremendous damage while building lots of meter. If your rival guards correctly, they'll almost certainly use advancing guard to push Iron Man back out. Iron Man's fast flight startup is very useful here; if an attack like standing H is pushed out, Iron Man remains vulnerable for a long time, but by flight canceling, you can avoid this period. Simply unfly or perform air S to return Iron Man back to earth quickly. If you happen to fly cancel in the right place, Iron Man won't lose any ground at all! (See Advanced Tactics for more information.) If your competitor doesn't use advancing guard for some reason, you can ground chain to your heart's content (all the way up to crouching H rocket if you like) before activating flight to go for an overhead. Air S simply makes Iron Man fall back to earth, but air ↘ + H, S can also be used for a double overhead that catches foes if they try to block just one air attack, then return to crouching guard. Be careful about spacing: depending on where you fly canceled and fell on the target with air S, combo follow-ups will be limited. When in doubt, the most consistent solution is to chain crouching M, standing H CANCEL Repulsor Blast M. Flight combos like **Combo II** also work and are much better, but they are more difficult to perform, especially on short notice.

Iron Man has such good assists (Unibeam especially; Repulsor Blast on certain teams) that you might end up with him as your anchor, using X-Factor in a last-ditch effort. If you realize Iron Man is going to be the beneficiary of X-Factor, try not to just use it cold; try to confirm into it. If you have bars stocked for Iron Avenger, you can wait for the opposition to do something foolish that Iron Avenger can successfully plow through; activate X-Factor first and buffer Iron Avenger during the X-Factor screen freeze. During lv.3 X-Factor, dashing forward to tack on Smart Bomb H into Proton Cannon after Iron Avenger leads to *1,234,600 damage* off what is basically a reversal! If it's ever down to one-on-one and you have at least four bars of meter left, you can just wait for the right moment to end it, basically.

If you happen to combo into Proton Cannon and it's not going to K.O. a character, mash Proton Cannon for a while, then X-Factor cancel it and dash (or wavedash, distance depending) forward to juggle your adversary with an X-Factor-boosted Proton Cannon! For this to work, you *must* get close enough for the frame 3 hit of Proton Cannon to juggle them after the first one. For a simpler but much more costly X-Factor cancel, pop X-Factor toward the end of Proton Cannon and perform Iron Avenger.

The speed boost of X-Factor also makes Unibeams much more appealing, especially if your rival has already used up their X-Factor, which means they won't be able to negate the huge chip damage X-Factor Unibeam spam can inflict. Smart Bombs also travel faster and in a longer arc, making them more useful from farther distances. Bombs away!

COMBO USAGE

I. CR. L, M, ST. H, CR. H CANCEL ↓↙← + S, AIR M, M, H, ↓ + H, S, LAND, IMMEDIATE FORWARD JUMP, AIR M, M, ↓ + H, S, LAND, CR. M, S CANCEL FORWARD SUPER JUMP, AIR M, M, H, ↓ + H, S, LAND, FORWARD DASH, →↓↘ + H OTG CANCEL ↓↘→ + ATK ATK (MASH ATK)

720,900 damage, 35% meter gain

Here's an ideal combo from point-blank crouching L or M. Although you can open with a jump-in attack or two and still score the full combo, the positioning requirement means you're most likely to start this combo after an empty triangle jump directly into an opponent. Since crouching H is now cancelable, many new combo avenues are open for Tony Stark, but chaining from standing H to crouching H is only consistent up close. At least standing H itself is no longer so finicky; it now works from pretty much anywhere after crouching M. Speed through the low-altitude flying chain and most of the jumping chain as quickly as possible, but pause briefly between air ↓ + H and air S during the jump. This is so your rival descends far enough to be juggled by crouching M, S.

This combo is possible on everyone, but keeping your competitor low enough for crouching M before the launcher is difficult on smaller characters. To make things easier, you can land from the jumping chain and perform Proton Cannon immediately. The third-frame hit of Proton Cannon (which basically hits in the same circle all around Iron Man as Repulsor Spread) juggles your target and ensures that the beam caps the combo off.

If you have at least 2.6 bars of meter at the beginning of the combo, you can replace the Proton Cannon at the end with Iron Avenger (cancel OTG Smart Bomb H to Iron Avenger *immediately*), then wavedash forward and OTG with Smart Bomb H into Proton Cannon for 1,221,100 damage! Ouch! If you have enough meter, you can convert one touch into a knockout against almost every single character with Iron Man. If you don't feel like adding a Proton Cannon, just OTG with Smart Bomb H, then wait for your foe's air recovery and go for an air throw! Even before this throw reset attempt, this deals over 960,000 damage (and only requires that you start the whole combo with 1.6 meters; the rest of the bar for Iron Avenger gets built during the combo).

COMBO USAGE CONT.

II. CR. (L), (M), ST. (H) [CANCEL] ⇒ ↓ ↙ ← + (S), AIR (M), (M), (H), ↓ + (H) [CANCEL] ⇒ ↓ ↙ ← + (S), FALLING AIR (H), LAND, IMMEDIATE FORWARD JUMP, AIR (M), (M), ↓ + (H), (S), LAND, CR. (M), (S) [CANCEL] ⇒ FORWARD SUPER JUMP, AIR (M), (M), (H), ↓ + (H), (S), LAND, FORWARD DASH, → ↓ ↘ + (H) OTG [CANCEL] ⇒ ↓ ↘ → + (ATK)(ATK) (MASH (ATK))

687,900 damage, 21% meter gain

This is a standard combo from crouching (L) or (M). Unlike **Combo I**, this isn't dependent on Iron Man being close, which makes this much more reliable after jump-in attacks. This combo is required if the opener doesn't strike an adversary who is right next to Iron Man; farther away, trying to chain into crouching (H) will miss and cause the combo to fail. Linking air (M) after fly canceling standing (H) is tight, but necessary; air (L) is a much, much easier link (Iron Man has one of the only four-frame air (L) attacks, after all), but it's only possible up close (in which case you might as well do **Combo I**, which is both easier and more damaging), and the whole point of this combo is to work from far away and more universally. The hardest part of this combo is probably working in every possible air (H); if you're having trouble, the easiest thing to do is to drop any instance of air ↓ + (H).

After unfly canceling air ↓ + (H) (or plain old air (H), for ease of use), IMMEDIATELY perform falling air (H) again. The key is to not really treat unfly and air (H) as distinct commands. Instead, think of it as one unbroken sequence, like plinking: ↓ ↙ ← + (S)~(H). When air actions are canceled with unfly, there is only one frame of recovery, so you can input (H) immediately. It may not seem like this is even possible at first, but it's definitely doable with consistency; just work on getting air (H) out instantly after Iron Man drops down from flight. You'll want to practice this anyway for one of Iron Man's best poking sequences. You have to use unfly air (H) in order to make the combo consistent (rather than just chaining to air (S) for the easy-mode method of dropping out of flight; air (H) allows Iron Man to land slightly faster and pops the opposing character up just a tiny bit higher than air (S), which allows the follow-up jumping attacks to work). As for the rest of the combo, simply perform it as quickly as possible, except for a (very) subtle delay between air ↓ + (H) and air (S) during the jump as during **Combo I**.

III. CR. (L), CR. (M), ST. (H), CR. (H) [CANCEL] ⇒ ↓ ↙ ← + (H), (H) (REPULSOR SPREAD) [CANCEL] ⇒ ↓ ↘ → + (ATK)(ATK) (MASH (ATK)) OR ↓ ↙ ← + (ATK)(ATK) (MASH (ATK)), WAVEDASH FORWARD, → ↓ ↘ + (H) OTG [CANCEL] ⇒ ↓ ↘ → + (ATK)(ATK) (MASH (ATK))

582,300 damage, 59% meter loss (or 1,004,300 damage, 349% meter loss)

Here's an easy combo into Proton Cannon from close range. Wait for all five hits of Repulsor Blast H before canceling to Repulsor Spread. Cancel Spread to Proton Cannon immediately; the beam must catch your competitors before they hit the ground. If you're near the corner, *don't* cancel Repulsor Spread to Proton Cannon; instead, dash forward and OTG the foe with Smart Bomb H, then cancel that into Proton Cannon.

If you have enough meter to go for Iron Avenger instead, then cancel from Repulsor Spread to Iron Avenger very late. If executed too early, your opponent may not have descended enough. After Iron Avenger, wavedash and OTG with Smart Bomb H; if you have meter, cancel into Proton Cannon!

IV. ANTI-AIR FLYING AIR (H) [CANCEL] ⇒ ↓ ↙ ← + (S), FALLING AIR (H), LAND, IMMEDIATE FORWARD JUMP, AIR (M), (M), ↓ + (H), (S), LAND, IMMEDIATE FORWARD JUMP, AIR (M), (M), ↓ + (H), (S), LAND, CR. (M), (S) [CANCEL] ⇒ FORWARD SUPER JUMP, AIR (M), (M), (H), ↓ + (H), (S), LAND, DASH, → ↓ ↘ + (H) OTG [CANCEL] ⇒ ↓ ↘ → + (ATK)(ATK) (MASH (ATK))

725,400 damage, 20% meter gain

Between the speed of Iron Man's flight activation, his newfound power to cancel crouching (H), and the indomitable nature of his air (M) and (H) attacks, it's common for opponents to be shot out of the sky at low altitude. How much you can actually embellish after landing from the flying air (H), unfly air (H) poking sequence depends on your competitor's actual position; the lower they are to the ground at first, the less you'll probably get. Cut off the last jumping loop, or go for a launcher or a combo into Repulsor Blast immediately upon landing if you're uncertain about the appropriateness of rejump juggles. As long as you get a loop of something or other into an air combo that leads to Proton Cannon, any anti-air sequence nets over 600,000 damage easily, and that's before considering the X-Factor, Iron Avenger, or follow-up THC possibilities.

V. CR. (L), (M), ST. (H) [X-FACTOR] ST. (H) [CANCEL] ⇒ ↓ ↙ ← + (S), AIR (M), (M), (H), ↓ + (H), (S), LAND, FORWARD JUMP, AIR (M), (M), ↓ + (H), (S), LAND, FORWARD JUMP, AIR (M), (M), ↓ + (H), (S), LAND, ST. (M) [CANCEL] ⇒ ↓ ↘ → + (ATK)(ATK) (MASH (ATK))

1,009,000 damage to point with lv.1 X-Factor, K.O. vs. any assist, meter neutral

Although crouching (H) rocket is improved, it can't hit both a point character and an assist simultaneously, so you'll have to omit it from combos if you realize you've caught two characters at once. That said, Iron Man doesn't need crouching (H) to severely damage or destroy two targets simultaneously. Even during lv.1 X-Factor, this is able to destroy any assist and deal over one million damage to point characters; at lv.2 X-Factor, the only point characters who'll survive are Hulk, Thor, and She-Hulk. During lv.3 X-Factor, no one survives!

ADVANCED TACTICS

KILLING ADVANCING GUARD WITH FLIGHT

By canceling an attack into flight just after your opponent uses advancing guard...

After your rival guards an attack and uses advancing guard, Iron Man normally gets pushed far away and must work to get in all over again. You can avoid this, though, if you activate flight just after your adversary uses advancing guard! This is because causing certain state changes just as advancing guard is taking effect negates the backward momentum it causes. In this case, advancing guard does actually push Iron Man backward for a frame or two, but then flight takes effect and stops the backward movement. Activate flight quickly enough after advancing guard, and Iron Man just stays right next to the opposing character. From here, going for an overhead of air (S) or air ⇩ + (H), (S) will be very surprising for a foe who expected some relief from Iron Man's assault.

...Iron Man won't be pushed anywhere!

COMBO APPENDIX

GENERAL EXECUTION TIPS

- Take care not to accidentally get an air exchange hit when chaining to air (S) just after using ⇧ + (H) or ⇩ + (H) in air combos
- When canceling OTG Smart Bomb H into Proton Cannon, you want the opening physical hit of Proton Cannon to strike *just after* every bomb has hit your opponent; cancel too soon, and the last bombs hit after the third-frame Proton Cannon hit, and your adversary inevitably flips out and gets ready to block the beam
- On the other hand, you must cancel OTG Smart Bomb H to Iron Avenger immediately
- And on yet another hand (you sure do have a strange body configuration), you must cancel Repulsor Spread to Iron Avenger *late* in order for it to work

THROW INTO CORNER, FORWARD DASH, ⇨⇩⇘ + (H) OTG, CR. (L), (M), ST. (H), CR. (H) CANCEL➔ ⇩⇙⇦ + (H), (H) (REPULSOR SPREAD), FORWARD DASH, ⇨⇩⇘ + (H) OTG CANCEL➔ ⇩⇘⇨ + (ATK)(ATK) (MASH (ATK))

Notes	Damage
Combo after throw or low altitude air throw into a corner	481,900 damage, 31% meter loss

CR. (M), ST. (H), (S) CANCEL➔ FORWARD SUPER JUMP, AIR (M), (M), (H), ⇩ + (H), (S), LAND, DASH, ⇨⇩⇘ + (H) OTG CANCEL➔ ⇩⇘⇨ + (ATK)(ATK) (MASH (ATK))

Notes	Damage
Simple launcher combo	661,100 damage, 37% meter loss

AS IRON MAN COMES IN: AIR (H) CANCEL➔ ⇩⇙⇦ + (S), (M), (M), (H) CANCEL➔ FORWARD AIRDASH, (H), (S) (IF ENEMY IS NEAR CORNER, LAND, ⇨⇩⇘ + (H) CANCEL➔ ⇩⇘⇨ + (ATK)(ATK) (MASH (ATK)))

Notes	Damage
—	Varies due to damage scaling

AS IRON MAN COMES IN: AIR (M), (H), ⇧ + (H) CANCEL➔ ⇧ + (ATK)(ATK) (UPWARD AIRDASH), (M), (M), (H) CANCEL➔ ⇩⇙⇦ + (S), DELAYED (M), (H) CANCEL➔ FORWARD AIRDASH, (M), (H) CANCEL➔ FORWARD AIRDASH, (M), (H) CANCEL➔ FORWARD AIR DASH, (S), LAND, ⇨⇩⇘ + (H) CANCEL➔ ⇩⇘⇨ + (ATK)(ATK) (MASH (ATK))

Notes	Damage
⇧ + (S) or ⇩ + (S) TAC to Iron Man, requires corner	Varies due to damage scaling

MAGNETO

"THE TIME FOR SUBTLETY IS PASSING. NOW IS THE TIME FOR CHANGE."

Bio

REAL NAME

Max Eisenhardt (born)

Erik Magnus Lehnsherr (public)

OCCUPATION

Conqueror, Mutant Terrorist

ABILITIES

Has the power to manipulate magnetism and metal at will. He can create magnetic barriers that are able to withstand nuclear explosions, and by altering geomagnetism, he can cause changes in the Earth's crust, and even ignite volcanoes.

WEAPONS

Anything that can be controlled through magnetism.

PROFILE

A survivor of the Auschwitz concentration camp during World War II, he developed the idea that genetically superior mutants should be the ones to rule over mankind. Fighting for the sake of mutantkind, he is a calculating character who stops at nothing to achieve his goals.

FIRST APPEARANCE

The X-Men #1 (1963)

POWER GRID

- 5 INTELLIGENCE
- 2 STRENGTH
- 5 SPEED
- 2 STAMINA
- 5 ENERGY PROJECTION
- 3 FIGHTING ABILITY

*This is biographical, and does not represent an evaluation of the in-game combat potential of this hero.

ALTERNATE COSTUMES

Overview

Vitality	850,000
Chain Combo Archetype	Marvel Series

X-Factor Boost	Damage	Speed
Level 1 (3 teammates remaining)	125%	115%
Level 2 (2 teammates remaining)	147.5%	122.5%
Level 3 (1 teammate remaining)	170%	130%

Your goal with Magneto is to push your challenger's character into the corner, and look for chances to connect with a throw. But if Magneto has beams, shockwaves, gravity things, and all this other stuff, why would you want to play him like a really mobile wrestler?

- **Clean hits with Magneto lead to combos that carry adversaries to the corner while building over a bar of hyper meter**
- **Scoring a throw deals half as much damage, but still results in a cornered foe and Magneto gains at least one bar via the combo after the throw**
- **Magneto's offensive momentum midscreen is killed by advancing guard without assists to help him, but throws can't be guarded and pushblocked, and advancing guard is less helpful to a cornered competitor**
- **Magneto's corner combos inflict terrific damage: at least 700,000 if you spend one bar of hyper meter, and possibly well over 900,000 if you use a lv.3 hyper combo or THC to a teammate**

How do you push adversaries into the corner with Magneto?

- **Using Electromagnetic Disruptor L, Magnetic Blast, Magnetic Shockwave, zoning assists, and the new Repulsion special move to create a wall that repels his opponents backward**
- **Attacking aggressively with throws and the tip of air Ⓗ, backed by interfering assists, when his foes are deterred from advancing**
- **Using a corner-carry combo off of any successful hit, including throws**

TUNING SINCE ORIGINAL MVC3

Since air Ⓗ and airdashing both behave differently in *UMvC3*, the "ROM" combo (super jump rising Ⓗ CANCEL down-forward airdash Ⓗ x8; it was more complicated in terms of timing/positioning, but that's the red meat) is mostly no longer possible midscreen. It's also harder (depending on the size of the challenger) for Magneto to perform repeated flying airdash Ⓗ air combos midscreen. (Both the ROM and flying airdash Ⓗ loops still work in the corner and sometimes midscreen, mostly on big adversaries; giant robots just aren't catching breaks lately, are they?)

Magneto is still a high-damage character, and he still rushes with the best of them. Triangle jump air Ⓛ still hits in about 19 frames, performed as quickly as possible; the change in airdash acceleration might make it *easier* for you to use triangle jump Ⓛ and Ⓗ now, especially from a normal jump (in particular, it is now much easier to triangle jump *backward* with air Ⓗ, which is a good close range feint). What he lost was the ability to carry any competitor into the corner from anywhere with the ROM loop, then hit them for another 10 seconds with the Hyper Gravitation corner loop, and finally cap it off with Gravity Squeeze for the assured knockout off a self-sufficient combo. Although that was only seen at high levels of play, it was still a bit much, and so it's gone. Magneto is still Pringles, though.

The Ⓛ and Ⓜ versions of Electromagnetic Disruptor have 5 and 4 more frames of recovery, respectively. EM Disruptor L is slightly less abusable from fullscreen, but many characters still have no answer for it simply by design. (Magneto is, after all, a sort of mutant demigod who can manipulate elements and fly, while Haggar is... uh, a determined politician with a pipe. It's not David and Goliath exactly, but...)

Magneto also gained three variations of a new class of special move that allows the momentum of adversaries to be altered (Storm, one of Magneto's best friends, at least as far as fighting games are concerned, got the other two moves like this). Competitors can be pushed out, pulled in, or slammed to earth. Between Magneto's considerable capabilities at both close and long range and the possibilities with assists, the existence of these moves serves only to strengthen the leader of the Brotherhood rather than to change his purpose.

- Air Ⓗ knocks Magneto's opponent back farther
- Airdash speed and distance reduced
- Recovery time on Disruptor L & M increased
- Magnetic Tempest and Gravity Squeeze are mashable
- Flight duration decreased to 106 frames from 120 frames
- New move: Fatal Attraction ← ↓ ↙ + Ⓛ pulls opponent toward Magneto
- New move: Repulsion ← ↓ ↙ + Ⓜ pushes challenger away from Magneto
- New move: Reverse Polarity ← ↓ ↙ + Ⓗ pulls foe down from the air
- Invulnerability removed from Magnetic Tempest

Screen	Command	Hits	Damage	Meter Gain	Startup	Active	Recovery	Advantage on Hit	Advantage if Guarded	Notes
1	Standing L	1	50,000	400	5	3	10	+1	0	Chainable into L attacks
2	Standing M	1	65,000	520	10	4	17	-2	-3	—
3	Standing H	1	83,000	664	8	7	26	—	-9	Knocks down

Crouching Basic Attacks

Screen	Command	Hits	Damage	Meter Gain	Startup	Active	Recovery	Advantage on Hit	Advantage if Guarded	Notes
1	Crouching L	1	43,000	344	6	3	9	+2	+1	Low attack, chainable into L attacks
2	Crouching M	1	70,000	560	9	4	19	-4	-6	Low attack, projectile has 1 low priority durability point
3	Crouching H	1	75,000	600	10	9	27	—	-12	Low attack, knocks down rival

Ground Special Attack—Launcher

Screen	Command	Hits	Damage	Meter Gain	Startup	Active	Recovery	Advantage on Hit	Advantage if Guarded	Notes
1	S (while standing or crouching)	1	90,000	720	8	5	23	—	-4	Launcher, not special- or hyper combo-cancelable

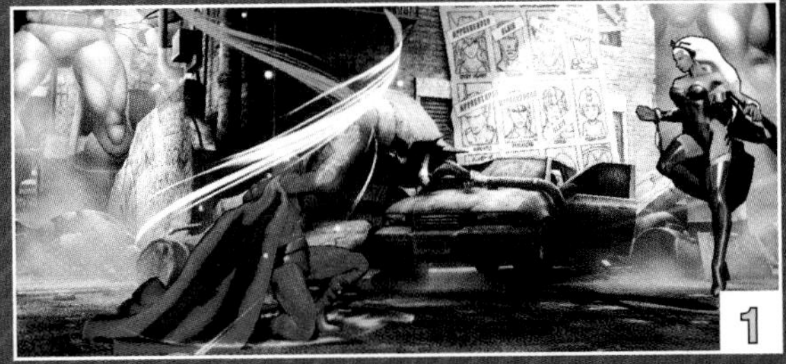

Air Basic Attacks

Screen	Command	Hits	Damage	Meter Gain	Startup	Active	Recovery	Advantage on Hit	Advantage if Guarded	Notes
1	Air L	1	48,000	384	6	3	18	+12	+11	Overhead attack
2	Air M	1	68,000	544	10	5	20	+17	+15	Overhead attack
3	Air H	1	83,000	664	10	7	19	+21	+19	Overhead attack

Air Ⓢ causes a hard knockdown when used in a launcher combo (this is sometimes called flying screen). When used outside of a launcher combo, air Ⓢ behaves mostly like another basic attack. Air exchange attacks, performed by inputting a direction plus Ⓢ, are only possible during a launcher combo. Exchange hits initiate team aerial combos by tagging in the next available character to continue the air combo.

Screen	Command	Hits	Damage	Meter Gain	Startup	Active	Recovery	Advantage on Hit	Advantage if Guarded	Notes
1	Air Ⓢ	1	90,000	720	11	6	19	+18	+16	Overhead attack, causes hard knockdown if used in launcher combo
2	Air ⇧ + Ⓢ (during launcher combo)	1	60,000	480	10	4	17	—	—	Tags in next available ally while lofting opponent upward
3	Air ⇨ or ⇦ + Ⓢ (during launcher combo)	1	50,000	400	10	4	Until grounded	—	—	Tags in next available ally while causing wall bounce, erases 1 hyper meter bar from foe
4	Air ⇩ + Ⓢ (during launcher combo)	1	50,000	400 + 10,000	11	5	20	—	—	Tags in next available ally while causing ground bounce, generates 1 hyper meter bar

1

2

3

4

MAGNETO

Throws

Throws are for snagging passive or blocking opponents. Since throws are active so quickly, you can also use them to preemptively toss opposing characters out of their offense. Combos are usually possible after throws, one way or another.

Screen	Command	Hits	Damage	Meter Gain	Startup	Active	Notes
1	⇨ + Ⓗ (ground)	4	80,000	800	1	1	Captures foe for 134 frames, Magneto may move after 90 frames
	⇦ + Ⓗ (ground)	4	80,000	800	1	1	Captures rival for 144 frames, Magneto may move after 91 frames
2	⇨ + Ⓗ (air)	4	80,000	800	1	1	Captures adversary for 152 frames, Magneto may move after 90 frames
	⇦ + Ⓗ (air)	4	80,000	800	1	1	Captures opponent for 163 frames, Magneto may move after 91 frames

1

2

As a Partner—Crossover Assists

Screen	Type	P1+P2 Crossover Combination Hyper Combo	Description	Hits	Damage	Meter Gain	Startup	Active	Recovery (this crossover assist)	Recovery (other partner)	Notes
1	Magneto—α	Magnetic Shockwave	Electromagnetic Disruptor L	1	90,000	720	35	11	120	90	Knocks down, beam durability: 1 frame x 5 low priority durability points
2	Magneto—β	Magnetic Tempest	Hyper Gravitation M	2	95,000	950	50	—	127	97	Captures foe, 2nd hit is inflicted if opponent is not struck while captured, 2nd hit knocks down, projectile has 3 low priority durability points
3	Magneto—γ	Magnetic Shockwave	Force Field L	1	100,000	800	28	20	119	89	Counter, assist vulnerable for 3 frames before counter activates, spinning knockdown if physical attack touches active frames, active frames nullify medium priority projectiles

1

2

3

Electromagnetic Disruptor is one of the best beams in the game, and beam assists are generally wonderful; Magneto—α is no exception (and, although Magneto had some recovery added to the Ⓛ and Ⓜ versions of EM Disruptor on point, his assist took no such hit). Pair this with any character who relies on zoning to bolster their long range assaults; pair this with any teleport-capable character to create instant, easy mix-ups when you call Magneto—α on one side, then immediately teleport to the other. With characters who can self-OTG, you can also frequently perpetuate a combo by scoring a hard knockdown (like after flying screen), then calling Magneto—α, then using an OTG move. Magneto's Electromagnetic Disruptor only hits once, keeping both hitstun decay and damage scaling down and probably putting your opponent in position for the combo to be continued.

Not only is it asking a lot for Magneto—β to actually hit a target outside of combos tailored just for the Hyper Grav assist, but you'll get Magnetic Tempest instead of Magnetic Shockwave in crossover combinations. This loses the OTG capability Magneto—α/—γ brings to the table for a team.

Magneto—γ grants Shockwave in crossover combinations, but it's not as useful as it would seem for being a counter assist. Magneto is a low-vitality character to begin with, and he's vulnerable when he lands, before he actually performs Force Field. If the challenger has *anything* active when Magneto touches down, Magneto just takes damage for no reason.

Snap Back

Screen	Command	Hits	Damage	Meter Gain	Startup	Active	Recovery	Advantage on Hit	Advantage if Guarded
1	↓↘→ + P1 or P2	1	50,000	500 - (-1 hyper meter bar)	2	4	20	—	0

Notes

On hit, snap back forces the opposing point character to be replaced by an assist. Opposing assist calls or tag outs are also locked out for 4 seconds

1

Special Moves

Screen	Name	Command	Hits	Damage	Meter Gain	Startup	Active	Recovery	Advantage on Hit	Advantage if Guarded	Notes
1	Electromagnetic Disruptor L	↓↘→ + Ⓛ	1	90,000	720	7	14	29	-2	-24	Knocks down, beam durability: 1 frame x 5 low priority durability points
	Electromagnetic Disruptor M	↓↘→ + Ⓜ	2	104,500	880	12	13	29	+2	-21	Knocks down, beam durability: 2 frames x 4 low priority durability points
	Electromagnetic Disruptor H	↓↘→ + Ⓗ	3	121,900	1080	17	15	24	+5	-19	Knocks down, beam durability: 3 frames x 4 low priority durability points
	Air Electromagnetic Disruptor L	(in air) ↓↘→ + Ⓛ	1	90,000	720	9	14	Until landing	-5	-26	Knocks down, beam durability: 1 frame x 5 low priority durability points
	Air Electromagnetic Disruptor M	(in air) ↓↘→ + Ⓜ	2	104,500	880	14	13	Until landing	+3	-20	Knocks down, beam durability: 2 frames x 4 low priority durability points
	Air Electromagnetic Disruptor H	(in air) ↓↘→ + Ⓗ	3	121,900	1080	21	15	Until landing	+10	-14	Knocks down, beam durability: 3 frames x 4 low priority durability points
2	Hyper Gravitation L	↓↙← + Ⓛ	2	95,000	950	26	—	35	+25	-22	Captures foe, 2nd hit is inflicted if opponent is not struck while captured, 2nd hit knocks down, projectile active for 15 frames, projectile has 3 low priority durability points
3	Hyper Gravitation M	↓↙← + Ⓜ	2	95,000	950	31	—	30	+31	-17	Captures adversary, 2nd hit is inflicted if competitor is not struck while captured, 2nd hit knocks down, projectile active for 15 frames, projectile has 3 low priority durability points
4	Hyper Gravitation H	↓↙← + Ⓗ	2	95,000	950	36	—	25	+31	-12	Captures opposing character, 2nd hit is inflicted if rival is not struck while captured, 2nd hit knocks down, projectile active for 15 frames, projectile has 3 low priority durability points

Special Moves continued

Screen	Name	Command	Hits	Damage	Meter Gain	Startup	Active	Recovery	Advantage on Hit	Advantage if Guarded	Notes
2	Air Hyper Gravitation L	(in air) ↓↙← + Ⓛ	2	95,000	950	30	—	36	+25	-24	Captures foe, 2nd hit is inflicted if opponent is not struck while captured, 2nd hit knocks down, projectile active for 15 frames, projectile has 3 low priority durability points
3	Air Hyper Gravitation M	(in air) ↓↙← + Ⓜ	2	95,000	950	35	—	31	+31	-19	Captures adversary, 2nd hit is inflicted if competitor is not struck while captured, 2nd hit knocks down, projectile active for 15 frames, projectile has 3 low priority durability points
4	Air Hyper Gravitation H	(in air) ↓↙← + Ⓗ	2	95,000	950	40	—	26	+31	-14	Captures opposing character, 2nd hit is inflicted if rival is not struck while captured, 2nd hit knocks down, projectile active for 15 frames, projectile has 3 low priority durability points
	Magnetic Blast L	(in air) ↑↗→ + Ⓛ	1	70,000	560	14	—	35	—	—	Knocks down airborne foe, recovers immediately when grounded, projectile has 5 low priority durability points
5	Magnetic Blast M	(in air) ↑↗→ + Ⓜ	1	70,000	560	18	—	31	—	—	Knocks down airborne opponent, recovers immediately when grounded, projectile has 5 low priority durability points
	Magnetic Blast H	(in air) ↑↗→ + Ⓗ	1	70,000	560	22	—	27	—	—	Knocks down airborne adversary, recovers immediately when grounded, projectile has 5 low priority durability points
	Force Field L	→↓↘ + Ⓛ	—	—	—	3	19	28	—	—	50 total frames, counter attack, active counter frames also nullify medium priority projectiles
6	Force Field M	→↓↘ + Ⓜ	—	—	—	8	19	29	—	—	55 total frames, counter attack, active counter frames also nullify medium priority projectiles
	Force Field H	→↓↘ + Ⓗ	—	—	—	12	19	30	—	—	60 total frames, counter attack, active counter frames also nullify medium priority projectiles
7	Force Field Counterattack	—	1	100,000	800	15	20	41	—	-37	Triggered if active frames of Force Field are struck with a physical attack, invincible from frames 1-75, spinning knockdown
8	Flight (in air OK)	↓↙← + Ⓢ	—	—	—	15	—	—	—	—	Activates flight mode, flight mode lasts for 106 frames
9	Fatal Attraction	←↓↙ + Ⓛ	—	—	—	7	23 (pulled)	11	—	—	Unblockable, pulls competitor toward Magneto, foe is free to act while being pulled
10	Repulsion	←↓↙ + Ⓜ	—	—	—	12	20 (pushed)	14	—	—	Unblockable, pushes opponent away from Magneto, adversary is free to act while being pushed
11	Reverse Polarity	←↓↙ + Ⓗ	—	—	—	16	10 (pulled down from air)	19	—	—	Unblockable, pulls airborne rival down to the ground, opposing character is free to act while being pulled down

1

Electromagnetic Disruptor: Magneto's beam has slightly more recovery at the end than it did in *MvC3*, but it's still one of the best ranged attacks. His EM Disruptor L starts traveling on frame 7 after input, and it crosses the entire field by frame 16. For comparison, most overheads aren't even that fast. When trying to control your challenger from fullscreen, or to preempt or stay even with zoning-oriented adversaries, EM Disruptor L should be the foundation of your efforts.

Because of its speed, grounded EM Disruptor is particularly good for hit checking opposing assists. If any EM Disruptor happens to knock down your competitor's assist, you have plenty of time to decide whether you'd like to cancel to Magnetic Shockwave to beef up the red damage inflicted (this doesn't work on point characters, since EM Disruptor doesn't cause a hard knockdown on them, but any hit is a brief hard knockdown on assists). This assist-punishing trick is more valuable if the assist is in the middle of the field, so Shockwave can carry them farther and hit more often. If the opposing assist is knocked down to the back of the screen, Shockwave only hits them once or twice; if EM Disruptor knocks them OFF screen, Shockwave might not hit at all.

If your opponent makes you nervous as you fire EM Disruptor, such as by airdashing just over it toward Magneto, cancel into Magnetic Shockwave to make Magneto safe against any character who doesn't have an invincible attack or quick teleport that can pass through Shockwave on reaction.

If you don't want to spend hyper meter or go for a reset at the end of air combos, finishing with standing Ⓗ canceled into EM Disruptor H is always a decent option (and can be canceled into Gravity Squeeze from anywhere, if you want to spend the meter).

Note that Electromagnetic Disruptor can only be used once per airborne period, after which Magneto will fall to earth unable to act or guard. Activate flight first if you want to shoot EM Disruptor repeatedly, or if you want to prevent Magneto from being helpless on the way down afterward.

Hyper Gravitation L 2

Hyper Gravitation M 3

Hyper Gravitation H 4

Hyper Gravitation: Magneto sends a magnetic snare out toward his rival; the heavier the version, the farther the magnetic snare travels, but the slower Magneto releases it.

Hyper Grav is a mainstay in corner combos, where it's possible to reliably juggle airborne foes with standing Ⓗ into Hyper Grav L leading into more corner shenanigans. In fact, you can make Magneto perform a so-called "Hyper Grav loop" on cornered competitors; see Advanced Tactics for more details. This can work midscreen, as well, but it's much harder.

The natural follow-up to Hyper Grav is either Magnetic Tempest (and then maybe a THC), or a short combo that leads into Gravity Squeeze (like the one mentioned in the EM Disruptor entry).

You can add Hyper Gravitation to combos midscreen either through the use of assists in combos (cause a hard knockdown, call an OTG assist and perform Hyper Grav), or by using air exchange to tag Magneto into the middle of a team aerial combo, letting him perform the auto-hit on the way in, then IMMEDIATELY airdashing down-forward and performing Hyper Grav L. (There are other ways, too; see the Combo Appendix.) Otherwise, it can be useful to occasionally "poke" with Hyper Grav H from mid to long range just to remind your opponent that you can send random snares their way. However, since Hyper Gravs themselves are easily destroyed by enemy projectiles, and because Magneto is wide open if Hyper Grav misses, this is not a baseline strategy that you can rely upon.

5

Magnetic Blast: This move is a diagonally-aimed magnetic projectile that can only be thrown while Magneto is airborne. The motion is unusual: while ↓↘→ fireball motions are second-nature to any fighting game player by now, ↑↗→ can be deceptively awkward, especially if you're trying to do something like use Mag Blast as soon as possible after a forward jump. Spend some time in Training Mode doing nothing but tossing Magnetic Blasts to get used to it. For another tip, whenever you're planning to throw a Mag Blast, try doing ↖ + (H) in midair first. One reason for this is to simply to sort of both "center" yourself and Magneto; since you're intentionally canceling air (H) into Magnetic Blast, the results are more predictable than if you tried to do Mag Blast by itself, failed, and somehow got another move on accident. The execution failures are then on your terms if they occur. Done correctly, and the air (H) barely even animates before Mag Blast, and starting at ↖ means that not only does the air (H) double as an option select air throw if your target happens to be in range, but it also makes it a natural motion to roll ↖↑↗→.

The angle of Magnetic Blast makes it very useful, since most characters can't deal particularly well with ranged threats that descend on them at a 45-degree angle. This is the same reason Akuma's air Go Hadou projectiles end up being so strong in any traditional *Street Fighter* title, where almost no one but him has that kind of ability. Get above your challenger and toss Mag Blast diagonally down at them, and Magneto is free to airdash in behind the projectile. Unlike beams, Mag Blasts do not dissipate if Magneto receives a hit after tossing them. You can also use Magnetic Blasts in variations of Magneto's air combos.

Magneto releases lighter versions of Magnetic Blast more quickly, but the projectiles travel more slowly. Heavier Magnetic Blasts take longer to toss, but they traverse the screen faster.

6

7

Force Field: For Magneto's counter move, he counters any physical hit that strikes him during active frames with his Force Field counterattack. The counterattack isn't assured; if your opponent triggered Force Field with an attack that recovers quickly, they may have time to guard the counterattack.

On hit, the Force Field counterattack causes a spinning knockdown; you can hyper combo cancel the recovery of the Force Field counterattack to capitalize. (You can also activate X-Factor.) During both the Force Field and the counterattack, Magneto is invincible to physical attacks, and incoming projectiles of medium priority or less become nullified. He can still be thrown, however.

In terms of application, you can use Force Field effectively against obvious assaults, such as repeated dive kick-type attacks (like the ones Wolverine, Trish, and others love to use) or square jump (H) spam. When your ground chains are guarded, you can also cancel crouching (H) into Force Field occasionally... most opposing players are aware that Magneto is punishable after a blocked slide, but you can deter this by occasionally mixing in Force Field. Overall, it's a better approach to just not have your slide blocked and to not play "chasing the queen" adding high-risk escapes to high-risk maneuvers, but it's worthwhile to do this kind of thing occasionally just to remind your competitors that you *might* do it.

Flight: Magneto's flight mode is invaluable for his mobility and air combos. Flight mode has been reduced slightly in duration since *MvC3* to cut down on Magneto's ability to stay airborne, flitting around with repeated flying airdashes. The duration reduction also slightly shortens Magneto's flight mode air combos.

Only with flight can Magneto airdash more than once per jump. This is done in one of two ways. You can cancel different directions of airdash into one another using normal inputs (↗ + ATK ATK, ↖ + ATK ATK, → + ATK ATK, and so on). Or, you can airdash in the same direction over and over using plink inputs (ATK ~ ATK, ATK ~ ATK, drumming two attack buttons on consecutive frames repeatedly while holding the direction you want to airdash—use (H) as the first button so your airdashes double as air throws! See Advanced Tactics for more details). You can use this in all sorts of ways, especially combined with using air (S) to drop from the flight whenever you want. From a flying position at normal jump height in near your rival, for example, you can airdash up-back then immediately back down-forward with air (S) to feint the backdash into a forward triangle jump. Air (S) makes Magneto land automatically, so if it hits, you'll be able to confirm and continue the combo from the ground. This is also extremely useful after taking a hit that causes Magneto to recover in the air; activate flight, then airdash away rapidly (while calling an assist that provides cover from the ground, if you have one), or feint airdashes away, then airdash aggressively at your foe with attacks.

8

Fatal Attraction, Repulsion, and Reverse Polarity: Along with Storm's new Fair and Foul Wind specials, these actions allow Magneto to push and pull adversaries around on a whim. Between Fatal Attraction and Repulsion, as with Storm's Foul/Fair Wind, the version that pulls opponents toward Magneto has both a slightly larger effect and occupies slightly less of Magneto's time than the version that pushes away. For Reverse Polarity, the move forces any competitor airborne between frames 16 and 26 to the ground.

Fatal Attraction 9

Repulsion 10

Reverse Polarity 11

These actions have no effect on assists, and they don't put your challenger into any actual kind of "stun" state, so they're still free to act. This means you won't want to use them for just any old reason, since that only gets Magneto into trouble. Depending on your team, you can couple the use of these actions with particular assists to make Magneto relatively safe and open up new avenues of opportunity.

For example, if a competitor such as Chris takes to the air to fire his Uzi, you can call some sort of assist that hits a long way laterally (like beams or Sentinel—α), then perform Reverse Polarity to haul him right back down and into the path of your assist. You'll be able to tack on an EM Disruptor to pile on, hit or guarded, and you're both back at fullscreen square one.

Or, from long range, you can call an assist like Chun-Li—γ, Chris—γ, or Dante—α, then perform Fatal Attraction. If your competitor is careless with their movement while Fatal Attraction sucks them in, they just may get clipped by the assist, giving you plenty of time to verify, dash forward, and launch them. As with Storm's Foul Wind, Fatal Attraction is also very useful to mess with adversaries who think they're going to fall or airdash onto Magneto. Perform an early preemptive Fatal Attraction after the opponent super jumps, and they'll be pulled clear over Magneto, and their air basic attacks whiff (unless it's something omnidirectional like Zero's air (H)).

These moves work at ANY time—while Reverse Polarity won't do anything to challengers who aren't airborne, Repulsion and Fatal Attraction can even push and pull competitors lying prone or recovering from a knockdown! In this manner, these moves can be very useful for devious resets. Fatal Attraction also allows you to squeeze a little more damage out of OTG Magnetic Shockwave by repositioning the opposing character closer to Magneto right before the hyper combo hits them off the ground.

Hyper Combos

Screen	Name	Command	Hits	Damage	Startup	Active	Recovery	Advantage on Hit	Advantage if Guarded	Notes
1	Magnetic Shockwave	↓↘→ + ATK ATK	6	327,800	14+1	44	56	—	-68	Frames 1-10 invincible, OTG-capable, hard knockdown
2	Magnetic Tempest (in air OK)	↓↙← + ATK ATK	40~80	275,400~ 330,700	4+23	77	29	—	-4	Knocks down, each rock has 1 high priority durability point, can be mashed for additional hits
3	Gravity Squeeze (level 3 hyper combo)	→↓↘ + ATK ATK	2~50	400,000~ 448,000	20+1	2	43	—	-30	Frames 1-10 invincible, OTG-capable, hard knockdown, unaffected by damage scaling, can be mashed for additional hits

Magnetic Shockwave: This creates a series of infinite-height energy columns that travel away from Magneto. If these pillars contact adversaries along the way, they'll be carried along with the wave. Thus, Magnetic Shockwave ends up dealing a lot more damage midscreen than near corners, where the columns quickly travel off the side of the playing field.

Magnetic Shockwave is most important for its defensive and anti-assist uses. When using Electromagnetic Disruptors to prod your challenger from far away and keep them out, they will probably eventually jump over your beam barrage. Here, they might airdash or fly forward and threaten Magneto, but you can just cancel the recovery of EM Disruptor to Magnetic Shockwave in order to insulate Magneto from most harm (your foe might still blow through with a teleport or a move that's invincible for a good period of time, like lv.3 hyper combos; in this case, you'll have to blow X-Factor to be safe—this can actually be bait against a teleporter—or just eat the punishment with a smile. You can't win 'em all). Your EM Disruptors also inevitably sometimes snipe opposing assists as they try to come on screen. On reaction to this, if the opposing assist is close to Magneto's side of the screen or in the middle of the playing field, cancel to Shockwave to punish the assist further and perhaps coax a bad mistake out of the opposing player's point character.

Shockwave can also end midscreen combos, and it is indirectly better at this than in original *MvC3* thanks to Fatal Attraction. After all, the closer your opponent is to Magneto when Shockwave hits, the better. Air combo your rival and cause flying screen, then perform Fatal Attraction to pull their body toward Magneto. Cancel to Magnetic Shockwave before they get up for the OTG. If you cause a hard knockdown in the corner, and you don't have an OTG assist handy to enable you to pop your competitor up into Hyper Grav CANCEL▶ Magnetic Tempest, then backdash away from the corner and perform Fatal Attraction canceled into Magnetic Shockwave. This ekes about ~55,000 more damage out of corner Shockwave than was possible in original *MvC3*.

Magnetic Tempest: Magnetic Tempest is used in combos, usually after Hyper Grav. Juggling into either Magnetic Tempest or Gravity Squeeze is the ultimate goal of most corner combos. Mash an attack input for increased damage.

If X-Factor is activated during Magnetic Tempest, the rocks dissipate right away. Since Magnetic Tempest combos involve the challenger being right next to Magneto, he'll be in position to dash and launch immediately. Hitstun decay becomes pretty severe in a combo by now, but you can use Magneto to immediately hand off to another character via a TAC, and then hitstun decay won't matter. Your next character can finish off both the team aerial combo and the current challenger character in X-Factor, and then be ready to mix the next competitor up.

Gravity Squeeze: Magneto's lv.3 hyper combo strikes wherever the opponent is on the 21st frame after input. An attack input can be mashed on hit for a little extra damage. Afterward, your foe is lobbed backward in a hard knockdown. Magneto can follow-up after this at the very least by juggling the opposing character with EM Disruptor; near corners, Magneto can actually dash in and use standing (H), (S) to launch the challenger before they hit the ground. Hitstun decay is high by the time you get to an air combo afterward, so the best you can usually do is to cause a hard knockdown in the corner. (With some assists, you can do better—for example, dash forward after Gravity Squeeze and juggle standing (H) CANCEL▶ EM Disruptor H while calling Dormammu—α, then cancel to Magnetic Tempest!)

Gravity Squeeze is OTG-capable, which makes it an excruciatingly easy way to add 400,000+ damage to any hard knockdown. It also combos after any standing (H), EM Disruptor, Hyper Grav, or Force Field counterattack. You might even choose to cause a long-lasting hard knockdown with one of Magneto's teammates, then tag him in to finish their combo with an immediate OTG Gravity Squeeze. Magneto's flexibility with adding Gravity Squeeze to any of his combos means he's always extra dangerous when he's packing surplus hyper meter.

Battle Plan

Magneto has a terrific air (H) and air (L) for rushing down challengers, but his ground attacks are actually not quick compared to the fastest pixies. So, you'll generally only want to attack on the ground behind the frame advantage that is provided by either a jump-in attack or an assist. Magneto works best with pinning assists, or assists that take up a lot of lateral space (and the longer they stay active, the better). Beam assists help Magneto's ranged game, as they do with anyone, but they don't tend to last long enough to give Magneto several free shots while his opponent guards, and they tend to keep your rival stuck in guardstun, which reduces the amount of ways they could screw up against an aggressive Magneto.

Ultimately Magneto works best with assists like Akuma—β and Sentinel—α. Backed by an assist like Akuma's projectile-invincible Tatsumaki, Magneto can be played in a proactive manner on offense; with Sentinel's drones, the play should be more laid-back and measured. (This is just as true if you select assists other than these, though your actual tactics may have to be altered slightly.) Both assists mentioned here are fragile and have to be covered in different ways, and Magneto is no ~~Sentinel~~ Thor, either, so the low vitality of the team also dictates how you should operate—carefully.

Magneto has an ideal means to cover Sentinel calls—standing with his back to the screen edge and performing EM Disruptor after calling Sentinel. If your foe does anything that makes you nervous, you can cancel to Magnetic Shockwave to protect both characters. After the drones are on screen and traveling, Magneto can catch up to them easily if you wavedash while they travel to your opponent's character. (Once Sentinel leaves, you are also safe to use Fatal Attraction to pull your adversaries forward into the drones, or execute Reverse Polarity to suck them down out of the sky into the drones.) As the opposing character is forced to block the drones one way or another, Magneto can then be made to alternate between dash-in crouching (L), triangle jump air (L), or empty triangle jump into crouching (L). Because Sentinel's drones force your competitor to sit still for so long, you have time to take two or three cracks at breaking down your rival's defense here. If your opponent weathers the storm and pushblocks Magneto back successfully, then it's time to create another space to call Sentinel and repeat the process. Other assists such as Captain America—α and Rocket Raccoon—α can be used for more or less the same purpose, although they occupy much less of the playing field.

By getting your challenger to guard an assist that holds them for a while, you'll buy yourself a chance to crack their shell.

Magneto's ranged powers are supplemented by new moves that let him reposition his adversary.

With an assist like Akuma—β, you can play more aggressively because Akuma cuts through so much stuff with his body (whereas Sentinel assist cuts through nothing, the robot just stands there beckoning for the drones—do robots need the pointing?—waiting for your challenger to nuke a giant, fragile target if you don't stop them). Instead of covering the assist call itself, your goal is to call the assist when you're already relatively close to your target, then react accordingly. Don't commit to an attack *while* you're dashing in and calling Akuma; wait to see the results of Akuma first. Otherwise, you might get both Magneto and Akuma caught at once. On the other hand, if Magneto isn't committed, you'll be able to block and pushblock if your adversary starts hitting Akuma; from here, you'll possibly be free to employ EM Disruptor, Hyper Grav H, or Magnetic Shockwave in order to stop them.

If Akuma starts hitting the opposing character, you can react in time to continue with a combo; if Akuma is guarded, your job is to force your challenger to keep guarding with either EM Disruptor, dash-in crouching (L), or a triangle jump mix-up so Akuma can leave safely.

Magneto also works well when paired with OTG-capable assists; the master of magnetism is fast enough and his combos are flexible enough to make just about any assist work. Off any OTG hit, you can continue the combo or easily link Hyper Grav to Magnetic Tempest to cap off a combo.

Magneto can be played to stalemate some characters with Electromagnetic Disruptors alone.

One big plus to landing a throw is that your challenger's incoming assist ends up whiffing harmlessly.

You can force incoming characters into situations where they're susceptible to an air throw or combo regardless of what they do.

With careful timing, you can use the new Repulsion special against a foe you've knocked down into the corner to prevent them from rolling out.

Without being backed by an assist who takes up a lot of space and gives Magneto chances to stage mix-ups without much risk, you'll have to take more advantage of Magneto's ranged tools, since rushing in mindlessly without cover is a good way to lose.

When in doubt, there is nothing wrong with attempting to zone your challenger with Electromagnetic Disruptor L and Magnetic Blast L. Shoot EM Disruptor at opponents who are directly across from Magneto; toss Mag Blasts down upon them from up above and far away. If you super jump backward and throw Mag Blast L as soon as possible, you'll have plenty of time afterward to either:

Airdash up-back and throw another Mag Blast L, then possibly activate flight to stay in the air longer, or fall to earth to get another bead on EM Disruptors and rushing in

Airdash down-forward, and attack behind the cover of Mag Blast L

Activate flight and airdash forward and down-forward repeatedly to either fall directly on a competitor with air (S) or pass over them to the other side

Mag Blasts are also very useful at normal jump height, if your challenger's team isn't constituted to completely dominate ground level (you're not going to get away with throwing many jump height Mag Blasts if Rocket Raccoon or Arthur are spamming projectiles while calling a Doctor Strange assist, for example). When he is this low to the ground, you have time to dash in with Magneto and combo after a Magnetic Blast hits from mid range (or, if Mag Blast is guarded, to triangle jump air (L), or empty triangle jump into throw or crouching (L), and so on). Throwing Magnetic Blast in this manner works as a sort of pseudo-assist, giving you a brief chance to attack without the risk of just running forward. At the very least, getting a Magnetic Blast out there assures you of adding an EM Disruptor H for your opponent to block right afterward, for a little chip damage and hyper meter gain.

Without an assist to help pin or Magnetic Blasts to attack behind, throws become especially important while playing Magneto. He's a fast character, extremely air-mobile, who can corner a competitor off any throw; whether you ground throw your challenger or air throw them, Magneto can manage to catch up and hit them while they're encased in magnetic rocks, and then it's corner carry combo time. Throws are important because without an assist to help him out, Magneto is fairly susceptible to being pushblocked. His overheads are good, but they're not really as fast as they look—characters who can jump and perform rising attacks as overheads are actually impossible to react to, while Magneto is merely very difficult. Magneto has a version of this, with instant overhead jumping air (M), canceled into triangle jump air (L), but it's difficult and misses many characters, especially if they're crouching (which they probably were, if jumping air (M) managed to hit them in the face). Your mix-ups between dash-in crouching (L) and triangle jump air (L)/(H) take on a totally different complexion once you can mix in surprise throw attempts reliably. Opponents waiting to use advancing guard to buy space end up getting snagged. Dashes can be crouch canceled into a throw attempt (be precise with your input to avoid accidentally getting an up-close ↓↘→ + (H)), while empty triangle jumps can naturally lead to a throw upon landing. (See the Advanced Tactics section for a means to install more than one air throw attempt into what looks like an empty triangle jump!)

So you've chased your challenger into the corner, either by pushing them back with Magneto's projectile prowess or with a corner carry combo. If the combo is still in progress when you get to the corner, try to find a way to finish with Hyper Grav L so that you can transition to the Hyper Grav loop (see Advanced Tactics) before tacking on a hyper combo or going for a reset. Depending on how the corner carry ended and whether Magneto has an OTG-capable assist handy, the best you can do may be to score a hard knockdown in the corner.

Once the opposing character rises, they'll be able to roll forward during ground recovery, but Magneto can be made to correct for that in multiple ways. If you have an assist like Sentinel—α handy, call it so the drones are occupying the space your challenger will roll forward into, then backdash as they roll forward. This gives them just enough room to put themselves into a confusing situation, while you still keep their backs to the corner. Alternatively, you can simply call an assist who can cover Magneto and pin the adversary, and then you can perform Repulsion as the target starts to roll forward. Magneto simply holds them in place, and then they'll be forced to guard the assist covering Magneto... and they'll still be in the corner, with Magneto right next to them with frame advantage!

Catching one or two sequences correctly with Magneto against a cornered competitor should result in a knockout. The next character falling in fresh also gets cornered. To cover a number of bases, the most consistent thing to do is to jump to meet them just as they come in with air (H) canceled into Magnetic Blast L. If they fall in mashing an attack trying to beat you out, this combos and allows you plenty of time to land and juggle with standing (H), (S) into an air combo. If they block, you'll still be right on top of them. If they use advancing guard, unless they do it immediately as air (H) hits (which is as likely an accident as anything else; using advancing guard against single attacks on reaction isn't reliable), Magneto lands before them! They're still stuck in the advancing guard animation in midair briefly, so Magneto is free to dash forward, then jump to air throw them before they land. Naturally, an air throw into the corner should mean a minimum of 450,000 damage, not counting THC or X-Factor possibilities.

Any of Magneto's combos can end with either standing (H) or a Hyper Grav; that means you can manufacture this scenario (new character falling in) with a snap back at the end of any combo (cancel st. (H) into snap back, or follow up Hyper Grav with st. (H) CANCEL snap back). If you are really in your challenger's head, and if they have assists with lots of red damage, then going for snap backs aggressively has more potential than taking guaranteed damage, provided you make your mix-ups pay off.

All this assumes all things go according to your Magneto gameplan, which won't be all the time. Your challenger may turn the tables and go after Magneto aggressively, banking on taking him out with just one solid combo into hyper combo, followed by THC. So you can't afford to be cavalier with Magneto's below-average vitality. The best anti-air against airdashing, jumping, and flying characters going for overheads and cross-ups is often to just try to air throw them. Failing that, Magneto's standing (L) actually makes a terrific hit-confirmable anti-air/anti-jump attack. The little energy flash Magneto creates with his hand is actually invincible (his hand and arm are vulnerable), like the similar effects created by Storm or Iron Man during basic attacks. On offense, use it instead of crouching (L) whenever you anticipate an adversary trying to jump away, or when you're attacking airborne challengers at low altitude. On defense, you can use it to try and tick incoming competitors out of their airborne attacks. As with crouching (L), just press the button two or three times whenever you use it to give yourself a chance to confirm whether the light attacks have caught your rival. If you do shoot an adversary down with standing (L) x2~3, launch immediately and go for a normal air combo or TAC. Be advised that standing (L) whiffs over the heads of small crouching characters. (And over Amaterasu, Arthur, Rocket Raccoon, and Viewtiful Joe while they're *standing!)* Finally, if you can manage to jump backward, air ↖ + (H) CANCEL Magnetic Blast L buys solid separation and a chance for Magneto to regain control, and backward triangle jump (H) actually comes out *faster* than forward triangle jump air (H) because of the new "hitch" in Magneto's down-back airdash. Even from a backward triangle jump, the attack still has good range.

"MINE IS THE POWER TO DESTROY—BUT I CHOOSE NOT TO. PROFIT FROM MY EXAMPLE."

COMBO USAGE

I. MIDSCREEN: CR. Ⓛ, Ⓛ, Ⓜ, Ⓗ, Ⓢ (CANCEL) FORWARD SUPER JUMP, IMMEDIATE AIR Ⓗ, PAUSE, (CANCEL) DOWN-FORWARD AIRDASH, PAUSE, AIR Ⓗ, LAND, FORWARD DASH, ST. Ⓗ, Ⓢ (CANCEL) FORWARD SUPER JUMP, AIR Ⓗ (CANCEL) FORWARD AIRDASH, AIR Ⓗ (CANCEL) ↓ ↙ ← + Ⓢ, AIR Ⓛ, Ⓗ (CANCEL) FORWARD AIRDASH, {AIR Ⓗ (CANCEL) FORWARD AIRDASH} REPEAT BRACKETS X5, AIR Ⓢ, LAND, (P1 OR P2) OTG-CAPABLE ASSIST, ↓ ↙ ← + Ⓗ (CANCEL) ↓ ↙ ← + (ATK)(ATK) (MASH (ATK)) OR ST. Ⓗ (CANCEL) ↓ ↘ → + Ⓗ (CANCEL) → ↓ ↘ + (ATK)(ATK) (MASH (ATK)), DASH IN ST. Ⓗ, Ⓢ (CANCEL) ← ↓ ↙ ↖ + Ⓗ

Requires OTG-capable assist (damage varies slightly based on assist), ~720,300 damage, ~124% meter gain (or ~945,000 damage, ~140% meter loss with Gravity Squeeze)

This combo carries your challenger corner-to-corner, and it requires an OTG-capable assist (if you simply end the combo at the hard knockdown, it still corners them while dealing a respectable 462,000 damage and building 117% hyper meter). From the middle of the playing field, this combo will already have your adversary in the corner by the time you get to the flight portion, and so it can work on every character; from closer to your own corner, they won't be in the other corner quite yet. This makes the air Ⓛ link after activating flight late in the combo unreliable or impossible on some mid-sized and almost all small characters:

Midscreen air Ⓗ to flight air combo unreliable on:

Arthur, Chun-Li, Deadpool, Doctor Strange, Felicia
Firebrand, Frank West, Phoenix*, Phoenix Wright
Rocket Raccoon, Spider-Man, Strider, Trish
Viewtiful Joe, Wolverine, X-23, Zero

*Not that it matters; this combo K.O.s Phoenix before the portion that doesn't work on her!

After the launch, you want to hit with air Ⓗ on the way up as soon as you can, but you want to pause before airdashing down-forward. This allows Magneto to rise as his victim drifts down slightly. After your late diagonal airdash, you then want to pause again, and link air Ⓗ on the way down as late as possible. After landing, you want to be able to have Magneto dash right into an opponent who's not very high off the ground, so standing Ⓗ to Ⓢ combos properly. This part can take some practice; it's easier (and trivially less damage) to simply land and perform crouching Ⓗ, Ⓢ instead. If this misses, you didn't position the rising and falling air heavy attacks properly. Take your time! (On big characters, you can squeeze in a second rep of super jumping air Ⓗ into airdash down-forward air Ⓗ, before dashing forward to relaunch.)

If the opening light attacks are guarded, then halt the combo and go for a throw, triangle jump air Ⓛ for an overhead, or **Combo I** again. If you think your challenger might try to jump away on the ground, or if they're airborne at low altitude already, open with standing Ⓛ x2 instead. If standing Ⓛ x2 strikes against an airborne competitor, just launch with Ⓢ immediately and proceed to the air combo portion without more ground attacks for the sake of consistency.

On small characters, you can perform everything up to where flight is, then do air Ⓢ for a hard knockdown instead. From here, dash forward and call the OTG assist, then perform Hyper Grav H into Magnetic Tempest. This is less damage, hyper meter, and pushback, but it's still totally worth doing, at around 696,100! Alternatively, see the Combo Appendix for a midscreen corner carry flight combo that does less damage, but is much easier and works on every character consistently.

Ending it with a hard knockdown short of the corner also opens up the chance to command dash upon landing with (ATK)(ATK), then perform Fatal Attraction canceled to Magnetic Shockwave. The dash, followed by Fatal Attraction, puts Magneto and his challenger right next to one another, making the most of Shockwave. This combo doesn't require the help of an OTG assist, and it allows Magneto to deal a relatively easy 548,900~576,900 damage on anyone in the cast.

II. CORNER ONLY: CR. Ⓛ, Ⓛ, Ⓜ, Ⓗ, Ⓢ (CANCEL) FORWARD SUPER JUMP, AIR Ⓗ, PAUSE, (CANCEL) DOWN-FORWARD AIRDASH, AIR Ⓗ, LAND, {UPWARD SUPER JUMP, AIR Ⓗ (CANCEL) DOWN-FORWARD AIRDASH, AIR Ⓗ, LAND} REPEAT BRACKETS X7, STANDING Ⓗ (CANCEL) ↓ ↙ ← + Ⓛ (CANCEL) ↓ ↙ ← + (ATK)(ATK) (MASH (ATK))

703,100 damage, 32% meter gain

The so-called "ROM" combo (a name appropriated from a similar up-and-down *MvC2* combo) is still around, but now it's only reliable in corners, where it still works on every character. After the launch, the first super jump repetition is not about speed, it's about position; as with **Combo I**, you want to hit with air Ⓗ ASAP on the way up, then let Magneto drift upward for a moment before airdashing down-forward. The difference here is that after airdashing down-forward, you want to strike with air Ⓗ immediately, so Magneto kind of wedges himself between them and the ground and pops his foe back up. From here, perform the seven follow-up reps as fast as you can; if they're in the right position, it's just about speed. (This combo is, strictly speaking, more work than absolutely necessary for this amount of damage, but hey, it looks rad—start off with triangle jump air Ⓗ to cr. Ⓗ before the launch, and you end up with a combo that is literally *22* heavy attacks in a row. In *MvC2*, he got by with a 5-fierce combo!)

After the final standing Ⓗ to Hyper Grav L, you can also opt to perform standing Ⓗ to EM Disruptor H to Gravity Squeeze. Or, you can just jab your opponent out of the Hyper Grav with standing Ⓛ, then go for an air throw back into the corner against their air recovery.

Whenever super jumping upward during this combo, it's most lenient to super jump up-back... but, this may increase your likelihood of accidentally performing a worthless Hyper Grav H instead of just getting upward-moving air Ⓗ. Super jumping straight up works fine, but it makes the timing slightly more exacting. You can use air Ⓜ in place of air Ⓗ during upward-moving portions of the combo, but this diminishes the usefulness to be less than much easier alternatives.

III. THROW / AIR THROW, WAVEDASH, CR. Ⓗ, Ⓢ (CANCEL) FORWARD SUPER JUMP, AIR Ⓗ (CANCEL) FORWARD AIRDASH, PAUSE, AIR Ⓜ, Ⓗ, LAND, {FORWARD JUMP, AIR Ⓗ (CANCEL) FORWARD AIRDASH, AIR Ⓜ, Ⓗ, LAND} REPEAT BRACKETS X2, ST. Ⓗ (CANCEL) ↓ ↘ → + Ⓗ (OR IN CORNER ↓ ↙ ← + Ⓛ (CANCEL) ↓ ↙ ← + (ATK)(ATK) AND MASH (ATK))

229,900 damage, 95% meter gain (or 468,100 damage and 9% meter loss with Magnetic Tempest ender in the corner)

Magneto can always follow up after a throw—you just might have to do it a bit differently depending on the position. After a forward ground throw, wavedash forward and slide into launcher with crouching Ⓗ, Ⓢ. After a backward ground throw, you can do the same thing, or simply use Hyper Grav H to pull your competitor over (backward throws, ground or air, keep them trapped longer than forward throws; on the ground, this gives Hyper Grav H time to retrieve them).

After low altitude air throws, you have time to land, dash forward, and slide into launch. If you didn't use up your airdash before the air throw, you can speed this up by airdashing down-forward and whiffing an attack to land faster.

Score an air throw above normal jump height, and you'll need to be quick to catch up to them. Again, if you didn't airdash before the air throw, airdash down-forward immediately while whiffing an attack. On landing, dash forward immediately to slide into launcher. If you already used up the airdash before the air throw, you'll have to use flight (airdashing closer for an air throw is very useful, so this is not unusual). After Magneto recovers from actually throwing them, activate flight. From here, you'll need to airdash two or three times in a row before using air Ⓢ to fall on the challenger and start a combo before they escape their magnetic shackles. To just airdash normally, you'll have to alternate directions (for the most consistency, use → + (ATK)(ATK) (CANCEL) ↘ + (ATK)(ATK), air Ⓢ on nearby challengers, and ↘ + (ATK)(ATK) (CANCEL) ↗ + (ATK)(ATK) (CANCEL) ↘ + (ATK)(ATK), air Ⓢ on faraway adversaries). If you can plink airdash consistently, hitting attack buttons on consecutive frames, you can just plink airdash down-forward back to the ground very quickly, and be ready to fall with air Ⓢ, then land and slide, and so on.

After launching a thrown challenger at midscreen, you can also proceed to the air combo portion of **Combo I**. Against a cornered opponent, you can proceed to either the ROM loop, the Hyper Grav loop (see Advanced Tactics), or a hybrid of the two.

MAGNETO

COMBO USAGE CONT.

IV. **CR. (L), (L), (M), (H), (S) CANCEL→ FORWARD SUPER JUMP, AIR (M), (M), (H) CANCEL→ FORWARD AIRDASH, AIR (H), (S), LAND, WAVEDASH FORWARD + P1 OR P2 WESKER—β OTG, ↓ ↙ ← + (H), (S) CANCEL→ FORWARD SUPER JUMP, AIR (M), (M), (H) CANCEL→ FORWARD AIRDASH, AIR (H), (S), LAND, ← ↓ ↙ + (L) CANCEL→ ↓ ↘ → + (ATK)(ATK) (OR → ↓ ↘ + (ATK)(ATK), MASH (ATK), FORWARD DASH ST. (H), (S) CANCEL→ UPWARD SUPER JUMP, AIR (H), (S))**

555,000 damage, 7% meter gain (self-sufficient for Shockwave ender) OR 898,600 damage, 165% meter loss with Gravity Squeeze ender

Without doing some fancy airdash and flight acrobatics, Magneto doesn't really have a reliable, universal, easy bread and butter combo for beginners or online play. Sure, you can just chain to launcher and then super jump cancel to Magnetic Shockwave, but that's not very meter-efficient. By using an OTG assist, he comes the closest to a worthwhile combo that's also easy (and viable for online play; things like the ROM or Hyper Grav loop simply aren't feasible on the intertubes). This allows him to relaunch for more meter, making the combo self-sufficient like his strongest solo combos. The Fatal Attraction at the end is intended to drag the floored foe forward, so more of Magnetic Shockwave hits. The damage for the combo varies depending on the OTG assist you select; Wesker—β is simply presented as a solid go-to to make any OTG combo work. (Wesker and Magneto also used to be best friends because of the THC glitch; with that gone, they remain close friends because they are really fond of each other's assists, but they do not make the best THC partners anymore. Make them the buns of the proverbial team sandwich with someone else as the meat, and don't think too much about how hard we forced that analogy.)

You can also simply perform Hyper Grav H CANCEL→ Magnetic Tempest directly off the OTG assist hit, which nets around 590,000 damage and results in a 31% meter loss, depending on the assist used. If you happen to have *two* OTG-capable assists along for the ride, you can add another super jump rep to this combo, or replace Shockwave with an OTG assist and Grav to Tempest. Packing two OTG-capable assists isn't the most reasonable strategy for team building or zoning, though.

V. **CR. (L), (L), (M), (H), (S) CANCEL→ FORWARD SUPER JUMP, AIR (H), PAUSE, CANCEL→ DOWN-FORWARD AIRDASH, AIR (H), LAND, DASH, (S) CANCEL→ ↓ ↘ → ↗ + (ATK)(ATK) X-FACTOR ↓ ↘ → + (ATK)(ATK)**

Requires X-Factor and midscreen, 663,800+ damage to point, 1,000,000+ to assist, 148% meter loss

If you realize you've caught both the opposing point character and their assist at midscreen, you can hurt them both quite a bit if you're willing to spend a couple bars while popping X-Factor. During lv.1 X-Factor, this combo deals around a million damage to any assist, so it knocks out most of the cast. The damage on a point character isn't amazing (at around 660,000), so save this for when it can either knock out two characters or a very important assist.

If you catch two characters near a corner, you can pop X-Factor, launch both characters, then just proceed to the repeated super jumping portion of **Combo II**. The so-called ROM is actually much easier to do in X-Factor because of Magneto's increased speed. Even during lv.1 X-Factor, the ROM can reach a million damage on point characters while knocking out any assist; at higher X-Factor levels, no character is going to survive. And rejoice, fans of original Magneto: during lv.2 & 3 X-Factor, Magneto is actually fast enough to do the midscreen ROM again! It's difficult, but possible.

If you catch single opponents near the corner during X-Factor, sometimes you can just repeat (standing (H) CANCEL→ Hyper Grav L, step forward). It's an infinite, but you need to be in at least lv.2 X-Factor for it to work on anyone except Sentinel and in lv.3 X-Factor for small characters. After a few repetitions of this loop to build meter and deal easy damage, cancel a Hyper Grav to Magnetic Tempest to score a knockout. In particular, keep this loop in mind if you end up with Magneto in a last-mutant-leader-standing situation, as lv.3 X-Factor makes this easy against anyone.

ADVANCED TACTICS

SCOOPS

By making a habit out of executing your airdashes, triangle jumps, and empty triangle jumps a certain way, you'll get way more air throws just as a matter of course.

Air throws are possible even 1 frame after leaving the ground, 1 frame before landing, and just as airdashes begin. By using a couple of tricks, you can install two air throw attempts into your empty Magneto triangle jumps, which helps tremendously when advancing on your adversary and trying to crack their shell. Jump forward, then airdash down-forward as soon as possible by inputting ↘ + (H)~(ATK). As Magneto descends, continue holding ↘ and tap (H) again before Magneto lands. Do this as quickly as possible.

This works because by delaying the non-(H) button press in the airdash command by only 1 frame, the game briefly thinks you are going for an air throw by holding a sideways direction plus (H) in midair. The other (ATK) input one frame later then reinterprets that command as an airdash, as a form of leniency. Go into Training Mode and turn on the input display and airdash over and over again, and you'll be surprised how often you're plink dashing already on *accident!* It's really difficult to hit two buttons on identical frames all the time, which is why this leniency is there to begin with.

Perform the command quickly, and input ↓ + (L) for crouching (L) when you land. (Or, land and do → + (H) for a *third* throw attempt!) Magneto should look like he's just empty triangle jumping forward spastically with no attack, before landing and going for a low combo (or throw). It's only natural that a competitor's reaction to overhead/empty jump mix-ups will be to try to get the heck outta dodge, but with this trick, you'll snag them automatically if they try to jump away. If you score an air throw, of course your crouching (L) will never happen, and you'll have time to prepare to follow up post-throw with a combo. If you happen to get your rival into the corner properly, you can proceed to the...

HYPER GRAVITATION CORNER LOOP

You can mix the Hyper Grav loop into your corner air combos, or you can just go for the loop as your general corner bread and butter.

When you combo into a Hyper Gravitation in the corner, you'll have a chance to go for a demanding, but rewarding, modular combo. Between the built-in capture period of Hyper Grav and the hardly-dwindling hitstun of air (H) and standing (H), this loop usually works for at least three reps even after lots of hits. Juggle into Hyper Grav somehow, then *immediately* super jump up-back as soon as Magneto can act after the Grav. Allow Magneto to drift just to the beginning of super jump height, then airdash down-forward with air (H), land and juggle with standing (H) canceled to Hyper Grav L, super jump up-back immediately, and lather, rinse, repeat.

The relatively simple three-hit combo portion into super jump must be performed very rapidly, but you must pause unusually long after super jumping. This causes the opposing character ensnared with Magneto to actually drift up with him, just as he begins to drag the screen to super jump height. If you don't let them drift upward slightly, the combo fails because the foe is too low in altitude for Hyper Grav L to snare him or her.

This loop can be repeated four times *at most* before it ceases to work (the more hits in the combo, the harder it becomes to loop, and in original *MvC3*, it could be looped twice as much), but in the meantime, it provides lots of extra damage and hyper meter for Magneto. Cap off the last Hyper Grav by canceling into Magnetic Tempest or Gravity Squeeze.

If all else fails for you in performing this combo, you're probably not hitting air (H) fast enough after down-forward airdashes. This combo is hard, but it's worthwhile.

Putting your competitor into a Hyper Grav in the corner can be accomplished by:

- Air combo near the corner into down-forward airdash (H), land, standing (H) [CANCEL] Hyper Grav L
- Air combo to flying air (H), cancel with "unflight," juggle with falling air (H), land, standing (H) [CANCEL] Hyper Grav L
- Throw the target into the corner, Hyper Grav (better: throw the foe, then perform an air combo into standing (H) into Hyper Grav L!)
- Ending an air combo with a hard knockdown, calling an OTG assist, then using Hyper Grav

ONCE YOU POP...

While Magneto's combos can be ended with hyper combos, you may also opt to cut combos short on purpose in order to set up situations where you can put your adversary right back into a combo with a throw or reset.

After snaring your challenger with Hyper Grav in a corner combo, for example, you can simply finish the combo with standing (L). Your rival gets forced to air recover right in front of Magneto; if they air recover neutral or backwards, jumping forward to air throw them on reaction is easy. Against big characters, you can air throw them no matter which way they air recover; against smaller foes, you won't be able to cover all your bases without also calling an assist to cover the space behind you in case they air recover forward over Magneto's head.

You can also combo into Hyper Grav, perform standing (L) while calling an assist who can cover a lot of space in front of you, like Dante—α or Rocket Raccoon—γ, then cancel to Repulsion. Your adversary won't go anywhere if they try to air recover forward, though they might expect to... and so they might try something that gets them hit by your assist.

While performing a combo for 400,000 damage isn't as beefy as going for 700,000+, if you can end the smaller combo such that you get a shot at another combo immediately, you can end up dealing much more damage overall. Meanwhile, you're not spending hyper meter on these "unfinished" combos, so there's more for Magneto and your whole team to play with.

COMBO APPENDIX

GENERAL EXECUTION TIPS

Getting better with Magneto combos is, in a way, about getting better at airdashing and moving around in *UMvC3* in general. He is a prototypical "Vs." character.

Practice attacking *immediately* after airdashing; fast enough to normal jump and triangle jump with air (H) and have it hit is a solid indicator. If you can't do that, you won't land the ROM or Hyper Grav loop consistently.

CR. (L), (M), (H), (S) [CANCEL] FORWARD SUPER JUMP, AIR (H), PAUSE, [CANCEL] DOWN-FORWARD AIRDASH, AIR (H), LAND, {FORWARD JUMP, AIR (H) [CANCEL] FORWARD AIRDASH, AIR (M), (H), LAND} REPEAT BRACKETS X3, ST. (H) [CANCEL] ↓↘→ + (H)

Notes	Damage
Simpler corner carry/general purpose combo than **Combo I**. Also a reliable X-Factor combo. Can replace EM Disruptor H ender with ↓↘→ + (ATK)(ATK) midscreen, or ↓↙← + (L) [CANCEL] ↓↙← + (ATK)(ATK) in corners	438,800, 113% meter gain (674,100 with Magnetic Tempest in corner)

CR. (L), (L), (M), (H), (S) [CANCEL] FORWARD SUPER JUMP, AIR (H) [CANCEL] FORWARD AIRDASH, AIR (M), (M) [CANCEL] ↓↙← + (S), AIR (L), (M), (H) [CANCEL] FORWARD AIRDASH, {AIR (H) [CANCEL] FORWARD AIRDASH} REPEAT BRACKETS X5, AIR (S)

Notes	Damage
Corner carry fly combo that works on everyone. Same enders are possible as **Combo I**.	384,800 damage, 105% meter gain (before possible follow-ups with OTG assists or Magnetic Shockwave/Gravity Squeeze

CORNER ONLY: CR. (L), (L), (M), (H), (S) [CANCEL] FORWARD SUPER JUMP, AIR (H) [CANCEL] DOWN-FORWARD AIRDASH, AIR (H), LAND, ST. (H) [CANCEL] ↓↙← + (L), (S) [CANCEL] FORWARD SUPER JUMP, AIR (H) [CANCEL] FORWARD AIRDASH, AIR (H) [CANCEL] ↓↙← + (S), AIR (L), (H) [CANCEL] FORWARD AIRDASH, AIR (H) [CANCEL] FORWARD AIRDASH, AIR (H) [CANCEL] [CANCEL] ↓↙← + (S), FALLING AIR (H), LAND, ST. (H) [CANCEL] ↓↙← + (L) [CANCEL] ↓↙← + (ATK)(ATK) (MASH (ATK))

Notes	Damage
—	~692,100 damage, 15% meter gain

GROUND THROW, DASH, JUMP, AND AIRDASH FORWARD, AIR (M), (H), LAND, CR. (L), (M), (H), (S) [CANCEL] FORWARD SUPER JUMP, AIR (H) [CANCEL] DOWN-FORWARD AIRDASH, AIR (H), LAND, {FORWARD JUMP, AIR (H) [CANCEL] FORWARD AIRDASH, AIR (M), (H), LAND} REPEAT BRACKETS X3, ST. (H) [CANCEL] ↓↙← + (L) [CANCEL] ↓↙← + (ATK)(ATK) (MASH (ATK))

Notes	Damage
—	495,600 damage, 16% meter gain

AFTER MAGNETO COMES IN: CANCEL AUTOHIT WITH IMMEDIATE DOWN-FORWARD AIRDASH, ↓↙← + (L) [CANCEL] ↓↙← + (ATK)(ATK) (MASH (ATK))

Notes	Damage
TAC combo to Magneto's Magnetic Tempest	Varies due to damage scaling

AFTER MAGNETO COMES IN: AIR (M), (M), (H) [CANCEL] ↓↙← + (S), AIR (L), (H) [CANCEL] FORWARD AIRDASH, {AIR (H) [CANCEL] FORWARD AIRDASH} REPEAT BRACKETS X5, AIR (S) (OR ANOTHER AIR EXCHANGE)

Notes	Damage
TAC combo to Magneto using ↑ + (S) or ↓ + (S)	Varies due to damage scaling.

M.O.D.O.K.

"THEY ONCE CALLED ME M.O.D.O.C.—BUT I'D MUCH RATHER BE 'KILLING' THAN 'COMPUTING!'"

Bio

REAL NAME

George Tarleton

OCCUPATION

Leader of A.I.M.,
Would-Be Conqueror,
Terrorist

ABILITIES

He is capable of various types of attacks using psionic abilities, and he also has superhuman calculating ability.

WEAPONS

Various weapons designed for killing outfitted into his hover-chair.

PROFILE

Formerly just a regular human, George was forced to become a living human experiment and was subsequently turned into M.O.D.O.K. (Mental Organism Designed Only for Killing). Calling himself the Scientist Supreme and using his vast intellect and psionic powers, he annihilated all those who were involved in his experiment.

FIRST APPEARANCE

Tales of Suspense #93 (1967)

POWER GRID

6	INTELLIGENCE
1	STRENGTH
1	SPEED
1	STAMINA
6	ENERGY PROJECTION
1	FIGHTING ABILITY

*This is biographical, and does not represent an evaluation of the in-game combat potential of this hero.

Vitality	*950,000*
Chain Combo Archetype	*Marvel Series*

X-Factor Boost	Damage	Speed
Level 1 (3 teammates remaining)	135%	105%
Level 2 (2 teammates remaining)	160%	110%
Level 3 (1 teammate remaining)	185%	115%

Your main goal when using M.O.D.O.K. is to push your opponents into the corner.

Why do you want to push the opposing character into the corner while playing as M.O.D.O.K.?

- **Placing M.O.D.O.K.'s Barrier (← ✣ Ⓗ) in front of a cornered opponent allows for mix-ups that are almost completely safe from retaliation**
- **M.O.D.O.K.'s attacks give him great combo opportunities in the corner, including the chance to land a large number of Analysis Cubes to power him up**

How does one push a competitor into the corner as M.O.D.O.K.?

- **Utilize moves to knock your rival off their feet, such as crouching Ⓗ or → ✣ Ⓗ**
- **Rely on low altitude fast airdashes, which give M.O.D.O.K. great opportunities to apply pressure**
- **Use assists and M.O.D.O.K.'s space-controlling projectiles to push opponents back**

Your secondary goal with M.O.D.O.K. is to control screen space and prevent your target from pressuring him into a corner.

Why do you want to prevent M.O.D.O.K. from being put in the corner?

- **M.O.D.O.K.'s slow movement speed and startup on most of his moves make it very difficult to maneuver when he's on the defensive**

How do you prevent M.O.D.O.K. from getting in the corner?

- **M.O.D.O.K.'s various projectiles can make any advancement unsafe for an adversary**
- **Use assists, such as Dante—α, to make competitors second-guess their approach toward M.O.D.O.K.**

Tuning Since Original MVC3

M.O.D.O.K. has received a few minor upgrades in *Ultimate Marvel vs. Capcom 3*, the most significant of which is the reduced recovery time on Analysis Cube. This projectile is the key to unlocking M.O.D.O.K.'s damage potential, and the reduced recovery time makes it easier to link after a successful Analysis Cube. Other changes include minor frame tweaks to his standing Ⓛ and air Ⓗ attacks, and the ability to mash his Killer Illumination hyper for added damage.

- **Air basic attacks can now be canceled into airdashes**
- **Active frames on standing Ⓛ reduced by half**
- **Air Ⓗ gains one frame of startup, but loses one frame of recovery**
- **Flight startup reduced by two frames**
- **Analysis Cube has five fewer recovery frames**
- **Killer Illumination can be mashed for extra damage**

Attack Set

Standing Basic Attacks

Screen	Command	Hits	Damage	Meter Gain	Startup	Active	Recovery	Advantage on Hit	Advantage if Guarded	Notes
1	Standing L	1	45,000	360	7	6	11	-1	-1	—
2	Standing M	5	67,100	800	10	9	17	+3	+3	Inflicts chip damage, fires 5 projectiles with 3 low priority durability points each
3	Standing H	1	80,000	640	16	10	20	+1	-4	Knocks down

Crouching Basic Attacks

Screen	Command	Hits	Damage	Meter Gain	Startup	Active	Recovery	Advantage on Hit	Advantage if Guarded	Notes
1	Crouching L	1	45,000	360	5	6	10	0	0	—
2	Crouching M	1	60,000	480	10	—	25	0	0	OTG-capable, projectile has 3 low priority durability points, the puddle created upon landing hits low, projectile is active for 60 frames
3	Crouching H	1	80,000	640	15	10	21	+3	-5	Low attack, jump cancelable

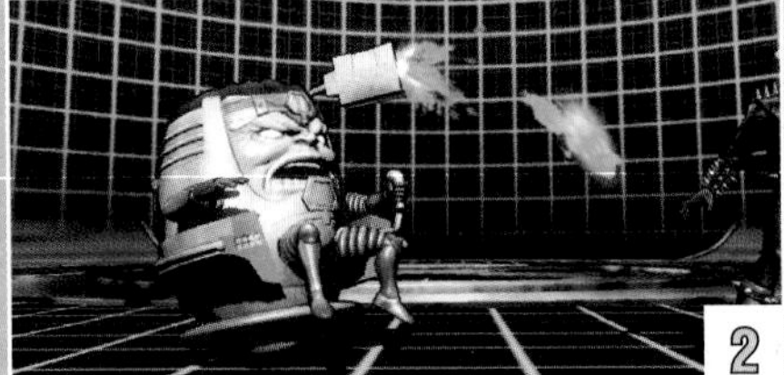
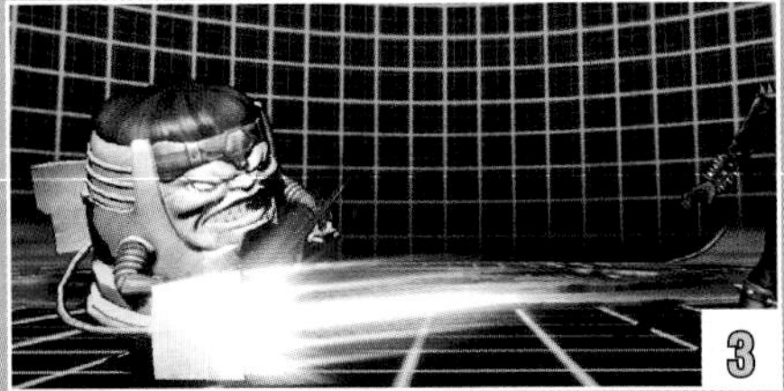

Ground Special Attack—Launcher

Screen	Command	Hits	Damage	Meter Gain	Startup	Active	Recovery	Advantage on Hit	Advantage if Guarded	Notes
1	S (while standing or crouching)	1	80,000	640	10	12	22	—	-8	Launcher, not special- or hyper combo-cancelable

Air Basic Attacks

Screen	Command	Hits	Damage	Meter Gain	Startup	Active	Recovery	Advantage on Hit	Advantage if Guarded	Notes
1	Air L	2~14	43,700-177,000	400	6	Until grounded	1	+11	+11	Overhead attack
2	Air M	1	70,000	560	10	10	16	-5	-5	Overhead attack
3	Air H	1	80,000	640	16	10	20	-8	-8	Overhead attack

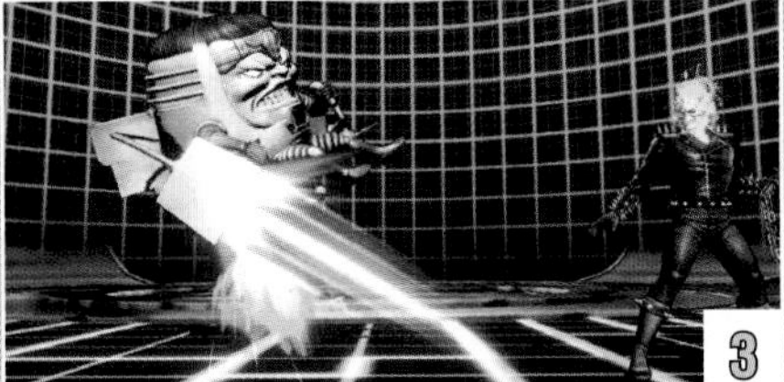

Air Special Attacks—Flying Screen and Air Exchange

Air Ⓢ causes a hard knockdown when used in a launcher combo (this is sometimes called flying screen). When used outside of a launcher combo, air Ⓢ behaves mostly like another basic attack. Air exchange attacks, performed by inputting a direction plus Ⓢ, are only possible during a launcher combo. Exchange hits initiate team aerial combos by tagging in the next available character to continue the air combo.

Screen	Command	Hits	Damage	Meter Gain	Startup	Active	Recovery	Advantage on Hit	Advantage if Guarded	Notes
1	Air Ⓢ	1	90,000	720	13	8	20	—	+18	Causes hard knockdown if used in launcher combo, causes ground bounce when performed at a low height
2	Air ⇧ + Ⓢ (during launcher combo)	1	60,000	480	15	7	Until grounded	—	—	Tags in next available ally while lofting opponent upward
3	Air ⇨ or ⇦ + Ⓢ (during launcher combo)	1	50,000	400	15	8	Until grounded	—	—	Tags in next available ally while causing wall bounce, erases 1 hyper meter bar from foe
4	Air ⇩ + Ⓢ (during launcher combo)	1	60,000	480	15	8	Until grounded	—	—	Tags in next available ally while causing ground bounce, generates 1 hyper meter bar

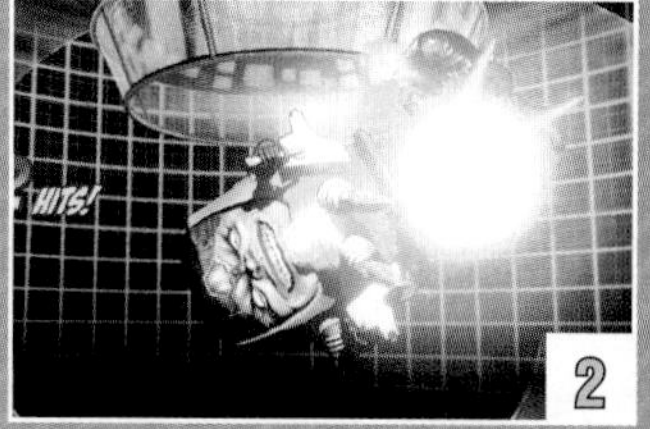

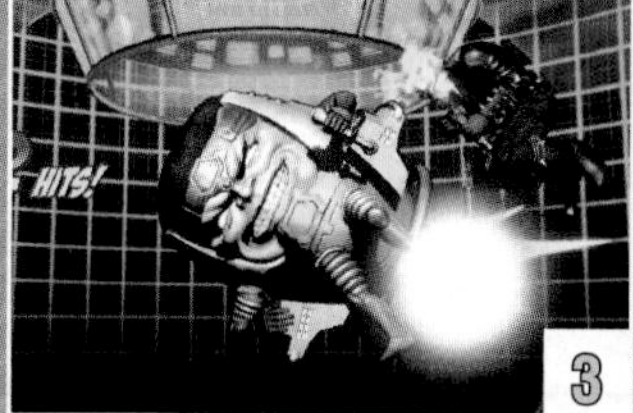

Command Attacks

Command attacks resemble basic attacks but have different chaining and canceling properties. It's usually possible to chain *into* a command attack from basic attacks, but most command attacks cannot be chained from or canceled themselves.

Screen	Name	Command	Hits	Damage	Meter Gain	Startup	Active	Recovery	Advantage on Hit	Advantage if Guarded	Notes
1	Force Beam	⇨ + Ⓗ	1	80,000	640	18	10	13	—	+3	Wall bounce, jump- cancelable
2	Barrier	⇦ + Ⓗ	—	—	—	30	—	15	—	—	Creates a shield that negates most attacks that are not hyper combos, projectile stays active for 122 frames
3	Big Barrier	(With Level of Understanding) ⇦ + Ⓢ	—	—	—	30	—	15	—	—	Creates a shield that negates most attacks that are not hyper combos, projectile stays active for 180 frames
4	Anti-Air Force Beam	⇖ + Ⓗ	1	80,000	640	18	10	13	+18	+3	Jump-cancelable

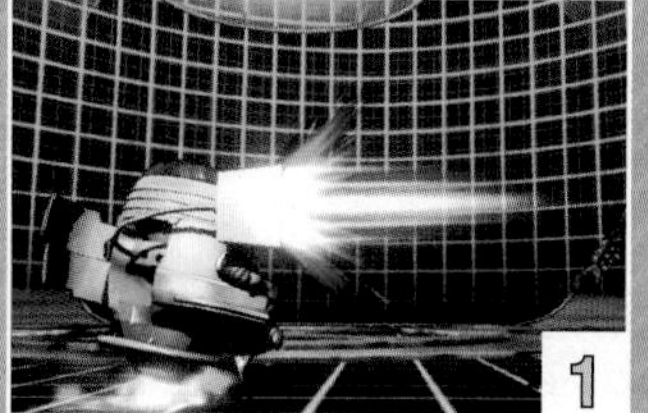

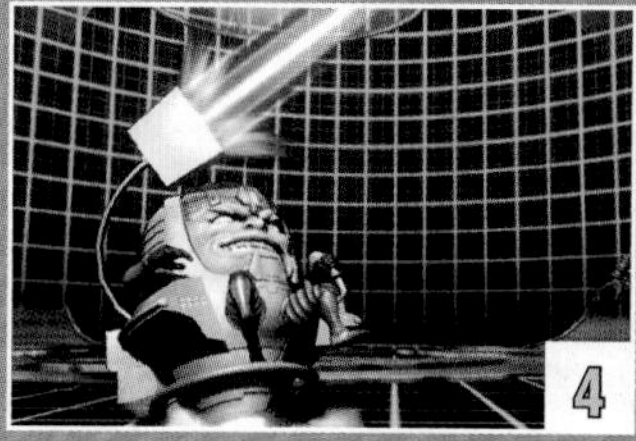

Throws

Throws are for snagging passive or blocking opponents. Since throws are active so quickly, you can also use them to preemptively toss opposing characters out of their offense. Combos are usually possible after throws, one way or another.

Screen	Command	Hits	Damage	Meter Gain	Startup	Active	Notes
1	⇨ + Ⓗ (ground)	2	80,000	800	1	1	Hard knockdown
	⇦ + Ⓗ (ground)	2	80,000	800	1	1	Hard knockdown
2	⇨ + Ⓗ (air)	1	80,000	800	1	1	Hard knockdown
	⇦ + Ⓗ (air)	1	80,000	800	1	1	Hard knockdown

M.O.D.O.K.

As a Partner—Crossover Assists

Screen	Type	P1+P2 Crossover Combination Hyper Combo	Description	Hits	Damage	Meter Gain	Startup	Active	Recovery (this crossover assist)	Recovery (other partner)	Notes
1	M.O.D.O.K.—α	Hyper Psionic Blaster	← + H	—	—	—	54	—	107	77	Creates a shield that negates most attacks that are not hyper combos, shield lasts 122 frames
2	M.O.D.O.K.—β	Hyper Psionic Blaster	Balloon Bomb M	1	80,000	640	64	—	117	87	Projectile lasts 182 frames, does not interact with other projectiles
3	M.O.D.O.K.—γ	Hyper Psionic Blaster	Psionic Blast M	4	103,000	960	44	20	108	78	Beam durability: 4 frames x 3 low priority durability points

1

2

3

All of M.O.D.O.K.'s assists are decidedly average, with no glaring benefits or detriments in comparison to the rest of the cast.

M.O.D.O.K.—α deploys a shield in front of your point character that can absorb a majority of attacks. If you're facing a zoning character throwing a stream of projectiles or if you're stuck in the corner, this assist can give you some much-needed breathing room as you plan your next attack. You can also use it offensively, allowing your own projectile characters to safely attack from a distance or lock down an opponent in the corner. The Barrier disappears if M.O.D.O.K. is hit during the startup frames of the assist, so try to cover his entry onto the field when calling him in.

M.O.D.O.K.—β releases a Balloon Bomb that floats to the center of the screen and remains active for 182 frames or until it hits an adversary. The assist version of Balloon Bomb is special: it ignores projectiles and even hyper combo beams! While not particularly useful for extending combos, the Balloon Bomb makes the center of the screen unsafe for your competitor and gives you more control over the arena.

M.O.D.O.K.—γ unleashes a Psionic Blast M at your foe. The most universally useful of M.O.D.O.K.'s assists, this beam travels the length of the screen, has a relatively quick startup time, and eats through most normal projectiles with its durability. Use the assist to cover the bottom area of the screen while your point character safely moves in from the air, or utilize it to pick up rivals after an OTG hit.

Snap Back

Screen	Command	Hits	Damage	Meter Gain	Startup	Active	Recovery	Advantage on Hit	Advantage if Guarded
1 	↓↘→ + P1 or P2	1	50,000	500 - (-1 hyper meter bar)	2	4	27	—	-5

Notes

On hit, snap back forces the opposing point character to be replaced by an assist. Opposing assist calls or tag outs are also locked out for 4 seconds

1

Special Moves

Screen	Name	Command	Hits	Damage	Meter Gain	Startup	Active	Recovery	Advantage on Hit	Advantage if Guarded	Notes
1	Battering Ram	S + ATK	1	90,000	720	13	10	23	-7	-7	Airborne from frame 1, can be performed in any direction
2	Psionic Blast L (in air OK)	↓↘→ + L	3	81,200	720	12	20	14	—	-4	Knocks down, beam durability: 3 frames x 3 of low priority durability points
2	Psionic Blast M (in air OK)	↓↘→ + M	4	103,000	960	20	20	16	—	-4	Knocks down, beam durability: 4 frames x 3 low priority durability points
2	Psionic Blast H (in air OK)	↓↘→ + H	5	122,600	1200	28	20	18	—	-4	Knocks down, fires diagonally downward in air, beam durability: 5 frames x 3 low priority durability points
3	Psionic High Blast	(With Level of Understanding) ↓↘→ + S	5	163,600	2000	28	20	18	+17	-9	Beam durability: 5 frames x 5 low priority durability points, staggers
4	Analysis Cube L (in air OK)	↓↙← + ATK	1	50,000	400	10	—	25	0	0	Charges Level of Understanding on hit, projectile has 1 low priority durability point, projectile stays active for 60 frames
4	Analysis Cube M (in air OK)	↓↙← + ATK	1	50,000	400	10	—	25	0	0	Charges Level of Understanding on hit, projectile has 1 low priority durability point, projectile stays active for 60 frames
4	Analysis Cube H (in air OK)	↓↙← + ATK	1	50,000	400	15	—	20	0	0	Charges Level of Understanding on hit, projectile has 1 low priority durability point, projectile stays active for 60 frames
5	Balloon Bomb L	→↓↘ + L	1	80,000	640	30	—	25	—	+1	Knocks down, projectile has 1 medium priority durability point, projectile stays active for 180 frames
5	Balloon Bomb M	→↓↘ + M	1	80,000	640	40	—	25	—	+1	Knocks down, projectile has 1 medium priority durability point, projectile stays active for 180 frames

Special Moves continued

Screen	Name	Command	Hits	Damage	Meter Gain	Startup	Active	Recovery	Advantage on Hit	Advantage if Guarded	Notes
5	Balloon Bomb H	⇨⇩⇙ + (H)	1	80,000	640	50	—	25	—	+1	Knocks down, projectile has 1 medium priority durability point, projectile stays active for 180 frames
	Air Balloon Bomb L	(in air) ⇨⇩⇙ + (L)	1	80,000	640	30	—	25	—	—	Knocks down, projectile has 1 medium priority durability point, projectile stays active for 180 frames
	Air Balloon Bomb M	(in air) ⇨⇩⇙ + (M)	1	80,000	640	40	—	25	—	—	Knocks down, projectile has 1 medium priority durability point, projectile stays active for 180 frames
	Air Balloon Bomb H	(in air) ⇨⇩⇙ + (H)	1	80,000	640	50	—	25	—	—	Knocks down, projectile has 1 medium priority durability point, projectile stays active for 180 frames
6	Jamming Bomb	(With Level of Understanding) ⇨⇩⇙ + (S)	1	80,000	800	50	—	25	—	+1	Reverses opponent's controls, homes in on target, projectile has 1 medium priority durability point, projectile stays active for 300 frames
7	Flight	⇩⇙⇦ + (S)	—	—	—	8	—	—	—	—	Lasts 300 frames

1

Battering Ram: M.O.D.O.K. charges forward with a head attack. You can also determine the direction by pressing the corresponding direction with the input. Outside of combos, you can employ it to move M.O.D.O.K. around the screen quickly. You may perform up to three Battering Rams during a jump or flight to keep M.O.D.O.K. in the air. It removes one attack repetition from Hyper Battering Ram if combined together into a combo.

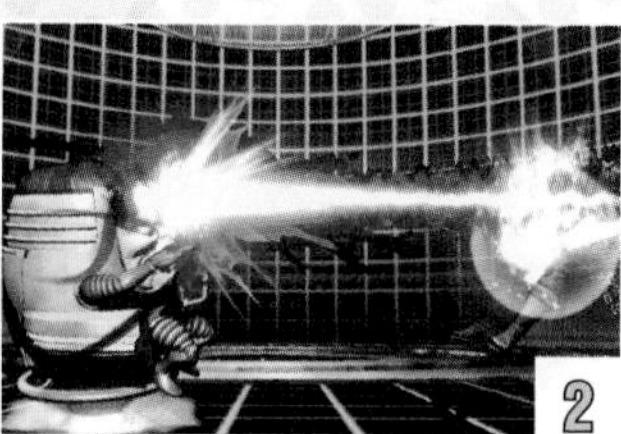
2

3

Psionic Blast and Psionic High Blast: This beam attack is great for controlling ground movement and countering an opponent's low priority projectiles. The (L) version has the fastest startup and chews through many low priority shots like Ryu's Hadoken or Taskmaster's arrows. For shots with higher durability, such as Arthur's Ax Toss, Psionic Blast M is your go-to attack. In the air, Psionic Blast H fires at a downward angle, enabling M.O.D.O.K. to hit grounded competitors from the safety of the skies.

You can perform Psionic High Blast after hitting a foe with an Analysis Cube. It is very similar to Psionic Blast H, except it cannot be performed in the air, it deals more damage, and it staggers the target. This stagger allows M.O.D.O.K. to follow up with a hyper combo attack or airdash in to begin a more damaging combo. All versions of Psionic Blast can be canceled into Hyper Psionic Blaster, but keep in mind that you cannot verify if the beam hits or not before doing so.

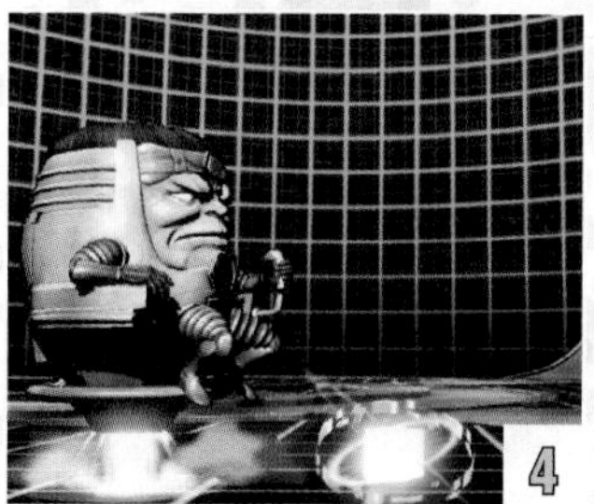
4

Analysis Cube: M.O.D.O.K. summons a small projectile that hovers in place for 60 frames. The button pressed determines the area where the cube appears: (L) deploys a cube at M.O.D.O.K.'s feet, (M) places a cube in the center of the screen at around jump height, and (H) places a cube at M.O.D.O.K.'s eye level on the opposite end of the screen. In the air, (L) places a cube immediately in front of M.O.D.O.K. below his feet, (M) places a cube at his eye level directly in front of him, and (H) places a cube above his head. The recovery time on this move has been reduced in *Ultimate Marvel vs. Capcom 3*, giving M.O.D.O.K. the ability to keep two cubes active on screen at once for a brief period of time.

The most basic use for Analysis Cube is to control screen space, while its secondary function is to power up M.O.D.O.K. Scoring a hit drains information from the opponent and gives M.O.D.O.K. one Level of Understanding (LOU). Up to nine LOUs can be stored, giving M.O.D.O.K. access to the Psionic High Blast, Jamming Bomb, and Big Barrier moves (each uses up one charge when performed), along with powering up his Hyper Psionic Blaster. With a full nine charges, Hyper Psionic Blaster can hit for 441,100 damage and leave a foe in a hard knockdown state! These benefits make landing Analysis Cube the foundation for most of M.O.D.O.K.'s gameplan.

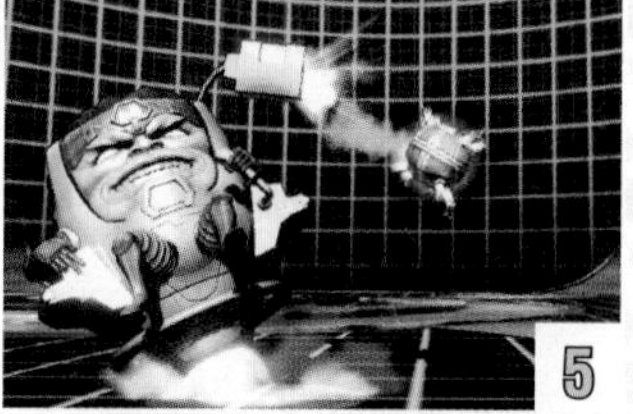
5

6

Balloon Bomb and Jamming Bomb: This attack fires a slow-moving bomb that stays active for 180 frames. Jamming Bomb L fires a bomb at M.O.D.O.K.'s feet that floats to stop right above his head. Jamming Bomb M launches a bomb above his head that floats down diagonally to almost the opposite corner of the screen. Jamming Bomb H homes in on the target for its entire duration. In air, Balloon Bomb L travels straight forward instead of floating upward, while the M and H versions behave the same. All bombs have 1 medium priority durability point, meaning it can stand up to most basic projectiles without exploding. Its long startup times mean that you can't haphazardly release bombs, so be sure to cover their deployment with an Analysis Cube or crouching (M).

Jamming Bomb requires one Level of Understanding to deploy, and once fired, it homes in on your rival and stays active for a whopping 300 frames. A successful hit places the foe in a special state that reverses their control scheme for nearly four seconds. This can be very difficult for an opponent to compensate for, making it a valuable method to cripple their defenses for a brief period of time. Jamming Bomb is a risky move: it cannot be performed in the air, and its large startup time means you need a great assist, such as Dante—α, to safely cover its deployment.

7

Flight: M.O.D.O.K. is unique among the flying characters of the cast. You can initiate flight with him by inputting ⇩⇙⇦ + (S) or by pressing ⇖, ⇧, or ⇗. The major difference is that with the standard flight input, you can cancel basic attacks into flight or initiate flight mode after a super jump. Performing an airdash or Battering Ram cancels flight mode, but M.O.D.O.K. can reenter flight mode one time before touching the ground if you input the flight command again. At 300 frames, M.O.D.O.K. has the longest flight duration in the game, enabling you to perform an unlimited number of aerial special moves during its duration.

Hyper Combos

Screen	Name	Command	Hits	Damage	Startup	Active	Recovery	Advantage on Hit	Advantage if Guarded	Notes
1	Hyper Psionic Blast (in air OK)	⇩⇘⇨ + ATK ATK	22~100	129,100~ 441,100	10+1	120	36	—	-30	Each charge of Level of Understanding up to 9 increases the number of hits and amount of damage Hyper Psionic Blaster deals, uses all existing charges of Psionic power, beam durability: 22 frames x 5 high priority durability points, hard knockdown
2	Hyper Battering Ram (in air OK)	⇩⇙⇦ + ATK ATK	3~15	72,700~ 305,000	4+4	11	24	—	-5	Pressing ATK repeatedly with a direction allows more hits and control of flight path
3	Killer Illumination	⇨⇩⇘ + ATK ATK	30~67	300,000~ 374,000	18+1	10	40	—	—	Frames 1-24 invincible, throw, hard knockdown, can be mashed for additional damage

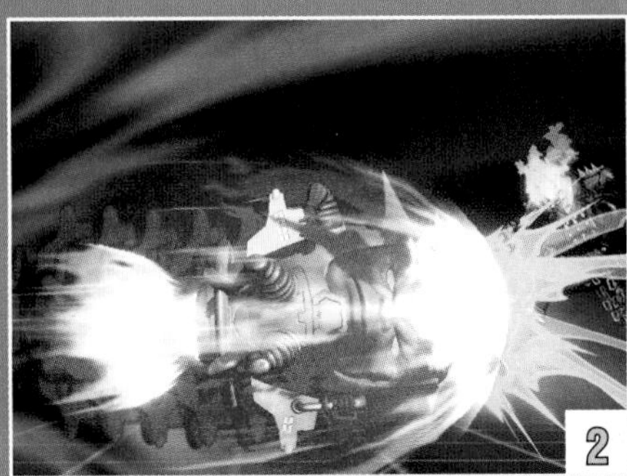

Hyper Psionic Blast: HSB is a fairly standard beam super unless it is powered up with Levels of Understanding obtained from Analysis Cubes. It's very useful in ranged combos or to punish opponents firing projectiles of their own. When powered up, Hyper Psionic Blast gains a considerable damage boost, but unless you've acquired seven to nine LOUs, Hyper Battering Ram is probably a better option for ending combos.

Hyper Battering Ram: M.O.D.O.K.'s second hyper combo is primarily his go-to combo ender. After activation, press ATK and any directional button to move M.O.D.O.K. in that direction and continue the attack up to five times. In nearly any situation where you can OTG an opponent with crouching M, following up with Hyper Battering Ram is an excellent damage option. However, remember that you lose one repetition of Hyper Battering Ram if the standard Battering Ram is used in the same combo.

Killer Illumination: A throw hyper combo with a very slow startup period, this is difficult to use for aggressive throw set-ups since an opposing character can simply jump away after activation. Instead, use its large invulnerability window to counter close range ground attacks, or THC into Killer Illumination from a hyper combo that leaves the opposing character in a hard knockdown state and use crouching M to continue to the combo. If it lands, you can OTG your foe after he or she recovers to add additional damage and possibly link into Hyper Battering Ram or Hyper Psionic Blast. In Ultimate Marvel vs. Capcom 3, Killer Illumination can be mashed to add additional damage.

Battle Plan

M.O.D.O.K.'s ⇨ + H attack is great for pushing opponents toward the corner.

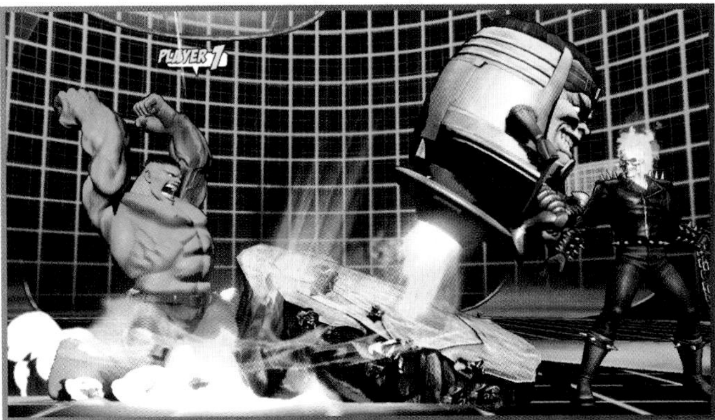

The right assist, such as Hulk—α, can help speed up the push to the corner.

With his wide body, unique flight mode, and a wide range of projectiles focused on space control, M.O.D.O.K. definitely ranks as one of the most unorthodox characters on the Ultimate Marvel vs. Capcom 3 roster. M.O.D.O.K.'s moves can be very slow, giving him a difficult time against faster characters. However, M.O.D.O.K. excels when he's in control of the momentum of a match, and he can decimate challengers in the corner. To fully realize M.O.D.O.K.'s potential, you need a good understanding of his projectiles and utilizing assists to make up for his weaknesses.

As discussed earlier, your goal with M.O.D.O.K. is to get his adversary into the corner. Accomplishing this goal can seem rather daunting the first time you take control of the floating chair because of M.O.D.O.K.'s slow rate of movement, so the first key is knowing how to get M.O.D.O.K. around the arena.

Unlike the rest of the cast, M.O.D.O.K. does not have a regular jump. Pushing ⇧ puts M.O.D.O.K. into a very low flight state. The short startup time of this method of flying allows M.O.D.O.K. to airdash almost instantaneously at low altitudes. Press ⇧ and immediately press any two ATK buttons to shoot M.O.D.O.K. across the screen. As he approaches his rival, press M or S. If the hit connects, you can follow up crouching H or ⇨ + H and guarantee that the opposing character ends up in the corner. If the hit is blocked, you should have plenty of frame advantage to begin another attack or call an assist to continue pushing your target back. Either way, you're closer to your goal.

Battle Plan continued

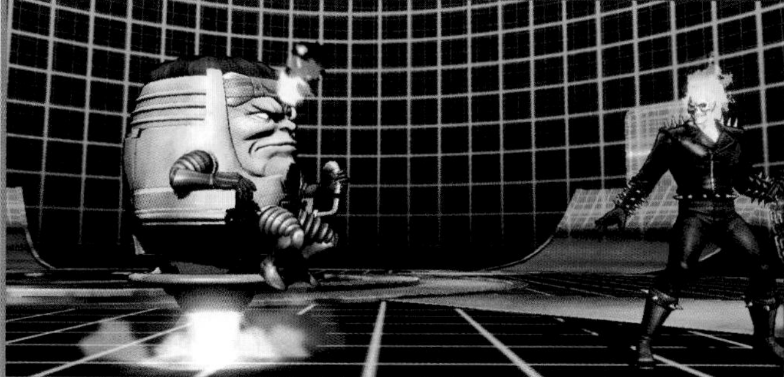
1 Level of Understanding

4 Levels of Understanding

Max (9) Levels of Understanding. Pay attention to M.O.D.O.K.'s headband to help keep track of your current LOU charges.

LOU is the key to unlocking M.O.D.O.K.'s more useful moves.

Assists that knock an opponent back or push them on block are also very helpful to getting your foe where you want them. Any beam assist or Hulk—α is great at this. Place an Analysis Cube M or Balloon Bomb M/H as you call the assist to prevent your competitor from jumping, and then have M.O.D.O.K. dash in as the hit connects to follow up with another attack.

Now that you have your opponent in the corner, your first focus should be to keep them there. With the cover of an assist or Balloon Bomb in the air, throw up a Barrier (⇦ + Ⓗ), or preferably a Big Barrier if you have LOU charges, to prevent your adversary from attacking M.O.D.O.K. This forces your challenger to jump if they want to escape; in this case, just have M.O.D.O.K. jump alongside them and hit them with a forward throw or Killer Illumination. From there, use crouching Ⓜ and follow up with ⇩ ⇙ ⇦ + Ⓛ CANCEL ⇩ ⇙ ⇦ + ATK ATK to deal a good chunk of damage and gain an extra Level of Understanding.

Once you've conditioned the other player to stop jumping, the real fun begins. Any attacks your foe does (besides hyper combos) will get eaten up by the Barrier, giving you free reign to do whatever mix-up you want: casually stroll forward and throw them (into a combo), use ⇗ + Ⓢ or ⇗ + Ⓗ for instant overheads (into a combo), or mix it up with a low-hitting crouching Ⓗ (into a BIG combo). You may want to consider omitting Hyper Battering Ram from your corner combos: other enders, like a simple crouching Ⓜ canceled into Barrier, allow you to place the enemy right in another mix-up!

When it comes to comboing opponents in the corner, the Analysis Cube plays a vital role. Off a single crouching Ⓗ, M.O.D.O.K. can easily gain 4-5 Levels of Understanding in a single combo. In the air, getting multiple cubes off in a single combo can be a trickier task. Since you can only have M.O.D.O.K. perform three aerial special moves in the air off a super jump, you need to have him enter flight mode to keep a combo going. There's a great trick to keep this going. Input the flight command, then ⇩ ⇙ ⇦ + Ⓢ, and plink Ⓛ afterward. The game accepts the single ⇩ ⇙ ⇦ motion, putting M.O.D.O.K. into flight mode and releasing an Analysis Cube immediately after! Aside from extending air combos, you can also utilize this maneuver to safely cover a quick flight getaway.

M.O.D.O.K. gets into a lot of trouble whenever an adversary can mount a serious offensive push. His slow movement and startup on a majority of his moves make it very difficult to react to faster characters breathing down his throat. Things can get hairy when M.O.D.O.K. is on the defensive, but that doesn't mean he doesn't have a few tricks up his sleeve to make it out alive.

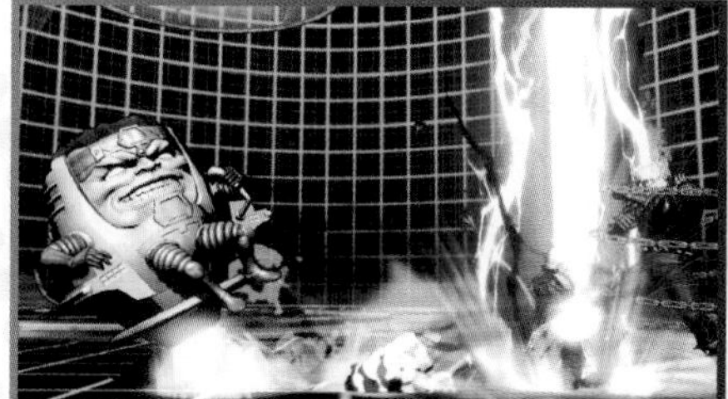
M.O.D.O.K. often needs a little help from assists to get out of a sticky situation. Dante—α is a great tool for him.

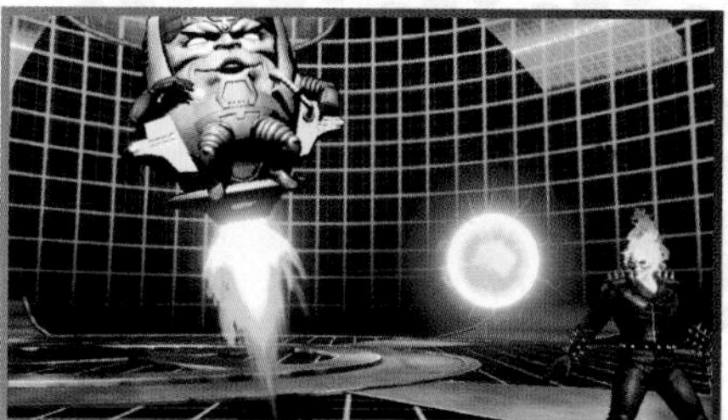
M.O.D.O.K.'s variety of projectiles can keep him safe from approaching opponents.

Having an assist that can keep the opposing character tied up for a long period of time is always useful. Dante—α is one of the best assists to pair with M.O.D.O.K. It creates a pillar that extends to the top of the screen, giving M.O.D.O.K. protection from rivals trying to get in anywhere from super jump height to the ground. If it connects, you can prepare an Analysis Cube to catch the flying target, tag them with a Jamming Bomb to alter the opponent's controls, or dash in to follow up with another attack. When guarded, you can easily reposition M.O.D.O.K.

Don't be afraid to have him take to the skies, either. M.O.D.O.K. has the longest flight time in the game, and this should be used to your advantage. Toward the top of the screen, competitors are forced to super jump to reach M.O.D.O.K., or burn through meter in the hopes of hitting him with a hyper combo. While your opponent is deciding what to do, you can call assists, fire Balloon Bomb H to home in on the target, or fire Psionic Blast H to rain beams down on grounded foes.

On the ground, advancing guard is M.O.D.O.K.'s best friend. He needs plenty of space to pull out his attacks, so use advancing guard to push a relentless enemy away from him. Once some space has been established, drop an acid puddle on the ground with crouching Ⓜ and immediately fire an Analysis Cube M to make the entire space between M.O.D.O.K. and his opponent a no-man's land. With this combination, your challenger can't dash or regular jump toward M.O.D.O.K., forcing them to think of another way in. Meanwhile, you have every option available to start M.O.D.O.K.'s assault anew.

If M.O.D.O.K. is stuck in the corner, you can have him deploy a Barrier to give him some added breathing room. With the Barrier up, M.O.D.O.K. can safely fire Psionic Blasts or deploy a Balloon Bomb to keep his opponent away as he waits for an assist to become available or waits for an opening to appear. He won't be safe forever, though. An adversary with fast projectiles or maneuverability can quickly close the gap and force M.O.D.O.K. back into a turtle situation. If M.O.D.O.K.'s rival butts up next to the Barrier, though, you can have M.O.D.O.K. snag the foe with a backward throw and turn the tides of battle!

COMBO USAGE

I. CR. Ⓗ CANCEL▶ FORWARD JUMP, FORWARD AIRDASH, AIR Ⓜ, LAND, Ⓢ CANCEL▶ FORWARD SUPER JUMP, AIR Ⓜ, Ⓗ, Ⓢ, LAND, FORWARD DASH, CR. Ⓜ CANCEL▶ ↓↙← + Ⓢ, FORWARD AIRDASH, AIR Ⓢ, LAND, ↓↙← + Ⓛ, Ⓢ CANCEL▶ FORWARD SUPER JUMP, AIR Ⓜ, Ⓜ, Ⓢ, LAND, CR. Ⓜ CANCEL▶ ↓↘→ + Ⓛ CANCEL▶ ↓↙← + ATK ATK, AFTER THE FIRST 3 HITS, ↗ + Ⓗ, ↗ + Ⓗ, ↑ + Ⓗ, ↑ + Ⓗ

687,300 damage, 4% meter loss

This bread and butter combo for M.O.D.O.K. takes advantage of his ability to airdash almost instantly in order to keep a combo going from midscreen. You'll need to practice airdashing quickly if you hope to keep the pressure on your opponent! However, you can forgo the airdashes entirely when performing this combo against a cornered competitor.

Your finger dexterity will be put to the test whenever you attempt to OTG a rival with crouching Ⓜ. You must cancel the attack after the slime shot is released, not when it connects. The following air attack or special move hits because you're able to begin moving before the slime puddle makes contact.

II. FORWARD JUMP, AIR Ⓢ, LAND ↓↙← + Ⓛ, CR. Ⓗ, → + Ⓗ CANCEL▶ ↓↙← + Ⓗ, WAVEDASH FORWARD TWICE, Ⓢ CANCEL▶ FORWARD SUPER JUMP, AIR Ⓜ, Ⓗ ,Ⓢ, LAND, FORWARD DASH, CR. Ⓜ CANCEL▶ ↓↙← + Ⓛ CANCEL▶ ↓↙← + ATK ATK, AFTER THE FIRST 3 HITS, ↗ + Ⓗ, ↗ + Ⓗ, ↑ + Ⓗ, ↑ + Ⓗ

639,000 damage, 38% meter loss

Air Ⓢ is a key component of M.O.D.O.K.'s pressure game. When performed at the moment M.O.D.O.K. leaves the ground for a jump, air Ⓢ acts as a very fast overhead attack. Once it connects, you must input ↓↙← + Ⓛ the second he lands to release the Analysis Cube in time to catch your opponent.

The trickiest timing comes when wavedashing toward the target after the Analysis Cube H attack. You must be very deliberate with your inputs in order to have M.O.D.O.K. reach his rival and connect with Ⓢ, or else it is fairly easy to drop the combo.

III. FRONT OR BACK THROW OR FRONT OR BACK AIR THROW, CR. Ⓜ CANCEL▶ ↓↙← + Ⓢ, FORWARD AIRDASH, AIR Ⓜ, LAND, Ⓢ CANCEL▶ FORWARD SUPER JUMP, AIR Ⓜ, Ⓗ, Ⓢ, LAND, FORWARD DASH, CR. Ⓜ, Ⓢ CANCEL▶ FORWARD SUPER JUMP, AIR Ⓜ, Ⓜ, Ⓢ, LAND, FORWARD DASH, CR. Ⓜ CANCEL▶ ↓↙← + Ⓛ CANCEL▶ ↓↙← + ATK ATK, AFTER THE FIRST 3 HITS, ↗ + Ⓗ, ↗ + Ⓗ, ↑ + Ⓗ, ↑ + Ⓗ

488,400 damage, 18% meter loss

M.O.D.O.K.'s ground and air throws give him plenty of time to OTG an opponent with crouching Ⓜ. You can input crouching Ⓜ CANCEL▶ ↓↙← + Ⓛ CANCEL▶ ↓↙← + ATK ATK for some quick damage, but if you're feeling bold, you should give this combo a try instead.

IV. CR. Ⓗ CANCEL▶ FORWARD JUMP, FORWARD AIRDASH, AIR Ⓢ, LAND, →↓↘ + Ⓛ X-FACTOR →↓↘ + Ⓛ, FORWARD DASH, Ⓢ CANCEL▶ FORWARD SUPER JUMP, AIR Ⓜ, Ⓜ, Ⓗ, Ⓢ, LAND, FORWARD DASH, CR. Ⓜ CANCEL▶ ↓↙← + ATK ATK, AFTER THE FIRST 3 HITS, ↗ + Ⓗ, ↗ + Ⓗ, ↑ + Ⓗ, ↑ + Ⓗ

870,100~1,111,100 damage, 14% meter loss or 11% meter gain

This combo utilizes Balloon Bombs and X-Factor to really amp up M.O.D.O.K.'s damage output. Just as with Combo I, you can forgo the airdashes when performing this combo against a cornered foe.

"I'M A MENTAL ORGANISM DESIGNED ONLY FOR KILLING... AND THAT'S WHAT I DO."

ADVANCED TACTICS

TAC CORNER CUBE COMBO CRAZINESS

Team aerial combos reset hitstun until M.O.D.O.K. touches the ground, allowing you to link up to nine cubes in one combo!

With M.O.D.O.K. in the secondary position, you can set up a very nasty combo in the corner, allowing him to acquire a full nine LOUs at once. Get the opponent into the corner, launch them into the air, and perform a ⇩ + Ⓢ TAC. This puts M.O.D.O.K. at maximum height with a freshly reset hitstun counter, allowing you to then perform the following combo:

Air Ⓗ CANCEL ⇩⇙⇦ + Ⓛ, air Ⓗ CANCEL ⇩⇙⇦ + Ⓛ, air Ⓜ CANCEL ⇩⇙⇦ + Ⓢ, air Ⓜ, Ⓜ, Ⓗ CANCEL ⇩⇙⇦ + Ⓛ, air Ⓜ CANCEL ⇩⇙⇦ + Ⓛ, air Ⓜ CANCEL ⇩⇙⇦ + Ⓛ, air Ⓜ CANCEL ⇩⇙⇦ + Ⓛ, air Ⓜ CANCEL ⇩⇙⇦ + Ⓛ, air Ⓜ CANCEL ⇩⇙⇦ + Ⓛ, air Ⓢ, land, cr. Ⓜ OTG CANCEL ⇩⇘⇨ + Ⓛ CANCEL ⇩⇘⇨ + ATK ATK

The timing is very strict on each repetition of this particular cube loop, although the trickiest part comes when you must activate flight. You must "plink" the Ⓜ input following the Ⓢ of the flight command, causing M.O.D.O.K. to deploy a cube immediately after flight is activated.

If you find yourself struggling with too many repetitions, cut straight to the air Ⓢ into crouching Ⓜ and follow up with ⇩⇙⇦ + Ⓛ CANCEL ⇩⇙⇦ + ATK ATK, and save your acquired Levels of Understanding for later in the battle.

COMBO APPENDIX

GENERAL EXECUTION TIPS

- Outside of combos, you can cover M.O.D.O.K.'s command flight with an Analysis Cube by plinking the appropriate ATK button immediately after inputting ↓ ↙ ← + Ⓢ
- In any case where you're OTG-ing an opponent with crouching Ⓜ, cancel into the next attack the moment the slime ball is released
- Practice airdashing immediately after jumping. This technique is crucial to M.O.D.O.K.'s combos and overall gameplan

→ ↓ ↘ + ATK ATK (MASH ATK), CR. Ⓜ CANCEL ↓ ↙ ← + Ⓢ, FORWARD AIRDASH, AIR Ⓢ, LAND, → ↓ ↘ + Ⓛ, Ⓢ CANCEL FORWARD SUPER JUMP, AIR Ⓜ, Ⓗ, Ⓢ, LAND, FORWARD DASH, CR. Ⓜ CANCEL ATK + Ⓢ CANCEL ↓ ↙ ← + ATK ATK, AFTER THE FIRST 3 HITS, ↗ + Ⓗ, ↑ + Ⓗ, ↖ + Ⓗ

Notes	Damage
This acts as a reversal against ground attacks	598,500 damage, 144% meter loss

AS MODOK COMES IN: AIR Ⓗ, Ⓢ, LAND, CR. Ⓜ CANCEL ↓ ↘ → + Ⓛ ↓ ↘ → + ATK ATK (MASH ATK)

Notes	Damage
⇧ + Ⓢ or ⇨ + Ⓢ or ⇩ + Ⓢ TAC to Modok	Varies based on damage scaling

AS MODOK COMES IN: AIR Ⓛ (3 HITS), Ⓗ CANCEL ↓ ↙ ← + Ⓛ, FALL A BIT, Ⓗ CANCEL ↓ ↙ ← + Ⓛ, {Ⓜ CANCEL ↓ ↙ ← + Ⓢ, Ⓜ} X 7, Ⓢ, LAND, CR. Ⓜ CANCEL ↓ ↘ → + Ⓛ CANCEL ↓ ↘ → + ATK ATK

Notes	Damage
Requires corner, ⇧ + Ⓢ TAC to Modok, instantly leads to a level 9 Hyper Psionic Blast	Varies based on damage scaling

AS MODOK COMES IN: AIR Ⓗ, ↓ ↙ ← + Ⓛ, AIR Ⓗ, ↓ ↙ ← + Ⓛ, AIR Ⓜ, ↓ ↙ ← + Ⓢ, Ⓜ, AIR Ⓜ, AIR Ⓗ, ↓ ↙ ← + Ⓛ, AIR Ⓜ, ↓ ↙ ← + Ⓛ, AIR Ⓜ, ↓ ↙ ← + Ⓛ, AIR Ⓜ, ↓ ↙ ← + Ⓛ, AIR Ⓜ, ↓ ↙ ← + Ⓛ, AIR Ⓜ, ↓ ↙ ← + Ⓛ, AIR Ⓢ, CR. Ⓜ, ↓ ↘ → + Ⓛ CANCEL ↓ ↘ → + ATK ATK

Notes	Damage
Requires corner, ⇩ + Ⓢ TAC to Modok, instantly leads to a level 9 Hyper Psionic Blast	Varies based on damage scaling

CR. Ⓗ CANCEL ↓ ↙ ← + Ⓛ, CR. Ⓗ CANCEL ↓ ↙ ← + Ⓛ, CR. Ⓗ CANCEL ↓ ↙ ← + Ⓛ, CR. Ⓗ, → + Ⓗ CANCEL ↓ ↙ ← + Ⓛ, ST. Ⓗ, → + Ⓗ CANCEL ↓ ↙ ← + Ⓗ CANCEL ↓ ↘ → + ATK ATK (MASH ATK), CR. Ⓜ CANCEL ↓ ↙ ← + ATK ATK, AFTER THE FIRST 3 HITS, ↗ + Ⓗ, ↑ + Ⓗ, ↖ + Ⓗ

Notes	Damage
Requires corner	813,300 damage, 131% meter loss

AIR Ⓢ, LAND, FORWARD DASH, ↓ ↙ ← + Ⓛ, CR. Ⓗ CANCEL ↓ ↙ ← + Ⓛ, CR. Ⓗ CANCEL ↓ ↙ ← + Ⓛ, CR. Ⓗ, → + Ⓗ CANCEL ↓ ↙ ← + Ⓗ CANCEL ↓ ↘ → + ATK ATK (MASH ATK), CR. Ⓜ CANCEL ↓ ↙ ← + ATK ATK, AFTER THE FIRST 3 HITS, ↗ + Ⓗ, ↑ + Ⓗ, ↖ + Ⓗ

Notes	Damage
Requires corner	823,300 damage, 130% meter loss

PHOENIX

"I'M SCARED... THERE'S A VOICE INSIDE THAT'S PUSHING ME TO KILL, TO DESTROY EVERYTHING...!"

Bio

REAL NAME
Jean Grey-Summers

OCCUPATION
Adventurer

ABILITIES
Telekinetic powers, as well as telepathy so strong she can control others' thoughts or force them into unconsciousness. Also serves as an avatar for the cosmic Phoenix Force.

WEAPONS
None

PROFILE
While returning from space, Jean was exposed to lethal levels of solar radiation. Her life was saved by the cosmic entity known as the Phoenix Force, though its power has at times consumed her to the point of evil as Dark Phoenix. Jean is married to Cyclops, leader of the X-Men.

FIRST APPEARANCE
The X-Men #1 (1963)

POWER GRID

3	INTELLIGENCE
2	STRENGTH
7	SPEED
7	STAMINA
7	ENERGY PROJECTION
4	FIGHTING ABILITY

*This is biographical, and does not represent an evaluation of the in-game combat potential of this hero.

ALTERNATE COSTUMES

1

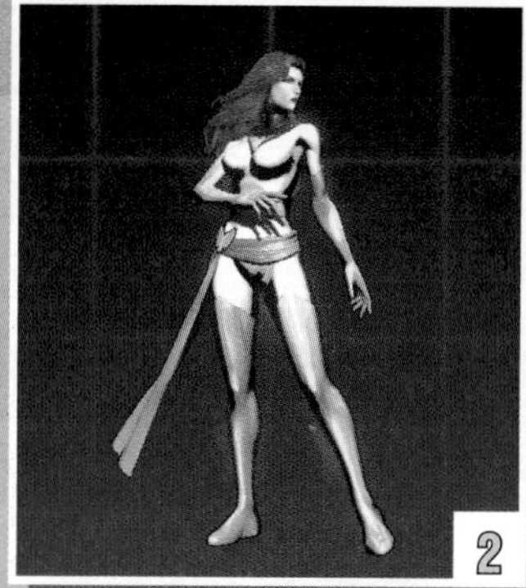
2

3

4

5

6

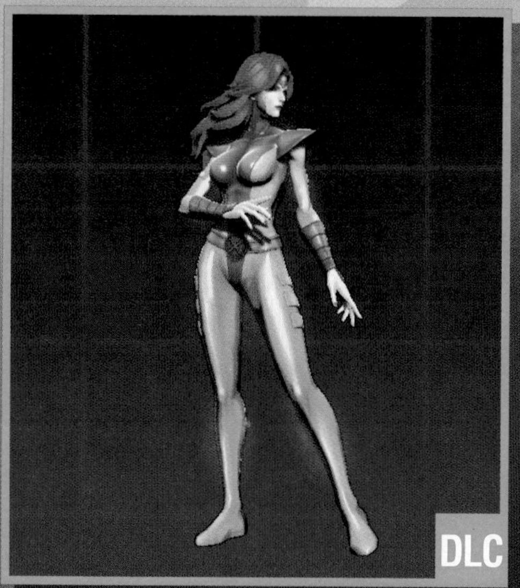
DLC

Overview

Vitality	375,000
Chain Combo Archetype	Hunter Series

X-Factor Boost	Damage	Speed
Level 1 (3 teammates remaining)	120%/135%	110%/115%
Level 2 (2 teammates remaining)	135%/170%	120%/130%
Level 3 (1 teammate remaining)	150%/200%	130%/145%

Your goal with Phoenix is to survive until your hyper meter reaches five bars. Why is this important?

- **Phoenix has the lowest vitality in the game by far, coming in at 375,000. She can be K.O.'d by every character in the game with a single combo**

However, once Dark Phoenix Rising is activated, Phoenix becomes arguably the most powerful character in the game, able to take out entire teams by herself. How is this goal achieved?

- **Staying out of the fight completely by never tagging in Phoenix or calling her as a crossover assist**
- **Letting her teammates build hyper meter through long combos, meter conservation, and team aerial combos**
- **Playing risk-free when Phoenix is in and getting her back to the sidelines as soon as possible**

Once you have Dark Phoenix Rising at the ready, your goal with Phoenix is to inflict as much damage as possible before getting K.O.'d.

Once Dark Phoenix Rising has been activated, your goal is to deal as much damage as possible while avoiding taking any yourself. Why is this the goal?

- **Dark Phoenix's destructive combos are enough to defeat most characters in one shot**
- **Dark Phoenix's health is gradually converted to red health, forcing you to take the initiative in ending the fight as soon as possible**

TUNING SINCE ORIGINAL MVC3

Phoenix was altered primarily to keep her from being able to throw air TK Shot H after air TK Shot H as a dominant, nigh-uncounterable strategy against many characters. As a result, Phoenix is only allowed one TK Shot per jump or super jump, and TK Shot H disappears if Phoenix is hit. Additionally, Phoenix's vitality has been lowered from 420,000 to 375,000.

The best way to deal with an opposing team featuring Phoenix is to force her in with a snap back, then mix her up as she falls in. If a Phoenix player blocks incorrectly, almost any combo will take her out. In original *MvC3*, Phoenix could negate the entry mix-ups of many characters by blocking the first thing they do against her entry, then airdashing upward and throwing TK Shot H one or twice before teleporting to safety. Phoenix players can no longer be so frivolous with relying on TK Shot H to keep them out of danger, and super jump height TK Shot H followed by a teleport is no longer possible.

So, it is basically just a little less built-in that Phoenix and Dark Phoenix will destroy so many characters by design, and the abuse of one move. Dark Phoenix also doesn't have it quite so easy, since she can no longer be made to get to super jump height to terrorize the other team with her beefed-up TK Shots with almost no danger to herself, unless the opponent happens to be named Magneto (who could Shockwave or Gravity Squeeze on reaction against that tactic).

Also, now that sideways TACs STEAL your meter, Phoenix is indirectly more susceptible to an opponent even when she's both offscreen and not in danger of being snapped in. Phoenix is a great character even without Dark Phoenix Rising, but never making a single mistake is asking a lot in a *Vs.* game. Phoenix was great, but Dark Phoenix was the goal of every single serious Phoenix player except one or two, and getting there is harder now.

Still, if either Phoenix or Dark Phoenix gets rolling on offense and takes out a character, she is as unassailable as ever dropping Traps and mixing up the new adversary falling in, and if you *do* make it to lv.3 X-Factor Dark Phoenix, you're still piloting the scariest, most high-risk, high-reward fighting game character ever conceived. She still can't control it!

- Vitality reduced to 375k from 420k
- Air TK Shot can only be used once per airborne period, unless flight is employed
- Air TK Shot does not recover until grounded, except if Phoenix is in flight mode
- Traps and Shots disappear if Phoenix is hit

Attack Set

Standing BasicAttacks

Screen	Command	Hits	Damage	Meter Gain	Startup	Active	Recovery	Advantage on Hit	Advantage if Guarded	Notes
1, 2	Standing L	1/2	30,000/+24,000	240/575	5/4	3/4	11	0/+4	-1/+1	Dark Phoenix fires 1 feather straight forward
3, 4	Standing M	1/4	46,000/+24,000 x 3	368/1219	8	3	16	0/-1	-1/-3	Dark Phoenix fires 3 feathers in a 90- degree arc
5, 6	Standing H	1/6	67,000/+24,000 x 5	536/1921	11/10	10	10	+4/+8	+3/+5	Dark Phoenix fires 5 feathers in a 180- degree arc

1

2

3

4

5

6

Crouching Basic Attacks

Screen	Command	Hits	Damage	Meter Gain	Startup	Active	Recovery	Advantage on Hit	Advantage if Guarded	Notes
1, 2	Crouching L	1/2	33,000/ +24,000	264/610	4/3	3	11	0/+4	-1/+1	Low attack/Dark Phoenix fires 1 feather straight forward
3, 4	Crouching M	1/4	50,000/ +24,000x3	400/1266	9	8	19	-8/-9	-9/-11	Low attack/Dark Phoenix fires 3 feathers in a 90- degree arc, at a 45-degree angle
5, 6	Crouching H	1/6	60,000/ +24,000x5	480/1841	12	4	23	—	-4/-11	Low attack, knocks down opponent/Dark Phoenix fires 5 feathers in a 90- degree arc, at a 45-degree angle

1

2

3

4

5

6

Ground Special Attack—Launcher

Screen	Command	Hits	Damage	Meter Gain	Startup	Active	Recovery	Advantage on Hit	Advantage if Guarded	Notes
1, 2	S (while standing or crouching)	1	80,000	640/921	10	5	21	—	-3/0	Launcher, not special- or hyper combo-cancelable

1

2

Air Basic Attacks

Screen	Command	Hits	Damage	Meter Gain	Startup	Active	Recovery	Advantage on Hit	Advantage if Guarded	Notes
1, 2	Air L	1/2	33,000/ +24,000	264/610	5	3	18	+16	+11/+14	Overhead attack/Dark Phoenix fires 1 feather straight forward
3, 4	Air M	1/4	47,000/ +24,000 x 3	376/1231	9/8	3	20	+17/+21	+16/+18	Overhead attack/Dark Phoenix fires 3 feathers in a 90- degree arc
5, 6	Air H	1/4	70,000/ +24,000 x 3	560/1496	8	11	17	+16/+14	+15/+12	Overhead attack/Dark Phoenix fires 5 feathers in a 180- degree arc, at a 90- degree angle

1

2

3

4

5

6

Air Special Attacks—Flying Screen and Air Exchange

Air Ⓢ causes a hard knockdown when used in a launcher combo (this is sometimes called flying screen). When used outside of a launcher combo, air Ⓢ behaves mostly like another basic attack. Air exchange attacks, performed by inputting a direction plus Ⓢ, are only possible during a launcher combo. Exchange hits initiate team aerial combos by tagging in the next available character to continue the air combo.

Screen	Command	Hits	Damage	Meter Gain	Startup	Active	Recovery	Advantage on Hit	Advantage if Guarded	Notes
1, 2	Air Ⓢ	1/6	70,000/ +24,000 x 5	560/ 1956	10	12	24	+16	+15	Causes hard knockdown if used in launcher combo/ Dark Phoenix fires 5 feathers in a 90- degree arc, at a -45-degree angle
3, 4	Air ⇧ + Ⓢ (during launcher combo)	1	60,000	480	10	7	19	—	—	Tags in next available ally while lofting opponent upward
5, 6	Air ⇨ or ⇦ + Ⓢ (during launcher combo)	1	50,000	400	9	3	20	—	—	Tags in next available ally while causing wall bounce, erases 1 hyper meter from opposing character
7, 8	Air ⇩ + Ⓢ (during launcher combo)	1	50,000	400 + 10,000	12	4	Until grounded	—	—	Tags in next available ally while causing ground bounce, generates 1 hyper meter

1

2

3

4

5

6

7

8

Command Attacks

Command attacks resemble basic attacks but have different chaining and canceling properties. It's usually possible to chain *into* a command attack from basic attacks, but most command attacks cannot be chained from or canceled themselves.

Screen	Name	Command	Hits	Damage	Meter Gain	Startup	Active	Recovery	Advantage on Hit	Advantage if Guarded	Notes
1, 2	Prominence Heel	⇨ + Ⓜ	1/4	50,000/ +24,000 x 3	400/ 1266	22	3	21	0/-6	-1/-8	Overhead attack/Dark Phoenix fires 3 feathers in a 60-degree arc, at a -30- degree angle
3, 4	Flare Sword	⇨ + Ⓗ	1/6	73,000/ +24,000 x 5	584/ 1990	15/14	5	24	-5/-1	-6/-4	Dark Phoenix fires 5 feathers in a 180-degree arc
3, 4	Air Flare Sword	(In air) ⇨ + Ⓗ	1/6	73,000/ +24,000 x 5	584/ 1990	15/14	5	9	+10	+9	Dark Phoenix fires 5 feathers in a 180-degree arc
5, 6	Burn Out Beak	(In air) ⇩ + Ⓗ	1/6	70,000/ +24,000 x 5	560/ 1956	15	Until grounded	7	+10	+9	Ground bounces airborne target, cannot be performed at very low altitudes/Dark Phoenix fires 5 feathers in a 90-degree arc, at a -90-degree angle
7	Phoenix Feathers	ATK and air Ⓢ as Dark Phoenix	1 each	24,000 each	230 each	—	—	—	—	—	Dark Phoenix fires feathers with any basic attack and air Ⓢ, each projectile has 5 durability points and is active 45 frames

1

2

3

4

5

6

7

Throws

Throws are for snagging passive or blocking opponents. Since throws are active so quickly, you can also use them to preemptively toss opposing characters out of their offense. Combos are usually possible after throws, one way or another.

Screen	Command	Hits	Damage	Meter Gain	Startup	Active	Notes
1	⇨ + Ⓗ (ground)	1	80,000/96,000	800/1152	1	1	Hard knockdown
1	⇦ + Ⓗ (ground)	1	80,000/96,000	800/1152	1	1	Hard knockdown
2	⇨ + Ⓗ (air)	1	80,000/96,000	800/1152	1	1	Hard knockdown
2	⇦ Ⓗ (air)	1	80,000/96,000	800/1152	1	1	Hard knockdown

1

2

As a Partner—Crossover Assists

Screen	Type	P1+P2 Crossover Combination Hyper Combo	Description	Hits	Damage	Meter Gain	Startup	Active	Recovery (this crossover assist)	Recovery (other partner)	Notes
1, 2	Phoenix—α	Phoenix Rage	TK Shot M	4/8	108,300/ 140,900	1024/ 1932	44	—	127	97	Projectile has 5 durability points, creates explosion hitbox upon destruction, explosion has 3 durability points and lasts for 15 frames or until single hit is used up /Dark Phoenix fires two TK Shots
3	Phoenix—β	Phoenix Rage	TK Overdrive L	4	103,000/ 123,700	960/1 380	32	14	111	81	Nullifies projectiles during active frames
4, 5	Phoenix—γ	Phoenix Rage	TK Trap H	1/3	90,000/ 162,500	720/ 1728	44	30	112	82	Trap has 5 durability points, projectile has 5 durability points/Dark Phoenix projectile is much larger, wall bounces competitor

1

2

3

4

5

When playing as Phoenix, the safest bet is to never call her as a crossover assist outside of combos. Because characters take extra damage when called as a crossover assist, it is very possible for Phoenix to be K.O.'d from one hyper combo or a few strong attacks.

TK Shot is a standard projectile crossover assist that you can use to extend combos or give long range support. TK Overdrive is also great for extending combos, but this can be extremely dangerous to call otherwise as she darts forward toward opposing characters. TK Trap has few uses, as it fires at an upward angle.

Snap Back

Screen	Command	Hits	Damage	Meter Gain	Startup	Active	Recovery	Advantage on Hit	Advantage if Guarded	Notes
1, 2	↓↙← + P1 or P2	1	50,000/ 60,000	500/ 720- (-1 hyper meter bar)	2	8	12	—	+6	On hit, snap back forces the opposing point character to be replaced by an assist. Opposing assist calls or tag outs are also locked out for 4 seconds

1

2

Special Moves

Screen	Name	Command	Hits	Damage	Meter Gain	Startup	Active	Recovery	Advantage on Hit	Advantage if Guarded	Notes
1, 2	TK Shot L (in air OK)	↓↘→ + L	2/4	80,300/ 128,800	696/ 1472	10	—	35 (until grounded in air, then 1 frame recovery)	-11/-7	-13/-9	Projectile has 5 low priority durability points, air version is OTG-capable, creates explosion hitbox upon destruction, explosion has 3 low priority durability points and lasts for 15 frames or until single hit is used up, projectile disappears if Phoenix is hit/Dark Phoenix fires 2 TK Shots
1, 2	TK Shot M (in air OK)	↓↘→ + M	4/8	108,300/ 141,300	1024/ 1932	20	—	35 (until grounded in air, then 1 frame recovery)	-7/-3	-8/-5	Projectile has 5 low priority durability points, air version is OTG-capable, creates explosion hitbox upon destruction, explosion has 3 low priority durability points and lasts for 15 frames or until single hit is used up, projectile disappears if Phoenix is hit /Dark Phoenix fires 2 TK Shots
1, 2	TK Shot H (in air OK)	↓↘→ + H	6/12	123,000/ 173,400	1280/ 2824	30	—	35 (until grounded in air, then 1 frame recovery)	-3/+1	-4/0	Projectile has 5 low priority durability points, homes in on opponent, explodes automatically after 120 frames, explosion has 3 durability points and lasts for 15 frames or until single hit is used up, projectile disappears if Phoenix is hit /Dark Phoenix fires 2 TK Shots

Special Moves continued

Screen	Name	Command	Hits	Damage	Meter Gain	Startup	Active	Recovery	Advantage on Hit	Advantage if Guarded	Notes
3, 4	TK Trap L	↓↙← + Ⓛ	1/3	90,000/ 162,500	720/ 1728	20	—	20	+4	+3/+7	Trap extends a hitbox vertically to ceiling, trap fires projectile upward at foe that crosses hitbox, trap disappears automatically after 300 frames or if another TK Trap L is created, each projectile has 5 low priority durability points, trap disappears if Phoenix is hit/Dark Phoenix trap hitbox and projectile are larger, projectile has 3 frames x 5 low priority durability points, knocks down rival
5, 6	TK Trap M	↓↙← + Ⓜ	1/3	90,000/ 162,500	720/ 1728	20	—	20	—	—	Trap extends a hitbox horizontally to screen edges, trap fires projectile forward at attacker that crosses hitbox, trap disappears automatically after 300 frames or if another TK Trap M is created, each projectile has 5 low priority durability points, trap disappears if Phoenix is hit /Dark Phoenix trap hitbox and projectile are larger, projectile has 3 frames x 5 low priority durability points, wall bounces adversary
7, 8	TK Trap H	↓↙← + Ⓗ	1/3	90,000/ 162,500	720/ 1728	20	—	20	—	—	Creates trap with no offensive hitbox, trap automatically fires projectile diagonally up-forward after 30 frames, projectile has 5 low priority durability points, trap disappears if Phoenix is hit /Dark Phoenix projectile is larger, has 3 frames x 5 low priority durability points, wall bounces competitor
9	TK Overdrive L	→↓↘ + Ⓛ	4	103,000/ 123,700	960/ 1380	8	14	19	—	-1/+2	Nullifies projectiles during active frames, knocks down
10	TK Overdrive M	→↓↘ + Ⓜ	4	103,000/ 123,700	960/ 1380	8	14	14	+17	+4/+7	Nullifies projectile during active frames, knocks down
9	TK Overdrive H	→↓↘ + Ⓗ	6	154,400/ 185,200	1584/ 2280	12	20	34	—	-21/-18	Nullifies projectile during active frames, knocks down
11	Teleportation	←↓↙ + ATK	—	—	—	10	—	20	—	—	—
12	Flight (in air OK)	↓↙← + Ⓢ	—	—	—	19	—	0	—	—	Puts Phoenix in flight mode, flight lasts for 102 frames, causes TK Shot to recover as if grounded

1

2

TK Shot: Phoenix throws a standard low-priority fireball that explodes on impact or when nullified. This explosion behaves as another projectile, lasting for another 15 frames, and has 3 points of low-priority durability.

TK Shot L releases the fastest, but has a velocity slower than that of TK Shot M. It is also the weakest of the three versions in terms of damage. However, TK Shot L is the projectile of choice when engaged in a long range firefight because of its quick startup time. The speed in which it travels makes it perfect for cross-ups, as well; a TK Shot L fired at long range travels slowly enough so Phoenix recovers before the projectile makes it to the opponent, creating a Teleport M cross-up opportunity.

When it comes to combos, the aerial version of TK Shot L should be your main projectile. It is OTG-capable and can be used to extend combos after a hard knockdown. It is also the most reliable version of TK Shot to use in air combos.

TK Shot M has twice the startup of TK Shot L but travels considerably faster and deals more damage, as well. If opposing players become used to the speed of TK Shot L, you can use TK Shot M to catch them off-guard. Though TK Shot M is OTG-capable, it can only be followed by Phoenix Rage because of its increased startup and speed, whereas there's time for a relaunch if TK Shot L is used to OTG instead.

TK Shot H has the slowest startup of the three, but it slowly homes in on opponents until 120 frames have passed (after which it explodes automatically) or Phoenix is hit. Because of its homing feature and increased damage, TK Shot H can be a headache for your competitors to deal with. You can also use it from afar to set up cross-ups with Teleport M or as cover fire for an approach.

As Dark Phoenix, all versions of TK Shot fire two projectiles simultaneously. Each shot is weaker individually, but they ultimately inflict more damage when both connect. As a result, TK Shot becomes much more difficult to avoid and does increased hitstun and blockstun.

3

4

TK Trap L: Phoenix sets a small trap on the floor, creating an invisible vertical tripwire. When an adversary crosses over the trap, a fiery projectile fires from the ground up to the top of the screen, hitting anything in its path. TK Trap L serves as a great defensive tool to stop any forward advances, since your opponent's only ways of dealing with the trap are to set it off or avoid it completely. Set down TK Trap L every chance you get to keep Phoenix as safe from aggressors as possible. Keep in mind that you can only set one TK Trap L at a time. If a second TK Trap L is set, the first trap disappears. Traps will also disappear if Phoenix is hit.

TK Trap L features a decent amount of hitstun; if you anticipate your rival getting hit by the trap, you can follow with another attack. You can use it in combos, as well.

As Dark Phoenix, TK Trap L deals considerably more damage and hitstun. → + Ⓗ canceled into TK Trap L can be looped several times, and TK Trap L can even be performed over and over in lv.3 X-Factor as a 100% damage combo!

5

6

TK Trap M: A horizontal version of TK Trap; Phoenix sets an aerial trap slightly above her head. Even though the invisible tripwire for the trap spans the screen's entire horizontal length, the trap can only fire forward from where it was originally placed. This makes it possible for the trap to be triggered from behind, causing it to whiff. Also note that the trap will disappear if Phoenix is hit.

In situations where you are in a position to set down a TK Trap defensively, setting down TK Trap L should have priority over TK Trap M. TK Trap M is generally easier to avoid than TK Trap L.

As Dark Phoenix, TK Trap M gains increased speed and range along with a wall bounce effect, making it one of her best attacks. After a connected TK Trap M, Dark Phoenix can teleport to the victim's position for a destructive combo. TK Trap M is an integral part of Dark Phoenix's arsenal, as is illustrated further ahead.

7

8

TK Trap H: TK Trap H behaves differently than the L and M versions because it is not triggered by the opposing character. Instead, TK Trap H is released automatically after 30 frames, firing up-forward at an angle. This attack has limited uses compared to TK Trap L and M, and it should be considered your last priority when setting traps in a defensive manner.

As Dark Phoenix, TK Trap H is given increased speed and damage like the other versions, as well as a wall bounce effect like TK Trap M. While it gains some use when used offensively or in setups, the other two versions of TK Trap have more utility overall.

TK Overdrive L/H: Phoenix launches herself at her target as a fiery torpedo, nullifying opposing projectiles. TK Overdrive is best used in long combos as a tactic to build meter for Dark Phoenix Rising. Even though it devours projectiles, it is extremely unsafe if blocked, leaving Phoenix open for an easy K.O. As Dark Phoenix, TK Overdrive gains no additional properties aside from extra damage. Use a crossover assist right before this attack to make it safe.

9

TK Overdrive M: TK Overdrive M is distinct from other versions of Overdrive in that it sends Phoenix upward at an angle, leaving her in a jumping state. Upon recovery, Phoenix is free to attack or perform special moves. You can also use it to extend combos.

10

11

Teleport: Phoenix can teleport near her adversaries in one of three positions: in front with Teleport L, behind with Teleport M, and directly above with Teleport H. Phoenix's Teleportation is extremely fast and can even be performed in the air. Both Teleport L and M are great ways to punish attacks or hyper combos that recover slowly. Ranged attackers such as Arthur or Hawkeye can no longer throw projectiles from fullscreen with confidence, since you can use Phoenix to punish them with Teleport M. Certain hyper combos can be avoided and punished with Teleport M, as well, such as Amaterasu's Okami Shuffle. Teleport M is also great for cross-ups when used in tandem with TK Traps, TK Shots, and crossover assists. Performing Teleport M right before a TK Shot L connects becomes unguardable on reaction; competitors must anticipate the cross-up and guard the other direction before the teleport. Mixing this up with Teleport L makes for a 50/50 guessing game!

Teleport H is different from L and M since it always causes Phoenix to reappear directly above her rival, regardless of their altitude. This makes it great for punishing foes who are raining projectiles from the sky. In some situations, Teleport H is better for punishing your foe than Teleport M. When an opponent is cornered Teleport M does not cross up anymore, so Teleport H into air ⇩ + Ⓗ becomes a more viable option for overcoming ranged attacks.

Flight: Phoenix's flight had undergone a slight change since original *MvC3*: she can no longer super jump, fly, then teleport, and have a chance of remaining in a flying state afterward. Flight is even more important to her now though, because Phoenix can no longer use air TK Shot multiple times in midair without flight. Use air TK Shot once and she drops like a stone, unable to guard. This also means she can no longer be made to jump, TK Shot, then teleport for a ready-made mix-up. You can produce more or less the same effect, however, by activating flight, firing a TK Shot, and then teleporting.

Flight is also useful to activate after air recovery, since you can airdash repeatedly while flying. This is useful for other characters to escape after they've been hit out of the air, though it's a little less important for Phoenix since if she was hit out of the air, it's unlikely she survived!

Hyper Combos

Screen	Name	Command	Hits	Damage	Startup	Active	Recovery	Advantage on Hit	Advantage if Guarded	Notes
1	Phoenix Rage (in air OK)	⇩⇘⇨ + ATK ATK	10	320,700/384,800	8+1	—	81	—	-38/-35	Frames 1-14 invincible, wall bounces opponent, beam durability: 10 frames x 5 high priority durability points
2	Healing Field	⇩⇙⇦ + ATK ATK	—	—	4+3	—	18	—	—	Creates Healing Field around Phoenix, Healing Field lasts for 600 frames, if foe is within Healing Field Phoenix regenerates red vitality, activating Healing Field while one is already active destroys the old Field and replaces it with new Field
3	Dark Phoenix Rising (Level 5 hyper combo)	When vitality is reduced to zero	1	0	30+0	4	0	—	+21	Activates automatically upon Phoenix's K.O. if 5 hyper meter bars stocked, frames 1-34 invincible, knocks down, restores Phoenix's health to 100%, permanently changes Phoenix into Dark Phoenix, Dark Phoenix on point gradually has vitality become red vitality

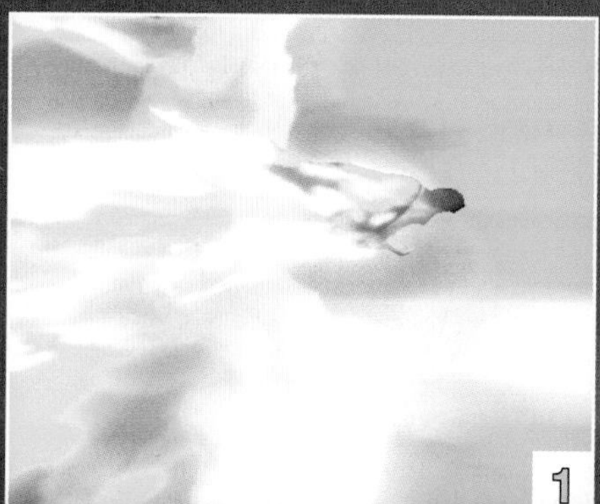

Phoenix Rage: Phoenix fires a screen-clearing projectile that causes huge damage and a wall bounce. It also sports a fairly long window of invulnerability during its startup, making it useful as a last-ditch effort to save Phoenix from an unavoidable hyper combo. Despite these perks, your hyper meter is best saved for Dark Phoenix Rising. Generally, only use Phoenix Rage if it will deal enough damage to score you a K.O. on your adversary.

Phoenix Rage is extremely unsafe if guarded. Be ready to THC or activate X-Factor if the opponent guards this hyper combo!

Healing Field: Phoenix envelops herself in a bright aura and heals red vitality rapidly so long as her competitor is within the aura. Because the life regeneration is so quick, close range damage is effectively halved for a much-needed boost in survivability. Healing Field is best used as Dark Phoenix, as meter needn't be saved after Dark Phoenix Rising occurs. If you need to regenerate red vitality before Dark Phoenix Rising, X-Factor is an alternative method to consider. You can use Healing Field for THCs, as well. Several hyper combos allow a continued combo if a THC into Healing Field is used.

Dark Phoenix Rising: Upon K.O., Phoenix automatically performs Dark Phoenix Rising if the hyper meter is totally full. This hyper combo covers a large portion of the space around Phoenix and knocks foes away without dealing any damage. Phoenix is invincible during the transformation.

Upon completion, Phoenix is resurrected as Dark Phoenix, with all life replenished. Dark Phoenix is considerably stronger than regular Phoenix (or, um, anyone); all attacks deal 20% more damage, all TK Shots are doubled, all TK Traps become much stronger, and all basic attacks are augmented with fiery feather projectiles, resulting in more hyper meter built per normal attack.

As a trade-off, all of Dark Phoenix's vitality is slowly turned into red vitality. To counter this, make use of Healing Field and X-Factor.

Battle Plan

Teleport M is your main way to cross competitors up. Teleport right before TK Shot makes contact.

TK Trap L cuts off frontal advances. Set it down whenever you get the chance!

The main goal as Phoenix is to build five bars of hyper meter to grant access to Dark Phoenix. Because of the hefty meter requirement, the battle begins at the character select screen! Choosing teammates for Phoenix is just as important as learning how to play the character. Characters who don't need hyper combos to be effective are ideal partners for Phoenix, as are characters with long, drawn-out combos that can build meter toward Dark Phoenix Rising. Amaterasu, Frank West, and Morrigan should also be considered when choosing characters to complement Phoenix because they possess meter-building crossover assists.

One of the fastest ways to build hyper meter is through team aerial combos. ⇩ + Ⓢ aerial exchange proves to be an invaluable resource, since it builds one whole bar of hyper meter if successfully performed. However, you can be sure that opposing players will be ready to counter a ⇩ + Ⓢ aerial exchange. As an alternative, you can use ⇧ + Ⓢ aerial exchange into a long, meter-building combo; characters with the ability to fly are especially good at this since their combos after an aerial exchange tend to be longer than those who cannot fly. On the other hand, if you find yourself caught in an air combo, be ready to counter with ⇦ or ⇨ + Ⓢ to avoid having your own meter taken away.

Conserving X-Factor is also important when playing a Phoenix-based team. Phoenix is extremely fragile and is very susceptible to chip damage, especially when she is forced in via snap back or teammate K.O. X-Factor serves as Phoenix's main defense against chip damage and should be used only in emergencies. If you find Phoenix in a dangerous position without five bars of hyper meter, you might want to consider activating X-Factor to keep her from being preemptively K.O.'d. X-Factor is also extremely important for Dark Phoenix, since it negates the red vitality conversion that Dark Phoenix suffers from. If you manage to save X-Factor for Dark Phoenix, you won't be disappointed; Dark Phoenix with X-Factor activated is a nightmare for competitors to deal with. She is almost certainly still the strongest character in the game, even with her adjustments.

Because of her low vitality and hyper meter dependency, Phoenix is best put in the third slot of the team. If Phoenix is forced into the match early without sufficient hyper meter built, your first priority should be to have her escape to safety. This is where Phoenix's mobility and defensive options come into play. Immediately employ advancing guard on any attacks that come your way, and retreat with backdashes, airdashes, and teleports if necessary. Once you've regained control of the match, tagging out right away isn't always the best option. Clever foes often wait for the tag, leaving Phoenix's teammate wide open for a huge combo or even a snap back to get Phoenix back in! Instead, try using TK Shot H or TK Trap L to cover your tag. There is nothing worse than saving Phoenix from danger only to have her put into another bad position!

Even though Phoenix is extremely vulnerable when forced in early, fighting back is an alternative to retreating, albeit a risky one. Combo opportunities should be taken if they present themselves! Take advantage of an opposing player's frenzy to K.O. Phoenix by using attacks like crouching Ⓜ and air ⇩ + Ⓗ. If used as an anti-air, crouching Ⓜ can often go right under enemy attacks, putting you in prime position to start a combo. If you are airborne, surprise foes below with air ⇩ + Ⓗ. This is also a good time to surprise your opponents with Teleport M. If they try to attack with a slower special move or hyper combo, use Teleport M to get to safety and punish your foe's laggy attack. If you manage to successfully land a hit, don't get greedy! Get Phoenix out as soon as possible via tag (which is usually safe after an air combo) or aerial exchange.

Once full hyper meter is achieved, you have a few choices. You can opt to switch in Phoenix early, fight until she is knocked out to activate Dark Phoenix Rising, then switch back out, finally giving her remaining teammates free reign over the hyper meter while saving Dark Phoenix herself as a measure of last resort. If your other two characters are defeated, Dark Phoenix likely enters the fight with some pre-built hyper meter for you to work with, and hopefully X-Factor, as well. This tactic gives you the most bang for your buck, hyper meter-wise, but isn't always possible, since it requires other teammates to not be K.O.'d.

Another option is to switch Phoenix in early and battle through the rest of the fight with Phoenix and Dark Phoenix. Phoenix on point is one of the strongest characters in the game with various offensive and defensive tools, and she is especially dangerous with crossover assists at her disposal. Her defensive game is made even stronger with crossover assists, and her offense can be fully unleashed since a K.O. activates Dark Phoenix Rising anyway! This means that you can take more risks when approaching and attacking. Dark Phoenix is even more of a threat with crossover assists, as well, and she is very capable of destroying the opposition without being switched back to the sidelines. This tactic works especially well with teammates who can fit the role of anchor on the team; if Dark Phoenix is lost, you can still rely on a strong anchor with X-Factor to clean up whatever Dark Phoenix didn't finish.

Yet another tactic to consider is saving Phoenix for last no matter what. An all or nothing tactic, this plan relies heavily on Dark Phoenix's destructive power with lv.3 X-Factor activated. You can take huge risks and play wildly with Phoenix's teammates in an attempt to win the fight without the use of Dark Phoenix. It doesn't matter so much if her teammates are K.O.'d or not, so you can take this opportunity to play a strong offensive game, pulling out all the stops! This isn't to say that an opportunity to win the fight should not be taken if it is presented early. If you are put in a position as normal Phoenix to K.O. your opponent's final remaining character at the expense of hyper meter and/or X-Factor, go for it if you are confident that you can end the match right then and there. Otherwise, you can still play it safe by waiting for Dark Phoenix Rising to occur before you activate X-Factor or spend further hyper meter.

The angle in which air H hits makes it perfect for square jumps!

In all three situations, you can shift from defense to offense with Phoenix, as long as Dark Phoenix Rising is ready to be activated. On offense, Phoenix has several weapons at her disposal. One of her main tools is triangle jump air L . Phoenix's air L attacks at a downward angle, making it ideal as an overhead attack. This becomes especially difficult to guard against when mixed with empty triangle jump crouching L . Both attacks are quick, making them hard for competitors to react to. You can also perform a square jump attack with air H . Phoenix's air H has a large, crescent-like hitbox, attacking both in front of and behind her. This makes it perfect for square jumps! If you manage to land a square jump air H , you can always follow with air ↓ + H . The target is sucked in toward you from the hitstun of the air H , allowing air ↓ + H to combo cleanly.

Phoenix's crouching M is invaluable at mid range. The distance it travels combined with the fact that Phoenix goes low enough to avoid many attacks make it an asset when trying to mount an offense. You can slide right under most projectiles and normal attacks with it, and it can be followed with crouching H , TK Shot L, or Teleport H to keep the momentum going.

Teleport M cross-ups are also a viable means of attack, and they can be utilized from a safe distance. Fire the slow-moving TK Shot L or TK Shot H before teleporting to set up cross-up opportunities. Even if the fireball is guarded after the Teleport M, you can use still use this position to rush down with low attacks, triangle jumps, and square jumps. For a particularly tricky attack, use the → + M Prominence Heel overhead immediately after teleporting to add another layer to the cross-up! Be careful, though, as a poorly timed Teleport M cross-up leaves Phoenix vulnerable because of its recovery time. If you feel the opposing player is anticipating your Teleport M and getting ready to counter with crouching L , try performing Teleport H into air ↓ + H instead to catch them by surprise.

Phoenix is a great rushdown character, but having Dark Phoenix Rising ready doesn't necessarily mean you must play offensively. Sometimes, frustrating your adversaries with defensive measures is a better option. TK Trap L is integral to this, and it should be performed whenever you get the chance. Once TK Trap L is set down, you can either set down TK Trap M for further coverage, or start firing TK Shots to force your opponent to make a move. Once they do, get ready to counter their change in gameplan with a surprise crouching M attack or Teleport M.

Once Dark Phoenix Rising is finally activated, the remaining characters and vitality of the opposing team must be evaluated. If there are still three characters to deal with, the initiative to attack must be taken because Dark Phoenix's vitality is slowly being converted to red. If there are only one or two low-vitality characters remaining, they are better dealt with from a distance to avoid the risk of a K.O. to Phoenix herself.

Playing a defensive game with Dark Phoenix isn't a bad idea. Since all TK Traps and TK Shots inflict significantly more damage, trying to get in close on a defensively played Dark Phoenix can take a huge toll on a foe's vitality. Dark Phoenix can still perform the same Teleport M cross-ups with TK Shots, but now they are even more difficult to avoid because there are two fireballs instead of one. TK Trap M becomes a real threat now, as well; if the target is hit by a TK Trap M, perform Teleport L on reaction to the wall bounce to combo for a K.O.

Perform standing H before special moves to use the feathers as cover.

A defensive measure not possessed by normal Phoenix is Dark Phoenix's standing H . After Dark Phoenix Rising, this attack is augmented with a fan-shaped blast of feathers firing in five directions, protecting Dark Phoenix from any frontal assaults. This attack alone shuts down many characters' offensive tools; a character like Tron has very few answers to Dark Phoenix standing still performing standing H over and over! To help Dark Phoenix's survivability, try to get accustomed to whiffing this attack before every special move performed if you can. The feathers are released immediately as the standing H is performed, so you can essentially add a fan of feathers to all special moves by canceling them from standing H .

Offense is where Dark Phoenix shines, since many of Dark Phoenix's combos lead to a K.O. The feathers produced by Dark Phoenix's basic attacks drastically increase the number of hits in combos, which assures that any combo will build an incredible amount of hyper meter. Dark Phoenix still has access to all the same offensive weapons as normal Phoenix, including triangle jumps and square jumps. Standing L and crouching L are greatly enhanced as Dark Phoenix. If pressed rapidly, they create a stream of projectiles which will push away guarding adversaries, while easily allowing you to hit confirm. If you see these feathers hitting your competitor, dash in and continue with a combo.

Some challengers decide to run away from Dark Phoenix, usually to wait out her X-Factor timer or to let the red vitality conversion consume her. In this situation, use TK Shot H to give chase. TK Traps are all much faster as Dark Phoenix and should be used to make the entire screen unsafe for opponents. TK Trap H can be useful against a fleeing foe, as well. It travels quickly at an angle that Phoenix cannot quickly get to without teleporting. The wall bounce effect added to TK Trap H after Dark Phoenix Rising helps immensely, as you can follow up any wall bounce with Teleport L or M for a combo opportunity.

Crouching M is a great way to approach your rivals.

Crouching M is also improved as Dark Phoenix. When performed, three feathers fire up, diagonally, and straight ahead for added coverage. Many opponents expect Dark Phoenix to approach via teleports or airdashing, but the horizontal distance crouching M covers makes it a viable tool for approaching, as well. If positioned properly, a crouching M canceled to Teleport M makes for a seemingly unguardable cross-up; as you teleport behind your competitor, the feathers strike their back as a cross-up! For proper positioning, try sliding back in after an advancing guard, then canceling it into Teleport M for the cross-up.

If your opponent has decided to corner themselves to avoid Teleport M, you can simply sit right outside their attack range, set a TK Trap L and TK Trap M to cover their escape, then fire TK Shot L repeatedly to safely chip away at their attempt to turtle. You can also use crouching L feather spam to get close for a throw attempt, which can be turned into a full combo via OTG air TK Shot L. If you think your adversary might try to avoid the throw by performing a throw escape or a jumping retreat, fake the throw attempt and instead go for crouching L to counter, which will catch them before they get off the ground if they hold up-back to jump. This can be further mixed with a forward dash into → + M . A cornered opponent is also more susceptible to triangle jump and empty triangle jump mix ups. If foes manage to escape your corner pressure, that's fine: you can use Teleport M for cross-ups again!

COMBO USAGE

I. **CR. Ⓛ, Ⓜ, Ⓗ, Ⓢ CANCEL FORWARD SUPER JUMP, AIR Ⓜ, Ⓜ, Ⓗ, ↓ + Ⓗ, LAND, ↓ ↙ ← + Ⓛ, FORWARD JUMP, AIR Ⓜ, Ⓗ, Ⓢ, LAND, ↓ ↘ → ↗ + Ⓛ OTG, LAND, → ↓ ↘ + Ⓗ**

19 hits, 386,300 damage, 79% meter gain

The main purpose of this combo is to build a large amount of hyper meter while inflicting a decent amount of damage. When super jumping, perform air Ⓜ, Ⓜ, Ⓗ, ↓ + Ⓗ quickly for the best results. You can also end this combo with Phoenix Rage, though this is not recommended if you are saving hyper meter for Dark Phoenix Rising.

II. **(CORNER REQUIRED) CR. Ⓛ, Ⓜ, Ⓗ, Ⓢ CANCEL FORWARD SUPER JUMP, AIR Ⓜ, Ⓜ, Ⓗ, ↓ + Ⓗ, LAND, ↓ ↙ ← + Ⓛ, FORWARD JUMP, AIR Ⓜ, Ⓗ, Ⓢ, LAND, ↓ ↘ → ↗ + Ⓛ, LAND, Ⓢ FORWARD SUPER JUMP, AIR Ⓜ, Ⓜ, Ⓗ, Ⓢ, LAND, ↓ ↘ → ↗ + Ⓛ, LAND, Ⓢ CANCEL FORWARD SUPER JUMP, AIR Ⓢ**

418,800 damage, 106% meter gain

On cornered competitors, Phoenix is able to perform even longer combos for building hyper meter. Make sure to perform the aerial attacks as quickly as possible to ensure the combo's success. Like many of Phoenix's combos, you can end this with Phoenix Rage, though this is only recommended if a K.O. is guaranteed. If not, your hyper meter is best saved for Dark Phoenix Rising.

III. **(AS DARK PHOENIX) CR. Ⓛ, Ⓜ, Ⓗ, → + Ⓗ CANCEL → ↓ ↘ + Ⓛ, CR. Ⓛ, ST. Ⓗ, → + Ⓗ CANCEL ↓ ↙ ← + Ⓛ, → + Ⓗ CANCEL ↓ ↙ ← + Ⓛ, → + Ⓗ, Ⓢ CANCEL FORWARD SUPER JUMP, AIR Ⓜ, Ⓜ, Ⓗ CANCEL ↓ ↘ → + ATK ATK**

1,043,900 damage, 127% meter gain

Dark Phoenix can easily perform 100% damage combos on most characters, as exemplified by this combo. More hyper meter is built than usual because of the feather projectiles, guaranteeing that Phoenix Rage becomes available to use at the end of this combo. For the best positioning, try delaying the → ↓ ↘ + Ⓛ after → + Ⓗ so that your opponent stays close to the ground.

IV. **(AS DARK PHOENIX) (CORNER REQUIRED) CR. Ⓛ, Ⓜ, Ⓗ, → + Ⓗ CANCEL → ↓ ↘ + Ⓛ, CR. Ⓛ, ST. Ⓗ, → + Ⓗ CANCEL ↓ ↙ ← + Ⓛ, ST. Ⓗ CANCEL ↓ ↙ ← + Ⓜ, ↓ ↙ ← + Ⓛ, ST. Ⓗ, → + Ⓗ CANCEL ↓ ↘ → + Ⓛ CANCEL ↓ ↘ → + ATK ATK**

1,125,000 damage, 139% meter gain

While Dark Phoenix combos are destructive regardless, they pack an extra punch in the corner. Linking the cr. Ⓛ after → ↓ ↘ + Ⓛ can take some getting used to, but it becomes second nature with some practice!

V. **(CORNER REQUIRED) FORWARD THROW, ↓ ↘ → ↗ + Ⓛ OTG, ST. Ⓗ, → + Ⓗ, Ⓢ CANCEL FORWARD SUPER JUMP, AIR Ⓜ, Ⓜ, ↓ + Ⓗ, LAND, ↓ ↙ ← + Ⓛ, Ⓢ CANCEL FORWARD SUPER JUMP, AIR Ⓜ, Ⓜ, Ⓗ, Ⓢ, LAND, ↓ ↘ → ↗ + Ⓛ OTG, → ↓ ↘ + Ⓗ**

292,100 damage, 97% meter gain

Forward throw is a great way to mix up your corner pressure with Phoenix. Wait until your adversary is as low to the ground as possible before launching with Ⓢ; the hitstun on → + Ⓗ gives you plenty of time to see if the positioning is just right.

"I WANTED YOU TO WIN. TO END MY THREAT ONCE AND FOR ALL. I HONESTLY DID."

ADVANCED TACTICS

I CAN'T CONTROL IT: DARK PHOENIX RISING COMBOS

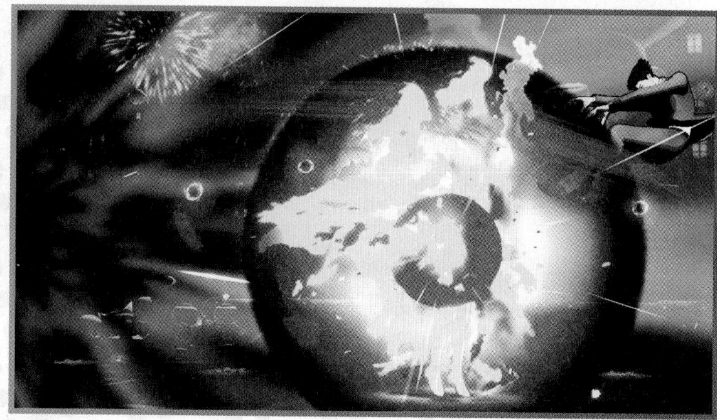

A combo off Dark Phoenix Rising gives you the upper hand right away.

Though Dark Phoenix Rising causes no damage, you can follow it with a combo if it is activated against a cornered or near-cornered competitor! If Dark Phoenix Rising is activated against a cornered opponent, immediately attack with a stream of crouching Ⓛ feathers to catch them for a combo. If you are near the corner upon activation, you can cancel Dark Phoenix Rising with X-Factor and perform a quick dash into crouching Ⓜ to catch the target before they hit the ground. At midscreen, the same technique can be used except with TK Overdrive L or H, which can be followed with crouching Ⓛ into a combo. Timing is key here!

DESTROYING WHOLE PLANETS: AFTER A K.O.

Coming in after a K.O. is the most dangerous position for your opponent to be in.

The key to Dark Phoenix's ability to destroy entire teams by herself lies in her deadly mix-up game on characters forced to join the fight after their partner is knocked out. With the use of TK Trap M, opposing players are forced to play a 50/50 guessing game in which one wrong guess can lead to another K.O. until the whole team is wiped out. To perform this, set down TK Trap M, wait for the fresh opposing character to set off the trap by falling in, then teleport just after the trap fires. The Trap's projectile is what you're actually using for the cross-up, so if you teleport to one side or the other *just* before the projectile hits their character, the opposing player doesn't have enough time to react. Basically, if your opposition blocks this tactic, it's luck, or you're being predictable with your timing, or your teleport choice. Use Teleport M and H for a cross-up, and employ Teleport L for a fake cross-up. If the trap hits, quickly dash or teleport into position to follow with a huge combo. If your adversary successfully guards the trap, you can seize control of the match by firing a stream of crouching Ⓛ projectiles, or performing Teleport M for another cross-up attempt.

Certain characters like Magneto and Storm can airdash upward to avoid falling into the invisible TK Trap M tripwire, while others can double jump to mess up your cross-up timing. This is one of the few scenarios where TK Trap H is extremely useful. Position and place TK Trap H so that it fires as soon as your foe appears, then place TK Trap M as normal and perform the teleport mix-up. Enemies trying to avoid TK Trap M instead get blasted by TK Shot H!

Because Teleport M cannot cross-up cornered opponents, an incoming character appearing in the corner does not fall victim as easily to TK Trap M setups. To counter this, immediately backdash after knocking out an adversary. If you move backward far enough, you can pull the screen backward to bring the playing field out of the corner. After doing so, you still have a moment to set TK Trap M down. Since the playing field has been moved, Teleport M can cross up as usual!

COMBO APPENDIX

GENERAL EXECUTION TIPS

When performing air combos, attack immediately after super jumping to ensure that the positioning is correct for ⇩ + Ⓗ to connect.

It is best to super jump straight up rather than forward during Phoenix air combos. Jumping straight up with Phoenix gives you the altitude you need for all hits to connect.

If you're having trouble with the tiger knee motion when performing air TK Shot to OTG, try performing the motion slowly. Only press Ⓛ when the entire motion is completed, all the way to ⇗ .

(AS DARK PHOENIX) CR. Ⓛ, Ⓜ, Ⓗ, ⇨ + Ⓗ CANCEL ⇩⇙⇦ + Ⓜ, ⇦⇩⇙ + Ⓛ, ST. Ⓗ, ⇨ + Ⓗ CANCEL ⇩⇙⇦ + Ⓛ, Ⓢ CANCEL FORWARD SUPER JUMP, AIR Ⓗ CANCEL ⇩⇘⇨ + ATK ATK

Notes	Damage
—	920,000 damage, 9% meter loss

CR. Ⓛ, Ⓜ, Ⓗ, ⇨ + Ⓗ CANCEL ⇩⇙⇦ + Ⓛ, ⇩⇙⇦ + Ⓛ, ⇩⇙⇦ + Ⓛ REPEAT

Notes	Damage
X-Factor level 2 or 3 required, works as Phoenix or Dark Phoenix	100% damage

SENTINEL

"THE PROGRAMMING OF THIS UNIT IS EVOLVING. CHANGING. ADAPTING. BECOMING... BASTION."

MODEL NUMBER
COTA-94

OCCUPATION
Mutant Hunter

ABILITIES
The Sentinel's strong, giant metal body boasts incredible power. It also has the abilities of flying and of tracking down mutants.

WEAPONS
Its primary weapons are the laser blasts (a special gene scrambler) it can fire from both its palms, as well as its fingertips. It can also release knockout gases.

PROFILE
Sentinel is a robot mutant hunter developed by Bolivar Trask, a scientist who felt that mutants were becoming a threat to mankind. Without developing their own artificial intelligence, Sentinels dutifully obey their orders, no matter who gives them.

FIRST APPEARANCE
The X-Men #14 (Sentinels, 1965), X-Men: Children of the Atom (COTA-94 model, 1994)

POWER GRID

- 1 INTELLIGENCE
- 4 STRENGTH
- 3 SPEED
- 5 STAMINA
- 6 ENERGY PROJECTION
- 4 FIGHTING ABILITY

*This is biographical, and does not represent an evaluation of the in-game combat potential of this hero.

ALTERNATE COSTUMES

Overview

Vitality	900,000
Chain Combo Archetype	2-Hits Limited

X-Factor Boost	Damage	Speed
Level 1 (3 teammates remaining)	130%	110%
Level 2 (2 teammates remaining)	150%	120%
Level 3 (1 teammate remaining)	170%	130%

Sentinel is an interesting hybrid: an offensive character that shouldn't be too close, and a beam-capable character that can't press that advantage against some characters. Your goal with Sentinel is to push your opponent to the corner while keeping them at proverbial arm's length, no closer than the reach of Sentinel's standing M. As a secondary goal, keep an eye out for chances to punish your foe's unprotected assist calls with Hyper Sentinel Force.

Sentinel is a gigantic and imposing killing machine. Why would you want to keep your adversary away?

- **Like Nemesis T-Type, Sentinel is too big for its own good. Characters with faster attacks (almost everyone) can beat Sentinel to the punch at close range, and it's easy for opponents to land instant overheads on crouching Sentinel by simply jumping and attacking**
- **Likewise, Sentinel has below-average vitality, and is easy to juggle. This model of Sentinel can't take chances. Master Mold doesn't make 'em like it used to**
- **Sentinel's own attacks are better at the edge of their ranges, where Sentinel's limbs are invulnerable and destroy projectiles. Staying at the edge of poke range also allows you to press a scary throw reach advantage—see Advanced Tactics for more information**

Why do you want the opposing character pushed into a corner?

- **Sentinel's combo damage potential is much stronger because combos can basically go on as long as you have hyper meter to spare and the willingness to spend it.**
- **Sentinel's Human Catapult command throw leads to bigger damage and meter gain opportunities**
- **Your foe has less space to backpedal away from Sentinel's long-reaching attacks and Human Catapult command throw, and advancing guard is less effective in pushing Sentinel away**

Finally, if the goal is both to keep your opponent away and to push them to the corner, how is that accomplished?

- **Forcing your adversary to guard either a long range assist or H mouthlaser, then activating flight and flying forward**
- **Cautiously wavedashing, jumping, and double jumping forward to gain ground**
- **Anticipating where your opponent will be and taking over that space with the invincible tip of one of Sentinel's M limbs**
- **Sensing when your opponent is playing passively and rushing in to grab them with Human Catapult**
- **Looking for opportunities to combo into Hard Drive, or to use its invulnerability to blow through an attack**

TUNING SINCE ORIGINAL MVC3

Sentinel saw more changes in *MvC3*'s early life than in the transition to *UMvC3*... The robot's vitality was lowered from 1.3 million to 905,000 in a patch shortly after the original game was released. Sentinel has it comparatively easy here. Sentinel can no longer combo OTG Rocket Punch L to Hyper Sentinel Force after an air combo, but being able to mash Plasma Storm for increased damage makes up for this.

Sentinel is one of the hardest-hit characters in terms of the damage of X-Factor being toned down, so it's no longer a guaranteed knockout every time a glowing, angry Sentinel even sneezes on an adversary with impossible-to-miss combos. Sentinel can still definitely accomplish ample mutant-killing in X-Factor, and X-Factor's speed boost is arguably more important to the robot than the damage (since it fixes the biggest disadvantage Sentinel has). It just takes more effort and better combos to do it this time around. No more easy mode launch, air M, H, S CANCEL death for Sentinel!

- **Vitality changed from 905,000 to 900,000**
- **Foes recover faster when hit by a Rocket Punch**
- **S launcher now has super armor (reduced from hyper armor)**
- **Plasma Storm can be mashed for more damage**

Attack Set

Standing Basic Attacks

Screen	Command	Hits	Damage	Meter Gain	Startup	Active	Recovery	Advantage on Hit	Advantage if Guarded	Notes
1	Standing L	1	70,000	560	7	3	28	-12	-15	Nullifies low priority projectiles during active frames
2	Standing M	1	100,000	800	14	3	32	-11	-15	Super armor from frames 6-15, nullifies medium priority projectiles during active frames
3	Standing H	5	102,300	1000	20	20	16	+6	-11	Hits fullscreen in 26 frames, chains to crouching H, deals chip damage, beam durability: 5 frames x 2 low priority durability points

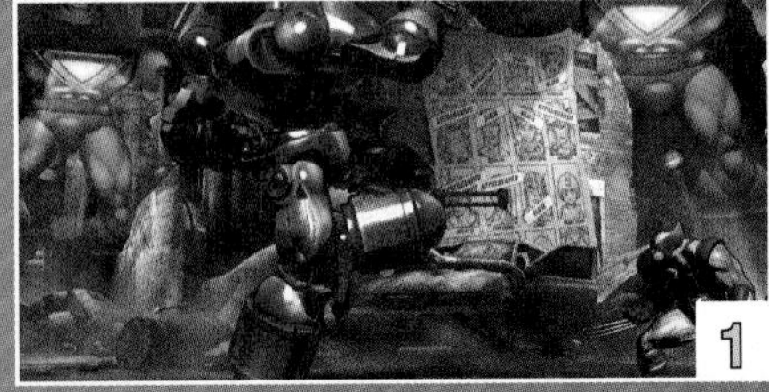
1

2

3

Crouching Basic Attacks

Screen	Command	Hits	Damage	Meter Gain	Startup	Active	Recovery	Advantage on Hit	Advantage if Guarded	Notes
1	Crouching L	1	70,000	560	9	3	25	-9	-12	Nullifies low priority projectiles during active frames
2	Crouching M	3	97,600	960	13	3(1) 4(1)4	30	—	-14	Low attack, super armor from frames 6-15, hits close range at 13 frames, mid range at 17 frames, nullifies medium priority projectiles during active frames
3	Crouching H	5	102,300	1000	20	20	16	+6	-11	Hits fullscreen in 26 frames, deals chip damage, beam durability: 5 frames x 2 low priority durability points

1

2

3

Ground Special Attack—Launcher

Screen	Command	Hits	Damage	Meter Gain	Startup	Active	Recovery	Advantage on Hit	Advantage if Guarded	Notes
1	S (while standing or crouching)	1	120,000	960	16	8	26	—	-8	Launcher, not super- or hyper combo- cancelable, super armor from frames 12-21, nullifies medium priority projectiles during active frames

1

1	Air L	1	75,000	600	8	6	22	+17	+14	Overhead attack, double jump- cancelable, nullifies low priority projectiles during active frames
2	Air M	1	100,000	800	12	4	32	+22	+18	Overhead attack, double jump- cancelable, nullifies medium priority projectiles during active frames
3	Air H	1	110,000	880	17	4	28	+25	+21	Overhead attack, nullifies medium priority projectiles during active frames

1

2

3

Air Special Attacks—Flying Screen and Air Exchange

Air S causes a hard knockdown when used in a launcher combo (this is sometimes called flying screen). When used outside of a launcher combo, air S behaves mostly like another basic attack. Air exchange attacks, performed by inputting a direction plus S, are only possible during a launcher combo. Exchange hits initiate team aerial combos by tagging in the next available character to continue the air combo.

Screen	Command	Hits	Damage	Meter Gain	Startup	Active	Recovery	Advantage on Hit	Advantage if Guarded	Notes
1	Air S	1	120,000	960	18	5	23	—	+18	Overhead, causes ground bounce, nullifies medium priority projectiles during active frames, causes hard knockdown if used in launcher combo
2	Air ⇧ + S (during launcher combo)	2	105,00	880	13	4	31	—	—	Tags in next available ally while lofting opponent upward
3	Air ⇨ or ⇦ + S (during launcher combo)	2	95,000	800	18	4	27	—	—	Tags in next available ally while causing wall bounce, erases 1 hyper meter bar from opposing character
4	Air ⇩ + S (during launcher combo)	2	95,000	800	18	4	27	—	—	Tags in next available ally while causing ground bounce, generates 1 hyper meter bar

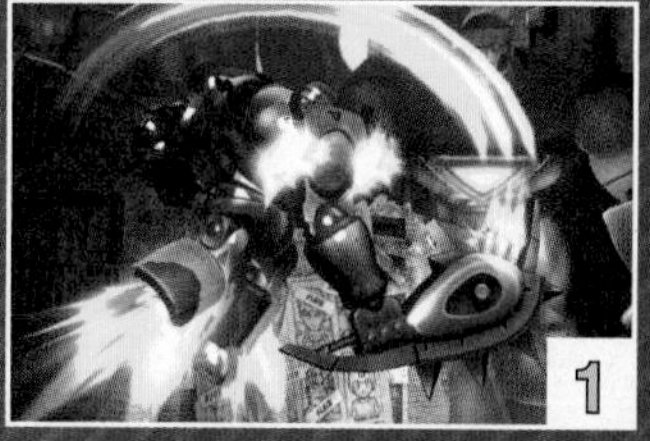
1

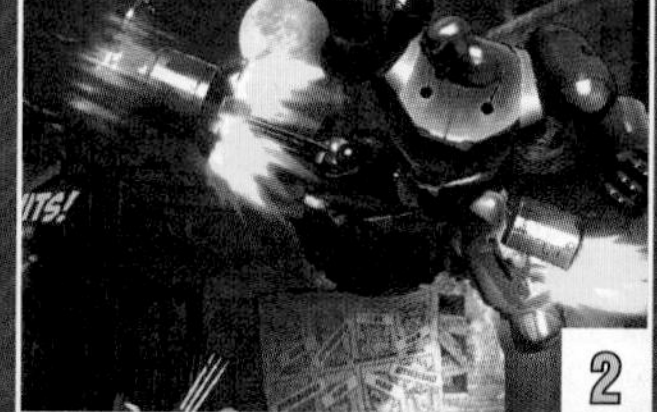
2

3

4

Throws

Throws are for snagging passive or blocking opponents. Since throws are active so quickly, you can also use them to preemptively toss opposing characters out of their offense. Combos are usually possible after throws, one way or another.

Screen	Command	Hits	Damage	Meter Gain	Startup	Active	Notes
1	⇨ + H (ground)	1	80,000	800	1	1	Hard knockdown
	⇦ + H (ground)	1	80,000	800	1	1	Hard knockdown
2	⇨ + H (air)	1	80,000	800	1	1	Hard knockdown
	⇦ + H (air)	1	80,000	800	1	1	Hard knockdown

1

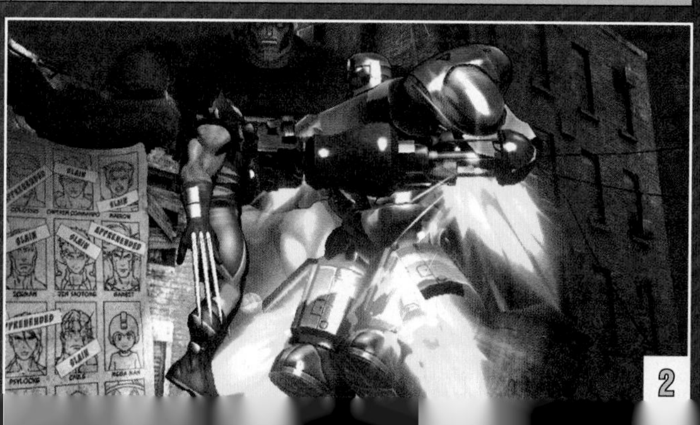
2

As a Partner—Crossover Assists

Screen	Type	P1+P2 Crossover Combination Hyper Combo	Description	Hits	Damage	Meter Gain	Startup	Active	Recovery (t his crossover assist)	Recovery (other partner)	Notes
1	Sentinel—α	Hyper Sentinel Force	Sentinel Force L	3	135,000	1200	45	—	146	116	Launches 3 projectile drones with 4 low priority durability points each, drones disappear if Sentinel is hit
2	Sentinel—β	Hyper Sentinel Force	Sentinel Force H	1~15	25,000 per bomb	200 per bomb	80	—	111	81	OTG- capable, 3 drones drop 5 bombs each, each projectile has 1 low priority durability point
3	Sentinel—γ	Plasma Storm	Rocket Punch L	1	130,000	1040	42	8	130	100	Knocks down, OTG-capable, nullifies medium priority projectiles during active frames

1

2

3

On paper, all three of Sentinel's assists have potential uses. Sentinel—β takes up more space than just about any other assist, and it is the least interruptible of the three. Sentinel—γ is a fast, hard-hitting OTG-capable assist with long reach, and the fist plows through most projectiles just like Sentinel's limbs on point. In practice, however, Sentinel—α has too many advantages to pick one of the others unless you are REALLY building a team to a specific purpose. (There are lots of characters with OTG-capable assists... why waste Sentinel's assist to gain that ability?)

The drone assist occupies so much screen real estate for so long that it's hard to pass up. This assist is one of the best in the game for enabling both offensive *and* defensive strategies (drones are almost required in order to play rushdown characters like Magneto, Wolverine, and Zero to full potential, and they help characters like Rocket Raccoon and Taskmaster control the center of the screen even more strongly). Indeed, this assist is so useful that it's a reason to put Sentinel on your team all by itself (and it certainly doesn't hurt that Sentinel is a strong character anyway and a beefy lv.3 X-Factor anchor, if it comes to that). Just keep an eye on Sentinel's vitality and cover the assist whenever possible, since assists are knocked out more easily than point characters. Losing Sentinel early on a team where the robot provides the primary assist means you've basically lost half or more of your offensive AND defensive abilities for the match. (Call the drones just before you force your target to guard a long range attack or beam such as Magneto's Electromagnetic Disrupter or Taskmaster's ⇨ + Ⓗ Web Swing, and you've more or less assured a safe exit for assist Sentinel.)

Finally, no matter which assist you pick, Sentinel has a terrific crossover counter... it just doesn't involve waiting around for the actual assist attack! Guard an attack, crossover counter to Sentinel with ⇨ + P1orP2, then perform Hard Drive *before Sentinel lands and does the counter.* This is expensive, costing two bars of meter, but it can be worth it. For example, if your opponent is trying to K.O. one of your characters with a beam hyper combo, they'll be very surprised when the tables are turned as Sentinel is countered into play with an invincible hyper combo that travels across the full screen! This trick can also be used to K.O. low-vitality characters who let you block something with enough recovery to guarantee that Hard Drive makes contact with them. Opponents are typically very surprised when you finish them off this way, and the mere threat that you might counter to an invincible hyper combo sometime later can influence decisions that they make against you for essentially the rest of time.

Snap Back

Screen	Command	Hits	Damage	Meter Gain	Startup	Active	Recovery	Advantage on Hit	Advantage if Guarded
1	⇩⇘⇨ + P1orP2	1	50,000	500 (-1 hyper meter bar)	2	3	32	—	-9

Notes

On hit, snap back forces the opposing point character to be replaced by an assist. Opposing assist calls or tag outs are also locked out for 4 seconds

1

Special Moves

Screen	Name	Command	Hits	Damage	Meter Gain	Startup	Active	Recovery	Advantage on Hit	Advantage if Guarded	Notes
1	Rocket Punch L	⇩⇘⇨ + Ⓛ	1	150,000	1200	18	8	38	-10	-20	Knocks down, OTG-capable, nullifies medium priority projectiles during active frames
2	Rocket Punch M	⇩⇘⇨ + Ⓜ	1	150,000	1200	18	8	38	-10	-20	Knocks down, nullifies medium priority projectiles during active frames
3	Rocket Punch H	⇩⇘⇨ + Ⓗ	1	150,000	1200	18	8	38	-10	-20	Knocks down, nullifies medium priority projectiles during active frames
1	Air Rocket Punch L	⇩⇘⇨ + Ⓛ	1	150,000	1200	16	8	32	-4	-14	Knocks down, OTG-capable, nullifies medium priority projectiles during active frames
2	Air Rocket Punch M	⇩⇘⇨ + Ⓜ	1	150,000	1200	16	8	32	-4	-14	Knocks down, nullifies medium priority projectiles during active frames
3	Air Rocket Punch H	⇩⇘⇨ + Ⓗ	1	150,000	1200	18	8	32	-4	-14	Knocks down, nullifies medium priority projectiles during active frames
4	Sentinel Force L	⇩⇙⇦ + Ⓛ	3	135,400	1200	21	—	54	+29	+26	Launches 3 projectile drones with 4 low priority durability points each, drones disappear if Sentinel is hit
5	Sentinel Force M	⇩⇙⇦ + Ⓜ	3	135,400	1200	21	—	54	+24	+23	Launches 3 projectile drones with 4 low priority durability points each, drones disappear if Sentinel is hit
6	Sentinel Force H	⇩⇙⇦ + Ⓗ	1~15	25,000 per bomb	200 per bomb	56	—	29	+19	+15	OTG-capable, 3 drones drop 5 bombs each, each projectile has 1 low priority durability point

Special Moves

Screen	Name	Command	Hits	Damage	Meter Gain	Startup	Active	Recovery	Advantage on Hit	Advantage if Guarded	Notes
7	Human Catapult L	⇨⇩⇘ + Ⓛ	1	120,000	1200	2	1	43	—	—	Throw attack, causes hard knockdown
	Human Catapult M	⇨⇩⇘ + Ⓜ	1	140,000	1400	6	1	39	—	—	Throw attack, causes hard knockdown
	Human Catapult H	⇨⇩⇘ + Ⓗ	1	160,000	1600	10	1	35	—	—	Throw attack, causes hard knockdown
8	Flight (in air OK)	⇩⇙⇦ + Ⓢ	—	—	—	17	—	—	—	—	Enters or exits flight mode, flight lasts 104 frames

Rocket Punch L 1

Rocket Punch M 2

Rocket Punch H 3

Sentinel Force L 4

Sentinel Force M 5

Sentinel Force L & M: Each version of Sentinel Force summons three drones, which act as projectiles (although they'll all disappear like a beam if an opponent hits Sentinel). The drones can be useful to put onscreen against opposing characters that don't have durable projectile threats, even though it's not the best idea against someone like Doctor Doom who can just cut through all the drones with his Plasma Beam, nor against teleport-capable characters that can simply teleport above or behind Sentinel. An ideal time to summon drones is immediately after knocking out (or snapping out) the current opposing point character... there will briefly be no one on screen to interrupt Sentinel and, by the time their new character falls into play, Sentinel is free to move alongside the drones (though, like the Sentinel—α drones assist, Sentinel Force drones all vanish if Sentinel takes damage).

Using Sentinel Force L to summon downward-angled drones may encourage your competitor to try jumping, super jumping, or flying above the fray, which puts them in position for you to use jumping or flying air Ⓜ. Using Sentinel Force M to summon upward-angled drones may encourage your adversaries to just crouch under Sentinel's little helpers at fullscreen. Wavedash forward and grab such passive opponents with Human Catapult.

Grabbing your foe with Human Catapult at midscreen, far from corners, presents a prime chance to summon TWO sets of Sentinel Force drones, if you want to force the rising opponent to guard for a while (and assuming you are not consistent enough with repeated wavedashes to make OTG Rocket Punch L feasible after Human Catapult midscreen, which is not an unreasonable assumption). If Sentinel has a teammate with a good long range assist, call that character into the fray, as well.

6

Sentinel Force H: Instead of firing three drones as battering rams, Sentinel Force H sends out three drones as carpet bombers. Each drone releases five small bombs, for a total of 15 bombs blanketing the area. Unlike Sentinel Force L & M, this version cannot be interrupted after Sentinel summons the drones, and the drones themselves cannot be destroyed. This version is much slower to fire than the others, though, and it's unlikely that enough of the bombs end up hitting to make the damage comparable to other attacks. On the other hand, it's possible to start a combo off of the bomb hits if Sentinel is close enough.

Rocket Punch: Sentinel players can direct its signature attack upward (Ⓗ), straight across (Ⓜ), or downward (Ⓛ). The fist that rockets away from Sentinel has no vulnerable hitbox, and it can plow intact through any low priority projectile it touches, with the exception of Chris's grenades. (If the fist strikes a medium priority projectile, both the Rocket Punch and the medium priority projectile become mutually nullified). The downward-aimed L version, whether airborne or grounded, is OTG-capable, which gives Rocket Punch its primary purpose: extending combos after a hard knockdown. To OTG foes after a hard knockdown with air Rocket Punch L, execute the move with a tiger knee motion: ⇩⇘⇨⇗ + Ⓛ. After the OTG hit, Rocket Punch can be canceled into Hard Drive or Plasma Storm.

When finishing midscreen combos with OTG Rocket Punch L, keep in mind you'll often have to wavedash forward to get close enough. Wavedash using command dashes (ATK ATK, ⇩, ATK ATK), so you don't accidentally whiff Human Catapult instead of getting the Rocket Punch you want at the end of the second dash.

Don't be too tempted to use Rocket Punches as pokes. If Rocket Punches are guarded, or if they miss altogether, Sentinel is left wide open for retaliation. Cancel guarded Rocket Punches to Hyper Sentinel Force to make Sentinel safe. Instead of poking with Rocket Punches, use Sentinel's Ⓜ attacks. This achieves the same effect, using safer attacks that can be hit-confirmed into combos.

7

Human Catapult: Human Catapult L is active in 2 frames, while a regular throw accomplished with ⇨/⇦ + Ⓗ is active in 1 frame. However, Human Catapult has a LOT more range than a normal throw (especially if you kara-cancel into it; see Advanced Tactics). Screwing up a throw attempt is bad for Sentinel either way, whether you whiff a Human Catapult grab or get a close-range standing Ⓗ instead of a regular throw. At least Human Catapult is unbreakable when it connects.

Sentinel's command grab increases in value near corners, where painful follow-up combos are possible. The M or H versions of Human Catapult are slower than the L version, but they deal more damage and allow for more follow-ups since your target is hurled higher into the air. Normally, you'll want to use Human Catapult L because of its fast startup. Human Catapult H can be useful after ticking with Ⓛ attacks up close; cancel late during the Ⓛ tick to Human Catapult H, so Human Catapult H reaches its active throwing frames just as your competitor recovers from guarding and becomes throwable.

It's possible to land huge combos off of midscreen Human Catapult L by calling the right assist just before performing the grab. Iron Man—β, Rocket Raccoon—γ, and Trish—β are perfect examples. The opponent gets ejected into the assist instead of being volleyed across the whole playing field, and this pins them point-blank long enough for Sentinel to recover and start a launcher combo. This approach is risky, however; if you whiff the grab or if your opponent simply interrupts it with their own attack before they are snagged, there's a good chance they'll catch both characters, Bob's your uncle, and you've just lost two-thirds of your team trying to get fancy with a command grab combo. The risk/reward is up to you, but generally it's best to not get too greedy; simply accept the positional advantage and the chance to briefly move in and call drones/assists for free that a successful Human Catapult represents.

However, there are equally team-oriented ways to capitalize on midscreen Human Catapults without taking unnecessary risks. If the next teammate has an OTG-capable hyper combo, you can perform Hyper Sentinel Force just as the opposing character hits the ground, then team hyper combo cancel to something like Storm's Hailstorm or Magneto's Magnetic Shockwave. The follow-up hyper combo pops your rival up and into the Hyper Sentinel Force drones, while also tagging in the new character. Similarly, if one of Sentinel's teammates has a hyper combo that OTGs during crossover combinations, you can simply dash forward and press P1+P2 for the whole team to take part.

8

Flight: During flight, Sentinel's stabilizing jets emit blue flames rather than yellow, and the robot can maneuver freely. Flight mode ends if ⇩⇙⇦ + Ⓢ is input again, if Sentinel is hit, if air Ⓢ is used, or if 104 frames elapse. Both the activation and manual cancelation of flight interrupts basic attacks, which enables quick aerial poking along with many damaging combos. Interrupting the recovery of blocked or whiffed basic attacks with flight also helps make Sentinel's laggy actions somewhat safer.

Sentinel is surprisingly maneuverable while flying, and it makes a smaller target with legs retracted and flight jets powered on than when standing on the ground. But since guarding isn't possible while flying, be careful regardless.

Hyper Combos

Screen	Name	Command	Hits	Damage	Startup	Active	Recovery	Advantage on Hit	Advantage if Guarded	Notes
1	Plasma Storm	↓↘→ + ATK ATK	20~39	282,200~337,400	10+1	81~92	25	—	-8	Knocks down opponent, can be mashed for extra damage, beam durability: 20 frames x 3 high priority durability points
2	Hard Drive (air only)	↓↘→ + ATK ATK (in air)	12	275,400	10+1	42(1)13	In recovery until landing	—	-5	Frames 1-70 invincible, last hit causes spinning knockdown that ignores hitstun decay
3	Hyper Sentinel Force	↓↙← + ATK ATK	9	306,000	10+1	—	84	—	+15	Frame 8-14 invincible, knocks down, 9 projectiles with 3 high priority durability points each

1

Plasma Storm: Plasma Storm is Sentinel's primary combo ender. Any grounded Sentinel combo that ends with Rocket Punch (basically, every Sentinel combo) allows you to tack on Plasma Storm. Mash ATK buttons during this hyper combo to increase the damage and number of hits. You can also link Plasma Storm after landing a Hard Drive or Hyper Sentinel Force hyper combo near the corner; either perform Plasma Storm right away after the previous hyper combo recovers, or (for slightly more damage, meter, and challenge) link a Rocket Punch first, then cancel into Plasma Storm.

2

Hard Drive (in air): During Hard Drive, Sentinel propels itself across the entire playing field in a straight line. Hard Drive is the only move Sentinel has with total invulnerability (Sentinel's limbs are never vulnerable during attacks like standing M or Rocket Punch, but the robot's body can be struck). Hard Drive is able to even travel cleanly through hyper combo beams! In the air, Sentinel players can use Hard Drive on reaction to punish anything that happens directly across from Sentinel. From the ground, performing Hard Drive with a "tiger knee motion" of ↓↘→↗ + ATK ATK is the closest thing Sentinel has to a reversal. Even if your foe guards it, or if Hard Drive sails clear over them, this technique usually travels so far and so fast that Sentinel isn't vulnerable. (Although some characters may catch Sentinel with fast, far-reaching lv.3 hyper combos.)

Aside from Hard Drive's use as a kind of reversal, you can insert this move into just about any combo that involves an air Rocket Punch—just cancel the Rocket Punch into Hard Drive. Instead of ending combos with OTG Rocket Punch L into Plasma Storm, you can use OTG tiger knee air Rocket Punch L into Hard Drive. This inflicts slightly less damage, but it almost always puts the enemy into the corner.

The last hit of Hard Drive causes a lengthy spinning knockdown. This allows Sentinel to continue a combo after knocking its rival into the corner with Hard Drive. The simplest thing to do is to launch with S, but hitstun decay usually means that whatever air combo you attempt gets cut short. With spare meter, you can simply juggle after Hard Drive with Plasma Storm, or Rocket Punch to Plasma Storm.

You can also link Hard Drive into another Hard Drive, or even into tiger knee Rocket Punch canceled into Hard Drive! As long as Hard Drive strikes properly so that the last hit causes the spinning knockdown again, you can continue juggling Rocket Punches and hyper combos.

3

Hyper Sentinel Force: This is Sentinel's safest hyper combo, since the drones come out after the hyper combo cutscene—even if Sentinel is struck. There are three waves of drones, with three drones in each wave. This makes Hyper Sentinel Force one of the best anti-assist hyper combos. If the opposing player calls an assist at mid to long range without covering it directly (e.g., forcing you to guard something, like a long range beam), simply activate Hyper Sentinel Force. That assist eats the damage of up to nine drones, with a 1.5x damage boost against the assist. When jockeying with your competitor for position at mid to fullscreen, stay twitchy and be ready to activate Hyper Sentinel Force on reaction to almost any assist coming out.

Hyper Sentinel Force can no longer follow up OTG Rocket Punch L after an air combo, but it still works in several other ways. For example, M canceled into Rocket Punch L canceled into HSF works. HSF also still works when canceling into it from Rocket Punch L OTG after Human Catapult.

"REPORT TO MASTER MOLD... TARGET: ELIMINATED. AWAITING FURTHER INSTRUCTION..."

Battle Plan

Sentinel's size makes it difficult for the robot to avoid attacks on the ground, and Sentinel certainly can't crouch under anything.

Not a great situation.

Sentinel's basic attacks are frightening, but slow. Every attack has an invulnerable hitbox that extends well away from Sentinel's body. Standing and crouching Ⓜ have super armor—during a certain period, they can absorb a single hit without being interrupted. Sentinel's Ⓢ launcher has super armor now too (this is actually down from original *MvC3*, where it had hyper armor). However, super armor on Ⓜ attacks doesn't kick in until the 6th frame of startup, and super armor on Ⓢ isn't active until frame 12.

The super armor properties of Ⓜ attacks and Ⓢ launcher are more effective from mid range, where the armor may catch an opponent who is dashing in with an attack. From close range, where your adversary has already established striking distance, whatever the opposing player does offensively will probably interrupt these attacks before they even arrive at their armor frames. These laggy moves are also much less safe when guarded up close than when guarded from the edge of their ranges. The same thing holds true of using Plasma Storm or Hyper Sentinel Force on the ground against close-range, aggressive enemies. If your rival is attacking anyway, they're probably going to interrupt the hyper combos in the first few frames, so insult is just added to injury as you lose a bar of hyper meter while Sentinel is getting hit anyway.

Therefore, point-blank, reliable options against an aggressive opponent are absent. Sentinel is reliant mostly on universal defensive options. Sparring with Sentinel's Ⓛ attacks is asking for trouble; they are Sentinel's only attacks with underwhelming hit areas, and they are still slower than the fast attacks of almost anyone else. Rather than trying for Ⓛ attacks that are inevitably out-prioritized, or armor attacks that are interrupted before they reach armor frames anyway, rely on successful guarding and advancing guard to reclaim breathing room. To try taking a little more initiative, you can sneak a throw or Human Catapult L into gaps in your opponent's close-range offense. If you're desperate to escape, tiger knee Hard Drive is the closest thing Sentinel has to a get-out-of-trouble-free card, and it's not even free: it costs a bar of hyper meter, the opponent may throw or low attack you out of pre-jump frames or before Hard Drive actually comes out, and Hard Drive isn't actually totally safe (but it does a good impression of it most of the time).

Additionally, while Sentinel has strong long-range tools like Ⓗ lasers, Sentinel Force drones, and Hyper Sentinel Force, if it comes down to a beam battle against certain characters, the robot is going to lose. Doctor Doom is the prototypical example of a character that usually gets ahead of Sentinel in the beam war. Against projectile-centric characters like Ryu and Akuma, Sentinel can win the fireball war when they don't have meter, but when they're loaded, the advantage tilts back in the favor of their fullscreen hyper combo beams. Additionally, some small characters, like Rocket Raccoon and Amaterasu, are a big problem for Sentinel because they can simply avoid anything the robot does while maintaining their own fullscreen offense. Some matches need to be covered by assists or other members of the team.

These characters can't crouch to avoid standing Ⓗ. Fire away!

Captain America	**Iron Man**	**Nemesis T-Type**	**Tron**
Hulk	**M.O.D.O.K.**	**Sentinel**	

These characters can duck under BOTH lasers, even crouching Ⓗ. Hold your fire!

Amaterasu	**Firebrand**	**Phoenix**	**Viewtiful Joe**
Arthur	**Frank West**	**Rocket Raccoon**	**Wolverine**
Felicia	**Morrigan**	**Strider**	

This is not to mention the fact that teleport and flight-capable characters completely skirt attempts at a ranged game and turn it into a liability. If you abuse lasers against the wrong enemies, it won't be uncommon to see Dante, Dormammu, Strider, Vergil, et al falling out of a teleport onto a soon-to-be-decommissioned Sentinel, which is now uselessly whiffing Ⓗ laser in the wrong direction. Flight characters can just stay above the fray; characters who can both fly and airdash can super jump above Sentinel's beams and drones and activate flight, then airdash repeatedly and unpredictably to get at Sentinel as desired.

So, while spamming Ⓗ lasers canceled into drones while calling Doctor Doom—β (or other strategies to that effect) annihilates poor characters like Haggar who don't have an answer at all, or poor players who gladly cooperate with running into your mindless barrage over and over before calling you a cheap player, that strategy won't cut the mustard against attentive, reactive opponents. It also won't work against characters that have easy answers, like an overpowering beam or fast teleport. (Sentinel Force drones are definitely an asset to almost any team, just not as much when Sentinel is on point; Sentinel—α is one of the game's strongest assists.)

A couple dashes away is far enough to threaten with Ⓗ lasers while still being close enough to dash forward to poke with the tip of standing or crouching Ⓜ. Any version of Sentinel's grounded Ⓜ and Ⓗ attacks can be hit-confirmed into Rocket Punch (and then Hyper Sentinel Force) from this distance or closer, and crouching Ⓜ can be chained into Ⓢ launcher even from just inside max range. On guard or whiff, you can cancel any of these attacks into flight, allowing Sentinel to either reposition or to transition to direct offense.

Two dashes away also puts Sentinel at the right range to threaten with dash forward kara-cancel Human Catapult. This serves as a counterpoint when opponents are scared of dash-in crouching Ⓜ. See Advanced Tactics for more on the kara-canceled grab.

Your challenger may opt to take to the skies, rather than worrying about whether Sentinel might spit lasers, dash forward with invincible fists, or dash forward into a grab with outrageous reach. That's fine, though—if you think that your competitor might try to jump or super jump from a couple dashes away (or if you react just as they leave the ground), jump forward and double-tap air Ⓜ right away. Since you're pressing Ⓜ twice, Sentinel naturally chains into another air Ⓜ if the first one connects. If successful, you have plenty of time to verify it's working and double jump into a stylish ground bounce combo; see combo VII.

If you poke with something like the tip of standing Ⓜ and cancel into flight, you're in roughly the same situation. Air Ⓢ here causes Sentinel to fall right back to earth, while ground bouncing overeager foes who tried to dash in after flying Sentinel. Or, flying air Ⓜ at this low altitude snags jumping enemies, and it can also be hit-confirmed into a ground bounce combo. See Advanced Tactics for more on using Sentinel's flight mode.

What all this means is that while Sentinel is an offensive character, you'll want to stay about a dash or two away from your rival at mid range, rather than trying to get in their face.

In addition to poking with (M) attacks on the ground, you can jump forward from a dash away and stomp with air (H).

From one dash away, you're in range to use the tips of (M) attacks, to kara-cancel standing (H) into a long range Human Catapult, or to jump forward with an overhead air (H) stomp.

None of these attacks is particularly fast or tricky when you look at them in a vacuum. It's the mixing up between them that causes one or the other to work. Opponents who are scared of crouching (M), which is Sentinel's only low attack and most important attack in general, are opening themselves up to eating air attacks or Human Catapult.

As a mix-up to zoning from one dash away, occasionally dash and attack with standing (L) chained to crouching (M). Crouching (M) strikes three times, with brief dead periods in between hits. Opposing players MUST keep holding down-back to continue blocking all of crouching (M). If they rise too early or try to jump out, the later hits still catch them, and you can still chain to launcher. This opens the door to use dash-in (L) as a tick before chaining to standing (H) and kara-canceling into Human Catapult H (the standing (H) is there only to add range to the throw, and the laser should not actually fire—see Advanced Tactics). No one is going to consistently use advancing guard after blocking just one initial (L) attack; where they will start advancing guard is while guarding follow-up attacks. So by dashing forward, ticking with (L), then timing Human Catapult H to snare your targets just as they become throwable after blocking, you can score unbreakable throws against adversaries who are too focused on not eating crouching (M). Naturally, once they're also worried about Human Catapult H, crouching (M) itself tends to have a higher rate of success when you go for it (opponents who anticipate a command grab and attempt to jump immediately after blocking (L) eat crouching (M) if you go for the chain instead).

Crouching (M) can chain successfully into (S) from slightly farther than standing (M), and it leads into air combos that deal over 600,000 damage and are meter self-sufficient. With surplus meter handy for THC handoffs, or by using X-Factor, it's easy to see how clean Sentinel hits should lead to knockouts against all but the heartiest opposing characters. Chances may be hard to come by, so you must make them count. If you strike with the very tip of standing (M) and chain to (S), it usually whiffs, so when you poke with standing (M), stick to canceling into flight or into a Rocket Punch canceled to Hyper Sentinel Force for chip damage or assist punishment.

Sentinel's armored moves help expose overly aggressive opponents.

Human Catapult used effectively is the scariest weapon Sentinel has.

With Sentinel's damage output and propensity for cornering enemies, you frequently attain a position to mix up a new character that is forced to fall in after their teammate was knocked or snapped out. Sentinel players have an interesting conundrum here: they can go for a lot of chip damage by filling the screen with garbage, or they can go for a "naked" mix-up against the new character, but they can't really do both. Both approaches are good in different situations.

For pinning, summon Sentinel Force M early while Sentinel has the screen to itself, then call the assist you brought along that deals the most chip damage. This should be timed and positioned so that the assist and the drones meet the new character just as they fall onto the screen at normal jump height. Summon another set of drones for free while your rival is trapped blocking (Sentinel Force L if you want to rush in and go for jumping air (H) or flying air (L) overheads; Sentinel Force M if you want to rush in and go for Human Catapult), then proceed back to your normal plan, having chipped the new character a little, gained a little meter, and still kept your opponent in the corner. The upside is small, but the downside is non-existent.

For chip damage, do the same thing, then cancel the second set of Sentinel Force drones into Hyper Sentinel Force. This is already going to deal decent chip damage; if you'd like to go all-in (such as near the end of a close round), cancel Hyper Sentinel Force with X-Factor, call your best chip assist again, then immediately cancel another set of Sentinel Force M drones into another HSF. With their character pinned, the opposing player is forced to think about popping X-Factor to avoid excessive chip damage. If they don't have X-Factor, they'll just have to eat it.

For much more potential, but also more risk, Sentinel can mix its adversary up directly. An opponent falling in fresh is a captive audience, and Sentinel's scary but slow armored moves are much more effective as a result. They HAVE to fall to the ground, and the only thing opposing players can do to change this is to use some sort of air mobility option or air special move if they have it. If you anticipate them airdashing upward to avoid the issue altogether, super jump and air throw them right back into the corner. Overzealous competitors who fall in using attacks can be severely punished by having them fall onto the armor frames of either (S) launcher (which beats nearly anything), or crouching (M). Forcing enemies to land on crouching (M) sometimes is crucial to making Human Catapult work when you try to grab them instead. Opponents who want to jump again as soon as they touch the ground and are worried about a throw soon get caught by crouching (M). Eventually, the opponent starts feeling afraid to do anything when their new characters fall in versus Sentinel, and that's when you should start timing Human Catapult to snare them just as they land.

Attacking a fresh character while in flight mode doesn't present much of a mix-up opportunity. Sure, if the opposing character eats flying air (M), (M) while falling in can take them for a ride, but if they're going to let that hit them, then they're also going to fall for (S) launcher and crouching (M) sweep. Those attacks have armor as insurance, as well as an unbreakable counterpoint in Human Catapult. If you attack while flying, on the other hand, your opponent just has to worry about guarding left or right and breaking air throws. That's actually less threatening than if Sentinel had just stood there waiting for them to fall in... But, this changes with the right assist. Backed by something like Dante—α or Storm—γ, flying Sentinel can cross your opponent up by calling the assist on one side, then flying over or under the opposing character to the other side (say, under them into the corner, just as they fall away from it). You can mix this up by sometimes staying on the same side, rather than crossing over. If the assist hits from either side, react by ground bouncing your competitor with air (S), which also automatically makes Sentinel land. From here, you can launch them into the combo of your choice. If they guard the assist properly, they're still stuck in mid-air next to a flying Sentinel that has frame advantage.

COMBO USAGE

I. Ⓢ CANCEL FORWARD SUPER JUMP, AIR Ⓗ CANCEL ↓↙← + Ⓢ, PAUSE, AIR Ⓛ, Ⓗ CANCEL ↓↙← + Ⓢ, PAUSE, FALLING AIR Ⓗ, LAND, PAUSE, Ⓢ CANCEL FORWARD SUPER JUMP, AIR Ⓗ CANCEL ↓↙← + Ⓢ, AIR Ⓛ, Ⓜ, Ⓗ, Ⓢ, LAND, WAVEDASH, ↓↘→ + ATK ATK OTG (MASH ATK)

835,200 damage, 5% meter gain

A clean Sentinel launcher leads to incredible damage with a self-sufficient combo. If you have meter left over to THC to another mashable hyper combo, your opponent is probably done. After Ⓢ launcher into super jump, strike with air Ⓗ canceled into flight as soon as possible. After flight, wait as long as possible before linking flying air Ⓛ, Ⓗ, then wait again after "unflying" air Ⓗ into falling air Ⓗ, and again between landing and launching again with Ⓢ. The purpose of inserting the pauses is to allow your adversary's body to drift down slightly, making the rest of the combo possible. Otherwise, they'll end up too high for either falling air Ⓗ or for the relaunch afterward to strike properly.

This combo works on every member of the cast, but landing the flight chain during the second super jump rep requires perfect positioning on tiny characters like Rocket Raccoon (or even Deadpool or Spider-Man). For an easier time, forego using flight and simply perform an air chain to Ⓢ for the hard knockdown. (If you're not sure of positioning, just use Ⓜ, Ⓗ, Ⓢ or even just Ⓗ, Ⓢ for consistency. The relaunch combo should also be simplified if you used several hits to chain into the first launcher, or if the combo started with the ground bounce of air Ⓢ.)

To trade damage for a cornered opponent, wavedash and OTG with tiger knee air Rocket Punch L (↓↘→↗ + Ⓛ) canceled into Hard Drive. If they're already near the corner, catch them after Hard Drive with Rocket Punch L into mashed Plasma Storm for 971,600 damage. (Or, meter permitting, execute another tiger knee Hard Drive, then a Rocket Punch into Plasma Storm to inflict around 1.15 million damage!)

II. →↓↘ + Ⓛ, DASH-IN ST. Ⓛ, Ⓜ, Ⓢ CANCEL SUPER JUMP FORWARD, AIR Ⓜ, Ⓜ, Ⓗ CANCEL ↓↙← + Ⓢ, AIR Ⓛ, Ⓜ, Ⓗ CANCEL ↓↙← + Ⓢ, FALLING AIR Ⓜ CANCEL DOUBLE JUMP, AIR Ⓗ, Ⓢ, LAND, ↓↘→ + Ⓛ OTG CANCEL ↓↘→ + ATK ATK (MASH ATK)

Requires corner, 654,700 damage, 21% meter gain

This unbreakable grab combo works when Sentinel is close enough to the corner to dash in and juggle standing Ⓛ after Human Catapult L. This is no farther than one dash away from the corner. The tricky part is just catching your competitor before they hit the ground after the throw. Perform every step as quickly as possible. If a surplus meter is almost ready when you get to the OTG, finish with tiger knee Rocket Punch L OTG canceled into Hard Drive, then juggle Rocket Punch into Plasma Storm for 790,200 damage. By inserting extra Rocket Punches between hyper combos in the corner, you can sometimes build enough meter to keep the combo going, whereas simply continuing from one hyper combo to the next would run out of bar.

If you land Human Catapult L too far from the corner to juggle afterward, just OTG with Rocket Punch L. With an assist like Trish—β, you can call the assist and then OTG the opposing character with Rocket Punch, so they pop up into the assist and the combo can continue without using hyper meter. If you don't have an assist to pop them up, you'll have to cancel Rocket Punch L to Hyper Sentinel Force or Plasma Storm (or X-Factor) to get more damage. At least landing Hyper Sentinel Force in this situation allows Sentinel to launch its target into the corner immediately afterward. If you then air combo to air Ⓢ, tiger knee air Rocket Punch L OTG to Hard Drive, then link Rocket Punch to Plasma Storm, you'll have all three Sentinel hyper combos in one sequence! (Along with at least 850,000 damage.)

III. →↓↘ + Ⓗ, IMMEDIATE JUMP FORWARD, AIR Ⓜ, Ⓜ CANCEL DOUBLE JUMP, AIR Ⓜ, Ⓗ, Ⓢ, LAND, Ⓢ CANCEL SUPER JUMP, AIR Ⓜ, Ⓜ, Ⓗ CANCEL ↓↙← + Ⓢ, AIR Ⓛ, Ⓛ, Ⓜ, Ⓜ, Ⓗ, Ⓢ, LAND, ↓↘→ + Ⓛ OTG CANCEL ↓↘→ + ATK ATK (MASH ATK)

Requires corner, 752,100 dmg, 59% meter gain

After performing Human Catapult H near a corner, it's possible to build a sizable amount of meter while also dumping some of it into your victim. Normal jump forward immediately after the throw recovers, but pause briefly before chaining air Ⓜ, Ⓜ. After ground bouncing and then launching your rival, perform the air and flight combo portion as quickly as possible.

Like most Sentinel combos, if you have surplus meter, you can score more damage after the hard knockdown. Finishing with a tiger knee Rocket Punch L OTG to Hard Drive, then Rocket Punch CANCEL Plasma Storm results in 875,100 damage!

Human Catapult H into the corner also lets you involve teammates without using meter. Tag a character who can OTG into a giant combo by themselves, like Dante or Doctor Doom, and let it rip...

IV. FORWARD OR BACKWARD THROW, DASH, ↓↘→ + Ⓛ OTG CANCEL ↓↙← + ATK ATK X-FACTOR ↓↙← + Ⓢ, FLY FORWARD, AIR Ⓜ, Ⓗ, Ⓢ, LAND, Ⓢ CANCEL SUPER JUMP FORWARD, AIR Ⓜ, Ⓜ, Ⓗ, Ⓢ, LAND, ↓↘→ + Ⓛ OTG CANCEL ↓↘→ + ATK ATK (MASH ATK)

1,130,500 damage with lv.1 X-Factor, 73% meter loss

Even with X-Factor toned down, angry red Sentinel is no joke. If you combo into Hyper Sentinel Force, you can still opt to make any combo ferocious by canceling the beginning of Hyper Sentinel Force into X-Factor, then flying forward to cause a ground bounce with air Ⓜ, Ⓗ, Ⓢ just as the last wave of HSF drones juggles the enemy.

That's just an example of confirming X-Factor within a combo, though. Normally, you'll just dash, OTG with Rocket Punch L, then cancel to Plasma Storm for 453,700 damage.

COMBO USAGE CONT.

V. CR. Ⓜ CANCEL ↓↘→ + Ⓛ X-FACTOR JUMP FORWARD, AIR Ⓗ, Ⓢ, LAND, DASH, ST. Ⓜ, Ⓢ CANCEL FORWARD SUPER JUMP, AIR Ⓜ, Ⓜ, Ⓗ CANCEL ↓↙← + Ⓢ, AIR Ⓛ, Ⓜ, Ⓜ, Ⓗ, Ⓢ, LAND, DASH, ↓↘→ + Ⓛ OTG CANCEL ↓↘→ + ATK ATK (MASH ATK)

X-Factor hit-confirm for two characters, 2,841,200 damage with lv.1 X-Factor, 295% meter gain

It's not as easy as it used to be, but Sentinel can still definitely toast entire teams at once with the right chance. This hit-confirm off of crouching Ⓜ gives you plenty of time to see that you've caught their point and assist together, so you can combo to Rocket Punch L, then cancel to X-Factor and erase two-thirds of the other team. No assist character survives this combo; the only point character who can survive is Thor.

VI. CR. Ⓜ, Ⓢ CANCEL FORWARD SUPER JUMP, AIR Ⓜ, Ⓜ, Ⓗ CANCEL ↓↙← + Ⓢ, AIR Ⓛ, Ⓗ X-FACTOR AIR Ⓜ, Ⓗ CANCEL ↓↙← + Ⓢ, FALLING AIR Ⓜ CANCEL FORWARD DOUBLE JUMP, AIR Ⓜ, Ⓗ, Ⓢ, LAND, DASH, ↓↘→ + Ⓛ OTG CANCEL ↓↘→ + ATK ATK (MASH ATK)

X-Factor hit-confirm for two characters, 2,320,900 damage with lv1 X-Factor, 226% meter gain

If you're too hard-wired into launching after crouching Ⓜ connects, you can still fit in an air X-Factor combo that can take out any assist and almost any point character.

VII. FLYING AIR Ⓜ CANCEL ↓↙← + Ⓢ, FALLING AIR Ⓜ CANCEL DOUBLE JUMP FORWARD, AIR Ⓜ, Ⓢ, LAND, DASH, ST. Ⓜ, Ⓢ CANCEL SUPER JUMP FORWARD, AIR Ⓜ, Ⓜ, Ⓗ CANCEL ↓↙← + Ⓢ, AIR Ⓛ, Ⓜ, Ⓗ, Ⓢ, LAND, DASH, ↓↘→ + Ⓛ OTG CANCEL ↓↘→ + ATK ATK (MASH ATK)

Airborne target, 811,100 damage, 30% meter gain

Whenever Sentinel catches an airborne target with air Ⓜ as a poke, it's party time. This is just one example, taken from a natural flying poke sequence: flying air Ⓜ canceled with unfly into falling air Ⓜ is a safe poke with enormous reach. Sentinel players should often cancel blocked Ⓜ attacks into flight in order to be safer and reposition Sentinel on the ground; this is also a natural time to poke with flying air Ⓜ, then unfly falling air Ⓜ just over the opposing character's head. If they happen to jump and get snagged by the two-hit combo, you can easily hit-confirm and double jump forward to continue.

No matter how you hit your opponents with attacks in midair, whether it's flying air Ⓜ or just a super jumping air Ⓛ, or whatever, the important thing is to make it to air Ⓢ for the ground bounce. Get that far, and virtually anything you do after launching deals scores of damage.

ADVANCED TACTICS

KARA-CANCEL HUMAN CATAPULT

You can extend the reach on Sentinel's Human Catapult throw by canceling into Human Catapult from standing Ⓗ. Cancel standing Ⓗ before Sentinel actually fires the mouthlaser. Sentinel takes a step forward during the startup of standing Ⓗ, so this translates into the command grab having horrifying range. How horrifying? The places where characters stand at the start of a match if they don't move is about right. If Sentinel is made to backdash from point-blank range, then perform the kara grab, it will work. In fact, from all the way across the playing field, wavedash once (with both dashes being full-length), and Sentinel is at the edge of kara grab range!

Make sure the opposing player is worried about cr. Ⓜ and air attacks, and they're sure to fall for dash-in kara-cancel Human Catapult.

Human Catapult H has the most range and offers the most follow-up potential, but Human Catapult L is active much faster and only loses a pixel or two in range anyway. Near a corner, every strength of Human Catapult leads to big damage. When using the kara grab on its own, the L version is best because of its speed. However, when chaining into the kara grab from a tick Ⓛ (standing Ⓛ, standing Ⓗ CANCEL →↓↘ + Ⓗ), the extra startup on the H version is actually what makes the trick work.

It's possible to follow up after Human Catapult midscreen with perfect wavedashing, but it's tough and inconsistent. With certain assists in Sentinel's back pocket, you can simply call the assist just as you go for the grab to score a big combo anywhere. Given that Human Catapult is inescapable, this is especially useful near corners, against characters falling in after their teammate is knocked/snapped out, and against opponents who just finished guarding the assist of Sentinel's partner.

HIT THEM WITH THE TIMBERLANDS: THE FLYING ROBOT

Sentinel's air moves are about controlling space and anticipating where your adversary wants to go.

Using flight effectively is different than playing a strict ground game. In terms of movement, Sentinel has one of the most agile flight modes, and the robot keeps momentum briefly when changing directions in midair. It's important to take advantage of this freedom by avoiding attacks and not staying in obvious places (like directly across from a character packing a beam hyper combo, or directly over someone who can call Dormammu—β, and so on).

For adversaries underneath Sentinel, flying air (L) is the fastest and best attack. Air (H) works, as well, and it certainly hits hard (and chains to air (S) easily for a launcher opportunity), but it's considerably slower. At low altitudes, the closest thing Sentinel has to a fast overhead is swooping in with flying air (L), (L). On hit, you can unfly and link falling (M) before landing and continuing on the ground (if guarded, go for crouching (M) or Human Catapult). Flying (L) isn't fast or tricky at all if you simply activate normal flight from the ground; Sentinel has a forced "rising" period before it can move or act. However, if you tiger knee flight activation (↓↙←↖ + (S)) so that you press (S) just as Sentinel leaves the ground, you'll get super jump flight instead and at a very low altitude! Although Sentinel's jets are still blue, this removes the totally obvious visual cue that Sentinel has started flying. This can be particularly good after dropping drones and an assist on a foe who is in the corner... It may be hard for them to see flying air (L) in this situation in time!

With Sentinel's enormous air (M), you can poke in the air ahead of where you think your opponent may go next, farther than any other character in the game. Flying (M) canceled to unfly falling (M) is perfect to place in front of or above a foe at long range. If they run into it, you can confirm into a huge combo from all but the most awkward of positions by double jump canceling the falling air (M) and chaining into a ground bounce. If you're relatively close, you can double jump and chain air (M), (H), (S). From farther away, you'll need to eliminate air (H). Depending on positioning, some improvisation may be required, but remember that you have longer than you probably think when chaining or linking Sentinel air attacks. Slow down and take your time until the flight combos come naturally.

Whenever you want to leave flight in a hurry, air (S), the "frying pan," acts as a shield that also happens to create a ground bounce. Use it whenever you'd like to return to terra firma in relative safety (for example, poking with standing (M), canceling to flight, then immediately returning to earth with (S)). If your opponent does something foolish like dash into the frying pan, good for you—free launcher!

It's extremely important to note that characters who recover in midair after being hit are in a normal jump state, even if they were thrown to the top of the playing field. Activating flight from this position allows Sentinel to reestablish mid to long range, while calling assists from a very unusual position. This is the main way Sentinel can take back momentum if the opposing player lands a hit.

COMBO APPENDIX

GENERAL EXECUTION TIPS

Don't rush into super jumping after launching with (S). Pause before super jumping, and then pause again briefly before attacking in midair, so your target levels off somewhat with their upward trajectory. Super jump too early or attack in midair too early, and Sentinel gets stationed in the wrong position for certain combos to work consistently.

Air (H) causes tons of hitstun, especially during super jumps. Don't rush linking after air (H) CANCEL flight. Pause and let your opponent drift down slightly. The timing is lenient until hitstun decay starts kicking in hard.

Air (M), (M) can be chained very slowly air-to-air and still combo. Give yourself time to verify the hits so you can score a ground bounce with air (S).

ST. (L), CR. (M), (S) CANCEL FORWARD SUPER JUMP, AIR (M), (M), (H), (S), LAND, DASH, ↓↘→ + (L) OTG CANCEL ↓↘→ + (ATK)(ATK) (MASH (ATK))

Notes	Damage
Simplest combo from fastest ground move	641,100, 29% meter loss

FLYING AIR (L), (L) CANCEL ↓↙← + (S), FALLING AIR (L), LAND, ST. (L), CR. (M), (S) CANCEL FORWARD SUPER JUMP, AIR (M), (M), (H) CANCEL ↓↙← + (S), AIR (L), (L), (M), (M), (H) CANCEL ↓↙← + (S), FALLING AIR (M) CANCEL FORWARD DOUBLE JUMP, AIR (H), (S), LAND, DASH, ↓↘→ + (L) OTG CANCEL ↓↘→ + (ATK)(ATK)

Notes	Damage
Low altitude overhead (on block, double jump cancel falling air (L) and go for air (H), (S))	658,300, 43% meter gain

P1 or P2 ROCKET RACCOON—γ + ST. (H) CANCEL →↓↘ + (L), (S) CANCEL SUPER JUMP FORWARD, AIR (M), (M), (H) CANCEL ↓↙← + (S), AIR (L), (L), (M), (H), (S), LAND, ↓↘→ + (L) OTG CANCEL ↓↘→ + (ATK)(ATK) (MASH (ATK))

Notes	Damage
Midscreen kara throw	671,800, 11% meter gain

ST. (H) CANCEL →↓↘ + (L), ↓↘→ + (L) OTG CANCEL ↓↙← + (ATK)(ATK), (S) CANCEL SUPER JUMP, AIR (M), (M), (H) CANCEL ↓↙← + (S), AIR (L), (M), (H), (S), LAND, ↓↘→↗ + (L) OTG CANCEL ↓↘→ + (ATK)(ATK), ↓↘→↗ + (L) CANCEL ↓↘→ + (ATK)(ATK), ↓↘→ + (L) CANCEL ↓↘→ + (ATK)(ATK) (MASH (ATK))

Notes	Damage
Kara throw, corner only; smoke if ya got 'em!	1,010,800, 297% meter loss

FLYING AIR (H) CANCEL ↓↙← + (S), FALLING AIR (H), LAND, DASH + P1 or P2 WESKER—β, ST. (M) CANCEL ↓↙← + (S), AIR (S), DASH, ST. (M), (S) CANCEL FORWARD SUPER JUMP, AIR (M), (M), (H) CANCEL ↓↙← + (S), AIR (L), (M), (H), (S), LAND, DASH, ↓↘→ + (L) OTG CANCEL ↓↘→ + (ATK)(ATK)

Notes	Damage
If opponent guards and does not use advancing guard, this works as a pseudo unblockable	840,500, 28% meter gain

SHE-HULK

"HOW MANY LADIES MADE THE CUT FOR BOTH THE AVENGERS AND THE FANTASTIC FOUR? YOU'RE LOOKING AT HER."

Bio

REAL NAME

Jennifer "Jen" Walters

OCCUPATION

Lawyer, Adventurer

ABILITIES

Like her cousin Hulk, Jennifer possesses great strength, durability, endurance, and a healing factor. Unlike her cousin, she almost always retains her full intelligence and personality as She-Hulk.

WEAPONS

None

PROFILE

Jennifer is the cousin of Robert Bruce Banner, the Hulk. After being gravely injured, she received a blood transfusion from Banner that allowed her to transform into She-Hulk. Her transformation extends as far as her personality, going from meek and mousy to strong-willed and confident.

FIRST APPEARANCE

The Savage She-Hulk #1 (1980)

POWER GRID

3 INTELLIGENCE
7 STRENGTH
3 SPEED
6 STAMINA
1 ENERGY PROJECTION
4 FIGHTING ABILITY

*This is biographical, and does not represent an evaluation of the in-game combat potential of this hero.

ALTERNATE COSTUMES

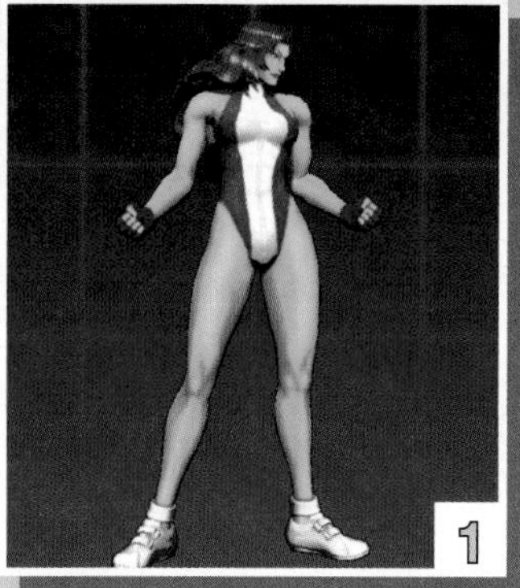
1

2

3

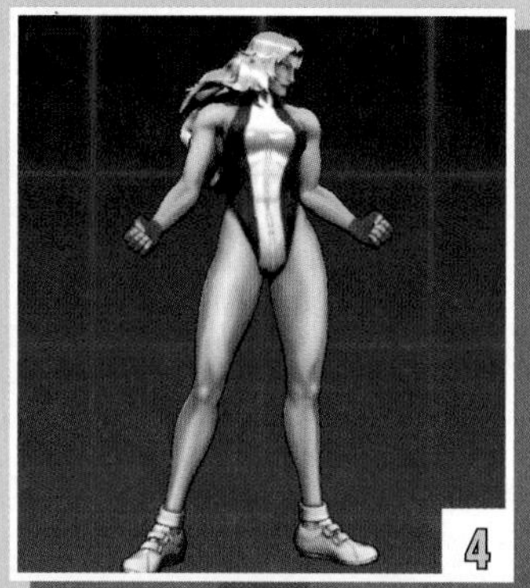
4

5

6

DLC

Overview

Vitality	1,150,000
Chain Combo Archetype	Marvel Series

X-Factor Boost	Damage	Speed
Level 1 (3 teammates remaining)	130%	110%
Level 2 (2 teammates remaining)	150%	120%
Level 3 (1 teammate remaining)	170%	130%

True to her character, She-Hulk isn't much interested in fighting from long range; she takes a very direct approach, getting up close and personal and brawling with the best of them. Naturally, your goal when using She-Hulk is to get within point blank range.

Why do you want to do this?

- When up close She-Hulk can threaten with her Heavy Strike L and Heavy Strike H; throw attacks that lead into massive damage if hit
- Enemies that try to evade Heavy Strike throw attacks open themselves up to getting hit low-hitting crouching attacks, air throws and the anti-air Heavy Strike M
- She has a fast overhead with frame advantage that can lead to combos, which is especially threatening when your foe is already in guardstun from a crossover assist
- She-Hulk has no zoning tools whatsoever. She isn't a threat unless she's close

How does She-Hulk achieve close range with her competitors?

- Forcing the enemy to guard a crossover assist
- Using She-Hulk's excellent wavedash to quickly close the distance
- Normal jumping forward while guarding, then using She-Hulk's excellent air Ⓗ to act as an air throw attempt, an air-to-air attack that leads into a combo, and an air-to-ground attack that leads into a combo
- Using a charged Chariot's hyper armor to muscle her way in
- Using Runners' Start to combat advancing guard

TUNING SINCE ORIGINAL MVC3

A successful tournament character early in original *MvC3's* lifespan, She-Hulk was weakened in three significant ways: crouching Ⓛ no longer chains into itself, limiting her ability to punish opponents for attempting to use advancing guard. Her fearsome crouching Ⓗ attack travels a much shorter distance, removing her ability to react to nearly anything and convert into major damage. Finally, her Senton aerial attack can no longer be canceled into a TAC attack, which was used to extend her combos for more damage in hard knockdown situations.

On the positive side, staying in the Runners' Start stance for 60 frames now enables a hyper armor version of her Chariot dash, giving She-Hulk an almost surefire way to close the distance against the opponent given enough time. She-Hulk also gains a brand new command normal that fills in some of the void left behind from her old crouching Ⓗ attack: the long range Lights Out!

- Crouching Ⓛ no longer chains into other Ⓛ attacks
- Crouching Ⓗ travels a much shorter distance
- Senton can no longer be canceled into TAC
- New Command Move: Lights Out! (← + Ⓗ)
- Chariot gains hyper armor if Runner's Start is charged for 60 frames
- Runner's Start can now transition into Torpedo more quickly
- Runner's Start can now transition into Clothesline more quickly
- Clothesline now wall bounces an airborne opponent
- Emerald Cannon now travels forward
- The damage of Taking out the Trash can now be increased by adding directional inputs on the controller

Attack Set

Standing Basic Attacks

Screen	Command	Hits	Damage	Meter Gain	Startup	Active	Recovery	Advantage on Hit	Advantage if Guarded	Notes
1	Standing Ⓛ	1	55,000	440	7	4	11	+1	-2	—
2	Standing Ⓜ	1	70,000	560	8	4	15	+2	-2	—
3	Standing Ⓗ	1	90,000	720	10	4	17	+5	+1	—

Crouching Basic Attacks

Screen	Command	Hits	Damage	Meter Gain	Startup	Active	Recovery	Advantage on Hit	Advantage if Guarded	Notes
1	Crouching Ⓛ	1	48,000	384	7	3	11	+2	-1	Low attack, chains into standing Ⓛ
2	Crouching Ⓜ	1	67,000	536	9	4	19	-2	-6	Low attack
3	Crouching Ⓗ	1	80,000	640	13	10	23	—	-11	Low attack, knocks down, press ⇨ between frames 21-30 to cancel into Chariot, press ⇦ between frames 21-30 to cancel into Catapult

Ground Special Attack—Launcher

Screen	Command	Hits	Damage	Meter Gain	Startup	Active	Recovery	Advantage on Hit	Advantage if Guarded	Notes
1	Ⓢ (while standing or crouching)	1	90,000	720	10	3	26	—	-7	Launcher, not special- or hyper combo-cancelable

Air Basic Attacks

Screen	Command	Hits	Damage	Meter Gain	Startup	Active	Recovery	Advantage on Hit	Advantage if Guarded	Notes
1	Air Ⓛ	1	55,000	440	6	8	17	+13	+10	Overhead attack
2	Air Ⓜ	1	70,000	560	7	4	26	+18	+14	Overhead attack
3	Air Ⓗ	1	85,000	680	9	4	26	+21	+17	Overhead attack

Air Special Attacks—Flying Screen and Air Exchange

Air Ⓢ causes a hard knockdown when used in a launcher combo (this is sometimes called flying screen). When used outside of a launcher combo, air Ⓢ behaves mostly like another basic attack. Air exchange attacks, performed by inputting a direction plus Ⓢ, are only possible during a launcher combo. Exchange hits initiate team aerial combos by tagging in the next available character to continue the air combo.

Screen	Command	Hits	Damage	Meter Gain	Startup	Active	Recovery	Advantage on Hit	Advantage if Guarded	Notes
1	Air Ⓢ	1	90,000	720	10	4	27	+18	+14	Causes hard knockdown if used in launcher combo
2	Air ⇧ + Ⓢ (during launcher combo)	1	60,000	480	9	4	Until grounded	—	—	Tags in next available ally while lofting opponent upward
3	Air ⇨ or ⇦ + Ⓢ (during launcher combo)	1	50,000	400	10	Until grounded	1	—	—	Tags in next available ally while causing wall bounce, erases 1 hyper meter bar from foe
4	Air ⇩ + Ⓢ (during launcher combo)	1	50,000	400	10	4	Until grounded	—	—	Tags in next available ally while causing ground bounce, generates 1 hyper meter bar

1

2

3

4

Command Attacks

Command attacks resemble basic attacks but have different chaining and canceling properties. It's usually possible to chain *into* a command attack from basic attacks, but most command attacks cannot be chained from or canceled themselves.

Screen	Name	Command	Hits	Damage	Meter Gain	Startup	Active	Recovery	Advantage on Hit	Advantage if Guarded	Notes
1	Greeting Punch	⇨ + Ⓗ	1	90,000	720	25	3	15	+8	+4	Overhead attack, press ⇨ between frames 21-32 to cancel into Chariot, press ⇦ between frames 21-32 to cancel into Catapult
2	Senton	(in air) ⇩ + Ⓗ	1	100,000	800	20	Until grounded	19	—	+1	Overhead attack, OTG-capable, 1 hit of super armor during frames 14-26, knocks down
3	Wall Jump	Jump backwards against wall, then press ⇗	—	—	—	8	—	—	—	—	Performs a wall jump, may initiate aerial attacks or movements after 8th frame
4	Lights Out!	⇦ + Ⓗ	1	130,000	1040	30	5	62	—	-45	Wall bounce, can chain into Ⓢ

1

2

3

4

Throws

Throws are for snagging passive or blocking opponents. Since throws are active so quickly, you can also use them to preemptively toss opposing characters out of their offense. Combos are usually possible after throws, one way or another.

Screen	Command	Hits	Damage	Meter Gain	Startup	Active	Notes
1	⇨ + Ⓗ (ground)	1	80,000	800	1	1	Hard knockdown
	⇦ + Ⓗ (ground)	1	80,000	800	1	1	Hard knockdown
2	⇨ + Ⓗ (air)	1	80,000	800	1	1	Hard knockdown
	⇦ + Ⓗ (air)	1	80,000	800	1	1	Hard knockdown

1

2

As a Partner—Crossover Assists

Screen	Type	P1+P2 Crossover Combination Hyper Combo	Description	Hits	Damage	Meter Gain	Startup	Active	Recovery (this crossover assist)	Recovery (other partner)	Notes
1	She-Hulk—α	Emerald Cannon	Torpedo	1	75,000	600	47	8	117	87	Low attack, OTG-capable, causes spinning knockdown
2	She-Hulk—β	Emerald Cannon	Clothesline	1	90,000	720	53	4	140	110	1 hit of super armor during frames 45-56, crumples for 124 frames on hit, causes spinning knockdown versus airborne foe
3	She-Hulk—γ	Emerald Cannon	Somersault Kick M	2	114,000	960	30	11	132	102	Causes spinning knockdown

1

2

3

She-Hulk—α is her most versatile assist, providing both a low attack and an OTG. This makes it an obvious choice for a majority of teams. You can use the low attack provided by this assist simultaneously with an overhead attack to create an unblockable attack. The OTG aspect works well with any character that requires an assist to continue combos after hard knockdowns, although it does have quite a bit of startup, which you must take into account when performing combos.

She-Hulk—β can be useful for the crumple it provides and can absorb one hit with super armor for several frames. However, it is slow to come out, making it a subpar defensive assist despite the super armor. It's also difficult to use outside of very basic combos, making it an awkward assist to use. It's important to note that the assist version of Clothesline is different from the normal version: the assist version does not wall bounce an airborne enemy.

She-Hulk—γ is very fast and covers a wide frontal area. The opposing character is knocked airborne, but the height where the foe recovers is low enough that most characters can convert into a combo if they can react to the hit. This assist may be useful in some teams but is still less useful than She-Hulk—α overall due to Torpedo's applications outside of combos.

Snap Back

Screen	Command	Hits	Damage	Meter Gain	Startup	Active	Recovery	Advantage on Hit	Advantage if Guarded
1	↓↘→ + P1 or P2	1	50,000	500 - (-1 hyper meter bar)	2	3	18	—	+1

Notes

On hit, snap back forces the opposing point character to be replaced by an assist. Opposing assist calls or tag outs are also locked out for 4 seconds

1

Special Moves

Screen	Name	Command	Hits	Damage	Meter Gain	Startup	Active	Recovery	Advantage on Hit	Advantage if Guarded	Notes
1	Heavy Strike L	↓↘→ + L	1	56,000	560	10	1	25	—	—	Throw, stuns foe for 120 frames
2	Heavy Strike M	↓↘→ + M	1	56,000	560	9	4	23	—	—	Throw, only hits airborne opponents, stuns rival for 120 frames
3	Heavy Strike H	↓↘→ + H	2	106,400	1064	20	6	20	—	—	Throw, stuns competitor for 120 frames
	Somersault Kick L	→↓↘ + L	1	100,000	800	8	10	21	-6(-3)	-9(-4)	Press → between frames 34-38 to cancel into Chariot, press ← between frames 34-38 to cancel into Catapult
4	Somersault Kick M	→↓↘ + M	2	133,000	1120	6	11	39	-12(-7)	-26(-21)	Press → between frames 51-55 to cancel into Chariot, press ← between frames 51-55 to cancel into Catapult
	Somersault Kick H	→↓↘ + H	3	162,500	1440	4	13	59	-29(-8)	-49(-38)	Press → between frames 66-75 to cancel into Chariot, press ← between frames 66-75 to cancel into Catapult
5	Runner's Start	↓↓ + S	—	—	—	9~60	—	—	—	—	Can be charged for 60 frames to automatically transition into a hyper armor version of Chariot, pressing S any time from frame 10 and onward causes She-Hulk to go into a 5-frame recovery period
6	Chariot	(During Runner's Start) →	—	—	—	1	Until touching opponent or wall	—	—	—	Charging Runner's Start for 60 frames gives Chariot hyper armor
7	Torpedo	(During Chariot) L	1	80,000	640	9	8	24	+4	-10	Low attack, OTG-capable, spinning knockdown, cancels into Runner's Start
8	Clothesline	(During Chariot) M	1	110,000	880	15	4	37	—	-19	1 hit of super armor during frames 7-18, crumples for 124 frames on hit, causes wall bounce against airborne opponents, cancels into Runner's Start

Special Moves continued

Screen	Name	Command	Hits	Damage	Meter Gain	Startup	Active	Recovery	Advantage on Hit	Advantage if Guarded	Notes
9	Somersault Kick+	(During Chariot) Ⓗ	2	133,000	1120	6	10	35	-7(-2)	-21(-16)	Press ⇨ between frames 46-50 to cancel into Chariot, press ⇦ between frames 46-50 to cancel into Catapult
10	Emergency Stop	(During Chariot) Ⓢ	—	—	—	5	—	—	—	—	Returns She-Hulk to neutral state
11	Catapult	(During Runner's Start) ⇦	—	—	—	26	—	—	—	—	She-Hulk jumps back and then leaps forward off the wall, stays airborne for frames 27-65, may initiate any Catapult maneuver during that time, cannot air guard during jump's entire duration
12	Shooting Star	(During Catapult) Ⓛ	1	90,000	720	6	Until grounded	8	—	+11	Ground bounce
13	Flying Drop Kick	(During Catapult) Ⓜ	1	110,000	880	10	Until grounded	15	—	+6	Wall bounce
14	Diving Senton	(During Catapult) Ⓗ	1	110,000	880	12	Until grounded	19	—	+1	1 hit of super armor during frames 14-26, ground bounce, OTG-capable
15	Emergency Landing	(During Catapult) Ⓢ	—	—	—	—	—	Until grounded, 5 frames of ground recovery	—	—	She-Hulk's forward momentum stops, and she falls straight down

Heavy Strike L 1

Heavy Strike M 2

Heavy Strike H 3

Heavy Strike: Heavy Strike is a crucial part of She-Hulk's mix-up game. All three versions of Heavy Strike put the opponent in a dizzy state when the move connects, allowing She-Hulk to follow up with a full combo. However, She-Hulk's damage gets scaled by approximately 25% more immediately following the throw.

Heavy Strike L grabs grounded adversaries, making it excellent for tick throw setups. It has fairly good range and can be canceled from basic attacks. This means that if the opposing player ever fails to advancing guard a basic attack, She-Hulk can threaten to cancel her recovery with a delayed Heavy Strike L. Competitors must use a 5 frame or faster attack or jump into the air to beat this. This technique is particularly useful with crouching Ⓗ, as this attack is normally punishable by most characters when executed at close range.

Heavy Strike M grabs airborne rivals while She-Hulk herself remains grounded. This is mainly used as a reset tool after your foe air recovers from a combo. It is very useful to use after an OTG with Torpedo, especially in the corner. Heavy Strike M is extremely powerful against characters with low air mobility. Although opposing players can attack She-Hulk out of this with fast attacks, this tactic can be risky for them because of She-Hulk's other threats like air throws or her Taking out the Trash hyper combo.

Heavy Strike H causes She-Hulk to dash forward and attempt a throw against a grounded opponent. You can employ this move to combat advancing guard against a cornered rival.

4

Somersault Kick: This is a fast attack with a high amount of active frames. All versions of this attack can be punished if guarded, but Somersault Kick L is difficult or impossible for most characters to punish if canceled into Catapult by holding back. You can use this to bait your competitor's attempts to punish She-Hulk, and then you can counter with a Catapult follow-up of your own.

5

Runner's Start: She-Hulk remains in Runner's Start until you press ⇦ for Catapult or ⇨ for Chariot, or until 60 frames elapse. After 60 frames, She-Hulk automatically begins Chariot, but with hyper armor. She can also press Ⓢ after eight frames in Runner's Start to cancel it. You can use this to cancel all basic attacks, Light's Out! Torpedo, and Clothesline to reduce the recovery of these moves. Doing so gives She-Hulk heavy frame advantage on several of these attacks.

Chariot 6

Torpedo 7

Clothesline 8

Somersault Kick + 9

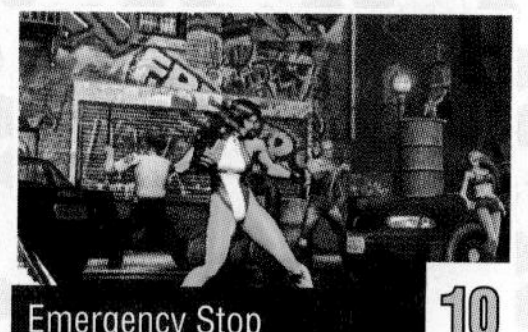
Emergency Stop 10

Chariot: She-Hulk begins running quickly forward, and if she charged Runner's Start for 60 frames, she gains hyper armor for the duration of Chariot. Press Ⓢ at any point to cancel Chariot.

Pressing Ⓛ during Chariot causes She-Hulk to attack with Torpedo. This attack hits low and is OTG-capable. This attack is primarily used to OTG after a launcher combo. It can be canceled into Runner's Start upon hitting OTG, immediately followed by Chariot into Emergency Stop, and finally Ⓢ to relaunch. This is She-Hulk's primary way to relaunch, but it can only be done early in combos. Hitstun decay causes opponents to air recover too soon for this technique to work effectively (or at all) after 10 hits.

Because of its armor property, Clothesline can be useful to catch adversaries and their assist at the same time if you can predict them, causing a crumple stun against both characters. Doing so enables She-Hulk to deal massive damage and likely KO the assist (and possibly the point character, as well). This is also useful after Heavy Strike to enable jump air Ⓜ, Ⓗ, Ⓢ combo loops.

You can utilize Somersault Kick+ in a similar fashion to Somersault Kick. If you see your foe jumping at you during Chariot, this can be a useful option as an anti-air attack. If it's blocked, you can attempt to bait and punish a counterattack by canceling to Catapult when landing.

Catapult 11

Shooting Star 12

Flying Drop Kick 13

Diving Senton 14

Emergency Landing 15

Catapult: She-Hulk jumps to the wall behind her and then launches herself forward toward the opposing character. She can alter her trajectory by using the different follow-up attacks or Emergency Landing. Catapult's main use is to avoid ground attacks on startup and bait anti-air attacks after the wall jump.

Shooting Star causes ground bounce and alters She-Hulk's trajectory to a much steeper decline. It also recovers much more quickly than the other Catapult attacks.

Flying Drop Kick causes wall bounce and makes She-Hulk lose almost all forward velocity and rapidly drop to the ground. This can be useful for punishing rivals who attempt to wavedash underneath your Catapults.

Diving Senton is similar to Senton. It also ground bounces, but once used, it continues forward with the same momentum. This move also has one hit of super armor from frames 14-26, making it useful against adversaries who attempt to anti-air you. The downside is that it has substantial startup compared to the other two attacks.

Emergency Landing makes She-Hulk immediately halt her trajectory and begin falling straight to the ground, though she is vulnerable until she lands. This is mainly used when you believe it would be risky to continue with any of the follow-up attacks to Catapult and want to land safely across the screen.

Hyper Combos

Screen	Name	Command	Hits	Damage	Startup	Active	Recovery	Advantage on Hit	Advantage if Guarded	Notes
1	Emerald Cannon	↓↘→ + ATK ATK	1	120,000	10+4	8	62	—	-48	Wall bounce, hard knockdown
2	Emerald Impulse	(During Emerald Cannon) ↓↘→ + S	1	120,000	26	31	41	—	—	Hard knockdown
3	Emerald Disaster	(During Emerald Impulse) ↓↘→ + S	1	120,000	46	22	21	—	—	Hard knockdown
4	Taking out the Trash	→↓↘ + ATK ATK	10	260,000	4+3	88~92	93~154	—	—	Frames 1-8 invincible, air throw, wall bounce
5	Road Rage (Level 3 Hyper Combo)	↓↙← + ATK ATK	3	180,000~ 400,000	18+0	1	3	—	—	Frames 1-19 invincible, throw, projectile has 4 high priority durability points, projectile cannot be destroyed

Emerald Cannon: This is primarily used as a combo ender, providing high damage for a level 1 hyper combo if all three attacks hit. You must input ↓↘→ + S during the first and second attacks to get subsequent attacks. This hyper combo is also excellent for beginning a THC because the last attack places the opposing character in a prime position for most hyper combos in the game. If a wall bounce was already used, the first hit does not wall bounce, making the second and third attacks unable to connect.

1

2

3

Taking out the Trash: This is a great anti-air throw hyper combo with invincibility frames that enable it to defeat nearly any airborne attack. This is also an excellent reset tool that you can use similarly to Heavy Strike M, but it is less vulnerable to counter attack. The only drawback is that it uses up your wall bounce: Emerald Cannon cannot be used in the follow-up combo to its full effect, making it an optimal time to utilize TAC or a reset combo.

4

5

Road Rage: As She-Hulk's level 3, this is a unique ground throw hyper combo. It has a fairly long startup at 18 frames, making it somewhat difficult to land. However, if your opponent is in a grounded state within range that allows them to be thrown once the super freeze happens, there is no escaping. If the throw connects, She-Hulk can actually follow up with OTG Torpedo and use Runners' Start canceling to launch her adversary, and since this hyper combo is only three hits, damage scaling remains very light!

What makes this hyper combo throw unique is that if your foe manages to avoid being thrown, a car that counts as a projectile with 4 high priority durability points will travel across the screen, making it very difficult for the competitor to punish She-Hulk even if she misses the throw.

"HEY, NO HARD FEELINGS, RIGHT? GIVE ME A CALL IF YOU EVER NEED A GOOD LAWYER."

Battle Plan

She-Hulk has difficulty against zoning characters and relies on assists to combat them, making her less than optimal as an anchor. She-Hulk is best as a point character for many reasons. She makes an excellent meter builder, as she has fairly damaging meter-less combos that she can connect from a variety of attacks. Furthermore, all these combos can easily lead into favorable reset situations, allowing her to take out many characters fairly quickly if she manages to successfully land a reset combo. Finally, her THC potential with Emerald Cannon is amazing, as it can be followed by a majority of hyper combos in the game, allowing for highly damaging combos when meter is used. When She-Hulk isn't on point, she makes for an amazing assist with her She-Hulk—α. This attack can provide an OTG to characters who need help with relaunch combos, but it also provides a low attack that can be used simultaneously with a high attack from the point character, creating an unblockable setup.

She-Hulk needs to be at close range to threaten her opponent. Consequently, this means that characters with strong zoning tools give her the hardest time. Her safest way to close the distance is to simply wavedash forward when there is any opportunity to do so. While advancing forward from afar, concentrate on trying to reactively jump forward over long range threats like projectiles and beams. Whenever you direct She-Hulk to jump forward, always immediately hold back on the controller after the ⇗ input: this allows you to move forward and guard at the same time. While it's obviously best to jump over threats entirely, guarding them low to the ground is the next best thing; She-Hulk will recover immediately after touching the ground, which usually results in a very significant reduction to guardstun. Immediately begin advancing forward to further close the distance!

Charge Runner's Start for 60 frames to gain hyper armor on Chariot, then charge through enemy projectiles and beams to close in on the opposing character!

Another method to close the distance is to charge Runner's Start for 60 frames, then use Chariot's hyper armor to blow through any threats in your way, often allowing for a free combo using Torpedo or Clothesline. If guarded, canceling these attacks into Runners' Start will cause She-Hulk to end up with as much as a five-frame advantage. If your competitor becomes accustomed to blocking this, you can simply cancel Chariot with Emergency Stop and immediately go for Heavy Strike L for a throw into full combo! You can use Somersault+ to combat adversaries who attempt to attack you from the air. Finding time to charge Runner's Start for a full second can be difficult against any character with projectiles, it's sometimes worth it to throw a teammate under the bus: call an assist that will jump in front of She-Hulk to soak up some damage immediately going into Runners' Start, buying you some precious time. If the other player doesn't have access to projectiles, but is still playing it safe by hanging back, simply charging Runners' Start across the screen is a great way to break the stalemate.

Once you manage to maneuver She-Hulk into range to attack with air (H) things get a bit easier. Jumping forward while guarding, then pressing ⇦ + (H) + (P1orP2) is a powerful option-select that covers a ton of bases:

- **Enemies in the air within range will get grabbed by an air throw, allowing for a follow-up combo**
- **If your foe breaks the air throw, they will drop directly into your crossover assist, allowing an immediate mix-up**
- **Air (H) will come out if the opponent is out of range, allowing you to chain to air (S) and transition into a combo**
- **If the enemy guards the air (H) your assist will pin them in place, allowing you to dash forward and establish point blank range**
- **If the other player elects to stay on the ground they'll have a ton of difficulty anti-airing air (H) due to its enormous hitbox; your assist will pin them in place shortly after**

The most consistent way for your opponent to stop the air (H) option select is to have an attack that beats it, of which there aren't many. To counter this, simply jump forward and guard, calling your crossover assist just before impact. Your assist will still be invincible coming while She-Hulk is guarding the attack, and will usually punish the enemy's vulnerable recovery. If your adversary instead tries to back out of range of She-Hulk's air (H), simply continue to press forward and push them farther back towards the corner.

Once She-Hulk is able to close on her opponent, she has a plethora of options to begin her offense and crack her rival's defense. While you can no longer chain crouching (L) for hit confirms, crouching (L) still has moderate speed, possesses amazing range for a light attack, and gives She-Hulk a +2 frame advantage. This tactic remains excellent for advancing guard baits and tick throw setups: if the opponent tries to use advancing guard on the single crouching (L) attack, perform a late chain into crouching (M), (H). This will leave a short gap in guardstun, which will often cause the enemy to get a crouching attack instead of advancing guard, which then gets counterhit by She-Hulk's crouching (M) attack. Verify the hits and chain into the (S) launcher for a combo. If the other player isn't trying to use advancing guard against your single (L) attacks, use the opportunity to set up a throw mix-up.

She-Hulk's Heavy Strike grabs cause a dizzy state on the opponent, allowing for big damage. While not particularly fast command throws, you can use this slower startup to cancel the recovery of basic attacks very late with Heavy Strike L, possibly baiting out punish attempts. You can utilize Heavy Strike H to combat advancing guard, especially in the corner. In midscreen, it can be risky to attempt this because She-Hulk can be pushed too far for Heavy Strike H to connect with her target. The move is most consistent when your crouching (H) is pushblocked, allowing the forward momentum to negate some of the distance caused by advancing guard. Furthermore, it must be done later than if done in the corner, giving your opponent more time to react and move. In the corner, advancing guard distance pushed is lessened, making Heavy Strike H likely to land if your foe does not specifically counter it, such as by jumping. You can also cancel basic attacks earlier with Heavy Strike H, allowing for only very small gaps for your adversary to react. Just keep in mind that timing the throw is different depending on whether your opponent utilizes advancing guard or not. If opposing players often attempt to have their characters jump away from your throws, you can use Heavy Strike M or Taking out the Trash to grab them out of the air.

Use crouching (L) frequently to train your opponent to block low, then hit them with a Greeting Punch overhead to score a combo!

She-Hulk's Greeting Punch (⇨ + (H)) overhead attack, adding another element to her mix-up game. Like nearly all overheads, this attack has slow startup, so it's best used in situations where you have a lot of frame advantage: force your foe to guard a crossover assist, then immediately drop a Greeting Punch on their head! When guarded, Greeting Punch provides a +4 frame advantage, giving She-Hulk free reign to apply any mix-up following this attack as long as the other player doesn't use advancing guard. In the likely event that they do, simply hold forward on the controller to cancel Greeting Punch into Chariot and run back into fighting range. This overhead leaves She-Hulk with 8 frames of advantage if it hits, allowing you to link a crouching (L) afterwards and go into a combo.

Crossover assists aren't only a great way to set up Greeting Punch, forcing the enemy to guard them puts you in a position of power where your options suddenly become much more powerful:

- **Greeting Punch overhead timed to hit immediately after the assist, forcing the opponent to guard high**
- **Low-hitting basic attacks will hit the other player if they are guarding high or trying to jump away**
- **Heavy Strike grabs your rival if they are concentrating on guarding the high/low mix-up**
- **Jumping forward and using option select air ⇦ + (H) will air throw your foe if they try to jump, and can also cross-up if they stay on the ground**

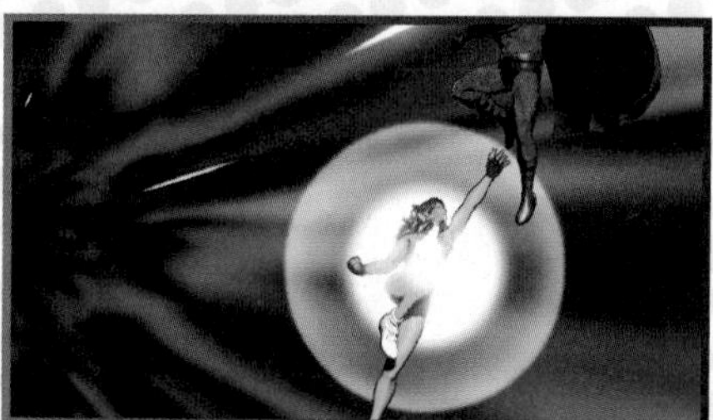

OTG with Torpedo after a hard knockdown to set up an air reset, then react to your opponent's air recovery and grab him out of the air!

Once you manage to score a combo, She-Hulk has excellent reset options that can be difficult for most characters to deal with. These setups typically begin with the OTG-capable Torpedo after a hard knockdown. This makes your rival air recover. Let Torpedo naturally recover. She-Hulk will be positioned below and slightly in front of her foe as they recover. From here, you can go for a Heavy Strike M if you don't expect that your opponent is going to attack after air recovering. However, this tactic cannot win against fast attacks that your competitor uses after air recovering. To counter this, you can use Taking out the Trash, which has the invincibility to blow through any attacks that lack invincibility. But, this limits your follow-up combo due to using a wall bounce; if the ensuing combo does not finish off the enemy, simply set up another reset!. The last option is to go for an option select air throw with ⇦ + (H) + (P1orP2). Even if the other player breaks the air throw, they will be forced to guard the assist and allow for an even better mix-up!

Defensively, She-Hulk has limited options. She mainly relies on advancing guard to stop her opponent's offense. Option select air throws are also great against jumping adversaries since the throws can instantly give you the offensive initiative. Taking out the Trash is also great against any airborne foes if they lack any air hyper combos. You can also use Road Rage if your rival is leaving gaps in their blockstrings.

COMBO USAGE

I. CR. Ⓛ, Ⓜ, Ⓗ, Ⓢ [CANCEL] SUPER JUMP FORWARD, AIR Ⓜ, Ⓜ, Ⓗ, Ⓢ, LAND, ↓↓ + Ⓢ [CANCEL] → [CANCEL] Ⓛ [CANCEL] ↓↘→ + ATK ATK [CANCEL] ↓↘→ + Ⓢ [CANCEL] ↓↘→ + Ⓢ, ↓↓ + Ⓢ [CANCEL] → [CANCEL] Ⓛ

609,800 damage, 40% meter loss

This is a basic She-Hulk combo that provides good damage that is relatively easy in comparison to some of her more difficult combos. Hit the first air Ⓜ quickly, but space the rest of the attacks out since they allow her to land sooner after the air Ⓢ, giving her more time to OTG with Torpedo. Buffer ↓↓ as She-Hulk is about to land and press Ⓢ right after she lands, then immediately press → to begin Chariot, then press Ⓛ to Torpedo as soon as she is within range of the opposing character.

II. CR. Ⓛ, Ⓜ, Ⓗ, Ⓢ [CANCEL] SUPER JUMP FORWARD, AIR Ⓗ, Ⓢ, LAND, ↓↓ + Ⓢ [CANCEL] → [CANCEL] Ⓛ [CANCEL] ↓↓ + Ⓢ [CANCEL] → [CANCEL] Ⓢ, Ⓢ [CANCEL] SUPER JUMP FORWARD, AIR Ⓗ, Ⓢ, LAND, ↓↓ + Ⓢ [CANCEL] → [CANCEL] Ⓛ [CANCEL] ↓↘→ + ATK ATK, ↓↘→ + Ⓢ, ↓↘→ + Ⓢ, ↓↓ + Ⓢ [CANCEL] → [CANCEL] Ⓛ

679,300 damage, 28% meter loss

This is similar to the first combo, but with a relaunch. Delay the air attacks as long as possible to allow She-Hulk to land with enough time to Torpedo. After the first knockdown, you'll need to use Runner's Start to cancel Torpedo to allow you to be able to relaunch. Remember that in the corner, you do not need to hold → after canceling Torpedo with Runner's Start.

III. ↓↘→ + ATK, ↓↓ + Ⓢ [CANCEL] → [CANCEL] Ⓜ [CANCEL] ↓↓ + Ⓢ [CANCEL] ← [CANCEL] Ⓗ, JUMP STRAIGHT UP, AIR Ⓜ, Ⓗ, Ⓢ, LAND, JUMP FORWARD, AIR Ⓜ, Ⓗ, Ⓢ, LAND, Ⓢ [CANCEL] SUPER JUMP FORWARD, AIR Ⓜ, Ⓜ, Ⓗ, Ⓢ, LAND, ↓↓ + Ⓢ [CANCEL] → [CANCEL] Ⓛ [CANCEL] ↓↘→ + ATK ATK [CANCEL] ↓↘→ + Ⓢ [CANCEL] ↓↘→ + Ⓢ, ↓↓ + Ⓢ [CANCEL] → [CANCEL] Ⓛ

577,500~588,700 damage, 8~13% meter gain

Heavy Strike is a strong part of She-Hulk's offense. A successful grab gives you a huge window to land nearly any attack. So to follow up, you have a crumple with Clothesline, which is then canceled into a Catapult followed by a ground bounce with Diving Senton. Immediately jump and attack with air Ⓜ, and then delay the following air attacks as much as possible so the opponent stays low enough and She-Hulk has enough time to land for the Ⓢ launch.

IV. → + Ⓗ [CANCEL] → [CANCEL] Ⓛ [CANCEL] ↓↓ + Ⓢ [CANCEL] → [CANCEL] Ⓢ, Ⓢ [CANCEL] SUPER JUMP FORWARD, AIR Ⓗ, Ⓢ, LAND, ↓↓ + Ⓢ [CANCEL] → [CANCEL] Ⓛ [CANCEL] ↓↓ + Ⓢ [CANCEL] → [CANCEL] Ⓢ, Ⓢ [CANCEL] SUPER JUMP FORWARD, AIR Ⓗ, Ⓢ, LAND, ↓↓ + Ⓢ [CANCEL] → [CANCEL] Ⓛ [CANCEL] ↓↘→ + ATK ATK, ↓↘→ + Ⓢ, ↓↘→ + Ⓢ, ↓↓ + Ⓢ [CANCEL] → [CANCEL] Ⓛ

736,600 damage, 25% meter loss

This is an alternative combo that begins with Greeting Punch that trades meter gain for higher damage. By holding → during Greeting Punch, She-Hulk automatically cancels into Chariot, allowing her to combo into Torpedo, then utilizes the Torpedo cancel relaunch twice. This combo is identical to Combo II once the first launch happens.

V. AIR THROW, LAND, ↓↓ + Ⓢ [CANCEL] → [CANCEL] Ⓛ [CANCEL] ↓↓ + Ⓢ [CANCEL] → [CANCEL] Ⓢ, Ⓢ [CANCEL] SUPER JUMP FORWARD, AIR Ⓜ, Ⓜ, Ⓗ, Ⓢ, LAND, ↓↓ + Ⓢ [CANCEL] → [CANCEL] Ⓛ [CANCEL] ↓↘→ + ATK ATK, ↓↘→ + Ⓢ, ↓↘→ + Ⓢ, ↓↓ + Ⓢ [CANCEL] → [CANCEL] Ⓛ

478,900 damage, 40% meter loss

She-Hulk can get amazing damage off air throws if she chooses to expend meter. Even if you choose to forgo the Torpedo cancel relaunch and immediately cancel Torpedo to Emerald Cannon, this combo deals 448,400 damage, though with a significantly higher meter cost at 80% meter loss.

VI. →↓↘ + ATK ATK, DASH FORWARD, CR. Ⓗ, Ⓢ [CANCEL] SUPER JUMP FORWARD, AIR Ⓗ, Ⓢ, LAND, ↓↓ + Ⓢ [CANCEL] → [CANCEL] Ⓛ [CANCEL] ↓↓ + Ⓢ [CANCEL] → [CANCEL] Ⓢ, Ⓢ [CANCEL] SUPER JUMP FORWARD, AIR Ⓗ, Ⓢ, LAND, ↓↓ + Ⓢ [CANCEL] → [CANCEL] Ⓛ

393,000 damage, 38% meter loss

While Taking out the Trash is a very powerful anti-air, its follow-up damage is somewhat limited unless you utilize a THC after the first hit of an Emerald Cannon ender. Dash immediately after recovering so that She-Hulk is close enough for crouching Ⓗ to hit.

VII. ↓↙← + ATK ATK, ↓↓ + Ⓢ [CANCEL] → [CANCEL] Ⓛ [CANCEL] ↓↓ + Ⓢ [CANCEL] → [CANCEL] Ⓢ, Ⓢ [CANCEL] SUPER JUMP FORWARD, AIR Ⓗ, Ⓢ, LAND, ↓↓ + Ⓢ [CANCEL] → [CANCEL] Ⓛ [CANCEL] ↓↓ + Ⓢ [CANCEL] → [CANCEL] Ⓢ, Ⓢ [CANCEL] SUPER JUMP FORWARD, AIR Ⓗ, Ⓢ, LAND, ↓↓ + Ⓢ [CANCEL] → [CANCEL] Ⓛ [CANCEL] ↓↘→ + ATK ATK [CANCEL] ↓↘→ + Ⓢ [CANCEL] ↓↘→ + Ⓢ, ↓↓ + Ⓢ [CANCEL] → [CANCEL] Ⓛ

931,000 damage, 332% meter loss

If She-Hulk manages to land her Road Rage throw, it can lead to huge damage, though it requires very heavy meter usage. After Road Rage finishes, you have a lot of time to land the follow-up Torpedo, so don't feel too rushed and just make sure you get it out.

ADVANCED TACTICS

HEAVY STRIKE DAMAGE SCALING AVOIDANCE

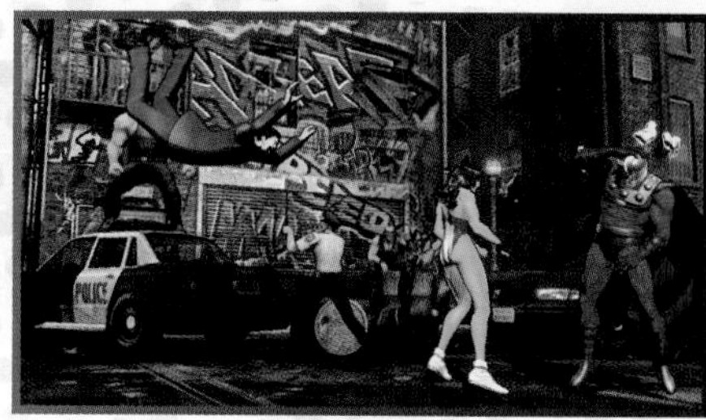

Tag in your partner to get more damage after a Heavy Strike!

Heavy Strike causes any follow-up attacks from She-Hulk to begin scaling by an additional 20%, somewhat limiting the amount of damage she can inflict. However, you can avoid this additional damage scaling by tagging in a different character, allowing the follow-up combo to do full damage, scaled by only the amount of hits from Heavy Strike!

TORPEDO CANCEL RELAUNCHES

Since Senton can no longer be TAC canceled, She-Hulk lost one of her methods of relaunching opponents. However, she still has a method of relaunching her rivals without the use of an assist. When hitting an adversary, OTG with Torpedo, immediately cancel to Runner's Start with ⇩ ⇩ + (S) on hit. An efficient way to cancel Torpedo to Runner's Start quickly is to execute Torpedo with ⇩ + (L), then simply input another ⇩ + (S) to complete the Runner's Start command. Next, immediately hold ⇨ and quickly press (S) twice once She-Hulk begins running, which will cause her to use Emergency Stop followed immediately by the launcher. The whole input sequence looks like this:

- ⇩ ⇩ + (S) to go into Runner's Start stance
- ⇨ immediately to go into Chariot
- ⇩ + (L) to hit with the OTG-capable Torpedo
- ⇩ + (S) to cancel into the second Runner's Start stance
- ⇨ immediately to use Chariot again
- (S), (S) quickly to cancel Chariot and launch!

Cancel an OTG Torpedo with Runner's Start and then Emergency Stop to reduce the recovery of Torpedo and allow a relaunch with (S)!

All of this happens extremely fast and only works early in combos, usually with fewer than approximately 10 hits before the relaunch. Keep in mind that Runner's Start has a 9 frame startup period before you can do anything, including canceling with Emergency Stop.

SHE-HULK

COMBO APPENDIX

GENERAL EXECUTION TIPS

- She-Hulk's combos require precise timing. Learn the rhythm of the combos to master them
- She-Hulk's aerial combos often require you to delay attacks so that she can land with enough time to perform her Torpedo OTG
- She-Hulks Torpedo cancel relaunches require very quick inputs (three presses of (S) within a total of 15 frames). Make sure you have your hand in a comfortable position to press this button quickly

CR. (L), (M), (H), (S) [CANCEL] SUPER JUMP FORWARD, AIR (M), (M), (H), (S), LAND, DASH FORWARD, JUMP FORWARD, CALL TASKMASTER—α, ↓ + (H), (S) [CANCEL] SUPER JUMP FORWARD, AIR (M), (M), (H), (S), LAND, ↓ ↓ + (S) [CANCEL] → [CANCEL] (L) [CANCEL] ↓ ↘ → + (ATK)(ATK) [CANCEL] ↓ ↘ → + (S) [CANCEL] ↓ ↘ → + (S), ↓ ↓ + (S) [CANCEL] → [CANCEL] (L)

Notes	Damage
Relaunch combo with Senton and Taskmaster—α assist	675,700 damage, 13% meter gain

AIR THROW, LAND, ↓ ↓ + (S) [CANCEL] → [CANCEL] (L) [X-FACTOR] DASH FORWARD, JUMP FORWARD, AIR (H), (S), LAND, JUMP FORWARD, AIR (M), (H), (S), LAND, (S) [CANCEL] SUPER JUMP FORWARD, AIR (M), (M), (H), (S), LAND, ↓ ↓ + (S) [CANCEL] → [CANCEL] (L) [CANCEL] ↓ ↘ → + (ATK)(ATK) [CANCEL] ↓ ↘ → + (S) [CANCEL] ↓ ↘ → + (S), ↓ ↓ + (S) [CANCEL] → [CANCEL] (L)

Notes	Damage
Delay first air (H) long enough to keep the opposing character low to the ground. Slight delay between air (M), (H), (S)	X-Factor level 1, 800,900 damage, 17% meter gain

↓ ↓ + (S) [CANCEL] → [CANCEL] (M), JUMP STRAIGHT UP, AIR (S), LAND, JUMP FORWARD, AIR (M), (H), (S), LAND, JUMP FORWARD, AIR (M), (H), (S), LAND, (S) [CANCEL] SUPER JUMP FORWARD, AIR (M), (M), (H), (S), LAND, ↓ ↓ + (S) [CANCEL] → [CANCEL] (L) [CANCEL] ↓ ↘ → + (ATK)(ATK) [CANCEL] ↓ ↘ → + (S) [CANCEL] ↓ ↘ → + (S), ↓ ↓ + (S) [CANCEL] → [CANCEL] (L)

Notes	Damage
Alternative to Senton Dive after Clothesline	710, 200 damage, 0% meter gain

← + (H) [CANCEL] ↓ ↓ + (S) [CANCEL] → [CANCEL] (S), (S) [CANCEL] SUPER JUMP FORWARD, AIR (H), (S), LAND, ↓ ↓ + (S) [CANCEL] → [CANCEL] (L) [CANCEL] ↓ ↓ + (S) [CANCEL] → [CANCEL] (S), (S) [CANCEL] SUPER JUMP FORWARD, AIR (H), (S), LAND, ↓ ↓ + (S) [CANCEL] → [CANCEL] (L) [CANCEL] ↓ ↘ → + (ATK)(ATK) [CANCEL] ↓ ↘ → + (ATK)(ATK) (DANTE THC, MASH (ATK))

Notes	Damage
THC is useful to get higher damage if wall bounce is already used in a combo	818,500 damage, 134% meter loss

↓ ↓ + (S) [CANCEL] → [CANCEL] (H) (2 HITS) [X-FACTOR], LAND, JUMP FORWARD, AIR (H), (S), LAND, AIR (M), (H), (S), LAND, AIR (M), (H), (S), LAND, (S) [CANCEL] SUPER JUMP FORWARD, AIR (H), (S), LAND, ↓ ↓ + (S) [CANCEL] → [CANCEL] (L) [CANCEL] ↓ ↘ → + (ATK)(ATK) [CANCEL] ↓ ↘ → + (S) [CANCEL] ↓ ↘ → + (S), ↓ ↓ + (S) [CANCEL] → [CANCEL] (L)

Notes	Damage
Starting a combo with Somersault+ using air X-Factor cancel	953,400 damage, 25% meter gain

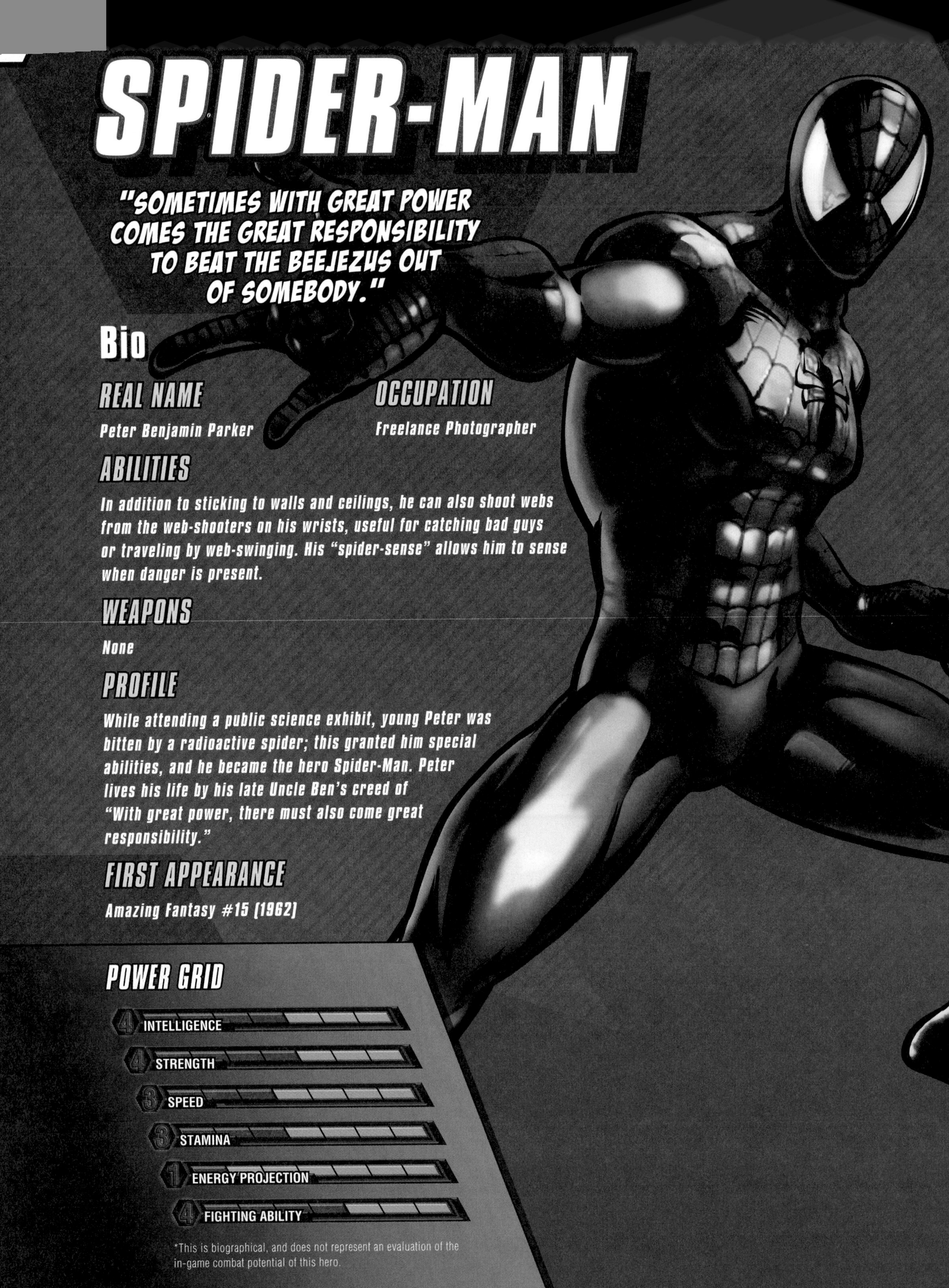

SPIDER-MAN

"SOMETIMES WITH GREAT POWER COMES THE GREAT RESPONSIBILITY TO BEAT THE BEEJEZUS OUT OF SOMEBODY."

Bio

REAL NAME

Peter Benjamin Parker

OCCUPATION

Freelance Photographer

ABILITIES

In addition to sticking to walls and ceilings, he can also shoot webs from the web-shooters on his wrists, useful for catching bad guys or traveling by web-swinging. His "spider-sense" allows him to sense when danger is present.

WEAPONS

None

PROFILE

While attending a public science exhibit, young Peter was bitten by a radioactive spider; this granted him special abilities, and he became the hero Spider-Man. Peter lives his life by his late Uncle Ben's creed of "With great power, there must also come great responsibility."

FIRST APPEARANCE

Amazing Fantasy #15 (1962)

POWER GRID

4	INTELLIGENCE
4	STRENGTH
3	SPEED
3	STAMINA
1	ENERGY PROJECTION
4	FIGHTING ABILITY

*This is biographical, and does not represent an evaluation of the in-game combat potential of this hero.

ALTERNATE COSTUMES

Overview

Vitality	900,000
Chain Combo Archetype	Marvel Series

X-Factor Boost	Damage	Speed
Level 1 (3 teammates remaining)	125%	115%
Level 2 (2 teammates remaining)	145%	125%
Level 3 (1 teammate remaining)	165%	135%

Spider-Man is a melee character armed with several tools for fighting and approaching from long range. Even though he can be annoying from a distance, your goal is to get him close to his opponent for an opportunity to land big combos. Why this goal?

- **Spider-Man's quick attacks, Web Swing pressure, square jumps, and triangle jumps are best utilized at close range**
- **Spider-Man's combos deal a decent amount of damage on their own without the help of a THC**

How is this goal achieved?

- **Using Web Ball L and Web Glide to set your adversary up for an approach**
- **Performing Web Swing H so that it is guarded at maximum range, granting frame advantage for continued pressure**
- **Luring the opponent close by frustrating them with ground and air Web Ball L combined with Web Throw L/M and a long range crossover assist**

TUNING SINCE ORIGINAL MVC3

Spider-Man now has the ability to cancel all special moves (except Web Throw) into Web Glide, expanding his attack options. In addition, Web Glide is now OTG-capable, allowing for combos not previously possible. The damage on Web Throw has been increased, but it scales much differently than before.

- Normal and special moves can be canceled into Web Glide
- Web Glide is OTG-capable
- Crawler Assault recovery reduced, and the move is now mashable
- Web Throw L damage increased
- Web Throw M and H damage decreased

Attack Set

Standing Basic Attacks

Screen	Command	Hits	Damage	Meter Gain	Startup	Active	Recovery	Advantage on Hit	Advantage if Guarded	Notes
1	Standing Ⓛ	1	43,000	344	4	3	9	+2	+1	—
2	Standing Ⓜ	1	60,000	480	8	3	15	+1	-1	—
3	Standing Ⓗ	1	70,000	560	10	6	24	-6	-8	—

1

2

3

Crouching Basic Attacks

Screen	Command	Hits	Damage	Meter Gain	Startup	Active	Recovery	Advantage on Hit	Advantage if Guarded	Notes
1	Crouching Ⓛ	1	40,000	320	6	2	11	+1	0	Low attack, chains into standing Ⓛ
2	Crouching Ⓜ	1	57,000	456	5	6	18	-5	-7	—
3	Crouching Ⓗ	1	67,000	536	10	7	37	—	-22	Low attack, knocks down

1

2

3

Ground Special Attack—Launcher

Screen	Command	Hits	Damage	Meter Gain	Startup	Active	Recovery	Advantage on Hit	Advantage if Guarded	Notes
1	Ⓢ (while standing or crouching)	1	80,000	640	9	4	26	—	-8	Launcher, not special- or hyper combo-cancelable

1

Air Basic Attacks

Screen	Command	Hits	Damage	Meter Gain	Startup	Active	Recovery	Advantage on Hit	Advantage if Guarded	Notes
1	Air Ⓛ	1	44,000	352	5	3	22	+11	+10	Overhead attack
2	Air Ⓜ	1	60,000	480	7	4	17	+16	+14	Overhead attack
3	Air Ⓗ	1	70,000	560	10	8	16	+19	+17	Overhead attack

1

2

3

Air Special Attacks—Flying Screen and Air Exchange

Air Ⓢ causes a hard knockdown when used in a launcher combo (this is sometimes called flying screen). When used outside of a launcher combo, air Ⓢ behaves mostly like another basic attack. Air exchange attacks, performed by inputting a direction plus Ⓢ, are only possible during a launcher combo. Exchange hits initiate team aerial combos by tagging in the next available character to continue the air combo.

Screen	Command	Hits	Damage	Meter Gain	Startup	Active	Recovery	Advantage on Hit	Advantage if Guarded	Notes
1	Air Ⓢ	1	78,000	624	9	8	11	+16	+14	Overhead attack, causes hard knockdown if used in launcher combo
2	Air ⇧ + Ⓢ (during launcher combo)	1	35,000	280	7	10	Until grounded	—	—	Tags in next available ally while lofting foe upward
3	Air ⇨ or ⇦ + Ⓢ (during launcher combo)	1	35,000	280	7	10	Until grounded	—	—	Tags in next available ally while causing wall bounce, erases 1 hyper meter bar from opponent
4	Air ⇩ + Ⓢ (during launcher combo)	1	50,000	400	10	8	Until grounded	—	—	Tags in next available ally while causing ground bounce, generates 1 hyper meter bar

1

2

3

4

Command Attacks

Command attacks resemble basic attacks but have different chaining and canceling properties. It's usually possible to chain *into* a command attack from basic attacks, but most command attacks cannot be chained from or canceled themselves.

Screen	Name	Command	Hits	Damage	Meter Gain	Startup	Active	Recovery	Advantage on Hit	Advantage if Guarded	Notes
1	Wall Jump	Jump backward against wall, then press ⇗	—	—	—	—	—	—	—	—	Performs a wall jump, may initiate aerial attacks or movements after 8th frame

1

Throws

Throws are for snagging passive or blocking foes. Since throws are active so quickly, you can also use them to preemptively toss opposing characters out of their offense. Combos are usually possible after throws, one way or another.

Screen	Command	Hits	Damage	Meter Gain	Startup	Active	Notes
1	⇨ + Ⓗ (ground)	1	80,000	800	1	1	Hard knockdown
	⇦ + Ⓗ (ground)	1	80,000	800	1	1	Hard knockdown
2	⇨ + Ⓗ (air)	1	80,000	800	1	1	Hard knockdown
	⇦ + Ⓗ (air)	1	80,000	800	1	1	Hard knockdown

1

2

As a Partner—Crossover Assists

Screen	Type	P1+P2 Crossover Combination Hyper Combo	Description	Hits	Damage	Meter Gain	Startup	Active	Recovery (this crossover assist)	Recovery (other partner)	Notes
1	Spider-Man—α	Crawler Assault	Web Ball L	1	10,000	100	40	—	121	91	Stuns for 34 frames on hit, projectile has 5 low priority durability points
2	Spider-Man—β	Crawler Assault	Web Swing H	1	90,000	720	44	20	114	84	—
3	Spider-Man—γ	Crawler Assault	Spider Sting M	1	80,000	640	35	21	137	107	—

Spider-Man has few uses as a crossover assist. You can use Spider-Man—α Web Ball to complement a ranged offensive, and the move can be followed with a combo if the projectile connects. Spider-Man—β Web Swing launches forward with a kick attack that causes adversaries to recover in the air, and it can be used in combos. Because of its forward momentum, this crossover assist is easily punished and should be used with caution. Spider-Man—γ Spider Sting has no frames of invulnerability when called as a crossover assist, so its use as an anti-air is limited. However, using Spider-Man—γ as a crossover counter does grant Spider Sting with a short window of invulnerability upon startup, making it useful for turning the tide against an overly offensive opponent.

Snap Back

Screen	Command	Hits	Damage	Meter Gain	Startup	Active	Recovery	Advantage on Hit	Advantage if Guarded
1	↓↘→ + P1 or P2	1	50,000	500 - (-1 hyper meter bar)	2	6	24	—	-8

Notes

On hit, snap back forces the opposing point character to be replaced by an assist. Opposing assist calls or tag outs are also locked out for 4 seconds

Special Moves

Screen	Name	Command	Hits	Damage	Meter Gain	Startup	Active	Recovery	Advantage on Hit	Advantage if Guarded	Notes
1	Web Ball L (in air OK)	↓↘→ + L	1	10,000	100	16	—	29	+5	-13	Captures foe for 34 frames on hit, projectile has 5 low priority durability points
	Web Ball M	↓↘→ + M	1	10,000	100	22	—	33	+10	-17	Captures rival for 43 frames on hit, projectile has 5 low priority durability points
	Web Ball H	↓↘→ + H	1	10,000	100	28	—	38	+15	-22	Captures competitor for 53 frames on hit, projectile has 5 low priority durability points
	Air Web Ball L	(in air) ↓↘→ + L	1	10,000	100	18	—	29	—	—	Captures target for 34 frames on hit, projectile has 5 low priority durability points
	Air Web Ball M	(in air) ↓↘→ + M	1	10,000	100	22	—	35	—	—	Captures adversary for 43 frames on hit, projectile has 5 low priority durability points
	Air Web Ball H	(in air) ↓↘→ + H	1	10,000	100	26	—	41	—	—	Captures opponent for 53 frames on hit, projectile has 5 low priority durability points
2	Spider Sting L	↓↘→ + L	1	70,000	560	7	21	20	-1	-19	Knocks down
	Spider Sting M	↓↘→ + M	1	80,000	640	9	21	26	-5	-25	Knocks down
	Spider Sting H	↓↘→ + H	1	90,000	720	11	21	44	-23	-43	Knocks down
3	Spider Bite	(During Spider Sting) H	1	45,000	400	3	3-8	Until grounded, 1 frame ground recovery	—	—	Input H between frames 17-23 of Spider Sting H, ground bounce
4	Web Swing L (in air OK)	←↓↙ + L	1	70,000	560	12	10	6	+15	+6	Air version is overhead attack, knocks down
	Web Swing M (in air OK)	←↓↙ + M	1	80,000	640	16	16	6	+9	0	Air version is overhead attack, knocks down
	Web Swing H (in air OK)	←↓↙ + H	1	90,000	720	20	20	2	—	0	Air version is overhead attack, knocks down
5	Web Throw L	→↘↓↙← + L	3	176,000	1760	20	—	27	—	-15	Hard knockdown, projectile has 3 low priority durability points
	Web Throw M	→↘↓↙← + M	3	123,200	1232	16	—	26	—	-10	Hard knockdown, projectile has 3 low priority durability points
	Web Throw H	→↘↓↙← + H	3	123,200	1232	14	—	25	—	-4	Hard knockdown, projectile has 3 low priority durability points
6	Web Glide (can be directed, in air OK)	S + ATK	1	20,000	160	16 (upward), 18 (downward)	Until contact	—	+19	+17	Holding ↗, ↘, ↙, or ↖ fires the shot at an angle in the corresponding direction, Spider-Man instantly recovers in air upon contact, OTG-capable projectile has 1 low priority durability point

1

Web Ball: Spider-Man fires a projectile that temporarily incapacitates his opponent. The speed of the projectile and length in which the adversary is incapacitated is determined by the strength of the attack: (L) travels the slowest, releases the fastest, and captures for 34 frames, while (H) travels the fastest, releases the slowest, and captures for 53 frames. Web Ball is Spider-Man's main way of threatening a rival from a distance, and you can use it as a way to control space on the ground. Fire a Web Ball (L) to clear the way, then have Spider-Man dash after it to close in on the opposing character. If the Web Ball connects, dash forward with a combo. If performed in the air, Spider-Man fires the projectile down at 45-degree angle, making it great for an annoying air-to-ground attack. You can have Spider-Man fire a maximum of two Web Balls in the air (three if X-Factor is activated in the air), and you can use them in tandem with his airdash, Web Glide, and Spider Swing to keep him airborne for a long period of time.

Spider Sting 2

Spider Bite 3

Spider Sting: Spider Sting launches Spider-Man up for an uppercut attack. If connected or guarded, Spider Sting can be followed with Spider Bite for a ground bounce and hard knockdown. The strength of the attack used determines the altitude, speed, and damage of this special move; (H) reaches the highest and does the most damage but is the slowest to recover, while (L) is the weakest and doesn't reach as high. Spider Sting is an integral part of Spider-Man combos, and you can follow all three versions with a combo during the ground bounce.

Spider Sting has no window of invulnerability, limiting its use as an anti-air attack. It also has an awful amount of recovery time, making it highly punishable if whiffed or guarded. Perform Spider Sting early to use it as an anti-air effectively, and cancel into Web Glide if guarded (see the Advanced Tactics section for more details).

4

Web Swing: Spider-Man swings forward with a kick and recovers in the air. The strength of the attack used determines the damage and distance of the swing, with (H) having the largest swing. After recovering, all normal jump actions are available, including attacking, guarding, or calling a crossover assist. Upon connecting, Web Swing causes massive hitstun, allowing for you to perform extended combos with air (M), (H), (S) (or air (H), (S) delayed slightly). If the kick is guarded during the later active frames, Web Swing grants frame advantage, and you can follow it with air attacks for overhead offensive pressure.

Although Web Swing can be guarded high or low normally, the aerial version is considered overhead and must be guarded high. To exploit this, you can modify Web Swing with a tiger knee motion of ←↓↙↖ to perform an aerial Web Swing low to the ground that must be guarded high. If you are having trouble performing this, try doing the motion slowly and pressing (ATK) very slightly after ↖ so that (ATK) is pressed during the three pre-jump frames of the super jump. Note that this technique is harder to connect on smaller opponents.

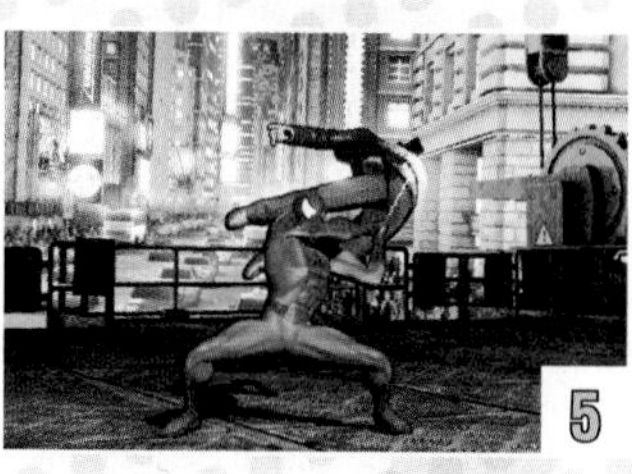

5

Web Throw: Spider-Man fires a long web projectile that grabs and tosses adversaries from a distance, causing a hard knockdown. Web Throw deals a hefty amount of damage for a projectile attack and can be fired in different directions depending on the strength of the attack used. Web Throw L fires the web straight across, traveling the entire distance of the screen horizontally. Web Throw M shoots upward at a 45-degree angle, cutting off a competitor's approach from the sky. Web Throw H fires straight up and is often used in combos from a launcher. A successful Web Throw can be followed with down-forward Web Glide OTG for a combo or Maximum Spider, so long as it is not performed in a combo heavily affected by hit decay.

6

Web Glide: Web Glide is Spider-Man's primary means of aerial mobility and is the equivalent to the 8-way airdash that characters like Nova or Doctor Doom possess. You can shoot Web Glide in one of three directions on the ground: ↖, ↑, or ↗; inputting (ATK) + (S) on the ground without any direction defaults to the forward-moving Web Glide. When Spider-Man is in the air, you can shoot Web Glide in four directions: ↙, ↖, ↗, ↘. Upon attaching to a wall or to a foe, Spider-Man then zips forward toward his mark and is free to attack or guard during the duration of the dash. Attacking an opponent with the glide causes a small amount of hitstun/guardstun and damage, allowing for combos after the web hits. Web Glide is also OTG-capable, giving Spider-Man increased combo potential. You can follow a Web Glide OTG with Maximum Spider, provided that hit decay has not heavily affected the previous combo.

Web Glide is not only good for moving around the screen but is also beneficial for setting up triangle jumps with a grounded up-forward Web Glide. You can also utilize it as a projectile to limit a competitor's movement due to the hitstun and guardstun it produces. Opponents closing in at normal jump height will have their approach cut off and even their attacks interrupted if shot with a grounded up-forward Web Glide. If you are having Spider-Man approach from the sky, aim a down-forward Web Glide at the target to set them up for the incoming aerial assault.

Hyper Combos

Screen	Name	Command	Hits	Damage	Startup	Active	Recovery	Advantage on Hit	Advantage if Guarded	Notes
1	Maximum Spider (in air OK)	↓↘→ + (ATK)(ATK)	15	271,600	7~23+4	8~11	68	—	-54	Invincible until Spider-Man reaches the wall, hard knockdown
2	Crawler Assault	→↓↘ + (ATK)(ATK)	8~16	292,100~350,400	20+4	3(5)3(5)3(5)3(5)3(5)3(5)3(5)3(10)5	41	—	-25	Frames 1-26 invincible, last hit wall bounces, can be mashed for additional hits
3	Ultimate Web Throw	→↘↓↙← + (ATK)(ATK)	1	300,000	29+3	15	76	—	—	Frames 1-20 invincible, air throw, hard knockdown

1

Maximum Spider: Spider-Man jumps to the back wall, then homes in on the opposing character for a series of aerial attacks into a hard knockdown. Spider-Man always travels to the wall behind him, so Maximum Spider's startup varies depending on Spider-Man's distance relative to the back wall, the fastest startup being with his back right next to the wall. Though the automatic tracking on Maximum Spider is fairly accurate, this hyper combo has a whopping 68 frames of recovery if unsuccessful, leaving Spider-Man open to the most damaging punish that his adversary can muster. Maximum Spider is mainly used in combos off Web Swing or Web Throw and can also be used midair. Use it only when you know it is going to connect, or when you have a safe THC to follow with.

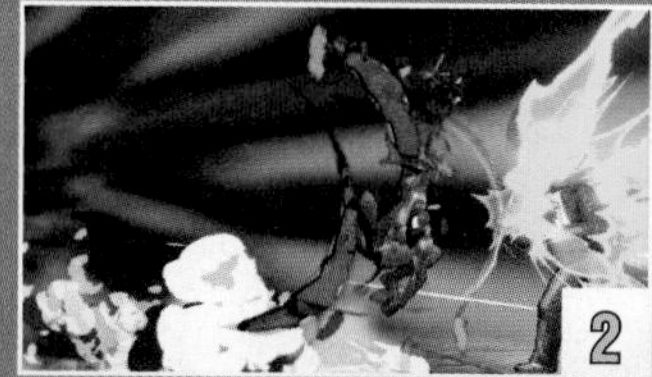

2

Crawler Assault: Spider-Man performs a barrage of attacks that causes a wall bounce and hard knockdown. Spider-Man is invulnerable for the first 26 frames of this hyper combo, but its slow startup makes it difficult to reliably blow through attacks. Its invulnerability frames are best utilized as a THC ender when another of your characters' hyper combos is about to be out-prioritized by an opposing hyper combo. After connecting with Crawler Assault, you can follow with a combo midscreen by simply dashing after the wall bounce, or follow in the corner with an aerial down-forward Web Glide OTG into a combo. Crawler Assault can be mashed for additional damage.

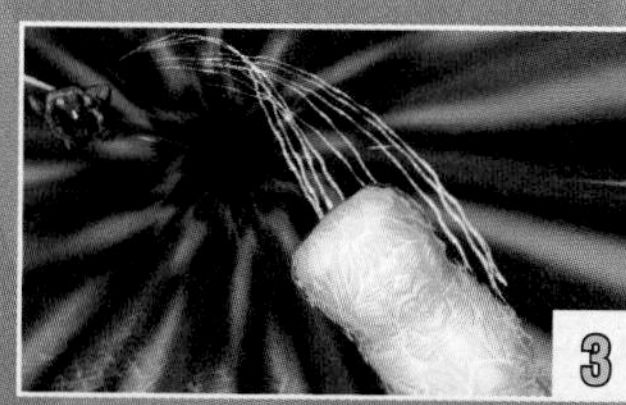

3

Ultimate Web Throw: Ultimate Web Throw is an air throw that only connects on aerial opponents and causes a hard knockdown. This hyper combo comes with certain restrictions in connecting it. Ultimate Web Throw completely ignores grounded adversaries, leaving them free to punish after Spider-Man's invincibility frames have worn off. In addition, since this hyper combo is considered a throw, it cannot be connected on opponents who are in hitstun or guardstun. Despite these restrictions, Ultimate Web Throw has a large area of effect, catching any competitors who are in its range. Use it at the end of combos that have been heavily affected by hit decay, or as a counter to a rival approaching at normal jump height. After connecting, you may follow with an aerial down-forward Web Glide OTG to give the hyper combo an added kick in damage.

Battle Plan

Use Web Ball and crossover assists to control the pace of the match from a distance.

Mix Web Ball L with Web Throw M to cover all angles of attack.

Spider-Man is most effective at close range, where players can use his quick attacks and Web Swing pressure to overwhelm opponents. Given this, it's in your best interest to get Spider-Man close to the opposing character, whether it means having him approach or luring the adversary in. While Spider-Man isn't necessarily a threat from fullscreen, he does have various tools and options to control the match from a distance. Becoming both familiar and comfortable with Spider-Man's mobility and learning the optimal range to use Web Swing are key for Spider-Man players.

From a distance, your goal is to harass competitors by using Web Ball and Web Throw with crossover assists. Though Web Ball L is usually the best version to use because of its quick startup and slow velocity, mixing it with the other two versions of Web Ball along with Web Throw L can be good to throw your rival off. Web Ball isn't the most durable projectile, however, so it's good to mix in aerial Web Ball for another angle of attack. If your challenger is firing more durable projectiles, jump and retaliate with aerial Web Ball L. If the projectile ever connects, your rival is incapacitated long enough for you to dash forward and perform a combo.

Once your opponent starts jumping more often to avoid the projectiles, you can use Web Throw M, Spider Sting, and air throws to counter their movement. Web Throw M fires at a 45-degree angle upwards to cut off an aerial approach. Air attacks can also be stopped with Spider Sting, but it is important to perform it early since it has no frames of invulnerability. You get a combo opportunity if Spider Sting connects, and it can be made safe with a Web Glide cancel. Learning to combo off air throws is important because Spider-Man can do decent damage off air throws with Web Glide OTG into a combo or Maximum Spider.

Guarding Web Swing during its later active frames yields frame advantage.

If assaulting from long range with Spider-Man's webs isn't enough to lure your target close, you can choose to use Web Ball as a shield to approach instead. You can fire Web Ball L at a distance, then either wavedash behind it or cancel it into a forward Web Glide to get in close. Aerial Web Ball L can be canceled into Web Glide for an approach, as well. When approaching with Web Glide, it is optimal to have your challenger either guarding Web Ball or the Web Glide projectile so that they are pinned down for the incoming assault. Use a crossover assist while approaching with Web Ball and Web Glide to apply pressure and cover your advance.

At mid range, Web Swing H becomes a viable tool in approaching. It reaches about half of the screen's length and has decent priority. If your opponent guards Web Swing H during the later active frames, you are granted heavy frame advantage and can follow with overhead air attacks before landing.

Web Swing H is susceptible to air throws if incorrectly spaced, so use a crossover assist to cover your Web Swing H if you are unsure of its spacing. Even at mid range, a connected Web Swing leads to a big combo, so be sure to practice the optimal spacing of Web Swing H.

Once you get into range, you can use Spider-Man's quick basic attacks and Web Swing pressure to fish for an opening. Standing (L) has a speedy 4 frames of startup and is great for interrupting the opposing character's own basic attacks at close range. To counter advancing guard, use Web Swing M to maintain positioning. As with most characters, keep the enemy's low guard in check with crouching (L). Conditioning your opponent to guard crouching (L) is important because much of Spider-Man's offense is comprised of square jumps, triangle jumps, and Web Swing overheads.

Square-jumping with (H) is better at mid range because of its horizontal, outward angle.

Web Glide isn't just for mobility! Use it offensively at close range in combos or to set up an overhead attack.

Once your opponent is conditioned to guard low, you can mix in Web Glide triangle jumps, square jumps, aerial Web Swing (L) (performed with a tiger knee motion), and Web Swing overheads to score an overhead attack. You can cancel basic attack chains into Web Swing L or M, then follow with air (M), (H), (S) for an overhead attack that works even if the Web Swing connects. During this sequence, use a crossover assist to protect Spider-Man from air throws after a guarded Web Swing, if possible. Web Swing is also a good way of combating advancing guard because of its forward momentum.

During offensive pressure, you can cancel basic attacks into Web Glide forward for a triangle jump. Even though it's not as fast as other characters' triangle jumps, the momentum from the glide allows for multiple air attacks before landing, making it tricky to guard properly. After conditioning your adversary to guard low, cancel a basic attack string into Web Glide. Then cancel the glide into air (M), (M), (H), which must be guarded high.

You can use Spider-Man's airdash to perform square jumps with air (H) or (S). After normal jumping, perform an airdash canceled into air (H) or (S). Air (H) is better to use if square-jumping outside of close range, while the angle in which air (S) strikes is better to use when square-jumping at close range. Your attack retains whatever momentum the airdash has the moment it is canceled, so canceling the airdash toward the beginning of its duration gives you the down-forward momentum ideal for a square jump. As with triangle jumps and Web Swing overheads, square jumps are best used when your competitor has been conditioned to guard low via crouching (L).

Aside from his fighting abilities, Spider-Man is also great at running away if necessary. When cornered, the quickest way to get away is to super jump and airdash with (ATK)(ATK) or ⇨⇨. Alternatively, you can use Web Glide to get away, though it has longer startup than an airdash. If you ever need to stall your rival (such as during the foe's X-Factor or a time-out situation), Spider-Man can use any combination of Web Ball, Web Glide, Web Swing, or an airdash to stay at high altitudes for a long period of time.

COMBO APPENDIX

GENERAL EXECUTION TIPS

When performing an OTG with Web Glide, cancel the glide with air (H) as soon as possible to allow enough time for it to connect before Spider-Man lands

For combos with Web Swing, weaker air attacks are easier to link than stronger ones due to faster startup. If you are having trouble connecting aerial basic attacks after Web Swing, try a different attack chain beginning with a weaker basic attack to alleviate the timing restriction

(AFTER A TAC) AIR (M), (H) CANCEL ➡ ↗ + (ATK) + (S), (H) CANCEL ➡ ←↓↙ + (H) CANCEL ➡ ↓↘→ + (ATK)(ATK)

Notes	Damage
⇧ + (S) or ⇨ + (S) or ⇩ + (S) TAC to Spider-Man	Varies based on damage scaling

CR. (L), (M), (H) CANCEL ➡ →↓↘ + (H) (DURING SPIDER STING) (H), CR. (H), (S) CANCEL ➡ FORWARD SUPER JUMP, AIR (M), (M), (H) CANCEL ➡ ←↓↙ + (L), (H), (S)

Notes	Damage
Character-specific combo for Arthur and Rocket Raccoon	557,900 damage, 42% meter loss

COMBO USAGE

I. CR. (L), (M), (H) [CANCEL] ← ↓ ↙ + (L), AIR (M), (M), (S), LAND, ST. (H) [CANCEL] → ↓ ↘ + (H) (DURING SPIDER STING) (H), CR. (H), (S) [CANCEL] FORWARD SUPER JUMP, AIR (M), (M), (H) [CANCEL] ← ↓ ↙ + (H) [CANCEL] ↓ ↘ → + (ATK ATK)

602,100 damage, 15% meter loss

Here's a bread and butter combo that breaks the 600,000 damage mark. After ← ↓ ↙ + (L), timing air (M), (M), (S) so that your opponent is as low to the ground as possible allows the next part of the combo to connect properly. Note that this combo does not work against Arthur or Rocket Raccoon because of their size. See the Combo Appendix for a special combo against these characters.

II. CR. (L), (M), (H) [CANCEL] ← ↓ ↙ + (L), AIR (M), (M), (S), LAND, ST. (H) [CANCEL] ← ↓ ↙ + (H), AIR (M), (M), (S), LAND, ST. (H) [CANCEL] → ↓ ↘ + (H) (DURING SPIDER STING) (H), CR. (H), (S) [CANCEL] FORWARD SUPER JUMP, AIR (M), (M), (H), DELAYED (S), LAND, [P1 or P2], ← ↓ ↙ + (H) [CANCEL] ↓ ↘ → + (ATK ATK)

683,100 damage, 26% meter gain

This combo can be used if you have an OTG-capable crossover assist such as Wesker—β or X-23—β. Delay air (S) at the end of the air combo to give Spider-Man enough time to land and call your crossover assist.

III. FRONT OR BACK AIR THROW, ↘ + (ATK) + (S), AIR (H) ON THE WAY DOWN, LAND, CR. (H) [CANCEL] → ↓ ↘ + (H) (DURING SPIDER STING) (H), CR. (H), (S) [CANCEL] FORWARD SUPER JUMP, AIR (M), (M), (H) [CANCEL] ← ↓ ↙ + (H) [CANCEL] ↓ ↘ → + (ATK ATK)

445,200 damage, 35% meter loss

Timing is crucial in performing a combo off an air throw. After the Web Glide, you should perform air (H) as soon as possible so that it has enough time to start up and connect before Spider-Man lands. Once this is mastered, the rest of the combo is standard fare.

IV. (AGAINST AN AIRBORNE OPPONENT) FORWARD JUMP, AIR (M), (M), (H), (S) [CANCEL] ← ↓ ↙ + (L), (H), DELAYED (S), LAND, ST. (M), (S) [CANCEL] FORWARD SUPER JUMP, AIR (M), (M), (H) [CANCEL] ← ↓ ↙ + (H) [CANCEL] ↓ ↘ → + (ATK ATK)

597,700 damage, 28% meter loss

The angle of air (M) makes it a great attack to use against an aerial opponent as anti-air, such as when a new character is coming in after a K.O. Delay air (S) in the sequence after the Web Swing to ensure that your target is as close to the ground as possible, allowing for the standing (M) to properly connect.

V. (AGAINST AIRBORNE OPPONENT) → ↘ ↓ ↙ ← + (ATK ATK), FORWARD JUMP, ↘ + (ATK) + (S), AIR (H) ON THE WAY DOWN, LAND, (S) [CANCEL] FORWARD SUPER JUMP, AIR (M), (M), (H) [CANCEL] ← ↓ ↙ + (H) [CANCEL] ↓ ↘ → + (ATK ATK)

778,900 damage, 164% meter loss

Ultimate Web Throw has invulnerability, but it runs out well before the attack comes out. However, it creates a giant hittable area in front of Spider-Man that shields him, making it possible to use it preemptively against low altitude jumps. After the Web Glide, perform air (H) as soon as possible so that it has enough time to connect before you touch the ground.

VI. (MIDSCREEN REQUIRED) → ↓ ↘ + (ATK ATK) (MASH (ATK)), FORWARD DASH, ST. (M), CR. (H) [CANCEL] ← ↓ ↙ + (L), AIR (M), (M), (S), LAND, ST. (H) [CANCEL] → ↓ ↘ + (H) (DURING SPIDER STING) (H), CR. (H), (S) [CANCEL] FORWARD SUPER JUMP, AIR (M), (M), (H), DELAYED (S), LAND, [P1 or P2], ← ↓ ↙ + (H) [CANCEL] ↓ ↘ → + (ATK ATK)

758,400 damage, 105% meter loss

This combo takes advantage of the ground bounce that Crawler Assault produces. Delay air (S) at the end of the air combo to allow enough time for Spider-Man to land, then call an OTG-capable assist to continue the combo.

VII. CR. (L), (M), ST. (H) [X-FACTOR], FORWARD DASH, CR. (M), (H) [CANCEL] ← ↓ ↙ + (L), AIR (H), DELAYED (S), LAND, ST. (H) [CANCEL] → ↓ ↘ + (H) (DURING SPIDER STING) (H), CR. (H), (S) [CANCEL] FORWARD SUPER JUMP, AIR (M), (M), (H) [CANCEL] ← ↓ ↙ + (H) [CANCEL] ↓ ↘ → + (ATK ATK)

826,000~1,049,400 damage, 11~42% meter loss

If you need a guaranteed K.O. and have X-Factor available, use this combo after hit-confirming with crouching (L), (M), (H). Be sure to adjust the timing on your inputs to compensate for the speed boost granted during X-Factor, especially level 3.

ADVANCED TACTICS

THIS ONE'S FOR J.J.: WEB GLIDE CANCELING

All of Spider-Man's special moves (except Web Throw) can be canceled into Web Glide at any point during their startup, recovery, or active frames, adding an extra dimension to Spider-Man's game overall. Spider Sting can be used without fear of punishment, and Web Ball L can be canceled into Web Glide for a covered approach. Canceling Web Ball into Web Glide is also useful for countering an opponent who has jumped over a poorly timed Web Ball. Web Glide canceling remains true for aerial special moves, as well. Web Swing can be canceled into Web Glide at super jump height, which can then be followed with an airdash to stall your adversary. Aerial Web Ball L can be canceled into Web Glide, which can then immediately be canceled into another Web Ball L to frustrate your competitor.

Web Glide canceling allows for many possibilities. Cover a Web Glide approach by canceling it from Web Ball L.

STORM

"I WILL NOT LOSE SO LONG AS THE RAINS AND THE WINDS ARE MINE TO COMMAND!"

Bio

REAL NAME

Ororo Iqadi T'Challa [née Munroe]

OCCUPATION

Queen of Wakanda, Adventurer

ABILITIES

Storm commands the weather— she can freely manipulate atmospheric temperature, pressure, humidity, etc. She also can control the surrounding atmosphere, create hurricanes, or even shoot lightning.

WEAPONS

None

PROFILE

Though she survived the ordeal, Ororo's parents died when a plane crashed into their home. Being buried under rubble proved a traumatic experience that would leave her with severe claustrophobia. Orphaned, she became a street thief in order to get by. She was later recruited by Charles Xavier, and decided to put her powers to use for good as a member of the X-Men.

FIRST APPEARANCE

Giant-Size X-Men #1 (1975)

POWER GRID

2	INTELLIGENCE
2	STRENGTH
3	SPEED
2	STAMINA
5	ENERGY PROJECTION
4	FIGHTING ABILITY

*This is biographical, and does not represent an evaluation of the in-game combat potential of this hero.

ALTERNATE COSTUMES

1

2

3

4

5

6

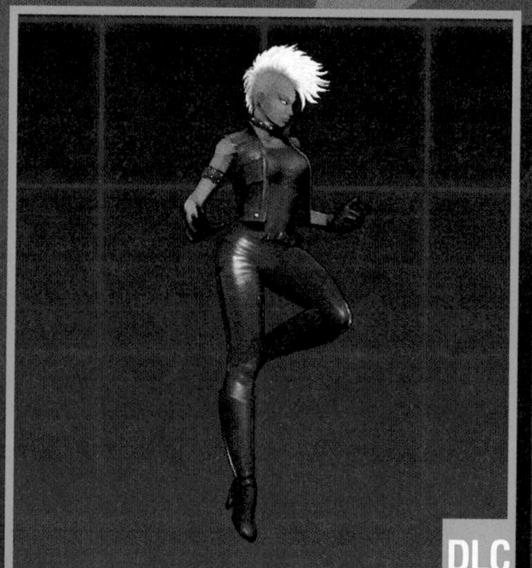

DLC

Overview

Vitality	850,000
Chain Combo Archetype	Hunter Series

X-Factor Boost	Damage	Speed
Level 1 (3 teammates remaining)	125%	115%
Level 2 (2 teammates remaining)	140%	130%
Level 3 (1 teammate remaining)	155%	145%

Storm can fulfill a variety of roles depending on her placement in a team and the needs of her teammates. You can play both keepaway and rushdown, and it's easy for you to switch Storm between these positions as needed. In the end, though, Storm most naturally lends herself to being played as a rushdown character. Her primary goal is to get right up close and personal with her adversary. Storm is an effective rushdown fighter because:

- **She can cross the playing field on the ground or in the air in a flash, especially with X-Factor active, and she can mix up between low and high quickly**
- **Her jump-cancelable basic attacks and airdash allow her to keep up pressure after being guarded or pushed away with advancing guard**
- **Her throws all lead to hyper combo or crossover combination opportunities**
- **One of her new moves, Foul Wind, actually pulls foes in from half the field away**
- **While she has very good stalling and keepaway abilities, she doesn't actually deal much damage with her projectiles. Their purpose is more to pester her opponents than to seal a win with consistent use. Her ranged attacks all also leave her wide open if they whiff, which is not great for the fragile goddess**

Storm has low vitality, and she doesn't inflict as much damage or build as much hyper meter as some aggressive characters. To offset this, Storm has a complete set of long range tools for feeling out the opposing character. Aggressive players frequently find that they have more success when they balance their aggression with periods of pretending not to be aggressive!

From far away, Storm has a large suite of threats with which to harangue an opponent:

- **Her Whirlwind projectile is slow to fire, but it can win out in ranged situations where no other projectile can**
- **Lightning Sphere and Double Typhoon are useful tools to attack an adversary that is below and a full screen away, an awkward angle from which most characters have no plan**
- **Hail Storm, while slow to start up, hits the whole screen instantly after the hyper combo cutscene, and Elemental Rage can be directed to strike *any* location at ground level in only 10 frames**
- **Crossover combinations with Storm—α or Storm—β let you fry assists from fullscreen on reaction, or easily OTG after hard knockdowns with any character.**

Storm's hyper meter building isn't the best, and you are likely to burn hyper combos outside of combos more than the average character while using her (see also: Akuma), so she usually doesn't generate surplus meter on her own. On a team where meter is generated and saved by other teammates, Storm becomes that much more useful because of terrific hyper combos and the flexibility they grant Storm with TACs, THCs, and crossover combinations.

TUNING SINCE ORIGINAL MVC3

Apart from the obvious addition of unique special moves that push or pull the enemy, Storm's most significant changes come from universal modifications to the game itself. With the THC glitch gone, Storm loses one of the main ways she contributed to a team (Elemental Rage being one of the most friendly THC glitch hyper combos in original *MvC3*). Her meter gain has also been slightly reduced, but that's true of most characters. She gains a buff in the form of being able to mash (ATK) for more damage on two of her hyper combos and in being able to use X-Factor in midair, but again, every other character got those changes, too.

However, Storm did lose two quirks that made her unique before: calling assists after floating during a super jump and passing through some characters in certain positions on the ground.

- **New Moves: Fair Wind and Foul Wind**
- **Storm can no longer call crossover assists after floating during a super jump**
- **Storm can no longer cancel the recovery of air Double Typhoon with Lightning Attacks**
- **Hail Storm and Lightning Storm can be mashed for extra damage**
- **Storm's floating posture has been altered, and she can no longer pass directly through certain small characters**

Attack Set

Standing Basic Attacks

Screen	Command	Hits	Damage	Meter Gain	Startup	Active	Recovery	Advantage on Hit	Advantage if Guarded	Notes
1	Standing Ⓛ	1	33,000	264	5	3	8	+3	+2	Chain-cancelable into Ⓛ attacks
2	Standing Ⓜ	1	55,000	440	9	11	10	-2	-4	Jump- cancelable
3	Standing Ⓗ	1	70,000	560	15	12	5	+7	+5	—

Crouching Basic Attacks

Screen	Command	Hits	Damage	Meter Gain	Startup	Active	Recovery	Advantage on Hit	Advantage if Guarded	Notes
1	Crouching Ⓛ	1	30,000	240	5	3	8	+3	+2	Low attack, chain-cancelable into Ⓛ attacks
2	Crouching Ⓜ	1	53,000	424	9	10	12	-3	-5	—
3	Crouching Ⓗ	1	67,000	536	13	11	14	—	-3	Low attack, knocks down, jump- cancelable

Ground Special Attack—Launcher

Screen	Command	Hits	Damage	Meter Gain	Startup	Active	Recovery	Advantage on Hit	Advantage if Guarded	Notes
1	Ⓢ (while standing or crouching)	1	80,000	640	13	12	11	—	-1	Launcher, not special- or hyper combo-cancelable

STORM

Air Basic Attacks

Screen	Command	Hits	Damage	Meter Gain	Startup	Active	Recovery	Advantage on Hit	Advantage if Guarded	Notes
1	Air (L)	1	35,000	280	4	3	18	+10	+9	Overhead attack
2	Air (M)	1	53,000	424	11	6	19	+17	+15	Overhead attack
3	Air (H)	1	68,000	544	12	7	19	+19	+17	Overhead attack

1

2

3

Air Special Attacks—Flying Screen and Air Exchange

Air (S) causes a hard knockdown when used in a launcher combo (this is sometimes called flying screen). When used outside of a launcher combo, air (S) behaves mostly like another basic attack. Air exchange attacks, performed by inputting a direction plus (S), are only possible during a launcher combo. Exchange hits initiate team aerial combos by tagging in the next available character to continue the air combo.

Screen	Command	Hits	Damage	Meter Gain	Startup	Active	Recovery	Advantage on Hit	Advantage if Guarded	Notes
1	Air (S)	1	75,000	600	13	15	11	+16	+14	Overhead attack, causes hard knockdown if used in launcher combo
2	Air ⇧ + (S) (during launcher combo)	2	105,00	880	12	4	22	—	—	Tags in next available ally while lofting opponent upward
3	Air ⇨ or ⇦ + (S) (during launcher combo)	2	95,000	800	12	4	22	—	—	Tags in next available ally while causing wall bounce, erases 1 hyper meter bar from foe
4	Air ⇩ + (S) (during launcher combo)	2	95,000	800	13	4	22	—		Tags in next available ally while causing ground bounce, generates 1 hyper meter bar

1

2

3

4

Throws

Throws are for snagging passive or blocking opponents. Since throws are active so quickly, you can also use them to preemptively toss opposing characters out of their offense. Combos are usually possible after throws, one way or another.

Screen	Command	Hits	Damage	Meter Gain	Startup	Active	Notes
1	⇨ + (H) (ground)	6	80,000	800	1	1	Hard knockdown
	⇦ + (H) (ground)	6	80,000	800	1	1	Hard knockdown
2	⇨ + (H) (air)	6	80,000	800	1	1	Hard knockdown
	⇦ + (H) (air)	6	80,000	800	1	1	Hard knockdown

1

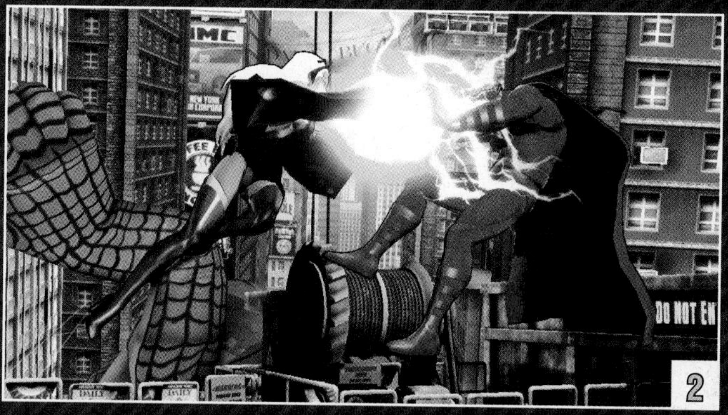

2

As a Partner—Crossover Assists

Screen	Type	P1+P2 Crossover Combination Hyper Combo	Description	Hits	Damage	Meter Gain	Startup	Active	Recovery (this crossover assist)	Recovery (other partner)	Notes
1	Storm—α	Hail Storm	Whirlwind M	5	102,300	1000	44	—	129	99	Whirlwind active for 30 frames, 5 projectiles with 3 low priority durability points each
2	Storm—β	Hail Storm	Double Typhoon M	6	140,300	1440	87	—	107	77	OTG-capable, typhoon active for 30 frames, beam durability: 6 frames x 5 low priority durability points
3	Storm—γ	Lightning Storm	Lightning Attack ⇗	1	60,000	480	37	13	121	91	—

Each of Storm's assists might see use on the appropriate team. Storm—α provides the general purpose assist. Like Storm's Whirlwind M on point, this unique projectile extends just short of fullscreen, while interrupting almost any threat along the way. It pushes rivals away whether on hit or block; you can use this to your advantage intentionally whenever you're pushing your opponent out with zoning teams or helping to push your adversary to the corner with aggressive setups. However, this pushback effect makes Storm—α less obviously useful in combos and for offensive pressure, the way more typical beams function.

Storm—β is one of the slowest assists to act in the game, and so it requires a lot of lead time (such as after scoring a hard knockdown, or either snapping out or knocking out the opposing point character) or plenty of cover in order to actually deploy it safely. It's OTG-capable, but using it for that purpose in combos requires tailoring combos to the assist rather than using assists to strengthen existing combos. At least, like Storm—α, this assist gives her Hail Storm within crossover combinations.

Since Hail Storm is both OTG-capable and one of the fastest-acting hyper combos *after* its hyper combo cutscene, having Storm—α or Storm—β in an assist slot and enough hyper meter for everyone to participate creates devastating crossover combinations. Just score a hard knockdown with *any* character, then immediately activate a crossover combination from anywhere on the screen. Hail Storm ensures that the target is both popped off of the ground and held in place. Pick teammates for Storm who have hyper combos that play well with Hail Storm in hyper combos to maximize this approach.

Storm—γ becomes active the quickest, strikes the most directly, opens the way for potential cross-ups by calling it just as you fly or jump over a foe, and reloads the fastest. It also lets you cancel directly into Lightning Storm if you use a crossover counter to bring Storm in. Unfortunately, Storm—γ also comes with Lightning Storm in crossover combinations, instead of Hail Storm. How important the Lightning Attack assist is to the other members of the team, and whether someone else already has an OTG-capable hyper combo for crossover combinations, dictates whether this trade-off is worth it.

Snap Back

Screen	Command	Hits	Damage	Meter Gain	Startup	Active	Recovery	Advantage on Hit	Advantage if Guarded
1	⇩⇘⇨ + P1 or P2	1	50,000	500 (-1 hyper meter bar)	2	5	12	—	+5

Notes

On hit, snap back forces the opposing point character to be replaced by an assist. Opposing assist calls or tag outs are also locked out for 4 seconds

Special Moves

Screen	Name	Command	Hits	Damage	Meter Gain	Startup	Active	Recovery	Advantage on Hit	Advantage if Guarded	Notes
1	Whirlwind L	⇩⇘⇨ + L (in air ok)	3	67,000	600	15	—	30 (air: 35)	0 (air: -5)	-2 (air: -7)	Whirlwind active for 22 frames, 3 projectiles with 3 low priority durability points each
2	Whirlwind M	⇩⇘⇨ + M (in air ok)	5	102,300	1000	20	—	37	+4 (air: +3)	+7	Whirlwind active for 30 frames, 5 projectiles with 3 low priority durability points each
3	Whirlwind H	⇩⇘⇨ + H (in air ok)	7	130,200	1400	25	—	40	+13 (air: +12)	+13 (air: +13)	Whirlwind active for 38 frames, 7 projectiles with 3 low priority durability points each
4, 5, 6	Double Typhoon	⇩⇙⇦ + ATK (in air ok)	6	140,300	1440	63	—	15 (air: until grounded)	+40	+21	OTG-capable, Typhoon active for 30 frames, beam durability: 6 frames x 5 low priority durability points
7	Lightning Attack 1~3x	S + ATK up to 3 times (can be directed, in air OK)	1~3	80,000 per attack	640 per attack	13 (15 once airborne)	13	25 or until grounded	—	-16	Knocks down, can cancel into subsequent attacks from frames 18-34, attack puts Storm in airborne state, air version requires minimum jump height: 4 frames
8, 9, 10	Lightning Sphere	⇨⇩⇘ + ATK (in air)	5	110,100	976	20	—	40	-1	-3	Minimum jump height: 4 frames, projectile has 5 low priority durability points, on hit or once destroyed creates burst with beam durability: 20 frames x 5 low priority durability points

Special Moves continued

Screen	Name	Command	Hits	Damage	Meter Gain	Startup	Active	Recovery	Advantage on Hit	Advantage if Guarded	Notes
11	Flight	↓↙← + (S)	—	—	—	22	—	—	—	—	Flight lasts for 99 frames
12	Fair Wind	→↓↘ + (S)	—	—	—	13	24	19	—	—	Pushes opposing character away from Storm for 24 frames
13	Foul Wind	←↓↙ + (S)	—	—	—	13	27	1	—	—	Pulls target toward Storm for 27 frames

Whirlwind L 1

Whirlwind M 2

Whirlwind H 3

Whirlwind: Whirlwind is a unique ranged attack that causes individual typhoons to swirl up across the screen in a staggered sequence. Each typhoon is actually its own projectile; if your competitor destroys one of them, it has no effect on the others. This means that Whirlwind, if released safely, disrupts almost anything in its path, projectiles, point characters, and assists alike. It can even pierce through M.O.D.O.K.'s barrier. However, like a beam, every stage of Whirlwind disappears if Storm takes a hit.

The (L) version creates three tornadoes that reach to mid range. The (M) version creates five tornadoes that reach almost fullscreen. The (H) version creates seven tornadoes that stretch across the entire playing field. The lighter the version, the shorter the startup and recovery periods.

Whirlwind is a big time commitment, but it's great if you can get it out there. If the opposing player didn't beat Storm to the punch with firing a projectile, very few actions can beat Whirlwind after it's released. And each individual tornado within Whirlwind pushes your rival back whether on hit or guard, and in turn, the next tornado pushes them farther down the line—Whirlwind H pushes the opposing character all the way across the screen! (Storm—α assist is very useful for this purpose, if your plan is to keep your foes away defensively or drive them into a corner aggressively.)

You can use Whirlwind in combos, most notably employing Whirlwind H to combo into Hail Storm from a ground chain at midscreen. There are better things to do in ground combos, though. (And during X-Factor, Whirlwind's travel speed goes up so much that Whirlwind to Hail Storm won't even work most of the time anyway.) And for zoning wars, Whirlwind L and M don't have sufficient deterring power or range. For both combos and zoning, stick to Whirlwind H. If you don't have time to release Whirlwind H in a given matchup, take to the skies, or approach your opponent aggressively instead.

Double Typhoon L 4

Double Typhoon M 5

Double Typhoon H 6

Double Typhoon: Double Typhoon takes over a second to summon, but once released, it creates a vertical cyclone that extends to just under super jump height. Double Typhoon is OTG-capable, although its lengthy startup prevents it from having much use outside of air throw follow-ups or specialized assist combos. Double Typhoon also boasts tremendous low priority projectile durability. Its behavior is similar to Dormammu's Purification pillars—Double Typhoon is really just an extremely sturdy vertical beam (though it does not extend to the ceiling as Purification does; Double Typhoon won't hit opponents at super jump height).

You can only use Double Typhoon once per airborne period, and the move makes Storm drop like a stone after release. To avoid this, activate flight before performing air Double Typhoon. Storm will still be flying when it's done, so you'll avoid the dangerous penalty.

Double Typhoon takes so long to activate that it's hard to use otherwise. It's not advisable at ground level unless you have a lot of time to yourself, like if the opposing player just started guarding your assist, or if you're placing a Double Typhoon over the area that a new character is about to fall in after a knockout.

7

Lightning Attack: Lightning Attack is an airborne special move that you can aim in any direction, like Storm's airdash. Lightning Attack can be canceled into itself at any point, whether on whiff, hit, or block, up to two times per use. The subsequent Lightning Attacks can be redirected, which is important because of the odd angles at which this attack can hit in midair.

You can only use Lightning Attack once per airborne period, and Storm falls straight down afterward, unable to act or guard. This is just like after using Double Typhoon in midair, and you have the same away around it: activate flight just before using Lightning Attacks. After the flight period ends, you'll fall to earth able to block or act as normal. (Or even able to perform Lightning Attack again!) Alternatively, if you don't want to do that, just make sure to redirect stages two and three of the Lightning Attack away from danger, back to the ground.

Although it's not quite Wolverine's Drill Claw, you can use ↘ Lightning Attack as a kind of triangle jump if you'd like to give your challenger a different look. If it hits close to the ground, you can link afterward with standing (M) into an extended combo. You can also use Lightning Attacks as a kind of hit-confirmable aerial poke (imagine if Street Fighter's Fei Long had Rekka-Kens in eight directions). If Lightning Attack hits, you can tack on Lightning Storm, or (for a little more oomph) you can cancel the third Lightning Attack with X-Factor, Lightning Attack three more times, then finally cap it off with Lightning Storm. A decent THC from here, if feasible, can knock out most characters.

Lightning Attack is not safe if guarded, so don't use it as a poke on its own unless you call a crossover assist first to provide cover, or if you have a plan for redirecting stages two and three on block.

Lightning Sphere L 8

Lightning Sphere M 9

Lightning Sphere H 10

Lightning Sphere: Lightning Sphere is a projectile that Storm can only throw while airborne. It can be directed up-forward ((H)), straight forward ((M)), or down-forward ((L)). Once Lightning Sphere actually connects with an opposing point character, assist, projectile, or beam, it expands into a larger sphere of ball lightning. This is the portion that actually deals damage (the initial spark is just a delivery system), but it also has astounding projectile durability. When competitors are capable of outgunning Storm's Whirlwind H, you can opt to take to the air and shoot diagonally down at them with Lightning Sphere L. Interestingly, while opponents who guard the Lightning Sphere explosion and use advancing guard find their characters pushed back slightly; their advancing guard has no effect on Storm! Throw a Lightning Sphere they're forced to block, and you're assured of gaining ground. When jumping, try not to use up your airdash before using Lightning Sphere, so you can airdash immediately after releasing it.

Apart from projectile durability and immunity to advancing guard, Lightning Sphere's other notable characteristic is the slow speed of the projectile, which allows Storm to cover awkward angles relatively well. For example, after jumping, flying, and performing Double Typhoon from far away, you can throw Lightning Sphere L. This makes it hard for your rival to get at you for a few seconds, unless they're right on top of you from the start. Finally, note that Lightning Sphere travels MUCH faster and is a better aggressive tool during X-Factor.

11

Flight: Storm's flight mode is a central part of her arsenal. While flying, Storm can airdash repeatedly, canceling airdashes into each other. This is useful whether you want Storm to run away, rush in, or escape after being knocked into the air. Either alternate different directions of airdashes (↗ + ATK ATK, ↘ + ATK ATK), or use plink airdashes to wavedash in the same direction across the sky (ATK~ATK, ATK~ATK, separating the button presses by 1 frame instead of hitting them simultaneously).

Since Storm falls without being able to block or act after performing air Double Typhoon or air Lightning Attack, flight is important for her to be able to use these moves in the air freely, without handing an opportunity to a watchful foe. If you perform these moves while Storm is flying, she won't be so helpless when falling to the ground afterward, and she can guard or attack as normal.

Storm's flight mode also enables air combos that involve canceling air (H) into airdash repeatedly. This is crucial to increasing the damage of her air combos that aren't preceded by a bunch of jump loops that make long air combos impossible anyway. It greatly increases her usefulness as the second or third stage of TACs.

12

Fair Wind: During Fair Wind, Storm uses the power of the wind to push her competitor away from her. This works no matter where her foe is or what they're doing. Blocking, attacking, jumping, any action your opponent is performing has its momentum altered by Fair Wind. Like Foul Wind, this is best when used to alter the jump trajectory of an opposing character when the opposing player doesn't expect it. Both Fair and Foul Wind have no effect on opposing assists, and neither puts your rival into any kind of stun or interruption—they can still act as normal; their trajectory is just altered against their will.

Fair Wind nudges an opponent for a slightly shorter duration (and thus a slightly shorter length) than Foul Wind, and it takes more of Storm's time to execute. This is compensated by Fair Wind pushing your adversary away rather than pulling them in. Use this to bolster ranged tactics, like using Fair Wind after calling Doctor Doom—β to ensure that the opponent is kept far away and is forced to deal with Doctor Doom's tracking missiles.

13

Foul Wind: Foul Wind suctions the opposing character toward Storm. Much more useful than Fair Wind, Foul Wind has both a larger effect on Storm's opponent (moving them closer toward Storm than Fair Wind pushes them away) and requires less time commitment. It also has more devious, damaging applications. The most basic use—if your competitor super jumps forward from fullscreen distance, looking to close the gap, use Foul Wind while they're at super jump height, and they'll be pulled clear over Storm. After they pass over her, their air basic attacks face the wrong direction, unless they fly or use a special move. Without doing anything, they'll land just on the other side of Storm, in prime position for you to immediately go for a launcher, an instant float overhead, a low combo, or a throw.

Coupled with the right assist, you can be more aggressive with Foul Wind use instead of just waiting to mess with airborne adversaries. From what seems like a safe distance to the opposing character, call an assist that takes up decent space and allows Storm to combo afterward, then immediately perform Foul Wind. The opponent is suctioned into the assist regardless of what they're doing. If they get hit, either cancel Foul Wind to Hail Storm, or launch and capitalize with an air combo.

Like Fair Wind, Foul Wind doesn't actually stun the enemy whatsoever, so don't get too predictable or careless with its use. Your competitor may simply wait for you to drag them in, then slide in with a basic attack, hoping to catch both Storm and her assist!

Both Fair Wind and Foul Wind can be hyper combo canceled; this can be useful if you drag your target into an assist and want to cancel to Hail Storm, or perhaps to rarely use Foul Wind "unsafely" before canceling into the quick Elemental Rage as the foe is dragged in thinking they can retaliate. Needless to say, be ready to THC away from Storm or activate X-Factor if this parlor trick fails.

Hyper Combos

Screen	Name	Command	Hits	Damage	Startup	Active	Recovery	Advantage on Hit	Advantage if Guarded	Notes
1	Hail Storm	↓↙← + ATK ATK	35~69	282,900~ 338,800	40+1	80	1	—	+7	Can be mashed for extra damage, knocks down, OTG-capable, airborne after frame 12, beam durability: 25 frames x 1 high priority durability points
2	Lightning Storm	↓↘→ + ATK ATK	15~29	289,000~ 344,400	18+1	50	53	—	-42	Can be mashed for extra damage, knocks down, beam durability: 15 frames x 1 high priority durability points
3	Elemental Rage	→↓↘ + ATK ATK	15	266,900	8+2	23	32	—	-28	Knocks down, OTG- capable, causes wall bounce, projectile has 5 high priority durability points

1

Hail Storm: Hail Storm has slow startup, but it hits nearly the entire playing field and is OTG-capable. After any air combo to flying screen where Storm lands about the same time as her adversary, perform Hail Storm immediately and mash ATK to add great damage. (If Storm lands much later than the opponent, you'll have to use Elemental Rage instead.) Any air throw can lead to Hail Storm on landing, too. Although slow to start, after the hyper combo cutscene, Hail Storm hits instantly. Combined with the whole hitting-the-entire-screen thing, this makes Hail Storm one of the best—if not THE best—hyper combo for using in THCs in the game. Any other character can find a way to hyper combo handoff to Hail Storm.

THCing from a fast hyper combo to Hail Storm also makes for a completely safe way to tag out another character for Storm. Try to time the handoff when your opponent happens to call an assist for heavy red damage. Remember that the most damage you can squeeze out of the end of any combo is to use a snap back to force in a badly hurt assist. Hail Storm happens to also be one of the best hyper combos for inflicting chip damage (especially with lv.3 X-Factor active), which is great against low-vitality foes.

Having Hail Storm as part of your team's crossover combination is probably the most important reason to consider Storm—α or Storm—β as your assist type. Hail Storm works well with literally any other two hyper combos, dealing good damage on guard or hit, and pinning opposing point and assist characters anywhere on screen.

Storm receives a significant indirect buff in *UMvC3* thanks to air X-Factor... combo to Hail Storm, cancel it with X-Factor (the rest of the Hail Storm still occurs!), then Hail Storm again! Oddly, your button presses still count as mashing for the damage on the first Hail Storm while it's going on, even though Storm is free to move after X-Factor. If you happen to catch the opposing player's assist and point together with a "random" Hail Storm, X-Factor cancel then wavedash in to launch both characters as the first Hail Storm ends. Air combo to a hard knockdown, then Hail Storm again! Good-bye, two characters, off a fullscreen guess. If their point character guards correctly but you catch their assist, you probably won't be able to X-Factor and dash in during Hail Storm (the point character can advancing guard Storm away), but you can X-Factor and just Hail Storm again to ice the assist.

2

Lightning Storm: Lightning Storm is Storm's standard air combo ending hyper combo. Almost any time you combo into Lightning Attack, you can hyper combo cancel into Lightning Storm. (At the end of very long combos, such as launching after several jump loops, hitstun decay may cause Lightning Attack into Lightning Storm to fail.) Mash ATK to maximize the damage. Lightning Storm is extremely unsafe if guarded, so save it for combos exclusively, and be careful not to embarrass yourself by getting this hyper combo instead of Elemental Rage after a hard knockdown, or when trying to punish challengers who make mistakes far away.

3

Elemental Rage: You can direct Elemental Rage to four points on screen. For it to strike point-blank next to Storm, input the command and do nothing. To deploy Elemental Rage one dash away from Storm, hold L; two dashes away, hold M. Hold H to strike with Elemental Rage all the way across the playing field.

For its range, Elemental Rage is active in an insanely short amount of time. Its most useful application is to treat it like you would the beam hyper combos of Akuma or Dormammu—if you see your opponent start a lengthy action, you can snag them with this from anywhere. You can also use the move to punish anything your adversary does that leaves them at worse than -10, which is not a small list of actions. As just one pertinent example, Storm can block Magneto's Electromagnetic Disrupter projectile, then instantly punish him from full screen with Elemental Rage!

Like Hail Storm, Elemental Rage is OTG-capable, and it's fast enough to sweep opponents up after throws on the ground. Because of its speed and flexibility, it also works well in THCs (though Hail Storm is almost always still better, unless the wall bounce caused by Elemental Rage helps the next stage of the THC, such as handing it over to Dormammu's Stalking Flare).

Battle Plan

Airdash up to super jump height and fly to call assists, maneuver, and use projectiles from the top of the screen.

Storm players can easily manipulate opponents who super jump in predictably by using Foul Wind. If they start clamming up, waiting for the vortex, you can simply air throw them.

Storm is a character best used for attacking an opponent directly, but that doesn't make her the same as, say, Wolverine, whose only plan is "move forward." Storm's low vitality and ranged tools mean that you should take a more measured approach by feeling your opponent out, baiting them into making mistakes, and letting the match come to you rather than resorting to brute force (which is a good way to get some of the more fragile characters torn up). You also need to try to land some glancing hits with Lightning Spheres, wind attacks, and assists, since she is generally not self-sufficient when it comes to hyper meter in her combos.

Although she's tailored for aggression, building a team around "runaway Storm" is an approach that can work. Storm can be used to play *very* hard to get; that was one of the main reasons she was the best overall character in *MvC2*. However, she can't build hyper meter by whiffing eight million air fierce attacks at the top of the screen anymore. Enter the three meter-building assists (Amaterasu—γ, Frank West—γ, and Morrigan—γ)! Even though Storm can't super jump, float, then call assists anymore, she can still get assists out there while at super jump height. Jump and then airdash upward, and voila, you're at super jump height but still able to call assists. From here, if the opposing character is a safe distance away, just call the meter assist, throw one or two Lightning Spheres, and activate flight. By now, the meter assist is ready to go again, and you can throw a Double Typhoon or more spheres. If your opponent is too close for comfort underneath Storm, don't call a helpless meter-building assist right on top of the opposing character. Activate flight, airdash repeatedly all the way to the other side of the playing field, *then* call your meter-building assist.

Between assist calls and whatever glancing hits you score with projectiles while running away, you should generate a hyper meter bar every two or three calls. A running Storm is much more threatening when she's armed with hyper meter… anytime you feel you can get away with Hail Storm's 40-frame startup, you can throw it out there on a whim from fullscreen (you can cancel into it from Whirlwind H first too, though this telegraphs the Hail Storm somewhat). Hail Storm deals solid chip damage if guarded, and it can deal huge damage to careless point characters or badly timed assists if not. It's also completely safe if guarded. Return to your regularly scheduled running and spamming of meter assists afterward.

You can stall with Storm in this fashion with or without the meter assist; you'll just have a lot more meter to toss around with random Hail Storms if you brought Amaterasu, Frank West, or Morrigan along. Other assists work better if your plan is to disrupt or actually force enemies to block attacks, rather than to just be terribly annoying while building bar. Ground-level beams hold enemies long enough to ensure super jump height Double Typhoon is put onscreen safely, for example. They'll also help Storm win projectile wars when ground Whirlwind H is too slow… get above the foe's barrage, call your beam assist during a likely gap, then toss Lightning Sphere L.

If the opposing player tries to retaliate against Storm's run away tactics by chasing her aggressively in the air—that only plays into your hands. An opponent who is prone to super jumping forward is an opponent that can be taken advantage of badly by using Fair Wind and Foul Wind to screw with their jump arcs. You can also use Lightning Attacks as a pseudo-safe poke against airborne competitors. If the first stage is guarded, you can redirect Storm away to safety; if it hits, the three stages of Lightning Attack give you plenty of time to verify and cancel to Lightning Storm.

During all this running, whenever your opponent guards either an assist or Lightning Sphere L, that's a chance for Storm to move into close range even from all the way across the screen. If your rival uses advancing guard against an assist or Lightning Sphere, it has no effect on Storm's forward progress. From a normal jump height Lightning Sphere L, just airdash forward and fall with air ⇨ + Ⓗ. If flight is active, airdash in repeatedly, then fall on the target with air Ⓢ, which naturally ends flight with an overhead and puts you at point-blank range. At ground level, you can simply use Foul Wind to pull your adversary in close while they're blocking your assist anyway. Using Foul Wind while your opponent is unoccupied is suicide (unless you're trying to get cute baiting them into doing something Elemental Rage can beat out), but using it while they're stuck in guardstun or hitstun from your assist is fine. You can also time Foul Wind to drag the target into an assist that must be guarded either high or low (for example, Nova—β or Phoenix Wright—γ), then strike at the other level with Storm.

Meanwhile, while trying to keep an opposing character out, your best poke options are the tip of Storm's Ⓢ launcher or the tip of instant float air ⇨ + Ⓗ (see Advanced Tactics). The little whirlwinds created by Storm's basic attacks represent her attack hitbox, but she's only vulnerable on her actual limbs, not on the whirlwind part. Think of the range of your attacks as being where the whirlwind portion strikes, rather than where Storm's limbs do. As a bonus, when poking with Ⓢ launcher, you can easily convert full air flight combos on a successful hit. If instant float air Ⓗ hits an airborne foe at low altitude, such as a character jumping or airdashing in, you can land and link st. Ⓜ, proceeding into a full jump loop or flight air combo! Similarly, if you happen to jump forward with air ⇨ + Ⓗ to go for an air throw, but you end up hitting your opponent with air Ⓗ in midair instead, cancel the hit into an airdash straight down, so you can juggle them and start a combo with standing Ⓜ.

Triangle jump air Ⓛ gives Storm a fast, reliable overhead that strikes any crouching character.

Storm is not vulnerable on the whirlwind portion of her attacks, and Ⓢ launcher is only -1 if guarded, making the tip of Ⓢ a safe poke that leads to a full combo on hit!

When you're up close on the ground, the best chain to open with is crouching Ⓛ, standing Ⓜ, crouching Ⓗ. This is plenty of time to hit-confirm, and the last two attacks are both jump-cancelable. This enables Storm's best combos, and it also gives you options for mixing your opponent up or regaining ground after Storm has been blocked and/or pushed away with advancing guard.

Realistically, you won't be cutting the chain combo short to jump cancel standing Ⓜ on reaction to advancing guard… chaining to crouching Ⓗ for a combo must be done too quickly. If the opposing player uses advancing guard as they block standing Ⓜ, you will probably be pushed out while crouching Ⓗ whiffs, and whiffed moves cannot be jump canceled. At least their extended guardstun following advancing guard ensures that you aren't punished for this; you simply lose momentum.

However, if you make it to crouching H and *then* the opponent uses advancing guard, you have time to react. Jump cancel crouching H, then airdash forward (a "square jump") immediately with air S or air ⇨ + H, and you're right back on top of them with a high-priority overhead attack.

If your competitor blocks all the way to crouching H and still didn't use advancing guard, now you're in prime position to leverage Storm's strongest mix-up. This time when you jump cancel the sweep, you're right above your rival in the air. From here, you can:

- **Quickly overhead them with triangle jump air L**
- **"Empty" triangle jump in with no attack, then land and throw**
- **Quickly overhead your foe with instant float air S or air ⇨ + H (see Advanced Tactics)**
- ***Instantly* overhead the opposing character with jump forward instant air L; following up with a combo requires that you call an assist a fair bit earlier, so it's timed to hit just after the rising L**
- **Delay an overhead by floating briefly, then attack with ⇨ + H or ⇖ + ATK + S (this counterhits your foe if they are desperate to use advancing guard and hit buttons too early; this may also trick your opposition into returning to crouching guard, if they expect Storm to land more quickly, as is usually the case. If they jump, this technique air throws them)**
- **Call an assist that pins the target, then airdash forward over their head**
- **Toss Lightning Sphere L diagonally down at them; Storm isn't pushed away if your opponent guards and pushblocks against this attack**

Any option except the throw can lead right back into the cr. L, st. M, cr. H chain. A ground throw can lead to Elemental Rage or a crossover combination. An air throw, if you happen to score one as an option select, has more potential (using ⇨ + H instead of just H while in the air is for the sole purpose of scoring throws, or breaking them, if you happen to be in range). You can simply use Hail Storm, or call an OTG-capable assist and launch, or use Double Typhoon L and then jump forward to combo with air H into Lightning Attacks into Lightning Storm.

If you're feeling cautious, you can also use jump cancels to transition easily back to stalling. Jump cancel *backward*, airdash up-back, then call an assist and activate flight. From here, you can throw Lightning Spheres diagonally at your foe, or put a Double Typhoon on screen. If you want to feign cowardice and then change gears, use flight to airdash repeatedly right back in (hopefully while the assist you called runs some sort of interference at ground level; an assist like Sentinel—α occupies foes long enough for you to airdash several times all the way to the other side of the opponent, then land, then still go for cr. L or an overhead on the target as they block the assist from behind).

When you land a hit with the main chain, you can make Storm embellish her combos quite a bit. Between jump-cancelable basic attacks, instant float, an airdash, and directable Lightning Attacks, Storm has scads of possible jump loop variations. These combos aren't just flashy, they're necessary; Storm's biggest weakness is her ability to build hyper meter. Her normal jump height loops and her flight air combos aren't icing on the cake; they're necessary for her to tread water. In any case, Storm's bread and butter combos are trickier than those of many characters, but remember that she's more about playstyle and the flexibility she brings to a team than the direct damage that she can inflict.

Storm would be nasty against new characters coming in after a snap back or knockout just with her normal mix-ups and the invincible tip of her launcher. Lightning Sphere pushes her over the top, however. Remember, Storm is unaffected by advancing guard against Lightning Sphere! So, while awaiting a character falling in fresh, jump and throw horizontal Lightning Sphere M so your opponent is forced to guard it as the first thing they do. Forcing them to guard when they fall in means they can be thrown afterward (characters who fall in doing absolutely nothing are immune to throws until they land), so the simplest thing to do is airdash forward after releasing Lightning Sphere—Storm then ends up in midair next to her adversary—then air throw them just after they exit guardstun. If you have an assist that can cover you on failure, call it just before the throw. If you time this properly, opposing players don't have a prayer of mashing out of this with air attacks unless they have 4 frame air L (such as Nova, Iron Man, or Storm herself). The opponent is put into a position where the best they can hope for consistently is a throw break, after which, depending on your assist, they may be pinned into a cornered mix-up from Storm immediately anyway.

Advancing guard against Lightning Sphere has no effect on Storm! Force new characters to guard Lightning Sphere, then air throw or go for a point-blank mix-up after they finish blocking.

Storm is extremely dangerous if other characters hand her plenty of bar to use (or if she generates extra through TACs).

This same tactic can also work against competitors midscreen, if you happen to throw a normal jump height Lightning Sphere M and they jump into it. You can even set it up purposefully by ending Storm juggles midscreen by throwing a Lightning Sphere toward the opponent's air recovery. If you're on target, they're forced to guard, advancing guard means nothing, and you're free to go for a reset or air throw!

The meter limitations Storm has are irrelevant if someone else is generating it for her. Storm is great in the same kind of last-ditch situation that Akuma, Dormammu, Phoenix, etc. thrive under: loaded with lots of hyper meter and lv.3 X-Factor ready. If you make it here and your opponent has already used up their X-Factor, show no mercy: pop lv.3 X-Factor and Hail Storm, Hail Storm, Hail Storm! Even one-on-three Storm can turn the tide in the right situation... let's say the first Hail Storm catches an errant assist and nukes it, and then you chip out a second character with several Hail Storms? Suddenly, one-on-three is one-on-one, if they can't counter by using their own X-Factor (such as if the reason they got such a lead was by popping X-Factor early). Meanwhile, any clean Storm hit should lead to a combo that deals at least 800,000 damage and possibly much more. Don't mess with nature.

COMBO USAGE

1. CR. L, ST. M, CR. H CANCEL FORWARD JUMP, IMMEDIATE ↘ + S + ATK, LAND, ST. M, CR. H CANCEL FORWARD JUMP, AIR H, S CANCEL FORWARD AIRDASH, AIR H, LAND, ST. M, H, S CANCEL FORWARD SUPER JUMP, AIR M, M, H, S, LAND, ↓ ↙ ← + ATK ATK OTG (MASH ATK)

605,600 damage, 19% meter loss

Both standing M and crouching H are jump-cancelable, so you can transition into another triangle jump air L or instant float air attacks (or fake either of those then go for a throw) if the opposing character guards. If they use advancing guard, you can jump cancel and square dash back in with air ➡ + H or air S. When this combo connects, the extra work involved with the ground-level jump and airdash loops goes mostly toward helping build meter, an area Storm lacks. If you don't at least do jump height loops or flight airdash loops with Storm, you're always going to be wanting for hyper meter.

Between jump cancels, instant float, airdashes, low-altitude Lightning Attacks back to the ground, and crossover assists, Storm has enormous variation on what she can do off a clean ground-level hit. This is one example of a consistent combo that works on everyone (including off an initial overhead, like triangle jump air L or instant float air S), and builds decent meter.

This combo has the distinct advantage of working in any level of X-Factor while being meter-self-sufficient (and dealing 876,300 / 980,300 / 1,085,500 damage at each level!). Storm's increased speed forces a minor change: you'll want to jump straight up, rather than forward, for the jump portions of the combo. Also, although Storm becomes crazy fast, you don't have to do the beginning portions as fast as you think. You do want to perform the super jump air combo as fast as possible, however.

COMBO USAGE CONT.

II. Ⓢ CANCEL SUPER JUMP FORWARD, PAUSE, AIR Ⓗ CANCEL FORWARD AIRDASH, AIR Ⓗ CANCEL ↓↙← + Ⓢ, AIR Ⓛ, Ⓗ CANCEL FORWARD AIRDASH, AIR Ⓗ CANCEL FORWARD AIRDASH, AIR Ⓗ CANCEL FORWARD AIRDASH, AIR Ⓗ CANCEL FORWARD AIRDASH, AIR Ⓗ, Ⓢ, LAND, ↓↙← + ATK ATK OTG (MASH ATK)

611,900 damage, 47% meter loss

This combo works if preceded by overheads and ground chains, but in that case, it's more worthwhile to go for combo I or other jump height variations to build more meter. This combo is best after poking with Ⓢ launcher.

Eight-way airdash characters can usually only airdash once per airborne period. During flight, this restriction disappears, so by transitioning to flight in a Storm air combo, you can loop air Ⓗ canceled to forward airdash, back to air Ⓗ, and so on. This goes a long way toward improving the damage and meter gain of Storm's air combos (her air chain being really picky and puny compared to most; Lightning Attack combos being limited in follow-ups; and Lightning Sphere combos being rad, but more trouble than they're worth). Flight lasts for just under two seconds, so it's possible to squeeze five or six heavy attacks at most. After up to five repetitions of airdash air Ⓗ, finish with air Ⓢ for a hard knockdown.

The first trick here is linking air Ⓛ after activating flight. This only works in short combos where hitstun decay hasn't kicked in yet. (Don't plan on flight combos after jump height loops unless you're in lv.2 or lv.3 X-Factor.) Storm's flight has slower startup than for other characters who use flight in air combos, so if you're having trouble with it, you're probably pressing Ⓛ way too early.

The second is being able to airdash air Ⓗ into your rival five times in a row without slipping under them. You give yourself a lot of help here if you hit with the initial air Ⓗ after launching as *high* in the air as possible. In other words, super jump immediately after launching, but wait as long as you can before attacking on the way up. Assuming you did that, the key is that the *slower* you do this combo, the better it works! Cancel air Ⓗ hits into airdash immediately, but then pause before the next air Ⓗ hits. Storm's air Ⓗ pops her target up slightly, but it also causes enough hitstun so they'll drift back down, if you give them the chance. Hit air Ⓗ too fast, and they'll be popped successively higher, until air Ⓢ on the end is guaranteed to miss. Slow down, though, and this combo should become second nature.

Storm's lateral airdash travels very far, but as long as you're letting the opposing character's body drift downward, Storm won't slip under them—she'll just push them back toward the corner, as though dashing into them on the ground. In X-Factor, as Storm's airdashes achieve ludicrous speed, this combo is still possible, but it is much more difficult as to be unreliable at lv.2 or lv.3.

This is also a great team aerial combo starter, just by using direction + Ⓢ in place of the hard knockdown. If the next character can extend into a hyper combo, you can THC Storm right back in with Hail Storm! Ouch. Especially if you start the TAC with ↓ + Ⓢ, this move always builds enough hyper meter to work, no matter what you do with the next character. Using teammates creatively in this manner goes a long way toward compensating for Storm's slightly below-average damage and hyper meter building.

When you TAC *to* Storm from another character, this is the combo you want to attempt (without the pre-flight airdash, though; either fly into air Ⓛ immediately off the exchange hit, or perform one air Ⓗ and then fly). This is also possible if you happen to catch the enemy in the gut with air Ⓗ air-to-air, but you'll want to finish with Lightning Attacks into Lightning Storm rather than air Ⓢ in that situation, as you won't get a hard knockdown or air exchange hit since the combo didn't start with a launcher.

III. P1 or P2 CHRIS—γ, THROW OR LOW ALTITUDE AIR THROW, CHRIS'S GRENADE HITS, DASH, ST. Ⓗ, CR. Ⓗ CANCEL FORWARD JUMP, AIR Ⓗ, Ⓢ CANCEL FORWARD AIRDASH, AIR Ⓗ, LAND, ST. Ⓜ, ST. Ⓗ, Ⓢ CANCEL FORWARD SUPER JUMP, AIR Ⓜ, Ⓜ, Ⓗ CANCEL FORWARD AIRDASH, AIR Ⓗ CANCEL Ⓢ + ATK X3 CANCEL ↓↘→ + ATK ATK (MASH ATK)

431,700 damage, 1% meter gain!

Whether off a front or back ground throw, Storm can always tack on Elemental Rage for 307,300 damage. And, off any air throw, Storm has time to land and Hail Storm for 367,600. Either of these costs her a hyper meter bar without building any of it back, though. If you have an assist handy that lasts long enough to hit your opponent just as Storm finishes the throw but before they hit the ground in a hard knockdown (or if the assist lasts long enough to OTG afterward), you can immediately proceed into a combo to recoup some of the meter you'll use. Alternately, you can use the opportunity to turn the jumping loops into an air throw opportunity; see Advanced Tactics for more details.

IV. CR. Ⓛ, ST. Ⓜ, CR. Ⓗ CANCEL FORWARD JUMP, IMMEDIATE ↘ + Ⓢ + ATK, LAND, ST. Ⓗ, CR. Ⓗ CANCEL UPWARD JUMP, AIR Ⓗ, Ⓢ CANCEL AIRDASH FORWARD, AIR Ⓗ, LAND, ST. Ⓗ, CR. Ⓗ CANCEL UPWARD JUMP, AIR Ⓗ, Ⓢ CANCEL AIRDASH FORWARD, AIR Ⓗ, LAND, Ⓢ CANCEL FORWARD SUPER JUMP, AIR Ⓜ, Ⓜ, Ⓗ, Ⓢ, LAND, ↓↙← + ATK ATK (MASH ATK)

1,094,700~1,212,100 damage, 41~56% meter gain (lv.2/3 X-Factor)

With the extra speed granted by higher levels of X-Factor, Storm gains access to new combos. She's fast enough to easily link standing Ⓗ after a down-forward Lightning Attack at low altitude; she's also fast enough to substitute standing Ⓗ for standing Ⓜ as the landing link in her jump loops. The timing of her jumping airdash loops is not the same as outside of X-Factor, or even X-Factor level 1; although Storm is faster, you'll actually want to do things *slower*, so she doesn't get out of hand and squirt past her rival.

"I HAVE LED THE X-MEN IN MANY A BATTLE. WORKING IN A TEAM COMES NATURALLY TO ME."

STORM

ADVANCED TACTICS

INSTANT FLOAT OVERHEADS

Using instant float for overheads allows you to give your opponent a different look when fishing for combos.

Tap or hold ⇧ while Storm is airborne to make her float. This kills all upward momentum and begins a slow descent. Only Rocket Raccoon is also capable of this trick. Apart from obvious uses for hovering in the air longer than your adversary anticipates, float also enables fast, extremely low altitude overheads. This is because floating can be performed as early as the 4th frame after Storm begins to jump, the first frame after she leaves the ground.

To execute this, tap any upward direction twice very quickly. Try to be precise, and tap up again cleanly after just one upward tap for the initial jump. If you get errant inputs, Storm may end up jumping and then immediately airdashing upward or sideways.

Once float begins, you can input attacks immediately, so once you're floating at low altitude, it's just a matter of hitting a button. Air Ⓛ during instant float whiffs over many crouching characters and doesn't cause enough hitstun in this situation to follow up with a ground combo consistently. Stick to using air Ⓜ, ⇨ + Ⓗ, or Ⓢ. Why ⇨ + Ⓗ when Storm doesn't actually have an air ⇨ + Ⓗ command attack? The better to option select a throw or throw break, if your opponent happens to jump.

Once you feel comfortable performing instant float air moves on their own, you can mix them into combos and mix-ups. Anytime your rival guards crouching Ⓗ, you can jump cancel and immediately float, then have a quick overhead heading for a target who was just blocking low.

SHADES OF MVC2: WHO FINISHES COMBOS?

You can use Foul Wind to create some very confusing post-air recovery situations.

Instead of launching near the end of Storm ground loop combos, you have an interesting chance to let the opposing character hang themselves and reset to another combo. Storm combos inevitably eventually lead to a standing or crouching Ⓗ before a launcher. Instead of launching, call an assist that occupies a lot of aerial screen space, like Rocket Raccoon—γ, then cancel the heavy attack to Foul Wind. Since you didn't launch after Ⓗ, the opponent air recovers at normal jump height in front of Storm, just as she sucks them forward with Foul Wind and as her assist arrives.

Depending on whether your rival air recovers forward, backward, or in place, and depending on which assist you use (Rocket Raccoon is just a useful suggestion... there are many possibilities), this can have lots of different effects, but the important part is that they can be virtually unblockable on reaction. After all, Foul Wind sucks them forward, and they're air recovering, so it's quite possible that they may cross just past Storm, running into her assist on the other side.

To add another layer to the mix-up, you can dash under them as they air recover, and call an assist while using Foul Wind from the other side... or call the assist from the original side, then dash under, then use Fair or Foul Wind as appropriate. Finally, you can opt to do nothing, let them flip out, then jump and air throw them. If you finished a ground combo with crouching Ⓗ, you can also jump cancel backward and fire Lightning Sphere. If you vary your approach and use assists that hit lots of normal jump height screen space, this approach is basically guaranteed to hit the opposing character a lot of the time, in the same way that using Wolverine Berserker Slash mix-ups well is essentially unguardable on reaction. In this way, Storm can pile on damage without being totally reliant on tacking on her hyper combos.

COMBO APPENDIX

GENERAL EXECUTION TIPS

Executing normal jump height loops is just a matter of doing all the steps as soon as possible. Practice until they are ingrained in muscle memory.

Whenever launching to a variation of the standard air Ⓜ, Ⓜ, Ⓗ, Ⓢ chain, perform the rising air Ⓜ hits as soon as possible on the way up.

On the other hand, when performing air combos where the first hit is air Ⓗ, such as when canceling to flight, perform the first air Ⓗ as late and high as possible.

CR. Ⓛ, Ⓜ, Ⓗ, Ⓢ CANCEL➡ FORWARD SUPER JUMP, AIR Ⓜ, Ⓜ, Ⓗ, Ⓢ, LAND, ⇩⇙⇦ + ATK ATK OTG (MASH ATK)

Notes	Damage
Simple Hail Storm combo	541,600, 62% meter loss

CR. Ⓛ, Ⓜ, Ⓗ, Ⓢ CANCEL➡ FORWARD SUPER JUMP, AIR Ⓜ, Ⓜ, Ⓗ CANCEL➡ FORWARD AIRDASH, AIR Ⓗ CANCEL➡ {Ⓢ + ATK} X3 CANCEL➡ ⇩⇘⇨ + ATK ATK (MASH ATK)

Notes	Damage
Simple Lightning Storm combo. Necessary Lightning Attack direction in the air combo varies depending on your opponent's position	566,300, 43% meter loss

CR. Ⓛ, ST. Ⓜ, CR. Ⓗ CANCEL➡ FORWARD JUMP, IMMEDIATE ⇘ + Ⓢ + ATK, LAND, ST. Ⓜ CANCEL➡ FORWARD JUMP, IMMEDIATE ⇘ + Ⓢ + ATK, LAND, ST. Ⓜ, Ⓗ, Ⓢ CANCEL➡ FORWARD SUPER JUMP, AIR Ⓜ, Ⓜ, Ⓗ CANCEL➡ FORWARD AIRDASH, AIR Ⓗ CANCEL➡ {Ⓢ + ATK} X3 CANCEL➡ ⇩⇘⇨ + ATK ATK (MASH ATK)

Notes	Damage
Necessary Lightning Attack direction in the air combo varies depending on the opposing character's position	596,200, 16% meter loss

AIR THROW, ⇩⇙⇦ + Ⓛ OTG, FORWARD JUMP, AIR Ⓗ CANCEL➡ ⇗ + Ⓢ + ATK CANCEL➡ ⇩⇘⇨ + ATK ATK (MASH ATK)

Notes	Damage
More elaborate air throw follow-up than naked Hail Storm; less damage but much more meter gain	337,300, 53% meter loss

SUPER-SKRULL

"YES, I FOUGHT FOR HUMANITY DURING SECRET INVASION. BUT DON'T READ TOO MUCH INTO THAT."

Bio

REAL NAME

Kl'rt

OCCUPATION

Soldier of the Skrull Empire

ABILITIES

Together with the Skrull ability of shapeshifting, Kl'rt is also capable of hypnotism. He has all the powers of the Fantastic Four, and can utilize them at the same time.

WEAPONS

None

PROFILE

A genetically-engineered super soldier created by the Skrulls to defeat the Fantastic Four, who stopped their invasion of Earth. His pride and tendency to look down on others is not unique to him, but a characteristic of the Skrull race in general.

FIRST APPEARANCE

Fantastic Four #18 (1963)

POWER GRID

- 2 INTELLIGENCE
- 6 STRENGTH
- 5 SPEED
- 6 STAMINA
- 6 ENERGY PROJECTION
- 4 FIGHTING ABILITY

*This is biographical, and does not represent an evaluation of the in-game combat potential of this hero.

ALTERNATE COSTUMES

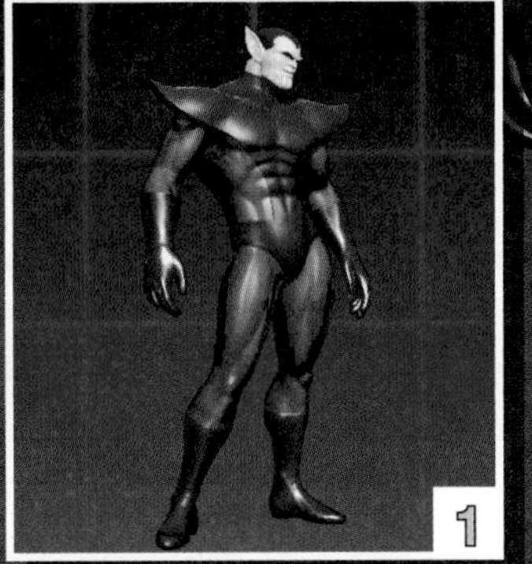

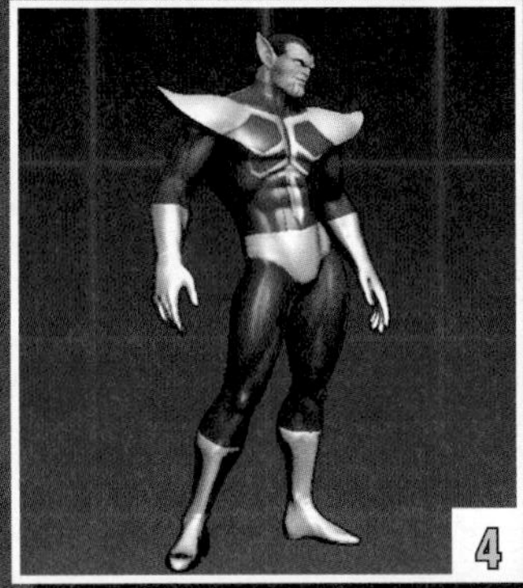

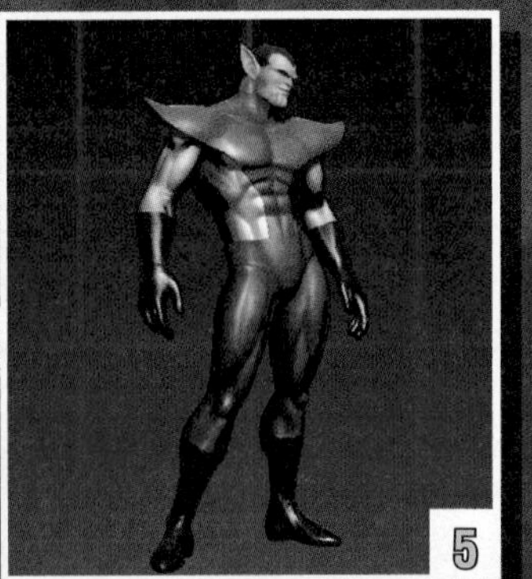

Overview

Vitality	1,000,000
Chain Combo Archetype	Hunter Series

X-Factor Boost	Damage	Speed
Level 1 (3 teammates remaining)	130%	110%
Level 2 (2 teammates remaining)	147.5%	122.5%
Level 3 (1 teammate remaining)	165%	135%

Your primary goal with Super-Skrull is to get within range of his Elastic Slam special move.

Why would you want to focus on being in range of Elastic Slam?

- Elastic Slam is an unblockable throw with incredible range, with two versions that can grab either airborne or grounded opponents
- Lack of hitbox on Super-Skrull's arm means Elastic Slam M can pass through most basic attacks and projectiles
- Super-Skrull has many OTG-capable moves, allowing you to create high damage combos off a successful Elastic Slam
- Being in range of Elastic Slam forces your competitor to make a choice; they cannot sit and play passively

How do you get Super-Skrull within range of Elastic Slam?

- Forcing your adversary into the corner, where their options for escaping Elastic Slam are very limited
- Utilizing lockdown crossover assists to force your foe into blocking, then getting into position for a mix-up
- Using Super-Skrull's unique airdash in conjunction with Brutal Pile Bunker and Stone Dunk to approach the target
- Using Meteor Smash with crossover assists to quickly close the distance on your rival

TUNING SINCE ORIGINAL MVC3

Super-Skrull received several minor tweaks in *Ultimate Marvel vs. Capcom 3*, the most obvious addition is the ability to perform Meteor Smash in the air. The super armor capabilities of Orbital Grudge now kick in two frames earlier, and he can no longer block while airdashing. Each of his hyper combos has changed slightly, as well: Inferno can be mashed for more damage, active and recovery frames of Skrull Torch have been tweaked, and Death Penalty no longer requires a specific combination of buttons to determine its landing area.

- Super-Skrull can no longer guard while in the middle of an airdash
- Meteor Smash can be performed in air
- Orbital Grudge super armor properties activate two frames faster
- Inferno is mashable for added damage
- Skrull Torch active frames increased
- Death Penalty automatically homes in on your opponent's location and no longer requires a specific button combination to determine where the attack lands

Attack Set

Standing Basic Attacks

Screen	Command	Hits	Damage	Meter Gain	Startup	Active	Recovery	Advantage on Hit	Advantage if Guarded	Notes
1	Standing Ⓛ	1	50,000	400	6	3	11	0	-1	Low attack
2	Standing Ⓜ	2	72,000	640	9	4	21	-4	-5	—
3	Standing Ⓗ	1	90,000	720	13	4	17	—	+2	Ground bounces foe

Crouching Basic Attacks

Screen	Command	Hits	Damage	Meter Gain	Startup	Active	Recovery	Advantage on Hit	Advantage if Guarded	Notes
1	Crouching Ⓛ	1	45,000	360	6	3	12	-1	-2	—
2	Crouching Ⓜ	1	75,000	600	8	3	18	+8	-3	Slightly launches opponent
3	Crouching Ⓗ	1	80,000	640	11	4	24	+5	-5	Low attack, knocks down rival

Ground Special Attack—Launcher

Screen	Command	Hits	Damage	Meter Gain	Startup	Active	Recovery	Advantage on Hit	Advantage if Guarded	Notes
1	Ⓢ (while standing or crouching)	1	100,000	800	11	4	24	—	-5	Launcher, not special- or hyper combo-cancelable

Air Basic Attacks

Screen	Command	Hits	Damage	Meter Gain	Startup	Active	Recovery	Advantage on Hit	Advantage if Guarded	Notes
1	Air Ⓛ	1	55,000	440	6	3	14	+10	+9	Overhead attack
2	Air Ⓜ	1	75,000	600	9	3	19	+17	+16	Overhead attack
3	Air Ⓗ	1	85,000	680	11	7	18	+19	+18	Overhead attack

Air Special Attacks—Flying Screen and Air Exchange

Air Ⓢ causes a hard knockdown when used in a launcher combo (this is sometimes called flying screen). When used outside of a launcher combo, air Ⓢ behaves mostly like another basic attack. Air exchange attacks, performed by inputting a direction plus Ⓢ, are only possible during a launcher combo. Exchange hits initiate team aerial combos by tagging in the next available character to continue the air combo.

Screen	Command	Hits	Damage	Meter Gain	Startup	Active	Recovery	Advantage on hit	Advantage if guarded	Notes
1	Air Ⓢ	1	90,000	720	15	4	15	+16	+15	Overhead attack, causes hard knockdown if used in launcher combo
2	Air ⇧ + Ⓢ (during launcher combo)	1	60,000	480	9	3	19	—	—	Tags in next available ally while lofting opponent upward
3	Air ⇨ or ⇦ + Ⓢ (during launcher combo)	1	50,000	400	13	4	17	—	—	Tags in next available ally while causing wall bounce, erases 1 hyper meter bar from foe
4	Air ⇩ + Ⓢ (during launcher combo)	1	50,000	400 + 10,000	13	4	17	—	—	Tags in next available ally while causing ground bounce, generates 1 hyper meter bar

1

2

3

4

Command Attacks

Command attacks resemble basic attacks but have different chaining and canceling properties. It's usually possible to chain *into* a command attack from basic attacks, but most command attacks cannot be chained from or canceled themselves.

Screen	Name	Command	Hits	Damage	Meter Gain	Startup	Active	Recovery	Advantage on Hit	Advantage if Guarded	Notes
1	Elastic Punch	⇨ + Ⓗ	1	90,000	720	15	4	22	-2	-3	—
2	Stone Smite	Standing Ⓗ (hold)	1	120,000	960	52	6	22	—	-5	OTG-capable, wall bounces rival, jump-cancelable, not special- or hyper combo-cancelable, inflicts chip damage
3	Rolling Hook	⇨⇨⇨ + Ⓗ	1	130,000	1040	24	3	24	—	-4	Hard knockdown, inflicts chip damage
4	Worm Squash	⇩⇩ + Ⓗ	1	37,800	378	1	2	29	—	—	Only hits grounded foes, not special- or hyper combo-cancelable, adversary remains grounded
5	Flame Kick	Crouching Ⓗ (hold)	1	110,000	880	48	4	34	—	-15	OTG-capable, spinning knockdown, jump cancelable, not special- or hyper combo-cancelable, inflicts chip damage
6	Brutal Pile Bunker	Air ⇩ + Ⓗ	2	115,000	960	15	Until landing*6	16	—	-9	Overhead attack, OTG-capable, floor bounces, knocks down, not special- or hyper combo-cancelable, inflicts chip damage
7	Stone Dunk	Air Ⓢ (hold)	1	120,000	960	37	6	22 (or until grounded, then 1 frame of recovery)	—	+21	Overhead attack, ground bounces target, not special- or hyper combo-cancelable, inflicts chip damage
8	Elastic Uppercut	⇖ + Ⓗ	1	90,000	720	15	4	22	-2	-3	—

1

2

3

4

5

6

7

8

Throws

Throws are for snagging passive or blocking opponents. Since throws are active so quickly, you can also use them to preemptively toss opposing characters out of their offense. Combos are usually possible after throws, one way or another.

Screen	Command	Hits	Damage	Meter Gain	Startup	Active	Notes
1	⇨ + Ⓗ (ground)	1	80,000	800	1	1	Hard knockdown
	⇦ + Ⓗ (ground)	1	80,000	800	1	1	Hard knockdown
2	⇨ + Ⓗ (air)	1	80,000	800	1	1	Hard knockdown
	⇦ + Ⓗ (air)	1	80,000	800	1	1	Hard knockdown

1

2

As a Partner—Crossover Assists

Screen	Type	P1+P2 Crossover Combination Hyper Combo	Description	Hits	Damage	Meter Gain	Startup	Active	Recovery (this crossover assist)	Recovery (other partner)	Notes
1	Super-Skrull—α	Inferno	Stone Smite	1	120,000	960	58	6	113	83	OTG-capable, wall bounces opponent
2	Super-Skrull—β	Inferno	Orbital Grudge M	6	140,300	1440	39	19	114	84	super armor from frames 37-51, knocks down adversary
3	Super-Skrull—γ	Skrull Torch	Tenderizer H	10	121,600	1536	42	3(4)3(4)3(4)3(4)3(4) 3(5)3()3(4)3(9)3	117	87	Knocks down foe

1

2

3

Outside of Elastic Slam and Meteor Smash, Super-Skrull's special attacks are not particularly great, and of course, the same thing can be said of his assist abilities. Super-Skrull's assists are generally only useful in certain situations, making an assist choice difficult for players choosing to place Super-Skrull in the second or third slot on a team.

Super-Skrull—α replicates the Stone Smite move, which is one of Super-Skrull's more useful command attacks. It covers a large area of the screen, is OTG-capable, and causes a wall bounce if it hits. However, its slow startup time and lack of invincibility allows Super-Skrull—α to be easily punished by a projectile or hyper combo, unless the point character is already in the middle of a combo.

Super-Skrull—β is based on Orbital Grudge M. Its forward momentum and super armor frames make it a tempting choice for some teams. Orbital Grudge super armor activates two frames faster in *Ultimate Marvel vs. Capcom 3*, but the added startup time of this assist makes it difficult to use as an effective counter.

Super-Skrull—γ is based on Tenderizer H, releasing a barrage of punches upward from Super-Skrull's location. While this moves dishes out a large number of hits and knocks down foes, it's generally impractical to use in combos. The damage scaling reduction caused by landing a full Tenderizer is more likely to cause you to deal less damage in the long run than your point character would do otherwise. Super-Skrull—γ can come in handy against incoming characters, forcing them to block as they enter the match and creating a potential throw mix-up situation.

Snap Back

Screen	Command	Hits	Damage	Meter Gain	Startup	Active	Recovery	Advantage on Hit	Advantage if Guarded
1	↓↘→ + P1 or P2	1	50,000	500 - (-1 hyper meter bar)	2	4	17	—	+2

Notes

On hit, snap back forces the opposing point character to be replaced by an assist. Opposing assist calls or tag outs are also locked out for 4 seconds

1

Special Moves

Screen	Name	Command	Hits	Damage	Meter Gain	Startup	Active	Recovery	Advantage on Hit	Advantage if Guarded	Notes
1	Orbital Grudge L	↓↘→ + L	3	94,800	840	10	11	30	+1	-10	Knocks down opponent, 1 hit of super armor during frames 8-17
	Orbital Grudge M	↓↘→ + M	6	140,300	1440	15	19	22	+8	-4	Knocks down foe, 1 hit of super armor during frames 13-27
	Orbital Grudge H	↓↘→ + H	9	171,100	2016	20	20	21	+10	-8	Knocks down rival, 1 hit of super armor during frames 18-34
2	Fatal Buster	(During Orbital Grudge) ↓↙← + H	1	70,000	560	15	4	37	—	-18	Wall bounces adversary, hard knockdown
3,4,5	Tenderizer (in air OK)	ATK)))	10	121,600	1536	18	3(4)3(4) 3(4)3(4) 3(4)3(5) 3(4)3(4) 3(9)3	25	—	-5	Knocks down competitor, L version is OTG-capable, all hits besides final cause hard knockdown, final hit of L version ground bounces
6,7,8	Elastic Slam	↓↙← + ATK	5	180,000	1800	21	1	44	—	—	Throw attack, hard knockdown
9	Meteor Smash (in air OK)	→↓↘ + ATK	2	125,000	1040	22	26*3	32	—	-21	Frames 6-19 invincible, OTG-capable, hits overhead, knocks down target

1

Orbital Grudge: Super-Skrull spins forward in a whirling fury of stone and fire. The length of the spin is determined by which ATK button is used. All three versions have super armor properties, but the super armor kicks in progressively slower with increased strengths. All versions of Orbital Grudge can be canceled into Fatal Buster.

In *Ultimate Marvel vs. Capcom 3*, the super armor effect of Orbital Grudge now kicks in two frames faster than in the original release. Super armor for Orbital Grudge L takes effect after eight frames, so you can now feasibly use it to combat certain basic attacks and projectiles.

2

Fatal Buster: Super-Skrull follows up Orbital Grudge with a massive uppercut that wall bounces your opponent and leaves them in a hard knockdown state. Its lengthy recovery time makes it difficult to chain the wall bounce into a combo, but it's not impossible. From midscreen, you can have Super-Skrull dash forward and juggle S launcher into a combo, or follow up Fatal Buster with an OTG-capable Meteor Smash and hyper combo cancel into Inferno.

Tenderizer L 3

Tenderizer M 4

Tenderizer H 5

Tenderizer: Combining the powers of Mr. Fantastic and The Thing, Super-Skrull unleashes a barrage of rock-encrusted punches. The L version directs the punches at a downward angle, M punches straight ahead, and H directs the punches at an upward angle. Tenderizer L is OTG-capable and is the fastest way to extend combos from midscreen. The final hit of Tenderizer L ground bounces your foe, allowing you to follow up with the Skrull Torch hyper combo. You can even use it to create an infinite combo (see the Advanced Tactics section). However, in most OTG situations, you'll want to use Meteor Smash, since it leads to more damaging combos.

The use of Tenderizer outside of combos is not advisable. Opponents can easily use advancing guard to push Super-Skrull back and punish the attack. Always be wary of pushing too many buttons when playing Super-Skrull!

Elastic Slam L 6

Elastic Slam M 7

Elastic Slam H 8

Elastic Slam: Elastic Slam is an unblockable command throw that is the most important tool in Super-Skrull's arsenal. The L and M versions both reach in front of Super-Skrull with varying range. Elastic Slam L has a range of about three character widths, while Elastic Slam M can reach about five character widths at the expense of a small dead zone right next to Super-Skrull's body. The H version of Elastic Slam grabs adversaries out of the air and serves as a great way to reset foes coming out of air recovery or create a simple mix-up with the other two versions.

Any version of Elastic Slam can lead to an easy combo—try Meteor Smash into Inferno for 527,500 damage, essentially forcing your competitor to stay off the ground at all times! The M version of Elastic Slam can sometimes be used on reaction if your opponent throws a mid range projectile. Super-Skrull's hand lacks a hitbox, allowing it to pass through the projectile cleanly to grab the opposing character.

9

Meteor Smash: Super-Skrull's Meteor Smash allows you to land OTG hits from anywhere on the screen. Used in almost all of Super-Skrull's combos that lead into Inferno, Meteor Smash is a huge contributor to Super-Skrull's high damage output. One of Super-Skrull's big changes in *Ultimate Marvel vs. Capcom 3* is that you can now also perform Meteor Smash in the air, giving Super-Skrull the ability to dodge incoming attacks as well as some easier combos. Outside of combos, you can use the delayed invulnerability of Meteor Smash to escape the corner against characters too slow to punish it—like Haggar or Nemesis. You can also occasionally use it as a counter against zoning projectile attacks, a surprise anti-air against super jumping opponents, or even as a surprise cross-up. When used with a slow long range projectile assist like Doctor Doom—β or Sentinel—α, Meteor Smash can be a great way to start offensive pushes: call the assist, attempt to cross your opponent up with Meteor Smash, then continue with a combo as the assist's attacks begin to hit! However, without the proper assist back-up, it's advisable to use Meteor Smash sparingly outside of combos since it is very unsafe if guarded.

The button used to determine the final destination of Meteor Smash is screen-relative; L lands on the left side of the screen, M in the middle, and H on the far right side of the screen.

Hyper Combos

Screen	Name	Command	Hits	Damage	Startup	Active	Recovery	Advantage on Hit	Advantage if Guarded	Notes
1	Skrull Torch	⇩⇘⇨ + ATK ATK (in air OK)	30	293,200	10+1	62	Until grounded, then 1 frame of recovery	—	-11	Frames 4-19 (4-11 in air) invincible, knocks down foe, Super-Skrull can be directed up or down using the controller
2	Inferno	⇩⇙⇦ + ATK ATK (in air OK)	50~99	284, 100~340, 400	10+2	57	14	+5	-22	Beam durability: 50 frames x 3 durability points, all hits except for final hit cannot be advancing guarded, can be mashed for additional hits
3	Death Penalty	⇨⇩⇘ + ATK ATK	13	450,000	20+6	8	45	—	-24	24 frames invincibility, OTG-capable, hits overhead

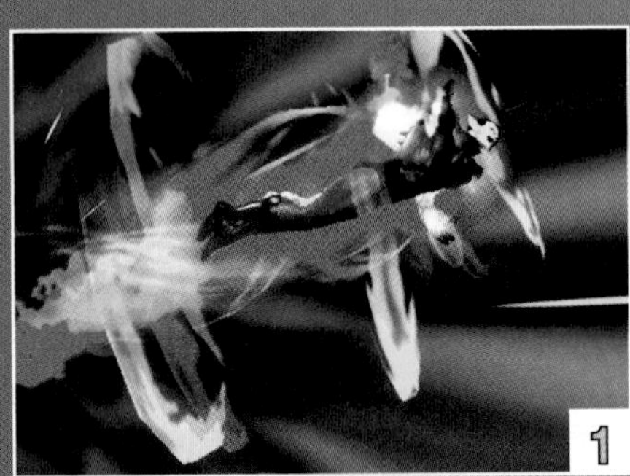

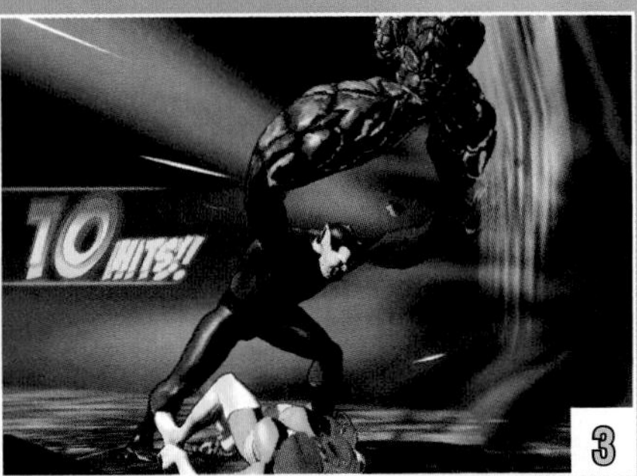

Skrull Torch: Flame On! Super-Skrull does his best Johnny Storm impersonation and turns himself into a flaming missile that flies across the screen and can be directed using the controller. Skrull Torch may simply be viewed as a combo finisher after Tenderizer, but it has a high number of invincibility frames and fast traveling speed that make it an effective tool for taking risks to catch opposing characters.

It's also one of the only defensive deterrents Super-Skrull has when facing aggressive adversaries who like to get close. You can activate Skrull Torch either on the ground or in the air, but just be sure that you have an extra gauge of hyper meter to perform a team hyper combo if your rival blocks.

Inferno: Super-Skrull unleashes the full fury of his flame power! Inferno has a huge area of effect, but it is also slow and does not have invincibility. Inferno is difficult to use outside of combos, but it's not too big of a detriment since most of Super-Skrull's combos end with an Inferno anyway. The damage potential of Inferno has been increased in *Ultimate Marvel vs. Capcom 3*, since it can now be mashed out for additional damage.

Death Penalty: Death Penalty is essentially a level 3 hyper combo version of Meteor Smash—they are both used to land OTG hits from anywhere on the screen. It's also one of the more damaging level 3 hyper combos in the game, so ending extended combos with Death Penalty is advised if it can successfully K.O. your opponent.

It's important to note that while Death Penalty is instantly invincible, the period of invulnerability ends before Super-Skrull reappears on the screen. When used to counter projectiles from all the way across the screen, Super-Skrull can occasionally get stopped cold in his tracks by an errant crossover assist attack.

Previously, different combinations of attack buttons were used to determine where Death Penalty would land. This is no longer required in *Ultimate Marvel vs. Capcom 3*—regardless of the two ATK buttons used to activate Death Penalty, the hyper combo eventually finds its mark.

Battle Plan

Super-Skrull's command attacks, paired with a slow projectile assist, offer a great way to get close in on your competitor.

Use Meteor Smash to cross up opponents, putting Super-Skrull in a perfect spot for Elastic Slam L.

Super-Skrull may have all of the powers of the Fantastic Four at his disposal, but the most valuable of the four is Mr. Fantastic's stretching ability—represented in this game by the Elastic Slam. Elastic Slam has a great range, but you still need to put some work in with Super-Skrull to get him within range of this powerful command throw. Luckily, there are a few techniques that are sure to help.

First, Super-Skrull has the option of covering distance by coming in from the air. His airdash only travels in one direction—diagonally upward—and should keep him safe from most grounded attacks. Have Super-Skrull jump into the air, activate his airdash, and then hold down (S) to come at your foe with a fully charged Stone Dunk. It covers a large area of the screen below Super-Skrull, can be used to cross up your opponent, and causes a ground bounce on the target if it hits, allowing you to follow up with a combo. Brutal Pile Bunker is also useful from an airdash, quickly dropping Super-Skrull to the ground with a punch that also ground bounces your rival. Brutal Pile Bunker has a -4 frame advantage on block, so unless your opponent has a quick jab, Super-Skrull should be able to block in time. Alternatively, you can airdash toward your rival and input ⇨ + (H) as you come in. While not a command move of any type, ⇨ + (H) counts as an air throw attempt and air (H) can beat most anti-air attacks.

On the ground, Super-Skrull has a couple more options to quickly close the distance. The first is to simply wavedash toward your adversary. Super-Skrull has a very fast wavedash that, when executed properly, can get Super-Skrull within range of Elastic Slam M in less than a second. Rolling Hook ⇨⇨⇨ + (H) is another option, since it covers a full screen's worth of distance and causes a wall bounce on hit.

All of these options are greatly enhanced with a slow, long range assist such as Doctor Doom—β or Sentinel—α. Super-Skrull relies heavily on these types of assists to create cross up situations or to make his moves safer. For example, calling Sentinel—α immediately before performing a Meteor Smash causes the drones to hit just as Super-Skrull lands his attack. If the assist is blocked, you can set up the next offensive move—such as an Elastic Slam—or if the assist hits, you just received an opening for a massive combo opportunity!

Make mix-up attempts safer by utilizing assists.

Once you're in range to grab your opponent with Elastic Slam, setting up mix up opportunities is going to be key for Super-Skrull's strategy. The easiest Elastic Slam mix up comes from poking at your rival with standing (L). Doing this gives your rival a few options, each of which can be countered. Begin by staggering the hits so that the added timing can strike opponents trying to use advancing guard. Standing (L) also hits low, so it can catch adversaries trying to jump away. Any time during your standing (L) prods, cancel into Elastic Slam L to punish your opponent for doing nothing. Should the standing (L) attacks hit, use that opportunity to start up the combo of your choice!

Successfully catching your target with Elastic Slam H is a bit of a guessing game. If you think your opponent is expecting Elastic Slam L or M and is going to jump away, call out an assist to cover Super-Skrull as you attempt to grab them with Elastic Slam H. If your adversary blocks, they'll be forced into guardstun while the assist attack plays out and keeps Super-Skrull safe from harm. Should your opponent jump and get caught in Elastic Slam, well, you've just earned yourself another combo opportunity. All versions of Elastic Slam are risky attacks if avoided, so be sure to cover your attempts at every opportunity.

Nearly every time you force your opponent to guard a crossover assist, you can immediately put your competitor into an Elastic Slam mix-up. From wherever Skrull may be on the ground, react to the assist making contact, then immediately have Skrull dash forward and use Elastic Slam M or H. This lets you be threatening without being in the range of crouching (L)!

Super-Skrull has very few options to protect a failed Elastic Slam grab. If you've got the meter to burn, you can cancel the Elastic Slam into Inferno and then team hyper combo to another character. Otherwise, you have to cancel out of Elastic Slam with X-Factor and hope you can capitalize on the added boost. X-Factor is never something you want to waste, so keep your options open as best you can.

Orbital Grudge super armor kicks in earlier in Ultimate Marvel vs. Capcom 3. Take advantage of this to punish your foes!

You can use Meteor Smash's invincibility can be used to escape sticky situations… if you're careful.

Super-Skrull struggles a bit when it comes to maintaining a solid defense. Very few of his normal, command, and special moves are useful for escaping a bad situation, but knowing what tools are useful is paramount when the momentum of a match starts going the opposing player's way.

In *Ultimate Marvel vs. Capcom 3*, Super-Skrull lost his ability to block during an airdash. This made what was once a valid escape plan now nearly useless for that purpose. For air defensive options, you have to rely heavily on air throws instead. Luckily, with the added ability to perform Meteor Smash in the air, you can option select an air throw. As you head toward your opponent, input ⇨ + (H) and cancel it into Meteor Smash, and if the attacker is in range, they'll be snagged by the air throw; otherwise, Meteor Smash is activated instead to send Super-Skrull away to safety. Alternatively, you can meet opponents in the air with a (M), (H), (S) chain that should keep Super-Skrull safe until he is grounded on block, or lead into a big combo if it connects.

If Super-Skrull gets trapped in the corner, salvation may lie in Meteor Smash and Orbital Grudge L. Meteor Smash is invincible from the 6th frame, allowing you a chance to have Super-Skrull escape the corner if you can time it to start between enemy attacks. Be sure to push the right (ATK) button: you wouldn't want to escape just to come right back down in the corner you were trying to escape!

Orbital Grudge L has super armor properties that start on the eighth frame of the attack, much sooner than in original *MvC3*. A 2 frame speed up may seem small on paper, but in practice, it means that Orbital Grudge is now more useful and viable to chew through an opponent's offense. If the attack is guarded, you can mix up with a delayed Fatal Buster to catch competitors trying to punish the Orbital Grudge.

In the end, however, the safest defense option for Super-Skrull is to utilize advancing guard to get your rivals off your back, and keep a sharp eye out for opportunities to air throw your attacker.

COMBO USAGE

I. ST. (L), CR. (M), CR. (H), (S) CANCEL⇨ FORWARD SUPER JUMP, AIR (M), (M), (H), (S), LAND, {IF THE ENEMY IS MIDSCREEN, → ↓ ↘ + (H) CANCEL⇨ ↓ ↙ ← + (ATK)(ATK) (MASH (ATK))} OR {IF THE ENEMY IS CORNERED, FORWARD JUMP, AIR ↓ + (H), (S) CANCEL⇨ FORWARD SUPER JUMP, AIR (M), (M), (H), (S), LAND, → ↓ ↘ + (H) CANCEL⇨ ↓ ↙ ← + (ATK)(ATK) (MASH (ATK))}

689,900~737,300 damage, 40% meter loss or 4% meter gain

This basic Super-Skrull combo has variable endings based on Super-Skrull's position after the first air (M), (M), (H), (S) chain. Delay the air (S) hit to the last possible moment to ensure the air ↓ + (H) will connect and put Super-Skrull in range to launch with (S). Otherwise, it's possible that the launcher attack will whiff entirely.

Should your challenger block standing (L), crouching (M), chain into a delayed standing (H). If it connects, transition into (S) and continue the combo, or chain standing (H) and kara-cancel into ↓ ↙ ← + (L) before it connects. Standing (H) leaves you at a frame advantage when blocked, so continue your offense in that case.

II. ST. (L), CR. (M), (H), (S) CANCEL⇨ FORWARD SUPER JUMP, AIR (M), (M), DELAYED (H), DELAYED (S), LAND, ST. (H) (HOLD), WAVEDASH FORWARD TWICE, (S) CANCEL⇨ FORWARD SUPER JUMP, AIR (M), (M), (H), (S), LAND, {→ ↓ ↘ + (H) CANCEL⇨ ↓ ↙ ← + (ATK)(ATK) (MASH (ATK))} OR {↓ + (H) (HOLD) CANCEL⇨ ↓ ↙ ← ↖ + (ATK)(ATK) (MASH (ATK)), LAND, ↓ ↙ ← + (ATK)(ATK) (MASH (ATK))}

746,400~917,800 damage, 4% meter gain or 100% meter loss

Here's a more damaging, but much harder to execute, midscreen combo that pummels your foe to the closest corner. After the first launch, you must delay the input of both air (H) and (S) to ensure that Super-Skrull lands as quickly as possible. This gives you enough time to fully charge Stone Smite. After the wall bounce, launch your rival with (S) again, then perform the following air chain at the peak of Super-Skrull's jump. If timed correctly, you should have just enough time to land a fully charged crouching (H). When the flaming sweep hits, cancel it into a jump and then Inferno by inputting ↓ ↙ ← ↖ + (ATK)(ATK) in one smooth motion. Doing the aerial version of the hyper combo causes Skrull to recover faster, giving you just enough time to juggle with another Inferno.

If performed near a corner, it's possible that Stone Smite can send your adversary flying over Super-Skrull's head. In this case, remember to reverse your input directions and input the appropriate button to correctly land Meteor Smash.

COMBO USAGE CONT.

III. ↓ ↙ ← + (ATK), → ↓ ↘ + Ⓗ ⇒ ↓ ↙ ← + (ATK)(ATK) (MASH (ATK))

517,500 damage, 72% meter loss

Super-Skrull's command grab is an essential part of his battle plan. This simple combo ensures you'll remove at least half of an opponent's life from a single Elastic Slam.

IV. FRONT AND BACK GROUND OR AIR THROW, → ↓ ↘ + Ⓗ ⇒ ↓ ↙ ← + (ATK)(ATK) (MASH (ATK))

456,500 damage, 82% meter loss

Similar to **Combo III**, this variation starts with an air throw instead of Elastic Slam. It does less damage than the Elastic Slam variant, but any extra damage is always a plus.

V. FORWARD SUPER JUMP, INSTANT ↓ + Ⓗ, FORWARD DASH, ST. Ⓛ, CR. Ⓜ, CR. Ⓗ, Ⓢ ⇒ FORWARD SUPER JUMP, AIR Ⓜ, Ⓜ, Ⓗ, Ⓢ, LAND, → ↓ ↘ + Ⓗ ⇒ ↓ ↙ ← + (ATK)(ATK) (MASH (ATK))

656,400 damage, 33% meter loss

Super-Skrull's Burning Pile Bunker (air ↓ + Ⓗ) isn't just a handy OTG attack, but it can also serve as a fast overhead attack with ground bounce properties. Take advantage of this move to catch unaware adversaries and chain into this damaging combo for minimal meter loss.

VI. → → → + Ⓗ, → ↓ ↘ + Ⓗ ⇒ ↓ ↙ ← + (ATK)(ATK) (MASH (ATK))

562,700 damage, 80% meter loss

Rolling Hook is a great tool for covering a lot of ground quickly. If the hit connects, quickly perform Meteor Smash H into Inferno for a good chunk of damage. Competitors may anticipate this move and attempt to call an assist to stop Super-Skrull, but Rolling Hook is more than likely going to catch the assist character, as well, leading to an even greater advantage for you!

VII. ST. Ⓛ, CR. Ⓜ, Ⓗ, Ⓢ ⇒ FORWARD SUPER JUMP, AIR Ⓜ, Ⓜ, DELAYED Ⓗ, DELAYED Ⓢ, LAND, ST. Ⓗ (HOLD), WAVEDASH FORWARD TWICE, Ⓢ ⇒ FORWARD SUPER JUMP, AIR Ⓜ, Ⓜ, Ⓗ, Ⓢ, LAND, → ↓ ↘ + Ⓗ ⇒ ↓ ↙ ← + (ATK)(ATK) (MASH (ATK)) [X-FACTOR] ↓ ↙ ← + (ATK)(ATK) (MASH (ATK))

990,500~1,055,300 damage, 100% meter loss

This punishing combo is a slight variation of **Combo II** that is nearly a guaranteed K.O. against a majority of the cast. The X-Factor cancel into a second Inferno at the end of the combo leaves a large chunk of X-Factor duration left to use against the next character on your opponent's team. However, only utilize this combo when you're certain it is going to K.O. your adversary; otherwise, you'll burn valuable X-Factor time trying to get the last few hits needed to finish the job on your current foe.

VIII. ↓ ↙ ← + (ATK), → ↓ ↘ + Ⓗ [X-FACTOR], WALK FORWARD, Ⓢ ⇒ FORWARD SUPER JUMP, AIR Ⓜ, Ⓜ, Ⓗ, Ⓢ, LAND, → ↓ ↘ + Ⓛ ↓ ↙ ← + (ATK)(ATK) (MASH (ATK))

823,600~975,500 damage, 14~3% meter loss

Another X-Factor combo that can be started from Elastic Slam, this combo can also be started from normal and air throws for less damage.

ADVANCED TACTICS

ELASTIC SLAM RESETS

Super-Skrull has a great chance to grab an airborne opponent out of air recovery, leading to a quick Meteor Slam CANCEL ▶ Inferno combo.

With Super-Skull's vast array of moves that can cause wall bounces, ground bounces, and are OTG-capable, it is pretty easy to find yourself in a combo where you've used two launchers, and an OTG Meteor Smash causes an adversary to air recover instead of being knocked down. You can capitalize on this by grabbing your rival out of air recovery with Elastic Slam H!

The easiest reset you can practice is a fairly simple combo: Ⓛ, Ⓜ, Ⓗ CANCEL ▶ cr. Ⓛ CANCEL ▶ ⇩⇙⇦ + Ⓗ. You can perform this combo anywhere on the screen and get a feel for the timing of grabbing opponents out of air recovery. Be sure to follow up the Elastic Slam with Meteor Smash and hyper combo cancel into Inferno.

The Elastic Slam H grab out of air recovery is never guaranteed, however. Characters with fast aerial move options like eight-way dashes can easily escape the attempt. Character who air recover forward can escape the grab every time, and this gives your competitor the opportunity to severely punish Super-Skrull while he recovers from the whiffed grab. Luckily, the natural tendency for most opposing players is to air recover backwards, and this is much more difficult to escape the long arm of the Skrull Empire!

CRISIS ON INFINITE SUPER-SKRULL COMBOS

The timing is very strict, but it's possible to unleash Tenderizer L right as Super-Skrull leaves the ground, preventing the last hit from coming out and leaving your opponent in a hard knockdown state.

Super-Skrull has an infinite combo that works against cornered foes in a hard knockdown state. The combo itself looks simple on paper, but the execution is a bit trickier: ⇩ + Ⓗ (charge) CANCEL ▶ jump CANCEL ▶ Ⓛ)) (repeat)

The trickiest part of this combo is timing the three Ⓛ inputs to trigger Tenderizer L at the exact moment Super-Skrull leaves the ground. To time the hits, watch for Super-Skrull's leg to connect with his challenger and press Ⓛ twice. Immediately after, press ⇗, and input the final Ⓛ command as soon as Super-Skrull's feet hit the ground. This is the trickiest part of the loop, but when done correctly, the final hit of Tenderizer L is canceled by Super-Skrull touching the ground, negating the ground bounce and leaving his opponent in a hard knockdown state. Super-Skrull is now free to repeat the loop with another Flame Kick.

After four to five repetitions, Super-Skrull gets pushed too far back for the Flame Kick to connect. When you think you're outside of the hit zone, simply dash cancel into Flame Kick to close the distance and continue the loop.

After seven to eight repetitions, damage scaling will have kicked in to a point where Super-Skrull is hardly dealing any damage to his rival. Luckily, at this point, Super-Skrull has built three bars of hyper meter off of the loop and can most likely finish of the opponent. Follow the last air Tenderizer L with a grounded Tenderizer L and cancel into Death Penalty. The infinite combo pays for itself, and you've got one fewer enemy to worry about!

COMBO APPENDIX

GENERAL EXECUTION TIPS

Delay hitting with air Ⓗ and Ⓢ at the end of aerial chains for as long as possible to ensure enough time to follow up with Super-Skrull's OTG-capable charge attacks.

After placing your opponent in a hard knockdown state, be aware of their position on the playfield if you plan on following up with Meteor Smash. Pressing the wrong attack button ruins the combo and potentially puts Super-Skrull at a disadvantage.

AS SUPER-SKRULL COMES IN: AIR Ⓗ, Ⓢ, →↓↘ + Ⓜ CANCEL ▶ ↓↙← + ATK ATK (MASH ATK)

Notes	Damage
⇧ + Ⓢ or ⇨ + Ⓢ TAC to Super-Skrull, ⇨⇩⇘ + Ⓜ must be done before Skrull touches the ground from the first jump	Varies based on damage scaling

FRONT THROW, ST. Ⓗ (HOLD) CANCEL ▶ VERTICAL JUMP, AIR Ⓢ (HOLD), LAND, FORWARD DASH, CR. Ⓜ, Ⓗ, Ⓢ CANCEL ▶ FORWARD SUPER JUMP, AIR Ⓜ, Ⓜ, Ⓗ, Ⓢ, LAND, ↓ + Ⓗ (HOLD) CANCEL ▶ ↓↙←↖ + ATK ATK (MASH ATK)

Notes	Damage
Requires corner	753,200 damage, 118% meter loss

CR. Ⓛ, CR. Ⓗ, Ⓢ CANCEL ▶ FORWARD SUPER JUMP, FORWARD AIRDASH, AIR Ⓗ, Ⓢ, LAND, ST. Ⓗ (HOLD) CANCEL ▶ FORWARD JUMP, AIR Ⓢ (HOLD), LAND, FORWARD DASH, CR. Ⓜ, Ⓗ, Ⓢ CANCEL ▶ FORWARD SUPER JUMP, AIR Ⓜ, Ⓜ, Ⓗ, Ⓢ, LAND, ↓ + Ⓗ (HOLD) CANCEL ▶ ↓↙←↖ + ATK ATK (MASH ATK), LAND, ↓↙← + ATK ATK (MASH ATK)

Notes	Damage
Requires corner	958,300 damage, 106% meter loss

ST. Ⓛ, CR. Ⓜ, Ⓗ, Ⓢ CANCEL ▶ FORWARD SUPER JUMP, AIR Ⓜ, Ⓜ, DELAYED Ⓗ, DELAYED Ⓢ, LAND, ST. Ⓗ (HOLD), WAVEDASH FORWARD TWICE, Ⓢ CANCEL ▶ FORWARD SUPER JUMP, AIR Ⓜ, Ⓜ, Ⓗ, Ⓢ, LAND, →↓↘ + ATK ATK

Notes	Damage
—	916,200 damage, 206% meter loss

ST. Ⓛ, CR. Ⓜ, Ⓗ, Ⓢ CANCEL ▶ FORWARD SUPER JUMP, AIR Ⓜ, Ⓜ, DELAYED Ⓗ, DELAYED Ⓢ, LAND, ST. Ⓗ (HOLD), WAVEDASH FORWARD TWICE, Ⓢ CANCEL ▶ FORWARD SUPER JUMP, AIR Ⓜ, Ⓜ, Ⓗ, Ⓢ, LAND, {↓ + Ⓗ (HOLD) CANCEL ▶ FORWARD JUMP, Ⓛ)), LAND, FORWARD DASH} X ∞

Notes	Damage
Requires corner, once the first hit connects, the combo continues indefinitely	Damage varies depending on the amount of loops performed

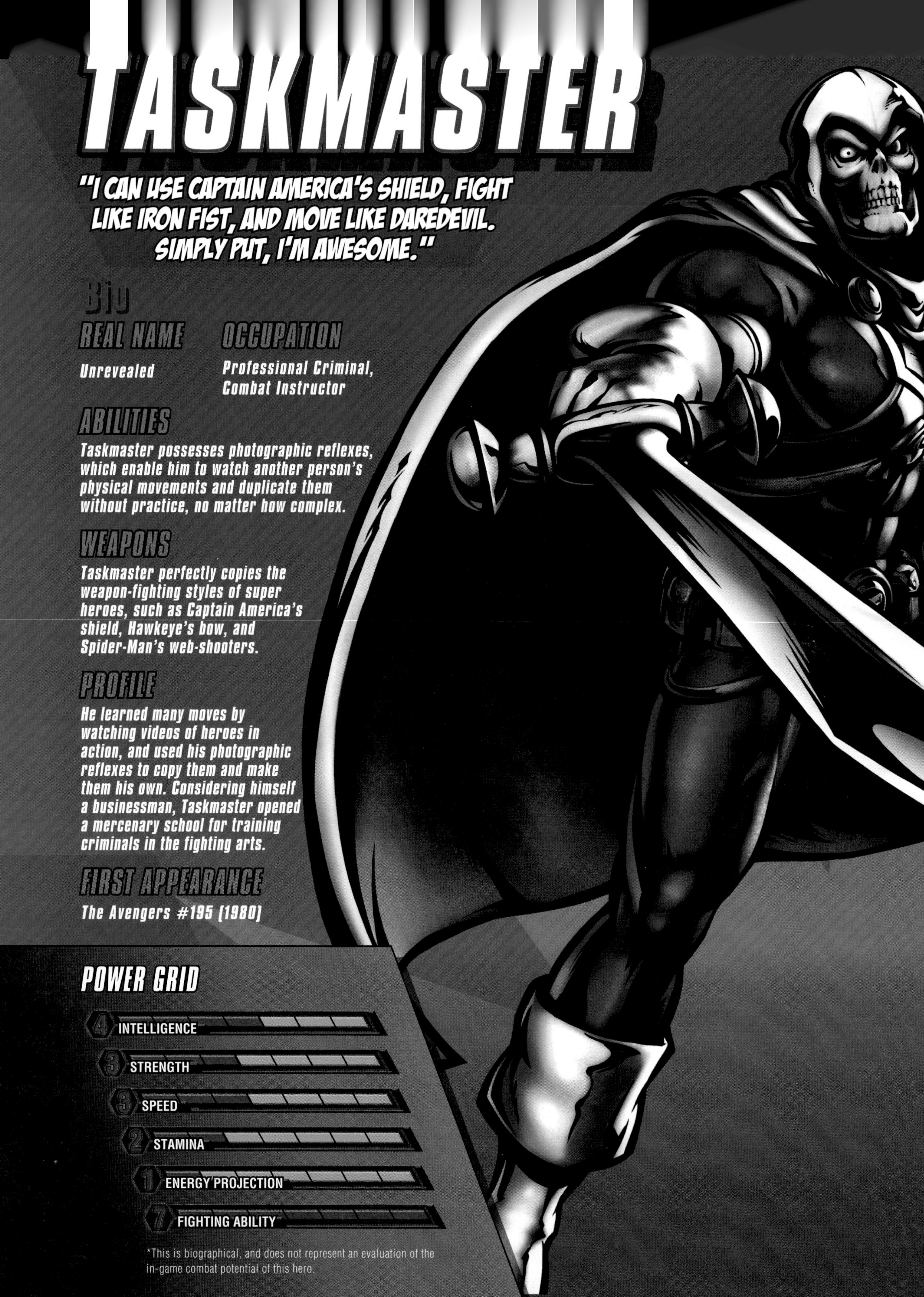

TASKMASTER

"I CAN USE CAPTAIN AMERICA'S SHIELD, FIGHT LIKE IRON FIST, AND MOVE LIKE DAREDEVIL. SIMPLY PUT, I'M AWESOME."

Bio

REAL NAME

Unrevealed

OCCUPATION

Professional Criminal, Combat Instructor

ABILITIES

Taskmaster possesses photographic reflexes, which enable him to watch another person's physical movements and duplicate them without practice, no matter how complex.

WEAPONS

Taskmaster perfectly copies the weapon-fighting styles of super heroes, such as Captain America's shield, Hawkeye's bow, and Spider-Man's web-shooters.

PROFILE

He learned many moves by watching videos of heroes in action, and used his photographic reflexes to copy them and make them his own. Considering himself a businessman, Taskmaster opened a mercenary school for training criminals in the fighting arts.

FIRST APPEARANCE

The Avengers #195 (1980)

POWER GRID

4 INTELLIGENCE

3 STRENGTH

3 SPEED

2 STAMINA

1 ENERGY PROJECTION

7 FIGHTING ABILITY

*This is biographical, and does not represent an evaluation of the in-game combat potential of this hero.

Vitality	1,100,000
Chain Combo Archetype	Marvel Series

X-Factor Boost	Damage	Speed
Level 1 (3 teammates remaining)	130%	110%
Level 2 (2 teammates remaining)	155%	115%
Level 3 (1 teammate remaining)	180%	120%

Taskmaster is well-rounded character who can produce big damage at close range or from a distance. Your main goal is to play a keepaway game using Aim Master with the help of crossover assists. Why this goal?

- **The damage, range, and guardstun/hitstun produced from Aim Master make it a great tool for forcing opponents to get closer. It is possible for adversaries to take heavy damage before ever getting close to Taskmaster**
- **Attempts at advancing on Taskmaster can be countered with the speed, priority, and damage potential of Charging Star**
- **If Aim Master isn't enough to overpower your rival's long—range game, you can use Guard Master H to counter opposing projectiles, further limiting your opponent's options from fullscreen**

How can this goal be achieved?

- **Using Aim Master's varying firing angles with projectile crossover assists to cut off your competitor's means of approaching while simultaneously causing heavy chip damage**
- **Countering the opposing character's advances with Charging Star after they become frustrated with dealing with Aim Master**
- **Retreating by jumping back with Aim Master M**

TUNING SINCE ORIGINAL MVC3

Taskmaster's returned with several changes in *Ultimate Marvel Vs. Capcom 3*. Sting Master has been added to his pool of special moves, and Web Swing can now be canceled into Aim Master or Legion Arrow at any time. The damage on Aim Master and Legion Arrow has been reduced, though Legion Arrow can now be mashed for more damage, effectively nullifying its damage reduction.

- **Aim Master damage reduced**
- **New Move: Sting Master ↓ ↘ → + S causes hard knockdown**
- **Web Swing now cancelable with Aim Master or Legion Arrow**
- **Initial Legion Arrow damage reduced, but it is now mashable for more damage**
- **Aim Master H arcs lower**
- **Air Aim Master H causes less Hover**
- **Charging Star knocks opponent further back, but not as high**
- **Taskmaster hovers less during jumping H**

Attack Set

Standing Basic Attacks

Screen	Command	Hits	Damage	Meter Gain	Startup	Active	Recovery	Advantage on Hit	Advantage if Guarded	Notes
1	Standing L	1	48,000	384	5	3	10	+2	+1	—
2	Standing M	2	72,000	640	8	2(1)3	17	0	-2	—
3	Standing H	1	90,000	720	11	3	20	+2	0	—

1

2

3

Crouching Basic Attacks

Screen	Command	Hits	Damage	Meter Gain	Startup	Active	Recovery	Advantage on Hit	Advantage if Guarded	Notes
1	Crouching L	1	45,000	360	5	3	14	-2	-3	Low attack
2	Crouching M	1	65,000	520	8	3	19	-2	-4	Low attack
3	Crouching H	1	80,000	640	10	3	23	-2	-3	Knocks down

1

2

3

Ground Special Attack—Launcher

Screen	Command	Hits	Damage	Meter Gain	Startup	Active	Recovery	Advantage on Hit	Advantage if Guarded	Notes
1	S (while standing or crouching)	1	90,000	720	9	5	30	—	-12	Launcher, not special- or hyper combo-cancelable

1

Air Basic Attacks

Screen	Command	Hits	Damage	Meter Gain	Startup	Active	Recovery	Advantage on Hit	Advantage if Guarded	Notes
1	Air L	1	50,000	400	5	3	15	+13	+12	Overhead attack
2	Air M	1	68,000	544	7	4	17	+16	+14	Overhead attack
3	Air H	2	92,500	800	11	4	21	+20	+18	Overhead attack

1

2

3

Air Special Attacks—Flying Screen and Air Exchange

Air Ⓢ causes a hard knockdown when used in a launcher combo (this is sometimes called flying screen). When used outside of a launcher combo, air Ⓢ behaves mostly like another basic attack. Air exchange attacks, performed by inputting a direction plus Ⓢ, are only possible during a launcher combo. Exchange hits initiate team aerial combos by tagging in the next available character to continue the air combo.

Screen	Command	Hits	Damage	Meter Gain	Startup	Active	Recovery	Advantage on Hit	Advantage if Guarded	Notes
1	Air Ⓢ	1	90,000	720	11	3	27	+17	+15	Overhead attack, causes hard knockdown if used in launcher combo
2	Air ⇧ + Ⓢ (during launcher combo)	1	60,000	480	7	10	Until grounded	—	—	Tags in next available ally while lofting opponent upward
3	Air ⇨ or ⇦ + Ⓢ (during launcher combo)	1	50,000	400	11	4	Until grounded	—	—	Tags in next available ally while causing wall bounce, erases 1 hyper meter bar from foe
4	Air ⇩ + Ⓢ (during launcher combo)	1	50,000	400 + 10,000	10	8	Until grounded	—	—	Tags in next available ally while causing ground bounce, generates 1 hyper meter bar

1

2

3

4

Command Attacks

Command attacks resemble basic attacks but have different chaining and canceling properties. It's usually possible to chain *into* a command attack from basic attacks, but most command attacks cannot be chained from or canceled themselves.

Screen	Name	Command	Hits	Damage	Meter Gain	Startup	Active	Recovery	Advantage on Hit	Advantage if Guarded	Notes
1	Web Swing	⇨ + Ⓗ (in air OK)	1	80,000	640	11	13	16	+7	-6	Knockdown, recovers in air neutral state, can only be performed one time while in air
2	Charging Star	⇦ + Ⓗ	1	95,000	760	6	9	29	—	-15	Immune to low and medium priority projectiles and beams during frames 4-18, knocks down, may be chained into Ⓢ

1

2

Throws

Throws are for snagging passive or blocking opponents. Since throws are active so quickly, you can also use them to preemptively toss opposing characters out of their offense. Combos are usually possible after throws, one way or another.

Screen	Command	Hits	Damage	Meter Gain	Startup	Active	Notes
1	⇨ + Ⓗ (ground)	2	80,000	800	1	1	Hard knockdown
	⇦ + Ⓗ (ground)	2	80,000	800	1	1	Hard knockdown
2	⇨ + Ⓗ (air)	1	80,000	800	1	1	Hard knockdown, drops foe directly underneath Taskmaster
	⇦ + Ⓗ (air)	1	80,000	800	1	1	Hard knockdown, drops opponent directly underneath Taskmaster

1

2

As a Partner—Crossover Assists

Screen	Type	P1+P2 Crossover Combination Hyper Combo	Description	Hits	Damage	Meter Gain	Startup	Active	Recovery (this crossover assist)	Recovery (other partner)	Notes
1	Taskmaster—α	Legion Arrow L+M	Aim Master L	3	135,000	1200	45	9	113	83	Each projectile has 3 low priority durability points
2	Taskmaster—β	Legion Arrow L+H	Aim Master M	3	135,000	1200	45	9	118	88	Each projectile has 3 low priority durability points
3	Taskmaster—γ	Legion Arrow M+H	Aim Master H	3	135,000	1200	45	9	123	93	OTG-capable, each projectile has 3 low priority durability points

1

2

3

All three of Taskmaster's crossover assists perform a different version of Aim Master, and all versions are fully charged with three arrows. Taskmaster—α performs Aim Master L. It can be used as long range support for characters who lack a projectile of their own, or to add to a character's long range game. It is also great for cross-ups with teleports or other special moves that cross up, such as X-23's Mirage Feint M or Zero's Hienkyaku M. Taskmaster—β performs Aim Master M, and you can use it to cover the upward angle in which many projectile characters cannot normally fire. Taskmaster—γ performs Aim Master H, which rains arrows down on opponents. The arrows fall individually in different positions, covering a large sum of space. This crossover assist is great for setting up any character's offense or for anti-air support.

Snap Back

Screen	Command	Hits	Damage	Meter Gain	Startup	Active	Recovery	Advantage on Hit	Advantage if Guarded
1	↓↘→ + P1 or P2	1	50,000	500 - (-1 hyper meter bar)	2	3	20	—	0

Notes

On hit, snap back forces the opposing point character to be replaced by an assist. Opposing assist calls or tag outs are also locked out for 4 seconds

1

Special Moves

Screen	Name	Command	Hits	Damage	Meter Gain	Startup	Active	Recovery	Advantage on Hit	Advantage if Guarded	Notes
1	Aim Master L (can be charged, in air OK)	↓↘→ + L	1~3	50,000~135,400	400~1200	13~21	1~9	37~21	-13~+3	-15~+1	Each projectile has 3 low priority durability points
2	Aim Master M (can be charged, in air OK)	↓↘→ + M	1~3	50,000~135,400	400~1200	13~21	1~9	42~26	-18~-2	-20~-4	OTG-capable, each projectile has 3 low priority durability points
3	Aim Master H (can be charged, in air OK)	↓↘→ + H	1~3	50,000~135,400	400~1200	13~21	1~9	47~31	-23~-7	-25~-9	OTG-capable, each projectile has 3 low priority durability points
4	Guard Master L	↓↙← + L	2	100,000	1000	5	20	20	—	—	Counterattack, counters high attacks, hard knockdown
4	Guard Master M	↓↙← + M	2	100,000	1000	5	20	20	—	—	Counterattack, counters low attacks, hard knockdown
4	Guard Master H	↓↙← + H	1	Varies	Varies	5	20	20	—	—	Counter attack, reflects some projectiles and nullifies beams, reflected projectiles deal their normal damage
5	Sword Master L	→↓↘ + L	1	50,000	400	31	5	22	—	-4	Knocks down
6	Head Butt	(When Sword Master L is blocked) H	1	30,000	240	24	5	16	+4	—	Unblockable
7	Lights Out	(During Head Butt) ↓↘→ + H	2	60,000	450	15	5	1	—	—	Unblockable, hard knockdown
5	Sword Master M	→↓↘ + M	1	50,000	400	44	5	22	—	-4	Knocks down
6	Head Butt	(When Sword Master M is blocked) H	1	30,000	240	24	5	16	+4	—	Unblockable
8	Below the Belt	(During Head Butt) M	1	28,000	224	13	5	21	-1	-3	—
9	Low Kick	(During Below the Belt) H	1	30,000	240	20	5	16	+4	+2	Low attack
7	Lights Out	(During Low Kick) ↓↘→ + H	2	70,000	700	15	5	1	—	—	Unblockable, hard knockdown
5	Sword Master H	→↓↘ + H	1	50,000	400	57	5	22	—	-4	Knocks down

Special Moves continued

Screen	Name	Command	Hits	Damage	Meter Gain	Startup	Active	Recovery	Advantage on Hit	Advantage if Guarded	Notes
6	Head Butt	(When Sword Master H is blocked) (H)	1	30,000	240	24	3	18	+4	—	Unblockable
8	Below the Belt	(During Head Butt) (M)	1	28,000	224	13	3	23	-1	-3	—
9	Low Kick	(During Below the Belt) (H)	1	30,000	240	20	4	17	+4	+2	Low attack
10	Shield Bash	(During Low Kick) (H)	1	25,000	200	21	3	22	0	-2	—
11	Knee Kick	(During Shield Bash) (M)	1	31,000	248	18	4	17	+4	+2	—
7	Lights Out	(During Knee Kick) ↓↘→ + (H)	2	80,000	800	15	5	1	—	—	Unblockable, hard knockdown
12	Sting Master	↓↘→ + (S)	2	113,000	1130	15	3	28	—	-3	Hard knockdown

Aim Master L 1

Aim Master M 2

Aim Master H 3

4

Aim Master: Taskmaster fires arrows that can be charged by holding the button down: performing Aim Master without charging fires one arrow, two levels of charge fires two arrows, and a full charge fires three arrows. Aim Master L fires straight forward and reaches fullscreen. Aim Master M fires at an angle and can be used to shoot foes closing in at normal jump height. Aim Master H fires upward before raining down in a parabola shape. You can use it to shoot your adversaries out of the sky or hold grounded opponents in place to set up an offense.

You can use Aim Master in the air, as well. Aerial Aim Master L fires straight forward and is used for air-to-air combat. Aerial Aim Master M fires downward at an angle and is OTG-capable. It is a great air-to-ground attack to use while jumping forward to pressure your rival or jumping backward to cover a retreat. Aim Master H fires almost straight down and can lead to tricky set-ups when used in conjunction with a crossover assist. The air versions of Aim Master M and H are both OTG-capable.

Aim Master is one of Taskmaster's primary ways of attacking. A fully charged set of arrows deals 135,400 points of damage (above average for a projectile) and can be charged fast enough to use regularly. Aim Master L and aerial Aim Master M should be used liberally at a distance on the ground, but Aim Master L is unsafe if guarded at close range, so be careful when using it anywhere other than from long range.

Guard Master: Taskmaster raises his shield and counters incoming attacks for a 20-frame duration. Guard Master counters different kinds of attacks based on the strength of the button used: Guard Master L counters mid attacks, Guard Master M counters low attacks, and Guard Master H counters projectiles. A successfully connected Guard Master L or M can be followed with an aerial Legion Arrow OTG. Guard Master H reflects projectiles back at opponents, though certain projectiles (such as beams) can only be nullified. Note that Guard Master does not counter hyper combos.

5

6

7

8

9

10

11

Sword Master: Sword Master is a slow slash attack that causes a soft knockdown. If it is guarded, you can follow it with the unguardable Head Butt attack, which you can then follow by a predetermined set of attacks based on which version of Sword Master was guarded. All three versions of Sword Master guarded lead to a hard knockdown when executed to their full extent, and you can follow them with Legion Arrow OTG for extra damage. Sword Master's startup varies based on the button used. Sword Master L is the fastest but has the weakest extensions, while Sword Master H has the longest startup but the most damaging extensions. Opponents can avoid the unguardable Head Butt by using advancing guard against the initial slash, so Sword Master is best used with the help of a crossover assist to hold foes in place for unguardable damage.

12

Sting Master: Sting Master is a melee attack that skewers competitors before sending them into a hard knockdown state. You can follow it with Legion Arrow OTG after connecting, like Guard Master and Sword Master. Sting Master has too much startup and recovery to be relied upon at close-quarters, but it is easily used in combos.

Hyper Combos

Screen	Name	Command	Hits	Damage	Startup	Active	Recovery	Advantage on Hit	Advantage if Guarded	Notes
1	Legion Arrow L+M	↓↘→ + L M	25~50	289,400~ 347,500	10+1	77	44	—	-22	Hard knockdown, each projectile has 1 high priority durability point, can be mashed for additional hits
	Legion Arrow L+H	↓↘→ + L H	25~50	289,400~ 347,500	10+1	77	44	—	-22	Hard knockdown, each projectile has 1 high priority durability point, can be mashed for additional hits
	Legion Arrow M+H	↓↘→ + M H	25~50	289,400~ 347,500	10+1	77	44	—	-22	Each projectile has 1 high priority durability point, OTG-capable, can be mashed for additional hits
	Air Legion Arrow L+M	(in air) ↓↘→ + L M	25~50	289,400~ 347,500	10+1	78	Until grounded	—	-22	Each projectile has 1 high priority durability point, can be mashed for additional hits
	Air Legion Arrow L+H	(in air) ↓↘→ + L H	25~50	289,400~ 347,500	10+1	77	Until grounded	—	-22	Hard knockdown on airborne opponents, each projectile has 1 high priority durability point, OTG- capable, can be mashed for additional hits
	Air Legion Arrow M+H	(in air) ↓↘→ + M H	25~50	289,400~ 347,500	10+1	77	Until grounded	—	-22	Hard knockdown on airborne adversaries , each projectile has 1 high priority durability point, OTG-capable, can be mashed for additional hits
2	Aegis Counter	↓↙← + ATK ATK	13	250,000	5+0	25	19	—	—	5 frames of invincibility, counters non-beam/ projectile attacks

1

2

Legion Arrow: Taskmaster fires a stream of arrows for mashable damage. Like Aim Master, you can aim Legion Arrow depending on the buttons pressed, and you can utilize this move both on the ground and in the air. While on the ground, L + M fires straight, L + H fires up at an angle, and M + H fires straight up before raining back down. In the air, L + M fires straight, L + H fires down at an angle, and M + H fires straight down.

Legion Arrow adds big damage to combos long and short and is also useful for shooting down aerial opponents, punishing crossover assists, punishing guarded or whiffed hyper combos, or blowing through enemy projectiles. However, Legion Arrow is unsafe if guarded at close range, so only use it up-close if you know it is going to hit. Additionally, Legion Arrow takes time to reach far distances, so foes can punish it with a teleport on reaction. These drawbacks aside, Legion Arrow is a great hyper combo and is a staple of Taskmaster's arsenal of attacks. If your adversary manages to jump over Aim Master L, cancel it into Legion Arrow to counter their punish.

Aegis Counter: Aegis Counter is a counterattack hyper combo that can catch any physical attack (hyper combos included) and can be followed with aerial Legion Arrow OTG for more damage. It has a period of invulnerability during its startup and can be used to counter an incoming hyper combo that is otherwise unavoidable, as long as it is physical. Aegis Counter is easily punishable during recovery and is also vulnerable to projectiles and throws, so it is not ideal to use this hyper combo recklessly.

Since Aegis Counter can be canceled into from special moves, use it for covering a dodged Aim Master L. You can also cancel into it when using Taskmaster for a crossover counter. Use a crossover counter into Taskmaster against an aggressive opponent and quickly cancel into Aegis Counter to stop their assault. Aegis Counter is great for THC setups, as well: if your competitor counters your hyper combo with an opposing hyper combo, quickly THC to Aegis Counter to stop your rival's hyper combo. Be mindful of the opponent's hyper meter, however; the opposing character can perform another THC to a projectile hyper combo to counter this tactic. Aside from using it as a counter, you can also employ Aegis Counter as a THC to continue a combo, provided that the previous hyper combo knocks your target high enough.

"I'LL SEND YOU A BILL FOR THE LESSON!"

Battle Plan

Increase the threat of Taskmaster's ranged attacks with the help of a crossover assist.

Ignore projectile attacks with Charging Star. Cancel into it from a forward dash for added distance.

Taskmaster is a well-rounded fighter who is effective at close or far range. The damage and range of a fully charged Aim Master is enough to make Taskmaster a serious threat at fullscreen, while the utility of Charging Star (⇦ + Ⓗ) and Web Swing (⇨ + Ⓗ) come into play at mid to close range. If you have the life lead as Taskmaster, don't be afraid to sit on the lead while fighting from a distance with Aim Master.

A large portion of Taskmaster's effectiveness is owed to Charging Star. With a mere 6 frames of startup, Charging Star is faster than most characters' Ⓜ and Ⓗ basic attacks, and it is immune to low and medium durability projectiles while active. It also covers a decent amount of horizontal range that you can extend by canceling into it from a forward dash. Charging Star is special move-cancelable and can be chained into Ⓢ upon connecting. It also boasts great priority, and you can rely on it to blow through an opponent's basic attacks and aerial assaults with ease.

As a downside, Charging Star is extremely unsafe if guarded. Competitors can either punish with a full combo while it recovers or go for a throw since Taskmaster is usually right next to the opposing character if guarded. Taskmaster has a few options if Charging Star is guarded, however. You can delay canceling the charge's recovery with Ⓢ as a frame trap for a would-be punish, though Ⓢ is also unsafe if guarded. You can also cancel Charging Star into Aim Master L, which is punishable if guarded at close range and interruptable if charged fully. Your best bet is to cover Charging Star with a crossover assist. Crossover assists may be called during Charging Star's recovery, so you can cover Taskmaster by inputting ⇦ + Ⓗ, P1 or P2, Ⓢ (or a special move) for a safe attack sequence depending on the crossover assist used.

At long range, Aim Master is your primary go-to attack and can always be canceled into Legion Arrow for a combo as long as it is hit-confirmed early. Aim Master L reaches fullscreen and is great for forcing your opponent to make a move. Clearing the floor with Aim Master L, air Aim Master M, and a ranged crossover assist forces your adversary to either burn meter in an attempt to retaliate or attack from the sky at an angle. Once your rivals start jumping to avoid Aim Master L, you can start using Aim Master M and air throws to keep them in check. You can have Taskmaster Legion Arrow OTG off any air throw, and you can even OTG with Aim Master H into a combo if the air throw is performed at normal jump height. If you have a life lead, there is no reason to risk getting close as Taskmaster; simply sit on the lead and fight at a distance with Aim Master to maintain your lead. Once your challenger is lured in, change it up by countering with standing Ⓗ, Web Swing, or Charging Star.

Taskmaster recovers before the arrows from Aim Master H rain down, allowing you to go in for a mix-up.

Taskmaster is vulnerable to air throws after Web Swing, so cover it with a crossover assist.

At mid range, you can use Web Swing as a means of starting offense. Web Swing is similar to Charging Star in that it launches Taskmaster forward, has good priority, and can be hit-confirmed into a combo. You can also perform Web Swing in the air, so it is commonly used in air combos. It recovers in the air, allowing for combos or continued pressure from the air when guarded on the ground. Crossover assists can be called at any time during Web Swing like a basic attack, so use crossover assists to pin opponents down after they guard Web Swing, then fall with air Ⓗ to keep the pressure going. This technique is also great for setting up unguardable attacks with a low crossover assist: time your low-hitting crossover assist so that it hits at the same time as a falling air Ⓗ follow-up to a guarded Web Swing. This attack is punishable by air throws, however, so be careful when using it without the cover of a crossover assist.

You can only perform Web Swing once in the air, so don't rely on it to keep Taskmaster in the air for long periods of time. However, using Web Swing on the ground does allow for another Web Swing upon recovery, since the ground swing does not use up the one aerial Web Swing that you are allowed. Web Swing can also be canceled into Aim Master (see the Advanced Tactics section for details).

Aim Master H becomes a threat at mid range, as well. Taskmaster recovers before the arrows of a charged Aim Master H rain down, so they can be used as a means of setting your rival up for a Web Swing, Charging Star, or wavedash to get into striking distance. The arrows from a fully charged Aim Master H all fall in a slightly different position, creating a spread that covers a lot of ground. Use a crossover assist to protect Taskmaster during the startup on the charge, then follow the arrows with a dash into melee range. You can react to Aim Master H if it connects with Charging Star for a combo, as well.

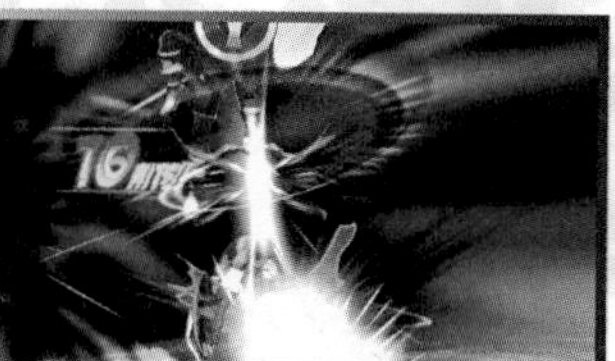

You can follow any of Taskmaster's throws with Legion Arrow OTG.

At close range, Taskmaster's crouching Ⓛ is a safe way to attack. It has long reach and starts up in a speedy 5 frames. Any chain of basic attacks started from crouching Ⓛ can always be chained into Charging Star for a combo. If guarded, you can either continue with a ground chain covered with a crossover assist, or mix up between another crouching Ⓛ or throw attempt. Standing Ⓜ and Ⓗ are great attacks, as well. The range and priority of these attacks is attributed to Taskmaster's sword, and they are not easy for your adversaries to deal with at close range.

You can follow either of Taskmaster's ground throws with Legion Arrow OTG, adding to Taskmaster's already strong up-close options. Dash in, cancel the dash with a crouch, then attempt the throw. If you think your opponent might attempt to counter the throw with a quick attack, use crouching Ⓛ instead for a counter-hit. Competitors trying to jump away from the throw attempt are tagged by crouching Ⓛ during the jump's startup frames if timed correctly. Attempts at jumping away from a throw attempt are also stopped with an air throw.

Charging Star has added uses at close range. Take advantage of its priority by blowing through your adversary's attempt to fight back. You can cancel into Charging Star from any basic attack, and you can use it after baiting your rival's attack for a counter-hit. Appear to be vulnerable during the recovery of a slower attack (such as standing Ⓗ), then interrupt your opponent's punishment attempt with a delayed Charging Star. Once your target fears Charging Star, you can get away with using slower-recovering moves and attack strings that are otherwise punishable when guarded.

Canceling from a basic attack can also be used with Web Swing, though it is better used as a means of keeping your offense flowing rather than starting a combo because of its slower startup. Cover the swing with a crossover assist, then continue pressure with a falling air Ⓗ, which puts Taskmaster into position for a crouching Ⓛ or throw mix-up. Web Swing is also a great alternative to Charging Star since it is better suited for combating advancing guard. Incorporate Web Swing into your offense to stay close against foes who constantly use advancing guard.

In the corner, Taskmaster's melee attacks are only harder to deal with. All throws become more difficult for challengers to escape from, and you can use Web Swing to keep opponents from using advancing guard for breathing space. The ranges on Taskmaster's basic attack and Charging Star are also great for keeping the pressure on cornered competitors. The usual crouching Ⓛ or throw mix-up is also applicable in the corner.

COMBO USAGE

1. CR. Ⓛ, Ⓜ, Ⓗ, → + Ⓗ, AIR Ⓜ, Ⓜ, → + Ⓗ, Ⓜ, Ⓜ, Ⓢ, LAND, ST. Ⓜ (2 HITS), Ⓗ, ← + Ⓗ, DELAYED Ⓢ CANCEL⇒ FORWARD SUPER JUMP, Ⓜ, Ⓜ, Ⓗ (2 HITS), → + Ⓗ, Ⓜ, Ⓜ, Ⓢ, LAND, VERTICAL JUMP ↓ ↘ → + Ⓗ (CHARGE) CANCEL⇒ ↓ ↘ → + ⓂⒽ (MASH ATK)

665,000 damage, 40% meter gain

A standard bread and butter combo, this combo always carries the opponent to the corner, so air ↓ ↘ → + ⓂⒽ always connects. When chaining into ← + Ⓗ, you must perform it very late to ensure that your foe never drops behind Taskmaster. If you are having problems with it, going straight into Ⓢ after standing Ⓜ, Ⓗ works, as well.

COMBO USAGE CONT.

II. FRONT OR BACK THROW, ↓ ↘ → ↗ + ⓂⒽ (MASH ATK)

396,500 damage, 92% meter loss

Taskmaster can perform Legion Arrow after any throw. The timing on this combo isn't very difficult; just be sure to input ⓂⒽ slightly after ↓ ↘ → ↗ so that Taskmaster is off the ground when the hyper combo is performed. Pressing ⓂⒽ too early might result in an accidental grounded Legion Arrow, which is easily punishable.

III. FRONT OR BACK AIR THROW, ↓ ↘ → + Ⓗ CANCEL ↓ ↘ → + ⓂⒽ (MASH ATK)

419,000 damage, 88% meter loss

Though Taskmaster can combo off an air throw with air ↓ ↘ → + Ⓗ, land, ← + Ⓗ, the strict positioning and timing required make this impractical for regular use. Furthermore, performing Legion Arrow right away does comparable damage to a launch combo off an air throw anyway, though it builds no meter. If you have no meter to spare, go for the launch combo. Otherwise, use this combo as your main air throw combo.

IV. (AGAINST AIRBORNE ENEMY) FORWARD JUMP, AIR Ⓜ, Ⓜ, Ⓗ (2 HITS), → + Ⓗ, Ⓜ, Ⓗ (2 HITS), Ⓢ, LAND, ST. Ⓜ (2 HITS), Ⓗ, ← + Ⓗ, DELAYED Ⓢ CANCEL FORWARD SUPER JUMP, AIR Ⓜ, Ⓜ, Ⓗ (2 HITS), → + Ⓗ, Ⓜ, Ⓜ, Ⓢ, LAND, {WHEN MIDSCREEN, FORWARD JUMP, AIR ↓ ↘ → + ⓁⒽ (MASH ATK)} OR {WHEN ENEMY IS CORNERED, VERTICAL JUMP ↓ ↘ → + Ⓗ (CHARGE) CANCEL ↓ ↘ → + ⓂⒽ (MASH ATK)}

617,000~654,900 damage, 17~29% meter gain

The angle of air Ⓜ makes it a great attack to use against an aerial opponent as anti-air, such as when a new character is coming in after a K.O. The version of Legion Arrow used at the end of the combo depends on positioning. Use ⓂⒽ in the corner and ⓁⒽ midscreen.

V. (AGAINST AN ENEMY'S ATTACK) ↓ ↙ ← + Ⓛ OR Ⓜ, FORWARD JUMP, AIR ↓ ↘ → + ⓁⒽ (MASH ATK)

400,700 damage, 90% meter loss

Even though Legion Arrow may miss several hits if your competitor isn't hugging a screen edge, this combo is still useful for capitalizing off a successful Guard Master. Note that you can also pair this combo with Aegis Counter for 427,700 damage and 200% meter loss.

VI. (WHEN ENEMY IS GUARDING) → ↓ ↘ + Ⓗ CANCEL Ⓗ CANCEL Ⓜ CANCEL Ⓗ CANCEL Ⓗ CANCEL Ⓜ CANCEL ↓ ↘ → + Ⓗ CANCEL {IF ENEMY IS MIDSCREEN, ↓ ↘ → ↗ + ⓁⒽ (MASH ATK)} OR {WHEN ENEMY IS CORNERED, ↓ ↘ → + ⓂⒽ (MASH ATK)}

452,100 damage, 78% meter loss

This is Taskmaster's standard unblockable combo. If memorizing the sequence of attacks is too troublesome for you, the Head Butt follow-ups can actually be mashed with continuous presses of Ⓜ and Ⓗ. Even then, it's still important to input ↓ ↘ → + Ⓗ after the fifth hit of the combo.

VII. CR. Ⓛ, Ⓜ, ST. Ⓗ X-FACTOR FORWARD DASH, CR. Ⓜ, Ⓗ, → + Ⓗ, AIR Ⓜ, → + Ⓗ, Ⓗ (2 HITS), DELAYED Ⓢ, LAND, ST. Ⓜ (2 HITS), Ⓗ, DELAYED ← + Ⓗ, Ⓢ CANCEL FORWARD SUPER JUMP, AIR Ⓜ, Ⓜ, Ⓗ (2 HITS), → + Ⓗ, Ⓜ, Ⓢ, LAND, VERTICAL JUMP, ↓ ↘ → + ⓂⒽ (MASH ATK)

1,066,200~1,425,600 damage, 58~116% meter gain

If you need a guaranteed K.O. and still have X-Factor available, this combo is enough to K.O. most characters in level 1 X-Factor and will K.O. any character in level 3 X-Factor. Although Taskmaster's speed is increased during X-Factor, it's fairly easy to adjust to the timing on the combo, despite the speed boost.

VIII. (IN OR NEAR CORNER) CR. Ⓛ, Ⓜ, ST. Ⓗ, ← + Ⓗ, Ⓢ CANCEL SUPER JUMP STRAIGHT UP, AIR Ⓜ, Ⓗ (2 HITS), → + Ⓗ, AIR Ⓜ, Ⓗ (2 HITS), Ⓢ, LAND, VERTICAL JUMP ↓ ↘ → + Ⓗ (CHARGE), LAND, ← + Ⓗ CANCEL ↓ ↘ → + Ⓢ, VERTICAL JUMP ↓ ↘ → + Ⓗ (CHARGE) CANCEL ↓ ↘ → + ⓁⒽ (MASH ATK), LAND, ↓ ↘ → ↗ + ⓂⒽ (MASH ATK)

877,500 damage, 95% meter loss

Usually, performing ← + Ⓗ in the corner during a combo causes Taskmaster to switch sides with his opponent, making it impossible to link two Legion Arrow hyper combos. With this combo, ↓ ↘ → + Ⓢ is used to end the combo with your adversary still in the corner, making the double Legion Arrow possible. Perform the second Legion Arrow as soon as Taskmaster lands from the first one with a tiger knee motion.

ADVANCED TACTICS

PICK YOUR POISON: OPTION SELECTS

At close range, go with ← + Ⓗ for a back throw. You'll either get the throw…

…or Charging Star!

An option select is an input or series of inputs used to produce an advantageous outcome in a situation where several different things can occur depending on positioning and the opposing player's action. Taskmaster has a few different option selects that are relatively easy to perform.

When in throwing range of an adversary, go for a back throw with ← + Ⓗ. If positioning and timing allow for a successful back throw, then the throw gets performed. If, for whatever reason, the throw attempt is unsuccessful, Charging Star gets performed instead. In addition, the ← input can possibly lead to guarding a quick mid-attack from your foe. This option select is great to use after your rival guards a crossover assist; press ← + Ⓗ the moment your opponent recovers from the guardstun of a crossover assist.

In a close-range air-to-air situation, press → + Ⓗ for an air throw attempt. If the air throw is unsuccessful, Taskmaster Web Swings instead, which can lead into a combo if connected or offensive pressure if guarded. This option select can be used on the ground, as well, as an alternative to the Charging Star option select.

Another air-to-air option select is performed with ← + Ⓗ CANCEL → + Ⓗ. With this option select, you'll either get the back air throw or air Ⓗ canceled into Web Swing. If the air throw is performed, the cinematic of the throw negates the → + Ⓗ input, and you can proceed to follow with Legion Arrow OTG. If you get the air Ⓗ instead, it then gets canceled into Web Swing, which you can follow with a combo or added offensive pressure if connected or guarded respectively.

With all three option selects, Taskmaster has the advantage whether the throw is successful or not. Learning to properly utilize these option selects is an integral part of Taskmaster's game overall. Cover Charging Star and Web Swing with a crossover assist if possible to limit your competitor's options in punishing these attacks.

WEB SWING CANCELS

At maximum range, a Web Swing canceled with maximum speed brings Taskmaster close to his target in an instant!

New to *Ultimate Marvel Vs. Capcom 3* is the ability to cancel Taskmaster's Web Swing into Aim Master or Legion Arrow. Canceling Web Swing into Aim Master makes for some interesting mobility options for Taskmaster depending on when the swing is canceled.

Canceling Web Swing early provides only a little forward momentum and can be used as a fake-out; cancel with Aim Master L on the ground or in the air at long range for a fake-out attack or at mid range for offensive pressure. Canceling the swing as late as possible provides a slight up-forward momentum and is a great follow-up to a guarded Web Swing. At super jump height, cancel a Web Swing late with Aim Master M or H to keep Taskmaster's air mobility from being too predictable while adding another angle of attack from the sky. On the ground, use the upward momentum of a late cancel to fire Aim Master M at a distance.

Canceling halfway through Web Swing is especially useful because the middle portion of the swing produces the most forward momentum. If performed correctly, Taskmaster gains the speed of an airdash and can travel almost the entire length of the screen! On the ground, cancel Web Swing halfway with Aim Master L as a means of approach. A charged Aim Master will not fire before Taskmaster lands in this situation, so it is best to use only one arrow of Aim Master when performing the Web Swing cancel on the ground. At normal jump or super jump height, cancel with a fully charged Aim Master M or H depending on positioning. You can use a Web Swing cancel at maximum speed to quickly get in on your rival, and you can make this safe with a long range crossover assist. You can also employ it as a way to get Taskmaster out of the corner.

Timing is crucial when trying to produce the desired effect from a Web Swing cancel. Once you've mastered this technique, Taskmaster's mobility options are increased dramatically, improving his effectiveness overall.

COMBO APPENDIX

GENERAL EXECUTION TIPS

When performing combos with air Ⓗ, land, ← + Ⓗ, the transition from air Ⓗ to ← + Ⓗ must be done somewhat slowly. Let the entire animation of air Ⓗ go through before attempting any ground attacks

(AFTER TAC) AIR Ⓜ, Ⓗ, → + Ⓗ, Ⓗ, Ⓢ, LAND, ↓↘→↗ + ⓁⓂ (MASH ATK) OR ↓↘→↗ + ⓂⒽ (MASH ATK)

Notes	Damage
↑ + Ⓢ or → + Ⓢ or ↓ + Ⓢ TAC to Taskmaster	Varies based on damage scaling

↓↘→ + Ⓛ CANCEL ↓↘→ + ⓁⓂ (MASH ATK) XF VERTICAL JUMP, AIR ↓↘→ + ⓁⒽ (MASH ATK)

Notes	Damage
—	674,400 damage, 188% meter loss

CR. Ⓛ, Ⓜ, ST. Ⓗ, ← + Ⓗ XF {← + Ⓗ CANCEL ↓↘→ + Ⓛ (CHARGE)} X ∞

Notes	Damage
Requires corner, looping segment can be performed indefinitely until the opponent is K.O.'d or X-Factor expires	Varies based on the number of hits it takes to K.O. opposing character

CR. Ⓛ, Ⓜ, ST. Ⓗ, {← + Ⓗ CANCEL ↓↘→ + Ⓢ, VERTICAL JUMP DELAYED ↓↘→ + Ⓗ (CHARGE), LAND}

Notes	Damage
Sequence in bracket may be looped 8 times	688,400 damage

THOR

"IT IS SAID ONE DAY MY LIFE SHALL BE CLAIMED BY RAGNAROK. TODAY IS NOT THAT DAY."

REAL NAME

Thor Odinson

OCCUPATION

Warrior, Adventurer

ABILITIES

Trained as a warrior, Thor excels at hand-to-hand combat, sword fighting, and throw techniques. With his other-worldly stamina and superhuman strength, ordinary attacks have no effect on him.

WEAPONS

Thor wields Mjolnir, a hammer forged from uru metal. Mjolnir is virtually unbreakable, and allows Thor to command the powers of the storm: rain, thunder, and lightning.

PROFILE

Thor is the son of Odin, ruler of Asgard, the home of the gods. Known as the strongest warrior in Asgard, his prideful ways were reformed after spending time living as a human. Currently, he is a member of the Earth's mightiest heroes, the Avengers.

FIRST APPEARANCE

Journey into Mystery #83 (1962)

POWER GRID

- 2 INTELLIGENCE
- 7 STRENGTH
- 7 SPEED
- 6 STAMINA
- 6 ENERGY PROJECTION
- 4 FIGHTING ABILITY

*This is biographical, and does not represent an evaluation of the in-game combat potential of this hero.

ALTERNATE COSTUMES

Overview

Vitality	1,250,000
Chain Combo Archetype	2-Hit Limited

X-Factor Boost	Damage	Speed
Level 1 (3 teammates remaining)	140%	100%
Level 2 (2 teammates remaining)	170%	100%
Level 3 (1 teammate remaining)	200%	100%

Thor is a highly mobile throw-based character. Your goal when playing Thor is to get him close to his opponent and force them to guess between a throw and combo starter.

Thor is most effective at close range because:

- Mighty Hurricane can be used on the ground or in the air, and both versions lead to high-damage combos. This gives you another way to stop adversaries who attempt to jump away from Thor at close range
- His airdash and flight give him great air mobility and offensive options that are unusual for a grappling-based character
- His Mighty Spark is too slow for a sustained ranged offense, and it also completely misses a large amount of crouching characters

How do you establish and maintain close range with Thor?

- Use flight and airdashes to pass over ground attacks and projectiles
- Use instant air Mighty Strike L at mid range
- Use assists to cover your approach
- Use Mighty Spark L against characters with little to no zoning capability to bait them into jumping toward Thor

TUNING SINCE ORIGINAL MVC3

Thor's Mighty Strike and Mighty Smash now take less time to charge and gain super armor when fully charged, which improves his offense and can make it difficult for unsuspecting opponents to counter these attacks. His combos now deal even more damage due to Mighty Tornado gaining extra damage when mashed. Mighty Punish now has 100% startup invincibility, making it much more effective as a defensive move at close range. He can no longer be hit out of this hyper combo during the first few startup frames as he could before.

- Ⓜ attacks do not push the enemy backwards as far
- Mighty Spark now causes more hitstun against airborne opponents
- Charged Mighty Strike startup reduced. Fully charged version gains one hit of super armor from frames 28-44
- Charged Mighty Smash H startup time reduced. Fully charged version gains one hit of super armor from frames 32-48
- Mighty Tornado is mashable for extra damage
- Mighty Punish is now invincible from frames 1-6, has more active frames, and knocks the enemy down for a longer period of time

Attack Set

Standing Basic Attacks

Screen	Command	Hits	Damage	Meter Gain	Startup	Active	Recovery	Advantage on Hit	Advantage if Guarded	Notes
1	Standing Ⓛ	1	65,000	520	8	3	23	-8	-10	—
2	Standing Ⓜ	1	90,000	720	13	3	30	-10	-13	—
3	Standing Ⓗ	1	110,000	880	18	2	36	-7	-12	Knocks down

1

2

3

Crouching Basic Attacks

Screen	Command	Hits	Damage	Meter Gain	Startup	Active	Recovery	Advantage on Hit	Advantage if Guarded	Notes
1	Crouching Ⓛ	1	63,000	504	7	3	24	-9	-11	Low attack
2	Crouching Ⓜ	3	97,600	960	13	12	19	-2	-5	Low attack
3	Crouching Ⓗ	1	105,000	840	16	4	36	—	-14	Low attack, knocks down

1

2

3

Ground Special Attack—Launcher

Screen	Command	Hits	Damage	Meter Gain	Startup	Active	Recovery	Advantage on Hit	Advantage if Guarded	Notes
1	Ⓢ (while standing or crouching)	1	110,000	880	11	4	28	—	-6	Launcher, not special- or hyper combo-cancelable

1

Air Basic Attacks

Screen	Command	Hits	Damage	Meter Gain	Startup	Active	Recovery	Advantage on Hit	Advantage if Guarded	Notes
1	Air Ⓛ	1	68,000	544	6	8	17	+16	+14	Overhead attack
2	Air Ⓜ	1	85,000	680	13	4	27	+21	+18	Overhead attack
3	Air Ⓗ	1	100,000	800	16	Until grounded or contact	1	+24	+21	Overhead attack

1

2

3

Air Special Attacks—Flying Screen and Air Exchange

Air (S) causes a hard knockdown when used in a launcher combo (this is sometimes called flying screen). When used outside of a launcher combo, air (S) behaves mostly like another basic attack. Air exchange attacks, performed by inputting a direction plus (S), are only possible during a launcher combo. Exchange hits initiate team aerial combos by tagging in the next available character to continue the air combo.

Screen	Command	Hits	Damage	Meter Gain	Startup	Active	Recovery	Advantage on Hit	Advantage if Guarded	Notes
1	Air (S)	1	110,000	880	14	5	37	+21	+18	Causes hard knockdown if used in launcher combo
2	Air ⇧ + (S) (during launcher combo)	1	60,000	480	15	4	Until grounded	—	—	Tags in next available ally while lofting opponent upward
3	Air ⇨ or ⇦ + (S) (during launcher combo)	1	50,000	400	13	4	Until grounded	—	—	Tags in next available ally while causing wall bounce, erases 1 hyper meter bar from foe
4	Air ⇩ + (S) (during launcher combo)	1	50,000	400 + 10,000	16	4	Until grounded	—	—	Tags in next available ally while causing ground bounce, generates 1 hyper meter bar

1

2

3

4

Throws

Throws are for snagging passive or blocking opponents. Since throws are active so quickly, you can also use them to preemptively toss opposing characters out of their offense. Combos are usually possible after throws, one way or another.

Screen	Command	Hits	Damage	Meter Gain	Startup	Active	Notes
1	⇨ + (H) (ground)	2	80,000	800	1	1	Throws foe upward, then hard knockdown
	⇦ + (H) (ground)	2	80,000	800	1	1	Throws opponent upward, then hard knockdown
2	⇨ + (H) (air)	2	80,000	800	1	1	Throws adversary directly under Thor, hard knockdown
	⇦ + (H) (air)	2	80,000	800	1	1	Throws rival directly under Thor, hard knockdown

1

2

As a Partner—Crossover Assists

Screen	Type	P1+P2 Crossover Combination Hyper Combo	Description	Hits	Damage	Meter Gain	Startup	Active	Recovery (this crossover assist)	Recovery (other partner)	Notes
1	Thor—α	Mighty Thunder	Mighty Spark M	7	114,100	1672	47	22~27	124	94	Initial spark lasts 20 frames, beam durability: 3 frames x 5 low priority durability points
2	Thor—β	Mighty Tornado	Mighty Smash	2	95,000	800	37	5(16)10	114	84	Causes ground bounce
3	Thor—γ	Mighty Tornado	Mighty Strike M	2	133,000	1120	44	11	126	96	Nullifies low and medium priority projectiles during active frames

1

2

3

Thor—α is a fairly strong beam attack, and the slow startup can be less important if used for the purposes of augmenting a character's zoning game or filling in gaps of an offense. The slow startup does make it somewhat ineffective at covering a character's approach at fullscreen against a zoning character, and it can be easily punished.

Thor—β causes ground bounce, automatically making it a useful combo tool, especially late in combos when hitstun decay is a major factor. You can use it late in combos to get in extra hits or allow hyper combos to connect when it would otherwise be impossible. It also comes out fairly quickly and has a large amount of active frames, so you can employ it at close range to fill gaps in your offense.

Thor—γ nullifies low and medium priority projectiles during its active frames, but Thor flies forward at an upward angle, making it less than ideal as a projectile-clearing tool. You can utilize it as an anti-air, but it is slow to come out and lacks any invincibility. The weird positioning it leaves the opposing character in also makes it difficult to use as a combo tool.

Snap Back

Screen	Command	Hits	Damage	Meter Gain	Startup	Active	Recovery	Advantage on Hit	Advantage if Guarded
1	⇩⇘⇨ + P1 or P2	1	50,000	500- (-1 hyper meter bar)	2	2	36	—	-12

Notes

On hit, snap back forces the opposing point character to be replaced by an assist. Opposing assist calls or tag outs are also locked out for 4 seconds

1

THOR

Special Moves

Screen	Name	Command	Hits	Damage	Meter Gain	Startup	Active	Recovery	Advantage on Hit	Advantage if Guarded	Notes
1	Mighty Spark L	⇩⇘⇨ + L	3	90,700	1056	15	19	12	+8	+5	Initial spark lasts 10 frames, beam durability: 1 frame x 5 low priority durability points
	Mighty Spark M	⇩⇘⇨ + M	7	123,000	1792	23	32	3	+16	+12	Initial spark lasts 20 frames, beam durability: 3 frames x 5 low priority durability points
	Mighty Spark H	⇩⇘⇨ + H	11	154,000	2648	30	45	0	+18	+14	Initial spark lasts 30 frames, beam durability: 5 frames x 5 low priority durability points
2	Air Mighty Spark L	(in air)⇩⇘⇨ + L	3	97,000	1056	13	19	9	+4	-4	Initial spark lasts 10 frames, beam durability: 1 frame x 5 low priority durability points
	Air Mighty Spark M	(in air)⇩⇘⇨ + M	7	123,000	1792	21	32	4	+8	-2	Initial spark lasts 20 frames, beam durability: 3 frames x 5 low priority durability points
	Air Mighty Spark H	(in air)⇩⇘⇨ + H	11	154,000	2648	28	45	0	+13	+1	Initial spark lasts 30 frames, beam durability: 5 frames x 5 low priority durability points
3	Mighty Smash L	⇨⇩⇘ + L	2	133,000	1120	12	6(17)3	28	—	-4	Hard knockdown
	Mighty Smash M	⇨⇩⇘ + M	2	160,000	1360	12	6(17)3	33	—	-9	Causes ground bounce, hard knockdown
	Mighty Smash H (Can be charged)	⇨⇩⇘ + H	5~7	203,700~ 226,100	1840~ 2160	13~33	6(19)3 (6)8~12	13~9	+20	+9~8	OTG-capable, fully charged version adds more hits and hitstun and gains super armor for frames 32-48
4	Mighty Strike L (Can be charged)	⇦⇩⇙ + L	2~3	133,000~ 175,900	1120~ 1600	20~31	11~11 (1)11	23~12	+13	-18~-7	Knocks down, nullifies low and medium priority projectiles during active frames, fully charged version gains 1 hit of super armor from frames 28-44 and extra hit
5	Mighty Strike M (Can be charged)	⇦⇩⇙ + M	2~3	133,000~ 175,900	1120~ 1600	20~31	11~11 (1)11	23~10	+4	-6~+5	Knocks down, nullifies low and medium priority projectiles during active frames, fully charged version gains 1 hit of super armor from frames 28-44 and extra hit
6	Mighty Strike H (Can be charged)	⇦⇩⇙ + H	2~3	133,000~ 175,900	1120~ 1600	20~31	11~11 (1)11	23~10	=4	-8~-7	Knocks down, nullifies low and medium priority projectiles during active frames, fully charged version gains 1 hit of super armor from frames 28-44 and extra hit
4	Air Mighty Strike L (Can be charged)	(in air)⇦⇩⇙ + L	2~3	133,000~ 175,900	1120~ 1600	20~31	11~11 (1)11	15~1	+10	+2~+14	Knocks down, nullifies low and medium priority projectiles during active frames, fully charged version gains 1 hit of super armor from frames 28-44 and extra hit
7	Air Mighty Strike M (Can be charged)	(in air)⇦⇩⇙ + M	2~3	133,000~ 175,900	1120~ 1600	20~31	11~11 (1)11	15~1 (or until grounded, then 11 frames recovery)	+10	+13	Knocks down, nullifies low and medium priority projectiles during active frames, fully charged version gains 1 hit of super armor from frames 28-44 and extra hit
8	Air Mighty Strike H (Can be charged)	(in air)⇦⇩⇙ + H	2~3	133,000~ 175,900	1120~ 1600	20~31	11~11 (1)11	15~1 (or until grounded, then 11 frames recovery)	+10	+13	Knocks down, nullifies low and medium priority projectiles during active frames, fully charged version gains 1 hit of super armor from frames 28-44 and extra hit
9	Mighty Hurricane L (in air OK)	⇨⇘⇩⇙⇦ + L	1	130,000	1300	5	1	40	—	—	Throw, hard knockdown
	Mighty Hurricane M (in air OK)	⇨⇘⇩⇙⇦ + M	1	150,000	1500	3	1	42	—	—	Throw, hard knockdown
	Mighty Hurricane H (in air OK)	⇨⇘⇩⇙⇦ + H	1	180,000	1800	1	2	43	—	—	Throw, hard knockdown
10	Flight (in air OK)	⇩⇙⇦ + S	—	—	—	30	—	—	—	—	Flight mode duration: 90 frames
11	Mighty Speech	⇩⇩ + H (hold down)	—	—	40 per frame	18	—	22	—	—	Charges hyper meter by 40 points per frame, can be canceled into from special moves

1

2

Mighty Spark: Mighty Spark is mainly used to combat enemy zoning and to zone out opposing characters with little to no zoning capability. Mighty Spark L has the fastest startup and is overall the most useful version for all purposes. Mighty Spark M and H have lengthy startup and active frames, but all versions have very little recovery. All versions leave Thor at a frame advantage on block or hit, and if connected at close range, they can lead to a full combo. Be aware that most mid-sized characters can duck under Mighty Spark, and some smaller characters can even avoid it while standing.

3

Mighty Smash: You can use Mighty Smash to punish projectiles at medium range. All versions are unsafe if an opponent guards this attack while airborne. Mighty Smash L causes hard knockdown and is safe when guarded against most characters. Those with 4 frame attacks can punish Mighty Smash L.

Mighty Smash M causes both ground bounce and a hard knockdown, making it very useful both as a combo starter and a combo tool. However, this version is easily punished and should not be used recklessly.

Mighty Smash H's most important aspect is that it is OTG-capable, allowing you to combo into Mighty Tornado after a hard knockdown. This is also the safest version of Mighty Smash, leaving Thor at a significant frame advantage if guarded. It also gains one hit of super armor if fully charged. These two attributes also make this a good mid range attack in anticipation of an opponent using a projectile or beam attack.

4

5

6

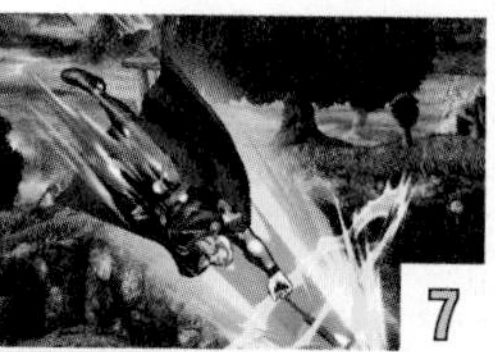
7

8

Mighty Strike: Mighty Strike nullifies low and medium priority projectiles and beams during active frames, making it a useful tool for combatting zoning characters. However, the ground versions of this attack have high recovery and are all easily punishable. To avoid this, use instant air versions of this attack using the input ← ↓ ↙ ↖ + ATK. Instant air Mighty Strike L is particularly effective, allowing Thor to progress forward through projectiles while remaining relatively safe. All versions now gain one hit of super armor when fully charged, making this attack an even more effective mid range tool.

9

Mighty Hurricane: This is Thor's command throw that makes him deadly at close range. Mighty Hurricane L has the most range but sacrifices startup speed. Range decreases but speed increases as you progress in strength of attack used, with Mighty Hurricane H having only one startup frame but requiring Thor to be right next to his target. The fast startup on Mighty Hurricane H makes it an excellent punish against unsafe moves or adversaries who attempt to leave gaps in their offense. You can also use this attack to cancel the recovery of your basic attacks and grab competitors attempting to punish them.

10

Flight: Flight allows Thor to stay airborne for 1.5 seconds (90 frames). During flight, the normal restrictions on specials or airdashes during airborne periods disappear, which allows Thor to airdash repeatedly in midair. Realistically, about four to six airdashes are possible before flight ends. You can use this technique to quickly advance or retreat across the screen.

11

Mighty Speech: This special move increases your team's hyper meter as long as the button is held down. This move has significant startup and recovery, so it's best used when there is no risk of being attacked, such as after a hard knockdown. This move can be very useful if Thor is being played as a meter builder, or if you choose to forgo ending combos with Mighty Tornado and instead opt to end them with hard knockdowns that give Thor ample time to charge meter.

Hyper Combos

Screen	Name	Command	Hits	Damage	Startup	Active	Recovery	Advantage on Hit	Advantage if Guarded	Notes
1	Mighty Tornado (in air OK)	↓ ↘ → + ATK ATK	15~29	321,600~382,700	20+2	85	58(air: 30 or until grounded)	—	-35	Final hit knocks down for grounded version, beam durability: 15 frames x 1 high priority durability points, can be mashed for additional hits
2	Mighty Thunder	→ ↓ ↘ + ATK ATK	4	383,700	24+14	40	63	—	-71	OTG-capable, knocks down, each projectile has 1 high priority durability point
3	Mighty Punish	→ ↘ ↓ ↙ ← + ATK ATK	2	310,000	4+0	2	23	—	—	Frames 1-6 invincible, throw

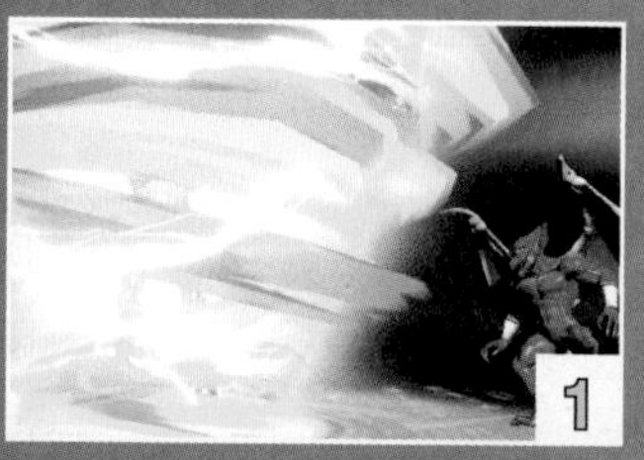
1

Mighty Tornado: This is Thor's primary combo ender that deals massive damage for a level 1 combo. This hyper combo is a very versatile combo tool because it can be performed in the air, as well. The grounded version causes opponents to fall until grounded, making it very useful for THC combos. Thor's aerial version of this move allows challengers to air recover, but Thor recovers much sooner to compensate.

2

Mighty Thunder: This attack is mainly used for OTG combos when you do not have time to land a charged Mighty Smash H to OTG, such as after Mighty Smash L, since you can hyper combo cancel to Mighty Thunder. You can also use it against competitors who are trying to super jump toward Thor or adversaries attempting to use an aerial zoning game.

3

Mighty Punish: This move now has full startup invincibility, making it excellent on defense as well as offense. You can employ it to punish any opponent who uses a hyper combo at close range, as well as stop your rivals from becoming predictable with their offense. Unlike Mighty Tornado, you cannot follow up with a combo after this throw. However, you can THC just as the last attack hits, which results in a very damaging THC combo. Since there are only two hits in this hyper combo, you can also cancel into a non-physical hyper combo, such as a power-up like Wolverine's Berserker Charge, that allows you to then follow up with a very damaging combo!

Battle Plan

Thor's Mighty Spark is good for combating projectiles and would be a good zoning tool if not for the fact that most characters can crouch under the beam.

Thor relies on getting close to his opponents to become a true threat, and this frequently requires help from crossover assists. His own assists, while decent, are not among the best in the game, making him less than ideal as an anchor. Instead, consider Thor for a meter builder or meter user for your team. Thor is actually a very good meter builder and point character if you choose to forgo some damage in order to build some meter using Mighty Speech or attempting a reset combo, and his Mighty Tornado can easily THC into another hyper combo for big damage.

Since Thor must be at close range to be effective, most characters with strong zoning capabilities will attempt to keep him at long range most of the time. Luckily, Thor has more options than your standard "grappler" to combat zoning, and he is surprisingly mobile in the air.

At long range, you can use Thor's Mighty Spark to combat enemy projectiles. You can have Thor spam Mighty Spark L remarkably fast. The only reason this is not a reliable zoning tactic is that most characters can completely avoid Mighty Spark by ducking. Against the unfortunate few characters who cannot duck Mighty Spark, spamming Mighty Spark L at fullscreen can very effective at controlling the ground space and forcing the opposing character to take to the air.

Battle Plan continued

Against characters with a strong ground-based zoning game, you can have Thor jump, then airdash up and utilize his flight mode. This brings Thor to super jump height, but since he only used a normal jump, you can still call assists at any time during this airborne period. From here, you can very quickly close the distance with Thor by airdash canceling quickly across the screen. Once Thor enters flight, an example input would be ↗ + (ATK)(ATK) CANCEL ↘ + (ATK)(ATK) CANCEL ↗ + (ATK)(ATK) CANCEL ↘ + (ATK)(ATK). All these inputs are done very quickly, and if done correctly, Thor zigzags horizontally across the screen. You can cancel any of these airdashes and flight mode by pressing air (H) to have Thor fall toward the opponent with a high priority air attack, or use Mighty Strike M if you suspect your competitor might attempt to repel you with a projectile or beam attack.

Thor can call assists while in flight mode as long as he doesn't activate it during a super jump.

At mid range, Thor gains different options for approaching. One potent option against characters who rely on projectiles and beams is to use an instant air Mighty Strike L by inputting ← ↓ ↙ ↖ + (L). This causes Thor to perform air Mighty Strike L immediately after leaving the ground. Not only does this attack plow through any projectiles or beams during its active frames (except hyper combos), but it also leaves Thor at a +2 frame advantage (+14 if you can manage to fully charge Mighty Strike). If it connects, you can continue into **Combo II**. If it is blocked, you can continue into a three-way mix-up between air (L) as an overhead attack or landing and going directly into crouching (L) for a low attack (both lead to **Combo I**), or landing and attempting to throw with Mighty Hurricane (which leads to **Combo III**). Do not become too predictable with Mighty Strike L, however, as opponents can jump to guard the attack while airborne. This allows your rival to recover immediately upon landing, leaving Thor at a massive frame disadvantage.

Instant air Mighty Strike L is potent at mid range, plowing through projectiles during its active frames, leading into a combo if it connects or leaving Thor at a frame advantage if it gets blocked.

Another strong option for Thor at both mid-range and short range is to utilize his 8-way airdash to create a very fast overhead attack while gaining a short distance very quickly, called a triangle jump. To do this, forward super jump, then immediately input ↘ + (ATK)(ATK), then (L). This method of triangle jumping is faster than simply doing a normal jump due to a height requirement of Thor's airdash. A normal jump would require 11 frames to reach the height requirement, while a super jump only requires five frames. If air (L) connects, you can continue with **Combo I**. If your competitor manages to guard air (L), you can apply mix-up pressure by following up with either cr. (L) or Mighty Hurricane, forcing your adversary to guess. Thor's air (L) has a large hitbox that allows it to be used in cross-ups. This makes Thor the only character that can easily threaten with both triangle jump overheads and cross-ups! Force your adversary to guard a crossover assist, then mix-up a triangle jump from a backwards jump to stay in front, and from a straight up jump to cross-up.

Once you have had Thor achieve close range, you'll need to discourage your opponent from jumping away from him. Do this by utilizing crouching (L) to hit your foes during their pre-jump startup frames, or follow them with a jump and grab them with air Mighty Hurricane leading into **Combo IV**. Once you have trained your opponent to stay on the ground, you can attempt Mighty Hurricane grabs while they try to block.

Unfortunately, nearly all of Thor's basic attacks are punishable when guarded. Luckily, Thor possesses a few ways to compensate for this weakness. One method is to bait a punish attempt with a slightly delayed chain into a stronger basic attack, such as standing (H). This becomes extra potent with the use of his Kara Mighty Hurricane (see the Advanced Tactics section for more info). If Thor is close enough, you can delay canceling into Mighty Hurricane or Mighty Punish to grab challengers as they attempt to punish Thor. You can also cancel into safe special moves like Mighty Spark L.

Once you manage to land a combo, you can forgo finishing with a hyper combo to take a chance at a reset combo. Thor has two main set-ups for resets. The first set-up involves finishing an aerial combo with air Mighty Strike L, then airdashing ↗ toward your opponent. This puts Thor in a perfect position to apply a mix-up regardless of which way his rival air recovers. You can go for air Mighty Hurricane to lead into **Combo IV**. The only escape for your adversary is for them to attack with a fast or invincible attack. If you suspect they might attempt to go after you with a fast attack, you can counter this by attacking with (L), (S) CANCEL ← ↓ ↙ + (M) and cancel into Mighty Tornado if the attacks connect.

Utilize resets to save meter and inflict massive damage on your opponent.

Another reset set-up is to use Mighty Smash H after a hard knockdown, then forward super jump followed by an immediate forward airdash. From here, you can either go for air Mighty Hurricane into **Combo IV** if you think your opponent might attempt to guard or execute air (L), (S) CANCEL ← ↓ ↙ + (M) if you think they might try to attack. At this height, it can be converted into a full combo, as well (see the first combo in Combo Appendix). This works better in the corner, since your rival can escape either of the above options by air recovering backward at midscreen.

Mighty Punish has full startup invincibility now, enabling it to put a quick halt to an opponent's offense.

Defensively, Thor has decent options. Aside from utilizing advancing guard to give him space, Thor's throws can give the opposing character a reason to think twice about attacking Thor at close range. His Mighty Hurricane H has a lightning-fast 1 frame startup, meaning it can punish any gaps your competitor leaves in their offense if they are at close range. Similarly, Mighty Punish now has full startup invincibility, and unlike most other throw hyper combos, it requires only one meter, allowing you to THC if you happen to miss the throw. It also has no post hyper combo screen freeze startup frames, making it impossible for adversaries to react after the hyper combo screen freeze. This makes it an extremely useful defensive move both for stopping predictable attack patterns and for punishing reckless ground-based hyper combos at close range. Even outside of Thor's grab range, you can use Mighty Punish defensively with its invincibility frames to THC into a more appropriate hyper combo.

COMBO APPENDIX

GENERAL EXECUTION TIPS

- **After (S) launchers, bring your air combo early but delay follow-up hits slightly if you intend to end with air (S) hard knockdown into OTG fully charged Mighty Smash H**
- **When canceling into Mighty Tornado, do so as soon as possible, or else opponents may air recover before Mighty Tornado connects**
- **Linking attacks after Mighty Spark can be more difficult than chain combos. If you are having trouble, press the follow-up attack button twice rapidly to maximize your chances of connecting the attack for a combo**

(AGAINST AIRBORNE OPPONENT) AIR (L), (S) CANCEL ← ↓ ↙ + (M) (2 HITS), LAND, CR. (H) CANCEL → ↓ ↘ + (M), (S) CANCEL FORWARD SUPER JUMP, AIR (H) CANCEL ← ↓ ↙ + (L) (2 HITS) CANCEL ↓ ↘ → + (ATK)(ATK) (MASH (ATK))

Notes	Damage
Must be done at about normal jump height. Ideal reset combo after OTG Mighty Smash H	774,200 damage, 25% meter loss

CR. (L) CANCEL ↓ ↘ → + (L), CR. (L), (H) CANCEL → ↓ ↘ + (M), (S) CANCEL FORWARD SUPER JUMP, AIR (M), (M), (H), (S), LAND, → ↓ ↘ + (H) (HOLD (H) UNTIL FULLY CHARGED) CANCEL ↓ ↘ → + (ATK)(ATK) (MASH (ATK))

Notes	Damage
Cr. (L) can chain to Mighty Spark L and be linked into another cr. (L), allowing a full combo	610,100 damage, 10% meter loss

ST. (H) CANCEL → ↓ ↘ + (M), (S) CANCEL FORWARD SUPER JUMP, AIR (M), (M), (H) CANCEL ← ↓ ↙ + (L) CANCEL ↓ ↘ → + (ATK)(ATK) (MASH (ATK))

Notes	Damage
A delayed st. (H) can be used to bait and counter hit punishes against a blocked cr. (L)	741,300 damage, 36% meter loss

CR. (L), (M) (X-FACTOR) CR. (L), (H) CANCEL → ↓ ↘ + (M), (S) CANCEL FORWARD SUPER JUMP, AIR (M), (M), (H), (S), LAND, → ↓ ↘ + (H) (HOLD (H) UNTIL FULLY CHARGED) CANCEL ↓ ↘ → + (ATK)(ATK) (MASH (ATK))

Notes	Damage
Hit confirm into X-Factor combo	X-Factor level 1, 1,090,300 damage, 40% meter gain

COMBO USAGE

I. CR. Ⓛ, Ⓗ CANCEL ➡⬇↘ + Ⓜ, Ⓢ CANCEL FORWARD SUPER JUMP, AIR Ⓜ, Ⓜ, Ⓗ CANCEL ⬅⬇↙ + Ⓛ CANCEL ⬇↘➡ + ATK ATK (MASH ATK)

726,400 damage, 31% meter loss

This is Thor's go-to combo against a ground-based foe, and it's ideal for following up triangle jump air Ⓛ or Mighty Spark L. Mighty Tornado must be canceled immediately following the second hit of air Mighty Strike L, or your opponent will be able to air recover. If this is difficult, you may cancel Mighty Strike L to Mighty Tornado after only one hit for a minor damage and meter loss.

II. ⬅⬇↙↖ + Ⓛ (2 HITS), AIR Ⓛ, LAND, ST. Ⓛ CANCEL ➡⬇↘ + Ⓜ, Ⓢ CANCEL FORWARD SUPER JUMP, AIR Ⓜ, Ⓜ, Ⓗ CANCEL ⬅⬇↙ + Ⓛ (2 HITS) CANCEL ⬇↘➡ + ATK ATK (MASH ATK)

680,100 damage, 23% meter loss

This combo can be somewhat difficult to perform due to some precise timing at a few points. The first point is immediately following the first air Mighty Strike L. Thor recovers while still airborne, allowing him to connect with air Ⓛ. He then lands almost immediately after connecting air Ⓛ, allowing you to immediately follow up with standing Ⓛ canceled into Mighty Smash M. This must all be performed very quickly, or your opponent will air recover.

III. ➡↘⬇↙⬅ + ATK, CR. Ⓛ, Ⓜ (3 HITS) CANCEL ➡⬇↘ + Ⓜ, Ⓢ CANCEL FORWARD SUPER JUMP, AIR Ⓜ, Ⓜ, Ⓗ, Ⓢ, LAND, ➡⬇↘ + Ⓗ (HOLD Ⓗ UNTIL FULLY CHARGED) CANCEL ⬇↘➡ + ATK ATK (MASH ATK)

566,500-616,500 damage, 12-7% meter loss

Thor's Mighty Hurricane allows you to follow up with a full combo, making his mix-ups very potent. Thor should have ample time to land cr. Ⓛ after recovering and converting into the full combo. You'll want to delay the timing on the Ⓜ, Ⓜ, Ⓗ, Ⓢ chain slightly so that Ⓢ hits as low to the ground as possible, allowing fully charged Mighty Smash H to hit. Charging Mighty Smash H is necessary to enable Mighty Tornado to connect after the OTG. You can forgo the Ⓜ after the initial cr. Ⓛ to get slightly more damage but less meter.

IV. (AGAINST AIRBORNE OPPONENT) AIR ➡↘⬇↙⬅ + ATK, CR. Ⓗ CANCEL ➡⬇↘ + Ⓜ, Ⓢ CANCEL FORWARD SUPER JUMP, AIR Ⓜ, Ⓜ, Ⓗ, Ⓢ, LAND, ➡⬇↘ + Ⓗ (HOLD Ⓗ UNTIL FULLY CHARGED) CANCEL ⬇↘➡ + ATK ATK (MASH ATK)

664,200-714,200 damage, 23%-18% meter loss

When you are performing air Mighty Hurricane against airborne adversaries, opponents bounce higher than normal, giving you enough time to have Thor land a much more damaging cr. Ⓗ and better scaling into the rest of the combo, making the air Mighty Strike L an overall better finisher unless you plan to THC.

V. GROUND THROW, CR. Ⓛ, Ⓜ CANCEL ➡⬇↘ + Ⓜ, Ⓢ CANCEL FORWARD SUPER JUMP, AIR Ⓜ, Ⓜ, Ⓗ, Ⓢ, LAND, ➡⬇↘ + Ⓗ (HOLD Ⓗ UNTIL FULLY CHARGED) CANCEL ⬇↘➡ + ATK ATK (MASH ATK)

428,200 damage, 20% meter loss

You don't need to use Thor's basic throws often thanks to his powerful command throws, but you can easily follow up his ground basic throws exactly the same way Thor does his Mighty Hurricane. However, this combo deals less damage because of basic throw damage scaling.

VI. CR. Ⓛ, Ⓗ CANCEL ➡⬇↘ + Ⓜ, Ⓢ CANCEL FORWARD SUPER JUMP, AIR Ⓜ, Ⓜ, Ⓗ, Ⓢ, LAND, ➡⬇↘ + Ⓗ (HOLD Ⓗ UNTIL FULLY CHARGED) CANCEL ⬇↘➡ + ATK ATK (MASH ATK)

701,200 damage, 23% meter loss

Here's an alternative version of **Combo I** that is superior for THC combos because the ground-based version of Mighty Tornado causes opponents to fall until grounded. Delay the launcher chain combo long enough so that you have enough time to fully charge Mighty Smash H.

ADVANCED TACTICS

MIGHTIER HURRICANE (KARA-CANCEL)

Using kara-cancels with Thor's basic Ⓗ attacks can greatly increase the range of your Mighty Hurricane, allowing Thor to threaten with these from even farther away.

Thor can use the initial forward momentum of some of his attacks to increase the range of his Mighty Hurricane. Thor has two basic attacks that are worthwhile for this technique. The first is standing Ⓗ, which moves Thor forward a moderate amount of distance. The technique is performed by pressing standing Ⓗ, then immediately inputting the motion ➡↘⬇↙⬅ + ATK. If done correctly, Thor begins swinging his hammer but cancels the attack into his Mighty Hurricane just before it hits. The other basic attack is crouching Ⓗ. This attack grants far greater range when canceled into Mighty Hurricane, but the timing for the kara-cancel is less forgiving than standing Ⓗ. Utilizing this technique can give let you grab opponents who thought they were at a safe range from Thor's Mighty Hurricane. Furthermore, since standing and crouching Ⓗ chained from crouching Ⓛ is a natural counterhit set-up, just the animation of Thor swinging his hammer can make adversaries instinctively block, allowing Thor's Mighty Hurricane to connect.

WOLVERINE

"YOU WANNA TRY YOUR LUCK AGAINST THE WOLVERINE?"

Bio

REAL NAME

James Howlett

OCCUPATION

Adventurer

ABILITIES

A specialist in close-quarters combat, Wolverine's healing factor gives him that extra edge in a fight. In addition to his fighting abilities, he is also fluent in multiple languages.

WEAPONS

Claws coated in virtually indestructible adamantium, which he can freely release from both hands. The claws are part of his skeleton, which is also coated in adamantium.

PROFILE

Beneath his gruff and crude exterior lies a noble spirit who genuinely treasures his comrades. However, in the face of his enemies, he is merciless, often employing extreme measures in his methods.

FIRST APPEARANCE

The Incredible Hulk #180 (1974)

POWER GRID

2	INTELLIGENCE
4	STRENGTH
2	SPEED
4	STAMINA
1	ENERGY PROJECTION
7	FIGHTING ABILITY

*This is biographical, and does not represent an evaluation of the in-game combat potential of this hero.

Vitality	950,000
Chain Combo Archetype	Hunter Series

X-Factor Boost	Damage	Speed
Level 1 (3 teammates remaining)	125%	115%
Level 2 (2 teammates remaining)	145%	125%
Level 3 (1 teammate remaining)	165%	135%

Your goal with Wolverine is to get into close range with frame advantage, ideally with access to a crossover assist.

When up close to an opponent, Wolverine gains access to his fearsome Berserker Slash mix-ups. Since Berserker Slash has lost all invincibility in *Ultimate Marvel vs. Capcom 3*, Wolverine must now be at frame advantage to effectively prevent getting hit out of the mix-up.

- **Wolverine's Berserker Slash is a self-contained mix-up: depending on the distance to the target and which version of the attack is performed, it can hit as either a cross-up or a frontal attack**
- **Berserker Slash cannot be guarded correctly on reaction; the opposing player must commit to a guess**
- **With the right circumstances, hitting with a Berserker Slash leads to a full combo**
- **In most cases, a character cannot avoid the Berserker Slash mix-up by jumping; the competitor simply gets hit out of the air, allowing you a free combo**

How does Wolverine get into range to threaten with Berserker Slash?

- **Using Wolverine's fast wavedash to cover distance safely, while still being able to guard incoming attacks**
- **Normal jumping over threats that stop Wolverine from wavedashing across the ground**
- **Advancing behind the cover of a long range crossover assist**

TUNING SINCE ORIGINAL MVC3

Many fans agreed that Wolverine was one of the top three characters in *Marvel vs. Capcom 3*. His ease of use, high damage, and invincible Berserker Slash combined to make him a threat at all skill levels!

The largest change to Wolverine's gameplay involves the Berserker Slash: it no longer has any sort of invincibility, which makes Wolverine players work much harder to get through long range defenses. It also forces Wolverine players to deal with an opposing player's long range attacks and tactics. These players can constantly press buttons while their character is far away in an attempt to fake you out or hit you.

The other major changes to Wolverine's gameplay are more indirect: level 1 X-Factor has been substantially weakened, drastically reducing Wolverine's ability to K.O. two characters in the first few moments of a match. Wolverine's primary crossover assist, Akuma—β, has also been significantly weakened to result in an overall less powerful Wolverine.

On the flip side, Wolverine gains a new special attack in Berserker Rage, and the damage of both his Berserker Barrage X and Fatal Claw hyper combos actually has increased significantly! While Wolverine players must work harder to mix opponents up now, they are still working with a character that has all the tools to win at a high level.

- All invincibility removed from Berserker Slash
- New special attack: Berserker Rage ATK
- Berserker Barrage additional hits now launch an opponent into the air
- Tornado Claw active and recovery frames tweaked
- Berserker Barrage X now can be mashed for additional damage
- Fatal Claw now can be mashed for additional damage

Attack Set

Standing Basic Attacks

Screen	Command	Hits	Damage	Meter Gain	Startup	Active	Recovery	Advantage on Hit	Advantage if Guarded	Notes
1	Standing Ⓛ	1	53,000	424	4/4	3/3	11/8	0/+3	-1/+2	—
2	Standing Ⓜ	1	67,000	536	6/5	3/3	22/17	-6/-1	-8/-3	—
3	Standing Ⓗ	1	95,000	760	11/9	4/4	24/18	+11/+17	-6/0	Knocks down opponent

1

2

3

Crouching Basic Attacks

Screen	Command	Hits	Damage	Meter Gain	Startup	Active	Recovery	Advantage on Hit	Advantage if Guarded	Notes
1	Crouching Ⓛ	1	48,000	384	6/5	3/3	12/9	-1/+2	-2/+1	Low attack
2	Crouching Ⓜ	1	70,000	560	7/6	3/3	19/14	+15/0	-5/0	Knocks opponent into the air
3	Crouching Ⓗ	1	78,000	624	12/10	4/4	20/15	—	-2/+3	Low attack, knocks down

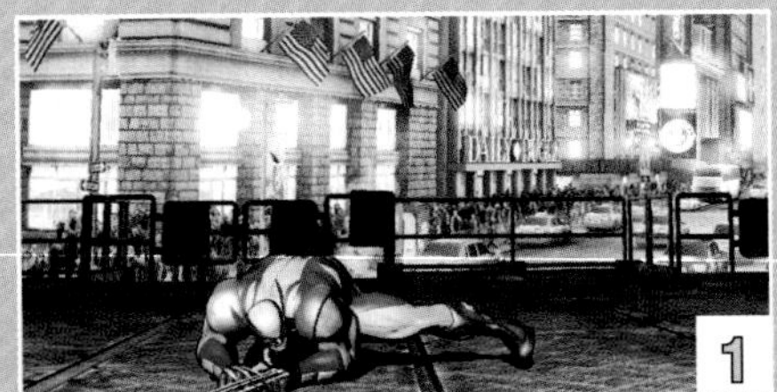
1

2

3

Ground Special Attack—Launcher

Screen	Command	Hits	Damage	Meter Gain	Startup	Active	Recovery	Advantage on Hit	Advantage if Guarded	Notes
1	Ⓢ (while standing or crouching)	1	80,000	640	9/7	4/4	27/21	—	-9/-3	Launcher, not special- or hyper combo-cancelable

1

Air Basic Attacks

Screen	Command	Hits	Damage	Meter Gain	Startup	Active	Recovery	Advantage on Hit	Advantage if Guarded	Notes
1	Air Ⓛ	1	50,000	400	4/4	7/6	12/9	+9/+9	+8/+8	Overhead attack
2	Air Ⓜ	1	70,000	560	6/5	3/3	24/18	+13/+14	+12/+11	Overhead attack
3	Air Ⓗ	1	80,000	640	8/7	2/2	26/20	+17/+15	+14/+13	Overhead attack

1

2

3

Air Special Attacks—Flying Screen and Air Exchange

Air Ⓢ causes a hard knockdown when used in a launcher combo (this is sometimes called flying screen). When used outside of a launcher combo, air Ⓢ behaves mostly like another basic attack. Air exchange attacks, performed by inputting a direction plus Ⓢ, are only possible during a launcher combo. Exchange hits initiate team aerial combos by tagging in the next available character to continue the air combo.

Screen	Command	Hits	Damage	Meter Gain	Startup	Active	Recovery	Advantage on Hit	Advantage if Guarded	Notes
1	Air Ⓢ	1	90,000	720	11/9	4/4	21/16	+16	+14	Causes hard knockdown if used in launcher combo
2	Air ⇧ + Ⓢ (during launcher combo)	1	25,000	200	8/7	2/4	26/16	—	—	Tags in next available ally while lofting opponent upward
3	Air ⇨ or ⇦ + Ⓢ (during launcher combo)	1	40,000	320	6/5	2/2	23/21	—	—	Tags in next available ally while causing wall bounce, erases 1 hyper meter from foe
4	Air ⇩ + Ⓢ (during launcher combo)	1	60,000	480 + 10,000	11/9	4/4	21/15	—	—	Tags in next available ally while causing ground bounce, generates 1 hyper meter

1

2

3

4

Command Attacks

Command attacks resemble basic attacks but have different chaining and canceling properties. It's usually possible to chain *into* a command attack from basic attacks, but most command attacks cannot be chained from or canceled themselves.

Screen	Name	Command	Hits	Damage	Meter Gain	Startup	Active	Recovery	Advantage on Hit	Advantage if Guarded	Notes
1	Cross Slash	(During st. Ⓜ hit) Ⓛ	1	64,000	480	3/3	2/2	17/13	0/+4	-2/+2	Pulls opponent toward Wolverine
2	Sliding Claw	⬂ + Ⓜ	1	70,000	560	10/8	8/7	21/16	—	-12/-6	Low attack, OTG-capable, soft knockdown
3	Brutal Claw	(During air Ⓜ hit) Ⓛ	1	64,000	480	3/3	3/3	29/22	+15/+14	+13/+13	Overhead attack
4	Diving Kick	Air ⇩ + Ⓗ	1	75,000	600	8/7	Until Grounded	10/8	—	+11 maximum	Staggers opponent on counterhit, ground bounces airborne opponent

1

2

3

4

Throws

Throws are for snagging passive or blocking opponents. Since throws are active so quickly, you can also use them to preemptively toss opposing characters out of their offense. Combos are usually possible after throws, one way or another.

Screen	Command	Hits	Damage	Meter Gain	Startup	Active	Notes
1	⇨ + Ⓗ (ground)	5~9	60,000~100,000	600~1,000	1	1	Can be mashed for additional hits
	⇦ + Ⓗ (ground)	5~9	60,000~100,000	600~1,000	1	1	Can be mashed for additional hits
2	⇨ + Ⓗ (air)	6~10	60,000~100,000	600~1,000	1	1	Can be mashed for additional hits
	⇦ + Ⓗ (air)	6~10	60,000~100,000	600~1,000	1	1	Can be mashed for additional hits

1

2

As a Partner—Crossover Assists

Screen	Type	P1+P2 Crossover Combination Hyper Combo	Description	Hits	Damage	Meter Gain	Startup	Active	Recovery (this crossover assist)	Recovery (other partner)	Notes
1	Wolverine—α	Fatal Claw	Tornado Claw M	3	94,800	840	30/24	11/9	135/126	106/83	Knocks down opponent
2	Wolverine—β	Berserker Barrage X	Berserker Slash M	1	100,000	800	44/35	3/3	121/114	91/71	Attack automatic re-aligns ally in opposing character's direction, knocks down opponent
3	Wolverine—γ	Berserker Barrage X	Berserker Barrage M	4	103,000	960	33/26	16/13	117/112	87/69	—

1

2

3

Wolverine's crossover assist attacks were fairly subpar in *Marvel vs. Capcom 3*. This hasn't changed much in *Ultimate*.

For the most part, you'll want to choose Wolverine—γ for the Berserker Barrage assist. It isn't great, but it can do a fairly decent job of keeping your opponent in blockstun long enough to set up a strong offense. If it hits, it generally carries your target too far away to continue a combo from it, unless the opposing character was in the corner.

Some characters have very specific combo requirements, such as needing an assist that brings the opponent high into the air. Dante's a good example of this, since he generally needs help converting his air throw into a full combo. For very specialized situations like these, you may want to look into picking Wolverine—α for the Tornado Claw. Otherwise, this assist is generally best avoided.

Berserker Slash in assist form doesn't cross up on its own, making its usefulness to a team questionable at best. Wolverine can momentarily increase his speed with the Berserker Charge hyper combo, then tag out to permanently increase the speed of all of his assist attacks. Even so, you won't see much of an increase in utility. Unfortunately, Wolverine's new Berserker Rage attack did not become one of his three assists. It would have been great for Wolverine to gain an assist similar to Chun-Li's Hyakuretsukyaku!

Snap Back

Screen	Command	Hits	Damage	Meter Gain	Startup	Active	Recovery	Advantage on Hit	Advantage if Guarded
1	↓↘→ + P1⇔P2	1	50,000	500 - (-1 hyper meter bar)	2	3	28	—	-10
Notes									
On hit, snap back forces the opposing point character to be replaced by an assist. Opposing assist calls or tag outs are also locked out for 4 seconds									

1

Special Moves

Screen	Name	Command	Hits	Damage	Meter Gain	Startup	Active	Recovery	Advantage on Hit	Advantage if Guarded	Notes
1	Berserker Barrage L	↓↘→ + L	2-4	66,500 – 104,900	560 - 960	6/5	7~16/ 6~13	25/20	-4/+2	-6~8/0~-1	Can be mashed for additional two hits, additional hits knock down opponent
	Berserker Barrage M	↓↘→ + M	4-6	103,000 – 134,100	960 - 1360	9/7	16~25/ 13~20	25/20	-5/+3	-7~8/+1~-1	Can be mashed for additional two hits, additional hits knock down opponent
	Berserker Barrage H	↓↘→ + H	6-8	131,000 – 156,100	1344 - 1744	13/10	24~24(1)9/ 19~19(1)7	25~26/ 20~21	-6/0	-8/-2~-1	Can be mashed for additional two hits, additional hits knock down opponent
2	Tornado Claw L	→↓↘ + L	3 - 7	81,200 – 131,200	720 – 1360	6/5	11~11(1)5(1)5/ 9~9(1)10	26~32/ 20~23	+3~+14/ +12~+21	-18/-8	Can be mashed for additional hits, knocks down
	Tornado Claw M	→↓↘ + M	4 - 10	103,000 – 164,300	960 - 1920	6/5	11~18(1)7(1)5/ 9~28	35~30/ 27~22	+5~+32/ +8~+25	-28/-16	Can be mashed for additional hits, knocks down
	Tornado Claw H	→↓↘ + H	5 - 11	122,600 – 177,700	1200 - 2160	6/5	12~17(1)5(1) 5(1)3(1)7/ 9~34	45~22/ 39~18	+8~+17/ +1~+30	-38/-24	Can be mashed for additional hits, knocks down
3	Drill Claw (in air OK)	S + ATK	1	80,000	640	16/13	14/11	25/19	+18/+20	+9/+11	Can be directed using the controller, knocks down opponent, on hit or guard Wolverine recovers in neutral state in air, on whiff does not recover until Wolverine lands
4	Berserker Slash L	↓↙← + L	1	100,000	800	18/14	3/3	24/18	—	-10/-5	Can pass through opponents from frame 1-10, attack automatically re-aligns in opposing character's direction, knocks down opponent
	Berserker Slash M	↓↙← + M	1	100,000	800	20/16	3/3	26/20	—	-12/-6	Can pass through opponents from frame 1-12, attack automatically re-aligns in opposing character's direction, knocks down opponent
	Berserker Slash H	↓↙← + H	1	100,000	800	22/17	3/3	27/21	—	-13/-7	Can pass through opponents from frame 1-15, attack automatically re-aligns in opposing character's direction, knocks down opponent
5	Berserker Rage L	L (rapidly)	5~18/ 4~16	81,700~169,200/ 68,600~162,200	800~ 2880	11/9	29/23	14/11	+9/+8	+7/+6	Can be mashed for additional hits
	Berserker Rage M	M (rapidly)	5~24/ 4~26	81.700~183,400/ 68,600~187,400	800~ 3840	11/9	29/23	14/11	+9/+8	+7/+6	Can be mashed for additional hits
	Berserker Rage H	H (rapidly)	5~52/ 4~46	81,700~239,400/ 68,600~227,400	800~ 8320	11/9	29/23	14/11	+9/+8	+7/+6	Can be mashed for additional hits

Berserker Barrage: The Berserker Barrage, formerly Wolverine's signature move in older games, is now difficult for Wolverine players to use effectively outside of combos. It's very unsafe if guarded, and it is also difficult to cover with crossover assists due to the long duration of the attack. There aren't many reasons to pick Berserker Barrage over the amazing Berserker Slash.

In combos, Berserker Barrage can be useful for adding damage in situations where hitstun has scaled severely, making it impossible to combo into Fatal Claw. In these situations, you can simply tack on Berserker Barrage H, then hyper combo cancel to Berserker Barrage X for good damage.

Berserker Barrage can be mashed for additional hits and damage, but in *Ultimate Marvel vs. Capcom 3*, the additional hits now immediately knock your foe into the air. This doesn't have any noticeable effect on juggle combos, however.

Tornado Claw: The Tornado Claw may look like a Shoryuken-esque attack, but unfortunately, it does not have any invincibility to speak of. This makes its usefulness very limited: it's not great as an anti-air, it cannot be used to break out of your opponent's offensive patterns, and it's still incredibly unsafe if guarded. However, the Tornado Claw has one very specialized use—it's the key component of the incredibly difficult Fatal Claw loop combos! See the Combo Appendix section for details.

Mashing buttons while Tornado Claw is hitting results in substantially more damage, but it also causes Wolverine to travel higher into the air. In *Ultimate Marvel vs. Capcom 3*, there are various changes to the active and recovery frame numbers of the Tornado Claw attacks, but these changes don't seem to have any major practical effects.

Drill Claw: While Drill Claw is Wolverine's only special attack that is accessible while jumping, it's still generally used only in combos. In combos, the Drill Claw conveniently bounces the opposing character up near Wolverine, allowing an easy Diving Kick combo, which in turn leads into a ground bounce for more punishment.

You can aim Drill Claw in all eight directions, as well as redirect it off of walls. Outside of combos, the Drill Claw is generally safe as long as Wolverine makes contact with the opponent. In this case, Wolverine bounces backwards in a neutral state, allowing you access to actions such as guarding, Diving Kicks, or even another Drill Claw! If the Drill Claw misses your foe completely, Wolverine becomes completely vulnerable to punishment all the way until he reaches the ground. Don't use Drill Claw as a substitute for an airdash!

Wolverine has a powerful mix-up using Drill Claw against new characters coming into the playing field. Check the Advanced Tactics section for more details!

Berserker Slash: Your most important attack by far, the Berserker Slash causes Wolverine to run forward a distance specific to the attack button pressed. While running forward, Wolverine can run straight through the opposing character to get behind them. After running the specified distance, Wolverine automatically attacks in the direction of the opponent. In other words, you can use the Berserker Slash to either cross up your opponent or hit your foe from the front!

A simple, yet incredibly effective mix-up, the Berserker Slash is simply too fast for human opponents to be able to consistently guard correctly on reaction. For the most part, players simply must commit to guarding in a specific direction ahead of time.

While the Berserker Slash is technically unsafe if guarded, few characters can consistently punish it due to the awkward range left between the two characters after it finishes. Also, you should always cover Berserker Slash by a crossover assist, or cancel the move into Berserker Charge or X-Factor. Doing any of the above not only allows you to convert any Berserker Slash mix-up into a full combo if it hits, but it also leaves you at frame advantage if guarded!

In original *Marvel vs. Capcom 3*, the Berserker Slash was completely invulnerable whenever Wolverine's shadows were visible. This gave the attack incredible utility, and it was the answer to practically every potential problem Wolverine could face. But in *Ultimate Marvel vs. Capcom 3*, the Berserker Slash isn't invincible at all, which forces Wolverine players to deal with many situations that never bothered them before.

Berserker Rage: A brand new attack for *Ultimate Marvel vs. Capcom 3*, Berserker Rage is very similar to Chun-Li's Hyakuretsukyaku. Unfortunately, it's also worse than Hyakuretsukyaku in nearly every way.

It's difficult to find a use for Berserker Rage in Wolverine's general gameplan: it adds a large amount of hitstun and damage scaling to Wolverine's combos, and it pushes Wolverine away if it is guarded. If your opponent is guarding, you'll almost always want to use crouching Ⓛ or Berserker Slash instead. Berserker Rage does leave Wolverine at a large frame advantage if guarded, but the opposing player can easily choose to use advancing guard to push him away.

It only takes three consecutive button presses to execute Berserker Rage; make sure to control your button presses to avoid performing this move on accident! Don't mash!

Hyper Combos

Screen	Name	Command	Hits	Damage	Startup	Active	Recovery	Advantage on Hit	Advantage if Guarded	Notes
1	Berserker Barrage X	↓↘→ + ATK ATK	17~34	286,200~343,600	13+3	71(13)4	29	—	-10	Invincible from frame 1-7, knocks down opponent. Can be mashed for additional hits
2	Fatal Claw (in air OK)	↓↙← + ATK ATK	13~26	302,100~362,500	9+8	50	37	—	-17	Knocks down opponent, air version does not recover until landing. Can be mashed for additional hits
3	Berserker Charge	↓↓ + ATK ATK	—	—	4+0	—	8	—	—	Puts 30% speed-up effect on Wolverine for 400 frames, hyper combo gauge does not fill while speed-up effect is active, Berserker Charge cannot be activated while speed-up is already active
4	Weapon X (Level 3 hyper combo)	→↓↘ + ATK ATK	27	440,000	16+1	17	15	—	—	21 frames invincibility, hard knockdown

Berserker Barrage X: Like the regular Berserker Barrage, you should typically only use the hyper combo Berserker Barrage X at the end of long combos where hitstun scaling won't let you combo into Fatal Claw.

On the flipside, in *Ultimate Marvel vs. Capcom 3*, Berserker Barrage X is now mashable for significantly more damage (still less than a mashed Fatal Claw, however). Berserker Barrage X is also much more conducive to set up a THC to another teammate, as the opposing character will be much lower to the ground.

Berserker Barrage X has a small amount of invincibility frames before super flash occurs, which has situational use in blowing through attacks. However, this isn't recommended, since it's very difficult to properly time the attack in this manner. You're much more likely to eat a full combo and also lose an entire hyper combo bar for your efforts.

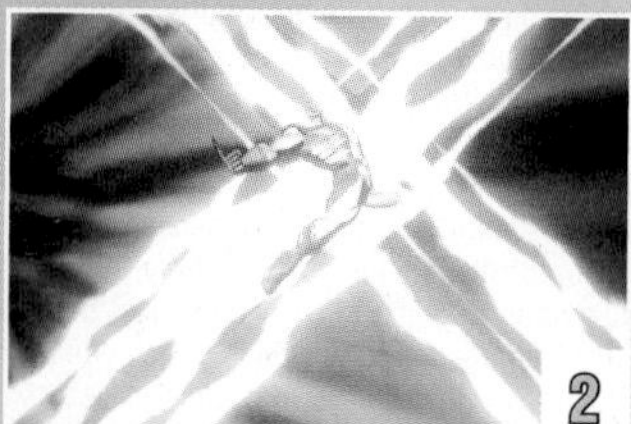

Fatal Claw: With its ability to be performed in the air, Fatal Claw is the preferred combo ender for Wolverine. It also inflicts significantly more damage than Berserker Barrage X!

One of the few improvements that Wolverine received in *Ultimate Marvel vs. Capcom 3*, you can now mash Fatal Claw to deal much more damage to your target. A fully mashed Fatal Claw inflicts a ridiculous 362,500 damage!

A weakness of the Fatal Claw is that it does not allow you to THC to a teammate for very long after the final hit lands. This generally leaves your opponent much too high up in the air for most hyper combos to connect properly. You can string together several Fatal Claws in one combo, guaranteeing a K.O. on any character. See the Combo Appendix section for details.

Outside of combos, the Fatal Claw doesn't have much use other than allowing Wolverine to THC out safely: super jump into the air, activate Fatal Claw, then THC to a different teammate's safe hyper combo!

Hyper Combos continued

3

Berserker Charge: Activating Berserker Charge puts Wolverine in a state where he becomes 30% faster for 400 frames. This effect stacks with the speed-up effect of X-Factor!

Use Berserker Charge primarily with a hyper combo canceling a Berserker Slash; if the Berserker Slash hits, you can capitalize and go into a full combo. If the Berserker Slash is guarded, it is still +7 if hyper combo canceled into a Berserker Charge. From there, you can still salvage the situation by immediately mixing up your opponent.

Wolverine does not build any hyper combo gauge bars at all while Berserker Charge is active. This is a significant detriment, as landing a combo while in Berserker Charge state causes you to lose one to two bars, all while your opponent is gaining bars by getting hit! Of course, this doesn't mean that you should refrain from using Berserker Charge after Berserker Slash; just use it in moderation so you don't find yourself at a massive hyper combo bar differential compared to your opponent.

Tagging in another teammate while Berserker Charge is active retains the speed-up effect while Wolverine remains inactive, giving you access to crossover assists that are 30% faster. This isn't quite as cool as it seems, however, since Wolverine's assists are still fairly lacking even with increased speed.

Generally, you won't want to activate Berserker Charge purely for the increased speed; it's mainly used to cancel Berserker Slash. However, activating Berserker Charge while already using X-Factor makes a huge difference: the combined speed-up boost is enough to allow jumping Ⓛ to combo into Drill Claw! This allows you to combo off of an instant overhead jumping Ⓛ against every character in the game! Previously, players could have Wolverine use Berserker Charge in THC combos to trigger the THC glitch, allowing for easy 100% damage combos. In *Ultimate Marvel vs. Capcom 3*, this glitch has been removed.

4

Weapon X: Like most level 3 hyper combos, you should use Weapon X primarily at the end of long combos because it causes massive, unscaled damage. It has a fair amount of invulnerable frames on startup, allowing you to use it to blow through certain attacks and hit your opposition. However, the invulnerable window after Wolverine starts dashing forward is very brief: only five frames. You can't use Weapon X to go through projectiles from afar, but you can employ it in point-blank situations to beat other hyper combos.

Battle Plan

Wolverine must close the distance to his competitor primarily with ground dashes and normal jumps.

Use a crossover assist to get close if you have to, but this forces you to use Berserker Charge in order to capitalize off of a Berserker Slash.

Though his crossover assist has been weakened, Akuma—β is still one of Wolverine's best partners. Ryu—β is pretty good, too!

Sentinel—α is great for pinning opponents down for long periods of time. This lets you set up instant overheads, as well as Berserker Slash cross-ups!

When using Wolverine, you really want to try to get close enough to your opponent so you can threaten with a Berserker Slash mix-up. Wolverine has no practical air mobility options to speak of: Drill Claw is much too unsafe for moving around. As such, you need to get in close the old-fashioned way: wavedashing forward on the ground while normal jumping over defensive threats.

Wavedashing normally with Wolverine frequently causes you to accidentally activate Berserker Charge (⇩, ⇩ + ATK ATK). To mitigate this, cancel your dashes with ⇘ on the controller instead of ⇩. This ends up looking like ⇨ + ATK ATK, ⇘, ⇨ + ATK ATK, ⇘ ...

Wavedashing with Wolverine also has to be performed much slower than with most characters, as Wolverine travels most of the distance in the latter portion of his dash. To get the most out of his wavedash, simply cancel the forward dash by pressing ⇘ much later than you normally would. Increased ground control now becomes necessary to position Wolverine closer to the opposing character!

Ideally, you'll want to close the distance on your opponent without using crossover assists; this lets you set up Berserker Slashes that are covered by the assist attack, allowing for combos if the slash hits and frame advantage if the slash is blocked. But realistically, this technique is often difficult, so at times, you should settle for simply forcing your opponent to guard a crossover assist. This gives you the frame advantage you'll need to freely set up a Berserker Slash mix-up and cancel into Berserker Charge. Crossover assists that nullify projectiles are greatly preferred; see the following section for details.

Once you manage to work your way into the range of Diving Kick, things become considerably easier. Diving Kick is fast and beats or trades with most anti-air attempts. It's also very difficult to air throw! If it counterhits, it causes a stagger state on your foe, which allows for easy conversion into a combo, and if it hits an airborne opponent, it causes a ground bounce state for a combo! If guarded, Diving Kick leaves you at a highly varied frame advantage situation: the lower the Diving Kick hits, the more frame advantage you have. Ideally, aiming at the feet of your target can give you up to 11 frames of advantage! Conversely, aiming the Diving Kick at the top of your opponent's head places you in disadvantage territory, which leaves you open to guaranteed ground throws and snap backs. In more extreme cases, opposing players who intentionally guard a Diving Kick in the air by jumping back at the last second can actually punish it with a full combo. Be careful with your Diving Kick placement!

Calling a crossover assist simultaneously with Diving Kick is a strong tactic: the assist starts hitting almost immediately after your opponent recovers from the guardstun of the divekick, giving you the frame advantage you'll need to set up a Berserker Slash.

Typically, you'll find that the Diving Kick counterhits both the opposing player's point character and crossover assist character. When this happens, don't hesitate to immediately use your X-Factor. When you get a lucky break like this, use the damage boost from X-Factor to K.O. both characters at the same time with a single basic combo. Happy birthday!

Wolverine reaches his full potential only when backed up with the right crossover assists. He needs the help of an assist to do the following critical things:

- **Combo after Berserker Slash without having to use Berserker Charge**
- **Convert air throws and ground throws into full combos**
- **Nullify projectiles to allow Wolverine to get near zoning opponents**
- **Place the opponent in large amounts of guardstun from afar, setting up a mix-up**

Out of all the assists in the game, only Akuma—β fills all four of these roles extremely well. He also keeps the number of hits in a combo low, resulting in more damage. Akuma—β causes much less hitstun in *Ultimate Marvel vs. Capcom 3*, but he is still the best overall assist to pair with Wolverine.

Iron Man—α and Doctor Doom—α both fill all four roles nicely, as well, and these characters also give you a fullscreen threat for the opposing player to deal with. However, both of these assists hit eight times, significantly reducing the damage in your combos.

Sentinel—α isn't great for nullifying projectiles, and he can't be used to combo from throws at all. However, Sentinel—α is arguably the best assist in the game for placing your foe in huge amounts of guardstun. This sometimes makes it much easier for you to close the distance against your opponent, and it also allows you to establish the threat of overheads! See the Advanced Tactics section for details.

Other honorable mentions:

- **Ryu—γ causes much more hitstun than Akuma—β, but he doesn't nullify projectiles.**
- **Arthur—β is a little more difficult to combo off of, but this is still very possible with practice. He also becomes much more powerful with Gold Armor!**
- **Ghost Rider—α and Iron Fist—γ don't nullify projectiles or place your opponent in a ton of blockstun, but their single-hit attacks allow for the most damaging combos!**
- **Hawkeye—α is a faster version of Arthur—β, but many characters can crouch under his arrows.**

Battle Plan continued

Now that the Berserker Slash is not invincible anymore, you'll have to do more work to ensure that your opponent doesn't press buttons. The simplest way to accomplish this is to pressure your opponent with crouching L attacks. Using advancing guard against a single crouching L attack is very difficult, and it is practically impossible to do purely on reaction. If the opposing player is trying to use advancing guard against your crouching L attacks, simply place a longer delay between the kicks; your opponent then likely gets a crouching H attack instead of an advancing guard, causing them to be counterhit by your crouching L. From here, verify the hit with another crouching L or two before going into a full combo.

Being able to cross the opposing player up with Berserker Slash while still having an assist available is the best scenario for Wolverine players!

Stagger the timing of your crouching L attacks to catch opponents attempting to use advancing guard. If they aren't pressing any buttons, break their defenses by canceling into a Berserker Slash L!

Dash forward and use standing H to counter attempts to stop your Berserker Barrage with normal attacks!

If the opposing player chooses not to use advancing guard, simply cancel one of your crouching L attacks into Berserker Slash L to cross them up. This is nearly impossible to guard on reaction; if your opponent commits to guarding the other way, they'll instead get hit by your delayed crouching L kicks.

Ideally, you'll want to call your crossover assist just before attacking with Berserker Slash; this lets you convert a successful hit into a full combo without having to cancel into Berserker Charge. If the Berserker Slash is guarded, your opponent will still be in guardstun from the crossover assist, giving you plenty of frame advantage to dash forward and put your foe in a second mix-up.

If you don't have the luxury of having a crossover assist available when doing a Berserker Slash, you'll have to cancel it into Berserker Charge to get any real damage from a successful hit. A successful hit leads into a full combo (see Combo Usage section) that is damaging, but it doesn't gain any hyper combo gauge bars whatsoever. You should avoid being left without any hyper combo bars to work with!

A guarded Berserker Slash that is canceled into Berserker Charge still results in a +7 frame advantage. See the Advanced Tactics section for details on how to maximize this situation.

You can still threaten your opponent with a cross-up Berserker Slash from much farther ranges, but first, you'll have to convince the opposing player to stop pressing buttons. Getting your challenger to guard a long range crossover assist is the easiest way to accomplish this, but it forces you to use a Berserker Charge to capitalize heavily. Simply jumping forward and quickly using Diving Kick generally beats most ground-based attempts to keep you away. Any Diving Kick hit in this situation generally is a counterhit, leading to an easy conversion to a combo. Players who are repeatedly pressing crouching L to stop Berserker Slashes can often stop and guard a Diving Kick on reaction; in this situation, dashing forward and hitting your opponent with the tip of standing H works very well. Standing H has a very strong set of collision hitboxes, with Wolverine's vulnerable area sitting well behind his attacking area. Cancel the standing H into forward Drill Claw, then use Diving Kick to go into a full combo.

If your adversary instead attempts to avoid your offense by jumping away, the simplest solution is to immediately mix them up with a cross-up Berserker Slash H or a non-cross-up Berserker Slash M. But keep in mind that certain characters have large air attacks that can beat both of these options, such as Nemesis T-Type's air H. Against these characters, you'll want to aggressively dash forward and attempt an air throw. Air throws can lead to a full combo, depending on the crossover assists you are using. See the Combo Appendix for details.

COMBO USAGE

I. CR. L, CR. L, ST. M, ST. H, S (CANCEL) → FORWARD SUPER JUMP, AIR M, M, H (CANCEL) → ATK + S, ↓ + H, LAND, ST. H, S (CANCEL) → FORWARD SUPER JUMP, AIR M, M, L, H (CANCEL) → ATK + S, ↓ + H (OR (CANCEL) → ↓ ↙ ← + ATK ATK, MASH ATK)

470,300~661,000 damage, 99% meter gain

Wolverine's famous "easy" combo. When the opening crouching L x 2 is guarded, follow up with a throw, delayed crouching L into Combo I again, or cancel into Berserker Slash L to cross up your opponent. If you're trying to combo after Wolverine's Diving Kick, replace crouching L with standing L, which is faster and makes the incoming link easier. Starting this combo with standing L also allows it to catch low-altitude triangle jumps for similar damage.

Performing this combo without the second crouching L results in 681,500 damage.

II. ↓ ↙ ← + ATK (CANCEL) → ↓ ↓ + ATK ATK, DASH, CR. M, ST. H, ST. S (CANCEL) → FORWARD SUPER JUMP, AIR M, M, H (CANCEL) → ATK + S, ↓ + H, LAND, ST. H, ST. S (CANCEL) → FORWARD SUPER JUMP, AIR M, M, H (CANCEL) → ATK + S (CANCEL) → ↓ ↙ ← + ATK ATK, MASH ATK

730,800 damage, 192% meter loss

Canceling the Berserker Slash into the Berserker Charge allows for a follow-up combo if it hits. Dash forward as quickly as possible after the Berserker Charge activation to ensure that you're in range for the juggle hits. You can input the dash earlier than you think!

III. WITH BERSERKER CHARGE ACTIVATED, CR. L, CR. M, ST. H (CANCEL) → ↓ ↙ ← + L, CR. M, ST. H (CANCEL) → ↓ ↙ ← + M, CR. M, ST. H (CANCEL) → ↓ ↙ ← + M, FORWARD DASH, ST. M, S (CANCEL) → FORWARD SUPER JUMP, AIR M, M, H (CANCEL) → ATK + S (CANCEL) → ↓ ↙ ← + ATK ATK, MASH ATK

771,700 damage, loses 100% meter (in addition to the cost of activating Berserker Charge)

This small loop takes advantage of the Berserker Charge speed-up effect for extra damage. The opening crouching M, standing H (CANCEL) → ↓ ↙ ← + L combo bumps your opponent high enough into the air for another crouching M to hit. If the opposing player has a tendency to attack after guarding your Berserker Slashes, you'll be landing this combo quite often.

IV. CR. L, CR. L, ST. M, ST. H, S (CANCEL) → FORWARD SUPER JUMP, AIR M, M, H (CANCEL) → ATK + S, ↓ + H, LAND, ST. H (CANCEL) → ↓ ↘ → + H (rapid) (CANCEL) → → ↓ ↘ + ATK ATK

859,700 damage, 220% meter loss

This basic method of landing Wolverine's level 3 hyper combo deals heavy damage, but it's not always worth the meter use. Save it for instances when you need to make a big comeback, or when you're fighting the opposing player's final team member.

WOLVERINE

COMBO USAGE CONTINUED

IV. CR. L, CR. L, ST. M, ST. H, S CANCEL FORWARD SUPER JUMP, AIR M, M, H CANCEL ATK + S, ↓ + H, LAND, ST. H CANCEL ↓↘→ + H)) CANCEL →↓↘ + ATK ATK

859,700 damage, 220% meter loss

This basic method of landing Wolverine's level 3 hyper combo deals heavy damage, but it's not always worth the meter use. Save it for instances when you need to make a big comeback, or when you're fighting the opposing player's final team member.

V. CR. L, CR. L, ST. M, ST. H, S CANCEL FORWARD SUPER JUMP, AIR M, M, H CANCEL ATK + S, ↓ + H, LAND, X-FACTOR, ST. H, S CANCEL FORWARD SUPER JUMP, AIR M, M, L, H CANCEL ATK + S CANCEL ↓↙← + ATK ATK

862,900~1,024,900 damage, 10~27% meter gain

This combo gives you plenty of time to decide whether or not to activate X-Factor, perfect for situations when you manage to catch two enemies with any random hit. Usually, you'll be able to take out both characters in one fell swoop! If you have trouble hitting the airborne enemy after the air ↓ + H hits, try actually canceling the dive kick's landing recovery period with X-Factor to give yourself more time.

VI. THROW OR AIR THROW, WAVE DASH FORWARD, ↘ + M CANCEL X-FACTOR, ST. M, ST. H, ST. S CANCEL SUPER JUMP FORWARD, AIR M, M, H CANCEL ATK + S, ↓ + H, LAND, ST. H, S CANCEL SUPER JUMP FORWARD, AIR M, M, L, H CANCEL ATK + S CANCEL ↓↙← + ATK ATK, MASH ATK

848,100~1,073,400 damage, 26~63% meter gain

If you land a throw against the last character on your opponent's team, or if you're behind and you need momentum, OTG your target with ↘ + M, then immediately cancel it into X-Factor. If you're fast, you can juggle your foe with standing M, H, S before they touch the ground again. Note that you only need to dash forward after the throw if you go for one of Wolverine's ground throws; his air throws leave him directly next to his foe.

VII. WITH X-FACTOR AND BERSERKER CHARGE ACTIVATED, INSTANT AIR L CANCEL ↘ + ATK + S, ↓ + H, LAND, ST. H, S CANCEL FORWARD SUPER JUMP, AIR M, M, H CANCEL ATK + S CANCEL ↓↙← + ATK ATK

773,100~1,020,300 damage, 100% meter loss (in addition to activating Berserker Charge)

This combo only works when both Berserk Charge and X-Factor are activated. It's intended to act as a very fast overhead opening attack. When guarded, continue a basic offensive pattern once you land from air ↓ + H. There's a high likelihood that you'll still be powered up when it's blocked, so you can even go for another instant overhead air L.

"YOU LOST, I WON. DEAL WITH IT, BUB."

ADVANCED TACTICS

INSTANT OVERHEADS

When using Wolverine, you must often employ X-Factor to finish off certain problematic characters early. When you use X-Factor in this way, you may want to think about activating Berserker Charge before the next character comes in: when both X-Factor and Berserker Charge are active, hitting your opponent with an overhead air L immediately after leaving the ground becomes a combo starter. Simply cancel the air L into Drill Claw, then Diving Kick, then proceed as normal. With the damage boost from X-Factor, this combo inflicts a ton of damage and likely instantly K.O. any characters with less than 800,00 health!

As an alternative, you can simply use an "instant overhead" air L, then immediately cancel into an aerial X-Factor and continue the combo! This is a much bigger gamble because you cannot verify the instant overhead air L to hit before canceling into X-Factor, but the surprise factor is much higher. The resulting combo also deals at least one million damage points! If your opponent guards the instant overhead air L, mix the opposing player up again with an overhead air M attack, or simply land and go low with crouching L.

If your opponent is guarding a multi-hit crossover assist, simply going for an instant overhead air L is an incredibly strong tactic. The assist combos after air L hits, allowing you to combo into a Drill Claw, then Diving Kick!

Activating Berserker Charge while already in X-Factor adds an incredibly scary overhead threat to Wolverine's offense.

Against very large characters, you can use air S as an instant overhead attack, then immediately cancel into Drill Claw for a free combo. Instant overhead air S works against the following characters:

Captain America	**Haggar**	**Sentinel**	**Nemesis T-Type**	**Doctor Strange**
Doctor Doom	**Hulk**	**She-Hulk**	**Ghost Rider**	

COMBO APPENDIX

GENERAL EXECUTION TIPS

- When performing chain combos, be careful not to spam inputs carelessly or you'll produce Berserker Rage on accident
- After activating Berserker Charge or X-Factor, attack as soon as possible after the screen freeze to keep a combo going. You can dash and attack with crouching Ⓜ after Berserker Charge sooner than you think!

THROW OR AIR THROW, FORWARD WAVE DASH, CALL AKUMA—β, ↘ + Ⓜ, FORWARD DASH, Ⓢ CANCEL➜ FORWARD SUPER JUMP, AIR Ⓜ, Ⓜ, Ⓗ CANCEL➜ ATK + Ⓢ, ↓ + Ⓗ, LAND, ST. Ⓗ CANCEL➜ ↓↘→ + Ⓗ)) (CANCEL➜ ↓↙← + ATK ATK, MASH ATK)

Notes	Damage
Throw combo using Akuma—β	438,400 damage

WITH X-FACTOR LEVEL 2 OR 3 ACTIVATED, CR. Ⓛ, CR. Ⓜ, ST. Ⓗ CANCEL➜ ↓↙← + Ⓛ, CR. Ⓜ, ST. Ⓗ CANCEL➜ ↓↙← + Ⓜ, CR. Ⓜ, ST. Ⓗ CANCEL➜ ↓↙← + Ⓜ, FORWARD DASH, ST. Ⓜ, ST. Ⓗ, Ⓢ CANCEL➜ FORWARD SUPER JUMP, AIR Ⓜ, Ⓜ, Ⓗ CANCEL➜ ATK + Ⓢ, ↓ + Ⓗ, LAND, ST. Ⓗ, Ⓢ CANCEL➜ FORWARD SUPER JUMP, AIR Ⓗ, Ⓢ, LAND, ↘ + Ⓜ

Notes	Damage
Damaging loop combo using level 2 or 3 X-Factor	1,350,400~1,595,700 damage, builds 2 meters

FORWARD JUMP, INSTANT AIR Ⓛ CANCEL➜ X-FACTOR, AIR Ⓜ, ST. Ⓜ, CR. Ⓜ, ST. Ⓗ, Ⓢ CANCEL➜ FORWARD SUPER JUMP, AIR Ⓜ, Ⓜ, Ⓗ CANCEL➜ ATK + Ⓢ, ↓ + Ⓗ, LAND, ST. Ⓗ, Ⓢ CANCEL➜ FORWARD SUPER JUMP, AIR Ⓜ, Ⓜ, Ⓛ, Ⓗ CANCEL➜ ATK + Ⓢ CANCEL➜ ↓↙← + ATK ATK

Notes	Damage
Instant overhead air Ⓛ into X-Factor combo	1,013,900~1,322,200 damage, 33-74% meter gain

WHEN USING AN ALTERNATE TEAMMATE, ACTIVATE A TAC WITH ↑ + Ⓢ, THEN AS WOLVERINE COMES IN PERFORM AIR Ⓜ, Ⓜ, Ⓗ CANCEL➜ ↗ + ATK + Ⓢ, ↓ + Ⓗ, LAND, Ⓢ CANCEL➜ FORWARD SUPER JUMP, AIR Ⓜ, Ⓜ, Ⓗ, Ⓢ, LAND, CALL PHOENIX—β, ↘ + Ⓜ, ↓↘→ + Ⓗ)) CANCEL➜ ↓↙← + ATK ATK

Notes	Damage
Optimal ender from upward TAC	—

WHEN USING AN ALTERNATE TEAMMATE, ACTIVATE A TAC WITH → + Ⓢ OR ↓ + Ⓢ, THEN AS WOLVERINE COMES IN, PERFORM AIR Ⓜ, Ⓜ, Ⓗ CANCEL➜ ↗ + ATK + Ⓢ CANCEL➜ ↓↙← + ATK ATK

Notes	Damage
Optimal ender from forward TAC	—

FORWARD JUMP, INSTANT AIR Ⓢ CANCEL➜ ↘ + ATK + Ⓢ, ↓ + Ⓗ, LAND, CR. Ⓜ, ST. Ⓗ, Ⓢ CANCEL➜ FORWARD SUPER JUMP, AIR Ⓜ, Ⓜ, Ⓛ, Ⓗ CANCEL➜ ATK + Ⓢ CANCEL➜ ↓↙← + ATK ATK

Notes	Damage
Combo from instant overhead air Ⓢ on large characters	648,100

CR. Ⓛ, CR. Ⓜ, ST. Ⓗ, Ⓢ CANCEL➜ FORWARD SUPER JUMP, AIR Ⓜ, Ⓜ, Ⓗ CANCEL➜ ATK + Ⓢ CANCEL➜ ↓↙← + ATK ATK CANCEL➜ X-FACTOR, ↓ + Ⓗ, LAND, ST. Ⓗ, Ⓢ CANCEL➜ FORWARD SUPER JUMP, AIR Ⓗ CANCEL➜ ATK + Ⓢ CANCEL➜ ↓↙← + ATK ATK

Notes	Damage
1 million damage combo with level 1 X-Factor	1,026,900

ST. Ⓜ, CR. Ⓜ, ST. Ⓗ, Ⓢ CANCEL➜ FORWARD SUPER JUMP, AIR Ⓜ, Ⓜ, Ⓗ CANCEL➜ ATK + Ⓢ, ↓ + Ⓗ, LAND, ST. Ⓗ, Ⓢ CANCEL➜ FORWARD SUPER JUMP, AIR Ⓜ, Ⓜ, Ⓗ, Ⓢ, LAND, CALL DANTE—β, ↘ + Ⓜ, {→↓↘ + Ⓛ (3 HITS) CANCEL➜ ↓↙← + ATK ATK} X 5

Notes	Damage
The Fatal Claw loop! When the opposing character soars over Wolverine after juggling with →↓↘ + Ⓛ (must hit three times) CANCEL➜ ↓↙← + ATK ATK, reverse the command for the follow-up Tornado Claw to compensate. If Fatal Claw hits as high as possible without sacrificing hits, you'll recover in time to juggle with repeated Tornado and Fatal Claws until your meter is depleted	800,000~1,400,000

SALVAGING A BERSERKER CHARGE

If you attack with Berserker Slash and it is guarded, canceling into Berserker Charge leaves you at a +7 frame advantage at a relatively close distance. This also applies if your opponent activates advancing guard before the Berserker Charge super flash! From here, you have three major options:

If Berserker Slash to Berserker Charge is guarded, use your +7 frame advantage to try to salvage the mix-up!

- Dash forward and attack with crouching Ⓛ. This beats all attempts from the opposing player to stick out any ground normal attacks. Jumping away helps avoid this.
- Immediately performing Berserker Slash M crosses up opposing players who sit there and guard low. It also crosses up opponents attempting to jump away. If you hit an opponent jumping away with Berserker Slash M, the speed bonus from Berserker Charge allows you to dash forward and get a full juggle combo. To combo against a grounded opponent, call a crossover assist before performing Berserker Slash M.
- If you think your challenger is going to jump and block in the opposite direction, counter with an immediate Berserker Slash L. This also leads to a full combo if hit.

If your opponent uses advancing guard after the super flash, the situation changes a bit. The additional guardstun gives you enough time to dash forward and hit them with crouching Ⓛ before they can even jump away. However, advancing guard in this situation pushes Wolverine back a very miniscule distance; not enough to cross up with Berserker Slash M. If you want to cross up in this situation, you'll have to dash forward and use Berserker Slash L.

CHINATOWN MIX-UP

When a new character is coming in, Wolverine has a nearly invisible mix-up using upwards Drill Claw!

When a new character enters the playing field, you have an incredibly simple and effective mix-up at your disposal. Simply run directly under your foe and attack with upwards Drill Claw while the opposing character is coming in. The timing of the Drill Claw determines whether the attack must be guarded in the cross-up direction or not, but it's impossible to visibly distinguish!

After the Drill Claw, call your crossover assist and use Diving Kick. If the Drill Claw hits, you can convert into a full combo. If the Drill Claw is guarded, your opponent then gets pinned in place by the Diving Kick and the crossover assist. Mix your challenger up with Berserker Slash, crouching Ⓛ, or instant overhead Ⓛ.

Best of all, this Drill Claw mix-up beats nearly all attempts by the opposing player to press buttons; the Drill Claw beats all normal aerial attacks on the way in, and it also cleanly hits attempts to airdash or fly away.

X-23

"I... I AM NOT A WEAPON!"

Bio

REAL NAME

Laura Kinney

OCCUPATION

Adventurer

ABILITIES

Due to her extensive training as a top-secret operative, X-23 is a master of multiple forms of martial arts, and is an expert in assassination techniques.

WEAPONS

Two claws in each hand and one in each foot, all made from virtually indestructible adamantium, which she can use freely.

PROFILE

Cloned from a damaged Wolverine gene sample, X-23 was created for one reason: to be the perfect killing machine. For years, she proved herself a notable assassin, though a series of tragedies eventually led her to Wolverine and the X-Men, with whom she now seeks to turn her life around.

FIRST APPEARANCE

NYX #3 (2004)

POWER GRID

2	INTELLIGENCE
2	STRENGTH
3	SPEED
4	STAMINA
1	ENERGY PROJECTION
6	FIGHTING ABILITY

*This is biographical, and does not represent an evaluation of the in-game combat potential of this hero.

ALTERNATE COSTUMES

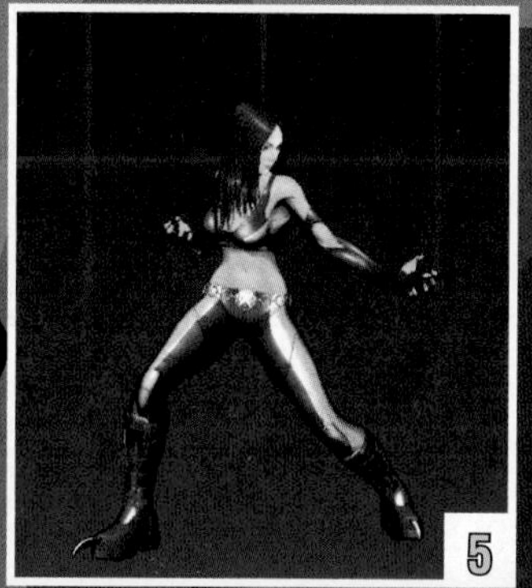
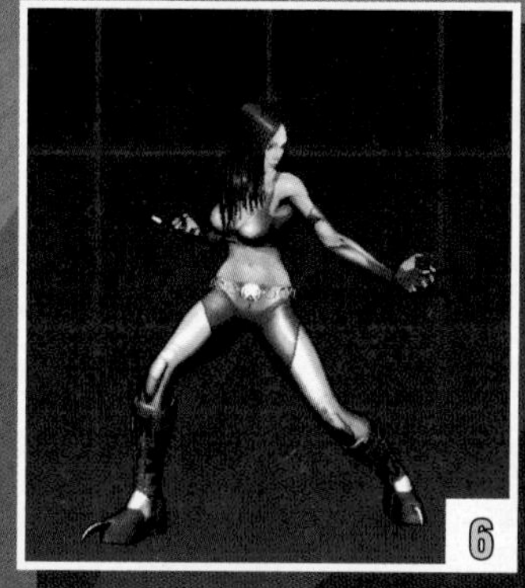

Overview

Vitality	830,000
Chain Combo Archetype	Hunter Series

X-Factor Boost	Damage	Speed
Level 1 (3 teammates remaining)	120%	120%
Level 2 (2 teammates remaining)	140%	130%
Level 3 (1 teammate remaining)	160%	140%

X-23 is a melee character; her effectiveness is heightened at close range. She benefits greatly from the help of crossover assists, so she is best placed first or second on a team. Your main goal with X-23 is to get her close, with the secondary goal of cornering her opponent. Why is this effective?

- X-23 has few options from fullscreen. The majority of her damage will be scored at point-blank range
- All of X-23's special moves move her forward, making it difficult for her rivals to push her away with advancing guard
- Mirage Feint M and Decapitating Slice become particularly deadly against a cornered adversary

How can these goals be achieved?

- Using a crossover assist to cover Neck Slice, Ankle Slice, and Mirage Feint
- Approaching from the sky with Talon Attack and ↓ + (H)
- Canceling attacks with Mirage Feint and Neck Slice to stay within close range

TUNING SINCE ORIGINAL MVC3

X-23 gains the ability to cancel Crescent Scythe and Mirage Feint into Talon Attack, increasing her offensive options. In return, her vitality has been decreased from 880,000 to 830,000. The rate at which X-23's air basic attacks decay hitstun is increased, reducing the number of rejump loops you can attempt with her, thus slightly reducing her damage output and meter gain. Damage has been added to Rage Trigger (with mashing) and Silent Kill, somewhat compensating for this change.

- Vitality decreased from 880,000 to 830,000
- Can cancel into Talon Attack from any aerial special move
- Rage Trigger is mashable
- Silent Kill 100,000 damage increase

Attack Set

Standing Basic Attacks

Screen	Command	Hits	Damage	Meter Gain	Startup	Active	Recovery	Advantage on Hit	Advantage if Guarded	Notes
1	Standing L	1	40,000	320	4	3	11	-1	-1	Chains into standing and crouching L
2	Standing M	2	54,000	480	5	2(2)3	19	-4	-5	—
3	Standing H	1	68,000	544	9	4	21	+1	-3	Knocks down

Crouching Basic Attacks

Screen	Command	Hits	Damage	Meter Gain	Startup	Active	Recovery	Advantage on Hit	Advantage if Guarded	Notes
1	Crouching L	1	35,000	280	5	3	13	-3	-3	Low attack, chains into standing and crouching L
2	Crouching M	2	50,400	448	6	7	16	-2	-3	Low attack
3	Crouching H	1	63,000	504	10	4	20	—	-2	Low attack, knocks down

Ground Special Attack—Launcher

Screen	Command	Hits	Damage	Meter Gain	Startup	Active	Recovery	Advantage on Hit	Advantage if Guarded	Notes
1	S (while standing or crouching)	1	80,000	640	8	4	27	—	-9	Launcher, not special- or hyper combo-cancelable

Air Basic Attacks

Screen	Command	Hits	Damage	Meter Gain	Startup	Active	Recovery	Advantage on Hit	Advantage if Guarded	Notes
1	Air L	1	40,000	320	4	3	16	+9	+9	Overhead attack
2	Air M	1	50,000	400	6	3	22	+16	+15	Overhead attack
3	Air H	1	70,000	560	11	3	22	+18	+17	Overhead attack

Air Special Attacks—Flying Screen and Air Exchange

Air Ⓢ causes a hard knockdown when used in a launcher combo (this is sometimes called flying screen). When used outside of a launcher combo, air Ⓢ behaves mostly like another basic attack. Air exchange attacks, performed by inputting a direction plus Ⓢ, are only possible during a launcher combo. Exchange hits initiate team aerial combos by tagging in the next available character to continue the air combo.

Screen	Command	Hits	Damage	Meter Gain	Startup	Active	Recovery	Advantage on Hit	Advantage if Guarded	Notes
1	Air Ⓢ	1	70,000	560	11	3	22	+18	+14	Causes hard knockdown if used in launcher combo
2	Air ⇧ + Ⓢ (during launcher combo)	1	45,000	360	11	4	Until grounded	—	—	Tags in next available ally while lofting opponent upward
3	Air ⇨ or ⇦ + Ⓢ (during launcher combo)	1	35,000	280	11	5	Until grounded	—	—	Tags in next available ally while causing wall bounce, erases1 hyper meter bar from foe
4	Air ⇩ + Ⓢ (during launcher combo)	1	45,000	360	11	4	Until grounded	—	—	Tags in next available ally while causing ground bounce, generates 1 hyper meter bar

Command Attacks

Command attacks resemble basic attacks but have different chaining and canceling properties. It's usually possible to chain *into* a command attack from basic attacks, but most command attacks cannot be chained from or canceled themselves.

Screen	Name	Command	Hits	Damage	Meter Gain	Startup	Active	Recovery	Advantage on Hit	Advantage if Guarded	Notes
1	Falling Claw	(in air) ⇩ + Ⓗ	1	68,000	544	8	Until grounded	10	+7	+6	Cancelable into TAC attack or ⇩ ⬃ ⇨ + ATK

Throws

Throws are for snagging passive or blocking opponents. Since throws are active so quickly, you can also use them to preemptively toss opposing characters out of their offense. Combos are usually possible after throws, one way or another.

Screen	Command	Hits	Damage	Meter Gain	Startup	Active	Notes
1	⇨ + Ⓗ (ground)	3	80,000	800	1	1	Hard knockdown
	⇦ + Ⓗ (ground)	3	80,000	800	1	1	Hard knockdown
2	⇨ + Ⓗ (air)	3	80,000	800	1	1	Hard knockdown
	⇦ + Ⓗ (air)	3	80,000	800	1	1	Hard knockdown

As a Partner—Crossover Assists

Screen	Type	P1+P2 Crossover Combination Hyper Combo	Description	Hits	Damage	Meter Gain	Startup	Active	Recovery (this crossover assist)	Recovery (other partner)	Notes
1	X-23—α	Rage Trigger	Neck Slice	1	80,000	640	42	7	119	79	—
2	X-23—β	Rage Trigger	Ankle Slice	1	80,000	640	44	4	114	84	Low attack, OTG-capable
3	X-23—γ	Rage Trigger	Crescent Scythe H	3	108,300	960	29	9	154	124	Knocks down

1

2

3

X-23—α Neck Slice is a standard attack with no special properties. X-23—β Ankle Slice is one of the few crossover assists that must be guarded low, making it useful to complement rushdown or for unguardable setups. This crossover assist is OTG-capable, as well, making it useful for any character to extend combos. X-23—γ Crescent Scythe has a large hitbox but does not have invincibility, decreasing its usefulness. However, it does has a very small window of invincibility when used as a crossover counter. If you are guarding an attack at close range, you can bring in X-23 via crossover counter, and X-23—γ will beat out any opposing attack (unless it happens to be more invincible than Crescent Scythe!). You can then proceed to cancel Crescent Scythe's recovery with Talon Attack L into a combo.

Overall, calling X-23 as a crossover assist should be kept to a minimum due to her low vitality.

Snap Back

Screen	Command	Hits	Damage	Meter Gain	Startup	Active	Recovery	Advantage on Hit	Advantage if Guarded
1	↓↘→ + P1 or P2	1	50,000	500 - (-1 hyper meter bar)	2	4	21	—	-3

Notes

On hit, snap back forces the opposing point character to be replaced by an assist. Opposing assist calls or tag outs are also locked out for 4 seconds

1

Special Moves

Screen	Name	Command	Hits	Damage	Meter Gain	Startup	Active	Recovery	Advantage on Hit	Advantage if Guarded	Notes
1	Neck Slice (can be charged)	↓↘→ + L	1~3	85,000~135,400	680~1200	18~37	9~12	14~11	0~+30	-1~0	Charged version staggers, charged version causes spinning knockdown if it hits aerial adversary
2	Ankle Slice (can be charged)	↓↘→ + M	1~3	85,000~135,400	680~1200	20~39	4~7	22~19	-3~+27	-4~-3	Low attack, charged version staggers and is OTG-capable
3	Decapitating Slice (can be charged)	↓↘→ + H	3	120,000	1200	26~45	8	23	—	—	Throw, knocks down, charged version has increased range
4	Talon Attack L	(in air) ↓↘→ + L	1	90,000	720	15	Until grounded	11	+10	+9	Hard knockdown when used in air combo after S launcher, can be canceled into from any aerial special move
5	Talon Attack M	(in air) ↓↘→ + M	1	90,000	720	15	13	13	-3	-4	Can be canceled into from any aerial special move
6	Talon Attack H	(in air) ↓↘→ + H	1	90,000	720	15	13	13	-3	-4	Can be canceled into from any aerial special move
7	Crescent Scythe L (in air OK)	→↓↘ + L	1	85,000	680	5	8	33 (in air – until grounded)	+1	-19	Knocks down
	Crescent Scythe M (in air OK)	→↓↘ + M	2	104,500	880	5	11	40 (in air – until grounded)	-5	-25	Knocks down
	Crescent Scythe H (in air OK)	→↓↘ + H	3	119,200	1056	5	12	59 (in air – until grounded)	-23	-46	Knocks down
8	Mirage Feint L (can be charged)	↓↙← + L	—	—	—	3	—	14	—	—	Charging state starts on frame 4 if button is held, pressing S during charge cancels feint
9	Mirage Feint M (can be charged)	↓↙← + M	—	—	—	3	—	25	—	—	Charging state starts on frame 4 if button is held, pressing S during charge cancels feint
10	Mirage Feint H (can be charged)	↓↙← + H	—	—	—	6	—	7	—	—	Can use air attacks during active frames, charging state starts on frame 7 if button is held, pressing S during charge cancels feint

1

Neck Slice: X-23 launches forward with a slice attack. If L is held down, you can charge Neck Slice for added damage, hitstun, and range. An uncharged Neck Slice reaches halfway across the screen, while a fully charged Neck Slice covers three-quarters of a screen's distance, making it a great way to get close. A successfully connected Neck Slice cannot be followed by basic attacks for a combo, but you can hit-confirm into Rage Trigger for decent damage. More importantly, a successful Neck Slice puts X-23 right where she wants to be—right next to her opponent. Neck Slice can be punished with a throw if guarded, so it is important to use this attack in tandem with a crossover assist to make it safe. A fully charged Neck Slice causes a stagger if connected, allowing for a combo opportunity. A charged Neck Slice also causes a hard knockdown on aerial rivals. Even though a charged Neck Slice can still be punished by a throw, you have enough time to have X-23 jump away from a throw attempt. Jump away from the throw attempt, and then counter with an air ↓ + H or Talon Attack L.

2

Ankle Slice: Ankle Slice is a low-hitting version of Neck Slice. A fully charged Ankle Slice is OTG-capable, making it a staple in X-23's combos. A charged Ankle Slice causes opponents to stagger, leaving them open for a full combo. Ankle Slice suffers from the same punishment options as Neck Slice, so it is best used either in combos or while covering with a crossover assist. You can cancel into Rage Trigger for decent damage if Ankle Slice connects.

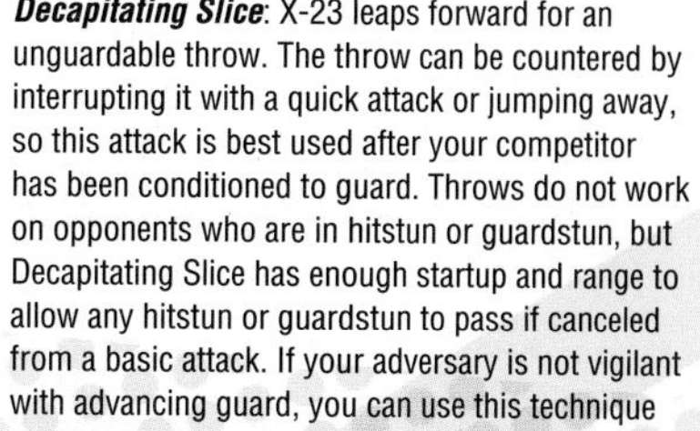
3

Decapitating Slice: X-23 leaps forward for an unguardable throw. The throw can be countered by interrupting it with a quick attack or jumping away, so this attack is best used after your competitor has been conditioned to guard. Throws do not work on opponents who are in hitstun or guardstun, but Decapitating Slice has enough startup and range to allow any hitstun or guardstun to pass if canceled from a basic attack. If your adversary is not vigilant with advancing guard, you can use this technique to score free damage. Because of Decapitating Slice's horizontal range, your opponent's advancing guard will not push X-23 away far enough out to avoid Decapitating Slice in the corner.

Talon Attack L 4

Talon Attack M 5

Talon Attack H 6

Talon Attack: Talon Attack is a flying kick that serves as X-23's main way of manipulating her aerial movement. Talon Attack L travels downward at an angle and can only be punished if guarded in the air. Talon Attack M flies straight, covering a large amount of horizontal distance. Talon Attack H sends X-23 flying upward at an angle, making it great for escaping corners. Talon Attack M and H recover in the air, so it is possible to attack or guard after recovering. Talon Attack L is commonly used as a combo ender and has the same hard knockdown property as air Ⓢ if used after first launching an opponent. Note that all versions of Talon Attack can be canceled into from Crescent Scythe at any time. Also, you may only use Talon Attack once in the air.

7

Crescent Scythe: X-23 flips forward with a crescent-shaped slice attack. The range and damage of Crescent Scythe differ depending on the button used, with Ⓗ being the strongest. This attack has no invincibility, so you must perform it early if used as an anti-air attack.

A whiffed or guarded Crescent Scythe leaves X-23 wide open for punishment. However, you can mitigate this by canceling into any version of Talon Attack. Stop foes who are approaching from the sky with Crescent Scythe H, then cancel into Talon Attack L or M to reverse their momentum!

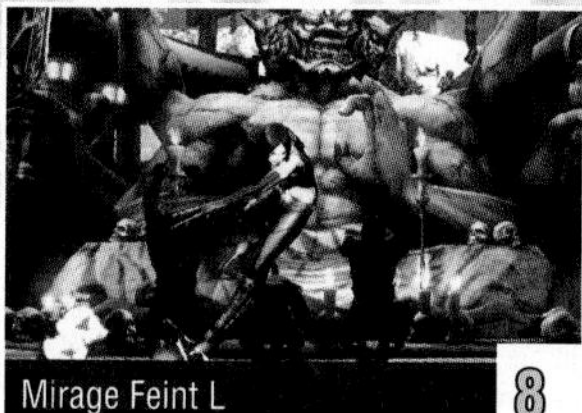
Mirage Feint L 8

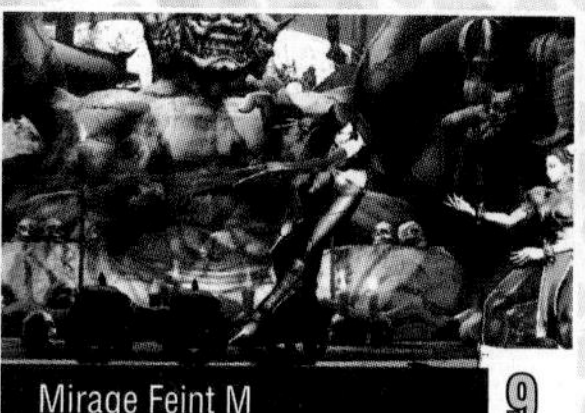
Mirage Feint M 9

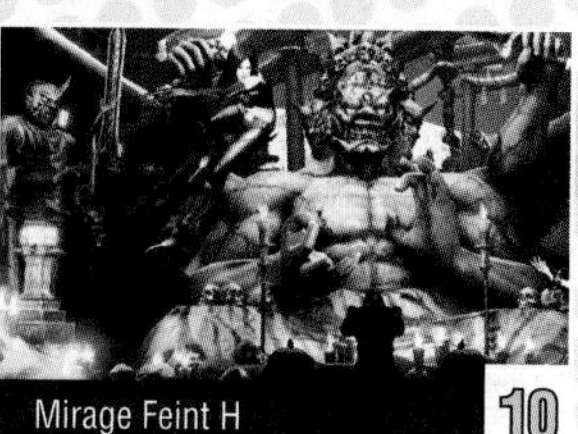
Mirage Feint H 10

Mirage Feint: Mirage Feint is a quick hop that you can employ for movement or set-ups. Mirage Feint L is a small hop and can be canceled from a guarded basic attack (such as standing Ⓗ) to stay close. Mirage Feint M travels the farthest of the three and can pass through opponents for a cross-up (this works in the corner, as well). Mirage Feint H is different because X-23 performs a small jump instead. During this jump, air basic attacks and special moves are available.

You can charge all three versions of Mirage Feint with their corresponding ATK button. The feint can be charged indefinitely, though a charged Mirage Feint has no special properties. While charging, the move can be canceled altogether by pressing Ⓢ. Take advantage of this option to cut down the recovery time of basic attacks (see the Advanced Tactics section for more details).

Hyper Combos

Screen	Name	Command	Hits	Damage	Startup	Active	Recovery	Advantage on Hit	Advantage if Guarded	Notes
1	Rage Trigger	↓↘→ + ATK ATK	13~26	245,400~ 294,600	13+2	16(13)24 (10)10	44	-12	-29	Frames 1-19 invincible, can be mashed for additional hits
2	Weapon X Prime	→↓↘ + ATK ATK	14	280,900	24+1	33	38	—	-50	Frames 6-64 invincible
3	Silent Kill (Level 3 Hyper Combo)	↓↙← + ATK ATK	2	400,000	20+9	290	—	—	—	Frames 6-29 invincible, X-23 becomes invisible upon activation, pressing Ⓢ when near the opposing character activates special unblockable attack and ends Silent Killer

1

Rage Trigger: Rage Trigger is combo-friendly and is X-23's main way of ending combos. It has a short period of invulnerability for blowing through close range attacks. Rage Trigger is extremely unsafe if guarded, so save its use for combos or reversals.

2

Weapon X Prime: If successfully connected, X-23 performs a barrage of melee attacks for a soft knockdown. Weapon X Prime is not as usable in combos as Rage Trigger because of its startup time. However, it has a considerably longer window of invincibility than Rage Trigger, and you can use it to counter projectile hyper combos from fullscreen. Utilize the move to THC to and from the other characters on your team and also to counter hyper combos at a distance.

3

Silent Kill: Upon activation, X-23 becomes invisible and has access to an unguardable cinematic attack performed by pressing Ⓢ. X-23 reappears either when the timer runs out or after successfully connecting the unguardable attack. Although she becomes extremely difficult to deal with, X-23 is not invulnerable while invisible; don't become careless after activation!

The unguardable Ⓢ attack is not considered a throw, so it can be connected on opponents who are in hitstun or guardstun. This allows you to perform standing Ⓗ CANCEL Ⓢ for unavoidable damage. Competitors must either fight blindly or run away during the duration of Silent Kill. If your rival does manage to escape initially, remember that X-23 has full access to all her attacks and crossover assists while invisible.

Battle Plan

Mirage Feint M covers nearly half the screen horizontally. Use it with the help of a crossover assist to approach.

Your main goal when using X-23 is to get her close to her attacker. She has no way of dealing damage from across the screen, so all effort should be put into getting X-23 into striking range. Once she is at mid to close range, X-23's hand-to-hand prowess shines!

You can have X-23 approach her foes in several different ways. The main way to approach is with a frontal assault utilizing X-23's "Slice" special moves. Neck Slice and Ankle Slice cover half a screen's distance uncharged, and they cover almost the entirety of the screen when fully charged. Neck Slice has a large hitbox and can be covered with a crossover assist to push forward safely. A fully charged Neck Slice is better to use if possible because of its increased range and hitstun. Charging Neck Slice has quite a bit of startup, so use a crossover assist to protect X-23 before attempting it. As your rivals become conditioned to dealing with Neck Slice, you can then mix up between Ankle Slice and Decapitating Slice to keep your opposition guessing. If the opposing character is not vigilant with advancing guard or low guarding, use Ankle Slice and Decapitating Slice for a possible combo opening while pushing the opposing character into the corner.

Mirage Feint is also a great way to close the distance between X-23 and her competitor. Mirage Feint M covers more ground than her forward dash and rivals it in speed, as well. Cover your advance with a crossover assist, then perform Mirage Feint M to get X-23 near the opponent. Mirage Feint L only hops a short distance, but you can use its short recovery time to lead into a Mirage Feint M, which then puts X-23 in attacking range. Mirage Feint H doesn't cover as much ground as Mirage Feint M, but it allows a crossover assist call while X-23 is in the air. Instead of performing Mirage Feint L to Mirage Feint M, try performing Mirage Feint L to Mirage Feint H with a crossover assist during the jump to keep X-23's mobility from being too obvious.

In addition, the short hop of Mirage Feint can be canceled into Talon Attack to travel even farther. You can surprise your challenger by performing a Mirage Feint L or M, canceling into Talon Attack M, then coming out of the Talon Attack with air Ⓗ for a heavily offensive approach. You can also use this for a tricky cross-up with Mirage Feint M. After crossing an opponent up with Mirage Feint M, immediately perform Talon Attack L for a quick dive attack from behind!

You can also utilize X-23's Talon Attack to have her approach from the sky. All versions of Talon Attack propel X-23 forward, with Talon Attack M and H traveling particularly far. This makes it possible for X-23 to approach at unusual angles. For example, you can follow a Talon Attack M or H with ⇩ + Ⓗ upon recovering to have X-23 drop directly on top of her adversaries. You can also simply attack with air Ⓢ after a Talon Attack M or H for a combo attempt. If you think your opponent is ready for an aerial assault, you can opt to guard after a Talon Attack M or H to avoid retaliation. If you have a long range crossover assist, you can call it, then quickly jump and perform Talon Attack M or H. Doing this at high altitudes is sneaky because your rival won't be able to see the crossover assist since the screen will be focused on X-23 flying in the air and not at the action on the ground! At mid range, you can use Talon Attack L not only as an offensive means of approach, but as a great way to punish projectiles, as well.

Cornered opponents are not safe from a Mirage Feint M cross-up!

Once close, you can utilize the speed of X-23's standing and crouching Ⓛ to mount an offense. Guarded attack strings can be canceled into Mirage Feint, Neck Slice, Ankle Slice, or Decapitating Slice depending on how your competitor behaves. If your foe is content in guarding X-23's onslaught, call a crossover assist during a guarded attack string, then cancel into Mirage Feint M for a cross-up while your teammate attacks from behind. You can also take advantage of an overly defensive opponent by opening them up with Decapitating Slice. To combat advancing guard, use Mirage Feint and Neck Slice to move back into position. Mix this up with Ankle Slice to check their low guard. Mirage Feint H becomes a threat at close range, as well. You can cancel your basic attacks into Mirage Feint H, then continue the assault with air attacks that must be guarded high. You can also cancel Mirage Feint H into Talon Attack L to continue the pressure.

Once cornered, enemies must deal with even more shenanigans! Mirage Feint M always crosses up cornered opponents, so they must then worry about guarding left or right in addition to the high/low mix-up produced by Ankle Slice and Mirage Feint H. Cornered challengers also fall victim to Decapitating Slice much easier, since advancing guard does not create enough distance for the opposing character to avoid the throw. Counter attempts at advancing guard with Neck Slice or Mirage Feint to keep your rival cornered. If you have an assist that locks the opponent down for an extended period of time, the corner is a great time to utilize it to set up Silent Kill!

COMBO USAGE

I. CR. Ⓛ, Ⓛ, ST. Ⓗ CANCEL ↓↙← + Ⓗ, AIR Ⓜ, Ⓗ, LAND, FORWARD JUMP, AIR Ⓜ, Ⓜ, Ⓗ, Ⓢ CANCEL ↓↘→ + Ⓛ, LAND, ST. Ⓜ (2 HITS), Ⓢ CANCEL FORWARD SUPER JUMP, AIR Ⓜ, Ⓜ, Ⓗ, ↓ + Ⓗ CANCEL →↓↘ + Ⓛ CANCEL ↓↘→ + Ⓛ, LAND, ↓↘→ + Ⓜ (CHARGE) CANCEL ↓↘→ + ATK ATK (MASH ATK)

604,500 damage, 8% meter gain

This is X-23's standard bread and butter combo. This combo has trouble working against smaller character like Rocket Raccoon, in which case, you should perform st. Ⓗ CANCEL ↓↙← + Ⓗ, air Ⓜ, Ⓗ, land, st. Ⓗ CANCEL ↓↙← + Ⓗ, air Ⓜ, Ⓗ CANCEL ↓↘→ + Ⓛ, land, st. Ⓜ (2 hits), Ⓢ into the remainder of the launch combo.

II. ↓↘→ + Ⓗ, ST. Ⓗ CANCEL ↓↙← + Ⓗ, AIR Ⓜ, Ⓗ, LAND, FORWARD JUMP, AIR Ⓜ, Ⓜ, Ⓗ, Ⓢ CANCEL ↓↘→ + Ⓛ, LAND, ST. Ⓜ (2 HITS), Ⓢ CANCEL FORWARD SUPER JUMP, AIR Ⓜ, Ⓜ, Ⓗ, ↓ + Ⓗ CANCEL →↓↘ + Ⓛ CANCEL ↓↘→ + Ⓛ, LAND, ↓↘→ + Ⓜ (CHARGE) CANCEL ↓↘→ + ATK ATK (MASH ATK)

577,300 damage, 15% meter gain

This combo is similar to **Combo I**, but it starts with Decapitating Slice. If you are having problems linking st. Ⓗ after ↓↘→ + Ⓗ, st. Ⓜ gives a few extra frames of leniency to juggle properly.

III. FRONT OR BACK AIR THROW, LAND, ATK ATK (FORWARD DASH), ↓↘→ + Ⓜ (CHARGE) CANCEL ↓↘→ + ATK ATK (MASH ATK)

345,900 damage, 80% meter loss

It's best to use ATK ATK to forward dash in this situation instead of →→ to avoid an accidental →↓↘ motion when attempting the ↓↘→ + Ⓜ.

IV. (WHILE ENEMY IS AIRBORNE) FORWARD JUMP, AIR Ⓛ, Ⓜ, Ⓗ CANCEL →↓↘ + Ⓛ CANCEL ↓↘→ + Ⓛ, LAND, ST. Ⓜ (2 HITS), Ⓢ CANCEL FORWARD SUPER JUMP, AIR Ⓜ, Ⓜ, Ⓗ, ↓ + Ⓗ CANCEL →↓↘ + Ⓛ CANCEL ↓↘→ + Ⓛ, LAND, ↓↘→ + Ⓜ (CHARGE CANCEL ↓↘→ + ATK ATK (MASH ATK)

601,600 damage, 17% meter loss

This combo is good to use in air-to-air situations. When a new character is incoming after a knock out, use air Ⓛ to interrupt their attack and go straight into this combo.

COMBO USAGE CONT.

V. CR. Ⓛ, ST. Ⓜ (2 HITS), CR. Ⓜ (2 HITS) [X-FACTOR] ST. Ⓜ (2 HITS), Ⓗ [CANCEL] ↓↙← + Ⓗ, AIR Ⓜ, Ⓗ, LAND, FORWARD JUMP, AIR Ⓜ, Ⓜ, Ⓗ, Ⓢ, LAND, FORWARD JUMP, AIR Ⓜ, Ⓗ, Ⓢ [CANCEL] ↓↘→ + Ⓛ, LAND, Ⓢ [CANCEL] FORWARD SUPER JUMP, AIR Ⓜ, Ⓜ, Ⓗ, ↓ + Ⓗ [CANCEL] →↓↘ + Ⓛ [CANCEL] ↓↘→ + Ⓛ, LAND, ↓↘→ + Ⓜ (CHARGE) [CANCEL] ↓↘→ + ATK ATK (MASH ATK)

897,800~1,162,100 damage, 47~92% meter gain

X-Factor allows for an extended bread and butter combo with an extra re-jump. If you're looking for a guaranteed K.O. and still have X-Factor available, this should be your go-to combo. X-23 becomes much quicker in X-Factor, so you should adjust your inputs accordingly.

ADVANCED TACTICS

MIRAGE FEINT CANCEL

You can charge all three versions of Mirage Feint by holding down the button used to perform it. This charge can be canceled at any time by pressing Ⓢ. With this, you can cancel the recovery of basic attacks by canceling them into Mirage Feint, then quickly press Ⓢ to cancel the Mirage Feint. For example, you can perform a Mirage Feint cancel with standing Ⓗ [CANCEL] ⇩⇙⇦ + Ⓜ. Once Ⓜ is pressed for the Mirage Feint, hold it down and press Ⓢ immediately afterward, almost simultaneously.

If performed correctly, the recovery time of the basic attack used is reduced drastically, and it even grants heavy frame advantage if used with Ⓜ and Ⓗ attacks. It is possible to loop standing Ⓛ, Ⓜ, Ⓗ several times by Mirage Feint canceling Ⓗ, which is normally not possible.

SILENT, BUT DEADLY

Hold your opponent in place with a crossover assist, then perform the unguardable Silent Kill attack with Ⓢ!

Because Silent Kill is an unguardable attack and not a throw, you can perform various set-ups on cornered foes that are virtually inescapable. Lockdown-heavy crossover assists such as Amaterasu—β Cold Star or Doctor Strange—β Eye of Aggamato can be used to hold your challengers in place for the unguardable attack. Attacks that linger onscreen even if the original character is no longer in play (such as Trish's Round Harvest or Phoenix's TK Trap) can be used to keep adversaries from escaping Silent Kill, as well. This is especially useful after a K.O. when a new character is coming in; foes will fall haplessly into X-23's clutches! If meter isn't an issue, you can follow Silent Kill with a combo to guarantee a K.O. Use this to turn the tides in battle!

COMBO APPENDIX

GENERAL EXECUTION TIPS

When performing →↓↘ + Ⓛ [CANCEL] ↓↘→ + Ⓛ during air combos, delay the ↓↘→ + Ⓛ for optimal positioning

(AFTER TAC) AIR Ⓜ, Ⓗ [CANCEL] →↓↘ + Ⓗ [CANCEL] ↓↘→ + Ⓛ, LAND, ↓↘→ + Ⓜ (CHARGE) [CANCEL] ↓↘→ + ATK ATK (MASH ATK)

Notes	Damage
⇧ + Ⓢ or ⇨ + Ⓢ or ⇩ + Ⓢ TAC to X-23	Varies based on damage scaling

(AFTER TAC) AIR Ⓜ, Ⓗ [CANCEL] →↓↘ + Ⓛ [CANCEL] ↓↘→ + Ⓜ, LAND, ↓↘→ + Ⓜ (CHARGE) [CANCEL] ↓↘→ + ATK ATK (MASH ATK)

Notes	Damage
Requires corner, ⇧ + Ⓢ or ⇩ + Ⓢ TAC to X-23	Varies based on damage scaling

CR. Ⓛ, Ⓛ, ST. Ⓗ [CANCEL] ↓↙← + Ⓗ, AIR Ⓜ, Ⓗ, LAND, FORWARD JUMP, AIR Ⓜ, Ⓜ, Ⓗ, Ⓢ [CANCEL] ↓↘→ + Ⓛ, LAND, ST. Ⓜ (2 HITS), Ⓢ [CANCEL] FORWARD SUPER JUMP, AIR Ⓜ, Ⓜ, Ⓗ, ↓ + Ⓗ [CANCEL] →↓↘ + Ⓛ [CANCEL] ↓↘→ + Ⓛ, LAND, CALL WESKER—β, ↓↘→ + Ⓛ (CHARGE), Ⓢ [CANCEL] FORWARD SUPER JUMP, AIR Ⓗ [CANCEL] →↓↘ + Ⓗ [CANCEL] ↓↘→ + ATK, LAND, ↓↘→ + Ⓜ (CHARGE) [CANCEL] ↓↘→ + ATK ATK (MASH ATK)

Notes	Damage
An assist combo that illustrates a method of increasing X-23's damage output and meter gain	708,600 damage, 52% meter gain

↓↘→ + Ⓛ (CHARGE), FORWARD JUMP, AIR ↓ + Ⓗ, LAND, ST. Ⓛ, Ⓗ, [CANCEL] ↓↙← + Ⓗ, AIR Ⓜ, Ⓗ, LAND, FORWARD JUMP, AIR Ⓜ, Ⓜ, Ⓗ, Ⓢ [CANCEL] ↓↘→ + Ⓛ, LAND, ST. Ⓜ (2 HITS), Ⓢ [CANCEL] FORWARD SUPER JUMP, AIR Ⓜ, Ⓜ, Ⓗ, ↓ + Ⓗ [CANCEL] →↓↘ + Ⓛ [CANCEL] ↓↘→ + Ⓛ, LAND, CALL WESKER—β, ↓↘→ + Ⓛ (CHARGE), Ⓢ [CANCEL] FORWARD SUPER JUMP, AIR Ⓗ [CANCEL] →↓↘ + Ⓗ [CANCEL] ↓↘→ + ATK, LAND, ↓↘→ + Ⓜ (CHARGE) [CANCEL] ↓↘→ + ATK ATK (MASH ATK)

Notes	Damage
—	650,900 damage, 23% meter gain

↓↙← + ATK ATK, Ⓢ, LAND, FORWARD DASH, ST. Ⓛ, Ⓜ (2 HITS), Ⓗ [CANCEL] ↓↙← + Ⓗ, AIR Ⓜ, Ⓗ [CANCEL] ↓↘→ + Ⓛ, LAND, ST. Ⓜ (2 HITS), Ⓢ [CANCEL] FORWARD SUPER JUMP, AIR Ⓜ, Ⓜ, Ⓗ, ↓ + Ⓗ [CANCEL] →↓↘ + Ⓛ [CANCEL] ↓↘→ + Ⓛ, LAND, ↓↘→ + Ⓜ (CHARGE) [CANCEL] ↓↘→ + ATK ATK (MASH ATK)

Notes	Damage
Requires corner. After landing from Silent Kill, you must dash forward st. Ⓛ immediately for the juggle. You may instead call an OTG assist after recovering from Silent Kill to make this combo easier and to make it viable midscreen	858,900 damage, 319% meter loss

ACTIVATE LEVEL 2 OR 3 X-FACTOR, {↓↘→ + Ⓛ (CHARGE), ↓↘→ + Ⓛ (CHARGE)} X ∞

Notes	Damage
Once the first hit connects, you may repeat this loop indefinitely until X-Factor expires	Damage varies depending on the number of loops performed

AKUMA

"MY SKILLS ARE UNPARALLELED!"

Bio

REAL NAME

Akuma

OCCUPATION

Fighter

ABILITIES

While his basic fighting style is based on Ansatsuken, same as Ryu, he has mastered his own style known as "Satsui no Hadou."

WEAPONS

None

PROFILE

A fighter who took on the name of "Master of the Fist." He seeks a true battle to the death with Ryu, and to make him into a worthy opponent, he tries to lead Ryu down the path of the "Satsui no Hadou."

FIRST APPEARANCE

Super Street Fighter II Turbo (1994)

POWER GRID

3	INTELLIGENCE
4	STRENGTH
2	SPEED
3	STAMINA
6	ENERGY PROJECTION
7	FIGHTING ABILITY

*This is biographical, and does not represent an evaluation of the in-game combat potential of this hero.

ALTERNATE COSTUMES

Overview

Vitality	750,000
Chain Combo Archetype	Marvel Series

X-Factor Boost	Damage	Speed
Level 1 (3 teammates remaining)	132.5%	107.5%
Level 2 (2 teammates remaining)	155%	115%
Level 3 (1 teammate remaining)	177.5%	122.5%

While Akuma is a fairly powerful point character, his amazing Tatsumaki Zankukyaku assist lets him really shine as a dedicated assist character. As an assist character, Akuma can power through projectile walls, enhance offense, and change the flow of a round in an instant.

But, as a dedicated assist character, what happens to Akuma when he's on his own? There will no doubt be situations in which Akuma has to fight for himself, so it's necessary to learn where and how Akuma is effective as a point character and how to best take advantage of his abilities.

Akuma's greatest strengths lie in his strong up-close game. When in close while using Akuma, you can easily mix your opponent up by:

- **Using Akuma's Zugaihasatsu overhead to hit the opposing character and chain straight into combo**
- **Dashing in with crouching L to hit an adversary afraid of Zugaihasatsu**
- **Throwing a blocking competitor and continuing to combo with Hyakki Gojin or Tenma-Gozanku Ungyo**
- **Crossing your target up by calling an assist, then teleporting or using aerial Tatsumaki Zankukyaku**

How can you get Akuma close to his foe?

- **Advancing by using Zanku Hadoken and Hyakki Goho**
- **Forcing him through projectiles with Tatsumaki Zankukyaku H**
- **Super jumping and using a mix of Zanku Hadoken and Tenmakujinkyaku**
- **Jumping forward with option select air Ⓗ + Tatsumaki Zankukyaku L to stop jumping opponents**
- **Using his wavedash to speedily approach a grounded attacker**

When getting close is impossible for Akuma, he can still deal considerable damage to both characters as an assist using Messatsu-Gohado Ungyo and Tenma-Gohado Ungyo. The damage on these beam hyper combos adds up quickly and the combos are fast and easy to connect, and they can be used on reaction to fullscreen projectiles. When Akuma has meter, he can force opponents to play passively and safely, since the Ungyo hyper combos can destroy assists. Akuma can also evade the opposing character's attacks and quickly punish with a Tenma-Gohado Ungyo, giving Akuma a threat you can use to advance on your adversary's position.

TUNING SINCE ORIGINAL MVC3

Akuma's main role was as the primary crossover assist on most teams. In *Ultimate MvC3*, the Tatsumaki Zankukyaku assist now functions the same as the special move normally does, inflicting much less hitstun. It is still a top-class assist, however, except you need to react quickly to successfully combo off a hit. Akuma was given a great new tool in that Hyakkishu and all of its follow-ups can now be performed in the air, giving Akuma additional aerial mobility and combo options, particularly from air throws.

- **Vitality down to 750,000 from 800,000**
- **Tatsumaki Zankukyaku crossover assist causes less hitstun; now is identical to the normal version of Tatsumaki Zankukyaku M**
- **Hyakkishu can now be performed in air**
- **Tatsumaki Zankukyaku L now inflicts slightly less hitstun**
- **Messatsu-Gohado Agyo can now be mashed for additional damage**
- **Messatsu-Gohado Ungyo can now be mashed for additional damage**
- **Tenma-Gozanku Agyo can now be mashed for additional damage**
- **Tenma-Gozanku Ungyo can now be mashed for additional damage**
- **Raging Demon can now be mashed for additional damage**

Attack Set

Standing Basic Attacks

Screen	Command	Hits	Damage	Meter Gain	Startup	Active	Recovery	Advantage on Hit	Advantage if Guarded	Notes
1	Standing L	1	53,000	424	6	3	6	+6	+5	Chains into L attacks
2	Standing M	2	72,000	640	9	5	14	+4	+2	—
3	Standing H	1	88,000	704	8	4	18	+3	+1	—

Crouching Basic Attacks

Screen	Command	Hits	Damage	Meter Gain	Startup	Active	Recovery	Advantage on Hit	Advantage if Guarded	Notes
1	Crouching L	1	48,000	384	5	2	11	+2	+1	Low attack, chains into L attacks
2	Crouching M	1	75,000	600	6	3	14	+3	+1	—
3	Crouching H	1	85,000	680	8	4	25	—	-6	Low attack, knocks down

Ground Special Attack—Launcher

Screen	Command	Hits	Damage	Meter Gain	Startup	Active	Recovery	Advantage on Hit	Advantage if Guarded	Notes
1	S (while standing or crouching)	1	90,000	720	7	3	21	—	-1	Launcher, not special- or hyper combo-cancelable

Air Basic Attacks

Screen	Command	Hits	Damage	Meter Gain	Startup	Active	Recovery	Advantage on Hit	Advantage if Guarded	Notes
1	Air L	1	53,000	424	8	9	7	+9	+8	Overhead attack
2	Air M	1	70,000	560	10	3	19	+14	+12	Overhead attack
3	Air H	1	88,000	704	10	3	23	+15	+13	Overhead attack

Air Special Attacks—Flying Screen and Air Exchange

Air (S) causes a hard knockdown when used in a launcher combo (this is sometimes called flying screen). When used outside of a launcher combo, air (S) behaves mostly like another basic attack. Air exchange attacks, performed by inputting a direction plus (S), are only possible during a launcher combo. Exchange hits initiate team aerial combos by tagging in the next available character to continue the air combo.

Screen	Command	Hits	Damage	Meter Gain	Startup	Active	Recovery	Advantage on Hit	Advantage if Guarded	Notes
1	Air (S)	1	90,000	720	8	4	16	+17	+15	Causes hard knockdown if used in launcher combo
2	Air ⇧ + (S) (during launcher combo)	1	60,000	480	10	4	Until grounded	—	—	Tags in next available ally while lofting opponent upward
3	Air ⇨ or ⇦ + (S) (during launcher combo)	1	50,000	400	10	3	Until grounded	—	—	Tags in next available ally while causing wall bounce, erases 1 hyper meter from foe
4	Air ⇩ + (S) (during launcher combo)	1	50,000	400	9	4	15	—	—	Tags in next available ally while causing ground bounce, generates 1 hyper meter

1

2

3

4

AKUMA

Command Attacks

Command attacks resemble basic attacks but have different chaining and canceling properties. It's usually possible to chain *into* a command attack from basic attacks, but most command attacks cannot be chained from or canceled themselves.

Screen	Name	Command	Hits	Damage	Meter Gain	Startup	Active	Recovery	Advantage on Hit	Advantage if Guarded	Notes
1	Zugaihasatsu	⇨ + (M)	2	81,000	720	21	4	19	-1	-3	Overhead attack, causes ground bounce against airborne adversary
2	Senpukyaku	⇨ + (H)	1	100,000	800	18	5	16	+10	+2	Knocks down rival
3	Tenmakujinkyaku	(in air) ⇩ + (M)	1	80,000	640	14	Until grounded	8	+11	+9	Not special- or hyper combo-cancelable

1

2

3

Throws

Throws are for snagging passive or blocking opponents. Since throws are active so quickly, you can also use them to preemptively toss opposing characters out of their offense. Combos are usually possible after throws, one way or another.

Screen	Command	Hits	Damage	Meter Gain	Startup	Active	Notes
1	⇨ + (H) (ground)	1	80,000	800	1	1	Hard knockdown
	⇦ + (H) (ground)	1	80,000	800	1	1	Hard knockdown
2	⇨ + (H) (air)	1	80,000	800	1	1	Hard knockdown
	⇦ + (H) (air)	1	80,000	800	1	1	Hard knockdown

1

2

As a Partner—Crossover Assists

Screen	Type	P1+P2 Crossover Combination Hyper Combo	Description	Hits	Damage	Meter Gain	Startup	Active	Recovery (this crossover assist)	Recovery (other partner)	Notes
1	Akuma —α	Messatsu-Gohado Agyo	Gohadoken M	1	90,000	720	38	—	141	111	Projectile has 5 low priority durability points
2	Akuma—β	Messatsu-Goshoryu	Tatsumaki Zankyaku M	3	132,600	1200	32	17(6)6	110	80	Knocks down opponent, destroys low and medium priority projectiles during active frames
3	Akuma —γ	Messatsu-Gohado Agyo	Hyakkishu M, Hyakki Gojin	1	90,000		59	11	93	63	Overhead attack, ground bounces airborne competitor, OTG-capable

Akuma—α Gohadoken has the same properties as Akuma's Gohadoken M, which makes it a decent projectile assist. While it isn't as useful as Doctor Doom —α or Arthur —β for offensive characters, it can add some additional firepower to a pure projectile team.

Akuma—β Tatsumaki Zankukyaku is Akuma's stand-out assist and is one of the best assists in the game because it performs numerous functions: it hits in front and behind, almost every character can use it to extend combos, it only hits three times (lessening damage scaling), it hits for a long time (making it useful in mix-ups), it keeps opponents in guardstun long enough for you to perform a high-low mix-up, and it completely destroys projectiles! This assist is the primary reason to use Akuma, as it makes virtually every team better.

Akuma—γ Hyakki Gojin is one of the only overhead assists in the game and can be used to create mix-ups that are completely unblockable! Unfortunately, Hyakki Gojin takes a long time to come out, so you'll need considerable time to perform this mix-up without endangering Akuma. It's very possible to build a team that can fully utilize this assist, but this requires some experimentation.

Snap Back

Screen	Command	Hits	Damage	Meter Gain	Startup	Active	Recovery	Advantage on Hit	Advantage if Guarded
1	↓↘→ + P1 or P2	1	50,000	500 - (-1 hyper meter bar)	2	4	18	—	+1

Notes

On hit, snap back forces the opposing point character to be replaced by an assist. Opposing assist calls or tag outs are also locked out for 4 seconds

Special Moves

Screen	Name	Command	Hits	Damage	Meter Gain	Startup	Active	Recovery	Advantage on Hit	Advantage if Guarded	Notes
1	Gohadoken L	↓↘→ + L	1	90,000	720	14	—	28	-4	-6	Projectile has 5 low priority durability points
	Gohadoken M	↓↘→ + M	1	90,000	720	14	—	31	-7	-9	Projectile has 5 low priority durability points
	Gohadoken H	↓↘→ + H	1	90,000	720	14	—	34	-10	-12	Projectile has 5 low priority durability points
2	Zanku Hadoken L	(in air) ↓↘→ + L	1	90,000	720	10	—	35	+11	+10	Projectile has 5 low priority durability points, if Akuma lands while still in recovery, then add 6 frames of ground recovery
	Zanku Hadoken M	(in air) ↓↘→ + M	1	90,000	720	10	—	40	+11	+10	Projectile has 5 low priority durability points, if Akuma lands while still in recovery, then add 6 frames of ground recovery
	Zanku Hadoken H	(in air) ↓↘→ + H	1	90,000	720	10	—	45	+11	+10	Projectile has 5 low priority durability points, if Akuma lands while still in recovery, then add 6 frames of ground recovery
3	Goshoryuken L	→↓↘ + L	1	90,000	720	6	14	24	-2	-15	Invincible from frames 1-6, airborne from frame 7, knocks down opponent
	Goshoryuken M	→↓↘ + M	2	118,000	1000	4	5(1)10	30	-4	-23	Invincible from frames 1-7, airborne from frame 5, knocks down foe
	Goshoryuken H	→↓↘ + H	3	132,600	1200	3	6(1)10	44	-18	-36	Invincible from frames 1-10, airborne from frame 5, knocks down adversary
4	Tatsumaki Zankyaku L	↓↙← + L	1	110,000	880	8	7	18	—	-1	Knocks down rival, destroys low and medium priority projectiles during active frames, airborne from frame 8
	Tatsumaki Zankukyaku M	↓↙← + M	3	132,600	1200	8	17(6)6	14	+11	+3	Knocks down competitor, destroys low and medium priority projectiles during active frames, airborne from frame 8
	Tatsumaki Zankukyaku H	↓↙← + H	5	166,200	1680	8	41(6)6	16	+9	+1	Knocks down target, destroys low and medium priority projectiles during active frames, airborne from frame 8

Special Moves continued

Screen	Name	Command	Hits	Damage	Meter Gain	Startup	Active	Recovery	Advantage on Hit	Advantage if Guarded	Notes
5	Air Tatsumaki Zankukyaku L (in air OK)	(in air) ⇩⇙⇦ + L	1	110,000	880	5	28	Until grounded, 6 frames of landing recovery	+13	+12	Destroys low and medium priority projectiles during active frames
	Air Tatsumaki Zankukyaku M (in air OK)	(in air) ⇩⇙⇦ + M	3	124,000	1120	5	18(4)6	Until grounded, 6 frames of landing recovery	+13	+12	Destroys low and medium priority projectiles during active frames
	Air Tatsumaki Zankukyaku H (in air OK)	(in air) ⇩⇙⇦ + H	5	159,600	1600	5	42(4)6	Until grounded, 6 frames of landing recovery	+13	+12	Destroys low and medium priority projectiles during active frames
6	Hyakkishu L (in air OK)	⇦⇩⇙ + L	—	—	—	—	—	37/Until grounded	—	—	Airborne from frame 1, Hyakkishu attacks can be performed from frame 14 on
	Hyakkishu M (in air OK)	⇦⇩⇙ + M	—	—	—	—	—	42/Until grounded	—	—	Airborne from frame 1, Hyakkishu attacks can be performed from frame 14 on
	Hyakkishu H (in air OK)	⇦⇩⇙ + H	—	—	—	—	—	53/Until grounded	—	—	Airborne from frame 1, Hyakkishu attacks can be performed from frame 14 on
7	Hyakki Gosho	(during Hyakkishu) L	1	100,000	800	9	4	15	—	+...12	Overhead attack, ground bounces foe
8	Hyakki Gojin	(during Hyakkishu) M	1	90,000	720	14	Until grounded	8	+...13	+...11	Overhead attack, ground bounces airborne adversaries, OTG-capable
9	Hyakki Goho	(during Hyakkishu) H	1	90,000	720	10	—	Until grounded	—	—	Projectile has 5 low priority durability points, automatically aligns with rival
10	Ashura Senku	⇨⇩⇘ or ⇦⇩⇙ + S	—	—	—	14	—	20	—	—	Invincible from frames 14-30

1

Gohadoken: Akuma's ground projectile is best used from fullscreen range because its slow recovery leaves Akuma vulnerable, allowing opponents who jump over the projectile to deal big damage.

Depending on the button pressed, Gohadoken travels across the screen at different speeds: L is the slowest, and H is the fastest. Each version of Gohadoken deals the same damage and inflicts 27,000 damage if guarded, which is nice for free chip damage. If an adversary is forced to block a Gohadoken, another can be thrown fairly safely, unless your competitor can hyper combo through it.

You should avoid trying to win a long range firefight with Gohadoken, since it only has 5 low priority durability points, which many long range characters can easily overpower. Extra care should be taken when throwing Gohadokens against characters with teleports because the long recovery of the projectile leaves Akuma vulnerable to characters who can quickly get behind him.

If a Gohadoken hits, you can easily tack on some extra damage by immediately hyper combo canceling into a Messatsu-Gohado combo from anywhere on the screen for free damage!

2

Zanku Hadoken: The aerial version of Gohadoken is an angled projectile aimed down toward the ground and is Akuma's go-to move for approaching distant opponents. The button pressed determines where the projectile is aimed: the L version is aimed almost completely downwards, while the H version travels nearly across the screen. The M version is best utilized when Akuma is super jumping, as it goes far enough to hit the opposing character from that height and is also angled so that it can block jumping competitors.

You should use these moves when normal jumping forward toward most adversaries. Against foes with a quick projectile that can nullify Zanku Hadoken, like Magneto and Arthur, you should have Akuma super jump and fire a Zanku Hadoken, and then follow it up with an aerial Hyakkishu into Hyakki Goho, or a Tenmakujinkyaku if you think your challenger is going to try to dash under Akuma. Note that the stronger versions of Zanku Hadoken have more recovery, which can leave Akuma vulnerable during a super jump if thrown at the wrong time. Generally, throw the projectile immediately after beginning a super jump.

Akuma can only throw one Zanku Hadoken per jump, even after one has recovered during a super jump. Akuma can act again after Zanku Hadoken has recovered, however, so follow up with a Hyakkishu move, Tenmakujinkyaku, or an aerial Tatsumaki Zankukyaku.

3

Goshoryuken: This variation on the classic "dragon punch" gives Akuma a valuable invincible attack that costs no meter, which you can use to interrupt your opponent's offense. Goshoryuken L is only invincible during its 6 frame startup time, while Goshoryuken M & H remain invincible well past their startup frames, with 7 and 10 frames of invincibility, respectively. Goshoryuken M has a startup time of only 4 frames, which is fairly fast, but Goshoryuken H has an amazingly quick startup time of only 3 frames, making it one of the fastest striking moves in the game and allowing it to punish any move that is -3 or greater!

If Akuma has meter, you can hyper combo cancel Goshoryuken H on the second hit into Tenma-Gozanku Agyo or Ungyo to make it completely safe, giving him an invincible attack that is very difficult for your foes to punish! If your opponent blocks the Goshoryuken, then the hyper combo cancels the recovery period, making Akuma safe; if your adversary is hit, the two attacks combo together, giving Akuma solid damage off a safe and invincible move!

4

Tatsumaki Zankukyaku: This spinning attack doesn't just go through projectiles; it destroys them! Starting from frame 8 and during all active frames, all projectiles that hit Akuma are completely destroyed, allowing Akuma to slice through zoning attacks in an instant!

Tatsumaki Zankukyaku L is safe if guarded to everything but 1 frame command throws and deals 33,000 points of chip damage, making it a powerful pressure tool against opponents, especially when they are in the corner. It's also Akuma's single most damaging attack, so you should use it in combos whenever possible. Tatsumaki Zankukyaku M & H give frame advantage if guarded, but your adversary can punish them by using advancing guard against the second-to-last hit, so be careful when using those moves from midscreen.

If Tatsumaki Zankukyaku M or H hit the target while the opposing character was in the corner, you can immediately go into a combo by hitting the S launcher; the move gives you ample time to verify that the attack hits, then confirm into Akuma's basic aerial combo. Against many characters, you can have Akuma combo into S from midscreen!

5

Air Tatsumaki Zankukyaku: The aerial version of Akuma's powerful Tatsumaki Zankukyaku allows Akuma to easily control space in the air, and it hits on both sides of Akuma, making it an excellent cross-up! Aerial Tatsumaki Zankukyaku also destroys projectiles only 5 frames after you perform the attack, making it an excellent tool for approaching zoning characters.

Like the ground version, air Tatsumaki Zankyaku L deals 110,000 points of damage, making it the most damaging single hit attack that Akuma has, so use it in combos whenever possible.

After performing air Tatsumaki Zankukyaku, Akuma is completely vulnerable until he lands or hyper combo cancels into Tenma-Gozanku Agyo or Ungyo. So when normal jumping at an opponent, use air Tatsumaki Zankukyaku L, and use air Tatsumaki Zankukyaku H when super jumping to make sure Akuma's safety is ensured until he hits the ground.

Hyakki Gosho: One of the three attacks that can only be performed during Hyakkishu, Hyakki Gosho is a short-range overhead punch that ground bounces the target on hit. Of the three Hyakkishu attacks, Hyakki Gosho is the least useful outside of combos because it has very limited range and few active frames.

7

Hyakki Gosho is most useful in combos, where you can use it to ground bounce your competitor. Outside of combos, the best way to use Hyakki Gosho is after an adversary is forced to block a normal jump attack—perform an air basic attack while calling a crossover assist, then cancel the jump attack into Hyakkishu L then Hyakki Gosho. This lets you keep up pressure while performing low-risk mix-ups. Hyakki Gosho is safe on block, allowing you to keep up your offense without risk of punishment!

9

Hyakki Goho: This Hyakkishu attack allows Akuma to throw a fireball in the middle of Hyakkishu simply by pressing Ⓗ. This attack is a major part of Akuma's offense, since it lets him advance under the cover of an air projectile, and if the opposition is forced to block Hyakki Goho, Akuma is at frame advantage! Being a Hyakkishu move, you can alter your gameplan on the fly by using Hyakki Gojin against an adversary trying to dash under Akuma, or by using Hyakki Gosho against a competitor attempting to meet Akuma in the air.

This move is mostly identical to Zanku Hadoken; it inflicts 27,000 points of chip damage when blocked, and Akuma can only throw one per Hyakkishu. After Akuma throws the projectile, he cannot act until he hits the ground, putting him in great peril if your rival evades the projectile.

You can also employ this attack to create two midair projectiles, which can create enough of a wall to stop most characters from destroying Akuma's fireballs! Throw a Zanku Hadoken during a super jump, then perform air Hyakkishu and Hyakki Goho immediately after to rain down Hadokens on your opponent!

Hyakkishu: When you perform this attack, Akuma jumps into the air and is granted access to the three powerful Hyakki attacks. Hyakkishu is primarily a tool to assist Akuma's offense, as he quickly moves forward and at any time can use one of the Hyakki attacks to attack opponents. Hyakkishu can now be performed in the air, which gives Akuma a semi-double jump, as well as the ability to throw two projectiles during a single jump.

6

Hyakkishu L only travels a short distance and is lower than a normal jump. The M version is essentially the same as his normal jump, while the Hyakkishu H travels across half the screen and goes very high, but not quite as high as a super jump. Primarily, you'll want to use Hyakkishu L in close-range situations, and employ Hyakkishu H to advance against zoning characters.

In the air, each Hyakkishu attack travels about half as far and high as the ground versions. As such, air Hyakkishu L barely moves upward at all! When canceled from a jumping attack, the Hyakkishu jump is barely off the ground. Consequently, you can use it in tricky double overhead attacks and can even create entirely unblockable situations with low-hitting crossover assists!

Unlike a normal jump, once Hyakkishu has sent Akuma into the air, he cannot guard and can only perform one of the Hyakki attacks or Tenma-Gozanku Agyo or Ungyo, so be careful when using it in situations where the opposing character can hit Akuma.

Hyakki Gojin: This Hyakkishu attack is an energy-infused dive kick that, unlike Tenmakujinkyaku, is an overhead attack and allows you to combo into additional damage when it hits. Hyakki Gojin is best used in combination with super jumping and using Hyakki Goho; if you think your opponent is going to try to dash under Akuma, use Hyakki Gojin instead of Hyakki Goho to dive down and cut them off!

8

You can also use Hyakki Gojin to extend Akuma's combos, as it is OTG-capable and ground bounces when hitting a grounded foe. You can use this fullscreen and after an air throw, but if it hits your rival just before they're about to stand up, it causes the competitor to ground recover instead of ground bouncing. If this happens, use it as an opportunity to continue attacking your challenger; use the overhead Zugaihasatsu, or cross up your opponent by calling a crossover assist, then switching sides with Ashura Senku!

10

Ashura Senku: Akuma's teleport causes him to quickly move to the left or right, depending on which direction the command is performed. Ashura Senku isn't recommended as an escape tool; while it has only 4 frames of recovery, it has 14 frames of startup, making it easily thwarted when Akuma is on the ground.

When covered by an assist, Ashura Senku becomes a powerful mix-up tool because it allows Akuma to quickly travel through his opponent, making it difficult to see which side of his competitor Akuma is on! Ashura Senku can even travel through an adversary in the corner, and it is a great way to open up the target and land one of Akuma's huge damage combos.

Ashura Senku can be hyper combo canceled at any time, allowing Akuma to teleport close to his foe and then cancel into an inescapable Raging Demon!

Hyper Combos

Screen	Name	Command	Hits	Damage	Startup	Active	Recovery	Advantage on Hit	Advantage if Guarded	Notes
1	Messatsu-Gohado Agyo	↓↙→ + ATK ATK	48~96	285,600~312,900	7+1	76	50	-18	-20	Can be mashed for additional damage, each projectile has 5 high priority durability points
2	Messatsu-Gohado Ungyo	↓↙→ + ATK ATK, hold H (mash ATK after beam begins)	25~50	260,300~312,500	7+1	80	46	—	-34	Knocks down opponent, can be mashed for additional damage, beam durability: 25 frames x 1 high priority durability points
3	Tenma-Gozanku Agyo	(in air) ↓↙→ + ATK ATK	48~96	285,600~342,900	7+2	76	16	-5	+3	Can be mashed for additional damage, each projectile has 5 high priority durability points
4	Tenma-Gozanku Ungyo	(in air) ↓↙→ + ATK ATK, hold H (mash ATK after beam begins)	25~50	260,300~312,500	7+2	80	13	—	-1	Knocks down adversary, can be mashed for additional damage, OTG-capable, beam durability: 25 frames x 1 high priority durability points
5	Messatsu-Goshoryu	→↓↙ + ATK ATK	9	292,000	13+3	14(6)14(6)14	40	-4	-22	Invincible from frames 1-21, knocks down rival
6	Raging Demon (Level 3 Hyper Combo)	L, L, →, M, H	15~30	465,000~510,000	5+0	40	4	—	—	Invincible from frames 1-39, throw attack, hard knockdown, can be mashed for additional hits

Messatsu-Gohado Agyo: During this hyper combo, Akuma unleashes a flurry of high priority projectiles angled to cover most of the screen in front of him! While this hyper combo potentially deals more damage than the Ungyo version and can be mashed for an additional 27,300 damage on top, most of the projectiles miss the opposing character by flying over the foe's head or into the ground.

his hyper combo is useful outside of combos as an approach tool, since the projectiles tay on the screen after Akuma has finished throwing them, allowing him to move in on is competitor under the cover of this hyper combo. Advancing guard can negate the ffectiveness of this technique, but it can be useful in a pinch, especially when Akuma oesn't have assists to help him cross the screen.

Tenma-Gozanku Agyo: The aerial version of Akuma's barrage of projectiles hyper is much more useful than the grounded version, because the spread of projectiles has a much higher chance of connecting with the opposing character and can be mashed for up to 57,300 additional points of damage! Generally, most projectiles will still miss your target, meaning that Tenma-Gozanku Ungyo is recommended in many situations.

This hyper combo really shines in combos, however: Akuma can end an air combo with Tenma-Gozanku Agyo, then tack on an additional Messatsu-Gohado Ungyo or Tenma-Gozanku Ungyo after he lands! For more details on these combos, check the Combo Usage section.

You can also use Tenma-Gozanku Agyo as a close range pressure tool, as Akuma is left at +3 frame advantage after he makes an adversary block this move from up close: make an opponent guard the hyper combo, then perform an aerial mix-up with aerial Hyakkishu!

Messatsu-Goshoryu: This hyper combo is invincible for 21 frames, making it an excellent way to avoid chip damage from a competitor's hyper combos. If an opponent is too close to Akuma when performing a raw hyper combo, immediately perform Messatsu-Goshoryu and blow through their attack. In combos on the ground, Messatsu-Goshoryu generally does less damage than Messatsu-Gohado Ungyo, and many of the hits whiff adversaries who are not on the ground or close to it. Additionally, the move will only fully connect during very specific THCs, making this hyper best used strictly as a counterattack.

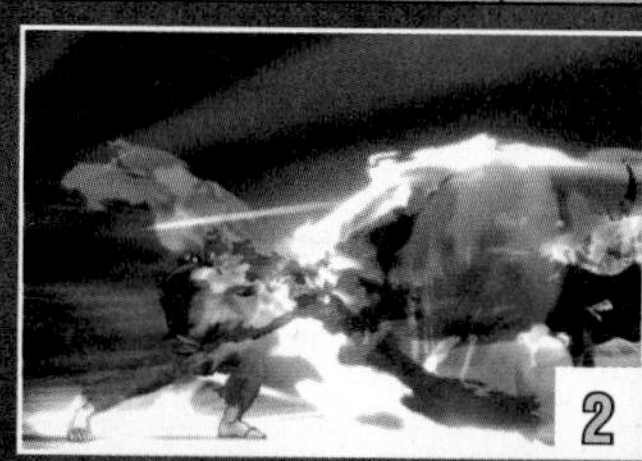

Messatsu-Gohado Ungyo: This hyper combo allows Akuma to shoot a fast, powerful high priority beam across the screen, damaging any adversaries caught in its path. This hyper combo starts up in only 8 frames, allowing Akuma to easily punish projectile-throwing rivals from fullscreen!

Whenever Akuma has meter, opponents should throw projectiles with caution, since Akuma players can easily cancel any move Akuma is performing into Messatsu-Gohado Ungyo and blast through any projectiles on the screen. You can also use this hyper to hit an assist from across the screen; if you see one come out, let this hyper rip! If it hits and Akuma has X-Factor available, cancel into X-Factor and fire off another Messatsu-Gohado Ungyo! This combo does up to 547,500 points of damage at level 1 X-Factor, and when this is combined with the damage bonus against assists, it can sometimes be enough for an instant K.O.!

Be wary of performing this hyper combo close to your opponent in situations where this hyper isn't guaranteed to hit, as it is -34 when guarded. Characters with fast, fullscreen moves like Magneto and Ryu can punish Akuma from fullscreen, but most characters will be able to punish it if they're close!

Tenma-Gozanku Ungyo: The aerial version of Akuma's beam hyper combo fires downwards at an angle and is OTG-capable, making it a very useful tool in Akuma's offense. It can also be mashed for an additional 52,200 points of damage, it does solid chip damage, and leaves Akuma at only a -1 frame disadvantage after it's over, making it completely safe! Since Tenma-Gozanku Ungyo only covers a small portion of the screen, characters with horizontally aimed projectile hyper combos like Taskmaster and Ryu can easily hit Akuma during the middle of the hyper combo, so take special care when playing against those characters.

Raging Demon: This level 3 hyper is an incredibly fast moving throw that can be mashed for an additional 45,000 damage, for a grand total of 510,000 damage! If you perform this hyper fairly close to your rival, the opposing character will be unable to escape, giving Akuma big guaranteed damage! Raging Demon is also invincible for 39 frames, so you can utilize it to blow through enemy attacks.

When performing this attack, make sure not to hit your opponent with an attack while entering the inputs; if your competitor is hit before Raging Demon is performed, they can easily jump away from the attack, rendering the attack useless. Raging Demon can also be used in THCs to catch blocking foes off guard; use an advancing hyper combo like Spencer's Bionic Arm to get close to the opponent, and at the last second, THC into Raging Demon for a gimmicky trick!

Battle Plan

Akuma's Tatsumaki Zankukyaku assist can completely negate projectiles, opening up space to start the attack!

Tatsumaki Zankukyaku can hit opponents from behind, effectively trapping your foe in the corner.

While Akuma can be a strong point character worth building a team around, he really shines on a team that takes advantage of his excellent Tatsumaki Zankukyaku assist. This assist maintains the properties of Akuma's Tatsumaki Zankukyaku M, which is already a powerful advancing tool in its own right!

Akuma—β's Tatsumaki Zankukyaku assist is versatile enough to be used in all stages of the game, from at long range to close up. From long range, calling Akuma at the right time can completely pierce through a zoning opponent's projectile attacks. Akuma isn't invincible when he comes out; even though his assist can destroy projectiles, if Akuma contacts a projectile attack before the attack comes out, he'll simply get hit and return to the bench. To use Akuma effectively, wait for a break in your competitor's zoning; every zoning character has a gap in their projectiles at some point. If Akuma is safely out and performing Tatsumaki Zankukyaku, your adversary can only hit Akuma with a projectile hyper combo, allowing your point character to dash in and close the distance.

Akuma should be called very carefully against characters like Taskmaster and Ryu who can cancel their projectiles immediately into their long range hyper combos. Tatsumaki Zankukyaku will only destroy low and medium priority projectiles, so characters who can quickly hyper combo cancel into projectile hyper combos can seriously damage Akuma. Akuma only has 750,000 health, making him one of the most fragile characters; an errant assist call can potentially get him eliminated in one combo.

At mid range, you can use Akuma's assist to simply take up most of the screen, since it stays on the screen for a long time and hits both in front of and behind Akuma. Characters attempting to jump over Akuma generally get hit in the back by Tatsumaki Zankukyaku, which allows nearly every character to land a huge combo. Also, if an opponent is forced to guard Akuma, he creates a golden opportunity for you to immediately launch an offensive; the three hits of Tatsumaki Zankukyaku place your rival in a surprisingly long amount of guardstun, during which advancing guard is ineffective. Capitalize on this by dashing in and using any mix-up attacks your character may have, such as overheads or cross-ups!

The Tatsumaki Zankukyaku is even more effective when directly integrated into a mix-up. Calling Akuma—β first, then using a quick side-switching special move like teleports or Wolverine's Berserker Slash can be a nightmare for the opposing player to defend against: Akuma makes contact with the enemy immediately after your point character has switched sides, scoring a hit unless your opponent was guarding in the opposite direction! Akuma then proceeds to hit three times with Tatsumaki Zankukyaku, giving you plenty of time to capitalize with a juggle combo. Akuma—β's assist is also great for turning quick overhead attacks into combo opportunities, but this is more difficult midscreen, because Akuma often carries your rival's character a long distance away.

You can also use Akuma's Tatsumaki Zankukyaku assist to extend many characters' combos, since it hits for a long time, letting you combo from things that normally have too much recovery, like Wolverine's Berserker Slash and Zero's Sentsuizan. The assist also only hits three times, which lessens the damage and hitstun scaling incurred by successive attacks!

Akuma can keep the pressure on by jumping over projectiles and firing one of his own!

Throw a Zanku Hadoken while super jumping, then immediately perform Tenmakujinkyaku to quickly approach fullscreen opponents!

When you are forced to fight with Akuma, you should try to get him in close as quickly as possible. Stuck in a long range firefight, Akuma doesn't have the arsenal he needs to compete against more dedicated projectile throwers, and most characters can quickly close the distance against him and put him on the defensive. Gohadoken only has 5 low priority durability points, which is only useful against characters who can't overpower them, like Rocket Raccoon or Zero, as well as against characters without advanced movement options, such as Haggar and Frank West. The recovery on Gohadoken is fairly long, however, making it easy for characters to slowly put Akuma on the defensive by jumping over them. If Akuma is forced into a firefight, try to catch your adversary and their assist on screen at the same time with the Messatsu-Gohado Ungyo beam hyper combo; chances are you can catch both of them at the same time, inflicting massive damage to the assist. Even if it doesn't K.O. the assist, it'll do considerable damage, which should keep them on the bench for long enough that they won't be a problem for a few precious seconds.

If you must play Akuma on point, try to pair him up with a crossover assist with slow-moving projectiles: Sentinel—α, Rocket Raccoon—α, or Arthur—β are all great choices. These types of assists not only bolster Akuma's long range game, they also function as covering fire to allow Akuma to quickly close the distance and place his foe in long enough guardstun to set up easy mix-ups. Characters with fullscreen hyper combos make good partners for Akuma in general: he will often be hitting with beam hyper combos from fullscreen, and these characters can be used in THCs for extra assist-destroying potential.

In most situations, Zanku Hadoken and Hyakki Goho prove more useful than Akuma's ground projectile, as it allows him to remain mobile while tossing fireballs. Having Akuma jump forward while tossing projectiles is a great way to safely gain distance on your opponent; the fireballs effectively act as a shield from the front, making this difficult for foes to stop by conventional means. From farther away, you can advance a much longer distance by using Hyakkishu H immediately followed by Hyakki Goho. Making contact with a projectile leaves Akuma with a huge amount of frame advantage; if Akuma is close enough, you'll be able to immediately dash in and perform a mix-up, or start a combo if the fireball hits the opposing character! When attacking your challenger with aerial projectiles, be sure to use the proper versions of the attacks so as to not toss a fireball behind the opponent; Akuma is vulnerable after an aerial projectile all the way until he reaches the ground, allowing for an easy combo for your adversary. To help mitigate this, play it safe and use weaker versions of Zanku Hadoken or Hyakkishu. This can still be thwarted if your foe dashes forward unexpectedly, moving clear under both Akuma and his projectile and leaving him open for a combo. To prevent this, use Tenmakujinkyaku or Hyakki Gojin: Akuma abruptly dives straight down onto his rival and cuts them off, allowing for a big combo!

Some characters with high-powered projectile attacks can make it very difficult for you to have Akuma bully his way in with aerial projectiles. Against these characters, try changing the angle of your approach: super jump forward and use Zanku Hadoken L on the way up to cover your descent. This tactic completely bypasses any ground control your competitor possesses and forces them to change up their game. The Zanku Hadoken will also have recovered well before Akuma lands, allowing you to perform a Tatsumaki Zankukyaku L on the way down to hit opponents trying to dash under Akuma. This tactic still allows your rival to get away from the corner by dashing under Akuma, so you'll want to omit the aerial projectile and drop down with Tenmakujinkyaku at times.

Once Akuma has reached midscreen, you can start mixing in aerial Tatsumaki Zankukyaku along with Zanku Hadoken; normal jump forward and press ⇨ + H + P1 or P2 to simultaneously perform an air throw attempt, an air H basic attack, and a crossover assist. Immediately after the kick extends, cancel into air Tatsumaki Zankukyaku H to complete the option-select: you'll get an air throw if your opponent is near and a combo if air H hits your rival out of a jump. Grounded competitors are then typically forced to guard the Tatsumaki Zankukyaku, then the crossover assist. This allows you to quickly have Akuma dash in and perform a mix-up! Even better, when this tactic is used from up close, the Tatsumaki Zankukyaku crosses up your challenger!

Akuma can teleport behind his opponent while calling an assist to create a cross-up that is very difficult for foes to block.

You can use Aerial Hyakkishu very low to the ground, and when combined with a low-hitting crossover assist, you can set up completely unblockable situations!

If you can manage to get Akuma up close to his opponent, there are many tools you can use to have Akuma mix up his rival and open them up for huge damage. His easiest mix-up involves using his quick Zugaihasatsu overhead, which hits twice and chains directly into the S launcher for a combo. While the S launcher is completely safe if guarded, an opponent using advancing guard against Zugaihasatsu causes the launcher to completely whiff, leaving Akuma wide open. To prevent this, simply verify that the two hits of the overhead are hitting before you chain into S! If Zugaihasatsu is blocked, cancel into Tatsumaki Zankukyaku M. It's +3 advantage on block, and you can utilize it to keep pressure on your adversary. You can also tack on an S launcher against any character if it hits in the corner!

A competitor making use of advancing guard can easily put a stop to Akuma's offense, forcing you to begin the approach process over from the beginning. To defeat advancing guard, use delayed crouching L attacks spaced farther apart than what you may be accustomed to; opponents trying to use advancing guard against single L attacks will likely mistime it, instead getting a crouching H attack. This then gets counterhit by your crouching L attacks, allowing you to convert into Akuma's massively damaging combos.

By using Akuma's Ashura Senku while calling an assist, Akuma can quickly cross up his opponent, opening them up for a combo. Use any assist that covers the ground horizontally, including assists that Akuma can use to close distance like Doctor Doom's Plasma Beam and Rocket Raccoon's Spitfire Twice! Simply call the assist before performing Ashura Senku; if it hits, you can easily convert the assist's hit into a juggle combo, and if it's blocked, Akuma generally remains covered by the assist with frame advantage, allowing you to keep up your offense. If blocked, try to slip in Zugaihasatsu while your competitor is blocking the assist! Ashura Senku has considerable startup and is vulnerable for 14 frames before Akuma teleports through his target, and it only travels across half the screen, so make sure your adversary isn't in position to hit Akuma out of Ashura Senku's startup.

To counter opponents trying to jump away from your offense, use the aforementioned air ⇨ + H + P1 or P2 CANCEL Tatsumaki Zankukyaku H option select: scoring an air throw in this manner is great, but a wrong guess still results in a cross-up situation that also forces your foe to guard your assist. Proceed to go right into another mix-up!

If your rival is intent on staying on the ground, jump forward and attack with a late air S canceled into air Hyakkishu L, then use Hyakki Gosho. The L version of air Hyakkishu causes Akuma to perform a very short hop, allowing you to perform a very quick double overhead! If combined with Wesker's low-hitting assist Samurai Edge (Lower Short), you can create a very quick completely unblockable setup with Akuma! Simply call Wesker the same time S is pressed, then cancel into Hyakkishu L to open up any grounded foe!

"I SEEK THE ULTIMATE POWER! I WILL NOT BE STOPPED BY MERE MORTALS!"

COMBO USAGE

I. CR. Ⓛ, ST. Ⓗ, → + Ⓗ, DASH, CR. Ⓜ, ST. Ⓗ, Ⓢ CANCEL SUPER JUMP, AIR Ⓜ, Ⓜ, Ⓗ, Ⓢ, ← ↓ ↙ + ATK CANCEL (DURING HYAKKISHU) Ⓜ, DASH, CR. Ⓗ, Ⓢ CANCEL SUPER JUMP, AIR Ⓜ, Ⓜ, Ⓗ CANCEL AIR ↓ ↙ ← + Ⓛ CANCEL ↓ ↘ → + ATK ATK (HOLD Ⓗ) MASH ATK

706,700 damage, 12% meter gain

After the first launcher, stagger the timing of the air Ⓜ, Ⓜ, Ⓗ, Ⓢ chain to make sure Akuma lands shortly after the opponent. This gives you more time to hit with the Hyakki Gojin. Performing Hyakkishu in the air makes it significantly easier to ground bounce your adversary in time.

You'll need to be able to judge the distance after inflicting the hard knockdown— in the corner, Hyakkishu L works all the time, but at midscreen, you'll generally need to use Hyakkishu M, which involves stricter timing. If the Hyakki Gojin hits too late, Akuma does not ground bounce the opposing character.

II. (CORNER REQUIRED) CR. Ⓛ, ST. Ⓗ, → + Ⓗ, CR. Ⓜ, ST. Ⓗ, → + Ⓗ CANCEL ↓ ↙ ← + Ⓛ CANCEL CR. Ⓜ, CR. Ⓗ, Ⓢ CANCEL SUPER JUMP, AIR Ⓜ, Ⓜ, Ⓗ, Ⓢ, ← ↓ ↙ + Ⓛ CANCEL (DURING HYAKKISHU) Ⓜ, CR. Ⓗ, Ⓢ CANCEL SUPER JUMP, AIR Ⓗ CANCEL ↓ ↙ ← + Ⓛ CANCEL ↓ ↘ → + ATK ATK (HOLD Ⓗ) MASH ATK

746,400 damage, 31% meter gain

This combo adds more hits in the corner, but it is slightly more difficult. Cancel the second Senpukyaku into Tatsumaki Zankukyaku as quickly as possible to give yourself enough time to juggle the crouching Ⓜ attack.

III. → + Ⓜ, Ⓢ CANCEL SUPER JUMP, AIR Ⓜ, Ⓜ, Ⓗ, Ⓢ, ← ↓ ↙ + Ⓗ CANCEL (DURING HYAKKISHU) Ⓜ, DASH, CR. Ⓗ, Ⓢ CANCEL SUPER JUMP, AIR Ⓜ, Ⓜ, Ⓗ CANCEL ↓ ↙ ← + Ⓛ CANCEL ↓ ↘ → + ATK ATK (HOLD Ⓗ) MASH ATK

631,600 damage, 12% meter loss

This combo hits directly off Akuma's Zugaihasatsu overhead.

Zugaihasatsu chains directly into the Ⓢ launcher and is two hits, giving you ample time to verify that the overhead is hitting before you go chain into the launcher.

IV. BACKWARDS OR FORWARDS AIR THROW, AIR ← ↓ ↙ + Ⓛ CANCEL (DURING HYAKKISHU) Ⓜ, DASH, CR. Ⓜ, CR. Ⓗ, → + Ⓗ, Ⓢ CANCEL SUPER JUMP, AIR Ⓜ, Ⓜ, Ⓗ, Ⓢ, ← ↓ ↙ + Ⓛ CANCEL (DURING HYAKKISHU) Ⓜ

264,900 damage, 67% meter gain

This combo costs no meter, so you should use it whenever Akuma needs to conserve or build meters for other characters on his team.

Any Akuma combo can be ended with a second OTG Hyakki Gojin to conserve meter. You can add a hyper combo to this combo by replacing the final Ⓢ with air Tatsumaki Zankukyaku L into Tenma-Gozanku Ungyo, for a total of 465,200 points of damage but a 38% loss in meter.

Ending the combo with Hyakki Gojin causes your opponent to instantly ground recover, giving you a chance to mix your rival up and catch them off guard with Zugaihasatsu or an Ashura Senku with assist cross-up!

V. CR. Ⓛ, ST. Ⓗ, → + Ⓗ, DASH, CR. Ⓜ, ST. Ⓗ, Ⓢ CANCEL SUPER JUMP, AIR Ⓜ, Ⓜ, Ⓗ, Ⓢ, ← ↓ ↙ + ATK CANCEL (DURING HYAKKISHU) Ⓜ, DASH, CR. Ⓗ, Ⓢ CANCEL SUPER JUMP, AIR Ⓜ, Ⓜ, Ⓗ CANCEL AIR ↓ ↙ ← + Ⓛ CANCEL ↓ ↘ → + ATK ATK MASH ATK, AIR ↓ ↘ → + Ⓗ, LAND ↓ ↘ → + ATK ATK (HOLD Ⓗ) MASH ATK

879,100 damage, 75% meter loss

This combo uses two hyper combos and does incredible damage, enough to knock out many characters in the game without the use of an assist!

This combo won't work if your opponent is in the corner after the Hyakki Gojin OTG, or if Akuma is just outside of the corner. To get your adversary out of the corner, perform Hyakkishu immediately after landing; Akuma hits the target with Hyakki Gojin and then lands on the other side of his foe, letting you finish the combo.

If Hyakki Gojin doesn't switch sides with the opposing character, you must perform a slightly different combo, which can be found in the Combo Appendix.

ADVANCED TACTICS

WHO NEEDS FRIENDS, ANYWAY?

To turn the tables, look for opportunities to blast both the point and assist character with Messatsu-Gohado Ungyo, then activate X-Factor and do it again!

While Akuma—β is a very powerful assist, that also means he's going to be in situations where he'll have to fight by himself with no crossover assists once his teammates are gone.

Unless you have a guaranteed chance to knock out a character with a combo, it's generally best to save X-Factor until Akuma's by himself; if the only way to save a character is by activating level 2 X-Factor to avoid chip damage, it's probably best to let that character get knocked out so Akuma can use X-Factor level 3 by himself.

Once Akuma is in X-Factor, you should use Tatsumaki Zankukyaku L fairly liberally, as it's incredibly fast, completely safe on block, inflicts 58,500 points of chip damage, and can lead to massive damage on hit. Tatsumaki Zankukyaku L combos into itself at X-Factor level 3, allowing you to connect up to eight in a single combo for 1,111,600 points of damage, which is enough to take out almost every character in the game! Against Thor, Haggar, Tron, and Nemesis T-Type, cancel the eighth Tatsumaki Zankukyaku L into Tenma-Gozanku Agyo to finish them off, dealing a total of 1,503,500 damage!

Once you've scared your challenger into blocking Tatsumaki Zankukyaku, look for a chance to dash in and throw out Zugaihasatsu, which is incredibly fast at X-Factor level 3 and can lead into an instant-knockout combo!

It's very common for your opponent to try to jump away in the face of an angry level 3 X-Factor Akuma. Be ready to switch it up and go for an air throw by using option-select air ⇨ + Ⓗ canceled into Tatsumaki Zankukyaku H!

If chasing down your rival is proving difficult, you may want to simply try to chip them into oblivion with multiple beam hyper combos; during X-Factor level 3, each beam hyper combo guarded results in 285,700 points of damage! Just be sure not to get punished; if your adversary's character is capable of punishing the ground version of the beam, you'll have to stick with the aerial version.

It's best to hold off on activating X-Factor as long as possible and look for a chance to connect with Messatsu-Gohado Ungyo. If it hits, or hits an assist, activate and then immediately throw out another Messatsu-Gohadou Ungyo, which will be a combo against both your opponent's point character and their assist. This deals 598,000 damage to the point character and 898,500 damage to the assist; enough to instantly knock out most assists!

UNLEASH THE POWER OF THE RAGING DEMON!

Raging Demon is completely invincible for 39 frames, allowing Akuma to blow through many attacks in the game!

Akuma's Raging Demon level 3 hyper combo is a throw that moves forward, and if performed close to an opposing character who isn't in the air, it cannot be avoided once the hyper combo has been performed. Properly used, it can be extremely effective not only as a throw, but also as a mix-up tool!

Raging Demon is completely invulnerable for 39 frames and travels across almost the entire screen, allowing it to beat nearly any move on the ground, including long range attacks like Doctor Doom's Plasma Beam and Magneto's Electromagnetic Disruptor!

When playing with Akuma and his teammates, you can also set up Raging Demon in several ways that are guaranteed to catch an adversary off guard the first time they see it. You can even create inescapable set-ups using THC: perform a hyper combo that moves directly to your competitor, like Spencer's Bionic Arm; if your rival blocks it, wait a moment, then THC into an inescapable Raging Demon! If your opponent avoids a hyper combo like Ryu's Shinku Hadoken, cancel into Raging Demon and punish the target for trying to punish you!

Since Akuma can hyper combo cancel his Ashura Senku, you can have him teleport through his challenger and then hyper combo cancel to an inescapable Raging Demon. This is great to use against new characters entering the playing field!

A flashy way to land a Raging Demon is to hyper combo cancel the startup frames of Zugaihasatsu: chain basic attacks into the overhead, then quickly input the Raging Demon command before the Zugaihatsu hits your rival. This is for style points more than anything—performing chains of basic attacks gets you pushed away by advancing guard more often than not.

After hitting Raging Demon, Akuma is left at extreme frame advantage. As long as you can guess the direction your adversary will ground recover, you can immediately follow the Raging Demon with an easy mix-up: dash in the direction of your foe, call a crossover assist, then immediately perform Ashura Senku to cross up, Zugaihasatsu to hit overhead, or crouching Ⓛ to hit low.

COMBO APPENDIX

GENERAL EXECUTION TIPS

- Perform OTG Hyakki Gojin as fast as possible to combo.
- When performing Raging Demon, be sure not to press Ⓜ before ⇨ ; perform the motion slowly and deliberately
- OTG Hyakki Gojin in the corner will switch sides unless you backdash before inputting Hyakkishu

CR. Ⓛ, ST. Ⓗ, ⇨ + Ⓗ, DASH, CR. Ⓜ, ST. Ⓗ, Ⓢ CANCEL SUPER JUMP, AIR Ⓜ, Ⓜ, Ⓗ, Ⓢ, ⇦⇩⇙ + ATK CANCEL (DURING HYAKKISHU) Ⓜ, DASH, CR. Ⓗ, Ⓢ CANCEL SUPER JUMP, AIR Ⓜ, Ⓜ, Ⓗ CANCEL AIR ⇩⇙⇦ + Ⓛ CANCEL ⇩⇘⇨ + ATK ATK MASH ATK, Ⓢ, LAND, AIR ⇩⇘⇨ + ATK ATK (HOLD Ⓗ) MASH ATK

Notes	Damage
Akuma two hyper combo corner variation. Ⓢ must be pressed immediately after the first hyper is performed. OTG with second hyper combo!	870,600

(CORNER REQUIRED) CR. Ⓛ, ST. Ⓗ, ⇨ + Ⓗ, ⇦⇩⇙ + Ⓛ CANCEL (DURING HYAKKISHU) Ⓛ, {JUMP Ⓜ, Ⓗ, Ⓢ CANCEL AIR ⇩⇘⇨ + Ⓛ} X 2, JUMP Ⓜ, Ⓗ, Ⓢ CANCEL AIR ⇩⇙⇦ + Ⓛ, LAND Ⓢ CANCEL SUPER JUMP, AIR Ⓜ, Ⓗ CANCEL AIR ⇩⇙⇦ + Ⓛ CANCEL AIR ⇩⇘⇨ + ATK ATK MASH ATK, Ⓢ, LAND, AIR ⇩⇘⇨ + ATK ATK (HOLD Ⓗ) MASH ATK

Notes	Damage
Outside of the corner, start with cr. Ⓛ, st. Ⓜ, repeat the rest of the combo	975,700

(X-FACTOR 3) {⇩⇙⇦ + Ⓛ} X 7, ⇩⇙⇦ + Ⓛ CANCEL ⇩⇘⇨ + ATK ATK MASH ATK

Notes	Damage
Without hyper combo, deals 1,111,600 damage; add on hyper to knock out characters with more health than that	1,503,500

AMATERASU

"NO TIME TO LICK YOUR WOUNDS, AMMY. WE HAVE TO FIND OROCHI!"

Bio

REAL NAME

Amaterasu Okami

OCCUPATION

Sun God

ABILITIES

Amaterasu is able to perform 13 types of miracles with the Celestial Brush. She also wields three divine weapons.

WEAPONS

Amaterasu employs three divine weapons: the Thunder Edge, the Devout Beads, and the Solar Flare. Each weapon possesses unique attributes, giving Amaterasu a variety of options in battle.

PROFILE

100 years ago, Amaterasu sealed away True Orochi but lost her physical form due to injuries sustained in battle. Her spirit was contained within a statue, and she was later resurrected, although without her Celestial Brush powers. She began a journey to restore beauty to Nippon while regaining her powers. To the average person, she appears as an ordinary wolf.

FIRST APPEARANCE

Okami (2006)

POWER GRID

7	INTELLIGENCE
1	STRENGTH
3	SPEED
3	STAMINA
6	ENERGY PROJECTION
5	FIGHTING ABILITY

*This is biographical, and does not represent an evaluation of the in-game combat potential of this hero.

ALTERNATE COSTUMES

1

2

3

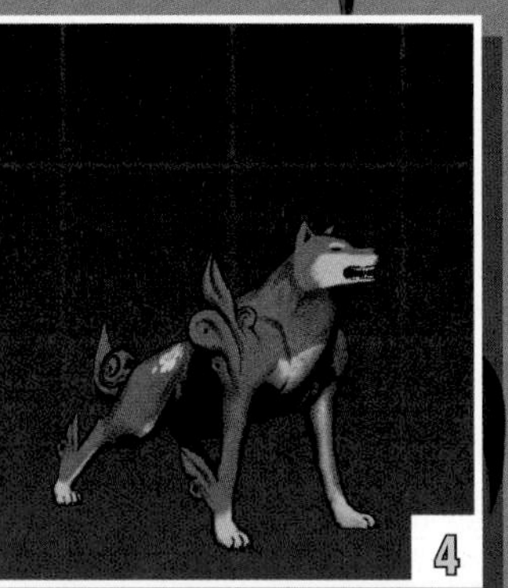
4

5

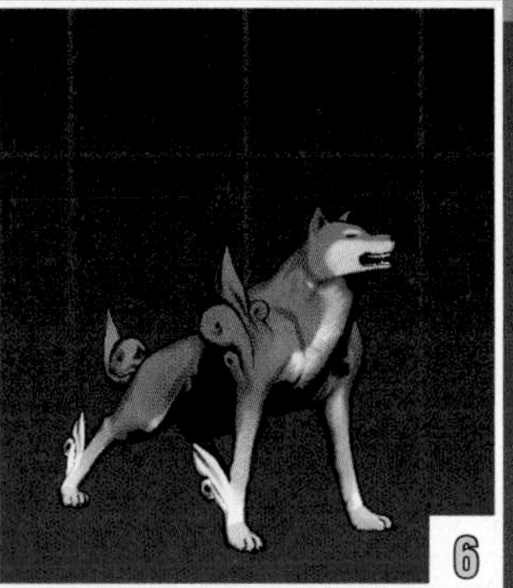
6

DLC

Overview

Vitality	800,000
Chain Combo Archetype	Marvel Series

X-Factor Boost	Damage	Speed
Level 1 (3 teammates remaining)	120%	120%
Level 2 (2 teammates remaining)	140%	130%
Level 3 (1 teammate remaining)	160%	140%

Amaterasu is a versatile character who can adapt to any situation on the fly. She is a powerhouse on both offense and defense, and she can effectively run away from danger, as well! Ultimately, your goal with Amaterasu is to push your competitor into the corner. Amaterasu benefits from a cornered opponent because:

- The pressure that Amaterasu can put on her rivals during Solar Flare mode is even more difficult to deal with when they are in the corner
- She has extended combo potential in the corner
- Her airdash covers a lengthy distance, making it easier to move back in after being pushed out with advancing guard

You can achieve this goal by:

- Pushing opposing characters into the corner with offensive pressure stemming from standing Ⓜ
- Keeping her offense going by using her airdash
- Using Thunder Edge L and her various versions of air Ⓗ to force adversaries into the corner

TUNING SINCE ORIGINAL MVC3

Amaterasu can no longer guard during her airdash. Competitors can be more prepared, knowing she doesn't have an option besides attacking. This should encourage Amaterasu players to be more measured, and less reckless, feinting airdashes often by jumping at full screen, airdashing, then immediately falling to earth with air Ⓗ. This places the vine graphic over the screen, the visual signal an Ammy airdash is coming, but she'll still be at full screen. The more often you do this, the more often you'll actually get to airdash in when you don't fake it. In addition, the hitstun on her attacks have been reduced overall. Some of her old combos no longer work properly as a result, such as Thunder Edge instant overhead air Ⓛ to ↘ + Ⓗ. Amaterasu also receives an indirect buff, since X-Factor now provides her a speed boost!

- Amaterasu can now use Weapon Change in the air.
- Amaterasu is now unable to block during the duration of her airdash.
- Standing Ⓛ is now -1 frame advantage on hit/block from +1/0
- Standing Ⓜ is now -1 frame advantage on hit/block from +1/-1.
- Standing Ⓗ (Solar Flare) is now +2 frame advantage on hit from +4.
- Standing Ⓗ (Thunder Edge) is now +1 frame advantage on hit from +3.
- Standing Ⓗ (Devout Beads) is now -9 frame advantage on hit from -7.
- Crouching Ⓛ is now -2 frame advantage on hit/block from 0/-1.
- Crouching Ⓜ has 3 more active frames and 3 less recovery frames.
- Crouching Ⓜ is now -1 frame advantage on hit from +1.
- Power Slash is now +6 frame advantage on hit from +8.
- Hitstun on air ↘ + Ⓗ has been reduced; canceling into Glaive Chop on a grounded opponent will no longer combo.

Attack Set

Standing Basic Attacks

Screen	Command	Hits	Damage	Meter Gain	Startup	Active	Recovery	Advantage on Hit	Advantage if Guarded	Notes
1	Standing Ⓛ	1	30,000	240	3	2	11	-1	-1	—
2	Standing Ⓜ	1	50,000	400	6	6	12	-1	-1	—
3	(With Solar Flare) Standing Ⓗ	1	60,000	480	8	4	16	+2	+2	Jump- cancelable
4	(With Thunder Edge) Standing Ⓗ	1	80,000	640	13	4	17	+1	+1	—
5	(With Devout Beads) Standing Ⓗ	4	79,500	800	15	4	30	-9	-9	—

Crouching Basic Attacks

Screen	Command	Hits	Damage	Meter Gain	Startup	Active	Recovery	Advantage on Hit	Advantage if Guarded	Notes
1	Crouching Ⓛ	1	28,000	224	4	2	12	-2	-2	Low attack
2	Crouching Ⓜ	1	50,000	400	7	6	12	-1	-1	Low attack
3	(With Solar Flare) Crouching Ⓗ	1	60,000	480	9	4	16	—	+2	Low attack, knocks down, jump- cancelable
4	(With Thunder Edge) Crouching Ⓗ	1	80,000	640	13	4	19	—	-1	Low attack, knocks down
5	(With Devout Beads) Crouching Ⓗ	4	79,500	800	13	4	26	—	-5	Low attack, knocks down

Ground Special Attack—Launcher

Screen	Command	Hits	Damage	Meter Gain	Startup	Active	Recovery	Advantage on Hit	Advantage if Guarded	Notes
1	Ⓢ (while standing or crouching)	1	70,000	560	7	6	18	—	-2	Launcher, not special- or hyper combo-cancelable

Air Basic Attacks

Screen	Command	Hits	Damage	Meter Gain	Startup	Active	Recovery	Advantage on Hit	Advantage if Guarded	Notes
1	Air Ⓛ	1	35,000	280	4	4	14	+8	+8	Overhead attack
2	Air Ⓜ	1	48,000	384	7	3	20	+13	+13	Overhead attack
3	(With Solar Flare) Air Ⓗ	1	60,000	480	9	5	20	+17	+17	Overhead attack
4	(With Thunder Edge) Air Ⓗ	1	90,000	720	17	4	17	+17	+17	Overhead attack
	(With Thunder Edge) hold air Ⓗ	1	110,000	880	36	4	17	—	+17	Overhead attack, , can cause multiple ground bounces in one combo
5	(With Devout Beads) Air Ⓗ	4	79,500	800	18	5	18	+17	+17	Overhead attack

Air Special Attacks—Flying Screen and Air Exchange

Air Ⓢ causes a hard knockdown when used in a launcher combo (this is sometimes called flying screen). When used outside of a launcher combo, air Ⓢ behaves mostly like another basic attack. Air exchange attacks, performed by inputting a direction plus Ⓢ, are only possible during a launcher combo. Exchange hits initiate team aerial combos by tagging in the next available character to continue the air combo.

Screen	Command	Hits	Damage	Meter Gain	Startup	Active	Recovery	Advantage on Hit	Advantage if Guarded	Notes
1	Air Ⓢ	1	70,000	560	11	3	22	+14	+14	Knocks down, causes hard knockdown if used in launcher combo
2	Air ⇧ + Ⓢ (during launcher combo)	2	105,00	880	13	—	Until grounded	—	—	Tags in next available ally while lofting opponent upward, projectile has 10 durability points and lasts for 30 frames
	Air ⇨ or ⇦ + Ⓢ (during launcher combo)	2	95,000	800	13	—	Until grounded	—	—	Tags in next available ally while causing wall bounce, erases 1 hyper meter bar from foe, projectile has 10 durability points and lasts for 30 frames
	Air ⇩ + Ⓢ (during launcher combo)	2	95,000	800	13	—	Until grounded	—	—	Tags in next available ally while causing ground bounce, generates 1 hyper meter bar, projectile has 10 durability points and lasts for 30 frames

1

2

Command Attacks

Command attacks resemble basic attacks but have different chaining and canceling properties. It's usually possible to chain *into* a command attack from basic attacks, but most command attacks cannot be chained from or canceled themselves.

Screen	Name	Command	Hits	Damage	Meter Gain	Startup	Active	Recovery	Advantage on Hit	Advantage if Guarded	Notes
1	Reflector Chain Combo Ichi	(With Solar Flare) ⇨ + Ⓗ	1	60,000	480	12	4	18	0	0	Chains into Ⓢ
	Reflector Chain Combo Ni	(during Reflector Chain Combo Ichi on contact) ⇨ + Ⓗ	1	60,000	480	12	4	19	-1	-1	Chains into Ⓢ
	Reflector Chain Combo San	(during Reflector Chain Combo Ni on contact) ⇨ + Ⓗ	1	60,000	480	12	4	19	-1	-1	Chains into Ⓢ
	Reflector Chain Combo Shi	(during Reflector Chain Combo San on contact) ⇨ + Ⓗ	1	60,000	480	12	4	20	-2	-2	Chains into Ⓢ
	Solar Flare Attack	(during Reflector Chain Combo Shi on contact) ⇨ + Ⓗ	1	60,000	480	12	4	21	-3	-3	Chains into Ⓢ
2	Glaive Chain Combo Ichi (can be charged)	(With Thunder Edge) ⇨ + Ⓗ	1	80,000/ 100,000	640/ 800	14/47	5	18/17	-1/+28	-1/0	Staggers when fully charged
	Glaive Chain Combo Ni (can be charged)	(during Glaive Chain Combo Ichi on contact) ⇨ + Ⓗ	1	80,000/ 100,000	640/I 800	15/47	5	17	0/+25	0	Staggers when fully charged
	Glaive Chain Combo San (can be charged)	(during Glaive Chain Combo Ni on contact) ⇨ + Ⓗ	1	80,000/ 100,000	640/ 800	15/47	5	17	0/+25	00	Staggers when fully charged
	Thunder Edge Slash (can be charged)	(during Glaive Chain Combo San on contact) ⇨ + Ⓗ	1	80,000/ 100,000	640/ 800	15/47	5	18	—	-1	Knocks down, staggers when fully charged
3	Rosary Chain Combo Ichi	(With Devout Beads) ⇨ + Ⓗ	4	79,500	800	17	5	27	-4	-11	—
	Rosary Chain Combo Ni	(during Rosary Chain Combo Ichi on contact) ⇨ + Ⓗ	4	79,500	800	17	5	21	+2	-5	—
	Rosary Chain Combo San	(during Rosary Chain Combo Ni on contact) ⇨ + Ⓗ	4	79,500	800	17	5	21	+2	-5	—
	Rosary Chain Combo Shi	(during Rosary Chain Combo San on contact) ⇨ + Ⓗ	4	79,500	800	17	5	22	+1	-6	—
	Devout Beads Whip	(during Rosary Chain Combo Shi on contact) ⇨ + Ⓗ	4	79,500	800	17	5	23	—	-7	Knocks down
4	Thunder Edge Stab (can be charged)	(With Thunder Edge, in air) ⇙ + Ⓗ	1	90,000/ 120,000	720/960	11/43	Until contact with ground	43	-22/+6	-22	Staggers when fully charged, can be canceled into aerial special attacks

1

2

3

4

Attack Set continued

Throws

Throws are for snagging passive or blocking opponents. Since throws are active so quickly, you can also use them to preemptively toss opposing characters out of their offense. Combos are usually possible after throws, one way or another.

Screen	Command	Hits	Damage	Meter Gain	Startup	Active	Notes
1	→ + Ⓗ (ground)	2	80,000	800	1	1	Hard knockdown
	← + Ⓗ (ground)	2	80,000	800	1	1	Hard knockdown
2	→ + Ⓗ (air)	2	80,000	800	1	1	Hard knockdown
	← + Ⓗ (air)	2	80,000	800	1	1	Hard knockdown

As a Partner—Crossover Assists

Screen	Type	P1+P2 Crossover Combination Hyper Combo	Description	Hits	Damage	Meter Gain	Startup	Active	Recovery (this crossover assist)	Recovery (other partner)	Notes
1	Amaterasu —α	Okami Shuffle	Solar Flare	—	—	—	31	24	96	66	Nullifies certain beam attacks, reflects low priority projectiles
2	Amaterasu —β	Okami Shuffle	Cold Star	8	113,600	1280	42	8(9)43	125	95	Each projectile has 1 low priority durability point
3	Amaterasu —γ	Okami Shuffle	Bloom	—	—	3000	25	—	180	150	—

Amaterasu's vitality is below average, so special care must be taken when using her crossover assists. Amaterasu—α Solar Flare's usefulness as a crossover assist is diminished because Amaterasu appears behind the point character rather than the front. Amaterasu—γ Bloom is a rare crossover assist type that grants a boost of 30% hyper combo gauge bar every time it is used. It can be useful on teams that can effectively utilize hyper combo meter, but its speed leaves something to be desired compared to the similar Morrigan—γ. Amaterasu—β Cold Star is by far her most useful crossover assist. Amaterasu performs Cold Star Ⓗ when summoned, making it more difficult to punish than her other two crossover assist choices. It also pins her competitor down for an extended period of time, leaving the adversary vulnerable to whatever mix-ups her teammates might have at their disposal.

Snap Back

Screen	Command	Hits	Damage	Meter Gain	Startup	Active	Recovery	Advantage on Hit	Advantage if Guarded
1	↓↘→ + P1 or P2	1	50,000	500 (-1 hyper meter bar)	2	6	12	—	+4

Notes

On hit, snap back forces the opposing point character to be replaced by an assist. Opposing assist calls or tag outs are also locked out for 4 seconds

Special Moves

Screen	Name	Command	Hits	Damage	Meter Gain	Startup	Active	Recovery	Advantage on Hit	Advantage if Guarded	Notes
1	Head Charge L	(in air) ↓↘→ + Ⓛ	1	70,000	560	13	15	13	-6	-6	—
2	Head Charge M	(in air) ↓↘→ + Ⓜ	1	70,000	560	13	15	13	-6	-6	—
3	Head Charge H	(in air) ↓↘→ + Ⓗ	1	70,000	560	18	Until hit or grounded	50	—	-7	Causes ground bounce
4, 5, 6	Power Slash	↓↙← + ATK	1	80,000	640	10	—	25	+6	+6	On contact with foe or hostile projectile, produces a projectile with 4 low priority durability points

Special Moves continued

Screen	Name	Command	Hits	Damage	Meter Gain	Startup	Active	Recovery	Advantage on Hit	Advantage if Guarded	Notes
7	Weapon Change	⇩⇩ + (ATK) (in air OK)	—	—	—	10	—	—	—	—	The strength used determines what weapon you change to: (L) for Solar Flare, (M) for Thunder Edge, and (H) for Devout Beads
8	Fireworks	(With Solar Flare) ⇨⇩⇘ + (L) or (M)	—	150,000	1500	6	15	7	—	—	The (M) version shifts into a counter throw if a high attack makes contact with the shield, the (L) version counters low attacks, holding the button increases its counter duration, hard knockdown
9	Solar Flare	(With Solar Flare) ⇨⇩⇘ + (H)	1	—	—	4	17	7	—	—	Nullifies certain beam attacks, reflects low priority projectiles
10, 11, 12	Thunder Edge (Can be charged)	⇩⇘⇨ + (ATK)	1	100,000/ 150,000	800/ 1200	12/33	6/11	20/16	+1/—	-1/+1	Knocks down when fully charged
13	Glaive Chop	(in air, with Thunder Edge) ⇩⇘⇨ + (S)	8	88,600	1120	21	Until hit or grounded + 8	31	+8	-14	This attack contains 12 projectile points, resets the 1 ground bounce per combo rule
14	Cold Star L	(With Devout Beads) ⇩⇘⇨ + (L)	1~8	20,000 per projectile	160 per projectile	13	1~101	22~32	-1~-11	-1~-11	Each projectile has 1 low priority durability point
15	Cold Star M	(With Devout Beads) ⇩⇘⇨ + (M)	1~8	20,000 per projectile	160 per projectile	13	1~96	22~35	-1~-14	-1~-14	Each projectile has 1 low priority durability point
16	Cold Star H	(With Devout Beads) ⇩⇘⇨ + (H)	1~8	20,000 per projectile	160 per projectile	18	1~92	33	-12	-12	Each projectile has 1 low priority durability point

Head Charge: An aerial attack where Amaterasu charges in one of three directions. The (L), (M), and (H) versions of this attack travel ⇗, ⇨, and ⇩, respectively. Use Head Charge L and M as a means of offensive approach. You can also use Head Charge L to make Amaterasu run away from her adversaries by Head Charging to the top of the playing field. This is great for waiting out temporary power-ups such as X-Factor or Ryu's Hado Kakusei. Head Charge H causes a ground bounce on hit and is useful for extending combos. Head Charge can be used a maximum of three times in the air. Like Power Slash, Head Charge is usable in all three of Amaterasu's attack modes.

Head Charge L 1

Head Charge M 2

Head Charge H 3

Power Slash: A floating projectile materializes in front of Amaterasu. The strength of the button used determines the position where the paper appears. Appearing directly in front of her, Power Slash L serves as a mid-range attack that Amaterasu players can use both offensively and defensively. If connected at this range, you can follow Power Slash L with standing (M) for a combo.

Power Slash L 4

Power Slash M 5

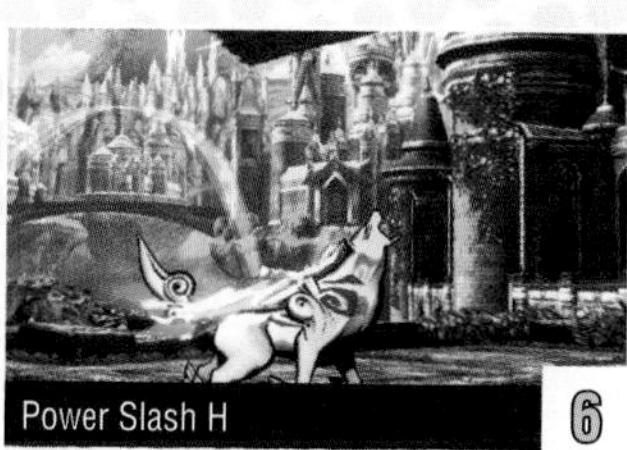
Power Slash H 6

The (M) and (H) versions of Power Slash appear higher than the (L) version and should be primarily used for defensive measures. Attackers jumping in on Amaterasu can be deterred with Power Slash M, while foes dropping down directly above her head are stopped by Power Slash H. These two versions of Power Slash stay on screen for a long period of time because of their slow downward descent. Therefore, Amaterasu players can use them as a trap of sorts for opposing characters trying to get into striking distance. Used like this, Power Slash H is especially useful for covering tag-outs; put it onscreen, then simply use a crossover attack to bring in another character. If your opponent tries to retaliate, the paper will probably protect you. Because of its quick startup and recovery, you can use Power Slash quite liberally without much risk. This attack is usable in all three of Amaterasu's attack modes.

7

Weapon Change: You can change Amaterasu's mode of attack by inputting ⇩⇩ + (ATK). Weapon Change M is used to switch to Thunder Edge, while the (H) version changes to Devout Beads. Amaterasu's default mode, Solar Flare, can be changed into from the other two modes with ⇩⇩ + (L). Weapon Change is extremely fast and can even be used in the middle of combos, followed by a standing (M) to continue the combo. Using Weapon Switch in the air causes Amaterasu to hover briefly to switch weapons, stopping any forward or backward aerial momentum. Note that this action counts toward Amaterasu's maximum of three special moves in the air. Even though Weapon Change is relatively safe, performing Power Slash M or H first to put a paper out for cover further decreases Ammy's vulnerability.

Being able to use Weapon Change in midair opens new possibilities for feints and transitions to aggression. She's free at act in midair after a Weapon Change; you can fake an airdash and then change weapons by jumping, airdashing, then immediately using weapon change. This could be used to fake an incoming airdash while simultaneously changing to Devout Beads for a stronger long range position, for example. On the other hand, you can also just jump, Weapon Change, then see what the opponent does. Since you didn't use your airdash yet in this case, you can come out of the midair Weapon Change by airdashing forward with an attack. In this way, you can shift to offense with terrific aerial attacks like Thunder Edge air (H) even if Ammy left the ground in a different attack mode!

8

Fireworks: Available only in Solar Flare mode, Fireworks acts as a counter to physical attacks. Once the ⇨⇩⇘ + (L) or (M) input is performed, the attack button used may be held down to keep the shield out indefinitely. If an attack comes into contact with the shield, Amaterasu instantly grabs her opponent for an aerial slam into a hard knockdown. You can then follow this slam with a combo by immediately performing Weapon Change M, airdashing forward, then performing air ⇘ + (H) CANCEL▶ ⇩⇘⇨ + (S). You can then cancel the Glaive Chop into Okami Shuffle, or continue the combo with standing (M), (S) for an air combo. Fireworks L catches high and mid attacks, whereas the (M) version counters low attacks. While both versions of Fireworks are able to counter special moves, they have no effect on hyper combos.

9

Solar Flare: Amaterasu puts up a green shield that reflects projectiles. Certain projectiles, such as beams, are not reflected but instead nullified completely. Solar Flare is ineffective against hyper combo projectiles. You can generate the shield indefinitely by holding down Ⓗ. This move alone forces projectile-centric characters to deal with Amaterasu differently than other characters, since she can just roll her puppy-dog eyes at her foe and keep Solar Flare going, then start using Cold Star to shoot right back at them when they're hesitant.

Thunder Edge L 10

Thunder Edge M 11

Thunder Edge H 12

Thunder Edge: Exclusive to Thunder Edge mode, Amaterasu charges forward with a glaive attack of the same name. Thunder Edge L is a straightforward attack that is used for combos and offensive pressure. The farther away it is used, the more frame advantage you get, increasing combo potential. Thunder Edge M travels at an upward diagonal angle and recovers in the air, making it possible to continue with air attacks. Thunder Edge H strikes straight up and is used as a defensive maneuver against opponents falling on top of Amaterasu's head. You can easily cancel Thunder Edge M and H into Okami Shuffle in order to maximize damage.

You can charge all three versions of Thunder Edge by holding down the ATK button used to perform the move. A fully charged Thunder Edge causes increased damage and hitstun. Because of the increased hitstun produced, it is possible to juggle off a charged Thunder Edge. If you think the opposing player might interrupt your attempt at a fully charged Thunder Edge, you can always release it early as a surprise attack!

13

Glaive Chop: An aerial attack only available during Thunder Edge mode, Glaive Chop comes straight down with a devastating chop. The impact of the blow also produces a bolt of thunder, and both strikes inflict damage on enemies. Glaive Chop perfectly complements an OTG ↙ + Ⓗ for a ground bounce. If used early in a combo, it can be followed with standing Ⓜ, Ⓢ. In combos where hit decay has already taken its course, Glaive Chop is best canceled into Okami Shuffle.

This is a terrific move, and it makes Amaterasu's self-OTG combos possible, but don't rely on it too frequently as an attack in an of itself, because it's unsafe if guarded. Be ready to hyper cancel into Okami Shuffle to protect Ammy if the opponent is ready to retaliate.

Cold Star L 14

Cold Star M 15

Cold Star H 16

Cold Star: Amaterasu fires an icy projectile that quickly travels the length of the screen. Pressing the attack button additional times allows you fire up to eight shots as a rapid stream or as delayed shots. Firing a single shot results in considerably faster recovery compared to when more are added. Each individual ice projectile has only a single low priority durability point. Cold Star L shoots straight ahead and is used as a long range attack. Cold Star M shoots at a 45-degree angle diagonally, blasting enemies out of the sky. Cold Star H is unique because it causes Amaterasu to slightly jump up before shooting diagonally toward the ground. Use this move in a firefight to hop over your target's projectiles while shooting some of your own.

If Cold Star connects anywhere besides maximum distance, you can cancel into Okami Shuffle for added damage. When doing this, it is important to cancel into the hyper combo early, since the window to combo Okami Shuffle is relatively small. After Okami Shuffle, harass your adversary further with Cold Star L as they recover from their knockdown for added chip damage.

Hyper Combos

Screen	Name	Command	Hits	Damage	Startup	Active	Recovery	Advantage on Hit	Advantage if Guarded	Notes
1	Okami Shuffle (in air OK)	↓↘→ + ATK ATK	1 + 35 + 18 + 1	70,000 + 10,000 x 35 + 7,000 x 18 + 80,000	18+4	184	4	—	+1	First projectile has 10 high priority durability points, second set of projectiles have 3 high priority durability points each, third set of projectiles have 5 high priority durability points each, last projectile has 5 high priority durability points, causes hard knockdown
2	Vale of Mist (in air OK)	↓↙← + ATK ATK	—	—	20+1	—	27	—	—	Slows your opponent's movement speed by 33%, slow duration lasts 300 frames
3	Divine Instruments (level 3 hyper combo)	→↓↘ + ATK ATK	25	400,000	8+2	15	35	—	-28	Frames 1-19 invincible, knocks down, Amaterasu ends in Thunder Edge mode

1

Okami Shuffle: With its quick startup and various applications, Okami Shuffle is Amaterasu's most practical hyper combo. The duration of the hyper combo is actually that of four phases—Amaterasu starts with a fiery blast, follows with a hail of ice, continues with a lightning storm, and finishes with a bolt of thunder. Each phase has a slight pause in between, so opposing characters defending are not in true guardstun. Also note that Okami Shuffle's hitbox and range is determined by the position of the screen, not the position of Amaterasu; the center of the screen is where Okami Shuffle appears, even if Amaterasu is not on the screen upon activation.

You can use Okami Shuffle in a variety of situations, making it Amaterasu's "go to" hyper combo. Rely on this move for ending combos, THCs (both from and into), punishing foes at long distances (including super jump height), and punishing crossover assists. It is even useful when used as part of a crossover combination because of its long duration. Your point character can often be controlled long before Okami Shuffle has ended, making it possible to OTG off the hard knockdown that the last phase causes.

Though Okami Shuffle is relatively safe when guarded, many characters can punish Amaterasu between the varying phases. The space behind Amaterasu is safe for opponents during the hyper combo, so characters with a teleport can easily punish her by teleporting behind her between the first two phases. A guarded Okami Shuffle at close to medium range is also punishable by dashing forward and air throwing Amaterasu between phases. Other characters can punish Amaterasu depending on their hyper combos, so it is best to not use this hyper combo randomly.

2

Vale of Mist: Amaterasu slows all adversaries down for a short period of time while her own speed is unaffected. Because of the extended hit stun this creates, you can perform certain special combos that are only available during this hyper. An advanced technique to use is to perform a combo ending in Power Slash L CANCEL▶ Vale of Mist into a THC of your choice. The next teammate coming in then reaps the benefits of Vale of Mist. Experiment with various THCs to perform otherwise impossible combos!

3

Divine Instruments: Amaterasu's level 3 hyper combo, Divine Instruments makes for high, unscaled damage at the end of long combos. It also sports a sizable window of invulnerability, making it ideal for blowing through an opposing character's offense.

Battle Plan

Make use of all three of Amaterasu's weapon changes for maximum effectiveness.

Power Slash can be used in any of Amaterasu's three modes.

Amaterasu's main strength is her versatility; she can fight effectively in close, from afar, in the air, or on the ground, and she can switch from offense to defense seamlessly. Some of her best attacks, such as standing/crouching Ⓜ and Power Slash, are usable in all three of her attack modes. All attack modes also have access to her unique three-way airdash that can travel forward, up-forward and down-forward. Combined with Head Charge, this gives Amaterasu strong mobility options in all three modes. Though it is possible to rack some wins using only one attack mode, Amaterasu's true potential is unlocked by utilizing different attack modes depending on the situation and character match-up.

Solar Flare: Solar Flare mode is best used for close-quarters combat. This stance has the combo-friendly ⇨ + Ⓗ attacks, as the other modes do not allow a launch after successful Ⓗ chains, nor are they special or hyper-cancelable. Solar Flare mode ⇨ + Ⓗ combo chains cause a substantial amount of hit and blockstun and build a good amount of hyper combo meter, and the first Ⓗ is jump-cancelable to help with mix-ups and offensive strings. Another strength of the Solar Flare mode is the air Ⓗ chain: Ammy can airdash in and press Ⓗ repeatedly when above the opponent's head. Depending on the timing this may cross up the opponent's character, and will typically break any airthrow attempts your adversary may try to stop the airdash. The speed of Amaterasu's crouching Ⓛ and the range/priority of her standing Ⓜ further complement the short-range style of Solar Flare mode.

Air Ⓗ is a great attack and should be your main aerial threat in Solar Flare mode. Air Ⓗ should always be performed with an input of ⇨ + Ⓗ to option select an air throw. If air Ⓗ connects or is guarded, continue with another air Ⓗ or two before landing. If you are in range for a throw, the ⇨ + Ⓗ input ensures the throw will be performed. Follow this with a forward ground dash into standing Ⓜ or Okami Shuffle if the air throw is performed at a high altitude.

By adding Fireworks to the equation, Amaterasu becomes a close-quarters monster. The true power of Fireworks is not the counter itself, but the hesitation that it produces in adversaries. By countering an enemy attack only once or even just showing the opponent Fireworks, competitors start thinking twice about attacking Amaterasu. In situations where a rival decides to stop their attack because Fireworks is being performed, take advantage of Fireworks' fast recovery time to let go of the counter and mix it up between crouching Ⓛ or a throw.

Threaten opponents with Fireworks... then surprise them with an attack or throw!

Thunder Edge: Thunder Edge mode boasts increased range over Solar Flare mode, as well as a wider variety of special attacks to utilize. Though Thunder Edge mode's ⇨ + Ⓗ chain attacks are not cancelable like Solar Flare mode's, Thunder Edge mode's standing Ⓗ is special move-cancelable and has huge priority and range. Also, you can charge each attack of Amaterasu's ⇨ + Ⓗ glaive attacks by holding down Ⓗ for increased damage and hitstun. Air Ⓗ can also be charged, causing a ground bounce for extended combos. Charging air Ⓗ fully also causes Amaterasu to stop moving in midair briefly, and this is a basic attack, and thus doesn't count against Amaterasu's air specials. By combining your actions here, Amaterasu can stay in the air for a very long time. This can be terrific if you want to burn some time safely while your opponent's X-Factor or their hyper combo power-up state dwindles away, for example. Super jump, charge air Ⓗ fully, airdash up-forward, charge air Ⓗ *again*, then perform Head Charge L upward x3, then charge air Ⓗ AGAIN! All told, Amaterasu can hang at the top of the screen longer than anyone else.

Take advantage of the huge range of Thunder Edge mode standing Ⓗ.

Thunder Edge mode is far from a runaway stance, though. Combining air ⬂ + Ⓗ, air charged Ⓗ, and Glaive Chop with airdashes and Head Charges, Amaterasu's air mobility can be made unpredictable for your opponent. Both aerial ⬂ + Ⓗ and air charged Ⓗ are special move-cancelable, granting even more control of the skies. You can stall at high altitudes using special attacks, then surprise enemies with a sudden ⬂ + Ⓗ. Air ⬂ + Ⓗ is great for offensive pressure; though it has a great deal of recovery, this can be mitigated though the use of special move cancels. If the dive attack hits, cancel into Head Charge H into a combo. If guarded, cancel into Head Charge M (which can then be followed by air Ⓛ) or an aerial Weapon Change to avoid punishment. Finally, Thunder Edge air Ⓗ out of an airdash is worth mentioning as one of the game's best air-to-ground attacks, bar none. It has huge range, the glaive itself is invincible, it can be made to strike in front of or behind opponents ambiguously by using it just as Amaterasu passes over them during an airdash, and on a successful hit it leads directly into the damaging **Combo II**. Because of this, although she loses Fireworks in Thunder Edge mode, Ammy is at her strongest on offense when wielding the giant blue glaive. Thunder Edge air Ⓗ is also excellent defensively, and can be used from far away to preemptively control the space your enemy wants to be in.

Amaterasu gains added air mobility during Thunder Edge mode with attacks like air ⬂ + Ⓗ.

Devout Beads: Amaterasu fights at a distance during Devout Beads mode. With its whip attacks and Cold Star, Devout Beads mode has the longest reach of the three modes. The three variations of Amaterasu's grounded whip attacks all have different ranges and properties. Standing Ⓗ covers the largest area of space and can be followed with crouching Ⓗ for a knockdown. Use this to cover the area in front of Amaterasu, as well as the area above her in which attackers may come in jumping or airdashing. Crouching Ⓗ is a far-reaching low attack used to surprise opponents by checking their low guard, though it cannot be followed by any attacks. ⇨ + Ⓗ commands the least amount of space control but attacks for a whopping 20 hits when all five whip attacks are connected. Though it is not cancelable, the hitstun is consistent enough to simultaneously call an assist for extra damage.

Attack from a distance with Devout Beads mode.

Learn the different ranges and uses of Amaterasu's Devout Beads whip attacks. Devout Beads mode is ideal for keeping out heavy-hitting brawlers, or for sitting on a life lead. At maximum range, you can keep opposing characters out of range by predicting their movements and countering with the appropriate version of Cold Star. If competitors get too close for comfort, use the whip attacks in conjunction with Power Slash and crossover assists to push your foe back out. This is also a good opportunity to use Power Slash as a means to cover a Weapon Change to Solar Flare mode, which is more suitable for up-close combat. The huge hitbox on Amaterasu's air Ⓗ during Devout Beads mode can be abused by using it while jumping backwards for a quick retreat.

Learn the different ranges and uses of Amaterasu's Devout Beads whip attacks.

"GOOD JOB, AMMY! I KNEW YOU COULD DO IT! LET'S GET BACK TO KAMIKI VILLAGE!"

COMBO USAGE

I. SOLAR FLARE CR. L, ST. M, H CANCEL → + HHHHHS CANCEL FORWARD SUPER JUMP, AIR M, M, H, H, H CANCEL ↓↘→ + H, LAND, ST. M, S CANCEL FORWARD SUPER JUMP, M, H, H, H, S

378,800 damage, 102% meter gain

Your go-to bread and butter during Solar Flare mode, this combo is easy to perform and nets a good amount of damage and hyper meter. After the second S input, you can opt to super jump cancel into Okami Shuffle by canceling the launcher with a tiger knee motion of ↓↘→↗ + ATK ATK. Ending with Okami Shuffle instead of the relaunch deals around 522,500 damage at a net cost of 22% meter loss.

II. THUNDER EDGE CR. L, M, H CANCEL ↓↘→ + L, ST. L, M, H CANCEL ↓↘→ + L, ST. M CANCEL S CANCEL FORWARD SUPER JUMP, AIR M, M, S, ↘ + H OTG CANCEL ↓↘→ + S (2 HITS) CANCEL ↓↘→ + ATK ATK

~573,500 damage, 20% meter loss

This is Amaterasu's main bread and butter combo in Thunder Edge mode. Learning the timing on linking attacks after ↓↘→ + L is paramount to this combo. Don't rush; you have more time than you think! In addition, sometimes you will end up on the other side of the opponent after air ↘ + H depending on the overall timing and positioning during the combo. To mitigate confusion, keep in mind you have a lot of time to cancel the ↘ + H into ↓↘→ + S, so use that time to adjust if you have unexpectedly switched sides mid-combo.

III. DEVOUT BEADS CR. L, ST. M, S, FORWARD SUPER JUMP, AIR H (4 HITS) CANCEL ↓↘→ + H, AIR H (4 HITS), LAND, ST. M, S CANCEL ↓↘→↗ + ATK ATK

~458,900 damage, 57% meter loss

This can be your go-to combo in Devout Beads mode. It is a fairly simple combo for a decent amount of damage. Delay the falling air H so that the st. M will properly connect, and then super jump cancel the S launcher into Okami Shuffle with either a tiger knee motion, or (with "auto super jump" set to ON in options) just hold S after the launcher, and perform Okami Shuffle quickly while holding S (but before the super jump actually happens)

ADVANCED TACTICS

OH MY GODDESS: SQUARE JUMPS

Solar Flare mode air H makes for tricky cross ups when used during a forward air dash.

Take enemies by surprise with the range of Thunder Edge mode air H.

Players can use Amaterasu's airdash offensively via square jumps. In Solar Flare mode, perform a normal jump, airdash, and quickly do an air L, M for an overhead attack. If the airdash is allowed to travel a short moment longer, you can achieve a tricky cross-up with square jump air H. In Thunder Edge mode, super jumping airdash H can be a very ambiguous cross-up because of its exaggerated hitbox. You can also square jump in place with Thunder Edge mode air H as a defensive tool to protect from frontal assaults. Devout Beads mode square jump air H can be used both offensively and defensively, since its range is similar to Thunder Edge mode's air H.

HOWL AT THE MOON: INSTANT OVERHEAD

Perform an air L immediately after leaving the ground from a normal jump for an instant overhead.

During X-Factor or Vale of Mist, Amaterasu can perform a deadly instant overhead attack in Thunder Edge mode. At close range, perform an air L immediately after leaving the ground to hit a crouching opponent. This can then be followed with air ↘ + H CANCEL Glaive Chop, then either Okami Shuffle or standing M, S to an air combo. Once your rivals are conditioned to this maneuver, mix it up by faking the instant overhead and attacking with crouching L instead. Both attacks are too fast to react to, forcing competitors to make a 50/50 guess to successfully guard.

Alternatively, you can attack your opponent with an instant overhead air L, then immediately cancel that into X-Factor to hit your opponent with a surprise combo. This is a fairly big gamble, however; there's no way to verify if the opponent's character got hit by the air L before canceling into X-Factor.

IV. SOLAR FLARE CR. Ⓜ, ST. Ⓗ, CR. Ⓗ CANCEL ⇨ ↓↓ + Ⓜ, THUNDER EDGE ST. Ⓜ, Ⓗ CANCEL ⇨ ↓↘→ + Ⓛ, ST. Ⓜ, Ⓗ CANCEL ⇨ ↓↘→ + Ⓛ, ST. Ⓜ, Ⓢ CANCEL ⇨ FORWARD SUPER JUMP, AIR Ⓜ, Ⓜ, Ⓢ, ↘ + Ⓗ OTG CANCEL ⇨ ↓↘→ + Ⓢ

598,700 damage, 12% meter loss

At mid range, cr. Ⓜ and st. Ⓜ will be your combo starters of choice due to their extended range over cr. Ⓛ. If the cr. Ⓜ attack is guarded, you can continue with → + ⒽⒽⒽⒽⒽ instead to keep the pressure on.

V. FORWARD THROW OR LOW ALTITUDE FORWARD AIR THROW, (SOLAR FLARE DASH FORWARD Ⓜ, Ⓢ CANCEL ⇨ FORWARD SUPER JUMP, AIR Ⓜ, Ⓜ, Ⓗ, Ⓗ, Ⓗ CANCEL ⇨ ↓↘→ + Ⓗ, LAND, Ⓢ CANCEL ⇨ SUPER JUMP, AIR Ⓜ ,Ⓗ, Ⓗ, Ⓗ, Ⓢ) *OR* (THUNDER EDGE DASH FORWARD Ⓜ, Ⓢ CANCEL ⇨ SUPER JUMP, AIR Ⓜ, Ⓜ, Ⓢ, ↘ + Ⓗ OTG CANCEL ⇨ ↓↘→ + Ⓢ CANCEL ⇨ ↓↘→ + (ATK ATK))

224,100 damage, 74% meter gain OR 381,800 damage, 54% meter loss

This is an important combo to master as forward throws are easy to mix-up into during Amaterasu's offense. You are going to be hitting → + Ⓗ a lot of the time in any position anyway, after all. As soon as the cinematic for the throw ends, get the dash input ready and hit with the st. Ⓜ a moment before the enemy hits the ground. The forward-lunging hitbox of st. Ⓜ makes the timing on the beginning of this combo forgiving.

VI. FORWARD OR BACKWARDS AIR THROW, ↓↘→ + (ATK ATK)

22 hits, 324,800 damage, 92% meter loss

Any air throw, front or back, can be followed by an aerial Okami Shuffle. Forward air throws cannot always be followed with a dash forward st. Ⓜ due to altitude, so Okami Shuffle can always be used as a consistent follow up. The faster the ↓↘→ + (ATK ATK) is performed after the throw cinematic has ended, the more likely the Okami Shuffle is to connect.

VII. SOLAR FLARE →↓↘ + Ⓛ VS. A JUMPING ATTACK (OR →↓↘ + Ⓜ VS. A LOW ATTACK), AIRDASH, ↓↓ + Ⓜ, AIR ↘ + Ⓗ OTG CANCEL ⇨ ↓↘→ + Ⓢ, ST. Ⓜ, Ⓢ CANCEL ⇨ ↓↘→↗ + (ATK ATK)

511,300 damage, 61% meter loss

A successfully landed Fireworks L or M has a long window of opportunity afterwards for a combo. For easy, guaranteed damage, you can go straight into ↓↘→ + (ATK ATK) immediately after Fireworks as well. The ↘ + Ⓗ dive can be fully charged for extra damage.

COMBO APPENDIX

GENERAL EXECUTION TIPS

When performing air combos with Amaterasu, input attack commands as fast as possible for the best results.

AIR Ⓛ, ↘ + Ⓗ CANCEL ⇨ ↓↘→ + Ⓢ, ST. Ⓜ, Ⓢ, SUPER JUMP, AIR Ⓜ, Ⓜ, Ⓢ, ↘ + Ⓗ OTG CANCEL ⇨ ↓↘→ + Ⓢ CANCEL ⇨ ↓↘→ + (ATK ATK)

Notes	Damage
Instant overhead setup during Vale of Mist or X-Factor.	441,200 damage, 18% meter loss

CR. Ⓛ, Ⓜ, Ⓗ CANCEL ⇨ ↓↘→ + Ⓛ, ↓↘→ + Ⓛ, ↓↘→ + Ⓛ, ↓↘→ + Ⓛ, ↓↘→ + Ⓛ, ↓↘→ + Ⓛ, Ⓢ, AIR Ⓢ, ↘ + Ⓗ OTG CANCEL ⇨ ↓↘→ + (ATK ATK)

Notes	Damage
Requires Vale of Mist and Thunder Edge mode. If mid-screen, reverse the motion for the 2nd through 6th loops of Thunder Edge, since you will be continually crossing the opponent up.	716,300 damage, 0% meter gain

CR. Ⓛ, Ⓜ, ST. Ⓗ, → + ⒽⒽⒽⒽⒽ, Ⓢ, FORWARD SUPER JUMP, AIR Ⓜ, Ⓗ CANCEL ⇨ ↓↓ + Ⓜ, AIR Ⓜ, Ⓢ, LAND, FORWARD JUMP, ↘ + Ⓗ CANCEL ⇨ ↓↘→ + (ATK ATK)

Notes	Damage
Air combo involving Weapon Change.	509,900, 27% meter gain

CR. Ⓛ, Ⓜ, ST. Ⓗ, → + ⒽⒽⒽⒽⒽ, Ⓢ, FORWARD SUPER JUMP, AIR Ⓜ, Ⓜ, Ⓗ, Ⓗ, Ⓗ CANCEL ⇨ ↓↘→ + Ⓗ, LAND, ST. Ⓗ CANCEL ⇨ →↓↘ + (ATK ATK)

Notes	Damage
Involves lv.3 hyper combo	769,100, 227% meter loss

ARTHUR

"YOU HAVE THE AIR... OF A DEMON!"

Bio

REAL NAME

Arthur

OCCUPATION

Knight

ABILITIES

Can rapidly hurl spears, swords, etc. toward his enemies. When wearing gold armor, he gains the ability to use magic.

WEAPONS

His inventory includes large lances, swords, fire bottles, bombs, boomerang scythes, the Swallow Blade, vine whips, etc.

PROFILE

The legendary knight who jumped into the demon world all by himself to save the princess who had been kidnapped by Satan. While best known for his dauntless courage in the face of terrifying monsters and life-threatening traps, he also enjoys wearing strawberry-print boxer shorts. Though he looks like an old man, he's really only 28 years old.

FIRST APPEARANCE

Ghosts 'n Goblins (1985)

POWER GRID

2 INTELLIGENCE

2 STRENGTH

2 SPEED

1 STAMINA

1 ENERGY PROJECTION

4 FIGHTING ABILITY

*This is biographical, and does not represent an evaluation of the in-game combat potential of this hero.

ALTERNATE COSTUMES

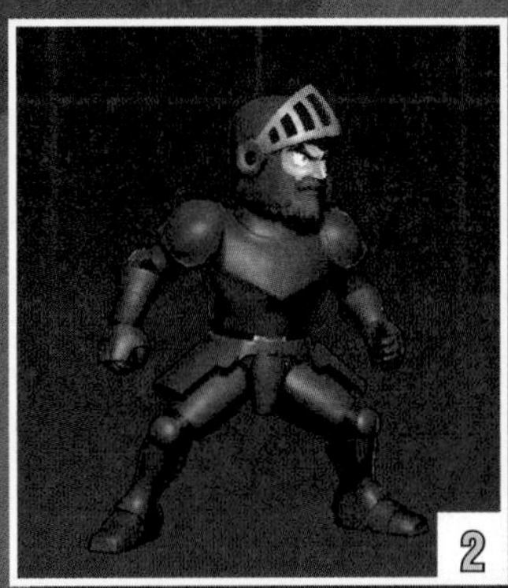

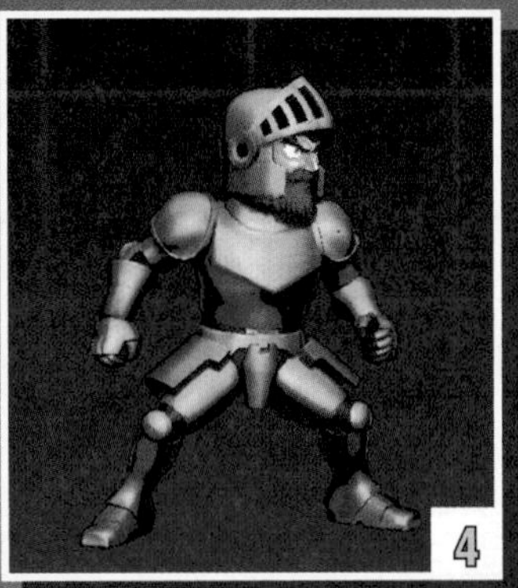

Overview

Vitality	850,000
Chain Combo Archetype	Marvel Series

X-Factor Boost	Damage	Speed
Level 1 (3 teammates remaining)	125%	115%
Level 2 (2 teammates remaining)	145%	125%
Level 3 (1 teammate remaining)	165%	135%

Your goal with Arthur is to keep attacking opponents far across the screen.

Why do you want to keep your adversaries far away while playing as Arthur?

- Arthur's huge assortment of projectile attacks are very effective at controlling the entire area of the screen below super jump height
- Projectiles that hit the target can be canceled into Goddess' Bracelet for a strong reactionary combo from fullscreen
- Each successful attempt to keep your competitor away builds a lot of hyper combo gauge, which fuels Arthur's powerful For The Princess hyper combo
- Arthur's close range defense leaves much to be desired, and it often forces you take a large risk to reestablish control of the match

How does one keep opposing characters away using Arthur?

- Jumping and using Air Dagger Toss, then immediately landing and using Lance Toss to cover the entire vertical height of the screen
- Using a long range crossover assist to bolster Arthur's control over the ground
- Reacting to super jumps with either air throws or by forcing your adversary to land into Air Dagger Toss again
- Staying out of the corner by occasionally pushing toward your opponent with projectiles, or by super jumping over the opposing character when the opportunity presents itself

Arthur has a secondary goal that comes into play when the primary goal isn't working: establish point-blank range!

As a slow and immobile projectile character, why would Arthur want to be close to his rival?

- Arthur's new and improved air Ⓢ gives him access to an easy instant overhead that leads into a combo
- Instant overheads can be mixed up with a low-hitting crouching Ⓛ or Ⓜ, creating a mix-up that is impossible for opponents to react to
- This mix-up gives Arthur a way to force large amounts of damage onto the opposing character, creating comebacks
- Some zoning characters with several aerial projectile attacks give Arthur an inordinate amount of trouble from long range; switching it up and going after these characters is often a better option

If he's slow and immobile, how do you achieve point-blank range with Arthur?

- Using the Ⓢ-canceled Air Scatter Crossbow technique to cover a large distance quickly
- Jumping forward and using Air Fire Bottle Toss
- While keeping an attacking opponent at bay, unexpectedly super jumping forward and attack with air Ⓢ
- In Golden Armor state, super jumping forward and use Air Scatter Crossbow

TUNING SINCE ORIGINAL MVC3

Not a lot of changes were made to Arthur in *Ultimate Marvel vs. Capcom 3*. However, one simple improvement drastically changes Arthur's game: air Ⓢ now immediately causes Arthur to drop down from his jump. This gives him a huge offensive option with the threat of lightning-fast instant overheads that lead into full combos, and it also greatly improves his mobility!

- Health increased from 800k to 850k
- Air Ⓢ is now OTG-capable
- Air Ⓢ causes Arthur to drop down instantly
- Extra hit of flame on Fire Bottle Toss

Attack Set

Standing Basic Attacks

Screen	Command	Hits	Damage	Meter Gain	Startup	Active	Recovery	Advantage on Hit	Advantage if Guarded	Notes
1	Standing L	1	30,000	240	6	3	11	0	-1	Chain-cancelable into L attacks
2	Standing M	1	48,000	384	12	3	23	-5	-7	Has autoguard property versus mid/high attacks throughout active frames
3	Standing H	1	65,000	520	14	5	22	-3	-5	—

Crouching Basic Attacks

Screen	Command	Hits	Damage	Meter Gain	Startup	Active	Recovery	Advantage on Hit	Advantage if Guarded	Notes
1	Crouching L	1	28,000	224	7	2	12	0	-1	Chain-cancelable into L attacks
2	Crouching M	1	45,000	360	10	3	22	-4	-6	Low attack
3	Crouching H	1	63,000	504	15	4	24	—	-6	Low attack, knocks down

Ground Special Attack—Launcher

Screen	Command	Hits	Damage	Meter Gain	Startup	Active	Recovery	Advantage on Hit	Advantage if Guarded	Notes
1	S (while standing or crouching)	1	70,000	560	9	4	31	—	-13	Launcher, not special- or hyper combo-cancelable

Air Basic Attacks

Screen	Command	Hits	Damage	Meter Gain	Startup	Active	Recovery	Advantage on Hit	Advantage if Guarded	Notes
1	Air L	1	30,000	240	7	9	10	+9	+7	Overhead attack
2	Air M	1	47,000	376	9	3	22	+16	+13	Overhead attack
3	Air H	1	63,000	504	11	5	20	+16	+14	Overhead attack

Air Special Attacks—Flying Screen and Air Exchange

Air Ⓢ causes a hard knockdown when used in a launcher combo (this is sometimes called flying screen). When used outside of a launcher combo, air Ⓢ behaves mostly like another basic attack. Air exchange attacks, performed by inputting a direction plus Ⓢ, are only possible during a launcher combo. Exchange hits initiate team aerial combos by tagging in the next available character to continue the air combo.

Screen	Command	Hits	Damage	Meter Gain	Startup	Active	Recovery	Advantage on Hit	Advantage if Guarded	Notes
1	Air Ⓢ	1	65,000	520	12	Until grounded	5	+9	+7	OTG-capable, causes hard knockdown if used in launcher combo
2	Air ⇧ + Ⓢ (during launcher combo)	1	60,00	480	10	4	Until grounded	—	—	Tags in next available ally while lofting opponent upward
3	Air ⇨ or ⇦ + Ⓢ (during launcher combo)	1	50,000	400	11	3	Until grounded	—	—	Tags in next available ally while causing wall bounce, erases 1 hyper meter bar from opposing character
4	Air ⇩ + Ⓢ (during launcher combo)	1	50,000	400 + 10,000	12	Until grounded	5	—	—	Tags in next available ally while causing ground bounce, generates 1 hyper meter bar

1

2

3

4

Command Attacks

Command attacks resemble basic attacks but have different chaining and canceling properties. It's usually possible to chain *into* a command attack from basic attacks, but most command attacks cannot be chained from or canceled themselves.

Screen	Name	Command	Hits	Damage	Meter Gain	Startup	Active	Recovery	Advantage on Hit	Advantage if Guarded	Notes
1	Cross Sword	⇦ + Ⓗ	1	70,000	560	26	—	24	-1	-3	Not special- or hyper combo- cancelable, projectile disappears if Arthur gets hit, projectile has 5 low priority durability points
2	Lance Charge	⇨ + Ⓗ	1	70,000	560	20	11	15	-2	-4	—

1

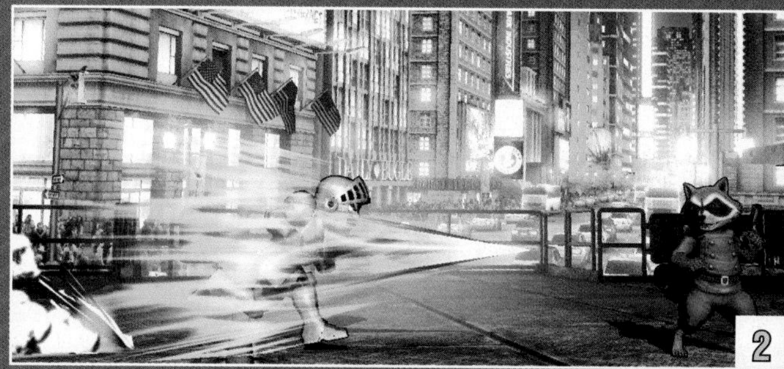
2

Throws

Throws are for snagging passive or blocking opponents. Since throws are active so quickly, you can also use them to preemptively toss opposing characters out of their offense. Combos are usually possible after throws, one way or another.

Screen	Command	Hits	Damage	Meter Gain	Startup	Active	Notes
1	⇨ + Ⓗ (ground)	1	80,000	800	1	1	Hard knockdown
	⇦ + Ⓗ (ground)	1	80,000	800	1	1	Hard knockdown
2	⇨ + Ⓗ (air)	1	80,000	800	1	1	Hard knockdown
	⇦ + Ⓗ (air)	1	80,000	800	1	1	Hard knockdown

1

2

ARTHUR

As a Partner—Crossover Assists

Screen	Type	P1+P2 Crossover Combination Hyper Combo	Description	Hits	Damage	Meter Gain	Startup	Active	Recovery (this crossover assist)	Recovery (other partner)	Notes
1	Arthur—α	Goddess' Bracelet	Heavenly Slash	1	80,000/ 110,000	640/880	31	8	134	104	Knocks down, causes spinning knockdown during Golden Armor state
2	Arthur—β	Goddess' Bracelet	Dagger Toss	3	108,300/ 149,000	960/1320	34	21	125	95	Creates 3 projectiles, each with 3 low durability points, each projectile has 5 low durability points during Golden Armor state and pierces through opponents
3	Arthur—γ	Goddess' Bracelet	Fire Bottle Toss	1~6/ 1~7	40,000~93,500/ 40,000~132,500	320~960/ 320~1376	44	—	128	98	OTG-capable, bottle staggers a rival, bottle has 5 low priority durability points, each hit of flame has 1 low priority durability point. During Golden Armor state, bottle has 2 frames x 5 low priority durability points, each hit of flame has 3 low priority durability points

1

2

3

Arthur's crossover assist attacks are exceptional, and this factor alone is reason enough to put Arthur on a team! While Dagger Toss and Fire Bottle Toss are strong assists on their own, they have the potential to become game-changing; it's possible for Arthur to permanently stay in Golden Armor state as an assist character! To accomplish this, activate the Golden Armor hyper combo while Arthur is the point character, then simply tag him out to a teammate any way you like. The 20-second timer before Golden Armor state freezes until Arthur becomes the point character again!

Depending on your team, getting Golden Armor Arthur assist might even be your first goal.

Arthur—β's Dagger Toss is the most well-rounded of the three assist types, and it is a big asset to any team. The three daggers add up to 9 combined projectile durability points to help deal with zoning characters, they don't excessively scale combos because they are only three hits, and they remain an active fullscreen threat for a long time!

While in Golden Armor state, the Dagger Toss assist becomes ridiculous: 15 combined projectile durability points is enough to beat the output of most zoning characters in addition to their own crossover assists! Even better, the daggers continue to travel even after hitting an opponent; they'll hit both the point and the assist character!

Arthur—γ's Fire Bottle Toss is also amazing, but it is a little bit more specialized than Dagger Toss: the flames are much slower and have less range but place your target in a huge amount of guardstun. This assist is more suited for offensive characters who don't have an inordinate amount of trouble closing the distance with their opponents. Unfortunately, you'll have to take care not to be too close to the opposing character when using this assist; directly hitting with the bottle prevents the flames from appearing.

In Golden Armor state, the Fire Bottle Toss assist no longer has that weakness; you can directly hit your adversary with the bottle and still reap the benefits of the wall of flames. The increased amount of flames of the Golden Armor version remains an active threat for such a long time that the flames essentially give you complete control over the next several moments in the fight!

Compared to the other two assists, Arthur—α's Heavenly Slash is much more difficult to use effectively. The Golden Armor version places your competitor in a tremendous amount of hitstun that is great for combos but is much too specialized in use when compared to the other two assists.

Snap Back

Screen	Command	Hits	Damage	Meter Gain	Startup	Active	Recovery	Advantage on Hit	Advantage if Guarded
1	↓↙→ + P1 or P2	1	50,000	500 - (-1 hyper meter bar)	2	5	22	—	-5

Notes

On hit, snap back forces the opposing point character to be replaced by an assist. Opposing assist calls or tag outs are also locked out for 4 seconds

1

Special Moves

Screen	Name	Command	Hits	Damage	Meter Gain	Startup	Active	Recovery	Advantage on Hit	Advantage if Guarded	Notes
1	Dagger Toss	↓↘→ + L	1~3	40,000~ 108,300/ 55,000~ 149,000	320~ 960/ 440~ 1320	10	—	28-32	-2~6	-4~8	Pressing L during the recovery period cancels into another Dagger Toss, up to two times, each dagger has 3 low priority durability points. During Golden Armor state, each dagger has 5 low priority durability points and pierces through opponents
2	Lance Toss	↓↘→ + M	1~2/ 1	60,000~ 114,000/ 130,000	480~ 960/ 1040	13	—	28~32	0~-4	-2~6	Pressing M during the recovery period cancels into another Lance Toss, can only be canceled once, each lance has 5 low priority durability points. During Golden Armor state, only one lance can be thrown. Staggers on counterhit, projectile has 10 medium priority durability points and pierces through adversaries
3	Scatter Crossbow	↓↘→ + H	2/3	95,000/ 108,300	800/ 960	15	—	33/32	-9	-11	Each projectile has 3 low priority durability points. During Golden Armor state, 3 projectiles are fired with homing ability, with 5 low priority durability points each
4	Air Dagger Toss	(in air) ↓↘→ + L	1~3	40,000~ 108,300/ 55,000~ 149,000	320~ 960/ 440~ 1320	10	—	32	+23	+21	Pressing L during the recovery period cancels into another Dagger Toss, up to two times, each dagger has 3 low priority durability points. During Golden Armor state, each dagger has 5 low priority durability points and pierces through rivals
5	Air Lance Toss	(in air) ↓↘→ + M	1-2/ 1	60,000~ 114,000/ 130,000	480~ 960/ 1040	13	—	32	+25	+23	Pressing M during the recovery period cancels into another Lance Toss, can only be canceled once, each lance has 5 low priority durability points. During Golden Armor state, only one lance can be thrown. Staggers on counterhit, projectile has 10 medium durability points and pierces through competitors
6	Air Scatter Crossbow	(in air) ↓↘→ + H	2/3	95,000/ 108,300	800/ 960	15	—	30/until grounded, 1 frame ground recovery	+20	+18	Each projectile has 3 low priority durability points. During Golden Armor state, 3 projectiles are fired with homing ability, with 5 low priority durability points each
7	Shield Deflect	→↓↘ + L	—	—	—	5	26	15	—	—	Nullifies all projectiles, counters low/mid attacks, staggers foe
8	Heavenly Slash	→↓↘ + M	1	90,000/ 120,000	720/ 960	7	8	41	-18	-27	Knocks down, causes spinning knockdown during Golden Armor, invulnerable first 14 frames
9	Hellbound Slash	→↓↘ + H	2	104,000/ 132,000	880/ 1120	15	5(18)6	28	—	-11	First hit knocks down opponent, second hit causes hard knockdown, causes ground bounce during Golden Armor state
10	Fire Bottle Toss	↓↙← + L	1/6/ 8	40,000/ 93,500/ 143,000	320/ 960/ 1552	20	—	35	+15	-14	OTG-capable, bottle staggers foe, bottle has 5 low priority durability points, each hit of flames has 1 low priority durability point. During Golden Armor state, bottle has 2 frames x 5 low priority durability points, each hit of flame has 3 low priority durability points
11	Ax Toss	↓↙← + M	1/3	100,000/ 135,400	800/ 1200	20	—	38	-5	-7	Staggers opponent on counterhit, projectile has 10 low priority durability points. During Golden Armor state, all hits stagger foe, projectile has 3 frames x 3 medium durability points and pierces through adversaries
12	Scythe Toss	↓↙← + H	2/4	95,000/ 85,900	800/ 800	20	50	40	+2	-1	Scythe is in play for 50 frames, has 3 low priority durability points. During Golden Armor state, projectile has 5 low priority durability points
13	Air Fire Bottle Toss	(in air) ↓↙← + L	1/6/ 8	40,000/ 93,500/ 143,000	320/ 960/ 1552	20	—	Until grounded, 11 frames of grounded recovery	+38	+8	OTG-capable, bottle staggers the opponent, bottle has 5 low priority durability points, each hit of flame s has 1 low priority durability point. During Golden Armor state, bottle has 2 frames x 5 low priority durability points, each hit of flame has 3 low priority durability points
14	Air Ax Toss	(in air) ↓↙← + M	1/3	100,000/ 135,400	800/ 1200	20	—	Until grounded, 11 frames of grounded recovery	+22	+20	Staggers opponent on counterhit, projectile has 10 low priority durability points. During Golden Armor state, all hits stagger opponent, projectile has 3 frames x 3 medium durability points and pierces through opposing characters
15	Air Scythe Toss	(in air) ↓↙← + H	2/4	95,000/ 85,900	800/ 800	20	—	Until grounded, 11 frames of grounded recovery	+28	+27	Scythe is in play for 50 frames, has 3 low priority durability points. During Golden Armor state, projectile has 5 low priority durability points

Dagger Toss: Arthur throws a single dagger with 3 low priority durability points. Tapping (L) again cancels Dagger Toss into a second one, and you can perform this move up to two additional times for three daggers total.

Dagger Toss travels slower and pushes back the opposing character a shorter distance than Lance Toss. They also both inflict the same amount of total chip damage, making Lance Toss the preferred projectile on the ground.

The Golden Armor version of Dagger Toss is a whole lot better: each dagger has 5 low priority durability points, substantially more damage, and pierces through opponents to hit assist characters, as well. Even so, you'll generally want to use the Golden Armor version of Lance Toss on the ground instead.

Lance Toss: Lance Toss fires a lance with 5 low priority durability points. Like Dagger Toss, tapping (M) again cancels Lance Toss into a second one. Only two lances can be thrown in this way.

On the ground, Lance Toss is generally superior to Dagger Toss. The lances travel faster across the screen, are more damaging, push your rival back farther, and cause longer guardstun.

Lance Toss is generally used immediately following an air projectile like Air Dagger Toss. This creates a solid wall of projectiles that covers the entire screen below super jump height. After your competitor guards the lances, immediately use Lance Toss again if you think your foe will attempt to dash forward.

The Golden Armor version of Lance Toss becomes a single flaming projectile with 10 medium priority durability points, destroying essentially all non-hyper combo projectiles. This gives you a huge advantage in nearly any long-range firefight that takes place on the ground!

The Golden Armor lance staggers the opposing player's character if it counterhits, and it also pierces through both the point and assist characters. The Golden Armor lance causes an enormous amount of guardstun, and in higher levels of X-Factor, the lance can singlehandedly keep your adversary in guardstun forever until they use advancing guard!

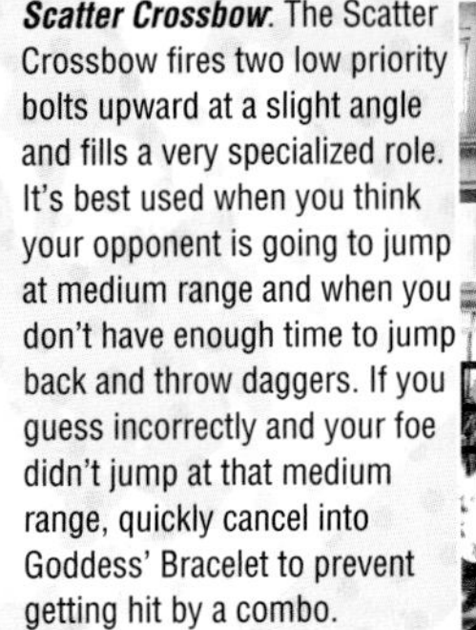

Scatter Crossbow: The Scatter Crossbow fires two low priority bolts upward at a slight angle and fills a very specialized role. It's best used when you think your opponent is going to jump at medium range and when you don't have enough time to jump back and throw daggers. If you guess incorrectly and your foe didn't jump at that medium range, quickly cancel into Goddess' Bracelet to prevent getting hit by a combo.

The Golden Armor version of Scatter Crossbow fires three projectiles with homing capabilities, making it an awesome tool. This gives you a great way to deal with pesky rivals firing projectiles down at super jump height!

Unfortunately, you won't be able to just repeatedly fire the homing bolts until Golden Armor expires: the homing bolts have a maximum turning radius and won't always be able to follow opposing characters who get around them.

Air Dagger Toss: Air Dagger Toss is the foundation of Arthur's zoning defense against opponents attempting to get close. It covers the entire "normal jump area" of the screen and recovers instantly on the ground, allowing Arthur to immediately follow it up with ground projectiles. Air Dagger Toss and ground Lance Toss combine to make up Arthur's "wall" tactic: causing large amounts of chip damage while limiting an encroaching player's options.

There's a proper timing for using Air Dagger Toss: start throwing daggers just before Arthur hits the peak of the jump. This creates an airtight wall of daggers that your competitor cannot jump between.

Air Lance Toss: Air Lance Toss is primarily used against other zoning characters who can fire projectiles downward from the air. Without Golden Armor, Arthur cannot aim projectiles up at opponents; Scatter Crossbow's angle isn't steep enough. Super jump up, and toss a lance their way!

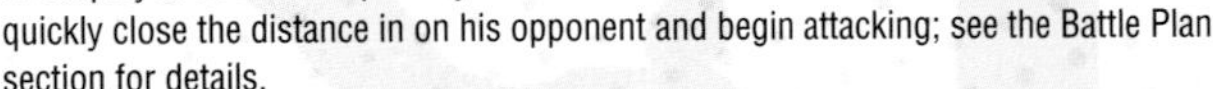

Air Scatter Crossbow: Arthur's main air-to-ground projectile, Air Scatter Crossbow fires downward at a slight angle that's handy for fullscreen fighting; jump over your target's projectiles and fire some crossbow bolts back at them!

Combined with Arthur's new (S)-canceling technique, Air Scatter Crossbow should be employed as Arthur's primary tool to quickly close the distance in on his opponent and begin attacking; see the Battle Plan section for details.

The Golden Armor version of Air Scatter Crossbow does not recover until Arthur lands back on the ground. While super jumping forward and using Air Scatter Crossbow is a great way to close the distance against his rival, be aware that it leaves Arthur completely open to any sort of counterattacks that nullify projectiles.

Shield Deflect: An odd special attack, Shield Deflect is a counter-type move that counters all attacks besides overheads; if timed well, Arthur deflects an attack with the shield and places his opponent in a stagger state for a combo. Arthur doesn't actually attack his adversary when the counter is triggered. The five frame startup time makes Shield Deflect difficult to use effectively, but the high reward on a successful counter can sometimes be worth the risk.

Due to the long recovery period of Shield Deflect, converting a successful counter into a combo can sometimes be difficult. If it seems impossible at the range you're currently in, you may want to think about simply hyper combo canceling directly into Goddess' Bracelet.

Shield Deflect has a strange quirk: Arthur has no vulnerable hitboxes behind the shield at all during the counter, making it effective against certain cross-up mix-ups like Wolverine's Berserker Slash.

Shield Deflect also nullifies projectiles, but the usefulness of this is extremely situational. In circumstances where an unavoidable projectile is coming toward Arthur, try using Shield Deflect to avoid chip damage. Shield Deflect does not nullify any hyper combo projectiles, however. There is no difference in the Golden Armor version of Shield Deflect.

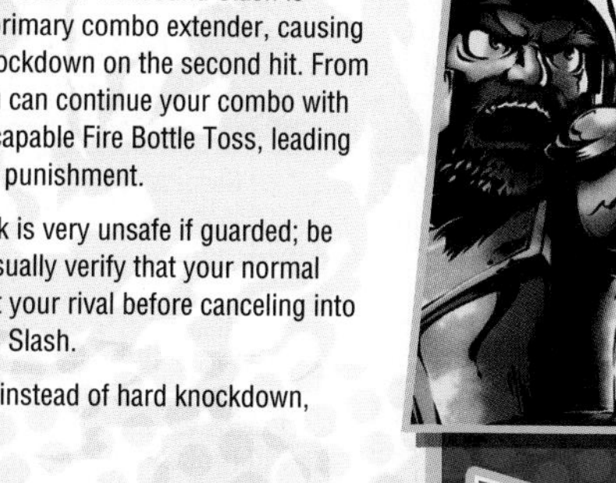

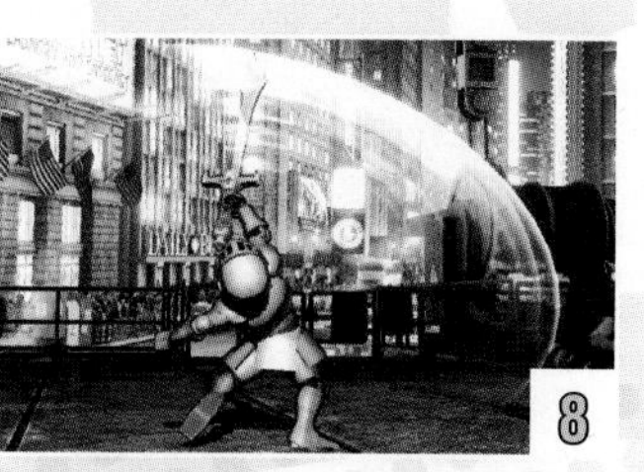

Heavenly Slash: A fairly quick slash that covers a large area, Heavenly Slash can sometimes be used as an anti-air attack. However, it is incredibly unsafe if guarded from the air or ground, and it also results in low reward if it successfully hits your foe.

The Golden Armor version of Heavenly Slash always causes soft knockdown and is unaffected by hitstun scaling. This allows you to perform a loop combo with level 2 or 3 X-Factor that can K.O. any character!

Hellbound Slash: Hellbound Slash is Arthur's primary combo extender, causing a hard knockdown on the second hit. From there, you can continue your combo with the OTG-capable Fire Bottle Toss, leading into more punishment.

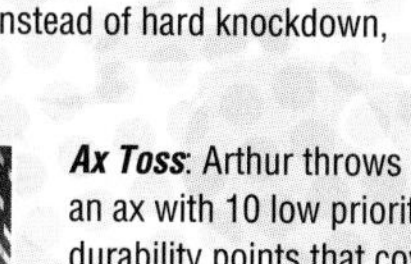

This attack is very unsafe if guarded; be sure to visually verify that your normal attacks hit your rival before canceling into Hellbound Slash.

The Golden Armor version causes a ground bounce state instead of hard knockdown, which affects the composition of Arthur's combos.

Fire Bottle Toss: Arthur throws a bottle that creates an OTG-capable wall of flames when it hits the ground. The bottle causes a stagger state if it makes contact directly with an opponent, but it doesn't create the wall of flames. This property can sometimes get you into a lot of trouble if Arthur ends up hitting his adversary's crossover assist character!

The flames of the Fire Bottle Toss travel across the ground slowly and hit several times. This results in a large amount of guardstun for your opponent!

However, you'll generally only use the ground version of Fire Bottle Toss as an OTG-capable attack in combos; to actually attack with it and capitalize off of the long guardstun, you'll want to use the air version. New to *Ultimate Marvel vs. Capcom 3*: Fire Bottle Toss has a sixth hit of flames. This results in even more hitstun and guardstun!

The Golden Armor version of Fire Bottle Toss always hits the ground and creates flames regardless of whether or not it strikes the opposing character. The flames also travel much farther and produce more hits! However, the bottle itself is also thrown farther—this makes Arthur's OTG combo in the corner impossible because the bottle is thrown off of the screen.

Ax Toss: Arthur throws an ax with 10 low priority durability points that covers a large area of the screen. Ten durability points is a lot, but for that purpose, you'll want to use Lance Toss instead; while they both output the same amount of durability points, Lance Toss has a much faster startup speed.

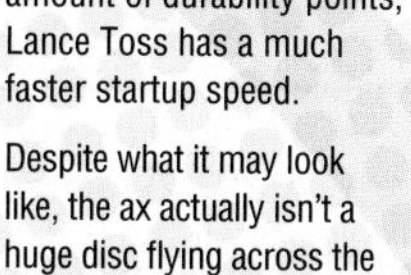

Despite what it may look like, the ax actually isn't a huge disc flying across the screen. Instead, it's a smaller projectile spiraling forward at an odd trajectory; it's entirely possible for the ax to go over and around small crouching opponents. The game only allows one ax projectile in play at a time. This prevents Arthur from using an air Ax Toss directly followed by a ground Ax Toss.

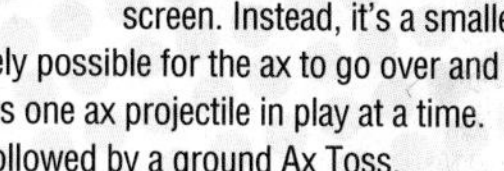

The primary purpose of Ax Toss is to put a slow-moving projectile onto the screen that covers a lot of space. This is useful for timing purposes, such as after connecting with an Air Lance Toss at super jump height; everything else travels across the screen too quickly and passes under your competitor.

As opposed to the standard version of Ax Toss, the Golden Armor version actually is a large disc! The ax becomes a medium priority projectile that follows a much more predictable pattern, arcing upwards before dropping back down and travelling across the ground. Use this attack whenever your target gets within medium range to effectively shield yourself from all angles of attack.

Scythe Toss: Another projectile that is primarily used in combos, Scythe Toss pulls opponents toward Arthur if it hits, allowing for additional hits to be tacked on afterward. Strangely, Scythe Toss pushes adversaries very far away if guarded. This is unfortunate, since it would've allowed for a very easy set-up for Arthur's instant overhead attacks!

Most of Arthur's attacks are unsafe if guarded against a cornered opponent; verify that your competitor is guarding and cancel into Scythe Toss instead to reduce your frame disadvantage to a single frame.

Humorously, the Golden Armor version of Scythe Toss is actually inferior to the regular version! It doesn't improve upon anything of note, and its additional hits only cause more hitstun and damage scaling!

Air Fire Bottle Toss: A great offensive tool, use Fire Bottle Toss while jumping toward the opposing character to gain ground and trap the foe in guardstun. Do this unexpectedly during your zoning defense to keep from backing up into your own corner!

Something to be wary of: the thrown bottle is destroyed on contact with the opponent's character, preventing the flames from appearing. While this is generally fine when you hit the opposing point character, it becomes much more of a liability when you toss a bottle onto an enemy crossover assist: Arthur will be completely vulnerable in the air while the opposing point character is able to attack due to the lack flames. The Golden Armor version of Air Fire Bottle Toss eliminates this risk; the bottle will always hit the ground and create flame regardless of what's in its way.

Air Ax Toss: If used late while jumping forward, the air version of Ax Toss can be another tool for Arthur to gain ground on his opponent. If your rival jumps into an Air Ax Toss used in this way, you can sometimes convert that hit into a full juggle combo!

Since Air Ax Toss travels so slowly and covers a large area, it creates great cover for an S-canceled Air Scatter Crossbow to traverse the rest of the screen!

The Golden Armor Air Ax Toss is a little strange: the ax still does the upward parabolic arc, but it then travels forward in a straight line at the height it was thrown from. This essentially makes it an extremely slow horizontal projectile.

Air Scythe Toss: You can use the Air Scythe Toss as an odd combo starter when jumping toward an opponent at medium range; if it hits, the opposing character gets pulled in for an easy conversion into a full combo.

Unfortunately, there aren't a lot of situations where this move successfully hits, so generally stick with Air Fire Bottle Toss or Ⓢ-canceled Air Scatter Crossbow for your offensive needs.

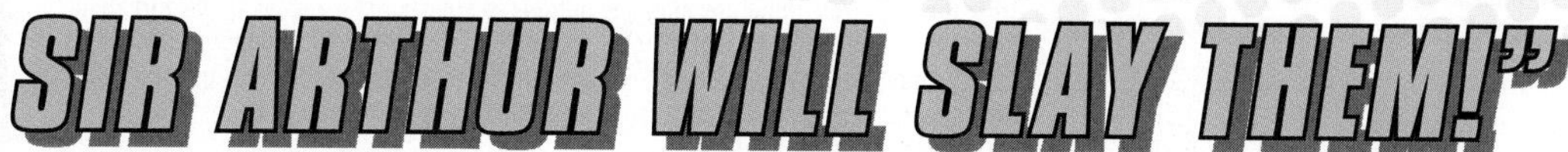

Hyper Combos

Screen	Name	Command	Hits	Damage	Startup	Active	Recovery	Advantage on Hit	Advantage if Guarded	Notes
1	Goddess' Bracelet	↓↘→ + ATK ATK	20-40	281,800-338,700	15 +1	112	5	+18	+16	Frames 1-10 invincible, can jump and double jump during active frames, each projectile has 2 high priority durability points, can be mashed for extra damage
2	Golden Armor	↓↙← + ATK ATK	—	—	20 +2	—	—	—	—	Frames 1-20 invincible, upgrades Arthur's armor state one level, Golden Armor lasts for 1200 frames. Golden Armor cannot be activated while Arthur is already in Golden Armor state. After Golden Armor state expires, Arthur is immediately placed in a hard knockdown state, also in no-armor state
3	For the Princess	→↓↘ + ATK ATK	10	400,000	15 +5	150	70	—	-62	Frames 1-229 invincible, hard knockdown

Goddess' Bracelet: Goddess' Bracelet quickly fires 20 fireballs, recovering quickly enough to leave Arthur at a huge frame advantage. There's enough advantage to continue combos afterward, and you can even perform another Goddess' Bracelet from all the way across the screen!

Goddess' Bracelet also has a fair amount of invincibility during its startup frames, and you can use it in sticky defensive situations when your opponent is getting too close for comfort. However, it only pushes your rival backwards a very short distance if guarded; use the frame advantage to get more projectiles onto the screen and push your competitor away!

The most common use of Goddess' Bracelet is to hyper combo cancel ground Lance Toss hits on reaction to any stray hits for strong damage. You must react fairly quickly for this to work, but it's generally safe to try. If it's guarded from far away, consider immediately tagging to another teammate across the screen; it's generally safe against all but the fastest attacks!

Arthur can jump and double jump while the fireballs are being thrown, allowing you to adjust on the fly to opponents that are being lifted too high. You can also mash for extra damage.

Golden Armor: The activation of Golden Armor has a large amount of invincibility, making it great to use for defensive purposes. It still has a small window of vulnerable recovery at the end, however, so you can't use it to prevent getting hit by hyper combos.

Activating Golden Armor upgrades Arthur's armor level by one. Arthur's armor hierarchy and their effects are as follows:

Level 1: No-armor state (receives 30% more damage)
Level 2: Regular Armor state (default)
Level 3: Golden Armor state (powers up all special attacks)

Being in Golden Armor state gives Arthur access to some incredibly powerful tools, such as powered-up versions of Lance Toss and Scatter Crossbow. See the appropriate attack descriptions for details.

Golden Armor state lasts for 20 seconds, after which Arthur immediately goes into hard knockdown in no-armor state. If the opposing player's character has access to strong OTG-capable options, this is like a ticking time bomb—try to get Arthur out of play before this happens!

Getting Arthur out of play while in Golden Armor state is actually a great strategic move, since it gives you access to Arthur's incredible Golden Armor crossover assists!

For the Princess: One of the best level 3 hyper combos in the game, For The Princess hits absolutely everything below super jump height, all while having a huge amount of invulnerability. This gives Arthur an awesome tool for catching both point and assist characters, generally resulting in a K.O. for both characters if you cancel into X-Factor!

While For The Princess has more than enough invincibility to be used defensively, it's incredibly unsafe if guarded. However, if canceled into X-Factor, the dragons continue attacking and keep your opponent in guardstun. Use this opportunity to pile on some free chip damage, threaten with an instant overhead, or safely tag in a teammate!

If For The Princess successfully hits your target, canceling into X-Factor allows for a damaging combo—you can do almost anything you want while the dragons are flying around and likely K.O. the opposing character! See the Combo Appendix section for details.

For The Princess is also OTG-capable, but using it in that manner is generally not an efficient use of hyper combo gauge bars. Using Fire Bottle Toss to Goddess' Bracelet is generally the better option.

Battle Plan

Keeping opponents away with Arthur largely centers around Arthur's "wall" tactic: jump into the air and use Air Dagger Toss, then immediately follow it up on the ground with Lance Toss. If performed correctly, you'll send a solid wall of projectiles toward your competitor with no gaps to jump between, and no ways to get around it besides super jumping or teleporting. If the opposing character doesn't avoid the wall, they're forced to guard at least two lances for good chip damage and hyper combo gauge gain. If your adversary gets hit by any of the projectiles, the lances generally hit, as well. Verify the hits, and then cancel into Goddess' Bracelet!

After every wall of projectiles, you can immediately jump back and repeat the sequence. However, opponents who immediately dash forward on the ground can gain a lot of distance and leave you in an uncomfortable position afterward. You have two main options to counter this: calling a crossover assist before throwing the daggers, or immediately using Lance Toss again.

If you do find yourself at an uncomfortable distance after a wall sequence, a good option is to suddenly attack your foe by super jumping toward them and dropping on them with air (S). Regardless of whether it is guarded or not, you'll prolong the time it takes for your opponent to back you into the corner!

If you ever make an incorrect read and are at risk of the opposing player closing the distance, immediately cancel to Goddess' Bracelet to retain control of the match. While your opponent is guarding the fireballs, evaluate your options at your current distance and react accordingly. The massive frame advantage from Goddess' Bracelet gives you an opportunity to attack a nearby competitor with air (S), or call a crossover assist and send another wave of projectiles.

Frustrated opponents typically super jump toward you in an attempt to get around your projectile defense. If you have plenty of room to spare before reaching the corner, counter this by simply jumping back and forcing your adversary to land in another wall of projectiles! Alternatively, you can try to get under your opponent to get away from the corner by using → + (H) or super jumping forward and using air (S). If you end up directly under your target, you can attempt an air throw, or an anti-air combo using the autoguard properties of standing (M).

Arthur is very weak to teleports, especially opponent-relative ones. He has no great ways to deal with them other than to simply stop firing projectiles in anticipation, which in turn allows the opposing character to freely dash forward across the ground. If you do manage to read an incoming teleport, be sure to punish it as hard as possible with a full combo! If your opponent's teleport causes them to end up in the air, be ready to anti-air with standing (M); it's very unlikely that your rival will emerge from the teleport without pressing any buttons. If your target manages to teleport while you're throwing projectiles on the ground, immediately cancel into Goddess' Bracelet to keep yourself safe from retaliation. Against characters with teleports, it's generally best to abandon the keepaway strategy; you'll have to either take the fight to them, or simply get Arthur out of the playing field.

Air Dagger Toss immediately followed by ground Lance Toss covers the entire screen below super jump height.

Verify that any ground Lance Toss hits into Goddess' Bracelet for easy damage!

While slow and difficult to time correctly, standing Ⓜ has autoguard properties that allows you to effectively anti-air your opponents and continue into a full combo!

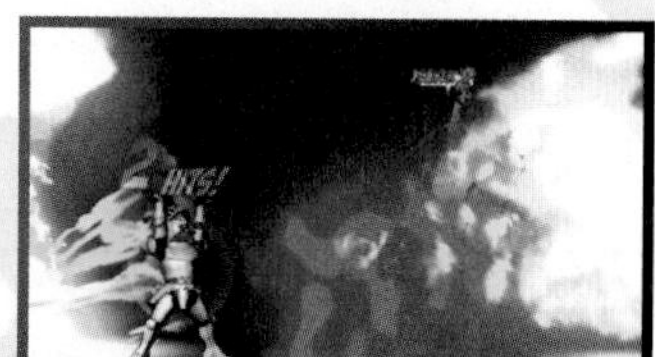

Opponents who skillfully use crossover assists can stick to Arthur for prolonged periods of time and prevent you from pushing them away with advancing guard. Counter this by using the invincible For The Princess attack to hit both characters!

If you find yourself up against the corner, or if you make an incorrect guess and let your competitor near, you'll have to make due with Arthur's comparatively weak in-close options. Your first choice should be to use the universal defensive options: advancing guard and air throws. Ideally, you'll able to simply use advancing guard to push your opponent away. With what little time you've just earned for yourself, your best option is generally to immediately take to the air with a super jump. This allows you to escape the corner, or you can drop onto your rival's head with air Ⓢ and attempt to regain momentum.

While air throws are generally the most consistent anti-air, Arthur has an interesting alternative option in his standing Ⓜ: this attack can autoguard attacks once its active frames begin, allowing you to blow through aerial attacks and land a full combo! However, standing Ⓜ is a sluggish 12 frames, making it difficult to time properly against all but the most predictable air attacks. When in doubt, simply air throw or guard instead!

The invincible Goddess' Bracelet and Golden Armor hyper combos are two more options available to you. If your adversary is right next to you whiffing an attack during your Golden Armor activation, capitalize with either an immediate throw or a combo standing from standing Ⓛ.

Another useful universal option is the crossover attack, or "random raw tag" as it is known within the competitive community. While incredibly unsafe if guarded, the invincibility and overhead properties of a crossover attack make it an option with a very high success rate. If you notice your competitor attempting to bait a crossover attack out by intentionally leaving holes in the offense and waiting to guard the crossover attack, that's your cue to super jump out of there! Alternatively, you can be aggressive and attempt to start a combo with a low-hitting attack while your opponent is expecting an overhead!

Opposing characters often stick to Arthur for prolonged periods of time by using crossover assists. While this generally prevents you from pushing them away using advancing guard, it also presents a great opportunity: using the invincible For The Princess level 3 hyper combo often hits both characters in these situations, giving you the possibility of knocking out both characters in one fell swoop if you activate X-Factor!

When fighting against other zoning characters, you will usually be able to win projectile clashes on the ground with Lance Toss.

Characters who can fire projectiles downward from super jump height are a big headache. Counter this by super jumping and meeting them in the air with a Lance Toss!

Fighting against other long range characters requires a different set of strategies. If the opposing character primarily fires projectiles from the ground, Arthur can generally win that battle simply by relying on Lance Toss and its 10 combined durability points. However, a few characters like Doctor Doom or Chris Redfield can out-produce Lance Toss with their own dominant projectiles. In these situations, you can regain the upper hand by having Arthur jump over their projectiles and fire Air Scatter Crossbow across the screen. Immediately follow up with a ground Lance Toss to tack on some additional chip damage. This creates a simple guessing game: to counter Air Scatter Crossbow, your adversary must wait before firing, plowing through the weak Scatter Crossbow bolts and hitting Arthur out of the air. If they are doing this, simply use Lance Toss during their period of hesitation; they won't have time to blow through the lances with their projectiles anymore!

Opponents who can aim air projectiles downward from super jump height are much more difficult to deal with; Scatter Crossbow doesn't have a steep enough angle to reach opponents that high, and everything else Arthur has is purely horizontal. Against these characters, your best option is to super jump into the air with them and intercept them with Air Lance Toss.

Hitting a rival with a super jump Lance Toss from across the screen is essentially a pure guess that the opposing player will be in the air; if you're not confident, just throw a single lance instead of two. This allows Arthur to recover in the air with enough time to use Scatter Crossbow or Ax Toss on the way down from the super jump that your opponent must deal with.

Despite being a ticking time bomb, activating Golden Armor makes Arthur a much more formidable opponent in long range firefights; Lance Toss becomes a medium priority projectile, plowing through essentially all enemy shots and continuing on to hit both point and assist characters. Against characters who can fire projectiles downward from super jump height, Scatter Crossbow in Golden Armor state now homes in on the opponent's location to give Arthur a reliable way to hit adversaries at great heights.

Long range firefights typically involve the help of crossover assists, as well. This is another prime opportunity to catch both the opposing character's point and assist characters with For The Princess!

Still, there are going to be long range firefights that are simply too much of an uphill battle for Arthur to handle. In these cases, you'll have to fall back on a backup plan—get close to your rival and start some offense!

Air Ⓜ can be used as an instant overhead against every character in the game. Chain into an air Ⓢ to be able to go into a full combo!

Super jump forward and press Ⓢ on the way up, then immediately cancel into an Air Scatter Crossbow to quickly close the distance on your target!

Mounting an offense with Arthur in original *Marvel vs. Capcom 3* was largely considered to be too impractical due to Arthur's lack of movement options: he has an incredibly slow walking speed, no ground dashes, no airdashes, and the slowest jump in the game. However, his newly improved air Ⓢ goes a long way toward remedying his mobility issues—it causes Arthur to quickly drop down from his jump while still retaining his forward momentum!

The simplest way to take advantage of this is to super jump forward and press Ⓢ on the way up. Arthur then moves forward at about twice his normal rate of speed! If your opponent is within midscreen range of Arthur, super jumping and pressing Ⓢ allows you to begin your attack in a flash! Super jumping forward and pressing Ⓢ is generally the best way to approach adversaries who are at mid-range or closer.

A slightly less aggressive option against opponents at mid-range is to simply jump forward and use Air Fire Bottle Toss. The bottle shields Arthur from most defensive attacks, and the flames trap the opponent in guardstun for a long period of time. This is a great way to push your competitor back toward the corner.

Against rivals who are all the way across the screen, you can take advantage of Arthur's new "Ⓢ-canceling" technique. This is exactly what it sounds like: super jump forward, press Ⓢ on the way up, then immediately cancel air Ⓢ into a special attack like Air Scatter Crossbow! Using Ⓢ-canceled Scatter Crossbow, Arthur can quickly travel more than half of the screen's length while simultaneously hiding behind projectiles! If the projectiles make contact with his opponent, Arthur is left at a huge frame advantage, enough to link a ⇨ + Ⓗ for a full combo if in range!

Ⓢ-canceling Air Fire Bottle Toss is another strong tactic. This attack allows Arthur to be on the ground and moving around while the bottle is still going up in the air! Since there is considerably more startup time on Fire Bottle Toss, you must super jump considerably higher to be able to properly Ⓢ-cancel this attack. Be sure to practice up in Training Mode!

If Arthur is in Golden Armor state, super jumping forward and immediately using Air Scatter Crossbow is a simple way to get across the entire screen. However, if your opponent's character has anything to nullify the crossbow bolts, you'll be a sitting duck; the Golden Armor version of Air Scatter Crossbow does not recover until Arthur lands on the ground.

Once you do manage to get near your target, you'll want to mix up the low-hitting crouching Ⓛ or Ⓜ attacks with an instant overhead air Ⓜ. Jumping and immediately pressing Ⓜ functions as an incredibly fast overhead attack on every character in the game, including Rocket Raccoon! Chain the air Ⓜ into air Ⓢ, then immediately cancel air Ⓢ into any air ⇩⇘⇨ special attack. None of these attacks actually has enough time to execute before Arthur touches the ground, but this strategy can cut the landing recovery frames of the air Ⓢ short. This allows you to land and get a full combo from an overhead Ⓜ! The ability to land a full combo from instant overhead Ⓜ without the help of crossover assists is a huge boost to Arthur's game in *Ultimate Marvel vs. Capcom 3*!

Simply jumping forward and pressing Ⓢ right away also works as an overhead with much fewer inputs required. However, air Ⓜ has more range and is much less likely to get interrupted by your opponent; air Ⓢ can be performed so low that the opposing player can often interrupt it with crouching Ⓛ attacks! To mitigate this, you can super jump and immediately press Ⓢ instead, but that makes the overhead considerably slower. It also requires you to cancel into an air special attack to be able to continue with a combo.

COMBO USAGE

I. (MIDSCREEN REQUIRED, NOT GOLDEN ARMOR STATE) CR. L, M, ST. H, → + H CANCEL → → ↓ ↘ + H, ↓ ↙ ← + L OTG, ↓ ↙ ← + H, → + H, S CANCEL → SUPER JUMP, AIR M, M, H, S, LAND, ↓ ↙ ← + L OTG CANCEL → ↓ ↘ → + ATK ATK, MASH ATK, FORWARD JUMP, LAND, S

612,700 damage, 25% meter loss

Arthur's basic combos can dish out surprising damage for such a little guy! If the opening attacks are guarded, cancel any of the normal attacks into Dagger or Lance Toss to push your adversary away. If you're more concerned with staying near the enemy after a failed attack, add an additional crouching L to the beginning of this combo to give yourself a more flexible opening. This reduces overall combo damage slightly, but it gives you great offensive options: after guarding two crouching L attacks, you're still in range for an instant overhead air M (combo IV), a throw, or more crouching L attacks if your competitor is attempting to use advancing guard!

II. ↓ ↘ → + M CANCEL → M (SECOND LANCE TOSS) CANCEL → ↓ ↘ → + ATK ATK, MASH ATK, ↓ ↘ → + M CANCEL → ↓ ↘ → + ATK ATK, MASH ATK

635,800 damage, 185% meter loss

Opponents attempting to get around Arthur's walls of projectiles often end up getting hit by lances. If you're quick, you can visually confirm the lances hitting your rival before canceling into Goddess' Bracelet for a full combo from all the way across the screen! If the Goddess' Bracelet is guarded, you're still left at a very large frame advantage, so generally the only risk for trying is the loss of hyper combo gauge.

Linking two Goddess' Bracelet hyper combos together takes a bit of practice, especially with the Lance Toss in the middle! See the Advanced Tactics section for tips on how to master this useful combo.

III. (CORNER REQUIRED) CR. L, M, H, → ↓ ↘ + H CANCEL → ↓ ↙ ← + L OTG, → ↓ ↘ + H, ↓ ↙ ← + L OTG, S CANCEL → SUPER JUMP, AIR M, M, H, S, LAND, ↓ ↙ ← + L OTG CANCEL → ↓ ↙ ← + ATK ATK, MASH ATK, JUMP, LAND, S

568,700 damage, 35% meter loss

Arthur must perform different combos against cornered competitors due to most of the flames of Fire Bottle Toss travelling off of the screen. Unfortunately, his corner combo inflicts less damage than its midscreen variant.

COMBO APPENDIX

GENERAL EXECUTION TIPS

Whenever air S makes contact with the opposing character, cancel into a ↓ ↘ → special attack like Scatter Crossbow. The attack won't have time to come out, but it still removes all of the ground recovery of air S and makes it much easier to combo a crouching L afterwards.

When using Air Dagger Toss to keep adversaries away, start throwing the daggers just before the peak of Arthur's jump.

Wait until Arthur begins to go over the health bars before pressing S when performing an S-canceled Scatter Crossbow.

(GOLDEN ARMOR STATE) FORWARD JUMP, INSTANT AIR M, H CANCEL → ↓ ↘ → + H (MISSES), LAND, CR. L, M, ST. H, → + H, S CANCEL → FORWARD SUPER JUMP, AIR M, M, H CANCEL → ↓ ↙ ← + M, LAND, WALK BACK A STEP, S CANCEL → FORWARD SUPER JUMP, AIR M, M, H CANCEL → ↓ ↙ ← + M, LAND, WALK BACK A STEP, S CANCEL → FORWARD SUPER JUMP, AIR M, H, S, LAND, CALL DOCTOR DOOM— α, FORWARD JUMP, AIR S, LAND, ↓ ↘ → + ATK ATK (MASH), FORWARD JUMP

Notes	Damage
Instant overhead combo during Golden Armor state	701,800 damage, 77% meter loss

(HALF-SCREEN OR GREATER DISTANCE FROM OPPONENT, GOLDEN ARMOR STATE, X-FACTOR LEVEL 3) ↓ ↘ → + M X6

Notes	Damage
Try to force your opponent to guard as many Golden Armor Lance Toss attacks as possible when Arthur has level 3 X-Factor activated. If one happens to hit, you get to take out one character with ease	1,218,000 damage, 124% meter gain

(MIDSCREEN REQUIRED, GOLDEN ARMOR STATE, X-FACTOR LEVEL 2 OR 3) CR. L, M, ST. H, → + H CANCEL → → ↓ ↘ + M, [→ ↓ ↘ + M] X8

Notes	Damage
In level 2 X-Factor, juggling Arthur switches sides every fourth Heavenly Slash. In level 3 X-Factor, all characters switch sides after every two Heavenly Slashes	1,400,000 +damage, 200% +meter gain

(CORNER REQUIRED) CR. L, ST. M, H, → + H CANCEL → ↓ ↙ ← + L, ST. H CANCEL → ↘ + H, ↓ ↙ ← + L OTG, ST. H, S CANCEL → SUPER JUMP, AIR M CANCEL → DOUBLE JUMP, M, H, S, LAND, ↓ ↙ ← + L OTG CANCEL → ↓ ↘ → + ATK ATK, MASH ATK, JUMP, LAND, S

Notes	Damage
Requires competitor to be fully flush against the corner, inflicts slightly more damage than Arthur's normal corner combo	587,900 damage, 29% meter loss

AS ARTHUR COMES IN: AIR M, H, S, LAND, ↓ ↙ ← + L OTG CANCEL → ↓ ↘ → + ATK ATK MASH ATK, FORWARD JUMP

Notes	Damage
TAC to Arthur with ↑ + S or ↓ + S or → + S	Varies due to damage scaling

→ ↓ ↘ + ATK ATK CANCEL → X-FACTOR, JUMP FORWARD, ↓ ↙ ← + M, LAND, WALK FORWARD UNTIL NEAR OPPONENT, ST. H CANCEL → → ↓ ↘ + H, ↓ ↙ ← + L OTG, ↓ ↙ ← + H, → + H, S CANCEL → SUPER JUMP, AIR H, S, LAND ↓ ↙ ← + L OTG CANCEL → ↓ ↘ → + ATK ATK, MASH ATK, JUMP, LAND, S

Notes	Damage
Level 3 X-Factor combo starting from For The Princess	1,473,000, 7% meter gain

(GOLDEN ARMOR STATE) CR. L, M, ST. H, → + H, S CANCEL → FORWARD SUPER JUMP, AIR M, M, H CANCEL → ↓ ↙ ← + M, LAND, WALK BACK A STEP, S CANCEL → FORWARD SUPER JUMP, AIR M, M, H CANCEL → ↓ ↙ ← + M, LAND, WALK BACK A STEP, S CANCEL → FORWARD SUPER JUMP, AIR M, H, S, LAND, → ↓ ↘ + ATK ATK

Notes	Damage
—	853,000

IV. (MIDSCREEN REQUIRED, NOT GOLDEN ARMOR STATE) FORWARD JUMP, INSTANT AIR Ⓜ, Ⓗ CANCEL ↓↘→ + Ⓗ (MISSES), LAND, CR. Ⓛ, Ⓜ, ST. Ⓗ, → + Ⓗ CANCEL → ↓ ↘ + Ⓗ, ↓ ↙ ← + Ⓛ OTG, ↓ ↙ ← + Ⓗ, → + Ⓗ, Ⓢ CANCEL SUPER JUMP, AIR Ⓜ, Ⓜ, Ⓗ, Ⓢ, LAND, ↓ ↙ ← + Ⓛ OTG CANCEL ↓ ↘ → + ATK ATK, MASH ATK, FORWARD JUMP, LAND, Ⓢ

628,500 damage, 8% meter loss

This is an instant overhead combo that is the cornerstone of Arthur's offense. Perform air Ⓜ, Ⓢ as soon as you leave the ground for the jump, then cancel into a whiffed Air Scatter Crossbow to eliminate the ground recovery frames of air Ⓢ. This gives you enough time to comfortably link a crouching Ⓛ and continue with the combo. You're left at a frame advantage even if the air Ⓜ is guarded, so stage a secondary offense by immediately attacking again with instant overhead air Ⓜ or the low-hitting crouching Ⓛ.

V. AIR THROW, CALL MAGNETO—α WHILE IN THE AIR, DOUBLE JUMP FORWARD, AIR Ⓢ, LAND, Ⓢ CANCEL FORWARD SUPER JUMP, AIR Ⓜ, Ⓜ, Ⓗ, Ⓢ, LAND ↓ ↙ ← + Ⓛ CANCEL ↓ ↘ → + ATK ATK, MASH ATK, FORWARD JUMP, FORWARD JUMP

501,800 damage, 41% meter loss

The new OTG-capable properties of air Ⓢ allow Arthur to convert air throws into combos much more reliably in *Ultimate Marvel vs. Capcom 3*. Once the air throw recovers, double jump forward while calling an assist, then attack with Ⓢ to OTG your adversary. If timed correctly, OTG Ⓢ knocks the opposing character into the assist and allow for an immediate Ⓢ launch when you land. While this combo uses Magneto—α as an example, almost any crossover assist that isn't particularly slow should work.

VI. (CORNER REQUIRED, GOLDEN ARMOR STATE) CR. Ⓛ, Ⓜ, ST. Ⓗ, → + Ⓗ, Ⓢ CANCEL FORWARD SUPER JUMP, AIR Ⓜ, Ⓜ, Ⓗ CANCEL ↓ ↙ ← + Ⓜ, LAND, WALK BACK A STEP, Ⓢ CANCEL FORWARD SUPER JUMP, AIR Ⓜ, Ⓜ, Ⓗ CANCEL ↓ ↙ ← + Ⓜ, LAND, WALK BACK A STEP, Ⓢ CANCEL FORWARD SUPER JUMP, AIR Ⓜ, Ⓗ, Ⓢ, LAND, CALL OCTOR DOOM—α, FORWARD JUMP, AIR Ⓢ, LAND, ↓ ↘ → + ATK ATK, MASH ATK, FORWARD JUMP

697,500 damage, 108% meter gain

In Golden Armor state, Arthur throws the bottle a bit farther when using Fire Bottle Toss. This actually makes it much less useful for corner combos, as the bottle simply flies clear off of the screen! To compensate for this, you'll need to use a crossover assist to help end your corner combos while in Golden Armor state. This example combo uses Doctor Doom—α, but many other crossover assists also work.

After hitting your target with air ↓ ↙ ← + Ⓜ, you must hold back after landing to move in front of the opposing character again, otherwise, the follow-up Ⓢ will miss or nick them in a manner that's impossible to follow up after. After the final knockdown with air Ⓢ, call Doctor Doom—α as soon as you land, wait a moment, and then jump and perform air Ⓢ for the OTG. Perform ↓ ↘ → + ATK ATK the second you land to ensure it hits right after Doom's beam.

ARTHUR

ADVANCED TACTICS

BRACELETS FOR EVERYONE

Against an opponent on the ground, Arthur can link together an infinite number of Goddess' Bracelet hyper combos. This is an incredibly useful tool, as it allows for K.O. combos from all the way across the screen starting from a Lance Toss!

Arthur can link together as many as five Goddess' Bracelet hyper combos, but the timing is tricky.

However, the timing required to link Goddess' Bracelet hyper combos together takes some practicing. Here are some tricks to help you on your way:

Mash the P1 and P2 buttons together. This lets you get a crossover combination hyper combo as early as possible. If you only have one hyper combo gauge bar, or if Arthur is the only character left on your team, you'll link two Goddess' Bracelets together easily! Otherwise, you'll spend more hyper combo gauge bars in what is likely a very inefficient combo.

From fullscreen distance, the proper timing to start the next Goddess' Bracelet is exactly when the 17th fireball is hitting the opposing character. While the super flash cutscene of the Goddess' Bracelet is playing, look at the combo gauge in the HUD: add 17 to that, and time your next Goddess' Bracelet at precisely the point where the combo gauge reaches that number!

You can also mash Goddess' Bracelet for extra damage, which throws a bit of a wrench into the works. When mashed, Goddess' Bracelet is actually 40 hits instead of 20. This means that you should add 34 to the current combo as a reference point instead of 17. Make sure you're mashing well enough to actually get 34 hits in 17 fireballs, though!

SAVE THE LAST LANCE

It's a situation that's happened to almost all of us: the opposing player lands an early hit, activates X-Factor, and takes out your first character in a single combo. Sometimes you lose two characters in this way!

If your opponent has already used their X-Factor early in the match, level 3 X-Factor Arthur's Lance Toss can quickly decimate a whole team!

While Arthur's potential to score a comeback win is greatly increased in *Ultimate Marvel vs. Capcom 3* due to his air Ⓢ, he still can use a little help. If your competitor has used their X-Factor already, that help can come in the form of X-Factored, Golden Armored lances!

Golden Armor lances are an amazing projectile—they're fast, have medium priority against other projectiles, inflict good damage, can hit both the point and assist character, and cause a stagger state on counterhit! In level 3 X-Factor, they become ridiculous! If any Golden Armor lance hits the opponent from half-screen or farther, you can easily combo together up to five additional lances, knocking out any character! If your adversary happened to be calling a crossover assist, they get taken out, as well!

If your opponent guards a Golden Armor Lance Toss, throwing repeated lances actually keeps them infinitely stuck in guardstun. They can wiggle the controller all they want; their character will still be stuck on the ground guarding lances. Each lance guarded inflicts a whopping 78,000 chip damage during level 3 X-Factor, so it only takes seconds to take out a fully healthy character guarding lances.

There is only one way to escape the guardstun of Golden Armor lances: your competitor must use advancing guard as early as possible when guarding a lance and then attempt to jump away. If done properly, your opponent will use advancing guard, jump and guard the next lance in the air, then be able cleanly jump over the third lance. The timing of the advancing guard isn't particularly easy, so opponents often guard several more lances than they have to before they escape.

When your rival does manage to escape, you'll want to bring them back to ground level so that you can toss more lances at them. The easiest way to go about this is to use the homing bolts of Scatter Crossbow; the only universal way to avoid this is to super jump up into the air. If the opposing character has air mobility options, send some more crossbow bolts up to force your opponent to use all their options quickly. From there, you'll want to time your next Lance Toss so that your adversary lands right into it. From there, you can go to town tossing lances again!

CHRIS

"I'LL ROOT OUT BIO-TERRORISTS WHEREVER THEY MAY HIDE!"

Bio

REAL NAME

Chris Redfield

OCCUPATION

BSAA Operative

ABILITIES

He has plenty of experience with all types of weapons, and he is also skilled with knives and in hand-to-hand combat. He has good observational and perception skills, both of which are important for survival.

WEAPONS

Chris wields various firearms, such as handguns, sub-machine guns, shotguns, etc. He is also armed with a military-issue knife and machete.

PROFILE

Ever since the Raccoon City Incident, he has been fighting continuously against the spread of bioterrorism despite the dissolution of Umbrella. He is also searching for his former partner, Jill, whose whereabouts are unknown.

FIRST APPEARANCE

Resident Evil (1996)

POWER GRID

3	INTELLIGENCE
4	STRENGTH
2	SPEED
2	STAMINA
1	ENERGY PROJECTION
4	FIGHTING ABILITY

*This is biographical, and does not represent an evaluation of the in-game combat potential of this hero.

ALTERNATE COSTUMES

Overview

Vitality	1,100,000
Chain Combo Archetype	Marvel Series

X-Factor Boost	Damage	Speed
Level 1 (3 teammates remaining)	140%	100%
Level 2 (2 teammates remaining)	165%	105%
Level 3 (1 teammate remaining)	190%	110%

Your objective with Chris is to safely inflict chip damage on your opponent.

- Gun Fire M and air Gun Fire L are two of the most damaging attacks in the game in terms of chip damage
- Air Gun Fire L inflicts a ton of chip damage while giving Chris huge frame advantage to work with
- Adversaries attempting to avoid chip damage usually set themselves up to get hit by an air throw, which Chris can easily convert into big damage
- Chris doesn't have many reliable ways to force damage onto his rival; chip damage is generally his best way to inflict any damage at all

How does Chris go about safely chipping the opposing character?

- Using Gun Fire M and long range crossover assists from across the screen
- Attacking with Air Gun Fire L when closer
- Staying out of trouble by liberally using Grenade Toss L whenever his target is within striking distance
- Winning long range firefights with the sheer power of Gun Fire H and the evasive capabilities of Prone Position

TUNING SINCE ORIGINAL MVC3

Chris received a host of improvements in *Ultimate Marvel vs. Capcom 3*, the most notable of which give him vastly improved combos. The OTG-capable crouching Ⓗ is now special and hyper combo-cancelable, which is great because Chris has no shortage of attacks that cause hard knockdown! Combine that with his newly improved Sweep Combo, which now properly hits juggled opponents, and the damage of Chris' combos suddenly reaches into the upper echelons of the game! These changes not only drastically increase Chris' damage output from clean hits, they also allow Chris to get major damage after throws, air throws, and even Gun Fire H from all the way across the screen!

- Chris' dash no longer has an 11 frame window where it cannot be canceled
- Low Shot (→ + Ⓜ) is now special and hyper combo-cancelable
- Crouching Ⓗ is now special and hyper combo-cancelable
- Air Low Shot (air ↓ + Ⓗ) is special and hyper combo-cancelable
- First hit of Combination Punch H is now subject to hitstun scaling
- Startup frames on Prone Position have decreased from 27 to 10
- Canceling Prone Position back to standing is much faster
- Recovery frames on Prone Shot are substantially reduced
- Sweep Combo second hit now causes hard knockdown if ground bounce has already been used, 13-20th hit are now OTG-capable

Attack Set

Standing Basic Attacks

Screen	Command	Hits	Damage	Meter Gain	Startup	Active	Recovery	Advantage on Hit	Advantage if Guarded	Notes
1	Standing L	1	48,000	384	6	3	11	-1	-2	—
2	Standing M	1	65,000	520	8	3	18	-3	-4	—
3	Standing H	1	80,000	640	10	3	21	-1	-2	—

1

2

3

Crouching Basic Attacks

Screen	Command	Hits	Damage	Meter Gain	Startup	Active	Recovery	Advantage on Hit	Advantage if Guarded	Notes
1	Crouching L	1	45,000	360	6	3	13	-3	-4	Low attack
2	Crouching M	1	80,000	640	8	3	18	-3	-4	Low attack
3	Crouching H	1	90,000	720	17	2	19	+2	+1	Low attack, OTG-capable, inflicts chip damage, shot has 3 low priority durability points

1

2

3

Ground Special Attack—Launcher

Screen	Command	Hits	Damage	Meter Gain	Startup	Active	Recovery	Advantage on Hit	Advantage if Guarded	Notes
1	S (while standing or crouching)	1	80,000	640	9	4	27	—	-9	Launcher, not special- or hyper combo-cancelable

1

Air Basic Attacks

Screen	Command	Hits	Damage	Meter Gain	Startup	Active	Recovery	Advantage on Hit	Advantage if Guarded	Notes
1	Air L	1	50,000	400	5	5	19	+6	+5	Overhead attack
2	Air M	1	70,000	560	8	3	27	+12	+11	Overhead attack
3	Air H	1	90,000	720	10	3	26	+15	+14	Overhead attack

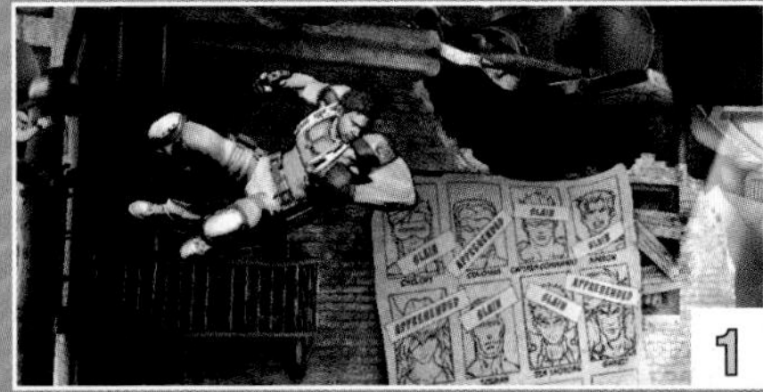
1

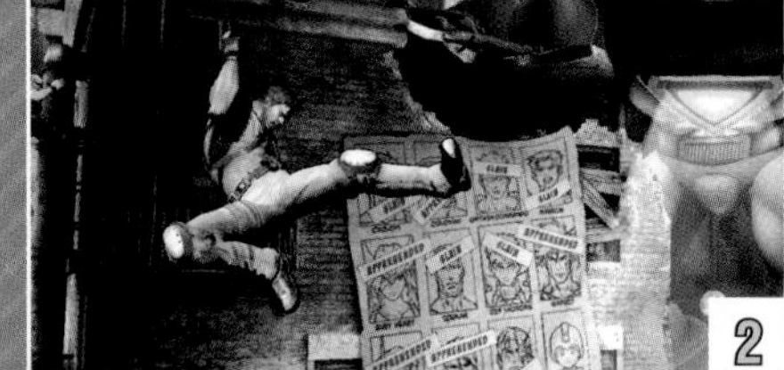
2

3

Air Special Attacks—Flying Screen and Air Exchange

Air Ⓢ causes a hard knockdown when used in a launcher combo (this is sometimes called flying screen). When used outside of a launcher combo, air Ⓢ behaves mostly like another basic attack. Air exchange attacks, performed by inputting a direction plus Ⓢ, are only possible during a launcher combo. Exchange hits initiate team aerial combos by tagging in the next available character to continue the air combo.

Screen	Command	Hits	Damage	Meter Gain	Startup	Active	Recovery	Advantage on Hit	Advantage if Guarded	Notes
1	Air Ⓢ	1	85,000	680	10	4	32	+18	+16	Causes hard knockdown if used in launcher combo
2	Air ⇧ + Ⓢ (during launcher combo)	1	60,000	480	10	4	Until grounded	—	—	Tags in next available ally while lofting an opponent upward
3	Air ⇨ or ⇦ + Ⓢ (during launcher combo)	1	50,000	400	8	4	Until grounded	—	—	Tags in next available ally while causing wall bounce, erases 1 hyper meter bar from opposing character
4	Air ⇩ + Ⓢ (during launcher combo)	1	50,000	400 + 10,000	10	6	Until grounded	—	—	Tags in next available ally while causing ground bounce, generates 1 hyper meter bar

1

2

3

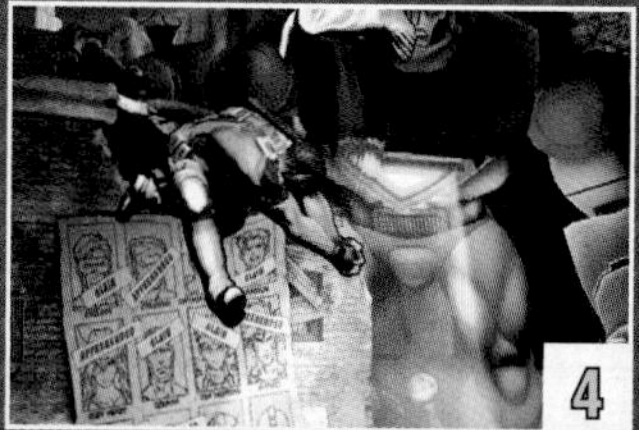
4

Command Attacks

Command attacks resemble basic attacks but have different chaining and canceling properties. It's usually possible to chain *into* a command attack from basic attacks, but most command attacks cannot be chained from or canceled themselves.

Screen	Name	Command	Hits	Damage	Meter Gain	Startup	Active	Recovery	Advantage on Hit	Advantage if Guarded	Notes
1	Low Shot	⇨ + Ⓜ	1	90,000	720	15	4	22	-3	-4	OTG-capable, inflicts chip damage, shot has 3 low priority durability points
2	Stun Rod	⇨ + Ⓗ	1	90,000	720	15	3	25	-5	-6	Inflicts chip damage
3	Flamethrower	⇦ + Ⓗ	9 - 25	110,000 – 171,200	1296~ 3600	20	17	22	0	-1	Cannot be canceled into, inflicts chip damage, button can be held for extra hits, not special-cancelable
4	Air Low Shot	Air ⇩ + Ⓗ	1	90,000	720	15	—	Until landing	+19	+18	Inflicts chip damage, shot has 3 low priority durability points

1

2

3

4

Throws

Throws are for snagging passive or blocking opponents. Since throws are active so quickly, you can also use them to preemptively toss opposing characters out of their offense. Combos are usually possible after throws, one way or another.

Screen	Command	Hits	Damage	Meter Gain	Startup	Active	Notes
1	⇨ + Ⓗ (ground)	1	80,000	800	1	1	Hard knockdown
	⇦ + Ⓗ (ground)	1	80,000	800	1	1	Hard knockdown
2	⇨ + Ⓗ (air)	2	80,000	800	1	1	Hard knockdown
	⇦ + Ⓗ (air)	2	80,000	800	1	1	Hard knockdown

1

2

As a Partner—Crossover Assists

Screen	Type	P1+P2 Crossover Combination Hyper Combo	Description	Hits	Damage	Meter Gain	Startup	Active	Recovery (this crossover assist)	Recovery (other partner)	Notes
1	Chris—α	Sweep Combo	Combination Punch H	2	131,000	1120	34	2(16)2	134	104	Hard knockdown
2	Chris—β	Grenade Launcher	Gun Fire M	8	125,00	1408	49	—	114	84	Each projectile has 1 low priority durability point
3	Chris—γ	Grenade Launcher	Grenade Toss L	1	117,000	1040	39	—	119	89	Spinning knockdown, projectile has 1 low priority durability point

Chris—β's Gun Fire M is his best all-around assist, and it is an asset to any team. It's basically a beam assist! Use it to bolster any character's long range zoning, use it as cover fire for an offensive character, use it in cross-up set ups; just use it a lot!

Grenade Toss L is a much more specialized assist; while it has the obvious application of being used for extra defense with zoning characters, you can also use it as a great way to extend combos! Midscreen, you can use Chris—γ for a single damaging hit that places your rival in a ton of aerial hitstun. In the corner, you can call Chris—γ simultaneously while pressing (S). From there, you can do a full aerial series ending with air (S), spike your opponent onto the landmine, then land and continue with your combo of choice.

Since the first hit of Combination Punch H is now subject to hitstun scaling, Chris—α is not nearly as useful in combos as he used to be. You can still cause a hard knockdown if you use the assist early enough in a combo, but it's difficult to recommend Combination Punch H over Grenade Toss L for similar purposes.

However, using a crossover counter to Chris —α can be a very strong tactic: Chris comes in fully invincible all the way until the first hitting frame of Combination Punch H. If this hits, you can convert that hit into a damaging combo! Combination Punch H is very unsafe if guarded, however, so try to only use this tactic in situations where it's guaranteed to hit, such as when guarding a non-invincible melee hyper combo.

Snap Back

Screen	Command	Hits	Damage	Meter Gain	Startup	Active	Recovery	Advantage on Hit	Advantage if Guarded
1	↓↘→ + P1 or P2	1	50,000	500 - (-1 hyper meter bar)	2	4	20	—	-2

Notes

On hit, snap back forces the opposing point character to be replaced by an assist. Opposing assist calls or tag outs are also locked out for 4 seconds

Special Moves

Screen	Name	Command	Hits	Damage	Meter Gain	Startup	Active	Recovery	Advantage on Hit	Advantage if Guarded	Notes
1	Combination Punch L	↓↙← + (L)	2	104,000	880	10	2(15)3	21	-1	-2	First hit staggers opponent
2	Body Blow	(During Combination Punch L) (L)	1	50,000	400	12	3	26	-3	-4	—
3	Heavy Blow	(During Body Blow) (M)	1	50,000	400	13	3	30	-5	-6	—
4	Payoff	(During Heavy Blow) (H)	3		1080	15	3(18)3(17)4	21	—	-3	Second hit knocks down foe, third hit wall bounces
5	Combination Punch M	↓↙← + (M)	2	122,000	1040	10	2(24)3	22	—	-3	First hit staggers rival, second hit knocks down, 4 frame gap on block between first and second hit
6	Magnum Combo	(During Combination Punch M) (H)	1	150,000	1200	22	—	37	—	-12	Wall bounces opposing character, hard knockdown, shot has 10 low priority durability points
7	Combination Punch H	↓↙← + (H)	2	131,000	1120	10	2(16)2	41	—	-20	Hard knockdown
8	Grenade Toss L	→↓↘ + (L)	1	130,000	1040	17	—	30	—	-7	Explosion is OTG-capable, spinning knockdown, landmine is created on 15th frame, landmine explodes on contact or persists for 90 frames before detonating, landmine can be detonated by projectiles from either player and also detonates whenever Chris receives damage, explosion has 1 medium priority durability point
9	Grenade Toss M	→↓↘ + (M)	1	150,000	1200	20	—	25	—	—	Grenade detonates after 90 frames, can bounce off of walls, can be detonated by projectiles and also detonates whenever Chris receives damage, causes spinning knockdown, is OTG-capable, explosion has 5 low priority durability points

Special Moves continued

Screen	Name	Command	Hits	Damage	Meter Gain	Startup	Active	Recovery	Advantage on Hit	Advantage if Guarded	Notes
10	Grenade Toss H	→↓↘ + Ⓗ	1+5	130,000 + 61,300	1040 + 600	25	—	26	—	—	Grenade detonates after 120 frames, can bounce off of walls, can be detonated by projectiles and also detonates whenever Chris receives damage, explosion causes spinning knockdown, is OTG-capable, creates flame pool upon detonation, flame pool lasts for 120 frames, explosion has 1 medium durability point, fire pool has 5 flames with 1 low priority durability point
11	Gun Fire L	↓↘→ + Ⓛ (in air OK)	10	129,900	1600	25	—	31	+7	+6	On counterhit, will stagger the foe if the first hit is a headshot. Each projectile has 1 low priority durability point
12	Gun Fire M	↓↘→ + Ⓜ (in air OK)	8	125,000	1408	25	13	22	+1	0	Fires 8 shots, each projectile has 1 low priority durability point
13	Gun Fire H	↓↘→ + Ⓗ (in air OK)	1	150,000	1200	22	—	34	—	-12	Wall bounces foe and causes hard knockdown, projectile has 10 low priority durability points
14	Air Gun Fire L	(in air) ↓↘→ + Ⓛ	10	129,900	1600	25	—	30 (or until grounded, then 1 frame recovery)	+36	+35	On counterhit, will stagger the foe if the first hit is a headshot. Each projectile has 1 low priority durability point
15	Air Gun Fire M	(in air) ↓↘→ + Ⓜ	8	125,000	1408	25	15	16 (or until grounded, then 1 frame recovery)	+21	+20	Fires 8 shots, each projectile has 1 low priority durability point
16	Air Gun Fire H	(in air) ↓↘→ + Ⓗ	1	150,000	1200	22	—	37 (or until grounded, then 1 frame recovery)	—	+19	Causes ground bounce, projectile has 10 low priority durability points
17	Prone Position	↓↓ + Ⓗ	—	—	—	10	—	5	—	—	Can move left or right while in Prone Position, exit Prone Position by tapping up on the controller
18	Prone Shot	(During Prone Position) Ⓗ	1	90,000	720	15	—	9	—	—	Not hyper combo-cancelable, projectile has 3 low priority durability points

1

Combination Punch L: Two punches that cancel into Body Blow with specific timing, the first hit causes a stagger state on your opponent. You can take advantage of this to easily hyper combo cancel into Grenade Launcher, but there are better combos and better means to accomplish this.

There is a very lenient 10 frame window to successfully cancel into Body Blow. The window begins immediately after the second punch connects.

Combination Punch L carries a 2 frame disadvantage if guarded, and it is generally punishable by throws from your competitor. It is difficult to punish this consistently, however, so it is sometimes worth the risk to immediately jump straight up after a Combination Punch L is guarded; if your opponent doesn't time their throw attempt correctly, they instead get a standing Ⓗ attack that probably misses completely. Come down with a jumping Ⓢ into a full combo! You'll want to be sure that the opposing player is attempting a throw, however; most opponents do not know the frame disadvantage of Combination Punch L and instead try to hit you with a crouching Ⓛ attack. While you can easily guard this, if you try to jump, you typically get hit instead.

Given that Combination Punch L leads to a host of follow-up hits, it's a little ironic that all of Chris' best combos do not utilize them. Usage of this attack is best kept for attempting to make guarded attack strings safer while inflicting a bit of chip damage.

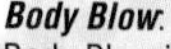

Body Blow: Body Blow is the singular follow-up to Combination Punch L, carrying a 4 frame disadvantage but at a slightly farther distance compared to Combination Punch L. This usually leaves Chris at a distance that is safe from both throw attempts, but unfortunately, that is not always the case. Even still, not very many characters have attacks or command throws with a 4 frame start-up or less, so ending attack strings with Body Blow is generally safe.

2

Body Blow cancels into Heavy Blow, also with a lenient 10 frame window. This window begins immediately after Body Blow hits the target.

3

Heavy Blow: Unlike Combination Punch L and Body Blow, Heavy Blow is very unsafe if guarded. It cancels into Payoff with a much stricter timing window: 5 frames immediately after Body Blow connects. The timing is earlier than what is intuitive, however; if you have trouble successfully canceling, try pressing Ⓗ a little earlier.

4

Payoff: The final attack of the Combination Punch L sequence causes wall bounce, is safe if guarded, and inflicts a lot of chip damage. However, all your adversary has to do is use advancing guard once, and Chris gets pushed halfway across the screen, punching air. This is incredibly unsafe!

Payoff is somewhat ironically named—it isn't exactly worth the time invested into learning the timing of this attack, given that Chris has many superior combo options.

5

Combination Punch M: Another punch series, the first hit of Combination Punch M causes a stagger state, and it is the preferred option to hyper combo cancel into Grenade Launcher. Both punches push your rival a fair distance away and leave Chris at a safe 3 frame disadvantage if guarded. However, there is a 4 frame window between the two punches; this allows your opponent enough time to jump into the air, guard the second punch while airborne, then immediately land and punish Chris with a full combo.

Combination Punch M can cancel into Magnum Combo with very specific timing: the timing window is 5 frames long, starting at 8 frames after the second punch connects. However, if you cancel into Magnum Combo on the last possible frame, it misses entirely!

Given Chris' new combo tools, Combination Punch M doesn't have much of a role in his gameplan. Chris has other more damaging combo options that cause far less hitstun scaling.

Magnum Combo: The follow-up to Combination Punch M causes wall bounce and a hard knockdown. Similar to Gun Fire H, it fires cleanly over the heads of most crouching adversaries, leaving Chris open for punishment.

Combination Punch H: Combination Punch H is another two-hit strike, only with no additional follow-up attacks. It causes a hard knockdown state and is an essential component of Chris' combos.

In *Ultimate Marvel vs. Capcom 3*, the first hit of Combination Punch H is now affected by hitstun scaling, allowing opponents to air recover between the first and second hits if performed late in a combo. This was clearly implemented to prevent ridiculous combo loops with the newly cancelable cr. H to Combination Punch H over and over!

Grenade Toss L: This is the cornerstone of Chris' defense; always try to have a landmine out whenever your competitor is closer than midscreen. The landmine explodes on contact, after 90 frames, or if Chris gets hit by the opposing character.

That last point is important—opponents hitting Chris up close detonate the landmine, generally blowing themselves up in the process. Chris can then juggle his rival and transition into a massive combo!

There are a few weaknesses to Grenade Toss L: adversaries with ranged attacks can safely hit Chris from afar and detonate the landmine. Characters with the ability to easily get behind Chris can also hit him without fear of the landmine. Lastly, it has a punishable 7 frame disadvantage if the initial mine placement is guarded.

Grenade Toss M: Chris throws a grenade that later explodes two-thirds of the distance across the screen. The grenade does not detonate on contact, but it still explodes if Chris gets hit, or if Chris manually shoots it with a projectile attack.

Grenade Toss M is usually used as a way to get an offensive threat onto the screen with the smallest time commitment—while Grenade Toss H and Gun Fire M are generally more effective, Grenade Toss M recovers more quickly.

Used creatively, you can also employ Grenade Toss M to set up throws! Use a crossover assist to pin your competitor in place while you toss a grenade under them. You'll have just enough time to wavedash forward and throw the opposing character before the grenade detonates, allowing for a big combo. If your target attempts to break the throw, jumping into the air causes them to get a standing H attack instead, which then promptly gets blasted by the grenade! Follow this technique up with a huge combo!

Grenade Toss H: Compared to Grenade Toss M, the H version has the following differences: it takes 30 frames longer to detonate, it both executes and recovers more slowly, and it leaves a giant pool of fire at the point of detonation!

Grenade Toss H is great against cornered opponents if you can manage to get your foe stuck in the flames, generally with the help of crossover assists or immediately after knocking out a character. If the opposing character gets stuck guarding in the pool of flames, they'll be at your mercy to guard several more special attacks, racking up a ton of chip damage.

Gun Fire L: The wide shotgun spread of Gun Fire L is primarily used preemptively from medium range to stop your adversary from jumping forward. Aside from having a landmine out, it's arguably Chris' strongest counter to airdashing opponents from afar.

You can use the spread fire of Gun Fire L to detonate Grenade Toss M or H, which is especially useful when canceled into from Low Shot (→ + M).

When used up close, most characters are still able to crouch directly under Gun Fire L and punish Chris, making this a poor choice to end guarded attack strings with.

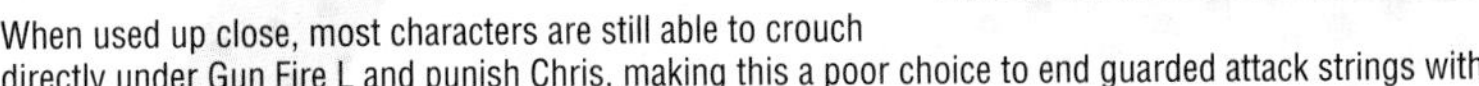

Gun Fire L has the odd property of staggering your target if the first pellet that connects is both a counterhit and a headshot. This is exceedingly rare when using the ground version of Gun Fire L, especially given that its main role is to counter your opposition's attempts to jump forward.

Gun Fire M: The main long range attacking option, Gun Fire M deals an impressive 52,800 points of chip damage. From across the screen, you'll want to force your adversary to guard this as often as possible. It also pushes the opposing character backward a large distance, making it great for ground control.

Gun Fire M has a total of 8 low priority durability points, certainly enough against most characters, but not great in firefights with other dedicated zoning characters. In long range matches, you'll want to match projectiles with Gun Fire H instead.

Gun Fire H: The magnum shot traverses the screen in an instant and has 10 low priority durability points, allowing Chris to simply power through most long range firefights. The bullet also pierces through both the opposing point and assist characters, knocking them both against the wall. This is a great opportunity to inflict massive damage on both characters!

If the magnum bullet hits, it causes a wall bounce and hard knockdown state, and Chris can convert that into a fullscreen combo for massive damage without even requiring hyper combo gauge!

Gun Fire H can be cleanly crouched under by most characters, so try to only use it in situations where it's guaranteed to hit your target.

Air Gun Fire L: Chris' go-to offensive tool, Air Gun Fire L inflicts a whopping 60,000 points of chip damage if all hits connect! Jumping shotguns recover immediately as Chris touches the ground, leaving him with a massive frame advantage of up to 38 frames. This gives you plenty of time to set up whatever you like: Grenade Toss H, a slow crossover assist like Sentinel—α, or even another jumping shotgun. If the shotgun hits the opposing character, you have all the time in the world to dash in and perform a combo. The combo's damage is massively scaled by the 10 hits of the shotgun, but it's still free damage and hyper combo gauge, and it carries your opponent all the way to the corner.

Since Chris is shielded by a mass of shotgun pellets, this attack is difficult for foes to counter without jumping directly over the blast. This opens your opposition up for air throw combos!

Like the ground version of Gun Fire L, the jumping version also has the chance to stagger opponents if you happen to get both a counterhit and a headshot. This is much more likely with the air version of Gun Fire L, however. When this happens, two jumping shotguns link together for a combo, allowing you plenty of time to visually verify the hits and dash forward for a full ground combo.

Air Gun Fire M: The aerial version of the machine-gun is OTG-capable, but given the new cancelable properties of cr. H and Low Shot, it isn't incredibly useful for that purpose anymore. When normal jumping, if you need an aerial projectile, it's generally preferable to use Air Gun Fire H, Air Low Shot, or Air Gun Fire L instead—there isn't enough time in a normal jump to fire all eight bullets.

However, super jumping forward and immediately using Air Gun Fire M is a strong tool for approaching your target. All eight bullets connect against a fullscreen opponent, and you'll still have enough time to fire an Air Low Shot before landing, adding up for some sizeable chip damage and a lot of frame advantage upon landing. This can easily be countered by foes wavedashing directly under Chris, however.

Air Gun Fire H: A strong all-around tool, the air version of the magnum shot inflicts 45,000 points of chip damage, causes a ground bounce state if hit, and is OTG-capable. This makes it great for combos in addition to general usage; if you manage to hit your opponent with Air Gun Fire H in a defensive situation, you can quickly convert that hit into a huge combo!

It's also good for fullscreen firefights: super jump straight up over your rival's projectiles and use Air Low Shot canceled into Air Gun Fire H for a quick damaging combo, or 72,000 points of chip damage if it is guarded.

As a general all-purpose tool, Air Gun Fire H does have some significant weaknesses when compared to Air Gun Fire L, however. The shotgun has a much wider spread of fire and also much more frame advantage if guarded. Air Gun Fire H maxes out at 20 frames of advantage compared to the 38-frame advantage of the air shotgun.

17

Prone Position: Activating Prone Position makes Chris go into his prone stance. From here, most projectiles pass harmlessly over him, while Chris can fire Prone Shot with impunity while calling crossover assists.

Prone Position absolutely dominates a large majority of the long range firefight matches in the game, since most characters don't have projectiles that they can angle downward far enough to hit Chris. These characters need to abandon the idea of a long range fight and approach Chris, something they typically aren't good at doing.

In *Ultimate Marvel vs. Capcom 3*, Prone Position has become significantly more useful: Chris can initiate and cancel out of Prone Position much more quickly. This makes it much less of a commitment to go into and out of the prone stance, and Chris becomes much less of a sitting duck when competitors do decide to move forward.

Prone Position also has another wackier use: see the Advanced Tactics section for details!

18

Prone Shot: Chris shoots at his target from Prone Position, causing chip damage while still going clear under most projectiles. Combined with a long range crossover assist, Prone Shot is incredibly difficult for most zoning characters to deal with.

Prone Shot received a marked improvement along with Prone Position in *Ultimate Marvel vs. Capcom 3*—the shot recovers much more quickly! This gives Chris a much more rapid rate of fire, and combined with the quick speed of canceling out of Prone Position, the ability to simply change tactics when the opposing player begins to make a move.

Hyper Combos

Screen	Name	Command	Hits	Damage	Startup	Active	Recovery	Advantage on Hit	Advantage if Guarded	Notes
1	Grenade Launcher	↓↘→ + ATK ATK	4	343,700	15+4	112	37	—	—	First hit incapacitates foe for 113 frames, does not incapacitate airborne foes, second hit causes spinning knockdown, third hit cause knockdown, fourth hit causes spinning knockdown, has homing capability, each projectile has 1 high priority durability point
2	Sweep Combo	→↓↘ + ATK ATK	22	290,400	10+2	4(10)3(27)8(27)17(20)7(43)20	53	—	-31	Second hit floor bounces foe, 21st and 22nd hits cause spinning knockdown
3	Satellite Laser (Level 3 Hyper Combo)	↓↙← + ATK ATK	27	445,500	35+1 (Lock On 14)	37	43	—	—	Invulnerable for (35+7) frames, creates a cursor to aim Satellite Laser, pressing any button fires, allows three shots within time limit, each shot is OTG-capable, time limit is 260 frames, each shot has 20 frames of startup

1

Grenade Launcher: Chris fires a single high priority grenade forward that freezes his opposition, then a homing grenade up into the air, finally followed by two more forward grenades. The homing grenade comes down last, effectively shielding Chris from all but invincible attacks and throws. This makes Grenade Launcher an effective tool for safely resetting the momentum in a match.

If the first freeze grenade hits Chris' target out of the air, it causes a hard knockdown, but the rest of the hyper combo does not connect in most situations. This makes its usage in juggle combos and THCs very limited. The homing grenade does do a good job of keeping Chris relatively safe, however. There are a few other ways to use this: using a THC immediately after Chris fires the homing grenade is a safe way to get Chris out of the game and another teammate in. Using a THC into Grenade Launcher is also a strong way to get another teammate out of the game.

While Grenade Launcher can indeed be used to win long range firefights, it's generally preferable to use Gun Fire H instead: fullscreen combos after a Gun Fire H hit actually lead to much more damage without costing a hyper combo gauge bar! Against a cornered opponent, you can hyper combo cancel into and link more hits after a Grenade Launcher, but it's a very meter-inefficient combo that inflicts barely more damage than a standard corner combo.

2

Sweep Combo: Sweep Combo sees a much more prominent role in *Ultimate Marvel vs. Capcom 3* as Chris' primary combo ender. The newly cancelable crouching Ⓗ attack allows you to tack this onto any combo ending with a hard knockdown, and improvements to the Sweep Combo allow it to be used in combos where you've already used a ground bounce.

While the second hit of Sweep Combo still causes a ground bounce state in *Ultimate Marvel vs. Capcom 3*, it now also causes a hard knockdown state if a ground bounce has already been used. This causes the shotgun portion of the hyper combo to miss completely, but the newly OTG-capable machine-gun portion then picks your adversary back up to get hit by the rest of it!

Sweep Combo allows for easy THC opportunities afterward; your opponent is left slowly spinning in the air at ground level all the way until they hit the ground. Combined with Chris' new combo potential, a single hit leading into a Sweep Combo with a THC is enough to K.O. most characters!

Satellite Laser: A strange level 3 hyper combo, Satellite Laser allows you to move a cursor onscreen and direct up to three OTG-capable shots of unscaled damage. The startup speed of Satellite Laser is remarkably slow, so you'll need to hyper combo cancel it from hard knockdown attacks like Combination Punch H and Gun Fire H.

3

Holding a button down during the activation of Satellite Laser determines where the cursor initially appears: Ⓛ puts the cursor in front of Chris, Ⓜ places it halfway across the screen, Ⓗ aims all the way across the screen, and not holding any button down at all causes the cursor to appear directly on top of Chris. This allows you to combo into Satellite Laser from anywhere on the screen! However, be sure not to press any other buttons until the Satellite Laser cutscene has finished; pressing buttons too early causes the cursor to show up on Chris!

Satellite Laser has a lot of invincibility, but most of it is used in its startup frames. It can generally only be used for this purpose to beat other hyper combos; everything else is simply too fast to react to.

Battle Plan

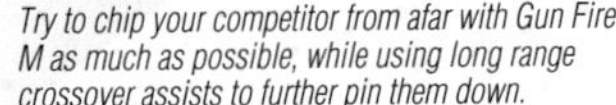
Try to chip your competitor from afar with Gun Fire M as much as possible, while using long range crossover assists to further pin them down.

If an encroaching opponent gets within striking range, try to have a landmine out at all times.

Most character matchups involve an opposing character trying to get close to Chris, while Chris is trying to force them to guard as many bullets as possible.

From afar, your gameplan revolves around Gun Fire M and long range crossover assists. Long range assists that remain active threats for a long period time are preferred, like Sentinel—α, Arthur—β, or even Ryu—β. These assists clog up the screen, are more difficult to avoid, and buy you more time for more shots of Gun Fire M.

Your rival must generally take to the air to avoid Gun Fire M. If the opposing character has limited air mobility options, simply delay your Gun Fire M a bit to force them to land into it and push them away again. If the competitor has mobility options like an airdash, you'll have to use Gun Fire L to reliably stop that type of approach. When stopped in this manner, it's very common for opponents to immediately jump again, so don't be afraid to use Gun Fire L several times in a row!.When your target eventually gets within half-screen distance, try to have a Grenade Toss L mine out at all times to cover yourself. Even if your opponent manages to hit Chris, the landmine explodes and hits Chris' opponent, as well. This is one of Chris' most damaging combo starters; juggle a crouching Ⓜ from the explosion, and go to town!

If your adversary does not have a projectile or a teleport, repeatedly doing Grenade Toss L followed by Gun Fire M is a great stalling tactic; laying down the landmine makes the machine-gun safe, and the machine-gun can push opponents far enough away to allow you to drop another landmine. Mix in crossover assists for even better results! Opponents without projectiles or teleports can generally only counter this tactic hitting with an attack that knocks down; they'll still get blasted by the landmine, but you won't be able to capitalize with a combo. From there, they can ground recover toward you and cover that last bit of distance.

If the opposing player starts doing this, simply stop using Gun Fire M and guard the opponent's knockdown attack instead. This causes them to still get hit by the landmine, which you can convert into a combo. Competitors jumping toward you without pressing a button are easily air thrown, which also goes into a full combo.

Another strong tactic against a mid range rival is to use the newly cancelable properties of the ⇨ + Ⓜ Low Shot: simultaneously call a crossover assist with Low Shot, then cancel Gun Fire L to prevent your foe from jumping, Gun Fire M to counter guarding, or Grenade Toss M or H for more aggressive play.

Alternatively, when your attacker gets into medium range, you can take this as an opportunity to suddenly begin attacking with Air Gun Fire L! This is especially powerful when your opponent is wary of landmines.

If the opposing character super jumps toward you, you'll want to place a landmine out to be waiting for them as they land. This forces them to come down without pressing a button, which in turn opens them up for another air throw.

If the opponent manages to get near you and begins to attack, use advancing guard as much as possible with the eventual goal of buying enough space to drop another landmine. This tactic buys you enough time to call a crossover assist while jumping away with Air Gun Fire L. When on defense, keep an eye out for opportunities to air throw, as well; not only are they among the most reliable anti-airs in the game, they're also one of Chris' main sources of damage!

Fighting against other dedicated projectile-based characters is simultaneously Chris' strongest point and biggest liability. Against most characters, Chris can dominate the long range match with the high durability and damage of Gun Fire H, along with the evasive properties of Prone Shot. However, some characters can float in the air at super jump height and rain down projectiles onto Chris. He generally doesn't have an answer to this other than to attempt to move in and establish an offense.

Most long range firefights revolve around the threat of Gun Fire H. If your adversary is firing any projectiles on the ground or at normal jump height, the magnum shot can generally slice cleanly through all projectiles and wall bounce any point and assist characters in its way. From here, you can convert into a damaging combo. See the Combo Usage section for details.

To combat Gun Fire H, your opponent can crouch directly under it before returning fire. In this situation, simply use Gun Fire M from across the screen to force an action out of your rival. A few characters are able to beat out Gun Fire H in a firefight, especially when they have a crossover assist backing them up. In these cases, you can simply use Prone Position to go clear under all of the incoming projectiles while pecking at the opposing character's feet with Prone Shot. When all the projectiles have flown by and the coast is clear, call a long range crossover assist to further frustrate your competitor. Between Prone Position and Gun Fire H, most characters have no choice but to either abandon the ranged game and go on offense, or take to the air and fire projectiles downward.

Gun Fire H has a high amount of durability points to win firefights with. It also leads to fullscreen combos!

The evasive properties of Prone Position give some characters fits; it forces them to either take to the air or to go on offense.

If your opponent decides to move in while Chris is in Prone Position, there's little to no risk involved; simply tap up on the controller to quickly cancel out of Prone Position and take advantage of Chris' newfound quickness in *Ultimate Marvel vs. Capcom 3*. Plop down a landmine, and proceed into standard defensive measures!

The fight becomes substantially more difficult against characters who can rain down projectiles from super jump height. If the opposing character can only fire one projectile in the air before falling, the best counter is to super jump toward the foe over their projectile and counter with air Gun Shot H. If it hits, you can quickly dash forward and launch your target for a combo. If your adversary can stay in the air and fire multiple projectiles down, then they'll be too high for any of Chris' guns to hit. Trying to maintain a long range fight in this case is futile, so you'll have to wavedash forward under the projectiles and try to get under your opponent. Go for an air throw on their way down, or lay down a landmine and set up your offense.

Air Gun Fire L is incredibly good; it deals a ton of chip damage while leaving you at a huge frame advantage!

Opponents trying to stop Chris' offense will inevitably jump. Counter this with an air throw into big damage.

Attacking with Chris midscreen can easily be summed up: jump in your rival's face and use the shotgun or the magnum, looking for opportunities to land an air throw all while pushing your target to the corner.

Air Gun Fire L is an amazing tool—it fires a gigantic spread of shotgun pellets in front of Chris, effectively making it impossible to anti-air except with invincible attacks. If guarded, it inflicts up to 60,000 points of chip damage and leaves you with a massive frame advantage of up to 38 frames. If it hits, you get to tack on a full combo that can carry your competitor to the corner!

When your jumping shotgun blasts are guarded, you have a number of simple options:

Jump forward and shotgun again

Use the massive frame advantage to call a crossover assist and use Grenade Toss H

Immediately use Gun Fire M against opponents who use advancing guard

Dash forward and mix up crouching Ⓛ with a throw

Wait on the ground in anticipation of the opposing character jumping forward to counter Air Gun Shot L, then do your own counter with Grenade Toss L or air throw

The most effective way to deal with Air Gun Fire L is to guard the blast in the air: the opponent recovers immediately upon touching the ground, drastically reducing guardstun and Chris' frame advantage. From there, the best option is to jump forward and meet Chris in the air with an attack or air throw. Counter this by having a landmine waiting for your foe when they land, or jump forward and air throw them yourself!

Against a cornered opponent, you can use the jumping shotgun a whole lot more due to advancing guard being weakened. This forces your attacker to make a move much more quickly, as the threat of nearly endless jumping shotguns is not an appealing one.

The corner allows you to get much more creative with Chris' offensive tools. Grenade Toss H in particular becomes much more deadly because you can force the opposing player to guard the following sequence: Low Shot pressed simultaneously with a crossover assist, cancel into Grenade Toss H, Gun Fire L to detonate the grenade and keep the opponent from jumping, then Gun Fire M as they are stuck in the pool of fire. Depending on the crossover assist used, this can amount up to 240,000 points of chip damage!

This is also a useful after knocking out a character. Before the next character comes in, use Grenade Toss H as many times as you can, force your adversary to guard Gun Fire L immediately as they enter the playing field, then tack on as many Gun Fire M shots as you can. When the fire begins to dissipate, call a long range crossover assist and move back in with jumping shotguns!

COMBO USAGE

CHRIS

I. CR. Ⓜ, ST. Ⓗ, → + Ⓗ CANCEL ⇒ ↓ ↙ ← + Ⓗ, WAVEDASH TWICE, OTG CR. Ⓗ CANCEL ⇒ ↓ ↙ ← + Ⓗ, FORWARD JUMP, AIR ↓ ↘ → + Ⓗ, LAND, → + Ⓗ, Ⓢ CANCEL ⇒ FORWARD SUPER JUMP, AIR Ⓜ, Ⓜ, Ⓗ, Ⓢ, LAND, FORWARD DASH, CR. Ⓗ CANCEL ⇒ → ↓ ↘ + ATK ATK

733,600 damage, 7% meter gain (or self sufficient for Sweep Combo ender)

Chris's main combo inflicts heavy damage while dragging his adversary across the screen, making it possible to transition into a corner variation (Combo II) if Chris is midscreen or closer to it. If air Ⓢ hits your opponent into a corner, perform a backwards jump Air Gun Fire H instead of a forward one. This ensures that the gun shot is properly positioned to hit the cornered competitor.

Crouching Ⓜ is Chris' preferred combo-starter in most cases: it has much farther range than crouching Ⓛ, and forgoing the crouching Ⓛ also substantially increases the total damage in the combo. However, don't hesitate to use crouching Ⓛ where speed is a factor—landing the hit is much more important than a few points of damage!

Try to get into the habit of verifying if your attacks are hit or guarded before the standing Ⓗ. Ending at standing Ⓗ is by far Chris' safest option: it has a 2 frame disadvantage and is out of range of most throws.

Chris doesn't have a great way to salvage his offense if his attacks are guarded without the help of a crossover assist. You can delay the → + Ⓗ hit to try to catch a rival pressing buttons, but this is a risky endeavor. If the → + Ⓗ is guarded, your safest bet is to cancel into Combination Punch L and roll the dice on whether or not your opponent can time their throw attempt well enough or not. If they are going for a throw, you can jump straight up while guarding. If they mistime the throw, they instead whiff a standing Ⓗ attack, allowing you to come down with air Ⓢ for a full combo.

II. (REQUIRES CORNER) CR. Ⓜ, ST. Ⓗ, → + Ⓗ CANCEL ⇒ ↓ ↙ ← + Ⓗ, OTG CR. Ⓗ CANCEL ⇒ ↓ ↙ ← + Ⓗ, OTG CR. Ⓗ CANCEL ⇒ ↓ ↘ → + Ⓗ, Ⓢ CANCEL ⇒ FORWARD SUPER JUMP, AIR Ⓜ, Ⓜ, Ⓗ, Ⓢ, LAND, {BACKWARDS JUMP, AIR ↓ ↘ → + Ⓗ, LAND, FORWARD DASH, Ⓢ CANCEL ⇒ FORWARD SUPER JUMP, AIR Ⓢ} OR {CR. Ⓗ CANCEL ⇒ → ↓ ↘ + ATK ATK}

605,100~776,900 damage, 107%~25% meter gain (or self-sufficient for Sweep Combo ender)

The corner variant of Chris' combo is both easier and more damaging! Of the two options shown, the first variation builds the most meter while still dealing strong damage. The second variation inflicts 176,000 more damage at the cost of a hyper combo gauge bar.

III. ↓ ↘ → + Ⓗ, WAVEDASH FORWARD 3 TIMES, OTG → + Ⓜ CANCEL ⇒ ↓ ↘ → + Ⓗ, FORWARD DASH, FORWARD JUMP, AIR OTG ↓ ↘ → + Ⓗ, LAND, → + Ⓜ CANCEL ⇒ ↓ ↘ → + Ⓗ

556,900 damage, 62% meter gain

Gun Fire H is used to counter most projectiles outright, or to punish mistakes from a distance. A successful hit leads to heavy damage from anywhere on screen, but you must wavedash as quickly as possible after the initial shot to move into range for the OTG Low Shot. When canceling the Low Shot, be sure to let the controller return to neutral before inputting the command for Gun Fire H to prevent accidentally getting Grenade Toss H instead.

IV. THROW OR AIR THROW, CR. Ⓗ CANCEL ⇒ ↓ ↙ ← + Ⓗ, WAVEDASH TWICE, OTG CR. Ⓗ CANCEL ⇒ ↓ ↙ ← + Ⓗ, FORWARD JUMP, AIR ↓ ↘ → + Ⓗ, LAND, → + Ⓗ, Ⓢ CANCEL ⇒ FORWARD SUPER JUMP, AIR Ⓜ, Ⓜ, Ⓗ, Ⓢ, LAND, FORWARD DASH, CR. Ⓗ CANCEL ⇒ → ↓ ↘ + ATK ATK

492,700 damage, 2% meter gain

Chris can get great damage from throws without the help of an assist. Shift into **Combo V** if the Combination Punches carry your adversary to the corner.

V. (REQUIRES CORNER) THROW OR AIR THROW, CR. Ⓗ CANCEL ⇒ ↓ ↙ ← + Ⓗ, CR. Ⓗ CANCEL ⇒ ↓ ↙ ← + Ⓗ, CR. Ⓗ CANCEL ⇒ ↓ ↘ → + Ⓗ, Ⓢ CANCEL ⇒ FORWARD SUPER JUMP, AIR Ⓗ, Ⓢ, LAND, CR. Ⓗ CANCEL ⇒ → ↓ ↘ + ATK ATK

535,300 damage, 9% meter loss

A corner variant of Chris' throw combos.

COMBO APPENDIX

GENERAL EXECUTION TIPS

After hitting Combination Punch H, input a dash immediately before jumping to get that extra distance you need.

To cancel Low Shot into Gun Fire H, return the controller to neutral before inputting the ↓ ↘ → motion; otherwise, you'll get Grenade Toss H on accident!

(AGAINST AIRBORNE OPPONENT) AIR M, H, S, LAND, ST. L, M CANCEL ➡ ↓ ↙ ← + H, JUMP FORWARD, AIR ↓ ↘ → + H OTG, LAND, → + H, S CANCEL ➡ SUPER JUMP, AIR M, M, H, S, LAND, CR. H OTG CANCEL ➡ → ↓ ↘ + ATK ATK

Notes	Damage
Air to air combo	659,700 damage

→ ↓ ↘ + L, (LANDMINE HIT), CR. M, ST. H, → + H CANCEL ➡ ↓ ↙ ← + H, JUMP FORWARD, AIR ↓ ↘ → + H OTG, → + H, S CANCEL ➡ SUPER JUMP, AIR M, M, H, S, LAND, DASH FORWARD, CR. H OTG CANCEL ➡ → ↓ ↘ + ATK ATK

Notes	Damage
Combo from errant landmine hit	749,800 damage

CR. L, M, ST. H, → + H CANCEL ➡ → ↓ ↘ + L, CR. L, M, ST. H, → + H CANCEL ➡ ↓ ↙ ← + H, JUMP FORWARD, AIR ↓ ↘ → + H OTG, LAND, → + H, S CANCEL ➡ SUPER JUMP, AIR H, S, LAND, DASH FORWARD, CR. H OTG CANCEL ➡ → ↓ ↘ + ATK ATK

Notes	Damage
Character-specific, you can continue a combo from a point-blank Grenade Toss L against some characters	692,700 damage

AIR ↓ ↘ → + H, DASH, CR. M, ST. H, → + H CANCEL ➡ ↓ ↙ ← + H, JUMP FORWARD, AIR ↓ ↘ → + M OTG, LAND, → + H, S CANCEL ➡ SUPER JUMP, AIR M, M, H, S, LAND, DASH, CR. H OTG CANCEL ➡ → ↓ ↘ + ATK ATK

Notes	Damage
Combo from a mid range Air Gun Shot H	695,000 damage

(WHEN THE ENEMY IS AT LONG RANGE AND NEAR A CORNER) ↓ ↘ → + H, WAVEDASH FORWARD 3 TIMES, OTG → + M CANCEL ➡ ↓ ↘ → + H, FORWARD DASH, FORWARD JUMP, AIR OTG ↓ ↘ → + H, LAND, → + H, S CANCEL ➡ FORWARD SUPER JUMP, AIR M, M, H, S, LAND, OTG ↘ + H CANCEL ➡ → ↓ ↘ + ATK ATK

Notes	Damage
A successful Gun Fire H hit leads to huge damage as long as the opponent's back is near a corner	819,400 damage, 11% meter loss

CR. M, ST. H, → + H CANCEL ➡ [X-Factor], ST. M, H, → + H, S CANCEL ➡ FORWARD SUPER JUMP, AIR M, M, H, S, LAND, FORWARD JUMP, AIR ↓ ↘ → + H, LAND, → + H, S CANCEL ➡ FORWARD SUPER JUMP, AIR M, H, S, LAND, CR. H CANCEL ➡ → ↓ ↘ + ATK ATK

Notes	Damage
An easy X-Factor combo that starts off of a verifiable opening	1,133,400~1,461,800 damage, 63%~115% meter gain

THROW OR AIR THROW, CR. H CANCEL ➡ ↓ ↙ ← + H CANCEL ➡ [X-Factor], WAVEDASH TWICE, OTG CR. H CANCEL ➡ ↓ ↙ ← + H, FORWARD JUMP, AIR ↓ ↘ → + H, LAND, → + H, S CANCEL ➡ FORWARD SUPER JUMP, AIR M, M, H, S, LAND, FORWARD DASH, CR. H CANCEL ➡ → ↓ ↘ + ATK ATK

Notes	Damage
An X-Factor throw combo that starts off of a verifiable opening	875,800~1,126,300 damage, 33~71% meter gain

(REQUIRES CORNER) CR. M, ST. H, → + H CANCEL ➡ ↓ ↙ ← + H, OTG CR. H CANCEL ➡ ↓ ↙ ← + H, OTG CR. H CANCEL ➡ ↓ ↘ → + H CANCEL ➡ ↓ ↙ ← + ATK ATK, OTG H, OTG H, OTG H, SATELLITE LASER ENDS, OTG CR. H CANCEL ➡ → ↓ ↘ + ATK ATK

Notes	Damage
A high damage corner combo that requires 4 meters-to use	1,155,400 damage, 324% meter loss

"I'LL BE DAMNED IF I LOSE ANOTHER PARTNER."

ADVANCED TACTICS

THAT FLOOR'S STILL KINDA DIRTY

After hitting sweep combo in the corner, the opponent will likely knockdown recover forward to try to get out of the corner.

If you didn't move at all, you can attack the opposing character from the front...

...or you can move forward slightly and attack them from the other side!

After Sweep Combo, the common reaction is to knockdown recover forward. If you do not move, the ground recovery roll just barely misses crossing up Chris. Standing still and hitting your opponent with a crouching Ⓛ attack is already pretty tricky! If you tap forward even slightly at the last second, Chris indeed gets behind the target, creating a deceiving mix-up.

If your adversary comes out of the roll concentrating on which side to guard, simply wait half of a beat and throw them. Very few characters can survive two successive combos from Chris!

If your opponent ground recovers backward, there aren't many great counter measures for that. Using Grenade Toss H is ideal, but that is very easily punished by an opposing character ground recovering forward. Since keeping your foe in the corner is more important than anything else, call an assist that can pin the opponent for ground recovering backward, all while positioning Chris for the above mix-up in case they go the other way.

THE LAZY MAN'S CROSS-UP DEFENSE

When opponents get behind Chris in Prone Position, the game treats it like he's getting up from a knockdown.

This makes him completely invincible for a moment...

...and sometimes able to punch fools in the face while they're vulnerable!

Ultimate Marvel vs. Capcom 3 is chock-full of dangerous offense based off of cross-ups. A lot of the better cross-ups are very low-risk, often even leaving the attacker at an advantage if guarded. Chris has a funky trick for these guys!

When an adversary gets behind Chris while he's in Prone Position, he is forced to stand back up. This act of standing up is treated as if he's rising from a knockdown. In other words, he's completely invincible until he's able to move!

However, if the opposing character does not cross Chris up, Chris can be hit from the front just like any other character can... assuming that the attack hits low enough to actually make contact with Chris.

Using Prone Position is a very aggressive way to counter cross-up happy players: read the cross-up attempt coming and get into Prone Position beforehand. When the cross-up attack completely whiffs through Chris' invulnerable body, react and punish accordingly! In some cases, you'll be able to land a full combo, but in most, you'll be able to get at least a guaranteed throw. Watch jaws drop as Dark Phoenix teleports behind you only to get her neck broken!

CHUN-LI

"YOU CAN'T BEAT ME WITH JUST BRUTE STRENGTH. GO AHEAD AND TRY."

Bio

REAL NAME

Chun-Li

OCCUPATION

Interpol Officer

ABILITIES

Extremely proficient in kung-fu, she is well-known for her varied and beautiful kicks more than her punches. Like Ryu, she is also able to utilize her spiritual energy in battle.

WEAPONS

None

PROFILE

She tirelessly continues her investigation to take down the criminal organization Shadaloo. While her strong sense of duty and obligation are readily apparent, she also longs to live the life of an ordinary woman.

FIRST APPEARANCE

Street Fighter II (1991)

POWER GRID

3	INTELLIGENCE
2	STRENGTH
3	SPEED
2	STAMINA
3	ENERGY PROJECTION
5	FIGHTING ABILITY

*This is biographical, and does not represent an evaluation of the in-game combat potential of this hero.

ALTERNATE COSTUMES

1

2

3

4

5

6

DLC

Overview

Vitality	850,000
Chain Combo Archetype	Marvel Series

X-Factor Boost	Damage	Speed
Level 1 (3 teammates remaining)	120%	120%
Level 2 (2 teammates remaining)	135%	135%
Level 3 (1 teammate remaining)	150%	150%

Your goal with Chun-Li is to achieve point-blank range against your opponent.

The extremely execution-heavy Chun-Li has access to a great mix-up at this range:

- Instant overhead Yosokyaku, which leads into a combo from anywhere on the screen
- The low-hitting crouching Ⓜ: a fast, ranged attack that leads into an even more damaging combo
- Chainable crouching Ⓛ attack, which can be delayed in an attempt to hit adversaries trying to use advancing guard
- Throws and air throws, which also lead into combos

How do you get Chun-Li into point-blank range?

- Using her ability to triple jump to approach from angles that are difficult to defend against
- Using the kara airdash technique to quickly airdash twice and cover a lot of ground
- Wavedashing forward on the ground when your competitor is expecting an aerial approach
- Advancing forward behind the cover of crossover assists
- Cornering a foe with the aid of her jump-cancelable normal attacks, and by hitting combos that can carry the opponent all the way into the corner

TUNING SINCE ORIGINAL MVC3

While Chun-Li received a number of improvements in the transition to *Ultimate Marvel vs. Capcom 3*, two stand out for having a much bigger impact than the rest: Yosokyaku (air ⇩ + Ⓜ) is now OTG-capable, giving you some execution-heavy ways to extend Chun-Li's combos and increase damage. While midscreen combos were eventually found that allow Chun-Li to combo into a Kikosho, the OTG-capable Yosokyaku allows her to land combos from her throws and air throws without the help of a crossover assist!

Chun-Li also received an entirely new special attack in her invulnerable EX Spinning Bird Kick, which is great for shutting down offensive rivals. Not to be ignored, her Kikosho hyper combo is now mashable— this adds a chunk of much-needed damage to her combos!

- Health increased from 800,000 to 850,000
- Yosokyaku is now OTG-capable
- New Move: EX Spinning Bird Kick. Hold ⇩ until flashing, ⇧ + ATK. Can also be performed in the air
- There is now a larger window to cancel Kikoken H to Kikoanken
- Tenshokyaku startup speed improved from 3 to 2 frames
- Air Tenshokyaku now recovers in neutral state instead of being vulnerable all the way until Chun-Li touches the ground
- Kikosho can be mashed for additional hits and damage
- Shichisei Ranka now automatically realigns with the opposing character if the foe goes behind Chun-Li after the initial hits

Attack Set

Standing Basic Attacks

Screen	Command	Hits	Damage	Meter Gain	Startup	Active	Recovery	Advantage on Hit	Advantage if Guarded	Notes
1	Standing Ⓛ	1	35,000	280	4	2	12	-1	-2	Chain-cancelable into Ⓛ attacks
2	Standing Ⓜ	1	50,000	400	6	3	16	-1	-2	—
3	Standing Ⓗ	1	70,000	560	10	3	18	+2	+1	Jump- cancelable

Crouching Basic Attacks

Screen	Command	Hits	Damage	Meter Gain	Startup	Active	Recovery	Advantage on Hit	Advantage if Guarded	Notes
1	Crouching Ⓛ	1	33,000	264	4	2	11	0	-1	Chain-cancelable into Ⓛ attacks
2	Crouching Ⓜ	1	48,000	384	6	3	14	+1	0	Low attack
3	Crouching Ⓗ	1	60,000	480	8	5	23	—	-6	Low attack, knocks down, jump-cancelable

Ground Special Attack—Launcher

Screen	Command	Hits	Damage	Meter Gain	Startup	Active	Recovery	Advantage on Hit	Advantage if Guarded	Notes
1	Ⓢ (while standing or crouching)	1	70,000	560	8	5	27	—	-10	Launcher, not special- or hyper combo-cancelable

Air Basic Attacks

Screen	Command	Hits	Damage	Meter Gain	Startup	Active	Recovery	Advantage on Hit	Advantage if Guarded	Notes
1	Air Ⓛ	1	40,000	320	4	3	16	+8	+7	Overhead attack, jump- cancelable
2	Air Ⓜ	1	55,000	440	6	6	18	+13	+12	Overhead attack, jump- cancelable
3	Air Ⓗ	1	70,000	560	8	4	18	+14	+13	Overhead attack, jump- cancelable

Air Special Attacks—Flying Screen and Air Exchange

Air Ⓢ causes a hard knockdown when used in a launcher combo (this is sometimes called flying screen). When used outside of a launcher combo, air Ⓢ behaves mostly like another basic attack. Air exchange attacks, performed by inputting a direction plus Ⓢ, are only possible during a launcher combo. Exchange hits initiate team aerial combos by tagging in the next available character to continue the air combo.

Screen	Command	Hits	Damage	Meter Gain	Startup	Active	Recovery	Advantage on Hit	Advantage if Guarded	Notes
1	Air Ⓢ	1	70,000	560	8	4	18	+15	+14	Causes hard knockdown if used in launcher combo
2	Air ⇧ + Ⓢ (during launcher combo)	1	25,000	200	8	4	18	—	—	Tags in next available ally while lofting foe upward
3	Air ⇨ or ⇦ + Ⓢ (during launcher combo)	1	40,000	320	8	4	18	—	—	Tags in next available ally while causing wall bounce, erases 1 hyper meter from opponent
4	Air ⇩ + Ⓢ (during launcher combo)	1	60,000	480	8	4	18	—	—	Tags in next available ally while causing ground bounce, generates 1 hyper meter

1

2

3

4

Command Attacks

Command attacks resemble basic attacks but have different chaining and canceling properties. It's usually possible to chain *into* a command attack from basic attacks, but most command attacks cannot be chained from or canceled themselves.

Screen	Name	Command	Hits	Damage	Meter Gain	Startup	Active	Recovery	Advantage on Hit	Advantage if Guarded	Notes
1	Kakukyakuraku	⇨ + Ⓗ	1	80,000	640	29	3	8	+12	+11	Airborne from frame 6, overhead attack, jump-cancelable, not special- cancelable
2	Yosokyaku	(In air) ⇩ + Ⓜ	1	65,000	520	4	11	6	—	—	Overhead attack, attack cancels into a diagonally up-forward bounce if hit, Chun-Li is in neutral state during bounce
3	Taunt	Select button	1	10,000	104	10	5	16	+2	+1	Cancelable into special moves, hyper combos, and Ⓢ
—	Wall Jump	Jump backward against the wall, then press ⬃	—	—	—	—	—	—	—	—	Performs a wall jump, may initiate aerial attacks or movement after 8th frame

1

2

3

Throws

Throws are for snagging passive or blocking foes. Since throws are active so quickly, you can also use them to preemptively toss opposing characters out of their offense. Combos are usually possible after throws, one way or another.

Screen	Command	Hits	Damage	Meter Gain	Startup	Active	Notes
1	⇨ + Ⓗ (ground)	1	80,000	800	1	1	Hard knockdown
	⇦ + Ⓗ (ground)	1	80,000	800	1	1	Hard knockdown
2	⇨ + Ⓗ (air)	1	80,000	800	1	1	Hard knockdown
	⇦ + Ⓗ (air)	1	80,000	800	1	1	Hard knockdown

1

2

As a Partner—Crossover Assists

Screen	Type	P1+P2 Crossover Combination Hyper Combo	Description	Hits	Damage	Meter Gain	Startup	Active	Recovery (this crossover assist)	Recovery (other partner)	Notes
1	Chun-Li—α	Kikosho	Kikoken L	1	50,000	400	43	—	126	96	Projectile lasts 88 frames, projectile has 5 low priority durability points
2	Chun-Li—β	Kikosho	Tenshokyaku M	5	101,400	1040	27	1(1)2 (3)1(5) 1(8)1	126	96	Knocks down foe
3	Chun-Li—γ	Hoyokusen	Hyakuretsukyaku H	10	97,300	1200	31	61	93	63	Knocks down opponent

The choice of which crossover assist type to assign to Chun-Li is an easy one: Chun-Li —γ's Hyakuretsukyaku is among the best assists in the game: it's incredibly fast and keeps your competitor in place for a long period of time. This makes it a natural fit for use in both combos and in offensive attack patterns! The Hyakuretsukyaku assist is no slouch on the defensive end of things, either: while it's not invincible, its quick speed and large attacking hitboxes can often interrupt an adversary moving in for the attack. Be sure to react accordingly and convert these hits into a combo!

Chun-Li —α's Kikoken L can be a useful asset to more defensive-minded teams; a slow-moving projectile on the screen is never a bad thing! Chun-li —β is best avoided; although it's a very fast assist that is only vulnerable for 1 frame before attacking, in practice, it is difficult to use for either defensive or offensive purposes.

Snap Back

Screen	Command	Hits	Damage	Meter Gain	Startup	Active	Recovery	Advantage on Hit	Advantage if Guarded
1	↓ ↘ → + P1⇔P2	1	50,000	500 - (-1 hyper meter bar)	1	4	17	—	+1

Notes

On hit, snap back forces the opposing point character to be replaced by an assist. Opposing assist calls or tag outs are also locked out for 4 seconds

Special Moves

Screen	Name	Command	Hits	Damage	Meter Gain	Startup	Active	Recovery	Advantage on Hit	Advantage if Guarded	Notes
1	Kikoken L	← ↙ ↓ ↘ → + L	1	50,000	400	19	—	26	-2	-3	Projectile lasts 88 frames, projectile has 5 low priority durability points
	Kikoken M	← ↙ ↓ ↘ → + M	1	70,000	560	19	—	26	0	-1	Projectile lasts 32 frames, projectile has 5 low priority durability points
	Kikoken H	← ↙ ↓ ↘ → + H	1	90,000	720	19	—	26	+2	+1	Projectile lasts 8 frames, projectile has 5 low priority durability points
2	Kikoanken	(During Kikoken H) H	1	100,000	800	19	5	18	—	+4	Causes crumple stun
3	Spinning Bird Kick L (in air OK)	↓ (charge), ↑ + L	2	76,000	640	9	20	27 (in air, until grounded)	-6 (in air, +28)	-15 (in air, +5)	Knocks down foe, air version has an additional 2 frames of grounded recovery
	Spinning Bird Kick M (in air OK)	↓ (charge), ↑ + M	3	94,800	840	9	30	24 (in air, until grounded)	+3 (in air, +28)	-12 (in air, +7)	Knocks down opponent, air version has an additional 2 frames of grounded recovery
	Spinning Bird Kick H (in air OK)	↓ (charge), ↑ + H	4	113,400	1056	9	40	21 (in air, until grounded)	+5 (in air, +30)	-8 (in air, +10)	Knocks down adversary, air version has an additional 2 frames of grounded recovery
4	EX Spinning Bird Kick	↓ (charge)(while flashing), ↑ + ATK	10	162,400	2000	9	35	26 (in air, until grounded)	+7 (in air, +25)	-6 (in air, +9)	Hold ↓ 90 frames to charge, invincible from frames 1-11, knocks down rival, not special- or hyper combo-cancelable
5	Hyakuretsukyaku L (in air OK)	L)))	4-10	51,500 – 107,200	48-0~ 1440	7	22	1	+24 (in air, +30)	+15 (in air, +15)	Knocks down competitor, can be mashed for additional hits
	Hyakuretsukyaku M (in air OK)	M)))	5-14	61,300 - 115,200	600~ 1680	7	22	1	+24 (in air, +31)	+14 (in air +16)	Knocks down foe, can be mashed for additional hits
	Hyakuretsukyaku H (in air OK)	H)))	8-19	85,100 – 130,600	960~ 2280	7	22	1	+24 (in air +33)	+12 (in air, +14)	Knocks down opponent, can be mashed for additional hits

Special Moves continued

Screen	Name	Command	Hits	Damage	Meter Gain	Startup	Active	Recovery	Advantage on Hit	Advantage if Guarded	Notes
6	Tenshokyaku L	→↓↘ + L	3	78,400	720	2	2(1)2 (4)3	19	+22	0	Airborne from frame 1, knocks down adversary
	Air Tenshokyaku L	(in air) →↓↘ + L	3	78,400	720	2	4(6)3	18	+25	0	Knocks down rival
	Tenshokyaku M	→↓↘ + M	5	101,400	1040	2	2(1)2 (3)1(5) 1(8)1	22	+27	-25	Airborne from frame 1, knocks down competitor
	Air Tenshokyaku M	(in air) →↓↘ + M	5	101,400	1040	2	4(5)2 (4)2(7)3	21	+26	-22	Knocks down foe
	Tenshokyaku H	→↓↘ + H	7	120,000	1360	2	2(1)1(5) 1(5)1(8) 1(5)1(8)3	13	+42	-38	Airborne from frame 1, knocks down opponent
	Air Tenshokyaku H	(in air) →↓↘ + H	7	120,000	1360	2	4(5)2(4) 2(7)2(4) 2(7)3	13	+44	-33	Knocks down adversary

Kikoken: Even though Chun-Li's signature projectile may look anemic in comparison to the other crazy projectiles in the game, the Kikoken L is a surprisingly useful tool! It moves very slowly across the screen, making it great for use as covering fire to advance behind, especially if you do not have a long range crossover assist handy. On the defensive end, repeated use of Kikoken L is surprisingly annoying for your opposition to get around, forcing your competitor to take to the air.

None of the Kikoken projectiles travel all the way across the screen: Kikoken L travels two-thirds of the distance of the screen while dealing the least damage, Kikoken M has half-screen reach and median damage, while Kikoken H barely travels a third of the screen and inflicts the most damage.

What this means to Chun-Li's gameplan is simple: use Kikoken L almost exclusively, with very situational use of Kikoken H in combos!

Kikoanken: You can cancel Kikoken H directly into Kikoanken by pressing H within the first 10 frames of the Kikoken's animation. It's not possible to get a "slow" Kikoanken by pressing H on the last possible frame; the startup speed of the attack is always 19 frames regardless.

Kikoanken is Chun-Li's most damaging single-hit attack, and it also causes a crumple stun state on your rival. This makes it ideal for use early on in combos before damage scaling becomes severe!

If guarded, Kikoanken leaves Chun-Li with 4 frames of advantage, letting her continue attacking afterward. However, opposing players typically start using advancing guard to push Chun-Li away instead of allowing her to repeatedly inflict chip damage with Kikoanken.

Spinning Bird Kick: One of the few attacks in the game that require a "charge," to perform the Spinning Bird Kick, you must first hold ↓ on the controller for at least 35 frames. Afterward, pressing ↑ along with an attack button executes the attack.

The ground version of the Spinning Bird Kick is difficult to use effectively; while it moves Chun-Li forward a long distance, it is very unsafe if guarded and has little payoff if it hits.

The air version of Spinning Bird Kick is much more useful, being a key component of Chun-Li's combos when performed as low to the ground as possible. Chun-Li recovers from the air version of Spinning Bird Kick a mere 2 frames after touching the ground, granting huge frame advantage when executed low to the ground. To perform a low-altitude Spinning Bird Kick, simply press the attack button a few frames after pressing ↑ on the controller; this tactic allows Chun-Li to jump into the air before performing the attack.

Chun-Li does not recover from air Spinning Bird Kick until she reaches the ground, so use of this attack any higher than extremely low altitudes is not recommended.

EX Spinning Bird Kick: A new special attack in *Ultimate Marvel vs. Capcom 3*, the EX Spinning Bird Kick is completely invulnerable for a large period of time, making it great for stopping offense oriented opponents in their tracks.

The EX version of the Spinning Bird Kick requires much more charge time than the regular version: 90 frames in total. To help notify you (and your rival!) when the EX Spinning Bird Kick is available, Chun-Li starts radiating a pink color.

The EX Spinning Bird Kick is unsafe if guarded. However, you can cancel the recovery frames into an invincible Hoyokusen hyper combo if your competitor attempts to retaliate.

This attack becomes much more powerful when used in the air, preferably at low altitudes; it then grants frame advantage if guarded and allows for combos if it hits!

Hyakuretsukyaku: Chun-Li's most useful, all-around special attack. Hyakuretsukyaku is fast and has great hitboxes that can beat most other attacks. If the attack hits, you can easily verify this and proceed into a combo. If guarded, Chun-Li is left at large frame advantage to work with, but your adversary will likely use advancing guard against this attack.

You can also have Chun-Li perform Hyakuretsukyaku in the air, which is useful both in combos and as a way to turn around and hit your target after airdashing behind them. Its multiple hits scales combos heavily, so it's best used near the end of a combo if possible.

Tenshokyaku: Chun-Li performs a number of kicks upward while rising into the air, but the usage of Tenshokyaku isn't what one might expect. Due to its newly increased speed in *Ultimate Marvel vs. Capcom 3*, this attack is actually best used as a way to punish guarded attacks that have at least 2 frames of disadvantage, which you can then convert into a combo. Of the three versions of the attack, Tenshokyaku L should be used almost exclusively due to its much quicker recovery.

The 2 frame startup speed of Tenshokyaku also makes it great for countering ground-based assaults: it usually interrupts or trades with anything thrown at it. In the event that it does get cleanly interrupted, Tenshokyaku puts Chun-Li in an airborne state on its first frame— this often makes it difficult for many characters to convert that hit into a combo. If guarded, Tenshokyaku leaves Chun-Li in the air and able to act, completely safe.

Also new to Chun-Li, the air version of Tenshokyaku recovers in a neutral state, leaving Chun-Li free to move. Previously, she was vulnerable all the way until she reached the ground!

Hyper Combos

Screen	Name	Command	Hits	Damage	Startup	Active	Recovery	Advantage on Hit	Advantage if Guarded	Notes
1	Kikosho	↓↘→ + ATK ATK	14~27	286,300~ 340,700	8+1	88	38	—	-32	Knocks down foe, beam durability: 14 frames x 3 high priority durability points, can be mashed for additional hits
2	Hoyokusen	↓↙← + ATK ATK	14	230,000	10+3	38(7) 34(7)6	42	—	-26	Invincible from frames 1-16, final hit is a launcher attack
3	Shichisei Ranka (level 3 hyper combo)	→↓↘ + ATK ATK	14	410,000	10+3	2(2)2(2) 2(2)2(20)3	27	—	-8	Invincible from frames 1-21, hard knockdown

Kikosho: Primarily used to end combos, the Kikosho is a fast hyper combo that covers a large area of the screen. Afterward, it allows for easy THC combos into nearly any other hyper combo in the game. New to *Ultimate Marvel vs. Capcom 3*, the Kikosho can now be mashed for additional damage!

Due to its relatively quick speed and huge area of effect, the Kikosho is also useful as a general utility hyper combo, countering several tactics from an opposing player. However, it is not invincible at all on its startup, and it is also very unsafe if guarded.

Hoyokusen: Fully invincible for 16 frames, Hoyokusen ends with a launcher attack to allow for follow-up combos afterward. Contrary to what one might think, Chun-Li players should generally avoid using Hoyokusen during combos because it adds a heavy amount of hitstun scaling to the entire combo while only marginally increasing the overall damage.

Instead, it should be used as a utility hyper combo for its invincibility; use it against obvious ground-based approaches or to cleanly beat other hyper combos on reaction.

Shichisei Ranka: This level 3 hyper combo has the same speed and range as the Hoyokusen, but it has slightly more invincibility to blow through opposing attacks. Shichisei Ranka's use should generally be restricted as a combo-ender that isn't subject to damage scaling; when used as an invincible attack, Hoyokusen actually results in more damage for less cost.

Battle Plan

Chun-Li's unique airdash is fast, but it doesn't travel very far...

...however, with the kara airdash technique, you can string two airdashes together to travel a surprising distance!

Before discussing any strategy, it should be mentioned that Chun-Li is a ridiculously execution-heavy character, likely more so than any other character in the game. To get the most out of Chun-Li, you need to constantly do difficult things, such as "kara" dashing to get near your opponent and executing low-altitude Spinning Bird Kicks and EX Spinning Bird Kicks for combos and for defense. Even the instant overhead Yosokyaku, which is the focal point of her offense, requires a combo that takes several hours of practice! If after reading this, you believe you have the patience and dedication required to truly get the most out of Chun-Li, read on!

In order to get her within point-blank range of a rival, you must take advantage of Chun-Li's large assortment of mobility options. While many characters in the game have access to a double jump, only Chun-Li and Viewtiful Joe have the ability to triple jump (well, Dante can in Devil Trigger mode if you want to count that). This allows Chun-Li to switch directions twice in the air, letting you have her do things like super jump forward, double jump backward to evade an anti-air attempt, then triple jump back toward her opponent again to begin attacking!

Triple jumps also allow Chun-Li to reach a great height while still in a normal jump state, giving access to crossover assists. This makes some interesting techniques possible, like triple jumping over all projectiles controlling the ground, calling a crossover assist to pin the target under you in place, then dropping in for the attack! Stay creative!

Chun-Li has a unique airdash, traveling 30 degrees downward at a very quick speed. It travels a much shorter distance when compared to most airdashes in the game, making it difficult to base an approach solely around the airdash.

The "kara" airdash technique helps remedy this—although airdashes normally can't be canceled directly into one another, you can both airdash twice in a row *and* get an option-select throw by first airdashing, then inputting → + H~ATK. This automatically kara-cancels a brief normal and an air throw attempt, neither of which you ever actually see, into a second airdash immediately. Simply drum → + H~ATK as fast as possible while your first airdash is in progress—also known as "plink" airdashing. This allows you to string two airdashes together and cover two-thirds of the screen's distance! This is an absolutely critical tool for Chun-Li; practice it in Training Mode until you can perform this tactic nearly 100% of the time!

Competitors worrying about Chun-Li's aerial approach eventually have to give up on ground control; it's pointless to fire projectiles and beams on the ground when Chun-Li is but a kara airdash or triple jump away from circumventing all of those projectiles and closing the distance. When your adversary stops giving you things to jump over, that's your cue to call a crossover assist and wavedash in on the ground!

Chun-Li is more reliant on crossover assists than other characters to close the distance and maintain offense against foes. Long range crossover assists such as Sentinel —α, Akuma —β, Rocket Raccoon —γ, and nearly any projectile-based assist are ideal teammates for her.

When you successfully reach point-blank range, Chun-Li's offense revolves around the threat of an instant overhead Yosokyaku performed immediately after leaving the ground. Impossible to guard on reaction, hitting the Yosokyaku allows you to immediately airdash with Chun-Li afterwards and combo an air Tenshokyaku L from the other side. From there, you can go into her execution-heavy Spinning Bird Kick loop combos! See the Combo Usage section for details.

Since it is impossible for an opponent to guard an overhead Yosokyaku on reaction, your competitor must simply commit to guarding high. To counter this, simply attack with the low-hitting crouching M attack instead. Leading in with a crouching M attack is a little unintuitive and may seem slow, but Chun-Li's crouching M has a very respectable 6 frames of startup: only a single frame slower than the average crouching L attack, and with a lot more range! From the crouching M, chain into a standing H and verify if the opposing character is guarding or not: if your opponent eats a hit, cancel into Kikoken H (to Kikoanken) and continue with a combo. If the attacks are guarded, jump cancel the standing H attack and airdash back in to continue your offense. Remember to call crossover assists to pin your adversary in place!

You can use Yosokyaku as an instant overhead attack against all opposing characters, and this move leads into a combo from anywhere on screen!

An opponent's use of advancing guard is one of Chun-Li's biggest problems. To combat this, stagger the timing of the chainable crouching (L) attack to mess up your opponent's timing!

Low-altitude EX Spinning Bird Kicks are a very powerful tool on defense. Completely invincible to stop your opponent's offense, they are safe if guarded and lead to a combo if they hit!

Tenshokyaku L has only 2 frames of startup, making it great for punishing attacks with slight disadvantage. You can then transition into a combo!

The overhead and low attack mix-up is best performed when you have a decent amount of frame advantage, usually after forcing your rival to guard a crossover assist. If the situation is more neutral, dashing in with Chun-Li's fast crouching (L) attack is a good way to establish control. Opponents who are wary of Chun-Li's Yosokyaku generally try to use advancing guard to try to push her away. However, using advancing guard on reaction to a single crouching (L) attack is nearly impossible to do. As such, you can perform two to three crouching (L) attacks with staggered timing; if the opposing player attempts to use advancing guard and mistimes it, they'll instead get a crouching (H) attack. This then is counterhit by Chun-Li's crouching (L) and allows you to verify and go into a full combo!

If your opponent wises up and stops trying to use advancing guard, you have several options available to you:

- **Throw the opposing character and go into a (difficult) combo**
- **Dash in and immediately attack with crouching (L) again, maintaining offense**
- **Manually buffer a dash with ⇨⇨ into the end of a crouching (L), then immediately jump and instant overhead with Yosokyaku**
- **Use crouching (M) to beat attempts to guard the Yosokyaku**
- **Super jump and immediately airdash behind your rival to cross them up with either crouching (L) or air Hyakuretsukyaku**

While you may spend a frustrating amount of time fighting against advancing guard and using jump-canceled attacks in an effort to stay in close, don't get discouraged! All of the advancing guard usage from your opponent is effectively pushing them farther back into the corner. Chun-Li's offense is much stronger against cornered competitors: advancing guard does not push her back nearly as far of a distance, and instant overhead Yosokyaku leads to a more damaging (and easier!) combo.

When defending against an assault from her adversary, Chun-Li actually has many more potent defensive options than the majority of the cast. Between Tenshokyaku L, EX Spinning Bird Kick, Hoyokusen, and Hyakuretsukyaku H, Chun-Li can give her aggressor much more to worry about than just advancing guard and air throws!

Tenshokyaku L executes in only 2 frames, making it one of the fastest attacks in the game that isn't a command throw. This is great for punishing attacks that have a -2 to -3 frame disadvantage! Hitting Tenshokyaku L leads to a combo and also punishes attacks from out of Chun-Li's throw range. Tenshokyaku L is also completely safe if guarded; attacking with Yosokyaku on the way down likely interrupts anything your opponent tries to do.

For attacks that have a disadvantage of -4 or more, punish with Chun-Li's fast crouching (L), resulting in a full ground combo. Between throws, Tenshokyaku L, and crouching (L), Chun-Li has a great number of moves that would otherwise be safe against other characters.

While Tenshokyaku L isn't invincible at all, its 2 frame startup causes it to beat most ground-based offenses, or at the very least trade. If Chun-Li gets hit out of Tenshokyaku L, she is in the air on the first frame, making it difficult for many characters to convert into a full combo.

The fully invincible Hoyokusen is great for just blasting through any ground-based offenses, and it is an option that your opponent must respect when approaching on the ground. Hitting with Hoyokusen leads into a full combo that builds back much of the hyper combo gauge used; see the Combo Usage section for details. Hoyokusen is incredibly unsafe if guarded, so be ready to THC to a safer teammate if possible.

One-frame air throws are still the best defense against airborne approaches, and in *Ultimate Marvel vs. Capcom 3*, you can finally convert these into a full combo while playing Chun-Li—without the help of a crossover assist!

A great option that works against both ground and air-based approaches is the fully invincible EX Spinning Bird Kick. The catch: you have to hold ⇩ on the controller for what seems like an eternity before having access to it. If your competitor stays close to Chun-Li primarily with jumping attacks, you won't be able to safely keep holding down on the controller for the requisite 90 frames. Once you do have it available, your adversary must take notice—a low-altitude EX Spinning Bird Kick is completely safe and leads into a combo if hit!

The following characters can crouch directly under a perfectly timed low-altitude EX Spinning Bird Kick:

- **Amaterasu**
- **Morrigan**
- **Phoenix**
- **Rocket Raccoon**

The ground version of EX Spinning Bird Kick is still a very strong tool, but the risk and the reward aren't quite as favorable. Hitting the target with the ground version of EX Spinning Bird Kick does not lead into a combo, and guarding it allows your opponent to retaliate with a combo. To help mitigate this, try hyper combo canceling the vulnerable recovery frames into an invincible Hoyokusen!

Another less glamorous alternative is to simply mash on the (H) button whenever you have a bit of space—Hyakuretsukyaku H can be very difficult for some characters to get around, and if it hits, you can easily verify and go into a combo!

Some character match-ups make it advantageous for a Chun-Li player to hang back and play defensively rather than trying to get close and force Yosokyaku mix-ups. In these situations, repeated use of Kikoken L provides a surprisingly solid ranged game for your adversary to deal with. Bolster this with crossover assists and an occasional backdash to help keep foes away.

To further frustrate offense oriented opponents, Chun-Li's ability to wall jump lets you stall the match for long periods of time. This is ideal for waiting out temporary power-ups like X-Factor or Wolverine's Berserker Charge. Normal jump back against the wall, wall jump forward, double jump back to the wall, wall jump yet again, triple jump back to the wall, and then wall jump a final time! From here, waste even more time by performing air Tenshokyaku H three times. Afterward, call a crossover assist to cover your descent, all while attacking with Yosokyaku on the way down to help prevent getting hit by an air throw.

COMBO USAGE

1. CR. (M), ST. (H) CANCEL ⇨ ← ↙ ↓ ↘ → + (H) CANCEL ⇨ (DURING KIKOKEN H) (H), ST. (H), CR. (H), (S) CANCEL ⇨ VERTICAL SUPER JUMP, AIR ↓ + (M), (H), (S), LAND, FORWARD DASH, VERTICAL JUMP, FORWARD AIRDASH, AIR ↓ + (M), (M), (M), (H), (S), LAND, (H)(H)(H) CANCEL ⇨ {↓ ↘ → + (ATK)(ATK) (MASH (ATK))} OR {→ ↓ ↘ + (ATK)(ATK)}

631,000~832,100 damage, 17~217% meter loss

Even Chun-Li's most basic combo is still difficult! With the new OTG-capable properties of Yosokyaku, Chun-Li can land decent damage off of this midscreen combo without an assist.

When the crouching (M), standing (H) opening is guarded, jump cancel it into a forward airdash (H), or chain into crouching (H) to Hyakuretsukyaku H. In the event that your foe uses advancing guard, jump-cancel the standing (H) attack and perform a kara airdash to move back into attack range.

Note that hitstun decay is high during this combo, which can easily cause the air attacks after OTG ↓ + (M) to whiff entirely. If this combo is preceded by a jump attack or assist hit of any sort, perform the Kikoanken and then immediately press (S) to launch your rival; omitting the (H) attacks should be just enough to keep the combo going. This also makes the entire combo much easier if you're starting off of the normal opening, so if you need lax timing, make this adjustment.

COMBO USAGE CONT.

11. CR. Ⓜ, ST. Ⓗ [CANCEL] ←↙↓↘→ + Ⓗ [CANCEL] (DURING KIKOKEN H) Ⓗ, DASH BACKWARDS, → + Ⓗ (HOLD ↓ FOR SPINNING BIRD KICK), ST. Ⓗ, CR. Ⓗ [CANCEL] JUMP, ↑ + Ⓗ (HOLD ↓ FOR SPINNING BIRD KICK), LAND, ST. Ⓗ, CR. Ⓗ [CANCEL] JUMP, ↑ + Ⓗ (HOLD ↓ FOR SPINNING BIRD KICK), LAND, CR. Ⓗ, [CANCEL] JUMP, ↑ + Ⓗ (HOLD ↓ FOR SPINNING BIRD KICK), LAND, Ⓗ)), MASH Ⓗ [CANCEL] {↓↘→ + ATK ATK (MASH ATK)} OR {→↓↘ + ATK ATK}

684,500 damage, 8% meter loss

This improved combo requires an extremely high level of execution, involving a lot of charge storing and fancy low-altitude Spinning Bird Kicks to work. However, this combo results in more damage, carries your adversary all the way into the corner, and is more consistent when mastered. Learning Spinning Bird Kick loops with Chun-Li takes time, but knowing how to do this pays dividends in the end!

After Kikoanken hits, immediately dash backwards and perform Kakukyakuraku (→ + Ⓗ) just as you start to move. This moves Chun-Li into a position that ensures Kakukyakuraku doesn't fly over her target's head. Immediately begin holding ↓ on the controller once the attack begins. After landing, store your charge by briefly letting the controller return to neutral to press standing Ⓗ, then immediately start charging ↓ again. Chain into crouching Ⓗ, then hold ↑ to jump cancel it.

The next tricky part of the combo requires you to perform a low-altitude version of the Spinning Bird Kick. After pressing ↑ to jump cancel the crouching Ⓗ attack, wait just a few frames to allow Chun-Li time to leave the ground before pressing Ⓗ again. If performed correctly, Chun-Li juggles her attacker with a low-altitude Spinning Bird Kick! Afterward, have Chun-Li juggle the opponent with your basic attack of choice before proceeding to juggle with another low-altitude Spinning Bird Kick!

While the Kakukyakuraku and the standing Ⓗ attacks add a fair amount of damage to the combo, they aren't necessary at all. Omitting those attacks entirely and simply concentrating on juggling low-altitude Spinning Bird Kicks still nets around 650,000 points of damage and carries your competitor to the corner.

ADVANCED TACTICS

THE TAC INFINITE

Chun-Li has a true infinite combo, but it has a ton of serious caveats.

When hitting with a team aerial combo, the new character coming in enjoys a brief period of time where hitstun scaling is completely reset and also does not advance at all until the character touches the ground. Given the right circumstances, Chun-Li never has to touch the ground at all, keeping her adversary locked in an infinite combo!

Now before you get excited, there are a number of limitations to the infinite combo:

- You must hit your target with two upward team aerial combos in the same combo
- You must have a teammate character who is able to increase the height of the target a fair amount during the combo
- Generally, one of your teammates must be knocked out

The goal is to get Chun-Li into play with a team aerial combo, then get the opposing character up to the very top of the playing field. From here, you can simply hit with Yosokyaku repeatedly while hugging the ceiling, completely unaffected by hitstun scaling.

So what gets a rival really high on the screen? Well, there's Chun-Li's own combos, using triple jumps, Hyakuretsukyaku H, and tons of Yosokyaku to bounce both characters up. After that, you have upward TAC attacks to launch the target to a great height. For the last bit, you'll have to rely on the combos of other characters. Characters like Viewtiful Joe, Dante (in Devil Trigger), and C. Viper have combos that happen at a much higher elevation than most.

Setting up the infinite combo works best if one character on your team has been knocked out. From here, you can start the combo with Chun-Li, gain a ton of height, upward TAC to a second character who will do their best to raise the height even farther, then finally upward TAC back into Chun-Li again!

While an experienced opponent is unlikely to let you hit two upward TACs in the same combo, this infinite gives you a great indirect effect: while your competitor absolutely cannot let you hit an upward TAC, you are free to drain meter from them with forward TACs, or gain an entire bar yourself with a downward TAC.

CHARGE IT TO THE GAME

Charge attacks can be stored for 8 frames. This allows you to do silly things like charge an EX Spinning Bird Kick...

...wavedash across the screen, making sure to never let go of the down direction for long...

...and then still be able to have access to the charge move!

Chun-Li's Spinning Bird Kick attacks require the ↓ direction on the controller to be held down for a period of time. This restricts a lot of your options: you can't move, you can't perform standing attacks, and you can't jump. However, the game allows you to retain your charge after letting go of the ↓ direction for up to eight frames. Presumably, this window exists to facilitate tools like Chun-Li's low-altitude Spinning Bird Kick. What probably wasn't intended—moving the controller back to ↓ continues to store the charge! This allows you to do a couple of fun yet execution-heavy things:

You can perform wavedashing by ATK ATK, then canceling with ↓, then ATK ATK again. As long as there aren't more than 8 frames between each ↓ input, this allows Chun-Li to wavedash while still having access to EX Spinning Bird Kick! While this isn't something you need to do often, it can be useful when used with the right crossover assists: call Sentinel —α, wavedash forward when your opponent is guarding the drones, then smack your rival with a low-altitude EX Spinning Bird Kick when they try to press a button!

An interesting thing to note: Chun-Li stops glowing pink as soon as the ↓ direction on the controller is released. Storing the charge by returning the controller to the ↓ position does not make Chun-Li glow again; you can wavedash across the screen with no indication that you have an EX Spinning Bird Kick locked and loaded.

The other, more practical use of storing charge is to add more damage to combos. Most of Chun-Li's combos involve Spinning Bird Kick loops—holding ↓ the entire time means that you'll have to completely omit standing Ⓗ from your combos. With stored charge, this is no longer an issue! You can do things like Kikoanken while holding ↓, very quickly release the charge to input the standing Ⓗ, back down to crouching Ⓗ to retain the charge, then jump cancel and still be able to perform the Spinning Bird Kick!

III. JUMP FORWARD, INSTANT ↓ + Ⓜ, AIRDASH, → ↓ ↘ + Ⓛ, LAND, JUMP FORWARD (HOLD ↓ FOR SPINNING BIRD KICK), AIR Ⓛ, Ⓜ, Ⓜ, Ⓗ, Ⓢ, LAND, CR. Ⓛ, Ⓜ, Ⓗ CANCEL ⇒ JUMP, ↑ + Ⓗ (HOLD ↓ FOR SPINNING BIRD KICK), LAND, CR. Ⓜ, Ⓗ CANCEL ⇒ JUMP, ↑ + Ⓗ (HOLD ↓ FOR SPINNING BIRD KICK), LAND, Ⓗ)), MASH Ⓗ CANCEL ⇒ ↓ ↘ → + ATK ATK (MASH ATK)

548,200 damage, 11% meter loss

Chun-Li can land a full combo from an instant overhead Yosokyaku, but this also requires a ton of practice! Immediately tap ATK ATK after hitting the Yosokyaku to airdash behind the opposing character, then combo into an air Tenshokyaku L from the other side. Note that the input command for Tenshokyaku must be performed in the opposite direction! After landing from Tenshokyaku L, immediately jump forward and perform the aerial chain combo while holding a ↓ charge. When you land, you'll have just barely enough time to juggle the crouching Ⓛ to be able to proceed into Spinning Bird Kick loops.

V. AIR FORWARD OR BACK THROW, AIRDASH, ↓ + Ⓜ (HOLD ↓ FOR SPINNING BIRD KICK) CANCEL ⇒ Ⓜ)), AIR Ⓗ, LAND, CR. Ⓜ, Ⓗ CANCEL ⇒ JUMP, ↑ + Ⓗ (HOLD ↓ FOR SPINNING BIRD KICK), LAND, CR. Ⓜ, Ⓗ CANCEL ⇒ ↑ + Ⓗ, LAND, Ⓗ)), MASH Ⓗ CANCEL ⇒ ↓ ↘ → + ATK ATK (MASH ATK)

453,000 damage, 26% meter loss

Using the OTG-capable Yosokyaku, Chun-Li can finally capitalize off of an air throw with a full combo!

VI. FORWARD OR BACK THROW, SUPER JUMP, AIRDASH, ↓ + Ⓜ (HOLD ↓ FOR SPINNING BIRD KICK) CANCEL ⇒ Ⓜ)), AIR Ⓢ, LAND, CR. Ⓜ, Ⓗ CANCEL ⇒ JUMP, ↑ + Ⓗ, LAND, CR. Ⓜ, Ⓗ CANCEL ⇒ ↑ + Ⓗ, LAND, Ⓗ)), MASH Ⓗ CANCEL ⇒ ↓ ↘ → + ATK ATK (MASH ATK)

465,000 damage, 21% meter loss

Hitting the Yosokyaku after a normal throw requires precise timing, but it can be mastered with practice. During throw animation, buffer a super jump with ↓ ↑ slightly early. After that, you'll have to time the airdash and the Yosokyaku; some people at BradyGames simply time the initial airdash, then mash ↓ + ⓁⓂ to perform this combo!

COMBO APPENDIX

GENERAL EXECUTION TIPS

- When juggling after a low-altitude Spinning Bird Kick, press the attack button much earlier than you think you are able to
- When canceling Yosokyaku into Hyakuretsukyaku M, simply input ↓ + Ⓜ))
- Perform the ← ↙ ↓ ↘ → motion for Kikoanken slowly; players often miss a diagonal input and get Kakukyakuraku (→ + Ⓗ) instead

→ ↓ ↘ + Ⓛ, (HOLD ↓ FOR SPINNING BIRD KICK), AIR Ⓢ, LAND, CR. Ⓜ, Ⓗ CANCEL ⇒ JUMP, ↑ + Ⓗ (HOLD ↓ FOR SPINNING BIRD KICK), LAND, CR. Ⓜ, Ⓗ, CANCEL ⇒ JUMP, ↑ + Ⓗ (HOLD Ⓗ FOR SPINNING BIRD KICK), LAND, CR. Ⓗ, CANCEL ⇒ JUMP, ↑ + Ⓗ, LAND, Ⓗ)), MASH Ⓗ CANCEL ⇒ ↓ ↘ → + ATK ATK (MASH ATK)

Notes	Damage
Tenshokyaku L can be used to punish attacks that have a frame disadvantage of -2 or more	539,800 damage, 24% meter loss

↓ ↙ ← + ATK ATK CANCEL ⇒ FORWARD SUPER JUMP, AIR ↓ + Ⓜ, Ⓗ, Ⓢ, LAND, FORWARD DASH, VERTICAL JUMP, FORWARD AIRDASH, AIR ↓ + Ⓜ, Ⓜ, Ⓜ, Ⓗ, Ⓢ, LAND, Ⓗ)) CANCEL ⇒ ↓ ↘ → + ATK ATK (MASH ATK)

Notes	Damage
Combo starting from an invincible Hoyokusen hyper combo	508,900 damage, 152% meter loss

CHARGE ↓ UNTIL YOU START FLASHING, JUMP, ↑ + ATK, LAND, CR. Ⓗ CANCEL ⇒ JUMP, ↑ + Ⓗ (HOLD ↓ FOR SPINNING BIRD KICK), LAND, CR. Ⓗ, CANCEL ⇒ JUMP, ↑ + Ⓗ (HOLD ↓ FOR SPINNING BIRD KICK), LAND, Ⓗ)), MASH Ⓗ CANCEL ⇒ ↓ ↘ → + ATK ATK (MASH ATK)

Notes	Damage
Combo starting from an invincible low-altitude EX Spinning Bird Kick	468,900 damage, 23% meter loss

CHARGE ↓ UNTIL YOU START FLASHING, ↑ + ATK CANCEL ⇒ X-FACTOR, LAND, CR. Ⓗ CANCEL ⇒ JUMP, ↑ + Ⓗ (HOLD ↓ FOR SPINNING BIRD KICK), LAND, CR. Ⓗ, CANCEL ⇒ JUMP, ↑ + Ⓗ (HOLD ↓ FOR SPINNING BIRD KICK), LAND, Ⓗ)), MASH Ⓗ CANCEL ⇒ ↓ ↘ → + ATK ATK (MASH ATK)

Notes	Damage
X-Factor combo from the ground version of EX Spinning Bird Kick	617,700~754,500 damage, 34~16% meter loss

AIR ↓ + Ⓜ X-FACTOR, Ⓗ, LAND, CR. Ⓜ, ST. Ⓗ CANCEL ⇒ ← ↙ ↓ ↘ → + Ⓗ CANCEL ⇒ (DURING KIKOKEN H) Ⓗ, ST. Ⓗ, CR. Ⓗ CANCEL ⇒ JUMP, ↑ + Ⓗ (HOLD ↓ FOR SPINNING BIRD KICK), LAND, CR. Ⓗ CANCEL ⇒ JUMP, ↑ + Ⓗ (HOLD ↓ FOR SPINNING BIRD KICK), LAND, CR. Ⓗ, CANCEL ⇒ JUMP, ↑ + Ⓗ (HOLD ↓ FOR SPINNING BIRD KICK), LAND, Ⓗ)), MASH Ⓗ CANCEL ⇒ ↓ ↘ → + ATK ATK (MASH ATK)

Notes	Damage
X-Factor combo from instant overhead Yosokyaku	881,700~1,093,400 damage, 3~28% meter gain

CR. Ⓜ, ST. Ⓗ CANCEL ⇒ ← ↙ ↓ ↘ → + Ⓗ CANCEL ⇒ (DURING KIKOKEN H) Ⓗ CANCEL ⇒ X-FACTOR, ST. Ⓗ, CR. Ⓗ CANCEL ⇒ JUMP, ↑ + Ⓗ (HOLD ↓ FOR SPINNING BIRD KICK), LAND, CR. Ⓗ CANCEL ⇒ JUMP, ↑ + Ⓗ (HOLD ↓ FOR SPINNING BIRD KICK), LAND, CR. Ⓗ, CANCEL ⇒ JUMP, ↑ + Ⓗ (HOLD ↓ FOR SPINNING BIRD KICK), LAND, Ⓗ)), MASH Ⓗ CANCEL ⇒ ↓ ↘ → + ATK ATK (MASH ATK)

Notes	Damage
Verifiable X-Factor combo from basic opening	887,000~984,400 damage, 6~11% meter gain

C.VIPER

"I DON'T DO OVERTIME. AND I DON'T PARTICULARLY LIKE REMATCHES, EITHER. SO WOULD YOU MIND ACCEPTING YOUR LOSS AND GOING HOME?"

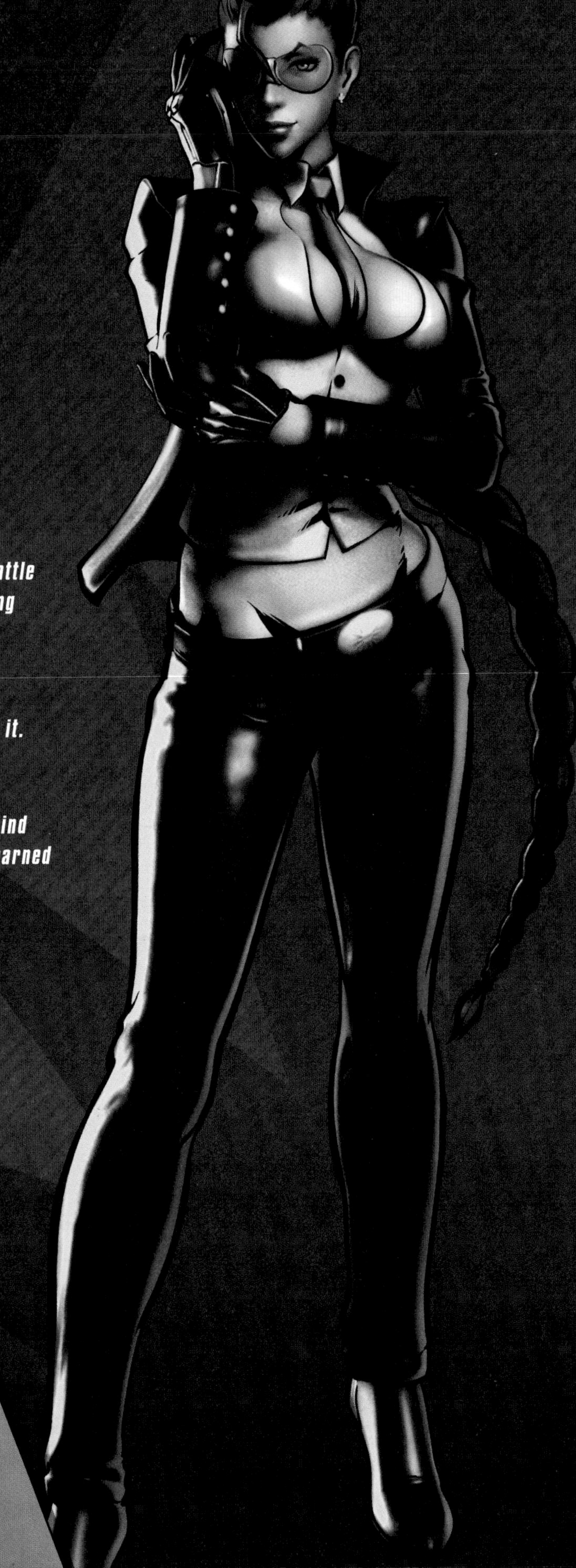

Bio

REAL NAME

Unknown

OCCUPATION

CIA Agent

ABILITIES

Has high physical abilities, complemented by her special battle suit equipped head to toe with weaponry. She uses a fighting style called "covert fighting tools," which she created.

WEAPONS

Her battle suit, which has various weapons integrated into it.

PROFILE

When it comes to work, she leaves honor and emotions behind and keeps it about business. Her diligence and efficiency earned her the nickname "Miss Perfect." However, in front of her daughter, she becomes a gentle, loving mother.

FIRST APPEARANCE

Street Fighter IV (2008)

POWER GRID

4	INTELLIGENCE
2	STRENGTH
3	SPEED
2	STAMINA
6	ENERGY PROJECTION
4	FIGHTING ABILITY

*This is biographical, and does not represent an evaluation of the in-game combat potential of this hero.

ALTERNATE COSTUMES

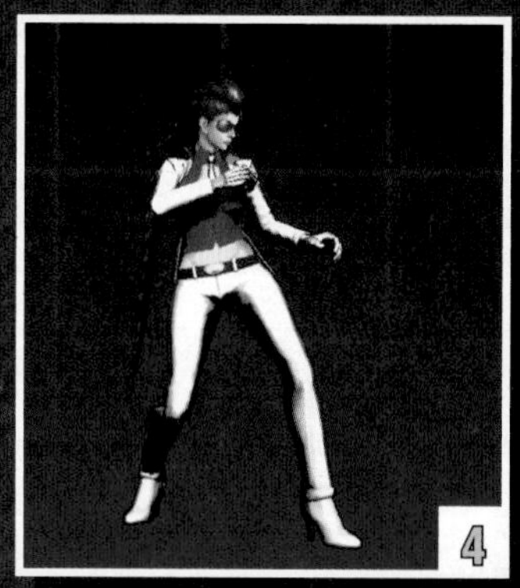

Overview

Vitality	900,000
Chain Combo Archetype	Marvel Series

X-Factor Boost	Damage	Speed
Level 1 (3 teammates remaining)	125%	115%
Level 2 (2 teammates remaining)	147.5%	122.5%
Level 3 (1 teammate remaining)	170%	130%

Your goal with C. Viper is to utilize her various tools to get her close to her opponent, the distance where she's most efficient. Why the simple goal?

- **Her Viper Elbow, triangle jump, and square jump offense is difficult to guard up close on reaction consistently, due to her speed as well as the angles of her air attacks**
- **Although a relatively difficult character to master execution-wise, she is capable of inflicting massive damage without using crossover assists or the corner**

For a melee character, C. Viper has a surprising number of tools to help her get close:

- **Seismic Hammer cancels to control space and to force movement from the opposing character**
- **Combining Seismic Hammer's jump cancel property with her eight-way airdash for versatile ways to engage her rival**
- **EX Thunder Knuckle to blow through projectiles, creating openings from fullscreen**
- **Thunder Knuckle M to advance and its Ⓢ-cancel to hit-confirm into her ground combos**
- **Focus Attack to absorb and counter attacks without being put into hitstun**

TUNING SINCE ORIGINAL MVC3

Aside from the addition of Optic Laser to her arsenal, C. Viper plays relatively similar to her previous counterpart. Her combos are now easier to perform due to the increased Ⓢ-cancel window on Thunder Knuckle.

- **The window to Ⓢ-cancel Thunder Knuckle has been increased**
- **C. Viper gained new special attack: Optic Laser**
- **Foes fall to ground faster after Burning Kick and air Burning Kick**
- **The forward momentum gained after super jumping and performing Ⓢ-canceled air Burning Kick has been reduced**

Attack Set

Standing Basic Attacks

Screen	Command	Hits	Damage	Meter Gain	Startup	Active	Recovery	Advantage on Hit	Advantage if Guarded	Notes
1	Standing L	1	40,000	320	5	3	10	0	-1	Low attack
2	Standing M	1	63,000	504	7	3	19	-4	-5	—
3	Standing H	1	75,000	600	9	3	22	-2	-3	—

1

2

3

Crouching Basic Attacks

Screen	Command	Hits	Damage	Meter Gain	Startup	Active	Recovery	Advantage on Hit	Advantage if Guarded	Notes
1	Crouching L	1	38,000	304	4	2	11	0	-1	—
2	Crouching M	1	60,000	480	7	3	20	-5	-6	Low attack
3	Crouching H	1	72,000	576	9	4	19	0	-1	—

1

2

3

Ground Special Attack—Launcher

Screen	Command	Hits	Damage	Meter Gain	Startup	Active	Recovery	Advantage on Hit	Advantage if Guarded	Notes
1	S (while standing or crouching)	2	75,000	640	8	5(3)6	24	—	-8	Launcher, not special- or hyper combo-cancelable

1

Air Basic Attacks

Screen	Command	Hits	Damage	Meter Gain	Startup	Active	Recovery	Advantage on Hit	Advantage if Guarded	Notes
1	Air L	1	43,000	344	6	3	15	+11	+10	Overhead attack
2	Air M	1	60,000	480	8	3	19	+16	+15	Overhead attack
3	Air H	1	73,000	584	7	3	24	+18	+17	Overhead attack

1

2

3

Air Special Attacks—Flying Screen and Air Exchange

Air (S) causes a hard knockdown when used in a launcher combo (this is sometimes called flying screen). When used outside of a launcher combo, air (S) behaves mostly like another basic attack. Air exchange attacks, performed by inputting a direction plus (S), are only possible during a launcher combo. Exchange hits initiate team aerial combos by tagging in the next available character to continue the air combo.

Screen	Command	Hits	Damage	Meter Gain	Startup	Active	Recovery	Advantage on Hit	Advantage if Guarded	Notes
1	Air (S)	1	75,000	600	9	4	23	+15	+14	Causes hard knockdown if used in launcher combo
2	Air ⇧ + (S) (during launcher combo)	2	105,00	880	8	5	43	—	—	Tags in next available ally while lofting opponent upward
3	Air ⇨ or ⇦ + (S) (during launcher combo)	2	95,000	800	8	3	20	—	—	Tags in next available ally while causing wall bounce, erases 1 hyper meter bar from foe
4	Air ⇩ + (S) (during launcher combo)	2	95,000	800	9	4	23	—	—	Tags in next available ally while causing ground bounce, generates 1 hyper meter bar

Command Attacks

Command attacks resemble basic attacks but have different chaining and canceling properties. It's usually possible to chain *into* a command attack from basic attacks, but most command attacks cannot be chained from or canceled themselves.

Screen	Name	Command	Hits	Damage	Meter Gain	Startup	Active	Recovery	Advantage on Hit	Advantage if Guarded	Notes
1	Viper Elbow	⇨ + (M)	2	65,000	520	22	4	13	+1	0	Overhead attack, chains into (S), may be canceled into a special move while in the air or during landing recovery
2	Focus Attack (can be charged)	(S) + (ATK)	1	70,000, 80,000 or 90,000	560, 640, or 720	25~77 (on release 12)	3	23	-3	-4	Attack charges minimum 14 frames, after the 6th frame up to the 5th (level 1 and 2) or 3rd (level 3) frame of recovery Viper has Hyper Armor, charging improves damage in three stages: release command during frames 1-30 for lv.1, frames 31-63 for lv.2, frames 64 and on for lv.3, lv.2/3 cause crumple, lv.3 version is unguardable, charging stance can be canceled into a dash or special move

Throws

Throws are for snagging passive or blocking opponents. Since throws are active so quickly, you can also use them to preemptively toss opposing characters out of their offense. Combos are usually possible after throws, one way or another.

Screen	Command	Hits	Damage	Meter Gain	Startup	Active	Notes
1	⇨ + (H) (ground)	12	80,000	800	1	1	Hard knockdown
	⇦ + (H) (ground)	12	80,000	800	1	1	Hard knockdown
2	⇨ + (H) (air)	12	80,000	800	1	1	Hard knockdown
	⇦ + (H) (air)	12	80,000	800	1	1	Hard knockdown

As a Partner—Crossover Assists

Screen	Type	P1+P2 Crossover Combination Hyper Combo	Description	Hits	Damage	Meter Gain	Startup	Active	Recovery (this crossover assist)	Recovery (other partner)	Notes
1	C. Viper —α	Emergency Combination	Thunder Knuckle H	1	80,000	640	29	7	130	100	Can be canceled with S when used as a crossover counter
2	C. Viper —β	Burst Time	Seismic Hammer	1	80,000	640	40	8	109	79	OTG-capable, can be canceled with S when used as a crossover counter, projectile has 5 low priority durability points
3	C. Viper —γ	Burst Time	Burning Kick	1	90,000	720	49	5	111	81	Overhead attack, can be canceled with S when used as a crossover counter, projectile has 5 low priority durability points

C. Viper has two generally useful crossover assists. C. Viper—β can be used as an OTG in combos, while C. Viper—γ counts as an overhead attack, great for opening up an opponent's ground defense. C. Viper—α can be used as a situational anti-air and as a crossover counter that leads to a combo (cancel it on hit by inputting S), but this is not recommended.

Snap Back

Screen	Command	Hits	Damage	Meter Gain	Startup	Active	Recovery	Advantage on Hit	Advantage if Guarded
1	⇩⇘⇨ + P1 or P2	1	50,000	500 (-1 hyper meter bar)	2	3	22	—	-3

Notes

On hit, snap back forces the opposing point character to be replaced by an assist. Opposing assist calls or tag outs are also locked out for 4 seconds

Special Moves

Screen	Name	Command	Hits	Damage	Meter Gain	Startup	Active	Recovery	Advantage on Hit	Advantage if Guarded	Notes
1	Thunder Knuckle L	⇩⇘⇨ + L	1	90,000	720	15	7	14	+2/+11	+1/+10	Projectile has 10 medium priority durability points, input S between frames 6-14 to cancel before hit, input S between frames 15-16 to cancel after hit. Second number in each frame field shows data when canceled
2	Thunder Knuckle M	⇩⇘⇨ + M	1	90,000	720	13	7	16	0/+11	-1/+10	Projectile has 10 medium priority durability points, input S between frames 3-12 to cancel before hit, input S between frames 13-14 to cancel after hit. Second number in each frame field shows data when canceled
3	Thunder Knuckle H	⇩⇘⇨ + H	1	100,000	800	5	7	44	-15/+24	-29/+10	Projectile has 10 medium priority durability points, input S between frames 1-4 to cancel before hit, input S between frames 5-6 to cancel after hit. Second number in each frame field shows data when canceled
4	Burning Kick L	⇩⇙⇦ + L	1	90,000	720	23	10	26	—	-14	Overhead attack, knocks down, projectile has 5 low priority durability points, input S between frames 7-14 to cancel before hit
4	Burning Kick M	⇩⇙⇦ + M	1	90,000	720	25	10	18	—	-6	Overhead attack, knocks down, projectile has 5 low priority durability points, input S between frames 9-16 to cancel before hit
4	Burning Kick H	⇩⇙⇦ + H	1	90,000	720	27	10	13	—	-1	Overhead attack, knocks down, projectile has 5 low priority durability points, input S between frames 10-17 to cancel before hit
4	Air Burning Kick L	(in air) ⇩⇙⇦ + L	1	80,000	640	21	10	Until grounded + 18	—	-6	Overhead attack, knocks down, projectile has 5 low priority durability points, input S between frames 6-11 to cancel before hit
4	Air Burning Kick M	(in air) ⇩⇙⇦ + M	1	80,000	640	19	10	Until grounded + 20	—	-9	Overhead attack, knocks down, projectile has 5 low priority durability points, input S between frames 6-11 to cancel before hit
4	Air Burning Kick H	(in air) ⇩⇙⇦ + H	1	80,000	640	17	10	Until grounded + 22	—	-11	Overhead attack, knocks down, projectile has 5 low priority durability points, input S between frames 6-11 to cancel before hit

Special Moves continued

Screen	Name	Command	Hits	Damage	Meter Gain	Startup	Active	Recovery	Advantage on Hit	Advantage if Guarded	Notes
5	Seismic Hammer	→↓↘ + ATK	1	80,000	640	16	8	35	-7	-18	Jump- cancelable after frame 19, projectile has 5 low priority durability points, input S between frames 6-11 to cancel before hit
—	Cancel	(during cancelable special) S	—	—	—	—	—	4/10	—	—	Thunder Knuckle and Seismic Hammer cancel recovery is 10 frames, Burning Kick cancel recovery is 4 frames
6	Optic Laser (can be charged)	ATK (hold down)	3	94,800	840	21	20	10	—	-7	Knocks down, requires 60 frames to charge, beam durability: 3 frames x 4 low priority durability points

Thunder Knuckle L: This is a mid range electrocuting poke attack. You can use this low-profile advancing move to duck under certain attacks while leading to combo opportunities. Make sure to utilize her S-cancel to combo from her Thunder Knuckle L on a confirmed hit. Also, canceling your ground basic attacks into this move is a good way to keep C. Viper in close quarters against her adversary.

Thunder Knuckle M: C. Viper performs a standing version of the Thunder Knuckle. Like Thunder Knuckle L, you can use this move to advance while being able to initiate combos by S-canceling. C. Viper sacrifices the low-profile property for a slightly faster startup over Thunder Knuckle L. This version of the Thunder Knuckle is preferably used in combos, while Thunder Knuckle L should be used on its own. Since both versions are S-cancelable, the difference in frame advantage on guard is practically non-existent.

Thunder Knuckle H: This attack shoots C. Viper diagonally up-forward into the air. It can be used as anti-air and is generally safe to use if it's S-canceled. You can also use it to initiate combos if it's canceled out of after a successful hit. Be careful with this attack, as it's unsafe when guarded if you don't cancel it; when used as anti-air, it must be done late and against low-altitude jumps in order for it to hit early enough for the S-cancel to be possible. This is difficult to do, so you may opt to save Thunder Knuckle H for combos only.

Burning Kick: These airborne flame kicks are considered overheads and must be guarded high. The L and M versions are unsafe when guarded, but they have a slightly faster startup. You can utilize Burning Kick H to start combos if followed by standing L on hit. The H version may also cross up opponents if performed point-blank; adding further flexibility to it, inputting S before Burning Kick H hits feints the attack, leaving Viper in front of the opposing character in an aerial state. From there, you can perform quick frontal air attacks against a rival expecting a hit from behind. Air versions of Burning Kick can be used in air combos or to change the trajectory and speed of her jumps. This move is generally safe to throw out at close range as long as the appropriate version is used, as the hittable portion of the flames is quite large in comparison to C. Viper's vulnerability.

Seismic Hammer: C. Viper slams the ground, causing an explosive pillar to appear, which actually counts as a projectile itself. The strength of the attack dictates where the explosion arises from. This is C. Viper's main zoning and spacing tool. It's OTG-capable and jump/super jump-cancelable on hit, when guarded, or when whiffed. The primary purpose of this move is to keep your opponent in check while allowing C. Viper to advance or retreat with her flexible air mobility options. You can also employ it as a proximity defense, such as against an incoming jump or airdash attack. It's also commonly used in combos (see **Combo I**). Since Seismic Hammer is jump-cancelable, and since pre-jump frames can be canceled into special moves, you can have C. Viper transition directly from Seismic Hammer into another Seismic Hammer, or into other special moves!

Optic Laser: Hold an attack button down until C. Viper's shades begin to flicker, then release the button to fire a horizontal optic blast at head height. Here's another one of C. Viper's zoning tools you can utilize to halt enemy advances near the ground. Most foes can crouch under the beam, as it is relatively high-profile, but it does stop foes from dashing briefly and may tag assists. There's only one version of this move, and only one can be charged at a time (holding more than one attack button does not allow you to fire more than one Optic Laser). Like with Zero's Buster Shot, you can swap the charge between buttons by starting to hold a different attack button down, and then releasing the first one; C. Viper continues charging her shades. Mix up your use of Seismic Hammer and Optic Laser to keep your adversary on his or her toes at a distance.

Hyper Combos

Screen	Name	Command	Hits	Damage	Meter	Startup	Active	Recovery	Advantage on Hit	Advantage if Guarded	Notes
1	EX Thunder Knuckle	⇩⬂⇨ + S (burns 1 bar of H.C. gauge)	1	150,000	1200 (-1 hyper meter bar)	10	38	28	—	-44	Crumples, frames 1-10 invincible, projectile has 10 medium priority projectile points, input S between frames 5-9 to cancel before hit, can be canceled into other EX attacks or hyper combos
2	EX Burning Kick	⇩⬃⇦ + S (burns 1 bar of H.C. gauge)	4	119,700 (20,000 x3 + 90,000)	1200 (-1 hyper meter bar)	9	10(5)5	20	—	-3	Knocks down, ignores hitstun decay, projectile has 5 low priority durability points, input S between frames 10-14 to cancel before hit, can be canceled into other EX attacks or hyper combos
	Air EX Burning Kick	(in air) ⇩⬃⇦ + S (burns 1 bar of H.C. gauge)	4	110,800 (20,000 x3 + 80,000)	1120 (-1 hyper meter bar)	6	10(5)5	Until grounded+16	—	-4	Knocks down, ignores hitstun decay, projectile has 5 low priority durability points, input S between frames 6-11 to cancel before hit, can be canceled into other EX attacks or hyper combos
3	EX Seismic Hammer	⇨⇩⬂ + S (burns 1 bar of H.C. gauge)	3	135,400	1200 (-1 hyper meter bar)	14	8	19	—	-5	Frame 1-16 invincible, knocks down, projectile has 5 low priority durability points, input S between frames 5-11 to cancel before hit, jump-cancelable after frame 19, can be canceled into other EX attacks or hyper combos
4	Emergency Combination	⇩⬂⇨ + ATK ATK	4	274,400	—	10+4	5(17)6 (13)6 (17)6	72	—	-74	Frames 1-36 invincible, third and fourth hits knock down, each punch nullifies 1 high priority projectile or beam (except Genmu Zero)
5	Burst Time	⇩⬃⇦ + ATK ATK	5	273,300	—	9+1	4(26)64	57	—	-99	Frames 6-13 are invincible, knocks down, OTG-capable, first attack hits low, first hit is a projectile with 100 high priority durability points
6	Viper Full Throttle	⇨⇩⬂ + ATK ATK (level 3 hyper combo)	22	430,000	—	10+0	10	49	—	-38	Frames 1-14 invincible, hard knockdown

EX Thunder Knuckle: C. Viper becomes a projectile and lunges fullscreen with a 10 medium durability point projectile attached to her fist. Use this to blow through projectiles to crumple your rival for combos (see the Combo Appendix), or to go through your opponent's up close attacks with its initial invincibility.

EX Burning Kick: This special version of Burning Kick is made for extending combos. With its special properties of forcing soft knockdowns and ignoring hitstun deterioration, this move usually finds a place near the end of stylish combos.

EX Seismic Hammer: An even bigger and faster version of C. Viper's Seismic Hammer, this is a mostly defensive move that you may also use in combos. It sports a high amount of invulnerability, covers a wider area, and even has a faster startup. Use under pressure to turn the tables and give C. Viper combo opportunities even while she is being attacked. Another great use of this move is for counter approaching hyper combos (at least ones with less invulnerability than EX Seismic Hammer).

Emergency Combination: This hyper combo possesses a ton of invulnerability on its startup, making it a great way to counter other hyper combos or attacks. It can also be useful in finishing ground combos, but it's less flexible in this regard than Burst Time. In most cases, you're better off using EX Seismic Hammer if you need an invincible reversal.

Burst Time: As C. Viper's main combo finisher, Burst Time is OTG-capable and has little use outside of combos, although it's extremely THC-friendly because the window to perform the next character's hyper combo extends all the way to your opponent's landing.

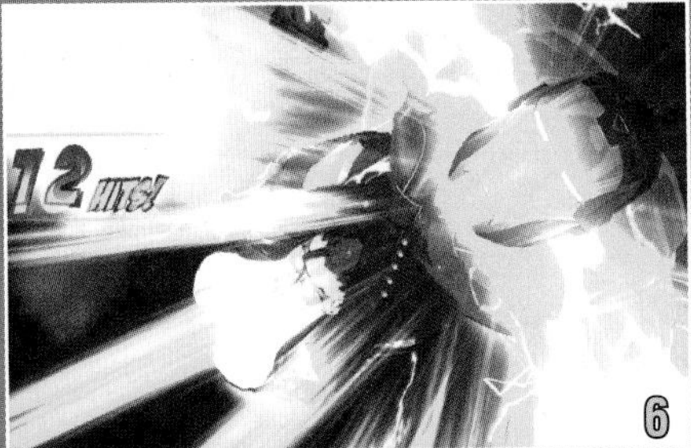

Viper Full Throttle: C. Viper shoots forward three-fourths of the screen distance and electrocutes her adversary for high damage. You can use this move in combos when preceded by Thunder Knuckle L or M either on the ground or in juggles. You can also utilize it similarly to Emergency Combination in countering other hyper combos or attacks. As a level 3 hyper combo, Viper Full Throttle is immune to damage scaling, and it always deals 430,000 damage.

Battle Plan

C. Viper has several tools to get around in the air, such as (S)-canceled Burning Kicks.

Performing Seismic Hammer in conjunction with her eight-way airdash (or double jump) is key in successfully engaging the opposing character with C. Viper. Properly using the correct version of Seismic Hammer to force your rival into a defensive posture presents C. Viper with easier opportunities to advance. An example of a standard advancing sequence would be using Seismic Hammer H on a foe who is a full screen away to force them to guard, then jump cancel it into a forward airdash to proceed with your offense. A more advanced technique is to cancel Seismic Hammer into itself repeatedly. This is a high-level technique and requires a bit of practice. Since Seismic Hammer is jump-cancelable, you can use the 3 pre-jump frames to cancel it into itself by tiger kneeing a second Seismic Hammer after the first. You'd think the motion for this would look like this: ⇨⇩⇘ + ATK ⇨⇩⇘⇨⇗ + ATK, and you'd be right, but there's an easier way to do it, thanks to the way inputs are buffered forward. Perform the first Seismic Hammer with ⇨⇩⇘⇨ + ATK, then repeat ⇩⇘⇨⇗ + ATK rapidly. You can repeat this sequence indefinitely as long as each subsequent motion is modified with ⇗ to register the jump cancel. A good way to practice this is to turn on "Input Display" in Training Mode to double-check your inputs after your attempts. If you're executing it correctly, the display should look similar to the notation provided here. Usually when an execution error occurs in the sequence, it's due to missing one of the crucial directions in the Seismic Hammer, either ⇩, ⇘, or ⇨. You can apply this technique to all of C. Viper's ground special moves, including Optic Laser (let go of ATK as soon you press ⇧ after the Seismic Hammer).

If your opponent ever uses advancing guard against your Seismic Hammers to push C. Viper out of firing range, you can use a similar jump cancelation technique to cancel into a forward dash. To do this, input ⇨⇩⇘ + ATK, then ⇧ ATK + (S) (hold) to cancel your pre-jump frames into Viper's Focus Attack, then cancel the charging animation into a forward dash. After the dash moves C. Viper back into range, perform another Seismic Hammer H to strike at your wary foe.

The opposing player's answer to Seismic Hammers is to either jump or match you with a beam of some sort. Jumps and projectiles can be lured out preemptively by faking it—input ⇨⇩⇘ + ATK CANCEL (S) to (S)-cancel the attack before its release. The Seismic Hammer flash occurs even during the feint, which may bait some players into taking action. When your opponent attempts a countermeasure just as the Seismic Hammer is released, you can usually cancel its recovery into a jump to air guard the incoming assault. This is the safest option when you're unsure of your foe's actions. Beams or other projectiles can be countered directly by canceling the Seismic Hammer at any time into ⇩⇘⇨ + (S), which plows through any low to medium priority projectile with ease. Aerial assaults are stopped by canceling into a forward jump and air throwing your competitor, or by canceling into Thunder Knuckle H with this command: ⇩⇘⇨⇗ + (H).

Some methods of countering your Seismic Hammer offense can be difficult to stop easily. Wolverine's Berserker Slash and air ⇩ + (H) are both examples of moves that effortlessly bypass your ranged attack. In these instances, it's best to use a combination of C. Viper's Focus Attack and EX Seismic Hammer to thwart these power plays. Her Focus Attack absorbs any incoming attack without stunning her, and you can then cancel into the invincible EX Seismic Hammer to counter your opponent's move (transition into **Combo VII** on hit). To do this, press and hold ATK + (S), release only (S) while continuing to holding ATK, then after your challenger's attack is absorbed, input ⇨⇩⇘ + (S) to blast them.

In the air, C. Viper has additional ways to stay airborne, aside from her double jump and airdash. If you utilize Burning Kick's (S)-cancel property, C. Viper can airdash (or double jump) and then Burning Kick (S)-cancel up to three times to remain in the air or to manipulate her jump trajectory. This works with both normal jumps and super jumps. Another technique with this cancel is to super jump up-forward, then perform an air Burning Kick H CANCEL (S) and attack on the way down to confuse your opponent with Viper's new trajectory.

Note that C. Viper's air basic attacks are double jump-cancelable, but not airdash-cancelable. Her airdashes propel her farther upward than her double jumps, however.

Once you've established your ground domination with C. Viper's Seismic Hammers and Optic Lasers, your opponent may be open to close range aggression. If you are able to move C. Viper in close and force the target to guard a ground mix-up, remember that C. Viper's crouching (L) is NOT considered a low attack and can be guarded high. Instead, use standing (L) or cr. (M) to initiate your attack sequences. Mix this up with her triangle jumps and Burning Kick H. To perform angled triangle jumps, first make C. Viper jump up or up-forward, and then dash down-forward. Attack immediately with air (L), air (H), or air (S). Airdashing straight back down to the ground instead of triangle jumping can be executed faster, making it more difficult for competitors to guard on reaction, although the straight-down airdash overhead can only be used if C. Viper is right next to her rival. Also note that only air (L) can be used in this version, since it's the only air move C. Viper has that has a fast enough startup to come out during her airdash straight down. Additionally, if you're in a good enough position and you've got your foe conditioned to guard low, you can go for C. Viper's Viper Elbow (⇨ + (M)). It's an overhead attack that chains into her (S) launcher. To execute the launcher, wait until the moment she lands from her elbow, and press (S). To make this combination safer so that you don't just whiff a launcher, you can cancel the first hit of her S into Thunder Knuckle M (which then may be canceled into a combo. See below).

C. Viper's (S)-cancel window during her Thunder Knuckles has been increased, making the move much easier to combo off of (while also making it safe on guard). For example, instead of starting her ground combos with standing (L), (M), (H) CANCEL ⇨⇩⇘ + (L), you can start them with standing (L), (M), (H) CANCEL ⇩⇘⇨ + (M) CANCEL (S), crouching (M), (H) CANCEL ⇨⇩⇘ + (L). This not only increases her damage potential but also gives you more time to confirm that the opposing character has been hit before completing your combo. It also allows you to keep C. Viper close, as Thunder Knuckle M is an advancing move.

Another important factor in C. Viper's offense is her air throw. Since your opponents will be afraid of you on the ground, it's important you go for air throws and capitalize on them as much as possible. Each one of C. Viper's throws can be led into a full combo, regardless of jump height. If your adversary is jump-happy, you may want to start using square jumps with (H). This is performed by jumping, then airdashing forward immediately followed by ⇨ + (H). This lets you apply pressure while at the same time threatening your challenger with an air throw, since if he or she jumps up, you automatically get a throw attempt when you press ⇨ + (H). See the Combo Appendix for follow-up combos off of throws and air throws.

C. Viper deals the most damage when she's close, so choose partners who help her clear the way to advance.

Use guardstun-heavy crossover assists like Amaterasu's Cold Star to hold your target in place for mix-ups.

As far as crossover assists go for C. Viper, she benefits most from ground clearing attacks to help her gain ground for her up-close offense. Crossover assists such as Magneto—α, Taskmaster—α, and Doctor Doom—α are all very handy for this purpose. She also benefits from crossover assists like Amaterasu—β, which holds opponents in place long enough for high/low mix-ups. As soon as you get your opponent to guard an assist up close, go for either a fast triangle jump (L), ⇨ + (M), ⇩⇗⇦ + (H), or just a plain crouching (M) CANCEL ⇩⇘⇨ + (M).

You may also opt to use defensive crossover assists in conjunction with her Seismic Hammers and Optic Lasers for fullscreen keepaway and zoning purposes. Crossover assists that go well with these moves include Doctor Doom—β, Nova—α, and Doctor Strange—α.

COMBO USAGE

1. ST. (L), (M), (H) CANCEL → ↓ ↘ + (L) CANCEL VERTICAL JUMP, FORWARD AIRDASH AIR (M), (S), LAND, ST. (M), (S) CANCEL SUPER JUMP, AIR (M), (M), (H) CANCEL DOUBLE JUMP, AIR (H), (S), LAND, → ↓ ↘ + ATK (OR WHEN NEAR A CORNER, CANCEL ↓ ↙ ← + ATK ATK)

405,000~591,000 damage, 24% meter loss

This is a simple combo for beginners and a safe damage outlet if lag is affecting your online play. After the final air (S), the follow-up → ↓ ↘ + ATK is done with a different strength depending on your rival's distance when they hit the ground. Use → ↓ ↘ + (M) when at the middle of the screen, and use → ↓ ↘ + (L) when your opponent is cornered.

COMBO USAGE CONT.

II. CR. Ⓜ, ST. Ⓗ CANCEL⇨ ↓ ↘ → + Ⓜ CANCEL⇨ Ⓢ (CANCEL ON HIT), CR. Ⓜ, ST. Ⓗ CANCEL⇨ → ↓ ↘ + Ⓛ CANCEL⇨ VERTICAL JUMP, FORWARD AIRDASH AIR Ⓜ, Ⓢ, LAND, ST. Ⓜ, Ⓢ (ONE HIT) CANCEL⇨ → ↓ ↘ + Ⓛ CANCEL⇨ VERTICAL JUMP, FORWARD AIRDASH AIR Ⓜ, Ⓢ, LAND, ST. Ⓜ, Ⓢ CANCEL⇨ SUPER JUMP, AIR Ⓜ, Ⓜ, Ⓗ CANCEL⇨ DOUBLE JUMP, AIR Ⓜ, Ⓗ, Ⓢ, WAVEDASH FORWARD, ↓ ↙ ← + ATK ATK (OR WHEN NEAR A CORNER, → ↓ ↘ + Ⓛ CANCEL⇨ ↓ ↙ ← + ATK ATK)

452,000~752,000 damage, 20% meter gain (self-sufficient for Burst Time ender)

Here's Viper's most used bread and butter combo, which builds just enough meter to tag on an optional Burst Time at the end. The Thunder Knuckle M is canceled by inputting Ⓢ just as it hits, allows for enough time for you to link a hit afterwards. Once you've launched your adversary into the air with the second → ↓ ↘ + Ⓛ, have C. Viper jump vertically or forward, then have her immediately airdash toward her opponent and attack with a delayed air Ⓜ, Ⓢ. To successfully land and juggle the target again after these hits, you must not hit too early, which causes your foe to be too high in the air, or too late, which causes the second Seismic Hammer L to miss entirely. Hit air Ⓜ, Ⓢ at a mid point during the airdash. Note that this second airdash Ⓜ, Ⓢ repetition is difficult to do. If ever in doubt, omit it from the combo and continue onward.

Near the end of the combo, after you've knocked your opponent to the floor with air Ⓜ, Ⓗ, Ⓢ, wavedash three times as quickly as possible in order to move into range for Burst Time.

When guarded, the canceled Thunder Knuckle M leaves you at a heavy frame advantage, enabling you to follow up with a throw, **Combo II**, or **Combo IV**. In fact, your competitor must push you away with advancing guard, or else they'll remain in guardstun as long as you repeatedly do cr. Ⓜ, st. Ⓗ CANCEL⇨ ↓ ↘ → + Ⓜ CANCEL⇨ Ⓢ. To compensate for attempts to push standing Ⓗ away, instead perform crouching Ⓜ CANCEL⇨ ↓ ↘ → + Ⓜ CANCEL⇨ Ⓢ, but cancel Thunder Knuckle before it hits, then throw your adversary. You can fake the Thunder Knuckle at any moment where you think your foe will use advancing guard against the previous attack to punish their attempt.

III. CR. Ⓜ, ST. Ⓗ CANCEL⇨ ↓ ↘ → + Ⓜ CANCEL⇨ Ⓢ (CANCEL ON HIT), CR. Ⓜ, ST. Ⓗ CANCEL⇨ ↓ ↘ → + Ⓜ CANCEL⇨ ↓ ↘ → + Ⓢ, → ↓ ↘ + Ⓛ CANCEL⇨ VERTICAL JUMP, FORWARD AIRDASH AIR Ⓜ, Ⓢ, LAND, ST. Ⓜ, ST. Ⓢ CANCEL⇨ → ↓ ↘ + Ⓛ CANCEL⇨ VERTICAL JUMP, FORWARD AIRDASH AIR Ⓜ, Ⓢ, LAND, ST. Ⓜ, Ⓢ CANCEL⇨ SUPER JUMP, AIR Ⓜ, Ⓜ, Ⓗ CANCEL⇨ DOUBLE JUMP, AIR Ⓜ, Ⓗ, Ⓢ, WAVEDASH FORWARD, ↓ ↙ ← + ATK ATK (OR WHEN NEAR A CORNER, → ↓ ↘ + Ⓛ CANCEL⇨ ↓ ↙ ← + ATK ATK)

834,400~858,400 damage, 61% meter loss

This combo uses two meters to deal heavy damage to the opposing character. It builds one meter during it despite the meter use at the beginning, so as long as you start with one meter, you'll be able to end with Burst Time. Be sure not to cancel into the EX Seismic Hammer when the sequence is guarded, since it's very unsafe to punishment.

IV. → + Ⓜ CANCEL⇨ Ⓢ CANCEL⇨ ↓ ↘ → + Ⓜ CANCEL⇨ Ⓢ (CANCEL ON HIT), CR. Ⓜ, ST. Ⓗ CANCEL⇨ ↓ ↘ → + Ⓜ CANCEL⇨ ↓ ↘ → + Ⓢ, → ↓ ↘ + Ⓛ CANCEL⇨ VERTICAL JUMP, FORWARD AIRDASH AIR Ⓜ, Ⓢ, LAND, ST. Ⓜ, ST. Ⓢ CANCEL⇨ → ↓ ↘ + Ⓛ CANCEL⇨ VERTICAL JUMP, FORWARD AIRDASH AIR Ⓜ, Ⓢ, LAND, ST. Ⓜ, Ⓢ CANCEL⇨ SUPER JUMP, AIR Ⓜ, Ⓜ, Ⓗ CANCEL⇨ DOUBLE JUMP, AIR Ⓜ, Ⓗ, Ⓢ, WAVEDASH FORWARD, ↓ ↙ ← + ATK ATK (OR WHEN NEAR A CORNER, → ↓ ↘ + Ⓛ CANCEL⇨ ↓ ↙ ← + ATK ATK)

802,700~826,700 damage, 64% meter loss

This high-damage combo starts off of Viper's command overhead, which has a cancelable recovery period. This period can be chained into Ⓢ, but only *after* the elbow hits; C. Viper must fully land from the elbow before you can input Ⓢ.

V. ↓ ↙ ← + Ⓗ, ST. Ⓛ, Ⓜ, Ⓗ, Ⓢ CANCEL⇨ → ↓ ↘ + Ⓛ CANCEL⇨ VERTICAL JUMP, FORWARD AIRDASH AIR Ⓜ, Ⓢ, LAND, ST. Ⓜ, Ⓢ CANCEL⇨ SUPER JUMP, AIR Ⓜ, Ⓜ, Ⓗ CANCEL⇨ DOUBLE JUMP, AIR Ⓜ, Ⓗ, Ⓢ, WAVEDASH FORWARD, ↓ ↙ ← + ATK ATK (OR WHEN NEAR A CORNER, → ↓ ↘ + Ⓛ CANCEL⇨ ↓ ↙ ← + ATK ATK)

620,600~644,600 damage, 10% meter loss

Burning Kick H is both an overhead and a cross-up at close distances, making this opening a valuable offensive option. However, it's completely unsafe when guarded, with your only method of escape being to cancel its recovery into an EX Seismic Hammer.

VI. ↓ ↘ → + Ⓢ, → ↓ ↘ + Ⓛ CANCEL⇨ VERTICAL JUMP, FORWARD AIRDASH AIR Ⓜ, Ⓢ, LAND, ST. Ⓜ, ST. Ⓢ CANCEL⇨ → ↓ ↘ + Ⓛ CANCEL⇨ VERTICAL JUMP, FORWARD AIRDASH AIR Ⓜ, Ⓢ, LAND, ST. Ⓜ, Ⓢ CANCEL⇨ SUPER JUMP, AIR Ⓜ, Ⓜ, Ⓗ CANCEL⇨ DOUBLE JUMP, AIR Ⓜ, Ⓗ, Ⓢ, WAVEDASH FORWARD, ↓ ↙ ← + ATK ATK (OR WHEN NEAR A CORNER, → ↓ ↘ + Ⓛ CANCEL⇨ ↓ ↙ ← + ATK ATK)

730,100~754,100 damage, 97% meter loss

Use this combo to punish projectiles from a distance. Even though it is unsafe when blocked, you can cancel its recovery into the invincible EX Seismic Hammer to thwart any punishment attempt. When your opponent guards in fear of the EX Seismic Hammer follow-up, cancel into a faked EX Seismic Hammer (→ ↓ ↘ + Ⓢ, Ⓢ) then go for a throw or low attack.

VII. → ↓ ↘ + Ⓢ CANCEL⇨ VERTICAL JUMP, AIRDASH DOWN-FORWARD, AIR Ⓗ, LAND, ST. Ⓗ CANCEL⇨ → ↓ ↘ + Ⓛ CANCEL⇨ VERTICAL JUMP, FORWARD AIRDASH AIR Ⓜ, Ⓢ, LAND, ST. Ⓜ, Ⓢ CANCEL⇨ SUPER JUMP, AIR Ⓜ, Ⓜ, Ⓗ CANCEL⇨ DOUBLE JUMP, AIR Ⓜ, Ⓗ, Ⓢ, WAVEDASH FORWARD, ↓ ↙ ← + ATK ATK (OR WHEN NEAR A CORNER, → ↓ ↘ + Ⓛ CANCEL⇨ ↓ ↙ ← + ATK ATK)

605,500~629,500 damage, 114% meter loss

The EX Seismic Hammer has enough invulnerability to plow through any incoming attack, making it valuable as a reversal. After canceling the EX Seismic Hammer into a vertical jump, wait a moment before the downward airdash to give your competitor time to fall. This ensures that they're close to the ground before air Ⓗ makes contact, allowing for the remainder of the combo to work.

VIII. THROW OR AIR THROW, → ↓ ↘ + Ⓛ [CANCEL] FORWARD JUMP, FORWARD AIRDASH AIR Ⓜ, Ⓢ, LAND, ST. Ⓜ, ST. Ⓢ [CANCEL] → ↓ ↘ + Ⓛ [CANCEL] VERTICAL JUMP, FORWARD AIRDASH AIR Ⓜ, Ⓢ, LAND, ST. Ⓜ, Ⓢ [CANCEL] SUPER JUMP, AIR Ⓜ, Ⓜ, Ⓗ [CANCEL] DOUBLE JUMP, AIR Ⓜ, Ⓗ, Ⓢ, WAVEDASH FORWARD, ↓ ↙ ← + ATK ATK (OR WHEN NEAR A CORNER, → ↓ ↘ + Ⓛ [CANCEL] ↓ ↙ ← + ATK ATK)

495,400~519,400 damage, 1% meter loss

When performing this combo off of a forward throw, make sure to cancel Seismic Hammer L into a forward jump. Otherwise, C. Viper won't be in range for the rest of the combo. If you have trouble doing it, trying starting the combo with EX Seismic Hammer instead, which leaves your rival closer to Viper for the follow-up hits.

IX. JUMP FORWARD, INSTANT AIR Ⓛ [X-FACTOR], AIR Ⓢ, LAND, CR. Ⓜ, ST. Ⓗ [CANCEL] ↓ ↘ → + Ⓜ [CANCEL] Ⓢ (CANCEL ON HIT), ST. Ⓜ, ST. Ⓗ [CANCEL] ↓ ↘ → + Ⓜ [CANCEL] ↓ ↘ → + Ⓢ, → ↓ ↘ + Ⓛ [CANCEL] VERTICAL JUMP, FORWARD AIRDASH AIR Ⓜ, Ⓢ, LAND, ST. Ⓜ, ST. Ⓢ [CANCEL] → ↓ ↘ + Ⓛ [CANCEL] VERTICAL JUMP, FORWARD AIRDASH AIR Ⓜ, Ⓢ, LAND, ST. Ⓜ, Ⓢ [CANCEL] SUPER JUMP, AIR Ⓜ, Ⓜ, Ⓗ [CANCEL] DOUBLE JUMP, AIR Ⓜ, Ⓗ, Ⓢ, WAVEDASH FORWARD, ↓ ↙ ← + ATK ATK (OR WHEN NEAR A CORNER, → ↓ ↘ + Ⓛ [CANCEL] ↓ ↙ ← + ATK ATK)

1,239,000~1,348,600 damage, 15% meter loss

This combo acts as a very quick overhead attack. Its cancelation into X-Factor cannot be verified on hit, so make sure you're willing to enter the mode regardless of whether it's guarded or not. Even if it is blocked, C. Viper ends up on top of her opponent in a powered-up state, so continue your attack.

X. CR. Ⓜ, ST. Ⓗ [CANCEL] ↓ ↘ → + Ⓜ [X-FACTOR], CR. Ⓜ, ST. Ⓗ [CANCEL] ↓ ↘ → + Ⓜ [CANCEL] ↓ ↘ → + Ⓢ, → ↓ ↘ + Ⓛ [CANCEL] VERTICAL JUMP, FORWARD AIRDASH AIR Ⓜ, Ⓢ, LAND, ST. Ⓜ, ST. Ⓢ [CANCEL] → ↓ ↘ + Ⓛ [CANCEL] VERTICAL JUMP, FORWARD AIRDASH AIR Ⓜ, Ⓢ, LAND, ST. Ⓜ, Ⓢ [CANCEL] SUPER JUMP, AIR Ⓜ, Ⓜ, Ⓗ [CANCEL] DOUBLE JUMP, AIR Ⓜ, Ⓗ, Ⓢ, WAVEDASH FORWARD, ↓ ↙ ← + ATK ATK (OR WHEN NEAR A CORNER, → ↓ ↘ + Ⓛ [CANCEL] ↓ ↙ ← + ATK ATK)

1,196,300~1,556,600 damage, 30% meter loss

This is a verifiable method of landing X-Factor damage. Go for this sequence when you manage to catch two of the opposing characters with a hit at the same time. Knocking them both out means that their final character may enter the screen when C. Viper is still powered up in X-Factor.

ADVANCED TACTICS

MOTHER KNOWS BEST: UNGUARDABLE LEVEL 3 FOCUS ATTACK

Since C. Viper's Focus Attack level 3 is an unguardable attack, there are ways to force an inescapable situation on your opponent. One way is to use a multi-hitting assist that puts your challenger into a long enough blockstun, such as Amaterasu—β, Doctor Strange—β, or Phoenix Wright—β. Another way to force the unguardable Focus Attack is to use a crossover combination with partners who have long hyper combos, and then have C. Viper X-Factor out of her hyper combo to perform the level 3 Focus Attack. This works with partners such as Dante (Million Dollars), Trish (Round Harvest), or Amaterasu (Okami Shuffle).

COMBO APPENDIX

GENERAL EXECUTION TIPS

- To cancel ↓ ↘ → + Ⓛ or Ⓜ, press Ⓢ as soon as the strike connects. Canceling as early as possible gives you sufficient time to link crouching Ⓜ afterward.
- If you are having trouble with → ↓ ↘ + Ⓛ [CANCEL] vertical jump, forward airdash air Ⓜ, Ⓢ, use ATK ATK for the airdash instead of → →. Delay air Ⓜ, Ⓢ so your opponent doesn't get too high for you to continue the combo.

AFTER C. VIPER COMES IN: AIR Ⓜ, Ⓜ, Ⓗ [CANCEL] DOUBLE JUMP, Ⓜ, Ⓗ, Ⓢ, WAVEDASH FORWARD, ↓ ↙ ← + ATK ATK (OR WHEN NEAR A CORNER, → ↓ ↘ + Ⓛ [CANCEL] ↓ ↙ ← + ATK ATK)

Notes	Damage
Team aerial combo handoff to C. Viper	Varies due to damage scaling

WHEN OPPONENT IS CORNERED, CR. Ⓜ, ST. Ⓗ [CANCEL] ↓ ↘ → + Ⓜ [CANCEL] Ⓢ (CANCEL ON HIT), CR. Ⓗ [CANCEL] ↓ ↘ → + Ⓜ [CANCEL] Ⓢ (CANCEL ON HIT), CR. Ⓗ [CANCEL] ↓ ↘ → + Ⓜ [CANCEL] ↓ ↘ → + Ⓢ, → ↓ ↘ + Ⓛ [CANCEL] VERTICAL JUMP, FORWARD AIRDASH AIR Ⓜ, Ⓢ, LAND, ST. Ⓜ, ST. Ⓢ [CANCEL] SUPER JUMP, AIR Ⓜ, Ⓜ, Ⓗ [CANCEL] ↓ ↙ ← + Ⓗ [CANCEL] Ⓢ (MISSES), Ⓜ, Ⓗ [CANCEL] DOUBLE JUMP, AIR Ⓜ, Ⓗ, Ⓢ, LAND, → ↓ ↘ + Ⓛ [CANCEL] ↓ ↙ ← + ATK ATK

Notes	Damage
↓ ↙ ← + Ⓗ [CANCEL] Ⓢ cancels the attack while moving you near your rival, enabling you to link into another air attack; this must be done as quickly as possible to work	863,000, 67% meter loss

DURING X-FACTOR LEVEL 3, CR. Ⓜ, ST. Ⓗ [CANCEL] ↓ ↘ → + Ⓜ [CANCEL] Ⓢ (CANCEL ON HIT), CR. Ⓜ, ST. Ⓗ [CANCEL] ↓ ↘ → + Ⓜ [CANCEL] Ⓢ (CANCEL ON HIT), CR. Ⓜ, ST. Ⓗ [CANCEL] ↓ ↘ → + Ⓜ [CANCEL] Ⓢ (CANCEL ON HIT), CR. Ⓜ, ST. Ⓗ [CANCEL] → ↓ ↘ + Ⓛ [CANCEL] VERTICAL JUMP, FORWARD AIRDASH AIR Ⓜ, Ⓢ, LAND, ST. Ⓜ, Ⓢ [CANCEL] SUPER JUMP, AIR Ⓜ, Ⓜ, Ⓗ [CANCEL] DOUBLE JUMP, AIR Ⓜ, Ⓗ, Ⓢ, LAND, → ↓ ↘ + ATK

Notes	Damage
A high damage combo that's viable only when X-Factor level 3 is activated. The improved speed allows you to link far more Thunder Knuckles together than normal	1,268,500 damage, 224% meter gain

CR. Ⓜ, ST. Ⓗ [CANCEL] ↓ ↘ → + Ⓜ [CANCEL] Ⓢ (CANCEL ON HIT), CR. Ⓜ, ST. Ⓗ [CANCEL] ↓ ↘ → + Ⓜ [CANCEL] ↓ ↘ → + Ⓢ, → ↓ ↘ + Ⓛ [CANCEL] VERTICAL JUMP, FORWARD AIRDASH AIR Ⓜ, Ⓢ, LAND, ST. Ⓜ, ST. Ⓢ [CANCEL] → ↓ ↘ + Ⓛ [CANCEL] VERTICAL JUMP, FORWARD AIRDASH AIR Ⓜ, Ⓢ, LAND, ST. Ⓜ, Ⓢ [CANCEL] → ↓ ↘ + ATK ATK

Notes	Damage
—	988,200 damage, 303% meter loss

DANTE

"DEMONS, SUPERHUMANS. MEH. SAME CRAP, DIFFERENT DAY."

Bio

REAL NAME

Dante

OCCUPATION

Devil Hunter

ABILITIES

In addition to his large sword and handguns, he can transform into a demon through his Devil Trigger ability. While transformed, he gains access to new powers.

WEAPONS

While best known for his large sword "Rebellion" and his personally hand-crafted guns "Ebony" and "Ivory," he can use weapons from any place and time—shotguns, dual swords, nunchaku, rocket launchers, etc.

PROFILE

Half-man half-demon born from the Legendary Dark Knight Sparda and his human wife, Eva. When he was still young, his mother was killed in a demon attack. To hunt down those responsible, he became a Devil Hunter and opened up a shop named "Devil May Cry."

FIRST APPEARANCE

Devil May Cry (2001)

POWER GRID

2	INTELLIGENCE
4	STRENGTH
3	SPEED
6	STAMINA
4	ENERGY PROJECTION
6	FIGHTING ABILITY

*This is biographical, and does not represent an evaluation of the in-game combat potential of this hero.

ALTERNATE COSTUMES

Overview

Vitality	900,000
Chain Combo Archetype	3-hit Alternating

X-Factor Boost	Damage	Speed
Level 1 (3 teammates remaining)	130%	110%
Level 2 (2 teammates remaining)	150%	120%
Level 3 (1 teammate remaining)	170%	130%

Your goal with Dante is to dominate your opponent from mid range, coercing mistakes and answering any situation with his unrivaled bag of tricks.You can control mid range with Dante for a variety of reasons:

- **His excellent anti-air and anti-ground basic attacks can preemptively control the space other characters want to invade**
- **Through advanced canceling tricks, you can convert Dante's hits from almost any range into full combos; you don't have to care about hitting with his standing Ⓛ combo starter deeply like most characters**
- **Successful hits can become ridiculous *Devil May Cry*-style combos involving a dozen different special moves**
- **In attacks like The Hammer, Dante has the tools to stop his rival from attempting to reverse his basic attacks**

Cracking your foe from mid range is accomplished by:

- **Attacking adversaries with standing Ⓛ and Ⓜ, which strike perfect places to stop targets coming in from the ground or the sky and can lead to full combos either way**
- **Canceling failed offensive or defensive pokes with Bold Move or Air Trick (ideally backed by an assist) to avoid punishment and keep momentum**
- **Sensing when your competitor is passive, then attacking aggressively with airdash attacks, airdash cross-ups, and Air Trick mix-ups backed by an assist**
- **Using advanced Bold canceling tricks to make Dante's combos work from almost any range and to turn → + Ⓗ Stinger into one of the game's longest-reaching, most threatening pokes**
- **Using Air Play and Hysteric to control the pace from farther than mid range, as the matchup permits**

TUNING SINCE ORIGINAL MVC3

The son of Sparda has arrived in *UMvC3* with his already dominant gameplan from the original version intact, yet he is almost like a new character in many subtle ways. His alternate specials are executed with a double-tap of the button rather than repeating the whole motion. The shortened command for alternate specials (just a second button press, one input, versus another motion then a button press, four inputs) makes Dante's tactics a lot easier to execute consistently in general, but some concessions have been made in his frame data to compensate for these changes, particularly with The Hammer, one of the most dominant attacks in *MvC3*.

Alterations to standing Ⓗ, Air Play, and Acid Rain force a revamp of what previously served as his main bread and butter combos. The removal of the THC glitch also means that THCing to Devil Trigger from another character's capture move (or performing a combo to Grapple, hyper canceling to Devil Trigger, then THC canceling to the next character's THC-glitch capable hyper) is no longer a virtually guaranteed knockout. Dante also generally gains a lot less hyper meter from his combos than he used to. In particular, multi-hitting sequences that are Dante staples, like Volcano to Beehive and Cold Shower to Prop Shredder, generate a lot less bar than before.

Air Ⓛ causes less hitstun. The change is enough that normal jump air Ⓛ chained to air Ⓜ is no longer a combo against an aerial rival. Dante players can no longer jump forward and start an option select by pressing the buttons to chain air Ⓛ, Ⓜ. When this chain was a two-hit combo, there was time to verify the result and either double jump cancel into a continued combo on hit, or airdash and perform another attack if air Ⓛ whiffed (which means air Ⓜ wouldn't have come out at all, and Dante is free to act again). Just air Ⓜ can still lead to a combo, but it doesn't give time to verify and perform something else if it whiffs. Air Ⓛ, Ⓜ still combos while Dante is super jumping.

- **Range of standing Ⓛ, Ⓜ, and Ⓗ are reduced**
- **Hitstun time and float properties adjusted for many moves**
- **The Hammer has frames 11-20 invincible (from 4-19)**
- **Air Play spark travels more quickly**
- **The re-juggle potential of Acid Rain has been reduced**
- **During Devil Trigger, Dante gains access to triple jump and double airdash**
- **All special movesthat required repeat motions (such as The Hammer, previously air ↓ ↘ → + Ⓛ ↓ ↘ → + Ⓛ) are performed with a repeat button press instead (now air ↓ ↘ → + Ⓛ Ⓛ).**
- **Million Dollars can be mashed for extra damage**

Attack Set

Standing Basic Attacks

Screen	Command	Hits	Damage	Meter Gain	Startup	Active	Recovery	Advantage on Hit	Advantage if Guarded	Notes
1	Standing Ⓛ	1	43,000	344	8	3	13	-2	-3	—
2	Standing Ⓜ	1	55,000	440	10	4	17	-2	-3	—
3	Standing Ⓗ	1	70,000	560	13	3	23	-3	-4	—

1

2

3

Crouching Basic Attacks

Screen	Command	Hits	Damage	Meter Gain	Startup	Active	Recovery	Advantage on Hit	Advantage if Guarded	Notes
1	Crouching Ⓛ	1	40,000	320	8	3	11	0	-1	Low attack, chainable to cr. Ⓛ
2	Crouching Ⓜ	1	50,000	400	11	2	20	-3	-4	Low attack
3	Crouching Ⓗ	4~19	50,000 + 10,000 each hit + 60,000	400 + 80 each hit + 480	15	1(7)4-34(21)4	39	-21	-21	Press Ⓗ rapidly on hit to inflict additional hits

1

2

3

Ground Special Attack—Launcher

Screen	Command	Hits	Damage	Meter Gain	Startup	Active	Recovery	Advantage on Hit	Advantage if Guarded	Notes
1	Ⓢ (while standing or crouching)	1	80,000	640	11	3	28	—	-9	Launcher, not special- or hyper combo-cancelable

1

Air Basic Attacks

Screen	Command	Hits	Damage	Meter Gain	Startup	Active	Recovery	Advantage on Hit	Advantage if Guarded	Notes
1	Air L	1	40,000	320	8	2	19	+12	+11	Overhead attack
2	Air M	1	58,000	464	11	3	22	+17	+16	Overhead attack
3	Air H	1	70,000	560	13	3	23	+18	+17	Overhead attack

1

2

3

Air Special Attacks—Flying Screen and Air Exchange

Air S causes a hard knockdown when used in a launcher combo (this is sometimes called flying screen). When used outside of a launcher combo, air S behaves mostly like another basic attack. Air exchange attacks, performed by inputting a direction plus S, are only possible during a launcher combo. Exchange hits initiate team aerial combos by tagging in the next available character to continue the air combo.

Screen	Command	Hits	Damage	Meter Gain	Startup	Active	Recovery	Advantage on Hit	Advantage if Guarded	Notes
1	Air S	1	90,000	720	23	Until grounded	20	—	-6	Hard knockdown
2	Air ⇧ + S (during launcher combo)	2	105,00	880	10	4	22	—	—	Tags in next available hero while lofting opponent upward
3	Air ⇨ or ⇦ + S (during launcher combo)	2	95,000	800	10	4	24	—	—	Tags in next available ally while causing wall bounce, erases 1 hyper meter bar from foe
4	Air ⇩ + S (during launcher combo)	2	95,000	800	12	Until grounded	0	—	—	Tags in next available ally while causing ground bounce, generates 1 hyper meter bar

1

2

3

4

Command Attacks

Command attacks resemble basic attacks but have different chaining and canceling properties. It's usually possible to chain *into* a command attack from basic attacks, but most command attacks cannot be chained from or canceledthemselves.

Screen	Name	Command	Hits	Damage	Meter Gain	Startup	Active	Recovery	Advantage on Hit	Advantage if Guarded	Notes
1	Stinger	⇨ + H	1	80,000	640	14	6	24	-2	-3	Wall bounce against airborne foes, Bold Move-cancelable, can chain to Million Stab, not special- or hyper combo- cancelable

1

DANTE

Ebony and Ivory Attacks and Sword Extensions

Dante's sword and his Ebony and Ivory handguns can be accessed as alternate versions or extensions of several attacks. These attacks can themselves be chained or linked into other moves that are not available otherwise, such as Prop Shredder. The purpose of most of these attacks is combo extension.

Rain Storm is Dante's OTG option after an air throw. See **Combo III**.

Cold Shower is one of the fastest OTG-capable moves in the game, allowing Dante to OTG after almost any hard knockdown. As a feature of advanced combos, it can be chained into Prop Shredder or Stinger lv.2 to keep the combo going.

Screen	Name	Command	Hits	Damage	Meter Gain	Startup	Active	Recovery	Advantage on Hit	Advantage if Guarded	Notes
1	Scat Shot	(H) (during frames 18-29 of standing (H))	2~4	20,000 per bullet	160 per bullet	(18+) 17	7	16	+9	+7	Can chain into PropShredder or Stinger, inflicts chip damage, each projectile has 1 low priority durability point, press (H) again for extra shots
2	Clay Pigeon	(H) anytime between contact and frame 40 (during (S) on hit or block)	2~10	25,000 per bullet	600 per bullet	(12+) 11	5~49	21	+1	0	Inflicts chip damage, each projectile has 1 low priority durability point, press (H) up to 6 more times for extra shots
3	Prop Shredder	(during frames 30-38 of Scat Shot, frames 20-36 of Cold Shower or frames 24-35 of Clay Pigeon) (S)	5	92,500	1000	(20+) 10	40	26	—	-10	Inflicts chip damage, super jump- cancelable on hit
Identical to Stinger	Stinger Lv.2	(during frames 30-38 of Scat Shot, frames 20-36 of Cold Shower or frames 24-35 of Clay Pigeon) → + (H)	1	80,000	640	(20+) 19	6	24	-2	-3	Wall bounce against airborne foes, Bold Move-cancelable, can chain to Million Stab, not special- or hyper combo- cancelable
4	Million Stab	(during frames 17-23 of Stinger or Stinger Lv.2) (H)))	6~16	5,000 per hit + 40,000	40 per hit +640	(17+) 3	10~39 (21)5	40	-23	-23	Inflicts chip damage, press (H) rapidly for extra hits
5	Weasel Shot	← + (H) (during frames 14-15 of standing (H))	2~6	20,000 per bullet	160 per bullet	(14+) 16	7~39	12~10	+14~+17	+14~+17	Inflicts chip damage, press (H) up to 3 more times for extra shots, each projectile has 1 low priority durability point
6	Rain Storm	(in air) (H)(H)	2~10	25,000 per bullet	200 per bullet	16	8~68	Until grounded	-2	-2	OTG-capable, inflicts chip damage, can cancel into Killer Bee, each projectile has 5 low priority durability points, press (H) up to five more times for extra shots
7	Cold Shower	↘ + (H)(H)	2~4	25,000 per bullet	200 per bullet	11	5~15	22	0	-1	OTG-capable, inflicts chip damage, can input (H) again for extra shots, can chain into Stinger or Prop Shredder, each projectile has 1 low priority durability point

1

2

3

4

5

6

7

Throws

Throws are for snagging passive or blocking opponents. Since throws are active so quickly, you can also use them to preemptively toss opposing characters out of their offense. Combos are usually possible after throws, one way or another.

Screen	Command	Hits	Damage	Meter Gain	Startup	Active	Notes
1	→ + H (ground)	5	80,000	800	1	1	Hard knockdown
	← + H (ground)	5	80,000	800	1	1	Hard knockdown
2	→ + H (air)	4	80,000	800	1	1	Hard knockdown
	← + H (air)	4	80,000	800	1	1	Hard knockdown

1

2

As a Partner—Crossover Assists

Screen	Type	P1+P2 Crossover Combination Hyper Combo	Description	Hits	Damage	Meter Gain	Startup	Active	Recovery (this crossover assist)	Recovery (other partner)	Notes
1	Dante—α	Million Dollars	Jam Session	10	90,800	1120	37	41	119	89	Knocks down, beam durability: 10 frames x 3 low priority durability points
2	Dante—β	Million Dollars	Crystal	4	120,300	1120	49	40	98	68	OTG-capable, each projectile has 3 low priority durability points
3	Dante—γ	Million Dollars	Weasel Shot	4	85,900	960	40	23	103	73	Each projectile has 1 low priority durability point

1

2

3

Dante doesn't have a mediocre assist, as each could find use on the right team. Dante—α provides a close range lockdown assist, which also has super jump height anti-air and mix-up capabilities. Dante—β provides an OTG assist, in case you absolutely must use Dante on your team and can't get the OTG capability elsewhere (Dante certainly doesn't need an OTG assist himself when he's on point). Crystal also has solid keep-out qualities when used against foes at mid range or farther. And Dante—γ is a weak, but quick, long range projectile assist. In the end, Dante—α is the easiest assist to recommend. It gives any character a cross-up against super jumping or flying characters simply by calling Dante and dashing underneath the airborne opponent; if Jam Session hits the target, some characters such as Sentinel and Wolverine can get up to the opposing character in time and use a ground bounce move to capitalize off the assist hit with a full combo. Dante—α is also great for pinning ground level adversaries, or for popping foes up if your character has an OTG-capable move of their own. For example, create a hard knockdown with Frank West, then call Dante—α right before using ↓ ↘ → + S for an OTG hit that bounces the opposing characterup into Dante's wicked shredding. In this case, Frank is able to finish a combo with an OTG Snapshot into another Snapshot (which puts Frank up to at least lv.3!), and still cancel into a hyper combo, thanks to Dante—α.

All three assists give Dante Million Dollars during crossover combinations (of course they do—he doesn't have another level 1 hyper combo that isn't a power-up state), which is actually quite good—Dante takes *forever* to finish Million Dollars compared to many hyper combos, so your point character may be free to move around and mix up your opponent or contribute to a combo while Dante continues to fire. The shorter your point character's hyper combo occupies them during crossover combinations involving Dante's Million Dollars, the better. For one example, see the Advanced Tactics in Spencer's chapter.

Snap Back

Screen	Command	Hits	Damage	Meter Gain	Startup	Active	Recovery	Advantage on Hit	Advantage if Guarded
1	↓ ↙ → + P1 or P2	1	50,000	- (-1 hyper meter bar)	2	4	22	—	-4

Notes

On hit,snap back forces the opposing point character to be replaced by an assist. Opposing assist calls or tag outs are also locked out for 4 seconds

1

Special Moves

Screen	Name	Command	Hits	Damage	Meter Gain	Startup	Active	Recovery	Advantage on Hit	Advantage if Guarded	Notes
1	Multi-Lock	⇩⇘⇨ + Ⓛ (hold Ⓛ to charge more orbs)	1~5	50,000 per shot	500 per shot	30+10	—	35	-5	-6	After first 30 frames of startup, each shot requires 40 frames of charging.Can move and call assists while charging, projectiles vanish if Dante is hit, each projectile has 5 low priority durability points.Once fired, projectile(s) wait 60 frames before seeking foe
2	Acid Rain	(During frames 5-24 of Multi-Lock) Ⓛ	3+15	30,000 x3 + 25,000 x 15	240 x 3 + 200 x 15	(5+)30	11	25	—	—	Fire 3 projectiles with 5 low priority durability points straight up for 35 frames, then splits into 5 smaller projectiles with 5 low priority durability points that fall to the ground in a spread
3	Crystal	⇩⇘⇨ + Ⓜ	4	35,000 per hit	280 per hit	25	—	30	+9	+8	Ice shards active for 42 frames, each projectile has 3 low priority durabilitypoints, OTG-capable
4	Million Carats	(During frames 5-21 of Crystal) Ⓜ	1	130,000	1040	(5+)18	23	25	—	-26	Knocks down, ignores hit stun decay, projectile has 5 medium priority durability points, OTG-capable
5	Hysteric	⇩⇘⇨ + Ⓗ	8	20,000 per hit	160 per hit	30	15	36	-14	-15	Each missile contains 1 low priority projectile point
6	Grapple	(during frames 15-27 of Hysteric) Ⓗ	1	60,000	600	(15+)15	19(14)	26	—	-37	Captures competitor, projectile has 5 low priority durability points
7	Reverb Shock	⇩⇙⇦ + Ⓛ	5	81,700	800	8	10(1)4	27	—	-9	Knocks down
8	Revolver	⇩⇙⇦ + Ⓜ	5	30,000 per hit	240 per hit	18	37(3)3	20	—	-1	Causes ground bounce
9	Jet Stream	⇩⇙⇦ + Ⓗ	6	153,900	1680	20	20	46	—	-48	Knocks down
10	Fireworks	(during frames 20-21 of Reverb Shock, frames 58-59 of Revolver, or frames 42-43 of Jet Stream) Ⓗ	26	10,000 per shot	80 per shot	(20+) 13	40	18	+4	+2	Each projectile has 5 low priority durability points
11	Crazy Dance	(during frames 22-23 of Reverb Shock, frame 57 of Revolver, or frames 45-46 of Jet Stream) Ⓢ	10	163,400	1634	(22+) 10	7	14	—	+1	Knocks down
12	Twister	⇨⇩⇘ + Ⓛ	10	97,300	1200	13	30	23	+5	-4	OTG capable, beam durability: 10 frames x 5 low priority durability points
13	Tempest	(during frames 15-54 of Twister) Ⓛ	10	129,900	1600	(15+) 18	20	30	—	-10	Knocks down, beam durability: 10 frames x 3 low priority durability points
14	Volcano	⇨⇩⇘ + Ⓜ	1	100,000	800	15	10	41	-22	-29	OTG-capable, jump- cancelable, nullifies medium priority projectiles
15	Beehive	(during frames 5-16 of Volcano) Ⓜ	9	106,600	1360	(5+)3	50(19)4	15	—	+3	Causes ground bounce
16	Jam Session	⇨⇩⇘ + Ⓗ	10	90,800	1120	13	41	27	0	-9	Knocks down, beam durability: 10 frames x 3 low priority durability points
17	Killer Bee	Air ⇩⇘⇨ + Ⓛ	1	80,000	640	18	Until Grounded	18	—	+1	Causes ground bounce
18	The Hammer	(during frames 5-16 of Killer Bee) Ⓛ	1	90,000	720	(5+) 19	3	Until grounded + 5	—	+16	Invincible from frames 11-20, overhead attack, hard knockdown
19	Air Play (can be charged)	(in air) ⇩⇘⇨ + Ⓜ	1/3/5	50,000/ 94,800/ 122,600	400/ 840/ 1200	9/25/ 41 + 6	—	14/ 19/ 23	+3/ +27/ +25	+2/ -1/ -3	Uncharged: projectile has 4 low priority durability points, Level 1 charge: beam durability: 3 frames x 3 low priority durability points, fully charged: beam durability: 5 frames x 3 low priority durability points
20	Sky Dance	(in air) ⇩⇘⇨ + Ⓗ	13	2 x 30,000 + 10 x 15,000 + 50,000	240 x 2 + 120 x 10 + 400	18	5(3)3(9) until grounded + 5	16	—	+1	Resets the 1 ground bounce per combo rule, hits 1-12 cause ground bounce, hit 13 causes knockdown
21	Air Trick	⇩⇩ + Ⓢ	—	—	—	11	—	11	—	—	Invincible from frames 11-15
22	Drive	⇩⇘⇨ + Ⓢ	2	80,000 + 70,000	640+560	32 (projectile: 36)	6	13	+5	+4	Projectile has 5 low priority durability points
23	Bold Move	Ⓢ + ATK	—	—	—	—	—	—	—	—	Airborne in a forward jump on 4th frame, cannot use air attacks until after 16th frame

1

Multi-Lock: Multi-Lock creates pink orbs that home in on the target after one second. Simply performing the motion creates one orb; hold Ⓛ longer to charge up to five orbs, which are all created whenever you release the button. Dante can move and jump normally while charging, and Multi-Lock can be released on the ground or in the air, but if any attacks or special movement options (Air Trick and Bold Move) are used, you'll lose the Multi-Lock charge and it won't fire.

In normal combat situations, Multi-Lock takes entirely too long to consider using, but it can be useful ifyour competitor is running away with super jumps or flight.Rather than having to chase them down or commit to Air Trick shenanigans, consider fully charging Multi-Lock to fire homing orbs at them. If you DO manage to fully charge Multi-Lock against a faraway foe, time Air Trick to teleport behind them just as Multi-Lock's homing lasers fire at your rival.

2

Acid Rain: Dante fires three pink bolts into the sky, which cause a flurry of lasers to rain down. The rising bolts can be used as anti-air against adversaries who are above Dante: if the rising bolts hit, then the laser rain drags the opposing character down afterward. Depending on your position, you can combo afterward with a chain into Ⓢ launcher. (It's far harder to reliably link Acid Rain into itself than in original *MvC3*, which alters a lot of the combos that were previously Dante's high-level bread and butter).

Acid Rain is most valuable used against new opposing characters forced to fall in after their teammates get knocked or snapped out. Fire Acid Rain early, while no opponents are on screen. Ideally, the downward laser rain should force the new competitor to guard in midair right after they appear onscreen, with Dante free to move on the ground underneath them. You can up the ante on the ensuing mix-up by canceling Acid Rain into Devil Trigger or X-Factor.

From here, you can either dash under your foe into a combo starting with standing Ⓜ, stay in front and go for a combo or throw, or dash under, jump vertically, then airdash back to the original side for a doublecross-up with air Ⓜ. Be careful with your timing on close range attacks here, since your adversary's safest escape route is to simply throw against a Dante player who leaves gaps. (For example, firing Acid Rain late so that Dante ends up attacking before the lasers provide cover.If the opposing player managed to throw Dante by then, Acid Rain becomes irrelevant. This gives your rival good incentive to try, so watch out.)

Crystal: Dante uses his Nunchaku to form ice shards on the ground. Crystal is OTG-capable and leaves Dante at a sizeable frame advantage if guarded, but Dante has no follow-up potential if his competitor uses advancing guard (and they will). Crystal is an example of a decent move stuck on a character who has better ones. To OTG foes after hard knockdowns,you should use Volcano and Cold Shower; to retain frame advantage if guarded, you should(ideally)use Stinger, Bold canceled into Reverb Shock canceled into Fireworks. Crystal does, however, create three huge ice shards that briefly and totally cover the area in front of Dante, while also potentially destroying incoming projectiles. Crystal is thus best used as relatively safe, preemptive space control from mid or long range; call an assist that will also bolster Dante's control of the screen before performing Crystal.

3

4

Million Carats: This extension to Crystal is also OTG-capable, and it sends your attacker into a close range spinning knockdown on contact, even if it picks them up off the ground. Million Carats leaves Dante at a punishable disadvantage if guarded. This makes it great for flashy combos, but limits its applications in a match.

5

Hysteric: Dante fires eight homing missiles that seek out his opponent. Hysteric has slow startup, so it won't win zoning wars against quick beam characters, and it isn't prudent up close in general. You wouldn't want to use it against someone like Akuma, Dormammu, or Ryu when he is loaded with hyper meter, either. But, when you have the time to use Hysteric safely from long range, it more or less guarantees control of the match for Dante for a moment, like a smaller version of Morrigan's Finishing Shower hyper combo. If the opposing character doesn't have a way to deal with it directly, you can keep them at bay by alternating between Hysteric and Air Play.

Apart from using Hysteric from long range to gain control of a match, you can use it aggressively as a kind of self-assist. Perform Hysteric, then cancel it with either Devil Trigger or X-Factor just after the eighth missile is fired. Dante is free to move immediately! Wavedash alongside the missiles, and you'll have time to verify and combo from the front if your competitor eats them, or use Air Trick to teleport behind your foe if they guard. Since they're stuck guarding the missiles, they won't be able to jump and air throw you out of the Air Trick teleport on reaction.

6

Grapple: Grapple pulls in your adversaries at ground level from fullscreen and puts them into position to be launched. The beginning looks the same as Hysteric, but then the Grapple travels much more quickly than Hysteric's homing missiles. Grapple first becomes active on the 30th frame after Hysteric began, and it hits fullscreen after about 48 frames, assuming you double tap Ⓗ immediately—Hysteric can be canceled into Grapple after inputting ⇩ ⬂ ⇨ + Ⓗ as soon as between 5 to 15 frames later (with the same result), or as late as 27 frames later (making Grapple that much slower).

Grapple can snag foes who expect to attack to stop Hysteric, or otherwise surprise opponents at long range. You can also insert it into flashy combos. It is extremely unsafe if guarded up close (or guarded at all by characters with fast fullscreen hyper combos).

7

Reverb Shock: Dante slides forward strumming his guitar, sending purple shockwaves around him. Reverb Shock is unsafe if guarded, but it can be made safe by chaining to the Fireworks extension by pressing Ⓗ just as Reverb Shock reaches the end of its hitting period (double or triple tap Ⓗ to be sure). You don't actually have to hit with Reverb Shock to chain to Fireworks—you can whiff Reverb Shock to Fireworks from long range to fill the screen with bullets. Because Reverb Shock is so fast, and because chaining to Fireworks makes it safe, you can use Reverb Shock as a close to mid range poke, as a blockstring ender, and as a method to get in from almost all the way across the screen: attack with ⇨ + Ⓗ Stinger, Bold canceled to Reverb Shock into Fireworks for a safe poke from enormous range! See Advanced Tactics for more on Bold canceling.

On hit only, you can chain Reverb Shock into Crazy Dance by pressing Ⓢ, but the timing is much stricter than for chaining Reverb Shock to Fireworks—Ⓢ must be pressed on the precise frame that Reverb Shock stops hitting. This is mostly not worth attempting unless you have no meter handy, or are going for style. (Which would be understandable; it's Dante, right? Sometimes you gotta style.)

8

Revolver: Revolver is a spinning attack that strikes several times and places a foe into a ground bounce at the end. You can easily combo into Revolver from Volcano, though the concept might sound difficult at first: Volcano is a special move and thus can't be canceled directly into other special moves, but it IS jump-cancelable… and the 3 pre-jump frames before a jump can be canceled into special moves, which prevents the jump from even happening. While that sounds complicated, the application is easy. Just hit with Volcano, then perform Revolver with ⇩ ⬀ ⇦ ⬂ + Ⓜ. Voila, the complicated-sounding jump cancel is built in, using a variant of the classic *Street Fighter* tiger knee motion.

Revolver, like Crystal, suffers from "Dante sure has a lot of good moves" syndrome. It's a good disease to have, to be sure. In the exact situation described here as a use for Revolver, to combo after Volcano, you should actually cancel Volcano into a forward jump, then chain air Ⓜ, Ⓗ and cancel to ⇩ ⬂ ⇨ + Ⓛ Killer Bee. This causes a ground bounce just like Revolver, while doing about 50,000 more damage and building more hyper meter. Sorry, Revolver. At least , you're still one of the best Beatles albums.

Jet Stream: Dante leaves a wake of flame as he travels the full length of the floor, blades outstretched. Jet Stream is most useful when you've created a ground bounce by OTGing a prone foe after a hard knockdown with Volcano chained into Beehive. Pause briefly before using Jet Stream to make Dante carry his adversary with him across the floor instead of slipping under too fast. Chain to Fireworks with (H) at the end, then cancel into a hyper combo. Jet Stream can chain into Crazy Dance with (S), but the timing is very strict—just as Jet Stream stops hitting.

Fireworks: Fireworks is an extension that can be chained into from Revolver, Reverb Shock, or Jet Stream by pressing (H) toward the end of those attacks. It showers the whole field with bullets, which deals good chip damage and leaves Dante with a very small frame advantage if guarded, so there's no reason not to chain into Fireworks if those attacks are blocked. Most combos that lead into Fireworks can be hyper combo canceled to Million Dollars or Devil Must Die for big damage.

Crazy Dance: An extension to Reverb Shock, Revolver, and Jet Stream that is executed by pressing (S) just as those attacks finish hitting. The timing is much less forgiving than for (H) to chain to Fireworks, and Crazy Dance cannot be hyper combo canceled, so save it for finishing combos in no-meter situations.

Twister: This move engulfs Dante in flames in a vertical column that reaches the top of normal jump height. The quick startup time is slightly misleading; the hitbox starts moving upward from Dante's feet on the 13th frame and travels until the 43rd frame. The flames don't actually protect Dante entirely until the 24th frame, and they don't reach the top of the screen until past the 30th frame.

All this means is that Twister is intended as an early anti-air against competitors falling from a super jump, or as an OTG combo tool. (Yes, this is Dante's only OTG-capable att… wait, nevermind. He's got that covered.) It's mildly unsafe if guarded. If it hits your opponent, you have plenty of time to see and chain to the Tempest follow-up by pressing (L) again.

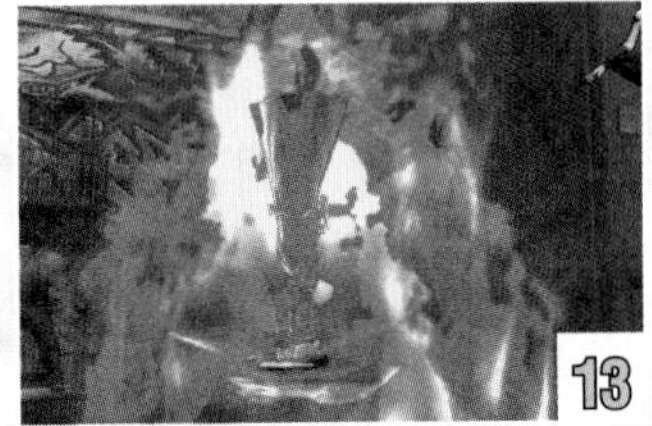

Tempest: The fiery follow-up to Twister. Don't rush: if Twister hits, there's plenty of time to confirm before double-tapping (L). A rival being hit by Twister gets dragged upward in the air, and then Tempest can launch them higher still. Near corners, if you time Tempest to keep the opposing character as high as possible after Twister, you can launch them afterward!

Because of two quirky features, Twister to Tempest has one marginal use besides fancy OTG combos into the corner. Both Twister and Tempest feature high beam durability, and while it's hard to see it, Dante actually leaps to the top of normal jump height during Tempest. Twister to Tempest can thus be used to stalemate some zoning characters from long range, since it destroys or avoids their projectiles. Gimmicky, with no upside (except that maybe someone will teleport into it… maybe), but possible.

Volcano: One of Dante's most important attacks. During this OTG-capable, jump-cancelable move, Dante brings his fist down with such force that the earth cracks.

As an OTG, this is one of Dante's best along with ↘ + (H)(H) Cold Shower. Foes who have been floored by a hard knockdown, such as after The Hammer or air (S), will be popped up, and they can be juggled by either the natural extension into Beehive by pressing (M) again or by jump canceling into air attacks.

For ground combat, it's important to learn to incorporate → + (H) Stinger, Bold canceled to Volcano in your ground combos. Using Stinger to Volcano in this way makes Dante's combos much more reliable from farther away, and increases his damage and hyper meter gain. See Advanced Tactics for more on Bold canceling.

Beehive: Beehive is the extension from Volcano executed by pressing (M) again. Be careful not to double tap (M) so fast that Volcano doesn't have a chance to strike! Dante unleashes a rapid-fire kick flurry, and he caps it off with an axe kick that ground bounces his opponent (unless a ground bounce was already used in the same combo, in which case, the foe ground recovers). From the ground bounce, the opposing character is in perfect position for you to launch them or juggle them laterally with Jet Stream.

Jam Session: A righteous peal across Dante's guitar sends a pinning purple column all the way to the ceiling of the playing field. Jam Session is narrower than it looks and unsafe if guarded up close, so save it for quick anti-air against competitors at super jump height above Dante. During lv.2 or 3 X-Factor, Jam Session can be linked into itself indefinitely.

Killer Bee: If you use this diving attack like a regular dive kick-type attack, it can get you into trouble, since it is unsafe if guarded. Its purpose is combo extension. It can be inserted after chaining to air (H) in combos, whether at normal or super jump height, for a ground bounce. You won't want to use it in combos after you've already expended a ground bounce with Beehive or Revolver.

The Hammer: The Hammer is an airborne double-handed smash that stems from Killer Bee, performed by inputting (L) again. The Hammer is an overhead attack that boasts brief full-body invincibility to cover the swing and the first couple of hitting frames. On hit, it causes a hard knockdown, and if guarded, it leaves Dante at a sizeable frame advantage.You can use The Hammer to crush expected anti-air attacks, or you can unleash it against foes recovering from knockdowns. Intimidating his competitors with The Hammer goes a long way toward enabling Dante to freely use Bold Move to cancel his ground chain combos.

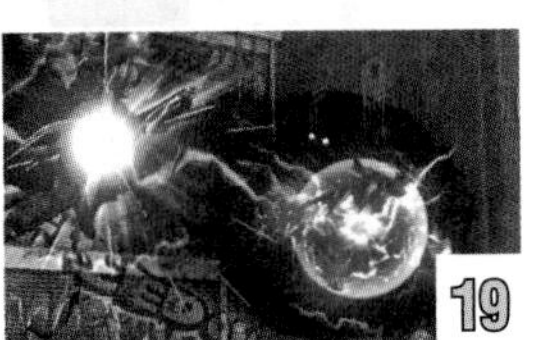

Air Play: During Air Play, Dante strums his guitar in midair, and a purple spark shoots forth, traveling diagonally downward at a shallow trajectory. Hold (M) during execution to charge the projectile before release, which increases its size and slows its speed. Air Play can only be used once per airborne period. This is a long range counterpoint to The Hammer; Air Play is a tool that asserts Dante's control above an opposing character. Air Play's angle of attack makes it ideal for firing at grounded beam characters that would outshoot Dante if he stayed at ground level. The recovery is fast, giving you time to airdash after the projectile or follow behind it on the ground, but since Air Play travels faster than in original *MvC3*, it's not as useful for this anymore. It is also no longer reliable in combos where it had become a staple, such as after Volcano jump canceled into air basic attacks. Still, from midrange, you can sometimes airdash in after Air Play and link air (M) if the spark hits the opposing character.

Sky Dance: Dante plummets to the ground in a spiraling, fiery dive. Sky Dance is intended to end simple air combos after air (H), and it can also be used as a fast overhead attack (perform it just off the ground at close range with ↓ ↘ → ↗ + (H)). Be careful not to abuse this technique, since if your adversary blocks correctly and uses advancing guard, Dante is left wide open for a counterattack.

Air Trick: Dante's teleport places him in the air directly behind his opponent, no matter where the rival is. After Air Trick, the situation is the same as during a point-blank normal jump, right down to Dante's options: he can still attack, use assists, airdash, or double jump.

After reappearing, mix your opponent up with air → + H (which gives you a chance for a throw or throw break if they jump) and The Hammer (which is partially invincible and therefore can defeat some attacks that would beat air H). Since Dante can airdash after Air Trick, you can have him airdash back over them with air M or The Hammer for a double cross-up! If you sense the opposing player might overcommit their team trying to escape the mix-up, you can also just backdash and either use Air Play or just wait and see if they give you something slow to punish heavily.

Dante is capable of calling assists, but this is a bad idea. If you're going to call an assist, do it BEFORE using Air Trick so at least if Dante gets hit, his assist isn't getting hit right along with him. That's what happens if you call an assist after Air Trick and then start getting hit.

Air Trick is a terrific tool, but it's not quite as tricky as it looks at first. After a ↓ ↓ + S input, Dante becomes invincible on the 11th frame and actually reappears, switches sides, and becomes vulnerable again on the 16th frame. Dante isn't actually free to act until the 20th frame, so the earliest you can get an attack out there is the 28th frame with air L, and you weren't going to do that (it would just whiff over a character's head, and air L chained to air M is no longer a natural combo during a normal jump). Using Air Trick into The Hammer, as one example, takes 46 frames minimum.

In the meantime, an attentive challenger watching for Air Trick only needs 4 frames to jump toward Dante and air throw him. In order to close the gap and use Air Trick successfully, you can't just use it overzealously against a neutral opponent. It's much tighter but still not all the way safe performed when you use → + H Stinger, Bold canceled into Air Trick. In order to stay on top of the opposing character using Air Trick safely, you'll have to accompany it with assists.

Drive: Dante pauses for a half-second before slashing with his sword, which sends a flame shockwave along the ground. Both the sword slash and the shockwave can strike. However, in just about any instance where you would want to put a projectile onscreen with Dante from the ground, Hysteric does the job faster and better. Drive fits in the pile with Crystal and Revolver; Dante's special moves that you can find a use for if you must, but you can also pretend that they don't exist.

Bold Move: Dante's most crucial movement technique. Bold Move is a command jump accomplished by pressing S + ATK. At first, this just looks like a jump. And lo, it is, mostly. Dante can be made to airdash, double jump, attack, and call assists (though he himself cannot act until the 16th frame after initiating Bold Move;this is slower than regular jumps, which allow actions on the 4th frame after input). Not too special, right?

Except that you can use Bold Move to cancel any of Dante's basic attacks, whether they hit or whiff. It can also be used to cancel Stinger. This allows Dante's opening chain attempts to be made relatively safe, and it transitions naturally into either a secondary offense with a forward airdash or backpedaling with a backdash and Air Play. Advanced execution techniques with Bold Move also enable Dante to perform combos and sequences not otherwise possible; see Advanced Tactics for more details.

Hyper Combos

Screen	Name	Command	Hits	Damage	Startup	Active	Recovery	Advantage on Hit	Advantage if Guarded	Notes
1	Million Dollars	↓ ↘ → + ATK ATK	28~ 55	254,200~ 301,100	10+1	137 (58)1	35	—	-14	Knocks down, can be mashed for extra damage, each projectile has 1 high priority durability point, final projectile has 5 high priority durability points
2	Devil Trigger	↓ ↙ ← + ATK ATK	—	—	4+0	—	4	—	—	Frames 3-4 invincible, attack power +15%,regenerates 2,000 red health per frame, grants access to Devil Trigger attacks, lasts 600 frames
3	Devil Must Die (level 3 hyper combo)	→ ↓ ↘ + ATK ATK	6	440,000	10+2	10	68	—	-56	Frames 1-21 invincibile, hard knockdown

Million Dollars: Dante uses Ebony and Ivory to unleash a stream of bullets into his attacker, capped off with a massive charged shell that sends them spinning. Million Dollars can be tacked onto the end of nearly any Dante combo, and ATK inputs can now be mashed during the hyper combo to maximize the damage. Using X-Factor to cancel Million Dollars into itself is among the game's easiest X-Factor hyper cancels; just activate X-Factor the instant after Dante fires the charged shell, then immediately perform Million Dollars again. (Broken tactics, pre-*MvC3* release!) You can also X-Factor cancel and use Air Trick immediately, to cause a hard knockdown with air S or The Hammer just as Dante's charged shell hits his foe. You can, of course, follow up after this hard knockdown with an OTG combo.

Although Million Dollars is active pretty quickly and you might catch players with their proverbial pants down guessing on it here and there, this is a bad habit. Opponents can jump out of the bullet stream as Dante charges the final shell and then punish him severely.

Devil Trigger: Devil Trigger transforms Dante into his devil form. Devil Trigger lasts for 10 seconds for Dante as a point character. During Devil Trigger, Dante deals 15% more damage, regenerates red vitality over time, and gains access to three new special moves: Air Raid, Thunder Bolt, and Vortex. New to *UMvC3*, Dante can also now either triple jump or double airdash during one jump period!

The only penalty is that Dante cannot generate hyper meter on point during this mode. The buffs are worth it, but if you don't like the fact that it is not building meter, you can activate Devil Trigger and then switch point characters (whether immediately by using another bar to THC from Devil Trigger, or by using a crossover attack or TAC to tag out).When Dante is tagged out, the Devil Trigger timer stops counting down, and Dante retains the Devil Trigger buffs indefinitely. Having Dante assists that regenerate red vitality and deal extra damage is no small benefit. The timer picks up where it left off if Dante becomes the point character again.

Devil Trigger is basically a mini X-Factor. After canceling an attack like Hysteric or Drive into Devil Trigger, use Air Trick to teleport to the other side of your competitor, covered by the projectiles. You can also cancel into Devil Trigger in the middle of some combos, then keep the combo going with a damage boost and new moves.

Devil Must Die: Dante's most powerful attack burns three bars of hyper meter and ignores damage scaling. Replacing Million Dollars with Devil Must Die at the end of just about any Dante combo turns it into a potential knockout blow, especially with X-Factor or Devil Trigger active.

Devil Must Die is invulnerable for the first 21 frames, and it strikes almost half the playing field away. Because of this, you can use it as a reversal on reaction to all sorts of things at the last second, including the hyper combo "freeze" that occurs at the beginning of an opponent's hyper combo.

Devil Trigger Attacks

Screen	Name	Command	Hits	Damage	Startup	Active	Recovery	Advantage on Hit	Advantage if Guarded	Notes
1	Air Raid	(in air, in Devil Trigger form) ↓↙← + Ⓢ	—	—	11	—	—	—	—	May be done while airborne, lasts 170 frames
2	Thunder Bolt	(in air, in Devil Trigger form) ↓↘→ + Ⓢ	8	130,700	10	25	6	+13	-1	OTG-capable, locks out opponent's advancing guard, beam durability: 8 frames x 1 low priority durability point
3	Vortex	(in air, in Devil Trigger form) →↓↘ + Ⓢ	5	141,100	14	20	8	—	+10	Frames 10-38 invincible, locks out foe's advancing guard, ignores hit stun decay

Air Raid: Air Raid is Dante's flight mode, available during Devil Trigger only. During flight, there's no restriction on the number of specials or airdashes that can be used. Conveniently, Devil Trigger Dante just happens to have access to a couple of particularly nasty air-only specials. By using flight, you can force your adversary to guard up to SEVEN Thunder Bolts instead of just three per airborne period: jump, dump two Thunder Bolts into the target, then activate Air Raid and very quickly pump out up to five more Thunder Bolts before Air Raid ends! This is a ton of damage, whether on hit or as chip.

You can also use Air Raid in Dante air combos for new possibilities, but this doesn't lead to anything earth-shattering; rather, it just allows mild embellishment. Devil Trigger is less about enabling new Dante combos (though it certainly does that) and is mostly about constant vitality regeneration, Thunder Bolt, and Vortex.

Thunder Bolt: It's a good thing for the rest of the cast that Dante doesn't have access to this move all the time. Devil Dante fires a stream of electricity downward at a 45-degree angle. The stream is fast and OTG-capable, leaves Dante at a frame advantage on hit, inflicts terrific damage on hit or guard, is easy to combo into and even links into itself as many times as you can manage, and is immune to advancing guard!The only reason this move doesn't have a kitchen sink is that Dante probably already has a kitchen sink hidden somewhere else in his movelist. Forcing your rival to block three of these attacks in a row is easy to accomplish and deals 165,600 damage; using Air Raid, you can force them to block a lot more at once.

Vortex: During Vortex, Devil Dante spirals across the entire screen laterally, totally invincible for most of his travel time. This move, like Thunder Bolt, ignores advancing guard, a very rare trait indeed. It leaves Dante at a frame advantage if guarded, and you can treat the move sort of like a mini Hard Drive (see Sentinel's hyper combos), "tiger kneeing" it to perform Vortex just off the ground with →↓↘↗ + Ⓢ. This gets Dante in for free with frame advantage from a fullscreen position! As with Thunder Bolt, Vortex fits easily into combos, and the opposing character can't do anything about you forcing them to guard three in a row.

Battle Plan

Dante's basic attacks are relatively slow (Dante's Ⓛ attacks hit in 8 frames... for the grossest contrast, Amaterasu's standing Ⓛ hits in 3 frames, and of course, normal throws are *1* frame). Avoid fighting in close unless you have frame advantage, such as after making your targets block a jump-in attack or an assist. Something like dash-in crouching Ⓛ might seem tempting because it's the path of least resistance for most characters, but not so for Dante. His crouching Ⓛ is slow, and it hits awkwardly on many characters (it usually whiffs completely around the feet of floating characters like Morrigan and Storm).

The ability to cancel whiffed basic attacks with Bold Move, Air Trick, or Reverb Shock lets Dante swing his big, high priority sword at will.

Instead of rushing in on the ground, play to Dante's strengths and fight at mid range. Right next to his opponent, Dante is very susceptible to throws and quicker basic attacks. But his speed deficiency is irrelevant from the tip of standing Ⓛ and Ⓜ pokes, and Dante's sword itself is invincible. And, pulling together tricks from all over Dante's enormous arsenal, you can score full combos even from max range with standing Ⓛ (see both **Combo II** and Advanced Tactics)! In short, aim for your rival with the tip of standing Ⓛ, rather than trying to dash in close.

In addition to their range and priority against grounded adversaries, standing Ⓛ and Ⓜ cut huge swaths through the airspace in front and above Dante and combo even against low altitude foes! Foes who are shot down out of airdash, flight, or jump attempts by standing Ⓛ, Ⓜ, or standing Ⓜ, Ⓗ give you time to verify the juggle and chain to Ⓢ for a launcher (see the aerial aside in **Combo II**). Since standing Ⓜ hits just above Dante's head, he can also dash under airborne competitors and strike with standing Ⓜ, Ⓗ. If this chain hits your opponent, you have time to pause and let them descend a little before chaining to Ⓢ launcher. Without the pause, your foe may be launched too high for a reliable air combo. It's good to pause before proceeding to Ⓢ launcher anyway; you don't have to chain to Ⓢ as fast as possible, and it's good to give yourself an extra moment to verify the hit. You *do not* want to have Dante's Ⓢ whiff or get blocked! Do not go for launchers frivolously! Verify them, and train yourself *not* to press Ⓢ otherwise. (This is good advice for any character with an unsafe launcher, which is most of the cast.)

With Dante's long chains giving plenty of time to visually confirm hits, there's no excuse for whiffing Ⓢ launcher.

While aiming with the tip of standing Ⓛ and Ⓜ, you'll inevitably whiff attacks, or they'll be guarded. An opposing character who blocks and uses advancing guard can also cause chain combo follow-ups to whiff. You can salvage Dante's whiffed, blocked, or advancing guarded attacks in several ways; whiffing basic attacks close to his rival is not the disaster for him that it is for most characters. Most simply, cancel failed chain combos into ↓↙← + Ⓛ Reverb Shock, then press Ⓗ for the Fireworks follow-up. This scores some chip damage and puts Dante back at square one, with very minor frame advantage. As a bonus, even if *every portion* of basic attack CANCEL➡ Reverb Shock CANCEL➡ Fireworks whiffs, the whole sequence still occurs!

For more variety and stronger potential, whiffed or guarded basic attacks can be canceled with Ⓢ + ATK Bold Move. (→ + Ⓗ Stinger can also be Bold canceled, but only on hit or block and not from a whiff; see Advanced Tactics for more information). Missed attacks immediately become new opportunities. The Bold Move command jump isn't as safe as conventional jumps, forcing Dante to wait 16 frames before acting or guarding, but this is still safer than whiffing an attack.

To be better safe than sorry, you can simply guard, or air dash backward and toss Air Play at your foe. You can also airdash forward and keep your offense going. For an air assault, Dante's most important attack is air Ⓜ. This move is double jump-cancelable, and not only hits with huge range in front of and just below airborne Dante, but it also works as a *wicked* cross-up if you jump and airdash over your opponent's head. Dante crosses over regardless, but depending on your timing, you can make air Ⓜ hit from the front or the back! You can perform this cross-up from a normal or super jump, but it proceeds slightly faster from a super jump since characters rise faster when super jumping; super jumping Dante rises to the altitude where airdashes are possible more quickly. Either way, airdash forward for the cross-up as soon as possible after leaving the ground.

Square dashing with Dante's airdash air Ⓜ and Ⓗ can lead to both frontal assaults and ambiguous cross-ups.

Air Ⓗ can also be used as an air attack, and it can also cross your attacker up, but the hitbox on air Ⓗ requires much more precision for this than air Ⓜ (you must descend just on the other side of an enemy for air Ⓗ to cross up, and it's not as ambiguous where it will actually hit as air Ⓜ). Air Ⓗ also can't be canceled with a double jump, so it doesn't lead to confirmable anti-air combos like air Ⓜ can (though that's irrelevant when you're airdashing, which prevents double jumping). When you go for air Ⓗ, always perform it with ⇨ + Ⓗ in order to air throw your rival (or break *their* throw) if they happen to be close enough. This is the reason to use air Ⓗ over Ⓜ from close ranges, to deter foes from just trying to jump and airthrow Dante. Don't over-press Ⓗ in midair, or you might accidentally produce Rain Storm, Dante's straight-down airborne Ebony and Ivory extension.

On the other hand, if you end up air throwing your competitor, you'll want to use Rain Storm on purpose to OTG them. With the right assist, it's possible to continue a combo after OTG Rain Storm, but it's difficult (see **Combo III** and the Combo Appendix).

You should be relentless about forcing your opponent to guard air Ⓜ and ⇨ + Ⓗ, whether after cross-up airdashes, airdashes to the front of your target, or after Air Trick. The opposing character should be worried about Dante's far-reaching and cross-up capable air basic attacks, so air specials are more likely to be effective when you mix it up. At any time while spamming aggressive airdashes, you can gear change to defense by airdashing backward and firing Air Play. If you think that the opposing player may attempt anti-air attacks to punish Dante, properly time your use of The Hammer to crush their attempt and lead to a full Dante combo.

If you catch airborne foes with air Ⓜ without airdashing, such as after using Bold Move and attacking with air Ⓜ out of a normal jump arc, you can double jump and link air Ⓜ, Ⓗ into Killer Bee for a ground bounce. If your opponent guards air Ⓜ, you can use the double jump to begin a secondary offense.

After knocking out an opposing character, perform Acid Rain early, so the new character is forced to guard it on the way in. Dashing to one side or the other with st. Ⓜ right under your target is very difficult for opponents to guard.

Dante's long combos naturally push opponents into the corner where they'll have extra trouble avoiding Dante's attacks. When adversaries are knocked out, especially near corners, get Acid Rain out early for a powerful mix-up against new characters falling in. Cancel into Devil Trigger or X-Factor to make the pressure more intense and the payoff greater.

Speaking of X-Factor, Dante can make great use of X-Factor whether it's early on in the match or a last-half-demon-standing situation. Because of his bulletproof standing chain combo string into Stinger (st. Ⓛ, Ⓜ, Ⓗ CANCEL ⇨ + Ⓗ), Dante gives you a veritable eternity to confirm whether you're hitting the opposing character and an assist, which is the ideal situation for popping X-Factor early. If you ever get the chance to knock out two characters at once, you take it.

Later on, once it's down to just Dante, any worry about conserving meter for teammates goes out the window, and you are free to stack Devil Trigger on top of lv.3 X-Factor. The vitality regeneration effect for both effects stacks, so X-Factor Devil Trigger Dante gains red vitality faster than anyone else! (…who is not Healing Field Phoenix.) Chipping with Thunder Bolt or just linking it into itself over and over becomes even sweeter in X-Factor, and it almost is an almost unbearably sexy option if your opponent has already burned their X-Factor. You are free to use any remaining hyper meter bars to keep Dante in Devil Trigger rather than saving for direct damage hyper combos as the anchor, since his combo damage is nuts already with Devil Trigger sitting on top of X-Factor, *and* he's capable of infinite damage anyway by linking Jam Session to Jam Session over and over… see the Combo Appendix. Dante only needs two surplus bars handed to him by fallen friends to power Devil Trigger for all of lv.3 X-Factor.

Saving resources for last-ditch Dante allows you to start his last hurrah with something ridiculous like Hysteric CANCEL Devil Trigger, Hysteric CANCEL ⇩⇩ + Ⓢ.

Devil Trigger is definitely still nice outside of X-Factor, but because Dante's hyper meter building is already reduced in *UMvC3*, and because competitors might actually be hacking away at your hyper meter actively with sideways TACs, it's perhaps better not to enter a mode that prevents more meter building unless you've built up several surplus bars to spend already. Saving a few bars for an assured knockout blow by ending a standard combo with Devil Must Die (or having it in your back pocket as an instant, half-screen, invincible reversal) is also too strong of an option to forsake.

Early on in a match, perhaps the best use of Devil Trigger is to get Dante out safely once he starts taking serious damage. Activate Devil Trigger (preferably at the end of a combo, but don't stick around too long fishing for the opportunity and accidentally get Dante all-the-way killed), then THC to your next character (preferably with a hyper combo that picks up where Dante left off). Now you're packing a Dante assist with a permanent damage buff and enhanced red vitality regeneration! Devil Trigger's timer doesn't tick down while Dante is tagged out! (Keep in mind that if assist Dante already has Devil Trigger active, you cannot THC *to* Dante using Devil Trigger.)

DANTE

COMBO USAGE

I. CR. Ⓛ, ST. Ⓛ, Ⓜ, Ⓢ CANCEL FORWARD SUPER JUMP, AIR Ⓜ, Ⓜ CANCEL DOUBLE JUMP Ⓜ, Ⓗ CANCEL ⬇⬊➡ + Ⓛ, LAND, Ⓢ CANCEL FORWARD SUPER JUMP, AIR Ⓜ, Ⓗ CANCEL ⬇⬊➡ + Ⓗ CANCEL ⬇⬊➡ + ATKATK (MASH ATK)

577,400 damage, 20% meter loss

Dante is a tough character to play to full potential, even with the alterations to his controls to bring him more within the reach of everyone. Even with the double-motions for alternate special moves gone, his top shelf material still requires Bold canceling and precise, rapid button inputs. This remains outside the reach of casual fans, but Dante still has effective, cool combos that don't require finger gymnastics. This simplified combo is good for beginners and online play. In the event that your opponent guards the first two or three hits of this combo, cancel into Bold Move to take to the air, then airdash forward to go for a cross-up, or pause, then chain to standing Ⓗ or ➡ + Ⓗ to lure out counterattacks. Instead of jumping with Bold Move or inserting a delayed Ⓗ hit into the chain, you can also cancel late into Air Trick to teleport behind an incoming counterattack. Apart from the side switch, Air Trick's brief invulnerability helps Dante flicker through many things the opposing player might try to do to retaliate.

If your adversary pushes you out with advancing guard after the first few hits, call a projectile assist and cancel your last whiffed hit in the chain into Air Trick to get right back in. If you'd rather not switch sides, such as when near corners, you can cancel with Bold Move and either airdash forward or use Air Play to slow things down.

II. ST. Ⓛ, Ⓜ, Ⓗ CANCEL ➡ + Ⓗ CANCEL ATK+Ⓢ CANCEL ➡⬇⬊ + Ⓜ CANCEL FORWARD JUMP, AIR Ⓜ, Ⓗ CANCEL ⬇⬊➡ + Ⓛ, LAND, Ⓢ CANCEL Ⓗ (ONLY 2 SHOTS) CANCEL Ⓢ CANCEL SUPER JUMP, ⬇⬊➡ + ⓁⓁ, LAND, ⬊ + ⒽⒽⒽ CANCEL ➡ + Ⓗ CANCEL ATK + Ⓢ CANCEL ⬇⬇ + Ⓢ, AIR Ⓢ, LAND, ➡⬇⬊ + ⓂⓂ (9 HITS) CANCEL ⬇⬊➡ + ATKATK (MASH ATK) OR ➡⬇⬊ + ATKATK

672,700~898,300 damage, 115% meter gain using Million Dollars ender

A hacked-up version of Dante's old *MvC3* loop combos, you can still get the party started, but Dante nets less meter and damage than he used to. The opening strike, standing Ⓛ, is considered one of the strongest combos starters in *MvC3* because of its long reach and ability to cleanly catch jumping targets.

For tips on Bold canceling, which is required for advanced Dante combos, see Advanced Tactics. After air ⬇⬊➡ + Ⓛ hits, wait until your rival falls a bit from the bounce before you input Ⓢ; this ensures they are low enough after the launch for the Clay Pigeon gunshots to hit. During the ⬊ + ⒽⒽⒽ CANCEL ➡ + Ⓗ ATK + Ⓢ segment, do not cancel Bold Move into ⬇⬇ + Ⓢ if you're near a corner; instead just do Bold Move to jump, then air Ⓢ. Finally, cancel Beehive at the end into a hyper combo *before* the final axe kick hit.

If you do strike an airborne assailant with standing Ⓛ when going for **Combo II**, you must launch instead of going for Stinger into Bold canceled Volcano; against aerial foes do st. Ⓛ, Ⓜ, Ⓗ, Ⓢ CANCEL vertical super jump, air Ⓜ CANCEL forward double jump, air Ⓗ CANCEL ⬇⬊➡ + Ⓛ, land, st. Ⓗ CANCEL ⬇⬋⬅ + Ⓛ CANCEL Ⓗ CANCEL ⬇⬊➡ + ATKATK (mash ATK).

COMBO USAGE CONT.

III. AIR THROW, AIR HHHHHHH (CALL TRON—β DURING 4TH HIT) CANCEL ↓↘→ + LL, LAND, ↘ + HHH CANCEL → + H CANCEL ATK + S CANCEL ↓↓ + S, AIR S, LAND, →↓↘ + MM (10 HITS) CANCEL ↓↘→ + ATKATK (MASH ATK) OR →↓↘ + ATKATK

374,100~631,100 damage, 84% meter gain

Dante can't normally inflict much combo damage off of an air throw besides just using Rain Storm, but with the right assist, combos like this become available. Input the command for the assist during the fourth gun shot, then cancel into The Hammer on hit 14. Don't feel bad if you have trouble scoring follow-up combos consistently after a Rain Storm OTG; the best Dante players in the world mess up Rain Storm, into assist, into Killer Bee all the time. It's hard!

IV. AIR S OR ↓↘→ + LL, ↘ + HHH CANCEL S CANCEL SUPER JUMP, ↓↘→ + LL, LAND ↘ + HHH CANCEL → + H CANCEL ATK + S CANCEL ↓↓ + S, AIR S, →↓↘ + MM, PAUSE, ↓↙← + H CANCEL H CANCEL ↓↘→ + ATKATK (MASH ATK)

523,200 damage, 97% meter gain

This OTG combo works after scoring a hit with either air S or The Hammer, either of which causes a hard knockdown. Air S has significantly more range and is easier to perform, while The Hammer has invulnerability and doesn't leave Dante vulnerable when he lands like air S.

You can get a double overhead and avoid the recovery period on air S by attacking with air S canceled into The Hammer! Even if you knock your opponent down right away with air S so The Hammer just whiffs, it recovers so quickly that there's still plenty of time to OTG with Cold Shower to Prop Shredder.

ADVANCED TACTICS

BOLD CANCELING

Dante's S + ATK command jump, Bold Move, can be used to interrupt his basic attacks on the ground. This is needed to make whiffed moves safe and to keep up momentum. Crucially, you can also use Bold Move to cancel Dante's exceptional ⇨ + H Stinger command attack on hit or block. The point is not to jump out of Stinger; the point is to then immediately cancel Bold Move's pre-jump frames into another special move. In practice, Bold Move is used as the go-between from Stinger to the next special.

This is easier than it sounds, thanks to Stinger only being Bold-cancelable on *contact*. (So, you can't Bold cancel too early and whiff the move entirely, like you can with basic attacks.) You can buffer the ATK + S command *very* early on during Stinger, and Bold Move will happen on the first possible frame after contact. When using Stinger on its own from mid range, you can buffer Bold Move as early as the 3rd frame; when chaining into Stinger, you can buffer Bold Move on the *2nd* frame! Basically, just input S + ATK as soon as you possibly can after ⇨ + H, well in advance of the actual hit, so you give yourself the maximum amount of time possible to perform the follow-up special move.

It can get even easier than that with the use of a plink input. Instead of pressing ATK + S and then inputting a separate command in just a handful of frames, input the command for the desired move, then press S *right* before you press the correct attack button. You should drum the buttons right after one another like with a kara cancel.

Once you're comfortable with Bold canceling Stinger, a whole new world of combo and mix-up possibilities opens up for Dante. The most useful follow-ups after Bold canceled Stinger:

VOLCANO:

⇨ + H CANCEL S + ATK CANCEL ⇨⇩⇘ + M, ⇗ *OR* ⇨ + H CANCEL ⇨⇩⇘ + S ~ M, ⇗

Using Stinger to Volcano gives you reliable ground combos into a jump cancel even from the edge of Dante's range (see Combo II). If guarded, you can still jump cancel Volcano to keep up your attack, but if your opponent uses advancing guard to push Dante out just before Volcano, Dante ends up whiffing the attack badly. Try to verify and end chains with one of the following options instead when a chain into Stinger is blocked.

BOLD MOVE:

S + ATK

Like with Bold canceling basic attacks, Dante simply jumps out of Stinger. You must wait a little bit longer to act than during a regular jump, however. Canceling standing H or ⇨ + H into Bold Move, then airdashing forward is a relatively safe means of following up blocked chains, and serves as a nice counterpoint to Air Trick.

REVERB SHOCK:

⇨ + H CANCEL S + ATK CANCEL ⇩⇙⇦ + L, H *OR* ⇨ + H CANCEL ⇩⇙⇦ + S ~ L, H

Stinger to Reverb Shock to Fireworks can be done even on whiff, and it is safe if guarded. This is the least risky follow-up after having an initial chain guarded.

AIR TRICK:

⇨ + H CANCEL ⇩ + S + ATK CANCEL ⇩ + S

If your rival guards Stinger, Bold canceling to Air Trick is extremely strong if you have an assist on the way out—they can advancing guard Stinger all they want, but it's not going to help them. On its own, Bold canceling Stinger (or standing H) to Air Trickis tighter than canceling to Air Trick from other basic attacks, but it's still not airtight. Aside from creating pressure after blocked Stinger on the ground, Bold canceling to Air Trick is vital to reliably catching midscreen opponents after OTGing them with ⇘ + HHH Cold Shower to ⇨ + H Stinger lv.2. Stinger creates a wall bounce against airborne or

Bold canceling allows Stinger, which is not special-cancelable, to be linked into special moves with Bold Move as a go-between.

Here, the opposing character pushblocks Dante's Stinger, but with an assist coming out and Bold canceled Air Trick switching sides on them, it doesn't matter.

juggled foes, so Bold canceling the Stinger to Air Trick lets Dante arrive next to them just after the wall bounce, where you can immediately strike with The Hammer or air S right back into a hard knockdown!

This command is easier than it sounds. Instead of trying to do ⇩⇩ + S quickly after ATK + S, the commands can be merged into one command that covers both bases. As soon as you input ⇨ + H, immediately input ⇩ + S + ATK, ⇩ + S. If performed quickly and precisely, you'll easily cancel to Air Trick from Stinger every time. Have fun with your new juggle/pressure toy.

DEVIL TRIGGER:

⇨ + H CANCEL S + ATK CANCEL ⇩⇙⇦ + ATKATK *OR* ⇨ + H CANCEL ⇩⇙⇦ + S ~ ATKATK

As a stylish, somewhat inefficient alternative to following up chain combos on hit with Stinger into Volcano, you can follow up with Stinger into Devil Trigger, *then* link to Volcano right after the hyper screen freeze and go about your business with a 15% damage buff. This is also all right if you want to tag a weak Dante out to regenerate red vitality with Devil Trigger, but you could extend the combo a lot further to gain hyper meter before doing that anyway. (Pretty much anywhere in our combos where Million Dollars is listed, you can just Devil Trigger and THC Dante out; combos that end in good position for Million Dollars almost certainly give the following character something to shoot at.)

GRAPPLE:

⇨ + H, pause, CANCEL S + ATK, ⇩⇘⇨ + H, H *OR* ⇨ + H, pause, CANCEL ⇩⇘⇨ + S ~ H, H

Juggling with Grapple is an alternative to following up the wall bounce of Stinger lv.2 (which is just Stinger used after certain Ebony and Ivory attacks, such as Scat Shot or Cold Shower) with Air Trick. Instead of going to them, you can Bold cancel to Hysteric, double tap H for the extension to Grapple, and bring them to you. This was more important in original *MvC3*, since this put the opponent into a captured state briefly and allowed Dante to Devil Trigger and then THC to a teammate to start the THC glitch.

HAMMER TIME

The sky did not fall. It was merely lowered slightly.

Yes, The Hammer had its invincibility adjusted to be shorter and to occur later on in the attack. But it's also a lot easier to perform now, which, depending on your execution, may result in a *more* effective (The?) Hammer. After all, were you inputting ⇩⇘⇨ + L⇩⇘⇨ + L perfectly every time? No, you weren't. This is still an incredible attack: a relatively fast (at around 24 frames until it hits, if you input ↓ ↘ → + Ⓛ Ⓛ perfectly), partially invincible overhead that causes a hard knockdown on hit and leaves Dante with big frame advantage on guard. Hsien-Ko players are tuning up the world's smallest violin for Dante players concerning The Hammer's adjustments.

The Hammer is best executed just off the ground with a tiger knee motion of ↓ ↘ → ↗ + Ⓛ Ⓛ. You want just a hint of a pause in between ↗ and the first Ⓛ input to ensure that Dante travels far enough so The Hammer doesn't whiff. Perform the motion from down to up-forward quickly, and it doubles as a super jump, which also helps with getting enough altitude for The Hammer to have time to come out before Dante lands again. Since Dante lands right after using The Hammer, he won't be pushed back too far if his opponent blocked The Hammer and used advancing guard. Coupled with the large frame advantage The Hammer creates on block, Dante can dash in for free after having The Hammer guarded. Because of this, just to be sure, you should have Dante dash after he lands *every* time you use The Hammer. In the case of advancing guard, you'll be right back where you started, in perfect position to try The Hammer again or to super jump and immediately airdash over your competitor to crossup with air Ⓜ or Ⓗ. And on a successful hit, you'll have plenty of time while dashing to to confirm and begin an OTG combo with ↘ + Ⓗ Ⓗ Cold Shower.

The Hammer is also useful after Air Trick, though you'll want to create a sizeable frame advantage with an assist or at least Hysteric CANCEL Devil Trigger before you try this.

This attack can also turn air Ⓢ, which is normally horribly unsafe when guarded, into a relatively safe double overhead, either hit of which leads into *Combo IV*. Attack your target with air Ⓢ, such as falling with it after Air Trick, but cancel air Ⓢ to The Hammer immediately on contact. Hit or guard, it doesn't matter; the important thing is not to let air Ⓢ hit the floor. If the opponent eats either attack, you get your combo!

DEVIL TRIGGER PLINK AIRDASHING

To improve your success with this technique, try drumming all three attack buttons one after the other as fast as you can. This can be applied to ground dashes wavedashes with most characters, too.

With Dante's Devil Trigger double airdash, you can add another layer to his mix-ups: after Air Trick, you can airdash over the enemy, then immediately airdash back for a *triple* cross-up. The double airdash also gives Dante more leeway in super jumping to aim Thunder Bolts at his adversary. Normally, you can't cancel an airdash into another airdash in the same direction, but you can with a form of kara-canceling.

If you press different attack buttons on consecutive frames (called "plinking"), the game interprets this as ATK ATK for a command dash. This works because virtually every basic attack in the game can be kara-canceled into a dash on the first frame. You can use this method to wavedash on the ground without actually inputting any directions (ATK ATK, ATK ~ ATK, ATK ~ ATK, ATK ~ ATK, etc.) This is true for airdashes as well, but normally, characters can't airdash more than once per airborne period. Of course, that's a different story during flight for airdash characters, or during Dante's Devil Trigger. This changes in Devil Trigger, where Dante can now use this trick to wavedash in midair, essentially. By airdashing once then inputting ATK ~ ATK precisely on consecutive frames during the dash, the airdash gets canceled into another airdash!

By using this technique, you make Devil Trigger Dante close the distance to his opponent or make it over to them for a cross-up from much farther away. This further presses the advantage Devil Trigger Dante already has over foes using advancing guard, thanks to Thunder Bolt and Vortex.

COMBO APPENDIX

GENERAL EXECUTION TIPS

Press ATK + Ⓢ as soon as possible after → + Ⓗ for more time to do Stinger Bold cancels.

Be precise with your Ebony and Ivory inputs; many combos are dependent on only landing a certain number of gunshots, when in reality, more could be mashed out.

After launching your target, you almost always want to hit their rising body as fast as possible, whether with super jump air Ⓜ or Clay Pigeon.

ST. Ⓛ, Ⓜ, Ⓗ CANCEL → + Ⓗ CANCEL X-FACTOR, ST. Ⓜ, Ⓗ, → + Ⓗ CANCEL ATK + Ⓢ CANCEL → ↓ ↘ + Ⓜ CANCEL FORWARD JUMP, AIR Ⓜ, Ⓗ CANCEL ↓ ↘ → + Ⓛ, LAND, Ⓢ CANCEL Ⓗ (2 SHOTS) CANCEL Ⓢ CANCEL SUPER JUMP, ↓ ↘ → + Ⓛ Ⓛ, LAND, ↘ + Ⓗ Ⓗ Ⓗ CANCEL → + Ⓗ CANCEL ATK + Ⓢ CANCEL ↓ ↓ + Ⓢ, AIR Ⓢ, LAND, → ↓ ↘ + Ⓜ Ⓜ (9 HITS) CANCEL ↓ ↘ → + ATK ATK (MASH ATK)

Notes	Damage
Verifiable means of linking X-Factor	1,034,700~1,330,000 damage, 164~200% meter gain

AIR THROW, AIR Ⓗ Ⓗ Ⓗ Ⓗ Ⓗ Ⓗ Ⓗ (14 HITS) CANCEL X-FACTOR, LAND, → ↓ ↘ + Ⓜ Ⓜ (10 HITS), ↘ + Ⓗ Ⓗ Ⓗ CANCEL → + Ⓗ CANCEL ATK + Ⓢ CANCEL ↓ ↓ + Ⓢ, AIR Ⓢ, LAND, → ↓ ↘ + Ⓜ Ⓜ (9 HITS) CANCEL ↓ ↘ → + ATK ATK (MASH)

Notes	Damage
Difficult air throw X-Factor combo. After OTG Rain Storm, must land and perform Volcano to Beehive immediately	700,900~875,900 damage, 115~127% meter gain

↓ ↘ → + ATK ATK (MASH ATK), X-FACTOR ON HIT 54, ↓ ↓ + Ⓢ, AIR Ⓢ, LAND, ↘ + Ⓗ Ⓗ Ⓗ CANCEL Ⓢ CANCEL SUPER JUMP, ↓ ↘ → + Ⓛ Ⓛ, AIR Ⓢ, LAND, ↘ + Ⓗ Ⓗ Ⓗ CANCEL → + Ⓗ CANCEL ATK + Ⓢ CANCEL ↓ ↓ + Ⓢ, LAND, → ↓ ↘ + Ⓜ Ⓜ (10 HITS), WAIT A MOMENT, ↓ ↙ ← + Ⓗ CANCEL Ⓗ CANCEL ↓ ↘ → + ATK ATK (MASH ATK)

Notes	Damage
—	986,200~1,289,600 damage,115%~127% meter gain

AS DANTE COMES IN: AIR Ⓜ CANCEL DOUBLE JUMP, AIR Ⓜ, Ⓗ CANCEL → ↓ ↘ → + Ⓛ, LAND, ST. Ⓗ CANCEL ↓ ↙ ← + Ⓛ CANCEL Ⓗ CANCEL ↓ ↘ → + ATK ATK (MASH ATK)

Notes	Damage
↑ + Ⓢ or → + Ⓢ TAC to Dante	Varies based on damage scaling

AS DANTE COMES IN: AIR Ⓜ, Ⓜ CANCEL DOUBLE JUMP, AIR Ⓜ, Ⓗ, Ⓢ, LAND, ↘ + Ⓗ Ⓗ Ⓗ CANCEL → + Ⓗ CANCEL ATK + Ⓢ, AIR Ⓢ, LAND, → ↓ ↘ + Ⓜ Ⓜ (10 HITS), PAUSE, ↓ ↙ ← + Ⓗ CANCEL Ⓗ CANCEL ↓ ↘ → + ATK ATK (MASH ATK)

Notes	Damage
↑ + Ⓢ or → + Ⓢ TAC to Dante on a cornered opponent	Varies based on damage scaling

ST. Ⓛ, Ⓜ, Ⓗ CANCEL → + Ⓗ CANCEL LV.2 OR 3 X-FACTOR, ST. Ⓜ, Ⓗ, → + Ⓗ CANCEL ATK + Ⓢ CANCEL → ↓ ↘ + Ⓜ CANCEL FORWARD JUMP, AIR Ⓗ CANCEL ↓ ↘ → + Ⓛ, LAND, Ⓢ CANCEL Ⓗ (2 SHOTS) CANCEL Ⓢ CANCEL → ↓ ↘ ↗ + Ⓗ, → ↓ ↘ + Ⓗ X ∞

Notes	Damage
Once the first Jam Session hits, all subsequent Jam Sessions combo indefinitely until your X-Factor meter runs out	1,300,000+

AIR THROW, AIR Ⓗ Ⓗ Ⓗ Ⓗ Ⓗ Ⓗ Ⓗ, LAND, → ↓ ↘ + Ⓛ CANCEL → ↓ ↘ + ATK ATK

Notes	Damage
Extremely hard assist-free air throw combo.Perform Rain Storm after falling a bit to drop closer to the ground, then do → ↓ ↘ + Ⓛ ASAP upon landing; cancel to Devil Must Die the second → ↓ ↘ + Ⓛ hits	580,700

FELICIA

"I'M FELICIA, THE MOST DANCINGIST, SINGINGIST WOMAN YOU'LL EVER MEET!"

Bio

REAL NAME

Felicia

OCCUPATION

Musical Star,
Sister of an Orphanage

ABILITIES

Can fight with feline abilities. She can also transform fully into a cat, although this is not really useful in battle.

WEAPONS

Fights with razor-sharp claws.

PROFILE

A cat woman who was taken in by a gentle sister, she is very kind and cheerful. She worked hard to achieve her dream of becoming a musical star. In order to help children who shared her circumstances, she now works as the sister of an orphanage.

FIRST APPEARANCE

Dark Stalkers (1994)

POWER GRID

2	INTELLIGENCE
2	STRENGTH
2	SPEED
3	STAMINA
1	ENERGY PROJECTION
4	FIGHTING ABILITY

*This is biographical, and does not represent an evaluation of the in-game combat potential of this hero.

ALTERNATE COSTUMES

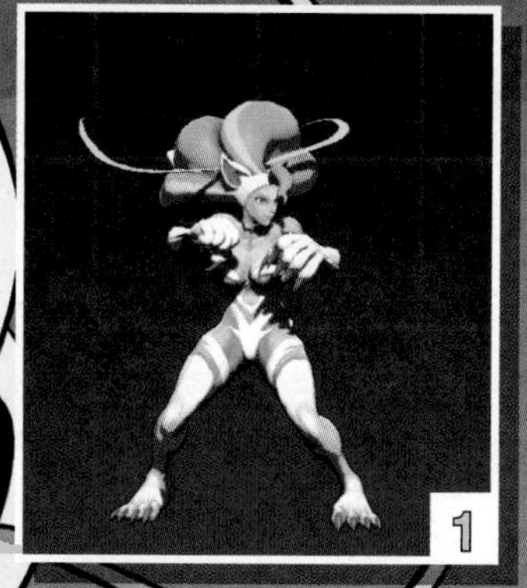

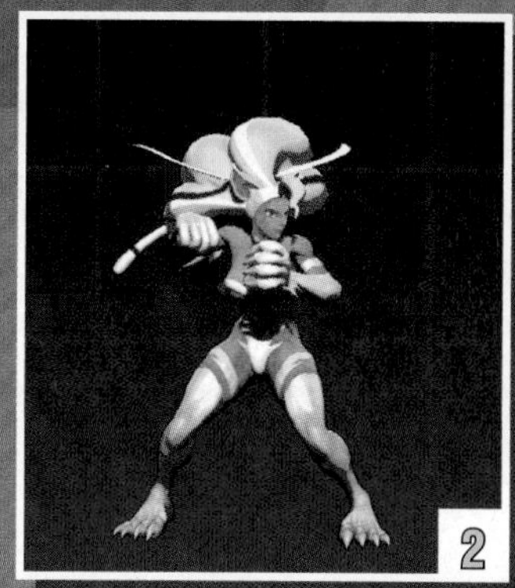

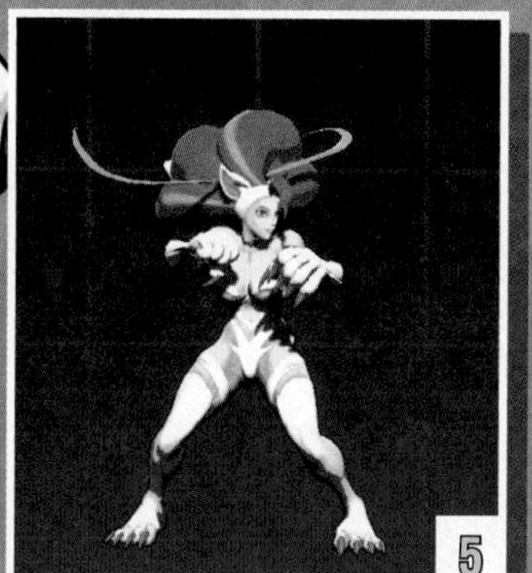

Overview

Vitality	880,000
Chain Combo Archetype	Hunter Series

X-Factor Boost	Damage	Speed
Level 1 (3 teammates remaining)	115%	125%
Level 2 (2 teammates remaining)	135%	135%
Level 3 (1 teammate remaining)	155%	145%

Your primary goal when playing as Felicia is to get within range to attack your opponent with crouching Ⓛ.

Why do you want to attack your adversary with crouching Ⓛ with Felicia?

- Between staggered crouching Ⓛ attacks and Cat Spike L, Felicia has two very strong options to punish her rival for attempting to use advancing guard, either of which leads into a combo
- Crouching Ⓛ catches competitors trying to jump away from Felicia
- Opposing characters wary of crouching Ⓛ open themselves up to being grabbed by the Hell Cat command throw, which also leads into a combo
- Even if your target guards several crouching Ⓛ attacks, it's still possible to salvage the mix-up with Felicia by using the large assortment of attacks that move her forward with frame advantage

How do you get within attack range of crouching Ⓛ?

- Using Delta Kick and air Delta Kick to quickly advance across the screen while avoiding threats, leaving Felicia with frame advantage
- Using Felicia's exceptional wavedash to close the distance when her foe is trying to deal with Delta Kick
- Calling long range crossover assists before wavedashing or using Delta Kick

Your secondary objective when using Felicia is to force your opponent into the corner.

Why do you want to force your adversary into the corner when playing as Felicia?

- Felicia's Kitty's Helper hyper combo can lead to unblockable setups in the corner
- Combos in the corner lead to a strong mix-up using Toy Touch, which in turn leads to more combos
- It becomes much easier to get within range of crouching Ⓛ
- Her high-pressure game in the corner forces her opponent to use advancing guard or jump, setting up opportunities to grab them with an air throw or the Hell Cat command throw

How do you force the opposing character into the corner as Felicia?

- Fighting advancing guard usage using Delta Kick M and Cat Spike M
- Effectively mixing in crossover assists into your offense to create a seamless flow of attacks
- Hitting your rival with combos!

TUNING SINCE ORIGINAL MVC3

Felicia has had some gaps in her offense filled in with the transition to *Ultimate Marvel vs. Capcom 3*. She can now perform Delta Kick in the air, giving her a much-needed aerial special move that opens up more combo and pressure opportunities. The recovery frames of Sand Splash have been greatly reduced, as well, and two of her hyper combos are now mashable for extra damage. On the other side of the coin, competitors now recover faster from her OTG-capable Toy Touch command attack, making it more difficult to combo afterward in long combos without the use of an assist or X-Factor. With the ground bounce properties of air Delta Kick, Felicia still inflicts more damage with her no-meter combos.

- Felicia's vitality increased to 880,00 from 875,000
- Toy Touch now causes less hitstun against airborne adversaries
- You may now perform Delta Kick in the air. The aerial version causes ground bounce if it hits against an airborne rival
- Recovery frames on Sand Splash reduced, Sand Splash H now hits two additional times, all versions are OTG-capable
- Dancing Flash and Please Help Me hyper combos can be mashed for additional damage

Attack Set

Standing Basic Attacks

Screen	Command	Hits	Damage	Meter Gain	Startup	Active	Recovery	Advantage on Hit	Advantage if Guarded	Notes
1	Standing L	1	35,000	260	4	3	10	0	-2	—
2	Standing M	1	55,000	440	7	3	16	-3	-3	—
3	Standing H	3	77,100	720	10	12	17	0	-2	—

1

2

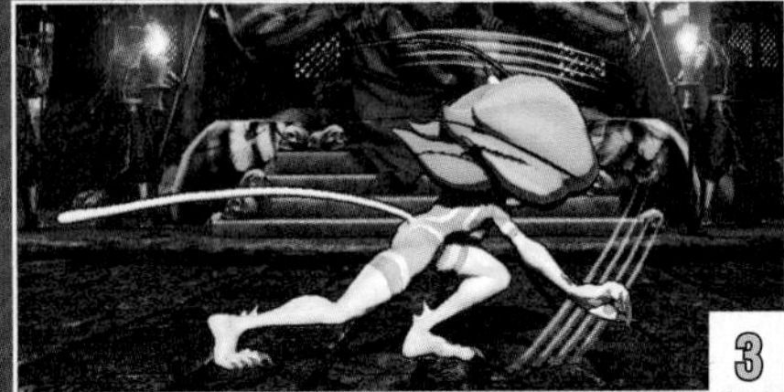
3

Crouching Basic Attacks

Screen	Command	Hits	Damage	Meter Gain	Startup	Active	Recovery	Advantage on Hit	Advantage if Guarded	Notes
1	Crouching L	1	44,000	352	5	2	11	0	-2	Low attack
2	Crouching M	1	53,000	424	7	3	18	-5	-5	—
3	Crouching H	1	65,000	520	10	4	26	—	-9	Low attack, knocks down

1

2

3

Ground Special Attack—Launcher

Screen	Command	Hits	Damage	Meter Gain	Startup	Active	Recovery	Advantage on Hit	Advantage if Guarded	Notes
1	S (while standing or crouching)	1	70,000	560	8	5	23	—	-7	Launcher, not special- or hyper combo-cancelable

1

Air Basic Attacks

Screen	Command	Hits	Damage	Meter Gain	Startup	Active	Recovery	Advantage on Hit	Advantage if Guarded	Notes
1	Air L	1	45,000	360	5	3	19	+10	+8	Overhead attack
2	Air M	1	55,000	440	8	4	29	+18	+14	Overhead attack
3	Air H	1	70,000	560	8	5	23	+16	+15	Overhead attack

1

2

3

Air Special Attacks—Flying Screen and Air Exchange

Air Ⓢ causes a hard knockdown when used in a launcher combo (this is sometimes called flying screen). When used outside of a launcher combo, air Ⓢ behaves mostly like another basic attack. Air exchange attacks, performed by inputting a direction plus Ⓢ, are only possible during a launcher combo. Exchange hits initiate team aerial combos by tagging in the next available character to continue the air combo.

Screen	Command	Hits	Damage	Meter Gain	Startup	Active	Recovery	Advantage on hit	Advantage if guarded	Notes
1	Air Ⓢ	1	70,000	560	9	4	33	+15	+13	Causes hard knockdown if used in launcher combo
2	Air ⇧ + Ⓢ (during launcher combo)	1	53,000	424	3	3	Until grounded	—	—	Tags in next available ally while lofting opponent upward
3	Air ⇨ or ⇦ + Ⓢ (during launcher combo)	1	37,000	216	8	4	Until grounded	—	—	Tags in next available ally while causing wall bounce, erases 1 hyper meter bar from foe
4	Air ⇩ + Ⓢ (during launcher combo)	1	53,000	424 + 10,000	9	6	Until grounded	—	—	Tags in next available ally while causing ground bounce, generates 1 hyper meter bar

1

2

3

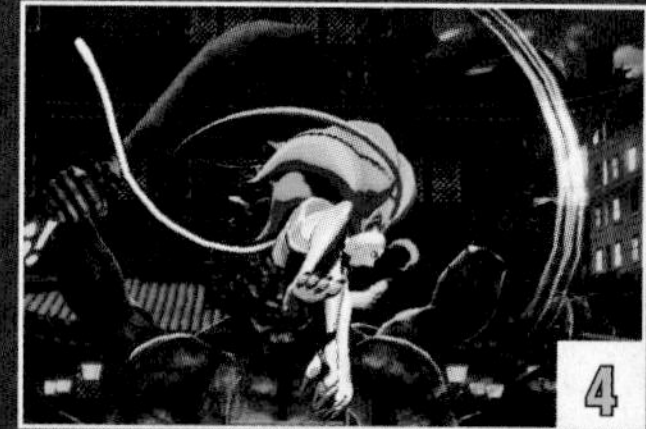
4

Command Attacks

Command attacks resemble basic attacks but have different chaining and canceling properties. It's usually possible to chain *into* a command attack from basic attacks, but most command attacks cannot be chained from or canceled themselves.

Screen	Name	Command	Hits	Damage	Meter Gain	Startup	Active	Recovery	Advantage on Hit	Advantage if Guarded	Notes
1	Toy Touch	⬂ + Ⓜ	1	50,000	400	8	3	20	-7	-7	Low attack, OTG- capable, jump- cancelable
2	Kitty Slash	⇦ + Ⓗ	2	74,000	6400	8	8	23	-3	-5	—
3	Wall Grab	When back is to a wall, jump toward it and hold ⇦	—	—	—	26	—	—	—	—	Felicia clings to a wall, input ⇨ during cling to perform wall jump, holding ⇦ causes her to slide down, may call assists during cling animation

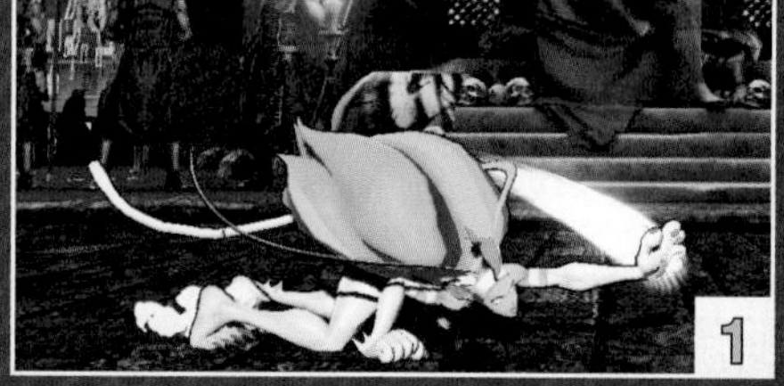
1

2

3

Throws

Throws are for snagging passive or blocking opponents. Since throws are active so quickly, you can use them to preemptively toss opposing characters out of their offense. Combos are usually possible after throws, one way or another.

Screen	Command	Hits	Damage	Meter Gain	Startup	Active	Notes
1	⇨ + Ⓗ (ground)	5~9	60,000~100,000	600~1000	1	1	Can be mashed for additional hits
	⇦ + Ⓗ (ground)	1	80,000	800	1	1	Causes hard knockdown
2	⇨ + Ⓗ (air)	1	80,000	800	1	1	Causes hard knockdown
	⇦ + Ⓗ (air)	1	80,000	800	1	1	Causes hard knockdown

1

2

As a Partner—Crossover Assists

Screen	Type	P1+P2 Crossover Combination Hyper Combo	Description	Hits	Damage	Meter Gain	Startup	Active	Recovery (this crossover assist)	Recovery (other partner)	Notes
1	Felicia—α	Dancing Flash	Rolling Buckler L + Rolling Slide	2	75,000	640	35	15(8)6	111	81	Second hit is a low attack
2	Felicia—β	Dancing Flash	Sand Splash M	3	81,300	720	42	12	118	88	OTG-capable, has 3 low priority durability points
3	Felicia—γ	Dancing Flash	Cat Spike M	1	90,000	720	50	3	113	93	Causes ground bounce on counterhit and against air adversaries

Felicia's crossover assists are fairly average, as far as their overall effectiveness. However, you can find a use for each of them in your team strategy.

Felicia—α performs Rolling Buckler L followed by Rolling Slide. You can use the low-hitting Rolling Slide in conjunction with overheads to create unblockable set-ups, making it incredibly useful in certain teams. You can also utilize it to bolster your team's overall offense just to pin the opposing character in place and make your offense more difficult to guard against.

Felicia—α is one of the rare assist types that is invincible on the first hitting frame when it is used as a crossover counter. Combined with the low hit for general use, this makes it easy to recommend over the others.

Felicia—β takes the form of Sand Splash M, generating two projectiles with 3 low priority durability points each that are OTG-capable. Theoretically, you can use Felicia—β to combat projectiles or extend combos, but this assist's slow startup makes that impractical in most situations.

Felicia—γ reproduces Cat Spike M. The greatest asset of this assist is its ability to cause a ground bounce on a counterhit or against an airborne foe. Against a grounded attacker, Felicia—γ causes a brief stagger that can be used to begin a combo. Overall, this assist is useful if your other two characters do not possess the ability to ground bounce an opponent.

Snap Back

Screen	Command	Hits	Damage	Meter Gain	Startup	Active	Recovery	Advantage on Hit	Advantage if Guarded
1	↓↘→ + 	1	50,000	500 - (-1 hyper meter bar)	2	12	17	—	-8

Notes

On hit, snap back forces the opposing point character to be replaced by an assist. Opposing assist calls or tag outs are also locked out for 4 seconds

Special Moves

Screen	Name	Command	Hits	Damage	Meter Gain	Startup	Active	Recovery	Advantage on Hit	Advantage if Guarded	Notes
1	Rolling Buckler L	↓↘→ + L	1	50,000	400	5	20	16	-32	-32	—
	Rolling Buckler M	↓↘→ + M	1	60,000	480	7	20	19	-32	-32	—
	Rolling Buckler H	↓↘→ + H	1	70,000	560	9	20	22	-32	-32	—
2	Neko Punch	(during Rolling Buckler) L	1	40,000	320	7	4	19	—	-2	Knocks down
3	Rolling Slide	(during Rolling Buckler) M	1	60,000	480	9	6	16	—	-4	Low attack, knocks down
4	Rolling uppercut	(during Rolling Buckler) H	3	108,300	960	3	10	24	-5	-13	Knocks down
5	Cat Spike L	→↓↘ + L	1	80,000	640	10	3	19	+4	+2	Ignores hitstun decay, staggers on counterhit
6	Cat Spike M	→↓↘ + M	1	90,000	720	20	3	14	+9	+7	Causes ground bounce on counterhit and against airborne rivals
	Cat Spike H	→↓↘ + H	1	100,000	800	25	3	23	—	-5	Causes ground bounce
7	Delta Kick L	←↓↙ + L	3	101,000	920	7	3(15)7	11	+8	+4	First hit knocks down opponent
	Delta Kick M	←↓↙ + M	3	101,000	920	7	3(15)9	10	+10	+6	First hit knocks down adversary
	Delta Kick H	←↓↙ + H	3	101,000	920	7	3(15)11	10	+12	+8	First hit knocks down competitor

Special Moves continued

Screen	Name	Command	Hits	Damage	Meter Gain	Startup	Active	Recovery	Advantage on Hit	Advantage if Guarded	Notes
8	Air Delta Kick L	⇦⇩⇙ + Ⓛ	3	101,000	920	7	3(15)Then active until grounded	7	—	+7	First hit knocks down foe, causes ground bounce if final hit hits airborne opponent
	Air Delta Kick M	⇦⇩⇙ + Ⓜ	3	101,000	920	7	3(15)Then active until grounded	7	—	+4	First hit knocks down target, causes ground bounce if final hit hits airborne adversary
	Air Delta Kick H	⇦⇩⇙ + Ⓗ	3	101,000	920	7	3(15)Then active until grounded	7	—	+10	First hit knocks down competitor, causes ground bounce if final hit hits airborne foe
9	Sand Splash L	⇦ (charge) ⇨ + Ⓛ	2	62,500	520	8	8	14	+4	+2	OTG-capable, projectile has 3 low priority durability points
	Sand Splash M	⇦ (charge) ⇨ + Ⓜ	3	82,700	720	12	13	14	+5	+2	OTG-capable, each projectile has 3 low priority durability points
	Sand Splash H	⇦ (charge) ⇨ + Ⓗ	5	115,800	1120	16	23	21	+8	+6	OTG-capable, each projectile has 3 low priority durability points
10	Hell Cat L	⇨⇘⇩⇙⇦ + Ⓛ	7	102,000	1020	5	1	25	—	—	Throw, hard knockdown
	Hell Cat M	⇨⇘⇩⇙⇦ + Ⓜ	10	126,000	1260	3	1	27	—	—	Throw, hard knockdown
	Hell Cat H	⇨⇘⇩⇙⇦ + Ⓗ	13	156,000	1560	1	2	28	—	—	Throw, hard knockdown
11	EX Charge	⇩⇩ + Ⓗ (hold down)	—	—	40 per frame	12	—	4	—	—	Charges hyper combo gauge
12	Cat & Mouse	ATK + Ⓢ	—	—	—	5	30	15	—	—	Invincible between frames 6~35, not hyper combo- cancelable

1

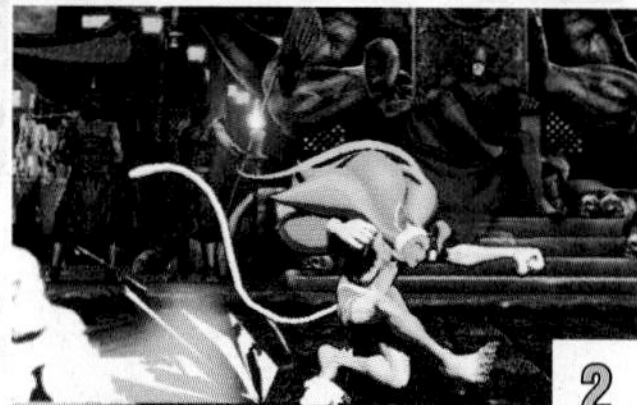
2

3

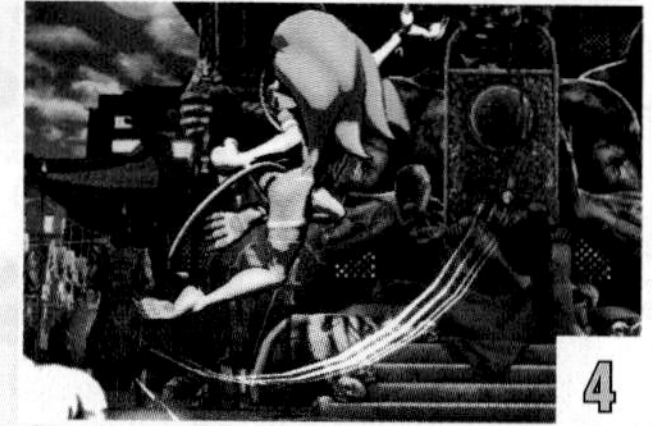
4

Rolling Buckler: Felicia does her best "blue hedgehog" impersonation in this rolling attack that is mainly used in combos. The distance Felicia rolls is determined by button strength: Ⓛ travels a quarter of the screen, Ⓜ travels half the length of the screen, and the Ⓗ version travels across three-fourths of the screen. All versions of Rolling Buckler leave Felicia at a terrible frame disadvantage, so unless you plan on directly canceling into a hyper combo, you'll want to use one of the three moves that can emerge with another button press.

Pressing Ⓛ during Rolling Buckler results in Neko Punch. It's the safest of all three Rolling Buckler enders, but it leaves Felicia at a -2 frame advantage and vulnerable to throws. A great move for low-altitude juggles, it can be hyper combo canceled into ⇩⇘⇨ + ATK ATK.

Pressing Ⓜ results in Rolling Slide, a low attack that can juggle the target on hit for more combos. It's definitely the best of the three Rolling Buckler enders in terms of utility, but keep in mind that it leaves Felicia at a -4 frame disadvantage on block and is highly susceptible to throws.

Finally, Ⓗ produces a Rolling Uppercut, the most damaging but least useful of the Rolling Buckler enders. Rolling Uppercut does not allow for combos after a hit and is insanely unsafe if guarded.

5

6

Cat Spike: Felicia leaps forward chasing after a ball and swipes with a powerful scratch attack. Cat Spike L travels the least amount of distance and staggers your competitor on a counterhit. Cat Spike L is very combo-friendly, but it is mainly used up close to counterhit opponents trying to use advancing guard against crouching Ⓛ. If guarded, Felicia maintains a positive frame advantage and can theoretically continue her offense, but her adversary then typically uses advancing guard on reaction to push her away.

Cat Spike M is used to stay close to cornered foes, pinning them in place and fighting the effects of advancing guard. You can also use it mid-combo, and it causes a ground bounce on counterhit or against an airborne attacker.

Cat Spike H, which travels the farthest out of all three, is designed to catch aerial rivals. It causes a ground bounce on grounded and aerial foes, but it can be difficult to use effectively. It's the only version of Cat Spike that leaves Felicia at a negative frame advantage on block, so use it in conjunction with air throws to increase its success rate.

7

Delta Kick: Easily Felicia's most important tool, Delta Kick allows Felicia to get near her opponent much more easily. On execution, Felicia attacks straight up into the air and then attacks with a kick at a downward angle. All three versions of the attack travel at different angles and must be aimed properly; it's very likely that Delta Kick goes flying over the head of a crouching competitor if you use the wrong version.

You can employ Delta Kick to clear most projectiles, and it is highly effective at keeping Felicia close to an adversary if they use advancing guard. The first hit of Delta Kick—as Felicia travels upward— knocks down her opponent. If only the final hit connects, the opposing character suffers a short stagger effect that allows you to follow through with a combo. Delta Kick also leaves Felicia at a positive frame advantage if guarded, making it one of her safest special moves.

8

Air Delta Kick: New to *Ultimate Marvel vs. Capcom 3*, air Delta Kick gives Felicia some much-needed air mobility options. You can now apply pressure from literally anywhere on the screen, and Felicia is always at a huge frame advantage after the attack. You can easily combo off a successful hit, or continue her offense if air Delta Kick is guarded. If the final hit connects against an airborne competitor, Felicia follows her challenger to the ground and creates a ground bounce. From here, you can relaunch the opposing character to extend combos. Against an airborne target, you can option select air Delta Kick H with an air throw by inputting ⇦⇩⇙⇦ + Ⓗ, making the attack attempt a bit safer.

Sand Splash: Felicia kicks sand in her opponent's face, generating short range projectiles that are one of Felicia's few options to combat projectiles at long range. The recovery time of Sand Splash has been reduced dramatically in *Ultimate Marvel vs. Capcom 3*, but it remains difficult to use effectively. Felicia needs to be close to her rival to hit them, and she has no shortage of alternative attacks that leave her at a better frame advantage.

Sand Splash H gains the addition of an extra hit, and all three versions are now OTG-capable. However, it's not very useful as an OTG attack because of the the small amount of hitstun it creates.

Hell Cat: Felicia's sharp command throw is a key component of her mix-up game and places her adversary in a hard knockdown state, leaving them vulnerable to Toy Touch OTG combos. Each version of Hell Cat has a slightly different range: the (L) version has the greatest range but deals the least amount of damage, while the (H) version has very little range but deals the most damage. Hell Cat L can reach the opposing character after 3-4 blocked light crouching attacks, while Hell Cat H can only grab the target after one.

Hell Cat H also has the least amount of startup time; as a 1 frame grab, it can beat any attack as long as it's in range. It's also great for punishing guarded attacks that leave Felicia at a +1 frame advantage or higher.

EX Charge: Input ↓ ↓ + (H) and then hold (H) to place Felicia in a crouched state that slowly charges her hyper combo meter. You cannot call assists or initiate attacks during the charge, although you can cancel into hyper combos or initiate Kitty's Helper kitten attacks. Although EX Charge can be performed behind the cover of assists, its best asset is the ability to cancel into it from basic attacks to reduce their recovery period—For example, crouching (M) leaves you at a -5 disadvantage when it hits normally, but canceling into EX Charge reduces this disadvantage to -1. Any attack whose combined active and recovery frames are greater than 17 benefits from this tactic; otherwise, Felicia is left at a greater disadvantage than she would be otherwise.

You can also use EX Charge to bait characters without projectiles, activating it at fullscreen to bait the character into coming toward Felicia. Alternatively, activate it against a retreating opponent to force them to come back.

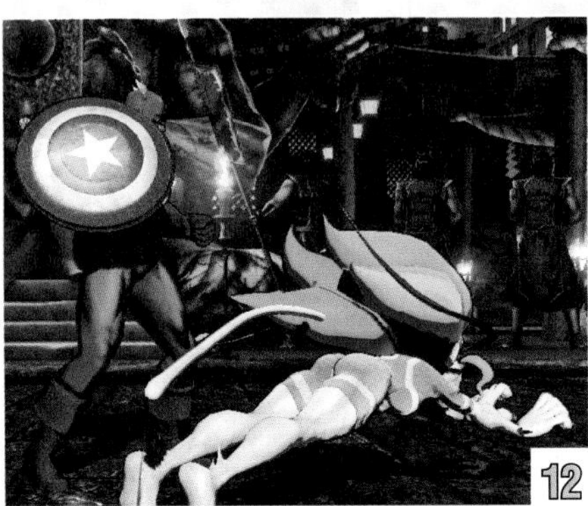

Cat & Mouse: A forward dash that is invulnerable for 24 frames after the initial 5 frame startup. Use this maneuver to pass through slow projectiles, escape corners, or create mix-up opportunities by first calling a crossover assist and then passing through your competitor! Cat & Mouse does have a heavy recovery period, so be wary about using it too often without the protection of an assist. Cat & Mouse will cross up foes who are cornered, putting Felicia into the corner in their place; call a pinning assist first to make this mix-up safer.

"DON'T BELIEVE THE RUMORS. WE DON'T ALWAYS LAND ON OUR FEET. I HAVE THE BRUISES TO PROVE IT!"

Hyper Combos

Screen	Name	Command	Hits	Damage	Startup	Active	Recovery	Advantage on Hit	Advantage if Guarded	Notes
1	Dancing Flash	↓↘→ + ATK ATK	12~23	246,700~ 290,000	8+1	27	19	+7	-26	Frames 9-16 invincible, knocks down, can be mashed for additional damaged
2	Kitty's Helper	→↓↘ + ATK ATK	—	25,000 (cat hit)	10+1	—	20	—	—	Summons helper for 600 frames, performing any attack causes cat helper to attack, cat attack is an overhead, has 30 frames of startup, 17 frames active, 7 frames recovery
3	Please Help Me (Level 3 Hyper Combo)	↓↙← + ATK ATK	30~73	400,000~ 443,000	4+16	7	71	—	-59	59 frames of invincibility, unaffected by damage scaling, knocks down, can be mashed for additional damage

Dancing Flash: Used mainly in combos, Dancing Flash can easily be linked into off of standing chains and some specials moves like Rolling Buckler. Due to changes in how hitstun works against airborne targets in *Ultimate Marvel vs. Capcom 3*, it is now very difficult to link a Toy Touch ↘ + (M) OTG hit into Dancing Flash after an air combo. This hyper combo also has a small window of invulnerability at startup, allowing it to pass through projectiles at long distances. You can slightly increase the damage output of Dancing Flash by mashing after the hyper combo connects.

Kitty's Helper: Felicia summons a friendly kitten to assist her during battle for 600 frames, or 10 seconds. Pressing an attack button causes the kitten to perform an overhead body splash that, when timed with low-hitting combos, creates unguardable situations that are vital to Felicia's corner strategy. Advancing guard has no effect on the kitten's attack, decreasing your rival's options to escape.

Unlike most power-up hyper combos, Felicia is able to build meter from her attacks while Kitty's Helper is active. The hyper combo ends when Felicia leaves the playing field or if another hyper combo is initiated.

Please Help Me: Upon activation, Felicia cries for the help of her fellow kitties, one of which pops in a short distance in front of Felicia. This level 3 hyper combo has a huge window of invulnerability, and you can use it to blow through your foe's obvious attempts to attack. While Please Help Me deals a decent amount of damage—and can be mashed to do even more—its three-bar cost is fairly steep compared to the utility of Kitty's Helper or Dancing Flash.

Battle Plan

When an adversary attempts to push Felicia back with advancing guard, send her right back in their face with Delta Kick M.

Felicia's crouching Ⓛ attack forms the foundation for your first offensive goal. Crouching Ⓛ does not push Felicia too far back from her opponent on block, allowing you to mix in a Hell Cat command grab, and it catches the opposing character should they attempt to jump. And if your rival decides to use advancing guard against Felicia's pokes, there are a couple of really good options to get her right back in her opponent's face. But the first thing you need to do is get within range of crouching Ⓛ to begin your mix-up game.

Proper use of wavedash techniques is the first obvious method to quickly close the distance. Felicia's wavedash is exceptionally quick, but proper execution is key to avoid accidentally initiating her EX Charge special. To avoid putting yourself in an awkward position, perform Felicia's wavedash by inputting ⇨ + ATK ATK, ⇘, ⇨ + ATK ATK. Remember to avoid inputting a down direction during inputs as well, to avoid accidentally performing a hyper combo. For an extra bit of protection, call in a projectile assist before starting the wavedash.

Delta Kick and air Delta Kick cover a lot of space very quickly, can be used to avoid projectiles, and leave Felicia at a positive frame advantage, making this move an excellent option for closing the distance. However, each version of Delta Kick comes down at a different angle, so it's very important that you become familiar with the distance that each version travels. Keep Felicia's distance to her competitor in mind when trying to get in with Delta Kick, and use the appropriate strength to get right in their face! Choose poorly, and you'll most likely end up flying straight over your rival's head.

Calling a projectile assist, such as Doctor Doom—α or Hawkeye—α, can help you immensely when using Delta Kick to close the distance between Felicia and her foe. While the opposing character is busy blocking the assist, Felicia can dive in from above, putting her in the perfect position to begin poking with crouching Ⓛ.

If your adversary guards Delta Kick and uses advancing guard, you have a few options available to you to keep the pressure on:

- **Immediately input ⇦⇩⇙ + Ⓜ to begin another Delta Kick. If your opponent presses a button after the advancing guard, you've scored a hit and can combo afterward. If they block the attack again, you're close enough to start the crouching Ⓛ pokes**
- **If your foe jumps back, wavedash forward and jump up to air grab them. You'll need to commit to this right away, so if your opponent is pressing buttons Felicia will likely run straight into them.**
- **You can use Cat Spike M ⇨⇩⇘ + Ⓜ as a high-damage counter, specifically against opposing players who begin mashing crouching Ⓛ themselves. If your competitor blocks the attack instead, Felicia still has a positive frame advantage to renew the assault.**
- **Against all other attacks, simply use crouching Ⓛ to cleanly counterhit your opponent and go into a combo**

A savvy opponent may consistently use advancing guard against your relentless assault of Cat Spike M and Delta Kick M. This can be a frustrating situation, but keep in mind that every time they push Felicia back, they're being pushed backward, as well, and you're getting closer to your secondary goal of forcing your opponent into the corner!

If your adversary is trying to use advancing guard against singular crouching Ⓛ attacks...

...then they will likely get counterhit by Cat Spike L or a delayed crouching Ⓛ attack! Once you've spooked your challenger into staying on the ground and guarding, grab them with Hell Cat H.

Once you're within range of Felicia's crouching Ⓛ, you can really start to open up her strong mix-up game. You'll need to make a decision to start with crouching Ⓛ, or if you're feeling bold, go immediately into Hell Cat H. Should you decide to play it safe, crouching Ⓛ may take longer to open up a defensive adversary, but you have several options to get you there.

Due to the fast properties of crouching Ⓛ, you can stagger out button presses and start playing mind games with your opposition. For example, advancing guard doesn't pose much of a problem for Felicia. With the hits staggered out, you can mitigate the push back from advancing guard and immediately cancel into Cat Spike L to close the distance. If the opponent attempts to use advancing guard during the crouching Ⓛ attacks, they'll most likely get a crouching Ⓗ attack and get counterhit instead. This puts their character into a stagger state, allowing you to follow up with the combo of your choice. If your competitor doesn't apply advancing guard, mix in Hell Cat after any number of crouching Ⓛ attacks to catch them off guard. Be mindful of your distance in relationship to your opponent, and use the appropriate version of Hell Cat to avoid whiffing the throw. Should your rival attempt to jump out of your staggered crouching Ⓛ assault, fearful of getting thrown, they'll be caught by the low-hitting attacks, and you may punish appropriately.

Be sure to mix up the attacks that you use to following up crouching Ⓛ so that your adversary doesn't begin to figure out your offense. Cat Spike L is easy to use advancing guard against on reaction, and this effectively ends your offensive momentum unless you called an assist first. If you find yourself the victim of advancing guard too often, you're not using Hell Cat enough! Get back in range, and use that command throw to keep your opponent on their toes!

You can also use Cat & Mouse in crouching Ⓛ range. Call in a projectile or lockdown assist, and then press Ⓢ + ATK to safely get Felicia to the opposite side of her foe. This adds a third element of cross-up defense into the equation! If the opponent guards the crossover assist Felicia will still generally have frame advantage afterwards, allowing you to resume your crouching Ⓛ offense.

The Kitty's Helper hyper combo really shines when the opposing character is in the corner.

Felicia's ability to apply pressure truly shines when she has her adversary in the corner. By using the grounded and air versions of Delta Kick, you can quickly close the distance from an advancing guard. You'll also have your opponent scared of the crouching Ⓛ mix-ups, and on top of that, you can create many opportunities to air throw or combo your rival as they try to jump out of the corner.

In situations where you have your opponent in a post-combo hard knockdown state, consider ending with Toy Touch ⇘ + Ⓜ. Thanks to one of the changes to Felicia in *Ultimate Marvel vs. Capcom 3*, you no longer have the option to cancel Toy Touch into Dancing Flash, so instead dash forward, jump, and attempt to air throw your target. Unless they neutral or forward air recover, you're likely to land the grab. If your foe anticipates this and tries to break the air throw, jump in from a little farther back and attack with air Ⓜ, Ⓗ, Ⓢ, which hits the opponent's air Ⓗ and allows you to continue with the combo.

Alternatively, if your competitor air recovers forward from the OTG hit, stay on the ground and wait until they're directly above Felicia, then jump straight up and air throw. Perform the air throw with ⇨ + Ⓗ, then immediately press Ⓢ and input the command for Delta Kick H. If the opponent gets grabbed, great! If not, you will either hit your opponent with a combo or land before them with frame advantage for further mix-ups.

The Kitty Helper hyper combo ⇨⇩⇘ + ATK ATK is your best friend when you have an adversary trapped in the corner. Activate it whenever you have a free moment—easily obtained by pinning your opponent down with an assist—and let the fur fly! Felicia's miniature companion stays on the screen for 600 frames, during which time you only need to concentrate on staying close to the opposing character with advancing guard-punishing techniques like delayed crouching Ⓛ attacks, Cat Spike L, and Delta Kicks. Any time you press an attack button, the kitten jumps into the air for a belly flop overhead attack. Combined with crouching Ⓛ attacks, this eventually leads into an unblockable hit. Once you confirm that the kitten has landed a hit, immediately convert it into a full combo.

COMBO USAGE

I. CR. Ⓛ, Ⓛ, ST. Ⓜ, ← + Ⓗ (2 HITS) [CANCEL] ⇒ ↓ ↘ → + Ⓗ (DURING ROLLING BUCKLER) Ⓜ, ST. Ⓛ, Ⓜ, ↘ + Ⓜ [CANCEL] ⇒ FORWARD JUMP, AIR Ⓜ, Ⓜ, Ⓗ, Ⓢ, LAND, Ⓢ [CANCEL] ⇒ FORWARD SUPER JUMP, AIR Ⓜ, Ⓜ, Ⓗ, [CANCEL] ⇒ ← ↓ ↙ + Ⓗ, LAND, {FORWARD DASH, ST. Ⓗ (3 HITS), Ⓢ [CANCEL] ⇒ FORWARD SUPER JUMP, AIR Ⓜ, Ⓗ, Ⓢ, LAND, ↘ + Ⓜ} OR {→ ↓ ↘ + Ⓛ [CANCEL] ⇒ ↓ ↘ → + ATK ATK}

464,600~588,600 damage, 121% meter gain or 5% meter loss

This is a basic combo with an easily verifiable opening. If crouching Ⓛ x 2 is guarded, follow up with ← ↓ ↙ + Ⓛ or **Combo I** again. In the event that your foe successfully uses advancing guard to push Felicia out, cancel into ← ↓ ↙ + Ⓜ to move back into attack range.

After Delta Kick connects, perform → ↓ ↘ + Ⓛ [CANCEL] ⇒ ↓ ↘ → + ATK ATK when your adversary is as low to the ground as possible. This is necessary to guarantee that Dancing Flash fully connects (a few hits here and there miss otherwise, though it still deals the majority of its damage).

When ↓ ↘ → + Ⓜ during Rolling Buckler M connects near the middle of the screen, Felicia often passes under her attacker to their backside. Be sure to reverse your remaining inputs to compensate. After canceling the first Toy Touch into a jump, perform air Ⓜ, Ⓜ, Ⓗ, Ⓢ as quickly as possible to ensure the last hit connects before landing.

In any instance where you end the combo with Toy Touch, immediately place the opponent in a mix-up by dashing forward, then performing a forward jump and go for either an air throw or a combo starting off of air Ⓛ.

II. CR. Ⓜ, ← + Ⓗ (2 HITS) [CANCEL] ⇒ → ↓ ↘ + Ⓛ, ST. Ⓛ, Ⓜ [CANCEL] ⇒ ↓ ↘ → + Ⓜ (DURING ROLLING BUCKLER) Ⓜ, ST. Ⓛ, Ⓜ, ↘ + Ⓜ [CANCEL] ⇒ FORWARD JUMP, AIR Ⓜ, Ⓜ, Ⓗ, Ⓢ, LAND, Ⓢ [CANCEL] ⇒ FORWARD SUPER JUMP, AIR Ⓜ, Ⓜ, Ⓗ, [CANCEL] ⇒ ← ↓ ↙ + Ⓗ, LAND, {FORWARD DASH, Ⓢ [CANCEL] ⇒ FORWARD SUPER JUMP, AIR Ⓜ, Ⓗ, Ⓢ, LAND, ↘ + Ⓜ} OR {→ ↓ ↘ + Ⓛ [CANCEL] ⇒ ↓ ↘ → + ATK ATK}

496,000~626,000 damage, 126~0% meter gain

This is a slightly more damaging variation of the previous combo. Unfortunately, you cannot lead it with a jumping attack unless the first crouching Ⓜ is omitted. Otherwise, hitstun decay ruins it. Also note that because of hitstun decay, both hits of ↓ ↘ → + ⓂⓂ do not combo properly unless the kick extension is initiated as soon as the roll hits.

III. → ↘ ↓ ↙ ← + Ⓗ OR AIR THROW, FORWARD DASH, ↘ + Ⓜ [CANCEL] ⇒ FORWARD JUMP, AIR Ⓜ, Ⓜ, Ⓗ, Ⓢ, LAND, Ⓢ [CANCEL] ⇒ FORWARD SUPER JUMP, AIR Ⓜ, Ⓜ, Ⓗ [CANCEL] ⇒ ← ↓ ↙ + Ⓗ, LAND, {FORWARD DASH, ST. Ⓗ (3 HITS), Ⓢ [CANCEL] ⇒ FORWARD SUPER JUMP, AIR Ⓜ, Ⓜ, Ⓗ, Ⓢ, LAND, ↘ + Ⓜ} OR {FORWARD DASH, ST. Ⓗ [CANCEL] ⇒ → ↓ ↘ + Ⓛ [CANCEL] ⇒ ↓ ↘ → + ATK ATK}

381,000~509,000 or 334,900~471,900 damage, 101% meter gain or 18% meter loss for → ↘ ↓ ↙ ← + Ⓗ opening, 98% meter gain or 26% meter loss for air throw opening

One of the key points of Felicia's offense is that she can convert nearly any throw into a full combo. The combo itself is nearly identical to her standard combos, but you may have to perform some precise wavedashes to be able to get into range of Toy Touch.

IV. WHEN THE ENEMY IS AIRBORNE, FORWARD JUMP, AIR Ⓛ, Ⓜ, Ⓜ, Ⓢ, LAND, Ⓢ [CANCEL] ⇒ FORWARD SUPER JUMP, AIR Ⓜ, Ⓜ, Ⓗ [CANCEL] ⇒ ← ↓ ↙ + Ⓗ, LAND, FORWARD DASH, {ST. Ⓗ (3 HITS), Ⓢ [CANCEL] ⇒ FORWARD SUPER JUMP, AIR Ⓜ, Ⓜ, Ⓗ, Ⓢ, LAND, ↘ + Ⓜ} OR {ST. Ⓗ (3 HITS) [CANCEL] ⇒ → ↓ ↘ + Ⓛ [CANCEL] ⇒ ↓ ↘ → + ATK ATK}

405,200~536,500 damage, 84% meter gain or 40% meter loss

This functions as your standard anti-air combo. When blocked, chain as far as air Ⓜ, Ⓜ, Ⓗ, Ⓢ, then land and go for the mix-up of your choice.

V. → ↓ ↘ + Ⓜ, ST. Ⓜ [CANCEL] ⇒ → ↓ ↘ + Ⓛ, ST. Ⓛ, Ⓜ [CANCEL] ⇒ ↓ ↘ → + Ⓜ (DURING ROLLING BUCKLER) Ⓜ, ST. Ⓛ, Ⓜ, ↘ + Ⓜ [CANCEL] ⇒ FORWARD JUMP, AIR Ⓜ, Ⓜ, Ⓗ, Ⓢ, LAND, Ⓢ [CANCEL] ⇒ FORWARD SUPER JUMP, AIR Ⓜ, Ⓜ, Ⓗ, [CANCEL] ⇒ ← ↓ ↙ + Ⓗ, LAND, {FORWARD DASH, ST. Ⓗ, Ⓢ [CANCEL] ⇒ FORWARD SUPER JUMP, AIR Ⓜ, Ⓗ, Ⓢ, LAND, ↘ + Ⓜ} OR {→ ↓ ↘ + Ⓛ [CANCEL] ⇒ ↓ ↘ → + ATK ATK}

537,100~667,100 damage, 127~1% meter gain

This combo starts off of Cat Spike M, which is a pressure tool used to stop advancing guard, fly over low attacks, and cross crouching adversaries up at close distances. You can verify whether the opening attack is blocked or not and shift into a secondary attack when it is.

VI. COUNTERHIT →↓↘ + Ⓛ, ← + Ⓗ CANCEL → →↓↘ + Ⓜ, ST. Ⓜ, ← + Ⓗ CANCEL → ↓↘→ + Ⓜ (DURING ROLLING BUCKLER) Ⓜ, ST. Ⓛ, Ⓜ, ↘ + Ⓜ CANCEL → FORWARD JUMP, AIR Ⓜ, Ⓜ, Ⓗ, Ⓢ, LAND, Ⓢ CANCEL → FORWARD SUPER JUMP, AIR Ⓜ, Ⓜ, Ⓗ, CANCEL → ←↓↙ + Ⓗ, LAND, {FORWARD DASH, Ⓢ CANCEL → FORWARD SUPER JUMP, AIR Ⓜ, Ⓗ, Ⓢ, LAND, ↘ + Ⓜ} OR {→↓↘ + Ⓛ CANCEL → ↓↘→ + ATK ATK}

532,100~667,100 damage, 126~7% meter gain

Cat Spike L is used to counterhit an opponent for pressing buttons during your crouching Ⓛ attacks. Its categorization as a special attack enables you to cancel into it with varied timing to help with this focus. A successful counterhit leads to a stagger and a giant opening.

VII. ←↓↙ + Ⓗ, ST. Ⓛ, Ⓜ, ← + Ⓗ CANCEL → ↓↘→ + Ⓜ (DURING ROLLING BUCKLER) Ⓜ, ST. Ⓛ, Ⓜ, ↘ + Ⓜ CANCEL → FORWARD JUMP, AIR Ⓜ, Ⓜ, Ⓗ, Ⓢ, LAND, Ⓢ CANCEL → FORWARD SUPER JUMP, AIR Ⓜ, Ⓜ, Ⓗ, CANCEL → ←↓↙ + Ⓗ, LAND, {FORWARD DASH, Ⓢ CANCEL → FORWARD SUPER JUMP, AIR Ⓜ, Ⓗ, Ⓢ, LAND, ↘ + Ⓜ} OR {→↓↘ + Ⓛ CANCEL → ↓↘→ + ATK ATK}

432,900~553,900 damage, 122% meter gain or 8% meter loss

This combo works only when Delta Kick hits from a distance. Use this technique to pass over low altitude fireballs.

FELICIA

ADVANCED TACTICS

PICKING THE PURR-FECT ASSIST

While Felicia can get around the screen really quickly, many of her approaches can be unsafe from long distances. To fill in this gap in her defense, Felicia can benefit greatly from a forward-moving projectile assist. Try out some of the following characters:

Doctor Doom—β	Ryu—β	Arthur—β
Hawkeye—α	Taskmaster—α	
Rocket Raccoon—α	Sentinel—α	

While Felicia becomes markedly better with any long range crossover assist, the slower-traveling ones are what make her shine brightest. Calling a slow assist like Rocket Raccoon—α before performing Delta Kick will force your opponent to guard the kicks, then immediately get stuck in further guardstun as the projectiles catch up. This lets you easily go right into a crouching Ⓛ or Hell Cat mix-up!

X-FACTOR LEVEL 2~3

Felicia is already one the fastest characters in the game, and under the influence of level 2 or 3 X-Factor, she becomes a real speed demon! The speed increase allows Felicia to chain together moves that normally could not be linked together. For example, Felicia's Delta Kick H becomes so fast in X-Factor that she can repeat it over and over again without her opponent ever leaving guardstun! Small and medium-sized characters can escape with a well-timed crouch or advancing guard for a small amount of breathing room, but larger characters like Nemesis or Sentinel are stuck unless they can initiate a crossover counter. With Kitty's Helper activated, however, you've pretty much got most characters totally locked down and absorbing massive amounts of chip damage. If you manage to score a hit on an adversary, see the Combo Appendix section for a simple infinite combo that you can use to eliminate anyone in the cast. It isn't too difficult for X-Factor Felicia to wipe out at least two characters before the bonus wears off.

COMBO APPENDIX

GENERAL EXECUTION TIPS

When performing air Ⓜ, Ⓜ, Ⓗ, Ⓢ after Toy Touch, do everything as rapidly as possible to gain enough time for the air Ⓢ to hit

After performing the air chain above, wait just slightly before juggling the Ⓢ launcher to ensure that the opposing character does not get too high into the air

AS FELICIA COMES IN: AIR Ⓜ, Ⓜ, Ⓗ CANCEL → ←↓↙ + Ⓗ, LAND, FORWARD DASH, ST. Ⓗ (3 HITS), Ⓢ CANCEL → FORWARD SUPER JUMP, AIR Ⓜ, Ⓗ, Ⓢ, LAND, ↘ + Ⓜ

Notes	Damage
⇧ + Ⓢ or ⇨ + Ⓢ TAC to Felicia	Varies based on damage scaling

AS FELICIA COMES IN: AIR Ⓜ, Ⓗ, Ⓢ, LAND, ↘ + Ⓜ

Notes	Damage
⇩ + Ⓢ TAC to Felicia	Varies based on damage scaling

CR. Ⓜ, ← + Ⓗ CANCEL → →↓↘ + Ⓛ X-FACTOR LEVEL 1, →↓↘ + Ⓛ, ST. Ⓜ, ← + Ⓗ CANCEL → ↓↘→ + Ⓜ (DURING ROLLING BUCKLER) Ⓜ, ST. Ⓛ, Ⓜ, ↘ + Ⓜ CANCEL → FORWARD JUMP, AIR Ⓜ, Ⓗ, Ⓢ, LAND, Ⓢ CANCEL → FORWARD SUPER JUMP, AIR Ⓜ, Ⓜ, Ⓗ, CANCEL → ←↓↙ + Ⓗ, LAND, {FORWARD DASH, CR. Ⓗ, Ⓢ CANCEL → FORWARD SUPER JUMP, AIR Ⓜ, Ⓗ, Ⓢ, LAND, ↘ + Ⓜ} OR {→↓↘ Ⓛ CANCEL → ↓↘→ + ATK ATK}

Notes	Damage
This is a verifiable opening into a level 1 X-Factor combo. While less damaging than the combo below, it's easier to do at level 1 than the other.	780,000~883,800 damage,147~19% meter gain

CR. Ⓜ, ← + Ⓗ CANCEL → →↓↘ + Ⓛ X-FACTOR, →↓↘ + Ⓛ X ∞

Notes	Damage
This X-Factor loop can now be done at any level, but it is very difficult to sustain it at level 1.	1,000,000+ damage, builds 3+ meters

HAGGAR

"IT'S MY JOB TO KEEP METRO CITY SAFE!"

Bio

REAL NAME

Mike Haggar

OCCUPATION

Mayor of Metro City

ABILITIES

Moves retained from his time as a pro-wrestler and his explosive power combine to make for dangerous attacks.

WEAPONS

Be it a steel pipe, a 2x4, or a hammer, any weapon he swings becomes extremely effective with his full force behind it.

PROFILE

Former professional wrestler who became the mayor of Metro City. Calling himself the "Fighting Mayor," he teamed up with his friends and took on the Mad Gear crime syndicate, paying back the destruction the gang had caused in spades.

FIRST APPEARANCE

Final Fight (1989)

POWER GRID

3	INTELLIGENCE
4	STRENGTH
2	SPEED
3	STAMINA
1	ENERGY PROJECTION
5	FIGHTING ABILITY

*This is biographical, and does not represent an evaluation of the in-game combat potential of this hero.

ALTERNATE COSTUMES

Overview

Vitality	1,200,000
Chain Combo Archetype	Marvel Series

X-Factor Boost	Damage	Speed
Level 1 (3 teammates remaining)	140%	100%
Level 2 (2 teammates remaining)	165%	105%
Level 3 (1 teammate remaining)	190%	110%

Your goal with Haggar is to achieve close range against an opponent while forcing them into the corner.

Why should you try to achieve close range with Haggar?

- Haggar has no long range attacks and requires close range to threaten his rival
- Haggar has dominant close range attacks that can lead to very damaging combos with little to no meter cost
- Haggar has dangerous throw mix-ups at close range

How do you achieve close range with Haggar?

- By wavedashing when it is safe, or behind the cover of a long range crossover assist
- Jumping at your opponent and using air ⬇ + Ⓗ when at mid range to discourage counterattacks
- Using crouching Ⓗ and then rolling forward in the direction of your opponent.

TUNING SINCE ORIGINAL MVC3

Haggar received few changes in *Ultimate Marvel vs. Capcom 3*. He can now OTG with his crouching Ⓗ, but it can now only be canceled by ➡ + Ⓗ. This gives him access to bigger combos with a wider array of assists than he had previously. As an assist, Haggar's—α assist, Double Lariat, has lost a significant amount of invincibility frames and no longer causes hard knockdown. This means that only 2 active frames of his attack have invincibility, making him much more vulnerable to attacks than before. The lack of hard knockdown makes him slightly less useful to characters who could follow with an OTG for big damage. Rapid Fire Fist has gained invincibility, giving Haggar a strong defensive option against out of combo hyper combos.

- Crouching Ⓗ is now OTG-capable
- Crouching Ⓗ now only chains to ➡ + Ⓗ and is no longer special or hyper-combo cancelable
- Haggar—α now only has 33 frames of invincibility and no longer causes hard knockdown
- Rapid Fire Fist now has 20 frames of invincibility

Attack Set

Standing Basic Attacks

Screen	Command	Hits	Damage	Meter Gain	Startup	Active	Recovery	Advantage on Hit	Advantage if Guarded	Notes
1	Standing L	1	65,000	520	7	3	16	-2	-3	—
2	Standing M	1	83,000	664	11	3	20	-1	-2	—
3	Standing H	1	100,000	800	14	4	21	—	+1	Ground bounces opponent

Crouching Basic Attacks

Screen	Command	Hits	Damage	Meter Gain	Startup	Active	Recovery	Advantage on Hit	Advantage if Guarded	Notes
1	Crouching L	1	62,000	496	8	3	14	0	-1	Low attack
2	Crouching M	1	80,000	640	12	3	21	-2	-3	Low attack
3	Crouching H	1	97,000	776	16	6	49	—	-29	Low attack, OTG-capable, puts Haggar in hard knockdown state, invincible after frame 50, knocks down foe, chains to ⇨ + H, not special- or hyper combo- cancelable

Ground Special Attack—Launcher

Screen	Command	Hits	Damage	Meter Gain	Startup	Active	Recovery	Advantage on Hit	Advantage if Guarded	Notes
1	S (while standing or crouching)	1	100,000	800	11	3	23	—	0	Launcher, not special- or hyper combo-cancelable

Air Basic Attacks

Screen	Command	Hits	Damage	Meter Gain	Startup	Active	Recovery	Advantage on Hit	Advantage if Guarded	Notes
1	Air L	1	58,000	464	7	Until grounded	1	+7	+6	Overhead attack
2	Air M	1	75,000	600	13	Until grounded	1	+19	+18	Overhead attack
3	Air H	1	100,000	800	16	Until grounded	1	+14	+13	Overhead attack

Air Special Attacks—Flying Screen and Air Exchange

Air Ⓢ causes a hard knockdown when used in a launcher combo (this is sometimes called flying screen). When used outside of a launcher combo, air Ⓢ behaves mostly like another basic attack. Air exchange attacks, performed by inputting a direction plus Ⓢ, are only possible during a launcher combo. Exchange hits initiate team aerial combos by tagging in the next available character to continue the air combo.

Screen	Command	Hits	Damage	Meter Gain	Startup	Active	Recovery	Advantage on Hit	Advantage if Guarded	Notes
1	Air Ⓢ	1	110,000	880	14	4	23	+19	+18	Causes hard knockdown if used in launcher combo
2	Air ⇧ + Ⓢ (during launcher combo)	1	60,000	480	13	3	17	—	—	Tags in next available ally while lofting opponent upward
3	Air ⇨ or ⇦ + Ⓢ (during launcher combo)	1	50,000	400	16	Until grounded	1	—	—	Tags in next available ally while causing wall bounce, erases 1 hyper meter from foe
4	Air ⇩ + Ⓢ (during launcher combo)	1	50,000	400 + 10,000	15	4	Until grounded, then 1 recovery frame	—	—	Tags in next available ally while causing ground bounce, generates 1 hyper meter

1

2

3

4

Command Attacks

Command attacks resemble basic attacks but have different chaining and canceling properties. It's usually possible to chain *into* a command attack from basic attacks, but most command attacks cannot be chained from or canceled themselves.

Screen	Name	Command	Hits	Damage	Meter Gain	Startup	Active	Recovery	Advantage on Hit	Advantage if Guarded	Notes
1	Steel Pipe	⇨ + Ⓗ	1	110,000	880	19	3	24	+10	+9	Staggers grounded adversaries, ground bounces airborne competitors, hard knockdown versus airborne rivals
2	Head Butt	(in air) ⇧ + Ⓗ	1	100,000	800	8	4	19	+16	+15	Overhead attack, causes dizzy state if attack counterhits a standing opponent, causes special knockdown state if counterhits airborne foe, hard knockdown, everything is OTG-capable
3	Air Steel Pipe	(in air) ⇩ + Ⓗ	1	120,000	960	14	3	29	—	+18	Overhead attack, ground bounces opponent, hard knockdown

1

2

3

Throws

Throws are for snagging passive or blocking opponents. Since throws are active so quickly, you can also use them to preemptively toss opposing characters out of their offense. Combos are usually possible after throws, one way or another.

Screen	Command	Hits	Damage	Meter Gain	Startup	Active	Notes
1	⇨ + Ⓗ (ground)	3~5	60,000~100,000	600~1000	1	1	Can be mashed for additional hits
	⇦ + Ⓗ (ground)	3~5	60,000~100,000	600~1000	1	1	Can be mashed for additional hits
2	⇨ + Ⓗ (air)	1	80,000	800	1	1	Hard knockdown
	⇦ + Ⓗ (air)	1	80,000	800	1	1	Hard knockdown

1

2

HAGGAR

As a Partner—Crossover Assists

Screen	Type	P1+P2 Crossover Combination Hyper Combo	Description	Hits	Damage	Meter Gain	Startup	Active	Recovery (this crossover assist)	Recovery (other partner)	Notes
1	Haggar—α	Giant Haggar Press	Double Lariat	3	108,300	960	32	45	121	91	Frames 1-33 invincible, converts 100,000 of Haggar's vitality into red vitality
2	Haggar—β	Giant Haggar Press	Violent Axe M	2	122,000	1040	42	5(12)4	110	80	Causes spinning knockdown
3	Haggar—γ	Giant Haggar Press	Steel Pipe	1	110,000	880	43	3	117	87	Ground bounces adversary, hard knockdown

1

2

3

Haggar—α, while not as strong as before, remains a strong defensive assist. The Double Lariat still stops most attackers in their tracks and allows combo follow-ups if you can react quickly enough. Characters with strong throw mix-ups can utilize this assist to create even deadlier mix-ups for their foes.

Haggar—β can be difficult to use. If used in combos, it knocks your opponent up, causing them to air recover a majority of the time and making it difficult to continue the combo. This does have some potential for air resets, but it is largely unnecessary.

Haggar—γ can be useful because it does provide a ground bounce. However, any characters who already use ground bounces in their combos naturally find this assist less useful.

All of Haggar's assists are fairly close range. Haggar—α is overwhelmingly the best option the majority of the time, since it is one of the few assists with invincibility frames and probably the best defensive assist in the game. Because of its invincibility frames, it also provides strong mix-up options to many characters in the cast.

Snap Back

Screen	Command	Hits	Damage	Meter Gain	Startup	Active	Recovery	Advantage on Hit	Advantage if Guarded
1	↓↘→ + P1 or P2	1	50,000	500 - (-1 hyper meter bar)	2	3	22	—	+5

Notes

On hit, snap back forces the opposing point character to be replaced by an assist. Opposing assist calls or tag outs are also locked out for 4 seconds

1

Special Moves

Screen	Name	Command	Hits	Damage	Meter Gain	Startup	Active	Recovery	Advantage on Hit	Advantage if Guarded	Notes
1	Violent Axe L	↓↘→ + L	1	110,000	880	15	4	22	+10	0	Spinning knockdown
2	Violent Axe M	↓↘→ + M	2	122,000	1040	18	5(12)4	17	+16	+5	First hit staggers opponent, second hit causes spinning knockdown
3	Violent Axe H	↓↘→ + H	3	160,600	1440	20	5(11)4 (14)3	19	—	+5	First hit staggers foe, third hit ground bounces
4	Hoodlum Launcher L	→↓↘ + L	2	140,000	1400	14	6	16	—	+4	Launcher attack
4	Hoodlum Launcher M	→↓↘ + M	2	140,000	1400	26	8	32	—	—	Launcher attack, throw attack
5	Hoodlum Launcher H	→↓↘ + H	2	140,000	1400	30	14	43	—	—	Launcher attack, air throw attack
6	Flying Piledriver L	→↘↓↙← + L	1	160,000	1600	5	1	30	—	—	Throw attack, hard knockdown
6	Flying Piledriver M	→↘↓↙← + M	1	190,000	1900	3	1	32	—	—	Throw attack, hard knockdown
6	Flying Piledriver H	→↘↓↙← + H	1	220,000	2200	1	2	33	—	—	Throw attack, hard knockdown
7	Skyhigh Back Drop L	(in air) →↘↓↙← + L	1	160,000	1600	5	1	35	—	—	Air throw attack, hard knockdown
7	Skyhigh Back Drop M	(in air) →↘↓↙← + M	1	190,000	1900	3	1	37	—	—	Air throw attack, hard knockdown
7	Skyhigh Back Drop H	(in air) →↘↓↙← + H	1	220,000	2200	1	2	38	—	—	Air throw attack, hard knockdown

Special Moves continued

Screen	Name	Command	Hits	Damage	Meter Gain	Startup	Active	Recovery	Advantage on Hit	Advantage if Guarded	Notes
8	Double Lariat	S + ATK	3	108,300	960	8	45	28	—	-31	40 frames invincibility, converts 100,000 of Haggar's vitality into red vitality, hard knockdown
9	Wild Swing	(in air) ↓ ↙ → + S	6~12	152,300~ 221,500	1523~ 2215	17	3	21	—	—	Deals more damage and more hits the higher Haggar is, hard knockdown

1

2

3

Violent Axe: All versions of Violent Axe leave Haggar safe or with a very strong frame advantage against grounded opponents, but all versions of this move have a very slow startup. The best use for this attack is during hit confirmed combos. Using this attack in blockstrings can be dangerous if your rival uses advancing guard before Violent Axe, leaving you wide open to a counterattack.

Violent Axe L is very useful early in combos, inflicting a large amount of damage in a single hit and allowing a follow-up juggle with standing L. You can use Violent Axe M in a combo after → + H, and it allows a follow-up juggle with standing M. Violent Axe H causes ground bounce, which allows for an easy follow-up but does not allow for future ground bounces in your combo.

Hoodlum Launcher: All three versions of Hoodlum Launcher launch your target and are super jump-cancelable. Hoodlum Launcher L is Haggar's primary launcher. It moves him closer to the opposing character and has +4 frame advantage when guarded, making it more useful overall than S as a launcher. You must use neutral super jump cancel to consistently follow all Hoodlum Launchers up with a launcher combo.

Hoodlum Launcher M is a throw with a similar startup animation, with a slight delay before Haggar charges forward. The fact that the animations are so similar makes it difficult for the opposing player to tell which version you are using.

4

5

Hoodlum Launcher H makes this mix-up even more deadly because Haggar has the same slight delay as Hoodlum Launcher M. However, with this version Haggar jumps forward with an air throw. This makes it difficult for your competitor to tell whether they should jump or stay grounded, because either option could lead to Haggar landing a throw into full combo! Hoodlum Launcher H is also useful for air resets!

6

Flying Piledriver: This is a close range command throw for Haggar that deals amazing damage. Weaker versions have more range, but less damage and more startup frames. With the new ability to self-OTG with his crouching H, this move has become much more useful. With the use of proper assists, Haggar can now convert this highly damaging command throw into a full combo!

Skyhigh Backdrop: This is basically an aerial version of Flying Piledriver, with all the same range, speed, and damage differences. You can also convert this attack to a full combo thanks to Haggar's new crouching H and the use of assists. This attack is useful as an air throw that foes cannot escape.

You can also whiff Skyhigh Backdrop in midair to halt Haggar's air trajectory. This can be done as many as three times in the air, substantially increasing his air time.

7

8

Double Lariat: This is Haggar's best defensive move, because it has a large amount of invincibility frames and requires the touch of only two buttons, allowing for faster input on reaction to attacks. If this attack connects, you can easily hit confirm by canceling into Rapid Fire Fist.

However, Double Lariat is very unsafe if guarded, and this attack completely misses on several crouching characters. If guarded or if your adversary is crouching under the attack, Haggar can cancel this attack into Final Haggar Buster once his foe leaves guardstun, punishing their attempt to punish Double Lariat.

Haggar has 100,000 of his vitality converted to red vitality when he performs this move, however, Haggar can perform this move when he has less than 100,000 vitality without dying.

9

Wild Swing: Haggar's main aerial combo ender, causing hard knockdown state. Wild Swing has the unique property of causing progressively more damage at higher altitudes. You can now follow this attack up with an OTG crouching H. When this attack is used with an assist, it can lead to an extended combo.

Hyper Combos

Screen	Name	Command	Hits	Damage	Startup	Active	Recovery	Advantage on Hit	Advantage if Guarded	Notes
1	Rapid Fire Fist	↓↙← + ATK ATK	12~45	276,800~ 414,700	10+5	3(21)4 (35)5	22	—	-1	Frames 1-20 invincible, can be mashed for extra hits, final hit ground bounces opponent, hard knockdown
2	Giant Haggar Press	→↓↙ + ATK ATK	1~8	200,00~ 328,400	5+16	16(4)44	30	—	-53	OTG-capable, final hit creates large explosion that has 10 high priority durability points, spinning knockdown, hard knockdown
3	Final Haggar Buster (Level 3 Hyper Combo)	→↘↓↙← + ATK ATK	8	450,000	8+0	1	34	—	—	Invincible from frames 1-10, throw attack, hard knockdown

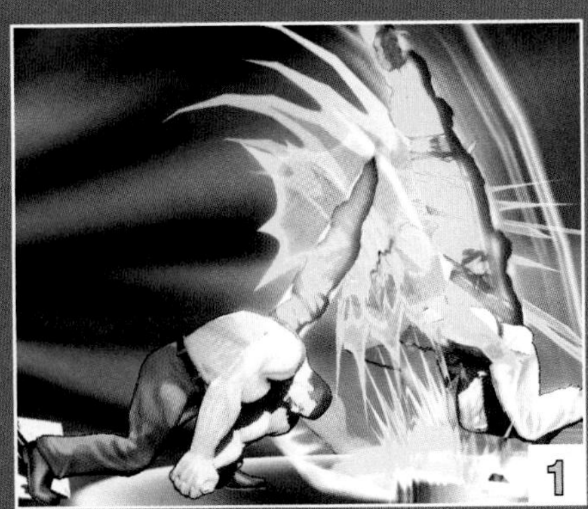

Rapid Fire Fist: Rapid Fire Fist is mainly used as a means to continue into a combo after a connected Double Lariat. It has enough invincibility frames to be used as a close range reversal, as well.

Mashing inputs before the first hit causes one of three "levels" of Rapid Fire Fist. Level 2 Rapid Fire Fist, identifiable by Haggar's eye gleaming, can be achieved with relatively light mashing, consists of 24 hits, and inflicts 346,400 damage. The level 3 version requires fairly rapid mashing and results in 30 hits and a whopping 381,100 damage! The level 3 version is identifiable by a red aura appearing behind Haggar.

Juggling with Rapid Fire Fist anywhere except early in a combo likely causes the opposing player to air recover before the final hit lands, making Haggar miss and leaving him vulnerable to punishment. Mashing for higher levels of Rapid Fire Fist during any juggle can potentially cause the last hit to miss regardless of when it is done in a combo. Although it may not seem intuitive, in juggles, you want to hit Rapid Fire Fist when your opponent is as high as the hyper combo allows, so you can ensure that the last hit connects.

Giant Haggar Press: Haggar goes into the air and then proceeds to fall toward his adversary. This move deals substantially more damage against airborne opponents. The last hit of this attack can OTG, so it can be tacked on the end of combos that end in hard knockdown for moderate damage, but the real use of this is to cancel this OTG hit into a THC for extra damage.

Haggar does have a way to combo into full damage with this hyper combo: super jump canceling an Ⓢ launcher attack. Perform this tactic by doing the motion →↓↘→↗ + ATK ATK. Haggar launches his rival, and then hits his foe for full damage on the way down!

Final Haggar Buster: This is Haggar's level 3 hyper combo, a grab that inflicts massive damage. Its 8 frame startup is rather slow for a hyper combo throw, but it has 10 frames of invincibility and a significantly long range to compensate. You can use this move defensively to blow through reckless attacks or hyper combos.

Now thanks to Haggar's new crouching Ⓗ OTG, he can convert this into a full combo combined with the use of an appropriate assist, allowing for even more punishment!

"JUST BE LUCKY YOU DIDN'T TOUCH MY DAUGHTER, OR ELSE YOU WOULD'VE SEEN ME WHEN I'M REALLY ANGRY!"

Battle Plan

Haggar—α is an amazing defensive assist and makes Haggar an asset to any team!

Haggar can find a spot on nearly any team, if only for the fact that he possesses one of the best defensive assists in the game. Aside from that, Haggar has some of the most damage non-meter combos and very high vitality, making him a good meter builder for a team. However, he has difficulties against opponents with strong zoning capabilities, especially without the use of a strong beam or projectile crossover assist. With all this in mind, Haggar is usually strongest in the second spot on a team, with a dedicated projectile or beam assist in the final spot. This allows him to be used as a defensive assist and helps ease the difficulty of using Haggar against zoning adversaries through the use of assists.

Haggar's Air Steel Pipe attack is a dominant attack that controls the immediate space in front of Haggar definitively.

Haggar needs to be close to his opponent to pose any real threat, so you'll need to close in on the opposing character. At mid range, Haggar's primary method of approaching his adversary is to jump forward and attack with ⇩ + Ⓗ attack, Air Steel Pipe. This attack has amazing priority and covers a large amount of space. The attack starts slightly behind his head and ends at a downward angle from his feet; this wide arc makes attacking Haggar while he is jumping a risky proposition. Normally, this attack would be susceptible to quick air throws, but you can option select an air throw by holding ⇖ + Ⓗ. If the attack connects, it ground bounces the opposing character, leaving you ample time to confirm the hit and continue into a full combo. Furthermore, Haggar's crouching Ⓗ makes using the ground bounce early less of an issue because you can now OTG with the use of an assist to get a large amount of damage.

Haggar's Head Butt is very fast and can be devastating as a counterhit, giving you ample time to convert this attack into a combo.

Also, if you suspect your opponent may jump, you can have Haggar jump and instantly use Head Butt to counter your opponent's movement. Similar to the strategy for Air Steel Pipe, you can air throw option select this with ⇙ + Ⓗ. This attack is very quick for a heavy attack with an 8 frame startup. If it manages to hit an airborne adversary as a counterattack, it puts the attacker in a special hard knockdown state that allows any attack to OTG! If it manages to hit as a counterattack on a grounded opponent, it makes the foe dizzy. This attack can also work as an instant overhead on some large characters, which can be chained into an air Ⓢ to allow Haggar enough time to land and convert into a full combo.

Another option is Haggar's ⇨ + Ⓗ attack, Steel Pipe. Similar to Air Steel Pipe, this attack has a wide arc and dominates the space immediately above and in front of Haggar, so it has a good chance to beat any close range attacks in these areas. If the attack connects, it causes Haggar's opponent to stagger, leaving them in hitstun for an extended period of time. This gives you ample time to confirm the hit and start a combo, such as Violent Axe L or Hoodlum Launcher L. Even if the attack is blocked, Haggar is at a massive frame advantage at +8. If your opponent doesn't use advancing guard against this attack, it gives you a prime opportunity to apply mix-ups afterwards, either with using a Hoodlum M/H mix-up or with dashing it and using Flying Piledriver.

Another riskier option is to use Violent Axe L. It does not have the dominating space control of the Steel Pipe attacks, but it is slightly faster. If it connects, you can juggle with a standing Ⓛ and continue into a full combo. On block, Haggar is completely safe, recovering the same frame as when your competitor has recovered from blockstun.

If the opposing player is playing very defensively and hesitantly, you can begin to use Hoodlum Launcher attacks at mid range. Using Hoodlum Launcher L leaves you at a +4 frame advantage, allowing you to apply mix-ups if your adversary doesn't use advancing guard. Even if your opposition does use advancing guard, Haggar's forward momentum can negate at least a portion of the advancing guard, leaving you in a good position to continue your offense. Once your rival is focused on blocking, you can use Hoodlum Launcher M to land a throw launcher into a big combo. If your foe tries to jump away from Haggar's Hoodlum Launcher M, you can start using Hoodlum Launcher H to punish your rival's jumps if you are close enough or if you have the opposing character cornered.

Haggar has an exceptionally difficult time against zoning opponents due to his lack of mobility or zoning ability. As such, your primary method of combating zoning adversaries is to use projectile or beam crossover assists during gaps in your foe's zoning game. Use this opportunity to wavedash behind your assist's attack to close the distance and start your offense with Haggar. Be wary when calling assists against characters who can easily punish your assists with a strong fullscreen hyper combo. Another option when calling assists is to super jump. Against some characters, this acts to protect your assist from horizontal hyper combos by threatening your competitor from above. If they attempt to punish your assist, you can land with an attack and punish them with a combo.

Haggar can put himself into a knockdown state with crouching Ⓗ and then roll forward past any projectiles or beams!

If Haggar lacks the appropriate assist on point, or otherwise cannot use them at the time for whatever reason, you must attempt to close the distance by employing some chicanery. If your opponent has several gaps while zoning, you can use these gaps to wavedash closer to your target and get in as close as possible. Haggar has high vitality and can afford to take some chip damage while closing the distance. Stay patient, and wait for mistakes and opportunities to move Haggar in.

If your opponent's zoning game is rather strong and does not present many opportunities to move forward, Haggar has a somewhat risky option to quickly close the distance. You can use Haggar's crouching Ⓗ to put him into a hard knockdown state. Once in this knockdown state, Haggar has the same rising options as if your rival had put him into a knockdown state. So, after performing crouching Ⓗ, you can hold ⇨ to roll toward your opponent. If your competitor is not expecting this, the opposing character may be vulnerable to a counterattack. However, if the opposing player can react to this, you must be ready to guard any attacks, but you will at least be closer to your target.

Once you are able to achieve close range with Haggar, he has some strong mix-up options that all can lead to damaging combos. Any throw from Haggar can potentially lead to a full combo. If Haggar is ever at close range, you can always threaten with his Flying Piledriver or Final Haggar Buster. If opponents attempt to escape by jumping, you can punish their retreat with Hoodlum Launcher H, Skyhigh Back Drop, or air throw. You can also use normal attacks with frame advantage or slight disadvantage to set up tick throws with Flying Piledriver or his ground throw. All of the mid range tactics work fairly well at close range, as well. However, you need to watch and determine how your rival reacts so you can use the appropriate attack to counter the opposing player's actions.

Haggar's Double Lariat is a strong defensive option.

If an opponent guards or crouches underneath your Double Lariat, use hyper combo cancels to land a level 3 hyper combo or make the attack safe!

Defensively, Haggar has high vitality, so you may be able to afford a few mistakes. His Double Lariat has a huge amount of invincibility frames, and you can use it at the cost of 100,000 vitality (which is converted to red vitality). If it lands, it can be canceled into Rapid Fire Fist or with X-Factor to convert into a combo. This makes it a great defensive option against a very aggressive adversary and can beat almost any basic attack your opponent sticks out. Double Lariat is also an excellent way to deal with teleporting characters, as it attacks on both sides of Haggar.

However, you must be careful with this attack because it is very unsafe if guarded. Furthermore, this attack completely misses on several characters when they are crouching. Luckily, you can use hyper combo cancelling to mitigate this vulnerability somewhat. If an opponent crouches under the attack, you can immediately cancel into Final Haggar Buster. Competitors will probably not send their character jumping in while Haggar is still spinning from the Lariat, causing the throw to connect. If your opponent blocks Double Lariat, you must wait until after they leave blockstun to cancel, leaving you only a short window to correctly land Final Haggar Buster. Another option is to cancel Double Lariat into Rapid Fire Fist to score some chip damage, then THC into a safe hyper combo.

COMBO USAGE

I. ST. (L), (M), → + (H), ↓ ↘ → + (L), ST. (L), (M) CANCEL → ↓ ↘ + (L) CANCEL SUPER JUMP STRAIGHT UP, AIR (M), (M), (H), ↓ + (H), LAND, → ↓ ↘ + (L) CANCEL SUPER JUMP STRAIGHT UP, AIR (M), (H), ↑ + (H) CANCEL ↓ ↘ → + (S), LAND, CR. (H)

615,300 damage, 122% meter gain

This is a basic combo for Haggar that utilizes his ground bounce with Air Steel Pipe to relaunch his opponent, resulting in large damage and a gain of 122% meter. It's important that after the Hoodlum Launcher, you have Haggar super jump straight up and not forwards. If Haggar goes forward, he ends up passing underneath his adversary and missing the attacks. Haggar can always land crouching (H) after any hard knockdown, and you can continue combos further with a proper assist.

II. AIR ↓ + (H), DASH, JUMP FORWARD, AIR (L), (M), (H), LAND, ST. (M) CANCEL → ↓ ↘ + (L) CANCEL SUPER JUMP STRAIGHT UP, AIR (M), (H), ↑ + (H) CANCEL ↓ ↘ → + (S), LAND, CR. (H)

537,800 damage, 82% meter gain

This is a solo combo after a ↓ + (H) ground bounce. The forward dash may not be required after the ground bounce if Haggar is close enough. If you have difficulty with the initial dash into air (L), (M), (H) part, you can simply do st. (M) CANCEL → ↓ ↘ + (L) instead for slightly less damage.

III. → ↘ ↓ ↙ ← + (ATK) OR AIR → ↘ ↓ ↙ ← + (ATK), CALL ROCKET RACCOON—α, CR. (H) CANCEL → + (H) CANCEL → ↓ ↘ + (L) CANCEL SUPER JUMP STRAIGHT UP, AIR (M), (M), (H), ↓ + (H), LAND, → ↓ ↘ + (L) CANCEL SUPER JUMP STRAIGHT UP, AIR (M), (H), ↑ + (H) CANCEL ↓ ↘ → + (S), LAND, CR. (H)

642,300 damage, 126% meter gain

With the use of certain assists and Haggar's new OTG-capable crouching (H), you can turn any hard knockdown throw into a damaging combo. You'll want to delay your crouching (H) slightly to give the assist enough time to strike after your crouching (H), giving you time to combo into your → + (H). If doing this after Skyhigh Back Drop or Final Haggar Buster, you may have to dash forward slightly while calling your assist, then canceling your dash with crouching (H).

IV. AIR THROW, LAND, DASH FORWARD, CR. (H) CANCEL → + (H) X-FACTOR ST. (L), (M) CANCEL → ↓ ↘ + (L) CANCEL SUPER JUMP STRAIGHT UP, AIR (M), (M), (H), ↓ + (H), LAND, → ↓ ↘ + (L) CANCEL SUPER JUMP STRAIGHT UP, AIR (M), (M), ↑ + (H) CANCEL ↓ ↘ → + (S), LAND, CALL ROCKET RACCOON—α, CR. (H) CANCEL → + (H), (S) CANCEL → ↓ ↘ → ↗ + (ATK)(ATK)

X-Factor level 1, 1,0777,000 damage, 72% meter gain

Normal throws scale down the damage of combos following them significantly, making this a prime time to use X-Factor to limit the amount of scaling on your follow-up combo. Make sure you X-Factor cancel immediately after the OTG crouching (H) hits and then immediately follow up with the standing (L). After the ↓ ↘ → + (S), call Rocket Raccoon—α and slightly delay your crouching (H) so that the second hit from the assist prevents the ground bounce, allowing you to connect the (S). Super jump cancel the (S) with the → ↓ ↘ → ↗ command to allow you to hit with the full damage of Giant Haggar Press. Without the second OTG follow-up, the combo causes 717,900 damage and has a 139% meter gain.

V. (S) + (ATK) CANCEL ↓ ↘ → + (ATK)(ATK), → ↓ ↘ + (L) CANCEL SUPER JUMP STRAIGHT UP, AIR (M), (M), ↑ + (H) CANCEL ↓ ↘ → + (S), LAND, CALL ROCKET RACCOON—α, CR. (H) CANCEL → + (H) CANCEL → ↓ ↘ + (L) CANCEL → ↓ ↘ → ↗ + (ATK)(ATK)

667,500 damage, 128% meter loss

This is a heavy damage combo off a Double Lariat. To make sure your rival does not air recover before the last hit, cancel Double Lariat with Rapid Fire Fists right as the foe begins to fall toward the ground. Don't mash for a higher level Rapid Fire Fist. After the last Hoodlum Launcher L, you must super jump cancel to get Giant Haggar Press to connect by inputting the motion → ↓ ↘ → ↗ + (ATK)(ATK).

ADVANCED TACTICS

HOODLUM LAUNCHER H RESETS

You can force an adversary into a difficult situation by purposely allowing them to air recover while near the ground, especially in the corner. This was somewhat difficult for Haggar to perform in *Marvel vs. Capcom 3*, but with the addition of his OTG-capable crouching Ⓗ, this setup has become much deadlier.

After a combo that ends with hard knockdown, call an assist and then press cr. Ⓗ [CANCEL] → + Ⓗ [CANCEL] ↓↘→ + Ⓛ. Your competitor air recovers shortly after being hit by your Violent Axe L. If your opponent air recovers neutral or back, you can then grab them out of the air with Hoodlum Launcher H. If the foe air recovers forward, you can jump and grab them with Skyhigh Back Drop or air throw. However, be wary using these resets against opposing characters with invincible air attacks, such as Sentinel's Hard Drive!

You can intentionally leave a combo unfinished while near the ground so that your opponent air recovers, allowing you to use Hoodlum Launcher H to begin a new combo!

CROSSOVER COUNTER ABUSE

Haggar's Double Lariat can beat most attacks and crossover assists

If an adversary becomes predictable in their attack patterns, teams with Haggar on them can take advantage of this and inflict massive damage.

COMBO APPENDIX

GENERAL EXECUTION TIPS

- When juggling Rapid Fire Fist after Double Lariat, try to hit your opponent with Rapid Fire Fist as high as possible
- Super jump cancel launchers to get full damage on Haggar Body Press with the command →↓↘→↗ + (ATK)(ATK)
- Always super jump straight up after Hoodlum launchers and hit with air Ⓜ as soon as possible

AIR ↓ + Ⓗ, DASH, JUMP FORWARD, AIR Ⓛ, Ⓜ, Ⓗ, LAND, ST. Ⓜ [CANCEL] →↓↘ + Ⓛ [CANCEL] SUPER JUMP STRAIGHT UP, AIR Ⓜ, Ⓗ, ↑ + Ⓗ [CANCEL] ↓↘→ + Ⓢ, LAND, CALL ROCKET RACCOON—α, CR. Ⓗ [CANCEL] → + Ⓗ [CANCEL] →↓↘ + Ⓛ [CANCEL] SUPER JUMP STRAIGHT UP, AIR Ⓜ, Ⓜ, ↑ + Ⓗ [CANCEL] ↓↘→ + Ⓢ, LAND, CR. Ⓗ

Notes	Damage
Using an assist to get full damage even when starting combo with ground bounce	687,200 damage, 137% meter gain

COUNTERHIT AIR ↑ + Ⓗ, LAND, Ⓜ, → + Ⓗ, ↓↘→ + Ⓛ, ST. Ⓛ, Ⓜ [CANCEL] →↓↘ + Ⓛ [CANCEL] SUPER JUMP STRAIGHT UP, AIR Ⓜ, Ⓜ, Ⓗ, ↓ + Ⓗ, LAND, →↓↘ + Ⓛ [CANCEL] SUPER JUMP STRAIGHT UP, AIR Ⓜ, Ⓗ, ↑ + Ⓗ [CANCEL] ↓↘→ + Ⓢ, LAND, CR. Ⓗ

Notes	Damage
Counterhit Head Butt against grounded opponent	650,000 damage, 125% meter gain

COUNTERHIT AIR ↑ + Ⓗ, LAND, ↓↘→ + Ⓛ, ST. Ⓛ, Ⓜ [CANCEL] →↓↘ + Ⓛ [CANCEL] SUPER JUMP STRAIGHT UP, AIR Ⓜ, Ⓜ, Ⓗ, ↓ + Ⓗ, LAND, →↓↘ + Ⓛ [CANCEL] SUPER JUMP STRAIGHT UP, AIR Ⓜ, Ⓜ, ↑ + Ⓗ [CANCEL] ↓↘→ + Ⓢ, LAND, CR. Ⓗ

Notes	Damage
Counterhit Head Butt against airborne competitor	607,300 damage, 110% meter gain

→↘↓↙← + (ATK)(ATK), CALL ROCKET RACCOON—α, CR. Ⓗ [CANCEL] → + Ⓗ [CANCEL] →↓↘ + Ⓛ [CANCEL] SUPER JUMP STRAIGHT UP, AIR Ⓜ, Ⓜ, Ⓗ, ↓ + Ⓗ, LAND, →↓↘ + Ⓛ [CANCEL] SUPER JUMP STRAIGHT UP, AIR Ⓜ, Ⓜ, ↑ + Ⓗ [CANCEL] ↓↘→ + Ⓢ, LAND, CR. Ⓗ

Notes	Damage
Level 3 hyper combo follow up	745,700 damage, 200% meter loss

GROUND THROW (MASH (ATK)), CALL ROCKET RACCOON—α, CR. Ⓗ [CANCEL] → + Ⓗ [CANCEL] →↓↘ + Ⓛ [CANCEL] SUPER JUMP STRAIGHT UP, AIR Ⓜ, Ⓜ, Ⓗ, ↓ + Ⓗ, LAND, →↓↘ + Ⓛ [CANCEL] SUPER JUMP STRAIGHT UP, AIR Ⓜ, Ⓜ, ↑ + Ⓗ [CANCEL] ↓↘→ + Ⓢ, LAND, CR. Ⓗ

Notes	Damage
Call assist while Haggar is throwing his rival to the ground	387,400 damage, 110% meter gain

COUNTERHIT AIR ↑ + Ⓗ, LAND, ST. Ⓜ, → + Ⓗ [CANCEL] ↓↘→ + Ⓛ, ST. Ⓛ, Ⓜ [CANCEL] →↓↘ + Ⓛ [CANCEL] SUPER JUMP STRAIGHT UP, AIR Ⓜ, Ⓗ, ↑ + Ⓗ [CANCEL] ↓↘→ + Ⓢ, LAND, CALL ROCKET RACCOON—α, CR. Ⓗ [CANCEL] → + Ⓗ [CANCEL] →↓↘ + Ⓛ [CANCEL] SUPER JUMP STRAIGHT UP, AIR Ⓜ, Ⓜ, ↑ + Ⓗ [CANCEL] ↓↘→ + Ⓢ, LAND, CALL WESKER—β, CR. Ⓗ [CANCEL] → + Ⓗ [CANCEL] →↓↘ + Ⓛ [CANCEL] →↓↘→↗ + (ATK)(ATK)

Notes	Damage
Double assist usage combo with super jump canceled hyper combo ender	915,000 damage, 66% meter gain

Ⓢ + (ATK) (XFC) ST. Ⓜ, Ⓢ [CANCEL] SUPER JUMP FORWARD, AIR Ⓜ, Ⓜ, Ⓗ, ↓ + Ⓗ, LAND, ST. Ⓜ, Ⓢ [CANCEL] SUPER JUMP FORWARD, AIR Ⓜ, Ⓜ, ↑ + Ⓗ, Ⓢ, LAND, CALL ROCKET RACCOON—α, CR. Ⓗ [CANCEL] → + Ⓗ, Ⓢ [CANCEL] →↓↘→↗ + (ATK)(ATK)

Notes	Damage
Double Lariat punish against two opposing characters	1,118,500 damage, 76% meter gain

HSIEN-KO

"WHAT ELSE DO I HAVE UP MY SLEEVES? NUH-UH! A GIRL'S GOTTA KEEP HER SECRETS, Y'KNOW!"

Bio

REAL NAME

Hsien-Ko

OCCUPATION

Priest (Senjutsu Style)

ABILITIES

A unique style of Chinese martial arts, blending techniques passed down though Senjutsu as well as hidden weaponry.

WEAPONS

Uses large steel talons, a gong, and other various weapons. She also uses an assortment of items, such as an Akuma doll, Vega's claw, Chun-Li's bracelets, etc.

PROFILE

Hsien-Ko and Mei-Ling are twin sisters who transformed into a jiangshi using Igyo Tenshin-no-Jutsu. They fight to save their mother's soul from the darkness. Hsien-Ko does the fighting, while Mei-Ling transformed into the charm on her hat in order to keep Hsien-Ko's powers under control.

FIRST APPEARANCE

Night Warriors (1995)

POWER GRID

2	INTELLIGENCE
3	STRENGTH
2	SPEED
3	STAMINA
1	ENERGY PROJECTION
4	FIGHTING ABILITY

*This is biographical, and does not represent an evaluation of the in-game combat potential of this hero.

ALTERNATE COSTUMES

Overview

Vitality	900,000
Chain Combo Archetype	Hunter Series

X-Factor Boost	Damage	Speed
Level 1 (3 teammates remaining)	125%	115%
Level 2 (2 teammates remaining)	145%	125%
Level 3 (1 teammate remaining)	165%	135%

When using Hsien-Ko, your goal is to keep your opponent at bay. Why is the goal to keep your adversary away?

Repeated use of Henkyo Ki can often seem like an impenetrable wall, keeping the opposing character at bay. Henkyo Ki H stops virtually all projectiles, shutting down most characters' long range game

Hsien-Ko is very slow, making it difficult to mount an offense with her. How can you keep your competition at bay with Hsien-Ko?

Stop ground advances cold with Henkyo Ki H, standing Ⓜ, standing Ⓗ, and Anki-Hou L

Use Anki-Hou M and ➔ + Ⓗ when opposing characters approach from the air

Tag opponents directly above Hsien-Ko's head with Anki-Hou H

TUNING SINCE ORIGINAL MVC3

Hsien-Ko can now jump cancel Rantetsu and Edoga, strengthening not only her combos but the utility of those attacks. New items have been added to Anki-Hou, as well.

Rantetsu (➪ + Ⓜ) is now jump-cancelable

Edoga (➪ + Ⓗ) is now jump-cancelable

Tenrai Ha can now be mashed for additional damage

Anki-Hou new items:

Oil drum (70,000 damage) 1 low priority durability point

Chunk of meat (70,000 damage, stagger) 1 low priority durability point

Cat doll (70,000 damage) 1 low priority durability point

Servbot snowman (70,000 damage, freeze visual effect) 1 low priority durability point

Chris' stun rod (70,000 damage, causes stagger and lightning effect) 1 low priority durability point

Samurai doll (70,000 damage, causes stagger) 1 low priority durability point

Reduced startup of cr. Ⓜ and decreased active frames

Jump attacks now cause the enemy to float less

Rantetsu can chain combo into Edoga

Increased untechable time from Edoga

Attack Set

Standing Basic Attacks

Screen	Command	Hits	Damage	Meter Gain	Startup	Active	Recovery	Advantage on Hit	Advantage if Guarded	Notes
1	Standing L	1	40,000	320	5	3	10	-1	-1	—
2	Standing M	1	60,000	480	7	5	20	-2	-2	—
3	Standing H	3	84,800	792	10	7	21	-1	-1	—

1

2

3

Crouching Basic Attacks

Screen	Command	Hits	Damage	Meter Gain	Startup	Active	Recovery	Advantage on Hit	Advantage if Guarded	Notes
1	Crouching L	1	40,000	320	5	3	12	-2	-2	Low attack
2	Crouching M	1	60,000	480	10	7	18	-8	-8	—
3	Crouching H	1	70,000	560	12	20	8	—	-5	Low attack, knocks down

1

2

3

Ground Special Attack—Launcher

Screen	Command	Hits	Damage	Meter Gain	Startup	Active	Recovery	Advantage on Hit	Advantage if Guarded	Notes
1	S (while standing or crouching)	1	75,000	600	11	5	21	—	-3	Launcher, not special- or hyper combo-cancelable

1

Air Basic Attacks

Screen	Command	Hits	Damage	Meter Gain	Startup	Active	Recovery	Advantage on Hit	Advantage if Guarded	Notes
1	Air L	1	42,000	336	6	6	18	+5	+7	Overhead attack
2	Air M	1	60,000	504	8	6	31	+11	+11	Overhead attack
3	Air H	3	84,800	792	13	12	26	+16	+16	Overhead attack

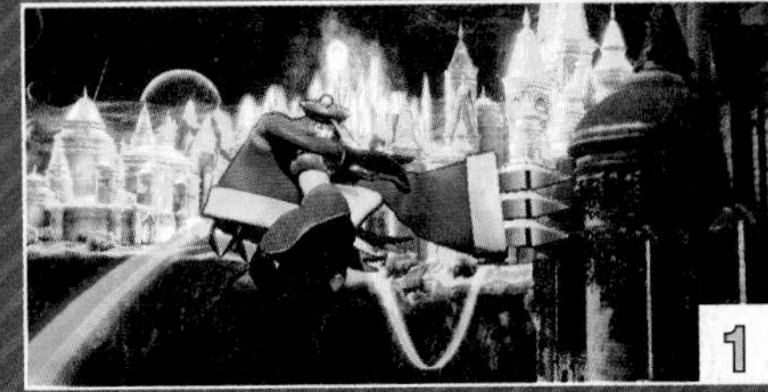
1

2

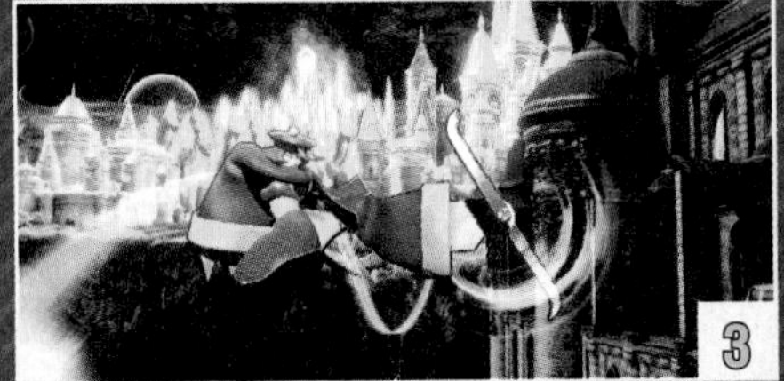
3

Air Special Attacks—Flying Screen and Air Exchange

Air Ⓢ causes a hard knockdown when used in a launcher combo (this is sometimes called flying screen). When used outside of a launcher combo, air Ⓢ behaves mostly like another basic attack. Air exchange attacks, performed by inputting a direction plus Ⓢ, are only possible during a launcher combo. Exchange hits initiate team aerial combos by tagging in the next available character to continue the air combo.

Screen	Command	Hits	Damage	Meter Gain	Startup	Active	Recovery	Advantage on Hit	Advantage if Guarded	Notes
1	Air Ⓢ	1	70,000	560	9	6	31	+15	+15	Causes hard knockdown if used in launcher combo
2	Air ⇧ + Ⓢ (during launcher combo)	1	60,000	480	13	9	31	—	—	Tags in next available ally while lofting opponent upward
3	Air ⇨ or ⇦ + Ⓢ (during launcher combo)	1	50,000	400	11	2	31	—	—	Tags in next available ally while causing wall bounce, erases 1 hyper meter bar from foe
4	Air ⇩ + Ⓢ (during launcher combo)	1	50,000	400 + 10000	11	2	31	—	—	Tags in next available ally while causing ground bounce, generates 1 hyper meter bar

1

2

3

4

Command Attacks

Command attacks resemble basic attacks but have different chaining and canceling properties. It's usually possible to chain *into* a command attack from basic attacks, but most command attacks cannot be chained from or canceled themselves.

Screen	Name	Command	Hits	Damage	Meter Gain	Startup	Active	Recovery	Advantage on Hit	Advantage if Guarded	Notes
1	Rantetsu	⇨ + Ⓜ	1	70,000	560	10	11	13	-6	-6	Jump-cancelable
2	Edoga	⇨ + Ⓗ	1	80,000	640	15	7	19	-3	-3	Jump-cancelable

1

2

Throws

Throws are for snagging passive or blocking opponents. Since throws are active so quickly, you can also use them to preemptively toss opposing characters out of their offense. Combos are usually possible after throws, one way or another.

Screen	Command	Hits	Damage	Meter Gain	Startup	Active	Notes
1	⇨ + Ⓗ (ground)	1	80,000	800	1	1	—
	⇦ + Ⓗ (ground)	1	80,000	800	1	1	—
2	⇨ + Ⓗ (air)	1	80,000	800	1	1	—
	⇦ + Ⓗ (air)	1	80,000	800	1	1	—

1

2

As a Partner—Crossover Assists

Screen	Type	P1+P2 Crossover Combination Hyper Combo	Description	Hits	Damage	Meter Gain	Startup	Active	Recovery (this crossover assist)	Recovery (other partner)	Notes
1	Hsien-Ko—α	Chireitou	Senpu Bu L	5	102,300	1000	53	35	117	86	—
2	Hsien-Ko—β	Tenrai Ha	Henkyo Ki M	1	70,000	560	36	—	124	93	Projectile has 5 low durability points, reflects other projectiles, disappears after 60 frames
3	Hsien-Ko—γ	Chireitou	Anki-Hou M	1	70,000-80,000	560-640	41	—	120	89	Bonsai tree and gold star stun for 120 frames, bombs cause hard knockdown, stun rod and samurai doll cause stagger, projectile has 1 low priority durability point

1

2

3

Hsien-Ko's assists are somewhat varied in their use, but one assist clearly stands above the rest. Use Hsien-Ko—α Senpu Bu to place your opponent in a huge amount of guardstun to both supplement offense and start combos. While normally Senpu Bu makes for a slightly better than average crossover assist, when combined with the Hyper Armor properties of Rimoukon it becomes an unstoppable force. Use it basically whenever Hsien-Ko is near her adversary to both hit the foe out of their offense and ensure that they do not press any buttons while on defense! Rimoukon with the Senpu Bu assist can be reason enough to place Hsien-Ko on your team!

Hsien-Ko—β as a crossover assist is not as useful as it is on point because Hsien-Ko appears behind the point character. This limits its usefulness as a projectile reflector. Hsien-Ko—γ Anki-Hou is a useful assist if your team requires long range support because it travels the entirety of the screen horizontally.

Snap Back

Screen	Command	Hits	Damage	Meter Gain	Startup	Active	Recovery	Advantage on Hit	Advantage if Guarded
1	↓↘→ + P1 or P2	1	50,000	500 (-1 hyper meter bar)	2	11	13	—	-1

Notes

On hit, snap back forces the opposing point character to be replaced by an assist. Opposing assist calls or tag outs are also locked out for 4 seconds

1

Special Moves

Screen	Name	Command	Hits	Damage	Meter Gain	Startup	Active	Recovery	Advantage on Hit	Advantage if Guarded	Notes
1	Anki-Hou	↓↘→ + ATK	1	70,000-80,000	560	17	—	28	-3	-6	H version is an overhead attack, Bonsai tree and gold star stun for 120 frames, cause special hard knockdown on airborne opponent in which all moves are OTG-capable. Bombs cause hard knockdown, inflict 80,000 damage and can be bounced around by attacks from either player. Stun Rod and Samurai Statue cause stagger. All projectiles have 1 durability point
2	Senpu Bu L (in air OK)	→↓↘ + L	5~10	102,300~162,400	1000-2000	29	35~70	1	+20	+20	Press L repeatedly for additional hits
	Senpu Bu M (in air OK)	→↓↘ + M	7~12	130,200~178,900	1400-2400	33	40~80	1	+22	+22	Press M repeatedly for additional hits
	Senpu Bu H (in air OK)	→↓↘ + H	8~13	142,100~185,900	1600-2600	37	40~90	1	+19	+19	Press H repeatedly for additional hits
3	Henkyo Ki L	←↓↙ + L	1	70,000	560	10	—	30	-18	-6	Projectile has 5 low priority durability points, reflects other low priority projectiles, disappears after 10 frames
	Henkyo Ki M	←↓↙ + M	1	70,000	560	12	—	32	-16	-10	Projectile has 5 low priority durability points, reflects other low priority projectiles, disappears after 60 frames
	Henkyo Ki H	←↓↙ + H	1	70,000	560	14	—	36	-14	-14	Projectile has 5 low priority durability points, reflects other low priority projectiles, disappears after 120 frames
	Air Henkyo Ki L	(in air)←↓↙ + L	1	70,000	560	10	—	28	—	—	Projectile has 5 low priority durability points, reflects other low priority projectiles, disappears after 10 frames

Special Moves continued

Screen	Name	Command	Hits	Damage	Meter Gain	Startup	Active	Recovery	Advantage on Hit	Advantage if Guarded	Notes
3	Air Henkyo Ki M	(in air)⇦⇩⇙ + Ⓜ	1	70,000	560	12	—	32	—	—	Projectile has 5 low priority durability points, reflects other low priority projectiles, disappears after 60 frames
	Air Henkyo Ki H	(in air)⇦⇩⇙ + Ⓗ	1	70,000	560	14	—	36	—	—	Projectile has 5 low priority durability points, reflects other low priority projectiles, disappears after 120 frames
4	Houten Geki L	⇨⇘⇩⇙⇦ + Ⓛ	8	96,000	960	9	2	18	—	—	Throw, hard knockdown
	Houten Geki M	⇨⇘⇩⇙⇦ + Ⓜ	12	144,000	1440	5	2	22	—	—	Throw, hard knockdown
	Houten Geki H	⇨⇘⇩⇙⇦ + Ⓗ	16	192,000	1920	2	2	25	—	—	Throw, hard knockdown

1

***Anki-Hou*:** Hsien-Ko hurls a seemingly random item to damage enemies. The game cycles through all of her available items every frame, making it theoretically possible (but extremely unlikely) to control the item that Hsien-Ko throws. These items include:

Standard items:

- **Axe**
- **Kunai**
- **Yashichi**
- **Chun-Li's bracelet**
- **Shuriken**
- **Cat doll**
- **Sword**
- **Chunk of meat**
- **Oil drum**

Bombs:

- **Bomb (nine seconds)**
- **Bomb (six seconds)**
- **Bomb (three seconds)**

Special items:

- **Snowman**
- **Chris' stun rod**
- **Samurai doll**
- **Bonsai tree**
- **Star**

Note that the oil drum is actually placed immediately before the snowman in the list of items; it does not have any special properties and was placed in the list of "standard items" for clarity.

The standard items listed have no special properties and act as regular projectiles. The bombs do not hit upon release; the timer on the bomb determines when the bomb explodes. Attacks from both Hsien-Ko and her opponent can send the bomb away, so it's possible for a bomb to explode in a different area than where it was initially thrown. With some foresight, you can capitalize on bomb explosions with a combo. If you see the opposing character near a bomb that is ready to explode, be ready with an attack! Keep in mind that the bomb explosion affects enemies only, so you don't have to worry about self-inflicted damage.

The snowman, samurai doll, and stun rod cause a greater amount of hitstun than the normal items. If you connect standing Ⓗ into one of these versions of Anki-Hou L, your adversary is stunned long enough for another standing Ⓗ.

The best items from Anki-Hou are definitely the bonsai tree and the star. If either of these items hits a standing opponent, they are put in a dizzy state for a brief period of time. At long range, the opposing character is too far for you to land a full combo, limiting your options to simply throwing another item. However, you can fully capitalize on a dizzy opponent when the bonsai tree or star hits at closer ranges.

But don't rely on these items for combos, since it is essentially impossible to determine which item will be thrown when Anki-Hou is performed. Rather, it is important to quickly recognize which item Hsien-Ko throws as soon as possible, so the proper follow-up can be performed. Expecting an oil drum and getting a bonsai tree instead can throw off your combo. Expecting a regular Anki-Hou L attack and getting a bomb can throw you off too! Therefore, learning which items behave in what ways and using the visual cue to quickly recognize the item can strongly improve your success with this attack.

Anki-Hou L boasts maximum horizontal distance, making it Hsien-Ko's farthest-reaching attack. Use it to harass foes from mid to long range. Anki-Hou M fires at a medium arc, making it perfect for attacking targets that are approaching from the air. Anki-Hou H tosses items straight up, which can hit opponents who are trying to attack Hsien-Ko from directly above. If the thrown item does not make contact with anything on the way up, it comes straight down in front of Hsien-Ko, hitting on the way down. Anki-Hou H is different in that it behaves as an overhead and must be blocked high. Given this, you can use it as an instant overhead on larger characters if the opposing character is right next to Hsien-Ko. Follow this with Chireitou or Tenrai Ha, or even X-Factor cancel into a combo!

2

***Senpu Bu*:** Senpu Bu is Hsien-Ko's primary way to start an offense. The button used determines the number of hits of the swing as well as the horizontal arc of the attack, with Senpu Bu H reaching the farthest. If connected, Senpu Bu can be followed up with falling air Ⓗ or Ⓢ. On guard, Senpu Bu puts Hsien-Ko in the perfect position to continue her assault. You can also mash the same button used to activate Senpu Bu for extra damage in the form of an added swing backward.

What is unique about Senpu Bu is that it completely ignores advancing guard. If Hsien-Ko merely touches her adversary with the Senpu Bu, they are unable to push her away, making it an excellent pressure tool. Senpu Bu recovers in the air, making it possible to follow up with aerial basic attacks, Senpu Bu, Henkyo Ki, or a crossover assist.

3

***Henkyo Ki*:** This is Hsien-Ko's most important attack. Henkyo Ki fires a slow-moving projectile from the gong, which stays on the screen for a long period of time. Henkyo Ki H can be fired quickly enough consecutively to have up to three on the screen at once, effectively controlling the space roughly three character lengths in front of her. When you use this move in conjunction with standing Ⓗ and ⇨ + Ⓗ, opposing players must find another way to move in on Hsien-Ko, since the space in front of her will only be cleared by a hyper combo.

The projectiles from the gong act as reflectors, sending any normal projectiles back at their originators. Certain projectiles, including beam-type attacks, are not reflected but instead are fully nullified by Henkyo Ki. This attack alone tilts long range firefights in Hsien-Ko's favor, forcing competitors to try another method of attack.

4

***Houten Geki*:** While Hsien-Ko players won't find many opportunities to use this attack, its damage potential makes up for it. Since Houten Geki causes a hard knockdown, you can easily perform Tenrai Ha afterwards for additional damage.

The startup and range of Houten Geki vary depending on the button used. Houten Geki L has the slowest startup but the longest range, while the Ⓗ version is the opposite. Houten Geki L has a significant amount of range, making it ideal to use after the opposing character guards a short string of attacks.

Hyper Combos

Screen	Name	Command	Hits	Damage	Startup	Active	Recovery	Advantage on Hit	Advantage if Guarded	Notes
1	Chireitou	↓ ↘ → + (ATK)(ATK)	1~6	60,000~ 317,700	30+5	145	44	—	-1~+18	OTG-capable, knocks down, each projectile has 1 high priority durability point
2	Tenrai Ha	↓ ↙ ← + (ATK)(ATK)	1~9	35,000~ 273,500	13+3	97-	39	—	-6	First hit is OTG-capable and an overhead attack, ground bounces the opponent, leaves the target in hard knockdown . Each projectile is OTG-capable, leaves the opponent in hard knockdown, and has 1 high priority durability point
3	Rimoukon	→ ↓ ↘ + (ATK)(ATK)	—	—	20+0	—	21	—	—	Hsien-Ko gains Hyper Armor status for 300 frames

Chireitou: Hsien-Ko draws forth a series of blades from underneath for a total of six hits. It is OTG-capable, making it useful for ending combos and inflicting more damage than Tenrai Ha. Hsien-Ko recovers early during the duration of the hyper combo, enabling her to tag to another teammate safely or even follow up with a super jumping (H) given that her positioning is correct.

It's important to note that Chireitou will not hit the opponent's character with all six blades if the foe is near the corner; the blades will be created off of the edge of the screen.

1

Tenrai Ha: Tenrai Ha sends spiked balls down directly in front of Hsien-Ko, leaving her rival in a hard knockdown state. Since the range of this hyper combo is limited to one spot, it is better to use than Chireitou when ending combos in the corner. If timed correctly, you can follow up Tenrai Ha with Chireitou or even another Tenrai Ha, so long as it is canceled from Henkyo Ki to prevent your opponent from ground bouncing. When used in this way, you can add as many Tenrai Ha hyper combos into a combo as you like! This attack is considered an overhead and must be blocked high.

2

3

Rimoukon: Rimoukon gives Hsien-Ko Hyper Armor for a six- second duration. Upon activation, Hsien-Ko is impervious to hitstun, letting her walk through most attacks unphased! While Hsien-Ko still takes damage in this mode, she retains the ability to guard attacks. Think Colossus's power-up hyper from *MvC2*. Opponents have no choice but to flee, since their attacks are easily countered while Rimoukon is in effect.

The properties of Rimoukon also carry over to Hsien-Ko as a crossover assist! When summoned, Hsien-Ko performs her crossover assist and can only be stopped if she is knocked out. Senpu Bu and Henkyo Ki are especially useful when augmented with Rimoukon, interrupting any incoming attacks without fail. Don't become too predictable with this tactic, however; because of the lack of hitstun, certain hyper combos end up dealing unscaled damage to Hsien-Ko since the hits won't register as combo hits. Effective ways to get Hsien-Ko to the sidelines with Rimoukon include a THC to a safe hyper combo upon activation, or covering a tag with Henkyo Ki H.

COMBO USAGE

I. (MID-SCREEN REQUIRED) CR. (L), ST. (M), CR. (M), (H), (S) CANCEL ➡ SUPER JUMP, AIR (M), (M), (S), LAND, ↓ ↘ → + (ATK)(ATK) OTG

483,900, 52% meter loss

You can use this combo as your go-to bread and butter combo. Because of the short range on Hsien-Ko's launcher, crouching (H) must be used right before, as it moves her forward so (S) can connect. If this combo is performed near the corner, it is better to end the combo with Tenrai Ha rather than Chireitou.

II. CR. (L), (M), (H), → + (H) CANCEL ➡ FORWARD JUMP, AIR (M), (S), LAND, CR. (M), (H), (S), SUPER JUMP, AIR (M), (M), (H), (S), LAND, ↓ ↘ → + (ATK)(ATK)

553,700 dmg, 30% meter loss

This combo utilizes Hsien-Ko's new ability to jump cancel Edoga. After the jump cancel, you can wait a long moment before performing the air (M), (S) so that your opponent isn't being juggled too high for the rest of the combo.

III. (CORNER REQUIRED) CR. (L), (M), (H), → + (H) CANCEL ➡ ← ↓ ↙ + (M), CR. (H), → + (H) CANCEL ➡ ← ↓ ↙ + (M), CR. (H), → + (H) CANCEL ➡ → ↓ ↙ + (M), CR. (H), (S) CANCEL ➡ FORWARD SUPER JUMP, AIR (H) (3 HITS), (S), LAND, ↓ ↙ ← + (ATK)(ATK)

588,800 dmg, 15% meter loss

In the corner, you can loop Edoga to Henkyo Ki M up to three times so long as your target is low to the ground. Hsien-Ko's corner combos deal more damage than her midscreen combos, so make sure to practice the Henkyo Ki loop!

IV. → ↓ ↘ + (L), AIR (H) (3 HITS), LAND, ST. (M), CR. (H), (S) CANCEL ➡ SUPER JUMP, AIR (M), (M), (H) (3 HITS), (S), LAND, ↓ ↙ ← + (ATK)(ATK) OTG

397,100 dmg, 44% meter loss

If Senpu Bu connects during offensive pressure, you can have Hsien-Ko fall with air (H) into a full combo. If you find that your adversary is too far to get the maximum damage from Tenrai Ha, try having Hsien-Ko walk or dash forward right before you perform the hyper combo.

Battle Plan

Hsien-Ko's strengths lie in her keep-away game. At mid to long range, Hsien-Ko can effectively keep her adversary away with a combination of basic attacks and special moves in conjunction with crossover assists. While this won't inflict large amounts of damage, you can capitalize on the opposing player's frustration while they are dealing with an obstacle course-like defense—this can cause them to make foolish mistakes.

You can easily control the ground with Hsien-Ko just by continually using Henkyo Ki H. Not only do your opponent's long range options become limited to nullified, but a ground approach gets cut off, as well. If your opposition is content with staying at maximum distance from Hsien-Ko, you can use Anki-Hou L with a long range crossover assist to keep the pace of the battle under control. Once enemies attempt to attack from the skies, Hsien-Ko can hold them off with Anki-Hou M. When competitors finally reach at least midscreen, you can deploy Hsien-Ko's farther-reaching melee attacks (such as standing (H), ⇨ + (H), and (M)). Cancel these attacks into more Henkyo Ki H to push your rival back to where they started. If you're persistent about using Henkyo Ki repeatedly, even if your rival jumps over a Henkyo Ki, they'll likely still land on top of the slow-moving projectile.

"Wall of Henkyo Ki" will stop opponents in their tracks.

Be wary of characters with extra mobility options, such as teleports or airdashes. If you become too complacent in your frontal defenses, a teleporting character can teleport behind Hsien-Ko and start a maximum damage combo. Thus, the best time to watch for teleports is when Henkyo Ki projectiles are on screen. Crouching (L) is fast enough to punish any ill-timed teleports.

Against airdashers, the (M) and (H) versions of Anki-Hou are very useful because they cut off the angles from which airdashers approach. However, they are most effective when used preemptively. If airdashing opponents are approaching from a 45-degree angle, try utilizing a Henkyo Ki "wall" by jumping and performing an aerial Henkyo Ki H, then landing and performing another Henkyo Ki H, blocking a substantial area of approach. You can use Edoga to stop enemies at this angle, as well. If the attack is blocked, cancel into a Henkyo Ki H. If it hits, jump cancel into a combo.

Hsien-Ko's airdash can be used as a means to both approach and escape, even though it is slower than most other airdashes in the game. You are also unable to guard during the entire duration of the airdash. To mitigate these weaknesses, use a defensive crossover assist such as Ghost Rider—β to cover a backwards airdash retreat, or a long range crossover assist such as Sentinel—α to help with a forward airdash approach.

A guarded Senpu Bu gives you substantial footing against foes.

If the battle manages to reach Hsien-Ko's immediate proximity, you have several up-close options to utilize. Both standing and crouching (L) are moderately fast and can be used as pokes to start a combo. If you want to create distance between Hsien-Ko and her competitor, you can perform a short combo (such as standing (L), (M), (H)) while simultaneously calling a crossover assist and ending with several gongs of Henkyo Ki. This creates sufficient space to continue keeping your opponent at bay.

Square jumping is another weapon at Hsien-Ko's disposal. Because of its slow speed, Hsien-Ko's airdash is better used as a means to attack rather than for its mobility. You can initiate a jump, quickly perform an airdash on the way up, and then immediately attack for a square jump attack that must be blocked high. At close range, square jumping with air (M), (S) is most effective, while square jumping with air (H) is best used when you need an attack that reaches farther. You can also utilize this technique to deal with opposing characters coming in with a low attack, since their attack is then easily dodged and countered. Mixing square jumps with crouching (L) keeps your competitors on their toes when it comes to their blocking skills.

ADVANCED TACTICS

USING HSIEN-KO'S FORWARD DASH

Hsien-Ko's forward dash behaves differently than other dashes in the game, mostly because it is more like a teleport than a dash. During the first 15 frames of the dash, Hsien-Ko does not actually move forward and is vulnerable to attack, though the move is still cancelable like any other dash. During the next 15 frames of the dash, Hsien-Ko disappears, becoming both invisible and invincible. If her foe is close enough, Hsien-Ko teleports to the other side for a cross-up. Because of its short traveling distance and vulnerability, the forward dash is best used as a mix-up tool. By first pinning down enemies with a crossover assist, you can create a tricky cross-up opportunity using the dash. You can also employ the technique against incoming characters after a K.O.

RUNNING AWAY

Hsien-Ko's aerial mobility is effective in situations where Hsien-Ko needs to run away. While she does specialize in defense, it can be extremely difficult for Hsien-Ko players to defend against a blazing fast level 3 X-Factor anchor! To get away, you can super jump to the top of the screen and stay at a high altitude by performing aerial Henkyo Ki and Senpu Bu multiple times. Senpu Bu in particular is great for wasting time because of the duration of the swing; make sure to mash the buttons during the Senpu Bu for double the swing time! Combine this with her airdash, and she can stall her opponent for a long period of time. Hsien-Ko can only perform three special moves in the air, so plan your escape carefully.

TEAM DYNAMIC

Even though Hsien-Ko isn't the strongest character on point, she can complement any team with the tools she offers while on the sidelines. Her most notable contribution to a team is her Senpu Bu crossover assist with Rimoukon activated. Other characters with strong offensive tools often find Hsien-Ko to be invaluable as a crossover assist because Senpu Bu is fairly easy to follow up with a combo, leading to big damage that Hsien-Ko is unable to deal on her own.

Having Hsien-Ko on your team makes your crossover combination OTG capable!

Having Hsien-Ko on the team also helps a team's crossover combination significantly since both of her offensive hyper combos are OTG-capable. Any teammate can easily perform a generic combo—launcher into air (M), (M), (H), (S), land, then crossover combination for big damage. This technique is more effective when used with characters that use particularly strong hyper combos during crossover combinations, such as Spencer's Bionic Arm or Dormammu's Chaotic Flame.

If Hsien-Ko's teammates have power-up hypers that recover quickly, Hsien-Ko can perform unguardable setups with them! At close range perform Tenrai Ha, then quickly THC to a power-up hyper such as Zero's Sougenmu or Arthur's Golden Armor. While the spiked balls are falling, strike the opposing character with a low-hitting attack. Since Tenrai Ha acts as an overhead, this setup is impossible to guard because your adversary is being assaulted both high and low simultaneously.

COMBO APPENDIX

GENERAL EXECUTION TIPS

Before performing an OTG with Tenrai Ha, walking or dashing can help you get into position for maximum damage.

When linking multiple Tenrai Ha, be sure to wait until the Tenrai Ha is completely finished before performing Henkyo Ki canceled into Tenrai Ha. Doing this too early can result in an accidental THC.

BACK THROW, ⇨ + (H), JUMP, AIR (L), (M), (H) (2 HITS), LAND, ST. (M), (S), SUPER JUMP, AIR (M), (M), (H), (S), LAND, ⇩⇙⇦ + ATK ATK OTG

Notes	Damage
	422,200 damage, 42% meter loss

⇨⇘⇩⇙⇦ + (H), ⇩⇙⇦ + ATK ATK OTG

Notes	Damage
Timing here is tight; get the half circle motion started right before Houten Geki ends	357,00 damage, 81% meter loss

CR. (L), (M), (H), ⇨ + (H) CANCEL ⇨⇩⇘ + (H), AIR (H) (3 HITS), LAND, ST. (M), (S), SUPER JUMP, AIR (M), (M), (H) (3 HITS), (S), LAND, ⇩⇙⇦ + ATK ATK OTG

Notes	Damage
Corner required	558,400 damage, 20% meter loss

MORRIGAN

"TRUST ME, I'M NOT AS DELICATE AS I MIGHT LOOK. I MIGHT BE THE ONE WHO ENDS UP BREAKING YOU IN HALF."

Bio

REAL NAME

Morrigan Aensland

OCCUPATION

Head of the Aensland House

ABILITIES

The large wings on her back can transform into tools, such as a jet booster, large sickle, drill, etc., as needed. She is also able to drain her opponent's energy, and create clones of herself.

WEAPONS

In addition to powerful magic, she can also utilize her wings, which are comprised of a collection of bats.

PROFILE

She is a succubus, a demonic creature able to seduce men. She is well-known for her voluptuous figure and her titillating clothing. Although she is the head of the Aensland House, one of the three major houses of the demon world, she often abandons her dull duties to go look for excitement.

FIRST APPEARANCE

Darkstalkers (1994)

POWER GRID

3	INTELLIGENCE
2	STRENGTH
3	SPEED
4	STAMINA
6	ENERGY PROJECTION
4	FIGHTING ABILITY

*This is biographical, and does not represent an evaluation of the in-game combat potential of this hero.

ALTERNATE COSTUMES

Overview

Vitality	950,000
Chain Combo Archetype	Hunter Series

X-Factor Boost	Damage	Speed
Level 1 (3 teammates remaining)	120%	120%
Level 2 (2 teammates remaining)	137.5%	132.5%
Level 3 (1 teammate remaining)	155%	145%

Morrigan is an unusual, high-execution character, not because she has exacting combos like Dante or C. Viper, but because merely moving around with her properly takes some getting used to. Morrigan's purpose is to attack her opponent from the air at mid range. This goal is not-so-subtly forced upon her by design:

- She lacks a conventional dash, and she instead rockets forward or backward off the ground if you input a ground dash command. There's no such thing as dash-in crouching Ⓛ for Morrigan! (See Advanced Tactics for her closest equivalent)
- She has three different types of airdashes: a lateral airdash of variable duration (release the input to end the airdash; continue holding the input to rocket all the way to one side or the other) and "parabola" airdashes both upward and downward
- Morrigan has a unique version of flight: unlike any other character, you can use the activation and deactivation of flight to cancel special moves when playing Morrigan!
- In addition to all her options for air mobility, Morrigan is equipped with fantastic aerial attacks for both a direct attack and cross-up antics

So, how does a Morrigan player go about assailing the opposition from up above?

- Using Soul Fists and air Soul Fists as a baseline to keep adversaries away and provoke reactions, and to set up positioning and provide cover for Morrigan's direct attacks
- Following up assists and fly-canceled Soul Fists with airdash tricks and air attacks
- Mixing in low attacks, low-hitting assists, and Vector Drain grabs where possible to give Morrigan's constant overhead threat more teeth
- When a hyper meter surplus is available, keeping Astral Vision active to double up Morrigan's attacks and projectiles

Morrigan also serves the seemingly mutually exclusive roles of both hyper meter battery and hyper meter user, at kind of the same time. Morrigan works as a battery because:

- Morrigan—γ is her recommended assist type. This meter-building assist is significantly faster than Amaterasu's or Frank West's; calling Morrigan assist allows her teammates to build hyper meter with very little effort, since all you have to worry about is keeping Morrigan safe or calling her where she's unlikely to be hit
- Her new ⬇ ⬊ ➡ + Ⓢ Soul Drain fireball siphons hyper meter bar away from the target, with double the potential meter payoff during Astral Vision
- You can extend Morrigan's combos for some time, building decent hyper meter if you hold off on using Morrigan's own hyper combos

However, you can easily make Morrigan use up any and all of the hyper meter she happens to build for a team; she is much more effective as a point character if you are willing to spend meter. Her hyper combos all have useful applications both for momentum and combos, but the price of admission is steep. Since Morrigan can eat meter as readily as she can produce it, and since picking her almost certainly means giving up a conventional assist, Morrigan teams work best when they are built with her in mind rather than just dropping her next to two other characters.

TUNING SINCE ORIGINAL MVC3

Unlike most flight characters, Morrigan's flight is actually improved. Faster flight startup leads to faster overheads, new and easier links after flight, and quicker flight-canceled specials, while slightly increased flight duration allows Morrigan to hover in the air with airdashes and Soul Fists just a tad longer. These changes only pour more cement on Morrigan's unique flight foundation. The addition of Soul Drain, a meter-draining version of Soul Fist, also adds more depth to Morrigan's frequent de facto role of battery.

Vector Drain now causes a longer hard knockdown, which allows for Morrigan to OTG by herself with immediate Shadow Servant. This is a significant upgrade from original *MvC3*, where she was reliant either on assists or crossover combinations as Morrigan—α to score damage off her unbreakable throw.

Darkness Illusion and Finishing Shower are now counted just like other special moves while Morrigan is airborne, so it is now impossible for her to loop Shadow Blade to hyper combo repeatedly in corner air combos.

- New move: Soul Drain ⬇ ⬊ ➡ + Ⓢ
- Vector Drain command throw and normal throws cause longer hard knockdown
- Soul Fist damage and hitstun increased
- Priority increased on air Ⓗ and air Ⓢ
- Longer flight duration (111 frames, from 106 frames)
- Faster flight startup (11 frames, from 15 frames)
- Finishing Shower missiles travel faster, Finishing Shower can be mashed for additional hits
- Finishing Shower and Darkness Illusion now subject to three special moves per airborne period restriction

Attack Set

Standing Basic Attacks

Screen	Command	Hits	Damage	Meter Gain	Startup	Active	Recovery	Advantage on Hit	Advantage if Guarded	Notes
1	Standing L	1	40,000	320	4	3	10	0	-2	Low attack
2	Standing M	1	55,000	440	8	4	13	+1	-1	—
3	Standing H	4	79,500	800	10	2(1)2(1)2(1)3	9	+11	+9	—

Crouching Basic Attacks

Screen	Command	Hits	Damage	Meter Gain	Startup	Active	Recovery	Advantage on Hit	Advantage if Guarded	Notes
1	Crouching L	2	52,500	480	4	2(3)2	10	0	-2	Chains into crouching L
2	Crouching M	1	53,000	424	8	4	16	-2	-4	Low attack
3	Crouching H	1	60,000	480	9	5	23	—	-7	Low attack, knocks down

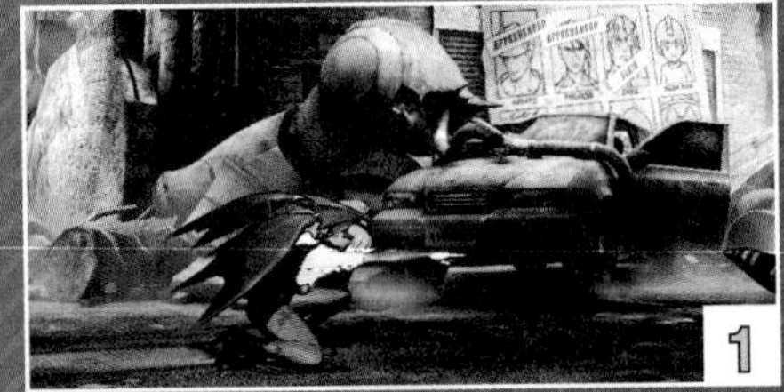

Ground Special Attack—Launcher

Screen	Command	Hits	Damage	Meter Gain	Startup	Active	Recovery	Advantage on Hit	Advantage if Guarded	Notes
1	S (while standing or crouching)	1	80,000	640	8	4	29	—	-12	Launcher, not special- or hyper combo-cancelable

Air Basic Attacks

Screen	Command	Hits	Damage	Meter Gain	Startup	Active	Recovery	Advantage on Hit	Advantage if Guarded	Notes
1	Air L	1	40,000	320	4	13	10	+6	+5	Overhead attack
2	Air M	1	55,000	440	7	4	26	+12	+10	Overhead attack
3	Air H	1	70,000	560	10	8	20	+14	+12	Overhead attack

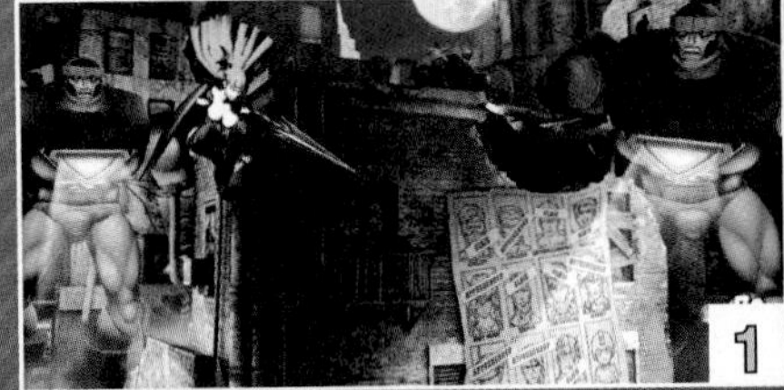

Air Special Attacks—Flying Screen and Air Exchange

Air Ⓢ causes a hard knockdown when used in a launcher combo (this is sometimes called flying screen). When used outside of a launcher combo, air Ⓢ behaves mostly like another basic attack. Air exchange attacks, performed by inputting a direction plus Ⓢ, are only possible during a launcher combo. Exchange hits initiate team aerial combos by tagging in the next available character to continue the air combo.

Screen	Command	Hits	Damage	Meter Gain	Startup	Active	Recovery	Advantage on hit	Advantage if Guarded	Notes
1	Air Ⓢ	3	89,900	840	5	23	18	+8	+6	Causes hard knockdown if used in launcher combo
2	*Air⇧ + Ⓢ (during launcher combo)*	1	55,000	440	11	5	Until grounded	—	—	Tags in next available ally while lofting opponent upward
3	Air⇨ or⇦ + Ⓢ (during launcher combo)	1	55,000	440	7	4	Until grounded	—	—	Tags in next available ally while causing wall bounce, erases 1 hyper meter bar from foe
4	Air⇩ + Ⓢ (during launcher combo)	1	55,000	440 + 10,000	10	8	Until grounded	—	—	Tags in next available ally while causing ground bounce, generates 1 hyper meter bar

1

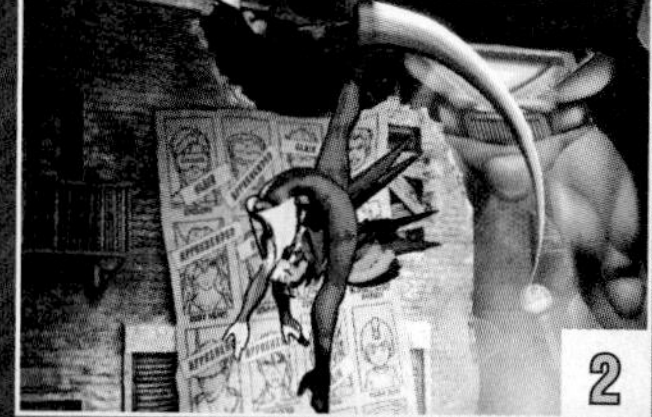
2

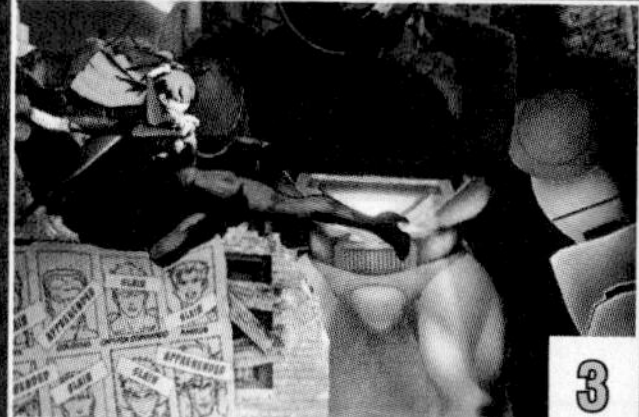
3

4

Command Attacks

Command attacks resemble basic attacks but have different chaining and canceling properties. It's usually possible to chain *into* a command attack from basic attacks, but most command attacks cannot be chained from or canceled themselves.

Screen	Name	Command	Hits	Damage	Meter Gain	Startup	Active	Recovery	Advantage on Hit	Advantage if Guarded	Notes
1	Splash Libido	⇨ + Ⓜ	1	70,000	560	12	6	22	+5	+3	Staggers opponent on counterhit
2	Deep Crescendo	⇨ + Ⓗ	1	70,000	560	11	5	29	-13	-13	Jump-cancelable, knocks down

1

2

Throws

Throws are for snagging passive or blocking opponents. Since throws are active so quickly, you can also use them to preemptively toss opposing characters out of their offense. Combos are usually possible after throws, one way or another.

Screen	Command	Hits	Damage	Meter Gain	Startup	Active	Notes
1	⇨ + Ⓗ (ground)	1	80,000	800	1	1	Hard knockdown
	⇦ + Ⓗ (ground)	1	80,000	800	1	1	Hard knockdown
2	⇨ + Ⓗ (air)	1	80,000	800	1	1	Hard knockdown
	⇦ + Ⓗ (air)	1	80,000	800	1	1	Hard knockdown

1

2

As a Partner—Crossover Assists

Screen	Type	P1+P2 Crossover Combination Hyper Combo	Description	Hits	Damage	Meter Gain	Startup	Active	Recovery (this crossover assist)	Recovery (other partner)	Notes
1	Morrigan—α	Shadow Servant	Shadow Blade H	5	102,300	100,000	27	15	132	102	Knocks down
2	Morrigan—β	Finishing Shower	Soul Fist L	1	70,000	560	39	—	128	98	Projectile has 5 low priority durability points
3	Morrigan—γ	Finishing Shower	Dark Harmonizer	—	—	3000	25	—	110	80	Fills hyper meter by 3000 points

1

2

3

Most "uppercut" type assists are not quite what they were in *MvC2*; assists are usually not a critical defensive measure (in fact, calling assists on defense is a great way to lose two characters at once if you don't block flawlessly). Morrigan—α is no different: while it might perhaps be used against someone airborne and above your point character or in particular combos, it doesn't really fill a vital niche on its own. It grants Shadow Servant in crossover combinations, which was important in original *MvC3* since it allowed for team combos after Vector Drain. Now, since the hyper combo version of Shadow Servant can do that on its own, that use for this assist has disappeared. Still, Morrigan—α remains somewhat noteworthy as one of the few invincible crossover counters. The first four active frames of the uppercut are invincible when you counter Morrigan in! If your challenger is close enough and vulnerable during those frames, they *will* be hit and carried into the sky with Shadow Blade. As with normal Shadow Blade, you can cancel the counter version into either flight (whether to go for an air combo on hit, or make Morrigan safer if the counter whiffs), or into Finishing Shower or Darkness Illusion for a hyper combo finisher.

Morrigan—β fires a Soul Fist projectile; you can use this similarly to other projectile assists, but the relatively low durability means that most beam and zoning characters can brush Soul Fist aside without much effort.

In the end, it's easy to recommend Morrigan—γ, one of only three meter-building assists in *UMvC3*. Amaterasu and Frank West also have assists that build up the hyper meter, but those meter assists are slower and consequently less safe than Morrigan's (during a meter assist the character just jumps out, poses, and then they leave; the shorter this takes, the better, obviously). Also, both Amaterasu and Frank West have *other* assists that are probably more useful to their team, whereas Morrigan's other assists are underwhelming anyway, and having the fastest meter assist is an irreplaceable, exclusive trait.

Snap Back

Screen	Command	Hits	Damage	Meter Gain	Startup	Active	Recovery	Advantage on Hit	Advantage if Guarded
1	↓↘→ + P1 or P2	1	50,000	500 - (-1 hyper meter bar)	2	6	26	—	-11

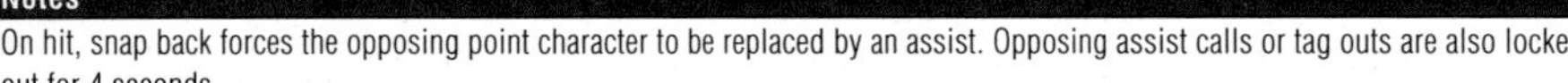

Notes

On hit, snap back forces the opposing point character to be replaced by an assist. Opposing assist calls or tag outs are also locked out for 4 seconds

1

Special Moves

Screen	Name	Command	Hits	Damage	Meter Gain	Startup	Active	Recovery	Advantage on Hit	Advantage if Guarded	Notes
1	Flight	↓↙← + S	—	—	—	11	—	1	—	—	Activates flight mode for 111 frames, may cancel any special move into flight
2, 3	Soul Fist	↓↘→ + ATK	1	70,000	680	15	—	36	-14	-16	Projectile has 5 low priority durability points
4	Air Soul Fist L	(in air) ↓↘→ + L	1	70,000	680	10	—	42	-6	—	Projectile has 5 low priority durability points
	Air Soul Fist M	(in air) ↓↘→ + M	1	70,000	680	10	—	45	-9	—	Projectile has 5 low priority durability points
5	Air Soul Fist H	(in air) ↓↘→ + H	1	70,000	680	10	—	48	-5	—	Projectile has 5 low priority durability points
6	Soul Drain (in air OK)	↓↘→ + S	1	85,000	3000	26	—	34	-12	-14	Projectile has 5 low priority durability points, steals 30% (3000 points) of meter from adversary
7	Shadow Blade L (in air OK)	→↓↘ + L	1	80,000	640	3	8	32/Until grounded, 11 frames ground recovery	-4	-19	Knocks down
	Shadow Blade M (in air OK)	→↓↘ + M	3	94,800	840	3	7	48/Until grounded, 11 frames ground recovery	-15	-30	Knocks down
	Shadow Blade H (in air OK)	→↓↘ + H	5	114,500	1120	3	15	50/Until grounded, 11 frames ground recovery	-21	-36	Knocks down

Special Moves continued

Screen	Name	Command	Hits	Damage	Meter Gain	Startup	Active	Recovery	Advantage on Hit	Advantage if Guarded	Notes
8	Vector Drain L	→↘↓↙← + Ⓛ	1	120,000	1200	5	2	20	—	—	Throw, hard knockdown
	Vector Drain M	→↘↓↙← + Ⓜ	1	150,000	1200	3	2	22	—	—	Throw, hard knockdown
	Vector Drain H	→↘↓↙← + Ⓗ	1	170,000	1200	1	2	24	—	—	Throw, hard knockdown

1

Flight: Lots of characters can fly, but for Morrigan, it's different. Flight is Morrigan's defining special move because Morrigan is the only fighting game character who can cancel the recovery of her SPECIAL MOVES with flight! Just as other flight-capable characters use flight activation (and flight deactivation, called "unfly") to interrupt basic attacks, so does Morrigan... but you can also fly cancel Soul Fists, Shadow Blades, and even Vector Drain grab attempts! When you fly cancel a special move, the 11 frame startup period for flight becomes, in effect, the previous special's recovery period. When you unfly cancel an air special, there is only 1 frame of recovery! (This ends up applying to just air Soul Fist and air Soul Drain; Shadow Blade is not unfly-cancelable, and Vector Drain can't be performed in midair.)

Other characters use flight for air combos, or for mobility, or to use more than three specials per jump—kind of modular tactics within their strategy, which don't trickle over into other things they do. But for Morrigan, flight essentially enables her whole gameplan by enhancing the safety and usefulness of all her specials. Without fly cancels, she's underwhelming, but with fly cancels, she's oddly the closest thing to *MvC2* Sentinel this game has—a character who requires more inputs just to transition between moves than they do to actually attack.

Fly canceling specials allows Morrigan to keep up in projectile output where she otherwise wouldn't; allows her to fire Soul Fists, and then craftily maneuver her in behind them; allows her to use Shadow Blade, and fly cancel to avoid hideous punishment on whiff or block; and allows her to cancel the whiff recovery of Vector Drain if the command grab fails. This is on top of the obvious added combo potential.

Since you can activate and deactivate flight once each per airborne period, that gives you two possible flight cancels each time Morrigan leaves the ground. For example, you can attempt Shadow Blade, confirm whether it misses the target, cancel into flight to avoid Shadow Blade's horrific recovery period, then shoot air Soul Fist and unfly cancel it so Morrigan falls safely back to the ground—and on Morrigan's way down, you still have her airdash left, in this example. Flight activation counts as a special move itself, so you can't fly if you've already used up three specials in a jumping period.

2

3

Soul Fist: Soul Fist is a standard low-priority, middling-durability projectile. It has the durability points of a fireball like Ryu's or Akuma's, and so Soul Fist clashes with those types of projectiles but usually loses out to beams. Soul Fist L and M travel horizontally, while Soul Fist H is fired at an up-forward angle. Soul Fist L is generally more useful than Soul Fist M since the projectile is slower and therefore stays on screen as a threat to the opposing character for a longer period of time.

The slow speed of Soul Fist L gives you time to have Morrigan dash forward, or have her jump and airdash forward behind the cover of the projectile. Call an assist along the way to prolong your offensive momentum. Against foes who can't overpower individual Soul Fists, Soul Fist L can be used repeatedly to control ground level; your opposition is forced to take to the air to go over the sea of Soul Fists. Use Soul Fist H and tiger knee air Soul Fist H as counterpoints to also cut off your adversary's routes through the air. Soul Fist H is also great for firing back at rivals who try to throw projectiles down from up above.

You can cancel Soul Fist's recovery by activating flight. This isn't worth doing if your plan is to Soul Fist L over and over, or if you want to follow Soul Fist L with an airdash (Morrigan isn't above the minimum height requirement to airdash after flying from the ground). What it is useful for is to transition to an aerial plan, or to fire air Soul Fist H. Unfly and land after Soul Fist H, and you're ready to fire Soul Fist L again.

4

5

Air Soul Fist: In a vacuum, air Soul Fist is more useful than ground Soul Fist, but the two versions of the projectile also complement each other. Firing down at your opposition is a more appealing proposition than trying to fight a ground war against beam characters. Air Soul Fist is also faster to fire than ground Soul Fist by 5 frames (air Soul Fist's recovery period is slightly longer, but this can be obviated by fly canceling). Shooting air Soul Fist H just off the ground with a tiger knee motion of ↓↘→↗ + Ⓗ is actually quicker to both fire and recover than Soul Fist L/M on the ground, although most characters can crouch under tiger knee air Soul Fist H even if it's performed as low as possible. Still, repeating tiger knee air Soul Fist H is an excellent way to control normal jump height, if you also call an assist to cover the ground. If you're worried about foes dashing under it, you can fly cancel air Soul Fist H and follow up with Soul Fist L or Soul Drain to fire a projectile at an angle into your opponent's path.

Coupled with Morrigan's unusual airdashes, which allow her to either rocket all the way to the side of a stage or swoop up or down in great parabolic arcs, fly-canceled air Soul Fist allows you to reposition her wherever you like on the stage, while covering the new territory. Fly-canceling and airdashing just after air Soul Fist also leads to chances to cross your competitor up without the use of an assist, or opportunities to extend air combos.

Air Soul Fist L and M fire at a 45-degree angle down-forward; air Soul Fist H fires straight across the screen. Morrigan is one of very few characters who possesses the option to fire from super jump height both laterally and downward with a projectile.

6

Soul Drain: This is Morrigan's new hyper meter-draining fireball. The presence of Soul Drain gives Morrigan another tool with which to contribute as a team battery (the role for which Morrigan—γ was previously part and parcel). However, because of its slow startup, Soul Drain is a supplemental projectile rather than a first option. The frantic pace of *UMvC3* is simply too quick for Soul Drain to be a primary tool.

Mix it in occasionally when firing fly-canceled Soul Fists, whether from the ground or the air. Launch Soul Fist first, then fly/unfly cancel and fire Soul Drain. The first Soul Fist in this example serves to cover Morrigan's Soul Drain startup. After releasing Soul Drain, you can treat it just like Soul Fist L, using the slow travel speed to Morrigan's advantage by following behind it, or by firing Soul Fist M to catch up with it.

On contact, Soul Drain sucks away nearly a third of a hyper meter bar from the competitor, adding it to Morrigan's team. Soul Drain doesn't have to hit the opposing point character—the effect still occurs if the fireball strikes an assist! That's actually a lot more likely during fireball skirmishes, since point characters can easily block the slow-moving projectile, especially if they recognize it is Soul Drain rather than Soul Fist (apart from Morrigan's extra-lengthy windup to throw the projectile, there is no other cue that Soul Fist L and Soul Drain are different).

During Astral Vision, Morrigan's shadow copies any of Morrigan's non-hyper combo actions, including Soul Drain. If you put a pair of fly-canceled Soul Drains out there, so will the shadow, and if your rival makes a mistake and runs into three or four of the projectiles, or if they call an assist who eats them, Astral Vision has paid for itself or more, while sapping a bar from your foe!

Despite its sluggish speed, you can combo into Soul Drain off of → + Ⓜ Splash Libido, though Morrigan must be closer to her foe than the max range of the move. It's also possible to THC into Astral Vision from certain other hyper combos and continue a combo starting with a double Soul Drain; as an example, you can THC from Spencer's Bionic Lancer to Astral Vision and fire Soul Drain to gain a bunch of meter back mid-THC.

7

Shadow Blade: Morrigan's uppercut lacks invincibility, so its primary use is for combo extension—finish air combos with Shadow Blade M canceled into Finishing Shower for solid damage anywhere. If you don't have hyper meter to spend, you can also combo into Shadow Blade, activate flight to cancel it, then immediately link another Shadow Blade or even flying basic attacks if your target is in the right position.

You can cancel Shadow Blade with flight activation, but it cannot be unfly canceled. If you perform Shadow Blade, fly, then perform Shadow Blade again, there's no way out of falling to the ground helplessly. Don't perform Shadow Blade during flight outside of combos.

Although it lacks invincibility, Shadow Blade travels very quickly, so it can be useful as an anti-air against targets up above; if it misses or if your attacker guards, you can fly cancel it to avoid the recovery period.

8

Vector Drain: Morrigan's command grab now leaves her foe in a hard knockdown state for slightly longer, allowing you to OTG with her Shadow Servant hyper combo. This is a significant improvement from original *MvC3*, where she generally had to have Morrigan—α as her assist type in order to follow throws with a crossover combination OTG. Yuck! Now you can pick Morrigan—γ like you wanted to anyway, and not have to worry about conforming yet another aspect of the team around Morrigan's prerequisites.

Vector Drain H is active in only 1 frame, but it has the shortest reach. Vector Drain L is slow by comparison, at 5 frames until the grab, but it has much more range. Still, Vector Drain H still out-reaches a regular throw, and it makes a great defensive option... if you block any enemy action that leaves them at -1 or worse, which is a considerably long list of things, you can simply Vector Drain H as soon as possible to retaliate. Tack on Shadow Servant if you like—this makes an ideal opening to use to THC to another character.

If the grab misses, you can cancel the whiff animation into flight! Fly canceling Morrigan's whiffed command throw into flight is even better now that flight has faster startup—see the Advanced Tactics section for more details.

Hyper Combos

Screen	Name	Command	Hits	Damage	Startup	Active	Recovery	Advantage on Hit	Advantage if Guarded	Notes
1	Finishing Shower (in air OK)	↓↘→ + ATK ATK	35~70	251,900~302,600	18+2	69	21	+13	+14	Missiles can be aimed up or down using the controller, each projectile has 1 high priority durability point, can be mashed for additional hits
2	Astral Vision	↓↓ + ATK ATK	—	—	10+6	—	13	—	—	Creates an Astral Vision that lasts for 590 frames, using a hyper combo ends Astral Vision
3	Shadow Servant	→↓↘ + ATK ATK	5	271,300	10+10	44	21	—	-45	Invincible from frames 1-29, OTG-capable, knocks down, each projectile has 5 high priority durability points
4	Darkness Illusion (Level 3 Hyper Combo, in air OK)	↓↙← + ATK ATK	33-35	405,000	16+0	79	Until grounded	—	-21	Invincible from frames 1-27, hard knockdown

1

Finishing Shower: Morrigan unleashes a hail of missiles that you can direct up or down by holding the desired direction. ATK can be mashed during the hyper combo to generate more missiles. For a reliable finisher to air combos, cancel Shadow Blade M into Finishing Shower, then hold ↑ and mash ATK. Morrigan recovers while the missiles are still on screen, so in air combos in the corner, you can actually continue hitting your adversary right after Finishing Shower. (The simplest follow-up is to just use air S for a hard knockdown, or direction + S to start a TAC—that's right, in the corner, you can score an air exchange *after* Morrigan's full air combo bread and butter!) Shadow Blade CANCEL Finishing Shower can no longer be repeated several times in the same corner air combo, since Finishing Shower now counts against the special actions available per jump.

Although Finishing Shower isn't anywhere near as fast as conventional beam hyper combos like Ryu's Shinkuu Hadoken or Dormammu's Chaotic Flame, it's still fast enough to use to regain control of a match or to punish assists. Because there are so many missiles, and because you can direct them after release, it's almost impossible for the opposing character to avoid Finishing Shower unless they teleport behind Morrigan right when it begins.

2

Astral Vision: Morrigan calls forth a shadowy copy of herself from the ether. After activation, this shadow stands on the OTHER side of the opponent, equidistant from the real Morrigan. It is perhaps the purest power-up hyper state: Morrigan can still build hyper meter, and the power-up state disappears if you tag Morrigan out or use one of her other hyper combos. Astral Vision is a statement that says the match will be all about Morrigan for the duration.

During Astral Vision, Morrigan's shadow duplicates any of her non-hyper actions. This even includes sequences like using fly cancels to throw double Soul Fists: Morrigan throws Soul Fists from one side, while the shadow throws Soul Fists from the other. The same is even true of Soul Drain projectiles, making it possible for Astral Vision to do much more than pay for itself if you can nail your competitor with three or more Soul Drains before the timer expires. Naturally, having a shadow throwing Soul Drains from the other side of the opposing character simultaneously makes the slow meter-draining projectile much more dangerous.

Note that characters have asymmetrical hitboxes—they are not necessarily vulnerable in the same proportions at their front as they are to their back. When attacking at close range with Astral Vision, this allows combos to be sustained that are not otherwise possible, since Morrigan's shadow hits the target at rare angles from behind. But it can also have unexpected effects, like causing the real Morrigan to miss a juggle because her double popped the enemy out of place.

3

Shadow Servant: This hyper combo serves as Morrigan's general-purpose reversal and OTG. It is not safe from retaliation if guarded, but Morrigan is invincible for the first whopping 29 frames, and most characters end up getting pushed too far back to punish Morrigan. The invincibility probably gives Shadow Servant its most important function: serving as Morrigan's "panic button."

Shadow Servant is also invaluable for its ability to OTG after any of Morrigan's normal throws, whether on the ground or in the air, or after her Vector Drain command grab. You can also use it to OTG after air combos at midscreen, or right after nailing your adversary with Darkness Illusion! Perform Shadow Servant as soon as possible in any of these circumstances.

Like Magneto's Magnetic Shockwave, Shadow Servant hits with columns that travel away from Morrigan (though they do not extend up to super jump height). This means that it's less effective when Morrigan is far away from a floored foe, or if the opposing character is in the corner. In the first case, several of the rising columns just whiff in front of the opposition before one finally OTGs them, and in the second case, the later stages of the hyper combo occur harmlessly off-screen.

4

Darkness Illusion: Morrigan's lv.3 hyper combo travels the full lateral length of the field, is possible on the ground or in the air, and is invincible for the first 27 frames. Although it has 16 frames of pre-freeze startup, it's instant afterward. On the ground, you can use it as a reversal on reaction to the screen freeze of virtually any opposing hyper combo, and in the air, it is easily inserted onto the end of combos.

Darkness Illusion causes a hard knockdown; if you feel like spending the meter, OTG with Shadow Servant immediately after the level 3!

If you miss with Darkness Illusion, Morrigan flies across the screen vulnerable for a long time. You can't THC away from lv.3 hyper combos, failed or not, but you CAN activate X-Factor off a failed lv.3.

Battle Plan

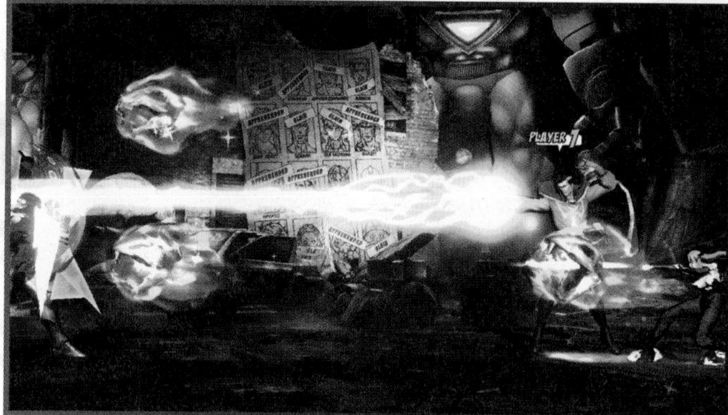

Soul Fists allow you to control the space in front of Morrigan; add in suitable assists and fly cancel tricks to enhance Soul Fist zoning.

Morrigan has dominant basic attacks for offense, but she lacks a ground dash, and her crouching (L) attack can be guarded standing. You'll run the risk of being extremely predictable if you don't set up some baseline expectations in your challenger, and you can't effectively threaten low in order to actually present real mix-ups without some semi-advanced tricks. Individually, Soul Fists seem underwhelming. But combine their slow speed with Morrigan's unique fly cancels and air mobility, and these projectiles underpin her efforts on both offense and defense.

Against opponents who simply aren't equipped to handle ranged threats, such as non-projectile characters or impatient players, you can fire Soul Fist L over and over. Soul Fist L (and Soul Drain, its meter-suctioning counterpart) travels very slowly, so you can put several of them on screen at once. If you can get a string of Soul Fists going, you've asserted horizontal control at ground level.

With fly canceling of specials, the possibilities grow more interesting and flexible. You can increase vertical coverage along the ground by quickly performing Soul Fist L canceled into flight, then air Soul Fist H canceled with flight deactivation, or unfly. The quicker air Soul Fist H will catch up to the slower Soul Fist L by the time they're approaching the other side of the screen, forming a sort of Soul Fist column. With some practice, you can perform this back-to-back repeatedly. Your Soul Fist wall forces opponents to super jump to get over the Soul Fist barrage. If they keep running into Soul Fists or they simply block, great—if it ain't broke, don't fix it. You are still controlling the match, eking out some chip damage, and building hyper meter in the process.

If you want to transition to offense, you can simply have Morrigan forward dash or jump and airdash right behind the cover of Soul Fist.

When Soul Fists from the ground are overmatched, take to the sky. Morrigan is even better at doubling up Soul Fists and using them as cover from up above.

UMvC3 has no shortage of characters and assists who pack projectiles and beams that can cut through Soul Fist without a problem, or at least prevent them from ever threatening the opposing point character. In these circumstances, you'll be forced to jump before going to work with Soul Fists. This is both very likely, given the kind of teams and characters who are popular, and perfectly acceptable to Morrigan, who is more at home in the air than on solid ground.

Get above your adversary from midscreen out or farther, then fire air Soul Fist L down at them. You can opt to simply repeat Soul Fist two more times, since Morrigan slowly drifts back down to the ground; this technique places three slow-moving fireballs in a lazy downward rain in front of where Morrigan lands. Attentive opposing players may use this as a cue to wavedash forward under both the projectiles and Morrigan herself, which puts her in a bad position during the descent.

So instead of just firing Soul Fist after Soul Fist, your default baseline should be to have Morrigan jump or super jump into the air, fire air Soul Fist L once or twice, then cancel Soul Fist recovery with flight activation. (If you normal jump or use Shadow Blade to take to the air, you'll have assists available later in the sequence, before Morrigan touches the ground again; otherwise, you'll have to call your assist before super jumping if you want it in play.) From here, Morrigan has a vibrant branching option tree for both aggressive play or keepaway. Depending on what her opponent's doing, Morrigan's proximity to them, and whether she's in a normal or super jump state during flight, you can choose to have her rush in or run at a whim.

Fly canceled Soul Fists provide essential cover for Morrigan's attacks.

Aggressive options after air Soul Fist L x1~2 CANCEL flight:

Immediate downward airdash, then go for air (S) as Morrigan draws close to her competitor; this is an overhead that hits her foe at roughly the same time or even just before Soul Fist. Air (S) automatically ends flight mode, leaving Morrigan right next to her rival on the ground. If air (S) and Soul Fist(s) hit the target, proceed to *Combo I* immediately

Immediate downward airdash, then do nothing so Morrigan completes the parabola dash and potentially ends up on the other side of the opposing character; in this case, Soul Fists and assists that haven't touched them yet become cross-ups! From the other side, you can simply have Morrigan fall from flight with air (S), or manually unfly with ⇩ ⇙ ⇦ + (S) and fall on the opposing character with air ⇨ + (H)

Immediate downward airdash, then manually input the flight command again to fall next to the opposing character. Start a chain with standing (L), a low attack that's active in 4 frames, immediately upon landing

Air Soul Fist M CANCEL unfly, immediate downward airdash. Same as any of the above, but appropriate from farther away; as with grounded Soul Fist L fly canceled to air Soul Fist H, this causes two Soul Fists of different speeds to more or less merge by the time they arrive at the target. Two projectiles make lovely cover for Morrigan to swoop in behind

Zoning options after air Soul Fist L x1~2 CANCEL flight:

Laterally airdash all the way to one side of the playing field or the other, as desired (if you cross over your rival, this changes the Soul Fist into a cross-up); whenever Morrigan arrives over your preferred landing zone, perform another Soul Fist L canceled with flight deactivation

Mix in Soul Drain shots. It's much more feasible to put a meter-stealing Soul Drain fireball out there if you safely released Soul Fist from an advantageous position just prior. This prevents the adversary's aggressive frontal assault from simply knocking Morrigan out of Soul Drain's lengthy startup; they'll have the first Soul Fist or two to contend with. Once you've safely put one Soul Drain on screen, you can treat it just like Soul Fist L and continue to repeat Soul Drains until your competitor gives you a reason to stop.

In addition to leaping to super jump height, you can also consider using Shadow Blade as a pseudo-jump that happens to hit on the way up—if your plan was to super jump and shoot Soul Fists at your foe anyway, you can get to super jump height without actually shifting the screen upward by performing Shadow Blade H, fly canceling at its apex, then firing Soul Fist L or H, as appropriate depending on the target's position. This Soul Fist can then be unfly canceled, leaving Morrigan free to airdash in behind the cover of the fireball or to toss another Soul Fist or Soul Drain. Meanwhile, although Morrigan achieves high altitude, she got there with a special move performed from the ground, so she's considered normal jumping—assists can be summoned!

The point of zoning with Soul Fists and of using Soul Fists as cover before airdash attacks is to give you a little margin for error. Running opponents through a Soul Fist gauntlet before you attack allows you to pick spots on your terms, rather than trying to force the issue too hard by going for airdash offense without establishing a presence.

When you do have your competitor on their heels, guarding Soul Fists or occupied by a beam or zoning assist, now is the time to attack aggressively. The downward parabola airdash usually works best for rushing; by canceling the airdash early with an attack, it's identical to a triangle jump, yet it works from an incredible distance away from the opposing character. When used a little bit later, just as Morrigan starts to swoop back upward, she'll only carry a little bit of that momentum into her attacks once you start your air chain, but it is still enough for her to hang in the air for one or two overhead attacks longer than perhaps your opponent expects. And if you wait all the way until Morrigan swoops upward, she's probably crossed clean over the target, creating interesting cross-up opportunities.

Morrigan airdashes off the ground instead of dashing conventionally; keep holding the dash input to continue dashing for longer. Her forward dash cannot be canceled with an attack for 15 frames; her backward dash cannot be canceled at all.

If you forward dash from close range, it has the same effect as an airdash, although it takes a little bit longer for Morrigan to act—she cannot guard or attack for the first 15 frames of her forward dash. Performing air Ⓛ or air Ⓢ as soon as possible leads to a 19 or 20 frame overhead. Flying from the ground is even faster: 11 frames of flight startup, for a 15 or 16 frame overhead. Very impressive, considering you can cancel into flight from blocked low attacks.

Morrigan has some of the best offensive basic attacks in the game, especially in the air. All of her Ⓛ attacks are active in 4 frames, and her incredibly fast air Ⓢ is only 1 frame slower than that. Air Ⓛ stays out for eons, active for 13 frames (hilariously long for an airborne light attack). Her air attacks are so fast, and the trajectory of some of her airdashes so shallow, that it's usually easy to perform two or three hit overhead chains when airdashing or jumping in toward an adversary, especially with air Ⓛ x2. This doesn't create much hitstun, though, so if you rush in with air Ⓛ, link standing Ⓛ into **Combo I** immediately upon landing. Morrigan's air attacks have excellent attack hitboxes, and Morrigan herself is usually balled up at the center of these attacks, much smaller herself than most combatants on screen.

Air Ⓗ can strike at very unusual angles.

Airdashing in with air Ⓜ or air Ⓗ works well also, especially with air Ⓗ; perform it with ⇨ + Ⓗ when airdashing in for the option select air throw potential, and try to aim this move just over the center of opposing characters. This is especially useful if you use an upward airdash to "leap" right on top of your foe. Depending on Morrigan's angle of descent and when you perform air Ⓗ, you can make it cross up (or not) very ambiguously. Jumping in with air Ⓜ or Ⓗ gives much more time than air Ⓛ to link upon Morrigan's landing, so start ground chains with crouching Ⓜ instead as long as you didn't have her jump in with air Ⓛ. This results in gentler damage scaling and hitstun decay in the following combo. If your competitor guards your aggressive airdash attack into ground chain, finish the chain with ⇨ + Ⓗ Deep Crescendo, which is jump- cancelable. After the jump cancel, you're in perfect position to have Morrigan airdash in again immediately for another overhead, or you can perform a lightning-quick empty triangle jump with air Ⓢ. Follow this with a ground guessing game to ratchet up your pressure (see the Advanced Tactics section).

If your opposition guards Morrigan's air attack and uses advancing guard to push her out, she won't be pushed back terribly far—you're close enough to have her super jump and airdash right back in, if you want to. You can also step forward and stick out ⇨ + Ⓜ Splash Libido to see if your opponent feels like getting counterhit by it. If she gets guarded and pushblocked during ground chains, Morrigan's momentum is usually stunted a little bit, unless you have an assist on the way out to keep your rival blocking, or unless the enemy pushblocked ⇨ + Ⓗ —in which case, you can simply jump cancel and get her right back in, as well.

When the tables are turned and the opposing player is dictating the pace against Morrigan, there are some answers that are specific to her. ⇨ + Ⓜ can interrupt anything an opponent does at ground level, or from a shallow air angle. There's always the temptation to use Shadow Servant if a challenger is getting in your face; the big invulnerability period at the beginning almost assures that anything they're doing, and any assist they're calling, gets stuffed and badly bruised. If you have a good partner in the next slot to THC to (ideally that partner will be safe whether Shadow Servant actually hits or not), you can make what seems like a "guess" end up being very lucrative. If your adversary is forcing you to guard attacks up close, be ready to go for Vector Drain H against gaps in their offense; any Vector Drain attempt can be option selected into flight activation and then Morrigan's air drill just by double-pressing Ⓢ right after finishing the Vector Drain command. If your foe is in range for Vector Drain, great; if Morrigan misses the grab, you barely have time to even perceive it, and a quick close-range follow-up overhead is built in. Otherwise, guard and use advancing guard effectively, and look for a gap during which you can super jump and airdash away, or at least backpedal with an instant backward airdash into air Ⓢ.

The use of Astral Vision makes Morrigan much more powerful, but just as with keeping Devil Trigger running for Dante or Sougenmu running with Zero, making this power-up hyper central to your strategy results in funneling most of your team's meter to Morrigan.

If Morrigan has free reign over the team's hyper meter, the free and easy use of Astral Vision makes her a much more dangerous character. Sure, you can't use hyper combos, but you won't need them to get solid damage, and Morrigan's offense is greatly improved—because her shadow attacks from point-blank behind the opposing character when Morrigan is at close range in front of them, their use of advancing guard will not be meaningful for several hits, as though you had just pinned with an assist like Chun-Li—γ. Since you're more or less assured a follow-up shot after the initial jump-in, you can virtually guarantee a hit *somewhere* by mixing up effectively between chains starting with standing Ⓛ and crouching Ⓜ, and impromptu flight cancels into immediate falling air Ⓢ. Having Morrigan's shadow active also makes Soul Fist and Soul Drain spam more effective—there is twice as much of it, after all. This is particularly hard to deal with for new characters falling in after their teammates are snapped or knocked out.

If the situation ever degrades to the point where Morrigan is all alone and X-Factor is still left, then there's no question about what to do: keep Astral Vision up and running, and go after the remaining enemy characters from hell to breakfast, succubus-style. Soul Fist projectiles are much faster during X-Factor, and Soul Drains becomes almost as fast as stock Soul Fists.

COMBO USAGE

I. CR. Ⓜ, Ⓗ, → + Ⓗ CANCEL⇒ FORWARD JUMP, AIR Ⓜ, Ⓜ, Ⓗ CANCEL⇒ ↓ ↘ → + Ⓗ CANCEL⇒ ↓ ↙ ← + Ⓢ, FORWARD AIRDASH, AIR Ⓗ, Ⓢ, LAND, CR. Ⓗ, Ⓢ CANCEL⇒ VERTICAL SUPER JUMP, AIR Ⓜ, Ⓜ, Ⓗ CANCEL⇒ → ↓ ↘ + Ⓜ CANCEL⇒ {↓ ↘ → + ATK ATK (MASH ATK, HOLD ↑ AFTER MISSILES BEGIN TO HIT)} OR {↓ ↙ ← + ATK ATK, LAND, → ↓ ↘ + ATK ATK OTG}

607,700~952,400 damage, 19%~319% meter loss

This is a flexible combo with variable endings. Crouching Ⓜ, Ⓗ, → + Ⓗ is the opening that keeps damage scaling to a minimum. It's most appropriate after airdashing in with air Ⓗ or air Ⓜ, which both give you plenty of time to have Morrigan land and link crouching Ⓜ. If she jumps in with air Ⓛ, you'll need to land her and use a chain of standing Ⓛ, Ⓜ, crouching Ⓜ, Ⓗ, → + Ⓗ. This increases meter gain but lowers overall damage. After jump canceling → + Ⓗ and performing air Ⓜ, Ⓜ, Ⓗ CANCEL⇒ ↓ ↘ → + Ⓗ, cancel Soul Fist into flight and immediately airdash forward. Attack with air Ⓗ, Ⓢ during the airdash as fast as possible. Once Morrigan lands, perform crouching Ⓗ once the opponent has drifted down next to Morrigan (but before they actually hit the dirt).

When the opening chain is guarded, cancel → + Ⓗ into a jump and airdash down toward your competitor to take another shot at cracking their shell, or upward dash over them while calling an assist. If you're looking for a more flexible opening, start this combo with crouching Ⓛ, which is a two-hit attack that's easy to verify and leaves Morrigan directly next to the target if guarded. Use this as an opportunity to go for Vector Drain and → + Ⓜ setups. The reason crouching Ⓛ isn't recommended as a general opener is that using it adversely affects damage scaling in combos. The same is true for air Ⓢ, but these attacks are still too powerful not to use sometimes.

For any air combo that ends in Finishing Shower in the corner, you should be able to tack on at least another hit or two—air Ⓢ for a hard knockdown, or direction + Ⓢ to start a TAC.

II. CR. Ⓜ, Ⓗ, → + Ⓗ CANCEL⇒ FORWARD JUMP, AIR Ⓜ, Ⓜ, Ⓗ CANCEL⇒ ↓ ↘ → + Ⓗ CANCEL⇒ ↓ ↙ ← + Ⓢ, FORWARD AIRDASH, AIR Ⓗ, Ⓢ, LAND, CR. Ⓗ, → + Ⓗ CANCEL⇒ FORWARD JUMP, AIR Ⓜ, Ⓜ, Ⓗ, Ⓢ, LAND, Ⓢ CANCEL⇒ VERTICAL SUPER JUMP, AIR Ⓜ, Ⓜ, Ⓗ CANCEL⇒ → ↓ ↘ + Ⓜ CANCEL⇒ {↓ ↘ → + ATK ATK (MASH ATK, HOLD ↑ AFTER MISSILES BEGIN TO HIT)} OR {↓ ↙ ← + ATK ATK, LAND, → ↓ ↘ + ATK ATK OTG}

614,700~975,100 damage, 6% meter gain or 294% meter loss (or self sufficient for Finishing Shower ender)

This low-hitting combo only deals slightly more damage than **Combo I**, but it builds enough meter to be self-sufficient for the Finishing Shower ender. However, because of the additional re-jump loop, this combo cannot be done with a jump attack preceding it. Use it whenever you go for a raw low, which isn't preempted by a jump-in.

III. (AGAINST AIRBORNE OPPONENT) FORWARD JUMP, AIR Ⓜ, Ⓜ, Ⓗ CANCEL⇒ ↓ ↘ → + Ⓗ CANCEL⇒ ↓ ↙ ← + Ⓢ, FORWARD AIRDASH, Ⓗ, Ⓢ, LAND, CR. Ⓗ, → + Ⓗ CANCEL⇒ FORWARD JUMP, AIR Ⓜ, Ⓜ, Ⓗ, Ⓢ, LAND, Ⓢ CANCEL⇒ VERTICAL SUPER JUMP, AIR Ⓜ, Ⓜ, Ⓗ CANCEL⇒ → ↓ ↘ + Ⓜ CANCEL⇒ ↓ ↘ → + ATK ATK (MASH ATK, HOLD ↑ AFTER MISSILES BEGIN TO HIT)

585,800 damage, 11% meter loss

This anti-air combo uses elements of **Combo II.** Leaping upward to meet encroaching airborne adversaries can be very effective if you can manage to score an air throw or start a full combo from low altitude. If air Ⓜ, Ⓜ, Ⓗ is guarded, chain into air Ⓢ to safely bring the opposing character to the ground behind frame advantage. You may be in position here to go for Vector Drain, or use → + Ⓜ Splash Libido to fish for a counterhit stagger (see **Combo**..., uh, see the next combo).

IV. COUNTERHIT → + Ⓜ, FORWARD DASH, AIR Ⓜ, Ⓗ, LAND, CR. Ⓜ, Ⓗ, → + Ⓗ CANCEL⇒ FORWARD JUMP, AIR Ⓜ, Ⓜ, Ⓗ CANCEL⇒ ↓ ↘ → + Ⓗ CANCEL⇒ ↓ ↙ ← + Ⓢ, FORWARD AIRDASH, Ⓗ, Ⓢ, LAND, Ⓢ CANCEL⇒ VERTICAL SUPER JUMP, AIR Ⓜ, Ⓜ, Ⓗ CANCEL⇒ → ↓ ↘ + Ⓜ CANCEL⇒ {↓ ↘ → + ATK ATK (MASH ATK, HOLD ↑ AFTER MISSILES BEGIN TO HIT)} OR {↓ ↙ ← + ATK ATK, LAND, → ↓ ↘ + ATK ATK OTG}

618,500~975,600 damage, 4~304% meter loss

Use → + Ⓜ to preemptively stop enemy attacks when you're at a frame advantage, such as after your rival guards your assist or jump-in attack. This goes hand-in-hand with her Vector Drain command throw, which is threatening enough to warrant an opponent's attempt to throw or attack it at close ranges. The needles Morrigan summons have a giant area of effect, and they act as an invulnerable shield to frontal attacks. This also means Splash Libido is good for preemptively stopping mid range ground attacks. → + Ⓜ causes a heavy stagger when it counterhits an incoming move, leaving you enough time to link into a forward dashing air Ⓜ, Ⓗ. It also leaves you at a frame advantage when guarded, so have no fear when using it.

COMBO USAGE CONT.

V. CR. M, H, → + H CANCEL ⇨ FORWARD JUMP, AIR M, M, H CANCEL ⇨ ↓ ↘ → + H [X-FACTOR], FORWARD AIRDASH, H, S, LAND, CR. H, → + H CANCEL ⇨ FORWARD JUMP, AIR M, M, H, S, LAND, S CANCEL ⇨ VERTICAL SUPER JUMP, AIR M, M, H CANCEL ⇨ → ↓ ↘ + M CANCEL ⇨ ↓ ↘ → + ATK ATK (MASH ATK, HOLD ↑)

877,700~1,025,200 damage, 15~34% meter gain

A verifiable X-Factor combo that's similar to **Combo II**. X-Factor's speed enhancement means this combo works even after a jump-in opener, unlike **Combo II**. Cancel air ↓ ↘ → + H into X-Factor just as you would normally cancel into flight.

VI. FRONT OR BACK AIR THROW OR → ↘ ↓ ↙ ← + ATK, → ↓ ↘ + ATK ATK [X-FACTOR], VERTICAL JUMP, FORWARD AIRDASH (TRAVEL TO THE ENEMY), AIR S, LAND, CR. H, → + H CANCEL ⇨ FORWARD JUMP, AIR M, H, S, LAND, S CANCEL ⇨ SUPER JUMP, AIR M, M, H CANCEL ⇨ → ↓ ↘ + M CANCEL ⇨ ↓ ↘ → + ATK ATK (MASH ATK, HOLD ↑)

976,600~1,169,300 damage, 107~79% meter loss

A verifiable X-Factor combo off of a ground or air throw. After doing → ↓ ↘ + ATK ATK, immediately activate X-Factor so that the blades get the damage boost. Have Morrigan jump vertically the second she's able, then at the peak of Morrigan's jump, airdash forward to chase down the opponent's juggled body. When you approach them, perform air S to begin the ground chain segment.

COMBO APPENDIX

GENERAL EXECUTION TIPS

- Practice alternating ↓ ↘ → and ↓ ↙ ← quickly and cleanly to improve fly cancels
- Practice getting the right airdash whenever you want, and getting air attacks as soon as possible afterward
- To combo Shadow Blade into Finishing Shower, you must hyper cancel the uppercut earlier than you think
- Don't attack immediately after launching and super jumping; pause to allow Morrigan to gain altitude first

→ ↘ ↓ ↙ ← + ATK, → ↓ ↘ + ATK ATK OTG

Notes	Damage
Shadow Servant gets more hits and damage midscreen. Heavier versions of Vector Drain deal more damage	332,500~427,700 damage, 73% meter loss

THROW OR AIR THROW, → ↓ ↘ + ATK ATK OTG

Notes	Damage
Shadow Servant gets more hits and damage midscreen	337,700 damage, 92% meter loss

AS MORRIGAN COMES IN: AIR M, H CANCEL ⇨ ↓ ↙ ← + S, M, H CANCEL ⇨ → ↓ ↘ + M CANCEL ⇨ ↓ ↘ → + ATK ATK (MASH ATK, HOLD ↑)

Notes	Damage
⇧ + S or ⇨ + S or ⇩ + S TAC to Morrigan	Varies due to damage scaling

CR. M, H, → + H CANCEL ⇨ ↓ ↘ → + H CANCEL ⇨ ↓ ↙ ← + S, AIR H CANCEL ⇨ ↓ ↘ → + H CANCEL ⇨ ↓ ↙ ← + S, LAND, FORWARD JUMP, AIR M, M, H CANCEL ⇨ ↓ ↘ → + H CANCEL ⇨ ↓ ↙ ← + S, FORWARD AIRDASH, H, S, LAND, S CANCEL ⇨ FORWARD SUPER JUMP, AIR M, M, H CANCEL ⇨ → ↓ ↘ + M CANCEL ⇨ ↓ ↘ → + ATK ATK (MASH ATK, HOLD ↑ TO DIRECT MISSILES), → ↓ ↘ + H

Notes	Damage
Requires corner	703,400 damage, 6% meter gain

WITH ASTRAL VISION ACTIVE, CR. M, H, → + H CANCEL ⇨ ↓ ↘ → + H CANCEL ⇨ ↓ ↙ ← + S, AIR H CANCEL ⇨ ↓ ↘ → + H CANCEL ⇨ ↓ ↙ ← + S, LAND, FORWARD JUMP, AIR M, M, H CANCEL ⇨ ↓ ↘ → + H CANCEL ⇨ ↓ ↙ ← + S, FORWARD AIRDASH, H, S, LAND, CR. H, S CANCEL ⇨ FORWARD SUPER JUMP, AIR M, M, H CANCEL ⇨ → ↓ ↘ + M CANCEL ⇨ ↓ ↘ → + ATK ATK (MASH ATK, HOLD ↑)

Notes	Damage
Requires Astral Vision; pause briefly between ⇨ + H and ⇩ ⇘ ⇨ + H to avoid producing ⇨ ⇩ ⇘ + H accidentally	781,100 damage, meter neutral

"MMM, THAT REALLY DID NOT SATISFY MY URGE. I'M GOING TO HAVE TO LOOK FOR SOMEONE ELSE TO TAKE CARE OF ME."

ADVANCED TACTICS

SUCCUBUS RUSHDOWN 101: WHIFFING AIR Ⓢ AND OS VECTOR DRAIN

Whiffing the air drill is Morrigan's fastest way to fake an overhead.

The fake overhead paves the way for an immediate low attack...

...or for Morrigan's inescapable Vector Drain grab! (Which leads back to an overhead naturally, if it is unsuccessful.)

Morrigan is kind of a walking (or is it gliding?) advanced tactic. She moves unconventionally, requiring more premeditation than other characters—she can't just dash around to reposition at close range, or go for dash in low short, or what have you. Your challengers, at least the smart ones, will know that Morrigan is a very air and flight-centric combatant. They're liable to default to guarding high, or even to simply jumping backward—after all, the threat of dash-in crouching low attacks or rapid-fire low attacks chained to catch jumpers, which is so devastating from other rushdown characters, is absent from Morrigan. So how do you threaten low, which makes your opponents hesitant to take evasive action, which in turn allows your overhead threats to succeed more often?

The first step is mastering empty triangle jump with whiffed air Ⓢ. Some rushdown characters can just airdash down-forward and do nothing for a built-in empty triangle jump. Not Morrigan: if you perform a downward airdash without attacking, she descends briefly before swooping back up into the air. This can be great for setting up left/right cross-ups with assists and fly-canceled Soul Fists, but it's not so great for establishing a high/low threat... unless you're packing a low-hitting assist, this doesn't threaten low whatsoever.

So, what about whiffing an air attack to end her airdash and cause her to land prematurely? This works, but it *only* works with her air Ⓢ drill—oddly, even though air Ⓜ and Ⓗ are both slower than air Ⓢ, they are *incapable* of being made to whiff on purpose during an aggressive airdash! The catch here is that in order to cause a triangle jump air Ⓢ to whiff, you must perform a downward dash as soon as possible after jumping, and then perform air Ⓢ as soon as possible after airdashing. Of course, you'll know if you did it correctly—Morrigan should just land abruptly, without hitting her adversary. If you didn't airdash low enough, or if you waited too long to press Ⓢ, the drill hits your competitor, and that's not what you are after here.

Once you're comfortable whiffing drill, you've got your overhead feint down. The second step is to mix up between standing Ⓛ, ⇨ + Ⓜ Splash Libido, and a Vector Drain H option select upon landing.

Standing Ⓛ is a low attack that is active in only four frames; it naturally chains directly into *Combo I* (or, practically any other combo Morrigan is capable of). If your rival guards and doesn't use advancing guard to push Morrigan away before you inevitably chain to ⇨ + Ⓗ, you can jump cancel and immediately airdash to overhead or fake overhead again.

The counterpoint to standing Ⓛ is Vector Drain H. Be careful performing Vector Drain here; the airdash into whiffed air Ⓢ must be done so quickly that it can be difficult to actually even perform Vector Drain immediately upon landing. In any case, perform Vector Drain with a motion of ⇨⬂⇩⬃⇦ + Ⓗ ~Ⓢ, Ⓢ. This is less complicated than it might look: just perform a backward half-circle into Ⓗ, then immediately double-tap Ⓢ. If your foe is in a throwable state after your whiffed air Ⓢ into Vector Drain, great! They'll be scooped up into Morrigan's warm embrace, and you can tack on Shadow Servant afterward if you like. If they are somehow NOT in a throwable state—like if they jumped, or if they'd exited guardstun or hitstun too recently, or if they're just out of range—the Ⓢ double-tap causes the Vector Drain whiff to be canceled into flight, which is then canceled into air Ⓢ. So, with this fast sequence, the best case scenario is a mix-up between a low attack or an unbreakable throw, and the worst-case scenario is that you get a built-in 16 frame overhead follow-up!

If you're worried that either of this options won't work up close, or if you're not certain about positioning (like if you are outside of Vector Drain range, due to a misplaced airdash or the opposing character's advancing guard), Splash Libido is always an option. This interesting spiked command attack extends unbeatable spears in front of Morrigan: while her body itself is vulnerable, the whole area covered by the Splash Libido needles is not. If your competitor is trying to attack, whether to preempt what they perceive as your overhead/low/throw mix-up, or if they're simply mashing on inputs hoping to get either a throw break or advancing guard, Splash Libido usually can counterhit them, which causes an obvious stagger. If you react by having Morrigan dash forward as soon as possible, you can start a full combo from here! (See *Combo VI*.)

RYU

"DEDICATE YOURSELF, AND ANYTHING IS POSSIBLE! HUMAN POTENTIAL IS TRULY LIMITLESS ..."

Bio

REAL NAME

Ryu

OCCUPATION

Fighter

ABILITIES

Utilizes a unique fighting style based on Ansatsuken, with elements of karate, judo, and taekwondo blended in. He is also able to utilize his spiritual energy.

WEAPONS

None

PROFILE

Ryu's name gained great recognition among martial artists after he defeated the Muay Thai king in a fight. However, instead of claiming his fame, Ryu began to wander the globe, hoping to become a true warrior. He continues his journey, engaging in battles with fighters he meets along the way.

FIRST APPEARANCE

Street Fighter (1987)

POWER GRID

2 INTELLIGENCE

3 STRENGTH

2 SPEED

3 STAMINA

5 ENERGY PROJECTION

5 FIGHTING ABILITY

*This is biographical, and does not represent an evaluation of the in-game combat potential of this hero.

ALTERNATE COSTUMES

1

2

3

4

5

6

DLC

Overview

Vitality	1,000,000
Chain Combo Archetype	Marvel Series

X-Factor Boost	Damage	Speed
Level 1 (3 teammates remaining)	135%	105%
Level 2 (2 teammates remaining)	160%	110%
Level 3 (1 teammate remaining)	185%	115%

Your goal with Ryu is to set up an offense centered on his improved Collarbone Breaker attack.

Ryu's Collarbone Breaker lends itself to a strong mix-up that you can exploit when your opponent becomes afraid of this attack.

- **Collarbone Breaker is an overhead attack that can chain directly into a launcher**
- **You can exploit this to land low-hitting crouching (L) attacks on rivals attempting to guard the overhead**
- **Competitors who become focused on blocking correctly can be thrown, which leads into OTG-capable Air Shinku Hadouken**
- **You can cross up your opponent with Ryu's Tatsumaki Senpukyaku L, adding yet another mix-up option that must be guarded**

How do you close on an adversary so you can apply Ryu's mix-ups?

- **Jump with air ⇨ + (H) (option-select throw) canceled into air Tatsumaki Senpukyaku L to cover both the air and ground**
- **If your opponent is focused on trying to stop the air Tatsumaki Senpukyaku L, use the opportunity to wave dash toward the opposing character**
- **Force rivals to guard crossover assists in order to reestablish positioning and apply mix-ups**
- **Keep opponents away with Hadoken, then suddenly attack once the opposing character gets within mid range**

TUNING SINCE ORIGINAL MVC3

Ryu received a large amount of new special attacks and hyper combos, but most of these can be difficult to utilize effectively. Collarbone Breaker can now be chained into (S) and is special and hyper-cancelable, which has vastly improved Ryu's offense. The Hado Kakusei and Shin Tatsumaki Senpukyaku attacks now give him better combos and damage output.

- **Forward and backward dashes are now cancelable after 4 frames—this previously was 11 frames**
- **Collarbone Breaker (➡ ✚ (M)) now chains into (S), is also special and hyper combo-cancelable**
- **New special attack Ren Hadoken: ⬇ ↘ ➡ ✚ (S) (mash) fires a stream of up to five short-ranged fireballs**
- **New special attack Baku Hadoken: ⬇ ↘ ➡ ✚ (S) (hold) fires a single fireball so fast that it's nearly invisible, also wall bounces the enemy**
- **New special attack Hado Shoryuken: ➡ ⬇ ↘ ✚ (S) powered up Shoryuken with increased invulnerability and adds additional blue flame hits**
- **New hyper combo Hado Kakusei: ⬇ ⬇ ✚ (ATK)(ATK) 15% speed boost and altered hyper combos**
- **New hyper combo Shin Hadoken: ⬇ ↘ ➡ ✚ (ATK)(ATK) during Hado Kakusei, ricochets off of walls**
- **New hyper combo Shin Tatsumaki Senpukyaku: ⬇ ↙ ⬅ ✚ (ATK)(ATK) during Hado Kakusei, creates massive cyclone**
- **Shinku Hadoken now can be mashed for additional damage**
- **Shinku Tatsumaki Senpukyaku now can be mashed for additional damage**

Attack Set

Standing Basic Attacks

Screen	Command	Hits	Damage	Meter Gain	Startup	Active	Recovery	Advantage on Hit	Advantage if Guarded	Notes
1	Standing Ⓛ	1	50,000	400	5/5	3/3	10/8	+3/+5	+1/+3	Chain-cancelable into Ⓛ attacks
2	Standing Ⓜ	1	75,000	600	8/7	3/3	21/18	-3/-1	-5/-3	—
3	Standing Ⓗ	1	90,000	760	10/9	3/3	21/18	+4/+7	+2/+5	—

Crouching Basic Attacks

Screen	Command	Hits	Damage	Meter Gain	Startup	Active	Recovery	Advantage on Hit	Advantage if Guarded	Notes
1	Crouching Ⓛ	1	45,000	360	5/5	2/2	11/9	+3/+5	+1/+3	Low attack, chain-cancelable into Ⓛ attacks
2	Crouching Ⓜ	1	68,000	544	8/7	3/3	19/17	-1/+1	-3/-1	Low attack
3	Crouching Ⓗ	1	80,000	640	10/9	4/4	26/23	—	-4/-1	Low attack, hard knockdown

Ground Special Attack—Launcher

Screen	Command	Hits	Damage	Meter Gain	Startup	Active	Recovery	Advantage on Hit	Advantage if Guarded	Notes
1	Ⓢ (while standing or crouching)	1	100,000	800	9/8	5/5	22/19	—	-1/+2	Launcher, not special- or hyper combo-cancelable

Air Basic Attacks

Screen	Command	Hits	Damage	Meter Gain	Startup	Active	Recovery	Advantage on Hit	Advantage if Guarded	Notes
1	Air Ⓛ	1	55,000	440	6/6	13/13	5/4	+9/+11	+7/+7	Overhead attack
2	Air Ⓜ	2	108,000	960	9/8	4/4	19/16	+19/+19	+17/+14	Overhead attack
3	Air Ⓗ	1	90,000	720	9/8	4/4	23/20	+23/+22	+21/+20	Overhead attack

Air Special Attacks—Flying Screen and Air Exchange

Air Ⓢ causes a hard knockdown when used in a launcher combo (this is sometimes called flying screen). When used outside of a launcher combo, air Ⓢ behaves mostly like another basic attack. Air exchange attacks, performed by inputting a direction plus Ⓢ, are only possible during a launcher combo. Exchange hits initiate team aerial combos by tagging in the next available character to continue the air combo.

Screen	Command	Hits	Damage	Meter Gain	Startup	Active	Recovery	Advantage on Hit	Advantage if Guarded	Notes
1	Air Ⓢ	1	95,000	760	9/8	8/7	19/17	+20	+18	Overhead attack, causes hard knockdown if used in launcher combo, not special- or hyper combo-cancelable
2	Air ⇧ + Ⓢ (during launcher combo)	1	60,000	480	8/7	7/7	17/14	—	—	Tags in next available ally while lofting opponent upward
3	Air ⇨ or ⇦ + Ⓢ (during launcher combo)	1	50,000	400	11/10	5/5	21/17	—	—	Tags in next available ally while causing wall bounce, erases 1 hyper meter bar from foe
4	Air ⇩ + Ⓢ (during launcher combo)	1	50,000	400	9/8	8/7	18/17	—	—	Tags in next available ally while causing ground bounce, generates 1 hyper meter bar

Command Attacks

Command attacks resemble basic attacks but have different chaining and canceling properties. It's usually possible to chain *into* a command attack from basic attacks, but most command attacks cannot be chained from or canceled themselves.

Screen	Name	Command	Hits	Damage	Meter Gain	Startup	Active	Recovery	Advantage on Hit	Advantage if Guarded	Notes
1	Collarbone Breaker	⇨ + Ⓜ	2	63,000	560	23/21	4/4	22/19	-3/-1	-5/-1	Overhead attack
2	Roundhouse Kick	⇨ + Ⓗ	1	95,000	760	13/12	3/3	21/18	+4/+7	+2/+5	—

Throws

Throws are for snagging passive or blocking opponents. Since throws are active so quickly, you can also use them to preemptively toss opposing characters out of their offense. Combos are usually possible after throws, one way or another.

Screen	Command	Hits	Damage	Meter Gain	Startup	Active	Notes
1	⇨ + Ⓗ (ground)	1	80,000	800	1	1	Hard knockdown
	⇦ + Ⓗ (ground)	1	80,000	800	1	1	Hard knockdown
2	⇨ + Ⓗ (air)	1	80,000	800	1	1	Hard knockdown
	⇦ + Ⓗ (air)	1	80,000	800	1	1	Hard knockdown

As a Partner—Crossover Assists

Screen	Type	P1+P2 Crossover Combination Hyper Combo	Description	Hits	Damage	Meter Gain	Startup	Active	Recovery (this crossover assist)	Recovery (other partner)	Notes
1	Ryu—α	Shinku Tatsumaki Senpukyaku	Shoryuken H	1	150,000	1200	27/25	14/14	132/125	102/88	Knocks down opponent
2	Ryu—β	Shinku Hadoken	Hadoken L	1	100,000	800	34/31	—	128/123	98/86	Projectile has 5 low priority durability points
3	Ryu—γ	Shinku Tatsumaki Senpukyaku	Tatsumaki Senpukyaku H	3	143,500	1280	37/34	17(6)6/15(6)6	115/108	85/72	Knocks down adversary

1

2

3

Ryu—γ is great for offensive support and combos. Fast and long ranged, it keeps an opponent in hitstun and guardstun for a considerable amount of time. Furthermore, it only has three hits, so it does not cause a large amount of damage scaling in combos. It is similar to the popular Akuma—β crossover assist, with the trade-off of inflicting more hitstun, but lacking the ability to nullify projectiles.

Ryu—β uses Hadoken L, which is a decent assist to have in general. This assist is more suited to increasing your zoning ability (or negating your competitor's zoning), but possesses substantially less combo utility than Ryu—γ

Ryu—α lacks the invincibility that the normal version of Shoryuken possesses. This makes it difficult to use effectively as a defensive move. It sends an adversary flying very high, also making its combo utility negligible.

You can permanently speed up all of Ryu's assists with Hado Kakusei. This makes Ryu—γ Tatsumaki Senpukyaku more potent due to the decreased startup, but it gives you less time to react to a successful hit.

Snap Back

Screen	Command	Hits	Damage	Meter Gain	Startup	Active	Recovery	Advantage on Hit	Advantage if Guarded
1	↓↘→ + P1 or P2	1	50,000	500 - (-1 hyper meter bar)	2	3	23	—	0

Notes

On hit, snap back forces the opposing point character to be replaced by an assist. Opposing assist calls or tag outs are also locked out for 4 seconds

1

Special Moves

Screen	Name	Command	Hits	Damage	Meter Gain	Startup	Active	Recovery	Advantage on Hit	Advantage if Guarded	Notes
1	Hadoken L	↓↘→ + L	1	100,000	800	10/9	—	35/31	-2/+2	-4/0	Projectile has 5 low priority durability points
	Hadoken M	↓↘→ + M	1	100,000	800	10/9	—	39/34	-6/-1	-8/-3	Projectile has 5 low priority durability points
	Hadoken H	↓↘→ + H	1	100,000	800	10/9	—	43/38	-10/-5	-12/-7	Projectile has 5 low priority durability points
2	Air Hadoken	(in air) ↓↘→ + ATK	1	100,000	800	14/13	—	38/33	-8/-2	-9/-4	Projectile has 5 low priority durability points
3	Ren Hadoken (rapid fire)	↓↘→ + S (rapidly press)	1~5	50,000~204,600	400~2000	21/19	—	42/36	-9/-3	-11/-5	Can be mashed to fire up to 5 projectiles, projectile remains active for 21 frames each projectile has 5 low priority durability points
	Air Ren Hadoken (rapid fire)	(in air) ↓↘→ + S (rapidly press)	1~5	50,000~204,600	400~2000	21/19	—	43/37	-1/+3	-3/+1	Can be mashed to fire up to 5 projectiles, projectile remains active for 21 frames each projectile has 5 low priority durability points
4	Baku Hadoken	↓↘→ + S (charge)	1	150,000	1200	53/48	—	37/33	—	-8/-4	Causes wall bounce, projectile has 5 low priority durability points
	Air Baku Hadoken	(in air) ↓↘→ + S (charge)	1	150,000	1200	53/48	—	33/29	—	+12/+13	Causes wall bounce, projectile has 5 low priority durability points
5	Shoryuken L	→↓↘ + L	1	100,000	800	3/3	14/14	25/20	-7/-2	-13/-8	Invincible from frames 1-2
	Shoryuken M	→↓↘ + M	1	120,000	960	3/3	14/14	33/27	-9/-4	-21/-15	Invincible from frames 1-5
	Shoryuken H	→↓↘ + H	1	150,000	1200	3/3	14/14	47/40	-19/-12	-35/-28	Invincible from frames 1-9

Special Moves continued

Screen	Name	Command	Hits	Damage	Meter Gain	Startup	Active	Recovery	Advantage on Hit	Advantage if Guarded	Notes
6	Hado Shoryuken	→↓↘ + Ⓢ	4	203,000	1760	28/25	14/14	34/28	+16/+22	-22/-16	Invincible from frames 1-30, projectile hits 3 times and has 1 low priority durability point
7	Tatsumaki Senpukyaku L	↓↙← + Ⓛ	1	90,000	720	13/12	6	23/19	—	-3/+1	Knocks down opponent
	Tatsumaki Senpukyaku M	↓↙← + Ⓜ	2	114,000	960	13/12	7(6)6/6(6)6	21/17	—	-1/+3	Knocks down competitor
	Tatsumaki Senpukyaku H	↓↙← + Ⓗ	3	143,500	1280	13/12	17(6)6/15(6)6	22/15	—	-2/+3	Knocks down adversary
8	Air Tatsumaki Senpukyaku L	(in air) ↓↙← + Ⓛ	1	100,000	800	13/12	20/18	Until grounded	—	—	—
	Air Tatsumaki Senpukyaku M	(in air) ↓↙← + Ⓜ	4	117,600	1120	13/12	26(4)6/23(4)6	Until grounded	—	—	—
	Air Tatsumaki Senpukyaku H	(in air) ↓↙← + Ⓗ	5	135,800	1360	13/12	36(4)6/32(4)6	Until grounded	—	—	—
9	Jodan Sokuto Geri L	←↓↙ + Ⓛ	1	100,000	800	14/13	5/5	30/25	—	-9/-4	Wall bounces rival
	Jodan Sokuto Geri M	←↓↙ + Ⓜ	1	100,000	800	16/14	5/5	32/28	—	-11/-7	Wall bounces target
	Jodan Sokuto Geri H	←↓↙ + Ⓗ	1	100,000	800	18/16	5/5	34/29	—	-13/-8	Wall bounces opponent

1

Hadoken: The "wave motion fist" executes and recovers more quickly than most projectiles, but this is offset by its low amount of durability points compared to that of strong zoning characters. Against aggressive characters, use Hadoken to control the ground, forcing your foe to jump over them. Each Hadoken inflicts 30,000 points of chip damage, so your adversary naturally wants to avoid them.

Hadoken L should be the primary version used; it has fastest recovery and slowest projectile speed, leaving the projectile on screen the longest and Ryu the least vulnerable. This allows you to best control screen space.

Hadoken H has the slowest recover but creates the fastest-moving projectile. Throwing Hadoken L immediately followed by Hadoken H from fullscreen does not leave your competitor much time to move in between the two projectiles. This is a useful tactic if you are trying to maximize chip damage, or prevent another long range character from being able to attack in-between the two fireballs.

2

Air Hadoken: The air version of Hadoken has considerably slower startup and recovery compared to the ground version, making it riskier to use. Its primary use should be from fullscreen in anticipation of the opposing player trying to advance in the air.

Performing air Hadoken by inputting a ↓↘→↗ + ATK motion can dramatically reduce the recovery on air Hadoken if done immediately off the ground, enough that you can actually combo a ground Hadoken H after an instant air Hadoken L.

3

Ren Hadoken: One of Ryu's new special attacks, mash the Ⓢ button to create up to five short range Hadoken projectiles. This attack is primarily used for extra damage in corner combos. Against a guarding foe, one use of advancing guard pushes Ryu too far away for the additional fireballs to land.

4

Baku Hadoken: Another new special attack, Baku Hadoken creates an invisible projectile with 5 low-priority durability points and wall bounces. It is difficult to use effectively, since the startup is slow and the durability is still exactly the same as a regular Hadoken. It's difficult to capitalize on the wall bounce outside of the corner with anything besides a Shinku Hadoken, unless you use Baku Hadoken at a low altitude by inputting ↓↘→↗ + Ⓢ. If done properly, Ryu lands on the ground and recovers immediately after releasing the projectile, allowing him to dash forward after the wall bounce and convert into a full combo.

5

Shoryuken: Shoryuken is one of the rare invincible special attacks in the game, making it great for stopping an opponent's offense. Shoryuken H inflicts the most damage and has the most invulnerability, making it the most useful version in most cases. However, if you have three meters, you can use Shoryuken M to combo into Shin Shoryuken.

You should be concerned with the recovery of this attack, since all three versions can be easily punished if guarded. To mitigate risk, cancel Shoryuken into the ground version of Shinku Hadoken. If it hits, aim the Shinku Hadoken upward for a quick 450,000 damage. If guarded, aim it forward, forcing your adversary to guard the beam and keeping Ryu safe.

6

Hado Shoryuken: Another new special attack, Hado Shoryuken has a huge amount of invulnerability, more than most hyper combos! However, it is much slower than a normal Shoryuken, limiting its use. This attack can be employed in situations where the huge amount of invincibility frames can be used to beat hyper combos that Shoryuken H won't beat.

7

Tatsumaki Senpukyaku: The ground version of Tatsumaki Senpukyaku is difficult to use effectively, since it is punishable by throws if guarded, but it doesn't reward you with much if it hits.

However, during Hado Kakusei state, all versions of Tatsumaki Senpukyaku grant frame advantage if guarded. There is also a damaging loop combo involving the L version.

8

Air Tatsumaki Senpukyaku: The air version of Tatsumaki Senpukyaku L is one of Ryu's best offensive assets. It immediately alters his trajectory, moving slightly up-forward a bit before dropping down. This attack grants massive frame advantage when guarded or on hit. Furthermore, it can be preceded by option-selected air (H) air throw attempts, leaving Ryu in a very favorable position if you snag your foe with an air throw, or if air (H) or Tatsumaki Senpukyaku L hits or is guarded. Tatsumaki Senpukyaku L can also cross up opponents! See the Advanced Tactics section for more information!

Air Tatsumaki Senpukyaku M and H travel across the screen, but they leave Ryu completely vulnerable until he reaches the ground. This can be mitigated in two ways. You can use the motion ↓↙←↖ + ATK to do it immediately off the ground, which gives massive frame advantage on hit or when guarded. In addition, the hits caused by all versions of air Tatsumaki Senpukyaku do not knock down grounded competitors, allowing a combo afterward if done correctly! The other method is to hyper combo cancel the air Tatsumaki Senpukyaku into air Shinku Hadoken.

9

Jodan Sokuto Geri: This attack is primarily a combo tool that causes wall bounce. Jodan Sokuto Geri L version causes your rival to bounce the shortest distance off of the wall, preferable in corner combos to prevent the target from bouncing over Ryu. Jodan Sokuto Geri H version causes the farthest bounce from the wall, making midscreen combos possible with some precise wavedashing. All versions of Jodan Sokuto Geri are slow and unsafe if guarded, but the stronger versions more than the L version. This makes it a poor attack to use outside of combos.

However, if you have slightly more than one hyper meter bar available, hyper combo canceling Jodan Sokuto Geri into Hado Kakusei results in a very damaging combo, and it also makes it much easier to capitalize off of a midscreen wall bounce. If Jodan Sokuto Geri is guarded, hyper combo canceling into Hado Kakusei leaves Ryu with up to a +4 frame advantage.

Hyper Combos

Screen	Name	Command	Hits	Damage	Startup	Active	Recovery	Advantage on Hit	Advantage if Guarded	Notes
1	Shinku Hadoken (in air OK)	↓↘→ + ATK ATK	25~50	261,700~ 313,900	18+1	80	23	+3	-8	Can be steered using the controller, holding up during the super flash causes beam to fire straight up, holding down during air version causes beam to fire straight down, knocks down opponent, downward version is OTG-capable, beam durability: 25 frames x 1 high priority durability point, can be mashed for additional hits
2	Shinku Tatsumaki Senpukyaku	↓↙← + ATK ATK	43~83	266,300~ 315,200	13+4	2(1)4(1)2(1)5(1)2(1) 5(1)2(1)5(1)2(1)5(1) 2(1)5(1)2(1)5(1)2(1) 5(1)2(1)5(1)2(1)5(1) 2(1)2(2)6	35	—	-12	Frames 1-17 invincible, last hit cause hard knockdown, can be mashed for additional hits
3	Hado Kakusei	↓↓ + ATK ATK	—	—	18+7	—	—	—	—	Puts a 115% speed-up effect on Ryu for 339 frames, Shin Hadoken and Shin Tatsumaki Senpukyaku can be activated while speed-up is active, Hado Kakusei cannot be activated while speed-up is already active
4	Shin Hadoken (in air OK)	(during Hado Kakusei) ↓↘→ + ATK ATK	25~50	290,800~ 349,300	18+1	80	23	+3	-8	Beam ricochets off the wall, standing beam ricochets upward toward the opposite wall, air beam ricochets downward toward the back wall, durability: 25 frames x 1 high priority durability points
5	Shin Tatsumaki Senpukyaku	(during Hado Kakusei) ↓↙← + ATK ATK	43~83	332,500~ 394~600	13+4	2(1)4(1)2(1)5(1)2(1) 5(1)2(1)5(1)2(1)5(1) 2(1)5(1)2(1)5(1)2(1) 5(1)2(1)5(1)2(1)5(1) 2(1)2(2)6	35	—	-12	Frames 1-17 invincible, last hit causes hard knockdown, can be mashed for additional hits
6	Shin Shoryuken (Level 3 Hyper Combo)	→↓↘ + ATK ATK	3	380,000	11+0	4	50	—	-28	Frames 1-22 invincible, hard knockdown

1

1

1

1

Shinku Hadoken: Ryu possesses one of the best beam hyper combos in the game due to the versatility of Shinku Hadoken. Before Ryu begins firing his beam, you can initially choose to fire it in one of two directions, depending on Ryu's position. If no direction is held, he fires Shinku Hadoken directly in front of him. If grounded, you can hold up to fire the beam directly upward. If in the air, you can hold down to fire the beam at a downward angle. Regardless of the direction fired, you can continue to change the direction of Ryu's beam slightly in any direction.

Furthermore, even if your rival guards this attack, it is nearly impossible to punish it. In fact, a majority of the cast can't punish it at all. It also pushes your adversary far away. This is particularly useful if you need breathing room to reestablish dominance.

This move is useful in and out of combos, and it has exceptional damage for a level 1 hyper combo now that it can be mashed for extra damage. In combos, it's a fantastic combo ender. The air version of Shinku Hadoken is one of the few horizontal beam hyper combos that can be performed at super jump height, and all versions are remarkably useful at putting a screeching halt to projectile and beam-based zoning characters. The air version is also OTG-capable!

It also has excellent THC synergy, both for starting and continuing into the next level of a THC. Shinku Hadoken can be used in THC combos from nearly any hyper combo!

Shinku Tatsumaki Senpukyaku: This hyper combo has a fair amount of invincibility that can be used as a long range alternative to Shoryuken in defensive situations, and it can now be mashed for extra damage. This hyper combo causes hard knockdown and, if you manage to land this in the corner, you can follow it with an OTG air Shinku Hadoken if you are quick. However, the direction in which Shinku Tatsumaki Senpukyaku sends the target is somewhat random.

Hado Kakusei: Ryu has gained a speed boost hyper combo in *Ultimate Marvel vs Capcom 3*: he gains a 15% speed boost for roughly 5.6 seconds when this hyper combo is activated. Ryu gains access to Shin Hadoken and Shin Tatsumaki Senpukyaku, but he loses access to Shinku Hadouken and Shinku Tatsumaki Senpukyaku for the duration. He also gets some freaky eyes! Unlike most power-up hyper combos, Ryu can still gain meter during Hado Kakusei to offset the short duration.

The primary use of this hyper combo is to cancel Jodan Sokuto Geri when performed in a midscreen combo to enable more damaging combos, but you can also use the move as a way to safely cancel otherwise unsafe special attacks.

Like most power-up states, if Ryu leaves gameplay while in Hado Kakusei state, he retains his powered-up state until he is the primary character again, granting his crossover assists the 15% speed increase.

Shin Hadoken: Only available during Hado Kakusei, this move temporarily replaces Shinku Hadoken. This hyper combo fires a horizontal beam that bounces off of the wall. Ironically, it's generally worse than the regular Shinku Hadoken because Shin Hadoken cannot be aimed; this prevents you from being able to use the OTG-capable air Shinku Hadoken to capitalize off of throws.

Shin Tatsumaki Senpukyaku: Only available during Hado Kakusei, this move temporarily replaces Shinku Tatsumaki Senpukyaku. This hyper combo is nearly identical to Shinku Tatsumaki Senpukyaku except for two major differences: it inflicts substantially more damage at 394,600 points, one of the strongest level 1 hyper combos in the game, and it also boasts a much higher vertical hitbox. These two differences make it ideal for ending all Hado Kakusei combos.

Shin Shoryuken: This attack is Ryu's level 3 hyper combo that deals unscaled damage, making it great for use at the end of a long combo. Also, on hit, Ryu recovers far sooner than when his competitor hits the ground, allowing you to continue with a juggle combo anywhere on the screen. Combined with 22 frames of invincibility, it can be a potent counter to opponents who use hyper combos recklessly against Ryu.

Battle Plan

When jumping, press ⇨ + H at the peak of the jump to get both an aerial attack and an air throw attempt…

…then input an option-select air Tatsumaki Senpukyaku L to cover all the other options!

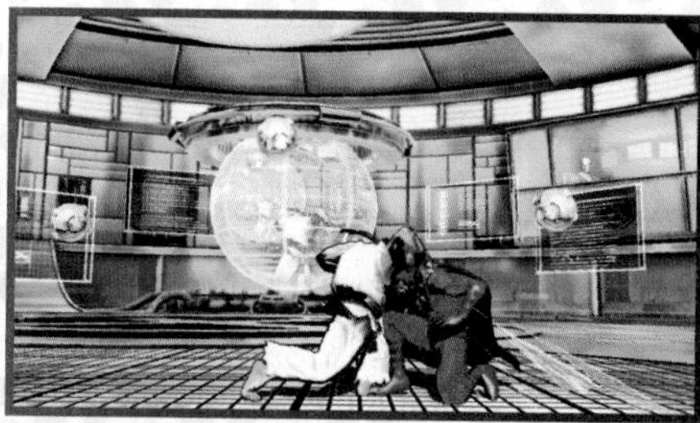

The Collarbone Breaker overhead attack leads to great damage if it hits, and it is the focal point of Ryu's offense.

Ryu works best when you have access to large amounts of meter, so using another character to build meter for him on a team is a good strategy for playing him. Ryu makes an excellent meter user and a fantastic anchor. You can use meter with Ryu to mercilessly punish careless assists with Shinku Hadoken. Also, Ryu with level 3 X-Factor and a full hyper meter can inflict massive amounts of chip damage.

When at mid range, usually your best option is to advance on the opposing character by using option select air H into air Tatsumaki Senpukyaku L: jump forward, press ⇨ + H on the way up, input ⇩ ⇙ ⇦ + L immediately after the kick extends. This allows you to air throw rivals who are nearby, come down with air Tatsumaki Senpukyaku L on ground competitors for huge frame advantage, and force airborne foes from farther away to guard both the air H and the air Tatsumaki Senpukyaku L.

Opponents may attempt to counter this by waiting with an anti-air. To counter adversaries waiting to anti-air your aerial assault, simply wavedash in and attack with crouching L to begin your close range offense.

Zoning attackers may try to keep you away with projectiles and beams. Your best bet is either to try to evade them, or punish them with Shinku Hadoken if they get careless and predictable with their zoning tactics.

Using projectile and beam crossover assists to guard your approach is always an option. If your opponent guards an assist, it gives you time to rush in and begin your mix-ups. Avoid reckless use of your crossover assist; however, you don't want to end up with your assist being punished for a huge amount of damage.

Once you manage to close in on your target, your offense with Ryu should be focused on setting up the overhead Collarbone Breaker ⇨ + M, which leads into damaging combos if it connects. When you have the opportunity to attack your rival, lead with either Collarbone Breaker or crouching L. If you attack with crouching L, you have several options to mix up your opponent with:

Staggered low-hitting crouching L chains, hitting competitors who attempt to use advancing guard. This also hits opponents attempting to jump away

Chain crouching L into the overhead Collarbone Breaker

Throw (into OTG air Shinku Hadoken)

Buffer a dash and do more staggered crouching L attacks to maintain pressure

It's possible to hit-confirm Collarbone Breaker's two hits and cancel into Jodan Sokuto Geri H on reaction. If the overhead is guarded, chain into Ryu's safe S launcher. If it is a little too difficult to confirm the hit, either press S every time regardless of hit or block, or do a weaker, faster version of Jodan Sokuto Geri. However, weaker versions of Jodan Sokuto Geri require a hyper combo cancel to Hado Kakusei to be able to capitalize with a combo fully, except in the corner, where Jodan Sokuto Geri L is always the best option.

Any crouching L or Collarbone Breaker hit can be verified and canceled into a Jodan Sokuto Geri for a big damage combo. If you have slightly more than one hyper meter bar, you can hyper combo cancel into Hado Kakusei and perform an even more damaging combo; see the Combo Usage section.

Ryu's Hadoken attacks are best used to control horizontal planes of the battlefield.

Air Shinku Hadoken is one of the only beam hyper combos in the game that can travel horizontally in the air; this makes it great for countering aerial projectiles!

While you have Ryu at long range against more aggressive characters, you'll want to rack up as much free chip damage and meter as you can; use Hadoken L to dominate the ground space and air Hadoken H in anticipation of long range jumps. Make use of long range projectiles and beam assists to assist in zoning when necessary.

If you've managed to successfully keep your competitor away with your Hadoken projectiles, consider hyper combo canceling into Shinku Hadoken whenever your foe gets uncomfortably close to Ryu, so you can push them back out. As long as you have meter to spare, you can use Shinku Hadoken to react to many tactics the opposing player uses to close the distance, racking up a decent amount of damage.

Almost inevitably, your foe eventually finds a way to close in and establish mid range. Once this happens, consider abruptly changing your pace to suddenly rush them down instead with option select air Ⓗ into air Tatsumaki Senpukyaku.

If you find yourself against another zoning character at long range, try to simply overpower them on the ground with repeated Hadoken L and H. Use assists carefully to help you win the long range firefight. It is important to know your opponent's projectile strengths, since Ryu can simply be outgunned by some of the other zoning characters in the cast. If your adversary can overpower you with their projectiles or beams, you'll have to either go on offense or attempt to discourage your foe's zoning by using meter to punish their projectile or beam use with Shinku Hadoken.

Some competitors may have the option to fire projectiles at a downward angle at Ryu from the air, allowing them to bypass your ground-based Hadokens while still pressuring you with air-based projectiles. Fortunately, Ryu has one of the best counters in the game to this strategy with air Shinku Hadoken. Alternatively, if your opponent is predictable, or you suspect they might start employing this tactic, you can just preemptively jump up and cover that area of the screen with a Hadoken to momentarily force your rival to stay grounded.

The invincible Shoryuken H is one of the best defensive tools in the game. Hyper combo cancel into Shinku Hadoken for lots of damage!

Air throws are essential to both Ryu's offense and defense.

While you have Ryu on defense, generally try to rely on advancing guard and air throws to keep your attacker at bay. Option select a Tatsumaki Senpukyaku L into all air throw attempts; this sometimes lets you suddenly turn the tables and gain the initiative. However, some aerial tactics are difficult to stop with an air throw, such as Wolverine's Diving Kick and Amaterasu's airdash air Ⓗ. Against these attacks, you may want to use Shoryuken to make your rival hesitate.

The invincible Shoryuken is one of the best defensive tools in the game—cancel into Shinku Hadoken for safety when your opponent guards it and tack on a lot of extra damage by aiming it upward when Shoryuken connects. Furthermore, Shoryuken only has 3 frames of startup, making it useful for punishing guarded attacks that are -3 or -4. However, if the frame disadvantage is -5 or greater, simply punish with crouching Ⓛ into a full combo.

Another defensive alternative is to use Shinku Tatsumaki Senpukyaku, which has more horizontal range and can be used to THC for more damage if it successfully hits or to a safe hyper combo if it is blocked.

COMBO USAGE

I. CR. Ⓛ, ST. Ⓜ, CR. Ⓗ, → + Ⓗ, Ⓢ CANCEL ⇒ FORWARD SUPER JUMP, AIR Ⓜ (2 HITS), Ⓗ CANCEL ⇒ ↓↘→ + Ⓢ, Ⓢ, Ⓢ, Ⓢ, Ⓢ CANCEL ⇒ ↓↘→ + ATK ATK (MASH ATK)

640,500 damage, 32% meter loss

This is a basic Ryu combo that should be relatively easy to master. Perform the air Ⓜ, Ⓗ with a slight delay after the Ⓢ launch. The target must be above Ryu's head for all five shots of ↓↘→ + Ⓢ to connect. If this combo is guarded, you can stop it at standing Ⓜ to leave it relatively safe from harm.

II. → + Ⓜ, Ⓢ CANCEL ⇒ FORWARD SUPER JUMP, AIR Ⓜ (2 HITS), Ⓗ CANCEL ⇒ ↓↘→ + Ⓢ, Ⓢ, Ⓢ, Ⓢ, Ⓢ CANCEL ⇒ ↓↘→ + ATK ATK (MASH Ⓢ)

558,200 damage, 50% meter loss

Ryu no longer needs X-Factor or an assist to combo after his overhead Collarbone Breaker. Chaining into Ⓢ is safe on guard unless Ryu is near a corner, in which case, your challenger can land a throw against it.

III. CR. Ⓛ, ST. Ⓜ, CR. Ⓗ, → + Ⓗ CANCEL ⇒ ←↓↙ + Ⓗ CANCEL ⇒ ↓↓ + ATK ATK, FORWARD WAVEDASH TWICE, CR. Ⓜ, ST. Ⓗ, → + Ⓗ CANCEL ⇒ ↓↙← + Ⓛ, ST. Ⓜ, Ⓗ, → + Ⓗ CANCEL ⇒ ↓↙← Ⓛ, →↓↘ + Ⓜ CANCEL ⇒ ↓↙← + ATK ATK (MASH ATK)

795,200 damage, 104% meter loss

Though seemingly costly, activating Hado Kakusei mid-combo allows you to improve your overall damage output while continuing to build meter. Shoryuken canceled into Shin Tatsumaki Senpukyaku can be performed without much fuss when you only have two or fewer bars. With three bars or more, use the special input: →↓↘↓↙ + Ⓜ, ← + ATK ATK. Otherwise, you will accidentally cancel into Shin Shoryuken.

IV. → + Ⓜ CANCEL ⇒ ←↓↙ + Ⓗ, WAVE DASH TWICE, CR. Ⓜ, ST. Ⓗ, → + Ⓗ, Ⓢ CANCEL ⇒ FORWARD SUPER JUMP, AIR Ⓜ (2 HITS), Ⓗ CANCEL ⇒ ↓↙← + Ⓗ (5 HITS) CANCEL ⇒ ↓↘→ + ATK ATK (MASH ATK)

606,600 damage, 19% meter loss

For a little extra effort, you can inflict slightly more damage off of a basic opening. After ←↓↙ + Ⓗ connects, you must wavedash forward with perfect timing in order to juggle with crouching Ⓜ. Near corners, this combo does not require any dashes, and you should use ←↓↙ + Ⓛ instead.

V. (AGAINST AIRBORNE OPPONENT) FORWARD JUMP, AIR Ⓜ (2 HITS), Ⓗ CANCEL ⇒ ↓↙← + Ⓗ CANCEL ⇒ ↓↘→ + ATK ATK (MASH ATK)

500,800 damage, 70% meter loss

A basic anti-air combo that's perfect for attacking an enemy who's entering the screen after snap back or character K.O. When blocked, cancel into ↓↙← + Ⓛ to safely land from the failed assault.

COMBO APPENDIX

GENERAL EXECUTION TIPS

After hitting Jodan Sokuto Geri H, manually buffer a dash input with → → to get the earliest possible dash. From there, you'll just need to wavedash once to be in range to have Ryu juggle his competitor.

After ground throwing the opponent, input ↓ ↘ → ↗ + ATK ATK much earlier than you think you can to be able to consistently hit the air Shinku Hadoken OTG.

To properly time juggle attacks after Shin Shoryuken, immediately dash forward and attack with standing M as Ryu disappears from the bottom of the screen.

FRONT AND BACK THROW OR FRONT AND BACK AIR THROW, AIR ↓ ↘ → + ATK ATK, HOLD ↓ (MASH ATK)

Notes	Damage
Input ⇩ ⬂ ⇨ ⬀ + ATK ATK to OTG after ground throws	379,800 damage, 92% meter loss

→ ↓ ↘ + H CANCEL ↓ ↘ → + ATK ATK, HOLD ↑ (MASH ATK)

Notes	Damage
Input ⇨ ⇩ ⬂ ⇨ + ATK CANCEL ATK ATK (mash ATK) if you have 3 or more hyper combo bars	449,800 damage, 88% meter loss

→ + M CANCEL ← ↓ ↙ + H CANCEL ↓ ↓ + ATK ATK, FORWARD WAVEDASH TWICE, CR. M, ST. H, → + H CANCEL ↓ ↙ ← + L, ST. M, H, → + H CANCEL ↓ ↙ ← L, → ↓ ↘ + M CANCEL ↓ ↙ ← + ATK ATK (MASH ATK)

Notes	Damage
The overhead variation of **Combo Usage III**	739,200 damage, 122% meter loss

CR. L, ST. M, CR. H, → + H CANCEL ← ↓ ↙ + H, FORWARD WAVEDASH TWICE, CR. M, ST. H, → + H CANCEL ↓ ↙ ← + L, → ↓ ↘ + M CANCEL → ↓ ↘ + ATK ATK, FORWARD DASH, CR. M, ST. H, → + H, S CANCEL VERTICAL SUPER JUMP, AIR H CANCEL ↓ ↙ ← + H CANCEL ↓ ↘ → + ATK ATK (MASH ATK)

Notes	Damage
Level 3 Ryu combo	1,099,100 damage, 383%% meter loss

CR. L, ST. M, CR. H, → + H CANCEL ← ↓ ↙ + H CANCEL ↓ ↓ + ATK ATK CANCEL X-FACTOR, WAVE DASH TWICE, CR. M, ST. H, → + H CANCEL ↓ ↙ ← + L, ST. M, H, → + H CANCEL ↓ ↙ ← L, → ↓ ↘ + M CANCEL ↓ ↙ ← + ATK ATK (MASH ATK)

Notes	Damage
Use special input at the end if you have 3 or more hyper combo bars. ⇨ ⇩ ⬂ ⇩ ⬃ + M, ⇦ + ATK ATK	1,070,400~1,359,700 damage, 80~48% meter loss

↓ ↙ ← ↖ + H, CR. L, ST. M, CR. H, → + H CANCEL ← ↓ ↙ + H, FORWARD WAVEDASH TWICE, CR. M, ST. H, → + H, S CANCEL FORWARD SUPER JUMP, AIR M (2 HITS), H CANCEL ↓ ↙ ← + H CANCEL ↓ ↘ → + ATK ATK (MASH ATK)

Notes	Damage
Opening Tatsumaki Senpukyaku must be done immediately off the ground	542,700 damage, 6% meter loss

ADVANCED TACTICS

CAN A WARRIOR GET A SHINKU?!

If you have three hyper meter bars, trying to do hyper combo cancel Shinku Hadoken from a Shoryuken usually causes you to get an accidental Shin Shoryuken instead.

In every Capcom fighting game is a system known as "input priority." Input priority governs what command to execute when two commands overlap closely. For example, performing ⇨ ⇩ ⬂ ⇨ gets interpreted as a ⇨ ⇩ ⬂ motion rather than a ⇩ ⬂ ⇨ motion.

This is a big problem for Ryu players because you often need to hyper combo cancel Shoryuken attacks quickly: if you have three hyper meter bars, trying to cancel Shoryuken with Shinku Hadoken usually gets you an accidental Shin Shoryuken instead! That's a lot of wasted meter, and a lot of free damage for your foe if they happened to guard the Shoryuken!

There are some ways to manipulate the game's input priority system into giving you the correct hyper combo. To cancel Shoryuken with Shinku Hadoken, perform the following inputs: ⇨ ⇩ ⬂ ⇨ + ATK CANCEL ATK ATK. The awkward motion still gives you a Shoryuken command due to input priority, but by the time you input ATK ATK, the original ⇨ command will be out of the input buffer. The game then only recognizes the ⇩ ⬂ ⇨ command, allowing for the hyper combo cancel to Shinku Hadoken!

Hado Kakusei combos involve hyper combo canceling a Shoryuken to a Shin Tatsumaki Senpukyaku. This is an even more awkward input: ⇨ ⇩ ⬂ ⇩ ⬃ + ATK CANCEL ⇦ + ATK ATK. Practice makes perfect!

SPINNING INTO TOWN

To add to Ryu's mix-up of low attacks, Collarbone Breaker, and throws, you can also cross up your adversary with air Tatsumaki Senpukyaku L!

Ryu has another slightly more difficult option mix-up option when you manage to get close enough to start his offense with crouching L. Air Tatsumaki Senpukyaku can cross up competitors, as well! Perform cross up air Tatsumaki Senpukyaku L by inputting ⇩ ⬃ ⇦ ⬁ ⇧ ⬀ + L; you get a combo if it hits and a huge frame advantage if guarded. This technique works best against smaller characters, or opponents who don't stand up to guard until a little later.

Against larger adversaries, jump and immediately press ⇨ + H to get an air throw attempt, then immediately cancel to air Tatsumaki Senpukyaku L before the kick even comes out to cross up players using large characters. This serves to both discourage foes from jumping and protecting you from air throws while also crossing up your opposition.

SPENCER

"EITHER DIE A HERO, OR LIVE LONG ENOUGH TO HAVE EVERYONE TURN ON YOU."

Bio

REAL NAME

Nathan Spencer

OCCUPATION

Former U.S. Government Operative (Dishonorably Discharged)

ABILITIES

Besides the bionic arm attached to his left shoulder, he is proficient with various firearms.

WEAPONS

In addition to his bionic arm, he also utilizes handguns, rifles, grenade launchers, etc.

PROFILE

Once a hero of the war against the Empire, he was branded a traitor and sentenced to death by his government following the Bionic Purge. However, with the emergence of a new bionic threat, he has answered the call to return to the battlefield.

FIRST APPEARANCE

Bionic Commando (1987)

POWER GRID

- 2 INTELLIGENCE
- 4 STRENGTH
- 2 SPEED
- 2 STAMINA
- 1 ENERGY PROJECTION
- 4 FIGHTING ABILITY

*This is biographical, and does not represent an evaluation of the in-game combat potential of this hero.

ALTERNATE COSTUMES

1

2

3

4

5

6

DLC

Overview

Vitality	1,050,000
Chain Combo Archetype	Marvel Series

X-Factor Boost	Damage	Speed
Level 1 (3 teammates remaining)	135%	105%
Level 2 (2 teammates remaining)	160%	110%
Level 3 (1 teammate remaining)	185%	115%

Your goal with Spencer is to get him close to his opponent while pushing them into the corner. Why is that the goal?

- **Spencer's only ranged tool consists of various forms of using his bionic arm for grapple attacks and movement**
- **Spencer's attacks and combos naturally push the opposing character to the corner, while Spencer builds a lot of hyper meter**
- **Against a cornered adversary, Spencer is capable of inflicting lots of pain, easily breaking 700,000 damage with only one hyper meter bar**

Spencer can approach and push his competitor to the corner in a few ways:

- **By approaching his opponent using dashes and grapple movement, covered by an assist**
- **By mixing your foe up between his low attacks, Spencer's → + Ⓗ overhead, and throws to score combos that carry a character to the corner**
- **By keeping an eye out for chances to blow through the opposing player's attacks using his Bionic Lancer**

TUNING SINCE ORIGINAL MVC3

Spencer has been altered only slightly since the last go-round. He has gained a new move, Bionic Bomber, which enhances his corner combo potential even further. He didn't, however, gain any mashable moves... Spencer's hits are more about quality than quantity, after all. He catches a mild nerf in terms of losing the ability to start the old THC glitch with his Bionic Maneuvers hyper combo, but he is hardly alone in losing access to the THC glitch. Catch your rival slipping near a corner, and you'll still make them pay plenty with new combos.

- **New Move: Bionic Bomber (in air)↓ ↘ → + Ⓢ**
- **Spencer's behavior after falling from air Swing Wire altered slightly**
- **Swing Wire travels more quickly**
- **Spencer floats higher after Zip Kick**
- **Startup of up-close Armor Piercer reduced to 3 (from 4)**
- **Wavedash speed improved**

Attack Set

Standing Basic Attacks

Screen	Command	Hits	Damage	Meter Gain	Startup	Active	Recovery	Advantage on Hit	Advantage if Guarded	Notes
1	Standing L	1	48,000	384	6	3	11	0	-1	Chains to standing L
2	Standing M	1	67,000	536	9	3	22	-6	-7	—
3	Standing H	1	88,000	704	12	3	21	0	-1	—

1

2

3

Crouching Basic Attacks

Screen	Command	Hits	Damage	Meter Gain	Startup	Active	Recovery	Advantage on Hit	Advantage if Guarded	Notes
1	Crouching L	1	45,000	360	7	3	10	+1	0	Low attack
2	Crouching M	1	70,000	560	8	3	21	-5	-6	—
3	Crouching H	1	80,000	640	13	4	19	—	0	Low attack, knocks down

1

2

3

Ground Special Attack—Launcher

Screen	Command	Hits	Damage	Meter Gain	Startup	Active	Recovery	Advantage on Hit	Advantage if Guarded	Notes
1	S (while standing or crouching)	1	90,000	720	10	4	26	—	-7	Launcher, not special- or hyper combo-cancelable

1

Air Basic Attacks

Screen	Command	Hits	Damage	Meter Gain	Startup	Active	Recovery	Advantage on Hit	Advantage if Guarded	Notes
1	Air L	1	45,000	360	6	3	15	+8	+6	Overhead attack
2	Air M	1	63,000	504	8	5	20	+11	+10	Overhead attack
3	Air H	1	83,000	664	10	5	21	+16	+17	Overhead attack

1

2

3

Air Special Attacks—Flying Screen and Air Exchange

Air Ⓢ causes a hard knockdown when used in a launcher combo (this is sometimes called flying screen). When used outside of a launcher combo, air Ⓢ behaves mostly like another basic attack. Air exchange attacks, performed by inputting a direction plus Ⓢ, are only possible during a launcher combo. Exchange hits initiate team aerial combos by tagging in the next available character to continue the air combo.

Screen	Command	Hits	Damage	Meter Gain	Startup	Active	Recovery	Advantage on Hit	Advantage if Guarded	Notes
1	Air Ⓢ	1	88,000	704	10	5	21	+16	+15	Causes hard knockdown if used in launcher combo
2	Air ⇧ + Ⓢ (during launcher combo)	1	60,000	480	10	3	23	—	—	Tags in next available ally while lofting opponent upward
3	Air ⇨ or ⇦ + Ⓢ (during launcher combo)	1	50,000	400	10	3	23	—	—	Tags in next available ally while causing wall bounce, erases 1 hyper meter bar from opposing character
4	Air ⇩ + Ⓢ (during launcher combo)	1	50,000	400	10	3	23	—	—	Tags in next available ally while causing ground bounce, generates 1 hyper meter bar

1

2

3

4

Command Attacks

Command attacks resemble basic attacks but have different chaining and canceling properties. It's usually possible to chain *into* a command attack from basic attacks, but most command attacks cannot be chained from or canceled themselves.

Screen	Command	Hits	Damage	Meter Gain	Startup	Active	Recovery	Advantage on Hit	Advantage if Guarded	Notes
1	⇨ + Ⓗ	1	90,000	720	21	3	22	+4	-2	Overhead attack, not special- or hyper combo- cancelable

1

Throws

Throws are for snagging passive or blocking opponents. Since throws are active so quickly, you can also use them to preemptively toss opposing characters out of their offense. Combos are usually possible after throws, one way or another.

Screen	Command	Hits	Damage	Meter Gain	Startup	Active	Notes
1	⇨ + Ⓗ (ground)	2	80,000	800	1	1	Hard knockdown
	⇦ + Ⓗ (ground)	2	80,000	800	1	1	Hard knockdown
2	⇨ + Ⓗ (air)	2	80,000	800	1	1	Hard knockdown
	⇦ + Ⓗ (air)	2	80,000	800	1	1	Hard knockdown

1

2

As a Partner—Crossover Assists

Screen	Type	P1+P2 Crossover Combination Hyper Combo	Description	Hits	Damage	Meter Gain	Startup	Active	Recovery (this crossover assist)	Recovery (other partner)	Notes
1	Spencer—α	Bionic Lancer	Wire Grapple L	1	20,000	200	34	17	117	87	Causes hard knockdown, projectile has 1 low priority durability point
2	Spencer—β	Bionic Lancer	Wire Grapple M	1	20,000	200	34	17	117	87	Pulls target down to ground and puts them in standing state, projectile has 1 low priority durability point
3	Spencer—γ	Bionic Lancer	Armor Piercer	1	130,000	1040	45	4	134	104	Causes wall bounce

You might find a use for each of Spencer's assists; the one you select depends on the needs and construction of the rest of your team. All three assists come equipped with Bionic Lancer for crossover combinations—not only does this add one single extremely damaging hit to any crossover combination, but it's also invincible, far-reaching, and very fast.

1

2

3

Spencer—α is a Wire Grapple that causes a hard knockdown at the feet of your point character. Long range characters equipped with lengthy attacks, quick projectiles, or durable beams can call Spencer—α just before their long range attacks turn what would have previously been glancing hits into full combos. The long range attack should end as Spencer's grapple strikes, then you can proceed to an OTG combo. You can do the same thing in combos. Note that just like Spencer's Wire Grapple L on point, most small characters can crouch under the grapple hook.

Spencer—β resembles his Come 'ere! attack in that instead of putting the opposing character into a hit state, it just places them on their feet in front of the point character. If you wait too long, they'll be free to act, just as after Come 'ere! when Spencer is on point. However, if you stick a meaty attack out over to where Spencer drags his foe, you can start a combo. This assist works as anti-air from outside of close range, and it can naturally enable and extend many combos.

Spencer—γ is Armor Piercer; unfortunately, Armor Piercer as an assist is always the slower 130,000 damage version. This assist can be very useful if your other characters would benefit from having a wall bounce assist to place in combos.

Snap Back

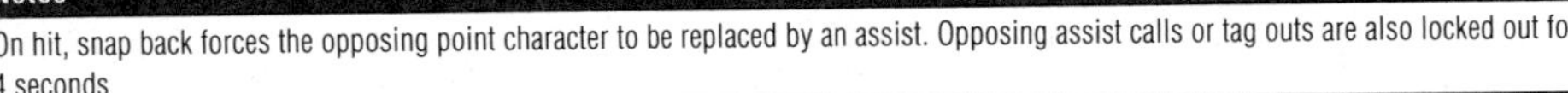

Screen	Command	Hits	Damage	Meter Gain	Startup	Active	Recovery	Advantage on Hit	Advantage if Guarded
1	↓↘→ + P1 or P2	1	50,000	500 - (-1 hyper meter bar)	9	2	21	—	-1
Notes									
On hit, snap back forces the opposing point character to be replaced by an assist. Opposing assist calls or tag outs are also locked out for 4 seconds									

1

Special Moves

Screen	Name	Command	Hits	Damage	Meter Gain	Startup	Active	Recovery	Advantage on Hit	Advantage if Guarded	Notes
1, 2, 3	Wire Grapple	↓↘→ + ATK	1	30,000	240	10	22	51	-33	-13	Projectile has 5 low priority durability points
4	Reel in Punch	(When Wire Grapple hits) L	1	72,000	720	—	—	—	—	—	Wire Grapple follow-up, hard knockdown
5	Zip Kick	(When Wire Grapple hits) M	1	90,000	900	—	—	—	—	—	Wire Grapple follow-up, wall bounce
6	Come' ere!	(When Wire Grapple hits) H	—	—	—	—	—	—	+2	—	Wire Grapple follow-up, pulls standing victim to Spencer
7, 8, 9	Air Wire Grapple	↓↘→ + ATK (in air)	2	120,000	1200	13	16	Until grounded	—	—	Projectile has 5 low priority durability points, causes wall bounce
10	Jaw Breaker	→↓↘ + ATK	1	35,000	350	5	1	31	—	—	Throw attack, hard knockdown
11	Smash Kick	(During Jaw Breaker M or H) H	2	94,500	1200	—	—	—	—	—	Jaw Breaker follow-up, causes wall bounce
11	Critical Smash	(During Jaw Breaker M or H, specific timing) H	2	157,500	2000	—	—	—	—	—	Jaw Breaker follow-up, causes wall bounce
12	Armor Piercer	↓↘→ + S	1	180,000 / 150,000 / 130,000	1440 / 1200 / 1040	3~8 / 21	6 (12) 4	41	—	-22	Hits on 3rd frame if adversary is nearby; 21st frame if not
13	Bionic Bomber	(in air) ↓↘→ + S	2	142,000	1200	35	Until grounded	22	—	+3	OTG-capable, knocks down, final hit creates explosion that can destroy projectiles
14	Swing Wire	On ground: Any non-downward direction + S + ATK; in air: any non-upward direction + S + ATK	1	10,000	—	11	Until opponent or screen edge hit	—	+9 air / -2 ground	+8 air / -3 ground	Spencer reels himself to wherever the grapple touches
15	Swing Grapple	In air: Any upward direction + S + ATK	—	—	—	—	—	—	—	—	Swing can be interrupted halfway through with basic attacks and air S

Wire Grapple: Spencer fires a grapple either straight ahead, diagonally up-forward, or straight up. The grapple itself counts as a projectile, and so it can clash with other projectiles, but if its durability points are expended then it can no longer hit your adversary.

Wire Grapple L 1

Wire Grapple M 2

Wire Grapple H 3

Wire Grapple L, which travels laterally, can be useful occasionally as a long range poke, as long as your opponent is not dominating ground level with projectiles. With the right assist you can perform H Come'ere!, follow-up, and score a full combo.

Wire Grapple M can work as a preemptive anti-air to snag competitors just as they leave the ground. If you lack an assist to make a combo off of Come 'ere! feasible, you can proceed off a successful Wire Grapple to M Zip Kick, and then continue a combo starting with a down-forward aimed Swing Wire at mid screen, or a chain to launch near the corner.

You can use Wire Grapple H as an anti-air for foes directly above, or it can combo if you launch an opponent who is in the air just over Spencer, then super jump cancel into it. This is useful to know, since performing Wire Grapple H into the L Reel in Punch follow-up causes a hard knockdown while ignoring damage scaling! Find a way to work in multiple vertical Wire Grapples to L follow-ups for tremendous damage in your combos.

On contact, Wire Grapple briefly stuns your target and awaits your input. Pressing an attack button initiates one of three follow-up attacks.

L Reel in Punch 4

M Zip Kick 5

H Come 'ere! 6

Reel in Punch, Zip Kick, and Come 'ere!: The follow-ups for a grounded Wire Grapple are activated by pressing L, M, or H upon a successful Wire Grapple hit. Zip Kick is the automatic follow-up for air Wire Grapple, and it is more useful in that situation; from grounded Wire Grapple, Reel in Punch and Come 'ere! have more potential.

Reel in Punch causes a hard knockdown, which allows Spencer to start a combo—dash forward and OTG with tiger knee air Wire Grapple M. This causes Zip Kick automatically, which leaves Spencer in the air in position to continue the juggle. Even something as simple as landing, performing Bionic Lancer immediately, then finishing with another OTG tiger knee Wire Grapple M deals 473,500 damage!

Come 'ere! simply pulls your adversary into close range while putting Spencer at a frame advantage of +2. On his own, Spencer needs more frame advantage than that in order to be scary or even safe while you have him on offense, so giving up the guaranteed damage of Reel in Punch for Come 'ere! is ill-advised. The story changes if Spencer is backed by an assist who lasts long enough to hit a foe after a successful Wire Grapple to Come 'ere! Examples of assists who work for this include Doctor Strange—β, Firebrand—α, and Trish—β. Call a long-lasting assist, then perform Wire Grapple. If it hits, tap H for Come 'ere!, and you get a free combo! If it doesn't, the assist helps cover Spencer's recovery.

Air Wire Grapple: In the air, Wire Grapple can be aimed either straight ahead, diagonally downward, or straight down. On hit, air Wire Grapple transitions to Zip Kick automatically, causing a wall bounce and leaving Spencer and his adversary in midair.

Air Wire Grapple L 4

Air Wire Grapple M 5

Air Wire Grapple H 6

Air Wire Grapple M and H are OTG-capable, and thus a staple in Spencer's combos. It's best used to OTG your opponent after air S has caused flying screen but BEFORE Spencer lands. This requires careful aim on the way down, but just force yourself to go for it, and it quickly becomes second nature. Use the M version midscreen and the H version in corners (or if you happen to end up at point-blank range during a midscreen combo).

If air Wire Grapple doesn't hit successfully, Spencer falls straight down, unable to block or act until landing. Astute players know this, and they can then simply wait to launch Spencer just before he lands. With careful timing, you can avoid this dangerous penalty. Input the S + ATK command for either Swing Wire or Swing Grapple JUST as a failed air Wire Grapple finishes retracting—the timing is strict—and you can cancel the end of the recovery of Spencer's air Wire Grapple into the grapple movement! This not only makes air Wire Grapple a safer option than it would be otherwise, but it leads to tactics on its own. For example, you can have Spencer get above a cornered competitor and guess on air Wire Grapple H straight down, knowing that if your fishing doesn't pay off, you can swing Spencer backward to safety or forward to create a jump-in offense.

10

Jaw Breaker: Spencer's command throw is active on frame 5 after input. It's relatively slow, for a throw; normal throws are active in 1 frame, as are many other command throws. Jaw Breaker also doesn't have extra range like many command throws do; it reaches about as far as a regular grab (despite Spencer lunging forward with his hand, his actual throwing hitbox doesn't even make it to his elbow).

Still, a successful Jaw Breaker leads to varied combo opportunities anywhere on screen, and there are tricks to landing it outside of just dashing in and hoping for the best. So, while Jaw Breaker is a mediocre "cold open" throw for starting your offense, you can layer it into your attack patterns to cover more bases. And although it's a tad slow, it still works fine against completely defensive and passive opponents because it's unbreakable on contact.

The L and M versions are almost identical, and these moves grab grounded adversaries. The H version is actually an air throw, aimed at airborne enemies. The hitbox for Jaw Breaker H is much more lenient than Jaw Breaker L and M, and Spencer can snag just about anything that's airborne and in the vicinity of his arm; imagine him holding a beach ball, and that's about right. So, while you'll need tricks to make Jaw Breaker L and M truly successful (see Advanced Tactics), Jaw Breaker H simply requires that you read that the opposing character is leaving the ground or that you react to their airborne actions. It can be especially useful against a captive audience, like fresh characters forced to fall in post-K.O.

A successful Jaw Breaker tosses the target into the air; afterward, they land in a hard knockdown. You can make Spencer start a juggle with M before your opponent hits the ground, or you can have Spencer OTG afterward with air Wire Grapple or Bionic Bomber. After Jaw Breaker M or H, you can follow up Jaw Breaker more directly with Smash Kick and Critical Smash.

11

Smash Kick / Critical Smash: The canned follow-up to Jaw Breaker M or H, these kicks are accomplished by pressing H after Spencer tosses his foe skyward with Jaw Breaker, but before his target stops ascending. Spencer leaps upward and delivers a powerful kick that wall bounces his victim. The difference between Smash Kick and Critical Smash is in timing—for Critical Smash, you must input H PRECISELY on the 33rd frame after the grab starts (or, the 11th frame after Spencer starts to smack his competitor into the air). Critical Smash inflicts heavier damage, and it creates a harder wall bounce that brings the target back closer to Spencer, so it's easier to follow up.

You'll know if you got Critical Smash from the obviously increased damage and the highlighted hit effect. You can't mash H to get Critical Smash—you must hit H on exactly the right frame. This is just longer than half a second after first landing the throw.

12

***Armor Piercer*:** This heavily damaging bionic arm attack varies slightly depending on how close your adversary is when you initiate it. From 3 to 8 frames after input, a hitbox appears and extends slightly farther every 2 frames, ending about one character width from Spencer. If your opponent breaks the path of this tripwire-like hitbox at any time during those 6 frames, Armor Piercer strikes on the very next frame. It gets slightly weaker as it travels, however: if Armor Piercer strikes on frames 3 or 4 it deals 180,000 damage; during frames 5 or 6, it deals 150,000 damage; during frames 7 and 8, it deals 130,000 damage. If your attacker hasn't "set off" a close range Armor Piercer after 8 frames, then Armor Piercer strikes on frame 21, inflicting 130,000 damage. You'll still get the wall bounce and decent damage, but this is obviously much slower.

Since Spencer has no basic attack faster than 6 frames, and since his Jaw Breaker throw grabs on frame 5, close range Armor Piercer is actually the fastest attack Spencer has that isn't a normal throw. It's also fast enough to link after Spencer's → + H overhead, which is important for making his mix-ups threatening. It's unsafe if guarded, however, so while it can work as a raw guess because of its speed, any guessing of this kind may get you into trouble as much as it helps. Be ready to hyper cancel to Bionic Lancer, then THC to a partner if the opposing player blocks and shows signs of retaliating.

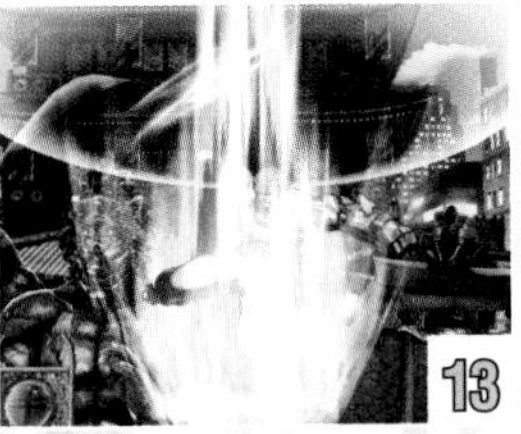
13

***Bionic Bomber*:** This diving, OTG-capable attack new to *UMvC3* gives you another tool to score OTG hits with Spencer in combos. The startup is extremely slow, so you'll want to start it as soon as possible after hard knockdowns. You can insert Bionic Bomber into just about any corner combo, or after tossing your foe with Jaw Breaker (forgo the Smash Kick follow-up, and just jump and perform Bionic Bomber on them during the hard knockdown).

Swing Wire 14

Swing Grapple 15

***Swing Wire and Swing Grapple*:** Spencer uses his bionic arm to get around, as well as to attack. Uses of Swing Wire and Swing Grapple in midair count against the three special moves per airborne period rule.

For Swing Wire, possible with S + ATK + any direction on the ground or any non-upward direction in the air, Spencer fires his grapple out (this is actually a projectile with low damage) then pulls himself to wherever it strikes—whether that's the floor or a screen edge, or the opposing character. Swing Wire cannot be interrupted once initiated, and while it allows Spencer to close in at odd angles and redirect himself at will, he'll usually be at a throwable disadvantage at a minimum when he uses Swing Wire to approach his adversary directly, unless he was up close already. Swing Wire is still his most important movement option, and it is vital for extending combos.

Swing Wire has a slightly bigger hitbox than Wire Grapple, but it still whiffs over the heads of certain crouching characters: Amaterasu, Frank West, and Rocket Raccoon.

During Swing Grapple, accomplished with S + ATK + any upward direction while airborne, Spencer fires the bionic arm diagonally upward to anchor on some unseen point and hurl him forward in a kind of double jump. You can interrupt Swing Grapple partway through with other grapples or attacks.

Hyper Combos

Screen	Name	Command	Hits	Damage	Startup	Active	Recovery	Advantage on Hit	Advantage if Guarded	Notes
1	Bionic Maneuvers	↓↘→ + ATK ATK	6	304,500	18+2	22	23	—	-22	Hard knockdown
2	Bionic Lancer	↓↙← + ATK ATK	1	250,000	4+3	10	50	—	-37	Frames 1-11 invulnerable, long spinning knockdown into hard knockdown

1

Bionic Maneuvers: Spencer's autocombo hyper combo is great for piling on damage, especially near corners where you're guaranteed a follow-up with tiger knee air Wire Grapple M or H, followed by even more juggling.

It's possible to juggle all the way into another Bionic Maneuvers hyper combo.

Bionic Maneuvers is one of the hyper combos that takes place in its own little cutscene; like lv.3 hyper combos or Storm's Elemental Rage, it cannot be canceled with X-Factor.

Like Wire Grapple L on the ground or Spencer—α, this grapple attack whiffs over the heads of small characters who are crouching. That's fine, since you shouldn't use Bionic Maneuvers outside of combos anyway!

2

Bionic Lancer: Spencer charges almost the full length of the screen with a ferocious, single-hit bionic punch. Bionic Lancer travels very quickly, and Spencer is invincible for the first 11 frames. This means you can use Bionic Lancer as an invincible punisher or reversal through almost anything, up to half the screen away.

The invincibility also makes Bionic Lancer great for educated guesses before you were going to THC anyway, especially if your opponent happens to call an assist while you wind up the big bionic punch.

After a hit, Bionic Lancer flings the target straight upward in a spinning knockdown. Afterward, they're laid out prone in a hard knockdown. After most Bionic Lancer hits, you should be able to OTG with tiger knee air Wire Grapple M. You can also opt to activate X-Factor or THC to keep the combo going.

About the only mean thing you can say about Bionic Lancer is that moves that have armor properties simply absorb it, since it's only one hit.

Battle Plan

Your goal with Spencer is to get him close to his opponent so he can hit them, which is pretty simple. Do that, and his other objective of pushing his adversary to the corner occurs naturally. Spencer doesn't have the movement, mix-up, or ranged tools of some characters; he doesn't have a teleport or a triangle jump, or a dive kick. What he does have are his Wire Grapples and Swing Wire, however, which allow him to engage the enemy in an unorthodox and unique manner.

You'll want to be patient when moving in on your rival. Wavedash and jump forward cautiously behind the cover of a beam assist, like Iron Man—α or Taskmaster—α. The cover of an assist also provides a chance to use horizontal Swing Wire on the ground or diagonal down-forward Swing Wire in the air to move into close range. Without the assist to cover Spencer, opposing characters can usually react to Swing Wire straight at them by throwing Spencer; Swing Wire leaves him at a disadvantage. Time an assist for when your competitor is already guarding, however, and you can get Spencer into close range.

Without an assist, or when your opponent is being particularly obstinate or evasive, you'll have to be less direct. Swing Wire and Swing Grapple are a big help because they allow you to redirect Spencer back and forth across the playing field in midair.

Swing Wire is vital for Spencer to get around, but beware of throws and air throws.

With the right assist to back it up, Wire Grapple is a useful long range poke.

Don't be predictable—perform backward Swing Wires into a screen edge that go nowhere, or zip back and forth repeatedly, so your adversary can't pin you down. Zipping away with Swing Wires is also your escape method after air recovery, much like how some characters can fly and then airdash away repeatedly.

At the end of Swing Wire and halfway through Swing Grapple, you can make Spencer perform other attacks. This is useful after zipping over attackers' heads with Swing Wire, so you can fall with an attack from the other side (preferably while an assist hits from the side you vacated); it's also vital in combos after a midscreen air Wire Grapple M hit (down-forward Swing Wire, air S just before Spencer lands, standing H, S, and so on).

When you anticipate running into another airborne character, or when Spencer's grapple movement has ended and he's about to fall in on them, rely on air ⇨ + H for attacking air to air or air to ground. This combines an option select air throw with an effective air attack. If you happen to score an air throw with Spencer, whether on reaction or as an option select, proceed to **Combo V**.

The effectiveness of Wire Grapples as pokes on their own is matchup-dependent. Many small characters can crouch under Wire Grapple L, lessening its value. Strong projectile characters won't give Spencer a place to squeeze in ground level grapples. Characters whose offense is based on calling an assist and then teleporting can annihilate Wire Grapple L attempts. Instead, success with using this high-risk, high-reward poke comes when your opponent is very conditioned to fear your use of Spencer's aggressive Swing Wire movement. Call an assist for cover and ⇨ + S + ATK to get in from fullscreen regardless of advancing guard, and your opposition should start to respect Spencer's wire animations. If you anticipate that your competitor might jump away at ground level, Wire Grapple M can come into play. Wire Grapple H is primarily used to juggle foes just above Spencer's head in certain combos, since damage scaling doesn't touch Wire Grapple H to Reel in Punch.

In matchups where getting ground level grapples out there is simply unfeasible, like against Arthur, you might instead get some mileage out of occasionally sniping at ground level projectile-based characters with normal jump height air Wire Grapple M. From almost a full screen away, this can lead to a full combo if you manage to snag your rival while they're busy tossing projectiles under Spencer. Spencer is unsafe after a whiffed air Wire Grapple, but the very end of recovery can be canceled into Swing Wire or Swing Grapple for a safe escape or a secondary assault.

While Wire Grapples aren't safe if whiffed or guarded, you can use that as intentional bait by canceling to Bionic Lancer to nail opponents who think they're going to punish a missed grapple. Be ready to THC to a safe hyper combo or activate X-Factor if Bionic Lancer is guarded too (though you can't always double down each time you make a punishable decision; sometimes, you just have to take the medicine if your adversary is ready to administer it). If your opponent guards Bionic Lancer and you *do* pop X-Factor to be safe, immediately go for either a low-hitting combo, or ⇨ + H for an overhead that you can link into Armor Piercer on a successful hit.

Can crouch under Wire Grapple L:

Amaterasu	**Frank West**	**Viewtiful Joe**	**Strider**
Arthur	**Morrigan**		**Wolverine**
Firebrand	**Phoenix**	**Rocket Raccoon**	**X-23**

While dancing with your opponent at mid range, edging for a clean hit up close, keep a keen eye out for your enemy to slip up and give you something to blow through with Bionic Lancer. This is actually just about everything, although some lv.3 hyper combos can out-invincible Spencer's invincible bionic arm. Bionic Lancer is invincible on the very first frame, so you can even use it on reaction to the hyper screen freeze of the opposing player's hyper combo! On hit, you have the option to K.O. them by X-Factor canceling into a nasty follow-up—see **Combo VIII.**

When you do establish close range, open up with a chain of crouching L, M. Try to stop there and confirm whether your competitor is blocking or not before proceeding further. If they are hit, chain to standing H, S for a launch, among any number of other options. If your adversary is guarding, you have a layered mix-up to apply here. By chaining to either ⇨ + H or crouching H, you can mix them up between high or low attacks. The ⇨ + H overhead can link to Armor Piercer in any situation and into light attacks on counterhit; see **Combo IV**. The other option is to pause slightly after crouching M, then chain to crouching H and kara-cancel into Jaw Breaker for a surprise command throw (see Advanced Tactics).

Bionic Lancer plows through virtually anything for the first 11 frames, and it is that rare hyper combo that is invincible from the first frame.

Right Hook and crouching L are Spencer's combo openers on the ground.

Alternately, you can go for crouching L again, or opt to do nothing and see if your challenger overextends themselves, doing something you can punish.

When your rival is on offense against Spencer, Bionic Lancer is obviously the biggest deterrent, but it is high risk and not an unlimited resource. Spencer's L attacks are too slow to beat out the primary pokes of most aggressive characters. Close range Armor Piercer is actually the fastest defensive asset Spencer has. Apart from an occasional educated guess for Armor Piercer or Bionic Lancer, try to stick with proper guarding and advancing guard. Against airborne opponents, standing L works as a surprisingly good anti-air; it chains into itself, so you can press it several times and confirm that it hits before proceeding to a follow-up combo or throw attempt depending on whether your competitor ate the L hits or blocked them. Jaw Breaker H is also an anti-air option if you're certain the opposing character is falling toward Spencer.

With just about any successful hit or combo taking your target into the corner or close to it, and with the strength of Spencer's corner combos, you often have a chance to pressure a fresh character falling in. Spencer also builds plenty of meter for you to use on snap backs if you want to force the situation. Through a simple setup, you can make Spencer's Jaw Breaker H extremely difficult to avoid for the new foe. Time a forward jumping air L to hit the fresh competitor just as they fall into the playing field; they should be forced to block immediately. Spencer then lands before they do, and you can perform Jaw Breaker H to snag them! If your opponent uses advancing guard on air L, you can still do this; you just need to dash forward with Spencer immediately when he lands, before performing Jaw Breaker H.

Jump and force fresh characters to guard air L ...

...then land and grab them with Jaw Breaker H!

From outside of the corner, opposing teammates that are forced to fall in can be met with a midair horizontal Swing Wire to force a close range situation right away. For a left/right mix-up, call a projectile or beam assist, then as the new character falls in, either Swing Wire forward at ground level *under* the new character, or jump and Swing Wire forward at jump height *over* the new character. Depending on your timing and your selection of assist, the point when your rival actually has to guard can be up for grabs.

COMBO USAGE

I. CR. L, M, ST. H, S CANCEL⇨ FORWARD SUPER JUMP, AIR M, M, H, S, ↓↘→ + M OTG, LAND, ↓↙← + ATK ATK, ↓↘→↗ + M

Midscreen only, 574,800 damage, 41% meter loss

An easy combo that only works when in the middle of the playing field; near corners, perform **Combo III** instead. The first OTG is done by pausing just after the air combo that ends in S, then performing air Wire Grapple M to OTG them while Spencer is on the way down. This generally puts adversaries in better post-wall bounce position for juggles than if you landed after air S, then did a tiger knee air Wire Grapple to OTG. A ↓↘→↗ + M tiger knee command is required for the final air Wire Grapple M, to OTG after Bionic Lancer. Since the wall bounce was used up already, the second Wire Grapple simply ends the combo.

If crouching L, crouching M is guarded, halt your combo and instead stage a secondary attack. Chain crouching M into → + H to go high, or crouching H to go low. You can also cancel crouching M into ATK + S to move directly next to your opponent for a throw opportunity; this is risky because of the frame disadvantage you're left at on guard, but it's still difficult for your competitor to react to at close range. This disadvantage doesn't matter if you cover Spencer's Swing Wire with an assist call, however.

II. CR. L, M, ST. H, S CANCEL⇨ FORWARD SUPER JUMP, AIR M, M, H, S, ↓↘→ + M, AIR ↘ + ATK + S, AIR S, LAND, ST. H, S CANCEL⇨ FORWARD SUPER JUMP, AIR M, M, H, S, LAND, ↓↘→↗ + M

Midscreen only, 488,700 damage, 104% meter gain

An extended midscreen variation that uses no hyper meter. This is typically used to build bar while pushing your rival into the corner. After the first air chain to air S, pause briefly on the way down, then use a well-aimed ↓↘→ + M before you land to OTG the opposing character. Then, just after recovering from the Air Wire Grapple M, perform ↘ + ATK + S so that Swing Wire's actual grapple travels under the target before juggling them, which holds them for Spencer to make contact with air S on the way in just before landing.

If the combo does carry your foe all the way to the corner instead of just close to it, you can add on more damage. Instead of another air Wire Grapple OTG after the second flying screen air S, perform ↓↘→ + S on the way down before landing to OTG with Bionic Bomber. Hyper combo cancel Bionic Bomber's landing to Bionic Maneuvers, then OTG *again* with tiger knee air Wire Grapple H to cap it off for 696,500 damage and 18% meter gain!

COMBO USAGE CONT.

III. CR. L, M, ST. H, S (CANCEL) FORWARD SUPER JUMP, AIR M, M, H, S, ↓ ↘ → + H OTG, LATE AIR S, LAND, FORWARD JUMP AIR M, H, S (CANCEL) ↘ + S + ATK, LAND, S (CANCEL) FORWARD SUPER JUMP, AIR M, M, H, S, ↓ ↘ → + S (CANCEL) ↓ ↘ → + ATK ATK, ↓ ↘ → ↗ + H

Corner only, 705,700 damage, 30% meter gain (self sufficient for Bionic Maneuvers ender)

Again, perform the falling air Wire Grapple OTG before landing. After ↓ ↘ → + H makes contact, Spencer flips backwards in midair. Perform a late air S during the flip, just before Spencer touches the ground. Then jump forward immediately and juggle your opponent with the air chain into down-forward Swing Wire. You may have to take a half-step away from the corner after landing but before relaunching, so that Spencer can keep the target from getting launched out of the corner instead of into it.

After launching your rival into the air and chaining M, M, H, S, perform ↓ ↘ → + S while Spencer is still in the air. This is not a cancel; you must wait for air S to fully recover before doing it.

For less meter but more damage and a flashier combo, you can take advantage of the lack of damage scaling on grounded Wire Grapple H to Come 'ere! You can only combo to super jump canceled Wire Grapple H from S when launching an adversary who is basically right above Spencer, which is exactly how they end up in this combo: flush above him in the corner. You can super jump cancel the final launcher in the corner into Wire Grapple H by either inputting ↓ ↘ → ↗ + H immediately, or (if "Auto super jump" is set to ON in options) by simply holding down S while inputting ↓ ↘ → + H. Either way, when the grapple hits, press L for the Come 'ere! follow-up, which leaves the foe in another hard knockdown. Jump and perform Bionic Bomber immediately to OTG, then cancel it into Bionic Maneuvers. Tack on tiger knee air Wire Grapple H for **765,600**! (And 16% hyper meter instead of 30%.)

IV. → + H, ↓ ↘ → + S, {FORWARD DASH, ST. M, H, S (CANCEL) FORWARD SUPER JUMP, AIR M, M, H, S, LAND, ↓ ↘ → ↗ + M} OR {FORWARD DASH, ST. M, H, (CANCEL) ↓ ↙ ← + ATK ATK, ↓ ↘ → ↗ + M}

541,800~623,200 damage, 71% meter gain or 58% meter loss

Linking Armor Piercer after Right Hook is technically a 1 frame link, but because *UMvC3* has a small input buffer that carries forward unused inputs, it's easier than it sounds. It's essential to add oomph to → + H with Armor Piercer into a combo when you land it. This combo does not work against Rocket Raccoon unless he's near a corner. It also doesn't work against Arthur, Viewtiful Joe, or Zero if Spencer's back is to a screen edge. In these cases, perform → + H, ↓ ↘ → + S (CANCEL) ↓ ↙ ← + ATK ATK, ↓ ↘ → ↗ + M instead.

V. AIR THROW, LAND, ↓ ↘ → ↗ + H, {↓ ↙ ← + ATK ATK, ↓ ↘ → ↗ + M} OR {WHEN OPPONENT IS CORNERED, AIR S, LAND, M, H, S (CANCEL) FORWARD SUPER JUMP, AIR M, M, H, S, ↓ ↘ → + S (CANCEL) ↓ ↘ → + ATK ATK}

367,500~454,400 damage, 80% meter loss or 17% meter loss

A simple combo off of Spencer's air throw. After the throw, it's possible to perform ↓ ↘ → + H before touching the ground, but the timing is tight. It's usually easier to land and do ↓ ↘ → ↗ + H.

VI. → ↓ ↘ + ATK (CANCEL) H (CRITICAL SMASH), FORWARD JUMP, AIR M, H, DELAYED S, LAND, FORWARD JUMP, AIR M, H, DELAYED S, LAND, ST. M, H {S (CANCEL) FORWARD SUPER JUMP, AIR M, M, H, S, ↓ ↘ → ↗ + M} OR {(CANCEL) ↓ ↙ ← + ATK ATK, ↓ ↘ → ↗ + M}

435,200~542,600 damage, 108% meter gain

This combo follows up a successful Jaw Breaker M or H. The damage data mentioned assumes that you land the Critical Smash variation, though it works even if you get Smash Kick instead. Smash Kick forces Spencer to dash forward before the initial jump. During the air M, H, S sequence, delay the S input slightly so that Spencer lands immediately after it hits. This ensures that the follow-up jump chain can connect.

VII. ↓ ↘ → + ATK, L (REEL IN PUNCH), WAVEDASH, ↓ ↘ → ↗ + M OTG, {LAND, ↓ ↙ ← + ATK ATK, ↓ ↘ → ↗ + M OTG} OR {IF FOE IS CORNERED: LATE AIR S, LAND, ST. M, H, S (CANCEL) FORWARD SUPER JUMP, AIR M, M, H, S, ↓ ↘ → + S (CANCEL) ↓ ↘ → + ATK ATK}

473,500~638,900 damage, 22% meter loss

When at a distance, attack with ↓ ↘ → + ATK after you've made an opponent hesitant with unpredictable Swing Wire movement. It's also useful as a long range punisher if the opposing player messes up badly. Take care to cover yourself with assists or pick your spots for Wire Grapple attempts carefully, as the recovery is horrendous. When doing the version near corners, after falling with late air S, land and take a half step away from the corner before starting the relaunch chain with standing M.

VIII. CR. L, M, ST. H (CANCEL) ↓ ↙ ← + ATK ATK (X-FACTOR) {UPWARD JUMP, AIR M, H, S (CANCEL) ↘ + S + ATK, LAND} X3 ST. M (CANCEL) ↓ ↘ → + S, S (CANCEL) FORWARD SUPER JUMP, AIR H, S, FALLING ↓ ↘ → + M OTG

1,012,100~1,246,600 damage, 56~107% meter gain (depending on X-Factor level; 1 bar must already be available for Bionic Lancer at the beginning)

This is a verifiable X-Factor combo that works at any level of X-Factor and starts off of a basic opening. The same combo follow-up after the X-Factor cancel of Bionic Lancer works from Bionic Lancer by itself if you use it to blow through your adversary's attack or punish them from far away. After Bionic Lancer to X-Factor, wait for the foe to start descending during the spinning knockdown to jump and meet them with the air chain into Swing Wire loops. If you jump upward to catch your rival properly from the Bionic Lancer, the Swing Wire loops can simply be done as quickly as possible.

ADVANCED TACTICS

KARA-CANCEL JAW BREAKER

You can extend the range on Jaw Breaker significantly by canceling into it from the very beginning of either standing Ⓗ or crouching Ⓗ. You want Jaw Breaker to emerge before those heavy attacks are actually capable of hitting. Be careful not to get → + Ⓗ Right Hook rather than just standing Ⓗ if going for the standing kara-cancel. It's generally easier and more consistent to go for crouching Ⓗ kara-canceled to Jaw Breaker anyway.

In guarded chain combos or after Ⓛ ticks, chain to crouching Ⓗ and cancel to Jaw Breaker immediately for a surprise unbreakable throw!

The easiest way to apply this is as a very strong tick throw: just chain standing or crouching Ⓛ into crouching Ⓗ, then cancel to Jaw Breaker before the sweep hits. This works even from the tip of the ranges for Spencer's Ⓛ attacks (you can even do it after chaining standing Ⓛ x3 if your target hasn't used advancing guard by then), and it doesn't require much timing—just do it as quickly as possible. Usually, you'll want to go for Jaw Breaker L or M to snag grounded adversaries, but if you expect they'll try to jump away from your close range offense, you can use Jaw Breaker H instead.

This isn't airtight, but it's very fast and difficult to react to; if your opponent counters correctly, it was as likely an accident as a solid reaction, such as if they mash attacks on autopilot expecting to advancing guard and they throw you instead. The most likely scenario is that the foe beats you to the punch with their normal throw or with a quick Ⓛ attack.

Apart from tick throws, kara Jaw Breaker can make Spencer's normal ground chain game much stronger. His typical ground opener is crouching Ⓛ, Ⓜ. If this is guarded, chaining to crouching Ⓗ or → + Ⓗ presents a high/low mix-up to your rival. Normally, Spencer is too far away after Ⓛ, Ⓜ is guarded for Jaw Breaker to connect in order to add a throw layer to the mix-up cake, but Jaw Breaker can reach if you chain to kara-canceled crouching Ⓗ. Unlike the tick kara throw from Ⓛ attacks, you'll want to pause just a split second after crouching Ⓜ is guarded before chaining to crouching Ⓗ CANCEL Jaw Breaker. If you chain to sweep and then necessarily kara-cancel right away, Jaw Breaker will be active while your adversary is still stuck in hitstun/blockstun and therefore immune to throws.

SPENCER AND CROSSOVER COMBINATIONS

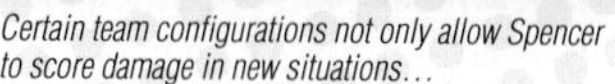

Certain team configurations not only allow Spencer to score damage in new situations...

...but they also let you continue his own combo afterward!

Bionic Lancer is fast, hard-hitting, and invincible, and none of that changes during a crossover combination. As a partner character, Spencer adds a long-reaching hit to any crossover combination. On point, since Bionic Lancer is just one hit, Spencer is free to act again really quickly. Paired with certain partners, this can lead to some interesting uses for crossover combinations.

With partners who have OTG-capable hypers, this opens the door for Spencer to (even more easily) add heavy damage to any hard knockdown, but in particular, one place he normally can't... after a normal ground throw. As an example, if Storm—α or β or Hsien-Ko—β is in the next slot, and Spencer's packing two hyper meter bars, you can ground throw, then just activate crossover combination (with Hsien-Ko—β, you'll need to dash forward immediately after the throw). The partner's hyper combo OTGs the opposing character up into Spencer's Bionic Lancer, and that's over 500,000 damage off a normal throw, anywhere.

This can be taken further with certain hyper combos that last a particularly long time, such as Amaterasu's Okami Shuffle or Dante's Million Dollars. These hyper combos strike for so long that you will be free to act with Spencer and keep the combo going after the crossover combination is over.

Combining the ideas, with a team like Spencer, Dante, and either Storm—α/β or Hsien-Ko—β, build at least three hyper meters, then score a normal throw on your opponent. Simply activate crossover combination (dash if you have Hsien-Ko), and the OTG-capable partner then pops the thrown foe up into both Bionic Lancer and Million Dollars. This deals heavy damage already, but most importantly, since Million Dollars takes forever, Spencer will be free to act *standing right next to the enemy*! Since Million Dollars sends the target into a spinning knockdown in two places, you can quickly perform Wire Grapple H to Reel in Punch (which is immune to damage scaling in combos!) at least twice before Million Dollars ends. All told, what's the damage? Approaching 900,000, confirmed off a throw. And this is just the beginning of the possibilities.

"I'VE LOST EVERYTHING, BUT I'M NOT GOING TO LOSE THIS FIGHT."

COMBO APPENDIX

GENERAL EXECUTION TIPS

You can perform Spencer's chains more slowly than most other characters. Verify off of crouching Ⓛ, Ⓜ!

Juggles after OTG air Wire Grapple M and H almost always work better if you perform them while falling after an air Ⓢ hard knockdown, rather than waiting to land and tiger knee the grapples.

In any situation where Bionic Bomber is being used, start it as early as possible.

AS SPENCER COMES IN: AIR Ⓜ, Ⓗ, Ⓢ, LAND, ↓↘→↗ + Ⓜ, {LAND, ↓↙← + ATK ATK, ↓↘→↗ + Ⓜ} OR {AIR Ⓢ, LAND, ↓↘→ + Ⓢ CANCEL ↓↘→ + ATK ATK, ↓↘→↗ + Ⓜ}

Notes	Damage
TAC with ↑ + Ⓢ or ↓ + Ⓢ	Varies based on damage scaling

→ + Ⓗ, ↓↘→ + Ⓢ CANCEL ↓↙← + ATK ATK CANCEL X-FACTOR, ST. Ⓜ, Ⓗ CANCEL ↓↙← + ATK ATK, ↓↘→↗ + Ⓜ

Notes	Damage
Basic X-Factor combo off overhead	933,000~1,101,500 damage, 152~142% meter loss

(REQUIRES CORNER) CR. Ⓛ, Ⓜ, ST. Ⓗ, CANCEL ↓↘→ + ATK ATK, ↓↘→↗ + Ⓗ, AIR Ⓢ, LAND, ST. Ⓜ, Ⓗ, Ⓢ CANCEL FORWARD SUPER JUMP, AIR Ⓜ, Ⓜ, Ⓗ, Ⓢ, ↓↘→ + Ⓢ OTG, LAND, ↓↘→ + Ⓢ CANCEL ↓↘→ + ATK ATK, ↓↘→↗ + Ⓗ

Notes	Damage
High-damage corner combo using Bionic Bomber. Connecting ↓↘→ + Ⓢ after Bionic Bomber requires perfect timing; if too difficult, instead cancel air ↓↘→ + Ⓢ to ↓↘→ + ATK ATK (reducing damage to 780,600)	800,200

TRISH

"YEAH, I'M ACTUALLY A DEMON SPAWN FROM HELL. BUT I'M ACTUALLY NOT A BAD GIRL WHEN YOU GET TO KNOW ME."

Bio

REAL NAME

Trish

OCCUPATION

Devil Hunter

ABILITIES

Excellent at fighting with guns and swords. She also wields lightning-based powers.

WEAPONS

She uses the great sword Sparda, once wielded by the legendary Dark Knight of the same name. She also has a pair of guns named "Luce & Ombra.

PROFILE

Originally created by a demon in order to lure Dante into a trap, she fell to her target's charms after working side by side with him, and betrayed the demon world. Now, she serves as Dante's partner in his business.

FIRST APPEARANCE

Devil May Cry (2001)

POWER GRID

2	INTELLIGENCE
5	STRENGTH
3	SPEED
6	STAMINA
4	ENERGY PROJECTION
4	FIGHTING ABILITY

*This is biographical, and does not represent an evaluation of the in-game combat potential of this hero.

ALTERNATE COSTUMES

Overview

Vitality	850,000
Chain Combo Archetype	3-Hits Alternating

X-Factor Boost	Damage	Speed
Level 1 (3 teammates remaining)	120%	120%
Level 2 (2 teammates remaining)	140%	130%
Level 3 (1 teammate remaining)	160%	140%

Your goal with Trish is to keep your foe at bay, harassing them with her long range and trap-oriented Trick moves while building up the hyper meter. You need to keep the opposing character away because:

- **Trish can hide behind the cover of her Trick "Hopscotch" and Trick "Peekaboo" traps both on the ground and in the air**
- **Covered by traps, you are more free to use her long range Low Voltage and Round Trip projectiles**
- **Coaxing her opponent to run into traps leads to free combo opportunities**

With hyper meter built up from the keepaway, Trish can greatly contribute to the efforts of her entire team:

- **By using Trick traps, Round Trip, or Round Harvest, then tagging out with a crossover attack (hold P1 or P2), Trish can hand off to another teammate in near total safety**
- **Her Round Harvest and Maximum Voltage hyper combos are ideal for punishing assists and chipping the foe from long range**
- **Round Harvest is one of the best hyper combos for crossover combinations**

Trish also has solid rushdown tools, useful when the opponent is passive or frightened, or when you have resources to burn. Trish becomes much scarier when she is either armed with X-Factor or has surplus hyper meter to keep Round Harvest reaping.

TUNING SINCE ORIGINAL MVC3

Changes to Trish were mostly to make her less capable of outright runaway tactics. She can only use Trick "Hopscotch" once per airborne period, so she can no longer super jump backward and reposition Hopscotch multiple times during the jump. But, she can still do this if you activate flight first, since special move limitations disappear while flying... although her flight duration has been slightly reduced to curb potential abuse of this tactic.

- **Flight mode time reduced from 120 frames to 100 frames**
- **Air Maximum Voltage is OTG-capable**
- **Maximum Voltage can be mashed for additional hits**
- **Trick "Hopscotch" can only be used once per airborne period**
- **Standing Ⓜ can now chain to crouching Ⓜ**

Attack Set

Standing Basic Attacks

Screen	Command	Hits	Damage	Meter Gain	Startup	Active	Recovery	Advantage on Hit	Advantage if Guarded	Notes
1	Standing L	1	38,000	304	5	3	8	+2	+2	Chains to crouching L
2	Standing M	1	50,000	400	9	4	17	-4	-4	—
3	Standing H	1	70,000	560	13	2	24	-3	-3	—
4	(During Round Trip or Round Harvest) Standing H	1	65,000	520	10	4	18	—	+1	—

1

2

3

4

Crouching Basic Attacks

Screen	Command	Hits	Damage	Meter Gain	Startup	Active	Recovery	Advantage on Hit	Advantage if Guarded	Notes
1	Crouching L	1	40,000	320	5	3	8	+2	+2	Low attack, chains into standing L
2	Crouching M	1	48,000	384	10	8	13	-4	-4	Low attack
3	Crouching H	1	68,000	544	13	4	22	—	-3	Low attack, knocks down
4	(During Round Trip or Round Harvest) Crouching H	1	65,000	520	11	7	19	—	-3	Low attack, knocks down

1

2

3

4

Ground Special Attack—Launcher

Screen	Command	Hits	Damage	Meter Gain	Startup	Active	Recovery	Advantage on Hit	Advantage if Guarded	Notes
1	S (while standing or crouching)	1	80,000	640	12	4	23	—	-4	Launcher, not special- or hyper combo- cancelable
2	(During Round Trip or Round Harvest) S (while standing or crouching)	1	70,000	560	9	4	23	—	-4	Launcher, not special- or hyper combo- cancelable

1

2

Air Basic Attacks

Screen	Command	Hits	Damage	Meter Gain	Startup	Active	Recovery	Advantage on Hit	Advantage if Guarded	Notes
1	Air Ⓛ	1	42,000	344	4	3	18	+11	+11	Overhead attack
2	Air Ⓜ	1	52,000	416	8	4	20	+13	+14	Overhead attack
3	Air Ⓗ	1	75,000	600	14	3	26	+16	+18	Overhead attack
Identical to Stiletto Kick	(During Round Trip or Round Harvest) Air Ⓗ	1	70,000	560	13	Until grounded	7	+12	+12	Cancelable into TAC attack, can be performed at low altitude

1

2

3

Air Special Attacks—Flying Screen and Air Exchange

Air Ⓢ causes a hard knockdown when used in a launcher combo (this is sometimes called flying screen). When used outside of a launcher combo, air Ⓢ behaves mostly like another basic attack. Air exchange attacks, performed by inputting a direction plus Ⓢ, are only possible during a launcher combo. Exchange hits initiate team aerial combos by tagging in the next available character to continue the air combo.

Screen	Command	Hits	Damage	Meter Gain	Startup	Active	Recovery	Advantage on Hit	Advantage if Guarded	Notes
1	Air Ⓢ	1	80,000	640	11	2	26	+15	+15	Causes hard knockdown if used in launcher combo
2	Air ⇧ + Ⓢ (during launcher combo)	1	60,000	480	9	6	16	—	—	Tags in next available ally while lofting opponent upward
3	Air ⇨ or ⇦ + Ⓢ (during launcher combo)	1	50,000	400	8	4	24	—	—	Tags in next available ally while causing wall bounce, erases 1 hyper meter bar from opposing character
4	Air ⇩ + Ⓢ (during launcher combo)	1	50,000	400	11	4	21	—	—	Tags in next available ally while causing ground bounce, generates 1 hyper meter bar

1

2

3

4

Command Attacks

Command attacks resemble basic attacks but have different chaining and canceling properties. It's usually possible to chain *into* a command attack from basic attacks, but most command attacks cannot be chained from or canceled themselves.

Screen	Name	Command	Hits	Damage	Meter Gain	Startup	Active	Recovery	Advantage on Hit	Advantage if Guarded
1	Stiletto Kick	(In air) ⇩ + Ⓗ	1	70,000	560	13	Until grounded	7	+12	+12
Notes										
Cancelable into TAC attack; cannot be performed at very low altitude										

1

Throws

Throws are for snagging passive or blocking opponents. Since throws are active so quickly, you can also use them to preemptively toss opposing characters out of their offense. Combos are usually possible after throws, one way or another.

Screen	Command	Hits	Damage	Meter Gain	Startup	Active	Notes
1	⇨ + Ⓗ (ground)	1	80,000	800	1	1	Hard knockdown
	⇦ + Ⓗ (ground)	1	80,000	800	1	1	Hard knockdown
2	⇨ + Ⓗ (air)	1	80,000	800	1	1	Hard knockdown
	⇦ + Ⓗ (air)	1	80,000	800	1	1	Hard knockdown

1

2

As a Partner—Crossover Assists

Screen	Type	P1+P2 Crossover Combination Hyper Combo	Description	Hits	Damage	Meter Gain	Startup	Active	Recovery (this crossover assist)	Recovery (other partner)	Notes
1	Trish—α	Round Harvest	Trick "Hopscotch"	1	70,000	560	44	—	117	87	Trap stays active for 300 frames, projectile has 1 low priority durability point
2	Trish—β	Round Harvest	Trick "Peekaboo"	1	10,000	100	34	—	127	97	Activates when glyph is touched, foes can attack the glyph to make it disappear, captures opponent for 53 frames, trap stays active for 300 frames, projectile has 3 low priority durability points
3	Trish—γ	Maximum Voltage	Low Voltage H	3	108,300	960	49	—	132	102	Each projectile has 3 low priority durability points

1

2

3

Trish's best assist is Trish—β, which calls her out to place Trick "Peekaboo." Peekaboo mostly functions as it does for Trish on point: a glyph is placed onscreen that remains for five seconds. The crucial difference is that the glyph *doesn't* disappear if either your point character or Trish is struck after she sets it! This is unlike Trish's Tricks on point, which disappear if she receives a hit. Call Trish—b preemptively to fortify a position, or call it when you believe your competitor is eager to jump or airdash in. Just like Trish on point, if your rival attacks the glyph, it simply disappears, but just like on point, you simply call Trish to summon it again.

Trish—α grants Trick "Hopscotch." This move is also good; it's just slightly slower and doesn't lend itself to follow-up combos as easily as Peekaboo.

Both Trish—α and Trish—β grant access to Round Harvest in crossover combinations. Because Trish releases Sparda and is free to act so quickly during Round Harvest, if you start a crossover combination with Trish on point, you are guaranteed to be able to move with Round Harvest locking your adversary down while up to two teammates pummel them, as well. This is a chance to contribute to the crossover combination's damage, while also getting a leg up on building back the hyper meter that has been expended.

Trish—γ provides the three-bolt version of Low Voltage and replaces Round Harvest with Maximum Voltage in hyper combos. This isn't bad, but if what you want from a character slot is a beam assist and beam hyper combo in crossover combinations, there are lots of choices, whereas only Trish can provide Trick traps via crossover assist. Trick assists not only help you protect your point character, but protect your *other assist*, as well!

Snap Back

Screen	Command	Hits	Damage	Meter Gain	Startup	Active	Recovery	Advantage on Hit	Advantage if Guarded
1	↓↘→ + P1 or P2	1	50,000	500 - (-1 hyper meter bar)	2	4	18	—	+1

Notes

On hit, snap back forces the opposing point character to be replaced by an assist. Opposing assist calls or tag outs are also locked out for 4 seconds

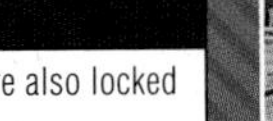

1

Special Moves

Screen	Name	Command	Hits	Damage	Meter Gain	Startup	Active	Recovery	Advantage on Hit	Advantage if Guarded	Notes
1	Low Voltage L (in air OK)	↓↘→ + L	1	70,000	560	15	—	35	-13	-13	Each projectile has 3 low priority durability points
2	Low Voltage M (in air OK)	↓↘→ + M	2	95,000	800	20	—	37	-15	-15	Each projectile has 3 low priority durability points
3	Low Voltage H (in air OK)	↓↘→ + H	3	121,900	1080	25	—	40	-18	-18	Each projectile has 3 low priority durability points
4	Trick "Hopscotch" (in air OK)	↓↙← + L	1	80,000	640	20	—	25	-2	-2	Projectile fires when opponent touches or passes over the glyph, glyph disappears if Trish is hit, trap stays active for 300 frames, projectile has 3 low priority durability points
5	Trick "Peekaboo" (in air OK)	↓↙← + M	1	10,000	100	10	—	35	+19	-13	Activates when glyph is touched, foe can attack the glyph to make it disappear, captures opponent for 53 frames, trap stays active for 300 frames, projectile has 3 priority durability points
6	Round-Trip (in air OK)	↓↙← + H	15~23	118,600	1800~2760	35	—	15	—	—	Blade advances for 40 frames or until durability points are used and then returns to Trish, projectile has 5 low priority durability points, St.H, Cr.H, and Air H, properties change until blade returns
—	Switch Sign (in air OK)	→↓↘ + ATK	—	—	—	10	—	10	—	—	Causes Round-Trip blade to hold its position momentarily
7	Air Raid (in air OK)	↓↙← + S	—	—	—	21	—	—	—	—	Flight mode, flight mode lasts for 100 frames

Low Voltage L 1

Low Voltage M 2

Low Voltage H 3

Low Voltage: This is Trish's projectile. All versions travel at the same speed. Low Voltage L is the fastest to fire and quickest to recover, but it fires only one bolt; on the ground, this travels at a height that unfortunately allows most characters to crouch under it. Thus, Low Voltage L should be used to stop forward dashes, rather than to zone. Low Voltage M fires two bolts, while Low Voltage H fires three; neither version can be crouched under on the ground, but Trish has longer startup and recovery, which leaves her more vulnerable.

The air versions fire bolts downward at a 45-degree angle. This is a difficult angle for most characters to deal with, which is one of the reasons Trish thrives in the air. Set Trick traps to cover Trish before you take to the air to fire Low Voltage.

4

Trick "Hopscotch": You can use this Trick both on the ground and in the air; either way, it has the same result. A glyph is placed on the floor right in front of Trish, which extends a slender vertical hitbox all the way to the top of the playing field. If an adversary passes over the glyph in any way, the glyph fires a bolt directly upward at them. Only one Hopscotch glyph can be active at a time; using it again erases the first glyph while producing a new one. The glyph disappears if the opposing character trips it, if five seconds pass, or if Trish is hit. Hopscotch can now only be used once per airborne period (unless you use it again during Air Raid). Hopscotch is less risky used in midair than on the ground, so this is a significant change. Hopscotch is also important to follow Stiletto Kick in Trish's air combos, and it is useful to place alongside Trick "Peekaboo" for fresh characters to fall toward.

If foes end up stuck high over Trish's head, such as when they are at air recovering at super jump height, you can place Trick "Hopscotch" just under them repeatedly. Each fresh glyph immediately fires another projectile at the challenger up above.

5

Trick "Peekaboo": Like Hopscotch, Peekaboo can be used on the ground or in the air, but it can only be used once per airborne period. Trick "Peekaboo" causes Trish to place a glyph in midair in front of her. If the competitor attacks this glyph, they simply destroy it; it also disappears after five seconds, or if Trish is hit. If your opponent runs into the glyph, they'll be captured long enough for Trish to capitalize with a full combo, or at least use Maximum Voltage from too far away to launch.

Trick "Peekaboo" is active very quickly, fast enough to use on reaction to aggressive movements that aren't coming in from point-blank range, such as long range airdashes.

Used in conjunction with Hopscotch, Peekaboo lets Trish control enough of the screen to attack more safely with Low Voltage.

6

Round-Trip and Switch Sign: After a startup lengthy compared even to Low Voltage H, Trish hurls Sparda across the screen like a boomerang. While Sparda is out of Trish's hands and in transit, her heavy basic attacks and launcher become kick attacks rather than sword swings, and air H isn't an overhead. Keep that in mind if Trish ends up next to her adversary during Round Trick, especially if you want to mix your opponent up.

On its own, you're unlikely to get Round Trip out safely very often. It's much easier to utilize while Hopscotch and Peekaboo are active nearby; it's also best to throw it from the air, so if your rival gets around it, they're still less likely to hit Trish at a clean angle. Throw Round Trip at normal jump height, so if it comes back to you at ground level, your adversary must deal with it.

The Switch Sign command can be input whenever Sparda is traveling to slow it down briefly. This is useful if Sparda runs into the target dead-on; time Switch Sign correctly, and Sparda slows down just as it starts hitting the opposing character, forcing the opposing player to guard. You'll up the damage or deal chip damage either way by using Switch Sign to drag the blade over them longer.

7

Air Raid: Trish's flight mode has had a hair of a second shaved off of her total flight time. This is to compensate for making Trish's flight mode even more important, since she can no longer use Hopscotch over and over again while in the air unless Air Raid is activated.

You can also use Air Raid to run or rush through the air very quickly with repeated airdashes. During flight, you can't cancel the same direction airdash into itself, but you can cancel airdashes in different direction. (In other words ↙ + ATK ATK, ↙ + ATK ATK, repeat works, but → + ATK ATK, → + ATK ATK doesn't work.) There's an exception: if you execute airdashes during flight with a "plink" command, it looks like an aerial wavedash, with the same direction dash canceled into itself! To perform this, input desired direction + ATK ~ ATK with the buttons separated by only one frame; in other words, drum two attack buttons one after another as quickly as possible. Performed over and over, you can use this tactic to wavedash across the sky while flying in a flash!

Hyper Combos

Screen	Name	Command	Hits	Damage	Startup	Active	Recovery	Advantage on Hit	Advantage if Guarded	Notes
1	Round Harvest	⇩⇙⇦ + ATK ATK	24	244,700	20+19	—	10	—	—	Projectile homes in on opponent for 120 frames, projectile has 1 high priority durability point, St.Ⓗ, Cr.Ⓗ, and Air Ⓗ properties change until blade returns, disappears if Trish is hit
2	Maximum Voltage (in air OK)	⇩⇘⇨ + ATK ATK	30~60	269,300~323,000	15+1	116	20	+2	+2	Each projectile has 1 high priority durability point, air version is OTG-capable, can be mashed for additional hits
3	Duet Pain (Level 3 hyper combo)	⇨⇩⇘ + ATK ATK	18	400,000	10+11	4	30	—	-11	Frames 1-22 invincible, unaffected by damage scaling, causes hard knockdown

Round Harvest: Round Harvest is Trish's biggest asset. After moderately lengthy startup (getting Round Harvest off in traffic is a little bit like looking for a place to fit in Storm's Hail Storm), Trish releases Sparda in a powered-up state. The giant demon blade homes in on the target unavoidably for two seconds. Like with Round Trip, Trish's launcher and Ⓗ attacks are kicks instead of sword swings, and air Ⓗ becomes Stiletto Kick and stops being an overhead. Sparda disappears and Round Harvest ends instantly if Trish takes a hit, but if she releases Sparda cleanly it's very unlikely.

If the opposing player guards Round Harvest and uses advancing guard repeatedly, Trish won't be able to approach her foe. But if you tag in or THC to another character in place of Trish just after she releases Sparda, the opponent's attempts to use advancing guard won't matter! The new character is then free to get right up close and personal with an adversary who is forced to guard Round Harvest. And if they're not guarding, great—continue the combo with the new character.

Maximum Voltage: Trish's projectile hyper combo shoots dozens of bolts across the screen. The ground version shoots laterally, which is great for zapping assists, chipping opponents, or continuing a full screen combo as Round Trip or Round Harvest hits a competitor. It's not quite the hyper combo beams of Akuma or Dormammu in terms of speed, but it's still fast enough to force your attacker to respect the threat.

Just like air Low Voltage, Air Maximum Voltage fires at a 45-degree angle downward. New to *UMvC3*, this air version is OTG-capable! Most obviously, this means Trish can score a decent OTG combo by herself after an air throw by airdashing and shooting at her opponent with air Maximum Voltage.

Air Maximum Voltage has no invulnerability, but because of its angle, it has another specific use: after guarding your competitor's attack with another character, you can crossover counter to Trish and IMMEDIATELY use air Maximum Voltage the instant Trish starts to "exist" as far as the game is concerned—don't wait for her to actually land and perform her assist attack as the counter! Many attacks, when guarded, are laggy enough that this ensures that Trish is basically firing directly into the face of an opposing character. If your opponent was pressuring you up close, the likelihood is also high that they might have called their assist for you to shoot at, too!

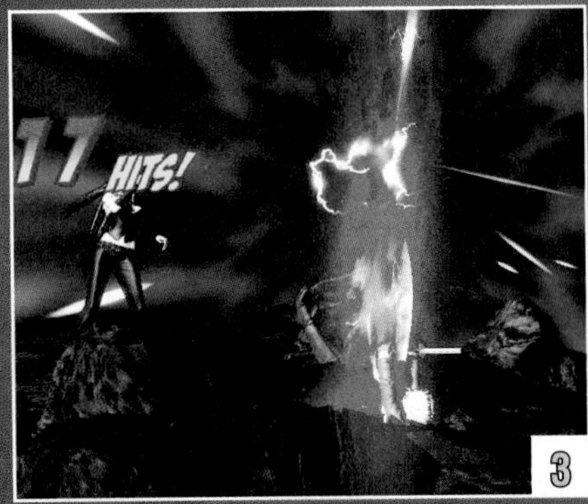

Duet Pain: Trish's lv.3 hyper combo allows her to tack on heavy damage to otherwise routine combos because it's unaffected by damage scaling. It's also invincible for the first 22 frames, giving Trish a good option to blow through things on reaction, like the hyper combo cutscene freeze of an opponent! The range is not quite that of similar lv.3 hyper combos like Dante's Devil Must Die or Iron Man's Iron Avenger, however.

"NO, I JUST LOOK LIKE DANTE'S MOTHER. YES, I KNOW HOW WEIRD THAT IS. DON'T REMIND ME."

Battle Plan

Both Tricks serve to cut off airspace for a foe, but Hopscotch does it in a pillar, while Peekaboo traps a localized area.

The payoff for being patient and waiting for foes to run into Peekaboo is high.

Trish is well-equipped for both rushdown and runaway. She can fly and double jump, her eight-way airdash enables both square and triangle jumps, and she has projectiles and traps galore. Her damage output is slightly below average, however, and so is her vitality, which skews her risk/reward in favor of leaning on her ranged tools a little more, at least at the beginning of a match. This helps you feel out the opposing player and sense whether they'll be weak to Trish rushdown, without getting Trish impaled finding out first-hand. This approach also builds hyper meter, especially if Trish brought a meter-building assist to the Hopscotch and Peekaboo party. This hyper meter can then either help out Trish's teammates or enable her to go on the offensive with Round Harvest.

Low Voltage travels really quickly, but it takes longer to actually fire than many main projectiles. This is especially true of the M and H versions, which are the ones you'll have to actually use on most characters, since the majority of characters can crouch under Low Voltage L. Low Voltage L should therefore be used when you want to stop ground movement like forward dashes; don't rely on it to send threats to a fullscreen opponent.

Fire away! These characters can't crouch under Low Voltage L:		These characters can *stand* under Low Voltage L!:	
Captain America	Ghost Rider	Amaterasu	Rocket Raccoon
C.Viper (sometimes)	M.O.D.O.K.		
Doctor Doom	Nemesis T-Type		
Doctor Strange	Ryu		
Haggar	She-Hulk		
Hulk	Spencer		
Iron Man	Thor		
	Tron		

Having to use Low Voltage M or H to threaten distant foes means Low Voltage can't be relied upon for zoning by itself, and it also means that Trish inevitably loses most projectile wars on the ground. That's fine, since her projectiles aren't for winning projectile wars. Instead, get above other beam and projectile characters at super jump height and fire Low Voltage down at an angle they can't cover. If your opponent is apt to dash forward in retaliation to your super jump (not an abnormal reaction), then super jump and place Trick "Hopscotch" before you take aim with Low Voltage. The aiming area of the Hopscotch glyph can be considered, in effect, a slim infinite column designed to protect Trish. If you have a special move action left on the way down, you can place Trick "Peekaboo" at low altitude before landing to supplement Hopscotch.

Against teleport and rushdown characters, who are less eager to duck back with beams and more eager to get at Trish's face, you can play more of a ground game. On the ground, it's Peekaboo you'll want out first, rather than Hopscotch. It comes out so quickly that you can use it as an early anti-air, and it covers perfectly the air entry angle for most aggressive characters. From behind Peekaboo, you can place Hopscotch to strengthen Trish's position before using Round Trip or Low Voltage to chip your opposition. In this capacity, Peekaboo sort of serves to give Trish time to use Hopscotch at all, since Hopscotch's startup on the ground is very risky to use against the fast characters of *UMvC3*.

The opposing player should be constantly harassed and reminded of the presence of Trick traps. Use these tactics well, and they can serve as mini-assists for Trish while also helping cover her own assists. Be diligent about keeping Peekaboo and Hopscotch active and in places beneficial to you. Hopefully during all this, you're keeping Trish and her assists out of trouble, while your competitor has to guard or get hit by bolts and traps. At some point, your opponent is going to get fed up and come after you full bore, one way or another. It's important to note that Trish has lost some capability in running away here since *MvC3*, but the functionality can replicated. She can no longer place Trick "Hopscotch" more than once during jump periods. So, she cannot Hopscotch, airdash, Hopscotch to reposition it under her, or put Hopscotch out multiple times in air blockstrings to both pressure a foe and leave a present for them even if they push away Trish with advancing guard.

Achieve super jump height by airdashing upward from a jump, and you'll still be able to call assists while retaining a position advantage. Pair this with a meter-building assist to up the payoff.

If you build surplus meter while running, feel free to dump it into errant assists in the form of Round Harvest or Maximum Voltage (or, Round Harvest into Maximum Voltage!).

Before, Trish could reposition Hopscotch much less deliberately. Now, this must be more premeditated. Jump, call an assist, airdash upward, and place both of Trish's Trick traps. This uses up her airdash and both of her Trick traps for the jump, along with two of the three possible special move actions per jump. It leaves one special move action left: this special move is spent activating Air Raid. Trish is now at super jump height and in Air Raid flight mode, having set Hopscotch and Peekaboo and called an assist. Since the whole thing started with a normal jump, she can still call assists, and since flight is active, she can airdash or use special moves regardless of using those actions up already! For example, you can then have Trish airdash backward, call the other assist (or the same one again, if it reloads fast enough), reposition your Trick traps if desired, then pepper the target with Low Voltage H while they're held back by Trick traps and your assists. Or, you can opt to go offensive, calling an assist on one side of the opponent before using repeated flight airdashes to get to the other side of them. From here, you can proceed to a close range offense backed by the frame advantage your assist (and possibly your Trick traps) created.

While setting all the traps, when the situation calls for it, Trish can rush just fine. When your opponent is passive or overly defensive, when you sense they're weak, when Trish has X-Factor active, or if getting up close and personal is just your thing, you can play Trish very aggressively. Trish also has strong rushdown tools like her Stiletto Kick diving attack, her excellent air basic attacks, and her crouching M slide.

Her fastest attack is air L, at 4 frames until active. This kick drives her fastest overheads, triangle jump air L and instant jumping air L (for more on instant jumping air L, see Advanced Tactics). Mix up between these, crouching L to **Combo I or II**, and throw at close range. If your adversary jumps away as you strike with these options, you will probably whiff. If you read that your opponent wants to escape, dash in with standing L or jump forward with air M, M instead (into **Combo V** on hit).

If your rival guards these attacks, they'll likely use advancing guard to push Trish away. Trish remains in striking distance, though. She's still in range to square jump right back in with air S or air ⇨ + H (for the option select air throw opportunity). Although this looks really scary, it's pretty telegraphed and easy to block; the opposing character just has to remain standing. As a counterpoint, you can wavedash immediately, then either attack low with crouching L or use instant jumping air L.

Of special note is her Stiletto Kick. This isn't an overhead, but it can cross the opposing player up, and advancing guard does very little to push Trish away after the dive kick is blocked. This helps create one of her Advanced Tactics, and it enables Trish players to basically spam Stiletto Kick. Sure, your opponent can block it all day, but they'd better not slip up. Beware of the standard counters to telegraphed divekick-type attacks: counter type moves and X-Factor guard cancels. (In this situation, opposing players block one of your obvious Stiletto Kicks, activate X-Factor immediately, then start hitting Trish before she lands. Brought to you by *MvC3* players trying to figure out how to deal with Wolverine!). Note that Stiletto Kick can be canceled on hit or guard before landing, or even when it whiffs, so you can keep your competitor on their toes by canceling blocked or whiffed Stiletto Kicks right above them into Trick "Hopscotch."

Anytime Trish is pushblocked away is also a natural time to drop Trick "Peekaboo" and transition right back to pestering your target from afar. Trish actually recovers slightly faster than her foe, so setting a trap is basically free after her jump-in is pushed away with advancing guard.

Advancing guard doesn't mean much when you want to advance with Trish.

Last-ditch Trish gains just enough speed to make her attacks much more effective mix-up weapons.

With X-Factor active, especially lv.2 or lv.3 X-Factor, Trish almost becomes a different character. With a significant damage boost, her below average damage goes away, and her rushdown attacks get even faster. She is much more likely to knock out opposing characters, and since her moves execute much faster, you have time to leverage a powerful mix-up against the next character coming in: knock a character out, then place Trick "Peekaboo" and Trick "Hopscotch" near where your adversary will land. Then, as they fall in, dash under them as they fall into the traps. Performed correctly, if the foe gets crossed up, the traps combo into each other and hold the target in place, where you can launch and K.O. another character!

Finally, just as opponents can use X-Factor to cancel guard and punish obvious Trish attacks like Stiletto Kick, you can do the same thing with Trish. Guard something obvious the opponent does, like a dive kick, then activate X-Factor and *immediately* open up with crouching M. The slide will take care of positioning worries for you, and allow you to chain into standing H, S. See the Combo Appendix for a possible follow-up combo.

COMBO USAGE

I. CR. Ⓛ, Ⓛ, Ⓜ, ST. Ⓗ CANCEL Ⓢ FORWARD SUPER JUMP, AIR Ⓜ, ↓ + Ⓗ CANCEL ↓↙← + Ⓛ, Ⓛ, Ⓜ CANCEL FORWARD DOUBLE JUMP, Ⓜ, Ⓗ, ↓ + Ⓗ CANCEL ↓↘→ + Ⓛ CANCEL ↓↘→ + ATK ATK (MASH ATK)

560,900+ damage, 33% meter loss

This easy, consistent Trish combo outputs moderate damage. If you anticipate that your rival is going to attempt jumping away, replace the opening crouching attacks with standing ones. This catches foes just as they leave the ground, while the crouching opener would miss. Try to stop short if your opponent is blocking after crouching or standing Ⓛ x2. If your opener is guarded, follow up with a throw, Combo I again, or an immediate triangle jump air Ⓛ or instant overhead air Ⓛ (see Advanced Tactics).

This combo provides a verifiable means of using X-Factor. Instead of ending with Stiletto Kick canceled to Low Voltage L to Maximum Voltage, simply cancel Stiletto Kick directly into Maximum Voltage, mash ATK for most of the duration, then X-Factor cancel and immediately perform air Maximum Voltage again. This nets around 775,900~826,800 damage. Not as efficient as many X-Factor combos, but if you use this to K.O. a character, you'll have plenty of X-Factor time left for the opposing player's next character. You cannot cancel Stiletto Kick into Low Voltage during this variation because of the three special moves per jump rule—you have to save one of them for the second Maximum Voltage.

II. CR. Ⓛ, Ⓛ, Ⓜ, Ⓗ CANCEL Ⓢ FORWARD SUPER JUMP, AIR Ⓜ, ↓ + Ⓗ (PAUSE ON HIT) CANCEL ↓↙← + Ⓛ, Ⓜ, Ⓗ, LAND, WAIT A MOMENT, ST. Ⓗ, Ⓢ CANCEL FORWARD SUPER JUMP, AIR Ⓜ, Ⓜ, Ⓗ, Ⓢ, LAND, WAVEDASH TWICE, ↓↘→↗ + ATK ATK (MASH ATK)

618,400 damage, 19% meter loss

This combo deals heavier damage and builds more hyper meter than Combo I, but it is more difficult, especially on small characters (near corners, it is much easier). The trick here is to hit your target as quickly as possible with air Ⓜ, ↓ + Ⓗ after the launch, but then pause for a split second before canceling Stiletto Kick to Trick "Hopscotch." If you cancel from Stiletto Kick to Hopscotch instantly on hit, Trish won't descend, and this stops the combo from working, or makes it inconsistent outside of corners. But, if Trish is given time to descend just a hair along Stiletto Kick's path, canceling to Hopscotch puts your adversary in perfect position for the follow-up air Ⓜ, Ⓗ. Of course, if Hopscotch doesn't combo at all, you waited too long!

III. (REQUIRES CORNER) CR. Ⓛ, Ⓛ, Ⓜ, Ⓗ CANCEL Ⓢ FORWARD SUPER JUMP, AIR Ⓜ, ↓ + Ⓗ CANCEL ↓↙← + Ⓛ, Ⓜ, Ⓗ, LAND, PAUSE, ST. Ⓗ, DOCTOR DOOM—β ASSIST + Ⓢ CANCEL FORWARD SUPER JUMP, AIR Ⓜ, Ⓜ, Ⓗ, Ⓢ, LAND, ↓↙← + Ⓗ, DOCTOR DOOM—β HITS, Ⓢ CANCEL VERTICAL SUPER JUMP, AIR Ⓢ, ROUND TRIP HITS, AIR Ⓢ, LAND, ↓↘→↗ + ATK ATK (MASH ATK)

710,100 damage, 12% meter gain (self sufficient for Maximum Voltage ender)

This complex combo shows an example of how assists can greatly help Trish's damage output. It works by timing Doctor Doom's Hidden Missiles assist to hit an opponent after they've been knocked down. This is done by calling the assist at the exact same time you perform the second Ⓢ launcher. After landing from the first air Ⓢ, immediately throw Round Trip, then once the missiles OTG the opposition, launch with Ⓢ and follow them into the sky. Perform a late air Ⓢ to spike your competitor directly into Round Trip (causing them to bounce into the sky again), then do air Ⓢ again while you plummet downward. After landing, you should have plenty of time to score the OTG air Maximum Voltage.

Since Doctor Doom is on your team in this example, note that if he's in the next slot, his Sphere Flame is one of the best hyper combos to THC into near corners. Lock and load, leader of Latveria! 900,000+ damage awaits.

IV. AIR THROW, FORWARD AIRDASH, AIR ↓↘→ + ATK ATK (MASH ATK)

377,800 damage, 92% meter loss

A basic air throw combo. After throwing your foe, airdash as soon as you're able, then perform ↓↘→ + ATK ATK just as you approach them. You can pop X-Factor just after the hyper combo ends and perform another ↓↘→ + ATK ATK for additional damage, but this isn't worth doing unless you're certain it'll K.O. the opposing character.

V. (AGAINST AN AERIAL OPPONENT) FORWARD JUMP Ⓜ, Ⓜ, Ⓗ, ↓ + Ⓗ, LAND, ST. Ⓛ, Ⓜ, Ⓗ, Ⓢ CANCEL FORWARD SUPER JUMP, AIR Ⓜ, Ⓜ, Ⓗ, Ⓢ, LAND, WAVEDASH FORWARD TWICE, ↓↘→↗ + ATK ATK (MASH ATK)

571,200 damage, 41% meter loss

An anti-air combo used to attack normal jump height airborne opponents. Double-tap Ⓜ on the way up during a forward jump without waiting to see if it hits. You'll get the chain and have time to verify into air Ⓗ to Stiletto Kick if air Ⓜ, Ⓜ comes out. If Trish whiffs the first air Ⓜ entirely, the second Ⓜ press does nothing, and Trish is free to act in midair. Depending on what your rival is doing and where they are, you can set Trick "Hopscotch" to be safe and stake a claim on land, Stiletto Kick to go on the attack if they're at the right angle, or airdash toward or away from your opponent, depending on your inclination.

ADVANCED TACTICS

CHILD OF MUNDUS: INSTANT JUMPING AIR L AND ANTI-ADVANCING GUARD RUSHDOWN

Jump at your adversary with instant jumping air L ...

...then use air ↓ + H to defeat advancing guard!

With a tight, aggressive sequence, Trish can negate use of advancing guard. The tactic starts with jumping right next to your opponent and striking with rising air L as soon as possible. You can input L as soon as 3 frames after inputting an upward direction for the jump, so press L immediately after pressing up-forward.

The next step is chaining into ↓ + H. You *don't* want to buffer this input by pressing ↓ + H early. For this to work properly, you must input air ↓ + H as soon as possible *after* their advancing guard actually starts pushing Trish back—preferably within 2 frames. Any longer than that, and air ↓ + H usually causes Trish to whiff ↓ + H.

If your rival doesn't use advancing guard, whether rising L hits or is guarded, whatever they do against the follow-up air ↓ + H won't matter. If they guard the divekick and use advancing guard, Trish is barely pushed back because she lands right away and stops backsliding. Whether they guard *or* employ advancing guard, Trish is left right next to them with frame advantage! If they *eat* the dive kick, well, great. Proceed to the combo of your choice.

If rising air L hits, ↓ + H won't cause a combo normally. It can combo on many standing characters if air L hits as a counterhit, though, which may occur frequently if your foe tries to throw or throw break at close range. However, it still won't work on small characters. You can also score combos by calling an assist before jumping with air L, so the assist hit can fill in the tiny gap between air L and air ↓ + H.

In lv.2 or 3 X-Factor, air L, ↓ + H becomes a natural combo, although Trish rises so quickly during these modes that air L whiffs on many small crouching characters, and on other characters, it only combos if it hits them while they're standing. It's still a very strong option, depending on the size of the opponent—mid-sized and large characters essentially aren't able to keep X-Factor Trish off of them.

When you are pressing a challenger on offense and sense they are scared of instant air L into Stiletto Kick (along with the other cornerstones of Trish's aggressive air game: square jump H, and triangle jump L and S), super jump and immediately triangle jump toward your adversary with air ↘ + H. Upon landing, attack immediately with crouching L or a throw.

Do this empty triangle jump as rapidly as possible; you don't want the screen to actually shift to super jump height, so air H actually whiffs. Trish should be so low in altitude by the time you press ↘ + H that Stiletto Kick can't occur, so the ↘ + H input produces a whiffed air H that doubles as an option select air throw. Because of slight command overlap with her Stiletto Kick, if you triangle jump using the command dash (↘ or ↙ + ATK ATK) using H as one of the buttons, Trish *always* produces an option select throw at the beginning of diagonal downward airdashes. If your opponent starts to jump away as you attempt this mix-up, you'll get a throw automatically. To sum up, this sequence lets you fake a high attack and then immediately go for a low, while giving yourself two chances to air throw without even thinking about it!

Layer mixing up between instant overhead air L and empty triangle jumps into low attacks, and you'll enhance the effectiveness of Trish's rushdown greatly.

HARVEST MOON

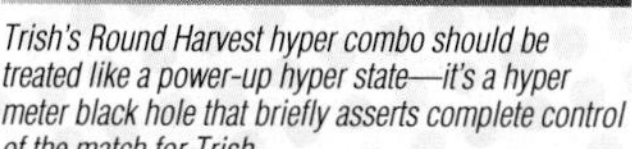
Trish's Round Harvest hyper combo should be treated like a power-up hyper state—it's a hyper meter black hole that briefly asserts complete control of the match for Trish.

Round Harvest is also effective in crossover combinations, especially when Trish is on point and free to act immediately!

The best time to use Round Harvest is whenever you find the time, really. If you can get it out there, your rival almost certainly has to deal with it, and if they call any assist, it gets chewed up. Beware of certain characters like Ghost Rider who have attacks that can easily reach through Sparda and hit Trish. Just like with Trick traps, Round Harvest disappears if Trish gets hit. Luckily, once it's actually over your opponent and spinning, that's a non-issue.

It's important to note Trish's heavy basic attacks and launcher are different when she doesn't have Sparda in hand. In particular, air H becomes a slightly altered version of Stiletto Kick and is no longer an overhead! If you want to attack high during Round Harvest, you need to use triangle jump air L or S. Alternate between using these and employing empty triangle jumps into crouching L. Round Harvest doesn't actually last that long—just two seconds—so make the most of the time.

It can be difficult to do anything to your adversary if they guard Round Harvest and start spamming advancing guard. In this situation, Trish gets pushed back no matter how good your wavedashing is. You can deal with this in a few ways. You can simply accept it, try to catch assists in Round Harvest (which you can follow up with Maximum Voltage for great risk-free punishment to the assist), and just fire Low Voltage H at the enemy a few times while they block Sparda.

Or, for a much bigger advantage, bring in another character, who can then rush your competitor down without being affected by advancing guard! To do this, either simply tag Trish out immediately after using Round Harvest, or THC from Trish's Round Harvest to the power-up hyper of another character (such as Firebrand's Luminous Body or Wolverine's Berserker Rage).

Between unguardable special moves like C.Viper's Focus Attack and Taskmaster's Sword Master chains, and various combinations of high or low attacks with high and low-hitting assists, you can do some very nasty things to characters who block Round Harvest and can't rely on advancing guard to save them. Unless they're prepared with an invincible crossover counter, there's nothing they can do to stop you from forcing the issue.

COMBO APPENDIX

GENERAL EXECUTION TIPS

- Chain from crouching L, L, M quickly during ground combos; the inputs can't be delayed.
- When using air M, ↓ + H in air combos, perform air M as soon as possible after super jumping.
- When using air M, M, etc. in air combos, wait a moment before attacking after launching.
- Perform airdashes diagonally downward with H as one of the buttons for built-in option select throws before triangle jumps.

AS TRISH COMES IN: AIR M, M CANCEL → FORWARD DOUBLE JUMP, M, H, ↓ + H CANCEL → ↓↘→ + L CANCEL → ↓↘→ + ATK ATK (MASH ATK)

Notes	Damage
TAC to Trish with ↑ + S or → + S or ↓ + S	Varies due to damage scaling

CR. L, L, M, ST. H CANCEL → S FORWARD SUPER JUMP, AIR M, ↓ + H, LAND, ST. L, M, H CANCEL → ↓↘→ + L CANCEL → →↓↘ + ATK ATK

Notes	Damage
Basic combo into Duet Pain	702,100 damage, 254% meter loss

CR. L, M, ST. H CANCEL → XF, CR. M, ST. H, S FORWARD SUPER JUMP, AIR M, ↓ + H, LAND, ST. L, M, H, S CANCEL → FORWARD SUPER JUMP, AIR M, M CANCEL → DOUBLE JUMP, AIR M, H, ↓ + H CANCEL → ↓↘→ + L CANCEL → ↓↘→ + ATK ATK (MASH ATK)

Notes	Damage
Stronger X-Factor combo than Combo I option, but uses more X-Factor time	750,600~1,027,900 damage, 1~31% meter gain

TRON

"IF IT'S NOT NAILED DOWN, IT'S MINE!"

Bio

REAL NAME

Tron Bonne

OCCUPATION

Air Pirate

ABILITIES

A mechanical engineering genius, she is able to create anything from small robots, such as the Servbots, to large aerial battleships. She is also able to pilot mechas.

WEAPONS

Utilizes the Servbots as well as mechas she has built. In the VS. series, she pilots a walking mecha battle tank called the Gustaff.

PROFILE

The only daughter of the Bonne family of air pirates, she is extremely prideful and is a sore loser. However, she can be charmingly awkward in front of someone she has a crush on, and values her family above all else. She travels the world in the hopes of getting rich quick, but her misadventures usually only end up adding to her debt.

FIRST APPEARANCE

Mega Man Legends (1997)

POWER GRID

6	INTELLIGENCE
5	STRENGTH
2	SPEED
5	STAMINA
1	ENERGY PROJECTION
3	FIGHTING ABILITY

*This is biographical, and does not represent an evaluation of the in-game combat potential of this hero.

ALTERNATE COSTUMES

1

2

3

4

5

6

DLC

Overview

Vitality	1,200,000
Chain Combo Archetype	Marvel Series

X-Factor Boost	Damage	Speed
Level 1 (3 teammates remaining)	135%	105%
Level 2 (2 teammates remaining)	160%	110%
Level 3 (1 teammate remaining)	185%	115%

When playing as Tron, your goal is to close on your opponent and force them into the corner.

Why would you want to close on your adversary when Tron pilots a big robot that throws Servbots and huge rocks?

- **Tron's true strength lies in her dominant air Ⓜ and Ⓗ attacks and her command throw mix-ups on the ground**
- **Tron can dominate the space around the corner, and the corner allows Tron's biggest combos while also making all her combos easier to perform**
- **Tron has difficulty against zoning characters. Keeping your rival in the corner denies them the space needed to effectively keep Tron away**

How do you approach your competitor and force them into the corner using Tron?

- **Using a low altitude airdash combined with air Ⓜ or Ⓗ**
- **Using low altitude air Bonne Strike to push the opposing character closer to the corner**
- **Using Bonne Strike with a projectile or beam crossover assist that can protect Tron's punishable recovery period**

TUNING SINCE ORIGINAL MVC3

Tron received a few significant changes in *Ultimate Marvel vs Capcom 3*. Probably the most significant was the change to Tron—β assist. It is now just as vulnerable as any other assist, changing it from one of the best assists in the game to an average one. Another significant change is that her air Ⓗ knocks opponents farther away, making it difficult to continue combos consistently outside of the corner without the use of Bonne Strike. Servbot Surprise Hyper is now mashable, which leads to a slight increase in her corner combo damage. Servbot Launcher gaining up to three attacks can lead to some good corner pressure. Bandit Boulder is now special/hyper-cancelable, and this can be useful in niche situations and short combos.

- Gustaff Flame is special/hyper-cancelable
- Bandit Boulder is special/hyper-cancelable after frame 35
- Servbot Launcher can be mashed to launch up to three Servbots
- Servbot Surprise Hyper can be mashed for additional hits
- Air Ⓗ knocks adversaries farther away
- Tron—β assist is now more vulnerable to attacks
- Increased length of hard knockdown caused by normal throw
- Increased jump cancel window of Gustaff Fire
- Bandit Boulder rock lift hitstun decreases with combo length
- Increased minimum damage scaling of special moves
- Lowered float of ground Bonne Strike
- Air Bonne Strike hitstun decreases with combo length
- Fixed Bonne Mixer and Shakedown Mixer so they can come out on an empty cancel

Attack Set

Standing Basic Attacks

Screen	Command	Hits	Damage	Meter Gain	Startup	Active	Recovery	Advantage on Hit	Advantage if Guarded	Notes
1	Standing L	1	55,000	440	7	3	12	+1	-1	—
2	Standing M	4	72,800	800	9	8	29	-10	-13	Nullifies medium priority projectile and beams
3	Standing H	1	100,000	800	15	30	31	—	-38	Knocks down opponent, nullifies medium priority projectile and beams

1

2

3

Crouching Basic Attacks

Screen	Command	Hits	Damage	Meter Gain	Startup	Active	Recovery	Advantage on Hit	Advantage if Guarded	Notes
1	Crouching L	6	65,600	960	8	13	18	-5	-7	Low attack
2	Crouching M	1	75,000	600	11	5	19	-3	-6	Low attack
3	Crouching H	4	95,500	960	11	9	16	—	+4	Low attack, knocks down, OTG- capable, can move forward or backward during attack, can cancel into Bandit Boulder, not special- or hyper combo- cancelable

1

2

3

Ground Special Attack—Launcher

Screen	Command	Hits	Damage	Meter Gain	Startup	Active	Recovery	Advantage on Hit	Advantage if Guarded	Notes
1	S (while standing or crouching)	1	100,000	800	8	5	38	—	-20	Launcher, not special- or hyper combo- cancelable

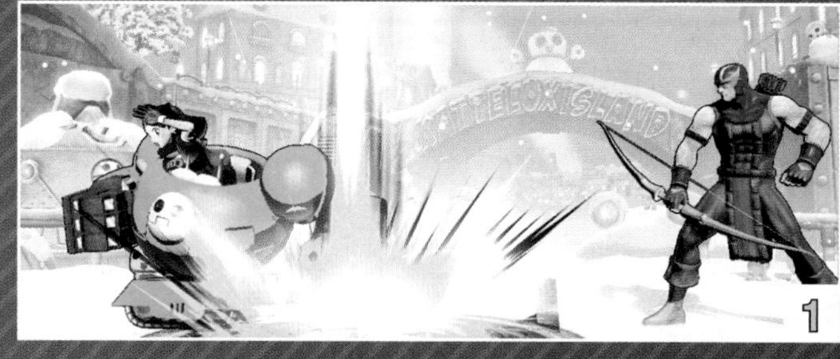
1

Air Basic Attacks

Screen	Command	Hits	Damage	Meter Gain	Startup	Active	Recovery	Advantage on Hit	Advantage if Guarded	Notes
1	Air L	3	69,300	720	9	6	21	+14	+11	Overhead attack
2	Air M	1	80,000	640	9	5	21	+17	+13	Overhead attack
3	Air H	1	100,000	800	15	Until grounded	3	—	+12	Overhead attack, knocks down opponent, nullifies medium priority projectiles and beams

1

2

3

Air Special Attacks – Flying Screen and Air Exchange

Air (S) causes a hard knockdown when used in a launcher combo (this is sometimes called flying screen). When used outside of a launcher combo, air (S) behaves mostly like another basic attack. Air exchange attacks, performed by inputting a direction plus (S), are only possible during a launcher combo. Exchange hits initiate team aerial combos by tagging in the next available character to continue the air combo.

Screen	Command	Hits	Damage	Meter Gain	Startup	Active	Recovery	Advantage on Hit	Advantage if Guarded	Notes
1	Air (S)	1	100,000	800	17	4	30	—	+15	Causes hard knockdown if used in launcher combo, ground bounces foe
2	Air ⇧ + (S) (during launcher combo)	1	60,000	480	9	5	Until grounded	—	—	Tags in next available ally while lofting opponent upward
3	Air ⇨ or ⇦ + (S) (during launcher combo)	1	50,000	400	15	Until grounded	1	—	—	Tags in next available ally while causing wall bounce, erases 1 hyper meter from opposing character
4	Air ⇩ + (S) (during launcher combo)	1	50,000	400 + 10,000	16	4	Until grounded	—	—	Tags in next available ally while causing ground bounce, generates 1 hyper meter

Command Attacks

Command attacks resemble basic attacks but have different chaining and canceling properties. It's usually possible to chain *into* a command attack from basic attacks, but most command attacks cannot be chained from or canceled themselves.

Screen	Name	Command	Hits	Damage	Meter Gain	Startup	Active	Recovery	Advantage on Hit	Advantage if Guarded	Notes
1	Gustaff Fire	⇨ + (M)	5	84,000	1000	12	20	17	-3	-6	5th hit is jump- cancelable, inflicts chip damage, nullifies medium priority projectile and beams during active frames
2	Bandit Boulder	⇨ + (H)	3	165,300	1520	15	5(15)1	21	+4	+1	Can be canceled into special or hyper after frame 35, inflicts chip damage, nullifies medium priority projectile and beams during first 5 active frames, rock can be held for 72 frames, projectile has 10 low priority durability points

Throws

Throws are for snagging passive or blocking opponents. Since throws are active so quickly, you can also use them to preemptively toss opposing characters out of their offense. Combos are usually possible after throws, one way or another.

Screen	Command	Hits	Damage	Meter Gain	Startup	Active	Notes
1	⇨ + (H) (ground)	1	80,000	800	1	1	Hard knockdown
	⇦ + (H) (ground)	1	80,000	800	1	1	Hard knockdown
2	⇨ + (H) (air)	1	80,000	800	1	1	Hard knockdown
	⇦ + (H) (air)	1	80,000	800	1	1	Hard knockdown

As a Partner—Crossover Assists

Screen	Type	P1+P2 Crossover Combination Hyper Combo	Description	Hits	Damage	Meter Gain	Startup	Active	Recovery (this crossover assist)	Recovery (other partner)	Notes
1	Tron—α	Servbot Surprise	Bonne Strike M	6	117,000	1200	33	14(1)2	110	80	Knocks down opponent
2	Tron—β	Servbot Surprise	Gustaff Fire (⇨ + Ⓜ)	5	102,300	1000	36	20	109	79	Nullifies low and medium priority projectile and beams during active frames
3	Tron—γ	Servbot Surprise	Bandit Boulder (⇨ + Ⓗ)	3	151,600	1360	38	5(16)1	113	83	Nullifies low and medium priority projectile and beams during first 5 active frames, projectile has 10 low priority durability points

Tron's assist choice is no longer obvious, since Tron—β is now vulnerable to attacks just like any other assist. Your choice of Tron assist is going to depend on your need and your team goal.

You can use Tron—α to extend combos, but it is best used late in combos because it hits six times. If used early in a combo, it could severely diminish the overall damage due to damage scaling. You can also use this assist to fill in small gaps in your team's offensive pressure, allowing you to sustain momentum for a longer period of time against an opponent.

Tron—β is short range but boasts a large number of active frames and the ability to nullify any projectiles and beams of medium priority or lower, and it provides a good amount of hitstun. This makes it strong for corner pressure and for extending combos. However, its use as a defensive assist has been severely limited by the increased vulnerability.

Tron—γ differs from the command attack version because the thrown boulder can travel fullscreen. Similar to Tron—β, it nullifies medium or lower priority projectiles and beams during the first 5 active frames (while she is picking up the boulder), and the thrown boulder has a hefty 10 durability points. This is useful against a zoning character because it can nullify their projectiles while providing Tron with a strong projectile of her own to help turn the battle to your advantage.

Snap Back

Screen	Command	Hits	Damage	Meter Gain	Startup	Active	Recovery	Advantage on Hit	Advantage if Guarded
1	⇩⬂⇨ + 	1	50,000	500 - (-1 hyper meter bar)	2	30	31	—	-38

Notes

On hit, snap back forces the opposing point character to be replaced by an assist. Opposing assist calls or tag outs are also locked out for 4 seconds

Special Moves

Screen	Name	Command	Hits	Damage	Meter Gain	Startup	Active	Recovery	Advantage on Hit	Advantage if Guarded	Notes
1	Bonne Strike L	⇦⇩⬃ + Ⓛ	4~8	75,900~118,400	720~1360	9	8~20(1)2	18	—	-7	Knocks down, can be mashed for extra hits
	Bonne Strike M	⇦⇩⬃ + Ⓜ	6~11	99,400~140,300	1040~1840	9	14~29 (1)2	18	—	-7	Knocks down, can be mashed for extra hits
	Bonne Strike H	⇦⇩⬃ + Ⓗ	8~15	118,400~160,400	1360~2480	9	20~41 (1)2	18	—	-7	Knocks down, can be mashed for extra hits
2	Air Bonne Strike L	(in air)⇦⇩⬃ + Ⓛ	4~8	75,900~118,400	720~1360	13	8~20 (1)2	Until grounded, 7 frames ground recovery	—	—	Knocks down, can be mashed for extra hits
	Air Bonne Strike M	(in air)⇦⇩⬃ + Ⓜ	6~11	99,400~140,300	1040~1840	13	14~29 (1)2	Until grounded, 7 frames ground recovery	—	—	Knocks down, can be mashed for extra hits
	Air Bonne Strike H	(in air)⇦⇩⬃ + Ⓗ	8~15	118,400~160,400	1360~2480	13	20~41(1)2	Until grounded, 7 frames ground recovery	—	—	Knocks down, can be mashed for extra hits
3	Beacon Bomb L	⇩⬂⇨ + Ⓛ	1	50,000	500	33	—	17	—	+5	Captures adversary for 82 frames on hit, projectile disappears after 16 frames, projectile has 1 low priority durability point
	Beacon Bomb M	⇩⬂⇨ + Ⓜ	1	60,000	600	43	—	16	—	+6	Captures rival for 82 frames on hit, projectile has 1 low priority durability point
4	Beacon Bomb H	⇩⬂⇨ + Ⓗ	1	70,000	700	33	—	17	—	+5	Captures competitor for 82 frames on hit, projectile has 1 low priority durability point

Special Moves continued

Screen	Name	Command	Hits	Damage	Meter Gain	Startup	Active	Recovery	Advantage on Hit	Advantage if Guarded	Notes
5	Servbot Launcher L	→ ↓ ↘ + (L)	1	70,000 per Servbot	560 per Servbot	18	—	37	-12	-15	Servbot projectile active for 50 frames, can be mashed to launch another Servbot after 30 frames for a total of 3 Servbots, projectile has 5 low priority durability points
	Servbot Launcher M	→ ↓ ↘ + (M)	1	70,000(per Servbot)	560 (per Servbot)	18	—	37	-12	-15	Servbot projectile active for 92 frames, can be mashed to launch another Servbot after 30 frames for a total of 3 Servbots, projectile has 5 low priority durability points
	Servbot Launcher H	→ ↓ ↘ + (H)	1	70,000(per Servbot)	560 (per Servbot)	18	—	37	-12	-15	Servbot projectile active for 68 frames, can be mashed to launch another Servbot after 30 frames for a total of 3 Servbots, projectile has 5 low priority durability points
6	Bonne Mixer L	→ ↘ ↓ ↙ ← + (L)	4	120,000	1200	5	1	41	—	—	Throw attack, hard knockdown
	Bonne Mixer M	→ ↘ ↓ ↙ ← + (M)	7	165,000	1650	3	1	43	—	—	Throw attack, hard knockdown
	Bonne Mixer H	→ ↘ ↓ ↙ ← + (H)	10	210,000	2100	1	2	44	—	—	Throw attack, hard knockdown

1

2

Bonne Strike: Bonne Strike can knock foes airborne and usually allows for follow-up attacks (standing (L) or (M) are best) that can lead into a full-blown combo. The downside is that the large amount of hits causes significant damage scaling on any following attacks. The most obvious use is to perform air Bonne Strike immediately after a successful air (H) to convert into a full combo.

When used on the ground and blocked, this move is normally unsafe. However, when Tron has at least three hyper gauge bars, you can make it risky for an adversary to attempt to punish this attack because you can cancel the recovery at any point with her Shakedown Mixer. You can also use Bonne Strike at very low altitudes to reduce the recovery on the move while making it safe or even gaining frame advantage!

3

4

Beacon Bomb: This attack is a poor zoning tool because of its long startup and recovery, along with the projectile's low durability. However, you can use this move to extend combos, most frequently as a setup to land Servbot Surprise. The most common ways to land Beacon Bomb during combos are after an assist or an air (S) ground bounce.

You can also use Beacon Bomb to convert stray crossover assist hits into full combos.

Servbot Launcher: Tron's robot Gustaff fires a Servbot toward the target at an upward angle. The Servbot slowly drift toward the ground for a short time before falling quickly the rest of the way. You can press (L), (M), or (H) following the first input to fire up to three total Servbots. Each press fires its corresponding version of the attack. Slowly spreading out the attacks and repeating the process can actually be difficult for some competitors to get past. Servbot Launcher M is the most versatile version, since it stays active the longest.

5

You can employ Servbot Launcher to pressure an incoming character after a K.O. Firing Servbot Launcher M three times gives you a chance to attack your rival while the opposing character is locked down by the descending Servbots. You can sometimes convert any Servbot hits into a combo. You can even time the Servbot attacks far enough apart so Tron can dash in and throw her target between Servbots.

Bonne Mixer: Bonne Mixer is a strong command throw that can be followed up with OTG attacks. However, it is difficult to follow up with Tron's own OTG attacks outside of the corner because it requires near-perfect wavedashing.

The version you select depends on your need. Bonne Mixer L has the most startup frames, but also has the most range. Bonne Mixer H has only 1 startup frame but has very limited range. Bonne Mixer M is in between the other two versions.

6

Keep in mind that you can use Bonne Mixer to cancel any basic attack. You can bait opponents into trying to punish unsafe basic attacks used up close, and cancel into Bonne Mixer for big combos!

Hyper Combos

Screen	Name	Command	Hits	Damage	Startup	Active	Recovery	Advantage on Hit	Advantage if Guarded	Notes
1	Servbot Takeout	↓↘→ + ATK ATK	41	251,800	10+6	—	83	—	-61	Frames 1-10 invincible, knocks down opposing character, projectile has 1 high priority durability point
2	Servbot Surprise	→↓↘ + ATK ATK	10~19	320,700~376,800	6+24	—	95	—	+24	Frames 4-7 invincible, knocks down foe, can be mashed for additional hits, huge Servbot is active for 10(22)65 frames
3	Shakedown Mixer (Level 3 hyper combo)	→↘↓↙← + ATK ATK	18	440,000	6+0	3	43	—	—	Frames 1-9 invincible, throw, hard knockdown

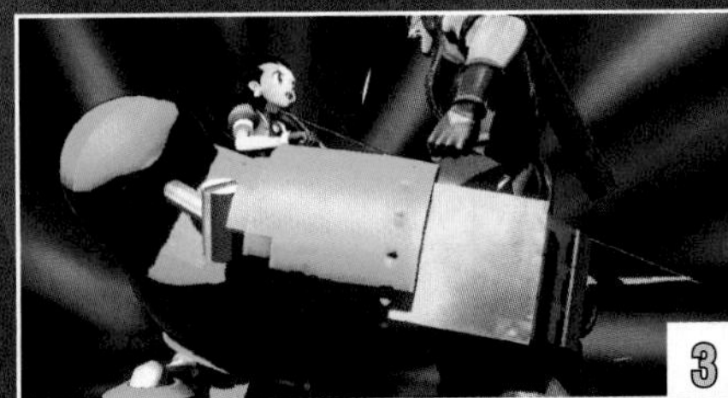

Servbot Takeout: This hyper combo serves mainly as a combo ender. It has massive recovery and cannot be canceled with X-Factor unless it successfully hits, even though it can still be canceled with a THC.

On a successful hit, you can X-Factor cancel this move to follow up with additional hits while the lunch rush keeps your attacker locked in hitstun.

Servbot Surprise: This hyper combo has a variety of uses. You can use it in combos after a Beacon Bomb or after standing (H) if your target is high enough off the ground. Furthermore, it leaves you with enough frame advantage to continue the combo afterwards!

This move can also be used on an incoming opponent after a snap back or character K.O. Tron then recovers while the giant Servbot is still active, allowing her to pressure her adversary immediately afterward!

Shakedown Mixer: Simply the threat of this level 3 hyper combo can change the whole dynamic of a match. It becomes risky for your opponent to attempt to punish any unsafe basic attack or special move because you can cancel them into Shakedown Mixer. It's impossible for the opposing character to do anything once the first 6 frames of startup have passed and the screen freeze animation has started, making it very difficult to react to. As a result, expect your competitors to jump often when you are close enough for this attack to be a threat. Use these opportunities to punish your foe for jumping with air throws and low attacks!

"SHOW SOME FEAR, THE BONNE FAMILY'S HERE! SERVBOTS! TIME TO WORK!"

Battle Plan

Tron can fit in any spot on a team. As a point character, she has high vitality and is nearly self-sufficient in terms of meter usage in combos. You can also inflict high damage combos without using meter if assists are available. However, you will probably have problems using her against characters who possess strong zoning games, so you need to be more reliant on assists to manage her in these fights. She also relies on assists to get her highest damaging combos. This makes her less than ideal as an anchor. She is the biggest threat when she has three hyper meter bars, so her strongest position on a team is probably as the main meter user, in the middle slot.

Air (H) is one of Tron's most dominant moves. It can nullify projectiles, it is active until grounded, and it can start a combo anywhere on screen.

Air (M) is another dominant attack with amazing range and decent startup speed.

Your goal with Tron is to get her close to the opposition to hit them or apply throw mix-ups. Either of these options naturally pushes the target to the corner due to the nature of her throws and combos. Successfully approaching an adversary to get in close, however, can be a trickier endeavor.

Tron's most dominant basic attack is her air (H). It is active the entire time she is airborne, hits to both her left and right, and also nullifies medium and low priority projectiles and beams. While it now knocks opponents farther away, you can still follow it up with a Bonne Strike M or H (ground or air) to convert any low altitude air (H) hit into a highly damaging combo. Airdash just before using air (H) and the momentum of the airdash will carry air (H) forward for a bit, before Tron falls straight down. If you perform air (H) after an airdash, Tron simply falls straight down. If you mix up between using air (H) during or just after an airdash, ideally from about the distance characters start from each other at the beginning of a match, this makes it difficult for an opponent to discern the correct direction to block. Immediately follow this move up with an air Bonne Strike M or H if against a grounded or low altitude opponent, which will be safe even on block, allowing for a throw mix-up. Air (M) is another dominant basic attack of Tron's. It has enormous reach in front of her and can also be used with airdashes to gain extra distance. You can then convert any successful hit into a full combo by chaining into air (H) or air (M), (H) and then landing to continue the combo.

Use Bandit Boulder to nullify projectiles...

...then call an assist while throwing the boulder, then cancel into Bonne Strike to begin your offense!

Another option for getting close to your opponent is the use of Bonne Strike. It has fast startup, covers ground quickly, and can lead into full combos. However, Bonne Strike has -7 frame advantage, and air Bonne Strike is in recovery until grounded. So how does this make Bonne Strike a viable option? One way is through the use of projectile or beam assists to cover Bonne during her recovery. It's best to use an assist that allows Tron to continue into a combo if any of the attacks hit. Another method is to use Bonne Strike instantly after jumping. You can do this by inputting ←↓↗↖ + (H). Finally, if you have three hyper bars, you can attempt to bait your rival into punishing your "unsafe" Bonne Strike, canceling your recovery into Shakedown Mixer right as your foe attacks!

Bonne Mixer and Shakedown Mixer are crucial components of Tron's mix-up offense.

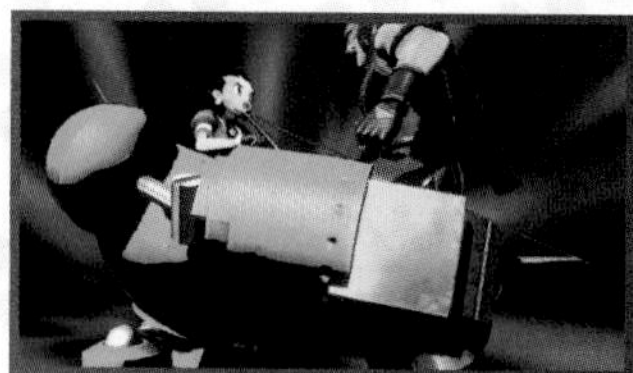

Just the threat of her ground command throws can lead to competitors making mistakes you can take advantage of.

Against zoning opponents who are able to put projectiles or beams on the screen constantly, Bandit Boulder may be a useful option, as it nullifies low and medium priority projectiles during its first 5 active frames. Call an assist at the same time, then release the boulder, and cancel into Bonne Strike H behind the cover of your assist and boulder! If you are lucky, Tron will get some stray hits, and you can end up scoring a big combo! However, be wary of characters who can cancel their attacks into fullscreen projectile or beam hyper combos very quickly. An adversary who notices your tactic could easily end up causing massive damage to both Tron and your assist!

Once you are close enough to threaten with Bonne Mixer or Shakedown Mixer, your options become much more dangerous, and you essentially force your opponent into making a guess. You usually have to read whether the opposing character will continue to stay grounded or attempt to jump. You must find a way to discourage your rival from jumping so you can increase the chances of landing a Bonne Mixer. The simplest option is to simply attack with an early low attack.

However, none of Tron's crouching attacks is particularly fast, so this is best done with enough frame advantage to offset the slow startup (like a very low altitude blocked Bonne Strike). Another option is to immediately jump forward and airdash with → + (H) ~ (ATK), then use air → + (H). For the airdash, your goal is to "drum" the (H) input one frame before the other attack input, so → + (H) registers for a single frame. This serves a dual purpose in that you get two chances to throw your opponent (airdash/throw option select with → + (H) ~ (ATK), and air → + (H)), and if your adversary doesn't jump, you likely cross them up with your air (H), allowing you to continue your pressure.

If you ever land any of Tron's normal throws or her Bonne Mixer, you can follow these moves up with highly damaging combos. Air throws present her strongest combo option midscreen, as you can immediately follow up with air (M) canceled into air Bonne Strike H and convert to a full combo. A normal ground throw requires either wavedashing into OTG or an assist OTG to follow up at midscreen. In the corner, a throw can be followed up with an immediate standing (M) before they even hit the ground. Bonne Mixer always require an OTG to follow with a combo, and it is somewhat difficult to follow up with midscreen. It requires you to do near perfect wavedashing into crouching (H). Following up with an OTG in the corner, however, is fairly easy. At midscreen, if your competitors ever break a ground throw attempt, you can immediately jump forward and press (S) at the apex of your jump for cross-up air (S), which scores a ground bounce that leads to a full combo on hit.

Tron is especially dangerous in the corner, since she gains even more options for controlling her opponent's movement.

Once you have your adversary in the corner, your options and damage with Tron improve greatly. Air (H) becomes even more dominant because it can shut down the air space above and in front of a character, making it difficult for them to escape the corner. Any air (H) attacks that hit no longer have to be followed up with Bonne Strike and instead can be followed up by single hit ground basic attacks, thus preventing early combo damage scaling. This can make the difference between a 1,000,000 and 750,000 damage combo. Furthermore, all her throws become much easier to follow up with a combo. You can also employ Servbot Launcher in conjunction with a projectile or beam assist to provide a huge frame advantage to work with. You can be extra sneaky with this by spreading out the last two Servbot launcher attacks just enough to be able to dash in and command grab your opponent between the Servbots!

Using Gustaff Fire is a great way to allow Tron to combat advancing guard and maintain offensive pressure.

If your blockstrings up close are being blocked and Tron is in danger of being pushed out of range, you can use Gustaff Fire and jump cancel the attack. From this, you can use your airdash attack/throw option selects or low altitude Bonne Strikes to continue the pressure!

COMBO USAGE

I. AIR (H) CANCEL→ ←↓↙ + (M), LAND, ST. (M) (3 HITS), → + (M) CANCEL→ FORWARD JUMP, AIR (M), (M), (H), LAND, ST. (M) (3 HITS), → + (M) CANCEL→ JUMP FORWARD, AIR (H), (S), LAND, ↓↘→ + (L), →↓↘ + (ATK)(ATK) (MASH (ATK)), ST. (H) CANCEL→ ↓↘→ + (ATK)(ATK)

725,700 damage, 96% meter loss

Tron's basic combo from a successful air (H) that requires no assists. Tron can almost always be made to land two hyper combos in any combo, provided you have the meter to spend, so high damage is guaranteed. This combo doesn't require any delays until the Servbot Surprise and should be performed as quickly as possible to ensure that your opponent does not flip out of the combo at any point.

Landing the standing (H) after Servbot surprise can be a bit tricky to time. Tron recovers slightly before the Servbot shrinks. The best visual cue is to watch for her satellite dish to begin retract; press (H) immediately after, and you should be able to continue the combo. You can visually confirm to see if the standing (H) hits before canceling into Servbot Takeout to make sure you don't waste a hyper meter bar and end up being punished hard for your mistake.

II. AIR (H) CANCEL→ ←↓↙ + (M), LAND, ST. (M) (3 HITS), → + (M) CANCEL→ FORWARD JUMP, AIR (M), (M), (H), LAND, (S) CANCEL→ FORWARD SUPER JUMP, AIR (M), (M), (H), (S), LAND, CALL SENTINEL—α, SLIGHT DELAY, CR. (H) (4 HITS), → + (H) CANCEL→ ↓↘→ + (H), JUMP FORWARD, AIR (H), (S), LAND, ↓↘→ + (L), →↓↘ + (ATK)(ATK) (MASH (ATK)), ST. (H) CANCEL→ ↓↘→ + (ATK)(ATK)

843,900 damage, 33% meter loss

While similar to the first combo, the use of an assist gives a substantial increase to Tron's damage potential along with increased meter building. You'll want to time your crouching (H) OTG to hit right as Sentinel points its finger, and time the ↓↘→ + (H) to hit right after the last Sentinel Drone hits the enemy. Using two assists can enhance Tron's damage and meter building even further. See the Combo Appendix for details.

COMBO USAGE CONT.

III. AIR Ⓗ, LAND, CR. Ⓜ, ST. Ⓗ, Ⓢ CANCEL FORWARD SUPER JUMP, AIR Ⓜ, Ⓜ, Ⓗ, Ⓢ, LAND, CALL SENTINEL—α, SLIGHT DELAY, CR. Ⓗ (4 HITS), → + Ⓗ CANCEL ↓ ↘ → + Ⓗ, FORWARD JUMP, AIR Ⓗ, Ⓢ, LAND, ↓ ↘ → + Ⓛ, → ↓ ↘ + ATK ATK, ST. Ⓗ CANCEL ↓ ↘ → + ATK ATK

Corner only, 972,100 damage, 68% meter loss

As mentioned before, Tron's damage becomes even stronger if you start one of her combos against a cornered foe. Here is the same air Ⓗ combo starter, but because of the corner, Tron is no longer dependent on a multi-hit move to convert the combo, and she can go for several hard-hitting, single hit attacks. This does require assist usage or X-Factor to fully realize the damage potential.

IV. AIR THROW, AIR Ⓜ CANCEL ← ↓ ↙ + Ⓗ, LAND, ST. Ⓜ, → + Ⓜ CANCEL FORWARD JUMP, AIR Ⓗ, Ⓢ, LAND, ↓ ↘ → + Ⓛ, → ↓ ↘ + ATK ATK (MASH ATK), ST. Ⓗ CANCEL ↓ ↘ → + ATK ATK

613,000 damage, 128% meter loss

This is Tron's solo air throw combo. Tron can still get great damage off air throws, and that can be improved significantly with the use of assists. The trickiest part of this combo is hitting the air Ⓜ immediately after the air throw. It has to be done immediately after the air throw happens in order to connect, or else your adversary ends up too far away for the air Ⓜ to hit. See the Combo Appendix for assist usage!

V. GROUND THROW, WAVEDASH, CR. Ⓗ (4 HITS), → + Ⓗ CANCEL ← ↓ ↙ + Ⓗ (MASH Ⓗ) CANCEL ↓ ↘ → + ATK ATK

411,400 damage, 49% meter loss

Tron's solo ground throw combo. It's difficult for her to do much else without the use of assists, but it is still solid damage for a simple throw combo. Delay the ← ↓ ↙ + Ⓗ slightly after Bandit Boulder so that you gain full hits, then cancel into Servbot Takeout immediately after the final hit of Bonne Strike. See the Combo Appendix for a more damaging assist combo!

VI. → ↘ ↓ ↙ ← + Ⓗ, DASH, CR. Ⓗ (4 HITS), → + Ⓗ CANCEL ← ↓ ↙ + Ⓗ (MASH Ⓗ) CANCEL ↓ ↘ → + ATK ATK

Corner only, 510,500 damage, 36% meter loss

Bonne Mixer H with a solo combo follow-up identical to her ground throw follow-up. This is technically possible to do midscreen but requires near perfect wavedashes along with a perfectly timed cr. Ⓗ. See the Combo Appendix for a more damaging assist combo!

VII. → + Ⓜ CANCEL ← ↓ ↙ ↖ + Ⓗ (MASH Ⓗ), LAND, Ⓢ CANCEL FORWARD SUPER JUMP, AIR Ⓜ, Ⓜ, Ⓗ, Ⓢ, LAND, CALL SENTINEL—α, SLIGHT DELAY, CR. Ⓗ (4 HITS), → + Ⓗ CANCEL ↓ ↘ → + Ⓗ, FORWARD JUMP, AIR Ⓗ, Ⓢ, LAND, ↓ ↘ → + Ⓛ, → ↓ ↘ + ATK ATK (MASH ATK), ST. Ⓗ CANCEL ↓ ↘ → + ATK ATK

776,600 damage, 56% meter loss

You can actually use Gustaff Fire to start a combo against grounded targets as well as airborne ones. Using the instant air Bonne Strike method described in Advanced Tactics, Gustaff Flame becomes a potent attack that allows you to continue pressure and land a very damaging combo if any of the attacks hit, while leaving you safe if the attacks are blocked!

ADVANCED TACTICS

INSTANT AIR BONNE STRIKE

Using Gustaff Fire jump canceled into instant air Bonne Strike is a potent offensive tool!

Tron's offense can be made far more dangerous through the use of very low altitude Bonne Strikes. The input for this motion is ⇦ ⇩ ⇙ ⇘ + ATK. When done correctly, you can eliminate a large amount of her recovery by landing almost immediately. If done on the first possible frame off ground, she actually ends up with a +1 frame advantage! When used in conjunction from the jump-cancelable Gustaff Fire, it can make for a very potent offense that even advancing guard can't really stop. You can also use Bonne Strike immediately after an air Ⓗ that is blocked by a grounded adversary. If any of these is done correctly, it's safe on block and leads to a free combo if it manages to hit!

COMBO APPENDIX

GENERAL EXECUTION TIPS

- Beacon Bomb has a slow startup. Take this into account when performing combos
- Buffer Bonne Strike before your air Ⓗ lands to ensure your Bonne Strike is performed in the air
- When doing Gustaff Fire into a jump canceled instant air Bonne Strike, delay the input for instant air Bonne Strike slightly, as the jump does not occur until after the last hit of Gustaff Fire

CR. Ⓛ (1 HIT), Ⓜ, ST. Ⓗ, Ⓢ CANCEL➤ FORWARD SUPER JUMP, AIR Ⓜ, Ⓜ, Ⓢ, LAND, CR. Ⓗ (4 HITS), → + Ⓗ CANCEL➤ ↓ ↘ → + ATK ATK

Notes	Damage
Simple combo starting with a low hit	576,100 damage, 31% meter loss

AIR Ⓗ, LAND, CR. Ⓜ, ST. Ⓗ, Ⓢ CANCEL➤ FORWARD SUPER JUMP, AIR Ⓜ, Ⓜ, Ⓗ, Ⓢ, LAND, CALL SENTINEL—α, SLIGHT DELAY, CR. Ⓗ (4 HITS), → + Ⓗ CANCEL➤ ↓ ↘ → + Ⓗ, FORWARD JUMP, AIR Ⓗ, LAND, ST. Ⓗ, Ⓢ CANCEL➤ FORWARD SUPER JUMP, AIR Ⓗ, Ⓢ, LAND, CALL DANTE—α + CR. Ⓗ (4 HITS), ↓ ↘ → + Ⓗ, FORWARD JUMP, AIR Ⓗ, Ⓢ, LAND, ↓ ↘ → + Ⓛ, → ↓ ↘ + ATK ATK (MASH ATK), ST. Ⓗ CANCEL➤ ↓ ↘ → + ATK ATK

Notes	Damage
Corner only, cr. Ⓗ after Sentinel—α should start the same time Sentinel points its finger. After first ↓ ↘ → + Ⓗ, delay air Ⓗ until Tron descends from the jump so there's time tolink st. Ⓗ, Ⓢ. Wait for cr. Ⓗ to recover before ↓ ↘ → + Ⓗ, or you end up canceling into Bandit Boulder instead. ↓ ↘ → + Ⓗ should hit just as Dante's Jam Session stops hitting the target	1,093,100 damage, 1% meter loss

AIR THROW FORWARD, AIR Ⓗ, LAND, ST. Ⓜ (3 HITS), → + Ⓜ CANCEL➤ FORWARD JUMP, AIR Ⓜ, Ⓜ, Ⓗ, LAND, ST. Ⓜ (3 HITS), Ⓢ CANCEL➤ FORWARD SUPER JUMP, AIR Ⓜ, Ⓜ, Ⓗ, Ⓢ, LAND, CALL SENTINEL—α, SLIGHT DELAY, CR. Ⓗ (4 HITS), → + Ⓗ CANCEL➤ ↓ ↘ → + Ⓗ, JUMP FORWARD, AIR Ⓗ, Ⓢ, LAND, ↓ ↘ → + Ⓛ, → ↓ ↘ + ATK ATK (MASH ATK), ST. Ⓗ CANCEL➤ ↓ ↘ → + ATK ATK

Notes	Damage
Corner only. If you are too low to the ground, you may have to use air Ⓜ instead of air Ⓗ. The rest of the combo is similar to Combo Usage II	794,900 damage, 30% meter loss

THROW FORWARD, ST. Ⓜ (3 HITS), → + Ⓜ CANCEL➤ FORWARD JUMP, AIR Ⓜ, Ⓜ, Ⓗ, LAND, ST. Ⓜ (3 HITS), Ⓢ CANCEL➤ FORWARD SUPER JUMP, AIR Ⓜ, Ⓜ, Ⓗ, Ⓢ, LAND, CALL SENTINEL—α, SLIGHT DELAY, CR. Ⓗ (4 HITS), → + Ⓗ CANCEL➤ ↓ ↘ → + Ⓗ, JUMP FORWARD, AIR Ⓗ, Ⓢ, LAND, ↓ ↘ → + Ⓛ, → ↓ ↘ + ATK ATK (MASH ATK), ST. Ⓗ CANCEL➤ ↓ ↘ → + ATK ATK

Notes	Damage
Corner only, ground throw version of above combo.	762,400 damage, 36% meter loss

→ ↘ ↓ ↙ ← + Ⓗ, CALL WESKER—β, DASH, CR. Ⓜ, ST. Ⓗ, Ⓢ CANCEL➤ FORWARD SUPER JUMP, AIR Ⓜ, Ⓜ, Ⓗ, Ⓢ, LAND, CALL SENTINEL—α, SLIGHT DELAY, CR. Ⓗ (4 HITS), → + Ⓗ CANCEL➤ ↓ ↘ → + Ⓗ, FORWARD JUMP, AIR Ⓗ, Ⓢ, ↓ ↘ → + Ⓛ, → ↓ ↘ + ATK ATK (MASH ATK), ST. Ⓗ CANCEL➤ ↓ ↘ → + ATK ATK

Notes	Damage
Corner Bonne Mixer combo. Wesker must be called immediately to land the OTG hit. Other assists can be used with Tron's cr. Ⓗ OTG, as well	854,700 damage, 49% meter loss

AIR Ⓗ X ← ↓ ↙ + Ⓗ, LAND, Ⓢ CANCEL➤ SUPER JUMP FORWARD, AIR Ⓜ, Ⓜ, Ⓗ, Ⓢ, LAND, CALL SENTINEL—α, SLIGHT DELAY, CR. Ⓗ (4 HITS), → + Ⓗ CANCEL➤ ↓ ↘ → + Ⓗ, JUMP FORWARD, AIR Ⓗ, LAND, ST. Ⓗ, Ⓢ CANCEL➤ SUPER JUMP FORWARD, AIR Ⓗ, Ⓢ, LAND, CALL DANTE——α, CR. Ⓗ (4 HITS), ↓ ↘ → + Ⓗ, JUMP FORWARD, AIR Ⓗ, Ⓢ, LAND, ↓ ↘ → + Ⓛ, ST. Ⓗ CANCEL➤ ← ↓ ↙ + Ⓗ (MASH)

Notes	Damage
A possible midscreen meter building combo. Delay the last Bonne Strike as long as possible to connect with full damage	639,100 damage, 219% meter gain

AIR Ⓗ, LAND, CR. Ⓜ, ST. Ⓗ, Ⓢ CANCEL➤ FORWARD SUPER JUMP, AIR Ⓜ, Ⓜ, Ⓗ, Ⓢ, LAND, CALL SENTINEL—α, SLIGHT DELAY, CR. Ⓗ (4 HITS), → + Ⓗ CANCEL➤ ↓ ↘ → + Ⓗ, FORWARD JUMP, AIR Ⓗ, LAND, ST. Ⓗ, Ⓢ CANCEL➤ FORWARD SUPER JUMP, AIR Ⓗ, Ⓢ, LAND, CALL DANTE—α, CR. Ⓗ (4 HITS), ↓ ↘ → + Ⓗ, FORWARD JUMP, AIR Ⓗ, Ⓢ, LAND, ↓ ↘ → + Ⓛ, ST. Ⓗ CANCEL➤ ← ↓ ↙ + Ⓗ (MASH Ⓗ)

Notes	Damage
Corner only. Same as above but in the corner, utilizing strong single hit moves at the beginning of the combo	792,000 damage, 218% meter gain

INSTANT AIRDASH

Use super jumps to reach the airdash height ceiling faster!

Tron's airdash cannot be done as soon as she leaves the ground. When normal jumping, she cannot airdash until frame 9 of her jump. This means that you must wait 9 frames until you start your offense! However, there is a trick that can allow you to execute this airdash faster. By super jumping, you can cut this wait to 5 frames! This is because there is a "height requirement" for most airdashes. Super jumping moves you higher faster, which allows you to execute your airdash sooner.

VIEWTIFUL JOE

"HENSHIN-A-GO-GO, BABY!"

Bio

REAL NAME

Joe

OCCUPATION

High School Student, Young Hero

ABILITIES

His VFX Power gives him abilities similar to camera effects seen in movies, such as the ability to slow down everything on the screen.

WEAPONS

Utilizes various weapons, including his Voomerang and Shocking Pink Bombs. With his beloved Six Machine, an aircraft capable of transforming into a robot or a cannon, he is ready for any battle.

PROFILE

Before becoming Viewtiful Joe, he was just a 17-year-old who loved the movies. His girlfriend Silvia often became angry over his immature ways.

FIRST APPEARANCE

Viewtiful Joe (2003)

POWER GRID

2	INTELLIGENCE
2	STRENGTH
5	SPEED
2	STAMINA
1	ENERGY PROJECTION
5	FIGHTING ABILITY

*This is biographical, and does not represent an evaluation of the in-game combat potential of this hero.

ALTERNATE COSTUMES

1

2

3

4

5

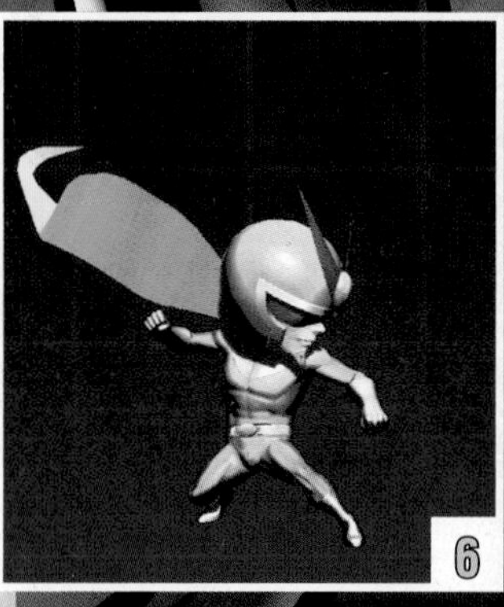
6

DLC

Overview

Vitality	950,000
Chain Combo Archetype	Hunter Series

X-Factor Boost	Damage	Speed
Level 1 (3 teammates remaining)	120%	120%
Level 2 (2 teammates remaining)	140%	130%
Level 3 (1 teammate remaining)	160%	140%

Much like the games he originated from, Viewtiful Joe is a quick, scrappy character that is at his best when he's up close and personal. As such, your primary goal as Viewtiful Joe is to achieve point-blank range against your opponent.

At point-blank range, Viewtiful Joe has a mix-up that is incredibly difficult for adversaries to guard against

- **Excellent Knuckle Punch (→ + Ⓜ) is an incredibly fast overhead attack that leads into combos on hit**
- **Air Ⓗ can be used as both an instant overhead and an air throw attempt, then canceled into Red Hot Kick H to lead into a combo on hit**
- **Airdashing forward and using air Ⓢ is a fast cross-up attack with an enormous hitbox**
- **Crouching basic attacks are all low-hitting and can be mixed in when the opposing character starts guarding high**

How do you achieve point-blank range when using Viewtiful Joe?

- **Airdashing forward and canceling into a low-altitude Voomerang L to quickly advance forward while firing projectiles**
- **Using plink airdashes to cover a lot of distance**
- **Forcing your foe to guard a crossover assist and moving in**
- **Attacking your rival with Red Hot Kick L or M from super jump height, then airdashing forward**
- **Using charged Voomerang L to pin your competitor in place momentarily, making it much easier to force them to guard a crossover assist**

Your secondary goal is to hit your opponent with the Viewtiful God Hand hyper combo

Why do you want to hit your adversary with Viewtiful God Hand?

- **Viewtiful God Hand places the opposing character in a slow state for 10 seconds**
- **Immediately after hitting Viewtiful God Hand, you can perform a strong mix-up of the low-hitting crouching Ⓛ or instant overhead air Ⓗ, which easily leads into a combo when your foe's character is in slow state**
- **Hitting a combo while your rival is in slow state can lead into another Viewtiful God Hand for another mix-up**

How do you hit your competitor with Viewtiful God Hand?

- **Have access to an OTG-capable crossover assist**
- **Use the OTG-enabled assist to end combos with Viewtiful God Hand instead of Desperado**

TUNING SINCE ORIGINAL MVC3

Viewtiful Joe has received some substantial improvements to his toolset in the transition to *Ultimate Marvel vs. Capcom 3*. First is the addition of the V-Dodge, a new move that makes Viewtiful Joe instantly invincible to strikes and projectiles, aiding both his offensive and defensive options. The recovery time on Shocking Pink has been drastically reduced, to the point of recovering almost instantly. Some of his hyper combos have received changes, as well, including OTG-capable properties for the air version of Desperado.

- **Vitality increased from 880,000 to 950,000**
- **New special move: V-Dodge (Ⓢ + ATK)**
- **Recovery frames on Shocking Pink have been reduced from 22 to 4**
- **Mach Speed can now be mashed for additional damage**
- **Air version of Desperado is now OTG-capable**

Attack Set

Standing Basic Attacks

Screen	Command	Hits	Damage	Meter Gain	Startup	Active	Recovery	Advantage on Hit	Advantage if Guarded	Notes
1	Standing L	1	38,000	304	4	3	11	-2	-3	Chains into standing L
2	Standing M	1	50,000	400	7	3	17	-3	-4	—
3	Standing H	1	65,000	520	9	3	21	-1	-3	—

Crouching Basic Attacks

Screen	Command	Hits	Damage	Meter Gain	Startup	Active	Recovery	Advantage on Hit	Advantage if Guarded	Notes
1	Crouching L	1	35,000	280	5	3	10	-1	-2	Low attack
2	Crouching M	1	48,000	384	8	3	17	-3	-4	Low attack, chains into standing M
3	Crouching H	1	60,000	480	9	13	21	—	-13	Low attack, knocks down

Ground Special Attack—Launcher

Screen	Command	Hits	Damage	Meter Gain	Startup	Active	Recovery	Advantage on Hit	Advantage if Guarded	Notes
1	S (while standing or crouching)	1	70,000	560	8	3	23	—	-5	Launcher, not special- or hyper combo-cancelable

Air Basic Attacks

Screen	Command	Hits	Damage	Meter Gain	Startup	Active	Recovery	Advantage on Hit	Advantage if Guarded	Notes
1	Air L	1	38,000	304	5	3	15	+8	+7	—
2	Air M	1	50,000	400	7	3	20	+12	+11	—
3	Air H	1	65,000	520	8	4	24	+15	+13	—

Air Special Attacks—Flying Screen and Air Exchange

Air Ⓢ causes a hard knockdown when used in a launcher combo (this is sometimes called flying screen). When used outside of a launcher combo, air Ⓢ behaves mostly like another basic attack. Air exchange attacks, performed by inputting a direction plus Ⓢ, are only possible during a launcher combo. Exchange hits initiate team aerial combos by tagging in the next available character to continue the air combo.

Screen	Command	Hits	Damage	Meter Gain	Startup	Active	Recovery	Advantage on Hit	Advantage if Guarded	Notes
1	Air Ⓢ	3	64,200	600	9	8	24	+14	+12	Causes hard knockdown if used in launcher combo
2	Air ⇧ + Ⓢ (during launcher combo)	1	60,000	480	8	5	22	—	—	Tags in next available ally while lofting foe upward
3	Air ⇨ or ⇦ + Ⓢ (during launcher combo)	1	50,000	400	7	3	20	—	—	Tags in next available ally while causing wall bounce, erases 1 hyper meter bar from opponent
4	Air ⇩ + Ⓢ (during launcher combo)	1	50,000	400 + 10,000	9	8	Until grounded	—	—	Tags in next available ally while causing ground bounce, generates 1 hyper meter bar

1

2

3

4

Command Attacks

Command attacks resemble basic attacks but have different chaining and canceling properties. It's usually possible to chain *into* a command attack from basic attacks, but most command attacks cannot be chained from or canceled themselves.

Screen	Name	Command	Hits	Damage	Meter Gain	Startup	Active	Recovery	Advantage on Hit	Advantage if Guarded	Notes
1	Excellent Knuckle Punch	⇨ + Ⓜ	1	50,000	400	13	3	23	-9	-10	Overhead attack

1

Throws

Throws are for snagging passive or blocking foes. Since throws are active so quickly, you can also use them to preemptively toss opposing characters out of their offense. Combos are usually possible after throws, one way or another.

Screen	Command	Hits	Damage	Meter Gain	Startup	Active	Notes
1	⇨ + Ⓗ (ground)	1	80,000	800	1	1	Hard knockdown
	⇦ + Ⓗ (ground)	1	80,000	800	1	1	Hard knockdown
2	⇨ + Ⓗ (air)	1	80,000	800	1	1	Hard knockdown
	⇦ + Ⓗ (air)	1	80,000	800	1	1	Hard knockdown

1

2

VIEWTIFUL JOE

As a Partner—Crossover Assists

Screen	Type	P1+P2 Crossover Combination Hyper Combo	Description	Hits	Damage	Meter Gain	Startup	Active	Recovery (this crossover assist)	Recovery (other partner)	Notes
1	Viewtiful Joe—α	Desperado	Voomerang L	1	70,000	560	39	—	125	95	Projectile has 5 low priority durability points
2	Viewtiful Joe—β	Mach Speed	Groovy Uppercut M	1	80,000	640	30	13	121	91	Knocks down opponent
3	Viewtiful Joe—γ	Desperado	Shocking Pink L	1	80,000	640	50	—	114	84	Bomb projectile has 1 low priority durability point, bomb takes 66 frames to detonate, explosion has 8 active frames, explosion projectile has 99 low priority durability points

1

2

3

Viewtiful Joe received a great deal of improvements to his overall toolset, but his assists remain unchanged. Each of his crossover assists is fairly average in its effectiveness.

Viewtiful Joe—α fires a Voomerang projectile that travels straight across the screen at ground level. It is a useful all-around assist that can aid both offensive and defensive characters.

Viewtiful Joe—β replicates Groovy Uppercut M, attacking at an upwards angle. It is the fastest of Viewtiful Joe's crossover assists, but it is also difficult to use effectively because of its short range.

Viewtiful Joe—γ releases a Shocking Pink bomb into the playfield. The projectile remains on screen for 66 frames before detonation, and it can be knocked around the playfield by any attack from you or your opponent. The explosion is OTG-capable and can set up some unique combo opportunities. You can also use this assist to increase your point character's offensive options, since part of the screen is temporarily unsafe for your adversary.

Snap Back

Screen	Command	Hits	Damage	Meter Gain	Startup	Active	Recovery	Advantage on Hit	Advantage if Guarded
1	↓↘→ + P1 or P2	1	50,000	500 - (-1 hyper meter bar)	2	3	22	—	-3

Notes

On hit, snap back forces the opposing point character to be replaced by an assist. Opposing assist calls or tag outs are also locked out for 4 seconds

1

Special Moves

Screen	Name	Command	Hits	Damage	Meter Gain	Startup	Active	Recovery	Advantage on Hit	Advantage if Guarded	Notes
1, 2	Voomerang L (can be charged)	↓↘→ + L	1~3	70,000~150,000	560~1200	10~66	—	34	-12	-14	Charged version homes in on your target, projectile has 5 low priority durability points, charged version has 3 frames x 3 low priority durability points
	Voomerang M (can be charged)	↓↘→ + M	1~3	70,000~150,000	560~1200	10~66	—	37	-15	-17	Charged version homes in on your rival, projectile has 5 low priority durability points, charged version has 3 frames x 3 low priority durability points
	Voomerang H (can be charged)	↓↘→ + H	1~3	70,000~150,000	560~1200	10~66	—	40	-18	-20	Charged version homes in on your competitor, projectile has 5 low priority durability points, charged version has 3 frames x 3 low priority durability points
	Air Voomerang L (can be charged)	(in air) ↓↘→ + L	1~3	70,000~150,000	560~1200	15~69	—	37	+20	+17	Charged version homes in on your adversary, projectile has 5 low priority durability points, charged version has 3 frames x 3 low priority durability points
	Air Voomerang M (can be charged)	(in air) ↓↘→ + M	1~3	70,000~150,000	560~1200	17~71	—	35	+20	+17	Charged version homes in on your foe, projectile has 5 low priority durability points, charged version has 3 frames x 3 low priority durability points
	Air Voomerang H (can be charged)	(in air) ↓↘→ + H	1~3	70,000~150,000	560~1200	19~73	—	33	+20	+19	Charged version homes in on your challenger, projectile has 5 low priority durability points, charged version has 3 frames x 3 low priority durability points
3	Shocking Pink (can be charged)	↓↙← + ATK	1	80,000	640	24	—	4	—	—	OTG-capable, bomb detonation damages both player character and foe, either player attacking the bomb causes it to move, bomb takes 66, 130, and 194 frames to detonate for the L, M, and H versions respectively, explosion has 8 active frames, causes spinning knockdown, bomb projectile has 1 low priority durability point, explosion has 99 low priority durability points

Special Moves continued

Screen	Name	Command	Hits	Damage	Meter Gain	Startup	Active	Recovery	Advantage on Hit	Advantage if Guarded	Notes
4	Red Hot Kick L	(in air) ↓ ↙ ← + L	1	80,000	640	12	Until grounded	23	+9	+7	Overhead attack, if Red Hot Kick makes contact with opponent, Viewtiful Joe bounces backwards in the air with 13 frames of recovery
5	Red Hot Kick M	(in air) ↓ ↙ ← + M	1	80,000	640	12	Until grounded	23	+9	+7	Overhead attack, if Red Hot Kick makes contact with adversary, Viewtiful Joe bounces backward in the air with 13 frames of recovery
6	Red Hot Kick H	(in air) ↓ ↙ ← + H	3	94,800	840	18	Until grounded	19	+2	0	—
7	Air Joe L	(in air) L (mash)	4	96,800	920	3	5(11)5 (3)4(7)5	6	—	—	Can be mashed for additional hits
	Air Joe M	(in air) M (mash)	5	119,700	1200	3	5(11)5 (3)4(7)5 (8)5	8	—	—	Can be mashed for additional hits
	Air Joe H	(in air) H (mash)	6	146,200	1560	3	5(11)5(3) 4(7)5(8) 5(15)5	21	—	—	Can be mashed for additional hits
8	Groovy Uppercut L	→ ↓ ↘ + L	1	80,000	640	8	13	14	+7	-6	Knocks down foe
9	Groovy Uppercut M	→ ↓ ↘ + M	1	80,000	640	6	13	13	+8	-5	Knocks down rival
	Groovy Uppercut H	→ ↓ ↘ + H	2	104,000	880	10	11(19)14	7	+20	0	First hit knocks down competitor, second hit causes spinning knockdown
10	V-Dodge	S + ATK	—	—	—	1	32	13	—	—	Invincible to everything except throws from frames 1-32, can be canceled into special moves and hyper combos

Voomerang: Viewtiful Joe's Voomerang is a useful general projectile attack with 5 low priority durability points. The Voomerang's trajectory changes depending on the strength of the button pressed. L travels directly forward, and is well-suited to combat most regular projectiles. M travels straight up from the point of release, and it can potentially be used to strike opponents jumping in. However, this is not a preferred strategy since you're better off trying to air throw your competitor. H curves around Viewtiful Joe before flying backward at an upward angle. This version is difficult to use effectively, but you can utilize it to catch characters trying to dash above Viewtiful Joe

Voomerang can also be performed in the air, changing the effective use of each version. Air Voomerang L is one of Viewtiful Joe's best tools, as it can be used either offensively to advance forward or defensively to thwart advancing opponents. Jump, airdash, and immediately use Voomerang L to toss the projectile and cover the moment Joe hits the ground! Air Voomerang M bends straight down, useful for approaching characters from super jump height. Super jump, airdash, and use Voomerang M to drop down on your adversary safely; if the foe hits Joe, the Voomerang then drops on their head and usually allows for a combo. Air Voomerang H bends around below Viewtiful Joe before traveling backward. Unlike the ground version, air Voomerang H is great for catching rivals trying to dash underneath an airborne Viewtiful Joe.

Voomerang (charged): All versions of Voomerang can be charged. A charged Voomerang has increased projectile durability and travels in the same direction as the uncharged versions. The projectile then homes in on an opponent and sticks to them for a few moments.

You can cover the time Viewtiful Joe is vulnerable while charging by super jumping and beginning the charge the second Viewtiful Joe leaves the ground by inputting ↓ ↘ → ↑ + ATK (hold). The Voomerang will be fully charged by the time Viewtiful Joe reaches the ground. Call in an assist to make this technique even safer.

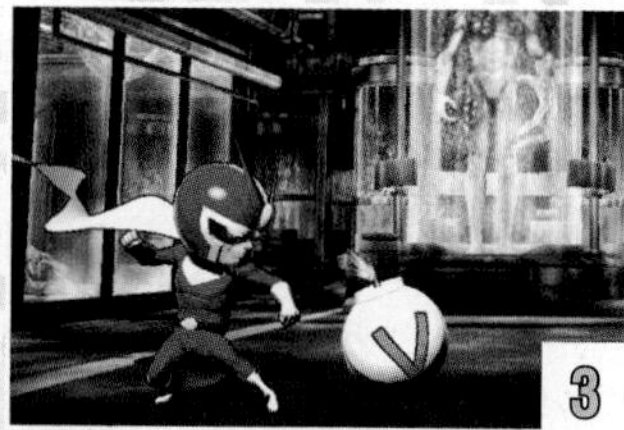

Shocking Pink: Viewtiful Joe drops a bomb with a variable fuse time depending on the attack button pressed. Until it explodes, both players can knock the bomb around the playfield. The bomb's explosion is OTG-capable and can damage both players.

In *Ultimate Marvel vs. Capcom 3,* the recovery time of Shocking Pink has been reduced to four frames—a nearly instant recovery time. This allows Shocking Pink to come into play more often and become a more prominent part of Viewtiful Joe's gameplan. For example, cancel guarded attacks into Shocking Pink to make your competitor unsure whether they can attack or not. The L version detonates quickly enough that opponent generally gets hit if they try to immediately attack; when they've been conditioned not to attack, drop one of the other two versions of the bomb to continue attacking while your foe remains passive and unsure of what to do next.

Viewtiful Joe can delay the release of a bomb by keeping the attack button held down, and can even control the timing of the explosion; see Advanced Tactics for more details.

Red Hot Kick L: This aerial attack sends Viewtiful Joe straight down, creating a decent opportunity to begin attacking an adversary from super jump height directly over their head. If Red Hot Kick L makes contact, Viewtiful Joe bounces backward in the air in a neutral state. Airdash forward after the bounce to continue your attack!

Red Hot Kick M: Viewtiful Joe travels downward at a 45-degree angle. Its properties are similar to the L version, except that Red Hot Kick M is most useful in the middle of air combos.

Red Hot Kick H: Although it travels in the same direction as Red Hot Kick M, this version hits multiple times and does not bounce backward on contact. This attack has some applications for combos and in general offense, since it is surprisingly safe if guarded.

7

Air Joe: Viewtiful Joe floats slowly back to the ground while attacking with a flurry of punches and kicks. Air Joe can be mashed to add extra duration. It's generally better to avoid using this move in combos, as it adds a lot of hitstun decay and damage scaling in return for little damage output.

Groovy Uppercut L 8

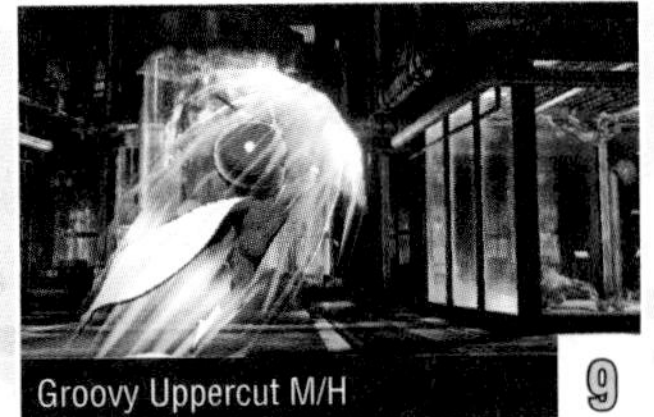
Groovy Uppercut M/H 9

Groovy Uppercut: Although you can use Groovy Uppercut as an effective anti-air, it does not have any invulnerability, which limits the overall effectiveness of this attack. The strength of each button determines its trajectory: L travels straight up, M launches at a 45-degree upward angle, and H hits twice, the final hit puts your opponent into a spinning knockdown. All three versions leave Viewtiful Joe in the air, allowing you to juggle your foe after a successful hit.

10

V-Dodge: Viewtiful Joe gets an effective new tool in *Ultimate Marvel vs. Capcom 3*! V-Dodge makes Viewtiful Joe invincible to everything but throws from the very first frame, and it can be canceled into special moves or hyper combos. V-Dodge can highly useful either offensive or defensively; any time your adversary is near you and tries to attack, activate V-Dodge and cancel into Groovy Uppercut M to punish and go into a combo! However, if you don't cancel V-Dodge into a special move or hyper combo, you are susceptible to attacks during its recovery period.

Hyper Combos

Screen	Name	Command	Hits	Damage	Startup	Active	Recovery	Advantage on Hit	Advantage if Guarded	Notes
1	Desperado (in air OK)	↓↘→ + ATK ATK	1	250,000	18+1	—	72	—	-52	Frames 1-15 invincible, air version is OTG-capable, projectile has 15 high priority durability points
2	Viewtiful God Hand	↓↙← + ATK ATK	2	145,000	10+2	4	34	+3	-17	Slows foe down by 25% for 600 frames
3	Mach Speed	→↓↘ + ATK ATK	15~28	252,000~286,000	8+4	3(7)80(9)4	49	—	-32	Frames 1-32 invincible, launcher, can be mashed for additional hits

1

Desperado: Viewtiful Joe summons his ship, the "Six Machine," to fire a large, high-durability projectile. Desperado does have some invulnerability, but it runs out before the move finishes starting up. It's generally used most effectively in the air to end combos. In *Ultimate Marvel vs. Capcom 3,* Desperado is now OTG-capable, useful for adding on some much-needed additional damage off on air throw.

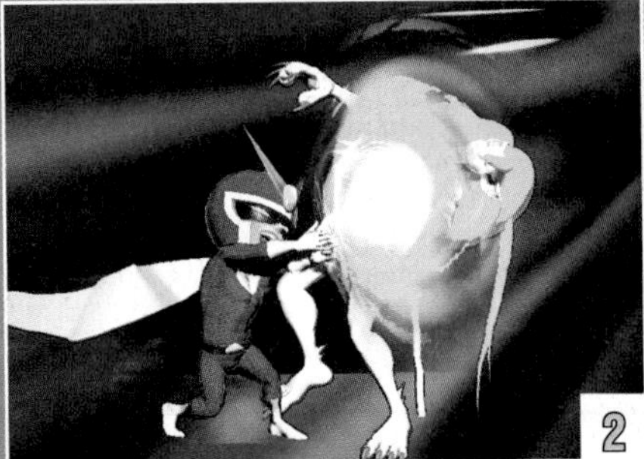
2

Viewtiful God Hand: This short ranged attack does little in the way of damage, but it leaves the opposing character in a slowed state for a solid 10 seconds. While in the state, everything your competitor does is slower, including recovering from hitstun; this allows for combos that are not possible otherwise. The slowed adversary is left standing right next to Viewtiful Joe and leaves Joe with a small frame advantage, leading to potential mix-up situations right off the bat. Ending combos with Viewtiful God Hand is a strong play if you don't have to sacrifice too much damage to your rival to do so.

Note that once Viewtiful God Hand connects with a target, you cannot team hyper combo-cancel the attack animation.

3

Mach Speed: This powerful hyper combo has a ton of invincibility, and it ends in a launcher that can lead into an air combo on hit. Mach Speed's invincibility and speed make it an excellent defensive hyper combo; it can pass right through beam hypers like Ryu's Shinku Hadoken with ease! Save Mach Speed for the end of damaging combos or to defend against enemy hyper combos—it is ridiculously unsafe if guarded. Mach Speed is mashable for more damage in *Ultimate Marvel vs. Capcom 3.*

"WHOA! SO YOU'RE, LIKE, A REAL HERO? FOR REAL?"

Battle Plan

Airdashing toward your opponent and throwing a Voomerang L is a great way to get in for a combo.

Viewtiful Joe has an excellent array of mobility options available to him, and you'll need to take advantage of all of them to accomplish your primary goal of getting with point-blank range of your rival. In the air, Viewtiful Joe has access to two airdashes and a triple jump. Only two other characters in the entire roster share these traits—Chun-Li and Devil Trigger mode Dante.

Triple jumping allows Viewtiful Joe to reach super jump height from a normal jump, granting him access to crossover assists. With the help of crossover assist, Viewtiful Joe can retain control of the ground while triple jumping over any projectiles that his opponent tosses out. Lock down your adversary with an assist and triple jump above their head, then come crashing down with an attack like Red Hot Kick H to begin your assault.

Viewtiful Joe's double airdash allows him to cover horizontal distance in the air rather quickly, especially when you incorporate plink airdashing into your game. Plinking refers to hitting separate buttons on consecutive frames, which the game interprets in interesting ways. In Viewtiful Joe's case, plinking allows you to cancel his airdash right into another airdash, which is not normally possible. You can install an option select air throw at the same time! First take to the air and airdash, and then perform → + Ⓗ~(ATK) mid-dash. Since you're hitting → + Ⓗ one frame before another (ATK) button, the game very briefly interprets this as both the start of air Ⓗ, and an air throw attempt. The (ATK) input on the next frame then kara cancels air Ⓗ into another airdash! Go into Training Mode and turn on the Input Display in order to view your inputs to master plink airdashing—performed properly, your button presses appear staggered, rather than simultaneous.Combined with an airdash, air Voomerang L is an excellent option to get close to your opponent. Cancel an airdash into ↓ ↘ → + Ⓛ to launch the projectile at a very low height, forcing your rival to either block the attack or absorb the hit. In either case, Viewtiful Joe is at a massive frame advantage, since he recovers immediately upon landing. Spam this technique from long distances while calling crossover assists to keep your foe pinned down and while simultaneously closing the distance!

Viewtiful Joe's options to close the distance in the air do not end there. You can plink airdash just above your target and use air Ⓢ for a cross up, or super jump, airdash, and use the downward trajectory of air Voomerang M to land an attack from above. If you're looking for a riskier way to cover a large amount of distance quickly, super jump and then attack with Red Hot Kick L or M. Once the hit connects, airdash once Viewtiful Joe recovers from the bounce caused by Red Hot Kick to get back in and continue applying pressure to your foe.

Any of the above tactics benefit greatly from crossover assists that can pin down the opposing character. Beam or multi-hit projectile assists like Iron Man—α or Amaterasu—β work great for this purpose at long ranges. Akuma—β, Dante—α, or Phoenix Wright—β are viable options, as well. Don't forget Viewtiful Joe's triple jump ability either: it may take slightly longer to ascend to super jump height, but you can call an assist before attacking.

If your opponent has caught on to your vast array of air shenanigans, they may start to counter your attempts to close the distance. However, now that you have them trained, you can flip the script on your assault tactics: instead of advancing toward your adversary through the air, wavedash forward along the ground to surprise your foe.

Use V-Dodge (Ⓢ + (ATK)) to avoid incoming attacks, and cancel into Groovy Uppercut M to punish!

Once you've closed the distance and gotten within point-blank range of your opponent, you can begin applying Viewtiful Joe's mix-up game, which can be almost impossible for opposing players to defend against consistently. Switch between the following tactics to keep your competitors guessing and break through their defenses:

Excellent Knuckle Punch (→ + Ⓜ) hits overhead. Cancel into Groovy Uppercut M to begin a combo

Jump and immediately press Ⓗ for an instant overhead attack, then cancel into Red Hot Kick H to return to the ground and continue the combo. Note you can option select an air throw by holding → as you press Ⓗ, in case your rival tries to jump away

Low-hitting crouching Ⓛ attacks can be chained together with slow timing. If your target tries to use advancing guard or jump away, cancel into V-Dodge to counter

While assaulting with crouching Ⓛ, mix in an Excellent Knuckle Punch for an easy overhead hit

Jump, then airdash as low as possible and cross up your foe with air Ⓢ

If all else fails, throw your opponent. Viewtiful Joe's ground throws lead to easy damage but do not lead into anything more damaging on their own

In addition to a strong mix-up, point-blank range means that Viewtiful Joe is within striking distance of his Viewtiful God Hand hyper combo. This hyper combo slows down your opponent by 25% and opens even more close-range mix-ups! For more information on what Viewtiful God Hand can do for you, see the Advanced Tactics section.

If you have a hard time getting within point-blank range, Joe still has quite a few options when it comes to long range battles. The airdash to air Voomerang L technique, for example, works just as well with a backdash to cover Viewtiful Joe as he retreats. Continue spamming this attacking until you give Joe enough breathing room to continue pursuing your primary goal.

Desperado can now hit OTG, allowing Viewtiful Joe to get more damage from an air throw.

When your opponent pushes Joe back to medium range and establishes their position there, surprise them by going on offense with airdash Ⓢ cross ups, or wavedash forward into crouching Ⓛ. Now you've turned the tides and can continue your point-blank mix-up strategies.

The new V-Dodge (Ⓢ + (ATK)) maneuver is invaluable against an adversary attacking Viewtiful Joe. Activate V-Dodge to avoid one of their attacks and immediate cancel into Groovy Uppercut M to put Viewtiful Joe on the offensive and swing the momentum of the battle in your favor.

Air throws are an important tool for Viewtiful Joe to take advantage of against airborne foes. In original *MvC3*, Viewtiful Joe could not deal much damage from a successful air throw, but in *UMvC3*, you can now hit with the OTG-capable Desperado hyper combo for some more respectable damage. Keep an eye out for airborne opponents nearby, and jump toward them with → + Ⓗ (CANCEL) ↓ ↙ ← + Ⓗ. If Viewtiful Joe is close enough to the opposing character an air throw will occur, and if not, air Ⓗ will be canceled into Red Hot Kick H for a relatively safe contingency plan!

The Mach Speed hyper combo serves as a way to get close and shut down aggressive competitors at the cost of a hyper meter. Its long invincibility window blows through most attacks and can even be used to counter beam hyper combos. Be mindful of your hyper meter bar and have at least two in reserve before randomly throwing out Mach Speed as a Hail Mary. Mach Speed is incredibly unsafe if guarded, in which case you'll need that extra bar to DHC to your teammate and avoid a heavy punish from your rival.

COMBO USAGE

1. CR. Ⓜ, ST. Ⓜ, Ⓗ, CR. Ⓗ (CANCEL) → ↓ ↘ + Ⓜ, AIR Ⓗ (CANCEL) FORWARD DOUBLE JUMP, Ⓜ, Ⓗ (CANCEL) ↓ ↙ ← + Ⓜ, ↓ ↙ ← + Ⓗ, LAND, ST. Ⓗ, Ⓢ (CANCEL) VERTICAL SUPER JUMP, AIR Ⓜ, Ⓜ, Ⓗ (CANCEL) FORWARD DOUBLE JUMP, Ⓜ, Ⓗ (CANCEL) FORWARD DOUBLE JUMP, Ⓜ, Ⓗ (CANCEL) ↓ ↙ ← + Ⓜ, ↓ ↙ ← + Ⓜ (CANCEL) ↓ ↘ → + (ATK)(ATK)

606,200 damage, 8% meter gain

Viewtiful Joe's bread and butter combo is highly effective, pays for itself in meter gain, and can be performed anywhere on the screen. However, there are two parts of this combo where the timing is a bit tricky. First, be careful of the timing for connecting the first air Ⓗ after Groovy Uppercut M: press the button too soon and the attack won't come out at all, too late and your adversary will have recovered from the previous hit. After Red Hot Kick H, you'll need to be vigilant to catch the opponent on time as they're falling for the relaunch.

If performing this combo at mid screen, there's a chance that Red Hot Kick H will place Viewtiful Joe on the opposite side of your adversary. This does not change the combo in the least, but remember to reverse your input directions to compensate.

COMBO USAGE CONT.

II. → + M ⇨ → ↓ ↘ + M, AIR H ⇨ FORWARD DOUBLE JUMP, M, H ⇨ ↓ ↙ ← + M, ↓ ↙ ← + H, LAND, ST. H, S ⇨ VERTICAL SUPER JUMP, AIR M, M, H ⇨ FORWARD DOUBLE JUMP, M, H ⇨ FORWARD DOUBLE JUMP, M, H ⇨ ↓ ↙ ← + M, ↓ ↙ ← + M ⇨ ↓ ↘ → + ATK ATK

588,100 damage, 6% meter loss

When you're harassing your opponent with low-hitting crouching L attacks at point blank range, mix in the overhead Excellent Knuckle Punch and begin this combo.

III. CR. M, ST. M, H ⇨ ↓ ↘ → + L ⇨ → ↓ ↘ + ATK ATK (MASH ATK) ⇨ VERTICAL SUPER JUMP, AIR M, M, H ⇨ FORWARD DOUBLE JUMP, M, H ⇨ FORWARD DOUBLE JUMP, M, H ⇨ ↓ ↙ ← + M, ↓ ↙ ← + M ⇨ ↓ ↘ → + ATK ATK

671,000 damage, 137% meter loss

Combo III takes advantage of the launcher attack at the end of the Mach Speed hyper combo. You'll need slightly less than two hyper meter bars in the bank before starting this combo. As you're mashing buttons to increase the damage of Mach Speed, be aware of when the hyper combo ends so you can follow up with the super jump cancel in time. Also, be sure you're not pressing buttons as you super jump, otherwise you'll catch your opponent too soon—or miss them entirely—and may not be able to finish the combo.

IV. FORWARD JUMP, INSTANT AIR H ⇨ ↓ ↙ ← + H ⇨ → ↓ ↘ + ATK ATK (MASH ATK) ⇨ VERTICAL SUPER JUMP, AIR M, M, H ⇨ FORWARD DOUBLE JUMP, M, H ⇨ FORWARD DOUBLE JUMP, M, H ⇨ ↓ ↙ ← + M, ↓ ↙ ← + M ⇨ ↓ ↘ → + ATK ATK

615,400 damage, 123% meter loss

Part of Viewtiful Joe's key offensive strategy is to be aggressive with airdashes into air S, Voomerang L, and air H. This combo starts with an air H attack after airdash, and keeps the good times rolling with a Red Hot Kick H into Mach Speed. Like in **Combo III**, be aware of the time it takes Mach Speed to complete so you can quit mashing buttons in time.

Depending on where you begin air H, there is a chance you can cross up your opponent with the attack. If the cross up occurs remember to reverse your inputs, otherwise Joe will begin the startup animation for Voomerang and fall to the ground without releasing the projectile.

V. FRONT OR BACK AIR THROW, LAND, ↓ ↘ → ↗ + ATK ATK

317,500 damage, 92% meter loss

The air version of the Desperado hyper combo gains OTG-capability in *Ultimate Marvel vs. Capcom 3*. Take advantage of this improvement to score some free damage off of a simple air throw. Practice the ↓ ↘ → ↗ + ATK ATK motion in training mode to get a feel for executing air Desperado the moment Joe leaves the ground. Alternatively, depending on how far the opponent has been thrown, you can allow Joe to fall slightly after the air throw and input ↓ ↘ → + ATK ATK on the way down to connect the hit.

VI. (AGAINST AIRBORNE ENEMY) FORWARD JUMP, AIR M, M, H ⇨ FORWARD DOUBLE JUMP, H ⇨ ↓ ↙ ← + M, ↓ ↙ ← + H, ST. H, S ⇨ VERTICAL SUPER JUMP, AIR M, M, H ⇨ FORWARD DOUBLE JUMP, AIR M, H ⇨ FORWARD DOUBLE JUMP, M, H ⇨ ↓ ↙ ← + M, ↓ ↙ ← + M ⇨ ↓ ↘ → + ATK ATK

554,500 damage, 12% meter loss

Take advantage of a jumping opponent using Joe's triple jump and snag them with this combo. The trickiest part with this combo is that you can't necessarily guarantee how high you'll be when you catch your opponent with the first air M, and if you connect ↓ ↙ ← + H at too high an altitude, you're opponent will air recover before the get within range of standing H. Otherwise, much like with **Combo I**, your big worry is catching the opponent with standing H as the fall after Red Hot Kick M.

VII. CR. M, ST. M, H ⇨ ↓ ↘ → + L XF FORWARD DASH, CR. M, ST. M, H ⇨ ↓ ↘ → + L ⇨ → ↓ ↘ + ATK ATK (MASH ATK) ⇨ VERTICAL SUPER JUMP, AIR M, M, H ⇨ FORWARD DOUBLE JUMP, M, H ⇨ FORWARD DOUBLE JUMP, M, H ⇨ ↓ ↙ ← + M, ↓ ↙ ← + M ⇨ ↓ ↘ → + ATK ATK

1,004,900 damage, 106% meter loss

Normally, the recovery time of Voomerang makes it useless for mid-combo usage. However, with an X-Factor cancel it can lead to huge damage. Activate X-Factor as soon as the Voomerang projectile connects and continue the combo. The same tip for following the launcher after Mach Speed in previous combos applies here, only now you must take into account for the X-Factor speed boots. Master this combo and you're guaranteed a K.O. against all but the mightiest of adversaries!

ADVANCED TACTICS

THE (VIEWTIFUL) HAND OF GOD

Viewtiful God Hand opens up a whole slew of new combo options.

Viewtiful God Hand is an amazing hyper combo to take advantage of. By slowing down his opponent by 25%, Viewtiful Joe gets to enjoy increased frame advantage on all of his moves, and a world of new combo opportunities becomes open to you. Landing Viewtiful God Hand can be accomplished with a fairly simple mix-up.

When you're within point-blank range of your adversary, start poking them with crouching Ⓛ, following up with an instant overhead air Ⓗ into Red Hot Kick H for a combo. Once Red Hot Kick H connects, cancel into ⇩ ⇙ ⇦ + ATK ATK to slow them down! Once your rival is slowed, you can link attacks that would not do so otherwise. For example, you can now combo standing Ⓛ attacks after a successful Red Hot Kick H into a full combo.

You can easily pull off a big combo into another Viewtiful God Hand. End your combo with an attack that results in a hard knockdown state, pick up the opposing character with an OTG-capable assist, and combo into another Viewtiful God Hand to keep the offense flowing!

SHOCKING PINK CONTROLLED EXPLOSIONS

Controlling the explosion of Shocking Pink bombs can leave your opponent questioning their available options.

Thanks to a drastically reduced recovery time, bringing Shocking Pink bombs into play has become a much more viable option in *Ultimate Marvel vs. Capcom 3.* However, there's still an issue with the bomb's detonation time and its ability to also damage Viewtiful Joe. Thankfully, there's a technique that allows you to detonate a bomb whenever you want!

You can normally delay the release of Shocking Pink by keeping the attack button held down, causing Viewtiful Joe to dribble the bomb like a mini-Pelé. By holding down another ATK button before releasing the first, Viewtiful Joe releases the bomb, but it will not explode. Keep the button held down as long as you like and kick the bomb around the playfield. When you're ready to set off the bomb, simply release the button. Combined with V-Dodge, you can place the bomb essentially anywhere you want on the ground as a trap and avoid the explosion from damaging Joe, too!

Use this technique to set up an alternative OTG method for Viewtiful Joe or to keep your opponent on their toes as this hot potato gets knocked around the playfield. You can even switch which ATK button is being held down to continue to hold back the explosion (similar to Zero's Mega Buster charge). The bomb only explodes if you release a button, if Viewtiful Joe gets hit, or if someone pauses and unpauses the game (which is totally cheating!).

COMBO APPENDIX

GENERAL EXECUTION TIPS

Joe excels at long air combos thanks to his triple jump, but beware of pushing too many buttons while in the air to avoid accidently executing Air Joe (ATK))).

Practice the timing of landing air Ⓗ after Groovy Uppercut M. It is key to consistently extending your ground combos into the air.

The launch attack after Mach Speed (→ ↓ ↘ + ATK ATK) can be used to tack on great deal of damage. Learn its timing to properly follow up after the hyper combo.

AS V. JOE COMES IN: AIR Ⓜ, Ⓗ CANCEL⇒ CANCEL⇒ FORWARD DOUBLE JUMP, Ⓜ, Ⓗ CANCEL⇒ FORWARD DOUBLE JUMP, Ⓜ, Ⓗ CANCEL⇒ ↓ ↙ ← + Ⓜ, ↓ ↙ ← + Ⓜ CANCEL⇒ ↓ ↘ → + ATK ATK

Notes	Damage
⇧ + Ⓢ or ⇨ + Ⓢ TAC to Joe	Varies based on damage scaling

AS V. JOE COMES IN: AIR Ⓗ CANCEL⇒ CANCEL⇒ FORWARD DOUBLE JUMP, Ⓜ, Ⓗ CANCEL⇒ FORWARD DOUBLE JUMP, Ⓜ, Ⓗ CANCEL⇒ ↓ ↙ ← + Ⓜ, ↓ ↙ ← + Ⓜ CANCEL⇒ ↓ ↘ → + ATK ATK

Notes	Damage
⇩ + Ⓢ TAC to Joe	Varies based on damage scaling

CR. Ⓜ, ST. Ⓜ, Ⓗ, CR. Ⓗ CANCEL⇒ → ↓ ↘ + Ⓜ, AIR Ⓗ CANCEL⇒ FORWARD DOUBLE JUMP, Ⓜ, Ⓗ CANCEL⇒ ↓ ↙ ← + Ⓜ, ↓ ↙ ← + Ⓗ, LAND, ST. Ⓗ, Ⓢ CANCEL⇒ VERTICAL SUPER JUMP, AIR Ⓜ, Ⓜ, Ⓗ CANCEL⇒ FORWARD DOUBLE JUMP, Ⓜ, Ⓗ CANCEL⇒ ↓ ↙ ← + Ⓜ, FORWARD AIRDASH, AIR Ⓢ, LAND, CALL WESKER—β, ↓ ↙ ← + ATK ATK

Notes	Damage
This illustrates an example combo that ends with the God Hand	533,200 damage, 5% meter gain

WITH VIEWTIFUL GOD FIST ACTIVE, FORWARD JUMP, INSTANT AIR Ⓗ CANCEL⇒ ↓ ↙ ← + Ⓗ, ST. Ⓜ, Ⓗ, Ⓜ, Ⓗ CANCEL⇒ ↓ ↘ → + Ⓛ CANCEL⇒ → ↓ ↘ + ATK ATK (MASH ATK) CANCEL⇒ VERTICAL SUPER JUMP, AIR Ⓜ, Ⓜ, Ⓗ CANCEL⇒ FORWARD DOUBLE JUMP, Ⓜ, Ⓗ CANCEL⇒ ↓ ↙ ← + Ⓜ, FORWARD AIRDASH, Ⓢ, LAND, CALL WESKER—β, ↓ ↙ ← + ATK ATK

Notes	Damage
—	647,100 damage, 124% meter loss

WITH GOD HAND ACTIVE, CR. Ⓜ, ST. Ⓜ, Ⓗ, Ⓜ, Ⓗ, Ⓜ, Ⓗ CANCEL⇒ ↓ ↘ → + Ⓛ CANCEL⇒ → ↓ ↘ + ATK ATK (MASH ATK) CANCEL⇒ VERTICAL SUPER JUMP, AIR Ⓜ, Ⓜ, Ⓗ CANCEL⇒ FORWARD DOUBLE JUMP, Ⓜ, Ⓗ CANCEL⇒ ↓ ↙ ← + Ⓜ, FORWARD AIRDASH, Ⓢ, LAND, CALL WESKER—β, ↓ ↙ ← + ATK ATK

Notes	Damage
—	657,200 damage, 122% meter loss

WESKER

"THIS WORLD SHALL BE MINE."

Bio

REAL NAME

Albert Wesker

OCCUPATION

Former S.T.A.R.S. Captain

ABILITIES

Having infected himself with a special virus, he gained several super-human abilities, such as being able to dodge bullets. In addition to his skills with firearms, he is also very knowledgeable about bioengineering.

WEAPONS

Uses many firearms.

PROFILE

A very calculating and dangerous individual, he will do anything to further his own gains. Having perfected the Uroboros Virus, he plans to infect the global population with it, leaving only the chosen ones, such as himself, to create a new world.

FIRST APPEARANCE

Resident Evil (1996)

POWER GRID

6	INTELLIGENCE
4	STRENGTH
5	SPEED
4	STAMINA
1	ENERGY PROJECTION
5	FIGHTING ABILITY

*This is biographical, and does not represent an evaluation of the in-game combat potential of this hero.

ALTERNATE COSTUMES

Overview

Vitality	1,000,000
Chain Combo Archetype	Marvel Series

X-Factor Boost	Damage	Speed
Level 1 (3 teammates remaining)	130%	110%
Level 2 (2 teammates remaining)	150%	120%
Level 3 (1 teammate remaining)	170%	130%

The objective with Wesker is to achieve close range against an opponent.

When in close, Wesker has access to incredibly powerful offensive options:

- **Phantom Move L used in conjunction with crossover assists can start combos from an unexpected cross-up.**
- **Mustang Kick is a one-frame command throw that leads to a full combo against opponents attempting to guard.**
- **Wesker's backwards air throw stops attempts to jump away from the mix-up and leads into a full combo.**
- **All of Wesker's combos end with an OTG ↘ + Ⓗ, which puts him in great position for subsequent mix-ups!**

How does one achieve close range with Wesker?

- **Wavedashing forward behind the cover of a crossover assist**
- **Beating your opponent at long range with Samurai Edge gunshots, forcing your challenger to come to you**
- **Carefully wavedashing forward while guarding and jumping over attacks**
- **Using Tiger Uppercut to counter long-range attacks and projectiles**

The secondary goal with Wesker is to get rid of his signature sunglasses: whenever Wesker's sunglasses are off, he deals an additional 15% damage on all of his attacks! See the Advanced Tactics section for details.

TUNING SINCE ORIGINAL MVC3

Widely regarded to be a top-class character in the original *Marvel vs. Capcom 3*, the Ultimate version of Wesker emerges with his gameplay surprisingly intact. The most significant weakening of Wesker's abilities involves the Samurai Edge (Horizontal Fire) (→ + Ⓗ): it does not bounce airborne opponents nearly as high anymore, making it nearly impossible to convert full-screen gunshots into full combos. Rhino Charge has lost its invulnerable startup, making it significantly less useful as a way to counter dive kicks and random hyper combos from an opponent.

However, Wesker has gained a significant improvement: losing his shades grants him a 10% speed boost and a 15% damage boost! This gives you a great reason to use Phantom Dance more often, which makes Wesker remove his specs!

- Vitality changed to 1,000,000 from 1,100,000.
- Air Ⓜ has one less frame of startup but gained one frame of recovery.
- Samurai Edge (Horizontal Fire) has one less frame of recovery.
- Jaguar Dash has three fewer startup frames, five more active frames, and three fewer recovery frames. Now -6 frame disadvantage on hit and -10 on block.
- Phantom Move recovery increased by one frame on the M and H versions.
- Rhino Charge now only invincible on frame 5 instead of 1-5.
- Cobra Strike is now cancelable into Phantom Move.
- Samurai Edge (Horizontal Fire) (→ + Ⓗ) does not bounce airborne opponents as high.
- Wesker now gains a 5% speed boost and 10% damage boost when his sunglasses are off.
- Wesker now gains a 10% speed boost and 15% damage boost when his sunglasses are broken.

Attack Set

Standing Basic Attacks

Screen	Command	Hits	Damage	Meter Gain	Startup	Active	Recovery	Advantage on Hit	Advantage if Guarded	Notes
1	Standing L	1	55,000	440	5	5	8	+2	+1	—
2	Standing M	1	73,000	684	8	2	22	-4	-6	—
3	Standing H	2	92,500	800	12	8	18	+2	0	—

Crouching Basic Attacks

Screen	Command	Hits	Damage	Meter Gain	Startup	Active	Recovery	Advantage on Hit	Advantage if Guarded	Notes
1	Crouching L	1	53,000	424	5	2	11	+2	+1	Low attack
2	Crouching M	1	75,000	600	8	5	14	+1	-1	Low attack
3	Crouching H	1	80,000	640	10	3	25	—	-5	Low attack, knocks down

Ground Special Attack—Launcher

Screen	Command	Hits	Damage	Meter Gain	Startup	Active	Recovery	Advantage on Hit	Advantage if Guarded	Notes
1	S (while standing or crouching)	1	100,000	800	10	3	21	—	-1	Launcher, not special- or hyper combo-cancelable

Air Basic Attacks

Screen	Command	Hits	Damage	Meter Gain	Startup	Active	Recovery	Advantage on Hit	Advantage if Guarded	Notes
1	Air L	1	55,000	440	5	8	16	+13	+12	Overhead attack
2	Air M	1	73,000	584	9	5	16	+17	+16	Overhead attack
3	Air H	1	88,000	704	11	7	18	+19	+17	Overhead attack

Air Special Attacks—Flying Screen and Air Exchange

Air Ⓢ causes a hard knockdown when used in a launcher combo (this is sometimes called flying screen). When used outside of a launcher combo, air Ⓢ behaves mostly like another basic attack. Air exchange attacks, performed by inputting a direction plus Ⓢ, are only possible during a launcher combo. Exchange hits initiate team aerial combos by tagging in the next available character to continue the air combo.

Screen	Command	Hits	Damage	Meter Gain	Startup	Active	Recovery	Advantage on Hit	Advantage if Guarded	Notes
1	Air Ⓢ	1	95,000	760	10	5	24	+16	+14	Causes hard knockdown if used in launcher combo
2	Air ↑ + Ⓢ (during launcher combo)	2	105,00	880	9	3	20	—	—	Tags in next available ally while lofting opponent upward
3	Air → or ← + Ⓢ (during launcher combo)	2	95,000	800	11	5	20	—	—	Tags in next available ally while causing wall bounce, erases 1 hyper meter bar from opponent
4	Air ↓ + Ⓢ (during launcher combo)	2	95,000	800	10	5	21	—	—	Tags in next available ally while causing ground bounce, generates 1 hyper meter bar

Command Attacks

Command attacks resemble basic attacks but have different chaining and canceling properties. It's usually possible to chain *into* a command attack from basic attacks, but most command attacks cannot be chained from or canceled themselves.

Screen	Name	Command	Hits	Damage	Meter Gain	Startup	Active	Recovery	Advantage on Hit	Advantage if Guarded	Notes
1	Samurai Edge (Horizontal Fire)	→ + Ⓗ	1	80,000	640	15	—	30	-6	-8	Not special- or hyper combo-cancelable; inflicts chip damage; projectile has 3 low priority projectile points; Ⓛ, Ⓜ or Ⓗ all cancel into respective Phantom Moves
2	Samurai Edge (Lower Shot)	↙ + Ⓗ	1	80,000	640	15	2	24	-1	-3	Low attack; OTG-capable; not special- or hyper combo-cancelable; inflicts chip damage; projectile has 3 low priority projectile points; Ⓛ, Ⓜ, or Ⓗ all cancel into respective Phantom Moves
3	Samurai Edge (Anti-surface)	Air ↓ + Ⓗ	1	80,000	640	15	—	Until landing	+23	+21	Not special- or hyper combo-cancelable; inflicts chip damage; projectile has 3 low priority projectile points; Ⓛ, Ⓜ, or Ⓗ all cancel into respective Phantom Moves

Throws

Throws are for snagging passive or blocking foes. Since throws are active so quickly, you can also use them preemptively to toss opposing characters out of an offensive stance. Combos are usually possible after throws, one way or another.

Screen	Command	Hits	Damage	Meter Gain	Startup	Active	Notes
1	→ + Ⓗ (ground)	2	80,000	800	1	—	Hard knockdown
	← + Ⓗ (ground)	2	80,000	800	1	—	Hard knockdown
2	→ + Ⓗ (air)	2	80,000	800	1	—	Hard knockdown
	← + Ⓗ (air)	2	80,000	800	1	—	Hard knockdown

As a Partner—Crossover Assists

Screen	Type	P1+P2 Crossover Combination Hyper Combo	Description	Hits	Damage	Meter Gain	Startup	Active	Recovery (this crossover assist)	Recovery (other partner)	Notes
1	Wesker—α	Phantom Dance	Ghost Butterfly	1	120,000	960	42	3	117	87	Wall bounces opponent
2	Wesker—β	Phantom Dance	Samurai Edge (Lower Shot)	1	80,000	640	39	2	116	86	OTG-capable; low attack; projectile has 3 low priority projectile points
3	Wesker—γ	Phantom Dance	Jaguar Dash + Jaguar Kick	3	116,400	1040	49	5(9)4	114	84	Knocks down

When using Wesker, the decision of which crossover assist type to pick is a no-brainer: Wesker—β and the OTG-capable, low-hitting Samurai Edge is one of the most useful assets a team could possibly have. This is clearly the best OTG-capable assist in the game, since it is lightning-quick and not does not cause any unwanted state like a ground bounce or wall bounce. It's one of the few low-hitting assists in the game, so Samurai Edge can be used to set up unblockable situations when used simultaneously with an overhead attack!

Snap Back

Screen	Command	Hits	Damage	Meter Gain	Startup	Active	Recovery	Advantage on Hit	Advantage if Guarded
1	↓↘→ + P1 or P2	1	50,000	500 (-1 hyper meter bar)	2	4	32	—	-13

Notes

Once hit, snap back forces the opposing point character to be replaced by an assist. Opposing assist calls or tag outs are also locked out for 4 seconds

Special Moves

Screen	Name	Command	Hits	Damage	Meter Gain	Startup	Active	Recovery	Advantage on Hit	Advantage if Guarded	Notes
1	Cobra Strike	↓↘→ + (L)	1	100,000	800	10	4	32	—	-13	Hard knockdown
2	Ghost Butterfly	↓↘→ + (M)	1	120,000	960	18	3	25	—	-5	Wall bounces; pressing (L), (M), or (H) all cancel into respective Phantom Moves
	Phantom Move L	(During Ghost Butterfly or Samurai Edge) (L)	—	—	—	11	—	20	—	—	—
	Phantom Move M	(During Ghost Butterfly or Samurai Edge) (M)	—	—	—	11	—	25	—	—	—
	Phantom Move H	(During Ghost Butterfly or Samurai Edge) (H)	—	—	—	11	—	20	—	—	—
3	Jaguar Dash	↓↘→ + (H)	5	122,600	1200	22	15	24	-6	-10	Can switch sides with foe on contact; (H) cancels into Jaguar Kick on hit
4	Jaguar Kick	(during Jaguar Dash) (H)	1	100,000	800	10	4	22	—	-3	Knocks down; can cancel into Cobra Strike
5	Mustang Kick	→↘↓↙← + ATK	2	120,000	1200	1	2	26	—	—	Throw; (M) version causes hard knockdown; (H) version wall bounces
6	Phantom Move L	→↓↘ + (L)	—	—	—	11	—	20	—	—	Invincible from frames 11-20
7	Air Phantom Move L	→↓↘ + (L)	—	—	—	11	—	35	—	—	Invincible from frames 11-31
8	Phantom Move M	→↓↘ + (M)	—	—	—	11	—	25	—	—	—
9	Air Phantom Move M	→↓↘ + (M)	—	—	—	11	—	40	—	—	—
10	Phantom Move H	→↓↘ + (H)	—	—	—	11	—	20	—	—	Invincible from frames 11-22

Special Moves continued

Screen	Name	Command	Hits	Damage	Meter Gain	Startup	Active	Recovery	Advantage on Hit	Advantage if Guarded	Notes
11	Air Phantom Move H	⇨⇩⇘ + Ⓗ	—	—	—	11	—	25-28	—	—	Invincible from frames 11-12
12	Tiger Uppercut L	⇦⇩⇙ + Ⓛ	—	—		5	15	11	—	—	Counters non-low physical attacks
	Tiger Uppercut L Follow-Up Attack	—	1	120,000	960	18	4	27	—	-8	Invincible from frames 1-18; launcher; can travel through foe; automatically aligns with foe
13	Tiger Uppercut M	⇦⇩⇙ + Ⓜ	—	—	—	5	15	11	—	—	Counters low physical attacks
	Tiger Uppercut M Follow-Up Attack	—	1	120,000	960	21	4	24	—	-5	Invincible from frames 1-20; wall bounces; can travel through foe; automatically aligns with foe
14	Tiger Uppercut H	⇦⇩⇙ + Ⓗ	—	—	—	5	13	13	—	—	Counters projectiles
	Tiger Uppercut H Follow-Up Attack	—	1	120,000	960	19	4	24	—	-5	Invincible from frames 1-18; wall bounces; can travel through foe; automatically aligns with foe

1

Cobra Strike: Useful in combos, Cobra Strike is a damaging single-hit attack that causes a hard knockdown. If used early enough in a combo, Cobra Strike allows you to pick up opponents with the OTG-capable Samurai Edge (Lower Shot) and continue with more punishment. You should attempt to include Cobra Strike into combos whenever you can, since it inflicts more damage than other combo variants, such as Ghost Butterfly.

New to *Ultimate Marvel vs. Capcom 3* is the ability to cancel Cobra Strike into the Phantom Move teleports. This makes it much easier to get close to your opponent afterward to hit with the Samurai Edge (Lower Shot): simply press Ⓛ to cancel, teleport right next to your challenger, and continue from there. However, this often positions Wesker behind the opposing player, so if you're trying to push your adversary to the corner, you may want to manually wavedash after hitting the Cobra Strike instead.

If the Cobra Strike is guarded, you can cancel into Phantom Move L or M to move away to safety. Un-canceled Phantom Moves can be very unsafe if guarded, if your opponent has an attack with enough range to reach you afterward. As an alternative, you can also cancel into Phantom Move Ⓗ in an attempt to keep your offense going, but an alert opponent can easily air throw you out of this tactic.

2

Ghost Butterfly: Another combo-based attack, Ghost Butterfly causes a wall bounce that allows you to easily extend your combos. Ghost Butterfly can combo in situations with slightly higher hitstun deterioration than Cobra Strike (with the accompanying Samurai Edge (Lower Shot) and juggle hits), so there are specific combos that call for this attack instead. Ideally, your combos should include both!

Ghost Butterfly can also be canceled into Phantom Move, which is useful both for combos and for safety if guarded.

3

Jaguar Dash: Jaguar Dash propels Wesker across the screen to attack his challenger. Even though it is not particularly fast, it can be useful as a long range punisher in very specialized situations. Jaguar Dash cancels into Jaguar Kick, which in turn cancels into Cobra Strike for a combo.

Wesker's newfound ability to cancel Cobra Strike into Phantom Move makes Jaguar Dash a much more interesting attack: calling an assist during the Jaguar Kick, then canceling into Cobra Strike and teleporting allows you to establish Wesker's offense at long range.

4

Jaguar Kick: A single-hit knockdown attack following the Jaguar Dash. Jaguar Kick cancels into Cobra Strike, and the move also has the peculiar ability to allow you to call assists during it, even though it's technically a special move. Always cancel the Jaguar Kick into Cobra Strike, since the Jaguar Kick can be punished by one-frame throws if guarded.

5

Mustang Kick: The Mustang Kick is a throw attack that leads to a full combo, making it the focal point of Wesker's close range offense. It only has a single frame of startup, which means it will beat any of your opponent's options that don't involve being in the air or being invincible.

Of the three versions, Mustang Kick L has the most range and causes a soft knockdown. This takes a bit of practice in order to convert to a combo, especially with the new change to Wesker's Samurai Edge (Horizontal Fire) gunshot attack. However, the Ⓛ version of the Mustang Kick also leads to the most damaging combo out of the three versions.

Mustang Kick M has slightly less range but causes a hard knockdown. Ironically, this isn't much easier to convert into a combo against a midscreen foe when compared to the Ⓛ version, and it leads to less damage. Mustang Kick H has the least range of the three, but it causes a wall bounce for very easy combos that result in less damage. A more difficult combo variation exists that inflicts slightly less damage than Mustang Kick L combos, but that defeats the purpose of using the Ⓗ version over the Ⓛ version!

Phantom Move L: Arguably Wesker's most important asset, Phantom Move L causes him to teleport forward a large distance. This serves three key purposes for Wesker: traveling forward a large distance quickly, going through projectiles, and getting behind an opponent.

Primarily, use Phantom Move L to get behind the opposing character. More accurately, employ this move to cross your opponent up in conjunction with crossover assist attacks. Break your adversary's defenses by calling a ranged assist, teleporting behind the opposition, then converting that hit into a full combo!

Unlike most other teleport-style moves in *Ultimate Marvel vs. Capcom 3*, Wesker's Phantom Moves send him to an area relative to his own current location. This makes it a little trickier to use than most teleports, since Wesker players must actually form a gameplan to get within range to cross up with Phantom Move L.

Phantom Move M: This version of Phantom Move teleports Wesker backwards a large distance, something you won't typically want to do. It's not useful as a mix-up to Phantom Move L: if you're timing your assist cross-ups with Phantom Move L well enough, your challenger needs to simply commit to guarding in the opposite direction ahead of time, not looking for any visual stimulus. When this is the case, simply dash forward and hit your opponent with a crouching (L) attack or a Mustang Kick!

Phantom Move M is most useful when canceled into from a Samurai Edge (Horizontal Fire): if your adversary avoids the gunshot by jumping over or dashing under it, simply teleport backwards to safety.

Phantom Move H: This version of Phantom Move teleports Wesker forward a short distance and up into the air. As Wesker is falling, he automatically aligns with his opponent and can perform attacks in the proper direction.

Usage of Phantom Move H is very similar to that of Phantom Move L, the two key differences being the shorter travel distance and the fact that Wesker ends up in the air. If your challenger doesn't expect the Phantom Move H, it's a great way to maintain offense without the aid of a crossover assist: drop onto the opposing character with a falling attack, and leverage that frame advantage into more offense. However, if alert opponents expect that the Phantom Move H is coming, they can counter with a guaranteed air throw. Still, it's a great tool when used sparingly, and it is significantly more difficult to guard against when the opposing player is cornered.

Air Phantom Move L: The aerial version of Phantom Move L has considerably more recovery time than the ground version, and it isn't used as easily for offensive purposes. In fact, its best use is often for stalling and running away from opponents!

Super jumping up to the top of the screen, then performing air Phantom Move L three times burns a lot of time off of the clock, making it great for waiting out timed power-ups like X-Factor or Wolverine's Berserker Charge!

Air Phantom Move M: One of Wesker's greatest strengths is his backwards air throw, which leads to full combos without requiring the help of an assist. This results in the need for Wesker players to aggressively guess when an opponent is going to jump and try to grab them out of it. If Wesker misses an air throw, he is left vulnerable in the air performing his aerial (H) attack. To help mitigate this, buffer the input for Phantom Move M into every air throw attempt.

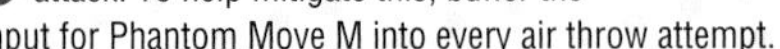

If your air throw attempt is successful, Wesker performs the throw animation, and your extra inputs are simply ignored. If your air throw attempt fails, you'll quickly cancel the startup frames of the air (H) into a backwards teleport, moving to safety. This isn't foolproof: air Phantom Move M has a number of non-invincible startup frames before Wesker teleports away. It's still vastly preferable to whiffing the air (H) right in your competitor's face, though!

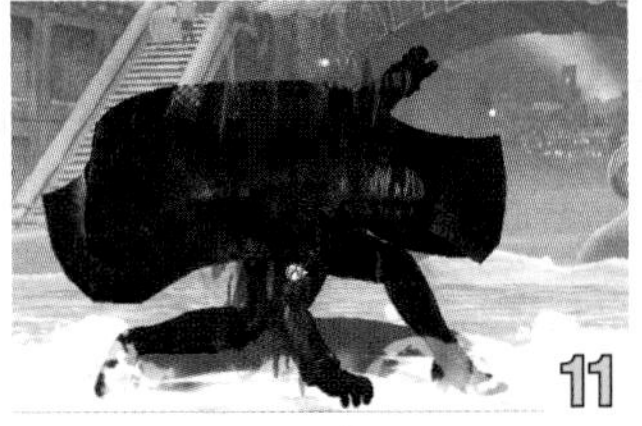

Air Phantom Move H: This maneuver teleports Wesker straight down to the ground, regardless of his current height in the air. This is useful in several situations, particularly for making Wesker's aerial Samurai Edge gunshots safer. Air Phantom Move H is also an essential tool for running away from your adversary: mixing air Phantom Move H in with your air Phantom Move L teleports keeps your movement patterns unpredictable, and your opponent must do drastically different things to counter the two options!

Although it's tempting, super jumping directly over your opponent and teleporting down with Phantom Move H isn't recommended; alert players will expect it (what else can Wesker threaten with up there?) and punish the teleport's recovery with a full combo. Simply falling from the super jump normally, keeping an eye out for breaking air throw attempts, is a much safer way to approach your opponent.

Tiger Uppercut L: The Tiger Uppercut attacks are counter attacks: after the initial startup frames pass, Wesker stands there waiting to accept an attack from the opponent. If the timing is correct and the right type of attack is received, then Wesker will receive no damage, automatically transitioning into an invincible Tiger Uppercut follow-up attack.

All of the Tiger Uppercut versions have five frames of startup, which isn't particularly fast. It's often too difficult to use a Tiger Uppercut on reaction to an opponent's attack, since you'll generally get interrupted out of the startup frames. Tiger Uppercuts are best used in anticipation.

Even if you successfully time a Tiger Uppercut to receive the proper type of attack, the follow-up attack isn't necessarily guaranteed to hit if your adversary's attack recovers quickly enough, or if the opposing player guards in the proper direction. If guarded, Wesker can sometimes be punished with a full combo depending on the speed of the opponent's attacks. With that said, since Tiger Uppercut attacks almost always cross up, the chances of your challenger guarding them are slim.

These counter attacks can be difficult to use effectively, but they can also be game-changers when used creatively. The ability to land a full combo off of a good read isn't something to dismiss!

Tiger Uppercut L counters all physical strikes besides hyper combos and low-hitting attacks. This makes it most useful against dominant aerial attacks like divekicks and Haggar's pipe. If the counter successfully triggers, Wesker teleports behind the opponent and performs a launcher attack for a free combo.

Tiger Uppercut M: Tiger Uppercut M triggers against low-hitting attacks and is generally difficult to set up in an actual match. Whenever low-hitting attacks are a threat, your target is generally right up in your face. When this is the case, you simply don't have time to pull off the five-frame startup of Tiger Uppercut M. In these situations, it's most prudent to simply guard low and look for opportunities to use advancing guard to push your adversary away.

13

14

If Tiger Uppercut M successfully triggers, Wesker teleports behind opposing characters and hits them for a wall bounce combo.

Tiger Uppercut H: Tiger Uppercut H triggers against projectile attacks, making it an alternate, interesting tool to deal with projectile-based zoning defense. If it triggers, Wesker teleports forward a medium distance before striking with a wall bounce attack. The unfortunate downfall of Tiger Uppercut H is that it doesn't have great range, and it requires you to work your way through projectiles into medium range. At this range, projectiles are much more difficult to react to in time use Tiger Uppercut. Even if you do successfully pull it off, slow-moving projectiles often have the opponent recover in time to guard the follow-up attack. Still, this remains an option you'll need to keep in mind against some difficult defenses to crack and in match-specific situations such as against Doctor Strange's Eye of Agamotto.

Hyper Combos

Screen	Name	Command	Hits	Damage	Startup	Active	Recovery	Advantage on Hit	Advantage if Guarded	Notes
1	Phantom Dance (in air OK)	↓↘→ + ATK ATK	Max 16	344,200	10+1	83	40	—	-20~-30	All hits cause soft knockdown
2	Rhino Charge	↓↙← + ATK ATK	1	250,000	5+0	16	28	—	—	Frame 5 invincible; counters all physical attacks including hyper combos; puts the opponent in a crumple stun state where the opposing character is still considered grounded
3	Lost in Nightmares	→↓↘ + ATK ATK (level 3 hyper combo)	12	450,000	6+8	5	30	—	-12	Invincible from frames 1-16; hard knockdown

1

2

3

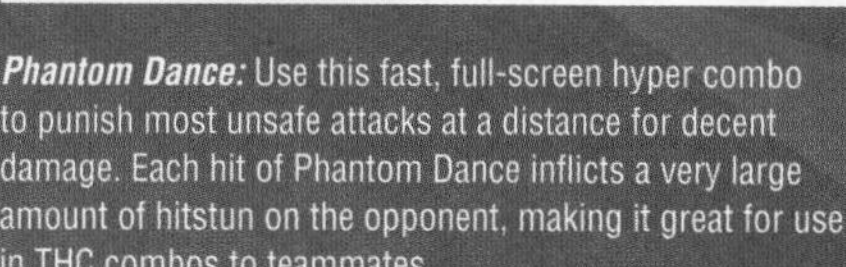

Phantom Dance: Use this fast, full-screen hyper combo to punish most unsafe attacks at a distance for decent damage. Each hit of Phantom Dance inflicts a very large amount of hitstun on the opponent, making it great for use in THC combos to teammates.

Phantom Dance is very unsafe if guarded, but there's a quirk to it: Wesker always reappears at the point where the hyper combo was started. After guarding several hits of Phantom Dance, your challenger is generally too far away to punish with anything besides fast, full-screen hyper combos. The exception is against cornered adversaries: they don't get pushed back anywhere from guarding the Phantom Dance attacks, so Wesker simply reappears directly in front of them for easy punishing.

Wesker removes his sunglasses whenever he performs Phantom Dance. New to *Ultimate Marvel vs. Capcom 3*, this character flavor touch now has a large effect on gameplay! Whenever Wesker does not have his sunglasses on, he becomes 10% faster and inflicts 15% more damage across the board! See the Advanced Tactics section for more details on Wesker's sunglasses and wacky ways to land the Phantom Dance.

Rhino Charge: Similar to the Tiger Uppercut attacks, Rhino Charge is a counter attack that triggers against all physical attacks, including overheads, low attacks, and even hyper combos! If successfully triggered, Wesker performs a guaranteed, single-hit, high-damage attack that leaves the opponent in a crumple stun state. From there, you can go into your combo of choice!

Substantially weakened in *Ultimate Marvel vs. Capcom 3*, Rhino Charge no longer has invincibility all the way until the active frames begin. This all but takes away its former role: countering hyper combos on reaction to the "super freeze" cutscene.

Rhino Charge is still a powerful tool that you should definitely unleash upon your challengers; its usage simply has changed to be much more similar to the Tiger Uppercut attacks.

Lost in Nightmares: Wesker's level 3 hyper combo is generally best used as a combo ender to finish off opponent characters. At 450,000 damage, Lost in Nightmares is one of the most damaging level 3 hyper combos in the game. If Wesker is without his sunglasses, Lost in Nightmares inflicts an insane 517,500 points of un-scaled damage!

Due to the loss of invincibility on Rhino Charge in *Ultimate Marvel vs. Capcom 3*, Lost in Nightmares also performs an increased role as an invincible hyper combo.

Battle Plan

Advancing forward behind the cover of a ranged assist is the easiest way to close the distance. However, this doesn't afford you the luxury of being able to cross your opponent up with a crossover assist attack.

Using Phantom Move L through zoning defenses is another option, but it gets much more complicated when projectile-using crossover assists are involved.

When using Wesker, your primary goal is getting close enough to the challenger to establish an offensive threat. Ideally, you'll want to establish medium range without using a crossover assist for cover; this allows you to threaten your adversary with a cross-up using both the assist and Phantom Move L to get behind your opponent. To accomplish this, you'll have to use Wesker's natural tools to get around defenses: a fast wavedash, jumping forward while guarding, Phantom Move L and H, and the occasional Tiger Uppercut.

Generally, the safest, surest way to close the distance on your opposition is to simply wavedash forward while keeping an eye for incoming attacks that must be guarded. When doing this, pay attention to your challenger's projectile-using tendencies, and identify gaps that you can safely jump over. You'll incur a fair amount of chip damage this way, and this process may be frequently tedious, but with enough patience, you should eventually close the gap to a distance where you can call an assist and cross up with Phantom Move L. From there, your opponent must change up their gameplan: if they continue trying to keep you out with projectiles, they run the risk of you getting behind them with Phantom Move L and starting a combo. If they don't commit to anything, you can simply wavedash forward and quickly cover the rest of the distance before beginning your offense.

For the less patient, calling a long range crossover assist for cover and wavedashing or using Phantom Move L is often a much easier way to cover ground; the tradeoff is that you lose the ability to cross your adversary up with Phantom Move L while attacking with the assist. Still, when up close, Wesker's assist-less offensive options are very formidable.

A team dedicated to zoning defense generally has a long range character in addition to a long range crossover assist, and these are much more difficult to quickly close the distance on: teleporting through one character's projectiles typically lands Wesker directly into another volley of projectiles from the other character. In these situations, Tiger Uppercut H becomes a much more attractive option. After triggering Tiger Uppercut H, Wesker becomes invincible, flies across the screen, and strikes with a wall bounce attack.

Super jumping toward the opposition is often a tempting option, but this usually just puts you in a bad situation: super jumping gives your adversary plenty of time to finish whatever they were doing and maneuver directly under you. From there, they can completely control the timing of when they want to air throw you, and you'll have to commit to falling down without pressing a button in order to be able to break the throw attempt. This allows the opposing player to perform a dangerous mix-up on you, dashing to either side of you and attacking before you land, then forcing you to choose a direction to guard in. If you must take to the air and super jump, try to find a safe spot away from your foe to teleport down using Phantom Move H. Attempting to drop directly onto the challenger with Phantom Move H is likely to get countered by a full combo if you're battling an alert opponent; what else can Wesker possibly threaten his competition with from way up there?

Crossing up an opponent with Phantom Move L while calling an assist is a key part of Wesker's offense.

If you get within striking range, and don't have your assist available, threaten your adversary with the Mustang Kick throw attack!

Opponents that are wary of the first two options often take to the air; snag them with a backwards air throw and convert to a full combo!

Once you do manage to close the distance on the opposing character, you'll want to take advantage of Wesker's mix-up options. At medium range, your best options all lead to combos:

Call a crossover assist and teleport behind your challenger using Phantom Move L. This beats everything besides jumping and pre-emptively guarding in the opposite direction.

Dash forward and attack with crouching Ⓛ. This is the most damaging option, but it only beats foes that are pre-emptively guarding in the opposite direction.

Dash forward and grab your adversary with Mustang Kick. This beats any attempt to guard on the ground, but it loses to jumping and general button-pressing.

Dash forward and attempt an air throw. This beats jumping, but it loses to everything else. Option select your air throw attempt into air Phantom Move M!

By and large, crossing up the opposing player with Phantom Move L while calling an assist has the highest success rate. While your opponent can take a huge risk and try to guard in the opposite direction, most players simply opt to jump away. This distills the mix-up into two options for the most part: assist cross-up, or dash forward and air throw. If your competitor decides to guard your assist cross-up, that leaves you at point-blank range and frame advantage!

If you manage to achieve point-blank range with frame advantage against your opponent, your best options change:

A perfectly timed Mustang Kick beats everything besides perfectly timed attacks faster than a five-frame startup, normal throws, and jumping.

Crouching Ⓛ beats any button pressing; it also beats pre-emptive jump attempts for big damage.

Air throws beat jumps.

Whenever opposing character leaves guardstun, they become invulnerable to throws for four frames. Other than basic throws, very few characters in the game have attacks that are faster than 5 frames; attempting to grab the opponent with a Mustang Kick on the fifth frame after guardstun has finished is an incredibly solid tactic. Practically anything your adversary can do in an attempt to avoid the Mustang Kick will get hit by crouching Ⓛ into huge damage!

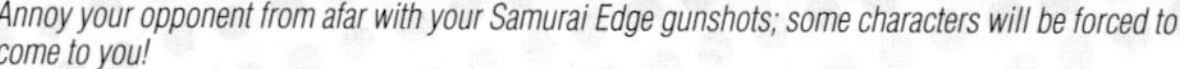

Annoy your opponent from afar with your Samurai Edge gunshots; some characters will be forced to come to you!

Up-close defense with Wesker is relatively generic: look for opportunities to air throw an opponent while using advancing guard against their grounded attacks!

WESKER

Wesker's long range gameplan:

Samurai Edge (Horizontal Fire) quickly fires a bullet across the screen at high altitude. Unfortunately, most characters can crouch directly under the bullet. New to *Ultimate Marvel vs. Capcom 3*, the Samurai Edge (Horizontal Fire) bounces airborne opponents to a much lower height. This prevents you from being able to convert full-screen Samurai Edge shots into combos using Phantom Move L.

Regardless, the Samurai Edge (Horizontal Fire) is a useful tool for controlling your opponent's options: unless the opposing player's character can dash directly under the bullet, it all but forces the character to sit still and crouch. This allows you to control the tempo of the fight: call a long-ranged crossover assist simultaneously with the gunshot, and maneuver to the desired distance between yourself and the challenger!

Characters that cannot crouch under Samurai Edge (Horizontal Fire):

Nemesis T-Type **Tron** **Hulk** **M.O.D.O.K.** **Sentinel**

The aerial Samurai Edge (Anti-Surface) is primarily used as a way to actively threaten opponents with chip damage from across the screen: super jump straight up and immediately press ⇩ + Ⓗ, then press Ⓗ again to cancel to Phantom Move H and teleport back down to the ground. When battling long range characters, wait until they fire a projectile at you, then super jump over it and take your free shot. Used effectively enough, the two long range Samurai Edge shots can force your opponent to switch up their gameplan, sometimes drastically enough to force them to come to you!

Against an enemy up-close, Wesker's defensive options are relatively standard: use advancing guard when possible, and look for opportunities to jump up and air throw your opponent. Remember to option select an air Phantom Move M into your air throw attempts. Simply input the Phantom Move M command immediately after every air throw attempt to make Wesker teleport backwards if the throw attempt fails.

At medium range, you have a bit more time to get tricky with your defense. You can actually counter most of your adversary's attempts to close the distance and attack you by calling an assist and using Phantom Move L. When this happens, your opponent has actually closed the distance for you!

If you want to gamble, wait for a good read and go for high damage using the Rhino Charge counter attack! Some of the risk of Rhino Charge can be mitigated by simply option selecting a THC to another, safer hyper combo if your teammate has one; if your opponent attacks into the Rhino Charge and triggers it, your THC input is simply ignored while Wesker is punching the opponent. If the opponent didn't bite, your THC input switches Wesker out to a teammate performing a (ideally) safe hyper combo.

You can also option select an X-Factor activation during Rhino Charge: if the counter doesn't activate, Wesker activates X-Factor and becomes able to guard safely. If your challenger is right next to you in this situation, coming out of the X-Factor activation with a one-frame Mustang Kick can beat anything your adversary does, short of jumping or performing an invincible attack.

COMBO USAGE

I. CR. Ⓛ, Ⓜ, Ⓗ [CANCEL] ↓↘→ + Ⓛ [CANCEL] Ⓛ (PHANTOM MOVE CANCEL), ↘ + Ⓗ, CR. Ⓜ, ST. Ⓗ (2 HITS) [CANCEL] ↓↘→ + Ⓜ [CANCEL] Ⓗ (PHANTOM MOVE CANCEL), AIR Ⓢ, LAND, CR. Ⓗ, Ⓢ [CANCEL] SUPER JUMP, AIR Ⓜ, Ⓜ, Ⓗ, Ⓢ, DASH, ↘ + Ⓗ

516,900 damage (594,600 damage without shades), 108% meter gain

Wesker's basic combo inflicts beefy damage all without using any hyper combo gauge bars! If the initial hits are guarded, canceling the crouching Ⓗ attack into Phantom Move H is an effective way to keep the offensive momentum, but an alert opponent can air throw you for your troubles. Ideally you'll want to call a crossover assist before canceling the crouching Ⓗ into Phantom Move L, crossing up your opponent and giving plenty of time to resume your offense if it is guarded.

The final Samurai Edge (Lower Shot) pops the opponent up into the air for a mix-up opportunity: grab them with an air throw, attack with air Ⓛ (into **Combo IV**), or call a crossover assist and cross up with Phantom Move L!

Samurai Edge (Lower Shot) can also be canceled into a crossover combination by pressing P1 + P2; while this may cost up to three hyper combo gauge bars, it's worth thinking about using this whenever the damage will be enough to finish off the enemy character.

II. →↘↓↙← + Ⓛ, DASH, CR. Ⓜ, ST. Ⓗ (2 HITS) [CANCEL] ↓↘→ + Ⓛ [CANCEL] Ⓛ (PHANTOM MOVE CANCEL), ↘ + Ⓗ, CR. Ⓜ, Ⓗ, Ⓢ [CANCEL] SUPER JUMP, AIR Ⓜ, Ⓜ, Ⓗ, Ⓢ, LAND, DASH, ↘ + Ⓗ

356,700 damage (410,300 without shades), no meter required, 93% meter gain

While the changes to Samurai Edge (Horizontal Fire) prevent Wesker's old Mustang Kick L combos from working, this variant still gets the job done quite nicely. Mustang Kick L recovers immediately as Wesker kicks the opponent, so manually buffer the forward dash by pressing →→ much earlier than what is intuitive.

COMBO USAGE CONT.

III. BACKWARDS AIR THROW, ↘ + (H), CR. (M), ST. (H) (2 HITS) CANCEL→ ↓↘→ + (M) CANCEL→ (H) (PHANTOM MOVE CANCEL), AIR (S), LAND, CR. (H), (S) CANCEL→ SUPER JUMP, AIR (M), (M), (H), (S), DASH, ↘ + (H)

261,100 damage (300,500 damage without shades), no meter required, 92% meter gain

Wesker is able to convert air throws into full combos with much more ease compared to most characters. While the combo itself doesn't inflict a ton of damage, it leads into another mix-up opportunity after hitting the final Samurai Edge (Lower Shot).

IV. AIR (L), (H), (S), LAND, JUMP FORWARD, AIR (L), (H), (S), LAND, ST. (M), (H) (2 HITS), (S) CANCEL→ SUPER JUMP, AIR (M), (M), (H), (S), LAND, DASH, ↘ + (H) OTG

453,200 damage (521,100 without shades), no meter required, 92% meter gain

This air-to-air combo is primarily used against opponents that constantly press buttons when in the air. Air (L) will beat them to the punch, and from there you can go on to inflict a sizeable amount of damage. To avoid getting hit by this combo your opponent must commit to simply guarding in the air; this opens them to air throws leading to **Combo III**!

The air (S) attacks must be slightly delayed in order to keep the opposing character above Wesker. Everything else should be performed as quickly as possible. If your opponent guards the initial air (L) attack continue with the aerial chain anyway; you'll land right next to your opponent with substantial frame advantage from the air (S) attack. Follow up with a mix-up of crouching (L) or Mustang Kick L.

V. ↓↙← + (ATK)(ATK), CR. (M), ST. (H) (2 HITS) CANCEL→ ↓↘→ + (M) CANCEL→ (H) (PHANTOM MOVE CANCEL), AIR (S), LAND, CR. (H), (S) CANCEL→ SUPER JUMP, AIR (M), (M), (H), (S), LAND, DASH, ↘ + (H) OTG

532,000 damage (611,700 without shades), 1 meter required, -22% meter gain

Rhino Charge is a great high-damage counter to predictable attacks that are otherwise hard to stop, such as Wolverine's Diving Kick and Nemesis' Angled Deadly Range. Follow it up with a simple combo that inflicts a ton of damage!

COMBO APPENDIX

GENERAL EXECUTION TIPS

The Ghost Butterfly cancel into a Phantom Move H must be performed late; wait until you see the strike actually hit before pressing the (H) button.

If you're not comfortable with the Phantom Move cancel, simply dash forward and juggle the opponent with cr. (M), cr. (H), (S) afterwards. The damage difference is marginal.

Linking a crouching (M) after an OTG Samurai Edge (Lower Shot) is integral to Wesker's more damaging combos, but the timing is fairly tight. Press the (M) once, attempting to time it properly, rather than trying to mash on the button and hoping it works. Practice is everything!

CR. (L), (M), (H) CANCEL→ ↓↘→ + (M), DASH, CR. (M), (H), (S) CANCEL→ SUPER JUMP, AIR (M), (M), (H), (S), LAND, DASH, ↘ + (H)

Notes	Damage
Easy combo, suitable for online play	469,000 damage, 79% meter gain

→↘↓↙← + (H), DASH, CR. (M), (H), (S) CANCEL→ SUPER JUMP, AIR (M), (M), (H), (S), LAND, DASH, ↘ + (H)

Notes	Damage
Easy Mustang Kick combo	323,200 damage, 65% meter gain

←↓↙ + (L) CANCEL→ SUPER JUMP, AIR (M), (M), (H), (S), DASH, ↘ + (H)

Notes	Damage
Combo from Tiger Uppercut L	375,800 damage, 42% meter gain

CR. (L), (M), (H) CANCEL→ ↓↘→ + (M), DASH, ↓↘→ + (L) CANCEL→ (L) (PHANTOM MOVE CANCEL), ↘ + (H), CR. (M), (H), (S) CANCEL→ SUPER JUMP, AIR (M), (M), (H), (S), LAND, DASH, ↘ + (H)

Notes	Damage
Slightly more damaging variant of basic combo, builds less hyper combo gauge. Dash with (ATK)(ATK) after hitting Ghost Butterfly to be able to perform Cobra Strike without accidentally executing Phantom Move L instead.	525,200 damage, 93% meter gain

←↓↙ + (M), WAVEDASH TWICE, CR. (M), (H), (S) CANCEL→ SUPER JUMP, AIR (M), (M), (H), (S), LAND, DASH, ↘ + (H)

Notes	Damage
Combo from Tiger Uppercut M or H	462,300 damage, 62% meter gain

(GLASSES OFF) CR. (L), (M), (H) CANCEL→ ↓↘→ + (L) CANCEL→ (L), ↘ + (H), CR. (H) CANCEL→ ↓↘→ + (L) CANCEL→ (L), ↘ + (H), CR. (M), (H), (S) CANCEL→ SUPER JUMP, AIR (M), (M), (H), (S), LAND, DASH, ↘ + (H)

Notes	Damage
Slightly optimized combo when Wesker does not have his sunglasses on	617,200 damage, 120% meter gain

CR. (L), (M), (H) CANCEL→ ↓↘→ + (L) CANCEL→ (L) (PHANTOM MOVE CANCEL), ↘ + (H) OTG, CR. (M), ST. (H) (2 HITS) CANCEL→ ↓↘→ + (M) CANCEL→ (H) (PHANTOM MOVE CANCEL), AIR (S), LAND, CR. (H), (S) CANCEL→ SUPER JUMP, AIR (M), (M), (H), (S), DASH, ↘ + (H), (X-FACTOR) →↓↘ + (ATK)(ATK)

Notes	Damage
Combo using level 1 X-Factor and Lost in Nightmares	1,101,900 damage, 191% meter loss

ADVANCED TACTICS

WESKER'S A JERK

After landing a combo, the OTG Samurai Edge (Lower Shot) leaves you in great position to immediately mix-up your opponent again.

After you have completed a combo with an OTG Samurai Edge (Lower Shot), your adversary quickly recovers in the air above you. This gives you a great opportunity to mix-up your opponent!

If your challenger recovers backwards:

Dashing forward, then attempting an air throw beats everything except guarding.

Dashing forward, then jumping forward from slightly farther away keeps Wesker out of throw range. Attacking with air L here punishes everything besides guarding, and it leads into a full combo.

Calling a crossover assist, then teleporting with Phantom Move L beats everything besides guarding in the opposite direction, and it airdashes upward. Attacking with air L is an incredibly strong option: you get a damaging combo if it hits (see the Combo Usage section for details), and if guarded, you end up with frame advantage at point-blank range unless the opponent uses advancing guard. Attacking with air L after the OTG shot essentially forces the opposing player to guard, which you can easily counter with backwards air throws.

If the opponent recovers forwards:

- Waiting until the challenger passes over you, then jumping toward them and attack with air L beats everything besides guarding.
- Waiting until the opponent recovers, then jumping back and air throwing beats everything besides teching throws and airdashes.
- Waiting until your adversary passes over you, then grabbing them with Mustang Kick when they land beats everything besides airdashes, air attacks that can cross up, and immediately jumping upon landing.

KEEP YO STUNNA SHADES OFF!

Find ways to slip Phantom Dance in early; you'll get a 15% damage boost and 10% speed boost for as long as Wesker remains in play!

New to *Ultimate Marvel vs. Capcom 3*, Wesker now gets a substantial 15% damage and 10% speed increase across the board whenever he doesn't have his sunglasses on! There are two ways to get rid of Wesker's shades:

- Use the Phantom Dance hyper combo, which removes Wesker's shades at the beginning of the animation.
- Get punched in the face a lot (the authors do not recommend this method).

There are also two ways for Wesker to get a new pair of sunglasses, which you don't want! By far, the most important way to lose Wesker's damage boost is to simply have Wesker leave gameplay in any way. This also includes using THCs or TACs!

The second way for Wesker to find another pair of shades is to simply press the Taunt button. If your gameplan includes frequent usage of taunts, Wesker might not be the ideal character for you!

If you don't think you're going to have to switch Wesker out any time soon, it's worth it to start thinking about how you're going to slip a Phantom Dance into the mix. The Phantom Dance hyper combo is generally safe to just throw out randomly, unless any of the following is true:

- The opponent has an invincible attack at their disposal.
- The challenger has a fast, full-screen hyper combo.
- Wesker starts the Phantom Dance close to a cornered adversary.

Of course, actually hitting your opponent with a Phantom Dance is vastly preferable to simply getting away with it safely. With that in mind, what are some good ways to land a Phantom Dance?

- THC to Phantom Dance from a teammate character's combo.
- Ending a combo with Phantom Dance against a cornered opponent. This leaves you in prime position to mix-up the opposing player afterwards! Against a midscreen adversary, forgoing the mix-up after a combo typically isn't worth the 15% damage boost.
- Cross your opponent up with Phantom Dance! See the following section for details.

PHANTOM DANCE SHENANIGANS

Phantom Dance used in a situation like this can cross up your competitor. Better yet, it might not! It's totally random!

While the random nature of Phantom Dance can often cause you to miss a few hits in combos, it can cause some incredibly unpredictable cross-ups outside of combos.

The simplest way to set up a Phantom Dance mix-up is to simply time the attack in a way so that the first hit misses against a midscreen challenger. Wesker flies past the opponent, bounces off of the wall, and hits the opponent in the back. Or, he might fly past the opposing player again and hit them in the front. It's impossible to react to!

There are a number of situations where you can take advantage of this:

- When the opponent jumps toward you
- After ending a combo with Samurai Edge (Lower Shot)
- Whenever your foe is recovering from a knockdown, such as after a normal ground throw

The other way to set up Phantom Dance mix-ups requires a lot less finesse: lead your opponent to the middle of the screen, and just do it! While bouncing around, Wesker often randomly crosses up the opposing player for hilarious results! If the opponent's character cannot easily punish midscreen Phantom Dances, this is a great way to get Wesker's sunglasses off. Alternatively, you can easily verify that the Phantom Dance has started to hit the adversary and cancel into a team hyper combo!

"THIS IS THE END OF HUMANITY AND THE START OF A NEW WORLD ORDER!"

WESKER

ZERO

"YOU CAN'T EVEN LAY A SINGLE SCRATCH ON ME. MOVE ON BEFORE YOU GET HURT."

Bio

REAL NAME

Zero

OCCUPATION

Maverick Hunter

ABILITIES

Has great physical ability as well as excellent skills with a variety of weapons. He is able to learn the abilities of the enemies he defeats and add them to his existing arsenal, making him even stronger than before.

WEAPONS

His primary weapons are the Z-Saber, an energy sword, and his Zero Buster, a weapon capable of firing energy shots.

PROFILE

Ever since he was found in a cave by Sigma, he has worked tirelessly as a Maverick Hunter. Beneath his cool exterior lies an extreme intolerance for evil; once he gets into a fight with a Maverick, he won't stop until his enemy has been mercilessly cut down. He is best friends with X of the Maverick Hunters' 17th Elite Unit.

FIRST APPEARANCE

Mega Man X (1993)

POWER GRID

3	INTELLIGENCE
2	STRENGTH
5	SPEED
2	STAMINA
5	ENERGY PROJECTION
5	FIGHTING ABILITY

*This is biographical, and does not represent an evaluation of the in-game combat potential of this hero.

Alternate Costumes

Overview

Vitality	830,000
Chain Combo Archetype	Marvel Series

X-Factor Boost	Damage	Speed
Level 1 (3 teammates remaining)	120%	120%
Level 2 (2 teammates remaining)	140%	130%
Level 3 (1 teammate remaining)	160%	140%

Your goal with Zero should be to apply offensive pressure to your opponent as much as possible and push their character to the corner.

Why do you want to apply offensive pressure and push your rival into the corner?

- Zero's strength stems from the vast array of offensive tools that allow you to maintain pressure and create combo opportunities
- Zero has low vitality and weak defensive tools. Staying on offense helps offset this disadvantage
- Zero's combo potential increases dramatically against a cornered foe. Zero also has excellent resets and option selects against cornered characters
- Zero's zoning tools are limited, making zoning an ineffective option against much of the cast

How does one get to close range and maintain offensive pressure with Zero?

- With the aid of assists, Hienkyaku allows him to maintain offense and can create mix-ups that are difficult to block. Through the use of Hienkyaku H, Zero is one of the few characters who can cross up an opponent in the corner
- Use Zero's level 3 Hyper Zero Buster to cancel out Hienkyaku L & M, and utilize Raikousen to create cross-ups that are difficult to block.
- Discerning use of instant Raikousens and Sentsuizan L, to make for mix-ups that are difficult to block
- Use of Sougenmu to create large offensive pressure and unblockable setups that can lead to large damage

Your secondary goal is to attack opponents from across the screen, keeping them at long distance.

Why use Zero's relatively weak zoning game when he is such an offense oriented character?

- Zoning is an effective strategy against adversaries who lack zoning tools or who have low mobility
- Zero's zoning tools and high mobility can be used to control the pace of the match and deny his foes offensive opportunities. This can force the opposing player to take large risks to avoid running down the clock

How do you use Zero's zoning tools effectively?

- Use Hadangeki L to control horizontal space; it has low recovery and slow movement. Zero can have several of these active at once
- Keep Hyper Zero Blaster charged at all times; it has quick startup, and level 3 causes knockdown and gives space to reestablish your zoning
- Use Sougenmu and Hadangeki L to virtually lock an opponent to the ground for the duration of Sougenmu
- Use Hienkyaku M to quickly dash under airborne rivals and create space

Tuning Since Original MVC3

Zero received few changes in *Ultimate Marvel vs. Capcom 3*, but he received two important changes to his level 3 Hyper Zero Blaster. It no longer causes hard knockdown, removing the ability to OTG after this move. To make up for this loss, level 3 Hyper Zero Blaster can be used to cancel the recovery of any special move, giving Zero the ability to make certain special moves safe and create new interesting mix-up opportunities. This is similar to Morrigan canceling her special moves with flight, or Spider-Man canceling his special moves with Web Zip.

As an indirect nerf, Zero can no longer be used as one of the strongest THC glitch characters; before, using the glitch to hand-off to Sougenmu Zero was a virtually assured knock out, and then a nasty mix-up on the next character.

- Hyper Zero Blaster (level 3) no longer causes hard knockdown
- Hyper Zero Blaster (level 3) can cancel any special move
- Sougenmu THC glitch has been removed
- Health increased to 830,000
- Decreased hit stun time on all normal attacks (Ⓛ, Ⓜ, and Ⓗ)
- Slightly increased horizontal air knockback from Shippuga
- Applied limit on number of air Hyper Zero Blaster that can be performed in one jump
- Ground recovery time increased after Sentsuizan
- Changed angle of Sentsuizan H
- Raikousen will go behind an opponent in the corner

Attack Set

Standing Basic Attacks

Screen	Command	Hits	Damage	Meter Gain	Startup	Active	Recovery	Advantage on Hit	Advantage if Guarded	Notes
1	Standing L	1	35,000	280	5	3	12	-2	-3	—
2	Standing M	1	53,000	424	7	3	19	-4	-5	—
3	Standing H	3	64,200	600	11	10	16	+1	0	—

Crouching Basic Attacks

Screen	Command	Hits	Damage	Meter Gain	Startup	Active	Recovery	Advantage on Hit	Advantage if Guarded	Notes
1	Crouching L	1	30,000	240	4	2	11	0	-1	Low attack
2	Crouching M	1	56,000	448	8	3	20	-5	-6	Low attack
3	Crouching H	1	70,000	560	13	5	18	—	-1	Knocks down

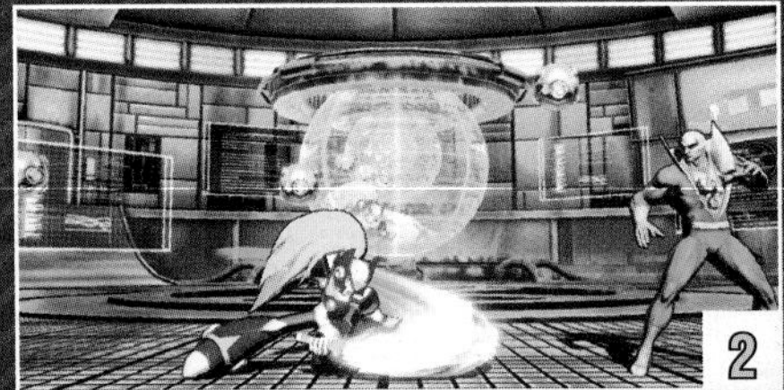
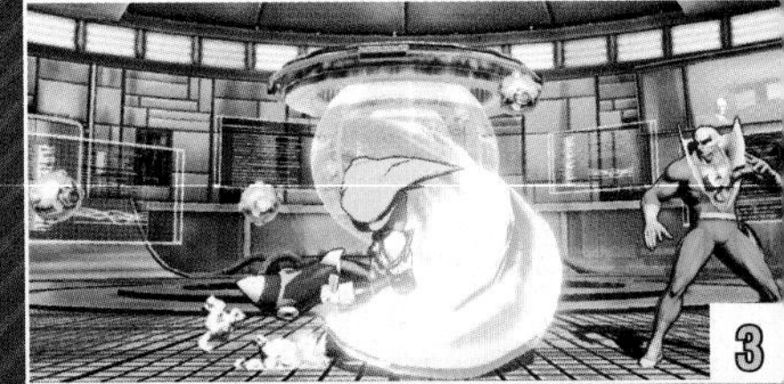

Ground Special Attack—Launcher

Screen	Command	Hits	Damage	Meter Gain	Startup	Active	Recovery	Advantage on Hit	Advantage if Guarded	Notes
1	S (while standing or crouching)	1	80,000	640	9	5	22	—	-5	Launcher, not special- or hyper combo-cancelable

Air Basic Attacks

Screen	Command	Hits	Damage	Meter Gain	Startup	Active	Recovery	Advantage on Hit	Advantage if Guarded	Notes
1	Air L	1	33,000	264	5	3	12	+10	+9	Overhead attack
2	Air M	1	55,000	440	8	3	19	+16	+15	Overhead attack
3	Air H	3	64,200	600	10	18	15	+18	+17	Overhead attack

Air Special Attacks—Flying Screen and Air Exchange

ir Ⓢ causes a hard knockdown when used in a launcher combo (this is sometimes called flying screen). When used outside of a launcher combo, air Ⓢ behaves mostly like another asic attack. Air exchange attacks, performed by inputting a direction plus Ⓢ, are only possible during a launcher combo. Exchange hits initiate team aerial combos by tagging in the next vailable character to continue the air combo.

Screen	Command	Hits	Damage	Meter Gain	Startup	Active	Recovery	Advantage on Hit	Advantage if Guarded	Notes
1	Air Ⓢ	1	75,000	600	13	9	17	+15	+14	Causes hard knockdown if used in launcher combo, overhead attack
2	Air ⇧ + Ⓢ (during launcher combo)	2	105,00	880	10	5	21	—	—	Tags in next available ally while lofting opponent upward
3	Air ⇨ or ⇦ + Ⓢ (during launcher combo)	2	95,000	800	13	7	18	—	—	Tags in next available ally while causing wall bounce, erases 1 hyper meter bar from opposing character
4	Air ⇩ + Ⓢ (during launcher combo)	2	95,000	800	10	5	21	—	—	Tags in next available ally while causing ground bounce, generates 1 hyper meter bar

1

2

3

4

Command Attacks

ommand attacks resemble basic attacks but have different chaining and canceling properties. It's usually possible to chain *into* a command attack from basic attacks, but most command ttacks cannot be chained from or canceled themselves.

Screen	Name	Command	Hits	Damage	Meter Gain	Startup	Active	Recovery	Advantage on Hit	Advantage if Guarded	Notes
1	Shippuga	⇨ + Ⓗ	3	77,100	720	14	7	17	+5	+4	Cancelable from any basic attack
2	Kuenzan	(in air) ⇩ + Ⓗ	3	64,200	600	9	18	9	+18	+17	Reverses the direction Zero spins

1

2

Throws

hrows are for snagging passive or blocking opponents. Since throws are active so quickly, you can also use them to preemptively toss opposing characters out of their offense. Combos re usually possible after throws, one way or another.

Screen	Command	Hits	Damage	Meter Gain	Startup	Active	Notes
1	⇨ + Ⓗ (ground)	6	80,000	800	1	1	Hard knockdown
	⇦ + Ⓗ (ground)	1	80,000	800	1	1	Hard knockdown
2	⇨ + Ⓗ (air)	7	80,000	800	1	1	Hard knockdown
	⇦ + Ⓗ (air)	2	80,000	800	1	1	Hard knockdown

1

2

As a Partner—Crossover Assists

Screen	Type	P1+P2 Crossover Combination Hyper Combo	Description	Hits	Damage	Meter Gain	Startup	Active	Recovery (this crossover assist)	Recovery (other partner)	Notes
1	Zero—α	Rekkoha	Ryuenjin H	5	102,300	1000	29	25	116	86	—
2	Zero—β	Rekkoha	Hadangeki M	1	70,000	560	32	—	126	96	Projectile has 3 low priority durability points
3	Zero—γ	Rekkoha	Shippuga (→ + H)	3	81,200	720	37	7	109	79	Inflicts chip damage

Zero's assists are mediocre at best, and because of Zero's low vitality, it's recommended that you use Zero's assists sparingly.

Zero—α is his Ryuenjin H. It lacks any invincibility frames, making it a lackluster defensive assist. It also hits five times, making it less than ideal for combos because of damage scaling. Finally, it positions the opposing character awkwardly, making it difficult for most characters to continue with an optimal combo afterwards.

You may find some usefulness and provide additional firepower to zoning teams with Zero—β, but the projectile is fast and only has 4 durability points, making it an inferior alternative to most projectile and beam assists. If Zero activates Sougenmu and is switched out to an assist character, this actually becomes a fairly strong projectile assist to back up a dedicated zoning character. However, this requires hyper meter use to set up, along with exposing the already low-vitality Zero to the possibility of taking damage as an assist.

Zero—γ is his Shippuga. This is most useful for characters that have an OTG attack themselves, but need an assist to extend the combo further. Unlike the normal version of the attack, Zero inflicts chip damage with his assist version. You can also use this assist to shore up gaps in a character's rushdown offense, but it has limited range and can be dangerous to use against a savvy adversary who can time advancing guard right before your assist, leaving Zero attacking the air and vulnerable to counterattack.

Snap Back

Screen	Command	Hits	Damage	Meter Gain	Startup	Active	Recovery	Advantage on Hit	Advantage if Guarded
1	↓↘→ + P1 or P2	1	50,000	500 (-1 hyper meter bar)	2	7	17	—	-2

Notes

On hit, snap back forces the opposing point character to be replaced by an assist. Opposing assist calls or tag outs are also locked out for 4 seconds

Special Moves

Screen	Name	Command	Hits	Damage	Meter Gain	Startup	Active	Recovery	Advantage on Hit	Advantage if Guarded	Notes
1	Hadangeki L	↓↘→ + L	1	70,000	560	17	—	25	-1	-2	Projectile has 3 low priority durability points
	Hadangeki M	↓↘→ + M	1	70,000	560	8	—	34	-7	-8	Projectile has 3 low priority durability points
2	Hadangeki H	↓↘→ + H	2	55,000 x 2	440 x 2	13	—	34	-7	-8	Each projectile has 3 low priority durability points
3	Ryuenjin L	→↓↘ + L	1	70,000	560	5	9	24	-10	-11	Knocks down
	Ryuenjin M	→↓↘ + M	3	81,200	720	5	15	21	-5	-6	Knocks down
	Ryuenjin H	→↓↘ + H	5	102,300	1000	5	25	21	-7	-16	Knocks down
4	Raikousen L	(in air) →↓↘ + L	5	102,300	1000	30	15	8~until grounded	+20	+17	Knocks down airborne foes, can pass through opponents
5	Raikousen M	(in air) →↓↘ + M	5	102,300	1000	30	15	Until grounded	+5	+4	Knocks down airborne adversaries, can pass through rivals
6	Raikousen H	(in air) →↓↘ + H	5	102,300	1000	30	15	Until grounded	-14	-15	Knocks down airborne foes, can pass through opponents
7	Hienkyaku L	↓↙← + L	—	—	—	5	—	25	—	—	Can pass through adversaries
8	Hienkyaku M	↓↙← + M	—	—	—	5	—	35	—	—	Can pass through rivals
9	Hienkyaku H	↓↙← + H	—	—	—	5	—	22	—	—	Can pass through opponents

Special Moves continued

Screen	Name	Command	Hits	Damage	Meter Gain	Startup	Active	Recovery	Advantage on Hit	Advantage if Guarded	Notes
10	Air Hienkyaku L	(in air) ↓ ↙ ← + L	—	—	—	—	—	—	—	—	Warps Zero to ground, can pass through foes
11	Air Hienkyaku M	(in air) ↓ ↙ ← + M	—	—	—	6	—	20	—	—	Can pass through competitors
12	Air Hienkyaku H	(in air) ↓ ↙ ← + H	—	—	—	6	—	21	—	—	Can pass through attackers
13	Sentsuizan L	(in air) ↓ ↘ → + L	—	—	—	1	—	15	—	—	—
14	Sentsuizan M	(in air) ↓ ↘ → + M	1	60,000	480	13	Until grounded	10	+9	+8	OTG- capable, causes hard knockdown if used in launcher combo
14	Sentsuizan H	(in air) ↓ ↘ → + H	1	80,000	640	18	Until grounded	10	+9	+8	OTG- capable, causes hard knockdown if used in launcher combo
15, 16	Hyper Zero Blaster level 1 (can be charged, in air OK)	ATK (hold down)	1/1/3	40,000	320	5	—	23	-6	-7	Requires 30 frames of charging, projectile has 2 low priority durability points
17, 18	Hyper Zero Blaster level 2 (can be charged, in air OK)	ATK (hold down)	1	70,000	560	5	—	23 (air: 15)	-4	-5	Requires 70 frames of charging, projectile has 4 low priority durability points
19, 20	Hyper Zero Blaster level 3 (can be charged, in air OK)	ATK (hold down)	3	108,300	960	5	—	23 (air: 15)	—	+2	Cancelable from any special move, requires 150 frames of charging, knocks down, beam durability: 3 frames x 3 low priority durability points

Hadangeki L/M 1

Hadangeki H 2

Hadangeki: Hadangeki is a projectile that can be used to create offense or to keep your adversary away. Hadangeki L is the most versatile version because of its fast recovery and slow traveling speed.

Offensively, Zero players can use this move against foes with dominant ground-to-ground basic attacks but poor zoning tools. As a result of the slow projectile speed and fast recovery, Zero can dash behind his Hadangeki L and follow up with a combo if it hits. If the opposing character jumps, you can react to this with a fast air throw.

Defensively, you can use this attack against less mobile characters that possess little to no zoning ability. It can be fired rapidly enough to make it virtually impossible for your opponent to advance on the ground. Zero can react to normal jumps with air throws if his adversary is close enough, or dash underneath an opposing character who attempts to approach Zero with a super jump.

When used in combination with Sougenmu, Hadangeki L spam can be very difficult for a competitor to escape once caught in hitstun or blockstun.

3

Ryuenjin: Ryuenjin lacks any invincibility frames to make it a strong defensive option. It has fairly fast startup at 5 frames, but it is highly punishable if blocked or whiffed. Zero's basic L attacks are as fast or faster and can lead to combos. Offensively, Ryuenjin has little combo potential except possibly to be canceled by a level 3 Hyper Zero Blaster.

Raikousen: Raikousen causes a knockdown against airborne opponents regardless of hitstun decay, making it an invaluable combo tool. You can also link it after a level 3 Hyper Zero Blaster if done quickly. Used with Sougenmu, you can employ the move in combos to keep your foe juggled in the corner until Zero runs out of meter or you choose to end the combo.

Raikousen L 4

Raikousen M 5

Raikousen H 6

You can also use Raikousen L and M to travel through an opponent at specific distances. Since the lightning appears with a slight delay after Zero's movement, it can create a cross-up for the opposing player that is difficult to block.

Hienkyaku L 7

Hienkyaku M 8

Hienkyaku H 9

Air Hienkyaku L 10

Air Hienkyaku M 11

Air Hienkyaku H 12

Hienkyaku: Hienkyaku remains a core aspect of Zero's gameplay. Hienkyaku L & M are Zero's primary means of combating advancing guard. It also serves as a very fast cross-up threat to your adversary when used with assists or canceled with level 3 Hyper Zero Blaster. All ground versions of Hienkyaku and air Hienkyaku M & H can also push opponents out of the corner, allowing for deadly mix-ups, especially when a new opposing character is forced in (either via snap back or the loss of a teammate).

You can take advantage of air Hienkyaku L after an air level 3 Hyper Zero Blaster to reach the ground quicker than normal and continue a combo. You can also use it to avoid a foe who attempts to combat Zero while he is airborne.

Sentsuizan L 13

Sentsuizan M & H 14

Sentsuizan: Sentsuizan is Zero's go-to OTG move for extending combos. With a fully charged Hyper Zero Blaster, Zero now has the ability to combo after his OTG on his own without the use of X-Factor or an assist. This attack is also good for achieving a hard knockdown during a launcher combo.

Sentsuizan L has very fast recovery and can be used as an instant overhead if done with the motion ↓↘→↗ + L, causing Zero to stop his jump just above the ground, which allows you to follow up with a quick air attack. It can also be used to simply extend Zero's air time for a short period of time. Keep in mind that he is limited to three special moves per jump.

15

17

19

Hyper Zero Blaster (level 1) 16

Hyper Zero Blaster (level 2) 18

Hyper Zero Blaster (level 3) 20

Hyper Zero Blaster: While the first two levels of this attack charge quickly, the true strength of this move is in the level 3 version. This attack can achieve a knockdown regardless of hitstun. While it has lost the ability to cause hard knockdown in *Ultimate Marvel vs. Capcom 3*, it can now be used to cancel any special move! Players can take advantage of this in a variety of ways. It can be used to cancel the recovery of unsafe moves. It can also be used offensively to create extremely fast cross-up attacks by canceling Hienkyaku or Raikousen the instant they switch sides. It can also be used to cancel Sentsuizan M or H after an OTG to continue a combo.

Hyper Combos

Screen	Name	Command	Hits	Damage	Startup	Active	Recovery	Advantage on Hit	Advantage if Guarded	Notes
1	Rekkoha	↓↘→ + ATK ATK	30	269,300	16+10	80	29	+1	-14	OTG- capable, knocks down, beam durability: 30 frames x 1 high priority durability points
2	Sougenmu	↓↙← + ATK ATK	—	—	10+1	—	1	—	—	Frames 9-10 invincible, creates shadow that mimics Zero 16 frames later, shadow lasts 300 frames, using any hyper combo causes shadow to disappear, Zero does not gain meter while Sougenmu is active
3	Genmu Zero (level 3 hyper combo)	→↓↘ + ATK ATK	1	350,000	10+1	—	57	—	-36	Frames 1-24 invincible, hard knockdown, projectile has 100 high priority durability points

1

2

3

Rekkoha: The ability of this hyper combo to OTG makes it a prime candidate for a combo ender. You'll have to start this hyper combo as soon as Zero lands for it to OTG because there is quite a bit of time before the beam hits the ground. It can also combo into itself with the use of X-Factor.

This hyper combo has a lengthy delay before the beam hits ground level and slowly pulls the opponent up when it hits, limiting the THC potential. Doing a THC into this is possible as long as there is enough hitstun or a hard knockdown for the beam to connect in time to continue the combo. Doing a THC from this move usually requires a hyper combo with an upward attack angle or fullscreen coverage. This requires you to choose Zero's partners carefully, or be stuck with limited THC use.

Sougenmu: Sougenmu creates a shadow that copies Zero's attack exactly 16 frames later. You can use this to create nearly unblockable high/low situations through air attacks followed by low attacks. You can also use it to increase Zero's zoning potential for a short period of time (though this is not recommended except in niche cases). If Zero somehow is no longer the point character while Sougenmu is active, Sougenmu remains active until Zero becomes the point character again, at which time it continues for the duration that was left when he became an assist character.

Sougenmu increases Zero's damage potential, especially in the corner. It can be used either to create big damage early in combos (Sentsuizan relaunch loop) or to extend combos beyond what hitstun decay would otherwise allow (Raikousen loop). These tactics are explained in detail later.

Genmu Zero: Zero's level 3 hyper combo boasts one of the strongest projectiles in the game. With 100 high priority durability points and lightning-fast travel speed, this huge projectile can plow through nearly any beam or projectile in its way. Thanks to its invincibility frames, you can use it to react to most enemy hyper combos. Genmu Zero also makes a good combo ender (usually after a level 3 Hyper Zero Blaster or Raikousen) because it ignores damage scaling.

Battle Plan

You'll want to keep your opponent in the corner as much as possible, where you have access to Zero's highly damaging Sougenmu combos.

Zero's play style favors maintaining pressure on your challenger as much as possible, while keeping the opposing character in the corner. He lacks strong defensive tools and has low vitality, so staying aggressive is the strongest option in most cases. Zero's offense relies heavily on the use of assists. Consequently, Zero is not a strong candidate for the anchor of a team. Instead, Zero performs best as the first or second character. Zero can do a decent job as a battery, but because his attacks are multi-hitting, you may find it difficult to produce high damage without meter. Zero's offense becomes a much bigger threat when he has access to an abundance of hyper meter against a cornered foe, giving him an avenue for his highly damaging Sougenmu combos.

How you begin your offense depends on the character you are facing off against, since characters with stronger zoning ability often try to keep Zero out and force him into bad situations. Using an assist to help initiate your offense is helpful but risky. A savvy competitor can severely punish your assist if you are careless.

Against characters with a dominant ground zoning game, it may be best to take to the air, to use your air Hienkyaku M and airdash to close the distance. Ideally, you should be above your opponent before you begin your assault. If so, you have several options depending on your height and what your adversary is doing. If you are fairly close to ground, or you suspect your opponent might attempt to jump to fight you in the air, an option select air Ⓗ/throw is a dominant option. Since air Ⓗ has a large number of active frames, this means even if your rival doesn't jump to meet you, you'll likely still be a threat nearly all the way to the ground. If your foe backdashes farther away from you or forward dashes under you, Raikousen L is an option to cross your opponent up if spacing permits. Keep in mind that Zero's airdash is relatively slow and easy to see coming, so plan accordingly.

Sentsuizan is a high priority air attack that can lead to full combos. Take care not to miss, since it does have slight recovery once you hit the ground!

If you are higher up, you can use Sentsuizan as a pseudo dive kick. Sentsuizan M gives you a steeper angle than Sentsuizan H, making it a better option if you are directly above your competitor. Sentsuizan H would be more useful if you still are not very close to your opponent or you expect your adversary to retreat backwards. If it hits, you can easily continue into a combo with crouching Ⓛ. If your foe is cornered and you have level 3 Hyper Zero Blaster charged, you can cancel Sentsuizan recovery into Hyper Zero Blaster. This can lead into highly damaging sequences, like Zero's Sougenmu Sentsuizan relaunch combo.

Against characters that have weak ground projectiles or lack them entirely, it may be best to use Hadangeki L or a projectile assist. You can then use the projectiles as cover to dash forward or use Hienkyaku. These projectiles, along with the range provided by Zero's Z-Saber, let him dominate the space in front of him against these types of characters. This forces your rivals to defend against your offense or take to the air. If your opponent attempts to super jump toward you, you can simply dash or Hienkyaku M under the opposing character and continue zoning with projectiles. You can also attempt to counter their jumps with an air throw option select. Air throws are a solid option for Zero because he can convert them into combos.

Zero's offense is largely based around using Hienkyaku L and M combined with projectile assists or Hyper Zero Blaster level 3, causing opposing players to guess the side where Zero will ends up.

Once you have gained the offensive initiative with Zero, a competent competitor usually attempts to escape. The most common method involves utilizing advancing guard to reset the situation. Thankfully, Zero possesses the means to counter advancing guard. If you have a projectile assist available, such as Sentinel—α, you can call your assist and use ground Hienkyaku L or M to regain lost ground while the projectiles protect you. Hienkyaku L places Zero in front of his adversary, whereas Hienkyaku M situates him behind his rival a majority of the time. Alternatively, you can use a level 3 Hyper Zero Blaster to cancel the recovery of the Hienkyaku, leading to an easy combo if landed at point-blank range. This is a strong option because Hienkyaku L and H initially look identical. This makes it difficult for your competitor to tell the side where Zero ends up; with perfect spacing, it's totally ambiguous for the opposition. However, you need a way of covering Zero's long period of vulnerability during Hienkyaku. Hienkyaku possesses no invincibility frames, and opposing characters recover before Zero does, allowing them to easily punish you. Hienkyaku H followed by an airdash can be used, as well, but it is fairly slow and gives a quick opponent a chance to escape. Another tricky, yet slightly risky option, is to use Hienkyaku H immediately followed by Raikousen L to cross up your adversary! This leaves Zero vulnerable for a while but can be useful if your opponent is hesitant or expecting your ground Hienkyaku mix-ups. Calling an assist before Hienkyaku H can help provide coverage during this vulnerability.

If you are airborne using a special move-cancelable normal attack when your opponent uses advancing guard, you can cancel the attack with air Hienkyaku M. Unlike the ground version, in this case, Zero rarely ends up behind his target. Again, an assist or level 3 Hyper Zero Blaster is required to make this safe. Another option here is to use Raikousen M, which can cross up your foe. You'll want to use this attack as low to the ground as possible to minimize recovery time. If done low enough, you can then follow up with a combo with crouching Ⓛ! Hienkyaku H into Raikousen L can be used, as previously mentioned.

If your opponent defends successfully, and is persistent about using advancing guard to push Zero away during blockstrings, you can put this knowledge to good use by delaying later hits in chain combos when guarded. The idea is to delay attacks so much that by the time the opponent goes to press attack buttons, expecting to pushblock, they'll have actually left guardstun. Their double button press then becomes an Ⓜ or Ⓗ attack, which your delayed attack will immediately counterhit! This works well with Zero because of his relatively fast attacks, the reach advantage provided by his Z-Saber, and the natural inclination of opposing players to want to push Zero away from them immediately.

If you find your competitor not using advancing guard often, Zero has further options to attempt to break a rival's defense. Zero's most effective mix-up remains Hienkyaku in tandem with a projectile or beam assist, or level 3 Hyper Zero Blaster. The goal is to cross up at the last possible moment before the assist's projectile or beam hits the opposing character, or to cancel the Hienkyaku with level 3 Hyper Zero Blaster as soon as it crosses up. However, you still have options when no assists are available. Raikousen L done at close range can cross up your opponent and lead to a combo. Another option is to use Sentsuizan L low to the ground by inputting ⇩ ⇙ ⇨ ⇗ + Ⓛ, then following up with air Ⓛ, Ⓜ for a fast overhead attack. Alternatively, you can land and immediately follow with crouching Ⓛ. These two options work well together because the startup animations of Sentsuizan and Raikousen look similar, making it difficult for the opposing player to predict which one you are using.

Use Raikousen to cross up your opponent and combat advancing guard!

Zero lacks any strong defensive options and must either rely heavily on advancing guard to create space or wait for gaps in your adversary's offense to regain offensive momentum. Trying for an option select air throw with ⇨ or ⇦ + Ⓗ against jumping opponents is usually a strong choice. You can almost always use Genmu Zero if an opponent recklessly uses any hyper combo you have a chance to react to, which brings their offense to a screeching halt. This is especially useful if the opposing player is trying to inflict chip damage through an otherwise safe hyper combo.

COMBO USAGE

I. CR. Ⓛ, Ⓜ, Ⓗ, Ⓢ CANCEL⇒ FORWARD SUPER JUMP, AIR Ⓜ, Ⓜ, Ⓗ (3 HITS), Ⓢ, LAND, CALL X-23—β, FORWARD DASH, Ⓢ CANCEL⇒ FORWARD SUPER JUMP, AIR Ⓜ, Ⓜ, Ⓗ, Ⓢ, LAND, ↓ ↘ → + ATK ATK

549,900 damage, 27% meter loss

It is difficult to land Zero's long combos at midscreen. There are numerous ways to store a buster shot for long air combos, but most of those combos now have consistency problems when not performed near a corner. As a result, it's best to pair Zero with a good assist to strengthen his midscreen combos (and ultimately make them much easier to do). An OTG assist, like X-23—β, works well for this, as do She-hulk—α and Wesker—β. It's also possible to use non-OTG-capable assists; call the assist, dash forward, then do ↓ ↘ → ↗ + Ⓗ to OTG your foe. If timed right, the assist hits soon after the dive, and you can launch the opposing character with Ⓢ again.

II. (CORNER REQUIRED) CR. Ⓛ (HOLD Ⓛ), Ⓜ, Ⓗ, Ⓢ CANCEL⇒ VERTICAL SUPER JUMP, AIR Ⓜ, Ⓜ CANCEL⇒ ↓ ↘ → + Ⓗ, LAND, VERTICAL JUMP, AIR ↓ ↘ → + Ⓗ CANCEL⇒ RELEASE Ⓛ, AIR Ⓢ, LAND, Ⓢ CANCEL⇒ FORWARD SUPER JUMP, AIR Ⓜ, Ⓜ, Ⓗ, Ⓢ, LAND, ↓ ↘ → + ATK ATK

622,700 damage, 17% meter loss

A corner combo that takes advantage of the new ability of level 3 Hyper Zero Blaster to cancel special moves. After the initial launch with Ⓢ, delay your link into air Ⓜ, Ⓜ slightly to give your Blaster more time to charge. Once your target has been knocked to the ground, OTG with air ↓ ↘ → + Ⓗ, then release Ⓛ to cancel into the shot. Be sure to cancel air ↓ ↘ → + Ⓗ before it touches the ground, or else Zero performs the ground version of the shot, making the air Ⓢ afterwards impossible.

III. FRONT AIR THROW, LAND, X-23—β, FORWARD JUMP, AIRDASH FORWARD, AIR Ⓜ, Ⓢ, LAND, ST. Ⓜ, Ⓢ CANCEL⇒ FORWARD SUPER JUMP, AIR Ⓜ, Ⓜ, Ⓗ, Ⓢ, LAND, ↓ ↘ → + ATK ATK

396,600 damage, 48% meter loss

An air throw combo that uses an assist. Call X-23 as you fall from the throw, then land, wait a moment, then jump forward and airdash forward. Be sure to let your jump gain a little height before the airdash, or else air Ⓜ, Ⓢ won't fully connect.

IV. (CORNER REQUIRED) CR. Ⓛ (HOLD Ⓛ), Ⓜ, Ⓗ, Ⓢ CANCEL⇒ VERTICAL SUPER JUMP, AIR Ⓜ, Ⓜ CANCEL⇒ ↓ ↘ → + Ⓗ, LAND, VERTICAL JUMP, AIR ↓ ↘ → + Ⓗ CANCEL⇒ RELEASE Ⓛ (IMMEDIATELY PRESS AND HOLD Ⓛ AGAIN), AIR Ⓢ, LAND, Ⓢ CANCEL⇒ FORWARD SUPER JUMP, AIR Ⓜ, Ⓜ, Ⓗ, Ⓢ, LAND, VERTICAL JUMP, AIR ↓ ↘ → + Ⓗ CANCEL⇒ RELEASE Ⓛ, → ↓ ↘ + Ⓛ (HOLD Ⓗ) CANCEL⇒ ↓ ↙ ← + ATK ATK, VERTICAL JUMP, AIR RELEASE Ⓗ, → ↓ ↘ + Ⓛ (HOLD Ⓗ), LAND, {→ ↓ ↘ → ↗ + Ⓛ, LAND} X 6, VERTICAL JUMP, AIR RELEASE Ⓗ

716,800+ damage, 9% meter gain

A complex combo that sets up a Raikousen loop via Sougenmu activation. After hitting your opponent with the second air ↓ ↘ → + Ⓗ OTG, cancel into the level 3 Hyper Zero Blaster and immediately perform air → ↓ ↘ + Ⓛ; hold Ⓗ after inputting the command. As soon as Zero lands from the Raikousen, hyper cancel into ↓ ↙ ← + ATK ATK. If done early enough, the lightning will still be hitting the target as you enter Sougenmu, giving you enough time to have Zero jump and fire a Hyper Zero Blaster. From there, perform the air Raikousen, land, then perform them repeatedly with the command → ↓ ↘ → ↗ + Ⓛ to do them as close to the ground as possible. After the final level 3 Hyper Zero Blaster has been released, you can perform another → ↓ ↘ + Ⓛ CANCEL⇒ ↓ ↙ ← + ATK ATK to start the loop all over again. You can continue this loop for as long as you have meter to spend on Sougenmu.

V. (CORNER REQUIRED) CR. Ⓛ (HOLD Ⓛ), Ⓜ, Ⓗ, → + Ⓗ (3 HITS) CANCEL⇒ ↓ ↙ ← + ATK ATK, Ⓢ CANCEL⇒ VERTICAL SUPER JUMP, AIR Ⓜ, Ⓜ CANCEL⇒ ↓ ↘ → + Ⓗ, LAND, Ⓢ CANCEL⇒ VERTICAL SUPER JUMP, AIR Ⓜ, Ⓜ CANCEL⇒ ↓ ↘ → + Ⓗ, LAND, Ⓢ, CANCEL⇒ VERTICAL SUPER JUMP, AIR Ⓜ, Ⓜ CANCEL⇒ ↓ ↘ → + Ⓗ, LAND, Ⓢ CANCEL⇒ VERTICAL SUPER JUMP, AIR Ⓜ CANCEL⇒ RELEASE Ⓛ, WAIT A MOMENT, ↓ ↘ → + Ⓗ, LAND, ↓ ↘ → + ATK ATK

772,000 damage, 174% meter loss

This is the Sougenmu relaunch loop. After hitting your adversary with air ↓ ↘ → + Ⓗ, the shadow version of the attack hits the foe OTG as Zero recovers, allowing you to launch them again.

VI. FRONT AIR THROW, AIRDASH FORWARD, ↓ ↘ → + Ⓗ CANCEL⇒ X-FACTOR, AIR Ⓜ (HOLD Ⓛ), LAND, ST. Ⓜ, Ⓢ CANCEL⇒ FORWARD SUPER JUMP, AIR Ⓜ, Ⓜ, Ⓗ, Ⓢ, LAND, X-23—β, FORWARD DASH, Ⓢ CANCEL⇒ VERTICAL SUPER JUMP, AIR Ⓜ CANCEL⇒ RELEASE Ⓛ, → ↓ ↘ + Ⓛ, LAND, Ⓢ CANCEL⇒ FORWARD SUPER JUMP, AIR Ⓗ, Ⓢ, LAND, ↓ ↘ → + ATK ATK

781,100~987,200 damage, 19~50% meter gain

A verifiable X-Factor combo that begins with a throw. Air ↓ ↘ → + Ⓗ should be canceled just as it makes contact with the opposing character; any lower, and there won't be enough time to do air Ⓜ. During the final Ⓢ launch, perform air Ⓗ as late as possible to ensure that Zero falls fast enough afterwards to OTG with ↓ ↘ → + ATK ATK.

VII. CR. Ⓛ, Ⓜ, Ⓗ, Ⓢ CANCEL⇒ FORWARD SUPER JUMP, AIR Ⓜ, Ⓜ, Ⓗ (3 HITS), Ⓢ, LAND, CALL X-23—β, FORWARD DASH, Ⓢ CANCEL⇒ FORWARD SUPER JUMP, AIR Ⓜ, Ⓜ, Ⓗ, Ⓢ, LAND, ↓ ↘ → + ATK ATK CANCEL⇒ X-FACTOR, ↓ ↘ → + ATK ATK

809,900~946,200 damage, 129% meter loss

A basic X-Factor combo. Though it uses two meters, the verifiable and optional X-Factor ending allows you to quickly finish off an opponent with plenty of X-Factor time left for the next competitor entering the screen.

ADVANCED TACTICS

CUTTING SHORT COMBOS

You can use Hienkyaku in many situations to put Zero into an advantageous situation that keeps opposing players guessing!

Many of Zero's attacks are multiple hits leading to damage scaling, hurting Zero's damage more than other characters. However, Zero has excellent options for you to reset combos into difficult to block mix-ups that can lead to further damage.

On the ground, the simplest option is to simply call an assist during a combo (one with enough to delay that the combo will end) and do Hienkyaku L or M immediately after to cross your target up. Your opponent likely expects you to continue the combo and may not look for a cross-up reset, and they'll block the wrong direction to guard the assist's attack!

You can utilize a similar tactic in air combos. Simply cancel an air Ⓜ into a Hienkyaku. Hienkyaku L takes Zero to the ground quickly, allowing you to call an assist while your competitor is still recovering and falling toward the ground. Most characters are forced to block this assist, providing you with a free mix-up. Hienkyaku H can be particularly confusing to adversaries who use neutral or backward air recovery after a reset in the corner. Zero goes over them and may—or may not!—end up stationed behind them as they fall. Zero can option select air throw with his air ⇨ + Ⓗ, or even attack once his opponent is grounded with air Ⓗ, depending on when the opposing character air recovered.

OPTION SELECTS

Against cornered foes, Zero can apply pressure without having to worry about whether opponents might attempt to leave the corner! Against a cornered adversary, Sentsuizan M is a strong offensive option…

But, if a rival attempts to leave, Sentsuizan's input changes to a Hienkyaku M, causing Zero to follow his competitor!

Since Zero's strongest damage options are in the corner, most floored opponents attempt to roll forward away from the corner. Due to the nature of his inputs in the air, he has excellent option selects that allow you to maintain pressure against opposing characters who have been knocked down, preventing an easy escape for them.

When your opponent is cornered, a strong option is to use Sentsuizan M as your target is standing or rolling. If your foe chooses to stay in the corner, they must then deal with a strong air attack that can lead to a highly damaging corner combo from Zero. However, if they choose to attempt to roll under Zero, your input becomes Hienkyaku M, allowing Zero to follow his rolling opponent and instantly apply air pressure with air Ⓗ. This works even better with delayed projectile assists like Sentinel—α.

You can use Raikousen M in a similar manner either in the corner or midscreen. If done low enough to the ground, Zero can follow up with a combo! However, be aware that using this move against a cornered opponent puts you in the corner instead, so this is best used with a lengthy projectile assist like Sentinel—α. This tactic decreases the difficulty of continuing the combo while also giving you time to get back out of the corner while your rival is forced to block the assist projectiles.

COMBO APPENDIX

GENERAL EXECUTION TIPS

Zero has several combos and mix-ups that require air specials to be executed very quickly and low to the ground. Simply add ⇗ to the end of the motion with a very slight delay before the button press.

You can continue charging Zero's blaster while switching the button used to charge. Simply hold down a different ATK button while the original ATK button is being held. You can then release the original ATK button to free it up for use!

Air Hyper Zero Blaster has very fast recovery. Any combos where a Raikousen or Hienkyaku follows an air level 3 Hyper Zero Blaster requires the Raikousen or Hienkyaku to be input immediately upon recovery.

AS ZERO COMES IN: AIR Ⓜ, Ⓜ CANCEL➡ ↓↘→ + Ⓗ, (IF YOU LAND IN A CORNER, ADD ↓↘→ + ATK ATK)

Notes	Damage
⇧ + Ⓢ or ⇨ + Ⓢ or ⇩ + Ⓢ TAC to Zero	—

(REQUIRES CORNER) CR. Ⓛ (HOLD Ⓛ), Ⓜ, Ⓗ CANCEL➡ →↓↘ + ATK ATK, ↓↘→↗ + Ⓗ CANCEL➡ RELEASE Ⓛ, Ⓢ CANCEL➡ FORWARD SUPER JUMP, AIR Ⓜ, Ⓜ, Ⓗ, Ⓢ, LAND, ↓↘→ + ATK ATK

Notes	Damage
A corner combo utilizing Zero's new OTG capabilities to easily launch Zero's opponent after his level 3 hyper combo. The opening string and Genmu Zero give just enough time to charge a level 3 Hyper Zero Blaster. When air ⇩ ⇖ ⇨ + Ⓗ hits, wait until it touches the ground before canceling into the shot	863,700 damage, 359% meter loss

"I ENJOY BATTLING WORTHY OPPONENTS SUCH AS YOU. IT KEEPS ME ON MY TOES AND MAKES ME THAT MORE EFFICIENT."

DLC

SHUMA-GORATH

"I AM HE WHO SLEEPS, BUT NOW AWAKENS!"

Bio

REAL NAME

Shuma-Gorath

OCCUPATION

Lord of Chaos, Master of the Great Old Ones, Ruler of a Hundred Dimensions

ABILITIES

Shuma-Gorath generates his own mystical power, but he also draws energy, mystical or otherwise, from others. Shuma-Gorath can release destructive blasts and can manipulate magical energy on a planetary scale. He can communicate telepathically and control others, even across dimensions.

WEAPONS

None

PROFILE

God of another dimension. As he is able to assume the form of whatever it is that people fear, he has no true form. Having taken a liking to Earth, he has tried to rule over the planet many times since the prehistoric age, but he has usually been thwarted by a shaman or magic user, such as Doctor Strange.

FIRST APPEARANCE

Marvel Premiere #5 (1972)

POWER GRID

INTELLIGENCE

STRENGTH

SPEED

STAMINA

ENERGY PROJECTION

FIGHTING ABILITY

*This is biographical, and does not represent an evaluation of the in-game combat potential of this hero.

ALTERNATE COSTUMES

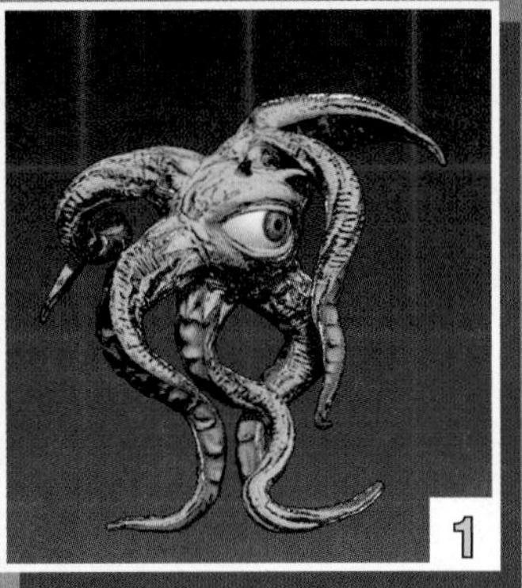
1

2

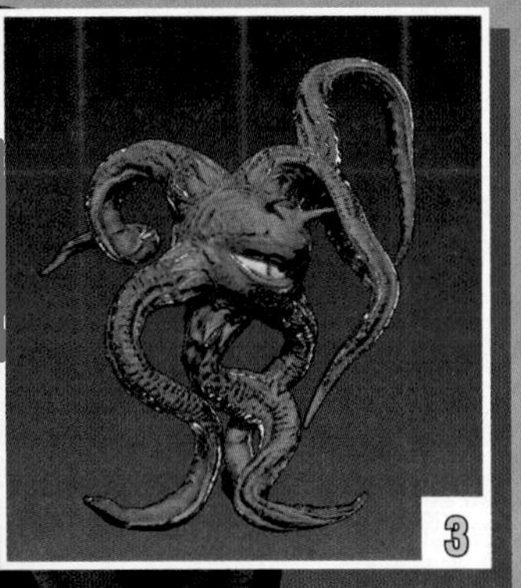
3

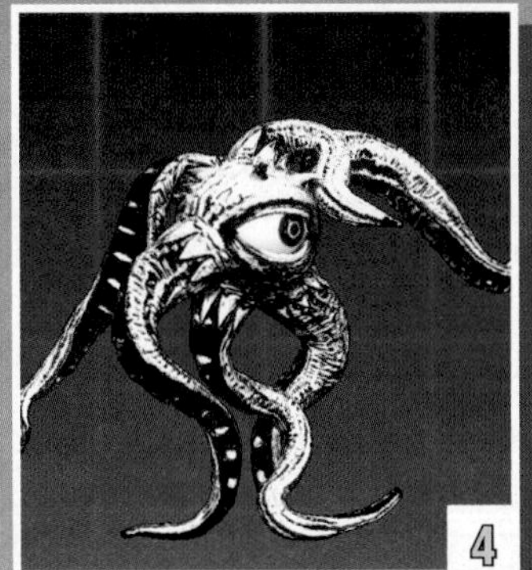
4

5

6

DLC

Overview

Vitality	950,000
Chain Combo Archetype	Hunter Series

X-Factor Boost	Damage	Speed
Level 1 (3 teammates remaining)	127.5%	112.5%
Level 2 (2 teammates remaining)	144.9%	125%
Level 3 (1 teammate remaining)	162.4%	137.5%

Though it may not be immediately obvious given Shuma-Gorath's aesthetics, his character archetype is essentially that of an up-close brawler. Your primary goal when playing as Shuma-Gorath is to get him within point-blank range of his opponent to perform mix-ups.

What sort of mix-ups do you perform at point blank range with Shuma-Gorath?

- **Air Mystic Smash and air Ⓢ can be used as instant overheads that lead into a combo**
- **His low-hitting, rapid fire crouching Ⓛ can be used to punish opponents for doing anything besides guarding low**
- **If his target is concentrating on guarding, Shuma-Gorath has powerful throws that can steal health and meter, as well as allow for combos afterward**
- **This distance puts Shuma-Gorath in range of his high-damage level 3 hyper combo, Chaos Dimension**

How do you close the distance against a rival to get Shuma-Gorath within point-blank range?

- **Airdashing into air Ⓜ to cross up your competitor**
- **Using air Mystic Smash to cover a good chunk of distance**
- **Utilizing Mystic Smash M & H, which allow Shuma-Gorath to quickly cover ground**
- **Hitting your opponent with Mystic Stare eyeball projectiles forces them to attack you in order to remove the eyeballs, or remain in place to block the explosion**
- **Using assists, such as Akuma—β, that lock down your rival and cover Shuma-Gorath's attempts to get in**

TUNING SINCE ORIGINAL MVC3

The lord of the Chaos Dimension did not receive any new moves in the transition to *Ultimate Marvel vs. Capcom 3*, but he did gain a few substantial buffs to his existing tools, greatly improving his up-close mix-ups and damage potential. Air Ⓢ loses its ability to hit OTG but now causes a hard knockdown state that allows you to combo after a non-launcher combo hit, making for an instant overhead that can be followed with a combo. Shuma-Gorath's command throw received some frame data tweaks, and you can now score an OTG hit with him after the throw, resulting in a full combo as well. Shuma's standard throw now steals meter as well as vitality from the opposing character.

- **Throws steal 2,000 points of opponent's hyper meter and 40,000 vitality, now inflict 40,000 damage instead of 80,0000**
- **Air Ⓢ is no longer OTG-capable. It now causes a hard knockdown state, even when used outside of launcher combos**
- **Devitalization deals more damage, has more active frames, and takes less recovery time. It is now possible to connect an OTG hit after Devitalization**
- **Hyper Mystic Smash is now mashable for additional damage**
- **Chaos Dimension is now mashable for additional damage**

Attack Set

Standing Basic Attacks

Screen	Command	Hits	Damage	Meter Gain	Startup	Active	Recovery	Advantage on Hit	Advantage if Guarded	Notes
1	Standing L	1	33,000	264	4	3	11	0	0	Cancels into L attacks
2	Standing M	2	62,000	560	5	2(2)3	19	-3	-3	—
3	Standing H	6	82,800	960	9	2(2)2(2)2(2)2(2)2(2)2	10	+12	+12	—

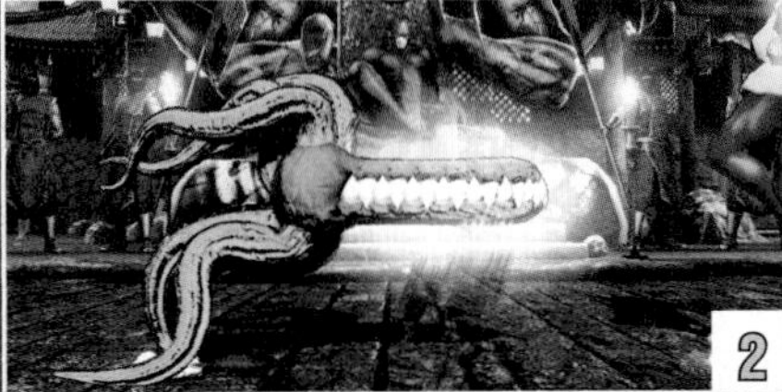
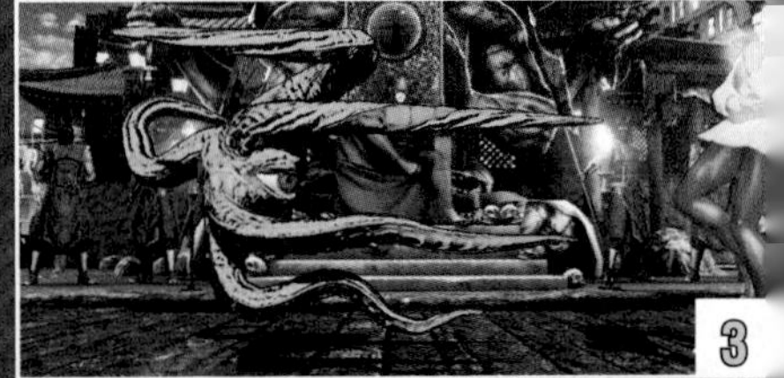

Crouching Basic Attacks

Screen	Command	Hits	Damage	Meter Gain	Startup	Active	Recovery	Advantage on Hit	Advantage if Guarded	Notes
1	Crouching L	1	33,000	264	5	3	13	-2	-2	Low attack, cancels into L attacks
2	Crouching M	2	63,000	560	6	3(1)4	15	—	0	Low attack, knocks down opponent
3	Crouching H	1	70,000	560	10	4	20	+7	0	Knocks down foe, jump- cancelable

Ground Special Attack—Launcher

Screen	Command	Hits	Damage	Meter Gain	Startup	Active	Recovery	Advantage on Hit	Advantage if Guarded	Notes
1	S (while standing or crouching)	1	75,000	600	7	4	28	—	-8	Launcher, not special- or hyper combo-cancelable

Air Basic Attacks

Screen	Command	Hits	Damage	Meter Gain	Startup	Active	Recovery	Advantage on Hit	Advantage if Guarded	Notes
1	Air L	1	38,000	304	4	3	16	+8	+8	Overhead attack
2	Air M	2	54,000	480	6	7	18	+17	+17	Overhead attack
3	Air H	1	75,000	600	11	4	21	+19	+19	Overhead attack

Air Special Attacks—Flying Screen and Air Exchange

Air (S) causes a hard knockdown when used in a launcher combo (this is sometimes called flying screen). When used outside of a launcher combo, air (S) behaves mostly like another basic attack. Air exchange attacks, performed by inputting a direction plus (S), are only possible during a launcher combo. Exchange hits initiate team aerial combos by tagging in the next available character to continue the air combo.

Screen	Command	Hits	Damage	Meter Gain	Startup	Active	Recovery	Advantage on Hit	Advantage if Guarded	Notes
1	Air (S)	1	80,000	640	8	Until grounded	22	—	-3	Overhead attack, causes hard knockdown, not special- or hyper combo- cancelable, causes hard knockdown if used in launcher combo
2	Air ⇧ + (S) (during launcher combo)	1	60,000	480	11	2	23	—	—	Tags in next available ally while lofting opponent upward
3	Air ⇨ or ⇦ + (S) (during launcher combo)	1	50,000	400	11	4	Until grounded	—	—	Tags in next available ally while causing wall bounce, erases 1 hyper meter from foe
4	Air ⇩ + (S) (during launcher combo)	1	50,000	400	11	4	Until grounded	—	—	Tags in next available ally while causing ground bounce, generates 1 hyper meter

1

2

3

4

Command Attacks

Command attacks resemble basic attacks but have different chaining and canceling properties. It's usually possible to chain *into* a command attack from basic attacks, but most command attacks cannot be chained from or canceled themselves.

Screen	Name	Command	Hits	Damage	Meter Gain	Startup	Active	Recovery	Advantage on Hit	Advantage if Guarded	Notes
1	Strange Gaze	⇨ + (H)	1	75,000	600	15	6	15	—	+3	Knocks down adversary
2	Air Strange Gaze	(in air) ⇧ + (H)	1	75,000	600	11	4	21	—	+19	Knocks down competitor

1

2

Throws

Throws are for snagging passive or blocking opponents. Since throws are active so quickly, you can also use them to preemptively toss opposing characters out of their offense. Combos are usually possible after throws, one way or another.

Screen	Command	Hits	Damage	Meter Gain	Startup	Active	Notes
1	⇨ + (H) (ground)	4	40,000	400 + 2000	1	1	Hard knockdown, steals 40,000 vitality and 2000 meter from foe
	⇦ + (H) (ground)	4	40,000	400 + 2000	1	1	Hard knockdown, steals 40,000 vitality and 2000 meter from opponent
2	⇨ + (H) (air)	4	40,000	400 + 2000	1	1	Hard knockdown, steals 40,000 vitality and 2000 meter from rival
	⇦ + (H) (air)	4	40,000	400 + 2000	1	1	Hard knockdown, steals 40,000 vitality and 2000 meter from target

1

2

As a Partner—Crossover Assists

Screen	Type	P1+P2 Crossover Combination Hyper Combo	Description	Hits	Damage	Meter Gain	Startup	Active	Recovery (this crossover assist)	Recovery (other partner)	Notes
1	Shuma-Gorath—α	Hyper Mystic Ray	Mystic Ray H	10	129,900	1600	52	30	95	65	OTG-capable, knocks down opponent, beam durability: 10 frames x 1 low priority durability points
2	Shuma-Gorath—β	Hyper Mystic Smash	Mystic Stare L	12	105,200	1440	46	—	120	90	Projectiles disappear after 29 frames, beam durability: 6 frames x 1 low priority durability points
3	Shuma-Gorath—γ	Hyper Mystic Smash	Mystic Smash L	8	113,600	1280	37	32	110	80	—

Shuma-Gorath's assists run the gamut from awesome to... well, not so great. Depending on the nature of your team, you'll most likely want to choose between Shuma-Gorath—α and Shuma-Gorath—γ.

Shuma-Gorath—α replicates his Mystic Ray H attack, sweeping the screen from bottom to top with a laser beam. This assist is excellent at temporarily locking down a huge portion of the playfield, potentially catching your opponent—and hopefully their assist character—in the middle of a move, or just forcing them to stay put while your point character moves in to attack. The beam is OTG-capable, as well, but its slow startup time requires you to call the assist as soon as possible to take advantage of this feature.

Shuma-Gorath—β fires a group of eyeballs that disappear after 29 frames, a very short range for a projectile assist. Due to its long startup time, this assist is practically useless in extended firefights or at long range. The eyeball projectiles do not stick to the target like they do when Shuma-Gorath is on point, but instead explode on impact.

Shuma-Gorath—γ is the fastest assist at his disposal. Mystic Smash L has an extremely short range, and it is mostly useful for holding an adversary in place for mix-ups because of its multiple hits. However, on contact, this move could work against you: the number of hits it adds to a combo may cause too much damage scaling to be helpful.

Snap Back

Screen	Command	Hits	Damage	Meter Gain	Startup	Active	Recovery	Advantage on Hit	Advantage if Guarded
1	↓↘→ + P1⇄P2	1	50,000	500 - (-1 hyper meter bar)	2	6	15	—	+3

Notes

On hit, snap back forces the opposing point character to be replaced by an assist. Opposing assist calls or tag outs are also locked out for 4 seconds

Special Moves

Screen	Name	Command	Hits	Damage	Meter Gain	Startup	Active	Recovery	Advantage on Hit	Advantage if Guarded	Notes
1	Mystic Stare L	← (charge), → + L	6/6	46,600/ 117,000	480/ 1200	22	—	23	+10	+10	Projectiles disappear after 29 frames, projectiles attach to opponent on hit and explode 180 frames later, Mystic Stare cannot be used while projectiles are attached to adversary, exploding projectiles are OTG-capable, attached projectiles disappear if Shuma-Gorath is hit, beam durability: 6 frames x 1 low priority durability points
1	Mystic Stare M	← (charge), → + M	6/6	46,600/ 117,000	480/ 1200	22	—	28	+5	+5	Projectiles disappear after 29 frames, on hit projectiles attach to competitor on hit and explode 180 frames later, Mystic Stare cannot be used while projectiles are attached to rival, exploding projectiles are OTG-capable, attached projectiles disappear if Shuma-Gorath is hit, beam durability: 6 frames x 1 low priority durability points
1	Mystic Stare H	← (charge), → + H	6/6	46,600/ 117,000	480/ 1200	22	—	33	0	0	Projectiles disappear after 29 frames, projectiles attach to foe on hit and , explode 180 frames later, Mystic Stare cannot be used while projectiles are attached to target, exploding projectiles are OTG-capable, attached projectiles disappear if Shuma-Gorath is hit, beam durability: 6 frames x 1 low priority durability points
2	Mystic Smash L	↓↘→ + L	8	113,600	1280	13	32	18	+2	+2	—
2	Mystic Smash M	↓↘→ + M	9	122,200	1440	15	36	18	+2	+2	—
2	Mystic Smash H	↓↘→ + H	9	122,200	1440	18	40	18	+2	+2	—

Special Moves continued

Screen	Name	Command	Hits	Damage	Meter Gain	Startup	Active	Recovery	Advantage on Hit	Advantage if Guarded	Notes
3	Air Mystic Smash L	(in air) ↓↘→ + L	6	117,000	1200	12	Until grounded	13	+7~10	+7~10	Overhead attack
	Air Mystic Smash M	(in air) ↓↘→ + M	7	130,200	1400	15	Until grounded	13	+7~10	+7~10	Overhead attack
	Air Mystic Smash H	(in air) ↓↘→ + H	8	142,100	1600	18	Until grounded	13	+7~10	+7~10	Overhead attack
4	Devitalization L	→↘↓↙← + L	2	130,000	1300	5	22	23	—	—	Throw, hard knockdown, negates single-hit projectiles during active frames
	Devitalization M	→↘↓↙← + M	2	160,000	1600	3	1(2)21	23	—	—	Throw, hard knockdown, negates single-hit projectiles during active frames
	Devitalization H	→↘↓↙← + H	2	190,000	1900	1	2(3)21	23	—	—	Throw, hard knockdown, negates single-hit projectiles during active frames
5	Mystic Ray L	↓ (charge), ↑ + L	6	93,500	960	22	30	9	-10	-10	Knocks down opponent, OTG-capable, beam durability: 6 frames x 1 low priority durability points
6	Mystic Ray M	↓ (charge), ↑ + M	8	113,600	1280	25	30	6	+12	+9	Knocks down adversary, OTG-capable, beam durability: 8 frames x 1 low priority durability points
7	Mystic Ray H	↓ (charge), ↑ + H	10	129,900	1600	28	30	3	+11	+9	Knocks down competitor, OTG-capable, beam durability: 10 frames x 1 low priority durability points

1

Mystic Stare: Shuma-Gorath fires a ring of six nasty little eyeballs that stick to his opponent on contact, and explode after 180 frames. The distance the eyeballs travel is determined by the strength of the button pressed: L travels about a quarter-length of the screen, M reaches half the length of the screen before disappearing, and H can hit a foe at fullscreen distance. The eyeball explosion is OTG-capable, which can be useful in corner combos if you time your attacks correctly.

This projectile has very little durability, and combined with the charge time required to start up the move, it is not recommended for firefights. You also cannot fire another Mystic Stare if the opposing character already has eyeballs attached to them. Eyeballs attached to an adversary disappear if Shuma-Gorath gets hit before they have a chance to explode.

Hitting your competitor with Mystic Stare puts the target in an awkward position. They can choose to become defensive and attempt to block the inevitable explosion; in this case, this is your opportunity to press the attack. Should your challenger choose to not respect the eyeballs, hang tight and defend until the explosion occurs. The explosion is your cue to go back on offense.

3

Air Mystic Smash: As an overhead attack, air Mystic Smash is one of Shuma-Gorath's most important tools in *Ultimate Marvel vs. Capcom 3*. Each attack button results in a different angle of attack: L travels at a very short range, M travels the farthest, and H is in-between the two and also slower. All versions of air Mystic Smash give Shuma a positive frame advantage if blocked, making it an excellent method for getting him closer to his opponent. You can also use this as an instant overhead into a combo by inputting ↓↘→↗ + ATK to execute the move the second Shuma-Gorath leaves the ground.

Mystic Smash: Shuma-Gorath compacts his body into a spiky ball and hurtles a distance across the screen depending upon the button pressed. Mystic Smash serves primarily as a means to cover ground while attacking your opponent.

2

Mystic Smash L travels a short distance forward. When used at point-blank range, Shuma-Gorath passes through his rival and ends up on the opposite side from where he started. Used with an assist, this can create some mix-up opportunities.

Mystic Smash M travels halfway across the screen before dropping straight down. Until Shuma-Gorath drops down, Mystic Smash M follows a similar trajectory to the H version of the move. This can create situations confusing for an opposing player, since they'll expect Shuma to travel straight over their heads. Instead, drop down on them and start attacking with crouching L to combo. Call a crossover assist before performing the move for added protection and coverage.

Mystic Smash H travels in a wide arc across the length of the screen. Unless your adversary is jumping or near a corner, Shuma-Gorath will most likely pass straight over their heads. It can be useful to combat advancing guard: should your challenger use advancing guard against one of your crouching L attacks, cancel into Mystic Smash H to close the gap quickly.

Devitalization: The frame data for Shuma-Gorath's command throw has been drastically changed in *Ultimate Marvel vs. Capcom 3*, including a huge increase in active frames and a big decrease in recovery time. This means it's now possible to score an OTG hit after Devitalization, allowing for full combos! Use this move to grab opponents who are blocking your staggered L attacks with using advancing guard. Because of the quick 1-frame startup time on the H version, you can also use Devitalization to punish guarded attacks.

4

Devitalization also nullifies single-hit projectiles during its active frames. By blocking projectiles this way, you'll avoid chip damage and pushback, and you'll gain 10% of your hyper meter bar.

Mystic Ray: Shuma-Gorath fires an OTG-capable beam from his eye that travels in a sweeping arc from down to up. The angle at which the beam ends is determined by the strength of the button pressed: L stops parallel to the ground, M ends at about a 45-degree angle, and H stops with the beam pointing straight up. Mystic Ray is a great zoning tool when combined with assist to cover its long startup time. During shorter combos, or with the aid of an assist, you can link Mystic Ray into Hyper Mystic Ray or Hyper Mystic Smash for increased damage.

Mystic Ray L 5

Mystic Ray M 6

Mystic Ray H 7

SHUMA-GORATH

DLC

Hyper Combos

Screen	Name	Command	Hits	Damage	Startup	Active	Recovery	Advantage on Hit	Advantage if Guarded	Notes
1	Hyper Mystic Smash	⇨⇩⇙ + ATK ATK	30~60	298,000~ 357,900	18+10	73	69	—	-42	Frames 16-41 invincible, OTG-capable, hard knockdown against airborne opponents, each projectile has 3 frames x 1 high priority durability points, can be mashed for additional hits
2	Hyper Mystic Ray	⇩⇘⇦ + ATK ATK	20	279,700	20+4	30(29)12	100	—	-88	Frames 1-18 invincible, OTG-capable, hard knockdown, 2 beams, beam durability: 20 frames x 1 high priority durability points
3	Chaos Dimension (Level 3 hyper combo)	⇩⇙⇨ + ATK ATK, Ⓗ	1	50,000	10+1	5	20	—	-1	Frames 1-15 invincible, knocks down rival, enters Chaos Dimension state, Chaos Dimension state lasts for 300 frames
4,5	Chaos Dimension Attack (in air OK)	(during Chaos Dimension state) Ⓗ	11~28	350,000~ 435,000	4	3	11	—	—	Unguardable, causes hard knockdown, can be mashed for additional hits

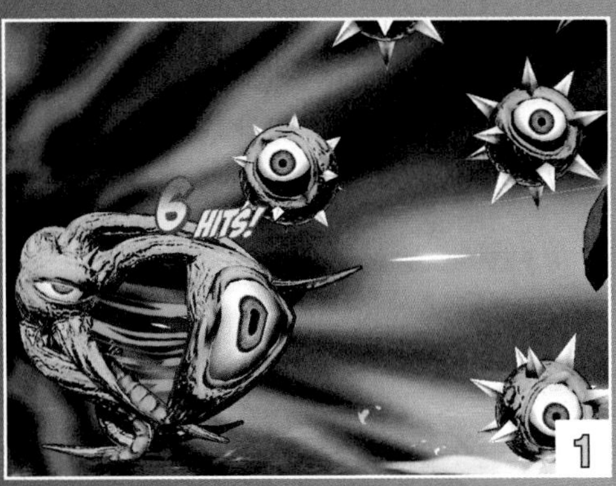

Hyper Mystic Smash: Shuma-Gorath channels his dark power and fires an onslaught of bouncing spiked Shuma-balls across the screen. Each Shuma-ball launches at a random angle, from traveling horizontally across the screen and disappearing quickly to moving in an almost totally vertical motion that keeps the Shuma-ball on the screen for a while. Hyper Mystic Smash is OTG-capable, and it is Shuma-Gorath's most damaging follow up after a combo or the Devitalization command throw. In *UMvC3*, Hyper Mystic Smash can be mashed to increase damage.

Hyper Mystic Smash has some invincibility, but this feature does not kick in until just before the screen freezes. Combined with a slow startup time, this can make Hyper Mystic Smash difficult for Shuma players to use on reaction against an opponent at close range. However, this hyper is difficult for an adversary to punish at longer ranges.

Hyper Mystic Ray: Hyper Mystic Ray fires two high-powered Mystic Rays in succession: the first ends at an angle comparable to Mystic Ray M, and the second ends at the same angle as Mystic Ray H. It has a lot of invincibility frames, which unfortunately end before the attack starts. Regardless, Hyper Mystic Ray is still a great defensive tool to stop competitors from attacking, and you can use its pre-attack invincibility frames to counter a foe rushing at Shuma with an attack. This is your go-to hyper combo for ending combos in the corner—Hyper Mystic Smash usually ends up sending a majority of the Shuma-balls over an opponent's head in this area.

Do not throw out this hyper combo at random because it's ridiculously unsafe on block and can easily be punished by any fullscreen hyper combo.

Chaos Dimension: Chaos Dimension is a level 3 hyper combo that begins with a quick invincible attack that knocks the target into the air and places Shuma-Gorath in a Chaos Dimension state that lasts for 300 frames (five seconds). In the Chaos Dimension state, all Ⓗ attacks become a quick unguardable attack that triggers a cutscene for massive damage. All you have to do is get Shuma-Gorath near the opposing player and hit them while they're in guardstun.

You have a choice after triggering Chaos Dimension and striking with the initial invincible attack: follow up with Ⓗ to deal big damage immediately, or attempt to go for a combo and pile on even more damage—at the risk of running out of time before you can connect with Ⓗ.

Chaos Dimension can result in guaranteed damage against an incoming character after a K.O. or snap back: activate Chaos Dimension before the new opponent comes in, and simply jump forward and press Ⓗ to ruin their day. For more information on using X-Factor to squeeze the most out of Chaos Dimension, see the Advanced Tactics section.

"THIS DIMENSION BELONGS TO ME NOW!"

Battle Plan

Shuma-Gorath may be the lord of the Chaos Dimension, but he's got a bit of a hill to climb in order to compete in the world of *Marvel vs. Capcom.* With a slow airdash, half of his special moves requiring charged inputs, and heavy reliance on assists, Shuma-Gorath doesn't have the wide breadth of tools that most of the cast enjoys. However, knowing how to manipulate the tools Shuma has available to get him within point-blank range can make him a worthy contender.

Air Mystic Smash M is a safe way to cover long distances.

Assists that stop your foe from attacking are perfect for getting your opponent in optimal range of Shuma-Gorath.

Mystic Smash, both air and ground versions, is the key foundation for your initial attempts to have Shuma-Gorath close the distance. On the ground, Mystic Smash H covers the most ground, and its wide arc can pass over projectiles. If you hope to hit your opponent with the attack, however, you must perform Mystic Smash H from around three-fourths of the screen. At fullscreen, Shuma falls short of his rival and is positioned in range for an easy punish. At half-screen or shorter, Shuma passes over the head of all but the largest characters and ends up a considerable distance behind his adversary. At closer distances, you'll want to rely on Mystic Smash M, which travels half the arc of the H-version before dropping straight down on the target's head.

In the air, Shuma-Gorath's airdash combined with air Mystic Smash M can cover as much ground as a grounded Mystic Smash H, with the added benefit of acting as an overhead attack against the opposing player. Air Mystic Smash M actually travels the farthest horizontal distance of all three attacks and is your best bet for catching opponents hanging out at the opposite end of the screen. Keep a sharp eye on your competitor's movements and be prepared to change the strength of the attack depending on their relation to Shuma. Air Mystic Smash covers more ground the higher Shuma-Gorath is in the air, so think about super jumping before performing the attack to gain maximum distance.

If you're having trouble getting Shuma-Gorath into a position to use Mystic Smash against a zoning attacker, remember that Shuma-Gorath's command throw can nullify single hit projectiles. Input → ↘ ↓ ↙ ← + ATK before the projectile hits, and Shuma absorbs the hit, negating all chip damage, avoiding pushback, and gaining 10% hyper combo meter in the process. Thanks to the small amount of blockstun created by absorbing a projectile, you may have enough time to transition into Mystic Smash after Devitalization recovers.

Unfortunately, most of these tactics are very unsafe without crossover assist coverage. A savvy opponent can easily hit Shuma-Gorath out of Mystic Smash with most attacks, and the amount of time Shuma hangs in the air allows competitors to simply move out of the way. Shuma-Gorath benefits the most from assists that force his foe to hunker down to avoid damage. Crossover assists to consider for Shuma-Gorath include: Akuma—β, Rocket Raccoon—γ, and Doctor Doom—α. Call an assist before you attempt any of above methods to get Shuma within his optimal range.

Once you've achieved point-blank range, Shuma-Gorath has some surprisingly strong mix-up tactics at his disposal. Begin your assault with the low-hitting crouching L. Stagger the timing of crouching L attacks to hit opponents trying to use advancing guard, or catch them if they try to jump away. Verify the crouching L hits and transition into a combo, or immediately perform another mix-up against a guarding opponent.

You may also choose to open up with an instant overhead air Mystic Smash L by inputting ↓ ↘ → ↗ + L, which begins the move the moment Shuma leaves the ground. This attack is also sure to catch rivals trained to block low from the staggered crouching L attacks. The instant overhead Mystic Smash is the most frightening tool Shuma-Gorath has at his disposal; it's too fast to guard on reaction, has good range, and allows for combos if hit. If guarded, you're left at point blank range with plenty of frame advantage to go into another mix-up if the opponent does not use advancing guard. Since it's unlikely that any competent player *won't* use advancing guard, concentrate on salvaging the situation and quickly closing the distance again— call your best crossover assist and immediately perform a low-altitude air Mystic Smash M by inputting ↓ ↘ → ↗ + M.

If your challenger continues to block your crouching L assault, you've got them in a prime position to grab with Devitalization. New to *Ultimate Marvel vs. Capcom 3*, Devitalization now leaves you with enough time to pick up the opponent with the OTG-capable Mystic Ray H, after which you can continue juggling! See the Combo Usage section for details.

The jump-cancel properties of crouching H can come in handy if the opposing player blocks one of your chain combos. After crouching H, immediately jump-cancel into an instant overhead air Mystic Smash L to stay within range of your adversary. Should your rival successfully use advancing guard on any of your normal attacks, cancel into Mystic Smash M instead to quickly regain lost ground.

Mystic Smash can quickly regain any ground lost when the opponent uses advancing guard.

Advancing guard should be the least of your worries when mixing up the opponent: if you find yourself getting pushed away too often from advancing guard, you're being to predictable in your offense. Vary the timing of your crouching L attacks more, use more overhead attacks, or go for more grabs. All three options are very strong tools with Shuma-Gorath; don't get fixated on just one attack!

Combined with an airdash, air M has a wide hitbox that can cross up adversaries.

Finally, you can attempt a cross-up using air M. Its amazingly wide hitbox makes it a prime candidate for some cross-up action. When close to your target, have Shuma-Gorath super jump into the air, airdash, and press M immediately. The distance Shuma-Gorath travels from the airdash is enough for air M to connect on the opposite side of his adversary, and chaining into a second air M allows you to continue with a combo. Shuma-Gorath won't always be in a prime position for his offensive game, and you'll need to know how to defend properly and avoid getting his tentacles tied in a knot.

You can rely on the invincibility of Shuma-Gorath's backward dash to avoid some attacks.

On the ground, you can employ Mystic Stare H to control horizontal space. Call an assist that covers air space (like Rocket Raccoon—γ) and fire off the ring of eyeballs. The opponent then gets forced to block the projectiles and assist, giving you a chance to try to close the distance again, or they'll end up with eyeballs stuck to them. In the event that your attackers find themselves with ticking eye-bombs stuck to their chests, they'll be forced to hang back and wait to block the inevitable explosion. There's also a chance that the opposing player might get aggressive in an attempt to hit Shuma and remove the eyes. In this case, stay on the defensive and bide your time till the eyeballs explode... either way, you're in a better position to continue your offense.

Assists can help Shuma-Gorath cover the charge time of his special moves.

You can use Mystic Ray M and H in a similar fashion, but with Shuma-Gorath controlling the air space instead of his assist. In this case, you'll need an assist that locks down the ground, such as Akuma—β, while Shuma fires his beam. An adversary who attempts to jump the assist gets caught by the Mystic Ray beam, and this lets you get Shuma-Gorath in the air to prep a Mystic Smash for closing the distance.

Shuma-Gorath's backdash has some frames of invincibility that you can use to dodge some fast-moving projectiles, although this can be difficult to time. His backdash takes 45 frames to complete, and it's only invulnerable from frames 12-31. For projectiles that travel quickly, such as Taskmaster's arrows, the window provides sufficient time to escape. Shuma can also pass through slower projectiles such as Ryu's Hadoken L, but he'll be hit during the recovery frames of his backdash animation. Use the tactic sparingly, and only when you're sure of the fired projectile's properties.

You have two primary options when facing opponents attempting to jump in on Shuma-Gorath's position: crouching H and an option-select air Mystic Smash H into air throw. Crouching H has a tall hitbox and covers a decent area around Shuma-Gorath, making it a very effective anti-air attack. Once you've confirmed the hit, you can jump-cancel into a combo. Air Mystic Smash H can be option selected into an air throw by simply inputting ↓ ↘ → (hold) + H. You'll either confirm the grab and gain some health and hyper meter, or you'll execute the air Mystic Smash that then allows you to follow up with a combo or continue your mix-up strategies.

COMBO USAGE

I. CR. Ⓜ (2 HITS), Ⓗ CANCEL BACKWARD JUMP, AIR ↓↘→ + Ⓜ, LAND, CR. Ⓗ CANCEL BACKWARD JUMP, AIR ↓↘→ + Ⓜ, LAND, CR. Ⓗ CANCEL CHARGE ←, → + Ⓛ, FORWARD DASH, Ⓢ CANCEL FORWARD SUPER JUMP, AIR Ⓜ (2 HITS), Ⓜ (2 HITS), Ⓗ, Ⓢ, LAND, FORWARD DASH (EYES DETONATE), Ⓢ CANCEL FORWARD SUPER JUMP, AIR Ⓗ, Ⓢ, LAND, ↓↙← + ATK ATK

634,800 damage, 5% meter gain

Shuma-Gorath's crouching Ⓜ attack has much more range than his crouching Ⓛ attack and is only a single frame slower, which often makes it more useful as an opening attack. Crouching Ⓜ pulls the enemy towards you— if this opening is guarded, you're in range to cancel into a late Devitalization H to grab the enemy, or chain into a delayed crouching Ⓗ to counter hit attempts to stop the throw. Jump-cancel the crouching Ⓗ into an immediate air Mystic Smash M for a quick overhead attack and to maintain offensive momentum.

Whenever possible, you should start this combo with staggered crouching Ⓛ attacks to more easily salvage your offense if the opening attacks are guarded: immediately perform an air Mystic Smash L overhead attack, grab them with Devitaliation H, cross-up by airdashing and using air Ⓜ, or keep them guarding with more crouching Ⓛ attacks! Adding two crouching Ⓛ attacks to the beginning of the combo only reduces the damage by a minimal 700 points.

There are two points to remember when learning this combo: after hitting crouching Ⓗ, you'll want to jump in a direction that won't cause Mystic Smash M to end up behind the opponent, usually this will be backwards, unless the combo was started from a long range crouching Ⓜ. After the Mystic Stare eyeballs detonate, wait for the opponent to fall a little before juggling with Ⓢ. This prevents the opponent from being too high in the air to hit with the final air Ⓢ attack.

II. ↓↘→↗ + Ⓛ, LAND, CR. Ⓜ (2 HITS), Ⓗ CANCEL BACKWARD JUMP, AIR ↓↘→ + Ⓜ, LAND, CR. Ⓗ CANCEL CHARGE ←, → + Ⓛ, FORWARD DASH, Ⓢ CANCEL FORWARD SUPER JUMP, AIR Ⓜ (2 HITS), Ⓜ (2 HITS), Ⓗ, Ⓢ, LAND, FORWARD DASH (EYES DETONATE), Ⓢ CANCEL FORWARD SUPER JUMP, AIR Ⓗ, Ⓢ, LAND, ↓↙← + ATK ATK

573,800 damage, 3% meter loss meter loss

The opening air Mystic Smash acts as an instant overhead, and is the centerpiece of Shuma-Gorath's offense. If guarded, attack with a low-hitting crouching Ⓛ, grab with Devitalization, or immediately do another instant overhead air Mystic Smash again.

III. FRONT OR BACK THROW, CHARGE ↓, ↑ + Ⓗ, {IF ENEMY IS MIDSCREEN, CR. Ⓜ (2 HITS), Ⓢ CANCEL FORWARD SUPER JUMP, AIR Ⓜ (2 HITS), Ⓜ (2 HITS), Ⓗ, Ⓢ} OR {IF ENEMY IS CORNERED, CR. Ⓗ CANCEL BACKWARDS JUMP, AIR ↓↘→ + Ⓜ, LAND, CR. Ⓗ CANCEL CHARGE ←, → + Ⓛ, Ⓢ CANCEL VERTICAL SUPER JUMP, AIR AIR Ⓜ, Ⓜ, Ⓗ, Ⓢ, LAND, FORWARD DASH (EYES DETONATE), Ⓢ CANCEL FORWARD SUPER JUMP, AIR Ⓗ, Ⓢ, LAND, ↓↙← + ATK ATK}

197,500~529,700 damage, 73~24% meter gain

Shuma-Gorath can use his normal throw to start combos, giving you an even more potent mix-up when up close. The Mystic Ray H must be done immediately after the throw recovers, or else you run the risk of the enemy ground recovering behind you and punishing with a combo of their choosing.

This same combo can be used from Devitalization or air Ⓢ. Against larger characters, the OTG-capable Mystic Ray H can be followed by crouching Ⓜ, Ⓗ into air Mystic Smash loops for much better damage.

IV. FRONT AIR THROW, AIR Ⓜ (1 HIT), Ⓜ (2 HITS), LAND, FORWARD JUMP, AIR Ⓜ (2 HITS), Ⓗ, ↑ + Ⓗ, LAND, CR. Ⓗ CANCEL BACKWARD JUMP, AIR ↓↘→ + Ⓜ, LAND, CR. Ⓗ CANCEL CHARGE ←, → + Ⓛ, FORWARD DASH, Ⓢ CANCEL FORWARD SUPER JUMP, AIR Ⓜ, Ⓜ, Ⓗ, Ⓢ, LAND, FORWARD DASH (EYES DETONATE), Ⓢ CANCEL FORWARD SUPER JUMP, AIR Ⓗ, Ⓢ, LAND, ↓↙← + ATK ATK

551,900 damage, 32% meter gain

Shuma-Gorath's air throw allows you to juggle opponents before they hit the ground. This allows you to perform one of the most damaging air throw combos in the game, gain some vitality back, and still enjoy a net profit in meter gain!

V. CR. Ⓜ (2 HITS), Ⓗ CANCEL BACKWARD JUMP, AIR ↓↘→ + Ⓜ, LAND, CR. Ⓗ CANCEL BACKWARD JUMP, AIR ↓↘→ + Ⓜ, LAND, CR. Ⓗ CANCEL CHARGE ←, → + Ⓛ, FORWARD DASH, Ⓢ CANCEL FORWARD SUPER JUMP, AIR Ⓜ (2 HITS), Ⓜ (2 HITS), Ⓗ, Ⓢ, LAND, FORWARD DASH (EYES DETONATE), Ⓢ CANCEL FORWARD SUPER JUMP, AIR Ⓗ, Ⓢ, LAND, ↓↙← + ATK ATK X-FACTOR ↓↙← + ATK ATK

856,800~918,800 damage, 5% meter gain

A simple X-Factor version of **Combo I** that adds damage to its end when it's needed. Using X-Factor with Shuma-Gorath in combos isn't normally recommended however; it's generally best to save it for Chaos Dimension set-ups. Don't hesitate to pop X-Factor if the ensuing combo will finish off the opponent's final character, though!

If you have three bars left over after vanquishing a character, activate the Chaos Dimension hyper combo to do some guaranteed X-Factor boosted damage against the next adversary. See the Advanced Tactics section for details.

ADVANCED TACTICS

CHAOS REIGNS

Chaos Dimension is the most damaging attack in Shuma-Gorath's arsenal. As a level 3 hyper combo, that damage comes at a great cost, but the ability to get a guaranteed hit against incoming characters makes it well worth the meter! After knocking an opponent out or hitting them with a snap back, immediately input ↓ ↘ → + ATK ATK to put Shuma in his Chaos Dimension state. Then simply jump forward and press H as the new character comes in, and watch as Shuma-Gorath uses his dark magic to bring the pain.

With X-Factor activated, the results can be even more damaging, putting your rival in a very dangerous starting position. Check out the various damage levels of Chaos Dimension:

Shuma-Gorath is guaranteed to send an incoming enemy into the Chaos Dimension.

- **No X-Factor: 350,000~435,000 damage**
- **Level 1 X-Factor: 446,300~554,000 damage**
- **Level 2 X-Factor: 507,000~630,700 damage**
- **Level 3 X-Factor: 568,700~715,000 damage**

That's a whole lot of guaranteed damage for the cost of three hyper meter bars. Don't forget to mash those attack buttons to pile on the extra damage!

COMBO APPENDIX

GENERAL EXECUTION TIPS

If you plan on following up air S with a Mystic Stare OTG hit, immediately begin holding ↓ after pressing S. Holding ↓ too soon can result in an unwanted TAC attempt.

When launching the enemy after a Mystic Stare eyeball detonation, wait until the opponent's character drops lower to the ground; this helps keep your foe low enough to hit with an air S attack

AS SHUMA-GORATH COMES IN: AIR H, ↑ + H CANCEL ↓ ↘ → + M

Notes	Damage
↑ + S or → + S or ↓ + S TAC to	Varies based on damage scaling

→ ↘ ↓ ↙ ← + H, CHARGE ↓, ↑ + H, (IF ENEMY IS MIDSCREEN, CR. M (2 HITS), S CANCEL FORWARD SUPER JUMP, AIR M (2 HITS), M (2 HITS), H, S) OR (IF ENEMY IS CORNERED, CR. H CANCEL BACKWARDS JUMP, AIR ↓ ↘ → + M, LAND, CR. H CANCEL CHARGE ←, → + L, S CANCEL VERTICAL SUPER JUMP, AIR M, M, H, S, LAND, FORWARD DASH (EYES DETONATE), S CANCEL FORWARD SUPER JUMP, AIR H, S, LAND, ↓ ↙ ← + ATK ATK)

Notes	Damage
Combo from Devitalization	369,000~701,200 damage, 68~19% meter gain

CR. M (2 HITS), H CANCEL FORWARD JUMP, AIR M (2 HITS), H, ↑ + H, LAND, FORWARD JUMP, AIR M (2 HITS), H, ↑ + H, LAND, FORWARD JUMP, AIR M (2 HITS), H CANCEL ↓ ↘ → + L, ↓ ↘ → + ATK ATK, CR. M (2 HITS), S CANCEL FORWARD SUPER JUMP, AIR M (2 HITS), M (2 HITS) CANCEL H (MASH ATK)

Notes	Damage
—	779,400 damage, 216% meter loss

FRONT AIR THROW, AIR M (1 HIT), M (2 HITS), LAND, FORWARD JUMP, AIR M (2 HITS), H, ↑ + H, LAND, FORWARD JUMP, AIR M (2 HITS), H, ↑ + H, LAND, FORWARD JUMP, AIR M (2 HITS), H CANCEL ↓ ↘ → + L, ↓ ↘ → + ATK ATK, CR. M (2 HITS), S CANCEL FORWARD SUPER JUMP, AIR M (2 HITS), M (2 HITS) CANCEL H (MASH ATK)

Notes	Damage
—	691,900 damage, 196% meter loss

DLC

JILL

"CHRIS... RACCOON CITY... S.T.A.R.S.... WHAT ARE THESE MEMORIES?"

Bio

REAL NAME

Jill Valentine

OCCUPATION

BSAA Operative

ABILITIES

Various abilities including masterful unlocking abilities, bomb disposal, hand-to-hand combat, and gun skills learned during American military training.

WEAPONS

Many different firearms, such as handguns, sub-machine guns, shotguns, rocket launchers, etc. She is also able to use military knives.

PROFILE

To save Chris during a fight, she threw herself off a cliff along with Wesker. Her body was never found and she was presumed dead; however, she survived the fall and was taken by Wesker for one of his experiments. After being subjected to the Uroboros tests, she was outfitted with a mind control device, making her into a puppet soldier.

FIRST APPEARANCE

Resident Evil (1996)

POWER GRID

2	INTELLIGENCE
2	STRENGTH
3	SPEED
2	STAMINA
1	ENERGY PROJECTION
4	FIGHTING ABILITY

*This is biographical, and does not represent an evaluation of the in-game combat potential of this hero.

Alternate Costumes

Overview

Vitality	850,000
Chain Combo Archetype	Hunter Series

X-Factor Boost	Damage	Speed
Level 1 (3 teammates remaining)	125%	115%
Level 2 (2 teammates remaining)	140%	130%
Level 3 (1 teammate remaining)	155%	145%

Your main goal with Jill should be to position Jill to force Feral Crouch mix-ups on her opposition. Jill doesn't have the best options from fullscreen, but her abilities begin to shine as she gets closer to the opposing character. Boasting long meter-building combos as well as THC-friendly hyper combos, Jill excels in close-quarters combat. Getting Jill near her competitor is advantageous because:

- **Jill's Feral Crouch mix-ups can be extremely difficult to defend against**
- **Jill can blow through her rival's offense with Feral Crouch Ⓗ (Somersault), leading to a full combo**

How can you get Jill get close to her opposition?

- **Using Arrow Kick to close the distance between Jill and the target**
- **Using forward Teleports to get close and up-forward Teleports to dodge projectiles**
- **Forcing your way in with the priority of her air basic attacks and crouching Ⓜ**

Tuning Since Original MvC3

Jill is relatively unchanged from her *MvC3* counterpart, but the removal of the "THC Glitch" indirectly reduces her damage output by a large margin. Jill's ability to X-Factor in the air makes for interesting combos when used during Machine Gun Spray.

Also, Jill—β Arrow Kick no longer causes hard knockdown.

Attack Set

Standing Basic Attacks

Screen	Command	Hits	Damage	Meter Gain	Startup	Active	Recovery	Advantage on Hit	Advantage if Guarded	Notes
1	Standing Ⓛ	1	33,000	264	4	2	12	0	-1	Chains into Ⓛ attacks
2	Standing Ⓜ	1	45,000	360	7	3	20	-4	-6	—
3	Standing Ⓗ	1	63,000	504	9	3	21	0	-2	—

1

2

3

Crouching Basic Attacks

Screen	Command	Hits	Damage	Meter Gain	Startup	Active	Recovery	Advantage on Hit	Advantage if Guarded	Notes
1	Crouching Ⓛ	1	30,000	240	5	2	11	+1	0	Low attack, chains into Ⓛ attacks
2	Crouching Ⓜ	1	43,000	344	8	12	16	-9	-11	Low attack, chains into standing Ⓜ
3	Crouching Ⓗ	1	60,000	480	9	3	26	—	-7	Low attack, knocks down

1

2

3

Ground Special Attack—Launcher

Screen	Command	Hits	Damage	Meter Gain	Startup	Active	Recovery	Advantage on Hit	Advantage if Guarded	Notes
1	Ⓢ (while standing or crouching)	1	70,000	560	8	3	24	—	-5	Launcher, not special- or hyper combo-cancelable

1

Air Basic Attacks

Screen	Command	Hits	Damage	Meter Gain	Startup	Active	Recovery	Advantage on Hit	Advantage if Guarded	Notes
1	Air Ⓛ	1	35,000	280	5	7	6	+11	+10	Overhead attack
2	Air Ⓜ	1	50,000	400	8	3	20	+16	+14	Overhead attack
3	Air Ⓗ	1	65,000	520	9	4	21	+19	+17	Overhead attack

1

2

3

Air Special Attacks—Flying Screen and Air Exchange

Air (S) causes a hard knockdown when used in a launcher combo (this is sometimes called flying screen). When used outside of a launcher combo, air (S) behaves mostly like another basic attack. Air exchange attacks, performed by inputting a direction plus (S), are only possible during a launcher combo. Exchange hits initiate team aerial combos by tagging in the next available character to continue the air combo.

Screen	Command	Hits	Damage	Meter Gain	Startup	Active	Recovery	Advantage on Hit	Advantage if Guarded	Notes
1	Air (S)	1	68,000	544	9	6	21	+16	+14	Overhead attack
2	Air ⇧ + (S) (during launcher combo)	2	105,00	880	10	3	19	—	—	Tags in next available ally while lofting foe upward
3	Air ⇨ or ⇦ + (S) (during launcher combo)	2	95,000	800	11	5	20	—	—	Tags in next available ally while causing wall bounce, erases 1 hyper meter bar from opponent
4	Air ⇩ + (S) (during launcher combo)	2	95,000	800	10	5	21	—	—	Tags in next available ally while causing ground bounce, generates 1 hyper meter bar

1

2

3

4

Command Attacks

Command attacks resemble basic attacks but have different chaining and canceling properties. It's usually possible to chain *into* a command attack from basic attacks, but most command attacks cannot be chained from or canceled themselves.

Screen	Name	Command	Hits	Damage	Meter Gain	Startup	Active	Recovery	Advantage on Hit	Advantage if Guarded	Notes
1	Reverse Roundhouse	⇦ + (H)	1	63,000	504	11	4	21	-1	-3	Chains from any basic attack
2	Sickle Kick	⇨ + (H)	1	65,000	52	23	3	12	+9	+7	Overhead, recovers in Feral Crouch

1

2

Throws

Throws are for snagging passive or blocking foes. Since throws are active so quickly, you can also use them to preemptively toss opposing characters out of their offense. Combos are usually possible after throws, one way or another.

Screen	Command	Hits	Damage	Meter Gain	Startup	Active	Notes
1	⇨ + (H) (ground)	2	80,000	800	1	1	Hard knockdown
	⇦ + (H) (ground)	2	80,000	800	1	1	Hard knockdown
2	⇨ + (H) (air)	2	80,000	800	1	1	Hard knockdown
	⇦ + (H) (air)	2	80,000	800	1	1	Hard knockdown

1

2

As a Partner—Crossover Assists

Screen	Type	P1+P2 Crossover Combination Hyper Combo	Description	Hits	Damage	Meter Gain	Startup	Active	Recovery (this crossover assist)	Recovery (other partner)	Notes
1	Jill—α	Machine Gun Spray	Cartwheel Kick	1	80,000	640	39	10	116	86	Ground bounces foe
2	Jill—β	Machine Gun Spray	Arrow Kick	1	100,000	800	44	9	119	89	Wall bounces adversary
3	Jill—γ	Machine Gun Spray	Somersault Kick	1	90,000	720	34	10	133	103	Knocks down competitor

Jill's melee-oriented offense is reflected in her crossover assists, as well. Jill—α Cartwheel Kick is fairly easy to start combos from, causing a ground bounce and knocking opponents slightly into the air. Jill—β causes a wall bounce into a hard knockdown, so it is great for cross-ups and extending combos. Somersault's invincibility is noticeably absent from the Jill—γ crossover assist. However, the attack retains all of its properties as a crossover counter, making it one of the best crossover counters in the entire game. It is invincible on startup and can be jump canceled or Feral Crouch canceled into a combo.

Snap Back

Screen	Command	Hits	Damage	Meter Gain	Startup	Active	Recovery	Advantage on Hit	Advantage if Guarded
1	↓↘→ + P1 or P2	1	50,000	500 (-1 hyper meter bar)	2	3	21	—	-2

Notes

On hit, snap back forces the opposing point character to be replaced by an assist. Opposing assist calls or tag outs are also locked out for 4 seconds

Special Moves

Screen	Name	Command	Hits	Damage	Meter Gain	Startup	Active	Recovery	Advantage on Hit	Advantage if Guarded	Notes
1	Flip Kick	↓↘→ + L	1	70,000	560	13	10	13	—	-1	Knocks down opponent, recovers in Feral Crouch
2	Cartwheel Kick	↓↘→ + M	1	80,000	640	15	10	21	—	-9	Ground bounces competitor, recovers in Feral Crouch
3	Arrow Kick	↓↘→ + H	1	100,000	800	20	9	27	—	-14	Wall bounces target, hard knockdown, Jill bounces backward in an airborne state if hit
4	Double Knee Drop L	(in air) ↓↘→ + L	1	70,000	560	18	Until grounded	11	+10	+8	Overhead attack, hard knockdown against airborne adversaries
4	Double Knee Drop M	(in air) ↓↘→ + M	1	80,000	640	23	Until grounded	11	+15	+13	Overhead attack, ground bounces airborne rivals, hard knockdown against airborne opponents if ground bounce is already used
4	Double Knee Drop H	(in air) ↓↘→ + H	1	90,000	720	30	Until grounded	14	+33	+5	Overhead attack, staggers grounded targets, ground bounces airborne rivals, hard knockdown against airborne opponents if ground bounce is already used
5	Fallen Prey	→↓↘ + L	2	98,000	980	8	2	31	—	-11	Low attack, hard knockdown, OTG- capable
6	Ensnarement	→↓↘ + M	2	98,000	980	10	3	28	—	-9	Hard knockdown
7	Position Exchange	→↓↘ + H	1	—	0	10	1	25	+4	—	Throw, switches sides with opposing characters
8	Feral Crouch	↓↓ + S	—	—	0	10	—	—	—	—	Cannot guard while in Feral Crouch, press S again to cancel
9	Low Sweep	(During Feral Crouch) L	1	45,000	360	8	4	26	-6	-8	Low attack, recovers in Feral Crouch, cancelable into special attacks and hyper combos
10	Jumping Roundhouse	(During Feral Crouch) M	1	85,000	680	20	3	23	—	-4	Wall bounces opponent
11	Somersault Kick	(During Feral Crouch) H	1	90,000	720	10	10	41	0	-29	Frames 1-14 invincible, knocks down target, jump- cancelable
12	Teleport	(During Feral Crouch) ←, ↘, ↑, ↗, or →/(During Mad Beast) input any direction	—	—	0	9	6	2	—	—	Frames 9-14 invincible, can pass through competitors, Teleport is cancelable into special moves and hyper combos at any time

1

Flip Kick: Jill performs a kick while doing a back flip, automatically leaving her in Feral Crouch stance. Flip Kick can be useful in combos, since it inflicts a large amount of hitstun, leaving the opposing character vulnerable in the air for a long period of time. Manually canceling Flip Kick into Feral Crouch with ⇩ ⇩ + (S) is important because it allows combos that are otherwise not possible, such as Flip Kick into Jumping Roundhouse, or even Flip Kick into another Flip Kick! You can also use it for offensive pressure, as it is a mere -1 frame advantage when guarded and a possible +11 frame advantage when canceled into Feral Crouch.

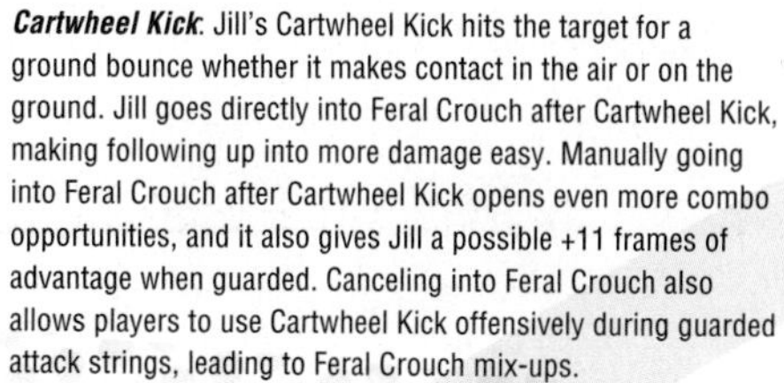

Cartwheel Kick: Jill's Cartwheel Kick hits the target for a ground bounce whether it makes contact in the air or on the ground. Jill goes directly into Feral Crouch after Cartwheel Kick, making following up into more damage easy. Manually going into Feral Crouch after Cartwheel Kick opens even more combo opportunities, and it also gives Jill a possible +11 frames of advantage when guarded. Canceling into Feral Crouch also allows players to use Cartwheel Kick offensively during guarded attack strings, leading to Feral Crouch mix-ups.

2

Cartwheel Kick also has a deceptive vertical hitbox, often bringing down opponents who are above Jill's head during a combo. Cartwheel Kick can always be relied upon during combos, as it resets the opposing character's positioning by placing the target directly in front of Jill. You can always follow up Cartwheel Kick with a Somersault for further combos.

3

Arrow Kick: Use Jill's Arrow Kick to quickly and offensively close the distance between Jill and her competitor. If it hits, Arrow Kick causes a wall bounce and leaves Jill in a jump state that you can use to follow up with a full combo in or near the corner. Though Arrow Kick seems airborne, Jill is considered grounded the entire time until it hits. Therefore, cancel Arrow Kick into Feral Crouch or a hyper combo if it misses or is guarded. Canceling a guarded Arrow Kick not only makes it safer to use, but it also leads to Feral Crouch mix-ups and frame traps due to the guardstun that Arrow Kick creates, leaving Jill at a +11 frame advantage.

When used in conjunction with any far-reaching crossover assist (such as a beam or projectile), Jill players can effectively control the ground and force Feral Crouch mix-ups. Keep in mind that Arrow Kick can only be canceled during its animation or when guarded, not when it hits.

4

Double Knee Drop: An aerial overhead attack, Jill drops straight down with a knee attack. This attack causes a staggering amount of hitstun (+34 on hit), making it extremely easy to follow up with a combo. The Double Knee Drop is also Jill's only aerial special move, and it can be used to change the trajectory of her air movement to keep its use from becoming too predictable. With this attack, you can punish opponents who are trying to set up an offense underneath Jill, such as dashing under for a quick cross-up. The (H) version of this move has considerably more startup than its (L) and (M) counterparts, so keep this in mind when using it as a mobility tool. You can also use Double Knee Drop as a combo follow-up to Jill's ⇨ + (H) overhead attack, making for an easy combo follow-up on hit.

5

Fallen Prey: A low-hitting attack that is OTG-capable, going directly into a throw if it hits. Add this move for extra damage after any hard knockdown, including aerial combos and ground/air throws. Unfortunately, while the opposing character is being thrown, they are invincible to all other attacks, making it nearly impossible for Jill players to use crossover assists to extend the combo. However, Viewtiful Joe—γ and Sentinel—β will connect after Fallen Prey if called immediately before performing it.

6

Ensnarement: Ensnarement causes Jill to toss her competitor behind her, causing a hard knockdown. Easy to land during combos, follow it up with Fallen Prey, Machine Gun Spray, or even a juggled (L) or (M) if the opposing character is tossed into the corner, leading to an extended combo opportunity. Because the opponent is put in a hard knockdown state, you can use Ensnarement simply to end combos as a positional tool—Jill's rivals are left to get up into any mix-ups that you may have ready.

7

Position Change: Once the opposing player is conditioned to guard your attacks, you can mix it up by using Position Change instead. A successfully landed Position Change can link into Jill's standing (L) for a full combo. The timing to successfully land the standing (L) attack is strict: the window is technically only a single frame, but the game allows you to input basic attacks two frames early, giving you a three-frame window. Once your target becomes wary of Position Change, you can use Jill's crouching (L) to hit their attempts at jumping away from the throw.

8

Feral Crouch: Much of Jill's offense stems from her Feral Crouch stance. During Feral Crouch, you gain access to three special moves unique to the stance, as well as Jill's Teleport. In addition, almost all of Jill's grounded basic attacks and special moves can be canceled into Feral Crouch. Even though Jill is unable to guard during this stance, continuing into Feral Crouch after hit/guarded special moves actually reduces the risks of Jill's offense because it avoids the recovery time of slower moves. Lastly, Jill is not limited to performing attacks unique to Feral Crouch during the stance, as she retains all her special moves and hyper combos at her disposal.

To be able to calculate for yourself what Jill's frame advantage is after canceling an attack into Feral Crouch, you can perform some simple math:

Add together the active and recovery frames of the attack

Add the sum to the attack's frame advantage

Subtract 11 (the total duration of the Feral Crouch, plus the one additional active frame of the canceled attack)

The difference is the new frame advantage of canceling the attack into Feral Crouch!

9

Low Sweep: Pressing (L) during Feral Crouch makes for a quick low attack that is special-cancelable as well as cancelable right back into Feral Crouch. If your competitor expects a high attack (such as Teleport straight up into air (H)) or wants to punish Jill's Feral Crouch, perform Low Sweep to surprise your opponent and hit for a combo.

If Low Sweep isn't canceled, Low Sweep automatically returns Jill to Feral Crouch.

10

Jumping Roundhouse: Jill delivers a roundhouse kick that causes a wall bounce. Unlike Arrow Kick, Jumping Roundhouse can be canceled into Feral Crouch both when guarded and if it hits, making follow-ups much easier. On hit, cancel into Feral Crouch to Teleport to follow up the wall bounce with any combo of your choice. When guarded, Roundhouse Kick causes the same amount of blockstun as Jill's other special moves, giving Jill a +11 frame advantage and making Feral Crouch mix-ups an ideal follow-up.

11

Somersault: Learning to properly use Jill's Somersault is paramount for offensive and defensive playing alike. Somersault is one of best special moves in the game. It is cancelable into Feral Crouch and jump-cancelable, it starts some of Jill's most damaging combos, it perfectly combos into either of her level 1 hyper combos, and it has a large window of invincibility. If timed correctly, you can even use Somersault to stop many opposing hyper combos!

On hit, Somersault can be canceled into Machine Gun Spray or Raven Spike, or jump canceled into her jump loop (normal jump into air (M), (M), (H), (S)). When guarded, players using Jill can jump cancel away to safety, jump cancel straight up or forward for continued pressure, or Feral Crouch cancel into any of her special moves to keep an adversary guessing.

12

Teleport: A staple of her arsenal, Jill can teleport out of Feral Crouch in one of five directions. It is invulnerable for a short period of time, and you can use it to quickly close distances, retreat from a dangerous position, or mix up your competitor by passing through their character. However, it should be noted that Jill isn't instantly invincible; there is a 9 frame vulnerable window before Jill becomes immune to harm.

The up-forward version of the Teleport automatically corrects Jill's direction if she happens to cross over her foe. Crossing up with up-forward Teleport into falling (H), or forward Teleport into crouching (L) can be a nightmare for opposing players to deal with. To mix it up further, inputting the command for Position Change during Feral Crouch causes Jill to Teleport toward her competitor and quickly cancel into the throw for unguardable damage.

Also, keep in mind that forward and up-forward Teleports always cross up if your target is close enough, even if the opponent is cornered.

Hyper Combos

Screen	Name	Command	Hits	Damage	Startup	Active	Recovery	Advantage on Hit	Advantage if Guarded	Notes
1	Machine Gun Spray	↓↘→ + ATK ATK	Max 22	196,200 (11,000 per bullet)	10+9	38	23	0	-3	Frames 1-20 invincible, OTG- capable, each projectile has 3 high priority durability points
2	Raven Spike	→↓↘ + ATK ATK	7	290,800	8+1	5	36	—	-19	Hard knockdown
3	Mad Beast (Level 3 hyper comb)	↓↙← + ATK ATK	—	—	10+1	—	1	—	—	Frames 1-10 invincible, leaves Jill in Mad Beast state for 600 frames, all movement becomes Feral Crouch Teleports during Mad Beast state, all special moves become cancelable into Teleports, able to crouch block only, able to perform up to 3 Teleports in air

1

Machine Gun Spray: Jill covers the screen with a spray of bullets. Touting 20 frames of invulnerability and quick startup, take advantage of Machine Gun Spray to get Jill out of a bind, plow through your adversary's offense, or chain as part of a combo. Because of its invulnerability and screen coverage, this hyper combo resets the pace of the battle in your favor.

To get full damage out of Machine Gun Spray, position Jill so that the opposing character is right next to her during the apex of her flip, which is about the height of a normal jump. Setting up Machine Gun Spray correctly can mean a difference of 100-200k damage. Canceling a Feral Crouch Somersault into Machine Gun Spray makes for an ideal combo finisher.

You can utilize the quick duration of the hyper combo in several different ways. With a slower crossover assist, you can call your crossover assist and immediately perform Machine Gun Spray before the assist even comes into play. Depending on the crossover assist, you can gain positional advantage and momentum from this technique if you have Jill recover before the duration of the crossover assist.

If Jill is on point, using crossover combinations is also a viable tactic. Chances are that Machine Gun Spray will recover faster than the hyper combos of Jill's teammates, letting you mount an offense while the opposing player is still dealing with the crossover combination. If the crossover combination is guarded, it's an opportune time to go for an overhead with → ↓ (H) or Feral Crouch Teleport mix-ups.

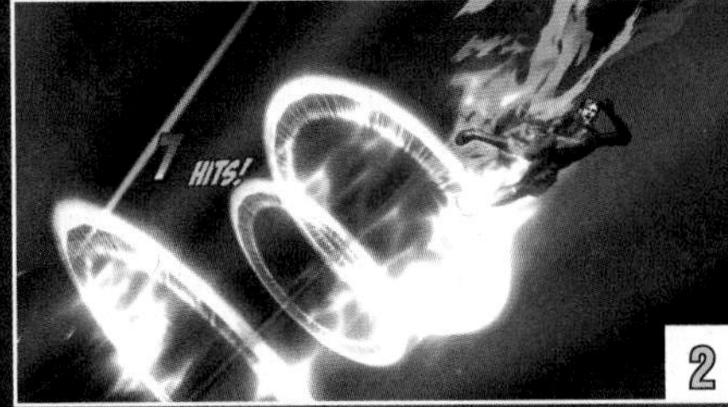

2

Raven Spike: Great for ending combos, Raven Spike sets your adversary up for easy THC combos. The vertical hitbox and speed of Raven Spike can be very deceptive, and you can use it defensively to catch your competitor off guard. When using it outside of combos, make sure you have a hyper combo to safely THC into, as Raven Spike has enough recovery for the opposing character to easily punish.

While Raven Spike used to be a great way to start the "THC Glitch" trick, in *Ultimate Marvel vs. Capcom 3*, the glitch has been completely removed. This essentially removes Jill's ability to knock out most characters with a single combo.

3

Mad Beast: Jill goes into a special stance that is unique in that:

- **All directional inputs are now Teleports, even in the air**
- **All special moves can now be canceled into Teleport**
- **All basic attacks can be canceled into Teleport**

Given that most of Jill's attacks are Teleport-cancelable, you can perform massive combos and resets during Mad Beast. In addition, Jill can still build meter during Mad Beast mode (unlike most other power-up hypers), and she retains her Mad Beast mode even if switched out to another teammate. Though Jill can still guard low during Mad Beast, she is unable to guard standing, and she is highly vulnerable during this mode. Therefore, utilizing Mad Beast either during combos or while your target is already pinned down minimizes the risk taken.

Since Teleport can be instantly canceled into special moves, this allows Jill to perform what looks like special moves canceled into other special moves: perform a special move, cancel it into Teleport, then immediately cancel the Teleport into a special move! This allows for fun combos that involve repeated alternating Flip Kicks and Cartwheel Kicks!

Battle Plan

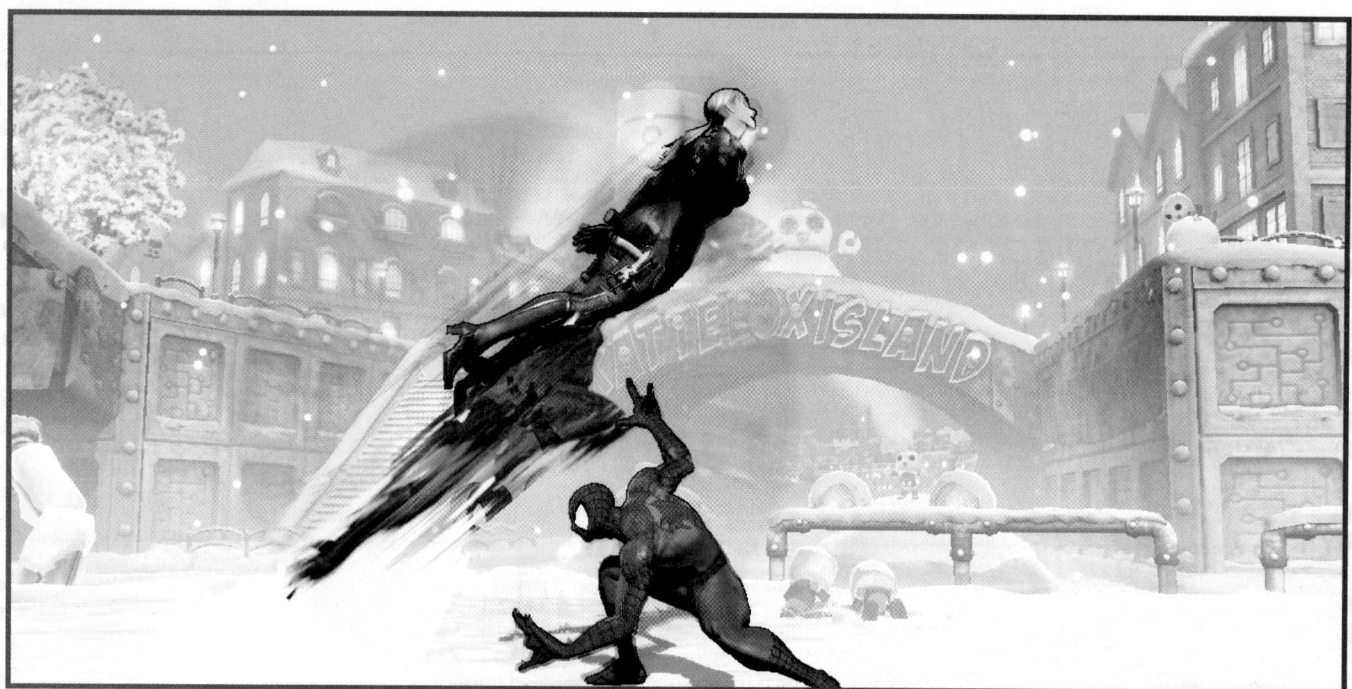

Attacks performed from an upwards-angled Teleport will always face the proper direction.

The majority of Jill's damage comes from her fighting abilities up close, so it is important to master closing the distance between Jill and her competitor.

You can approach this in several different ways. The most straightforward way is to simply wavedash or jump forward while using a crossover assist to cover your approach. Jill's overall speed and the priority of her jumping Ⓛ and Ⓜ attacks in an air-to-air situation force opponents to think twice about their counterattacks. Using Jill's crouching Ⓜ during a straightforward offensive can be useful, as well: not only does it force adversaries to guard low, but it also sneaks below most projectiles and even numerous basic attacks. You can cancel the slide into any special moves at any time. Cancel into Arrow Kick or Feral Crouch to Teleport for added distance, or perform crouching Ⓗ into Flip Kick or Cartwheel Kick for a combo if the slide hits.

You can also have Jill approach by using her Arrow Kick. Arrow Kick covers a significant distance, so use the move as a sort of offensive dash, tagging any opposing characters or crossover assists in its path. Since it is Feral Crouch-cancelable when guarded, it can be used to set up Feral Crouch mix-ups, too.

The fastest way that Jill can approach is via her Teleport. Teleport is Feral Crouch-cancelable, so Jill can traverse the screen quickly by performing a Teleport into Feral Crouch into yet another Teleport. This method of approach is especially vulnerable to crossover assists, so be wary of the type of crossover assists that the opposing player has at their disposal. The window of invulnerability that Teleport → possesses can be used to pass through projectiles, but it can be difficult to time consistently. As an alternative, you can use Teleport ↗ to dodge incoming projectiles, however it does not grant as much horizontal distance as Teleport → does.

Once close, you can utilize Jill's lightning-fast standing and crouching Ⓛ to start an offense. Crouching Ⓜ is also a great attack to start an offense. This slide attack goes under most projectiles and many basic attacks, as well. After your opponent is conditioned to guarding low, surprise them with → + Ⓗ for an overhead attack. Performing → + Ⓗ automatically puts Jill into Feral Crouch stance, so you can use the easy input technique (see the Advanced Tactics section) by holding down Ⓛ to link into Low Sweep, which can then be followed with ↓ ↘ → + Ⓛ or Ⓜ CANCEL ↓ ↓ + Ⓢ into a combo.

If your ground attack strings are ever guarded, cancel into Feral Crouch to begin Jill's strong mix-up game. Mix-ups via Feral Crouch will be your main source of doing damage. Feral Crouch mix-ups can be started by canceling into Feral Crouch from a guarded Arrow Kick or a guarded cr. Ⓛ, Ⓜ, st. Ⓗ. If your opponent uses advancing guard against either of these attacks, perform a Teleport → to get right back in for another attack string canceled into Feral Crouch.

Jill has many ways to open opponents up with Feral Crouch. Once foes realize advancing guard is useless against her Teleport, you can start using teleports to mix them up. Teleporting → at close range causes Jill to cross the opponent up, even in the corner. After teleporting, complete the cross-up attack with crouching Ⓛ, or use a crossover assist to complement the cross-up, which is faster if timed so that Jill crosses up the moment the crossover assist connects. This mix-up is not foolproof, however. An opponent who is mashing a quick Ⓛ attack can catch Jill during her teleport recovery. To counter this, you can teleport ↗ for an overhead cross-up instead. After the teleport, fall with air Ⓗ into a combo. ↗ teleports will cross-up even in the corner, and Jill will automatically face the correct direction so that subsequent attacks will never whiff. Opponents can counter this with an air throw, so inputting → + Ⓗ acts as an option select: an air throw attempt will be escaped, otherwise air Ⓗ will be performed for an overhead. If either of these mix-ups are guarded, you can perform another basic attack chain canceled into Feral Crouch to keep your offense flowing. A third mix-up to add to this is performing Low Sweep from Feral Crouch. If delayed slightly, Low Sweep acts as a frame trap to catch opponents who are either trying to jump out of the mix-up or counter with an attack of their own. If connected, cancel into ↓ ↘ → + Ⓛ CANCEL ↓ ↓ + Ⓢ to continue the combo. To keep your teleport mix-ups tight, make sure to hold the direction in which you wish to teleport immediately after your ↓ ↓ + Ⓢ input. This ensures that Jill will teleport as soon as Feral Crouch's startup frames have passed.

Some opponents will try to counter-attack the Feral Crouch mix-ups with quick attacks of their own. To counter this, you can perform a delayed Somersault from Feral Crouch. After canceling into Feral Crouch from a guarded attack, delay your Ⓗ input to allow your opponent's guardstun to pass, otherwise it will be a true guard string. If opponents try any sort of attack, the invulnerability on Somersault's startup will blow through their counter attempt. You can then jump cancel into her air loop (see Advanced section) into a combo.

Against an opponent who is well versed in guarding mix-ups, you can perform Position Change into a combo, which cannot be guarded. Once in Feral Crouch, input → ↓ ↘ + Ⓗ to perform Position Change. The → input will perform the teleport, while the rest of the Position Change input will cancel the teleport into the throw. Use this mix-up in conjunction with Teleport mix-ups and Somersault frame traps to cause the opponent's defense to crumble.

If you find your opponent trying to deal with Jill's mix-ups by staying off the ground with normal jumps, counter with an air Ⓗ option select. When attempting an air throw or simply attacking with air Ⓗ, always use a → + Ⓗ input. If air Ⓗ is guarded, continue with air Ⓢ and land into standing Ⓛ to mount a secondary offensive. If air Ⓗ is guarded, continue with air Ⓢ, then go into a jump loop (see the Advanced Tactics section). If you are close enough, → + Ⓗ will get you an air throw, which can be followed with Fallen Prey or Machine Gun Spray into a THC. You can also use the air-to-air priority of air Ⓛ and Ⓜ to beat out opposing aerial attacks, which can then lead into jump loops.

Against a cornered opponent, all Feral Crouch mix-ups are still viable, even the Teleport cross-ups. Enemies are most likely to use advancing guard when cornered, so use → Teleport to get back in.

COMBO USAGE

I. CR. Ⓛ, Ⓜ, ST. Ⓗ CANCEL ↓ ↓ + Ⓢ, FERAL CROUCH Ⓗ, FORWARD JUMP, AIR Ⓜ, Ⓗ, Ⓢ, LAND, FORWARD JUMP, Ⓜ, Ⓗ, Ⓢ, LAND, ST. Ⓜ, Ⓗ, ← + Ⓗ CANCEL ↓ ↘ → + Ⓜ CANCEL ↓ ↓ + Ⓢ, FERAL CROUCH ↑, AIR Ⓢ, LAND, ST. Ⓜ, Ⓗ, ← + Ⓗ CANCEL ↓ ↘ → + Ⓛ CANCEL → ↓ ↘ + ATK ATK

535,800 damage, 12% meter loss

Here's a great combo to use after landing a clean hit. The air Ⓜ, Ⓗ, Ⓢ jump loop can be done slowly for better positioning. Timing your hits so that your opponent is close to the ground is essential for the success of this combo.

II. → + Ⓗ CANCEL ↓ ↘ → + Ⓛ, CR. Ⓛ, Ⓜ, Ⓗ CANCEL ↓ ↘ → + Ⓛ, FERAL CROUCH Ⓛ CANCEL ↓ ↘ → + Ⓛ, FERAL CROUCH Ⓛ CANCEL ↓ ↘ → + Ⓜ, FERAL CROUCH Ⓗ CANCEL ↓ ↘ → + ATK ATK

595,800 damage, 47% meter loss

This combo acts as an easy follow-up to Jill's → + Ⓗ overhead attack. Try to hit the Feral Crouch Ⓛ as late as possible for this combo to fully connect.

III. CR. Ⓛ, ST. Ⓜ, CR. Ⓜ, ST. Ⓗ, CR. Ⓗ CANCEL ↓ ↘ → + Ⓛ CANCEL ↓ ↓ + Ⓢ, FERAL CROUCH Ⓜ CANCEL ↓ ↓ + Ⓢ, FERAL CROUCH →, UPWARD JUMP, AIR Ⓜ, Ⓗ, Ⓢ, LAND, ST. Ⓜ, Ⓗ, ← + Ⓗ CANCEL ↓ ↘ → + Ⓜ, FERAL CROUCH Ⓗ CANCEL ↓ ↘ → + ATK ATK

566,300 damage, 27% meter loss

Feral Crouch Ⓜ sends your adversary flying for a wall bounce, making it ideal to add to combos if you are looking to carry the target to the corner. The Feral Crouch canceling can be tricky at first, but with practice, it is manageable.

IV. (OPPONENT IN THE AIR) FORWARD JUMP, AIR Ⓜ, Ⓜ, Ⓗ, Ⓢ, LAND, UPWARD JUMP, AIR Ⓜ, Ⓜ, Ⓗ, Ⓢ, LAND, UPWARD JUMP, AIR Ⓜ, Ⓜ, Ⓗ, Ⓢ, LAND, ST. Ⓜ, Ⓗ, ← + Ⓗ CANCEL ↓ ↘ → + Ⓜ CANCEL ↓ ↓ + Ⓢ, FERAL CROUCH ↑, AIR Ⓗ, ST. Ⓜ, Ⓗ, ← + Ⓗ CANCEL → ↓ ↘ + ATK ATK

545,900 damage, 4% meter loss

This combo is great for incoming characters after a K.O. Between each jump loop, make sure to pause slightly before having Jill jump again to ensure that the opposing character is as low to the ground as possible. If you are having trouble with the timing, try using only air Ⓜ, Ⓗ, Ⓢ instead. Note that you can use this combo as an instant overhead against crouching larger characters like Nemesis, Sentinel, or Hulk so long as one repetition of the jump loop is omitted.

"I DON'T CARE IF YOU THINK I'M A MINDLESS PUPPET. ALL THAT MATTERS IS MY MISSION."

ADVANCED TACTICS

FERAL CROUCH EASY INPUT TECHNIQUE

Holding down (H) immediately after performing Feral Crouch ensures that the Somersault gets executed as quickly as possible.

Take advantage of input shortcuts to optimize the execution and timing of Jill's Feral Crouch attacks. For example, a combo of standing (L), (M), (H) [CANCEL] → Feral Crouch [CANCEL] → Somersault may be difficult to perform because of the pause between Feral Crouch and Somersault. Luckily, holding down an input during the startup frames of Feral Crouch causes the move to fire as soon as possible. Thus, in the previous combo, an alternate method for performing it is standing (L), (M), (H) [CANCEL] → Feral Crouch (hold (H)) [CANCEL] → Somersault. The Somersault fires at the first frame possible, guaranteeing the combo's success.

This method can be used to optimize the timing for two other approaches:

For Teleport cross-ups: standing (L), (M), (H) [CANCEL] → Feral Crouch (hold ↙) [CANCEL] → Teleport

To tighten frame trap offense timing: Arrow Kick [CANCEL] → Feral Crouch (hold (M)) [CANCEL] → Jumping Roundhouse [CANCEL] → Feral Crouch (hold (L)) [CANCEL] → Low Sweep [CANCEL] → Flip Kick

JUMP LOOP

Due to the angles of Jill's jumping attacks, players can loop her air chains during a normal jump. The typical combo is air (M), (M), (H), (S), land, repeat. Try to keep opponents as low to the ground as possible when performing the jump loop. This combo can be varied depending on the situation:

For continuing a combo after Somersault, the loop can be reduced to a slowly timed jumping (H), (S) to keep the opponent from going too high during the combo ((H) at the apex of the jump, (S) on the way down)

For an air-to-air attack at normal jump height, using air (L), (M), (H), (S) is useful due to the angle and speed of Jill's air (L) (L), (M) on the way up, (H), (S) on the way down)

During combos, one or two repetitions of air (M), (M), (H), (S) or air (M), (H), (S) can be used for extending damage and meter building

Furthermore, Jill's air (M) acts as an instant overhead against large characters such as Hulk or Sentinel. Given this, Jill's entire jump loop can be performed on large characters while they are crouching. Opponents are forced to play a high/low guessing game whenever Jill is near.

WHO'S NEXT?

Not every teleport in the game can cross up in the corner. Luckily, Jill's Teleport does!

Jill has several options to mix incoming opponents up after a K.O.

Against opponents who come in attacking immediately, Jill can counter their attack by doing a preemptive jump loop (air (L), (M), (H), (S))

Against adversaries who come in with a delayed attack, you can use Somersault to out-prioritize their attack

Opponents coming in defending fall prey to Feral Crouch mix-ups including ↑/↙/→ Teleport cross-ups and Teleport into Position Change.

COMBO APPENDIX

GENERAL EXECUTION TIPS

Somersault causes heavy hitstun. When jump canceling from it, you don't need to attack right away; delay your hits to make sure the positioning is correct.

Use the Feral Crouch easy input technique to make her combos easier.

If you are having trouble performing jump loops, try normal jumping straight up instead of forward to help with positioning.

CR. (M), ST. (M), (H), CR. (H), ← + (H) [CANCEL] → ↓↘→ + (M) [CANCEL] → ↓↙← + ATK ATK, ↓↘→ + (L) [CANCEL] → ↓↘→ + (M), ↓↘→ + (L) [CANCEL] → ↓↘→ + (M), ↓↘→ + (L) [CANCEL] → ↓↘→ + (M), ↓↘→ + (L) [CANCEL] → ↓↘→ + (M), ↓↘→ + (L) [CANCEL] → ↓↘→ + (M), ↓↘→ + (L) [CANCEL] → ↓↘→ + (M), ↓↘→ + (L) [CANCEL] → ↓↘→ + (M), ↓↘→ + (L) [CANCEL] → ↓↘→ + (M), ↓↘→ + (L) [CANCEL] → ↓↘→ + ATK ATK

Notes	Damage
Make sure not to cancel the ↓↘→ + (M) or ↓↘→ + (L) until the attack has connected; otherwise, you will accidentally Teleport. If you feel your rhythm starting to fade mid-combo, simply cancel any ↓↘→ + (L) into ↓↘→ + ATK ATK to get as much damage as possible	812,300, 32% meter gain

CR. (L), (M), (H) [CANCEL] → ↓↘→ + (L) [CANCEL] → ↓↓ + (S), FERAL CROUCH →, ST. (L), ST. (M), (H) [CANCEL] → ↓↘→ + (L) [CANCEL] → ↓↓ + (S), FERAL CROUCH →, ST. (M), (H), ← + (H) [CANCEL] → ↓↘→ + (M), FERAL CROUCH ↑, AIR (H), LAND, ST. (M), (H), ← + (H) [CANCEL] → ↓↘→ + (L) [CANCEL] → →↓↘ + ATK ATK

Notes:	Damage
If you execute this combo midscreen, each Teleport will cross up. Reverse inputs accordingly	489,700 damage, 26% meter loss

↓↘→↗ + (H), REPEAT

Notes:	Damage
This combo is an easy 100% damage combo if done in X-Factor. Requires corner	100% damage

It's not the size
of the toy
in the fight...
It's the size
of the fight
in the toy.
MARVEL
VS.
CAPCOM
3
Fate of Two Worlds
MiniMates
Coming in December
from Diamond Select Toys
www.diamondselecttoys.com
DIAMOND
SELECT TOYS
ARTASYLUM
MARVEL
www.marvel.com
©CAPCOM. Licensed for use by Diamond Select Toys. Diamond Select Toys and Collectibles is a trademark of Diamond Select Toys and
Collectibles, LLC. © 2011 Diamond Select Toys and Collectibles. All Rights Reserved. Art Asylum™, MINIMATES, and the Art Asylum Logo are

Official Strategy Guide

By Joe Epstein, Campbell Tran, Adam Deats, Daniel Maniago, Ian Rogers, Josh Richardson, and Logan Sharp

MARVEL CAPCOM®

www.marvel.com www.capcom.com

DK/BradyGames, a division of Penguin Group (USA) Inc.
800 East 96th Street, 3rd Floor
Indianapolis, IN 46240

ISBN: 978-07440-1354-2

Printing Code: The rightmost double-digit number is the year of the book's printing; the rightmost single-digit number is the number of the book's printing. For example, 11-1 shows that the first printing of the book occurred in 2011.

14 13 12 11 4 3 2 1

Printed in the USA.

BRADYGAMES STAFF

Publisher
Mike Degler

Editor-In-Chief
H. Leigh Davis

Licensing Manager
Christian Sumner

Operations Manager
Stacey Beheler

CREDITS

Senior Development Editor
Chris Hausermann

Sr. Book Designer
Brent Gann

Production Designer
Areva

Editorial Assistant
Angie Lawler

THE CREW AT BRADYGAMES WOULD LIKE TO THANK:

Brian Oliveira, Seth Killian, Steve Lee, Josh Izzo, and everyone at Capcom for their support and help with this project. Thanks to Chris Baker and everyone at Marvel involved in the approval process of this book.

A special thank you to our authors:

Joe "Dr. Deelite" Epstein

Campbell "Buktooth" Tran

Adam "Kamui" Deats

Daniel "ClockwOrk" Maniago

Ian "Cylus 51" Rogers

Josh "Lord Hedonism" Richardson

Logan "amodf" Sharp

Thanks so much for the long hours of data mining, combo testing, documenting, writing, proofing, and everything else that it took for you to put this massive body of work together. Without you, this book would not have happened. Thanks so much for grinding it out and making this book the best it could be. We wish you all the best!

-C

AUTHOR ACKNOWLEDGEMENTS:

JOE EPSTEIN:

Thanks to: Chris, Leigh, Mike, Brent, Areva, Angie, and the whole staff of BradyGames for continually indulging and abetting my lunacy; the co-authors whose toil made this possible (in particular Campbell and Adam, who went far above and beyond the call); the family and friends of each author for putting up with worrying whether they are alive anymore (yes, barely); members of the fighting game community for their unprecedented support (seriously, thank you); Logan, for the real-life crossover assist; and my dear Mia, for absolutely everything else.

CAMPBELL TRAN:

Thanks to the guide team for putting up with my bossiness and idealistic expectations, my friends for understanding why I dropped off the face of the planet for an extended period of time, the fighting game community for the continued support, my nine girls for getting me through my time of need, my good friend Garlic Jim for dropping by, Joe Camel for the assist, and Stella for keeping things interesting.

ADAM DEATS:

Another guide has finished up, and the cost for writing this one was high; my personal schedule included 18 hour work days and many lunch periods spent sleeping in my car. My drive to work under such conditions, a drive possibly fueled by erroneous logic, is the hungry readers who buy these books, and the camaraderie I feel with my fellow writers. Thank you Campbell for keeping us organized when you should've been developing games instead. Thank you Joe for writing my pet characters; you held on to my good ideas, improved upon what was there, and made them read like flowers and rainbows. I like flowers and rainbows. Thanks also goes to Chris Hausermann, Leigh Davis, Angie, Brent, Areva, and the remainder of the BradyGames crew for their support, book design, and thoughtful editing. I care about the work we do, I wouldn't be involved if I didn't. Finally, thanks goes to Seth Killian at Capcom for his stealthy support and handsome looks. You're a dreamboat, Seth, a dreamboat.

DANIEL MANIAGO:

First and biggest thanks go to Joe Epstein. Thank you so much not only for giving me the opportunity of a lifetime, but for teaching me some of the most important lessons in life that I might not have learned otherwise. Huge thanks to Campbell and Adam for putting up with me throughout the project, and to Josh, Ian, Chris, Leigh, and everyone at Brady and Capcom for making this book possible. Special thanks go to Bill Wellman, ShadyK, ytwojay, Wentinel, the Degen Den, James Chen, Pedro Avila, Mike Watson, Seth Killian, Brian Olivera, Mike Ross, Combofiend, Koogy, IFC Yipes, Project GiantSword and everyone else that makes the fighting game community awesome. Final thanks go to my family and Sue Jin Kim for always being there. Any complaints/hate mail may be sent to me online via Twitter (@mvcClockw0rk) or brokentier.com!

IAN ROGERS:

First, I'd like to thank Michelle and the kids for being so supportive while working on these very time consuming guides. I'd like to thank my fellow authors for working themselves ragged along with me. Thanks to BradyGames for allowing us to work on this guide. Thanks to our readers, we really hope you enjoy this guide and find it useful!

JOSH RICHARDSON:

Whew! This was quite the undertaking, and I've got a few people to thank for helping me through: Katie, for being patient with me while I disappeared for weeks at a time. My fellow co-authors for helping me get up to speed. Greg, Sam, James, and the rest of the Off Base Productions crew for all their support. Isotope for keeping my comics on hold. Southtown Arcade, who's ranbats keep me hungry for more Marvel (beware the luscious lips of M.O.D.A.M. y'all!). And finally, to the fighting game community for constantly evolving the game and sharing their knowledge. You rock!

LOGAN SHARP:

I couldn't have ever done anything without Vanessa, the second most important thing in my life behind our ridiculous cats. Also thanks to Joe, Adam and Campbell for giving me a shot at this guide, couldn't have done it without you!